W9-DIM-438

THE NEW INTERNATIONAL
GREEK TESTAMENT COMMENTARY

Editors
I. Howard Marshall
and
Donald A. Hagner

THE GOSPEL OF
MARK

THE GOSPEL OF MARK

A Commentary on the Greek Text

by

R. T. FRANCE

WILLIAM B. EERDMANS PUBLISHING COMPANY
GRAND RAPIDS, MICHIGAN / CAMBRIDGE, U.K.

THE PATERNOSTER PRESS
CARLISLE

© 2002 Wm. B. Eerdmans Publishing Co.

Published jointly 2002 in the United States of America by
Wm. B. Eerdmans Publishing Co.
255 Jefferson Ave. S.E., Grand Rapids, Michigan 49503
www.eerdmans.com

and in the U.K. by
Paternoster Press
P.O. Box 300, Carlisle, Cumbria CA3 0QS

All rights reserved. No part of this publication may be reproduced, stored in a retrieval
system, or transmitted in any form or by any means, electronic, mechanical,
photocopying, recording, or otherwise, without the prior permission of the publisher or a
license permitting restricted copying. In the U.K. such licenses are issued by the
Copyright Licensing Agency, 90 Tottenham Court Road, London W1P 9HE.

Printed in the United States of America

07 06 05 04 03 02   7 6 5 4 3 2 1

Library of Congress Cataloging-in-Publication Data

France, R. T.
The Gospel of Mark: a commentary on the Greek text / R. T. France.
p.   cm.   — (The New international Greek Testament commentary)
Includes bibliographical references and indexes.
ISBN 0-8028-2446-3 (alk. paper)
1. Bible. N.T. Mark — Commentaries.   I. Title.
II. New international Greek Testament commentary (Grand Rapids, Mich.)

BS2585.53.F73   2002
226.3′07 — dc21

2001053854

Paternoster ISBN 0-85364-576-0

In grateful memory of

MY FATHER

5.1.1908 – 13.5.2000

CONTENTS

CONTENTS

FOREWORD

Although there have been many series of commentaries on the English text of the New Testament in recent years, very few attempts have been made to cater particularly to the needs of students of the Greek text. The present initiative to fill this gap by the publication of the New International Greek Testament Commentary is very largely due to the vision of W. Ward Gasque, who was one of the original editors of the series. At a time when the study of Greek is being curtailed in many schools of theology, we hope that the NIGTC will demonstrate the continuing value of studying the Greek New Testament and will be an impetus in the revival of such study.

The volumes of the NIGTC are for students who want something less technical than a full-scale critical commentary. At the same time, the commentaries are intended to interact with modern scholarship and to make their own scholarly contribution to the study of the New Testament. The wealth of detailed study of the New Testament in articles and monographs continues without interruption, and the series is meant to harvest the results of this research in an easily accessible form. The commentaries include, therefore, extensive bibliographies and attempt to treat all important problems of history, exegesis, and interpretation that arise from the New Testament text.

One of the gains of recent scholarship has been the recognition of the primarily theological character of the books of the New Testament. The volumes of the NIGTC attempt to provide a theological understanding of the text, based on historical-critical-linguistic exegesis. It is not their primary aim to apply and expound the text for modern readers, although it is hoped that the exegesis will give some indication of the way in which the text should be expounded.

Within the limits set by the use of the English language, the series aims to be international in character, though the contributors have been chosen not primarily in order to achieve a spread between different countries but above all because of their specialized qualifications for their particular tasks.

The supreme aim of this series is to serve those who are engaged in the ministry of the Word of God and thus to glorify God's name. Our prayer is that it may be found helpful in this task.

I. Howard Marshall
Donald A. Hagner

Abbreviations

1. BOOKS OF THE BIBLE

Gn., Ex., Lv., Nu., Dt., Jos., Jdg., Ru., 1, 2 Sa., 1, 2 Ki., 1, 2 Ch., Ezr., Ne., Est., Job, Ps(s)., Pr., Ec., Ct., Is., Je., La., Ezk., Dn., Ho., Jo., Am., Ob., Jon., Mi., Na., Hab., Zp., Hg., Zc., Mal., Mt., Mk., Lk., Jn., Acts, Rom., 1, 2 Cor., Gal., Eph., Phil., Col., 1, 2 Thes., 1, 2 Tim., Tit., Phm., Heb., Jas., 1, 2 Pet., 1, 2, 3 Jn., Jude, Rev.

2. OLD TESTAMENT APOCRYPHA AND PSEUDEPIGRAPHA

Ben Sira	The Wisdom of Jesus ben Sira, or Ecclesiasticus
2 Bar.	*Syriac Apocalypse of Baruch*
1 Enoch	*Ethiopic Enoch*
2 Enoch	*Slavonic Enoch*
3 Enoch	*Hebrew Enoch*
2 Esdr.	2 Esdras
Jdt.	Judith
Jub.	*Jubilees*
1, 2, 3, 4 Macc.	1, 2, 3, 4 Maccabees
Pss. Sol.	*Psalms of Solomon*
Sib. Or.	*The Sibylline Oracles*
Sus.	Susannah
Test. Abr.	*Testament of Abraham*
Test. Ben.	*Testament of Benjamin*
Test Dan	*Testament of Dan*
Test Iss.	*Testament of Issachar*
Test. Job	*Testament of Job*
Test Levi	*Testament of Levi*
Test. Mos.	*Testament of Moses*
Test. Naph.	*Testament of Naphtali*
Test Sim.	*Testament of Simeon*
Test. Sol.	*Testament of Solomon*
Test. Zeb.	*Testament of Zebulun*
Tob.	Tobit
Wis.	Wisdom of Solomon

3. DEAD SEA SCROLLS AND RELATED TEXTS

CD	Cairo *Damascus Document*
1QH	*Hodayot (Thanksgiving) Hymns* from Qumran Cave 1
1QM	*Milḥamah (War Scroll)* from Qumran Cave 1
1QS	*Serek hayyahad (Rule of the Community)* from Qumran Cave 1
1QSa	Appendix A to 1QS *(Rule of the Congregation)*
4Q174	*Florilegium* from Qumran Cave 4
4Q246	*Apocryphon of Daniel* from Qumran Cave 4
11Q13	*Melchizedek Scroll* from Qumran Cave 11
11Q19	*Temple Scroll* from Qumran Cave 11

4. RABBINIC AND TARGUMIC LITERATURE

'Abod. Zar.	*'Abodah Zarah*
'Abot	*'Abot*
'Abot. R. Nat.	*'Abot de Rabbi Nathan*
'Arak.	*'Arakhin*
b.	Babylonian Talmud
B. Bat.	*Baba Batra*
B. Meṣ.	*Baba Meṣia*
B. Qam.	*Baba Qamma*
Ber.	*Berakhot*
Beṣah	*Beṣah (= Yom Ṭob)*
Ct. Rab.	*Canticles Rabbah*
'Eduy.	*'Eduyyot*
'Erub.	*'Erubin*
Ex. Rab.	*Exodus Rabbah*
Giṭ.	*Giṭṭin*
Ḥag.	*Ḥagigah*
Ḥul.	*Ḥullin*
Ket.	*Ketubbot*
Lv. Rab.	*Leviticus Rabbah*
m.	Mishnah
Mak.	*Makkot*
Meg.	*Megillah*
Mek. Ex.	*Mekilta on Exodus*
Mid.	*Middot*
Miq.	*Miqwa'ot*
Naz.	*Nazir*
Ned.	*Nedarim*
Neg.	*Nega'im*
Nid.	*Niddah*
Ohol.	*Oholot*
Parah	*Parah*
Pe'ah	*Pe'ah*

Pes.	*Pesaḥim*
Roš HaŠ.	*Roš HaŠanah*
Sanh.	*Sanhedrin*
Šab.	*Šabbat*
Šebi.	*Šebi'it*
Šebu.	*Šebu'ot*
Šeq.	*Šeqalim*
Sop.	*Soperim*
Soṭah	*Soṭah*
Suk.	*Sukkah*
t.	Tosefta
Ta'an.	*Ta'anit*
Tg. Ct.	*Targum on Canticles*
Tg. Ps-J.	*Targum Pseudo-Jonathan*
Ṭoh.	*Ṭoharot*
Yad.	*Yadayim*
Yom.	*Yoma*
Zeb.	*Zebaḥim*

5. NEW TESTAMENT APOCRYPHA
AND OTHER EARLY CHRISTIAN WRITINGS

Barn.	*Barnabas*
Chrysostom	Chrysostom
Hom. Mt.	*Homilies on Matthew*
1 Clem.	*1 Clement*
Did.	*Didache*
Epiphanius	Epiphanius
De Mens.	*De Mensibus*
Haer.	*Adversus Haereses*
Euseb.	Eusebius
H.E.	*Historia Ecclesiastica*
Gos. Pet.	*Gospel of Peter*
Gos. Thom.	*Gospel of Thomas*
Hermas	Hermas
Sim.	*Similitudes*
Vis.	*Visions*
Irenaeus	Irenaeus
Haer.	*Adversus Omnes Haereses*
Jerome	Jerome
De Vir Ill.	*De Viris Illustribus*
Ep.	*Epistles*
Justin	Justin Martyr
Apol.	*Apology*
Dial.	*Dialogue with Trypho*

Origen	Origen
Comm. Joh.	*Commentary on John*
Contra Cels.	*Contra Celsum*
Pol.	Polycarp
Tertullian	Tertullian
Adv. Marc.	*Adversus Marcionem*

6. OTHER JEWISH, CLASSICAL, AND HELLENISTIC LITERATURE

Dio Chrysostom	Dio Chrysostom
Orat.	*Orations*
Josephus	Josephus
Ant.	*Jewish Antiquities*
Ap.	*Against Apion*
Life	*Life of Flavius Josephus*
War	*The Jewish War*
Juvenal	Juvenal
Sat.	*Satires*
Philo	Philo of Alexandria
Abr.	*De Abrahamo*
Decal.	*De Decalogo*
Flacc.	*In Flaccum*
Leg. Gai.	*De Legatione ad Gaium*
Spec. Leg.	*De Specialibus Legibus*
Philostratus	Philostratus
VA	*Vita Apollonii*
Pliny the Elder	Pliny the Elder
Ep.	*Epistles*
Pliny the Younger	Pliny the Younger
Nat. Hist.	*Natural History*
P. Oxy.	*Oxyrhynchus Papyri*
Plutarch	Plutarch
Apophth. Lacon.	*Apophthegmata Laconica*
Tacitus	Tacitus
Ann.	*Annals*
Hist.	*Histories*

7. MODERN WORKS

ABD	*The Anchor Bible Dictionary,* ed. D. N. Freedman. 6 vols., New York: Doubleday, 1992
Aland	*Synopsis Quattuor Evangeliorum,* ed. K. Aland. Stuttgart: Württembergische Bibelanstalt, 1973[8]
ASNU	*Acta Seminarii Neotestamentici Upsaliensis*

ASTI	*Annual of the Swedish Theological Institute*
BAGD	*A Greek-English Lexicon of the New Testament and Other Early Christian Literature,* by W. Bauer, trans. and rev. by W. F. Arndt and F. W. Gingrich; 2d edn. rev. by F. W. Gingrich and F. W. Danker. Chicago: University of Chicago Press, 1979
BBR	*Bulletin for Biblical Research*
BDF	*A Greek Grammar of the New Testament and Other Early Christian Literature,* by F. Blass and A. Debrunner, trans. and rev. by R. W. Funk. Chicago: University of Chicago Press, 1961
BETL	Bibliotheca Ephemeridum Theologicarum Lovaniensium
Bib	*Biblica*
BJRL	*Bulletin of the John Rylands Library*
BT	*The Bible Translator*
BTB	*Biblical Theology Bulletin*
BZ	*Biblische Zeitschrift*
BZNW	Beihefte zur Zeitschrift für die neutestamentliche Wissenschaft
CBQ	*Catholic Biblical Quarterly*
DNTT	*The New International Dictionary of New Testament Theology,* ed. C. Brown. 3 vols., Exeter: Paternoster, 1975-78
EQ	*Evangelical Quarterly*
ETL	*Ephemerides Theologicae Lovanienses*
ExpTim	*Expository Times*
GP	*Gospel Perspectives: Studies of History and Tradition in the Four Gospels,* ed. R. T. France, D. Wenham, and C. L. Blomberg. 6 vols., Sheffield: JSOT Press, 1980-86
Henn.-Schn.	*New Testament Apocrypha,* by E. Hennecke, ed. W. Schneemelcher. ET, 2 vols., London: SCM, 1963, 1965
HeyJ	*Heythrop Journal*
HTR	*Harvard Theological Review*
ICC	International Critical Commentary
IEJ	*Israel Exploration Journal*
Int	*Interpretation*
ISBE	*The International Standard Bible Encyclopedia,* ed. G. W. Bromiley et al. 4 vols., Grand Rapids: Eerdmans, 1979-88
JBL	*Journal of Biblical Literature*
JETS	*Journal of the Evangelical Theological Society*
JJS	*Journal of Jewish Studies*
JSNT	*Journal for the Study of the New Testament*
JSNTS	Journal for the Study of the New Testament Supplements
JSOTS	Journal for the Study of the Old Testament Supplements
JSS	*Journal of Semitic Studies*
JTS	*Journal of Theological Studies*
LSJ	*A Greek-English Lexicon,* by H. G. Liddell and R. Scott, new edn. by H. S. Jones and R. McKenzie. Oxford: Oxford University Press, 1940 (supplement, ed. E. A. Barber, 1968)
MM	*The Vocabulary of the Greek Testament Illustrated from the Papyri and Other Non-Literary Sources,* by J. H. Moulton and G. Milligan. London: Hodder & Stoughton, 1930

N-A^{27}	*Novum Testamentum Graece,* 27th edn., ed. E. Nestle, K. Aland et al. Stuttgart: Deutsche Bibelstiftung, 1993
NovT	*Novum Testamentum*
NTS	*New Testament Studies*
RB	*Revue Biblique*
RSR	*Recherches de Science Religieuse*
SBLDS	Society of Biblical Literature Dissertation Series
SBLM	Society of Biblical Literature Monographs
SBT	Studies in Biblical Theology
Schürer	E. Schürer, *The History of the Jewish People in the Age of Jesus Christ,* rev. and ed. by G. Vermes, F. Millar, M. Goodman, and M. Black. 3 vols., Edinburgh: T. & T. Clark, 1973-87
SE	*Studia Evangelica*
SJT	*Scottish Journal of Theology*
SNT	Supplements to Novum Testamentum
SNTSM	Society for New Testament Studies Monographs
ST	*Studia Theologica*
Str-B	*Kommentar zum neuen Testament aus Talmud und Midrasch,* by H. L. Strack and P. Billerbeck. Vols. 1-4, München: Beck, 1922-28; vols. 5-6 by J. Jeremias and K. Adolph, München: Beck, 1956, 1961
TDNT	*Theological Dictionary of the New Testament,* ed. G. Kittel and G. Friedrich. ET, 9 vols., Grand Rapids: Eerdmans, 1964-74
TynB	*Tyndale Bulletin*
TZ	*Theologische Zeitschrift*
UBS^{4}	*The Greek New Testament,* 4th rev. edn., ed. B. Aland, K. Aland, et al. Stuttgart: Deutsche Bibelgesellschaft/United Bible Societies, 1993
VT	*Vetus Testamentum*
WUNT	Wissenschaftliche Untersuchungen zum Neuen Testament
ZNW	*Zeitschrift für die neutestamentliche Wissenschaft*

BIBLIOGRAPHY OF WORKS
REFERRED TO IN THIS COMMENTARY

(For standard reference works see the list of abbreviations at the beginning of this volume.)

The commentaries in section 1 are referred to in this commentary by author's name only. References to these commentaries (and to the standard works of reference) are not listed in the Author Index. Books in section 2 are referred to by author's name and initials and short title, articles in section 3 by journal, volume, and year of publication.

1. Commentaries on the Gospel of Mark

H. Anderson, *The Gospel of Mark* (New Century Bible). London: Oliphants, 1976.

F. Belo, *A Materialist Reading of the Gospel of Mark.* ET, Maryknoll: Orbis, 1981.

C. E. B. Cranfield, *The Gospel according to Saint Mark* (Cambridge Greek Testament Commentary). Cambridge: Cambridge University Press, 1959.

J. Gnilka, *Das Evangelium nach Markus* (Evangelisch-katholischer Kommentar zum NT). 2 vols., Zürich: Benziger Verlag/Neukirchen-Vluyn: Neukirchener Verlag, 1978, 1979.

E. P. Gould, *The Gospel according to St. Mark* (ICC). Edinburgh: T. & T. Clark, 1896.

R. A. Guelich, *Mark 1:1–8:26* (Word Biblical Commentary). Dallas: Word, 1989.

R. H. Gundry, *Mark: A Commentary on His Apology for the Cross.* Grand Rapids: Eerdmans, 1993.

E. Haenchen, *Der Weg Jesu: Eine Erklärung des Markus-Evangeliums und der kanonischen Parallelen.* 2d edn., Berlin: de Gruyter, 1968.

M. D. Hooker, *The Gospel according to St. Mark* (Black's NT Commentaries). London: A. & C. Black, 1991.

L. W. Hurtado, *Mark* (New International Biblical Commentary). Peabody, MA: Hendrickson, 1989.

W. L. Lane, *The Gospel according to Mark* (New International Commentary on the NT). Grand Rapids: Eerdmans, 1974.

S. C. E. Legg, *Novum Testamentum Graece, secundum Textum Westcotto-Hortianum: Euangelium secundum Marcum.* Oxford: Oxford University Press, 1935.

E. Lohmeyer, *Das Evangelium des Markus* (Kritisch-exegetischer Kommentar über das NT). 17th edn., Göttingen: Vandenhoeck & Ruprecht, 1967.

C. S. Mann, *Mark: A New Translation with Introduction and Commentary* (Anchor Bible). New York: Doubleday, 1986.

C. Myers, *Binding the Strong Man: A Political Reading of Mark's Story of Jesus*. Maryknoll, NY: Orbis, 1988.

D. E. Nineham, *The Gospel of St. Mark* (Pelican Gospel Commentaries). Harmondsworth: Penguin, 1969.

R. Pesch, *Das Markus-Evangelium* (Herders theologischer Kommentar zum NT). 2 vols., 3d edn., Freiburg: Herder, 1980.

E. Schweizer, *The Good News according to Mark*. ET, London: SPCK, 1971.

A. Stock, *The Method and Message of Mark*. Wilmington, DE: Michael Glazier, 1989.

V. Taylor, *The Gospel according to St. Mark*. London: Macmillan, 1952.

B. M. F. Van Iersel, *Mark: A Reader-Response Commentary* (JSNTS 164). Sheffield: Sheffield Academic Press, 1998.

2. Books

W. F. Albright and C. S. Mann, *Matthew* (Anchor Bible). New York: Doubleday, 1971.

L. C. Allen, *Psalms 101–150* (Word Biblical Commentary). Waco: Word, 1983.

D. C. Allison, *The End of the Ages Has Come: An Early Interpretation of the Passion and Resurrection of Jesus*. Edinburgh: T. & T. Clark, 1985.

A. M. Ambrozic, *The Hidden Kingdom: A Redaction-critical Study of the References to the Kingdom of God in Mark's Gospel*. Washington: Catholic Biblical Association, 1972.

D. E. Aune, *Prophecy in Early Christianity and the Ancient Mediterranean World*. Grand Rapids: Eerdmans, 1983.

————, *The NT in Its Literary Environment*. Cambridge: James Clarke, 1987.

M. Avi-Yonah (ed.), *Encyclopaedia of Archaeological Excavations in the Holy Land* Oxford: Oxford University Press, 1976.

K. E. Bailey, *Through Peasant Eyes*. Grand Rapids: Eerdmans, 1980.

E. Bammel (ed.), *The Trial of Jesus: Cambridge Studies in Honour of C. F. D. Moule* (SBT 13). London: SCM, 1970.

E. Bammel and C. F. D. Moule (ed.), *Jesus and the Politics of His Day*. Cambridge: Cambridge University Press, 1984.

R. J. Banks, *Jesus and the Law in the Synoptic Tradition* (SNTSM 28). Cambridge: Cambridge University Press, 1975.

M. Barth, *Ephesians 1–3* (Anchor Bible). New York: Doubleday, 1974.

S. C. Barton, *Discipleship and Family Ties in Mark and Matthew* (SNTSM 80). Cambridge: Cambridge University Press, 1994.

R. J. Bauckham, *Jude and the Relatives of Jesus in the Early Church*. Edinburgh: T. & T. Clark, 1990.

———— (ed.), *The Gospels for All Christians: Rethinking the Gospel Audiences*. Edinburgh: T. & T. Clark, 1998.

G. R. Beasley-Murray, *Jesus and the Kingdom of God*. Grand Rapids: Eerdmans, 1986.

————, *Jesus and the Last Days: The Interpretation of the Olivet Discourse* (incorporating revised editions of *Jesus and the Future*, 1954, and *A Commentary on Mark 13*, 1957). Peabody, MA: Hendrickson, 1993.

M. A. Beavis, *Mark's Audience: The Literary and Social Setting of Mark 4.11-12* (JSNTS 33). Sheffield: Sheffield Academic Press, 1989.

P. Benoit, *Jesus and the Gospel*. London: Darton, Longman & Todd, 1973.

K. Berger, *Die Amen-Worte Jesu* (BZNW 39). Berlin: de Gruyter, 1970.

E. Best, *The Temptation and the Passion: The Markan Soteriology* (SNTSM 2). Cambridge: Cambridge University Press, 1965 (2d edn., 1990, pagination unchanged).

————, *Following Jesus: Discipleship in the Gospel of Mark* (JSNTS 4). Sheffield: JSOT Press, 1981.

————, *Mark: The Gospel as Story*. Edinburgh: T. & T. Clark, 1983.

————, *Disciples and Discipleship: Studies in the Gospel according to Mark*. Edinburgh: T. & T. Clark, 1986.

G. B. Bilezikian, *The Liberated Gospel: A Comparison of the Gospel of Mark and Greek Tragedy*. Grand Rapids: Baker, 1977.

C. C. Black, *The Disciples according to Mark: Markan Redaction in Current Debate* (JSNTS 27). Sheffield: Sheffield Academic Press, 1989.

M. Black, *An Aramaic Approach to the Gospels and Acts*. 3d edn., Oxford: Oxford University Press, 1967.

J. Blinzler, *The Trial of Jesus: The Jewish and Roman Proceedings against Jesus Christ Described and Assessed from the Oldest Accounts*. ET, Cork: Mercier Press, 1959.

D. L. Bock, *Blasphemy and Exaltation in Judaism and the Final Examination of Jesus: A Philological-Historical Study of the Key Jewish Themes Impacting Mark 14:61-64* (WUNT 106). Tübingen: Mohr (Siebeck), 1998.

E. L. Bode, *The First Easter Morning: The Gospel Accounts of the Women's Visit to the Tomb of Jesus* (Analecta Biblica 45). Rome: Biblical Institute Press, 1970.

P. Bonnard, *L'Évangile selon Saint Matthieu*. Neuchâtel: Delachaux & Niestlé, 1963.

G. H. Boobyer, *St Mark and the Transfiguration Story*. Edinburgh: T. & T. Clark, 1942.

R. P. Booth, *Jesus and the Laws of Purity: Tradition History and Legal History in Mark 7* (JSNTS 13). Sheffield: JSOT Press, 1986.

J. W. Bowker, *The Targums and Rabbinic Literature*. Cambridge: Cambridge University Press, 1969.

————, *Jesus and the Pharisees*. Cambridge: Cambridge University Press, 1973.

S. G. F. Brandon, *Jesus and the Zealots*. Manchester: Manchester University Press, 1967.

K. E. Brower and M. W. Elliott (ed.), *'The Reader Must Understand': Eschatology in Bible and Theology*. Leicester: Apollos, 1997.

R. E. Brown, *The Gospel according to John* (Anchor Bible). New York: Doubleday, 1966.

————, *The Semitic Background of the Term 'Mystery' in the NT*. Philadelphia: Fortress, 1968.

————, *The Death of the Messiah: From Gethsemane to the Grave. A Commentary on the Passion Narratives in the Four Gospels*. London: Chapman, 1994.

F. F. Bruce, *This Is That: The NT Development of Some OT Themes*. Exeter: Paternoster, 1968

————, *The 'Secret' Gospel of Mark*. London: Athlone Press, 1974.

C. Bryan, *A Preface to Mark: Notes on the Gospel in Its Literary and Cultural Settings*. Oxford: Oxford University Press, 1993.

R. Bultmann, *The History of the Synoptic Tradition*. ET, Oxford: Blackwell, 1963.

R. A. Burridge, *What Are the Gospels? A Comparison with Graeco-Roman Biography* (SNTSM 70). Cambridge: Cambridge University Press, 1992.

G. B. Caird, *Jesus and the Jewish Nation*. London: Athlone Press, 1965.

J. Camery-Hoggatt, *Irony in Mark's Gospel: Text and Subtext* (SNTSM 72). Cambridge: Cambridge University Press, 1992.

G. S. Cansdale, *Animals of Bible Lands.* Exeter: Paternoster, 1970.

P. Carrington, *According to Mark: A Running Commentary on the Oldest Gospel.* Cambridge: Cambridge University Press, 1960.

D. A. Carson, *The Gospel according to John.* Leicester: Inter-Varsity Press, 1991.

M. Casey, *Aramaic Sources of Mark's Gospel* (SNTSM 102). Cambridge: Cambridge University Press, 1998.

H. C. C. Cavallin, *Life after Death, Part 1: An Enquiry into the Jewish Background.* Lund: Gleerup, 1974.

D. W. Chapman, *The Orphan Gospel: Mark's Perspective on Jesus.* Sheffield: JSOT Press, 1993.

J. H. Charlesworth (ed.), *The OT Pseudepigrapha.* London: Darton, Longman & Todd, vol. 1, 1983; vol. 2, 1985.

B. D. Chilton, *A Galilean Rabbi and His Bible: Jesus' Own Interpretation of Isaiah.* London: SPCK, 1984.

————, *God in Strength: Jesus' Announcement of the Kingdom.* Sheffield: JSOT, 1987.

M. J. Cook, *Mark's Treatment of the Jewish Leaders* (SNT 51). Leiden: Brill, 1978.

O. Cullmann, *Peter: Disciple, Apostle, Martyr. A Historical and Theological Study.* 2d edn., London: SCM, 1962.

————, *The Christology of the NT.* ET, London: SCM, 1963.

H. Cunliffe-Jones, *A Word for Our Time? Zechariah 9–14, the NT and Today.* London: Athlone Press, 1973.

P. L. Danove, *The End of Mark's Story: A Methodological Study.* Leiden: Brill, 1993.

D. Daube, *The NT and Rabbinic Judaism.* London: Athlone Press, 1956.

W. D. Davies and D. C. Allison Jr., *The Gospel according to Saint Matthew* (ICC). 3 vols., Edinburgh: T. & T. Clark, 1988, 1991, 1997.

J. D. M. Derrett, *Law in the NT.* London: Darton, Longman & Todd, 1970.

————, *Jesus' Audience.* London: Darton, Longman & Todd, 1973.

————, *Studies in the NT,* vol. 1. Leiden: Brill, 1977.

C. H. Dodd, *Historical Tradition in the Fourth Gospel.* Cambridge: Cambridge University Press, 1963.

S. E. Dowd, *Prayer, Power and the Problem of Suffering: Mark 11:22-25 in the Context of Markan Theology* (SBLDS 105). Atlanta: Scholars Press, 1988.

F. G. Downing, *Christ and the Cynics.* Sheffield: Sheffield Academic Press, 1988.

J. D. G. Dunn, *Baptism in the Holy Spirit: A Re-examination of the NT Teaching on the Gift of the Spirit in relation to Pentecostalism Today.* London: SCM, 1970.

————, *Jesus and the Spirit: A Study of the Religious and Charismatic Experience of Jesus and the First Christians as Reflected in the NT.* London: SCM, 1975.

————, *The Partings of the Ways between Christianity and Judaism and Their Significance for the Character of Christianity.* London: SCM, 1991.

T. Dwyer, *The Motif of Wonder in the Gospel of Mark* (JSNTS 128). Sheffield: Sheffield Academic Press, 1996.

E. E. Ellis, *The Gospel of Luke* (The Century Bible). London: Nelson, 1966.

C. A. Evans, *To See and Not Perceive: Isaiah 6:9-10 in Early Jewish and Christian Interpretation* (JSOTS 64). Sheffield: Sheffield Academic Press, 1989.

————, *Jesus and His Contemporaries: Comparative Studies.* Köln: Brill, 1995.

C. F. Evans, et al., *The New Testament Gospels.* London: BBC, 1965.

W. R. Farmer, *The Synoptic Problem.* New York: Macmillan, 1964; 2d edn., Dillsboro: Western North Carolina Press, 1976.

————, *The Last Twelve Verses of Mark* (SNTSM 25). Cambridge: Cambridge University Press, 1974.

W. Feneberg, *Der Markusprolog: Studien zur Formbestimmung des Evangeliums.* München: Kösel, 1974.

J. Finegan, *Handbook of Biblical Chronology.* Princeton, NJ: Princeton University Press, 1964.

————, *The Archeology of the NT.* Princeton, NJ: Princeton University Press, 1969.

J. A. Fitzmyer, *Essays on the Semitic Background of the NT.* London: Chapman, 1971.

————, *A Wandering Aramean: Collected Aramaic Essays.* Missoula: Scholars Press, 1979.

R. M. Fowler, *Loaves and Fishes: The Function of the Feeding Stories in the Gospel of Mark* (SBLDS 54). Chico, CA: Scholars Press, 1981.

R. T. France, *Jesus and the OT: His Application of OT Passages to Himself and His Mission.* London: Tyndale, 1971.

————, *The Gospel according to Matthew: An Introduction and Commentary.* Leicester: Inter-Varsity Press, 1985.

————, *The Evidence for Jesus.* London: Hodder, 1986.

————, *Matthew: Evangelist and Teacher.* Exeter: Paternoster, 1989.

————, *Divine Government: God's Kingship in the Gospel of Mark.* London: SPCK, 1990.

S. Freyne, *Galilee from Alexander the Great to Hadrian 323 BCE to 135 CE: A Study of Second Temple Judaism.* Wilmington: Glazier, 1980.

————, *Galilee, Jesus and the Gospels: Literary Approaches and Historical Investigations.* Dublin: Gill & Macmillan, 1988.

S. R. Garrett, *The Temptations of Jesus in Mark's Gospel.* Grand Rapids: Eerdmans, 1998.

B. Gärtner, *The Temple and the Community in Qumran and the NT: A Comparative Study in the Temple Symbolism of the Qumran Texts and the NT* (SNTSM 1). Cambridge: Cambridge University Press, 1965.

L. Gaston, *No Stone on Another: Studies in the Significance of the Fall of Jerusalem in the Synoptic Gospels* (SNT 23). Leiden: Brill, 1970.

T. J. Geddert, *Watchwords: Mark 13 in Markan Eschatology* (JSNTS 26). Sheffield: Sheffield Academic Press, 1989.

E. J. Goodspeed, *Problems of NT Translation.* Chicago: University of Chicago Press, 1945.

M. D. Goulder, *Midrash and Lection in Matthew.* London: SPCK, 1974.

L. Grollenberg, *Unexpected Messiah: or How the Bible Can Be Misleading.* ET, London: SCM, 1988.

R. H. Gundry, *The Use of the OT in St. Matthew's Gospel, with Special Reference to the Messianic Hope* (SNT 18). Leiden: Brill, 1967.

————, *Matthew: A Commentary on His Literary and Theological Art.* Grand Rapids: Eerdmans, 1982.

L. Hartman, *Prophecy Interpreted: The Formation of Some Jewish Apocalyptic Texts and of the Eschatological Discourse Mark 13 par.* Lund: Gleerup, 1966.

A. E. Harvey, *Jesus and the Constraints of History.* London: Duckworth, 1982.

V. Hasler, *Amen: redaktionsgeschichtliche Untersuchung zur Einführungsformel der Herrenworte 'Wahrlich ich sage euch'.* Zürich: Theologischer Verlag, 1969.

D. M. Hay, *Glory at the Right Hand: Psalm 110 in Early Christianity* (SBLM 18). Nashville: Abingdon, 1973.

B. W. Henaut, *Oral Tradition and the Gospels: The Problem of Mark 4* (JSNTS 82). Sheffield: Sheffield Academic Press, 1993.

M. Hengel, *Judaism and Hellenism: Studies in Their Encounter in Palestine during the Early Hellenistic Period.* ET, London: SCM, 1974.

————, *Property and Riches in the Early Church: Aspects of a Social History of Early Christianity.* ET, London: SCM, 1974.

————, *The Son of God: The Origin of Christology and the History of Jewish-Hellenistic Religion.* ET, London: SCM, 1976.

————, *Crucifixion in the Ancient World and the Folly of the Message of the Cross.* ET, London: SCM, 1977.

————, *The Charismatic Leader and His Followers.* ET, Edinburgh: T. & T. Clark, 1981.

————, *Studies in the Gospel of Mark.* ET, London: SCM, 1985.

————, *The Zealots: Investigations into the Jewish Freedom Movement in the Period from Herod until 70 A.D.* ET, Edinburgh: T. & T. Clark, 1989.

H. Hoehner, *Herod Antipas* (SNTSM 17). Cambridge: Cambridge University Press, 1972.

C. H. Holladay, *'Theois Aner' in Hellenistic Judaism: A Critique of the Use of This Category in NT Christology* (SBLDS 40). Missoula: Scholars Press, 1977.

J. W. Holleran, *The Synoptic Gethsemane: A Critical Study.* Rome: Universita Gregoriana Editrice, 1973.

M. D. Hooker, *Jesus and the Servant: The Influence of the Servant Concept of Deutero-Isaiah in the NT.* London: SPCK, 1959.

————, *The Son of Man in Mark.* London: SPCK, 1967.

————, *The Message of Mark.* London: Epworth, 1983.

M. Hubaut, *La parabole des vignerons homicides.* Paris: Gabalda, 1976.

J. M. Hull, *Hellenistic Magic and the Synoptic Tradition* (SBT 28). London:SCM, 1974.

J. Jeremias, *Infant Baptism in the First Four Centuries.* ET. London: SCM, 1960.

————, *The Parables of Jesus.* ET, London: SCM, 1963.

————, *The Eucharistic Words of Jesus.* ET, London: SCM, 1966.

————, *Abba. Studien zur neutestamentlichen Theologie und Zeitgeschichte.* Göttingen: Vandenhoeck & Ruprecht, 1966.

————, *The Prayers of Jesus* (SBT 6). ET, London: SCM, 1967.

————, *Jerusalem in the Time of Jesus: An Investigation into Economic and Social Conditions during the NT Period.* ET, London: SCM, 1969.

————, *New Testament Theology, vol. 1: The Proclamation of Jesus.* ET, London: SCM, 1971.

D. Juel, *Messiah and Temple: The Trial of Jesus in the Gospel of Mark* (SBLDS 31). Missoula: Scholars Press, 1977.

————, *Messianic Exegesis: Christological Interpretation of the OT in Early Christianity.* Philadelphia: Fortress, 1988.

S. P. Kealy, *Mark's Gospel: A History of Its Interpretation, from the Beginning until 1979.* New York: Paulist Press, 1982.

H. C. Kee, *Community of the New Age: Studies in Mark's Gospel.* London: SCM, 1977.

————, *Medicine, Miracle and Magic in NT Times* (SNTSM 55). Cambridge: Cambridge University Press, 1986.

W. H. Kelber, *The Kingdom in Mark: A New Place and a New Time.* Philadelphia: Fortress, 1974.

———— (ed.), *The Passion in Mark: Studies on Mark 14–16.* Philadelphia: Fortress, 1976.

F. Kermode, *The Genesis of Secrecy: On the Interpretation of Narrative.* Cambridge, MA: Harvard University Press, 1979.

J. D. Kingsbury, *The Christology of Mark's Gospel.* Philadelphia: Fortress, 1983.

E. F. Kirschner, *The Place of the Exorcism Motif in Mark's Christology, with Special Reference to Mark 3:22-30.* Unpublished Ph.D. dissertation, CNAA, 1988.

W. Klassen, *Judas: Betrayer or Friend of Jesus?.* London: SCM, 1996.

G. Klinzing, *Die Umdeutung des Kultus in der Qumrangemeinde und im NT.* Göttingen: Vandenhoeck & Ruprecht, 1971.

H.-W. Kuhn, *Ältere Sammlungen im Markusevangelium* (Göttingen: Vandenhoeck & Ruprecht, 1971.

M. Künzi, *Das Naherwartungslogion Markus 9.1 par.* Tübingen: Mohr, 1977.

D. Lamont, *Christ and the World of Thought.* Edinburgh, 1934.

S. Légasse, *Le Procès de Jésus.* Paris: Cerf, 1995.

R. H. Lightfoot, *History and Interpretation in the Gospels.* London: Hodder & Stoughton, 1935.

————, *Locality and Doctrine in the Gospels.* London: Hodder & Stoughton, 1938.

————, *The Gospel Message of St. Mark.* Oxford: Oxford University Press, 1950.

B. Lindars, *NT Apologetic: The Doctrinal Significance of the OT Quotations.* London: SCM, 1961.

E. Lohmeyer, *Galiläa und Jerusalem.* Göttingen: Vandenhoeck & Ruprecht, 1936.

R. N. Longenecker, *Biblical Exegesis in the Apostolic Period.* Grand Rapids: Eerdmans, 1975.

———— (ed.), *The Challenge of Jesus' Parables.* Grand Rapids: Eerdmans, 2000.

B. L. Mack, *A Myth of Innocence.* Philadelphia: Fortress, 1988.

R. J. McKelvey, *The New Temple: The Church in the NT.* Oxford: Oxford University Press, 1969.

A. H. McNeile, *The Gospel according to St. Matthew.* London: Macmillan, 1915.

J. L. Magness, *Sense and Absence: Structure and Suspension in the Ending of Mark's Gospel.* Atlanta: Scholars Press, 1986.

J. Mann, *The Bible as Read and Preached in the Old Synagogue,* vol. 1. Cincinnati, 1940.

T. W. Manson, *The Teaching of Jesus: Studies of Its Form and Content.* 2d edn., Cambridge: Cambridge University Press, 1935.

————, *The Sayings of Jesus.* London: SCM, 1949.

J. Marcus, *The Mystery of the Kingdom of God* (SBLDS 90). Atlanta: Scholars Press, 1986.

————, *The Way of the Lord: Christological Exegesis of the OT in the Gospel of Mark.* Edinburgh: T. & T. Clark, 1993.

C. D. Marshall, *Faith as a Theme in Mark's Narrative* (SNTSM 64). Cambridge: CUP, 1989.

I. H. Marshall, *Last Supper and Lord's Supper.* Exeter: Paternoster, 1980.

E. L. Martin, *Secrets of Golgotha.* Alhambra, CA: ASK, 1988.

R. P. Martin, *Mark: Evangelist and Theologian.* Exeter: Paternoster, 1972.

W. Marxsen, *Mark the Evangelist: Studies on the Redaction History of the Gospel.* ET, Nashville: Abingdon, 1969.

F. J. Matera, *The Kingship of Jesus: Composition and Theology in Mark 15* (SBLDS 66). Chico, CA: Scholars Press, 1982.

———, *NT Christology*. Louisville: Westminster John Knox, 1999.

U. Mauser, *Christ in the Wilderness* (SBT 39). London: SCM, 1963.

B. M. Metzger, *The Text of the NT: Its Transmission, Corruption, and Restoration*. 2d edn., Oxford: Oxford University Press, 1968.

———, *A Textual Commentary on the Greek New Testament*. London/New York: United Bible Societies, 1971.

R. P. Meye, *Jesus and the Twelve: Discipleship and Revelation in Mark's Gospel*. Grand Rapids: Eerdmans, 1968.

B. F. Meyer, *The Aims of Jesus*. London: SCM, 1979.

E. M. Meyers and J. F. Strange, *Archaeology, the Rabbis and Early Christianity*. London: SCM, 1981.

J. Ramsey Michaels, *Servant and Son: Jesus in Parable and Gospel*. Atlanta: John Knox, 1981.

G. Minette de Tillesse, *Le Secret Messianique dans l'Évangile de Marc*. Paris: Cerf, 1968.

D. J. Moo, *The OT in the Gospel Passion Narratives*. Sheffield: Almond, 1983.

G. F. Moore, *Judaism in the First Centuries of the Christian Era*. 3 vols., Cambridge, MA: Harvard University Press, 1927-30.

L. Morris, *Studies in the Fourth Gospel*. Exeter: Paternoster, 1969.

C. F. D. Moule, *An Idiom-Book of NT Greek*. 2d edn., Cambridge: Cambridge University Press, 1960.

———, *The Origin of Christology*. Cambridge: Cambridge University Press, 1977.

F. Neirynck, *Duality in Mark: Contributions to the Study of the Markan Redaction* (BETL 31). Leuven University Press, 1972.

G. W. E. Nickelsburg, *Resurrection, Immortality, and Eternal Life in Intertestamental Judaism*. Cambridge, MA: Harvard University Press, 1972.

D. E. Oakman, *Jesus and the Economic Questions of His Day*. New York: Mellen, 1986.

G. R. Osborne, *The Resurrection Narratives: A Redactional Study*. Grand Rapids: Baker, 1984.

R. V. Peace, *Conversion in the NT: Paul and the Twelve*. Grand Rapids: Eerdmans, 1999.

N. Perrin, *Jesus and the Language of the Kingdom: Symbol and Metaphor in NT Interpretation*. Philadelphia: Fortress, 1976.

C. Perrot, *Jésus et l'Histoire*. Paris: Desclée, 1979.

J. Piper, *Love Your Enemies: Jesus' Love Command in the Synoptic Gospels and in the Early Christian Paraenesis* (SNTSM 38). Cambridge: Cambridge University Press, 1979.

E. J. Pryke, *Redactional Style in the Marcan Gospel: A Study of Syntax and Vocabulary as Guides to Redaction in Mark* (SNTSM 33). Cambridge: Cambridge University Press, 1978.

Q. Quesnell, *The Mind of Mark: Interpretation and Method through the Exegesis of Mark 6,52* (Analecta Biblica 38). Rome: Biblical Institute Press, 1969.

H. Räisänen, *Die Mutter Jesu im NT*. Helsinki, 1969.

———, *The 'Messianic Secret' in Mark*. ET, Edinburgh: T. & T. Clark, 1990.

D. Rhoads and D. Michie, *Mark as Story: An Introduction to the Narrative of a Gospel*. Philadelphia: Fortress, 1982.

J. Richards, *But Deliver Us from Evil*. London: Darton, Longman & Todd, 1974.

A. Richardson, *The Miracle-Stories of the Gospels.* London: SCM, 1941.

H. Riesenfeld, *Jésus Transfiguré* (ASNU 16). Copenhagen: Munksgaard, 1947.

J. A. T. Robinson, *Redating the NT.* London: SCM, 1976.

—————— (ed. J. F. Coakley), *The Priority of John.* London: SCM, 1985.

J. M. Robinson, *The Problem of History in Mark* (SBT 21). London: SCM, 1957.

C. Rowland, *The Open Heaven: A Study of Apocalyptic in Judaism and Early Christianity.* London: SPCK, 1982.

D. S. Russell, *The Method and Message of Jewish Apocalyptic, 200 BC–AD 100.* London: SCM, 1964.

M. Sabbe (ed.), *L'Évangile selon Marc: Tradition et rédaction* (BETL 34). Leuven University Press, 1974.

W. Sanday and A. C. Headlam, *The Epistle to the Romans* (ICC). Edinburgh: T. & T. Clark, 1902.

E. P. Sanders, *The Tendencies of the Synoptic Tradition* (SNTSM 9). Cambridge: Cambridge University Press, 1969.

——————, *Paul and Palestinian Judaism.* London: SCM, 1977.

——————, *Jesus and Judaism.* London: SCM, 1985.

——————, *Judaism: Practice and Belief, 63 BCE–66 CE.* London: SCM, 1992.

—————— and M. Davies, *Studying the Synoptic Gospels.* London: SCM, 1989.

P. E. Satterthwaite, R. S. Hess, and G. J. Wenham (ed.), *The Lord's Anointed: Interpretation of OT Messianic Texts.* Carlisle: Paternoster, 1995.

T. E. Schmidt, *Hostility to Wealth in the Synoptic Gospels* (JSNTS 15). Sheffield: JSOT, 1987.

H.-H. Schroeder, *Eltern und Kinder in der Verkündigung Jesu.* Hamburg: Herbert Reich, 1972.

E. Schürer, *The History of the Jewish People in the Age of Jesus Christ,* rev. and ed. by G. Vermes, F. Millar, M. Goodman, and M. Black. 3 vols., Edinburgh: T. & T. Clark, 1973, 1979, 1986/1987.

H. Schürmann, *Das Lukasevangelium I.* Freiburg: Herder, 1969.

C. H. H. Scobie, *John the Baptist.* London: SCM, 1964.

J. Sergeant, *Lion Let Loose: The Structure and Meaning of St. Mark's Gospel.* Exeter: Paternoster, 1988.

A. N. Sherwin-White, *Roman Society and Roman Law in the NT.* Oxford: Oxford University Press, 1963.

W. T. Shiner, *Follow Me! Disciples in Markan Rhetoric* (SBLDS 145). Atlanta: Scholars Press, 1995.

P. F. Shuler, *A Genre for the Gospels: The Biographical Character of Matthew.* Philadelphia: Fortress, 1982.

M. Smith, *Clement of Alexandria and a Secret Gospel of Mark.* Cambridge, MA: Harvard University Press, 1973.

——————, *The Secret Gospel.* New York: Harper & Row, 1973.

——————, *Jesus the Magician.* London: Gollancz, 1978.

K. Snodgrass, *The Parable of the Wicked Tenants* (WUNT 27). Tübingen: Mohr, 1983.

B. Standaert, *L'Évangile selon Marc: Composition et Genre Littéraire.* Brugge: Sint Andriesabdij, 1978.

G. N. Stanton, *Jesus of Nazareth in NT Preaching* (SNTSM 27). Cambridge: Cambridge University Press, 1974.

E. Stauffer, *Jesus and His Story.* ET, London: SCM, 1960.

R. H. Stein, *An Introduction to the Parables of Jesus.* Philadelphia: Westminster, 1981.

K. Stendahl, *The School of St. Matthew and Its Use of the OT.* Uppsala, 1954.

N. B. Stonehouse, *The Witness of Matthew and Mark to Christ.* London: Tyndale, 1944.

C. H. Talbert, *What Is a Gospel? The Genre of the Canonical Gospels.* Philadelphia: Fortress, 1977.

J. E. Taylor, *John the Baptist within Second Temple Judaism.* London: SPCK, 1997.

W. R. Telford, *The Barren Temple and the Withered Tree* (JSNTS 1). Sheffield: JSOT Press, 1980.

————— (ed.), *The Interpretation of Mark.* 2d edn., Edinburgh: T. & T. Clark, 1995.

—————, *The Theology of the Gospel of Mark.* Cambridge: Cambridge University Press, 1999.

G. Theissen, *The Miracle Stories of the Early Christian Tradition.* ET, Edinburgh: T. & T. Clark, 1983.

—————, *The Shadow of the Galilean.* ET, London: SCM, 1987.

—————, *The Gospels in Context: Social and Political History in the Synoptic Tradition.* Minneapolis: Fortress, 1991.

C. P. Thiede, *The Earliest Gospel Manuscript?: The Qumran Papyrus 7Q5 and Its Significance for NT Studies.* Carlisle: Paternoster, 1992.

D. L. Tiede, *The Charismatic Figure as Miracle-Worker* (SBLDS 1). Missoula: Scholars Press, 1972.

M. A. Tolbert, *Sowing the Gospel: Mark's World in Literary-Historical Perspective.* Minneapolis: Fortress, 1989.

É. Trocmé, *The Formation of the Gospel according to Mark.* ET, London: SPCK, 1975.

C. M. Tuckett (ed.), *The Messianic Secret.* London: SPCK, 1983.

————— (ed.), *Synoptic Studies.* Sheffield: JSOT Press, 1984.

————— (ed.), *The Scriptures in the Gospels* (BETL 131). Leuven University Press, 1997.

N. Turner, *A Grammar of NT Greek, vol. 3: Syntax.* Edinburgh: T. & T. Clark, 1963.

G. H. Twelftree, *Christ Triumphant.* London: Hodder & Stoughton, 1985.

B. M. F. Van Iersel, *Reading Mark.* ET, Edinburgh, T. & T. Clark, 1989.

P. A. Verhoef, *The Books of Haggai and Malachi.* Grand Rapids: Eerdmans, 1987.

G. Vermes, *Scripture and Tradition in Judaism.* Leiden: Brill, 1961.

—————, *Jesus the Jew: A Historian's Reading of the Gospels.* London: Collins, 1973.

—————, *Jesus and the World of Judaism.* London: SCM, 1983.

H. C. Waetjen, *A Reordering of Power: A Sociopolitical Reading of Mark's Gospel.* Minneapolis: Fortress, 1989.

R. E. Watts, *Isaiah's New Exodus and Mark* (WUNT 88). Tübingen: Mohr Siebeck, 1997.

R. L. Webb, *John the Baptizer and Prophet: A Socio-Historical Study* (JSNTS 62). Sheffield:Sheffield Academic Press, 1991.

A. J. M. Wedderburn, *Beyond Resurrection.* London: SCM, 1999.

D. Wenham, *The Rediscovery of Jesus' Eschatological Discourse* (*GP,* vol. 4). Sheffield: JSOT, 1984.

—————, *Paul: Follower of Jesus or Founder of Christianity?.* Grand Rapids: Eerdmans, 1995.

S. Westerholm, *Jesus and Scribal Authority.* Lund: Gleerup, 1978.

J. Wilkinson, *Jerusalem as Jesus Knew It: Archaeology as Evidence.* London: Thames & Hudson, 1978.

J. F. Williams, *Other Followers of Jesus: Minor Characters as Major Figures in Mark's Gospel* (JSNTS 102). Sheffield: Sheffield Academic Press, 1994.

J. G. Williams, *Gospel against Parable: Mark's Language of Mystery.* Sheffield: JSOT, 1985.

W. Wink, *John the Baptist in the Gospel Tradition* (SNTSM 7). Cambridge: Cambridge University Press, 1968.

N. T. Wright, *Jesus and the Victory of God* (Christian Origins and the Question of God 2). London: SPCK, 1996.

W. H. Wuellner, *The Meaning of 'Fishers of Men'.* Philadelphia: Westminster, 1967.

F. Zimmermann, *The Aramaic Origin of the Four Gospels.* New York, 1979.

3. Articles

P. J. Achtemeier, 'Person and Deed: Jesus and the Storm-tossed Sea', *Int* 16 (1962) 169-176.

———, 'Toward the Isolation of Pre-Markan Miracle Catenae', *JBL* 89 (1970) 265-91.

———, 'The Origin and Function of the Pre-Markan Miracle Catenae', *JBL* 91 (1972) 198-221.

———, 'Miracles and the Historical Jesus: A Study of Mark 9:14-29', *CBQ* 37 (1975) 471-91.

B. Ahern, 'Staff or No Staff', *CBQ* 5 (1943) 332-37.

D. E. Aune, 'The Problem of the Genre of the Gospels: A Critique of C. H. Talbert's *What Is a Gospel?*', in R. T. France and D. Wenham (ed.), *GP,* 2. 9-60.

N. Avigad, 'A Depository of Inscribed Ossuaries in the Kidron Valley', *IEJ* 12 (1962) 1-12.

T. J. Baarda, 'Mark 9,49', *NTS* 5 (1958/9) 318-21.

———, 'Gadarenes, Gerasenes, Gergesenes and the "Diatessaron" Tradition', in E. E. Ellis and M. Wilcox (ed.), *Neotestamentica et Semitica* (FS M. Black). Edinburgh: T. & T. Clark, 1969, 181-97.

G. J. Bahr, 'The Seder of Passover and the Eucharistic Words', *NovT* 12 (1970) 181-202.

K. E. Bailey, 'The Fall of Jerusalem and Mark's Account of the Cross', *ExpTim* 102 (1990/1) 102-5.

E. Bammel, 'Crucifixion as a Punishment in Palestine', in E. Bammel (ed.), *Trial,* 162-65.

———, 'Markus 10,11f und das jüdische Eherecht', *ZNW* 61 (1970) 95-101.

———, 'The Titulus', in E. Bammel and C. F. D. Moule (ed.), *Politics,* 353-64.

———, 'The Trial before Pilate', in E. Bammel and C. F. D. Moule (ed.), *Politics,* 415-51.

J. M. G. Barclay, 'Mirror-reading a Polemical Letter: Galatians as a Test-case', *JSNT* 31 (1987) 73-93.

P. W. Barnett, '"Under Tiberius All Was Quiet"', *NTS* 21 (1974/5) 564-71.

J. Barr, '"Abba Isn't "Daddy"', *JTS* 39 (1988) 28-47.

C. K. Barrett, 'The House of Prayer and the Den of Thieves', in E. E. Ellis and E. Grässer (ed.), *Jesus und Paulus* (FS W. G. Kümmel). Göttingen: Vandenhoeck & Ruprecht, 1975, 13-20.

R. J. Bauckham, 'Synoptic Parousia Parables and the Apocalypse', *NTS* 23 (1976/7) 162-76.

———, 'Salome the Sister of Jesus, Salome the Disciple of Jesus, and the Secret Gospel of Mark', *NovT* 33 (1991) 245-75.

W. Bauer, 'The "Colt" of Palm Sunday', *JBL* 72 (1953) 220-29.

BIBLIOGRAPHY

N. A. Beck, 'Reclaiming a Biblical Text: The Mark 8:14-21 Discussion about the Bread in the Boat', *CBQ* 43 (1981) 49-56.

W. J. Bennett, 'The Herodians of Mark's Gospel', *NovT* 17 (1975) 9-14.

P. Benoit, 'Prétoire, Lithostroton et Gabbatha', *RB* 59 (1952) 531-50.

———, 'Les outrages à Jésus prophète (Mc xiv 65 par.)', in W. C. Van Unnik (ed.), *Neotestamentica et Patristica* (FS O. Cullmann; SNT 6). Leiden: Brill, 1962, 92-110.

K. Berger, 'Zur Geschichte der Einleitungsformel "Amen, ich sage euch"', *ZNW* 63 (1972) 45-75.

E. Best, 'Mark III.20, 21, 31-35', *NTS* 22 (1975/6) 309-19 (= *Disciples*, 49-63).

———, 'Mark's Narrative Technique', *JSNT* 37 (1989) 43-58.

J. N. Birdsall, 'Τὸ ῥῆμα ὡς εἶπεν αὐτῷ ὁ Ἰησοῦς: Mark xiv.72', *NovT* 2 (1958) 272-75.

———, 'The Withering of the Fig-Tree', *ExpTim* 73 (1961/2) 190-91.

D. A. Black, 'The Text of Mark 6.20', *NTS* 34 (1988) 141-45.

J. Blenkinsopp, 'The Oracle of Judah and the Messianic Entry', *JBL* 80 (1961) 55-64.

C. Bonner, 'Traces of Thaumaturgic Technique in the Miracles', *HTR* 20 (1927) 171-81.

G. H. Boobyer, 'The Eucharistic Interpretation of the Miracles of the Loaves in St. Mark's Gospel', *JTS* 3 (1952) 161-71.

———, 'Mark II.10a and the Interpretation of the Healing of the Paralytic', *HTR* 47 (1954) 115-20.

———, ' Ἀπέχει in Mark xiv.41', *NTS* 2 (1955/6) 44-48.

G. Bornkamm, 'Die Sturmstillung im Matthäus-Evangelium', *Wort und Dienst* (1948) 49-54; ET in G. Bornkamm, G. Barth, and H. J. Held, *Tradition and Interpretation in Matthew*. ET, London: SCM, 1963, 52-57.

F. H. Borsch, 'Mark xiv.62 and 1 Enoch lxii.5', *NTS* 14 (1967/8) 565-67.

L. C. Boughton, '"Being Shed for You/Many": Time-sense and Consequences in the Synoptic Cup Quotations', *TynB* 48 (1997) 249-70.

D. Brady, 'The Alarm to Peter in Mark's Gospel', *JSNT* 4 (1979) 42-57.

R. G. Bratcher, 'A Note on Mark XI,3', *ExpTim* 64 (1952/3) 93.

P. G. Bretscher, 'Exodus 4:22-23 and the Voice from Heaven', *JBL* 87 (1968) 301-11.

D. I. Brewer, 'Review Article: The Use of Rabbinic Sources in Gospel Studies', *TynB* 50 (1999) 281-98.

K. E. Brower, 'Mark 9:1: Seeing the Kingdom in Power', *JSNT* 6 (1980) 17-41.

———, 'Elijah in the Markan Passion Narrative', *JSNT* 18 (1983) 85-101.

———, '"Let the Reader Understand": Temple and Eschatology in Mark', in K. E. Brower and M. W. Elliott (ed.), *Reader*, 119-43.

R. E. Brown, 'The Pre-Christian Semitic Concept of "Mystery"', *CBQ* 20 (1958) 417-43.

———, 'The Semitic Background of the NT Mysterion', *Bib* 39 (1958) 426-48; 40 (1959) 70-87.

———, 'The Burial of Jesus (Mark 15:42-47)', *CBQ* 50 (1988) 233-45.

S. G. Browne, 'Leprosy: The Christian Attitude', *ExpTim* 73 (1961/2) 242-45.

F. F. Bruce, 'The Book of Zechariah and the Passion Narrative', *BJRL* 43 (1960/1) 336-53.

———, 'Render to Caesar', in E. Bammel and C. F. D. Moule (ed.), *Politics*, 249-63.

G. W. Buchanan, 'Jesus and the Upper Class', *NovT* 7 (1964) 195-209.

C. Burchard, 'Das doppelte Liebesgebot in der frühen christlichen Überlieferung', in E. Lohse (ed.), *Das Ruf Jesu und die Antwort der Gemeinde* (FS J. Jeremias). Göttingen: Vandenhoeck & Ruprecht, 1970, 39-62.

R. Buth, 'Mark 3:17 ΒΟΝΕΡΕΓΕΜ and Popular Etymology', *JSNT* 10 (1981) 29-33.

M. Casey, 'The Original Aramaic Form of Jesus' Interpretation of the Cup', *JTS* 41 (1990) 1-12.

———, 'The Date of the Passover Sacrifices and Mark 14:12', *TynB* 48 (1997) 245-47.

D. R. Catchpole, 'The Answer of Jesus to Caiaphas (Matthew xxvi.64)', *NTS* 17 (1970/1) 213-26.

———, 'The Synoptic Divorce Material as a Traditio-Historical Problem', *BJRL* 57 (1974/5) 92-127.

———, 'The "Triumphal" Entry', in E. Bammel and C. F. D. Moule (ed.), *Politics,* 319-34.

C. H. Cave, 'The Leper: Mark 1.40-45', *NTS* 25 (1978/9) 245-50.

C. P. Ceroke, 'Is Mark 2:10 a Saying of Jesus?', *CBQ* 22 (1960) 369-90.

C. B. Chavel, 'The Releasing of a Prisoner on the Eve of Passover in Ancient Jerusalem', *JBL* 60 (1941) 273-78.

B. D. Chilton, 'Jesus *ben David:* Reflections on the *Davidssohnfrage*', *JSNT* 14 (1982) 88-112.

H. L. Chronis, 'The Torn Veil: Cultus and Christology in Mark 15:37-39', *JBL* 101 (1982) 97-114.

D. M. Cohn-Sherbok, 'An Analysis of Jesus' Arguments concerning the Plucking of Grain on the Sabbath', *JSNT* 2 (1979) 31-41.

———, 'Jesus' Defence of the Resurrection of the Dead', *JSNT* 11 (1981) 64-73.

A. Y. Collins, 'The Appropriation of the Psalms of Individual Lament by Mark', in C. M. Tuckett (ed.), *The Scriptures in the Gospels,* 223-41.

L. W. Countryman, 'How Many Baskets Full? Mark 8:14-21 and the Value of the Miracles in Mark', *CBQ* 47 (1985) 643-55.

J. D. Crossan, 'Mark and the Relatives of Jesus', *NovT* 15 (1973) 81-113.

———, 'The Parable of the Wicked Husbandmen', *JBL* 90 (1971) 451-65.

B. Couroyer, 'De la mesure dont vous mesurez il vous sera mesuré', *RB* 77 (1970) 366-70.

R. J. Daly, 'The Soteriological Significance of the Sacrifice of Isaac', *CBQ* 39 (1977) 45-75.

F. W. Danker, 'Mark 8,7', *JBL* 82 (1963) 215-16.

———, 'The Literary Unity of Mark 14:1-25', *JBL* 85 (1966) 467-72.

D. Daube, 'Responsibilities of Master and Disciples in the Gospels', *NTS* 19 (1972/3) 1-15.

P. R. Davies and B. D. Chilton, 'The Aqedah: A Revised Tradition History', *CBQ* 40 (1978) 514-46.

S. L. Davies, 'Who Is Called Bar Abbas?', *NTS* 27 (1980/1) 260-62.

P. G. Davis, 'Mark's Christological Paradox', *JSNT* 35 (1989) 3-18.

B. Dehandschutter, 'La parabole des vignerons homicides (Mc., XII,1-12) et l'évangile selon Thomas', in M. Sabbe (ed.), *Marc,* 203-19.

G. Delling, 'Βάπτισμα, βαπτισθῆναι', *NovT* 2 (1957) 92-115.

J. D. M. Derrett, 'The Anointing at Bethany', *SE* 2 (1964) 174-82 (repr. in Derrett, *Law,* 266-75).

———, 'The Stone That the Builders Rejected', *SE* 4 (1968) 180-86.

———, 'Law in the NT: The Palm Sunday Colt', *NovT* 13 (1971) 241-58.

———, '"Eating Up the Houses of Widows": Jesus' Comment on Lawyers', *NovT* 14 (1972) 1-9.

BIBLIOGRAPHY

————, 'Figtrees in the NT', *HeyJ* 14 (1973) 249-65.

————, 'Salted with Fire: Studies in Texts: Mark 9:42-50', *Theology* 76 (1973) 364-68.

————, 'Allegory and the Wicked Vinedressers', *JTS* 25 (1974) 426-32.

————, 'ἦσαν γὰρ ἁλιεῖς (Mk. I 16): Jesus' Fishermen and the Parable of the Net', *NovT* 22 (1980) 108-37.

————, 'Why and How Jesus Walked on the Sea', *NovT* 23 (1981) 330-48.

K. E. Dewey, 'Peter's Curse and Cursed Peter (Mark 14:53-54, 66-72)', in W. H. Kelber (ed.), *Passion,* 96-114.

J. R. Donahue, 'Tax Collectors and Sinners: An Attempt at Identification', *CBQ* 33 (1971) 39-61.

G. Dow, 'The Case for the Existence of Demons', *Churchman* 94 (1980) 199-208.

F. G. Downing, 'The Resurrection of the Dead: Jesus and Philo', *JSNT* 15 (1982) 42-50.

F. Dreyfus, 'L'argument scripturaire de Jésus en faveur de la résurrection des morts (Marc, XII,26-27)', *RB* 66 (1959) 213-24.

J. Drury, 'The Sower, the Vineyard, and the Place of Allegory in the Interpretation of Mark's Parables', *JTS* 24 (1973) 367-79.

I. Duguid, 'Messianic Themes in Zechariah 9–14', in P. E. Satterthwaite, et al. (ed.), *Anointed,* 265-80.

D. C. Duling, 'Solomon, Exorcism, and the Son of David', *HTR* 68 (1975) 235-52.

J. D. G. Dunn, 'Jesus and Ritual Purity: A Study of the Tradition-History of Mark 7.15', in *Jesus, Paul and the Law.* London: SPCK, 1990, 37-60.

P. Ellingworth, 'Text and Context in Mark 10:2,10', *JSNT* 5 (1979) 63-66.

J. K. Elliott, 'The Conclusion of the Pericope of the Healing of the Leper and Mark 1.45', *JTS* 22 (1971) 153-57.

————, 'The Text and Language of the Endings to Mark's Gospel', *TZ* 27 (1971) 255-62.

————, 'The Anointing of Jesus', *ExpTim* 85 (1973/4) 105-7.

————, '*Ho baptizōn* and Mark 1.4', *TZ* 31 (1975) 14-15.

————, 'Is ὁ ἐξελθών a Title for Jesus in Mark 1:45?', *JTS* 27 (1976) 402-5.

E. E. Ellis, 'Deity-Christology in Mark 14:58', in J. B. Green and M. M. B. Turner (ed.), *Jesus of Nazareth: Lord and Christ* (FS I. H. Marshall). Grand Rapids: Eerdmans, 1994, 192-203.

V. Eppstein, 'The Historicity of the Gospel Account of the Cleansing of the Temple', *ZNW* 55 (1964) 42-58.

C. A. Evans, 'On the Vineyard Parables of Isaiah 5 and Mark 12', *BZ* 28 (1984) 82-86.

————, 'Jesus' Action in the Temple: Cleansing or Portent of Destruction?', *CBQ* 51 (1989) 237-70.

C. F. Evans, 'I will go before you into Galilee', *JTS* 5 (1954) 3-18.

A. Feuillet, 'Le sens du mot Parousie dans l'évangile de Matthieu', in W. D. Davies and D. Daube (ed.), *The Background of the NT and Its Eschatology* (FS C. H. Dodd). Cambridge: Cambridge University Press, 1956, 261-80.

————, 'La coupe et le baptême de la Passion', *RB* 74 (1967) 356-91.

————, 'Le "Commencement" de l'économie Chrétienne d'après He. 2:3-4, Mc. 1:1 et Ac. 1:1-2', *NTS* 24 (1978) 163-74.

J. A. Fitzmyer, 'The Aramaic Qorban Inscription from Jebel Hallet Et-turi and Mk 7:11/ Mt 15:5', *JBL* 78 (1959) 60-65.

————, 'The Use of *Agein* and *Pherein* in the Synoptic Gospels', in E. H. Barth and R. E. Cocroft (ed.), *Festschrift to Honor F. Wilbur Gingrich.* Leiden: Brill, 1972, 147-60.

————, 'Aramaic *Kepha* and Peter's Name in the NT', in E. Best and R. McL. Wilson (ed.), *Text and Interpretation* (FS M. Black). Cambridge: Cambridge University Press, 1979, 121-32.

H. Fleddermann, 'The Flight of a Naked Young Man (Mark 14:51-52)', *CBQ* 41 (1979) 412-18.

————, 'A Warning about the Scribes (Mark 12:37b-40)', *CBQ* 44 (1982) 52-67.

————, '"And he wanted to pass by them" (Mark 6:48c)', *CBQ* 45 (1983) 389-95.

C. Fletcher-Louis, 'The Destruction of the Temple and the Relativization of the Old Covenant: Mark 13:31 and Matthew 5:18', in K. E. Brower and M. W. Elliott (ed.), *Reader,* 145-69.

J. M. Ford, 'Money "bags" in the Temple (Mk 11,16)', *Bib* 57 (1976) 249-53.

R. T. France, 'The Servant of the Lord in the Teaching of Jesus', *TynB* 19 (1968) 26-52.

————, 'Mark and the Teaching of Jesus', in R. T. France and D. Wenham (ed.), *GP,* 1. Sheffield: JSOT Press, 1980, 101-36.

————, 'Chronological Aspects of "Gospel Harmony"', *Vox Evangelica* 16 (1986) 33-59.

R. W. Funk, 'The Looking-Glass Tree Is for the Birds; Ezekiel 17:22-24; Mark 4:30-32', *Int* 27 (1973) 3-9.

P. H. Furfey, 'Christ as *Tekton*', *CBQ* 17 (1955) 204-15.

P. J. Gannon, 'Could Mark employ *auton* in 3,21 referring to *ochlos* in 3,20?', *CBQ* 15 (1953) 460-61.

P. Garnet, 'The Baptism of Jesus and the Son of Man Idea', *JSNT* 9 (1980) 49-65.

L. Gaston, 'Beelzebul', *TZ* 18 (1962) 247-55.

B. Gerhardsson, 'The Parable of the Sower and Its Interpretation', *NTS* 14 (1967/8) 165-93.

C. H. Giblin, '"The Things of God" in the Question concerning Tribute to Caesar', *CBQ* 33 (1971) 510-27.

J. B. Gibson, 'The Rebuke of the Disciples in Mark 8:14-21', *JSNT* 27 (1986) 31-47.

————, 'Jesus' Refusal to Produce a "Sign" (Mark 8:11-13)', *JSNT* 38 (1990) 37-66.

T. F. Glasson, 'Davidic Links with the Betrayal of Jesus', *ExpTim* 85 (1973/4) 118-19.

A. M. Goldberg, 'Sitzend zur Rechten der Kraft: Zur Gottesbezeichnung Gebura in der frühen rabbinischen Literatur', *BZ* 8 (1964) 284-93.

H. Gollwitzer, 'Liberation in History', *Int* 28 (1974) 404-21.

M. D. Goulder, 'On Putting Q to the Test', *NTS* 24 (1977/8) 218-34.

————, 'The Order of a Crank', in C. M. Tuckett (ed.), *Studies,* 111-30.

K. Grayston, 'The Study of Mark XIII', *BJRL* 56 (1973/4) 371-87.

J. H. Greenlee, 'Εἰς μνημόσυνον αὐτῆς, "For her Memorial": Mt xxvi.13, Mk xiv.9', *ExpTim* 71 (1959/60) 245.

K. Grobel, 'He That Cometh after Me', *JBL* 60 (1941) 397-401.

J. J. Gunther, 'The Fate of the Jerusalem Church: The Flight to Pella', *TZ* 29 (1973) 81-84.

G. Hartmann, 'Markus 3,20f', *BZ* 11 (1913) 249-79.

A. E. Harvey, 'The Use of Mystery Language in the Bible', *JTS* 31 (1980) 320-36.

N. Q. Hamilton, 'Temple Cleansing and Temple Bank', *JBL* 83 (1964) 365-72.

P. B. Harner, 'Qualitative Anarthrous Predicate Nouns: Mark 15:39 and John 1:1', *JBL* 92 (1973) 75-87.

H. StJ. Hart, 'The Crown of Thorns in John 19.2-5', *JTS* 3 (1952) 66-75.

————, 'The Coin of "Render unto Caesar . . ." (A Note on Some Aspects of Mark

12:13-17; Matt. 22:12-22; Luke 20:20-26)', in E. Bammel and C. F. D. Moule (ed.), *Politics,* 241-48.

N. Hass, 'Anthropological Observations on the Skeletal Remains from Giv'at ha-Mivtar', *IEJ* 20 (1970) 49-59.

L. S. Hay, 'The Son of Man in Mark 2:10 and 2:28', *JBL* 89 (1970) 69-75.

M. Hengel, 'Mk 7,3 πυγμῇ: Die Geschichte einer exegetischen Aporie und der Versuch ihrer Lösung', *ZNW* 60 (1969) 182-98.

J. Héring, 'Zwei exegetische Probleme in der Perikope von Jesus in Gethsemane', in W. C. Van Unnik (ed.), *Neotestamentica et Patristica* (FS O. Cullmann; SNT 6). Leiden: Brill, 1962, 64-69.

J. D. Hester, 'Socio-Rhetorical Criticism and the Parable of the Tenants', *JSNT* 45 (1992) 27-57.

R. H. Hiers, 'Not the Season for Figs', *JBL* 87 (1968) 394-400.

B. Hollenbach, 'Lest They Should Turn and Be Forgiven: Irony', *BT* 34 (1983) 312-21.

M. D. Hooker, 'Trial and Tribulation in Mark XIII', *BJRL* 65 (1982/3) 78-99.

———, '"What Doest Thou Here, Elijah?": A Look at St Mark's Account of the Transfiguration', in L. D. Hurst and N. T. Wright (ed.), *The Glory of Christ in the NT.* Oxford: Oxford University Press, 1987, 59-70.

T. Ilan, 'Notes on the Distribution of Jewish Women's Names in Palestine in the Second Temple and Mishnaic Periods', *JJS* 40 (1989) 186-200.

H. M. Jackson, 'The Death of Jesus in Mark and the Miracle from the Cross', *NTS* 33 (1987) 16-37.

H. Jahnow, 'Das Abdecken des Daches Mc 2,4; Lk 5,19', *ZNW* 24 (1925) 155-58.

J. Jeremias, 'Markus 14:9', *ZNW* 44 (1952/3) 103-7.

———, 'Paarweise Sendung im NT', in A. J. B. Higgins (ed.), *NT Essays* (FS T. W. Manson). Manchester: Manchester University Press, 1959, 136-43.

———, 'Palästinakundliches zum Gleichnis vom Sämann', *NTS* 13 (1966/7) 48-53.

———, 'Zum nichtresponsorischen Amen', *ZNW* 64 (1973) 122-23.

E. S. Johnson, 'Mark viii.22-26: The Blind Man from Bethsaida', *NTS* 25 (1978/9) 370-83.

———, 'Is Mark 15.39 the Key to Mark's Christology?', *JSNT* 31 (1987) 3-22.

S. R. Johnson, 'The Identity and Significance of the *Neaniskos* in Mark', *Forum* 8 (1992) 123-39.

D. R. Jones, 'A Fresh Interpretation of Zechariah IX-XI', *VT* 12 (1962) 256-58.

L. E. Keck, 'Mark 3:7-12 and Mark's Christology', *JBL* 84 (1965) 341-58.

———, 'The Introduction to Mark's Gospel', *NTS* 12 (1965/6) 352-70.

———, 'Toward the Renewal of NT Christology', *NTS* 32 (1986) 362-77.

A. Kee, 'The Old Coat and the New Wine: A Parable of Repentance', *NovT* 12 (1970) 13-21.

H. C. Kee, 'Aretalogy and Gospel', *JBL* 92 (1973) 402-22.

———, 'The Terminology of Mark's Exorcism Stories', *NTS* 14 (1967/8) 232-46.

———, 'The Transfiguration in Mark: Epiphany or Apocalyptic Vision?', in J. Reumann (ed.), *Understanding the Sacred Text* (FS M. S. Enslin). Valley Forge: Judson, 1972, 137-52.

R. Kempthorne, 'The Markan Text of Jesus' Answer to the High Priest (Mark xiv.62)', *NovT* 19 (1977) 197-208.

A. Kenny, 'The Transfiguration and the Agony in the Garden', *CBQ* 19 (1957) 444-52.

P. Ketter, 'Zur Localisierung der Blindenheilung bei Jericho', *Bib* 15 (1934) 411-18.

BIBLIOGRAPHY

G. D. Kilpatrick, 'The Gentile Mission in Mark and Mk 13,9-10', in D. E. Nineham (ed.), *Studies in the Gospels* (FS R. H. Lightfoot). Oxford: Blackwells, 1955, 145-58.

————, 'Mk 13,9-10', *JTS* 9 (1958) 81-86.

————, 'Jesus, His Family and His Disciples', *JSNT* 15 (1982) 3-19.

J. D. Kingsbury, 'The "Divine Man" as the Key to Mark's Christology — The End of an Era?', *Int* 35 (1981) 243-57.

H.-J. Klauck, 'Die Frage der Sündenvergebung in der Perikope von der Heilung des Gelähmten (Mk 2,1-12 parr)', *BZ* 25 (1981) 223-48.

J. Knackstedt, 'Die beiden Brotvermehrungen im Evangelium', *NTS* 10 (1963/4) 309-35.

D. A. Koch, 'Inhaltliche Gliederung und geographischer Aufriss im Markusevangelium', *NTS* 29 (1983) 145-66.

H. Kosmala, 'The Time of the Cock-Crow', *ASTI* 2 (1963) 118-20; 6 (1968) 132-34.

S. Krauss, 'Das Abdecken des Daches Mc 2,4, Lc 5,19', *ZNW* 25 (1926) 307-10.

H. Kruse, 'Die "Dialektische Negation" als semitisches Idiom', *VT* 4 (1954) 385-400.

H.-W. Kuhn, 'Das Reittier Jesu in der Einzugsgeschichte des Markusevangeliums', *ZNW* 50 (1959) 82-91.

K. Lake, ''Εμβριμησάμενος and ὀργισθείς (Mark 1,40-43)', *HTR* 16 (1923) 197-98.

J. Lambrecht, 'Redaction and Theology in MK., IV', in M. Sabbe (ed.), *Marc,* 269-307.

G. W. H. Lampe, 'St. Peter's Denial', *BJRL* 55 (1972/3) 346-68.

————, 'The Two Swords (Luke 22:35-38)', in E. Bammel and C. F. D. Moule (ed.), *Politics,* 335-51.

S. Légasse, 'Approche de l'episode préévangélique des Fils de Zébédée', *NTS* 20 (1974) 161-77.

E. E. Lemcio, 'External Evidence for the Structure and Function of Mark iv.1-20, vii.14-23 and viii.14-21', *JTS* 29 (1978) 323-38.

F. Lentzen-Deis, 'Das Motif der "Himmelsöffnung" in verschiedenen Gattungen der Umweltliteratur des NT', *Bib* 50 (1969) 301-27.

W. L. Liefeld, 'Theological Motifs in the Transfiguration Narrative', in R. N. Longenecker and M. C. Tenney (ed.), *New Dimensions in NT Study.* Grand Rapids: Zondervan, 1974, 162-79.

A. T. Lincoln, 'The Promise and the Failure: Mark 16:7,8', *JBL* 108 (1989) 283-300.

B. Lindars, 'Matthew, Levi, Lebbaeus and the Value of the Western Text', *NTS* 4 (1957/8) 220-22.

————, 'Two Parables in John', *NTS* 16 (1969/70) 318-29.

O. Linton, 'The Demand for a Sign from Heaven (Mk 8,11-12 and parallels)', *ST* 19 (1965) 112-29.

H. K. McArthur, 'On the Third Day', *NTS* 18 (1971/2) 81-86.

————, 'Son of Mary', *NovT* 15 (1973) 38-58.

S. V. McCasland, 'Signs and Wonders', *JBL* 76 (1957) 149-52.

C. C. McCown, 'ὁ τέκτων', in S. J. Case (ed.), *Studies in Early Christianity.* Chicago: University of Chicago Press, 1928, 173-89.

————, 'Luke's Translation of Semitic into Hellenistic Custom', *JBL* 58 (1939) 213-20.

F. R. McCurley, '"And after Six Days" (Mark 9:2): A Semitic Literary Device', *JBL* 93 (1974) 67-81.

J. I. H. McDonald, 'Receiving and Entering the Kingdom: A Study of Mark 10,15', *SE* 6 (1973) 328-32.

R. McKinnis, 'An Analysis of Mark X,32-34', *NovT* 18 (1976) 81-100.

A. Mahoney, 'A New Look at "The Third Hour" of Mk 15,25', *CBQ* 28 (1966) 292-99.

E. S. Malbon, 'TH OIKIA AYTOY: Mark 2.15 in Context', *NTS* 31 (1985) 282-92.

———, 'The Poor Widow in Mark and Her Poor Rich Readers', *CBQ* 53 (1991) 589-604.

J. Mánek, 'Mark viii.14-21', *NovT* 7 (1964) 10-14.

T. W. Manson, 'The Cleansing of the Temple', *BJRL* 33 (1951) 271-82.

J. Marcus, 'Scripture and Tradition in Mark 7', in C. M. Tuckett (ed.), *The Scriptures in the Gospels,* 177-95.

I. H. Marshall, 'Son of God or Servant of Yahweh? — A Reconsideration of Mark 1:11', *NTS* 15 (1968/9) 326-36.

———, 'The Meaning of the Verb "to baptize"', *EQ* 45 (1973) 130-40.

B. A. Mastin, 'The Date of the Triumphal Entry', *NTS* 16 (1969/70) 76-82.

S. Masuda, 'The Good News of the Miracle of the Bread', *NTS* 28 (1982) 191-219.

H. Merkel, 'Peter's Curse', in E. Bammel (ed.), *Trial,* 66-71.

R. L. Merritt, 'Jesus Barabbas and the Paschal Pardon', *JBL* 104 (1985) 57-68.

R. P. Meye, 'Mark 4.10: "Those about him with the Twelve"', *SE* 2 (1964) 211-18.

———, 'Psalm 107 as "Horizon" for Interpretating the Miracle Stories of Mark 4:35–8:26', in R. A. Guelich (ed.), *Unity and Diversity in NT Theology* (FS G. E. Ladd). Grand Rapids: Eerdmans, 1978, 1-13.

O. Michel, 'Eine philologische Frage zur Einzugsgeschicht', *NTS* 6 (1959/60) 81-82.

D. L. Miller, 'EMΠAIZEIN: Playing the Mock Game (Luke 22:63-64)', *JBL* 90 (1971) 309-13.

J. V. Miller, 'The Time of the Crucifixion', *JETS* 26 (1983) 157-66.

P. S. Minear, 'Audience Criticism and Markan Ecclesiology', in H. Baltensweiler and B. Reicke (ed.), *NT und Geschichte* (FS O. Cullmann). Zürich: Theologischer Verlag, 1972, 79-89.

H. W. Montefiore, 'Josephus and the NT', *NovT* 4 (1960) 139-60, 307-18.

———, 'Revolt in the Desert? (Mark vi.30ff)', *NTS* 8 (1961/2) 135-41.

W. E. Moore, '"Outside" and "Inside": A Markan Motif', *ExpTim* 98 (1986/7) 39-43.

S. Morag, ''Εφφαθά (Mark vii.34): Certainly Hebrew, Not Aramaic?', *JSS* 17 (1972) 198-202.

S. Motyer, 'The Rending of the Veil: A Markan Pentecost?', *NTS* 33 (1987) 155-57.

W. J. Moulder, 'The OT Background and the Interpretation of Mark x.45', *NTS* 24 (1977) 120-27.

C. F. D. Moule, 'Mark 4:1-20 Yet Once More', in E. E. Ellis and M. Wilcox (ed.), *Neotestamentica et Semitica* (FS M. Black). Edinburgh: T. & T. Clark, 1969, 95-113.

J. B. Muddiman, 'Jesus and Fasting: Mark ii.18-22', in J. Dupont (ed.), *Jésus aux Origines de la Christologie* (BETL 40). Gembloux: Duculot, 1975, 271-81.

A. Negoita and C. Daniel, 'L'énigme du levain. Ad Mc. viii.15; Mt. xvi.6; et Lc. xii.1', *NovT* 9 (1967) 306-14.

J. E. and R. R. Newell, 'The Parable of the Wicked Tenants', *NovT* 14 (1972) 226-37.

J. O'Callaghan, 'Papiros neotestamentarios en la cueva 7 de Qumran?', *Bib* 53 (1972) 91-100. ET in *JBL* 91 (1972), supplement 2.1-14.

G. Ogg, 'The Chronology of the Last Supper', in D. E. Nineham et al., *History and Chronology in the NT.* London: SPCK, 1965, 75-96.

D. Palmer, 'Defining a Vow of Abstinence', *Colloquium* 5/2 (1973) 38-41.

D. W. Palmer, 'The Origin, Form and Purpose of Mark xvi.4 in Codex Bobiensis', *JTS* 27 (1976) 113-22.

P. B. Payne, 'The Order of Sowing and Ploughing in the Parable of the Sower', *NTS* 25 (1978/9) 123-29.

———, 'The Authenticity of the Parable of the Sower and Its Interpretation', in *GP*, 1.163-207.

———, 'The Seeming Inconsistency of the Interpretation of the Parable of the Sower', *NTS* 26 (1980) 564-68.

N. Perrin, 'The High Priest's Question and Jesus' Answer (Mark 14:61-62)', in W. H. Kelber (ed.), *Passion,* 80-95.

R. Pesch, 'Levi-Matthäus (Mc 2,14/Mt 9,9; 10,3): Ein Beitrag zur Lösung eines alten Problems', *ZNW* 59 (1968) 40-56.

N. R. Petersen, 'When Is the End Not the End? Literary Reflections on the Ending of Mark's Narrative', *Int* 34 (1980) 151-66.

J. Pobee, 'The Cry of the Centurion — A Cry of Defeat', in E. Bammel (ed.), *Trial,* 91-102.

I. Rabinowitz, '"Be Opened" = Ἐφφαθά (Mark 7,34): Did Jesus Speak Hebrew?', *ZNW* 53 (1962) 229-38.

———, 'ΕΦΦΑΘΑ (Mark VII.34): Certainly Hebrew, Not Aramaic', *JSS* 16 (1971) 151-56.

B. Reicke, 'Synoptic Prophecies on the Destruction of Jerusalem', in D. E. Aune (ed.), *Studies in NT and Early Christian Literature* (FS A. P. Wikgren). Leiden: Brill, 1972, 121-34.

J. H. Reumann, 'Psalm 22 at the Cross: Lament and Thanksgiving for Jesus Christ', *Int* 28 (1974) 39-58.

R. Riesner, 'Bethany beyond the Jordan', *TynB* 38 (1987) 29-63.

V. K. Robbins, 'Last Meal: Preparation, Betrayal and Absence (Mark 14:12-25)', in W. H. Kelber (ed.), *Passion,* 21-40.

A. de Q. Robin, 'The Cursing of the Fig Tree in Mark', *NTS* 8 (1961/2) 276-81.

K. Romaniuk, 'Car ce n'était pas la saison des figues (Mk 11,12-14 parr.)', *ZNW* 66 (1975) 275-78.

J. M. Ross, 'With the Fist', *ExpTim* 87 (1975/6) 374-75.

C. Roth, 'The Cleansing of the Temple and Zechariah XIV.21', *NovT* 4 (1960) 172-81.

H. H. Rowley, 'Jewish Proselyte Baptism and the Baptism of John', in his *From Moses to Qumran.* London: Lutterworth, 1963, 211-35.

H. P. Rüger, '"Mit welchem Mass ihr messt, wird euch gemessen werden"', *ZNW* 60 (1969) 174-82.

M. Sabin, 'Reading Mark 4 as Midrash', *JSNT* 45 (1992) 3-26.

H. Sahlin, 'Die Perikope vom gerasenischen Besessenen und der Plan des Markus-evangeliums', *ST* 18 (1964) 159-72.

E. P. Sanders, 'Priorités et dépendance dans la tradition synoptique', *RSR* 60 (1972) 519-40.

———, 'The Overlaps of Mark and Q and the Synoptic Problem', *NTS* 19 (1972/3) 453-65.

B. Schaller, '"Commits adultery with her" not "against her", Mark 10:11', *ExpTim* 83 (1971/2) 107-8.

F. A. Schilling, 'What Means the Saying about Receiving the Kingdom of God as a Little Child (Mk X.15; Lk XVIII.17)?', *ExpTim* 77 (1965/6) 56-58.

T. E. Schmidt, 'Cry of Dereliction or Cry of Judgment? Mark 15:34 in Context', *BBR* 4 (1994) 145-53.

————, 'Mark 15:16-32: The Crucifixion Narrative and the Roman Triumphal Procession', *NTS* 41 (1995) 1-18.

K. Schubert, 'Biblical Criticism Criticised: with Reference to the Markan Report of Jesus's Examination before the Sanhedrin', in E. Bammel and C. F. D. Moule (ed.), *Politics,* 385-402.

G. Schwarz, '"Aus der Gegend" (Mk v.10b)', *NTS* 22 (1975/6) 215-16.

E. Schweizer, 'Er wird Nazoräer heissen (zu Mc 1,24; Mt 2,23)', in W. Eltester (ed.), *Judentum, Urchristentum, Kirche* (FS J. Jeremias; BZNW 26). Berlin: Töpelmann, 1960, 90-93.

R. Scroggs and K. I. Groff, 'Baptism in Mark: Dying and Rising with Christ', *JBL* 92 (1973) 531-48.

A. Segal, '"He who did not spare his own son . . .": Jesus, Paul and the Akedah', in P. Richardson and J. C. Hurd (ed.), *From Jesus to Paul.* Waterloo: Wilfrid Laurier University Press, 1984, 169-84.

O. J. F. Seitz, 'The Future Coming of the Son of Man: Three Midrashic Formulations in the Gospel of Mark', *SE* 6 (1973) 478-94.

H. D. Slingerland, 'The Transjordanian Origin of St. Matthew's Gospel', *JSNT* 3 (1979) 18-28.

J. Slomp, 'Are the Words "Son of God" in Mark 1:1 Original?', *BT* 28 (1977) 143-50.

C. W. F. Smith, 'Fishers of Men: Footnotes on a Gospel Figure', *HTR* 52 (1959) 187-203.

————, 'No Time for Figs', *JBL* 79 (1960) 315-27.

K. R. Snodgrass, 'The Parable of the Wicked Husbandmen: Is the Gospel of Thomas Version Original?', *NTS* 21 (1974/5) 142-44.

T. Snoy, 'Marc 6,48: ". . . et il voulait les dépasser." Proposition pour la solution d'une énigme', in M. Sabbe (ed.), *Marc,* 347-63.

S. Sowers, 'The Circumstances and Recollection of the Pella Flight', *TZ* 26 (1970) 305-20.

E. Stauffer, 'Jeschua ben Mirjam (Mk 6,3)', in E. E. Ellis and M. Wilcox (ed.), *Neotestamentica et Semitica* (FS M. Black). Edinburgh: T. & T. Clark, 1969, 119-28.

R. H. Stein, 'A Short Note on Mark xiv.28 and xvi.7', *NTS* 20 (1973/4) 445-52.

————, 'Is the Transfiguration (Mark 9:2-8) a Misplaced Resurrection-Account?', *JBL* 95 (1976) 79-96.

J. E. Steinmueller, 'Jesus and οἱ παρ' αὐτοῦ (Mk 3,20-21)', *CBQ* 4 (1942) 355-59.

R. L. Sturch, 'The "ΠΑΤΡΙΣ" of Jesus', *JTS* 28 (1977) 94-96.

M. E. Thrall, 'Elijah and Moses in Mark's Account of the Transfiguration', *NTS* 16 (1969/70) 305-17.

É. Trocmé, 'Marc 9,1: prédiction ou réprimande?', *SE* 2 (1964) 259-65.

G. W. Trompf, 'The First Resurrection Appearance and the Ending of Mark's Gospel', *NTS* 18 (1971/2) 308-30.

P. Trudinger, 'The Word on the Generation Gap: Reflections on a Gospel Metaphor', *BTB* 5 (1975) 311-15.

C. H. Turner, 'ὁ υἱός μου ὁ ἀγαπητός', *JTS* (1925/6) 113-29.

N. Turner, 'The Translation of Μοιχᾶται ἐπ' αὐτήν in Mark 10,11', *BT* 7 (1956) 151-52.

G. H. Twelftree, 'ΕΙ ΔΕ . . . ΕΓΩ ΕΚΒΑΛΛΩ ΤΑ ΔΑΙΜΟΝΙΑ . . .', in *GP,* 6.361-400.

J. M. Van Cangh, 'Les Multiplication des pains dans l'évangile de Marc', in M. Sabbe (ed.), *Marc,* 309-46.

BIBLIOGRAPHY

P. W. Van der Horst, 'Can a Book End with γάρ? A Note on Mark xvi:8', *JTS* 23 (1972) 121-24.

A. Vanhoye, 'La fuite du jeune homme nu (Mc 14,51-52)', *Bib* 52 (1971) 401-6.

B. M. F. Van Iersel, '"To Galilee" or "in Galilee" in Mark 14,28 and 16,7?', *ETL* 58 (1982) 365-70.

———, 'The Sun, Moon and Stars of Mark 13,24-25 in a Greco-Roman Reading', *Bib* 77 (1996) 84-92.

J. Verheyden, 'Describing the Parousia: The Cosmic Phenomena in Mk 13,24-25', in C. M. Tuckett (ed.), *The Scriptures in the Gospels,* 525-50.

H. Wansbrough, 'Mark III.21 — Was Jesus out of His Mind?', *NTS* 18 (1971/2) 233-35.

T. J. Weeden, 'The Cross as Power in Weakness (Mark 15:20b-41)', in W. H. Kelber (ed.), *Passion,* 115-34.

———, 'The Heresy That Necessitated Mark's Gospel', *ZNW* 59 (1968) 145-58, repr. in W. R. Telford (ed.), *Interpretation,* 89-104.

D. Wenham, 'The Meaning of Mark iii.21', *NTS* 21 (1974/5) 295-300.

J. W. Wenham, 'How Many Cock-Crowings? The Problem of Harmonistic Text-Variants', *NTS* 25 (1978/9) 523-25.

K. D. White, 'The Parable of the Sower', *JTS* 15 (1964) 300-307.

J. Wilkinson, 'The Case of the Epileptic Boy', *ExpTim* 79 (1967/8) 39-42.

———, 'The Physical Cause of the Death of Christ', *ExpTim* 83 (1971/2) 104-7.

J. Winandy, 'Le logion de l'ignorance (Mc., XIII,32; Mt., XXIV,36)', *RB* 75 (1968) 63-79.

A. G. Wright, 'The Widow's Mites: Praise or Lament? A Matter of Context', *CBQ* 44 (1982) 256-65.

E. Yamauchi, 'Magic or Miracle? Diseases, Demons and Exorcisms', in *GP,* 6.89-183.

J. A. Ziesler, 'The Transfiguration Story and the Markan Soteriology', *ExpTim* 81 (1969-70) 263-68.

———, 'The Vow of Abstinence: A Note on Mark 14:25 and Parallels', *Colloquium* 5/1 (1972) 12-14.

———, 'The Vow of Abstinence Again', *Colloquium* 6/1 (1973) 49-50.

G. Zuntz, 'Ein Heide las das Markusevangelium', in H. Cancik (ed.), *Markus-Philologie: Historische, literargeschichtliche und stilistiche Untersuchungen zum zweiten Evangelium* (WUNT 33). Tübingen: Mohr, 1984, 205-22.

INTRODUCTION

ABOUT THIS COMMENTARY

I have tried to write the sort of commentary I like to use. Whether this is what other readers are looking for will depend on what they think a biblical commentary should be. But I hope there are enough other people who share my own expectations to make the enterprise worthwhile. Let me spell out what I mean.

This is, in my intention, a commentary on Mark, not a commentary on commentaries on Mark. I have commented on the matters which I regard as needing or deserving comment, and not necessarily on those which have been the traditional concern of other commentators. Much of the time the two coincide fairly closely, but I have not felt obliged to say something about every issue which other commentators have raised. My method has been first to write my own comments on each section of the text (moulded, of course, by many years' awareness of the issues which have been current in Marcan studies), and only after that to look at other studies and commentaries on that passage. Where this reading raised further issues to which I have wanted to draw attention, these most often appear in the footnotes.

My concern is with the exegesis of the text of Mark, not with theories about its prehistory or the process of its composition.[1] Where synoptic comparison is illuminating for understanding Mark's text, I have tried to take this into account, but my object has always been the understanding and appreciation of Mark's text as we have it rather than proposing explanations as to how and why Mark came to be different from or the same as Matthew or Luke. Nor have I generally felt it important to discuss which elements in a given passage may derive from earlier tradition and which from Mark's own contribution. It is the Greek text of the gospel, however it may have come about, that is the given factor around which all critical theories revolve, and it is the exegesis of that text, not the exploration of the theories, which is the aim of this commentary.[2]

---

1. In the terms used by Van Iersel, 15-21, this commentary therefore offers a 'synchronic' rather than a 'diachronic' approach to the text, though I do not personally find that terminology (and the literary theories which underlie it and are diagrammed by Van Iersel) either helpful or necessary.

2. I am thus happy to echo the three 'goal-specific requirements' which M. A. Tolbert, *Sowing,* 21-29, sets out for her interpretation of Mark under the headings 'Circumventing the

That is not to say, of course, that this commentary is written in a vacuum, in two important senses, one literary and the other historical. First, my approach to the text is inevitably the product of my own experience of gospel studies from the days when form criticism was dominant, through the discovery of the brave new world of redaction criticism, and on into the proliferation of more 'contemporary' literary approaches on offer today. I would not categorise myself under any particular 'school' of literary criticism, though I hope I have learned from several. If one word plays a central role in my understanding of a gospel exegete's task, it is probably 'narrative'. I come to Mark's gospel as a book waiting to be read and enjoyed for itself, a carefully compiled, flowing account of the story of Jesus and his disciples, intended to be read and appreciated as a literary whole rather than as a collection of discrete units which may be discussed in isolation from their setting in the total work. I have tried to avoid too much jargon, especially that which has clustered around much modern literary theory and has tended to alienate those who simply want to appreciate the text as it stands. I hope that my comments are those of a theologically sympathetic reader who aims to deploy literary common sense with historical sensitivity for the elucidation of a text which comes from a different world from ours.

I shall set out later in this introduction my understanding of the structure of the gospel as an effective 'Drama in Three Acts'; I have tried to approach each part of the book in the light of its place in the planned development of the whole. A division of the text into sections is necessary for commenting in detail, but I recognise that those divisions are mine, not Mark's, and have tried not to allow them to get in the way of an appreciation of the narrative flow of the drama as a whole. The verse-by-verse comment on details of the text which occurs within each section is intended as supplementary to the introductory comments on the section itself and to be read only in that light. In other words, reference only to what I have to say under a given verse number may not represent all or even the most important part of what I have to say about the significance of that verse in its setting.

The second sense in which this commentary is not written in a vacuum is that I have aimed to draw on and be guided by the exciting recent developments in our historical awareness of the world within which Mark's story is set, which have come to be known loosely under the title of the 'Third Quest'[3] of the historical Jesus. The historical and cultural context of first-century Palestine is probably better appreciated by the world of NT scholarship these days than it has ever been previously in modern times, partly through the discovery of new material, but chiefly through the greater readiness of NT scholars to explore

---

Vorleben' [the form in which the traditions existed before Mark drew on them], 'Circumventing Fragmentation', and 'Circumventing the *Nachleben*' [reading Mark as Mark, not as interpreted especially by Matthew and Luke].

3. The term was coined by N. T. Wright in his revision of S. Neill, *The Interpretation of the NT, 1861-1986* (Oxford: Oxford University Press, 1988), 379.

and benefit from what has long been available to them in Jewish and (to a lesser extent) classical studies. The result has been an impressive (though not, of course, unanimous) drawing together of data from a wide range of sources to help us see Jesus more as the people of his own time may have seen him. As a former classicist I have followed this scholarly movement with delight, and I believe that there are important insights to be gained for the exegesis of gospel stories from it. In this commentary I have tried where appropriate to draw in such historical insights to illuminate the events which form the subject of Mark's drama.

This commentary is in a series focused on the Greek text, and it has been a pleasure to be able to comment directly on Mark's words rather than having to work through (and sometimes disagree with) a published translation. I have assumed a working knowledge of NT Greek on the part of the reader, and so I have not translated the text into English, nor have I felt obliged to explain forms and idioms for the benefit of the beginner. But where exegesis required attention to be paid to grammatical, syntactical, or lexical issues I have included such comments, usually with a pointer to one or more of the standard reference works.

The Greek text I have commented on is the agreed text printed by the United Bible Societies' *Greek New Testament* (4th rev. edn., 1993) and the Nestle-Aland *Novum Testamentum Graece* (27th edn., 1993). The Textual Notes which precede the comments on most sections of the text discuss those variants which are selected for presentation in the textual apparatus of UBS[4], together with a few further variants which I felt worthy of comment. Given the extraordinarily rich range of textual witnesses for Mark's Gospel (catalogued with such care by S. C. E. Legg, *Novum Testamentum Graece: Evangelium secundum Marcum,* Oxford: Clarendon, 1935, a labour of love from which I have greatly benefited) it would have been possible to write much more extensive textual notes, but this would have been out of proportion in a commentary such as this, and so the careful selection process already undertaken by the editors of UBS[4] seemed a suitable basis from which to work.

The bibliography which precedes this introduction contains the works actually cited in this commentary, not necessarily all those which I have used and benefited from in its preparation. It does not claim to be a complete listing of all works of significance relating to Mark, and I have not taken it upon myself to compile detailed bibliographies for each section of the text, since this has already been done with great care by others whose commentaries remain available;[4] it would in any case have been impossible in my relative isolation from suitable library facilities in the later stages of writing. It may also be worth

---

4. The fullest relatively recent sectional bibliographies available to me are found in the German commentaries of Pesch (1976, 1977) and, less fully, Gnilka (1978, 1979) and in the English commentary of Guelich (1989, on Mark 1:1–8:26 only; the planned second volume by C. A. Evans following Guelich's sudden death was unfortunately not yet published when this commentary went to press). Gundry's massive commentary (1993), while it does not contain sectional bibliographies as such, discusses in the 'Notes' on each section an extraordinarily wide range of published interpretation.

mentioning that since this commentary has been ten years in the making, some books and articles which have been published during that period (notably the commentaries of Gundry, 1993, and of Van Iersel, 1998) will receive somewhat uneven attention; those who enjoy such pursuits may like to work out at what stage in the writing each of these commentaries became available to me.[5] The writing was completed in August 2000.

ABOUT THE GOSPEL OF MARK

This is not a full study of all the traditional questions of 'Introduction' relating to the Gospel of Mark. Such studies have been written by others at greater length than the introduction to a commentary allows. I think particularly of four studies, from different perspectives and representing different stages in the history of Marcan studies, which I have found valuable: R. P. Martin, *Mark: Evangelist and Theologian* (Exeter: Paternoster, 1972); E. Best, *Mark: The Gospel as Story* (Edinburgh: T. & T. Clark, 1983); M. Hengel, *Studies in the Gospel of Mark* (ET, London: SCM, 1985); and most recently C. Bryan, *A Preface to Mark: Notes on the Gospel in Its Literary and Cultural Settings* (Oxford: Oxford University Press, 1993). Detailed surveys of scholarly literature on Mark have also been supplied by S. P. Kealy, *Mark's Gospel: A History of Its Interpretation* (New York: Paulist Press, 1982), and W. R. Telford, *The Interpretation of Mark* (2d ed.; Edinburgh: T. & T. Clark, 1995), 1-61. In the light of these studies, I have no need or desire to reinvent the wheel. The following pages aim only to set out the basic outline of the understanding of Mark's book on which the following commentary will be based.

A. What Sort of Book?

The earliest titles we have for this book[6] call it ΕΥΑΓΓΕΛΙΟΝ ΚΑΤΑ ΜΑΡΚΟΝ, and there is general agreement that this designation derives from the term Mark uses in his own heading to the book, Ἀρχὴ τοῦ εὐαγγελίου. . . . There is, however, equally broad agreement that when Mark wrote those words he was not using εὐαγγέλιον to designate a literary genre, but simply to indicate the nature of the subject matter of his work: it is a presentation in written form of the 'good news' about Jesus which was and is the subject of the church's teaching and mission

---

5. The major commentary on Mark by Joel Marcus in the Anchor Bible series, replacing that of C. S. Mann, appeared too late to be taken into account in this work, though I hope that my extensive use of Marcus's *The Way of the Lord* (also published while this work was in progress) and of his other publications on Mark may have allowed me to anticipate some of the exegesis offered in his commentary.

6. On the titles of the gospels (and especially their early origin) see the important and ground-clearing study by M. Hengel, *Studies,* 64-84.

(see below on 1:1). Mark did not say to himself, 'I am now going to write a εὐαγγέλιον'; it was only as it became necessary for the church to find a suitable label for this category of literature, church books about Jesus, that Mark's heading provided them with one. Once the term had become established as a designation for the four canonical versions of the one εὐαγγέλιον (so that τὸ εὐαγγέλιον κατὰ Μάρκον is properly translated not 'the gospel[-book] by Mark' but 'the [one] gospel in Mark's version') it became available as a literary label for other works about Jesus which came to be written from the second century onwards, however different in character they may have been from the narrative 'gospels' of the first century. Hence the *Gospel of Thomas, Gospel of Peter, Gospel of Philip, Gospel of Truth, Gospel according to the Hebrews,* and the like. The term which for Mark had designated the (hitherto oral) message of the first-century churches had thus come to mean something like 'a church book about Jesus'.

But if Mark did not have a pre-existing literary genre called εὐαγγέλιον to conform to, how might he and those who first read his book have perceived its nature? It is a book about Jesus, a historical figure of the recent past, whom the writer wishes to introduce and commend to his readers, and he achieves this aim by telling the story of (part of) his life and his death together with a selection of his teaching.[7] Such a description sounds like what most people would call a biography. Fifty years ago we were drilled in the critical orthodoxy of the form-critical school which insisted that the gospels were not to be seen as biographies,[8] but since then there has been a massive swing in scholarly opinion on this point, and increasingly sophisticated study of the nature of biographical writing in the ancient world has led to a general recognition that, for all the distinctiveness of its Christian content and orientation, in terms of literary form Mark's book (and those of Matthew, Luke and John) would have seemed to an educated reader in the first century to fall into roughly the same category as the lives of famous men pioneered by Cornelius Nepos and soon to reach their most famous expression in the 'Parallel Lives' of Plutarch.[9] Of course there is no one

---

7. In comparison with the other first-century gospels Mark is often said to have little actual teaching of Jesus, even though he speaks more often than they do of Jesus as a teacher. But if the other gospels are ignored, Mark on his own contains quite a high percentage of teaching in comparison with other biographical writings of the period, certainly enough to support his emphasis on teaching as a characteristic activity of Jesus. See my article 'Mark and the Teaching of Jesus' in *GP*, 1.101-36, where I estimate (113) that 'some 40% of the verses of Mark contain sayings of Jesus with some "teaching" content, not to mention a further roughly 12% which consists of the narrative contexts required to introduce important sayings and dialogues . . . where the teaching is the *raison d'être* of the narrative'.

8. This view is still found, e.g., in Nineham, 35-36.

9. Among the more valuable attempts to set the gospels within this category of literature may be mentioned G. N. Stanton, *Jesus,* 117-36; C. H. Talbert, *Gospel;* P. L. Shuler, *Genre;* D. E. Aune, *Environment,* 17-76; idem, *GP,* 2.9-60 (a critique of Talbert); R. A. Burridge, *Gospels;* C. Bryan, *Preface,* 9-64. See also, however, the important corrective offered by M. A. Tolbert, *Sowing,* 59-79, to the effect that Mark belongs more in the category of popular literature than among the more 'elite' literary productions which scholars today necessarily use as a way into the ancient literary world.

comprehensive description of 'biographical' writing which would fit all the varied attempts in classical and Jewish literature to present the lives of famous people, and some scholars have found it necessary to subdivide the category into such types as encomium, Peripatetic, Alexandrian, and romantic biographies.[10] But somewhere within this broad range of βίοι the reader coming to Mark's book for the first time would be likely to feel that it belonged.[11]

But while to assign a book to a literary genre may help us to appreciate the parameters within which its original readers might have been expected to make sense of it, it is not to say all there is to be said about it. Genre is 'a dynamic, not a static, concept'.[12] Just as there is a wide variety among Graeco-Roman 'biographies', so Mark is his own master, not bound to follow a pattern laid down by someone else.[13] His book represents something distinctive within the field of biographical writing, in terms of its subject, its origin, and the use for which it was intended. Each of these deserves a brief mention here.

1. The Subject of Mark's Book

Lucas Grollenberg interestingly draws our attention to the account given by the German classical scholar Günther Zuntz of his first encounter with Mark's gospel. Thoroughly at home in the literature of the Roman empire, Zuntz, we are told, was nonetheless quite unfamiliar with Christianity and its literature, and thus came to Mark with a freshness of perception impossible to most modern Christian readers. His response thus represents, says Grollenberg, 'what this book must have looked like to an educated reader of the first century of our era'. Zuntz speaks of his 'strong impression' that 'something very important was being put forward here with a superior purpose and concentration throughout the book. . . . The style and content of the story arouse a feeling of otherness, a feeling that this is not a history like other histories, not a biography like other biographies, but a development of the actions, sayings, and suffering of a higher being on his way through this anxious world of human beings and demons.'[14] While

---

10. C. H. Talbert, *Gospel*, 92-98, proposes an alternative classification into five types depending not on literary features but on the perceived function of the biography (providing a pattern to copy; dispelling a false image; discrediting the subject by exposé, etc).

11. In a 1965 radio broadcast C. F. Evans (*Gospels*, 7ff.) posed the question 'What kind of a book is a gospel?' and proposed to answer it by considering the dilemma of a librarian in ancient Alexandria needing to find a suitable shelf-classification for the Gospel of Mark. In the light of a generation of study since then, there is now fairly general agreement that he would have placed it in his biography section.

12. P. L. Shuler, *Genre*, 25-28.

13. L. Alexander in R. J. Bauckham (ed.), *Gospels*, 105, rightly comments that in the matter of genre the gospels 'clearly made their own way in the world along their own well-greased social pathways, blithely independent of the literary canon and its self-appointed guardians'.

14. L. Grollenberg, *Messiah*, 59-60, translating Zuntz's account from H. Cancik (ed.), *Markusphilologie*, 207.

Zuntz attributes the 'feeling of otherness' to both style and content, it is the latter which dominates his comment. And I suspect that in the first century a reader familiar with other βίοι would have had a similar 'feeling of otherness', for the simple reason that Jesus is not like other people, and so a 'biography' of Jesus will also be 'not like other biographies', especially if it is written by one of his followers who believes him to be the Son of God and to be still alive as the object of unconditional allegiance, rather than a noble figure of the past to be imitated.

As for the 'style', I do not think that Zuntz can have meant that Mark's Greek style as such promoted a feeling of otherness, unless it be by its sheer lack of literary sophistication (and Semitic flavour?) in comparison with that of other biographers. I suspect he was thinking more of the whole conception of the book and of its capacity to shock and to subvert comfortable literary expectations. Thus, while there is no doubt that Jesus is the 'hero' of this story, Mark seems to make a point of portraying him as unrecognised and rejected, even humiliated, continually let down and eventually deserted by even his closest associates, and the eventual victim of a hostile establishment. If it were not for what Zuntz calls 'a last comforting lightning flash', this story, read outside the Christian context of faith and hindsight, would be that of a heroic failure. This is not the stuff of which ancient biography is made, unless it is intended (as Mark's is surely not) as satire. In this commentary I shall have occasion to remark frequently on Mark's love of paradox and avoidance of 'encomium' in his presentation of Jesus, and indeed also of his disciples. It is this rather than stylistic sophistication which contributes to the 'feeling of otherness' experienced by those who come to this extraordinary little book without the 'benefit' of Christian conditioning.

2. The Origin of Mark's Book

One of the most persistent features of early Christian tradition about Mark is the belief that its origin was connected with the apostle Peter. We shall have more to say about this tradition later, but here it is worth noting how Papias, as quoted by Eusebius (*H.E.* 3.39.15), describes the origin of the material which went into making this book (note that Papias, writing at the beginning of the second century, is himself quoting an earlier authority, 'the Elder';[15] it is not clear at what point in the quotation, if at all, Papias moves on from the Elder's report to his own comment):

> This is what the Elder used to say: Mark became Peter's interpreter and wrote accurately, though not in order (τάξει), all that he remembered of the things said or done by the Lord. For he had not himself heard the Lord or been his follower, but later, as I said, he followed Peter. Peter delivered teachings as

15. Gundry, 1029-34, argues that this 'Elder' is in fact the apostle John.

occasion required, rather than compiling a sort of orderly presentation (σύνταξιν) of the traditions about the Lord.[16] So Mark was not wrong in recording in this way the individual items as he remembered them. His one concern was to leave out nothing of what he had heard and to make no false statements in reporting them.

If this tradition from the beginning of the second century is to be taken seriously,[17] Papias (and/or 'the Elder') felt the need to apologise for Mark's lack of 'order' (perhaps especially in comparison with the work of Matthew, who according to a separate quotation of Papias which immediately follows the above in Eusebius's work [*H.E.* 3.39.16] did in fact 'put the traditions in order', τὰ λόγια συνετάξατο, in a way Peter and Mark had not), and explained it on the basis of the sort of material which he had available to him in the 'unsystematic' preaching of Peter. So if Mark's life of Jesus lacked the sophisticated literary structuring which might have been expected in a βίος, it was because he was doing the best he could with material which originated in occasional preaching and teaching, not in formal records or scholarly research. This characterisation of Mark's book as a rather haphazard collection of 'individual items' lacking in discernible 'order' is very much out of keeping with modern evaluations of Mark's literary skill and the narrative integrity of his work (it sounds more like the old days of form criticism with its dismissive portrayal of Mark the compiler as like a child threading beads). It reflects the literary tastes of Papias's time and culture (moulded in part by the growing popularity of the more 'systematic' gospels of Matthew, Luke and John) rather than an evaluation of Mark as an author on his own terms. But the point we need to note here is that the distinctiveness of Mark's work in comparison with other βίοι derives not only from its subject matter but from the genesis of its material in the living teaching tradition of the first-century church.

If Papias's information is correct, Peter, even if not 'systematic' enough for some tastes, must have been a lively preacher. The vivid narrative style and content of the Marcan stories may well derive as much from the way Peter used to tell them as from Mark's own skill as a raconteur.[18] The events are told and the teaching heard mainly from within the experience of the disciple group.

16. I have translated τὰ κυριακὰ λόγια by 'traditions about the Lord' rather than 'oracles' or 'sayings' of the Lord because it seems from the context that Papias is talking of the raw material for Mark's gospel as a whole ('the things said or done by the Lord') rather than only of the sayings material. See my *Matthew: Evangelist,* 58-60, for a discussion of the meaning of λόγια in the fragments of Papias.

17. M. Hengel, *Studies,* 47-53, gives a useful and very positive account of its status. The likely date of Papias's writing used to be placed about A.D. 140, but there is now a growing consensus that he wrote in the first decade of the second century; see Gundry, 1026-29.

18. Lane, 10-11, goes further and suggests that the overall outline of Mark's gospel corresponds to the content of the brief sermon outline ascribed to Peter in Acts 10:36-41. But the difference in scale of the two accounts, and the fact that the Acts 10 outline corresponds also to other early Christian kerygmatic outlines, renders this comparison less than compelling.

This means that Mark's book reflects not the distant evaluation of a scholarly admirer of Jesus but the subjective experience of one of those who shared most closely in the stirring and yet profoundly disturbing events of Jesus' public ministry and his confrontation with the Jerusalem establishment. And it reflects those experiences as they were passed on in the day-to-day teaching ministry, 'as occasion required', of a living community of the followers of Jesus (within which Mark no doubt himself also followed Peter as a recognised teller of the stories of Jesus). It is, perhaps, this grounding in the active life of the church which gives much of the special flavour (and 'feeling of otherness') to the 'good news' as told by Mark.

3. The Function of Mark's Book

It may seem obvious that a book is intended to be read. But modern scholars are apt to forget that in the ancient world not very many people *could* read. It has recently been estimated that literacy in the ancient Mediterranean world was probably 'no more than 10 percent, although the figure may have risen to 15 or 20 percent in certain cities'.[19] Unless Mark's work was designed only for the benefit of the small minority who could read,[20] he must have reckoned on its being experienced by most of his target group as an oral text, read aloud probably in meetings of the local church; E. Best describes it as 'preaching'.[21] Recent scholarship has increasingly recognised this factor, and it is relatively common these days to hear Mark discussed as an oral text, or at least as a text intended in part for oral presentation. The bulk of C. Bryan's useful *A Preface to Mark* is devoted to the question 'Was Mark written to be read aloud?' and his answer is a firm yes: 'Mark was designed for oral transmission — and for transmission as a continuous whole — rather than for private study or silent reading.'[22]

Various features of Mark's style seem to reflect such a purpose, notably his more expansive storytelling manner and his well-known penchant for repetition or for dual expressions where one would do (ὀψίας γενομένης, ὅτε ἔδυ ὁ ἥλιος, 1:32; τότε, ἐν ἐκείνῃ τῇ ἡμέρᾳ, 2:20; χρείαν ἔσχεν καὶ ἐπείνασεν, 2:25, etc.). Such features make for a more memorable text, and make it easier for the listener, who does not have the option of stopping and turning back to refresh his or her memory, to keep the flow of the narrative in mind.[23] The 'sandwich'

19. M. B. Thompson in R. J. Bauckham (ed.), *Gospels,* 66.

20. R. A. Burridge, in R. J. Bauckham (ed.), *Gospels,* 138, comments that the NT 'contains material of a different social level from that of most surviving classical texts, which tend to originate from the literate and ruling elites'. He goes on to suggest that the gospels are intended for 'audiences in the middle of the [social] scale' (140).

21. E. Best, *Story,* 38-41.

22. C. Bryan, *Preface,* 152.

23. E. Best, *JSNT* 37 (1989) 43-58, offers an insightful study of 'Mark's Narrative Technique' as an author who 'stood on the boundary between oral and written literature'. Cf. D. Rhoads

technique, to which we shall return later, is a well-tried device of the popular raconteur in order to hold the audience's attention.[24]

In recent years even in the literate Western world it has been increasingly realised how effective Mark's book is as an oral text. In Britain the solo recitations of the complete gospel (in the Authorised Version!) by Alec McCowan held theatre audiences spellbound, and similar presentations of the gospel in a single session have been undertaken by others in his wake. The translation of the full text of Mark which appears in D. Rhoads and D. Michie, *Story*, 7-34, was prepared especially for this purpose, using some untraditional English idioms in order to convey something of the effect of Mark's less than literary Greek style and the oral impact of the text.[25] Many have found that hearing the gospel in this way as a complete work has given them a new appreciation of its quality as storytelling on an epic scale.

Some have felt that the impact of the work could best be conveyed by describing it as 'drama'.[26] While few have wished to go as far as G. B. Bilezikian, *Gospel*, who sees Mark as consciously modelled on classical Greek tragedy, most readers and hearers who experience Mark as a whole discern a 'dramatic' quality in the careful development of the plot. In particular, there is a deliberate buildup of tension as various strands of opposing reactions to Jesus are brought together into a final powerful confrontation leading to the dénouement of Jesus' arrest, trial, and death, which fulfils the twin patterns of the plotting of Jesus' opponents and of his own prediction of his fate which have been built into the story from almost the beginning. It is in an attempt to represent this dramatic character of Mark that I shall set out the following description of the book as a 'Drama in Three Acts'.

To conclude these comments on the literary genre of Mark, however different it may seem from what we today expect a biography to be, it is surely rightly classified as a 'biography' within the broad category of lives of famous people which were produced in the ancient Graeco-Roman (and to a lesser extent Jewish) world. It tells the story of a recent historical figure in such a way as to commend the man and his message, and to summon those who read or hear it to follow him as his first disciples were called to do. But for those accustomed to laudatory biographies such as those of Cornelius Nepos Mark's gospel would at the same time create a 'feeling of otherness'. This distinctive character may be traced first to its subject matter, in that it is a Christian work

---

and D. Michie, *Story*, 44-62; C. Bryan, *Preface*, passim, especially 72-81, 126-35. There is a useful description of the function of repetition in an oral text, with special reference to the repeated passion predictions in Mark 8–10, in J. Camery-Hoggatt, *Irony*, 157-58.

24. On British television the comedian Ronnie Corbett is particularly known for this device.

25. A similar retranslation attempting to reproduce in English Mark's syntactical idiosyncrasies, awkward tense changes, and the like is found in H. C. Waetjen, *Reordering*, 27-61 (with explanation on xi-xii). The result sounds (to use his own words) even more 'eccentric, strange, even inept' than that of Rhoads and Michie.

26. So, e.g., E. Best, *Story*, 128-33.

inspired by the conviction that Jesus of Nazareth was more than just a great man, and that he remains alive as the worthy object of devotion and commitment; and yet, paradoxically, it presents this more-than-human figure as the object of rejection and humiliation culminating in the most shameful form of death. It is distinctive, secondly, in the nature of the material from which it is composed, the teaching and preaching tradition of a living church, so that the resultant work bears the marks of 'preaching'. And it is distinctive, thirdly, in that it seems to have been written not as a book to be read in private, as probably most literary biographies of the ancient world were, but as a text for oral presentation, in a style which might not satisfy the canons of sophisticated literature, but which communicates with vigour to a nonliterary audience.

B. Mark's Gospel as a 'Drama in Three Acts'

Attempts to explain the structure of Mark's book, while they differ considerably in detail, generally recognise a basically similar pattern of development of the plot. Probably the most widely accepted observation is that towards the end of chapter 8 there is a watershed created by Peter's recognition of Jesus as Messiah (8:29) and by Jesus' subsequent declaration that his messianic mission is to culminate in rejection and death (8:31), a fate which those who follow him must expect to share (8:34-38). Up to this point the story has been of Jesus' public ministry in and around Galilee, and of his disciples' gradual perception of who he is. After this point the story moves inexorably downhill to Jerusalem where the rejection and death are to take place, and the focus is less on public ministry than on the preparation of the disciples for what lies ahead. A further generally recognised turning point comes at the end of chapter 10, when Jesus and his followers arrive in Jerusalem and the predicted confrontation with the establishment begins.

As a result, the plot of the gospel (after the opening declarations in the 'prologue', usually defined as either 1:1-13 or 1:1-15) is often understood as consisting of three main stages, focused on three geographical locations, stage 1 in and around Galilee (up to roughly[27] 8:21), stage 2 on the road to Jerusalem (roughly 8:22–10:52), and stage 3 in the capital itself (from 11:1 on). Within each of these main stages various subsections may be discerned, most obviously with the movement from the period of Jesus' public activity in Jerusalem (chs. 11–12) to the passion narrative (chs. 14–16), with the discourse of chapter 13 as in some sense a bridge between the two. But the three-stage geographical progression is widely noted, and several interpreters have taken it to be the principal structural basis of Mark's story.[28]

27. For varying views on just where this section ends see below, p. 321 n. 28.

28. See, e.g., much of the second half of C. Bryan, *Preface*, especially pp. 82-84; B. Van Iersel, *Reading*, 19-26, and with more elaboration his commentary, 75-86. I would not, however,

This conclusion is the more probable when it is noted how artificial this geographical outline is. In Mark's account Jesus visits Jerusalem only once, and the whole story seems designed to build up to that visit: note the two references in the Galilean phase to Jerusalem as the place from which opposition comes (3:22; 7:1), and the references to the hostility of the Jerusalem establishment (even where the city is not named) which punctuate the journey from north to south (8:31; 9:31; 10:33-34). All this contrasts strongly with the pattern presented in the Gospel of John, which has Jesus making frequent journeys between Galilee and Jerusalem (generally in connection with Jewish festivals), so that even in the period before Jesus' dramatic entry to the city in Jn. 12:12-19 he seems in this gospel to have spent at least as much time in Judaea as in his own territory. This Johannine pattern seems historically more probable, in that most Galilean Jews made regular visits to Jerusalem at Passover time, and it would be surprising if Jesus, once his public ministry in the north had begun, had failed to attract notice on such visits to Judaea. Moreover, there are indications in Mark's own narrative that Jesus has in fact been in Jerusalem before the final week, such as his already existing links with his hosts in Bethany, with the owners of the donkey on the Mount of Olives and of the guest room in Jerusalem used for the 'Passover' meal. While there is perhaps enough material in Mark 11–12 to prompt the desire of the religious authorities to eliminate Jesus, their settled hostility (and Jesus' prior awareness of it) would be more adequately explained if he had already come to their attention before this final Passover visit. All this suggests that Mark's simple outline of an extensive ministry in and around Galilee followed by a lengthy and carefully marked journey southwards culminating in a single climactic visit to Jerusalem owes more to his dramatic reshaping of the story than to a naive recording of events just as they happened. We shall consider later whether this 'Galilee and Jerusalem' schema may properly be understood to have symbolic significance for Mark; but even as a purely geographical datum it looks like a structure deliberately imposed on the story.

That is why I find it appropriate to read Mark as 'A Drama in Three Acts'. This is not meant to suggest either that Mark designed it for 'performance' in three sections, or that it is possible to discern clear breaks between the 'acts'. It is an observation about how I discern the development of the plot, not about any indication Mark may have given of how he planned the structure of his text. Few early Christian writings offer explicit structural markers: the sequences of sevens in the Book of Revelation, and the recurrent formula which concludes

---

wish to follow Van Iersel, and still less his pupil B. Standaert, *Composition,* when they go far beyond the basic three-stage development of the story to find 'concentric' structure ('a composition in lines and circles', Van Iersel) throughout Mark's narrative, in detail as well as in the overall plot. Stock, 23-32, adopts Standaert's structure, prefacing it with an account of 'chiastic awareness' in Graeco-Roman literature (19-23) which has no immediately obvious bearing on Mark. While Mark's use of 'sandwich' compositions at several points in the gospel is well known and important (see below), to recognise the use of this technique at some points does not require us to discover concentric patterns where they are not obvious in the text.

the five major discourses in the Gospel of Matthew stand out as exceptions, and Mark offers nothing of the sort. It is not surprising, therefore, that there is disagreement among interpreters of Mark about just where one section ends and another begins: we shall note several examples of 'bridge' passages which defy easy structural placement. Even the point of transition from the Galilean ministry to the journey to Jerusalem (between 'Act One' and 'Act Two') is variously placed at 8:14, 8:22, 8:27, or 8:31, and good reasons can be offered for preferring each of these as the new beginning. It seems clear, then, that Mark did not write a text in sections, but a single flowing narrative, and that any structure we discern is a matter of our reading of the text, not of Mark's direction.

With that necessary caveat, I set out below the outline of the development of Mark's story which I have found it convenient to follow in commenting on his text. There is no symmetry about it,[29] only a 'narrative flow', within which the different elements are woven together to carry the reader forward towards the climax. This is a broad outline rather than a detailed breakdown of the text, in that most of the sections set out below contain a number of subsections which will be separately discussed in the commentary.

1:1	**The Heading**
1:2-13	**The Prologue: Setting the Scene — The Dramatis Personae**
1:14–8:21	**Act One: Galilee**
1:14-15	Introduction: The Essential Message of Jesus
1:16-20	The Formation of the 'Jesus Circle'
1:21-39	Preaching and Healing: General Impression (A Day in Capernaum)
1:40–3:6	Controversial Aspects of Jesus' Ministry
3:7-12	Wide Recognition of Jesus' Authority to Heal
3:13-35	Varying Responses to Jesus: Supporters and Opponents
4:1-34	*Explanatory discourse:* The Paradox of the Kingdom of God
4:35–5:43	Further Revelations of Jesus' Unique Authority
6:1-6	Not Everyone Is Impressed by Jesus

29. I have a rooted suspicion of neat, symmetrical patterns (particularly when bolstered with the name of 'chiasmus'!) which are 'discovered' in texts which do not on the surface present themselves in that form. See, e.g., E. E. Ellis, *Luke,* 30-37, proposing an analysis into three main sections, of which each of the first two divides into six sub-sections of six sub-sub-sections each, and the third into three sub-sections of six sub-sub-sections each. With regard to Mark a much less elaborate but still in my view artificial structural scheme is argued recently by R. V. Peace, *Conversion,* 110-56. He divides Mark (after the prologue) into two main parts (divided at 8:30), each of which has three 'units'; each unit is focused on a different title of Jesus (teacher, prophet, Messiah, Son of Man, Son of David, Son of God), the sequence representing the progressive christological enlightenment of the disciples. While the point about christological development is valuable, the demarcation into six units seems to me neither necessary to it nor well supported in itself, especially when Peace tries to discern in the text pointers to intended sectional divisions. The pointers he postulates (an abrupt shift in theme together with an attempt by Mark to provide a smooth transition; 136) are so flexible as to be discoverable at many other points in the gospel as well.

As I mentioned above, many of these sections contain within them a number of separate pericopes, which I have grouped together because they seemed to me to have a prima facie coherence of subject matter and/or of function in the development of the narrative. I shall explain such groupings in the commentary as each section is reached.

The only feature of my outline which needs to be commented on now is what I have labelled the two 'explanatory discourses', which fall roughly in the middle of Acts One and Three. It is generally noted that within Mark's gospel there are two prominent concentrations of teaching material in chapters 4 and 13 (the bases respectively of the third and fifth of Matthew's five discourse collections), but the significance of their placing within the overall narrative flow of the gospel is not always appreciated.[30] In chapters 1–3 Jesus' proclamation of the kingdom of God and his associated works of power have led to a wide variety of reactions, from the enthusiastic commitment of the disciples to the abu-

---

30. See, however, B. Van Iersel, *Reading*, 24-25, for a very brief recognition of the place of the two discourses as 'framed' within the Galilee and Jerusalem sections of the narrative respectively; the point is developed in his commentary, pp. 74, 110-13.

sive and sinister hostility of the scribes from Jerusalem. So far the narrative has moved on at a breathless pace, but now in chapter 4 Jesus sits down to explain what is happening, first to the crowd and then in more depth to the disciples. The parables explore what happens when the message of the kingdom of God is 'sown' and why people react to it so differently, and the explanation of why Jesus teaches in parables gives a new perspective against which to set his continuing ministry in the chapters that follow. Similarly, in chapters 11–12 there is a rapid sequence of encounters between Jesus and the religious authorities of Jerusalem, located in the courtyard of the temple and culminating in Jesus' prediction that the temple will be destroyed. The discourse on the Mount of Olives, for which Jesus again sits down, explains the significance of what is happening with special reference to the fate of the temple, but setting this more widely in terms of 'the end of the old order', the coming sovereignty of the Son of Man which will succeed the collapse of the present power structure.

The two discourses of chapters 4 and 13 thus allow the reader a pause in the otherwise rapid pace of the narrative to think through the implications of the story so far, and provide a theological framework for understanding the new thing that is happening with the coming of Jesus of Nazareth. The fact that each occurs roughly halfway through what I have termed Acts One and Three of the drama suggests that there may be a literary as well as a theological purpose in the discourses, to provide a narrative pause which gives the reader time to reflect on the events as they unfold. Why, then, is there no comparable discourse in the middle of Act Two? Even to ask the question in that form is to bestow on my three-act scheme an authority which it does not possess. I am not arguing that Mark consciously structured his work in three acts, and so he was under no obligation to create symmetrical patterns to conform to the structure which I have thought fit to discern in his work. But if the question is put more circumspectly in the form 'Why did Mark not feel the need for any other such explanatory discourse between chapters 4 and 13?' perhaps we might point to the less hectic narrative pace of Act Two, much of which, even if not structured in long, coherent discourses, consists less of public activity and more of teaching material addressed to the disciples. In this more 'discursive' part of the drama there is perhaps less need for a reflective pause.

For further comment on the coherence of the above groups of pericopes, and especially on the distinctive nature and function of Act Two as a whole, see the introductions to each section in the commentary.

C. Mark the Storyteller

There is a striking contrast between the embarrassment of Papias's Elder over Mark's lack of 'order' and the current tendency to pay tribute to the careful and effective way in which Mark's story is told. In the early centuries of Christianity Mark's gospel was so overshadowed by its more 'orderly', fuller, and more theologically explicit neighbours that had it not been for its prestige as the gospel deriving from Peter it might well have fallen out of use altogether.[31] Now that same gospel is everywhere praised for its powerful and thought-provoking portrayal of Jesus,[32] and (no doubt in large part owing to the general modern view that it was the earliest gospel to be written) is the acknowledged starting point for most explorations of Christian origins.[33] The difference in the estimate of Mark derives partly from the nineteenth-century reversal of the traditional view that Matthew was the earliest gospel, but also more recently from the appreciation that Mark's work is not to be evaluated primarily as a source of systematic teaching material but as a story. It is above all as a raconteur that Mark impresses and delights modern readers, as we may suppose his work also affected those who heard it in the first century.

The features which make Mark's book so easy to read are to a large extent those which are characteristic of 'oral literature'.[34] I have mentioned earlier his tendency to repetition or recapitulation and to dual expressions, thus enabling the reader/hearer to 'catch up' as the story surges forward. Many have commented on the pace at which the narrative moves, emphasised by Mark's famous overuse of the adverb εὐθύς both to signal narrative developments within a pericope and to link successive events closely with one another (42 uses, with 7 within the short sequence 1:16-31 alone); a similar effect is produced by his frequent use of ἤρξα(ν)το as an auxiliary verb, while πάλιν occurs 26 times to enable the reader to link a new incident with the previous story. The sense of rapid movement is enhanced by the fact that his narrative clauses are generally linked paratactically rather than subordinated into the adverbial clauses which a more sophisticated Greek stylist would have preferred.[35] His frequent use of the

31. The relatively slight (and decreasing) use of Mark is broadly indicated by the amount of space taken by each gospel in the listing of biblical references in patristic literature published by the Centre d'Analyse et de Documentation Patristiques under the title *Biblia Patristica* (Paris: Centre Nationale de la Recherche Scientifique, 1975ff.). The lists of references in the first two centuries give 27 pages of references to Mark against 70 for Matthew, 60 for Luke, and 37 for John, but in the third century Mark achieves a bare 10 pages, against 120 for Matthew, 41 for Luke, and 69 for John. The lack of use of Mark is indicated also by the fact that in the late fifth century Victor of Antioch found no commentary on Mark's gospel yet available.

32. This reevaluation of Mark's literary merit is quite recent. As recently as 1963 E. Trocmé, *Formation,* 72, could conclude a review of Mark's literary ability with the blunt verdict: 'The author of Mark was a clumsy writer unworthy of mention in any history of literature.'

33. Note, however, the significant exception of J. A. T. Robinson, *Priority,* 36-122, who argues that the Gospel of John is the closest to source both in its actual origins as the work of the son of Zebedee and also in the more intimately informed nature of its contents. John, according to Robinson, *Priority,* 23-24, 'goes back to source rather than sources'.

34. Cf. the account of Mark's 'Narrative Patterns' and 'Other Literary Features' in D. M. Rhoads and D. M. Michie, *Story,* 45-62.

35. Speaking of ancient education in rhetoric, E. Best, *Story,* 113, comments that 'Mark's Greek suggests that he never got beyond the primary stage'. Pesch repeatedly characterises Mark's work as 'unliterarisch' (Pesch, 1.25, 32, etc.). We shall have cause quite frequently in this commentary to note Mark's 'awkward', 'inelegant', or 'grammatically crude' forms of expression; it is for the reader to judge whether the impact of the narrative is reduced, or rather sometimes enhanced, by this lack of polish.

historic present tense (at least 150 times in Mark; Matthew's much longer text has only half as many, and Luke hardly any), particularly of the verb λέγω, adds to the lively, colloquial style of his narrative. Mark also quite frequently uses periphrastic verb forms (most notably ἦν with a present participle). These and other distinctive stylistic features of Mark[36] contribute to the liveliness and impact of his text, whether encountered orally or in writing.

The enjoyability of Mark's storytelling is enhanced by the more extensive use of descriptive detail than in the other gospels. Typically the Marcan version of a miracle story may be twice as long as the equivalent pericope in Matthew, simply because Mark is more vividly descriptive, while Matthew goes straight to the heart of the story. Notable examples include the digging of a hole in the roof in 2:4 (ignored by Matthew) and the graphic accounts of the subjects of exorcisms in 5:2-5 and 9:17-22. In the case of Legion (unnamed by Matthew) the whole descriptive section of the story is represented in Matthew only by the laconic comment that his two demoniacs were χαλεποὶ λίαν (Mt. 8:28). The three miracle stories which take up the whole of the 43 verses of Mark 5 are covered by Matthew in a mere 16 verses. Mark, it is clear, enjoys a good story and relishes the telling of it almost to the point of self-indulgence.

Much of the graphic detail in Mark's storytelling may derive simply from his imaginative skill as a raconteur. Even what are often claimed to be 'eyewitness touches' could be due to the storyteller's creativity rather than to personal memory or tradition. But the persistent church tradition which names Peter as the source of Mark's material points to a potential source for such 'eye-witness' elements, in the memory (enhanced perhaps by frequent telling of his tale?) of the person who was nearer to the heart of most of the events which Mark records than anyone else except Jesus himself. Vincent Taylor (135-39) gives a list (under the rather surprising title 'The Objectivity of the Gospel') of some 200 'elements peculiar to Mark' in the first six chapters of the gospel, most of which consist of additional details in the telling of the stories which Mark shares with one or more of the other evangelists, and many of which could be classed as the sort of thing an eyewitness might have been likely to remember, such as the 'digging out' of the roof in 2:4, the apparently unused boat provided in 3:9, Jesus 'looking round on those sitting in a circle around him' in 3:34, the boat in the storm ἤδη γεμίζεσθαι, while Jesus was 'in the stern' 'sleeping on the cushion' in 4:37-38, the description of the crowds sitting down in groups on the 'green grass', πρασιαὶ πρασιαί (looking like rows of vegetables?!) in 6:39-40, and so on. Of course none of this would be beyond the creativity of an imaginative novelist, but unless there are other reasons for doubting the tradition of

---

36. For a useful survey of Marcan stylistic peculiarities see Taylor, 44-54, and the following discussion (55-66) of how far these are the results of Semitic influence on Mark's Greek. Cf. Mann, 168-72, and the briefer account of 'Marcan Style and Oral Syntax' by B. W. Henaut, *Tradition*, 66-68, following W. H. Kelber.

Mark's dependence on Peter (see below), to trace such details to 'the tradition' (meaning Peter) is at least as plausible. Taylor himself concludes that 'the great majority of the items in the list have rather the appearance of graphic details recorded because they were given in the tradition'. If, as seems likely to me, his perception is valid, one of the reasons for the vividness of Mark's narrative may be that he followed a good master, who had both an eye for interesting detail and the personal memory to supply it. Mark tells a good story because Peter must have been a man worth listening to.

The same may be said of the psychological comments which occur from time to time in Mark, with regard to the thoughts and emotions both of Jesus and of his disciples. These, too, could be simply the fictions of an 'omniscient narrator', but if the traditional connection with Peter has any validity, there may be as much memory as art in such features as Jesus' anger and 'snorting' over the leper (1:41, 43) and his mental torture described in Gethsemane (14:33-34), or in the disciples' guilty silence in 9:34 and the graphic description of the scared and bewildered group who followed Jesus on the road to Jerusalem in 10:32. Whether by exploiting Peter's memory or by exercising his own imagination, Mark has contrived to give his readers the feeling of 'being there', and that is a large part of what makes his story so easy and rewarding to read.

In discussing some views of the structure of Mark above, I expressed doubt over the extensive discovery of 'chiastic' or 'concentric' patterns in his work. But while this may not be the right way to understand Mark's overall design of his work, everyone agrees that when it comes to the arrangement of some individual pericopes Mark is a past master at the narrative art of 'sandwiching' one story or scene within another (variously described also as interpolation, intercalation, dovetailing, framing, etc.). Sometimes, as in the most frequently cited case, the inclusion of the healing of the woman with a haemorrhage within the account of the raising of Jairus's daughter (5:21-43), this arrangement is not specifically Marcan, but is shared with the other synoptic evangelists. In such a case it is at least arguable, particularly if one does not assume a rigid pattern of Matthean and Lukan 'copying' from Mark, that the linking of the two stories derives not from Mark's creativity but from the tradition, simply because that is the way it happened and was remembered. But other Marcan sandwiches are peculiar to his gospel, or at least stand out more clearly in his narration, and here we may speak with more confidence of Mark's distinctive narrative style.

Not all Mark's sandwiches are of the same type. When Mark inserts a 'flashback' concerning the death of John the Baptist between the sending out of the Twelve and their return (6:7-30), this is formally a 'digression' from the narrative sequence, and I have so labelled it in the commentary. It serves to fill the narrative gap required between the disciples' going out and their return. But I shall argue in the commentary (see introductory notes both to 6:7-13, 30 and to 6:17-29) that it serves a more important purpose than that by setting the mission of Jesus and his disciples within the context of official hostility. The comment on Herod's view of Jesus as a 'second John' (6:14-16) remains within the narrative framework of the disciples' mission, and it is this note which gives rise to the 'flashback'. The effect is not just to fill a narrative gap, but also to establish an important link between the fates of John and of his 'successor', and thus to contribute to the reader's understanding of the dynamics of the story which will eventually culminate in Jesus' own death.

Most of Mark's sandwiches are created not by narrative 'flashback' but by the interweaving of contemporary events in such a way that one helps to interpret the other. Notable examples are the enclosure of the scribal accusation that Jesus is in league with the devil within the story of his own family's attempt to restrain him because they thought he was mad (3:21-35), the more complex interweaving of the destruction of the fig tree with the demonstration against the 'fruitless' temple (11:11-27), and the parallel scenes of the trial of Jesus and the 'trial' of Peter which are interwoven in 14:53–15:1. Each of these will be discussed in the commentary, and other examples will be noted.[37] It will be noticed that in the latter two cases it is not a matter of a simple three-part sandwich but of successive visits to the two parallel scenes, in each case involving not three but five phases. We might note also that the three-part sandwich in chapter 3 is itself enveloped within a wider picture, as the contrasting attitude of Jesus' committed followers is depicted immediately before the mention of his sceptical family (3:13-19) and then reintroduced within the concluding part of the sandwich (3:31-35) in order to provide a foil to the family's failure to understand Jesus. A further and more complex example is found in 14:1-12, where three scenes are set parallel to each other, with the devotion of the unnamed woman at Bethany enclosed between two phases of the plotting of the priests, the latter itself enclosed within two mentions of the arrival of the Passover festival.

All this suggests that 'sandwich' is too simple a term for what Mark is doing; nor are all his interweavings 'concentric'. Not only does he enclose one story within another, but he likes to set up parallel scenes and move the spotlight successively between them. This is a proven narrative and dramatic technique, to maintain interest and to allow the reader/hearer to gain a wider perspective on the constituent elements of the story, placing one alongside another so that they become mutually illuminating. By this means the reader is invited to compare and contrast the different estimates of Jesus made by the scribes, his family, and his disciples, to note the common elements in the fate suffered by John the Baptist and the 'second John', to speculate about the symbolic significance of the otherwise inexplicable destruction of the fig tree, or to contrast the responses of Peter and his master in the face of a threatening situation. And all this in addition to the sheer artistic satisfaction produced by well-crafted storytelling.

37. For further examples and discussion see also H. C. Kee, *Community,* 54-56.

Mark's sandwiches thus serve a variety of functions, literary and theological. But at the simplest level they create suspense, as the reader has to wait for the conclusion of one story until another has been told (this is most notable in the story of Jairus's daughter, left *in extremis* while Jesus deals with a much less pressing case). And suspense is woven into Mark's dramatic structure as a whole, as the elements of the plot are woven together into a gradually approaching climax, well signalled in advance, and yet so improbable in relation to the beginnings of the story that the reader approaches it with a sense of disbelief as well as of inevitability. For this is a story of paradox. Frank Kermode well summarises this point:

> The paradoxes continue: unmistakable public recognitions alternate with demands for and withdrawals into silence. Demons infallibly recognize him; disciples do not. The Law is now kept and now broken. The canons of purity are challenged; a purity which is itself accused of uncleanliness opposes and purges the unclean. If the general sense that there is a moment of special force in the eighth chapter is well founded, it must be so because so many of these paradoxes come together there in a great knot. But there are many knots; they occur in the riddling parables, in the frequent collocation of perceptive demons and imperceptive saints, in the delight and gratitude of the outsider who is cured, and the astonishment, fear, and dismay of the insiders.[38]

It is because these paradoxes are maintained, and never fully resolved in explicit explanations, that many people find Mark's book such a good read, tantalising, thought-provoking, and above all never dull. And, of course, for those who believe that 16:8 is the intended end of the book, the element of paradox reaches its highest point just as the story closes, and without resolution. In the commentary on chapter 16 I shall argue that that is one paradox too far, and that it was not Mark's intention to leave the reader in suspense at the end of the book. But on the way to his conclusion, whatever it may have been or been intended to be, suspense and paradox are the hallmarks of Mark's individual way of telling the story of Jesus.

D. The Message of Mark

Not long ago it was fashionable to explain Mark's message in negative terms, by postulating undesirable views and tendencies in the first-century church which he wrote his book to oppose. Thus we had titles like 'The Heresy That Necessitated Mark's Gospel'[39] or 'The Aversions Displayed by the Evange-

---

38. F. Kermode, *Genesis*, 141.
39. T. J. Weeden in *ZNW* 59 (1968) 145-58, repr. in W. R. Telford (ed.), *Interpretation*, 89-104.

list'.[40] With reference to such 'corrective' interpretations of Mark, E. Best[41] makes the naughty but perceptive comment:

> Underlying such views is the assumption that Mark is a polemical writing. . . . People have read the Gospel for centuries without this idea ever coming into their heads. It is probably a scholars' mirage created by the attitude they take up to other scholars' writings; they are so used to writing polemically against one another that they assume it is the only reason why people write!

At the time when such 'corrective' approaches were dominant, one of the prime contenders for the role of the 'heresy' opposed by Mark was a conception of Jesus which followed the Hellenistic ideal of the θεῖος ἀνήρ, the wonder-working philosopher whom his followers regarded as at least semidivine. This triumphalistic estimate of Jesus (and, by implication, of what it meant to follow him) was, it was alleged, in sharp contrast to Mark's message of a rejected, unrecognised, and suffering Messiah; his paradoxical portrait of a crucified Son of God was thus an attempt to redress the balance.[42] The remarkable failure of the disciples to understand the nature of Jesus' mission which is so prominent a feature of Mark's story was part of this strategy, intended to provoke Mark's readers to adopt the radical new perspective of the kingdom of God which the disciples so signally failed to grasp, and thus to repudiate the more superficially attractive but ultimately disastrous estimate of Jesus as merely a θεῖος ἀνήρ. Nowadays one hears much less about θεῖοι ἄνδρες, since recent scholarship has cast significant doubt on whether there ever was such a recognised category, and whether the term θεῖος ἀνήρ would have been generally understood in the sense in which modern scholars have used it.[43] It seems more likely that Mark's concern was not with so specific a concept, but with the very natural human reluctance to accept that the promised Messiah could suffer rejection by the Jewish leadership and that a Son of God could live unrecognised among human beings and die a shameful death. This reluctance, exemplified by the experience of Jesus' first disciples, was no doubt equally strong among many of Mark's po-

40. Heading of ch. 2 of E. Trocmé, *Formation,* pp. 87-137.

41. E. Best, *Story,* 45-46. Best's own approach is well summed up on 93: 'Mark is not a controversialist, least of all an academic controversialist, but a pastor.'

42. Anderson, 55, gives eloquent expression to this view of Mark's aim: 'Mark campaigns against balcony-type Christians who are too high for the mission and discipleship that in Mark's terms necessarily involve cross-bearing and self-sacrifice. Now they lose themselves in vain recollection and contemplation of the mighty works and glorious heavenly status of Christ. . . . Now captivated by the thrill of living, as they believe, in the last days, they claim a private lien on the divine authority of Jesus and seek to prove their own messianic status by performing outward signs and wonders. . . . Such exalted ones the Evangelist must bring down to earth and warn that the only authentic Christian way is the way of the suffering Son of man.'

43. Important discussions include D. L. Tiede, *Figure;* C. H. Holladay, *Theios Aner;* J. D. Kingsbury, *Int* 35 (1981) 243-57; W. von Martitz, *TDNT,* 8.338-40.

tential readers, but it seems an unnecessarily negative approach to depict his gospel as written specifically to refute such a 'heresy' rather than to focus on his more positive aim, to present Jesus as the master Mark understood him to be and to call on his readers to follow Jesus appropriately.[44]

One of the most single-minded recent approaches to understanding Mark's purpose is that of R. H. Gundry, whose commentary is entitled *Mark: A Commentary on His Apology for the Cross*.[45] In opposition to virtually all previous attempts to discern Mark's overriding theme or purpose (listed and summarily dismissed on p. 1 under the heading: 'The Gospel of Mark contains no ciphers, no hidden meanings, no sleight of hand'!), and with a robust disregard for the 'regnant view that Mark corrects the theology of glory with the theology of suffering', Gundry argues that the opposite is the case, that for Mark the suffering of the cross is subsumed into the authority and glory of God's triumphant Messiah. Even, indeed especially, in the account of Jesus' suffering and crucifixion the emphasis falls on his dignity and triumph: Mark 'has glorified the passion'. In reaction against earlier 'corrective' accounts of Mark's purpose, this is a stimulating redressing of the balance. But I doubt whether subsequent interpreters will agree that so single an overriding purpose has in fact governed Mark's complex narrative in all its parts, or that Mark wrote the gospel primarily not for church members but 'as religious propaganda to be performed before interested listeners, i.e., as a missionary message to be read in public especially for non-Christians'.[46]

Another type of overriding purpose is sometimes suggested in terms of Mark's desire to present Jesus in the light of a particular OT model.[47] Two recent examples may illustrate this approach, both of which have contributed a lot to our understanding of Mark, and will be drawn on frequently in this commentary. Joel Marcus, *The Way of the Lord* (1993), focuses on a series of passages where Mark takes OT texts as the basis for 'christological exegesis', often in the light of more subtle developments in postbiblical Jewish thought, and suggests that he is constructing a pattern of messianic fulfilment in conscious distinction from the Zealot ideology recently discredited through the failure of the revolt against Rome. R. E. Watts, *Isaiah's New Exodus and Mark* (1997), suggests that Mark focused more specifically on the Book of Isaiah with its hope of

---

44. S. E. Dowd, *Prayer,* 6-24, gives an interesting historical survey of the rise and fall of what she calls 'the now defunct consensus' that Mark's gospel was to be interpreted as 'an anti-miracle polemic'. A less extreme example of a 'corrective' purpose proposed for Mark (and one more securely anchored in what we know of first-century Christianity) is that outlined by R. P. Martin, *Evangelist,* 160-62, and developed in the following chapter, that Mark wrote to counter a distortion of Paul's kerygma which 'placed all the emphasis on Christ as a heavenly figure, remote from empirical history and out of touch with earthly reality'.

45. Gundry sets out his thesis in broad outline on pp. 1-15, and it is deployed constantly throughout the 1000 pages of commentary before being reprised on pp. 1022-26.

46. Gundry, 1026.

47. For some recent proposals of this type which have not so far proved influential (those of J. D. M. Derrett, W. Roth, H. M. Humphrey, and W. M. Swartley) see Van Iersel, 60-64.

a 'new Exodus', and tailored his presentation of Jesus to demonstrate the fulfilment of this hope.[48] While neither Marcus nor Watts would argue, I think, that *all* of Mark's gospel can be accounted for in terms of their theses, each understands this argument from scripture to be more than just a contributory factor alongside others.

From time to time a more immediate purpose for the gospel is suggested in the light of first-century events, such as Marxsen's view that Mark wrote in order to warn Jerusalem Christians to flee to Galilee before the city was destroyed, or Brandon's view that Mark wrote in Rome immediately after the war in order to distance Gentile Christianity from the embarrassment of its Jewish roots.[49] Such specific theories of Mark's aim have not met with general agreement, and as long as both the date and place of writing remain a matter of dispute no theory which depends on a specific time and place can expect to fare better.

It is in any case questionable whether it is realistic to expect to uncover so specific a purpose underlying the writing of a gospel. Few books, especially narrative books as contrasted, for example, with a Pauline letter, are written with so restricted an aim. Most scholars are therefore content to agree simply that Mark's aim was to write about Jesus, drawing on the information available to him, and that in the process a number of his personal concerns and the circumstances of the church within which he wrote will have guided his writing, without any of them being so dominant as to be (consciously or unconsciously) *the* purpose of the book.

For a first-century church leader or teacher to write about Jesus was not only to tell the personal story of the prophet from Nazareth, but also to explain what it meant to be his follower and to inspire others to play their proper part in the movement he founded. So most discussions of Mark's aim or message rightly revolve around the two broad areas of christology and discipleship, of who Jesus is and of what it means to follow him, and we may usefully adopt those two headings.

Christology

Discussions of NT christology used to focus almost exclusively on 'titles' (and in particular on the evolution of the 'big four' titles, Christ, Lord, Son of Man, Son of God). Much that is important emerges from such a study, but that is not the whole of christology, a point vividly made by Leander Keck: 'To reconstruct the history of titles as if this were the study of christology is like trying to

48. Watts has convincingly demonstrated that Isaiah plays a more dominant role within Mark's use of the OT than previous scholarship has recognised. Cf also R. Schneck, *Isaiah in the Gospel of Mark I–VIII* (Vallejo, CA: BIBAL, 1994), referred to by Watts, *Exodus*, 26-27; Schneck's work has not been available to me.

49. W. Marxsen, *Mark*; S. G. F. Brandon, *Zealots*.

understand the windows of Chartres cathedral by studying the history of coloured glass.'[50] What Mark has to say about Jesus goes far beyond his use of 'Christ', 'Son of Man', and 'Son of God', and to try to tie it down in a few defining sentences is to miss the point that the whole gospel, in its narratives as much as in its relatively few theological statements about Jesus, is 'christology'. His portrait of Jesus emerges untidily and with a rich profusion of elements as the narrative develops, so that it is at least as appropriate to sum up his christology in as broad and imprecise a phrase as 'Jesus as the one who cares'[51] as it is to focus on the 'christological titles'. As Frank Matera rightly concludes, 'None of these [the titles Messiah, Son of God, Son of Man] can be understood adequately apart from Mark's narrative; for the Christology is in the story, and through the story we learn to interpret the titles.'[52]

I mentioned above the theory of Richard Peace that Mark's gospel is designed in two main parts each containing three roughly equal sections each focused on a new 'title' of Jesus, so that the disciples' awareness of Jesus' role is progressively enhanced as each new title is introduced. The sequence, Peace argues, is as follows: Part I ('Messiah', 1:16–8:30) containing Unit 1, 'Jesus the Teacher', 1:16–4:34; Unit 2, 'Jesus the Prophet', 4:35–6:30; Unit 3, 'Jesus the Messiah', 6:31–8:30; Part II ('Son of God', 8:31–15:39) containing Unit 4, 'Jesus the Son of Man', 8:31–10:45; Unit 5, 'Jesus the Son of David', 10:46–13:37; Unit 6, 'Jesus the Son of God', 14:1–15:39.[53] I believe that this structure is neater than Mark intended, with the titles Son of Man and Son of God occurring prominently in the narrative before their designated units and large parts of several units having no obvious bearing on the title assigned to them. In places Mark's focus seems to be less on the disciples than on others (Jesus is recognised, or in 6:4 not recognised, as 'prophet' by people in general and Herod in particular rather than by disciples; it is not the disciples but the centurion to whom Jesus is revealed as 'Son of God' in 15:39); indeed, in the second half of the gospel the emphasis seems to be on what the disciples failed to perceive rather than on any increase in their christological understanding. In the end it is not so much the disciples as the readers who are the beneficiaries of the christological revelation which Mark has built into his narrative. But Peace's analysis makes a useful contribution: first, it widens the discussion beyond the three 'major' titles Messiah, Son of Man, and Son of God (though its structure leaves no place for the further important emphasis on Jesus as King of the Jews in ch. 15); second, it recognises that Mark's christological focus is located in

50. From L. E. Keck's stimulating article 'Toward the Renewal of NT Christology', *NTS* 32 (1986) 362-77, which deals with the study of titles especially on 368-70.

51. This is the title of a central chapter of E. Best, *Story* (55-65), which rightly occupies a more prominent place in his study than the brief and almost apologetic chapter headed 'christology' (79-82) in which Best deals with titles, but also protests against 'the attempt to force Mark into a christological pattern' (80).

52. F. J. Matera, *Christology*, 26.

53. R. V. Peace, *Conversion*, 116-22.

the narrative development rather than in isolated sayings, resulting in an incremental revelation of who Jesus is and what he has come to do.

Jesus appears from the outset of Mark's narrative as one who causes astonishment, as a figure of unprecedented authority. The improbably ready response of Peter, Andrew, James, and John to a stranger's call to discipleship (1:16-20) leads straight into an incident in Capernaum where both Jesus' teaching and his power over unclean spirits cause astonishment at his authority (1:22, 27), after which Jesus quickly becomes the talk of the town, and beyond (1:28, 32-33, 37, 45; 2:2, etc.). The pattern thus established runs throughout Act One, as both crowds and disciples try to make sense of this extraordinary 'teacher' and 'prophet', and miracle after miracle compounds the astonishment. The result is a division of 'christological' opinion which Mark graphically illustrates in the contrasting groups of chapter 3 and then explores through the explanatory discourse of chapter 4 with its emphasis on divided response, on insiders and outsiders, on the privileged insight of disciples and the puzzlement of the crowd, on what is hidden and what is to be revealed. But as the story goes on even the supposedly enlightened disciples are found to be still asking, 'Who is this?' (4:41), and increasing evidence of Jesus' supernatural authority seems not to lead to a corresponding progress in their understanding (6:52; 7:18; 8:14-21).

When at last the apparent breakthrough is made in Peter's use of the title ὁ Χριστός, all that has been gained seems lost again as Peter's interpretation of the term is shown to be the very opposite to the 'thoughts of God' (8:32-33). From that point on the insistent repetition of the image of the rejected and suffering Son of Man and of a kingdom of God in which the first are last and the last first leaves the disciples hopelessly at sea; even the extraordinary revelation of Jesus' heavenly glory on the mountain leaves the inner group of Peter, James, and John more confused than enlightened. In this the disciples represent not a particularly hostile or obtuse ideology, but the very natural human reaction to a divine plan which makes no human sense; their thoughts are, to use again the language of a saying which is crucial for understanding Mark's christological perspective, human rather than divine (8:33).

And yet Peter's words, even if not his thoughts, had been right, and Jesus' messianic arrival outside the walls of Jerusalem sets this openly proclaimed 'Son of David' (10:47-48; 11:10) in inevitable conflict with the current leadership in David's city. The old question 'Who is this?' thus takes on a new dimension, as it is no longer a matter of making sense simply of Jesus on his own, but now of fitting him into the established theology of the people of God, its divine calling, its story and its institutions, and of relating him to the power structure which Jerusalem has come to represent. Two dominant 'characters' in the story represent that structure, the imposing physical structure of the temple and the human leadership of ἀρχιερεῖς καὶ γραμματεῖς καὶ πρεσβύτεροι τοῦ λαοῦ for whom the temple is the symbol of their authority. From chapter 11 onward, therefore, the story revolves around the temple, both as location and as subject, and the members of the Sanhedrin with whom Jesus is locked in increasingly hostile dialogue. The issue of authority remains central, and the reader gradually becomes aware of a contrast between the actual power concentrated in the hands of the Sanhedrin and the real authority of the Messiah/Son of God who, though subject to their temporal power, is the one sent by his Father to dispossess them (12:6-9), the stone which the builders will reject but which will become the divinely laid cornerstone. Over against this new, God-built structure ('made without hands', 14:58) the existing temple and all that it symbolises is now redundant. The explanatory discourse of chapter 13 links the coming destruction of the temple with the enthronement of the Son of Man, and the words of Jesus at his final Passover meal speak of a new covenant and thus a newly constituted people of God which will result from his death.

Thus by the time Jesus is arrested, tried, and executed, the reader has the pieces in place to begin to construct a more far-reaching answer to the question 'Who is this?' than was apparent in the wonder-working prophet of Galilee, more far-reaching, too, than the simple application of a few 'christological titles' could convey. It is a christology which at all points overturns 'human thoughts', and which can be expressed in the closing scenes of the gospel only by the irony of a narrative which presents Jesus at the moment of his official condemnation at last openly declaring his supreme authority over those who presume to judge him (14:61-62), and allows the reader, even as Jesus is tortured and crucified, to hear in the repeated jibes of Pilate, his Gentile soldiers, the Jewish crowd, and the chief priests and scribes the ultimate truth about Jesus, that this dying Son of Man is in truth the King of the Jews. This title, previously hinted at in Jesus' ride towards the city and in the muted deployment of Davidic language, now in the penultimate chapter of the gospel comes into the open, and blended with the tearing of the temple curtain and the Gentile centurion's acclamation of Jesus as Son of God leaves the reader with a potent mixture of christological themes to assimilate. Mark's paradoxical story thus invites us to think God's thoughts, not human thoughts, and when we begin to do so it will come as no surprise to find that the end was not after all the end, and that the promise of resurrection which was the barely noticed coda to each of Jesus' passion predictions is the only possible way forward. The story has only just begun.

In this barest outline of some of the main aspects of Mark's christological narrative I began with the beginning of Act One, in Galilee. But of course Mark's gospel does not begin there. In the Prologue he has already provided the most blatant clues as to the significance of the person whose story he is about to tell: Messiah, Son of God, bringer of God's salvation, mightier than the returning Elijah, the one who both gives and receives the Spirit of God, the chosen one who comes to do battle with the powers of evil, and who has angels at his side. In much of the story that follows the ultimate dimensions sketched out in the prologue are not brought into the open, but all the time the reader knows what disciples, crowds, and chief priests do not, and so is in a position to develop a christology which to them was available only ἐν παραβολαῖς.

The categories in which I have tried to sketch out Mark's presentation of Jesus are much broader and less philosophical than the traditional concerns of systematic christology, what used to be called 'The Person of Christ' or 'The Doctrine of Incarnation'. To understand who Jesus is, for Mark, is primarily to understand what he has come to do, how he fits into the ongoing story of God's dealings with his people in the particular context of Tiberian Palestine.[54] That is not to say that Mark saw no relevance for Jesus beyond the world of the mid-first century, but he has written a story of Jesus, not a treatise on incarnation and atonement, still less an exploration of trinitarian orthodoxy. It may be legitimate to use aspects of his narrative to guide our thinking in these more abstract areas, but if we do so it must be in the recognition that, as far as his book allows us to judge, we are going beyond the perspective within which he wrote them. Mark's is a narrative christology.

Discipleship[55]

While obviously the primary focus of a book about Jesus must be, in the broadest sense of the term, christology, the Gospel of Mark is the story not merely of Jesus but of Jesus and his disciples. From the time of his first appearance beside the lake of Galilee in 1:16, Jesus is seldom alone. He calls people to join him, and as he travels about in and around Galilee he is constantly accompanied by a band of close associates, called μαθηταί, sometimes individually named but usually spoken of as a group. The selection of the essential group of twelve, to whom distinctively Mark applies the term μαθηταί,[56] from among a wider circle of supporters is given in 3:13-19 a prominence which may seem surprising in view of the fact that most of their names never occur again; it is not the individuals that Mark wants his readers to notice so much as the group and what they represent. Even though in the majority of incidents narrated the Twelve do not play a central role, they are always there as a silent presence, watching, learning, reacting, and gradually being moulded into the focused community who will become the spearhead of the new movement of the kingdom of God after Jesus has gone. During the journey to Jerusalem which makes up Act Two of the drama the main focus of Jesus' attention will be on their training, and their failure to understand both Jesus' own mission and the new values of the kingdom of God which he has come to establish will set up the tension which preoccupies the reader until the story swings into its final phase in Jerusalem. There the disciples will for a time be less in evidence, though always present, while Jesus engages in debate with the Jerusalem leadership, but the discourse

54. E. Best, *Story,* 79-82, rightly emphasises that Mark's christology is concerned not with identity but with activity. Jesus is understood primarily by what he does.

55. For a detailed survey and critique of redaction-critical studies of the disciples in Mark see C. C. Black, *Disciples.*

56. See p. 158 below.

of chapter 13 is directed to the central group of disciples to provide them with orientation for the future, and the passion story proper will begin with Jesus still closely involved with the disciples at the Passover meal and on the road to Gethsemane. It is only in Gethsemane that the band will be broken up, leaving Jesus alone for the remainder of the passion narrative, in striking contrast with the story up to this point. The disciples' desertion (further emphasised by Peter's abortive attempt to stay with Jesus, 14:54, 66-72) leaves the reader bewildered by the apparent undoing of all that Jesus has been so carefully building up throughout the narrative, but an unexpected 'flash forward' in Jesus' prediction on the road to Gethsemane (14:28) has left open a window of hope, and this hope is reasserted as the story (as we have it)[57] closes with the call to the disciples, and especially Peter, to rejoin the risen Jesus in Galilee.

The disciples (as a narrative subject) are thus a central element in Mark's story. While it may be an exaggeration to say that 'the theme which plays the controlling part in the unfolding of the Gospel of Mark is the conversion of the Twelve',[58] that statement does at least post a valuable warning against any tendency to view discipleship as only a side issue in this gospel, and to look for Mark's distinctive message only in his christology proper. Not that the two are ultimately separable, of course. It is in their discovery of and response to who Jesus is that the disciples occupy our attention; discipleship is the proper outcome of a healthy christology. But the story Mark tells is to a large extent the story of Jesus as seen by his disciples. It is the story of their gradual 'conversion', with its new insights and sacrificial commitments as well as its gaffes and failures. It is about how twelve ordinary men met Jesus and entered into a new dimension of living.

At the narrative level the disciples could not be ignored: the historical Jesus was not a lone teacher, but the leader of a small itinerant group. But Mark's focus on the disciples is not just a matter of historical reminiscence. They are far too prominent in his narrative for that. Mark is writing in the context of, and for the guidance of, those who are now the successors to that early group of followers of Jesus, those through whom the mission of the kingdom of God must now be carried forward as it has first been by those original disciples.

So Mark sets those first disciples before his readers as a guide to their own following of Jesus. Some of the time they are exemplary models to be imitated: in their wholehearted commitment as they leave everything to follow Jesus (1:18, 20; 2:14; 10:28-30), in their privileged insight into the secret of the kingdom of God (4:11), and in their sharing in Jesus' work of proclamation and deliverance (3:14-15; 6:12-13, 30). But more often they are negative models, in their fear and faithlessness (4:40; 6:49-50), their selfish ambition (9:34; 10:35-

---

57. I shall discuss the question of Mark's extraordinary ending in the commentary on 16:1-8, and shall argue that 16:7 suggests that 16:8 was not the intended end of the story, even though we now have no authentic text of Mark beyond that verse.

58. R. V. Peace, *Conversion*, 112, summing up the main emphasis of his study.

28

45), their spiritual failure (9:14-29), and their ultimate desertion of their master. Above all, despite the declaration of 4:11 that they have been given special insight, they prove repeatedly, and increasingly as the story goes on, unable to grasp the basic principles of Jesus' teaching and mission (6:52; 7:18; 8:14-21), so that what Jesus said about the outsiders in 4:11-12 becomes true also of the disciples in 8:17-18, and the main focus of Act Two is on the disciples' need for (but extraordinary failure to profit from) a drastic programme of re-education into the values of the kingdom of God (8:31–10:45 passim). Peter in particular is portrayed as a tantalising mixture of special insight (8:29) and extraordinary obtuseness (8:32-33; 9:5-6), a man whose boasted loyalty collapses into the most shameful betrayal (14:29-31, 66-72). And then there is Judas Iscariot as well.[59]

Mark's 'realism' with regard to the disciples is sometimes spoken of as if it were a personal vendetta, a sort of corporate character-assassination. Certainly Mark pulls no punches, but it is far from inconceivable that in real life a group of ordinary men caught up in such an extraordinary story should respond like that, as they confronted at first hand and without warning a revolution of ideas and values which much of the Christian church still struggles to comprehend after twenty centuries of conditioning. All the evidence we have from the first century agrees on the ultimate failure of the Twelve until the situation was reversed at Pentecost. What Mark has done is to allow his readers to trace the weaknesses which led to that failure, so that history might not be allowed to repeat itself.

The preceding paragraphs outlined what are by common consent the two most central areas for discussing Mark's message, his presentation of christology and discipleship, of who Jesus is and what it means to follow him. A number of other issues which arise in studying Mark's gospel must be mentioned more briefly.

The Kingdom of God[60]

At the opening of Act One Mark summarises the good news which Jesus brings in terms of the coming of the βασιλεία τοῦ θεοῦ (1:15).[61] In the commentary on that passage I will take up the background and meaning of the term, but here we must note that a phrase introduced with such emphasis in the opening account of Jesus' ministry may be expected to play a prominent role in the story as a

---

59. C. C. Black, *Disciples,* 41-46, usefully sets out the positive and negative elements in Mark's portrayal of the Twelve in general and Peter in particular.

60. On the view of B. L. Mack, *Myth,* that Mark's message revolves around a concept of the 'kingdom of God' derived from Cynic and Stoic ideas, see the comments of Gundry, 1022.

61. I have discussed Mark's use of the phrase and the theology underlying it in my *Divine Government.*

whole. For those who are familiar with the Gospel of Matthew, therefore, it is a surprise to discover that Mark uses the term only 14 times, five of which are concentrated in the section 10:13-27. But its importance in Mark's thinking is indicated by the fact that the first explanatory discourse (4:1-34), which helps the reader to grasp the whole nature of Jesus' ministry and its effects, centres around this term. Not only are two of the three story-parables explicitly introduced as illustrating the nature of the kingdom of God (4:26, 30), but the explanation of the other and leading story-parable is introduced by Jesus' pregnant saying about understanding τὸ μυστήριον τῆς βασιλείας τοῦ θεοῦ (4:11), which is therefore to be understood not only as the subject of this parable as well (and thus of all parables, 4:13) but as denoting the insight into the hidden purpose of God which distinguishes Jesus' true followers from 'those outside', and which it is the function of this discourse to explain.

So despite its open proclamation by Jesus (1:15), the kingdom of God is something which not everyone can understand; it lies beyond natural human perception because it is the kingdom *of God*. It takes people by surprise, as when the seed grows unnoticed, αὐτομάτη, and as when the easily overlooked mustard seed becomes a great plant. At the moment it is secretly at work, but one day it will be seen to have come ἐν δυνάμει (9:1); while already dynamically present (1:15), its full experience lies still in the future (14:25). In the meantime it will continue to challenge and overturn the natural expectations and values of disciples and opponents alike (10:13-27), calling them to a radical new allegiance (9:47) which will set them apart from those who can see things only from a traditional human point of view (12:34; 15:43).

The phrase ἡ βασιλεία τοῦ θεοῦ (probably best represented in English by 'God's kingship') thus encapsulates the paradox which we have already seen to lie at the heart of Mark's story. It is a μυστήριον, not in the sense that it is an obscure concept in itself, but in that it challenges and opposes every natural human valuation. As long as people continue to think human thoughts (8:33) they will never understand, still less become part of, the βασιλεία τοῦ θεοῦ. Mark's gospel is the story of how Jesus sowed this good seed into the varied soil of Roman Palestine, and of the varied way in which its human inhabitants responded. In particular it is the story of how one selected group of men were given privileged access to God's thoughts, and of their struggle, still largely unsuccessful even at the end of the story, to transcend their human thoughts so that the good seed of God's kingship might grow and flourish in them and through them until it could be seen to have come with power. When Mark's story closes that time seems to remain still in the future.

If this is how Mark understands the coming of the kingdom of God which is the context in which his hero's life and work are presented, it is no wonder that his story is throughout one of paradox.

Secrecy

The word μυστήριον is best translated 'secret', something which is available only to those to whom it has been revealed. Mark's single use of the term in 4:11 is a pointer to a theme which emerges in other words at many points in the gospel and has often been singled out as one of the main distinguishing marks of his presentation of the story of Jesus. It is most prominent in the four attempts by Jesus to prevent people from talking freely about his miracles (1:43-44; 5:43; 7:36; 8:26), attempts which are sometimes spectacularly unsuccessful (1:45; 7:36-37). Demons too, with their supernatural insight, are forbidden to reveal the truth about the one who has dispossessed them (1:25, 34; 3:12). Jesus is often depicted as deliberately avoiding public notice and acclaim (1:37-38; 5:40; 6:31-32, 45-46; 7:24, 33; 8:23; 9:30). But the pattern is not monochrome. The initial account of Jesus' Galilean ministry is of open proclamation and response (1:14-39). Much of the time Jesus seems to have no objection to public notice and comment on his miracles and even to invite it (2:8-12; 3:2-5; 5:19-20, 30-34; 10:46-52), and on his eventual arrival in Jerusalem deliberately draws attention to himself and his mission (11:1-10, 15-18), so that at his arrest he can make a point of his open activity in the temple (14:49).

Much of this could be accounted for at the historical level as reflecting Jesus' prudential management of crowd response in order to avoid unwelcome publicity and disturbance by insensitive popular acclaim such as is recorded in 1:45–2:2; 6:31, and in order to avoid drawing the hostile attention of the authorities (6:14-16) before the time had come for him to declare himself.[62] But the silencing of the supernatural testimony of the demons suggests that more is involved, and this further dimension is strengthened by the two commands to silence which concern not miracles but the truth about Jesus himself, his Messiahship (8:30) and his divine glory and status as God's unique son as revealed in the transfiguration (9:9). It should be noted, however, that these two commands are addressed not to the crowds but to the disciples. They (and the demons) have been let into the secret which has so far been withheld from people in general, and the time is not yet ripe for it to be more widely known. The time will come for what has been hidden to be revealed (4:21-22): Jesus will himself declare that he is Messiah and Son of God (14:61-62), and the prohibition on talking about the transfiguration is valid only until after the resurrection (9:9).

The varied nature of this evidence suggests that any simple theory of a Marcan secrecy motif is likely to be inadequate. Secrecy is not an issue in itself. It is rather a function of the nature of Jesus' message and ministry, which, as we have seen in the previous section, runs counter to conventional human values, even to those of traditional Jewish religious expectation. The constant misunderstandings even on the part of Jesus' closest disciples vividly illustrate the ba-

---

62. I shall develop this point in the commentary on 8:30; see pp. 330-31.

sis for Jesus' caution about allowing people, even disciples, to talk openly about the μυστήριον which only divine revelation could unveil to human insight, and which would eventually work itself out through the humanly incomprehensible means of a rejected and abandoned Messiah, a dying Son of God, and an empty tomb. In the light of the paradox of 'God's kingship' as Mark understands it, we need no 'conspiracy theory' (such as was proposed by William Wrede in 1901 and has been revamped in different ways by many others since) to explain his frequent emphasis on the need to avoid premature disclosure of the mysterious means by which God had chosen to implement it. The mustard seed will grow in its own time, but until then its significance will necessarily remain hidden from all but the few whose eyes God has opened. But one day they will be able to see that, despite apparent failure and delay, God's kingship has come with power.

Eschatology

In the 'Old Testament' sense of the word, Mark's gospel is full of eschatology. It is all about the fulfilment within history of the promises of God. The good news of the fulfilment of the Scriptures, which is signalled in the great opening salvo of prophetic testimony (1:2-3), is a recurrent theme throughout the story, not only with reference to Jesus' proclamation and demonstration of God's kingship, leading up to his 'Davidic' approach to Jerusalem, but also and especially in the apparent disaster which follows, as the Son of Man 'goes as it is written of him' (14:21; cf. 9:12; 14:49), so that eventually the stone rejected by the builders may be elevated to become the cornerstone (12:10-11), as through Jesus' death on behalf of many a new covenant is established and the people of God reconstituted (14:22-25).

This is eschatological language, but it is not the language of the end of the world but rather of a new beginning, of the world restored under God's kingship. The historical horizon which dominates Mark's gospel is apparently bounded by the coming destruction of the temple and all that it stands for and the indefinite period during which the newly regathered people of God will then continue to live under the authority of the enthroned Son of Man (see commentary especially on 13:24-27), a period during which the good news will continue to be proclaimed throughout the world (13:10; 14:9). I shall argue in this commentary that the passages about the 'coming of the Son of Man', which have traditionally been interpreted as referring to a parousia which will mark the end of earthly history (8:38; 13:26; 14:62) do not naturally carry such a meaning, but use the enthronement language of Dn. 7:13-14 to describe the imminent vindication of the rejected Son of Man and his authority at the 'right hand of power' (14:62). That authority, though located in heaven, is operative within earthly history.

Some interpreters, having reached this conclusion, therefore find no place in Mark for the traditional doctrine of the parousia or for any closure to earthly history.[63] This view has the attractive simplicity of Occam's razor, but seems to me to be vulnerable on two fronts. Firstly, the author of this gospel lived in a period when the Christian churches, as far as we can judge from the NT, and especially from the letters of Paul which predate the gospel, shared not only a theoretical belief in Jesus' return, but also an enthusiastic and sometimes disruptively imminent expectation of it. And Mark's gospel does not give the impression of a document derived from an esoteric group cut off from this mainstream Christian current of belief. Of course an author who shared this belief is not obliged to have included any expression of it in a work to which he judged it to be irrelevant. But given both the scale of Mark's work and his strong interest in the post-resurrection authority of Jesus, the parousia belief might naturally have been expected to emerge at some point in the story. And secondly, the gospel does include a passage which resembles closely the parousia language of the other synoptic gospels, the statement about the unknown day and hour and the need to keep awake so as to be prepared for an unexpected coming (13:32-37). I shall argue in the commentary that, even though the language of 13:24-31 is not that of parousia but of enthronement, in v. 32 the subject has changed, and that at this point Mark is looking further into the future. He does not use the term παρουσία as Matthew does in his lengthy expansion (24:36–25:46) of this part of the tradition, but the subject matter is the same. So while Mark's 'parousia section' is surprisingly brief, allusive and low key, I believe that that is what it is, and that Matthew did not misinterpret this little pericope when he used it as the basis for a substantial treatment of Jesus' parousia and the συντέλεια τοῦ αἰῶνος.

Galilee and Jerusalem

I mentioned above the apparently artificial scheme of Mark's narrative in that the geographical setting of the successive phases of the story (Act One in Galilee and surrounding regions, Act Two on the road to Jerusalem, Act Three in Jerusalem) is likely to be a drastic simplification of Jesus' actual historical movements. It provides an effective dramatic structure, marking the development of the plot towards its climax. But it has often been suggested that it also carries a symbolic significance, with Galilee and Jerusalem representing two poles in Mark's theology, so that the geography is the medium of his message. This approach to Mark's gospel, associated particularly with the work of Ernst Lohmeyer and R. H. Lightfoot,[64] has been widely discussed in recent study of the gospel.

63. So especially N. T. Wright, *Victory,* in his study of Mark 13 and parallels (339-68), though his pan-synoptic approach does not result in a direct exegesis of Mark 13:32-37 as such.

64. E. Lohmeyer, *Galiläa;* R. H. Lightfoot, *Locality.* Cf also W. Marxsen, *Mark,* Study Two.

It has gained impetus from the increasing recognition in recent scholarship of the considerable contrast, and sometimes hostility, between the two regions of Galilee and Judaea in NT times.[65] Briefly united under David and Solomon, the northern and southern parts of Israel broke apart again under Rehoboam, and from that time until the Maccabean conquests in the second century B.C. they remained separately governed provinces under the various successive empires. After the death of Herod the Great they were again politically divided, and by the time of Jesus Galilee was under the client king Herod Antipas, Judaea under direct Roman rule. The separate histories of the two areas had led to a separate sense of identity, with Galilee a much less securely Jewish territory. During the Maccabean wars it had been felt necessary to evacuate the remaining Jewish population of Galilee to Judaea for safety (1 Macc. 5:14-23), and the reestablishment of a Jewish population in parts of Galilee was apparently largely due to the military success of Aristobulus I at the end of the second century B.C. (Schürer, 1.217-18). But these quite conservatively Jewish areas of Galilee, in which most of Mark's first act is set, were surrounded by flourishing Gentile communities, so that southerners tended to regard Galilean Jews with some suspicion. The hostile territory of Samaria which separated the two districts increased the isolation of Galilee, and there is rabbinic evidence that Galilean Jews spoke a distinctly 'northern' form of Aramaic (cf. Mk. 14:70; Mt. 26:73). At the time of Jesus a Galilean in Jerusalem, however strong his Jewish credentials, would have felt and been perceived as to some degree a foreigner, and an easy target of suspicion.

This historical and sociological difference between Galilee and Jerusalem is important as background to the interpretation of some gospel incidents, and I shall draw attention to these in the commentary that follows. But the Galilee/Jerusalem schema of Mark's narrative derives not only from historical observation but also, in the view of many interpreters, from a symbolic value which he has built onto the two locations. While there are exceptions, in broad terms Act One, set in and around Galilee, is a story of open proclamation and response, with committed disciples and enthusiastic crowds, while Act Three, in Jerusalem, is a dismal story of conflict, rejection, and death. And in between is Act Two, the journey from Galilee to Jerusalem, which begins with the warning of rejection and suffering in Jerusalem and develops into a determined march towards death. While there are hostile scribes and Pharisees in Galilee, Jesus' mission continues undeterred there, even though two appearances of scribes *from Jerusalem* signal deeper danger ahead (3:22; 7:1). It is the Jerusalem establishment who in the end will effectively suppress the Galilean prophet and disband his group of Galilean supporters. The Galilean pilgrims who welcome Jesus' arrival at Jerusalem will prove no match for the Jerusalem crowd who will demand his execution. But

---

65. Summarised by G. Vermes, *Jew,* 42-57, and fully demonstrated by S. Freyne, *Galilee from Alexander* and *Galilee, Jesus and Gospels.*

even as Jesus approaches the cross, he can look forward to the day when the good news which was first preached in Galilee will again be preached throughout the world, even as the Jerusalem temple is destroyed (13:10; 14:9), and the two pointers forward again to Galilee which light up the gloom of the Jerusalem climax (14:28; 16:7) suggest that it is from Galilee that the renewed mission is to be launched (as indeed Mt. 28:16-20 records, and I shall argue that Mark may well also have envisaged; see on 16:1-8).

It is, of course, too simple to imagine that Mark's Galilee was peopled entirely by heroes and his Jerusalem entirely by villains, that Act One is all glorious triumph and Act Three all disaster. Mark can record rejection and doubt in Galilee and popular acclaim in Jerusalem. But the overall characterisation of Galilee as the place of proclamation and response and of Jerusalem as the place of conflict and rejection seems very deliberate. The distinctiveness of this as a Marcan theme is illustrated by the different ways in which Matthew and Luke seem to have reacted to it. Both adopt the same artificial narrative outline, but it appears that the symbolism with which Mark has invested it was congenial to Matthew but not to Luke, in that whereas Matthew has if anything intensified the symbolic significance of the contrast between Galilee and Jerusalem to the detriment of the latter (see his additional material in 4:12-16; 21:10-11; 28:11-20), Luke already in his gospel and much more in Acts clearly depicts Jerusalem as the church's true home.

Mark's geographical symbolism, if such it is, is not a matter of great theological weight; it is rather a vehicle of his dramatic retelling of the story of Jesus, serving to draw out the intensely opposite reactions which he provoked, the contrasting soils into which the good seed had to be sown. But insofar as Jerusalem, and especially the temple which stood at the heart of its life, represented the status quo which was threatened by Jesus' radical new message, its failure to respond and the disaster which awaits it mark a decisive shift in the theology of the people of God, which is to find its focus no longer in the city, the temple and its priesthood, but in the stone which the builders rejected and which has now become the foundation stone of a new temple not made with hands.

E. The Origin of the Book

This, then, is an account of Jesus as he was understood by a leader in a Christian church sometime soon after the middle of the first century. It is questionable how important it is for us to be any more specific than that, even if that should prove to be possible. Just when and where the book was written, and by whom, interesting as they must be to historical scholarship, are not questions which are likely to have a major impact on its exegesis. The evidence usually adduced as a means of answering these questions is derived from the character and content of the book itself, so that on this basis there is an inevitable circularity in any attempt to determine the book's meaning from its supposed place or time of origin. Only if the external evidence of early church traditions about the book's origin is given greater weight than arguments from internal characteristics can we expect to find much exegetical enlightenment from a discussion of its provenance, and modern scholarship has been virtually unanimous in playing down the significance of the external evidence (though I shall go on to suggest that this scepticism about early church traditions is not always justified).

Another reason for caution in expecting any great exegetical help from establishing the place and time of the book's origin relates to the purpose for which gospels were written. In much of twentieth-century scholarship it has been taken for granted not only that a gospel was written in the context of a particular local church situation but also that its aim was to speak specifically to that situation. So understood, the gospels are to be interpreted in a way similar to that of the Pauline epistles as local, contingent texts, not as intended for the universal circulation which was in fact to be their destiny. On this basis much modern study of the gospels (notable the 'corrective' approaches outlined above) has been similar to the practice of 'mirror-reading' Paul's epistles[66] in order to reconstruct the local situations and concerns to which they were directed, and exegesis of their contents has been based on that presumed reconstruction. But in 1995 an important query was placed against such an assessment of the literary character and purpose of the gospels by Richard Bauckham in his lecture 'For Whom Were Gospels Written?', and the subsequent development of his thoughts on the subject by colleagues has reinforced his argument that the supposed local focus of the gospels has been assumed rather than argued, and is in fact a rather improbable assumption.[67] If Bauckham is right, and I think he is, the relevance of the historical provenance of the gospel for its exegesis becomes significantly less, since its intended message is not specifically focused on, still less limited to, the local Christian community out of which it emerged.[68]

The comments that follow with regard to where, when, and by whom this book was written can therefore be quite brief, as they do not materially affect the main purpose of this commentary, which is the understanding of the text.

Early church traditions about Mark's gospel, beginning with Papias at the beginning of the second century (or rather with the 'Elder' whom Papias

66. The term was appropriately suggested by J. M. G. Barclay, *JSNT* 31 (1987) 73-93.

67. The original lecture, given at the British New Testament Conference at Bangor in September 1995, appears along with other essays developing its theme in R. J. Bauckham (ed.), *Gospels*.

68. An earlier pointer to a similar view is found in the proposal of M. A. Beavis, *Audience*, 171, that 'Mark was directed not only to the evangelist's church, but to the more general audience of early Christian missionary teaching/preaching'. Cf her conclusions on 175-76, which set this missionary teaching hypothesis in contrast with 'the critical consensus that the Gospels were written for a Christian audience only'. Cf Gundry's view noted above that Mark's gospel is to be understood as 'religious propaganda to be performed before interested listeners, i.e., as a missionary message to be read in public especially for non-Christians' (Gundry, 1026).

quotes, and thus reaching back into the first century),[69] agree, where they offer specific comment on these points, that the author was called Mark (this Mark being assumed[70] to be the same one who appears at various points in the NT as a companion and colleague of Barnabas, Paul, and Peter),[71] that he derived his material from the preaching of Peter, with whom he was closely associated, and that the work was compiled in Rome or, more generally, 'in Italy'. This account of the origin of the gospel is repeated with minor variations[72] in Papias, the Anti-Marcionite and Monarchian Prologues, Irenaeus, Clement of Alexandria, Tertullian, Origen, Eusebius, Ephraem, Epiphanius, and Jerome; where the place of writing is not specifically mentioned (Papias, Tertullian, and Origen), it is assumed on the basis of the link with Peter's ministry in Rome. The traditional association of Mark with the church of Alexandria is not allowed to detract from this general understanding of the gospel's origin: Eusebius, *H.E.* 2.15-16 explains that Mark came to Egypt after he had written his gospel in Rome, and Epiphanius, *Haer.* 6.10 says that Peter sent him there after he had written the gospel.[73]

The only significant discrepancy among these early patristic notices is over whether Mark wrote the gospel before or after Peter's death (which is normally dated A.D. 64 or 65). Modern scholars (perhaps because it better suits their preferred dating) tend to quote only Irenaeus's statement (*Haer.* 3.1.1) that Mark wrote μετὰ τὴν ἔξοδον *(post excessum)* of Peter and Paul; cf. the Anti-Marcionite Prologue, *post excessionem Petri.* But the assumption that these terms refer to Peter's *death* is not certain,[74] and is cast in doubt by the wording of the tradition in 'Ephraem's' commentary on the Diatessaron, where the Latin version reads *cum abiisset Romam,* which surely refers to relocation rather than death.

69. See pp. 7-8 above for the text and comments on its date.

70. As W. R. Telford, *Theology,* 10, rightly points out, this identification is not made by Papias, or indeed explicitly by anyone before Jerome, and Marcus was a very common Roman name. But it may reasonably be supposed that when 'Mark' is mentioned without further specification it is the well-known NT character who is in view. The patristic accounts of Mark's involvement with Peter in Rome do not, however, depend on his identification with John Mark of Jerusalem.

71. It is of course not certain that all the various mentions of 'Mark' in the NT refer to the same person, though the fact that the 'Mark' of 1 Pet. 5:13 is mentioned alongside 'Silvanus' in 5:12, and that Silvanus (Silas) was also a prominent associate of Paul, tends to confirm that the same man was involved with both Paul and Peter.

72. It is frequently stated, but without any reason given, that all the subsequent accounts are *dependent on* that of Papias, and the conclusion is then drawn that this multiplicity of witnesses can safely be boiled down to only one. This is not at all obvious, since none of the writers before Eusebius mentions Papias as a source of their information. The fact that they agree with the essence (though not the wording) of Papias's account by no means requires that they derived their information from him.

73. The assertion of Chrysostom that Mark wrote the gospel in Alexandria is generally regarded as the result of his misreading Eusebius's statement (*H.E.* 2.16.1) that Mark was sent to Alexandria to preach τὸ εὐαγγέλιον ὃ δὴ καὶ συνεγράψατο, which more naturally means that the book was written *before* his mission to Egypt.

74. See Mann, 75-76, taking up the earlier suggestion of T. W. Manson.

But even if Irenaeus did mean that Peter died before Mark's gospel was written, his view stands in contrast to a more widespread tradition that Peter was still alive when Mark wrote. Clement of Alexandria in his lost work *Hypotyposeis* (apud Eusebius, *H.E.* 6.14.6-7; 2.15.1-2, the latter specifying that the reference is to book 6 of the *Hypotyposeis*), reports both Peter's equivocal response on being informed of Mark's writing (μήτε κωλῦσαι μήτε προτρέψα-σθαι) and his endorsement of it (κυρῶσαι τὴν γραφὴν εἰς ἔντευξιν ταῖς ἐκκλησίαις).[75] Origen (apud Eusebius, *H.E.* 6.25.5) implies Peter's more direct involvement in the project when he says that Mark wrote ὡς Πέτρος ὑφηγήσατο αὐτῷ. Epiphanius, as noted above, says that Peter sent Mark to Egypt after he had written the gospel. Jerome (*Ep.* 120.11) appears to believe that Mark wrote at Peter's dictation *(evangelium Petro narrante et illo scribente compositum est),* and says that Peter approved and authorised the gospel *(De Viris Illustribus* 8). Both Eusebius and Jerome claim to have got their information on this point not only from Clement but also from Papias; while the text of Papias quoted by Eusebius does not specify that the writing was done during Peter's lifetime, this is only a brief extract from Papias's longer work, and it is arguable that even in these few words Papias's account of Mark writing down what he had heard Peter saying assumes that Peter was still alive at the time. In terms of both frequency and clarity of reference, therefore, the tradition that Peter was still alive when Mark wrote his gospel has decidedly the better of it, and if Eusebius and Jerome are to be believed, it is also the earliest attested view with Papias.[76] Whether this tradition is based on historical record or on the natural assumption that Peter must have been personally involved in the production of a gospel which was so firmly associated with his teaching must of course remain a matter of judgment.

The tradition of the early church then affirms consistently that this gospel was written by Mark in Rome as a record of Peter's teaching, most probably while Peter was still alive and therefore not later than the early sixties of the first century.

Modern scholarship has had a remarkable propensity to regard early church traditions of this nature as automatically suspect. Actual arguments against taking the traditions seriously are not so common. Rather, an alternative structure is created around a presumed later dating for the writing of the gos-

75. The letter of Clement which refers to the Secret Gospel of Mark (see below on 10:32-34) also states that the original (canonical) Gospel of Mark was written κατὰ τὴν τοῦ Πέτρου ἐν Ῥώμῃ διατριβήν and explains the origin of the 'Secret Gospel' as Mark's subsequent work when he went to Alexandria after Peter's death, taking his own and Peter's memoirs with him. A further reference in the Latin version of Clement's *Adumbrationes* on 1 Pet. 5:13 confirms Clement's view that Mark wrote the gospel *praedicante Petro evangelium Romae.*

76. The case is argued cogently by J. A. T. Robinson, *Redating,* 107-15, and supported by Gundry, 1041-43. M. Hengel, *Studies,* 2-6, argues, however, that Irenaeus represents the earlier view, and that the earlier dating by Clement et al. (but not, he thinks, by Papias, despite the contrary assertions of Eusebius and Jerome) was a later attempt to link the gospel more closely with Peter.

pels as a group, based partly on conjectural reconstructions of the relation of each gospel to first-century developments, in particular the fall of Jerusalem[77] and the presumed phases of the development of the church's internal concerns and external relations especially with Judaism. Such reconstructions tend to place gospel writing as an enterprise subsequent to the time of Peter, with Mark's gospel dating from A.D. 65 at the earliest and more likely A.D. 70 or later, and so the Petrine connection for this gospel is generally discarded as historically unviable.[78]

A significant factor in this general suspicion of early church beliefs on the writing of the gospels is no doubt the almost unanimous[79] patristic belief that Matthew's was the first gospel to be written. Since the middle of the nineteenth century this belief has been replaced by the priority of Mark. Only in recent years has the priority of Matthew been reasserted by a significant minority of NT scholars, and it remains true that the priority of Mark is the assumed starting point for most gospel studies at the beginning of the twenty-first century. If, then, patristic views were in error on this point, why should they be credited on other related issues? Their understanding of the origin of Mark is thus found guilty by association with their mistaken view of priority.

In contrast to this general scepticism, Martin Hengel's *Studies in the Gospel of Mark* offers a robust argument for taking the patristic accounts of Mark seriously. Hengel is particularly scornful of the repeated assertion that the gospels are 'anonymous'[80] documents, to which the names of 'authors' were conjecturally attached sometime in the second century. His study on 'The Titles of the Gospels'[81] argues that as soon as more than one written version of the εὐαγγέλιον was in circulation some label would be necessary in order to distin-

---

77. For a useful brief assessment of two famous but very different attempts to connect the writing of Mark's gospel with the events of the Jewish War and the fall of Jerusalem, those of W. Marxsen and of S. G. F. Brandon, see E. Best, *Story,* 28-34.

78. See below, p. 274 n. 75, for the assertion of J. O'Callaghan that a fragment of Greek text found in Qumran Cave 7 comes from the Gospel of Mark. If true, this would argue for a date for Mark (c. A.D. 50?) earlier than either modern scholarship or indeed early church tradition allows for, but the likelihood of O'Callaghan's identification being accepted seems extremely remote. The data are conveniently available in Lane, 18-21.

79. Papias, the earliest witness, is a possible dissenter from this view, in that his accounts of the origins of Mark and Matthew as quoted by Eusebius appear to speak of Matthew as producing an 'orderly' work in reaction against Mark's lack of 'order' (see above, pp. 7-8); the inference is not certain, however, particularly since we cannot be sure that the two accounts quoted by Eusebius in *H.E.* 3.39.14-16 occurred together in Papias's work, and in the order (Mark followed by Matthew) in which Eusebius gives them. See further my *Matthew, Evangelist,* 25-27.

80. It is of course true that all the gospels are 'anonymous' (in contrast with, e.g., the Pauline letters) in the formal sense that the author is not named within the text. But on that basis most modern books (including this commentary) are also 'anonymous': it is only on the title page and cover that the author is named. And ancient manuscripts regularly carried titles or colophons which might be expected to identify the work contained in them; it was in such titles rather than in the text itself that the author's name would be found.

81. *Studies,* 64-84.

guish them, and the only such labels we know are the traditional terms κατὰ Μαθθαῖον, κατὰ Μάρκον, etc., which are found with remarkable unanimity from as early as we can trace the titles of these books. Hengel points out how improbable it is that a late conjectural attribution could have produced such unanimity and left no trace of alternative attributions. He also quotes Tertullian, *Adv. Marc.* 4.2.3 as typical of the view that a 'gospel' not bearing the name of its author could not be accepted as authoritative. It is thus altogether improbable that gospel books could have circulated in the latter part of the first century without titles, and those titles took the form of a statement of authorship. The tradition that Mark was the author of this gospel therefore goes back even earlier than Papias, close to the time of the book's own composition.

On other aspects of the origin of Mark's gospel Hengel similarly finds the tradition of the early church more plausible than most modern critical alternatives. He opts for Irenaeus's dating after the death of Peter rather than the more widely supported earlier date outlined above, and suggests that the gospel originated in Rome in A.D. 69, being the work of 'a Jewish Graeco-Palestinian, John Mark, who was a missionary companion of Peter for some time'.[82] The frequently claimed connection of the gospel with Peter, attested from Papias on,[83] is to be taken seriously, and matches the character of the gospel.[84] As for the place of origin, Hengel declares that 'The constantly repeated assertion that the work was written in Syria-Palestine — most recently, Antioch has been mentioned — has no really serious basis. It has become a bad habit among New Testament scholars to repeat erroneous opinions unchecked so long that they become a general assumption.'[85] He cites in support of the traditional Roman origin[86] not only the regularly noted Latinisms[87] in Mark's Greek gospel (which in themselves could mostly be understood as reflecting the language of the Roman occupation in the East),[88] but also a number of features which

---

82. *Studies,* 28-30.

83. A further very early witness to the connection of Mark's gospel with Peter is probably to be found in Justin, *Dial.* 106.3, where he cites the naming of James and John as 'Boanerges, which means Sons of Thunder' (a feature found only in Mark 3:17, not in the other gospels) as written in Peter's memoirs.

84. *Studies,* 47-53; cf. the excursus by R. Feldmeier, 'The Portrayal of Peter in the Synoptic Gospels', *Studies,* 59-63.

85. *Studies,* 28. The most influential argument in favour of a Syrian origin has probably been that of H. C. Kee, *Community,* especially 100-105. More recently see G. Theissen, *Gospels,* 235-58, and the response to this by Van Iersel, 36-39.

86. For a recent careful defence of this traditional view see Van Iersel, 31-57.

87. The Latinisms are listed and discussed by Gundry, 1043-45. See also Van Iersel, 33-35, who adds to the normal vocabulary items two aspects of Mark's syntax (deviations from standard Greek word-order and the nonfinal use of ἵνα) which he claims betray the influence of Latin.

88. It is often stated that the Latinisms are military and economic terms suitable to an occupied territory, not the social and domestic vocabulary of Rome. Thus, e.g., H. C. Waetjen, *Reordering,* 13-15, following W. H. Kelber, *Kingdom,* 129, suggests an origin in a Gentile context in southern Syria. More specifically Waetjen argues that the gospel was written for 'rural gentile Christians [who] belonged to the lower-class strata of Roman-occupied Syria' (15).

would have been quite unnecessary or inappropriate to someone familiar with the situation in Palestine or Syria: λεπτὰ δύο, ὅ ἐστιν κοδράντης (12:42); αὐλῆς, ὅ ἐστιν πραιτώριον (15:16); and the description of the woman in 7:26 as Συροφοινίκισσα, not just Φοινίκισσα. The need to translate Aramaic terms into Greek for his readers, as Mark does on several occasions, also suggests that he wrote in an area where Aramaic was not familiar.[89]

I have concentrated on Hengel's arguments not because they are unanswerably right (though I think they have the better of it in terms of historical method)[90] but because they illustrate how questionable modern critical reconstructions of gospel origins, with their almost axiomatic dismissal of early church tradition as not worthy of serious consideration, may prove to be when examined in the light of historical realism. I do not wish to argue that any one view of the gospel's origins, even that of the early church fathers where they agree, is necessarily right, but rather to suggest that any exegesis which bases itself firmly on one particular theory of gospel origins is likely to be founded on shifting sand.

This commentary is not therefore based consciously on a particular theory of authorship, date, and location. While it will be clear from the above that I believe that Hengel's positive evaluation of early church tradition represents the more responsible critical option, I do not think that this belief has significantly coloured the exegesis offered here. The aspect of the gospel's origins which is most likely to have a bearing on exegesis is, I think, the tradition that its message and narrative content are related to the preaching of Peter, whether by direct derivation or through the author's thought having been moulded by his association with the leading apostle. At times I shall take this possibility into account. But I do not think that the exegesis offered would be much affected if the link between Mark and the principal eyewitness of the story of Jesus could be shown to be less direct and less contemporaneous than Papias believed it to be.

F. Mark in Relation to Matthew and Luke

One other aspect of tradition which may have an effect on exegesis belongs not to the tradition of the early church but to that of nineteenth- and twentieth-century scholarship: the theory of the literary relationships of the three Synop-

---

89. D. W. Chapman, *Orphan* (the argument of the book is summarised on p. 29), arguing that Mark wrote in Palestine about A.D. 50, explains the 'Roman' elements of the gospel on the assumption that he was writing not for his own church but for one 'only remotely familiar with the Holy Land' (later identified as Rome, pp. 203-5), and that the distant recipients added a few 'explanations' to Mark's text (see his ch. 10 for these proposed later additions; he lists them on pp. 201-2).

90. Hengel's overall approach is strongly supported by the more extensive study of Mark's origin by Gundry, 1026-45; Gundry bases his account firmly on the evidence of Papias' Elder, whom he identifies as the apostle John (though this identification is not essential to his argument).

tic Gospels which is presupposed. The importance of this issue for exegesis is illustrated by the startling difference in approach found in C. S. Mann's Anchor Bible commentary of 1986 when compared with virtually all other recent commentaries on Mark, since Mann believes in the priority of Matthew, and so interprets Mark as a deliberate revision of the material earlier recorded by Matthew. It may be useful, therefore, for me to set out at the beginning what view I take of synoptic relationships, so that the exegesis that follows can be assessed in the light of that prior assumption.

The introduction to a commentary is not the place for a full discussion of the Synoptic Problem. I have gone as far in that direction as I ever expect to do in print in my *Matthew, Evangelist and Teacher,* pp. 24-49. Here I simply summarise the main lines of that discussion, which still represents my understanding of the question, with the hope that any reader wanting further elaboration will be willing to find it there.

The publication of W. R. Farmer's *The Synoptic Problem* (1964) marked the first significant reopening of what had been generally regarded during the earlier part of the twentieth century as a closed question. The classical 'Streeterian' theory of the priority of Mark, the existence of a lost document Q, and the direct literary dependence of both Matthew and Luke on these two sources was assumed to have been demonstrated beyond reasonable doubt, even though a few Catholic scholars continued to argue for the priority of Matthew and the problem of the 'minor agreements of Matthew and Luke against Mark' had never quite been defused. Farmer's book not only raised significant doubts as to how far the now traditional two-source theory could in fact account for the very complex data of synoptic relationships, but also enthusiastically resurrected the nineteenth-century 'Griesbach Hypothesis' (priority of Matthew, use of Matthew by Luke, and Mark as the final 'mediating' gospel based on Matthew and Luke) as a radically different explanation which, among its other attractions, eliminated the need to postulate a hypothetical Q. Since 1964, therefore, debate on the Synoptic Problem has sprung to life again.

Forty years on it may safely be said that the two-source theory remains by far the most widely supported and assumed account of synoptic origins. But it no longer holds the field with the unquestioned dominance of the earlier part of the twentieth century. Radically oversimplifying the situation, we may observe that at least three other approaches have become widely established. One is the Griesbach Hypothesis itself, which has won a significant number of converts from a wide variety of theological and ecclesiastical backgrounds, though it remains very much a minority movement. Another is a tendency, while accepting the priority of Mark, to treat the documentary existence of Q with some scepticism, whether by denying the need for Q altogether (notably in the work of M. D. Goulder)[91] or less radically by preferring to speak of a 'Q' strand of tradi-

---

91. Goulder has argued for Luke's direct use of Matthew in a series of studies: *Midrash,* 452-71; *NTS* 24 (1977/8) 218-34; and in C. M. Tuckett (ed.), *Studies,* 111-30.

tion (some or all of it more likely oral than written) rather than of a single document.[92] The third is the view, promoted by E. P. Sanders[93] and developed by J. A. T. Robinson[94] among others, that both the two-source theory and the Griesbach Hypothesis (as well as other similarly 'neat' solutions to the Synoptic Problem) are a good deal too simple, and that the process by which our NT gospels were formed is likely to have been more complex and fluid than a matter of simple literary dependence of one writer on another. It is this third strand of thinking that I find most persuasive.

The essential basis for Robinson's view is well summarised in the following statement:

> We have been accustomed for so long to what might be called linear solutions to the synoptic problem, where one gospel simply 'used' another and must therefore be set later, that it is difficult to urge a more fluid and complex interrelation between them and their traditions without being accused of introducing unnecessary hypotheses and modifications. But if we have learnt anything over the past fifty years it is surely that whereas epistles were written for specific occasions (though they might be added to or adapted later), gospels were essentially for continuous use in the preaching, teaching, apologetic and liturgical life of the Christian communities. They grew out of *and with* the needs. One can only put approximate dates to certain states or stages and set a certain *terminus ad quem* for them, according to what they do or do not reflect. And at any stage in this development one must be prepared to allow for cross-fertilization between the ongoing traditions.[95]

This concept of 'cross-fertilisation' rather than a purely 'linear dependence' seems to me to take more realistic account of the likely growth of gospel traditions in the first-century churches, which were not sealed units but remained in contact with one another as Christians travelled around the eastern part of the empire — the sort of free movement of Christian leaders and teachers which is so graphically illustrated at a slightly later period in *Did.*

92. This looser understanding of 'Q' has interestingly developed in parallel with an opposite tendency among the supporters of a documentary Q towards greater definition by debating the supposed 'recensions' of Q, and the distinctive theology and development of the 'Q community'.

93. Sanders heralded this approach in 1969 in the conclusion to his *Tendencies*, where he called for 'a period of withholding judgments on the Synoptic problem while the evidence is resifted', and suggested that a new view would be 'more flexible and complicated than the tidy two-document hypothesis. With all due respect for scientific preference for the simpler view, the evidence seems to require a more complicated one' (278-79). The theme is developed in later articles in *RSR* 60 (1972) 519-40; *NTS* 19 (1972/3) 453-65, and in E. P. Sanders and M. Davies, *Studying*, 51-119. We may note especially the section in the latter book headed 'In Favour of Complicated Solutions' (97-100), followed by a survey of several such solutions (with diagrams); the conclusion is drawn that any solution which purports to explain every feature of synoptic relationships is suspect, and that 'there is no one answer which easily solves everything' (117).

94. J. A. T. Robinson, *Redating*, 92-117.

95. J. A. T. Robinson, *Redating*, 94.

11–12. In such a situation it would be natural for traditions about Jesus to be shared and compared, and for collections of what later came to be known as 'gospel' material to grow up in different locations, each in its own distinctive form but with constant opportunity for influence and expansion from traditions preserved in other church centres. Thus when a Matthew or a Luke came to compile the material about Jesus available to him, it would be a rich mixture of distinctive traditions preserved in his own church together with a more extensive range of material in common circulation among the churches, probably largely in oral form though no doubt with some written material available (hence perhaps the more verbatim agreements in parts of the 'Q' material), as indeed Luke 1:1 explicitly tells us.

Mark's situation was, according to church tradition, rather different, in that he had direct access to one major oral source of Jesus tradition, the teaching of Peter, and his recording of that tradition clearly provided Matthew and Luke with the most significant single component in their collections. In that sense, I would continue to maintain the priority of Mark and the likelihood that Matthew and Luke depended on him rather than vice versa. But that does not entail that at every point Mark's version of a given tradition must be the starting point for the synoptic development. It is entirely possible that the versions available to Matthew or Luke may have taken shape earlier than Mark's writing up of those same stories or sayings, and indeed also that Mark himself (and even Peter?) benefited from traditions coming from other church centres. Thus while I regard Mark as the earliest of the surviving gospels to be produced in its present form, it does not seem to me necessary to conclude that at all points Mark represents an earlier form of the tradition than that preserved in either Matthew or Luke.

Here is Robinson's understanding of the issue of literary 'priority' among the Synoptic Gspels:

> We must be open to seeing that the most primitive state of the triple, or 'Markan', tradition (as indeed most scholars would agree in relation to the double, or 'Q', tradition) is not consistently or exclusively to be found in any one gospel, to which we must then assign overall temporal priority. Rather I believe that there was written (as well as oral) tradition underlying each of them, which is sometimes preserved in its most original form by Matthew, sometimes by Luke, though most often, I would judge, by Mark. Hence the strength of the case for the priority of Mark, which is nevertheless overstated when this gospel is itself regarded as the foundation-document of the other two. The gospels as we have them are to be seen as parallel, though by no means isolated, developments of common material for different spheres of the Christian mission, rather than a series of documents standing in simple chronological sequence.[96]

96. J. A. T. Robinson, *Redating*, 94.

I would disagree with this estimate by Robinson only in that I would wish to give greater weight than he does to the tradition of Mark's dependence on Peter, which would seem to place Mark in a more 'privileged' position than Matthew or Luke with regard to his access to the apostolic tradition. In that case Mark is likely to have been less dependent on collecting traditions from a variety of sources, and his work is more likely to have been used as a primary source of Jesus traditions by the other two synoptic evangelists. I would thus lay greater emphasis on the 'priority' of Mark than Robinson's cautious words suggest, but would agree with him that this priority is not to be construed in terms of a simple linear dependence which entails that Mark's version of a given tradition must always be understood to be the starting point.

It is with this more 'untidy' understanding of synoptic relationships that the following commentary has been written. I do not think that in practice it will be significantly different from what I might have written under a more strictly 'Streeterian' banner, since my aim is to understand Mark as Mark, not primarily in relation to his supposed place in the development of the traditions. I shall not, of course, be echoing Mann's attempts to explain Mark as a deliberate recasting of Matthew, but since I am not commenting on Matthew neither will there be much cause to speak of what Matthew may have made of Mark. But these brief comments on the Synoptic Problem may help to explain why at times my comments may seem to treat the synoptic versions of a given tradition as parallel rather than derivative.

I do not believe that I have solved the Synoptic Problem, nor do I believe that anyone else has provided an explanation which does full justice to all the extraordinarily complex data. But the attraction to me of Robinson's typically unconventional approach is that it suggests that a full 'solution' is neither possible nor necessary, that any tidily defined scheme of literary dependence, whether as simple as Goulder's or as complex as Boismard's,[97] fails to do justice to the rich variety and cross-fertilisation of Jesus traditions which might reasonably be expected to have occurred within the living and mobile complexity of early Christian preaching and teaching across the eastern Mediterranean world of the first century. In the light of that situation, I do not need a solution to the Synoptic Problem.

---

97. For Goulder's advocacy of the order Mark — Matthew — Luke with no Q, see above, p. 42 n. 91. The theory of M.-E. Boismard is set out in P. Benoit and M.-E. Boismard (ed.), *Synopse des quatres évangiles en français,* Tome II (Paris: Le Cerf, 1972), and presented visually in a diagram which has a first row consisting of four (hypothetical) documents, A, B, C, Q, a second row containing intermediate editions of each of the four gospels, and a third row containing the final texts of the four gospels; arrows indicating dependence crisscross the diagram, so that each gospel depends on two or more of the intermediate gospels and each intermediate gospel on at least two of the sources (two of them also on other intermediate gospels). E. P. Sanders and M. Davies, *Studying,* 105-11, give a sympathetic account of Boismard's theory, but conclude that 'in explaining everything, Boismard takes us into the realm of conjecture, where everything is possible'.

COMMENTARY

THE HEADING (1:1)

1. The phrase υἱοῦ (τοῦ) θεοῦ is absent from the first hand of ℵ, but added by the original corrector (i.e., probably before the MS left the scriptorium). It occurs in all other uncials except Θ, but is absent from a number of patristic citations, notably from all of Origen's five citations. It is improbable that a Christian scribe would deliberately omit this key title, and not at all unlikely that it might be added to fill out an apparently bald heading with a more explicitly christological title. For this reason some editors do not accept the phrase as original. But the omission in the two uncial MSS may reasonably be ascribed to mechanical error (especially since it was immediately corrected in one of them), in the light of the sequence of six identical -ου endings, especially if copied from a MS in which the titles were conventionally abbreviated, thus

ΑΡΧΗΤΟΥΕΥΑΓΓΕΛΙΟΥῙῩ̄ Χ̄Ȳ ῩῩ̄(ΤΟΥ)Θ̄Ȳ

Origen's omission of the phrase 'the Son of God' may indicate that the shorter text was in circulation in Caesarea in the third century, especially since Θ in Mark generally reflects a similar ('Caesarean') text to that used by Origen. Patristic citations, however, may be selective, as is shown by the fact that in two places Irenaeus quotes the full text, but in one case the shorter. (C. H. Turner, *JTS* 28 [1927] 150, points out that Irenaeus's omission of the words in this case, and that of Victorinus in a similar context, are due to their preoccupation at that point with the identification of Mark as the lion, to which the phrase υἱοῦ θεοῦ is not germane!) The prominence of the title 'Son of God' in Mark's gospel ilt will be picked up in 1:11, and reappear climactically in 15:39) makes its presence in the heading intrinsically likely. (J. Slomp, *BT* 28 [1977] 143-50, offers a clear overview of the issue, inclining with some hesitation to support the shorter text.)

This apparently perfunctory heading is in fact made up of several very significant terms. It identifies the subject as Ἰησοῦς, one of the commonest of first-century Jewish names,[1] and hence identified when he appears in the narrative as

---

1. Ἰησοῦς is the Greek form of the OT name Joshua. Of the named characters who appear in the narrative of Josephus's *Life* (allowing for some uncertainty over whether in some cases he refers to the same or a different person) the commonest names are Jesus (4-6), Simon (3-5), Levi (4), Jonathan (3), and Herod (3). Four of the twelve High Priests who held office in the first century were called Jesus. For other Jesuses in the NT see Mt. 27:16-17 (reading, with Θ etc., Ἰησοῦν Βαραββᾶν); Lk. 3:29; Acts 7:45; 13:6; Col. 4:11.

Jesus *of Nazareth* (1:9), but here described instead by terms which indicate his role rather than his place in society. Χριστός will not occur frequently in this gospel (in contrast with the Pauline corpus), and in every occurrence (8:29; 9:41; 12:35; 13:21; 14:61; 15:32) carries a clearly titular sense, focusing on Jesus' perceived or claimed role as the Messiah. Here it is given added weight by the solemn introduction of the scriptural witness in vv. 2-3; the time of messianic fulfilment has arrived. The addition of υἱὸς θεοῦ (if it is an original part of Mark's text; see Textual Note) apparently takes Mark's heading beyond the sphere of Jesus' messianic function to focus on his identity at a more fundamental level. It is possible, of course, in the narrative situation of the gospel, to understand Χριστός and υἱὸς θεοῦ as virtual synonyms, in the light of 2 Sa. 7:14 and Ps. 2:7 together with the evidence from Qumran that at least some first-century Jews interpreted these texts messianically,[2] but in an editorial heading the phrase must reflect the more developed understanding of Jesus' divine sonship which was current in Mark's church. In this fuller sense it will form the central term of Mark's christology, twice declared by the voice of God himself (1:11; 9:7), acknowledged by the spiritual insight of demons (3:11; 5:7; cf. 1:24), coming to at least guarded expression in Jesus' own words about his role and status (12:6-8; 13:32; cf. 12:35-37?) before being made the basis of his climactic declaration before the supreme court of Israel (14:61-62), and finally coming into focus in the striking paradox of the centurion's 'confession' (15:39). In his heading, therefore, Mark has declared his hand, and set the framework in which we are to understand the story which follows, however strange we may find the way in which the Messiah/Son of God behaves and is received in Israel.

I have been assuming so far that v. 1 is intended to function as the heading to the whole book. It has, however, been taken as the heading only to the prologue, whether construed as 1:1-13 (so Cranfield, Lane) or 1:1-15 (so Guelich), or to the account of John the Baptist (so Hooker), or even merely to the scriptural material in vv. 2-3. There is an element of truth in each of these views. The καθώς which begins v. 2 indicates that v. 1 should not be regarded as syntactically free-standing, since καθώς does not normally introduce a new sentence, but links what follows with what precedes (except occasionally where there is a following οὕτως), and this is regularly the case with καθώς γέγραπται.[3] Vv. 2-3 are therefore, formally speaking, a scriptural comment on v. 1, rather than the beginning of a new section introducing John the Baptist. The function of vv. 2-3 is, however, to indicate the significance of John the Baptist, whose story immediately follows in vv. 4-8. This story in turn serves to introduce the account of Jesus' baptism, and in that account the title υἱὸς θεοῦ, declared in the opening verse, is dramatically taken up. A further key term of the first verse, εὐαγγέλιον, recurs prominently in vv. 14-15. In all

---

2. See below, p. 609 and n. 31 there.
3. So, e.g., J. Marcus, *Way*, 17-18, following R. A. Guelich. Cf. R. E. Watts, *Exodus*, 55-56.

50

these ways, then, v. 1 leads into the prologue. Formally speaking, it is not a mere 'title' for the book.

In its contents, however, v. 1 points far beyond the first part of chapter 1. It sets forth themes which the whole book will explore. The εὐαγγέλιον which Mark is about to proclaim is not limited to the prologue. The prologue is, as Mark states, only its beginning (ἀρχή). Theologically it 'begins' with the scriptural hopes set out in vv. 2-3; from the narrative point of view it 'begins' in the context of John's baptism (vv. 4-8); the true content of the good news 'begins' to be revealed in the events at and after Jesus' baptism (vv. 9-13); and the open declaration of the εὐαγγέλιον 'begins' as Jesus' Galilean ministry is launched in vv. 14-15. All of this is ἀρχὴ τοῦ εὐαγγελίου, and the rest of the book will fill out its content.[4] In separating off v. 1 as 'the heading' I am not therefore suggesting any lack of connection with the prologue which follows, and I am consciously overriding its formal syntactical link with v. 2. Its function is broader than its immediate syntactical status. In these words Mark is alerting his reader to the significance of all that is to follow. But it is typical of his urgency and lack of formal concern that rather than constructing a neat self-contained 'title' he cannot wait to 'begin' with that which he has so effectively signalled in the few breathless (and verbless!) words of v. 1.

Ἀρχή (with neither article nor verb) may seem a rather bald way to begin a book. It is, however, typical of biblical style.[5] Similarly anarthrous headings, also without main verb, open the Gospel of Matthew (Βίβλος γενέσεως . . .) and the Book of Revelation (Ἀποκάλυψις Ἰησοῦ Χριστοῦ . . .), and are common in the OT (see Pr. 1:1; Ec. 1:1; Ct. 1:1); most of the prophetic books have a similar verbless heading (Is., Je., Ho., Joel, Am., Ob., Na., Hab., Zp., Zc., Mal.), and all of these headings in the LXX except those for Jeremiah and Habakkuk characterise the following work by an anarthrous noun. (Cf. also the headings of the Psalms.) Mark's use of ἀρχή, however, is not directly paralleled in any of these headings. The nearest biblical parallel is Ho. 1:2, where, *after* the heading, the content of the prophecy is introduced by ἀρχὴ λόγου κυρίου πρὸς Ὡσηε.

It is sometimes suggested that, just as Matthew's opening words, Βίβλος γενέσεως, are designed to recall the reader to the beginning of the OT, so also the choice of ἀρχή as the opening word of Mark is intended, like John's Ἐν ἀρχῇ ἦν ὁ λόγος, to be heard as an echo of Gn. 1:1 (so, e.g., Anderson, Myers following D. Via). The function of ἀρχή in Mark is, however, quite different from that in Genesis and John. It does not refer to the beginning of all things,

---

4. It is sometimes suggested (Pesch, Stock; cf. A. Feuillet, *NTS* 24 [1978] 163-74) that the *whole* of Mark's book is to be seen as only the ἀρχή, since the post-Easter growth and preaching of the church will further advance the εὐαγγέλιον. (Cf. also below, p. 670 n. 2.) While this is theologically true (cf. ἤρξατο, Acts 1:1; Feuillet discerns the same idea in Heb. 2:3-4), it is reading too much into ἀρχή here to see it as intended to carry so much theological weight, rather than simply to introduce the book, 'Here begins'.

5. For other (nonbiblical) works beginning with Ἀρχή see BAGD 111b.

but is defined by the following τοῦ εὐαγγελίου. The parallel with Ho. 1:2 gives a more satisfactory account of its function, as literary rather than theological.

GNB usefully captures the function of v. 1, and its syntactical link through καθώς with the following biblical quotations, when it translates as follows:

> This is the Good News about Jesus Christ, the Son of God.
> It began as the prophet Isaiah had written: . . .

We have noted in the introduction that εὐαγγέλιον was not a recognised title for a literary genre at the time Mark wrote, and that Mark is generally credited with having initiated that usage, not by design, but by the fact that his use of the term in the heading of his work offered an obvious label to those who in due course found it necessary to refer in generic terms to this apparently new category of writing. In classical Greek (where it was normally plural, like our 'good news') it originally meant the reward given to the bearer of good news, and then came to refer to the good news itself. In the Hellenistic period there are examples of its use in a more specifically religious context, particularly in connection with the cult of the emperor, whose birthday, accession to power, and the like, even a forthcoming 'royal visit', were hailed as εὐαγγέλιον. In the LXX, however, the noun occurs clearly only in 2 Kgdms. 4:10,[6] where it is plural and refers to a messenger's reward (with no particularly religious meaning). The verb εὐαγγελίζομαι (occasionally εὐαγγελίζω) is slightly more common, as the normal translation of Hebrew biśśar, 'to bring good news', and this is used in the Psalms (e.g., 40:9; 96:2) and prophets (especially the classic Deutero-Isaianic texts, Is. 40:9; 52:7; 61:1) with a more clearly religious connotation; here the news is that of the establishment of God's reign, the good news of salvation.[7] The quasi-technical use of the singular εὐαγγέλιον to refer to the Christian message seems, however, to have been a new development (perhaps to be attributed to the influence of Paul, drawing on Hellenistic religious usage?), already firmly established in the letters of Paul (which account for 80% of NT uses of εὐαγγέλιον), and therefore presumably already current usage by the time Mark wrote his gospel.

Mark's book is intended, therefore, to pass on the good news about Jesus. This news has been hitherto the subject of primarily oral declaration (Mann therefore appropriately translates εὐαγγέλιον here as 'Proclamation'), but Mark's book is an attempt to communicate it in written form (though probably

---

6. The feminine form εὐαγγελία is used in 2 Kgdms. 18:20, 22, 25, 27; 4 Kgdms. 7:9 to refer to the good news itself, rather than the reward it produces. In 2 Kgdms. 18:22, 25 the syntax would allow εὐαγγελια to be read either as feminine singular or as neuter plural, but the consistent use of the same form throughout the passage seems preferable.

7. J. Marcus, Way, 18-21, argues therefore that in using this phrase Mark 'is hinting more broadly that his whole story of "the beginning of the gospel" is to be understood against the backdrop of Isaian themes'. The whole thesis of R. E. Watts, Exodus, supports this claim.

with a view to its being read orally in the congregation). εὐαγγέλιον denotes the content rather than the form of the book.

The genitive Ἰησοῦ Χριστοῦ may, in theory, be read either as subjective ('the good news proclaimed by Jesus Christ') or objective ('the good news about Jesus Christ'). Some commentators take up positions on one side or the other, but most prefer to have it both ways. Guelich will not allow this since 'one or the other emphasis has to dominate'. Syntactically this is no doubt true, but if Mark is deliberately exploiting the ambiguity of the genitive construction, he would not be the first to do so, and either sense is entirely appropriate; moreover, 'the gospel of God' in 1:14 allows the same suggestive ambiguity. There are no other uses in Mark of the genitive after εὐαγγέλιον; the noun used absolutely refers in three cases to a message to be believed (1:15) or proclaimed (13:10; 14:9) rather than to the act of proclamation, though in the remaining two uses (8:35; 10:29) either sense is possible. It is therefore probably more natural to read the genitive after εὐαγγέλιον here as objective (the gospel *about* Jesus Christ), and this is the more normal usage in the rest of the NT (though note to the contrary Rom. 2:16; 16:25, etc., and, denoting the *recipients* of the gospel, Gal. 2:7). But vv. 14-15 will make it clear that the εὐαγγέλιον is in fact *preached by* Jesus as well. Whatever the dictates of syntactical pedantry, I think it likely that Mark would have approved, and may well have intended, the *double entendre* which the genitive construction allows.

THE PROLOGUE (1:2-13)

Whereas most modern writers (and some ancient writers; e.g., Lk. 1:1-4) introduce a book with a separate preface setting out its nature and purpose, Mark appears, after the heading in 1:1, to launch straight into his story without further indication to the reader of what the book will be about. Most recent commentators agree, however, that the first part of that story stands apart to some extent, as more of a preface than merely the first scene of the drama.

It is often suggested that Mark's prologue is similar in conception to that of John, where the first eighteen verses set the scene for what follows, not merely by introducing John the Baptist and Jesus as the main characters around whom the story will begin, but also by offering a theological framework against which the story can be better understood. Central to John's introduction is the creative idea of Jesus as the Λόγος, yet in the rest of the Fourth Gospel there is no further mention of this idea (compare also the term χάρις, of central importance in Jn. 1:14, 16, and 17, but not used in the rest of the gospel). We have here then, perhaps, John's reflection on the significance of the story of Jesus, written after the rest of the gospel was finished, and using new language which represents the theological conclusions which John wants his readers to share with him.

The language of Mark's prologue is perhaps not so obviously distinct from that of the book as a whole (though see below on πνεῦμα and ἔρημος), but it is generally recognised these days as setting the scene in a similar way, through the introduction of the main dramatis personae in a context separate from that of the succeeding narrative. The main disagreement is as to the extent of this 'prologue', whether it concludes with v. 13 or v. 15.[8] That issue will be discussed later; for now I will treat v. 13 as the end of the prologue.

R. H. Lightfoot pioneered this view in British scholarship.[9] In a lecture in 1949 he argued against the decision of Westcott and Hort to place a major break in their Greek text after Mk. 1:8,[10] and proposed that Mk. 1:1-13 should be un-

---

8. W. Feneberg, *Markusprolog,* unusually defines the prologue as vv. 1-11.

9. Anticipated by N. B. Stonehouse, *Witness,* 5, where the function of 1:1-13 as prologue is simply assumed, not argued.

10. Few commentators now accept this division; exceptions are Haenchen and Gundry (who calls 1:1-8 the 'first pericope'). See R. E. Watts, *Exodus,* 94-95, for a response to Gundry on this point. C. Bryan, *Preface,* 85-88, treats 1:1-8 as 'prologue' on the grounds that the three pericopes

derstood as Mark's 'prologue or introduction', and that 'just as in John, the narrative proper only begins with the account of the Lord's activity in vv. 14 and 15, when he comes into Galilee with the announcement that the time is ripe, and God's promises are now in process of accomplishment'.[11]

Lightfoot argued this case from the contents of the passage rather than by noting more specific linguistic markers. But subsequent study has drawn attention to the fact that, just as Jn. 1:1-18 uses key terms not used in the rest of the gospel, so also does Mk. 1:2-13. The terms usually noted are πνεῦμα and ἔρημος.

Πνεῦμα. In the whole of the gospel after 1:13 there are only three references to the (Holy) Spirit (3:29; 12:36; 13:11), only one of which (3:29) relates (indirectly) to the role of the Spirit in the ministry of Jesus. Yet in these opening verses the Spirit is mentioned three times (1:8, 10, 12) and appears as a central figure in the launching of Jesus' ministry. This remarkable difference in focus suggests that Mark has something of importance to which he wishes to draw his readers' attention at the outset.

The eschatological outpouring of God's Spirit was a significant feature in OT expectation, as seen in Is. 32:15; 44:3; Ezk. 36:26-27; 39:29; Jo. 3:1-5 (EVV 2:29-32), and the quotation of the latter in Peter's Pentecost sermon (Acts 2:17-21) shows the importance of this expectation for early Christian understanding of the significance of Jesus' ministry. This expectation underlies the prediction of John the Baptist that an ἰσχυρότερος will come who βαπτίσει ὑμᾶς ἐν πνεύματι ἁγίῳ (v. 8). But the references to the Spirit in 1:10, 12 do not refer to a general outpouring, but to his specific involvement in the ministry of Jesus himself; here, too, there is a suggestive OT background, with the prophecy of a coming 'shoot from the stump of Jesse', on whom the Spirit of Yahweh would rest (Is. 11:2), and of the chosen Servant upon whom Yahweh has put his Spirit (Is. 42:1), the anointed herald of good news upon whom the Spirit has come (Is. 61:1).

By his emphasis on the role of the Spirit in 1:2-13, therefore, Mark alerts the reader at the outset of his gospel, in a way which will not be open to him in the narrative situation after 1:14, to the messianic significance of Jesus, both as the one who is himself empowered and directed by the Spirit in the fulfilment of his eschatological role, and also, remarkably, as the one who 'dispenses' the Spirit, a role which in the OT passages mentioned above was exclusively that of Yahweh himself. The christological implications of this latter point will be taken up in the commentary on 1:2-8. For the moment we note the function of

---

that make up vv. 9-15, while linked with vv. 1-8, are 'transitional, functioning as a kind of hinge, or series of hinges'. Myers apparently speaks of 1:1-15 as 'the prologue' (121-22), but in fact he treats 1:1-20 as the first 'act' (called the 'prologue', 112), and subdivides it into two 'scenes', 1:1-8 and 1:9-20.

11. R. H. Lightfoot, *Message,* 19; the argument for 1:1-13 as prologue takes up pp. 15-20. An important subsequent study reinforcing Lightfoot at several points is U. Mauser, *Christ,* 77-102.

the prologue in taking Mark's readers behind the scenes to see something of the theological dimensions of the story which is to follow. In the subsequent narrative we shall hear little of the Spirit, but the reader who has listened well to the prologue will be able to interpret the scenes in Galilee and Jerusalem in the light of this more ultimate wilderness perspective.

Ἔρημος. The 'voice' of Is. 40:3 cries ἐν τῇ ἐρήμῳ (1:3). It is therefore ἐν τῇ ἐρήμῳ that John the Baptist, as the embodiment of that voice, comes to preach (1:4), and the ἔρημος thus forms the scene for Jesus' baptism. Immediately afterwards it is εἰς τὴν ἔρημον that the πνεῦμα directs Jesus (1:12), and Mark rather labours the point by reminding us in 1:13 that Jesus was there ἐν τῇ ἐρήμῳ with Satan and the wild animals. In view of the fact that the noun ἡ ἔρημος does not occur at all in the rest of Mark's gospel, it seems that Mark is going to some lengths to make sure that the reader of his prologue notices its special location and draws the appropriate conclusions.

But what *are* the appropriate conclusions? Is there any special theological significance in a wilderness?

At the very least, it marks a distinctive location. The rest of Mark's story will be set in the context of normal life, with Jesus surrounded by ordinary people. From time to time he will seek out a quiet place to get away from it all (1:35; 6:31-32), though the crowds will usually manage to find him even there (1:45; 6:33-34). On one memorable occasion he will take three disciples with him onto a lonely hilltop (9:2-13), and there alone in the rest of the gospel will occur a revelation parallel to the one which takes place in the wilderness in 1:10-11. But that will be only a temporary interlude. Here in the prologue, however, Jesus' public activity has not yet begun, and the wilderness represents a separation from ordinary life. With v. 14 the scene will change, and Jesus will be thrust into a ceaseless round of activity among the villages of Galilee; but for the moment, in this remote location, we can focus on Jesus himself as he faces alone the task which lies ahead.

But ἡ ἔρημος has a much more positive significance than merely a withdrawal from ordinary life. It is Isaiah's prophecy of the voice ἐν τῇ ἐρήμῳ which provides the cue for Mark's emphasis on this location, and Mark was not the first to notice these words of Isaiah. It was this same text which provided the rationale for the foundation of the Essene community at Qumran, in that same wilderness of Judaea: 'They shall separate from the habitation of ungodly men and shall go into the wilderness to prepare the way of Him; as it is written, "Prepare in the wilderness the way of . . . , make straight in the desert a path for our God".'[12] Thus it was specifically ἐν τῇ ἐρήμῳ that the men of Qumran expected God to appear and vindicate their stand against the apostasy of the official priesthood in Jerusalem. It was the theologically correct location.

12. 1QS 8:13-14; cf. 9:19-21. Cf. Josephus, *Life*, 11-12 for the ascetic recluse Bannus with whom Josephus lived for three years κατὰ τὴν ἐρημίαν in the period shortly after the gospel narrative.

For the wilderness was a place of hope, of new beginnings.[13] It was in the wilderness that Yahweh had met with Israel and made them into his people when they came out of Egypt. That had been the honeymoon period, before the relationship became strained. 'I remember the devotion of your youth, your love as a bride, how you followed me in the wilderness, in a land not sown. Israel was holy to Yahweh, the first fruits of his harvest' (Je. 2:2-3). In the wilderness Israel experienced privation and danger, and learned through this testing period to trust in the provision and protection of their God; this is the message of Moses' great exhortation to Israel in the early chapters of Deuteronomy, summed up in Dt. 8 (and used as a model for Jesus' own wilderness experience in the Q temptation narrative). So as the prophets looked back to the comparative purity of Israel's wilderness beginnings, the hope grew that in the wilderness God's people would again find their true destiny. 'Behold, I will allure her, and bring her into the wilderness, and speak tenderly to her. . . . And there she shall answer as in the days of her youth, as at the time when she came out of the land of Egypt' (Ho. 2:14-15; cf. Ezk. 20:35-38). The voice in the wilderness (Is. 40:3-5) which introduces Deutero-Isaiah's great vision of restoration, is followed by the recurrent theme of a new Exodus, a new beginning in a wilderness transformed by the renewing power of Israel's God (Is. 41:18-19; 43:19-21; 44:3-4, etc.).[14]

It was this wilderness hope which inspired not only the men of Qumran to go out into the wilderness to wait for God's coming in power, but also several less otherworldly would-be leaders of Israel in the troubled days of the Roman occupation. Theudas, who appears in Acts 5:36, led his followers down to the Jordan (i.e., that same 'wilderness' area where John had baptised), where they were attacked and routed by the procurator Fadus (Josephus, *Ant.* 20.97-98). Later, under Felix, an Egyptian 'prophet' collected a band of freedom fighters around him in the wilderness before leading them in an ill-fated assault on Jerusalem (Josephus, *War* 2.261-63; *Ant.* 20.169-72; Acts 21:38). In introducing this latter story Josephus makes a more general reference to 'impostors and deceivers' in this period who 'persuaded the crowd to follow them into the wilderness,' with the promise of divine wonders as a token of coming deliverance

13. An alternative, and opposite, symbolism is sometimes suggested, that the wilderness is a hostile place, the abode of evil spirits. It is, of course, in the wilderness that Jesus meets with Satan and the wild animals (1:13), but the text suggests that this was because that was where Jesus already was rather than because that was the place to find Satan. It was later Christian tradition, based no doubt on the synoptic temptation narratives, that developed this connection, as ascetics like St. Antony of Egypt went out into the desert to struggle with demons. Evidence for this connection in Jewish thought is not impressive, however. Reference is usually made to Str-B 4.515-16, but in fact at that point Billerbeck simply lists 'wilderness and ruins' as one (minor) item in a list of locations attributed to demons, and offers as evidence only three passages in the Jerusalem Targum, and a talmudic passage (*b. Ber.* 3a) which refers not to the wilderness but to the ruins of Jerusalem. The intriguing little Q pericope Mt. 12:43-45 suggests that the expelled demon did not relish living in ἄνυδροι τόποι!

14. For a much fuller account of the significance of the wilderness in the OT and in subsequent Jewish thought see U. Mauser, *Christ,* 15-61. See also J. Marcus, *Way,* 22-29, laying particular emphasis on the Isaian theme of a new Exodus.

(*War* 2.258-60; *Ant.* 20.167-68).[15] No doubt strategic considerations contributed to the choice of a remote location for such movements, but at least as important probably was the conviction that the ἔρημος was, theologically speaking, the right place to expect a new beginning for the people of God.

So when Mark emphasises the wilderness location in 1:2-13, it is not only to signal that this part of the gospel operates on a different level from the story of real-life involvement which will follow, but also that the wilderness is itself a symbol of hope and fulfilment. Marxsen makes the point vividly: 'ἐν τῇ ἐρήμῳ qualifies the Baptist as the fulfiller of OT predictive prophecy. Put in exaggerated form, the Baptist would still be the one who appears "in the wilderness" even if he had never been there in all his life.'[16] Where else but ἐν τῇ ἐρήμῳ would you expect to see the drama of God's eschatological salvation begin?

The prominent use of the terms πνεῦμα and ἔρημος in 1:2-13 thus acts as a pointer (not necessarily consciously designed as such by the author) to the function of these verses. They offer the reader a glimpse behind the scenes before the drama begins. There is a larger-than-life dimension to these verses, with their sonorous quotation (unparalleled in the rest of Mark's gospel) of key prophetic texts, the presence and activity of the Spirit of God, the opening of heaven and the divine voice, and the tableau of cosmic conflict set out in vv. 12-13. And all this takes place on a separate stage from the main drama, in the wilderness, the place of eschatological hope. If v. 1 has already staked a daring theological claim with the titles Χριστός and υἱὸς θεοῦ, these verses raise expectation to a higher level.

But the 'events' recorded in vv. 2-13, while they have a public dimension (John the Baptist and the crowd are also there ἐν τῇ ἐρήμῳ), are not recorded as a public revelation of who Jesus is. There is no indication that anyone other than Jesus himself saw or heard what happened after his baptism (1:10-11), or that the crowd had any reason to identify him with the ἰσχυρότερος of John's prophecy. No one else witnessed the confrontation with Satan and the animals, or saw the angelic intervention. All that people saw was an unknown man from an obscure village joining the many others who responded to John's call to baptism. It is only Mark's readers who, as a result of his prologue, are in a position to see more clearly who Jesus is, and how the prophetic words of vv. 2-3 are now coming to fulfilment.

These first few verses are a kind of theological commentary on the rest of the narrative. In v. 14 we come down to earth with a bump, and the characters in the story become the normal, everyday inhabitants of Galilee. It is as though in vv. 1-13, Mark has allowed us to see Jesus from God's angle, and now the curtain falls, and we are among men and women who stumble around, wondering what is happening. But though the characters in the story are bewil-

15. He uses similar language in *War* 7.438 about a Jewish leader, Jonathan the weaver, in Cyrene shortly after the war.

16. W. Marxsen, *Mark,* 37-38.

dered, Mark does not intend us to forget the truth which he has uncovered in these opening verses.[17]

Mark's prologue thus functions rather like the first two chapters of Job (so Anderson, 63), in giving the reader a heavenly perspective which is denied to the actors in the story. (The only pericope later in the gospel which offers a similar perspective, again with an explicit declaration of Jesus' identity by the audible voice of God, is 9:2-13, which again is given a clearly 'remote' geographical location, 'a high mountain by themselves alone'.)

I have posited a clear break between vv. 13 and 14. From v. 14 on the Spirit and the wilderness are no longer mentioned, and the scene has shifted from the Judaean wilderness to the inhabited towns and villages of Galilee. John the Baptist, a central figure in the prologue, has now been removed from the stage. The heavenly visions and supernatural actors of vv. 10-13 are replaced by everyday scenes peopled by ordinary Galileans. Verses 14-15 introduce the preaching ministry of Jesus which is to be the focus of the first act of the drama. The story has begun.

Yet several recent commentators (Anderson, Pesch, Gnilka, Mann, Guelich) define the prologue as finishing not with v. 13, but with v. 15, thus including in it what I have described as the opening verses of Act One, after the shift of scene. This alternative view, which began to challenge Lightfoot's in the mid-seventies and is now probably at least as widely supported, derives from an article by L. E. Keck,[18] in which he argues that the key word in Mark's introduction is εὐαγγέλιον, which is 'the rubric under which Mark wants to place his material' (359). The occurrence of εὐαγγέλιον in 1:1 and 1:14-15 thus forms the framework of Mark's introduction. He notes also that the mention of John the Baptist in v. 14 serves to round out the relation between John and Jesus which has developed in vv. 7-9. Keck therefore concludes that vv. 1-15 form a rounded introductory paragraph, and the story proper begins with the call of the first disciples in 1:16-20. This finding then feeds into Keck's analysis of the first half of the gospel into three main sections, each of which begins with 'discipleship material' (1:16-20; 3:13-19; 6:7b-13).

J. R. Michaels[19] goes further and suggests a deliberately chiastic design in vv. 1-15, as follows:

'a. the *gospel* of Jesus Christ (vs. 1);
  b. John the Baptist *in the desert,* in fulfillment of Scripture (vss. 2-4);
    c. John *baptizing in the Jordan* (vss. 5-8);
    c. Jesus *is baptized in the Jordan* (vss. 9-11);
  b. Jesus *in the desert* (vss. 12-13);
a. the *gospel* of God (vss. 14-15).'

17. M. D. Hooker, *Message,* 16. The whole first chapter provides a useful popular guide to Mk. 1:1-13 as prologue.
18. L. E. Keck, *NTS* 12 (1965/6) 352-70.
19. J. Ramsey Michaels, *Servant,* 44.

59

This scheme undoubtedly draws attention to repeated themes in these opening verses, but proposals for such deliberate patterning of the text are notoriously subjective, and the enthusiastic search for 'chiastic structures' by some modern commentators has produced little consensus that Mark actually intended his work to be read in this way. Similarly, while Keck is right to observe the recurrence of 'discipleship material', it does not therefore follow that the three sections he singles out (there are other sections on discipleship in Mark!) are intended to mark the beginning of deliberately composed 'sections'. Our discussion of the structure of Mark has in fact suggested that, like most good storytellers, he is more concerned to achieve an effective flow and development of his plot than to encourage detailed structural analysis of this sort.

Whether or not vv. 14-15 are to be regarded as part of Mark's prologue is therefore probably not ultimately a matter of crucial importance;[20] but I would suggest that this recent trend towards designating 1:1-15 as the prologue loses much more than it gains for our appreciation of Mark's introduction to his book. It disguises both the clear shift of scene from the wilderness to Galilee and, more importantly, the change of focus of which that scene-shift is a symbol, from the 'behind-the-scenes' account of the significance of Jesus to the real-life setting of the story of his ministry.

What Keck's argument does draw to our attention, however, is the careful way in which the opening of the Galilee narrative in 1:14-15 picks up themes already introduced (εὐαγγέλιον, the relation of John the Baptist to Jesus, κηρύσσω, μετάνοια), and thus sets the story of Jesus' ministry clearly within the theological framework already established. In so doing vv. 14-15 act as a 'second introduction',[21] set now not in John's wilderness but in the villages of Galilee where the good news must make its real-life impact, and the Son of God must confront and overthrow the kingdom of Satan.

The Forerunner (1:2-8)

TEXTUAL NOTES

2. In place of the phrase ἐν (τῷ) Ἠσαΐᾳ τῷ προφήτῃ, which is in all the earlier uncials except A and W and in virtually all the primary versional evidence, Byzantine MSS follow A W in reading ἐν τοῖς προφήταις, an obvious 'correction' in view of the fact that the following composite quotation begins with words from Malachi.

4. The variants around the words ὁ βαπτίζων ἐν τῇ ἐρήμῳ (B) arise from the fact

---

20. The transitional nature of these verses is well illustrated by Van Iersel's decision to include them *both* in his first main section, 'Setting the Scene' (31), *and* in the second, 'A Man of Authority' (43).

21. So J. M. Robinson, *Problem*, 23.

that Mark uses the title Ἰωάννης ὁ βαπτίζων here, as in 6:14, 24, rather than the more common Ἰωάννης ὁ βαπτιστής (so regularly Matthew and Luke, and also Mk. 6:25; 8:28). Scribes who were familiar with the more usual form Ἰωάννης ὁ βαπτιστής failed to recognise the title, and so attempted to construe the sentence with βαπτίζων as a participle parallel to κηρύσσων, to describe John's activity. This resulted in the inclusion of καί after ἐρήμῳ to coordinate the supposedly parallel participles (all MSS except B 33 892 2427 and the Sahidic and some Bohairic MSS), and in most cases also the omission of ὁ before βαπτίζων (other MSS except ℵ L Δ and the remaining Bohairic MSS). See commentary for reasons for preferring the B text. (See further J. K. Elliott, *TZ* 31 [1975] 14-15.)

6. The D reading δέρριν, which echoes the term used for prophetic clothing in Zc. 13:4, lacks sufficient support to be accepted here, even though τρίχας might have been due to assimilation to Matthew.

8. The inclusion of ἐν before ὕδατι (Byzantine MSS, with A W etc.) is less well supported than before πνεύματι, and is probably due to a scribal desire to produce a parallel syntax for the two clauses. This argues in favour of the ἐν before πνεύματι, which is more strongly supported (lacking only in B L; versional evidence is necessarily indecisive in a matter of Greek syntax), even though it might be suspect as a harmonisation with Mt. 3:11; Lk. 3:16. The more obvious harmonisation by the addition of καὶ πυρί has, by contrast, surprisingly little support.

As was noted above, the quotations of vv. 2-3 are syntactically linked with v. 1 by the use of καθώς; it is through the fulfilment of these scriptural passages that the good news finds its beginning. The passages quoted are not, however, prophecies about the coming of the Messiah, but about one (a 'messenger', a 'voice') who is to precede the coming of *God* to judge and save,[22] and that forerunner is immediately identified in v. 4 as John the Baptist. The immediate fulfilment of these scriptural models is therefore to be found apparently not in Jesus but in John.[23]

John's function is to prepare the way, but for whom? Mal. 3:1 and Is. 40:3 speak of preparing for the coming of ὁ κύριος (which in the OT context can

22. The identification of the figures named in Mal. 3:1 ('I', 'my messenger', 'the Lord whom you seek', 'the messenger of the covenant') is disputed. I have argued (*Jesus and the OT*, 91-92 n. 31) that *mal'ākî, hā'ādôn* (an unusual term; 'the Lord' in English does *not* here represent *YHWH*), and *mal'ak-habbᵉrît* are all the same person. Most assume that *hā'ādôn* must be a divine title, and since the structure of the sentence suggests the identification of *hā'ādôn* with *mal'ak-habbᵉrît*, some argue that the latter is also a term for God, and so distinct from the *mal'āk* of the first clause (so, e.g., P. A. Verhoef, *Haggai and Malachi*, 287-90). On either interpretation, however, no third person is mentioned.

23. M. A. Tolbert, *Sowing*, 239-48, argues, however, that the referent throughout vv. 2-3 is Jesus, the only figure mentioned so far: John does not come into Mark's picture until v. 4. The application of these texts to John rather than Jesus is, she believes, a result of deliberate rethinking by Matthew and Luke. It is in some ways an attractive argument, if Mark is detached from the subsequent exegetical tradition of the church, but it has its problems especially in that Tolbert is obliged to postulate a clear break between vv. 3 and 4, whereas the immediate repetition of the wilderness location suggests that they are meant to be closely linked, and in the σου of v. 2, which she takes to refer not to Jesus but to the reader (addressed in the singular as in 13:14).

only mean God), and John predicts the arrival of one who is ἰσχυρότερος, and who will dispense the Spirit as the prophets had said that Yahweh would do in the last days. Thus vv. 2-8 appear to leave no room for a human figure in the eschatological drama other than John himself, the forerunner sent to prepare for the eschatological coming of God (though see below on the significance of the second person in Mark's version of Mal. 3:1). When in v. 9 an obscure Northerner ('Ιησοῦς ἀπὸ Ναζαρὲτ τῆς Γαλιλαίας) appears on the scene, it is not immediately obvious what connection he has with the role either of John the forerunner or of the expected ἰσχυρότερος, and it will be the function of vv. 10-13 to begin to spell this out. The rest of the book will continue to guide the reader to an answer to this question.

John the Baptist thus appears in these verses as both of supreme significance, as the subject of some of the most stirring prophecies of the OT, the first embodiment of the age of eschatological fulfilment, and at the same time in the clearly subordinate role of the herald and footman, sent on ahead to prepare for the arrival of the sovereign. This tension in the estimate of John, familiar to us from its explicit presentation in the Q passage Mt. 11:7-15; Lk. 7:24-28, and from the recurrent Johannine focus on John's role (Jn. 1:6-8, 15, 19-34; 3:25-30; 5:33-36), is not spelled out by Mark. While John will be mentioned from time to time in his story (2:18; 6:14-16; 8:28; 11:27-33), the only point at which he will be the focus of the narrative after 1:2-8 will be the strange digression in which Mark offers a dramatic account of the circumstances of his death (6:17-29). It is only in 1:2-8 that we find Mark's direct account of the significance of John.

We shall see below that John is here portrayed as a prophetic figure, and later in the gospel this same estimate will recur (6:14-16; 8:28; 11:32). According to one strand of Jewish belief,[24] prophecy had ceased with Malachi, whose book came to a close with the prediction of the return of Elijah to herald the Day of the Lord. To present John as a prophet was, therefore, for those who subscribed to this view of prophecy, a daring and far-reaching claim, made the more striking when the pericope begins with a quotation of Malachi's eschatological prediction, and still further when John is described in terms used in the OT to mark out the distinctive characteristics of Elijah (see on v. 6). John is thus even 'more than a prophet' (Mt. 11:9). His coming marks the beginning of the end.

It is clear from Josephus, *Ant.* 18.116-19 that John was a noticeable figure in his own right, a preacher of religious revival with a following sufficient to raise fears about his political intentions.[25] Mark recognises the importance of

24. D. E. Aune, *Prophecy,* ch. 5 (note especially pp. 103-6), has shown conclusively that this was not, as it is often presented, the view of all Jews by the NT period, but that of a limited rabbinic school.

25. For detailed recent studies of John as a figure in first-century Judaism (not merely in his NT role as a foil to Jesus) see R. L. Webb, *John;* J. E. Taylor, *John.* Taylor, *John,* 15-48, offers a detailed argument against the assumption commonly made that John, because of his wil-

his movement (v. 5), but for him it is only the ἀρχὴ τοῦ εὐαγγελίου. The emphatic scriptural testimonial with which Mark introduces John (the only such editorial quotation in the whole gospel) by its content directs attention not to John himself but to the one who will follow him.

2-3 This is essentially a combined quotation of Mal. 3:1 (with elements drawn from Ex. 23:20) and Is. 40:3, the whole being attributed to Isaiah presumably because the better-known Isaiah text, even though coming second, was the basis of the herald idea which links the two.[26] Once the two texts are brought together, it is natural that Mal. 3:1 opens the combined quotation, not only because the opening Ἰδού could hardly come in the middle, but also because the idea of God's appointed herald is more explicit in Mal. 3:1, while the more allusive language of Is. 40:3 forms an appropriate comment on it. We do not know of these two passages being brought together previously, but it is a natural link, not only on the basis of the phrase *pnh-derek* which occurs in both,[27] but also because they share more generally (with Mal. 3:23-24 [EVV 4:5-6]) the idea of a herald for the eschatological coming of God.[28] Matthew and Luke, by incorporating the Mal. 3:1 quotation in their later account of the significance of John (Mt. 11:10; Lk. 7:27) while leaving Is. 40:3 at this point, have weakened the effect of this massive opening scriptural salvo.

Once Ex. 23:20 has been linked with Mal. 3:1 (see below) there is also a wilderness connection in each passage, which in this context would be important for Mark. Indeed, Myers suggests that by omitting that part of Mal. 3:1 which envisages the Lord appearing *in the temple* and linking the passage instead to the wilderness location, Mark is already signalling the dismissal of the institutional life of Israel which will be a recurrent theme of his gospel.

---

derness location and the nature of his message, must have had significant links with the Qumran community. She goes on to suggest that John was most closely associated with the Pharisees.

26. The importance of Isaiah for Mark's work as a whole is pointed out by M. A. Beavis, *Audience,* 110, and is made the subject of a major study by R. E. Watts, *Exodus.* The latter suggests (88-90) that 1:2-3 is deliberately constructed on the familiar lines of the Marcan 'sandwich' technique, the Malachi/Exodus quotation being designedly inserted between the Isaiah attribution and the Isaiah quotation. Similarly, Stock speaks of the Malachi quotation as 'framed by Isaiah's name and Isaiah's words'.

27. This link is found in the Hebrew/Aramaic text but not in the LXX. J. Marcus, *Way,* 16, therefore suggests that the link had already been made in Mark's community rather than being made by Mark specifically for his Greek gospel.

28. J. Marcus, *Way,* 29, feels it necessary to defend this sense of 'preparing the way' against what he surprisingly calls 'the usual [interpretation]', that '"the way of the Lord" in Mark 1:3 is most often interpreted "ethically" to mean the way in which the Lord wants people to walk'. I cannot recall meeting such a view in relation to Mk. 1:3, and find it hard to believe that it is 'usual'. Marcus's own extended discussion of 'the way of the Lord' in Mark (*Way,* 29-47) effectively demonstrates its eschatological character as the Lord's own way (along which, as a 'secondary emphasis', people are also called to walk).

The Isaiah passage[29] is quoted in the LXX text, modified only by the substitution of αὐτοῦ for τοῦ θεοῦ ἡμῶν at the end; while this might be no more than a simplifying substitution of pronoun for noun, making no difference to the understanding of the text, it also, by avoiding the direct use of θεός, allows the Christian reader to understand the κύριος of the previous line to refer to Jesus. Mal. 3:1, however, has undergone drastic alteration, largely by conflation with the LXX text of Ex. 20:23, a passage which uses similar language about God sending a *mal'āk* (ἄγγελος) in front to prepare the way. The words ἀποστέλλω (LXX Mal. 3:1 has ἐξαποστέλλω) and πρὸ προσώπου σου (LXX Mal. 3:1 has πρὸ προσώπου μου in the *second* clause) correspond to LXX Ex. 23:20, and while κατασκευάσει τὴν ὁδόν is closer to the Hebrew text of Mal. 3:1, *ûpinnâ derek l^epānāy* (LXX has ἐπιβλέψεται, which depends on reading the verb as Qal, not Piel), the second person pronoun σου again echoes Ex. 23:20.

Ex. 23:20 is a prophecy not of God's eschatological coming but of his provision for Israel in the wilderness, but the similarity of the wording led to the two passages being associated also in Jewish exegesis,[30] and the wilderness connection (picked up in the following quotation from Is. 40:3) would make the conflation especially attractive to Mark in this context. The main change which results is that a prophecy which in Malachi spoke of Yahweh's *mal'āk* preparing the way before *me* (i.e., Yahweh) is now applied to some unspecified third person, 'you'. In Ex. 23:20 the 'you' was Israel; here we are left to assume, with Christian hindsight, that it is Jesus. In this light, the substitution of αὐτοῦ for τοῦ θεοῦ ἡμῶν in the quotation from Is. 40:3 seems more likely also to have a christological purpose. Thus a note which was absent from both Mal. 3:1 and Is. 40:3, the presence of a third person in addition to Yahweh and his forerunner, is hinted at by means of a creative textual conflation and an apparently insignificant change of noun to pronoun.[31]

4 ἐγένετο here functions like the Hebrew *way^ehî* to introduce a new scene, and a new actor on the stage. No background to introduce John is either given or needed; his title and the brief account of his activity in vv. 4-6 tell us all we need to know about him for Mark's purposes. The textual confusion (see Textual Note) is best explained by Mark's use of the title Ἰωάννης ὁ βαπτίζων (used by Mark alone) rather than the more familiar Ἰωάννης ὁ βαπτιστής used by Matthew and Luke, leading scribes to try to construe βαπτίζων as a participle parallel to κηρύσσων. If Mark had in fact written ἐγένετο Ἰωάννης βαπτίζων ἐν τῇ ἐρήμῳ καὶ κηρύσσων βάπτισμα μετανοίας, it is not easy to see why the al-

29. For the significance of Is. 40:3 in contemporary Jewish thought see J. E. Taylor, *John*, 25-29 (with special reference to its use at Qumran); R. E. Watts, *Exodus*, 82-84 (and cf. Watts's discussion of the text in its own canonical setting in *Exodus*, 76-82).

30. J. Mann, *Bible*, 479-80; cf. K. Stendahl, *School*, 50. See especially *Ex. Rab.* 23:20.

31. See J. Marcus, *Way*, 37-41, for the creative ambiguity of Mark's use of κύριος, which 'subtly combines a recognition of the separateness of the two figures with a recognition of their inseparability', so that 'where Jesus acts, there God is acting'.

ternative readings would have arisen. It would, moreover, have been a more clumsy form of expression, with baptism mentioned twice in parallel clauses, whereas if ὁ βαπτίζων is part of John's title the sentence reads more naturally. There is no obvious rationale for Mark's choice of title for John in the four other occurrences in the gospel (6:14, 24, 25; 8:28), especially since ὁ βαπτίζων and ὁ βαπτιστής are used in adjacent verses in 6:24, 25! But it may be that here he used the participial form as the more explanatory, functional introduction for a reader who might not previously know about John, and to whom therefore the more formal substantival term βαπτιστής (used of John, both in the NT and in Josephus, *Ant.* 18.116, and occurring nowhere else) might be unfamiliar.[32]

For the connotations of ἐν τῇ ἐρήμῳ (echoing the quotation of Is. 40:3) see the general introduction to 1:2-13 above. Geographically the term applies to uncultivated and uninhabited country, and the specific mention of the Jordan in v. 5 restricts the possibilities to the area between the lake of Galilee and the Dead Sea.[33] It is hard to be more specific, since there was little habitation in any of that region apart from Jericho, but the mention of crowds from Judaea and Jerusalem in v. 5 suggests the southern part of the valley, not far from the inflow to the Dead Sea, and therefore remote from Galilee. John's conflict with Antipas (6:14-18) and his death, according to Josephus, in Antipas's palace of Machaerus on the east of the Dead Sea, suggest that at least part of his ministry was on the east side of the Jordan, in Antipas's territory of Peraea. But we do not have the information to allow us to discover the exact location,[34] and Mark was more interested in the symbolic significance of the ἔρημος than in its geographical definition.

Mark summarises the whole focus of John's mission in the condensed phrase κηρύσσων βάπτισμα μετανοίας εἰς ἄφεσιν ἁμαρτιῶν. This condensation might suggest that the βάπτισμα was itself the object of his preaching, but it is clear from all the accounts we have of John both in the NT and in Josephus that his focus was rather on repentance in the face of the threat of divine judgment, and his object was not simply to get people baptised, but to call together the repentant and restored people of God for the imminent eschatological crisis.[35] Baptism was a symbol of repentance and of belonging to the true remnant of the people of God. But Mark singles it out as the focus of this thumbnail sketch, since it was the most distinctive feature of John's ministry, and the one by which he had come to be popularly known.

32. J. K. Elliott, *TZ* 31 (1975) 14-15, argues that Mark used ὁ βαπτίζων consistently, and that where ὁ βαπτιστής occurs in Marcan MSS it is a later correction.

33. J. E. Taylor, *John,* 42-48, usefully discusses John's location, emphasising that the Jordan valley area was 'wilderness' (uncultivated) but not 'desert' like the desert of Judaea west of the Dead Sea. (Her concern in context is to distance John from Qumran.)

34. R. Riesner attempts, in a detailed study based on Jn. 1:28, *TynB* 38 (1987) 29-63, to locate John's ministry in *northern* Transjordan (Batanaea).

35. For an excellent brief historical appraisal of John's mission see B. F. Meyer, *Aims,* 115-28.

βάπτισμα is an exclusively Christian word, which appears for the first time in the NT.[36] Its use in Rom. 6:4 shows that it was already current in Christian circles before Mark wrote (and indeed there is no evidence that any alternative way of referring to this central aspect of Christian ritual was ever in general use), so that he has no need to explain it to his Christian readers. Historically speaking, however, John's distinctive rite was a new phenomenon. Ritual washing was common enough, both in the OT and increasingly in later Judaism (see on 7:3-4). It was a prominent element in the religious life of Qumran, and its importance in mainstream Judaism is indicated by the increasing number of *miqwā'ōt* (ritual immersion baths) which archaeological discovery is revealing in Jerusalem and elsewhere in Palestine, as well as by a whole tractate entitled *Miqwā'ōt* in the Mishnah.[37] But these were all regular, repeated washings, whereas John was calling for a single, initiatory baptism, indicating the beginning of a new commitment.[38] For this many believe that the most likely Jewish precedent is the ritual cleansing by immersion of a Gentile on becoming a proselyte.[39] But John's baptism was for Jews; to ask them to undergo the same initiatory ritual as was required of a Gentile convert was a powerful statement of John's theology of the people of God, one which is reminiscent of the 'remnant' theology of the prophets. To be born a Jew was not enough; it was only by μετάνοια εἰς ἄφεσιν ἁμαρτιῶν that one could be truly counted among the people of God.[40]

μετάνοια is not a frequent term in Mark. The noun occurs only here, and the verb only twice, to express the content of the preaching of both Jesus and his disciples (1:15; 6:12). But while the technical term may not be used elsewhere, the focus of much of the gospel, especially in the teaching on discipleship in 8:27–10:45, is on the need for a reorientation to the paradoxical values of the kingdom of God. It is indeed those who are already disciples who are most often called to such reorientation: the 'new mind-set' for which Jesus calls

36. βαπτισμός occurs in a handful of medical texts of the second century A.D. and later. In the NT it occurs only in the plural, and refers (with the possible exception of Heb. 6:2) only to ritual washings other than baptism. βάπτισμα occurs only in the singular.

37. See J. E. Taylor, *John*, 58-64, for an interesting discussion of the concept of 'impurity'; she emphasises that 'There is nothing morally sinful about being impure. One cannot avoid it. Becoming impure happens quite naturally all the time.'

38. It has been suggested that the Qumran community practised an initiatory washing when new members joined the community. 1QS 3:4 refers to 'purification by cleansing waters', and 1QS 3:9 to 'flesh cleansed by being sprinkled with cleansing waters' in connection with someone entering the 'community of truth'. J. E. Taylor, *John*, 76-81, argues, however, that this initial washing was not truly initiatory 'since it was not the decisive step towards inclusion in the community, but only something resulting from a practice of righteousness accounted acceptable by God'.

39. See H. H. Rowley, in his *From Moses to Qumran*, 211-35; J. Jeremias, *Baptism*, 24-29. It continues to be debated, however, whether the practice was already established in the early first century. For a recent summary of the arguments see R. L. Webb, *John*, 122-30; Webb's own view is that its introduction was probably post-70. J. E. Taylor, *John*, 64-69, regards its use in the early first century as possible though not proven.

40. J. E. Taylor, *John*, 84-88, traces John's theology especially to the Book of Isaiah.

is not learned in a moment at the initial point of commitment, but requires a lifetime of μετάνοια. But it is to such a revolution of attitudes and values that Jesus will call people when he announces the coming of the kingdom of God, and μετάνοια appropriately expresses the idea. The continuity in this respect between the ministries of John and Jesus (and his disciples) is therefore noteworthy.

Josephus agrees that John's baptism was connected with ἄφεσις ἁμαρτιῶν, but offers an interesting and instructive comment on the nature of the connection.[41] John presented baptism, according to Josephus, *Ant.* 18.117, as meaningful not in itself, but only if *preceded* by a commitment to ἀρετή, in the form of δικαιοσύνη towards one another and εὐσέβεια towards God. Baptism should *not* then be used 'to gain pardon for their sins', but was merely a bodily mark of purity, 'indicating that the soul had already been cleansed by righteousness.' This sounds almost like a Protestant statement designed to guard against attributing to baptism a saving efficacy *ex opere operato*. Mark's words are much less cautious, and could be interpreted as making the ἄφεσις ἁμαρτιῶν an automatic result of accepting John's baptism. The intervening word μετανοίας, however, makes this a less plausible deduction, and the syntax does not allow any definite conclusion as to precisely how βάπτισμα, μετάνοια, and ἄφεσις ἁμαρτιῶν relate to one another in Mark's understanding of John's baptism,[42] still less in the context of Christian baptism. Mark's interest in any case was not primarily in John's sacramental theology, but in his role in the eschatological drama.

It is perhaps for this reason that Mark betrays no doctrinal embarrassment over the fact that Jesus, the Son of God, who is repeatedly described in the NT writings and in later Christian orthodoxy as sinless, nonetheless presented himself for a βάπτισμα μετανοίας εἰς ἄφεσιν ἁμαρτιῶν. This was clearly a problem for Matthew, who not only includes an explicit debate on the issue between John and Jesus (Mt. 3:14-15) but also, by omitting this phrase, avoids an explicit description of the meaning of John's baptism.

5 Mark's description of the wide appeal of John's preaching (even if there is an element of exaggeration in the πᾶσα and the πάντες) tallies with Josephus's account of 'others joining the crowd mightily stirred up by his preaching', leading to Antipas's preemptive strike to avert a popular uprising. The failure to mention Galilee (or indeed Peraea) may reflect Mark's understanding that John was baptising towards the southern end of the Jordan valley. It has the effect of making the appearance of Jesus ἀπὸ Ναζαρὲτ τῆς Γαλιλαίας in v. 9 the more striking; he is not part of the Judaean crowd, but a stranger from the far north.

---

41. J. E. Taylor, *John*, 94-100, discusses the connection between Josephus's account and the NT version.

42. J. E. Taylor, *John*, 98, concludes that 'the NT describes John's practice not as an immersion for the remission of sins (with a view to repentance), but as an immersion of repentance (for the remission of sins).'

In view of the clearly negative attitude towards Jerusalem in the rest of the gospel, it is important to notice that here and in 3:7-8 Mark recognises a popular response to the preaching of both John and Jesus among Judaeans. The opposition to Jesus which will be centred in Jerusalem comes primarily from its scribes (3:22; 7:1), and from the impressively listed οἱ πρεσβύτεροι καὶ οἱ ἀρχιερεῖς καὶ οἱ γραμματεῖς (8:31; 10:33; 11:27) who constituted the Sanhedrin, while ὁ ὄχλος remains convinced that John had been a prophet (11:32), and therefore still potentially amenable to the claims of Jesus as his successor (12:12, 37).

Myers (125-26) further suggests, however, that by picturing the crowds coming *from* Jerusalem *to* the ἔρημος Mark is making his own 'subversive' point. 'According to the dominant nationalist ideology of salvation history, Jerusalem was considered the hub of the world to which all nations would one day come. . . . Mark turns this "circulation" on its head: far from embarking on triumphal pilgrimage to Zion, the crowds flee to the margins, for purposes of repentance.' (Cf. above on 1:2 for a similarly 'subversive' note in the linking of Mal. 3:1 not with the temple but with the wilderness.)

The mode of baptism ἐν τῇ Ἰορδάνῃ ποταμῷ remains a matter of debate. The use of a permanent river suggests the need for more than a token quantity of water. The word βαπτίζω itself (BAGD translates 'dip, immerse', and gives as non-Christian usages, 'plunge, sink, drench, overwhelm') and the phrases ἐν τῷ ποταμῷ here and ἀναβαίνων ἐκ τοῦ ὕδατος (v. 10) probably suggest immersion.[43] In the light of the apparently immersion symbolism of Christian baptism (Rom. 6:3-5), it seems probable that its predecessor also involved immersion, despite the fact that Christian art traditionally depicts John baptising Jesus by pouring water over his head.[44] We do not, however, have any firm evidence for John's method, nor is it necessarily true that the mode was always the same.

Similarly, we cannot reconstruct a liturgical practice from the simple phrase ἐξομολογούμενοι τὰς ἁμαρτίας αὐτῶν; there is no indication whether the confession was silent or aloud, and if the latter to whom it was addressed; it is hazardous even to conclude from the use of the present participle that the confession formed part of the act of baptism. The phrase merely repeats what v. 4 has already told us about the significance of John's baptism.

Jewish ritual washing (including proselyte baptism) was generally self-administered,[45] so that the use here of the passive of βαπτίζω, with an agent (ὑπ'

43. Note, however, the argument of I. H. Marshall, *EQ* 45 (1973) 130-40, that in the light of the language about 'baptising in the Holy Spirit' in v. 8 there is at least room for doubt as to whether immersion is a necessary aspect of the meaning of βαπτίζω.

44. See, however, H. Schürmann, *Lukasevangelium I*, 156, 176 for archaeological evidence for affusion rather than immersion as the early Christian mode of baptism, and L. Goppelt, *TDNT*, 8.332, for affusion as the normal method of baptism both by John and in early Christianity.

45. J. E. Taylor, *John*, 50, finds 'the only known parallel outside the NT for anyone immersing someone else' in Josephus's account of the murder by drowning of the High Priest Aristobulus III (*War* 1.437; *Ant.* 15.55), but she is presumably referring only to the use of the Greek verb βαπτίζω, since on the next page she mentions a reference to one person immersing another in *m. Miqw.* 8:5.

αὐτοῦ), suggests a deliberate break with convention (and one which Christian baptism followed; cf. Jn. 4:1-2); cf. also the emphatically active formulation in v. 8, ἐγὼ ἐβάπτισα ὑμᾶς. This further reinforces the special significance of John's baptism, and the prophetic role of John himself.[46]

6 The description of John's clothing and diet serves further to reinforce his prophetic image.[47] ζώνην δερματίνην περὶ τὴν ὀσφὺν αὐτοῦ is virtually an exact quotation from 4 Kgdms. 1:8, describing the distinctive garb of Elijah, while the preceding phrase, ἐνδεδυμένος τρίχας καμήλου, while not echoing the LXX of that verse, represents a likely meaning of the Hebrew *ʾîš baʿal śēʿār* ('a man characterised by hair') as one wearing a cloak of animal hair.[48] John is therefore presented (and intended to present himself?) at least as a prophet (Zc. 13:4), and most likely as the returning Elijah.[49] This is the more likely in Mark's mind in the light of 1:2, with its quotation of Mal. 3:1, since that text was regularly read in conjunction with Mal. 3:23-24 (EVV 4:5-6), the prophecy of the eschatological coming of Elijah.[50] It will not be until 9:13 that Mark will get close to an explicit identification of John with Elijah (though cf. their linking in 8:28), but already there is a broad hint of this understanding of his role.

John's diet, if simple and monotonous, was nutritious. ἀκρίδες are the only type of insect permitted as food in the Mosaic law (Lv. 11:20-23; cf CD 12:14-15 for their use as food at Qumran, roasted or boiled); they are still eaten with relish by those in whose lands they flourish.[51] There is no basis in Greek usage for the traditional notion (born no doubt of Western squeamishness) that the word refers here not to locusts but to the carob or 'locust'-bean (hence called 'St. John's bread'). John may have been an ascetic, but he was not a vegetarian! His diet represents the attempt to live, like Bannus in the same area some years later, on 'food that grows by itself' (i.e., living off the land) (Josephus, *Life* 11).[52]

7 The subject of John's regular preaching has already been indicated in v. 4, but here Mark adds a more specific focus which brings us to the heart of

46. See R. L. Webb, *John,* 179-83, for a full discussion of the mode of John's baptism.

47. Stock, 49, offers interesting comments on the symbolic importance of clothing in Mark's narrative.

48. Many commentators have taken the *śēʿār* as a reference to his clothing, since a belt is not likely to have been his only or most conspicuous attire! Elijah's cloak was a notable feature of his equipment (1 Ki. 19:13, 19; 2 Ki. 2:8-14), and a hairy cloak was standard prophetic dress (Zc. 13:4). See further M. Hengel, *Leader,* 36 n. 71. The LXX, however, takes *ʾîš baʿal śēʿār* as a reference to his personal appearance, ἀνὴρ δασύς, a hairy man.

49. J. E. Taylor, *John,* 34-38, argues that the camel hair indicated a use of sackcloth to symbolise repentance rather than any link with Elijah. But see the next note.

50. J. E. Taylor, *John,* 213-14, suggests that the location of John's ministry just across the Jordan from Jericho had special significance as the place where Elijah had ascended to heaven (2 Ki. 2:4-12), and therefore perhaps the place where he was expected to appear again.

51. P. Bonnard, *Matthieu,* 34, provides culinary directions! For their food value see G. S. Cansdale, *Animals,* 242-44.

52. J. E. Taylor, *John,* 34, 40-41, draws attention to the similarities between John's asceticism and that of Bannus, and suggests that Bannus may have 'known of John's example and copied him'.

what for him constitutes John's ministry as the ἀρχὴ τοῦ εὐαγγελίου Ἰησοῦ Χριστοῦ rather than, as in Josephus, a movement of interest for its own sake. ὁ ἰσχυρότερός μου is not in itself a very specific phrase, though clearly it indicates superiority in some way. ἰσχυρός is as general a term as English 'strong', so that the context is left to determine the nature of his superiority. The context supplies two clues: first the image of the slave undoing the sandal thong, a social metaphor which still leaves open the question of what sort of superiority is involved;[53] and secondly the contrast of two levels of baptism (v. 8), which focuses the issue on the nature and spiritual efficacy of the newcomer's mission.

The Christian reader has no difficulty in recognising in this ἰσχυρότερος a pointer to Jesus, and we have seen from the textual variations introduced into the scriptural quotations in vv. 2-3 that Mark probably intended his readers to take it that way. But the point is worth repeating that neither the OT passages produced in vv. 2-3 as models for John's role as forerunner nor the specific role which he assigns to the ἰσχυρότερος in v. 8 could be expected in themselves to suggest a *human* figure. It is Yahweh who will follow the forerunner in both Mal. 3:1 and Is. 40:3, and in OT thought it is Yahweh himself who will pour out his Spirit in the last days (Is. 32:15; 44:3; Ezk. 36:26-27; 39:29; Joel 3:1-2 [EVV 2:28-29], etc.). It says a lot for the underlying christology of Mark's gospel that he can allow the Baptist's words, which in themselves point directly to the coming of God, to be read as referring to the human Jesus. For him, apparently, the coming of Jesus *is* the eschatological coming of God. The title υἱὸς θεοῦ which he included in his heading is already being shown to be more than just a synonym for Χριστός; the events which follow Jesus' arrival on the scene in v. 9 will underline the point.

For the time being, however, the coming one is incognito (and will remain so for the actors in the story, since the revelations in vv. 10-13 are not publicly available, but offered only to the privileged insight of the reader). John's enigmatic words would presumably, in the narrative context, be understood as a prophecy of God's eschatological coming; only Mark's readers have been given a hint that there is a human ἰσχυρότερος waiting in the wings. There is, therefore, a delicate ambiguity about the phrase ὀπίσω μου. It is generally taken in a temporal sense, 'after me', and this is a possible sense of ὀπίσω, but not its usual sense, especially when used with the genitive of a person, and following the verb ἔρχομαι. This collocation is frequent in the NT, and becomes almost a technical term for discipleship, parallel to ἀκολουθέω. See, e.g., 1:17, 20; 8:34; Mt. 10:38; Lk. 21:8; Jn. 12:19. This intriguing phrase is used of Jesus' relation to John the Baptist not only here and in the Matthew parallel (3:11), but also in Jn. 1:15, 27, 30. On this basis it seems likely that the NT writers, aware of the

---

53. Taking off the master's sandals was a slave's role, though interestingly one which was felt to be too low for a Hebrew slave (*Mek.* Ex. 21:2), and specifically excluded from the otherwise menial duties of a rabbi's disciple (*b. Ket.* 96a). John places himself below either (he is not fit to do what is too demeaning even for them) in relation to the ἰσχυρότερος.

relationship between John and Jesus before the imprisonment of the former, were willing to describe Jesus as the 'disciple' of John[54] — with the aim, of course, of immediately indicating that in this case the disciple is greater than his master. There would then be a striking irony in v. 7 — 'my *disciple,* whose sandal thong I am not fit to untie'! There has, of course, been nothing in Mark's narrative so far to indicate any such relationship between John and Jesus, and Jesus will appear on the scene in v. 9 apparently as a stranger from a distant province; it is only in the light of the Fourth Gospel's account of the earlier links between John and Jesus (and Luke's mention of their family relationship?) that any such nuance could be heard in ὀπίσω μου. The reader of Mark who knows nothing of this wider tradition would not be in a position to understand it as anything other than a statement of temporal sequence.

8 The aorist ἐβάπτισα is sometimes explained as a Semitism, based on the Hebrew use of the perfect with a present meaning. Others suggest that it reflects Mark's (or John's?) awareness that with the coming of Jesus John's ministry is now at an end. It is probably more natural to understand it simply in the narrative context as the correct tense for John to use when addressing those who have just been baptised by him.

The contrast between John's water baptism and the Spirit baptism which will be the role of the one still to come is a recurrent theme in the NT (see Mt. 3:11; Lk. 3:16; Jn 1:33 [cf. 1:26-27, 31]; Acts 1:5; 11:16; 19:1-6). In each case the implication is that water baptism is a preliminary rite, of lesser significance; it is the Spirit baptism which is the 'real thing', for which John's water baptism merely prepares the way, and without which John's ministry is incomplete. While there is a clear distinction between John's baptism and Christian water baptism (so that in Acts 19:1-6 the former needed to be supplemented by the latter, not merely by the receipt of the Spirit), the stress laid on the contrast by the NT writers, expressing it in terms of water and Spirit rather than in terms of the agent of baptism, suggests that they intended to imply that even Christian water baptism on its own is inadequate.

'Water' and 'Holy Spirit' are not natural opposites. The one is physical, the other spiritual, so that at the least the antithesis directs our attention to the contrast between the outward act of washing and a change effected at a more 'internal' level. Cf. the flesh/Spirit contrast of Jn. 3:1-8, where again the bringing together of water and Spirit in v. 5 reminds the reader irresistibly of the discussion of water baptism and Spirit baptism in 1:26-33. Water baptism alone remains at the level of 'flesh'. But the Christian reader is not likely to be content with a mere outward/inward contrast; the mention of πνεῦμα ἅγιον inevita-

54. So, e.g., K. Grobel, *JBL* 60 (1941) 397-401; C. H. Dodd, *Historical Tradition,* 272-74; J. A. T. Robinson, *Priority,* 182-83. J. R. Michaels, *Servant,* 19-22, rather melodramatically suggests that the synoptic evangelists found Jesus' status as John's disciple an embarrassment (hence the omission of any reference to their parallel baptising ministry, Jn. 3:22-24; 4:1-2), but John 'broke the conspiracy of silence'; the presence of ὀπίσω μου in Mark and Matthew hardly fits this view.

bly adds a further dimension to John's prediction. Its background lies, as mentioned above, in the prophetic hope that in the last days Yahweh would 'pour out' his Spirit on his people. This is not simply a hope of spiritual refurbishment, but of the active presence of God himself among his people. To say of one who is able thus to mediate the presence of God himself that he is ἰσχυρότερος than John is something of an understatement!

βαπτίζω is a natural word to use in connection with water: its origin as an intensive form of βάπτω, 'to dip', is reflected in its normal usage as 'to immerse, drench, soak', and we have seen above that it is likely that John's baptism did involve a literal immersion, or at least soaking, in water. But it is not apparently so natural a metaphor to use with πνεῦμα ἅγιον, since the Holy Spirit is not easily pictured as a pool or river. The OT language about 'pouring out' the Spirit does, however, indicate that 'liquid' metaphors were not felt to be inappropriate for the Spirit, and similar usage is found in 1QS 4:20-22. Elsewhere in the NT also the Spirit is spoken of in terms of water, whether poured out or drunk (Jn. 7:37-39; Acts 2:33; 10:45; 1 Cor. 12:13; Tit. 3:5-6). This indicates that the metaphor is perhaps less surprising than we might first think, but none of these 'liquid' references to the Spirit easily allows the idea of dipping or immersion.[55] It may be therefore that we should appeal to the occasional secular usage of βαπτίζω in the wider (metaphorical) sense of 'to overwhelm', without implying literal immersion.[56] It is perhaps more likely, however, that the use of this verb is dictated more by the formulation of the antithesis than by any natural metaphorical sense. In that case it would be hazardous to draw any theological conclusions with regard to the nature of Christian experience of the Spirit from the use of the verb βαπτίζω.

Similarly, the preposition ἐν should not be pressed into a quasi-pictorial view of Jesus' followers being 'immersed in' the Holy Spirit. The range of usage of ἐν is too broad for such specific exegetical conclusions. If the textual note above is right in reading ἐν with πνεύματι ἁγίῳ but not with ὕδατι, and if the latter dative is to be understood as instrumental, then the ἐν should probably be taken in a similar sense (though what that means in the case of the Holy Spirit is not immediately obvious). The antithesis focuses neither on the verb βαπτίζω nor on its syntactical links, but on the contrast between water and the Holy Spirit, and on the two different levels of efficacy in the ministries of John and his successor which they represent.

It is not appropriate therefore to look for a specific point at which the prediction of v. 8b was to be fulfilled. While the events of Acts 2 clearly bring its fulfilment into visible focus, it was in the whole experience of the early Christian movement, not simply in the events of that one day, that the

---

55. See, however, the comment of J. E. Taylor, *John,* 140, that in 1QS 4:20-21 'we do get a sense that the "sprinkling" involves a very thorough drenching in spirit. It is not a mild splash.' She suggests that John is thinking here of 'a torrential downpour from heaven'.

56. So I. H. Marshall, *EQ* 45 (1973) 137-40.

new relationship with God predicted by John as his successor's gift would be experienced.

Mark 1:8 and parallels shed little light on the modern Pentecostal concept of a 'Baptism in the Spirit' experienced by some Christians subsequent to conversion, as a second stage in discipleship. It is noteworthy that the only passages in the NT which use the phrase βαπτίζω ἐν πνεύματι ἁγίῳ[57] (the noun βάπτισμα is never used in this connection) are those which contrast this baptism with water baptism as practised by John (Mt. 3:11; Mk. 1:8; Lk. 3:16; Jn. 1:33; Acts 1:5; 11:16). The immediate reference is therefore not to a second stage of Christian experience, but to the authentic Christian experience as contrasted with the preliminary (pre-Christian) experience represented by John's water baptism. This suggests that, whatever the merits of this Pentecostal model for Christian experience, 'Baptism in the Spirit' is not an appropriate term to use for it, and Mark 1:8 and the other NT passages which speak of baptising in Holy Spirit are not a suitable point at which to seek to ground it in the NT.

The Declaration of the Son of God (1:9-11)

TEXTUAL NOTES

There are, not surprisingly, a number of MSS and versional variations designed to assimilate the text of Mark to the better-known parallel text of Matthew (ἠνοιγμένους for σχιζομένους; ἐπ' αὐτόν for εἰς αὐτόν; ἐν ᾧ for ἐν σοί — but, surprisingly, no significant MSS offer οὗτός ἐστιν for σὺ εἶ).

11. The absence of ἐγένετο after φωνή in ℵ* D Θ and a few Old Latin MSS would leave φωνή as a subject without a verb (unless ἠκούσθη is added, as in Θ); its omission may also be a matter of assimilation to Mt. 3:17, where, however, the presence of ἰδού makes the lack of a verb less difficult.

This pericope is normally entitled 'the Baptism of Jesus'. But the baptism itself is recounted with minimal detail in v. 9, while the rest of the pericope is devoted to a description of what Jesus saw and heard immediately afterwards. Within the scope of Mark's prologue, it is these disclosures which are of primary importance, and they form the high point of the prologue's presentation of the true identity of Jesus the Messiah. The only passage in the rest of the gospel which will offer a similarly exalted view of Jesus is the transfiguration story, where the voice of God will again be heard declaring the identity of Jesus in words almost the same as in 1:11, with the significant difference that then they will be addressed to three of Jesus' disciples, not, as here, to Jesus himself alone.

---

57. The inclusion of ἐν in Mark 1:8 is likely but not certain: see Textual Note above. The language of 1 Cor. 12:13 is more complex: while the phrase ἐν ἑνὶ πνεύματι probably refers to the Holy Spirit (as also the following ἓν πνεῦμα ἐποτίσθημεν), the phrase εἰς ἓν σῶμα intervening between ἐν ἑνὶ πνεύματι and ἐβαπτίσθημεν makes this a less clear reference to 'Baptism in the Holy Spirit'.

In this respect Mark's account of Jesus' baptism differs from that in the other three gospels. Matthew says not that Jesus *saw* the heavens opened and the Spirit descending, but that they *were* opened; and whereas the heavenly voice in Mark is addressed to Jesus in the second person, in Matthew it is a statement about Jesus in the third person, suggesting that John at least was intended to hear it. Luke, like Mark, has the declaration in the second person, but he also, like Matthew, states that the heavens *were* opened, and further that the Spirit descended on Jesus σωματικῷ εἴδει ὡς περιστεράν, again implying an event visible, potentially at least, to others besides Jesus. In the Fourth Gospel the 'public' nature of the experience is even more explicit, in that we hear John the Baptist describing how he saw the Spirit descend on Jesus, and drew the appropriate conclusions (Jn. 1:30-34). Each of the other gospels, then, in different ways, presents the postbaptismal revelation as one offered at least to John, and potentially to others. In Mark there is no sign of this. It is narrated purely as an experience *of Jesus,* recorded by Mark for the benefit of his readers, but not accessible to any of the other actors on the scene, not even, apparently, to John.

The form of the revelation is threefold. The 'tearing' of the heavens vividly indicates the supernatural dimension of the truth about to be declared about Jesus. The descent of the Spirit marks him out as the one anointed to bring good news, and confirms the divine presence and power in his mission. And the voice of God, with its echoes of OT messianic themes, commissions him to undertake his God-given role, but also, and much more importantly, identifies him as the Son of God, picking up the title already introduced by Mark in 1:1. When his task is accomplished, on the cross, there will again be a 'tearing' (the same verb, σχίζω) ἀπ' ἄνωθεν, and Jesus' identity as 'Son of God' will again be declared, though by a very different and unexpected voice (15:38-39).[58] For now, this dimension of Jesus' mission is declared to him alone (and to us, as we read Mark's account).

Since Mark here introduces Jesus into his narrative for the first time, we are given no indication of what consciousness, if any, he had before his baptism of either his mission or his unique relationship to God. The question is of interest to us, both for our attempts to write the biography of the historical Jesus and for christological debate. But Mark offers no retrospect from this point. His focus is entirely forward-looking. From his baptism on, whatever may have been the case before, Jesus is equipped with the knowledge that he is Χριστός and υἱὸς θεοῦ, and Mark's narrative will enable his readers to see those truths worked out on the earthly scene, and to assess with this privileged insight the

---

58. In view of the fact that two of the three elements of 1:10-11 are apparently echoed in 15:38-39, it is tempting to see the third, the descent of the Spirit, also picked up in the verb ἐξέπνευσεν in 15:37, 39. (This connection is made independently in two articles in *NTS* 33 [1987], by H. M. Jackson [30-31] and by S. Motyer [155-157]; cf. also J. Marcus, *Way,* 57.) This would, however, be to read too much out of the etymology of the verb, and could lead to doctrinal complications (the Spirit leaving Jesus on the cross?) which there is no sign that Mark intended to raise.

responses of the other actors in the story to whom this revelation has not yet been given.

9 καὶ ἐγένετο followed by a main verb (ἦλθεν) is a Semitic construction, unknown outside biblical Greek, derived from the Hebrew *wayᵉhî*. (ἐν ἐκείναις ταῖς ἡμέραις has an equally formal, 'biblical' ring; Mark stands in the tradition of the great chroniclers of the acts of God in the OT.) It introduces a new phase in the story and, in this case, a new actor in the drama. John's words, and the OT prophecies by which he has been introduced, have led us to expect the ἰσχυρότερος who is to follow, but his name has not yet been mentioned (except in the heading). Now he arrives, as abruptly as Elijah burst on the scene in 1 Ki. 17:1, with no indication of his human origins and status other than the bare descriptor 'of Tishbe in Gilead'. Similarly, Jesus comes ἀπὸ Ναζαρὲτ τῆς Γαλιλαίας, but we have no further information about his background or status in society (6:3 will offer a meagre supplement). As far as it goes, however, this little phrase is striking enough. It is hardly the sort of epithet for an ἰσχυρότερος. In contrast with the rest of the crowd, who come from Judaea and Jerusalem (v. 5), Jesus is from the north. We have noted in the Introduction[59] the mutual distrust between Judaea and Galilee, particularly when any religious issue was at stake. Jn. 7:40-52 illustrates the instinctive Judaean rejection of the idea of a prophet from Galilee, still more the possibility that the Messiah might come from the north. As for Nazareth, it was so insignificant a village that few in the south had even heard of it (it is not mentioned in the OT, the Talmud, or Josephus), and even a Galilean like Nathanael could dismiss it with a contemptuous Ἐκ Ναζαρὲτ δύναταί τι ἀγαθὸν εἶναι; (Jn. 1:46). Recent scholarship has increasingly recognised the extent of the difference, indeed the hostility, between the two provinces.[60] It will come to the surface in 14:67, 70, where the Jesus movement will be seen to be, from the point of view of Jerusalem, a distinctively Galilean movement. Among John's crowd of southerners Jesus ἀπὸ Ναζαρὲτ τῆς Γαλιλαίας seems an improbable candidate for the role of ἰσχυρότερος.

The other striking paradox is that Jesus, having arrived on the scene, immediately ἐβαπτίσθη . . . ὑπὸ Ἰωάννου. John has proclaimed one who will be himself a baptiser (v. 8), and indeed with a type of baptism which John cannot match. Yet here he is, being baptised by John. Mt. 3:14-15 will try to unravel this puzzle, but Mark is content to leave the paradox sharply posed by the juxtaposition of vv. 8 and 9 without any explanation. (Cf. on v. 4 above for Mark's lack of embarrassment over Jesus' acceptance of a βάπτισμα μετανοίας εἰς ἄφεσιν ἁμαρτιῶν.)

Commentators have speculated on the significance of Jesus' baptism, and

---

59. See above, pp. 34-35.

60. An important pointer was G. Vermes, *Jew,* ch. 2. Cf. also E. M. Meyers and J. F. Strange, *Archaeology,* 31-47. S. Freyne, *Galilee from Alexander,* provides a full account, and his *Galilee, Jesus and the Gospels* applies his research more directly to the NT.

have usually (and probably rightly) explained it either on the theological ground of the necessity for the saviour to be identified with those he comes to save (sometimes adding the perspective of vicarious 'sin-bearing' drawn from Is. 53) or on the more historical ground that by accepting baptism Jesus identified with the ideology of the Baptist's movement which was to be the launching pad for his own, making his baptism in effect a 'vote' for John's vision of a restored people of God. But such explanations have no obvious basis in the text of Mark. Such a textual basis has, however, been suggested by U. Mauser,[61] followed closely by Lane. Mauser notes Lohmeyer's observation that vv. 5 and 9 are 'genau gleich gebaut' and draws out their parallel formulation (verb of motion [ἐξεπορεύετο/ἦλθεν] — geographically defined subject [πᾶσα ἡ Ἰουδαία χώρα καὶ οἱ Ἱεροσολυμῖται πάντες/Ἰησοῦς ἀπὸ Ναζαρὲτ τῆς Γαλιλαίας] — being baptised — by John — in the Jordan). The contrasts are striking, but deliberate (many/one; Judaea/Galilee); the parallel formulation indicates that the one takes the place of the many. Thus Jesus, for Mark, 'does not divorce himself from the sins of his people, but is bound up with them'. This is ingenious, and theologically attractive, but it is questionable whether such ingenuity was either clear enough for Mark's readers to see the point, or present in Mark's own mind. By the time the reader reaches v. 9, the immediate background is John's prediction of the one who is to come, and the ἦλθεν of v. 9 is more likely to evoke an echo of the ἔρχεται of v. 7 than of the ἐξεπορεύετο of v. 5. It is on the coming of the ἰσχυρότερος, not the Judaean crowd, that our attention is now focused. Thus the paradox of the baptiser baptised (and of the ἰσχυρότερος with the wrong credentials) stands out in all its starkness, without theological alleviation.[62]

10 Here is the first use of Mark's characteristic adverb εὐθύς, which occurs 11 times in the first chapter alone, and 37 times in the narrative of the gospel as a whole, usually to introduce a new incident, or a dramatic new phase within an episode. (The other evangelists use it, or more commonly the more correctly adverbial form εὐθέως, with much more restraint.) It adds to the graphic force of the narrative, and serves to keep the reader/hearer alert and aware of the dramatic development of the story. Here, together with the phrase ἀναβαίνων ἐκ τοῦ ὕδατος, it links Jesus' vision closely with his baptism: the one leads directly into the other. It is as he takes the decisive step of identifying himself with John's restoration movement that his own role and identity are declared. His 'submission' to John's baptism becomes the occasion for his commissioning as the one for whom John has been preparing.[63]

---

61. U. Mauser, *Christ*, 93-95.

62. Hooker suggests that the metaphorical use of βαπτίζω in 10:38-39 indicates that Jesus' baptism is to be understood as linked with his death. Again, there can be no objection to the theology implied, but Mark gives no obvious hint of such a connection at this point, unless we may assume that his readers were already so familiar with this symbolism that any mention of baptism necessarily evoked it.

63. Pesch, 1.90, suggests that the correspondence of ἀναβαίνων and καταβαῖνον is intended to indicate that 'Jesus' messianic equipment comes not from John's baptismal water, but from heaven!'

The opening of heaven is a recurrent theme in biblical and other literature (Jewish and pagan) to indicate a vision which reaches beyond the earthly dimension (Ezk. 1:1; Jn. 1:51; Acts 7:56; 10:11; Rev. 4:1; 19:11).[64] Ezekiel's vision, also beside a river (and, according to one interpretation of the book's opening sentence, at the age of thirty; cf. Lk. 3:23), provides a suggestive OT parallel, where a vision of God and a divine voice commissioned him for his prophetic role. But the normal verb in such visions is ἀνοίγω, used also in the synoptic parallels here. Mark's use of σχίζω is vivid and unexpected. He may have chosen it simply for its dramatic impact, which is considerable. But two other reasons are suggested. The first is the possibility mentioned above, that Mark thus links this episode with the only other use of σχίζω in his gospel, of the tearing of the temple curtain in 15:38, a startlingly different and yet no less important moment of revelation of the Son of God at the other end of his earthly ministry. The other is that the same metaphor occurs in Is. 63:19 (EVV 64:1), in the prayer that God will 'tear the heavens and descend' in a supernatural intervention to restore his people's fortunes; but while the Hebrew *qāra'* would be well rendered by σχίζω, the LXX in fact uses ἀνοίγω, so that the allusion would be discernible only by those who knew Isaiah in Hebrew.[65]

The second element in Jesus' vision (καταβαῖνον is still governed by εἶδεν) is the descent of the Spirit. This fulfils the prophetic expectation of a messianic figure endowed with God's Spirit (Is. 11:2; 42:1; 61:1). This is, of course, a different strand of prophecy from that echoed in v. 8, of the widespread pouring out of God's Spirit on his people. It is more in line with the concept of the Spirit equipping special people for special tasks, as in 1 Sa. 16:13 (cf. Jdg. 3:10; 6:34, etc.). The combination of this gift of the Spirit with the concept of anointing in Is. 61:1 (as in 1 Sa. 16:13) makes it a particularly appropriate mark of the mission of Jesus the Χριστός (v. 1).

Of the six Marcan references to the Holy Spirit, three use the full phrase τὸ πνεῦμα τὸ ἅγιον (3:29; 12:36; 13:11); in 1:8 we had πνεῦμα ἅγιον without any article, but here and in v. 12 it is simply τὸ πνεῦμα, as often in the NT. This absolute use is best seen here as anaphoric (so BAGD 676b, 5.d.α), the Spirit here being the one already introduced in John's prediction. The one who is to

64. For a wide survey of the theme in the literature of the period see F. Lentzen-Deis, *Bib* 50 (1969) 301-27.

65. An Is. 63 background is argued by R. E. Watts, *Exodus,* 102-8. C. Perrot, *Jésus,* 184, 198 n. 17, suggests that the whole baptismal pericope draws on a midrashic reading of Is. 63: coming up out of the water and receiving the Spirit, Is. 63:11; the tearing of heaven, Is. 63:19; the descent of the Spirit, Is. 63:14 (LXX only); the designation 'son', Is. 63:8. (He explains the dove from Ps.-Philo as designating Jesus 'le prophète à la colombe'.) There are a number of weak links in this chain, and the whole is ingenious rather than convincing. J. Marcus, *Way,* 49-50, proposes a similar though more cautious set of links with Is. 63, and goes on (*Way,* 56-58) to follow Lohmeyer in arguing from this background that the baptism narrative in Mark is intended to be understood as an 'apocalyptic theophany', perceived as yet only by Jesus, but related by Mark so that his readers may recognise 'that in Jesus' baptism the eschatological theophany foretold in the Old Testament has occurred'.

baptise with the Holy Spirit is here himself equipped for that role, as the Spirit descends εἰς αὐτόν.

The range of meaning of εἰς is sufficient to allow it to be seen here as little different from the ἐπί used in the synoptic parallels (cf. Jn. 1:32-33); a literal meaning 'into' would make nonsense of, e.g., Mt. 27:30; Lk. 15:22; 24:5, and would not be easy to envisage on a more literal, 'adjectival' understanding of ὡς περιστεράν here (see below). It is indeed possible that Mark's choice of this preposition was more theologically determined: just as other NT writers will speak of the Spirit 'dwelling in' believers, so he comes to Jesus not just as a temporary equipment for a specific task, but as a permanent presence in his life. It is unwise, however, to draw far-reaching conclusions from a single use of a common and wide-ranging preposition, especially when we contrast the following scholarly verdicts: 'In the light of Markan usage elsewhere this almost certainly means "*into* him", with εἰς deliberately preferred to ἐπί';[66] 'Turner observes that, in Mark, the preposition *eis* ("into") frequently appears in places where one would expect to find some other preposition (e.g., *pros* ["to", "towards"]), so that "the full meaning of *eis* . . . cannot be insisted on" . . . grammatically it is as legitimate to translate *eis auton* in 1:10 as "towards him" or "upon him" as it is to translate it "into him".' [67] General usage of the preposition, even within Mark, is not likely to be decisive for this unique context. The apparent absurdity of the imagery whereby Jesus sees a bird descending *into* himself forms a more persuasive argument for taking εἰς here in the wider sense as roughly equivalent to ἐπί.

The phrase ὡς περιστεράν has offered a great deal of scope to scholarly ingenuity. As part of the description of what Jesus *saw,* it should have some visual content, though commentators do not agree whether it should be understood 'adjectivally' (looking like a dove) or 'adverbially' (as a dove descends). Anderson (78), following Keck, prefers the latter on the laudable grounds that it 'has the great merit of preventing us from being side-tracked into great symbolic subtleties that are not there in Mark'. On this view the Spirit descends 'in a dove-like way', but there is no immediately obvious point to the comparison; does it mean 'swooping', 'fluttering', or, more commonly, 'gently' (though those with experience of city pigeons might have doubts about this!)?[68] In any case, if Jesus *saw* the descent, he must have seen something, and the Spirit as such has no visible form. On the whole, therefore, it seems more likely that we should take ὡς περιστεράν (as Luke certainly did: σωματικῷ εἴδει ὡς περιστεράν) as describing the visual form in which Jesus saw the Spirit.

But why a *dove?* The Rabbis sometimes used the dove as a symbol of Israel (*b. Ber.* 53b; *b. Šab.* 49a; *Ct. Rab.* 1:15, 2; 2:14, 1; 4:1, 2), but it is not clear

66. J. D. G. Dunn, *Baptism,* 29 n. 22. E. J. Goodspeed, *Problems,* 52-54, argued strongly that εἰς here must have its normal meaning: the Spirit took possession of Jesus.

67. J. D. Kingsbury, *Christology,* 62-63, quoting N. Turner, *Grammar,* 256.

68. Cf. the dove encounter narrated by J. E. Taylor, *John,* 274-75: 'certainly not a gentle experience'.

why the Spirit should be in the form of Israel, and the most direct use of this symbolism in biblical literature is not encouraging: in Ho. 7:11 Ephraim is a 'silly dove' ready to be caught! Perhaps a reader aware of the baptism-flood typology which appears in 1 Pet. 3:20-21 might think, as did a few patristic writers, of Noah's dove (Gn. 8:8-12) flying over the waters of the flood, but again any link with the Spirit is obscure.[69] More probably the image may be derived from Gn. 1:2, where the participle $m^e raḥepet$, describing the Spirit 'hovering' over the waters at creation, apparently uses the imagery of a bird (though LXX ἐπεφέρετο does not represent this); but it is not until R. Ben Zoma (late first century A.D.) that we find a reference specifically to a dove in this connection (b. Ḥag. 15a; cf. b. Ber. 3a, a second-century reference to 'a divine voice, cooing like a dove'; Tg. Ct. 2:12 interprets the voice of the turtledove as 'the voice of the Holy Spirit').[70] Thus we are not aware of any ready-made dove symbolism at the time of Mark, and it seems futile to try to provide one. More probably the species of bird is not at issue, any more than it was in Gn. 1:2; the dove is mentioned simply as one of the commonest and most familiar birds. The vision was of the Spirit in the form of a bird coming to rest on (surely *not* 'into'; see above) the one whose role it was to be to 'baptise with Holy Spirit'.

11 Neither here nor in 9:7 are we told in so many words whose φωνή is heard. But whereas in v. 3 we heard a voice ἐν τῇ ἐρήμῳ, this one comes ἐκ τῶν οὐρανῶν, and the words spoken leave no room for doubt that the speaker is God himself.[71] These words are therefore of the highest importance; whatever the verdicts which people in Mark's story may reach on the question of 8:29, 'Who do you say that I am?', the reader is left with no option, when the identity of Jesus is twice declared explicitly on the highest possible authority.

God's voice declares that Jesus is his son. There is a danger, in the complex scholarly debates over the scriptural background and the precise connotations of the words used, that we fail to hear what the voice actually says. There are intriguing (if sometimes speculative) implications for the parameters of Jesus' mission to be drawn from the analysis of these ten pregnant words, but one thing is clear beyond doubt: Jesus is here explicitly identified in the terms used in Mark's heading, υἱὸς θεοῦ. In the narrative that follows there will be secrecy and paradox, but here in the prologue there is open declaration. The reader need be in no doubt, whatever the reactions of the actors in the story.

69. P. Garnet, *JSNT* 9 (1980) 49-65, offers an ingenious thought sequence whereby the dove is intended to link Jesus with Noah, and thus, via Enoch, with the Son of Man!

70. For an interesting account of Jesus' baptismal experience based on this imagery see C. Rowland, *Heaven*, 360-63.

71. Commentators sometimes describe this utterance as a *bat qōl*, the term used by some rabbis from the first century A.D. for the 'echo' of God's voice which was believed to be his occasional means of communication since the alleged cessation of prophecy. This was, however, felt to be an inferior substitute for the earlier direct communication (J. Jeremias, *Theology*, 80-82). Mark gives no hint of this concept, and perhaps would not be enthusiastic for a term which suggests a second-rate revelation.

Traditionally the words have been understood as combining phrases from Ps. 2:7, 'You are my son, today I have begotten you', and Is. 42:1, 'Behold my servant, whom I uphold, my chosen, in whom my soul delights'. Less popular as a 'source', but arguably closer to the actual words used, at least in the LXX, is Gn. 22:2, where Isaac is described as τὸν υἱόν σου τὸν ἀγαπητόν, ὃν ἠγάπησας.

One school of thought, represented by J. Jeremias,[72] derives the whole pronouncement from Is. 42:1, on the supposition that 'ὁ υἱός μου in the voice at the baptism represents the christological development of an original ὁ παῖς μου', together with the fact that ἀγαπητός occurs in the quotation of Is. 42:1 in Mt. 12:18, where other known Greek versions have ἐκλεκτός (this unique version in Matthew may, of course, be due to the influence of this baptismal text rather than to a known version of Is. 42).[73] There is no sign elsewhere in the NT, however, that the 'ambiguity' of παῖς led to υἱός-sayings being derived from Servant passages; while παῖς can mean 'child', it is not synonymous with υἱός.[74] Even if such an origin for the saying were possible, it should not in any case affect our exegesis of Mark, since his text uses υἱός, not παῖς, and by the time he wrote his gospel Ps. 2:7 was widely accepted as a messianic proof-text (Acts 13:33; Heb. 1:5; 5:5). We may therefore understand the heavenly pronouncement on the basis of Ps. 2:7 and Is. 42:1.

Ps. 2 celebrates the establishment of the king, apparently newly achieved ('today I have begotten you'), on Mount Zion, and promises his coming triumph, by the power of Yahweh, over all nations. The address 'You are my son' in v. 7 picks up Nathan's prophecy designating David's son and successor as the son of God (2 Sa. 7:14). These two OT passages were brought together in 4Q174 (also known as *Florilegium*) as messianic texts (though the text breaks off after the inclusion of Ps. 2:1, so that we cannot be certain that v. 7 was actually quoted). 4Q174, together with two less certain references at Qumran, provides the basis on which it is now generally agreed that 'son of God' could be used as a messianic title by the first century,[75] though the paucity of documentary evidence (and the lack of any outside Qumran) is surprising. But there is no doubt that Ps. 2:7 was understood in this sense in Jewish interpretation as well as in the early church. The voice from heaven thus hails Jesus in terms which echo the role of the conquering Messiah.[76]

72. *TDNT,* 5.701-2; *Theology,* 53-55. There is a comprehensive response in I. H. Marshall, *NTS* 15 (1968/9) 326-36.

73. J. Marcus, *Way,* 51-53, argues that Is. 42:1 is the most likely source of ἀγαπητός here.

74. παῖς means 'child' in 9 of its 24 NT occurrences, but in only one of these (Jn. 4:51) is there an indication of relationship such that υἱός could be substituted for it.

75. See below, p. 609 n. 31.

76. J. Marcus, *Way,* 59-69, traces 'trajectories' in Jewish interpretation of Ps. 2 which embrace not only an 'eschatological-messianic' dimension but also the themes of the cosmic battle and of heavenly kingship, and suggests that Mark has been influenced by Ps. 2 not only in the baptismal voice but also in the subsequent narrative, especially in the confrontation with Satan in 1:12-13 and the preaching of God's kingship in 1:14-15.

Is. 42:1 speaks of Yahweh's servant on whom he has put his Spirit. We shall note later the importance of the figure of the suffering servant of Yahweh in Is. 52:13–53:12 for Mark's presentation of Jesus' mission (see especially on 10:45; 14:24). It is commonly assumed that the allusion to Is. 42:1 here is a pointer towards that broader 'servant christology', drawing on an established Jewish expectation of a servant figure drawn from a sequence of related Deutero-Isaianic passages (the 'Servant Songs'); the classic statement of that view was by J. Jeremias, *TDNT,* 5.677-717. More recently there has been a strong move to dispute the significance of 'servant christology' for Jesus and the NT writers, most fully in M. D. Hooker, *Servant.* While Hooker has not convinced most scholars that Is. 42 and Is. 53 were not of central importance in NT christology, there is now more caution in speaking of a unified servant figure. Typical is D. Juel,[77] who argues that neither Jewish nor NT interpretation allows us to speak of a 'servant figure' as such, but that Is. 42 and Is. 53 were drawn into Jewish and Christian messianic thinking on the basis that the Messiah is occasionally referred to as Yahweh's 'servant' (Zc. 3:8; Ps. 89:38-39). It is wiser, therefore, to speak here not of a designation of Jesus as 'the Servant', as opposed to 'the Messiah' of Ps. 2:7, but rather of two contrasting strands in Jewish messianic thought which are here brought creatively together.

The servant of Yahweh portrayed in Is. 42:1-4 is a nonviolent figure who achieves justice *(mišpāṭ)* for the nations by patient faithfulness, under the direction of the Spirit of Yahweh. Cf. Mt. 12:17-21 for the quotation of this passage at length to justify Jesus' nonconfrontational style of ministry. The combination of this text with Ps. 2:7 thus offers a suggestive basis for Mark's presentation of the paradox of a suffering, unrecognised Messiah.

If we grant, then, that Ps. 2:7 and Is. 42:1 are echoed in this pronouncement, is there any need to appeal also to Gn. 22:2? The wording of Gn. 22:2 LXX taken on its own is, as we have noted, closer to that of Mk. 1:11 than the LXX of either of the other two passages cited, but whereas they were both clearly understood as messianic prophecies, the story of Isaac is at first sight less obviously relevant. There is some evidence, however, that by the first century A.D. Jewish theology had developed a doctrine of the binding *('ᵃqēdâ)* and submission of Isaac as the vicarious basis for Israel's redemption,[78] and some scholars believe that this Aqedah doctrine was picked up by NT writers to explain the purpose of the death of Jesus.[79] The NT evidence for Aqedah ideas is, however, not impressive. The christianised *Test. Levi* 18:6-7 apparently under-

77. D. Juel, *Exegesis,* 119-33.

78. Seen, e.g., in the versions of Gn. 22 in *Tg. Ps.-J.* (see J. W. Bowker, *Targums,* 224ff.); Josephus, *Ant.* 1.232; Ps.-Philo 18:5; 32:2-4. G. Vermes, *Scripture,* 193-227, argues that this theology was current in the first century A.D.; see, however, the cautionary comments of E. P. Sanders, *Paul,* 28-29, and the fuller discussion by P. R. Davies and B. D. Chilton, *CBQ* 40 (1978) 514-46.

79. The debate is usefully summarised by D. J. Moo, *The OT,* 325-28; see further R. J. Daly, *CBQ* 39 (1977) 45-75 (and for Mk. 1:11, 68-71); A. Segal in P. Richardson and J. C. Hurd (ed.), *From Jesus to Paul,* 169-84.

stands Jesus' baptism in the light of Gn. 22, but without obvious Aqedah connotations. Here in Mk. 1:11, even if an allusion to Gn. 22:2 was intended, the echo of that famous phrase merely suggests an analogy between the special relationship of Jesus to God and that of Isaac to Abraham, offering food for devotional thought without the need for a consciousness of the Aqedah doctrine to explain it.

The term ἀγαπητός, whether derived from LXX Gn. 22:2 (where it represents Hebrew *yāḥîd,* 'one and only') or simply used as a natural expression for a special family relationship, will be echoed not only in the parallel pronouncement at the transfiguration, but also in Jesus' parable of the vineyard, where the final messenger is contrasted with the earlier δοῦλοι as being a υἱὸς ἀγαπητός (12:6), and thus as unique (note the preceding ἕνα). It thus carries something of the theological weight of the Johannine μονογενής,[80] and contrasts Jesus as God's only Son with others (including the prophets symbolised by the δοῦλοι in the parable) who may think of God as 'Father' in a lesser sense.[81] ἐν σοὶ εὐδόκησα represents the *rāṣtâ napšî* of Is. 42:1, which is rendered by εὐδοκέω in the versions of Thdt, Aquila, and Symmachus (as well as by Mt. 12:18); LXX uses εὐδοκέω to translate *rāṣâ* elsewhere, but here he uses προσδέχομαι. Together with *beḥîrî,* 'my chosen' (LXX ὁ ἐκλεκτός μου), the phrase, like ἀγαπητός, indicates the unique status of Jesus; while God's people as a whole are 'chosen', Jesus as he undertakes the role of the servant in Is 42:1, enjoys a special relationship to God, and God here endorses both his person and his mission.[82]

The divine declaration, and the whole experience of which it forms a part, is not phrased in such a way as to suggest that Jesus at this point becomes something which he was not before. The pericope has sometimes been spoken of as marking Jesus' *adoption* as Son of God. Such a view cannot be derived from Mark's wording, but must be based on dogmatic considerations drawn from elsewhere. The voice declares what Jesus is, not what he has now become,[83] and the whole pericope functions rather as a tableau than as a narrative. If there is here an echo of Ps. 2:7, it may be significant that the part of that verse which speaks of a new status ('today I have begotten you') is not included in the allusion,[84] as it is in Acts 13:33, and there the reference is to the resurrec-

---

80. C. H. Turner, *JTS* (1925/6) 113-29, argues from classical and LXX usage that 'ἀγαπητὸς υἱός is rightly rendered "Only Son"'.

81. P. G. Bretscher, *JBL* 87 (1968) 301-11, argues that in the light of Ex. 4:22-23 the motif of God's 'beloved' (= 'firstborn' or 'only') son is to be seen primarily as marking Jesus as the true representative of Israel.

82. See B. D. Chilton, *Rabbi,* 128-31, for a fuller account of the background in Is. 42:1 especially in the light of related passages in the Targum.

83. J. Marcus, *Way,* 72-75, argues that εὐδόκησα is to be understood as a real past tense, 'I have been pleased' rather than 'I am pleased' (expressing what has just happened) and that the tense (based as it is on the Hebrew perfect and LXX aorist of Is. 42:1) 'implies God's preexistent *choice* of the Messiah, without deciding the question of exactly when Jesus *becomes* Messiah'.

84. Except in the Western text of Lk. 3:22 (not in Mark), rightly rejected as an expansion by a scribe who recognised the allusion to Ps. 2:7.

tion, not the baptism. Clearly for Mark Jesus does not have to wait until the resurrection to become God's son; he is so already, and there is no hint that even at his baptism this is a new factor. What is new here is the launching into the public exercise of the role for which he, as Son of God, is thus prepared.

The Context of Jesus' Mission (1:12-13)

I have avoided the normal title for this section, 'The Temptation of Jesus', partly to signal the need to read Mk. 1:12-13 in its own distinctive form, rather than as a scaled-down version of the Q Temptation narrative, and partly because in any case temptation as such appears only in the brief participial phrase πειραζόμενος ὑπὸ τοῦ Σατανᾶ, which is not the main focus of this intriguing little pericope. Historically speaking, of course, both Mk. 1:12-13 and the Q Temptation narrative must relate to the same experience, located immediately after Jesus' baptism and before the beginning of his public ministry in Galilee. Both mention the directive role of the Spirit, the wilderness location, the forty-day period, and temptation by Satan. In Mark, however, there is no specification of the nature of the πειρασμός, no reference to the recently affirmed title 'Son of God', no dialogue between Jesus and the devil, no quotation of Scripture, and therefore no overt link with the desert experiences of Israel described in Dt. 6–8. But the Marcan account is distinctive not only for its brevity, but also for the fact that its mere 30 words contain elements absent from the Q tradition: the repeated mention of the ἔρημος, the designation of the διάβολος (Q) as Σατανᾶς (though this name is used in Mt. 4:10), the clause καὶ ἦν μετὰ τῶν θηρίων, and the role of the angels (in Matthew but not in Luke).

I stated above that temptation is not the main focus of Mk. 1:12-13. The most striking feature in the words used is the repetition εἰς τὴν ἔρημον (v. 12), ἐν τῇ ἐρήμῳ (v. 13). The only active verbs have as their subjects not Jesus or Satan, but the Spirit (ἐκβάλλει) and the angels (διηκόνουν); as for Jesus, his experience is described in more 'static' terms: he 'was' (ἦν) in the wilderness being tempted, and he 'was' (ἦν) with the wild animals. The whole pericope is not one of movement (after the initial 'expulsion' by the Spirit) or of event, but rather a wilderness tableau (cf. the similar comment on 1:11 above). Just as the revelation by the Jordan enabled us to see beyond the everyday scene and to gain an impression of the supernatural dimension of Jesus' mission, so the scene in the wilderness (away from ordinary human contact) displays the dramatis personae of the coming conflict, not in terms of Jesus' human supporters and opponents, but in the superhuman dimension. The tableau neatly arranges them into two camps: on the one side, supporting Jesus, are the Spirit and the angels; on the other, Satan and the wild animals. The reader who remembers this scene when the story begins will be able to see Jesus' conflicts and triumphs in their true light, for behind the earthly scenes in Galilee and Jerusalem lies a supernatural conflict. From time to time its supernatural dimension will again come to the surface, when Jesus confronts demonic power, and when the privileged three disciples are allowed to see his heavenly glory on the mountain. But this opening scene reminds us that even in the human encounters of Jesus' ministry, there is another dimension, sharply brought to our attention in 8:33 when Peter's very human misunderstanding provokes Jesus to address him as Σατανᾶ.

Mark gives no indication of the outcome of the confrontation with Satan at this point. Best[85] argues that Jesus' rejection of the charge of complicity with Satan in 3:22-30, and in particular the image of the strong man bound in 3:27, requires us to infer that Satan has already been defeated, and he therefore locates that defeat in 1:12-13. In the second edition of *Temptation* (pp. xviii-xxiii) he recognises that few exegetes have followed him in this inference,[86] but maintains his view on the basis that Satan 'effectively disappears from the Gospel after 1.12f.'. While this is partially true with reference to actual occurrences of the word Σατανᾶς (though see below on 4:15; 8:33), it assumes a doubtful distinction between Satan and other agents of spiritual evil. The prominence of Jesus' encounters with demons in the rest of the gospel (beginning almost immediately in 1:21-28) convinces most interpreters that there remains a real conflict.[87] The outcome is consistently victory for Jesus, but the narratives do not suggest that there was no real contest. In the absence of any indication here of the outcome of Satan's πειρασμός, therefore, it is more appropriate to read these verses as a presentation of the dramatis personae than as the account of the decisive victory.

The sequence from the overt expression of God's acceptance of Jesus in 1:11 to his testing at the hands of Satan recalls the opening of the Book of Job, where God's affirmation of Job's blamelessness (Job 1:8) leads directly to Satan's challenge and testing.

12 καὶ εὐθύς again alerts the reader to a new scene, but the fact that the action is initiated by the same Spirit whose coming was at the centre of the previous scene, and that the context remains that of the ἔρημος, links the two closely together. The mission on which Jesus has just been launched through the coming of the Spirit is given further definition by the scene which follows. Whereas Matthew and Luke speak here of the 'leading' of the Spirit, Mark uses the more vivid verb ἐκβάλλει; the historic present (occurring here for the first of some 150 times in Mark) adds to the immediacy of the impact. While it would be an exaggeration to say that ἐκβάλλω always suggests violence (it does not in Mt. 9:38; Jn. 10:4; Jas. 2:25), it normally implies at least the possibility of resistance (the majority of uses in Mark are of expelling demons). This is unexpected here, where Jesus' willing acceptance

85. E. Best, *Temptation,* 10-27.

86. He lists them in n. 6, p. xxii.

87. The strength of this view is indicated by the fact that the discussion of 'The Temptations of Jesus' in Mark by S. R. Garrett contains only six pages specifically on 1:12-13 (*Temptations,* 55-60), the rest of the 181-page book being concerned with other πειρασμοί faced by Jesus (and to a lesser extent his disciples) throughout Mark's narrative.

of his God-given mission has been clearly implied in the words ἐν σοὶ εὐδόκησα, but perhaps serves to underline the seriousness of the coming conflict which will be inaugurated ἐν τῇ ἐρήμῳ. The use of ἐκβάλλω also reinforces the OT concept of the Spirit of God as a powerful force (cf Mi. 3:8). εἰς τὴν ἔρημον is also slightly odd, since the scene of Jesus' baptism has already been at the site of John's ministry ἐν τῇ ἐρήμῳ, but there were still people there, and now Jesus is being taken to a scene away from humanity altogether. The specific location within the general area of the uninhabited lands around the Jordan is of course impossible to determine.

13 τεσσαράκοντα ἡμέρας need be no more than a idiomatic expression for a long but limited period, and is so used elsewhere in the Bible (e.g., Gn. 7:4 etc.; Nu. 13:25; 1 Sa. 17:16; Jon. 3:4; Acts 1:3). 'In later Jewish lit. only 7 is a more common number than 40' (H. Balz, *TDNT,* 8.137). But specific biblical backgrounds to Jesus' forty-day retreat may be suggested in the 'forty days and forty nights' spent by Moses on Sinai (Ex. 24:18; 34:28; Dt. 9:9, etc.), or, with specific reference to the wilderness, Elijah's forty-day journey with supernatural provision (1 Ki. 19:8). The other most prominent biblical use of forty is also in connection with the wilderness, the forty years of wandering experienced by the Israelites after the Exodus. In the Q narrative, with its clear echoes of Dt. 6–8, the number 40 strongly suggests the latter symbolism. In Mark this is less obvious, but the close collocation with πειραζόμενος and the specific mention of the animals (see below), together with the strong focus on the ἔρημος throughout the prologue, indicate that he, too, saw the τεσσαράκοντα ἡμέραι as an echo of the period of Israel's wilderness experience. Echoes of Moses and Elijah, whose experiences were specifically of forty *days,* are not so clearly relevant to Mark's context here.

Israel's wilderness period was one of πειρασμός (LXX Dt. 8:2, 16 uses the verb ἐκπειράζω, and the whole of Moses' discourses in Dt. 1–11 presents the period as one of testing, in preparation for the establishment of the nation in Canaan), and now it is appropriate for the one who comes to deliver Israel himself to undergo an analogous 'testing'. The more positive sense of πειράζω as 'test', 'prove', rather than 'tempt', 'seduce' is frequent in biblical Greek (the verb occurs seldom in secular Greek, where the form πειράω is more common, with a similar range of meaning), and is recognised by the increasing tendency to refer to Jesus' wilderness experience as 'Testing' rather than 'Temptation'. The immediate agent of the πειρασμός is of course Satan, but the whole experience was initiated by the Spirit and is thus to be seen in a positive light. While the Q narrative spells out several Satanic suggestions ('temptations'), the initiative of the Spirit there also indicates the same positive overall view of the experience. Here in Mark where no specific 'temptations' are mentioned that sense seems clearer. This is not to suggest, of course, that Satan is in any way presented as on the side of God; his purpose is, no doubt, as in the Q narrative, to persuade Jesus to disobedience. But Mark here reflects the tension which runs throughout the biblical presentation of Satan as at the same time both implacably hostile to God and yet operating, despite himself, within God's overall sovereignty.[88]

The πειρασμός as such is, however, as noted above, not the focus of this scene. This is found rather in the hostile presence with Jesus in the wilderness of Satan and the wild animals, while the Spirit and the angels support him. The clause ἦν μετὰ τῶν θηρίων has been interpreted in two opposite senses. Several recent commentators[89] have been attracted by a patristic view that Jesus' presence with the animals represents a restoration of the harmony of Eden (Gn. 1:28; 2:19-20), before the Fall disrupted the peaceful coexistence of the human and nonhuman creation and turned the θηρία from friends to enemies. Such a reconciliation features in OT prophecy (Is. 11:6-9; 65:25; Ho. 2:18), and would therefore be a mark of the eschatological fulfilment (cf. 2 Bar. 73:6).

This verse, however, does not indicate the nature of Jesus' relationship with the animals in the wilderness. Guelich suggests that 'μετά with the genitive indicates that Jesus was living peacefully with the animals', but that is far from obvious; indeed, his appeal for support to BDF 227(2) rather backfires, since the first of the examples there given of 'expressions of association' is πολεμεῖν μετά! Wild animals are part of the imagery of dangerous places like the wilderness (Is. 13:21-22; 34:13-14 [where LXX has δαιμόνια for ṣiyyîm]; Ezk. 34:5, 25), and of Israel's wilderness experiences (Nu. 21:6; Dt. 8:15), and protection from them is one of the blessings promised to God's people (Ps. 91:11-13). The protective ministry of angels over against wild animals in that last passage forms a suggestive background to Mk. 1:13, even apart from its explicit quotation (without mention of the animals) in the Q tradition of the temptation. Biblical usage suggests, therefore, that θηρία are to be understood, where there is no indication to the contrary, as hostile and dangerous to humans, who need protection from them.[90] Indeed, that is precisely the point of the prophecies of Is. 11:6-9 etc., that the normal hostile relationship will one day be reversed. But there is no indication in Mk. 1:13 that that day has been

88. The theme of testing/temptation in biblical and postbiblical Jewish thought is usefully surveyed by S. R. Garrett, *Temptations,* 19-49, particularly exploring the delicate relationship between the agency of God and of Satan in relation to πειρασμός.

89. There has been an interesting movement of opinion on this point. Older commentators such as Gould, Rawlinson, and Lohmeyer do not even mention the idea. It is noticed with hesitation by Taylor, Cranfield, Anderson, and Hooker, and mentioned only to be dismissed by Haenchen, Lane (following Mauser) and Gundry. Nineham entertains it more positively, and it is the preferred option of Schweizer, Pesch, Gnilka, Mann, and Guelich. Van Iersel, however, sees in the wild animals only 'the absence of human beings'. S. R. Garrett, *Temptations,* 57-58, suggests that in Mark's intention the animals represented danger as in Ps. 91, but that 'early readers likely heard echoes of other biblical texts too', including the Adamic parallel. Myers takes the animals as reflecting the 'political symbolics' of Daniel and Revelation, where θηρία stand for the opposition to the rule of God.

90. The symbolic use of θηρία in Daniel and Revelation to represent the forces of evil in opposition to God reinforces this negative connotation. Best, *Temptation,* 8, further suggests the relevance of a reference to θηρία for readers in Rome faced with the possibility of facing fierce animals in the arena (similarly Stock).

reached. It is through the protection of the angels (as in Ps. 91:11-13) that Jesus is able to survive μετὰ τῶν θηρίων.

The 'alliance' between Satan and the animals is parallelled in *Test. Iss.* 7:7 and *Test. Ben.* 5:2, where the blessing promised to God's faithful people is that evil spirits will flee from them and wild animals will be afraid of them. Even closer to Mk. 1:13 is *Test. Naph.* 8:4: 'The devil will flee from you; wild animals will be afraid of you, and the angels will stand by you'. If, as seems likely, this is a Christian text based on Mk. 1:13, it indicates that a very early reader understood the wild animals as part of the opposing forces, not as a symbol of Edenic harmony. If not, it testifies to the background of thought against which Mark wrote this verse.

οἱ ἄγγελοι διηκόνουν αὐτῷ supplies the opposite side to the hostility of Satan and the animals. Jesus is not alone in his conflict (cf. Mt. 26:53 for the availability of angelic help). If angelic protection is afforded to all who 'make Yahweh their refuge' (Ps. 91:11-13), how much more to the Son of God? The nature of their 'service' is not spelled out, but διακονέω often refers to domestic provision (cf. 1:31), and the analogy of Elijah's wilderness experience (1 Ki. 19:4-8; cf. the 40 days of v. 8) suggests that their service included the provision of food and drink (in Mt. 4:11 the specific focus on his hunger in vv. 2-4 makes this the more probable).

87

ACT ONE: GALILEE (1:14–8:21)

After the introductory scene ἐν τῇ ἐρήμῳ, the narrative proper begins as Jesus leaves that remote setting and comes into the region where the bulk of his public ministry is to be located. The term 'Galilee' in our heading is, of course, imprecise. As the narrative progresses, Jesus will find his way into neighbouring areas (Decapolis, on the east side of the lake, and the Phoenician territory around Tyre and Sidon to the northwest) and among non-Jewish people. But he remains in the north, and for most of the time within Galilee proper; his only contacts with Judaea will be when he meets with scribes who have come to Galilee from Jerusalem (3:22; 7:1). The signalling of his intention to go to Jerusalem (8:31) will launch the second act, and the journey which begins in the far north at Caesarea Philippi and ends in Jerusalem will be the narrative framework of that act. This then prepares the way for the single visit to Jerusalem which takes up the final act of the drama, finishing with its enigmatic pointer back to Galilee (16:7; cf. 14:28).

This first and longest act therefore contains the bulk of Mark's account of Jesus' public ministry. As the repository for the many individual stories which Mark wants to include it is necessarily less tightly structured than the rest of the book, and to divide it into sections is to risk imposing a systematic framework on Mark's story which he did not intend. The narrative moves on rapidly from scene to scene, carrying the reader on by its own momentum rather than by any formal structural markers. The divisions used in the following commentary should be regarded therefore as designed more for the commentator's (and reader's) convenience than as reflecting a conscious 'table of contents' in the mind of Mark.

Nevertheless, certain groupings of material clearly are deliberately significant. To say that there is no clear overall plan such as allows the confident delineation of sections is not to deny that there is a carefully constructed *sequence* to the narrative, so that one pericope follows on another not by accident but by design, and there is much insight to be gained by observing the links between them. Moreover, the large block of teaching material in chapter 4 stands prominently in the middle of this act, offering the reader the opportunity to pause and reflect on the theological significance of what is going on (see introduction to chapter 4 below), in much the same way as the prologue has offered a basis for understanding before the narrative begins, and as the discourse of chapter 13 will allow a further pause for thought in the middle of the final act. We shall see, too, that, after the more programmatic overview of the Galilean ministry provided in 1:14-39, the focus in 1:40–3:35 is on the growth of opposition to Jesus' ministry, and on the resultant range of responses, from outright hostility to enthusiastic discipleship; this division of attitudes, neatly summarised in the tableau of insiders and outsiders in 3:31-35, forms the basis for the teaching about the mystery of the kingdom of God which follows in chapter 4. In chapters 5-8 there is a clear movement outward from Jesus' base in Capernaum not only to other parts of Galilee but also to regions outside Galilee proper, and especially into Gentile territory. 7:1-23 revolves around Jesus' radical pronouncement on the nature of purity, the issue which above all kept Jews and Gentiles apart, and from 7:24 onwards there appears to be a deliberate extension of Jesus' ministry to those outside Israel, marked especially by the notable 'repetition' of the miraculous feeding of a crowd but now in Gentile territory; the theme of 'bread' for those outside the 'family' (7:27-29) leads into this important incident, and indeed 'bread' runs as a thought-provoking theme throughout the latter part of Act One (6:35-44; 6:52; 7:28-29; 8:1-9; 8:14-21).

The whole Galilean part of the gospel, therefore, is far from haphazard, even if it lacks specific structural markers. Its varied contents are woven together so as to provide the basis for considering the crucial questions which will open Act Two, τίνα με λέγουσιν οἱ ἄνθρωποι εἶναι; . . . ὑμεῖς δὲ τίνα με λέγετε εἶναι;

But that point is still a long way off. For now it is Mark's aim to lead us to understand how the messianic mission of the Son of God, set out in theological perspective in the prologue, was worked out in practice among the inhabitants of the villages and smaller towns of Galilee.

INTRODUCTION:
THE ESSENTIAL MESSAGE OF JESUS (1:14-15)

TEXTUAL NOTE

14. The bulk of the Western and Byzantine witnesses include τῆς βασιλείας after εὐαγγέλιον. The considerable weight of MSS and versions in favour of this reading is, however, outweighed by its obvious character as an 'improvement' by avoiding the unusual phrase τὸ εὐαγγέλιον τοῦ θεοῦ, and substituting a phrase which not only picks up ἡ βασιλεία τοῦ θεοῦ from the next verse but also echoes the familiar Matthean idiom, τὸ εὐαγγέλιον τῆς βασιλείας (Mt. 4:23; 9:35; 24:14).

Mark will refer later to Jesus' characteristic activity as κηρύσσων (1:38, 39), and will record the essential mission of the disciples as κηρύσσειν (3:14), a mission to be continued subsequently as the εὐαγγέλιον is proclaimed also to other nations (13:10; 14:9). But in none of these passages will he specify the content of their proclamation. The reader is expected to know it, because here at the outset he has spelled it out. (There is a brief reminder in 6:12, where the content of the disciples' proclamation is summed up in the two words ἵνα μετανοῶσιν, echoing one element of the fuller summary in 1:15.) Verses 14-15 therefore play a crucial role in Mark's story, as the reference point for all subsequent mentions of the proclamation initiated by Jesus and entrusted by him to his followers. Here is the essential content of the εὐαγγέλιον to which the people of Galilee are summoned to respond.[1]

14 The use of παραδοθῆναι without qualification to describe the arrest and imprisonment of John is surprising in view of the lack of any background at this point in Mark's story to enable the reader to understand it. The verb may be used deliberately in this way in order to point forward to the use of the same verb to describe the fate of Jesus (9:31; 10:33; 14:41); the fates of John and Jesus will be closely linked in 9:12-13. No indication is given yet of the charge against John. This will be revealed in 6:17-18. For now the reader is expected to know it already, or must simply take it on trust. There is no place here to spell it out, since John himself is no longer in focus, and to delay over the details of his story at this point would distract attention from his successor, who now takes, and will retain, his place in centre stage. The role of the forerunner is over; the time of fulfilment has come.

To launch his mission in his home territory of Galilee is, of course, a major change of scene from that of John's preaching and baptism in the (southern?) Jordan valley. Down there, people had had to make a special journey to John, but now Jesus is going to where people are, in the inhabited areas of his own province. His occasional attempts (with only partial success) to escape from regular contact with people will be clearly marked as exceptions to his normal style of ministry. Generally he intends to be noticed. The note of secrecy which will become evident as the Galilean ministry progresses is notably absent at its beginning.

Galilee was part of the territory of Herod Antipas. Jesus is not, therefore, escaping from the reach of the ruler who, as we will later discover, was responsible for the arrest and death of John, and his activity, too, will in due course come to Antipas's attention (6:14-16); he will be no friend of Jesus either (8:15). The move to Galilee is not so much a tactical withdrawal as the appropriate way for Jesus, the Galilean, to begin his own independent and public ministry.

There is an important element of continuity between John and Jesus. The same participle κηρύσσων which described John's ministry (v. 4) now describes that of his successor, and at least one of the elements in that proclamation is the same (see below on μετανοεῖτε; Mt. 3:2; 4:17 go further in assimilating their message). Is Jesus then, too, just a herald of a future act of God? Verse 15, as

---

1. For the function of 1:14-15 within Mark's narrative structure see C. D. Marshall, *Faith*, 36-43.

we shall see, forbids this conclusion, and the OT background to the idea of κήρυγμα includes not only the forerunner motif which Mark has invoked with reference to John, but also the messianic herald of Is. 40:9; 52:7; 61:1, whose role is to announce εὐαγγέλιον (LXX uses εὐαγγελίζομαι in all these passages), and who is himself the Spirit-endowed Messiah.[2]

The εὐαγγέλιον which was announced in v. 1 as the subject of Mark's book, and which has been filled out in vv. 2-13 as the news of the coming of the Messiah, the Son of God, is now given more specific focus in the content of that Messiah's message. Jesus himself is, as the ambiguity of the genitive construction in v. 1 conveniently allowed, both the subject and the object of the good news. But here, with ὁ Ἰησοῦς already expressed as the subject of κηρύσσων, Mark uses the phrase τὸ εὐαγγέλιον τοῦ θεοῦ, which appears occasionally in Paul (Rom. 1:1; 15:16; 2 Cor. 11:7; 1 Thes. 2:2, 8, 9; cf. 1 Pet. 4:17), but is unique here in the gospels. As in v. 1, the genitive is ambiguous, and either sense ('good news about God' or 'good news coming from God') would again be intelligible here; there seems no more reason here than in v. 1 to insist that either sense is exclusively intended. 'God's good news' is a phrase with clear Christian meaning, and the fact that it does not occur more often is largely attributable to the fact that τὸ εὐαγγέλιον generally occurs as a phrase intelligible in itself without further definition (except for the peculiarly Matthean τὸ εὐαγγέλιον τῆς βασιλείας).

15 ὅτι here, and often in Mark, serves to introduce direct speech, as we would use inverted commas. πεπλήρωται ὁ καιρός does not occur in the parallel statement of Jesus' proclamation in Mt. 4:17 (surprisingly in view of Matthew's strong focus on fulfilment); Luke has no direct parallel, but the Nazareth sermon, which has the same programmatic function in his gospel, expresses the same idea of fulfilment (especially Lk. 4:21), if not the exact phrase. It is not in itself a technical term; the NT can speak of a καιρός being fulfilled in various senses (Lk. 21:24; Jn. 7:8; cf. Lk. 1:20). But in view of the clear eschatological note in the prologue the reference here is clearly to the fulfilment of prophetic hope in the time of messianic deliverance. The idea is not simply that an allotted time has elapsed (that would have been better expressed by χρόνος, as in Acts 7:23), but that the decisive moment (καιρός) has now arrived. The use of the perfect tense indicates that this is not an announcement of something future, even imminent; the state of fulfilment already exists. This will be significant in considering the meaning of the following clause.

Another perfect tense follows, ἤγγικεν. ἐγγίζω means 'to come near', and is used in the LXX of Is. 46:13; 51:5; 56:1 to express the nearness of God's saving action, but there is room for discussion over what the perfect tense should be understood to mean in this context. Unlike πληρόω, ἐγγίζω is a verb of motion. To state that that motion has been completed does not, it is sometimes sug-

---

2. See B. D. Chilton, *God in Strength,* 27-95, for an extended argument that Mk. 1:14-15 as a whole is to be understood in the light of the Isaiah Targum.

gested, determine whether the βασιλεία τοῦ θεοῦ is now present or merely imminent; to say that that which was far away 'has come near' is not to say that it has arrived, merely that the result of its 'coming near' is that it now *is* near. Thus, to use the classic terms of this long-running debate, this clause is understood to speak of an eschatology which is not yet realised, but about to be realised.

There are several problems about this interpretation. There is, of course, the obvious point that if its intention is to avert the apologetic embarrassment of a proclamation which turns out not to have been true, then it does so at the risk of evacuating the word 'near' of any real meaning. If Jesus is understood to have proclaimed as 'near' something which had still not arrived even at the time when Mark wrote his gospel (let alone 2,000 years later), this is hardly less of an embarrassment than if he claimed that 'it' was already present. But there are more exegetical difficulties. First of all, this sort of argument depends on identifying the βασιλεία τοῦ θεοῦ as some identifiable situation or event which 'arrives' at a particular time. I shall argue in a moment that this is to misunderstand the NT phrase. Secondly, whatever the theoretical possibilities (and it is clear that ἤγγικεν in an eschatological context *can* refer to that which remains future: Jas. 5:8; 1 Pet. 4:7), Mark's use of the perfect tense suggests that something more is intended than a statement of imminence, when he could well have used the present, ἐγγίζει (as in 11:1, in the spatial sense). The only other use of ἐγγίζω in Mark offers a suggestive parallel; in 14:42 the betrayer ἤγγικεν, and (v. 43) *while Jesus is still saying this* παραγίνεται Ἰούδας! (Cf. Lk. 21:8, where the claim ὁ καιρὸς ἤγγικεν is parallel with ἐγώ εἰμι, a statement referring to the present rather than the future.) Thirdly, and crucially, it is a hollow victory to conclude that ἤγγικεν in itself *could* mean that 'it' is not yet present when the preceding clause allows no such ambiguity; the καιρός *has been* fulfilled, so that the logic of the two parallel clauses fixes the point of reference as present rather than future. Jesus is not predicting some future event, but announcing the time of fulfilment (as in the σήμερον of Lk. 4:21).[3] This conclusion is strengthened when we remember the emphasis of the prologue on the role of John as the forerunner; it would be odd if the one who succeeds him also turns out to be no more than a herald of something which lies still in the future.[4]

If, therefore, I am required to decide whether Mk. 1:15 expresses a 'realised' or a 'futurist' eschatology, I must vote for the former.[5] I believe, however, that to put the question in that form is to misunderstand the whole thrust of Jesus' pronouncement. This is the first occurrence in Mark of the phrase ἡ

3. W. F. Albright and C. S. Mann, *Matthew*, 24-25, attempted to 'capture the urgency' of ἤγγικεν by translating it 'is fast approaching'. In his subsequent solo commentary on Mark, however, Mann has found it necessary to change it to 'is upon you' in order to convey the 'note of immediacy'.

4. The issue is well summarised by C. D. Marshall, *Faith*, 34-35.

5. A. M. Ambrozic, *Kingdom*, 21-23, conveniently sets out reasons for finding this meaning in ἤγγικεν.

βασιλεία τοῦ θεοῦ, and that phrase is notoriously open to varied interpretations, particularly in popular usage, but also among NT exegetes. Having devoted a brief publication to the use of the phrase in Mark (*Divine Government: God's Kingship in the Gospel of Mark;* London: SPCK, 1990), I hope I may be allowed here simply to summarise the argument of the first chapter of that book by affirming that, in the light of the widespread recognition that βασιλεία is essentially an abstract noun referring to the 'rule' or 'kingship' of God, the phrase ἡ βασιλεία τοῦ θεοῦ should not be read as a term with a single specific referent, whether a time, place, event, or situation. It is therefore not appropriate to ask whether 'the kingdom of God' is past, present, or future, as if it had a specific time-reference like 'the day of Yahweh'.[6] God's kingship is both eternal and eschatological, both fulfilled and awaited, both present and imminent (as indeed NT scholarship now almost universally recognises, after long and futile attempts to confine the breadth of NT language within a single time reference). The purely eschatological understanding of the phrase has led to unnecessary polarisation in the exegesis of this verse. To declare that God's kingship has come near is to say that God is now fulfilling his agelong purpose, rather than to point to a specific time or event which can be defined as either already present or still future, but not both.

With the beginning of Jesus' ministry, therefore, a new era of fulfilment has begun, and it calls for response from God's people. That response is summed up in the twin imperatives μετανοεῖτε καὶ πιστεύετε. Both verbs, and their cognate nouns, occur frequently throughout the NT to denote the basis of discipleship, and they are brought together for this purpose again in Acts 20:21. But while these terms became part of standard Christian 'conversion' vocabulary (μετανοέω, with its connotation of 'change', is perhaps the nearest NT Greek equivalent to English 'conversion', ἐπιστρέφω being less commonly used; Belo here translates it 'be converted'), there is no improbability in Jesus' use of them. Both verbs recall the regular prophetic call to Israel to return *(šûb)* to their covenant obedience and to be faithful to Yahweh. μετάνοια has already occurred as the burden of John the Baptist's message (v. 4), and while it is not used in the LXX to translate *šûb* it clearly expresses the same demand for a radical new direction. πιστεύω (generally used in the LXX to translate the hiphil of *'mn*) conveys more the sense of trust than of 'belief' in the merely intellectual sense. Its object here, however, is expressed not as God but as the εὐαγγέλιον. The construction πιστεύω ἐν does not occur elsewhere in the NT except perhaps in Jn. 3:15 (where, however, the ἐν could be instrumental with ἔχῃ ζωήν; in Eph. 1:13 there is a similar ambiguity); the more common form, especially in John, is πιστεύω εἰς. Both forms are probably reflections of Semitic idiom (πιστεύω

---

6. While N. Perrin may have overstated his case (*Language,* 29-34), I think he errs on the right side in his argument that 'the kingdom of God' functions in biblical literature not as a 'concept', with a single agreed referent, but as a 'tensive symbol', serving rather to evoke the biblical conviction of the sovereignty of God than to point to any specific manifestation of it.

ἐν occurs in LXX Ps. 77[78]:22 for trust in God, and in Ps. 105[106]:12 for trust in his words). πιστεύω ἐν τῷ εὐαγγελίῳ therefore probably denotes not only an intellectual acceptance that the 'news' is true, but a response of acceptance and commitment.[7] Just what that commitment involves is not yet spelled out; it will be the aim of the rest of Mark's book to explain it.

THE FORMATION OF THE 'JESUS CIRCLE' (1:16-20)

After the ringing announcement of vv. 14-15 we are prepared for stirring events of at least national, if not cosmic, importance. What we find is very different: '. . . Jesus wandering by the sea, bidding some common laborers to accompany him on a mission. The world seems very much intact!' (Myers, 131). A similar paradox has already occurred in v. 9 with the arrival of the ἰσχυρότερος in the form of Ἰησοῦς ἀπὸ Ναζαρὲτ τῆς Γαλιλαίας, a candidate for baptism, and in v. 12 with the sequel to the declaration of the Son of God taking the form of a spell in the wilderness with Satan and the animals. Mark's readers are being prepared not to expect the coming of God's kingship to conform to conventional standards of importance. Just as Jesus' followers will have to learn a value scale different from that of 'those who are reckoned as rulers of the nations' (10:42-45), so the Messiah himself refuses to assert his authority by an impressive show of divine (still less of worldly) pomp and pageantry. The kingdom of God comes not with fanfare but through the gradual gathering of a group of socially insignificant people in an unnoticed corner of provincial Galilee. The parable of the mustard seed (4:30-32) will merely put into words what has been happening in practice from the first days of Jesus' ministry, the launching of a movement of ultimately huge dimensions which yet in its beginnings is so unimpressive as to be barely noticeable on the world stage.

The calling of the first disciples necessarily comes right at the beginning of the narrative, because the story which has been announced as the εὐαγγέλιον Ἰησοῦ Χριστοῦ is in fact the story of the 'Jesus circle'. From now until Gethsemane Jesus appears in the narrative constantly accompanied by his disciples, and their training and development will be one of the main focuses of the story. They may, and often will, fail him and disappoint him, but their role is crucial to the achievement of his mission, for it is through this flawed and vulnerable group of people that God's kingship will be established. And it is in tracing their development as Jesus' disciples, both in its successes and in its more frequent failures, that Mark will expect his readers to find the basis, whether by example or by warning, for their own discipleship.

The four men here introduced will form the central core of the disciple group (1:29; 3:16-18; 13:3, and without Andrew 5:37; 9:2; 14:33). The story of

7. So C. D. Marshall, *Faith,* 49-53. For further comment on πιστεύω ἐν see ibid., 44-45, 54-56.

their call (set out as two parallel stories of two pairs of brothers), while reflecting the specific context of the fishing industry to which they belonged, represents the essential elements in discipleship; the relationship with Jesus (ὀπίσω μου/ἠκολούθησαν αὐτῷ), the active promotion of his mission (ἁλιεῖς ἀνθρώπων), and the total commitment to his cause (ἀφέντες τὰ δίκτυα/τὸν πατέρα). W. T. Shiner gives a detailed analysis of the elements which make up Mark's three call stories (1:16-18, 19-20; 2:14), demonstrating their close formal similarity while differing in detail.[8]

16 ἡ θάλασσα τῆς Γαλιλαίας and its shores will be the scene of much of the story up to 8:26. (Mark, Matthew and John refer to this relatively small inland stretch of fresh water as θάλασσα, reflecting local usage based on the OT: *yām-kinneret,* Nu. 34:11 etc., for which the LXX uses θάλασσα. Luke and Josephus more correctly call it λίμνη.) Jesus made his base in the lakeside town of Capernaum. Despite his title (10:47; 14:67; 16:6), he does not seem to have spent much time in Nazareth (6:1-6 is the only visit recorded by Mark). As a small village in the hills Nazareth offered very limited scope for proclamation of the good news, whereas the lake (or rather its west and north sides; the east and south were outside the province of Galilee), with its prosperous fishing industry and an active trade route running through Capernaum to the neighbouring tetrarchy of Philip, was the focus of the province's life. It is striking, however, that there is no record of Jesus ever visiting the two Hellenistic cities which dominated the province politically, Sepphoris (just four miles from Nazareth) and Tiberias (not far down the lakeshore from Capernaum). It was among the more traditionally Jewish population of the lakeshore that Jesus sought, and found, a response to his message of the kingdom of God.

Mark will consistently refer to the first named disciple as Σίμων until he formally introduces the name Πέτρος as given to him by Jesus (3:16); thereafter he will consistently use Πέτρος (except in Jesus' words, 14:37). According to Jn. 1:44 Σίμων and Ἀνδρέας came from Bethsaida, across the north end of the lake in the tetrarchy of Philip; the Greek name Ἀνδρέας (and that of their associate Philip, also from Bethsaida, Jn. 1:44; Σίμων is also a Greek name, but used as equivalent to the common Hebrew name *Šimʿôn*) suggests a family open to Hellenistic influences, but this would be nothing unusual at this period in Galilee either.[9] Whatever their origin, however, they had by now settled in Capernaum (v. 29), and were no doubt fishing in that vicinity. ἀμφιβάλλω is a shorthand term for fishing by means of an ἀμφίβληστρον (Mt. 4:18; δίκτυον, vv. 18, 19, is a more general term for 'net'), the circular casting net thrown out either from the boat or by a man wading into the lake.[10] The addition ἦσαν γὰρ

---

8. W. T. Shiner, *Follow,* 172-75, with chart of parallels on 173.

9. M. Hengel, *Judaism,* 1.61-65, gives ample evidence of the frequency of Greek names in Palestine generally by this period.

10. H. C. Waetjen, *Reordering,* 10 and 79, assumes that as 'net casters' Simon and Andrew own no boat, and so belong to a less affluent class than James and John, whose father owns a boat and employs workers, and who thus 'enjoy a kind of middle-class prosperity and

ἁλιεῖς should be unnecessary for anyone who knows the meaning of ἀμφιβάλλω (but perhaps some of Mark's readers, from a more urban background, did not?); its inclusion serves, however, to prepare the way for the declaration of their new role as ἁλιεῖς ἀνθρώπων.

17 δεῦτε is an adverb meaning 'here', 'hither', which is sometimes used to supplement an imperative or hortative verb in the plural (as in 12:7; cf. the parallel use of the singular equivalent δεῦρο, 10:21); it then has the effect of an invitation or summons. Here and in 6:31 no verb is expressed, and followed by an indication of place δεῦτε then has the effect of an imperative, 'come on' to the place indicated, in this case ὀπίσω μου. 'Here! Behind me!' would reproduce the idiom, but the use of δεῦρο and δεῦτε is more everyday and less dramatic than that version suggests. For ὀπίσω μου as a standard term for the disciple's position in relation to his teacher see above on v. 7; while that technical sense may be debated there, in this case it is unquestionable, especially followed by ἀκολουθέω as the response to the summons in the next verse. Simon and Andrew are being called to follow Jesus as their leader, in a relationship which went beyond merely formal learning to a full-time 'apprenticeship'.

It is misleading, however, to express this relationship in terms of a rabbi and his *talmîdîm*. M. Hengel[11] has argued persuasively that Jesus' call to his disciples fits the model rather of the 'charismatic leader' inaugurated by Elijah's call of Elisha (1 Ki. 19:19-21, a story which bears interesting comparison with this pericope). Rabbis did not call their followers; rather, the pupil adopted the teacher.[12] Jesus' peremptory summons, with its expectation of radical renunciation even of family ties, goes far beyond anything they would be familiar with in normal society. It marks him as a prophet rather than a rabbi.

If their relationship with Jesus is not simply that of a learner, neither is their new role to be simply that of teachers. They are to be ἁλιεῖς ἀνθρώπων. The metaphor is, in the circumstances, a natural one to choose, but its meaning is not spelled out. A similar metaphor is used in Je. 16:16, where Yahweh will send τοὺς ἁλιεῖς τοὺς πολλούς, who will 'fish out' (ἁλιεύσουσιν) his people. But the context there is of judgment — they are being caught to be punished, and they will not escape. Similarly threatening fishing metaphors are used in Am. 4:2; Hab. 1:14-17, and the imagery is natural enough: it is no blessing for a fish to be caught! In the context of 'good news' this can hardly be Jesus' meaning, nor does it correspond to the task the disciples will be given later in the gospel; the gesture of condemnation in 6:11 is not the primary purpose of their mis-

---

comfortability'. This is not a certain inference, and is in tension with the natural meaning of καὶ αὐτούς in v. 19, which is that James and John *like Simon and Andrew* were in a boat. (Waetjen's translation 'and (he saw) them in a boat', p. 28, is forced.) There is no reason to doubt the assertion of Lk. 5:3 that Simon did own a boat.

11. M. Hengel, *Leader,* passim.

12. Stock, 70, cites an interesting parallel, however, in Socrates' 'call' of Xenophon (Diog. Laert. 2.28).

sion.[13] There is no doubt an element of judgment involved in the observation that fishing divides the caught from the uncaught, a division which the ministry of Jesus and of his disciples will make clear. But the aim will be to gain more disciples, to rescue people *from* rather than catch them *for* judgment, and that must be the point of Jesus' metaphor, even if its positive intention corresponds more to the perspective of the fisherman than to that of the fish.[14]

18   καὶ εὐθύς in this case does not introduce a new scene. It may be intended to underline the immediacy of the new disciples' response, but it would be unwise to base too much on this feature, since in v. 20 the same phrase introduces Jesus' call rather than the disciples' following; its role is more to keep the story going with vigour than to comment on the specific nature of their response. ἀφέντες τὰ δίκτυα, and still more leaving their father in v. 20, symbolises the renunciation involved in following Jesus. He takes precedence over livelihood and family.[15] In practical terms there were clearly limits to this renunciation, at least for some disciples: Jn. 21:3 suggests that Simon retained the use of a boat and fishing tackle when occasion required (and the frequent use of a boat in Mark's story suggests that someone in the group still owned one), and in v. 29 we shall find the house of Simon and Andrew still available for their family, and used apparently as Jesus' base in Capernaum; nor did Simon sever all links with his family (1:30-31; cf. 1 Cor. 9:5), despite his sweeping claim in 10:28. But the abandonment of the nets does represent a decisive change of lifestyle; from now on their fishing will be of another kind.

Mark gives no explanation for the ready response of these four men to the call of a total stranger.[16] It is, presumably, a mark of the ἐξουσία of Jesus (which will be the focus of the subsequent narrative: 1:22, 27; 2:10) that he could make an outrageous demand without explanation and receive instant obedience. But the information of the Fourth Gospel that these men had been with Jesus previously as members of the group around John the Baptist (Jn. 1:35-42)

13. W. T. Shiner, *Follow,* 175-76, asserts that 'the disciples are never shown gathering people' within the gospel, and that Mark's readers would have had to infer the nature of 'people fishing' from their knowledge of the post-Easter ministry of Simon and Andrew. While it is true that Mark does not record the disciples' success in recruitment, the preaching of repentance in 6:12, while not necessarily resulting in further μαθηταί in the more limited sense, was surely intended to evoke a response to Jesus' message.

14. The background and meaning of the metaphor are exhaustively discussed by W. H. Wuellner, *Meaning.* C. W. F. Smith, *HTR* 52 (1959) 187-203, argues for the more negative sense here; cf. Lane. Myers goes further: 'Jesus is inviting common folk to join him in his struggle to overturn the existing order of power and privilege'. J. D. M. Derrett, *NovT* 22 (1980) 108-37, revives an early church interpretation which finds the OT background to the image in Ezk. 47:8-10 (to which he adds further, more obscure, allusions to the blessings on Zebulun and Naphtali in Gn. 49 and Dt. 33).

15. See S. C. Barton, *Discipleship,* 66-67, and his demonstration (23-56) that the renunciation of family ties for the sake of religious and philosophical pursuits is a familiar theme in both Jewish and Graeco-Roman literature.

16. W. T. Shiner, *Follow,* 183-86, contrasts Mark's call narratives in this respect with other call stories in ancient literature where 'there is no example of such an unmotivated call story'.

in the period before John's imprisonment (Jn. 3:24) adds a further illuminating dimension.

19-20 The call of the sons of Zebedee follows the same pattern as that of the first pair of disciples, though the narrative details differ. One notable feature is the mention of their father Ζεβεδαῖος both in introducing Ἰάκωβος by his patronymic and as being left behind in the boat. The former is no doubt partly due to the need to differentiate this Ἰάκωβος from his lesser-known namesake in the disciple group (3:18), but the fact that the two brothers are described both in the disciple list (3:17) and in their one separate appearance in the gospel (10:35) as οἱ υἱοὶ Ζεβεδαίου suggests that they were generally known and remembered by this title, so that the inclusion of their father in the story of their call added an attractive human touch. The inclusion of the μισθωτοί further reinforces the real-life scenario; this sort of additional narrative detail, ignored by the other evangelists, is typical of Mark. It also provides an incidental warning to us against the common assumption that Jesus' disciples were drawn from the lowest strata of society ('a dominated class', Belo); two of them came from a family which could employ workers.

καὶ αὐτούς seems redundant and awkward since it appears to identify the specific situations of the two sets of brothers, whereas in fact the first pair were ἀμφιβάλλοντες while the others were καταρτίζοντες τὰ δίκτυα (preparing the nets for the next fishing trip, by mending, cleaning, folding, etc.). If, however, it is taken only with ἐν τῷ πλοίῳ, it links the two calls by indicating that each set of brothers was in a boat (presumably not the same one, since Jesus moved on, προβὰς ὀλίγον, between the two encounters; Lk. 5:7-10 describes the sons of Zebedee as Simon's μέτοχοι/κοινωνοί, in a separate boat). The terms used for call and response are different this time: instead of Jesus' direct speech we have the verb καλέω, used here by Mark perhaps to recall its later church use as a quasi-technical term for the beginning of Christian life, for which the brothers serve as a model; and instead of ἀκολουθέω we return to the significant use of ὀπίσω which we met in Jesus' summons in v. 17. The use of ἀπέρχομαι, rather than the simple ἔρχομαι as in 8:34, adds to the sense of radical departure and a new beginning.

PREACHING AND HEALING:
GENERAL IMPRESSION (1:21-39)

This short collection of scenes in and around Capernaum is apparently constructed within the framework of a single twenty-four-hour period. Verses 29, 32, and 35, with their clear indications of sequence and of time, serve to hold the four episodes together, so that the narrative flows from the sabbath meeting in the synagogue, on to the close of that sabbath at sunset when it was permissible for sick people to be brought for healing, and then on to the early hours of the following morning, when Jesus and his disciples set out for a wider ministry in other Galilean locations. This 'day in Capernaum' combines within it all the main features of Jesus' Galilean ministry, teaching (vv. 21-22, 27), exorcism (vv. 23-26, 32, 34, 39), healing (vv. 30-31, 32-34), and proclamation (vv. 38-39). It thus forms a graphic overview of the general character of that ministry, as is also indicated by the presence within it of more general statements relating to the wider scene (vv. 28, 39), and by the inclusive terms used (πανταχοῦ, ὅλην, v. 28; πάντας, v. 32; ὅλη, v. 33; πολλούς, πολλά, v. 34; πάντες, v. 37; ὅλην, v. 39).

Throughout this sequence Jesus does not appear alone, but as leader of a group of followers, as 1:16-20 has led us to expect. Thus the linking verbs in vv. 21 and 29 are plural (εἰσπορεύονται, ἐξελθόντες ἦλθον), the scene in vv. 29-34 is set in and outside the house of Simon and Andrew, and the closing scene finds Jesus pursued by his disciples, and explaining to them how *we* must go on to a wider ministry. Yet within this communal setting, it is Jesus individually who is the focus of attention, he alone who teaches, who acts to exorcise and heal, and even in vv. 38-39, while it is 'we' who must move on, it is so that Jesus (singular) can fulfil *his* mission of proclamation. Later the disciples will share in his ministry, but for now it is Jesus alone who acts, and about whom the news goes out (v. 28). The overall impression is of his unique ἐξουσία, noticed and commented on by the people (vv. 21, 27), and exemplified not only in his miraculous activity but also in his unquestioned determination of the group's agenda (vv. 35-39).

A Power Encounter in the Synagogue (1:21-28)

TEXTUAL NOTES

21. A range of variants (noted in UBS[3] but not in UBS[4]) revolve around two points: the absence of εἰσελθών in ℵ C L Δ *f*13 and some Syriac and Coptic witnesses, and in Origen, with ἐδίδασκεν generally preceding rather than following εἰς τὴν συναγωγήν; and the inclusion of αὐτούς to provide an object for ἐδίδασκεν when it occurs at the end of the clause (D Θ and Latin versions). In view of Mark's use of εἰς for ἐν elsewhere (see commentary below) ἐδίδασκεν εἰς τὴν συναγωγήν may well be original (Origen twice quotes it in this form). The awkward idiom would naturally lead to correction by the addition of εἰσελθών, leaving ἐδίδασκεν to move to the end of the clause, where it was felt by some to need an object. This seems a marginally more likely explanation of the variants than the accidental omission of εἰσελθών before εἰς, creating an awkward idiom which then remained uncorrected in a wide range of MSS and versions.

27. After συζητεῖν, where UBS[4] reads πρὸς ἑαυτούς, Aland reads αὐτούς (following ℵ B); either idiom is possible (for πρός after συζητέω see 9:14, 16; for the absolute use see 12:28), but the weight of MSS evidence suggests the former, the ℵ B reading being designed to provide a subject for the infinitive (unnecessarily, since the preceding verb makes the subject clear enough). The rich variety of readings for the direct speech beginning τί ἐστιν probably represent attempts to give a smoother flow to Mark's vivid but unconventional syntax. The key elements, διδαχὴ καινή and κατ' ἐξουσίαν, appear in all witnesses, so that the essential meaning is not affected.

The framework of this pericope is a sabbath visit to the synagogue, where Jesus' teaching leaves the congregation amazed by his ἐξουσία, so that his reputation spreads far and wide. But woven in with this straightforward motif is the story of a dramatic exorcism, the first of four individually recorded by Mark, which offers a more visible display of ἐξουσία, and which leads to a remarkable exclamation by the congregation (v. 27) in which teaching and exorcism seem to be interdependent aspects of that ἐξουσία.

Exorcism is a prominent feature of Mark's account of Jesus. He speaks of it as distinct from a more general healing ministry, and includes four individual accounts of exorcisms (1:23-27; 5:1-20; 7:24-30; 9:14-29), all of which are vividly related, and two of which include a dialogue between Jesus and the demon(s) which reveals their privileged knowledge of who he is. But in addition he reminds his readers from time to time that these were only a few selected examples, and more general accounts of Jesus' exorcistic ministry occur in 1:32-34, 39; 3:11-12 (again with a 'christological' declaration by the demons), while in 3:22-30 the controversy between Jesus and the Jerusalem scribes is based on the recognition of his effectiveness as an exorcist. The disciples, too, engage in exorcism as part of their mission (3:15; 6:7, 13; cf. 9:38-40), but it is made clear that they can do so only as commissioned by Jesus (3:14-15), specifically empowered by him for this task (6:7) and 'in his name' (9:38-39). This all adds up to a substantial element in Mark's presentation of Jesus, and the christological implications of his power over demons are drawn out in 3:22-30, as well as in the titles which they ascribe to him in 1:24; 3:11; 5:7.

It is thus appropriate that the opening exposure of Jesus to the Galilean public should focus on an exorcism, making this his first recorded miracle. The fact that it occurs at a regular weekly synagogue meeting and in the context of Jesus' authoritative teaching indicates a degree of integration in Jesus' messianic mission which a spectacular but remote event such as in 5:1-20 would not suggest.

Jesus and his disciples were not the only exorcists in the Mediterranean world at the time (as indeed Mt. 12:27 recognises). Papyri give evidence of widespread interest in exorcism, and certain exorcism accounts in ancient literature are frequently mentioned, notably those concerning Eleazar (Josephus, *Ant.* 8.46-48), Apollonius of Tyana (Philostratus, *VA* 4.20), and an unnamed Syrian exorcist (Lucian of Samosata, *Philopseudes* 16). It would be a mistake, however, to assume that Mark's focus on exorcism is therefore unremarkable, and that similar accounts abound in the literature of the time. The conclusions reached by my student E. F. Kirschner from his survey of exorcism in ancient literature are worth quoting. While noting the frequent references to exorcism and to exorcistic techniques, showing that the practice was widespread, he goes on:

Despite the great amount of material referring to exorcism/demons in the literature surveyed, there are *very few narratives available*. It is mainly in the NT, particularly in the Gospel of Mark, that most of the narratives are found. . . . Even *fewer exorcistic figures,* to whom exorcism stories are clearly ascribed, can be found. Of these, one is obviously a *legendary figure* (Solomon), another is apparently *semi-legendary* (Apollonius), still another is referred to *only once* (Eleazar), while another despite his fame for dealing with demons is *never shown to be exorcizing a demon* (Ḥanina). The only exorcistic figure in the extant literature to whom a number of exorcism stories are ascribed and related in detail is the biblical figure of Jesus of Nazareth.[17]

We are not therefore entitled to assume that Mark's readers, on being confronted at the outset by an exorcism, would respond, 'But of course, that is what we would expect of any special religious figure.' They, and we, are expected to recognise here, as the synagogue congregation did, a remarkable new διδαχὴ κατ᾽ ἐξουσίαν.

21 The newly gathered 'Jesus circle' already operates as a defined group, so that the plural verb εἰσπορεύονται needs no expressed subject. The form Καφαρναούμ, representing Hebrew *kᵉpar naḥûm,* appears in the older MSS; Καπερναούμ appears to be a later form of the name. It was a significant lakeside settlement, sufficiently important to have a detachment of Roman troops (Mt. 8:5-13), a customs post (2:14), and a resident official described as βασιλικός (Jn. 4:46). Its population at the time may have been as high as 10,000; its συναγωγή, a predecessor of the imposing fourth-century building now visible, would therefore have held a considerable sabbath congregation. Mark's καὶ εὐθὺς τοῖς σάββασιν ἐδίδασκεν might suggest that this unknown man of Nazareth took the initiative in imposing himself on the congregation, but the right to teach in the synagogue was controlled by its leaders (Acts 13:15), and the fact that Jesus was invited or allowed to do so suggests that, despite the role of this pericope in Mark's narrative as Jesus' first public appearance, he had already been active in the area long enough to be known and respected.

The awkward expression ἐδίδασκεν εἰς τὴν συναγωγήν (for which see the Textual Note above) apparently combines the ideas of entering and then teaching. Mark uses εἰς similarly when we would have expected ἐν in 10:10; 13:9, in each case where previous entry is assumed but not expressed. (Taylor also cites 1:9, 39 to support this usage, but they are not such close parallels, as in 1:39 the verb of motion is expressed, and in 1:9 ἐβαπτίσθη includes the idea of going into the water.)

Mark uses διδάσκω (vv. 21, 22) and διδαχή (vv. 22, 27) to describe Jesus' typical activity (and διδάσκαλος as a title for him) more often than the other gospels, despite their greater length, and whereas Matthew and Luke allow Jesus to be addressed as διδάσκαλε (or ῥαββί) only by outsiders (and Judas),

17. E. F. Kirschner, *Place,* 29.

Mark includes the title freely as one appropriate for Jesus' disciples to use.[18] Teaching is therefore clearly for Mark an essential part of Jesus' messianic mission, and one which is uniquely appropriate to him (though, like other aspects of his mission, it can be shared by his disciples, 6:30). In this it appears to differ from 'proclamation', since κηρύσσω is used of the mission both of John the Baptist (1:4, 7) and of the disciples (3:14; 6:12; 13:10; 14:9), and even of those who spread eyewitness accounts of Jesus' miracles (1:45; 5:20; 7:36), while Mark's prominent use of the term in first introducing Jesus' own mission (1:14, 38-39) is not repeated in the rest of the gospel. It appears that once the good news has been launched anyone may be a 'herald', but 'teaching' is particularly the role of the authoritative Messiah.[19]

22 ἐκπλήσσομαι (6:2; 7:37; 10:26; 11:18) and similar verbs ([ἐκ]θαμβέομαι, 1:27; 9:15; 10:24, 32; [ἐκ]θαυμάζω, 5:20; 12:17; ἐξίστημι, 2:12; 5:42; 6:51) are used frequently by Mark to record the reaction of onlookers, and sometimes the disciples, to both the words and deeds of Jesus (cf. the frequent use of φοβέομαι in similar contexts).[20] They indicate the recognition of something out of the ordinary, and keep the reader aware of the unprecedented ἐξουσία of Jesus, and of the surprising and even shocking nature of some of the things he said. Here no specific details are given of what it was in Jesus' teaching which stirred such a reaction; there will be plenty of such detail later on. But the general statement that his ἐξουσία differentiated his teaching from that of the γραμματεῖς suggests that he is already expressing some of the radical ideas, boldly contradicting accepted halakhic teaching, which will appear later in relation to, e.g., the sabbath (2:23–3:6), the purity laws (7:1-23), or divorce (10:2-12). γραμματεῖς will be mentioned frequently in the gospel, almost always as opposed to Jesus (and, from 8:31, linked with the πρεσβύτεροι καὶ ἀρχιερεῖς to form the group who brought about his death); only in 12:28-34 is a γραμματεύς presented in a positive light. The role of the γραμματεῖς as recognised theological authorities is noticed in 9:11; 12:35, but only to move on to a new perspective which leaves theirs behind. They represent the old régime, challenged by the fresh new teaching of Jesus, ὡς ἐξουσίαν ἔχων, as 2:21-22 will graphically illustrate.

ἦν διδάσκων is a classic example of Mark's liking for periphrastic constructions, using either εἰμι or γίνομαι (see Taylor, 45, 62-63). Possible examples have already occurred in 1:4, 13, but in each of those cases it seems preferable to treat the main verb and the participle independently ('John the Baptiser

---

18. For details see my article in *GP*, 1.101-36, especially 103-12.

19. On the relation of κηρύσσω to διδάσκω in Mark see further R. P. Meye, *Jesus*, 52-60.

20. For a full study of a variety of related Marcan expressions see T. Dwyer, *Wonder.* Dwyer helpfully sets the theme against the context of the motif of 'wonder' and the numinous in Graeco-Roman and Jewish literature. His survey calls in question the common assumption that an expression of wonder was a stock element in the narration of a miracle or exorcism. It is more commonly so used in the NT, and may well therefore be a distinctively Marcan development. For this passage (including v. 27) see ibid., 92-99.

appeared in the wilderness, proclaiming'; 'Jesus was there in the wilderness, being tempted'); here we have a true periphrastic construction, no different in meaning from the simple imperfect ἐδίδασκεν in v. 21, but merely a stylistic variation. It is possible that the periphrasis is intended to enliven the presentation: 'for there he was, teaching them . . .'. But to discover such a purpose in every Marcan periphrasis would call for some ingenuity, and it is better to see this simply as a stylistic trait, quite natural in Semitic Greek. (See v. 39 for a probable close parallel.)

23 καὶ εὐθύς here serves to introduce a specific dramatic event within the more general scene set up in vv. 21-22. For αὐτῶν see on v. 39 below. The incident concerns ἄνθρωπος ἐν πνεύματι ἀκαθάρτῳ; the use of ἐν to denote being 'under the special influence of the spirit' (BAGD, 260a, I.5.d) offers a macabre counterpart to the idiom ἐν τῷ πνεύματι τῷ ἁγίῳ (12:36; cf. Lk. 2:27; 1 Cor. 12:3; Rev. 1:10). Mark uses πνεῦμα ἀκάθαρτον and δαιμόνιον with equal frequency, and clearly as synonyms (see 6:7 with 13; 7:25 with 26); πνεῦμα ἀκάθαρτον corresponds to the term *rûaḥ ṭum'â,* used frequently in rabbinic writings in the same sense (cf. Zc. 13:2). Apart from the technical verb δαιμονίζομαι (1:32; 5:15-16), he describes the relation of the spirit to its human 'host' by speaking of the latter either as being ἐν the spirit (here and 5:2) or as ἔχων the spirit (7:25; 9:17; cf. 3:22, 30), while the process of deliverance is always expressed in terms of the spirit 'coming out' or being thrown out. The exorcism passages all speak of the demon as an active personality, distinct from the 'host', and controlling the behaviour of the latter. In the more summary references to exorcism (1:34, 39; 3:11, 15; 6:7, 13; 9:38) the 'host' is not even mentioned (except as implied in the verb ἐκβάλλω); Jesus (or his disciples) is shown in direct confrontation with the demons. All this is the language of demon possession and of exorcism, not of mental illness, and the same point is reinforced by Mark's careful use of distinct terminology for Jesus' ministry of exorcism and of healing (see below on 1:32, 34).

Typical of such encounters is the vocal exchange (cf. 3:11-12; 5:7-13; 9:25-26), the demon's part in that exchange being expressed as a shout, (ἀνα) κράζω, here and in 3:11; 5:7; 9:26; this was no doubt one of the most memorable features for an onlooker, and is mentioned also in non-Christian texts (*Test. Sol.* 1:13; 3:4; 4:11).

24 τί ἡμῖν καὶ σοί; is an OT formula of disassociation (e.g., 2 Sa. 16:10; 19:22). When addressed to an actual or potential aggressor it has the force of 'Go away and leave me alone' (Jdg. 11:12; 1 Ki. 17:18). The demon assumes, without any word yet from Jesus, that his mission must be ἀπολέσαι ἡμᾶς; there is instant recognition that they are on opposite sides. It is surprising that the demon here speaks in the plural, whereas in 5:7, where the demons will be found to be numerous, this formula is in the singular. Perhaps there is the thought of a multiple possession here, but more likely this particular demon speaks in this initial encounter on behalf of the whole threatened fraternity.

The use of Jesus' title Ναζαρηνός (the form used consistently by Mark and occasionally by Luke, whereas Matthew, John, and usually Luke use Ναζωραῖος; see H. H. Schaeder, *TDNT,* 4.874-79 for the two forms and their origin) adds formality to the address and backs up the claim οἶδά σε τίς εἶ (the σε is redundant, giving οἶδα two objects, but the sense is clear and the expression memorable; for comparable constructions see 7:2; 11:32; cf. 2:1). Exorcists were believed to gain power by possession of the demon's name (see on 5:7-9), and perhaps the demon here attempts, to no avail, to reverse the process. But the worrying thing about Jesus is not his earthly origin, Ναζαρηνός, but his 'real' nature as ὁ ἅγιος τοῦ θεοῦ. Here, as in 3:11; 5:7, the demon displays a supernatural insight as yet denied to human actors in the story. The reader is expected to note it, and to adopt it despite the dubious source from which it comes. The title used in 3:11 and 5:7 will be that already declared in 1:1, ὁ υἱὸς τοῦ θεοῦ; the use of ἅγιος here is therefore surprising. It has an obvious appropriateness as contrasting Jesus' holy character with that of his opponent (ἀκάθαρτον), and it links Jesus with the πνεῦμα ἅγιον whose presence is to mark his messianic ministry (1:8), and is the basis of his power over demons (3:22-30). ὁ ἅγιος τοῦ θεοῦ does not seem to have been used in Jewish literature as a recognised title, though such language can be used for people who were in a specially close relationship with God (2 Ki. 4:9; Ps. 106:16). In the NT, however, similar expressions are used for Jesus in Acts 3:14; 4:27, 30 (cf. ὅσιος in 2:27; 13:35), while the actual title ὁ ἅγιος τοῦ θεοῦ appears in Jn. 6:69. In Lk. 1:35 the υἱὸς τοῦ θεοῦ who is to be born is described as ἅγιον. Here it serves, therefore, to convey the demon's awareness that he has come up against a superior spiritual power. If it is not yet a direct ascription to Jesus of the title ὁ υἱὸς τοῦ θεοῦ, it suitably prepares the reader for its use in 3:11; 5:7.[21]

25 There is a notable lack of 'technique' about this as about all the exorcism stories in the gospels when compared with the few extrabiblical exorcism accounts. Only in 5:9 does Jesus ask the demon's name, and even there he is not recorded as using it. There is no incantation, no ritual, no 'props' of any kind, simply an authoritative word of command. That seems to settle the matter.

ἐπιτιμάω occurs in the same way in an exorcism account in 9:25 and for Jesus' silencing of demons in 3:12. H. C. Kee[22] has shown, however, that it is not a technical term of exorcism, being remarkably absent from exorcism literature outside the NT, but that its background is in the Hebrew *gāʿar,* used in the OT for God's 'subjugating word' against his enemies, which is not just a verbal protest, but effectively brings them under his control. In Mark the verb is used for Jesus' authoritative silencing of unwelcome human utterance in 8:30, 33, and, strikingly, with reference to the natural elements (again as here with

---

21. It has been suggested, e.g., by E. Schweizer, in W. Eltester (ed.), *Judentum, Urchristentum, Kirche,* 90-93, followed especially by Pesch, that ὁ ἅγιος τοῦ θεοῦ derives from a play on the word Ναζαρηνός, based on its similarity to Ναζιραῖος, the term used for Samson in LXX A Jdg. 13:7; 16:17, where LXX B has ἅγιος θεοῦ. This seems both excessively tortuous and in any case unnecessary, given the obvious appropriateness of the term ἅγιος for Jesus in this context.

22. H. C. Kee, NTS 14 (1967/8) 232-46.

φιμόω), in 4:39 (see commentary there). ἐπετίμησεν here therefore describes the effective command expressed in the direct speech which follows (as indeed λέγων indicates) rather than representing a separate element in the encounter.

φιμόω appears in 1 Cor. 9:9; 1 Tim. 5:18 in its literal sense, 'to muzzle'; it is an obvious metaphor for silencing someone, and is so used in a variety of contexts (Mt. 22:12, 34; 1 Pet. 2:15); while the term occurs in some later magical texts, its more general usage suggests that there is no reason to interpret it here as esoteric jargon, still less to use the literal form of a muzzle to argue that the metaphor involves some idea of 'binding' the demon (see further on 3:27). 'Be muzzled' is simply a vivid, colloquial way of saying 'Shut up!'

It will become clear in 1:34 and 3:11-12 that Jesus' motive in silencing the demons was to prevent them from revealing who he was. This reticence may be explained simply by the desire to avoid being authenticated by such undesirable witnesses, or it may be part of the wider theme of Jesus' secrecy, seen in his commanding silence on the part of those whom he had healed or who had witnessed his healings (1:44; 5:43; 7:36; 8:26), and even requiring the disciples not to reveal his Messiahship (8:30) or his glory revealed in the transfiguration (9:9). See on 8:30 for a fuller discussion of the 'messianic secret', and cf. the Introduction, pp. 31-32. If at least part of the reason for secrecy was to avoid premature and misdirected popular adulation, the christological revelations by the demons would certainly be a potential embarrassment. In this passage, however, that issue is not prominent, and the 'muzzling' of the demon is rather a necessary part of the exorcism, putting a stop to its defiant shouting.

26 σπαράσσω (literally to 'tear', but sometimes used medically of convulsions) will also recur in 9:26 (cf. συνσπαράσσω, 9:20). Many features in Mark's exorcism stories indicate that a resident demon affected not only the thinking and words but also the physical behaviour of the 'host'. In this case no physical symptoms have been mentioned in introducing the victim, but the destructive power of the demon is displayed at the time of its expulsion. The convulsion and the loud cry (cf. on ἀνακράζω, v. 23) are a mark of desperate, but ineffectual, resistance. Jesus' 'subjugating word' must be obeyed, as is shown by the exact echo at the end of v. 26 of the command ἔξελθε ἐξ αὐτοῦ.

27 For the crowd reaction see on v. 22; θαμβέομαι is not significantly different in effect from ἐκπλήσσομαι. It indicates perhaps that exorcisms as such were not as commonplace as is often suggested, but also that Jesus' style of exorcism was strikingly different from any they were familiar with. The specific mention of ἐξουσία and the simple sequence ἐπιτάσσει . . . ὑπακούουσιν both differentiate the immediate success of Jesus' authoritative command from the more protracted struggle and uncertain outcome which may be assumed to have characterised some other attempts at exorcism (note the ignominious failure of such an attempt in Acts 19:14-16).

συζητέω means to discuss (so 9:10), often with the hostile connotation of 'dispute' (8:11; 9:14, 16; 12:28), but with πρὸς ἑαυτούς (see Textual Note) it denotes intense discussion among the congregation. διδαχὴ καινὴ κατ᾽ ἐξουσίαν picks up the terms of v. 22, but whereas there the basis of their surprise was indeed διδαχή, here it is the exorcism, as the following clause makes clear. The congregation thus discern an integration in the different aspects of Jesus' ministry, in which authoritative teaching and authority over demons cohere into a single ἐξουσία, which is unprecedented.[23] The adverbial καί ('even') indicates that it is the power over demons which is the more remarkable aspect of this authority; to teach people οὐχ ὡς οἱ γραμματεῖς is impressive enough, but when 'even' demons cannot resist him there is greater cause for συζήτησις. Thus the issue 'Who is Jesus?', which will increasingly dominate Mark's narrative, is already raised acutely in his first public appearance.

28 The wide spread of Jesus' reputation in Galilee will be a recurrent theme (see 1:33, 37, 45; 2:1-2; 3:7-9). Alongside the typically Marcan themes of secrecy and lack of recognition runs that of the popular teacher and healer. This tension will be progressively resolved by the recognition that the popular enthusiasm is at a relatively superficial level of understanding, so that in chapter 4 the enthusiastic crowd will be characterised as οἱ ἔξω in contrast with the much smaller group of disciples to whom understanding has been granted. But for now Jesus is a local celebrity. Mark's terms are expansive (πανταχοῦ εἰς ὅλην τὴν περίχωρον), but deliberately limited so far only to Jesus' home province (taking τῆς Γαλιλαίας as an epexegetic genitive, 'the neighbouring region, that is, Galilee', rather than 'the region around Galilee', or 'the part of Galilee around [Capernaum]', either of which is a possible meaning). The wider spread of his reputation will come in 3:7-8, and will lead to unpleasant repercussions in 3:22.

A Single Healing (1:29-31)

TEXTUAL NOTE

29. The singular verbs ἐξελθὼν ἦλθεν are well attested (B D W Θ f¹ f¹³ OL), but are more likely to be a correction of originally plural verbs (picking up from εἰσπορεύονται in v. 21) in view of the fact that Jesus alone is in focus in the preceding and following scenes.

A single exorcism is followed by a single healing, before the more general summary of Jesus' performance of both types of miracle in vv. 32-34. Both accounts therefore serve as specific examples to illustrate the wider exercise of Jesus' ἐξουσία in relation to human affliction. They are, however, remarkably different stories. One deals with demon possession and the other with physical

---

23. T. Dwyer, *Wonder*, 98-99, concludes that the pericope emphasises the 'eschatological breaking-in of the kingdom, manifested in authoritative teaching and subsequent exorcism'. He goes on to question the view of Lohmeyer and others that the crowd's amazement is in itself meant to be read negatively as indicating their lack of true faith.

illness. One is very public while the other takes place in private. The synagogue incident is told in dramatic terms, with loud cries and authoritative commands and an astonished crowd left wrestling with the question of this new teacher's credentials; the healing of Simon's mother-in-law, however, has a domestic simplicity which is quite matter-of-fact, concluding with the serving of a meal. Thus, whatever the impression we might gain from the more general summaries, Mark does not allow us to picture Jesus as a travelling 'healer' with a set technique, but as a man of ἐξουσία who responds as may be appropriate to differing needs as he meets them.

29 Mark's mention of a direct sequence from the synagogue to the house of Simon and Andrew means that in his narrative scheme it is still the sabbath. The issue of Jesus' right to heal on the sabbath will be raised directly in 3:1-6 (see the commentary there on the rabbinic rules), but already here we find him disregarding the conventional form, albeit in private. The people in general will correctly wait until sunset, and therefore the end of the sabbath, to bring their sick for healing (v. 32), but in private in the house Jesus does not wait, and there is apparently no one to object.

The four men mentioned are, so far, the whole disciple group; others will be added in 2:14 and 3:13-19. ἡ οἰκία Σίμωνος καὶ Ἀνδρέου seems likely to have been Jesus' 'home' in Capernaum, and thus the meeting place for the group. Mark will from time to time mention an οἰκία (7:24; 9:33; 10:10) or οἶκος (2:1; 3:20; 7:17; 9:28) as the place where they met, away from the crowds, and while in two of these cases his geographical notes indicate a different location (7:24; 10:10) the others are either specifically set in Capernaum (2:1; 9:33) or belong to the general Galilean ministry, which seems to be based there. Thus, while Mark may well have developed the literary use of 'the house' as a symbol of privacy and instruction, he seems to have based it on an actual family home where Jesus was known to have been resident. What was already a typical extended family (two brothers and a mother-in-law are mentioned, suggesting a sizeable ménage) thus became for a period even more crowded. (The identification of this house as underlying the octagonal Byzantine building uncovered by the Franciscans near the synagogue in Capernaum, while not proven, is entirely plausible.)[24]

30-31 This mention of Simon's mother-in-law is the only indication that at the time of his call he was married; nor do we know the family circumstances of any of the other disciples. Peter's wife is mentioned again at 1 Cor. 9:5. πυρέσσουσα and πυρετός are not very specific terms, no more so than our 'fever'; for ancient understanding and classification of fevers see K. Weiss, *TDNT*, 6.956-58. It was not necessarily a very serious complaint, though in Jn. 4:52 πυρετός is used of a complaint thought to be potentially fatal (4:47), and Luke's συνεχομένη πυρετῷ μεγάλῳ here sounds more dramatic. λέγουσιν αὐτῷ περὶ αὐτῆς may be no more than the natural imparting of information to a guest

24. See E. M. Meyers and J. F. Strange, *Archaeology*, 59-60, 114-16, 128-30.

in the home, but more likely it suggests that the four men are already aware, especially after the events in the synagogue, that Jesus has special power.

Jesus' healing method contrasts with the exorcism of the previous scene. Now Mark records no words of Jesus, but rather physical touch. Mark's records of physical healings frequently mention Jesus touching the patient (1:41; 5:41; 6:5; 7:32-33; 8:23-25) or being touched by them (3:10; 5:27; 6:56); in exorcisms, by contrast, where the issue is not primarily physical but spiritual, touch is not mentioned (except after the exorcism has been completed, 9:27). For physically lifting the patient up cf. 5:41; 9:27. The cure was, as usual, instant. For the term ἀφῆκεν with a fever as subject cf. Mt. 8:15; Lk. 4:39; Jn. 4:52; it is a natural idiom which need not imply a 'personification' of the fever. The completeness of the cure is emphasised by the clause καὶ διηκόνει αὐτοῖς: no period of convalescence was needed. While διακονέω has a wide range of meaning, in this context its basic sense of domestic provision seems most likely; she fulfilled what would have been the expected role of the mother-in-law in the family home, by serving up refreshments.

General Healing Ministry (1:32-34)

TEXTUAL NOTE

34. The addition of Χριστὸν εἶναι or the like at the end of the verse has wide attestation, but such an addition to the rather bald ᾔδεισαν αὐτόν would be a natural correction, derived from the Lucan parallel, whereas it is improbable that the more explicit Χριστὸν εἶναι would be omitted from a wide range of text-types if it were original.

The individual accounts of exorcism and healing in vv. 23-31 are followed by a more general account, still placed on the same day in Capernaum, but offering a broader impression of Jesus' ministry of deliverance. Other such summary passages (cf. v. 39; 3:10-12; 6:53-56) will continue to remind us that the specific incidents related are only a few samples from Jesus' total Galilean ministry, and the recurrent mention in this part of the gospel of his widespread reputation and of the persistent crowds who followed him around (1:28, 37, 45; 2:2; 3:7-9, 20; 4:1; 5:21, 24; 6:14-15, 31-34; 7:24; 8:1-3; 9:14-15, 30) will underline his popularity as a teacher and healer.

32 ὀψίας δὲ γενομένης, ὅτε ἔδυ ὁ ἥλιος is perhaps the best-known example of Mark's tendency to 'duality',[25] to use two expressions where one would suffice. The fact that in this case the first is shared with Matthew and the second with Luke has led to interesting traditio-historical discussion, being claimed as evidence both by proponents and by opponents of Marcan priority, but cannot ultimately prove anything. The specific mention of sunset is not otiose, since

---

25. F. Neirynck, *Duality*, is an extensive discussion of this phenomenon.

sunset marked the end of the sabbath and therefore the time when patients could be carried about and Jesus could legitimately undertake healing (see on 3:2 for rabbinic rules on sabbath healing). The aorist tense ἔδυ (Aland prefers the more Hellenistic form, ἔδυσεν, found in B D and a few minuscules), unlike Luke's δύνοντος τοῦ ἡλίου, suggests that they correctly waited until after sunset to begin bringing the patients. ἔφερον (impersonal imperfect) suggests a continuous stream of people.

Mark (unlike Luke, 4:40-41) distinguishes those who are ill (οἱ κακῶς ἔχοντες) from the possessed (οἱ δαιμονιζόμενοι). This distinction is to be seen also in the terms used for Jesus' action in v. 34: θεραπεύω for the ill, and δαιμόνια ἐκβάλλω for the possessed. This distinction is maintained throughout Mark's gospel, both in the description of the problem and in the words used for Jesus' act of deliverance; the two types of deliverance are again mentioned side by side in 3:10-11; 6:13, and whenever one or the other is in focus, the appropriate terms are used, without confusion.[26] We have noted at 1:30-31 above the difference in the description of Jesus' actions, with touch mentioned in many cases of healing but never in an exorcism, the latter being accomplished simply by a word of command, addressed directly to the demon (except in 7:24-30, where the victim was not physically present at the time), not to the 'host'. There is thus no indication in Mark of any confusion between the two conditions, still less of the idea that people in the ancient world naturally attributed all physical afflictions to demonic action.[27]

It is perhaps worth noting that here, and throughout the gospel, we have no indication that Jesus himself went out looking for patients. The language is always of their either being brought to him or taking the initiative in approaching him themselves. He was not engaged in a 'healing campaign'; healing and exorcism, important as they were in his total ministry, arose not so much by design as from a natural response to need as he encountered it, boosted by people's desire to benefit from his unique ἐξουσία.

33 There is no doubt an element of exaggeration in the phrase ὅλη ἡ πόλις, as in the πάντας of the previous verse. In view of the close proximity of the houses excavated at Capernaum, the number who could be gathered physically πρὸς τὴν θύραν on any one occasion would be relatively limited. Mark is talking in general terms; Jesus is the talk of the town, and his reputation for healing and exorcism (based, presumably, on more incidents than Mark has actually recorded, since the only public event so far has been the exorcism in the synagogue) is drawing a crowd of those in need. Indeed, whatever the physical limitations on a single evening's crowd, the inclusiveness of Mark's language may not far outrun the reality of public interest in a newly discovered local

26. The demon possession described in 9:14-29 is often identified as epilepsy (see comments ad loc.); whatever the merits of this modern diagnosis, it is not that of Mark, who uses consistently the language of possession and exorcism.

27. For this distinction in the gospel accounts generally see further G. Theissen, *Miracle-Stories*, 85-94.

healer and exorcist in a first-century provincial town in the Middle East. The dramatic events in the synagogue would provide the necessary trigger to popular excitement.

34 The use of πολλούς and πολλά here is in apparent tension with the πάντας of v. 32. Perhaps the number was too great to allow all to be dealt with immediately (hence the continuing search for Jesus, v. 37; so Pesch). Or is Mark thus suggesting that there were some who remained unhealed, and therefore inviting his readers to recognise that Jesus' healing and exorcism were not an automatic, quasi-magical process, but a matter of individual treatment, whose outcome was at least to some extent dependent on the faith of the person concerned? The importance of faith for both healing and exorcism (in the latter case on the part of the victim's family rather than the victim himself) is certainly a feature of this as of the other gospels (2:5; 5:34, 36; 7:29; 9:19, 23-24; 10:52; cf. 11:22-23). But Mark does not elsewhere suggest that Jesus' 'success' in healing and exorcism was either selective or partial, except in the special case of Nazareth, where the lack of faith resulted in the healing of only ὀλίγοι (6:5) rather than πολλοί. It is therefore more likely that πολλοί and πολλά here (which after all are terms which emphasise quantity rather than the opposite) focus on the effectiveness of Jesus' ministry rather than on any limitation, of which no other hint is given, and that therefore Mark intends no contrast between πάντας and πολλοί. For πολλοί as 'inclusive' rather than exclusive see J. Jeremias, *TDNT*, 6.540-42.

The phrase ποικίλαις νόσοις similarly indicates a comprehensive healing ministry. The primary sense of νόσος is a 'disease' rather than, e.g., a congenital deformity or disability, but it is unlikely that Mark here intends any such distinction. The range of healings recorded in this gospel alone indicates a broader view of Jesus' healing power: 'fever', 'leprosy', 'paralysis', 'a withered hand', 'a flow of blood', a deaf and dumb man, two blind men, and a recently dead girl are all specifically mentioned. Allowing for some diagnostic uncertainty, these complaints go well beyond the primary sense of νόσος, and suggest that ποίκιλος is no exaggeration. Jesus was not a specialist.

ἤφιεν is an imperfect form of ἀφίημι, which came to be treated as if it were not a compound (the simple ἵημι does not occur in NT Greek), and developed endings as if from the form ἀφίω (BDF, 69[1], 94[2]). For the silencing of the demons see above on v. 25. Here, more obviously than there, the reason lies in what the demons know about Jesus (though here, unlike in 1:25; 3:11; 5:7, we are not told explicitly what that knowledge is; see Textual Note). It is possible that the reason lies partly in the character of the witnesses: the truth about Jesus should not be spoken by 'unclean spirits'. But the wording ὅτι ᾔδεισαν αὐτόν suggests that the problem lies primarily in their knowing that which ought not to be revealed, and that therefore this verse, more clearly than v. 25, introduces the theme of the 'messianic secret' (on which see further on 8:30 and pp. 31-32 above).

The Mission Expands beyond Capernaum (1:35-39)

TEXTUAL NOTE

39. The substitution of ἐν ταῖς συναγωγαῖς for εἰς τὰς συναγωγάς (noted in UBS³, not in UBS⁴) would be an obvious correction both to provide a more natural preposition after κηρύσσων and also to assimilate to the parallel text in Mt. 4:23. If, then, we may assume that εἰς τὰς συναγωγάς is original, the question arises whether the reading of ἦλθεν before κηρύσσων is also a correction to provide a verb of motion before the εἰς, since ἦν κηρύσσων εἰς seemed a harsh construction. The situation would then be parallel to v. 21, where we suggested, on the basis of other Marcan usage of εἰς, that ἐδίδασκεν εἰς τὴν συναγωγήν was the original. By analogy, ἦν κηρύσσων εἰς τὰς συναγὰς αὐτῶν, which is surprisingly widely attested despite its awkwardness, should probably be seen as the original reading here.

These verses bring us to the end of the 24-hour period begun in v. 21. The scene is still Capernaum (or rather a quiet place near the town), but the focus is now wider. While the inhabitants of Capernaum want Jesus to stay, and the disciples apparently share that hope, Jesus' sense of mission compels him to leave an apparently fruitful and popular ministry in order to extend his proclamation of the kingdom of God through the rest of Galilee. We are thus introduced to the dominant pattern of Jesus' Galilean ministry as one of itinerant preaching; Capernaum will be his base, but he will be seen in most of Mark's narrative up to chapter 10 as constantly on the move.

Here for the first time we meet a recurrent theme of the gospel, that of the difference between Jesus' programme and his disciples' (and still more other people's) expectation. It is not just that he is one step ahead of them; his whole conception of how God's kingship is to be made effective is quite different from theirs. While they would naturally pursue the normal human policy of taking advantage of popularity and building on success on their own home ground, following Jesus will increasingly involve them in having to learn a new orientation. In this case, indeed, there is no hint yet that Jesus' onward drive will lead to anything other than growing popularity and response, but simply that the scope of his vision is broader than theirs. It will not be long, however, before a more ominous note begins to be heard.

35 πρωῒ ἔννυχα λίαν is a clumsy but graphic phrase meaning 'Very early next morning, while it was still quite dark'. (ἔννυχα is the neuter plural of the rare adjective ἔννυχος, 'at night', used as an adverb.) The purpose of such an emphatic note of time may be to indicate that even after a demanding day Jesus did not take a deserved rest, or it may be to explain how he was able to get out of the town without drawing a crowd. At any rate, the picture of Jesus seeking out a quiet place for extended prayer before the next phase of his mission sets an important perspective for the crowded narrative which will follow. While Luke makes more frequent mention of Jesus' habit of prayer (though surprisingly not at this point), Mark will remind us of it only at 6:46 and, of course, in

Gethsemane (14:32-42); perhaps, having offered this brief cameo at the outset, he expects his readers to take the prayer dimension of Jesus' ministry as read. Here, however, unlike 14:32-42, we are given no indication of the content of his prayer.

An ἔρημος τόπος here is clearly to be distinguished from ἡ ἔρημος in 1:1-13. It is close to Capernaum, presumably some secluded spot out of the town; the fact that the disciples could find him suggests that they may already have been in the habit of meeting there. Such retreats from the public arena are a recurring feature of the narrative, interspersed between periods of public exposure and the pressure of the crowds (cf. 1:45; 3:13; 6:31-32, 46; 7:24; 8:27; 9:2, 30-31).

36-37 The compound form καταδιώκω is not common, and often has a hostile sense. Here it presumably expresses the eager (and concerned, even disgruntled?) search of the disciples; they 'tracked him down'. The subsuming of the other disciples (presumably still only Andrew, James, and John) under the phrase οἱ μετ' αὐτοῦ (where the αὐτοῦ most naturally refers to Simon, not to Jesus) is interesting. It may, of course, be read as a reflection of a reminiscence by Peter himself underlying Mark's narrative ('I and my friends'), but in view of Mark's consistent depiction of Peter as the leading disciple, it is probably intended already to indicate his leadership. We are not told why πάντες ζητοῦσίν σε, but may reasonably assume that what is sought is a continuation of the teaching, healing, and exorcism which have marked Jesus' powerful impact on the life of Capernaum. The disciples assume, and the people are demanding, that things should continue as they have so impressively begun. But Jesus has other priorities; his primary mission is not to be a wonder-worker but to proclaim the kingdom of God.

38 The next focus of Jesus' mission is to be proclamation in αἱ ἐχόμεναι κωμοπόλεις. ἐχόμενος (middle) in the sense of 'next to', 'neighbouring', is a recognised Greek usage, occurring in Lk. 13:33; Acts 20:15; 21:26 for the next day, and in Heb. 6:9 in a less literal sense, but only here in the NT for physical location. κωμόπολις also occurs only here in the NT. Its technical meaning is a settlement which is more than a village but cannot claim the status of πόλις, but NT usage of κώμη and πόλις is not politically sophisticated, the terms sometimes being used interchangeably (see H. Strathmann, *TDNT*, 6.529-30). Mark seems to operate with some sort of hierarchy, in which Jerusalem and Gerasa (?) are, correctly, πόλεις (5:14; 11:19) while Bethsaida and Bethphage (?) are κῶμαι (8:23; 11:2); in general statements about the settlements of Galilee he sometimes uses πόλεις (1:45; 6:33), sometimes κῶμαι (6:6), and once the comprehensive phrase κῶμαι ἢ πόλεις ἢ ἀγροί (6:56), indicating a range of levels of social importance; twice he uses κῶμαι to emphasise that they are outside the main centres of population (6:36; 8:27). He has just referred to Capernaum as a πόλις (1:33), which suggests that he regards it as the most significant settlement of its area; the use of κωμοπόλεις here for its neighbours therefore perhaps serves to indicate that, while not mere κῶμαι, they are of a lower status than

Capernaum (cf. Mt. 11:20-24, where the πόλεις of Chorazin and Bethsaida, which must surely be among the κωμοπόλεις here referred to, are put in a separate category from Capernaum). Jesus is, therefore, deliberately moving from the centre of local influence into a rather more 'grassroots' ministry.

ἵνα κηρύξω picks up the opening description of Jesus' mission in 1:14-15; the good news needs to be heard, and people summoned to respond, as widely as possible. This is the specific purpose of Jesus' mission; εἰς τοῦτο ἐξῆλθον. In fact Jesus himself will not again be recorded as κηρύσσων after v. 39; this will be the role rather of his supporters and particularly of the Twelve, while Jesus will be portrayed more often as διδάσκων (see above on vv. 14-15, 22). But here at the beginning of the mission it is Jesus himself who acts as herald. ἐξῆλθον is, perhaps deliberately, ambiguous. In the narrative context its most obvious reference is to the 'departure' (ἐξῆλθεν, v. 35) from Capernaum which has been the cause of their concern. Less probably it might refer to Jesus' leaving Nazareth and coming into the open (1:14-15). But an instructed Christian reader is likely to see more in it than that, and the similar use of ἦλθον/ἦλθεν in Jesus' words in 2:17; 10:45 to express his essential mission suggests that Mark may have in mind already the concept of the 'coming into the world' of the pre-existent Son of God (cf. 1:24?) which is such a prominent feature of the Fourth Gospel (for ἐξῆλθον in this sense cf. Jn. 8:42; 16:27-28). Luke 4:43 apparently takes it in this sense.

39 For the periphrasis ἦν κηρύσσων (see Textual Note above) see on 1:22. It indicates the habitual activity into which Jesus now launched, as the next phase of his mission. For κηρύσσων εἰς (again see Textual Note) see on 1:21, ἐδίδασκεν εἰς; here, as there, the preposition assumes a verb of motion which has not been expressed, and the whole clause amounts to 'he was going to and preaching in their synagogues'. The addition of αὐτῶν after συναγωγάς (as in v. 23) has been understood, particularly in Matthew who uses this expression more commonly, as dissociating the author (and his readers) from the synagogue authorities, and thus as reflecting the conditions of the latter part of the first century, when church and synagogue had gone their separate ways. In this context, where the synagogue is the prime focus of Jesus' ministry, and there is no hint yet of the hostility to come, that seems a most unlikely inference. In 1:23 the αὐτῶν refers naturally to the congregation whose favourable reaction has just been noted, and here the κωμοπόλεις of v. 38 form an equally natural antecedent. From the locations actually mentioned by Mark (and the other evangelists) it seems unlikely that εἰς ὅλην τὴν Γαλιλαίαν should be pressed to imply a visit to every part of Antipas's northern territory; see on v. 16 for the areas in which Jesus' ministry seems to have been focused.

The addition of καὶ τὰ δαιμόνια ἐκβάλλων to Jesus' declared mission of κηρύσσων represents, as we have seen (above on vv. 21-28), a major element in Mark's understanding of Jesus' ministry. It is unusual in a summary passage for exorcism to be mentioned without healing, though this occurs also with regard to the mission of the disciples in 3:14-15; 6:7. It was, as we have seen in vv. 21-

113

28, the most spectacular demonstration of his messianic ἐξουσία, and no doubt the one which continued to draw most general attention.

CONTROVERSIAL ASPECTS OF JESUS' MINISTRY (1:40–3:6)

The departure from Capernaum (1:35-39) brings to a close the 'Capernaum sequence' which began at 1:21, and ushers in a series of incidents in the wider neighbourhood which will lead up to the next general summary of Jesus' ministry and its impact in 3:7-12. The scene is in fact still set in Capernaum for most of this section, explicitly in 2:1, and by implication probably in the mention of the customs post (2:14) and the house of its officer (2:15) and again of the synagogue (3:1). Scenes set beside the lake (2:13) or in the cornfields (2:23) should probably therefore also be understood to be in or close to Capernaum. But these incidents are presented as typical of the wider ministry introduced in 1:38-39, and the first incident is set outside the town (see on v. 40), and leads to a period of retreat from any πόλις (v. 45).

A feature which links the various stories in this section is the increasing awareness that not everyone welcomes Jesus' teaching and activity, and the section will conclude with the remarkable revelation of a consequent plot on his life (3:6). Opposition is explicit in 2:6-7, 16, 18, 24; 3:2, 6, and the contrast between Jesus' views and practice and existing models of piety leads to a striking statement of dissociation in 2:21-22. The inclusion of 1:40-45 under this same heading of 'controversial aspects of Jesus' ministry' may seem less obviously appropriate, but the language Mark uses, and especially the enigmatic εἰς μαρτύριον αὐτοῖς, serves to prepare for the more direct confrontations to follow, while the excessive popularity which results from this incident (v. 45) inevitably brings Jesus to the notice of those who will find him a threat.

Jesus' opponents are variously described in this section as γραμματεῖς (2:6), Φαρισαῖοι (2:24), οἱ γραμματεῖς τῶν Φαρισαίων (2:16), and οἱ Φαρισαῖοι μετὰ τῶν Ἡρῳδιανῶν (3:6), while in 2:18 and 3:2 no subject is expressed, though in the latter case they are presumably the Φαρισαῖοι who go out in v. 6. Mark therefore has in view the familiar combination of 'scribes and Pharisees', with apparently little clear distinction in principle between them, though the phrase οἱ γραμματεῖς τῶν Φαρισαίων correctly reflects the situation of the Pharisees as a party or association to which some (probably most) scribes belonged, but whose membership was broader than only formally trained scribes. All four gospels agree that Pharisees constituted the core of the opposition to Jesus during his active ministry (even though the Sadducean priests and elders who controlled the Jerusalem establishment necessarily took the lead in his final elimination), and the Synoptic Gospels all include scribes as leading actors in that opposition. The tendency of some modern interpreters, both Jewish and Christian, to portray Jesus as an orthodox Pharisee whose teaching and actions could have caused no offence in Pharisaic circles must thus depend on a wholesale rejection of the gospel accounts. It is true that Christian tradition, taking its cue from the gospels, has unjustifiably made 'Pharisee' into a pejorative term, in defiance of the high regard in which Pharisees were clearly held in Jewish circles at the time. But it is not necessary, in order to rebut that calumny, to pretend that therefore Jesus saw eye to eye with the Pharisees. Mark clearly intends us to understand that there was a basic difference of approach to religious observance and the interpretation of Scripture which became increasingly obvious from the first days of Jesus' public ministry, and which was sufficiently fundamental to cause them to view him as a dangerous influence which must be eliminated. There is a sufficiently clear continuity between this gospel perspective and the enigmatic later rabbinic (Pharisaic) references to Jesus apparently as a *mesith,* a false teacher who was trying to 'lead Israel astray', to suggest a basic historical probability in the gospels' portrayal of Jesus' confrontation with the Pharisees of his day.

Throughout this section the focus falls, as we expect, on Jesus himself, but the recurrent mention of his μαθηταί (first named as such in 2:15) reminds us that, while the disciples as yet have no function of their own (for this see 3:13-19; 6:7-13), the 'Jesus circle' continues, as in the last section, to operate as a unit. The behaviour of the disciples is the subject of the hostile questions addressed to Jesus in 2:18, 24, and conversely it is to the disciples that Jesus' behaviour is criticised in 2:16. The reply in each case, of course, comes from Jesus himself.

Leprosy: The Law of Uncleanness (1:40-45)

TEXTUAL NOTES

40. καὶ γονυπετῶν (αὐτόν) may have been omitted in D B W, some OL, and the Sahidic, either by accident (homoioteleuton) or because it was felt to be redundant after παρακαλῶν αὐτόν (a redundancy which would be typical of Marcan style), or because the parallel in Mt. 8:2 does not use the rather rare verb γονυπετέω, but rather προσκυνέω. The presence of the idea of kneeling, but in different words, in both Matthew and Luke, suggests that γονυπετῶν was used in Mark.

41. The reading ὀργισθείς is not widely attested (D and a few OL) but is so striking and 'improbable' that a correction to the 'safer' σπλαγχνισθείς would be very natural, whereas it is hard to see why anyone should introduce ὀργισθείς. The argument of Metzger (*Textual Commentary,* 76) that scribes did not find it necessary to remove other references to Jesus' anger in 3:5; 10:14 ignores the fact that in those passages, unlike here, there was obvious cause for anger. The lack of either participle in Matthew and Luke (and in two OL MSS of Mark) also suggests that they found ὀργισθείς rather than the more congenial σπλαγχνισθείς in the tradition.

An encounter with a leper raises not only the problem of illness but also that of the Levitical laws of purity. Jesus' willingness to touch the man suggests a lack of concern with ritual purity, or at least a deliberate preference for meeting need over ritual correctness, which points forward to the controversy over his involvement with τελῶναι καὶ ἁμαρτωλοί in 2:16-17. But at the same time he insists that the cured leper must correctly observe the OT purification rites, εἰς μαρτύριον αὐτοῖς. There is thus a delicate balance in this pericope, which sets up an intriguing tension with regard to Jesus' attitude to the ritual law; the issues it raises in principle will become increasingly significant as the controversies between Jesus and the scribes develop.

The story focuses on a meeting between two men, but in the background are the mysterious αὐτοί of v. 44, and in v. 45 the cured man's disobedience to Jesus' demand for silence results in much wider repercussions. J. Sergeant[28] suggests that Mark placed the pericope at this point in order to account, through the 'double disobedience' of the man, for the 'two currents of mounting trouble which combine to overwhelm the Galilean ministry: the opposition of the authorities, and the suffocating pressure of the crowds'. The 'double disobedience' depends on the questionable assumption that the man did not go to the priest as instructed. But Sergeant's suggestion does help to explain the role of the pericope at this point in the gospel. From here on we shall begin to see why 'the Galilean ministry is ground to a halt between the upper and nether millstones of official opposition and overwhelming popularity'.

40 No indication of place is given, but a λεπρός would necessarily be outside normal habitation (Lv. 13:46), and v. 45 indicates that at this point Jesus was not preaching in a town. It is generally agreed that λέπρα in the Bible is used for a wider range of diseases than 'true leprosy' (Hansen's disease), though including it;[29] this man will have been suffering from a disfiguring skin complaint which was thought to be contagious. (The version of this story in Egerton Papyrus 2 [text in Aland ad loc.] has the man explain: 'As I was travelling with lepers and eating with them in the inn I too became leprous'.) The detailed rules of Lv. 13–14 (still in force in Jesus' day, v. 44) are designed to distinguish malignant from nonmalignant forms of disease. Only those diagnosed as malignant resulted in exclusion from society (Lv. 13:45-46); Simon 'the Leper' (14:3) was presumably either suffering from a nonmalignant disease or, like this man, had been cured (by Jesus?) and officially declared 'clean'. Clearly this man's disease was malignant, and may well have been Hansen's disease. Leprosy was one of the most dreaded diseases, and regarded as practically incurable (hence the prominence of the supernatural element in OT stories about its imposition and cure: Ex. 4:6-8; Nu. 12:9-15; 2 Ki. 5:1-27; 2 Ch. 26:16-21; to cure it is on a par with raising the dead, 2 Ki. 5:7; *b. Sanh.* 47a).

The leper approached (ἔρχεται πρὸς αὐτόν) to within touching distance (v. 41), in defiance of the taboo. γονυπετῶν may even indicate that he took the

---

28. J. Sergeant, *Lion,* 44-45.

29. For a useful, nontechnical summary of the evidence see S. G. Browne, *ExpTim* 73 (1961/2) 242-45.

initiative even more boldly by himself touching Jesus, as clasping the knees of the one appealed to was a recognised gesture of supplication in Greek culture; in a Jewish context, however, γονυπετέω more likely means to fall on one's own knees before the person. The piling up of participles (παρακαλῶν . . . γονυπετῶν . . . λέγων) is typical of Mark's prolixity; it results in a sense of strong, urgent appeal. ἐὰν θέλῃς has sometimes been read as expressing real doubt about Jesus' interest in his condition: he fears that a leper, as a social outcast, will not be an attractive case for this famous healer. But this is to read too much into ordinary politeness and natural diffidence: to preface a request by 'if you would be so kind' is not normally to express doubt as to the outcome. What is noticeable is rather his unquestioning assumption of Jesus' ability to cure his condition. Jesus' reputation (v. 28) has reached even to this man cut off from society, and it is such that even leprosy, normally assumed to be incurable, comes under his ἐξουσία. καθαρίζω is used consistently as the regular term for cure in all gospel passages concerning leprosy (but never in connection with other complaints; for the distinction see especially Mt. 10:8; 11:5), since the ritual uncleanness which the disease brings is as serious a problem as the disease itself. To be healed is also to be restored to 'clean' society.

41 ὀργισθείς (see Textual Note) is sometimes explained as Jesus' response to the leper's ἐὰν θέλῃς; he is annoyed that anyone should doubt his willingness to help. If, as argued above, that was not the implication of ἐὰν θέλῃς, another cause for Jesus' anger must be sought, and it is not obvious[30] (hence the textual emendation to σπλαγχνισθείς).[31] The surprisingly strong language of v. 43 (ἐμβριμησάμενος, ἐξέβαλεν) is equally unexpected. It is sometimes proposed that Jesus was annoyed at an interruption to his preaching mission, but this seems totally out of character, and preaching and healing always go hand in hand. The suggestion that he objected to the leper's 'unlawful' approach cannot be right in view of his response by equally 'unlawful' touch and immediate healing; similarly, if Jesus was displeased at being asked to breech the 'messianic secret' by 'une manifestation anticipée de la gloire messianique',[32] his immediate compliance is hard to explain. Mark certainly wants us to understand that Jesus was emotionally affected by the encounter, but does not explain why. The most likely explanation is, perhaps, that the suffering caused by the disease, both physically and socially, moved Jesus not only to compassion but to anger at the presence of such evil in the

30. The suggestion that the subject of ὀργισθείς is not Jesus but the leper (K. Lake, *HTR* 16 [1923] 197-98) produces a very artificial change of subject after ἥψατο; it is something of an exegetical counsel of despair. C. H. Cave, *NTS* 25 (1978/9) 245-50 (following a suggestion of J. Weiss), sees ὀργισθείς as a survival from an earlier version of the story in which the leper asked Jesus to usurp the priestly prerogative of declaring the leper cured; Jesus was very properly horrified!

31. Haenchen, 94-96, is unusual among recent commentators in arguing strongly for σπλαγχνισθείς as the original.

32. G. Minette de Tillesse, *Secret,* 49-50, suggesting 8:33 as a parallel.

world; perhaps also over the insensitivity of the social taboo. That the anger was not directed against the man himself is implied by the immediate compassionate response.

The phrase ἐκτείνας τὴν χεῖρα αὐτοῦ is 'redundant' with ἥψατο (and is probably too common a phrase to be intended as an echo of 2 Ki. 5:11), but by including it Mark draws attention dramatically to the significance of this particular touch. Jesus often touched a patient in the course of healing, but leprosy, unlike most other diseases, carried ritual uncleanness, and to touch a leper would be to become unclean oneself (quite apart from the fear of physical contagion). For the principle of uncleanness contracted by touch see Lv. 11:24-40; 14:46-47; 15:5-12, 19-27; Nu. 19:11-16, etc. For the resultant social exclusion of the leper see Lv. 13:45-46, and the detailed provisions of the Mishnah tractate *Nega'im*. Jesus shows a similar disregard for social/ritual taboo in 2:15-17, and in 7:1-23 the whole issue of purity will be discussed, leading up to the famous pronouncement of 7:19 that all food is 'clean'. Here need takes precedence over convention (even when firmly based in the OT). It is, of course, a nice point whether to touch the leper did in fact render Jesus unclean when the touch was itself the means of his cure. The touch which should have made Jesus unclean in fact worked in the opposite direction.

42 This is a particularly impressive καὶ εὐθύς; while the extent of the man's disfigurement cannot be known, an immediately visible cure is extraordinary. The vivid anthropomorphism ἀπῆλθεν ἀπ' αὐτοῦ ἡ λέπρα (cf ἀφῆκεν αὐτὴν ὁ πυρετός in v. 31) suggests that the symptoms of the disease could be seen to vanish, leaving the man visibly καθαρός (for a similarly immediate cure of leprosy see 2 Ki. 5:14, and the converse in Nu. 12:10; 2 Ki. 5:27; cf. also Ex. 4:6-7). Jesus' healings (except in 8:22-26) are immediate, and even the disfigurement of leprosy is no exception.

43 Even given the weaker usage of ἐκβάλλω (see on v. 12), Mark's language is surprising. ἐμβριμάομαι (used classically to denote 'scarce-controlled animal fury')[33] indicates Jesus' strong emotion in Jn. 11:33, 38 (where it is used with τῷ πνεύματι and ἐν ἑαυτῷ), but in that context no 'object' of the emotion is expressed. In 14:5 a following dative supplies an 'object', and the sense is clearly one of expressed hostility towards the person mentioned. Here, as in Mt. 9:30, a dative follows similarly, but there is no clear reason why the persons concerned (in each case those who have just been healed by Jesus) should be the object of Jesus' disapproval, and so the verb is usually translated 'strictly charged' rather than 'scolded' or worse. But a note of anger is clearly present in the few uses of this word group in the LXX and the other versions of the OT.[34] Since both here and in Mt. 9:30 the verb precedes a command to silence which is then promptly dis-

---

33. C. Bonner, *HTR* 20 (1927) 174. H. C. Waetjen, *Reordering*, 87, speaks (slightly melodramatically?) of Jesus' 'blazing anger' here.

34. C. Bonner, art. cit., sums up the general usage of the verb as of 'violent rage accompanied by visible or audible manifestations of emotion'.

obeyed, it is possible that it reflects Jesus' knowledge of and displeasure at that still future response.[35] Together with εὐθὺς ἐξέβαλεν it does not suggest gentle treatment. (It is sometimes suggested[36] that these terms indicate an element of exorcism, perhaps in an earlier version of the story. But ἐμβριμάομαι does not occur in exorcism accounts,[37] and ἐκβάλλω is used of people as well as of demons [cf. 1:12; 5:40; 11:15]; its object here is the leper, not a demon. There is no evidence that leprosy was attributed to demon possession.)

44 The prohibition ὅρα μηδενὶ μηδὲν εἴπῃς is correspondingly strong (for ὅρα used to intensify a command cf. 8:15; for the pleonastic double negative cf. 5:3; 11:2, 14; 14:25; 15:4-5). We have seen already Jesus' determination to silence the demons who recognised him (1:34; cf. 1:25). Here we have for the first time his attempted silencing of those whose personal experience of his healing power would naturally lead them to talk about him (cf. 5:43; 7:36; 8:26). Interestingly, whereas we are left to assume that demons were effectively silenced, in the case of humans both here and in 7:36 the command is ignored. (It may in any case be questioned how realistic Jesus' command was: a cured leper restored to society was not an everyday occurrence, and the question of how it had happened could hardly be avoided.) The pragmatic reason for this secrecy is clearly spelled out in v. 45; publicity of this sort resulted in excessive, and probably misdirected, popular enthusiasm which was a serious hindrance to Jesus' mission. It is not clear yet whether this is a question of 'messianic secrecy', as we have not been informed that anyone (other than the demons) was speaking of Jesus in messianic terms. We shall return to this question on 8:30.

The one exception to the secrecy Jesus demands is to go to the priest and complete the necessary procedure for the restoration of a healed leper to society (Lv. 14:1-32). This καθαρισμός was a lengthy procedure, requiring eight days, not to mention the period taken to travel from Galilee to Jerusalem and back (even if there were a priest in the locality, the offerings must be made in the temple in Jerusalem; see *m. Neg.* 14 for the rabbinic regulations). Until it is completed he would presumably have little opportunity to talk about Jesus, as he would still be socially excluded (which is why Sergeant's idea, mentioned above, that he disobeyed this instruction as well is improbable). There must therefore be a time lag between vv. 44 and 45, even though Mark's flowing narrative suggests that the explosion of popularity was immediate.

Despite Jesus' own lack of concern for ritual purity in v. 41, he here insists on the correct observance of the OT regulations (ἃ προσέταξεν Μωϋσῆς). In this case, however, there was no conflict of interests, and indeed it was in the

---

35. So, e.g., J. F. Williams, *Followers,* 97-98.

36. For example, by J. M. Robinson, *Problem,* 40; H. C. Kee, *JBL* 92 (1973) 418.

37. In Bonner's search for thaumaturgical uses of the term (*HTR* 20 [1927]) there is no mention of exorcism. Kee's argument depends on the equation of ἐμβριμάομαι with ἐπιτιμάω.

man's own interest to fulfil his legal obligations, to provide formal proof of his cure and thus to be allowed back into society.

It is possible that that is all that is meant by εἰς μαρτύριον αὐτοῖς — a formal proof to 'them' (people in general) that he is cured. But the same phrase will occur twice more in Mark: in 6:11 it has a hostile sense, the shaking off of the dust from the disciples' feet being a μαρτύριον to (perhaps *against?*) those who refuse their mission; and in 13:9 it is again in a context of opposition, where the disciples, hauled up before governors and kings *for Jesus' sake,* will be there εἰς μαρτύριον αὐτοῖς. (For the generally hostile usage see H. Strathmann, *TDNT,* 4.502-4.) When we meet priests later in the gospel, it will be in the form of the ἀρχιερεῖς who take the lead in the opposition to Jesus, and so it is likely that here, too, the phrase εἰς μαρτύριον αὐτοῖς has a note of confrontation, the αὐτοί being the priestly establishment represented by the one ἱερεύς mentioned in v. 44.[38] It will be some time before Jesus himself appears in Jerusalem, but the arrival of this cured leper will serve advance warning of the activities of the Galilean prophet. It has also been seen in a more positive sense, 'as a proof that, despite my reputation, I do expect people to observe the law';[39] but that would seem both premature at this point in the narrative (Jesus has not yet acquired any such reputation) and misdirected, since the conflict over the law will arise with the scribes and Pharisees, not with the priests.

45 κηρύσσω is the word for spreading good news (vv. 14-15), and, however inconvenient for Jesus, the man's disobedient proclamation was, and was recognised as, good news.[40] It is not necessary, however, to read τὸν λόγον here as a technical term for preaching the Christian gospel; see on 2:2 for Mark's use of the phrase. We do not need to be told what were the πολλά which he proclaimed and the λόγος which he disseminated; their result in the massive popularity of Jesus is evidence enough.[41] εἰς πόλιν is probably gen-

---

38. Myers supposes a more directly hostile intention: the man has already been to the priests, who have rejected his plea to be declared clean; now Jesus sends him back with the purificatory offering as 'a protest against the entire purity apparatus, which the priests control'. The supposition that the man had previously approached the priests is curious; what would have been the point of his doing so before being cured?

39. So, e.g., D. W. Chapman, *Orphan,* 75-76.

40. It has been suggested, e.g., by J. K. Elliott, *JTS* 22 (1971) 153-57, that the subject of the first part of v. 45 is Jesus, not the leper. This is not only syntactically unlikely (ὁ δέ, following Jesus' instructions to the man, should mark a change of subject showing his response; the following αὐτόν would also be redundant if not marking a further subject change), but also reads oddly as it makes Jesus' difficulties through overpopularity self-inflicted. Elliott, *JTS* 27 (1976) 402-5, is obliged to rescue his suggestion by construing ὁ ἐξελθών as a 'title' of Jesus, a suggestion improbable in itself, and particularly difficult at the conclusion of a pericope in which Jesus has already been the subject, so that no new descriptive phrase is needed to introduce him.

41. Myers, following B. J. Malina, suggests that Jesus' exclusion from the towns was not by his own choice in order to avoid excessive popularity, but because he was now *persona non grata* since he was regarded as unclean as a result of his contact with the leper. Mark gives no hint of any such understanding, here or elsewhere. On the contrary, he continually stresses Jesus' massive popularity: 2:2; 3:7-8; 4:1; 5:21, 24; 6:31.

eral, 'into any town', rather than specific 'into Capernaum' (the only πόλις so far mentioned), though the latter was of course affected, as 2:1-2 will show. The fact that the next few pericopes will be set in town suggests either that Mark was consciously exaggerating, or that he does not intend the episodes to be taken as being in chronological sequence (though 2:1 does suggest that Jesus' return to Capernaum had not been φανερῶς). ἔξω ἐπ' ἐρήμοις τόποις represents, ironically, the area where the leper, before his cure, had been forced to live (Lv. 13:46). But even the ἔρημοι τόποι are no refuge from popularity, since even there ἤρχοντο πρὸς αὐτὸν πάντοθεν, just as is to happen later when Jesus seeks out an ἔρημος τόπος by choice rather than by necessity (6:31-34). Thus in a few quick strokes Mark has painted a powerful picture of Jesus' 'success' and of the problems it is already beginning to cause. It will be important to bear this popular response to Jesus in mind as the opposition develops in succeeding scenes; his opponents do not represent the majority opinion.

Healing and Forgiveness (2:1-12)

TEXTUAL NOTES

4. Προσενέγκαι and προσεγγίσαι are both well attested, and either is appropriate in context. προσεγγίσαι might have been substituted for the transitive προσενέγκαι, since no object is expressed; on the other hand, προσενέγκαι might be due to partial assimilation to the Lucan parallel εἰσενέγκωσιν αὐτόν.

5, 9. There is probably in context no real difference in meaning between the perfect ἀφέωνται and the present ἀφίενται. The former is the reading of the Lucan parallel, the latter (probably) of the Matthean. Either reading therefore may be due to assimilation. Most MSS are consistent in the two verses, though ℵ changes from perfect in v. 5 to present in v. 9. The more 'decisive tone' which Taylor claims as a reason for preferring ἀφίενται may equally have appealed to a scribe familiar with the Matthean present.

If the element of controversy was still largely latent in the story of the leper, with Jesus' return to Capernaum it comes into the open, in the first direct confrontation with scribes, and their accusation of blasphemy. The occasion is a public miracle of healing, which provides a further specific example of the healing of the sick in Capernaum which was described in general terms in 1:32-34. But what could have been a straightforward account of Jesus' power over physical illness is given a new dimension by his (apparently unsought) declaration of the forgiveness of sins, leading to the scribes' theological objection to his assumption of the divine prerogative. From that point on the healing itself becomes subsumed under the larger question of the extent of Jesus' ἐξουσία, and the christological implications of his bold claim to do what only God has the right to do are added to the impact of an instantaneous healing to produce an emphatic crowd reaction.

121

Mark has already commented on the contrast between Jesus and the scribes in 1:22. There it was his διδαχή which displayed an ἐξουσία on a different level from theirs, and the contrast in their styles of teaching and scriptural interpretation will be further developed in the remaining pericopes which build up to the decision to destroy Jesus in 3:6. But already in that first episode in the synagogue the unprecedented authority of Jesus' teaching could not be separated from his more tangible authority over demon possession, the two strands together constituting a διδαχὴ καινὴ κατ' ἐξουσίαν (1:27), and now again the boldness of his declaration of forgiveness is backed up by tangible evidence through physical healing. The scribes thus face a formidable challenge to their authority, and the reaction of the crowd suggests that it is in danger of being eroded completely. It is a sign of the seriousness of the situation that in due course the scribes from Jerusalem will resort to the rather desperate expedient of trying to impugn Jesus' exorcistic power as demonically inspired (3:22). Already the local scribes seem to be set on a collision course with Jesus, which his provocative public declaration in v. 5 does not seem designed to conciliate.

1 The tension between this notice of Jesus' return to Capernaum and the previous verse which said he could not openly enter any town is eased both by the phrase δι' ἡμερῶν ('sometime later'), implying a sufficient time lapse for the immediate excitement to die down, and also by the fact that he apparently succeeded in returning unnoticed (not φανερῶς, 1:45); with the discovery of his arrival the earlier enthusiasm revived.

The nominative participle εἰσελθών strictly requires us to take Jesus (understood) as the subject of ἠκούσθη, rather than taking the verb as impersonal ('it was heard'); the ὅτι clause then explains the content of the report, producing a 'double object' in much the same way as οἶδά σε τίς εἶ in 1:24 ('he was heard, that he was in the house'); it is an easily intelligible if syntactically awkward idiom (cf. BDF, 405[2]). Alternatively, εἰσελθών may be read as a 'dangling participle', grammatically unrelated to the main verb (so Taylor). The οἶκος, we are left to assume, is that of 1:29.

2 See on 1:33 for the limited space πρὸς τὴν θύραν in first-century Capernaum. It is clear from v. 4 that Mark intends us to picture Jesus as 'besieged' inside the house, with the crowd in the narrow street outside listening to his teaching as best they could. Here, instead of using διδάσκω, Mark uses a phrase which will recur in 4:33 and 8:32, λαλέω τὸν λόγον. In this phrase, and in 4:14-20, ὁ λόγος may well reflect later Christian usage, as a term for the Christian message. It would be wrong, however, to read it as a technical term in every occurrence; in 5:36; 9:10; 10:22 ὁ λόγος refers simply to the utterance just reported, and in 1:45 what the leper spread was not the Christian κήρυγμα but the news of his cure. There is no reason here to see any difference in meaning from Mark's more common use of διδάσκω/διδαχή. It is thus in the course of Jesus' teaching activity that this miracle, like the exorcism of 1:23-26, will occur; the two aspects of his ministry are kept firmly together.

3 Jesus' reappearance in Capernaum triggers the same response as in chapter 1, and another 'stretcher case' (cf. ἔφερον in 1:32) is presented. κράβαττον (vv. 4, 9-12; Matthew calls it a κλίνη, Luke a κλινίδιον) was a colloquial term for a basic poor person's bed (Acts 9:33), usually mentioned as being portable (6:55; Jn. 5:8-11; Acts 5:15). παραλυτικός describes the man's condition, inability to walk, without more specific indication of its cause, which might be through one of a number of paralysing diseases or through injury; Luke's term παραλελυμένος is no more specific. Whatever the cause, the man is unable to move about, and is clearly recognised by the crowd as seriously disabled (vv. 9-12).

4 It would not take much of a crowd to make it impossible to bring a stretcher case into a room in a normal Capernaum house.[1] Those which have been excavated have small rooms, seldom reaching to as much as five metres across (since the width was limited by the length of tree trunks available for roofing). The houses, like most in ancient Palestine, were single-storey structures with flat roofs accessible by an outside staircase. The roof was used for working and sometimes for sleeping, and so it was not flimsy in construction; wooden beams or branches were thatched with rush and daubed with mud.[2] Mark's description of how the men ἀπεστέγασαν τὴν στέγην ('unroofed the roof') therefore suggests a major demolition job, and the addition of ἐξορύξαντες, literally 'digging it out', adds to the graphic effect.[3] The modern reader naturally wonders whether Jesus continued teaching, and the crowd listening, while this noisy and dangerous activity went on over their heads (and what the owner of the house [Simon?] thought about it), but Mark does not satisfy our curiosity. His interest is rather, as a storyteller, to enable his readers to enjoy one of the more memorable incidents of Jesus' Galilean ministry, and to provide the basis for the response of Jesus in v. 5, ἰδὼν τὴν πίστιν αὐτῶν. Their desperate desire to get their friend to the one person who could help him is more important than either the awkwardness of the narrative situation or the damage to property (cf. the lack of concern for the economic loss of the owners of the pigs in 5:11-20).[4]

5 πίστις in Mark relates closely to miraculous power.[5] It is the expectation that God (11:22-24), or more often Jesus, can and will exercise supernatu-

---

1. For a brief description of the houses excavated in Capernaum see J. Wilkinson, *Jerusalem,* 26-30; E. M. Meyers and J. F. Strange, *Archaeology,* 58-60, 128-30.

2. For a fuller description see C. C. McCown, *JBL* 58 (1939) 213-16.

3. See Josephus, *Ant.* 14.459, for Herod's removal of house roofs in order to destroy the soldiers hiding below; he uses a similar verb, ἀνασκάπτω, 'to dig up'.

4. Mark gives no hint of the romantic idea that the entry via the roof was not a matter of necessity but of design, intended to prevent a presumed 'demon of paralysis' from discovering the doorway and thus being able to return. This proposal was made by H. Jahnow, *ZNW* 24 (1925) 155-58, on the basis of Indian beliefs, and despite its lack of culturally relevant support (see S. Krauss, *ZNW* 25 [1926] 307-10) is mentioned by many commentators and favoured by a few (notably Gnilka).

5. See the detailed study by S. E. Dowd, *Prayer,* 96-117, which also includes a study of faith and miracles in the non-Christian literature of the ancient world.

ral power to solve a practical problem, usually of illness or physical danger. It is in response to πίστις that Jesus will heal (5:34, 36; 9:23-24; 10:52), and its absence will be either the subject of a rebuke to those who are nevertheless miraculously rescued (4:40) or an actual limitation on his miraculous activity (6:5-6). Here we have no record of a verbal expression of faith, but the action of the man's friends is sufficient to indicate their confidence in Jesus' healing power (based already on ample evidence, 1:32-34), and their determination to draw on it for their friend's benefit.

In the case of demon possession, where faith is mentioned at all it is not that of the victim (who speaks only as the voice of the demon) but of a relative (9:22-24; in 7:24-30 the word πίστις is not used, but the concept is implied in the λόγος of v. 29); in physical healing, on the other hand, it is normally the patient whose faith is in focus (except in the case of Jairus's daughter, for obvious reasons). Here, however, faith is apparently exercised on behalf of another, while the patient himself remains inactive until v. 12, and is silent throughout. No reason for this is offered; clearly Mark does not have a fixed stereotype of how faith must relate to healing. It is possible that he intends to include the faith of the patient as well as of his friends in αὐτῶν[6] (his action in v. 12 is certainly an act of faith), but it is their action, not any indication of his own attitude (unless he is understood to have instigated their unorthodox approach to Jesus), which Jesus sees (ἰδών) and on which his response is based.

To modern ears Jesus' response seems inappropriate, so much so that many commentators have suggested that the story originally continued with v. 11, the words of healing which the friends clearly expected, and that an originally simple healing story has been complicated by the insertion of a discussion of forgiveness (so Bultmann, Taylor, Haenchen, Anderson, Gnilka, Pesch).[7] Such theories can seldom be proved either right or wrong, but are of limited exegetical value for the text of Mark as we have it.[8] Mark clearly believed that Jesus dealt with the condition of the paralytic by focusing first on his sins, and that in some way the forgiveness of sin and physical healing were interrelated (vv. 9-11). Nor would this have been so surprising to his original readers as it may be to us, since a link between illness and sin runs through much of biblical literature, as well as being widespread in the ancient world. In many OT texts healing and forgiveness are so closely related that it is hard to tell whether the language of healing is meant to be understood of physical illness or metaphorically for restored spiritual health (e.g., Pss. 41:4; 103:3; Is 53:4-6), but sometimes physical healing is clearly related to forgiveness of sin (2 Ch. 7:13-14; Is. 38:16-17) just as physical suffering can be attributed to the sin of the sufferer

6. So J. F. Williams, *Followers*, 99-101.

7. While most propose that the 'insertion' begins at v. 5b (thus eliminating any mention of forgiveness from the supposed original story), Pesch includes v. 5b in the miracle story, regarding vv. 6-10 as a secondary expansion of the theme. Similarly H.-J. Klauck, *BZ* 25 (1981) 223-48.

8. The integrity of the pericope and its effectiveness in the development of the narrative are well discussed by C. D. Marshall, *Faith*, 78-86.

(Nu. 12:9-15; 2 Ch. 26:16-21) or indeed to sin in the community (2 Sa. 24:10-15). That suffering is the result of sin in the general sense that the world's evils are traced to the Fall would have been generally agreed, but the Book of Job testifies to a strong reaction against the view that the suffering of an individual must necessarily be the result of his or her own sin. A similar balance is maintained in the NT, with some suffering and death being attributed to the specific sin of those concerned (Jn. 5:14; Acts 5:1-11; 1 Cor. 11:30; 1 Jn. 5:16), while in other places such a direct connection is denied (Lk. 13:1-5; Jn. 9:2-3; 2 Cor. 12:7; Gal. 4:13-14).

The link between healing and forgiveness in this case is clear, but the nature of the connection is more obscure. The explicit link in v. 10 is that the physical healing proves the authority of the Son of Man to forgive; otherwise healing and forgiveness are mentioned side by side without explicitly making the one dependent on the other. Even the comparison in v. 9 of the relative 'easiness' of the declaration of forgiveness and the healing command is left in the form of a question. Since Jesus did not normally preface a healing with a declaration of forgiveness, there must be some special reason for introducing the issue in this case. Three seem worth considering: (1) that Jesus was aware that this man's illness, unlike others, was directly attributable to his sin; (2) that the patient so understood it (whether rightly or wrongly), and so was looking for more than physical relief;[9] (3) that Jesus, intent on raising the issue of his authority with the scribes, took this opportunity to do so, even though it was not strictly necessary to the case. Of these, (3) sounds improbably artificial, especially in view of the lack of any indication hitherto that Jesus intended to invite confrontation; his withdrawal from public notice in 1:35-38, 45 rather suggests the opposite. Both (1) and (2) depend on access to the minds of the actors which the narrative does not allow us; either is plausible, but each must be speculative.

τέκνον is not a common form of address. In the gospels, apart from cases of actual family relationship,[10] it is used only once by Jesus in addressing his disciples (10:24). The unexpected degree of familiarity it implies is no doubt designed to provide reassurance (cf. 5:34, where θυγάτηρ has the same effect). ἀφίενται (or ἀφέωνται; see textual note above) is understood by the scribes as a performative utterance (see BDF, 320): Jesus is not simply stating a fact, but actually forgiving. In the subsequent dialogue Jesus will not correct their understanding of his intention, but rather reinforce it by linking his declaration with instantaneous healing. The word in itself need not carry such force; as a 'divine passive' it need mean no more than 'God forgives your sins', and the OT contains at least one such clear declaration by an authorised prophet (2 Sa. 12:13), while the role of the priest in the sacrificial ritual was to procure a restored relationship with God through atonement. But Jesus occupied no such authorised

9. Cf the general statement attributed to Rabbi Hiyya, 'A sick man does not recover from his sickness until all his sins are forgiven him' (b. Ned. 41a).
10. In Lk. 16:25 Abraham addresses the rich man, his (theoretical) descendant, as τέκνον.

position. A declaration of forgiveness in such a context was tantamount to as-suming the authority to forgive on God's behalf, and in v. 10 Jesus will make that claim explicit.

6 The presence of γραμματείς in the house where Jesus is teaching indi-cates that the lines of confrontation are not yet clearly drawn; it will be this in-cident which focuses their opposition. While διαλογίζομαι in Mark generally refers to verbal discussion (8:16-17; 9:33; 11:31), at this point he presents the scribes' misgivings about Jesus' words as still unspoken (ἐν ταῖς καρδίαις αὐτῶν), though clearly shared; it is Jesus who brings the issue into the open.

7 Their misgivings are expressed in the form of questions. The first and last clauses of the verse are clearly interrogative, while βλασφημεῖ, standing on its own between them, could as well be punctuated as a further question, setting up the theological issue to which the (rhetorical) question of the last clause will provide the apparently unavoidable answer. It is the third question, then, to which it is assumed only one answer can be given ('No one!'), which turns the whole interrogative sequence in effect into an unspoken accusation, and re-quires an affirmative answer to the question 'Is he blaspheming?' The Mishnah has a very tight definition of blasphemy, as the actual pronouncing of the divine name (*m. Sanh.* 7:5), and clearly Jesus has not done that, but it is clear that in the pre-70 period the term was used more broadly (see on 14:64). To claim to do what only God could do, and to constitute himself God's spokesman in de-claring sins forgiven, was to infringe the divine prerogative. Cf. the 'definition' of blasphemy in Jn. 10:33: ὅτι σὺ ἄνθρωπος ὢν ποιεῖς σεαυτὸν θεόν. Blasphemy is a capital offence (Lv. 24:10-16), and it will be on this charge that Jesus is eventually condemned (14:64), so the matter is serious. The use of εἷς, rather than μόνος as in Luke, perhaps carries the implication that what is at issue here is the defence of the Jewish creed that 'Yahweh is one' (Dt. 6:4). A man who claims to do what only God can do threatens that unique status, and that is blas-phemy.[11] See on v. 5 for how far Jesus' words necessarily carried this connota-tion; but if they could have been interpreted in a safely monotheistic sense, nei-ther the scribes nor Jesus takes that option.

8 ἐν ἑαυτοῖς and ἐν ταῖς καρδίαις ὑμῶν both underline the point already made in v. 6 that no spoken accusation has been offered. Jesus' awareness of their criticisms is thus not derived from hearing any words, but is something which he knows ἐν τῷ πνεύματι αὐτοῦ. Jesus' supernatural powers of discern-ment are not made explicit in Mark as often as in the other gospels (but see 5:30; 12:15), but this indication of them serves here to reinforce, even if only in passing, the extraordinary impression of ἐξουσία conveyed by this pericope as a whole. By bringing the issue into the open Jesus ensures that the christological implications of his claim to forgive sins are brought to public recognition, and it is this as much as the healing itself which contributes to the crowd's reaction in

11. E. E. Ellis provides a useful analysis of the nature of Jesus' claim vis-à-vis scribal views in J. B. Green and M. M. B. Turner (ed.), *Jesus of Nazareth: Lord and Christ,* 192-94.

v. 12. Whatever the claims of secrecy in the rest of the gospel, Mark does not here allow us to see Jesus as one anxious to hide his light under a bushel.

9 εὔκοπος is a rare adjective meaning 'easy'; the use of the comparative in setting up a question of probabilities is an idiom attested only in the sayings of Jesus, here, in 10:25 (with parallels), and in Lk. 16:17. In the latter two cases the argument is a negative one: the impossibility of one concept (a rich person entering the kingdom of God; a minor point of the law being annulled) is asserted by declaring it to be 'easier' for something admittedly impossible to happen (a camel going through the eye of a needle; heaven and earth disappearing). It is thus an *a fortiori* argument (cf. the rabbinic *qal waḥomer*). Here, too, we have an *a fortiori* argument, but this time it operates positively: if the more 'difficult' can be achieved, this guarantees the validity of the claim to do the 'easier'. The answer to Jesus' rhetorical question must therefore be that it is εὐκοπώτερον to say 'Your sins are forgiven', since that is the point to be proved (v. 10), and it will be proved by the successful utterance of the 'more difficult' command to the paralytic to get up and go. To regard the forgiveness of sins as 'easier' than healing a medical complaint may seem oddly out of keeping with biblical perspectives, but the argument does not focus on the inherent value of the acts themselves, but on their force as proof to a sceptical audience. A visible healing is 'hard evidence', whereas a merely verbal claim to forgive sins invites scepticism. To tell a paralysed man to get up and walk exposes the speaker to ridicule if it is not successful; but how can a claim to have forgiven sins be falsified?

For ἀφίενταί σου αἱ ἁμαρτίαι see on v. 5, and textual note. The command to the paralytic serves as a warning to those who make exegetical capital out of the difference between the present and aorist imperatives; ἆρον is correctly 'punctiliar', and περιπάτει 'linear', but it is not obvious why the present imperative ἔγειρε should be used for what must be a single action.

10 This is the first occurrence in Mark of the phrase ὁ υἱὸς τοῦ ἀνθρώπου. It will recur at 2:28, and then not again until the beginning of Act Two (8:31), when it will assume a central role, and appear a further 12 times in the gospel. It would be out of place in this commentary to attempt to survey the immense and increasingly complex scholarly debate over this term.[12] I shall assume a view which is well represented among recent scholarship (though no point is uncontroversial): (1) that Jesus used this term to refer to himself, and that it was recognised and reproduced by the evangelists as his distinctive self-designation; (2) that it derives at least in part from Dn. 7:13-14, and that that text is often relevant to exegesis of passages in the gospels which use the term, even though it is used much more widely than merely in conscious allusion to that passage; (3) that the term 'the Son of Man' as such was not in current use in Judaism as a messianic title, even though the messianic significance of Dn. 7 was recognised and developed in later Jewish literature; and (4) that therefore

---

12. There is a useful and fairly recent summary in W. D. Davies and D. C. Allison, *Matthew*, 2.43-52.

the distinctive use of 'the Son of Man' by Jesus derives from his own choice of a term with clear messianic overtones but without a ready-made nationalistic content such as was carried by 'Messiah' or 'Son of David'.[13]

It has often been suggested, however, that in the two occurrences of the phrase in Mk. 2 we have the survival of an earlier use, corresponding to normal Hebrew and Aramaic usage, whereby 'the son of man' simply refers to humanity in general. In that case Jesus would here be declaring, contrary to the scribes' assumption in v. 7, that a human being has the authority to forgive sins on earth (and in 2:28 that humanity is 'Lord of the sabbath', thus extending the thought of v. 27). But in view of the use of ὁ υἱὸς τοῦ ἀνθρώπου in the rest of Mark's gospel (and in the gospel tradition as a whole) it is surely inconceivable that he or his readers could have understood it in such a strikingly different sense at this point. (Note that in 3:28 where a generic sense is intended Mark conspicuously uses not the singular but the plural, οἱ υἱοὶ τῶν ἀνθρώπων.) Even in the telling of the story before Mark incorporated it in his gospel, the generic sense would be inappropriate, since the authority given to the Son of Man is proved by a miracle performed not by people in general but by this one Son of Man in particular, in such a way as to set him apart from the rest of humanity, who recognise a unique power at work, and ascribe glory to God (v. 12). The issue at stake in the whole pericope is that of the unique ἐξουσία claimed and exercised by Jesus. While no background has been given in the gospel so far for understanding this new title (though Mark's readers already had ample background in the church's usage), the dynamics of the passage are such that the title must be understood not primarily as identifying Jesus with the rest of humanity, but precisely as setting him apart.[14] Those who recognised in the title an allusion to Dn. 7:13-14 might be expected to get the point, since the figure there described is one to whom is given a unique authority over the peoples of the earth.[15]

13. In describing ὁ υἱὸς τοῦ ἀνθρώπου as a title not currently in use I am, of course, assuming that the *Similitudes of Enoch,* the only other Jewish writing of the period to develop a distinctively 'titular' use of the same phrase, was either not yet in existence at the time of Jesus' ministry (the debate on its date of origin, occasioned by lack of evidence for this section of the *Book of Enoch* among the Qumran texts, continues unresolved), or was not widely known in the circles in which I.. moved, and that the title was independently developed from Dn. 7:13-14 by Jesus and by the author of the *Similitudes.*

14. This specific background to the term is in danger of being lost when ὁ υἱὸς τοῦ ἀνθρώπου is represented in translation by an English phrase which emphasises primarily its lexical sense as a human being rather than its specific Daniel background: e.g., Mann's use of 'The Man', or even H. C. Waetjen's use (*Reordering,* passim) of 'the New Human Being'.

15. The lack of background for the title in the narrative context has led some (e.g., G. H. Boobyer, *HTR* 47 [1954] 115-20; Cranfield; C. P. Ceroke, *CBQ* 22 [1960] 369-90; Lane; L. S. Hay, *JBL* 89 [1970] 69-75) to suggest that the whole clause ἵνα δὲ εἰδῆτε ὅτι ἐξουσίαν ἔχει ὁ υἱὸς τοῦ ἀνθρώπου ἀφιέναι ἁμαρτίας ἐπὶ τῆς γῆς is not part of the dialogue, but an editorial aside by Mark to the reader (to whom, of course, the title will be familiar). This has several disadvantages: it creates the only editorial use of 'Son of Man' in the gospels; it places two unrelated asides side by side in the middle of a discourse; and it leaves the dialogue lacking its crucial point, Jesus' assertion of his own special ἐξουσία over against the scribes' query in v. 7.

The ἐξουσία which Jesus here claims is not merely that of declaring sins forgiven, but of forgiving (see on v. 5 for the distinction). This is exactly the way the scribes' unspoken thoughts have set up the problem in v. 7; they have in mind a distictively divine prerogative, and Jesus responds in their own terms, claiming to be able to exercise that divine right ἐπὶ τῆς γῆς. This phrase is added not so much to limit the ἐξουσία asserted (on earth but not in heaven), but rather to underline the boldness of the claim: forgiveness, hitherto thought to be an exclusively heavenly function, can now be exercised ἐπὶ τῆς γῆς because of the presence of ὁ υἱὸς τοῦ ἀνθρώπου (who according to Dn. 7:13-14 was to receive from God an authority to be exercised over all the earth).

The last three words of v. 10, λέγει τῷ παραλυτικῷ, have occasioned unnecessary concern. Their intrusion into an otherwise continuous speech of Jesus has been taken as a sign of the dislocation or composite origin of the text, attempting to smooth an otherwise awkward change of focus in the sayings of vv. 10 and 11, or picking up the same words from v. 5 to resume the healing story after the presumed insertion of vv. 5b-10 (see on v. 5 above). But this is too subtle. The ἵνα of v. 10 demands a main clause as its sequel, but v. 9 has already made it plain that that clause must be a command addressed to the paralytic, not to the scribes whom Jesus is currently addressing. A change of addressee at this point is therefore already built into the logic of the discourse, and Mark's inserted 'stage direction' is merely a help to the reader of a written text to follow the change of focus which would have been obvious in the event by the speaker's physical movement or gesture. Far from showing any dislocation, Jesus' words form a logically coherent sequence from v. 8b to v. 11, while Mark's insertion of λέγει τῷ παραλυτικῷ is an aside designed to help the reader of the written text to follow the movement of a three-cornered dialogue (cf. his asides, for different purposes, in 7:19 and 13:14).[16]

11-12 The effect of Jesus' words is immediate and public, as the preceding dialogue required; here, ἔμπροσθεν πάντων, is the visible proof of his ἐξουσία not only to heal physical illness but also *a fortiori* to forgive sins. Here there is no attempt, as in the case of the leper, to restrict publicity; Jesus has a point to make, and it is meant to be noticed. ἐξίστασθαι is parallel in meaning to the reaction to his first Capernaum miracle, ἐθαμβήθησαν (1:27). The inclusion of δοξάζειν τὸν θεόν, a phrase more typical of Luke than of Mark, may be intended to show that whereas the scribes took Jesus' words as a challenge to the prerogative of God, the crowd understood Jesus to be acting for God and with his approval. The main impression, as in 1:27, is that they are witnessing something unprecedented: οὕτως οὐδέποτε εἴδομεν. In terms of physical healing, of course, they *have* already seen similar things (1:32-34), but this time the declaration of the forgiveness of sins, and Jesus' bold defence of his right to do so, has added a new dimension.

16. For the suitability of the construction from a narrative point of view see C. D. Marshall, *Faith,* 80-82.

Disreputable Company (2:13-17)

TEXTUAL NOTES

14. Apart from unimportant differences in the spelling of Λευίν, the significant variation is the reading Ἰάκωβον in D Θ some OL etc., supported by Tatian (Origen says that Levi was mentioned as an apostle in 'some of the MSS' of Mark). This reading is presumably a harmonistic device arising from the fact that James 'the Less' is listed as τὸν τοῦ Ἀλφαίου in 3:18 (this is far more likely than the later introduction of the unknown Levi, whose name is in any case secure in the Lucan text). It also has the effect of substituting a known apostolic name for that of Levi, who appears in no apostolic list, though it is remarkable that there is no MS evidence for the obvious solution to this problem by assimilating to Matthew's Μαθθαῖον. (See further B. Lindars, NTS 4 [1957/ 8] 220-22.)

15-16. The reading of ℵ L Δ (cop^bo), making οἱ γραμματεῖς τῶν Φαρισαίων the subject of ἠκολούθουν, depends on understanding ἀκολουθέω in its basic sense ('they followed and saw') rather than in the more normal Marcan sense (just used twice in v. 14) indicating discipleship (Guelich accepts this reading). But on either reading the γραμματεῖς remain the subject of ἔλεγον in v. 16. The unusual phrase οἱ γραμματεῖς τῶν Φαρισαίων has not surprisingly been assimilated in many MSS to the familiar οἱ γραμματεῖς καὶ οἱ Φαρισαῖοι; the originality of the genitive form is indicated not only by its rarity but also by Luke's οἱ Φαρισαῖοι καὶ οἱ γραμματεῖς αὐτῶν.

16. ὅτι, following αὐτοῦ, is read only by B and a few other witnesses. It is syntactically awkward (see comments below), and is therefore accepted as the harder reading, while τί ὅτι (A and Alexandrian MSS), τί (Θ), and διὰ τί (ℵ D W etc.) are seen as corrections, the latter being an assimilation to Matthew and Luke as well as to the construction which follows in v. 18.

16. The addition of ὁ διδάσκαλος ὑμῶν in ℵ C L Δ etc. is due to assimilation to Matthew, and the second person plural form in a few minuscules to assimilation to Luke. The widespread addition of καὶ πίνει is probably also an assimilation to Luke, as well as reflecting a natural prolixity.

In this pericope the group of disciples (first referred to by that term in v. 15) is further augmented by a new recruit, in a way which is closely parallel to 1:16-20 (see the introduction to that section for the formal parallels). Hereafter there will be no further such call narratives; we are left to assume that the other members of the group were recruited in similar ways. This second call narrative, however, differs from the first not only in that the man's occupation is different, but also in that his position in society is strikingly different from that of the four fishermen. To call a τελώνης to join his group was a daringly provocative action, not only incurring the disapproval of the religious establishment, but also risking giving offence to the patriotic instincts of the common people. Jesus' disdain for the restraints which scribal convention placed on contacts with the religiously disreputable is then put beyond doubt by his going on to join a gathering of other such social outcasts in the house of this new recruit.

As in the last pericope, any suggestion that Jesus acted in ignorance or by mistake is dispelled by a direct challenge (this time spoken) from the scribes, to which again Jesus responds not with an apology but with a defence of his action: it is not only permissible for him to mix with such company; rather, it is the very purpose of his mission (with ἦλθον picking up the messianic ἐξῆλθον of 1:38). In this pericope then, as in the last, Mark allows us to see that the alienation between Jesus and the establishment is not a matter of misunderstanding or misrepresentation on the part of his opponents, but derives directly from his own deliberately chosen stance, which he has no intention of modifying in the face of their entirely predictable objections. There is a fundamental incompatibility between his agenda and theirs, as vv. 21-22 will shortly explain in graphic terms.

In this pericope, as in the previous one, there is a focus on sin and forgiveness, on exclusion and acceptance. Jesus' acceptance of the unacceptable serves not only the negative purpose of showing up the hostility and narrow exclusivism of the scribes, but also the positive purpose of indicating the revolutionary nature of the new situation in the kingdom of God. The meal where πολλοὶ τελῶναι καὶ ἁμαρτωλοὶ συνανέκειντο τῷ Ἰησοῦ καὶ τοῖς μαθηταῖς αὐτοῦ forms a vivid illustration of the inclusiveness of the new community of the forgiven, to which even, indeed especially, the most unlikely are called. It is likely that Mark saw in this rather special meal (note the implications of κατακεῖσθαι, συνανέκειντο, on which see comments below) a symbol of the messianic banquet; if so, the guest list is not at all what most Jews would have expected.

13 There is no direct narrative link with the preceding episode. This is a separate incident, though the convergence of the crowd and Jesus' continuing public teaching follow on naturally from the establishment of these motifs in all the Capernaum pericopes so far. The location is still Capernaum, as is indicated not only by the lakeshore setting but also by the presence of the τελώνιον, since Capernaum functioned as the border town between the tetrarchies of Antipas and of Philip. ἐξῆλθεν παρὰ τὴν θάλασσαν (together with παράγων, v. 14) reminds us of 1:16, where the same setting was used for the call of the first four disciples. It is not so obviously appropriate for a τελώνης as for fishermen, but a lakeside customs post would give its occupants access to travellers both by boat and by the road along the northern shore of the lake.

14 It is usually assumed that Λευί (Mark and Luke) is an alternative name for Ματθαῖος (Matthew), and that this individual is therefore the same who appears under the name Ματθαῖος in all the lists of the Twelve (and is at that point also identified as a τελώνης, Mt. 10:3). It would not be unusual for a person to have two names, whether both Semitic (Σίμων [Šimʿôn]/Πέτρος [Kēpāʾ])[17] or one Semitic and one Greek (Θωμᾶς [Tᵉʾômāʾ]/Δίδυμος). It is therefore not necessary to assume that an otherwise unknown man named Levi has been arbitrarily identified with Matthew by the first evangelist.[18] The sug-

---

17. Cf. the evidence from Nabataean inscriptions cited by Lane, 100-101 n. 29.
18. So R. Pesch, *ZNW* 59 (1968) 40-56.

gestion of Albright and Mann[19] that Levi was not so much a name as a tribal designation, 'the Levite', is unlikely in view of the common use of the name Levi at this time.[20] Taylor is attracted by the alternative reading Ἰάκωβον τὸν τοῦ Ἀλφαίου (see Textual Note), but it is hard to see how the name Levi might have been added if the original reference was to James (and Luke also has the name Levi here). That Levi/Matthew and James should each have had a father named Alphaeus is possible, though the name is not common; they may have been brothers, but in that case it is odd that they are not listed together, as the two pairs of brothers met in 1:16-20 regularly are.

The τελώνης was not a collector of the poll tax mentioned in 12:14, which was a direct Roman tax levied in Judaea since A.D. 6. In Galilee, which was not yet under direct Roman rule, a variety of taxes were levied by Antipas,[21] prominent among which were customs charged on goods in transit. It is probable that Levi was a local customs officer, perhaps working for a more powerful middleman who would be responsible to Antipas for the provincial customs revenue. The mention of πολλοὶ τελῶναι at his house (v. 15) suggests that he did not work alone, so that his abandonment of the τελώνιον did not necessarily leave it unguarded.

The account of his call is similar to that of the four fishermen, but here the verb ἀκολουθέω is used in both summons and response: it is increasingly a technical term for the disciple relationship. The narrative gives the same impression of immediate response and of reckless abandonment of the former way of life.

15 γίνεται κατακεῖσθαι αὐτόν is a Semitic turn of phrase; in 1:4 and 1:9 a Semitic ἐγένετο *(way^ehî)* was followed by a participle and an indicative verb respectively; here, as in 2:23, an infinitive supplies the real verbal content of the clause, while καὶ γίνεται serves to draw the reader's attention to this new development in the story. κατάκειμαι and κατακλίνομαι are used (like ἀνάκειμαι and ἀνακλίνομαι) specially for reclining at a meal (cf. the following συνανέκειντο). While there is no need to assume that every use of these terms denotes literally the Greek and Roman style of eating, reclining on couches around a central table, rather than the more traditionally Jewish sitting position,[22] this custom was probably quite widely followed in Palestine by this time, particularly for more formal or festive meals (and Luke calls this a δοχὴ μεγάλη). In using this more luxurious terminology, Mark may intend to hint at that greater messianic banquet which Jews expected at the end of the age.

Both αὐτόν and αὐτοῦ are potentially ambiguous. It is unlikely that both

19. W. F. Albright and C. S. Mann, *Matthew,* CLXXVII-CLXXVIII. Mann here translates Λευίν as 'the Levite'.

20. Levi appears as a name, not a tribal designation, of four (perhaps three) separate individuals in Josephus's *Life,* making it the third most common name in that work after Jesus and Simon.

21. For the taxation system in Galilee see H. Hoehner, *Herod,* 73-79; for a wider view of taxation in this period, E. Schürer, 1.372-76. See also J. R. Donahue, *CBQ* 33 (1971) 39-61.

22. See J. Jeremias, *Words,* 48-49.

refer to Levi, since then there would be no basis for the following mention of 'sitting with Jesus'. But all the other permutations are possible: Levi in Jesus' house, Jesus in Levi's house, or Jesus in his own house, joined by Levi and his friends. Since, however, Mark nowhere else refers to the house in Capernaum (which was in fact probably Simon's) as Jesus' house, it is more likely that we should understand that Jesus went to a meal in Levi's house (as indeed Luke explicitly states);[23] the offence is then not only in his company but in the place where he is seen eating.

The association of τελῶναι with ἁμαρτωλοί is found also in Mt. 11:19; Lk. 15:1 (cf. Lk. 18:10-14), and other mentions of τελῶναι in the gospels assume that they are despised as a class (Mt. 5:46; 18:17; 21:31-32 [with πόρναι]). Jewish literature supports this view of their social standing.[24] The collection system which enabled a local official to make a substantial profit by charging what he could get rather than a fixed sum inevitably led to public distrust and hatred of the profession, and the fact that they worked for an unpopular government added to their social ostracism. J. Jeremias has argued that the Jewish τελώνης, unlike the collector of the poll tax, was not obliged to enter unclean houses and therefore was not technically unclean in a ritual sense, so that to enter Levi's house put Jesus' moral standing rather than his ritual purity in question.[25] It may be doubted, however, how far most people (even most scribes?) saw this as a significant distinction.[26] It was, at any rate, company which no respectable religious teacher could keep. ἁμαρτωλοί may carry the more technical sense of those whose lack of observance of legal regulations placed them outside the 'pure' company which Pharisees kept (Mann here translates 'nonobservant Jews'), but the term is probably used in a more general sense, with the focus at least as much on moral as on ritual offence.

This is the first time Mark has used a collective noun for the members of Jesus' circle. From here on μαθητής will occur frequently in this sense. It does not relate exclusively to them, but is used equally of the adherents of John and of the Pharisees (v. 18). Its derivation from μανθάνω (and its Latin equivalent *discipulus*) may suggest a primarily intellectual bond of teacher and learner, but the usage of the term (as of the rabbinic *talmîd*) is broader than that. While Mark does not usually spell out the names and number of those he refers to as μαθηταί, so that it is not certain that he always restricts the term to the Twelve (see below on 3:13-19), it regularly denotes those who are Jesus' constant companions (ἵνα ὦσιν μετ' αὐτοῦ, 3:14), and on whose instruction and training he will increasingly concentrate, to the exclusion of the following crowds, as the narrative progresses.

23. E. S. Malbon, *NTS* 31 (1985) 282-92, argues that Jesus is entertaining the outcasts in his own house, and that Luke has deliberately changed the story to lessen Jesus' offence.

24. See J. Jeremias, *Jerusalem*, 310-12.

25. J. Jeremias, *Theology*, 110-11. See further J. R. Donahue, *CBQ* 33 (1971) 39-61.

26. R. P. Booth, *Purity*, 80-81, 110, disagrees with Jeremias's conclusion (though not in direct dialogue with him).

ἦσαν γὰρ πολλοὶ καὶ ἠκολούθουν αὐτῷ (the subject of which I take to be the same as in the preceding clause, πολλοὶ τελῶναι καὶ ἁμαρτωλοί, not the μαθηταί, as Cranfield; see also Textual Note above) is a typically Marcan piece of extra verbiage (absent from Matthew and Luke), conveying no specific new information, but heightening the scandal of Jesus' disreputable entourage. In view of the double use of ἀκολουθέω in v. 14, it is likely that Mark intends to indicate a degree of enthusiasm for Jesus similar to that which led Levi to leave the τελώνιον (though there is no indication that any of them, like Levi/Matthew, joined the travelling group of μαθηταί); here, if not among the scribes of the Pharisees, Jesus' message is falling on good soil.

16 While the expression οἱ γραμματεῖς τῶν Φαρισαίων ('Pharisee-lawyers', Mann) is unusual, it correctly represents the fact that within the larger Pharisaic party there were professional scribes, whose concern, even more than that of Pharisees in general, was to ensure correct observance of the law.[27] The basis of their objection is not spelled out, but the double mention of eating suggests that the key issue was that of purity, since it was by eating the wrong food or in the wrong place that defilement might be contracted. (It will be eating which raises the question again in the key discussion on purity in 7:1-23.) It is also true, however, that sharing a table with someone was recognised as a symbol of identification, so that the social as well as the ritual aspect of Jesus' conduct is involved. There is apparently no need to spell out the problem: it is taken for granted that to eat with τελῶναι καὶ ἁμαρτωλοί is unacceptable. The address of the objection to the disciples rather than to Jesus himself (conversely in 2:18, 23-24 it will be Jesus who is accosted with regard to the disciples' action) may indicate a reluctance for direct confrontation; cf. the silent criticism of v. 7. More likely it is a result of the narrative situation: they cannot get to Jesus himself because he is inside the house as guest of honour.

The syntax of their challenge is obscure. Assuming the reading ὅτι (see Textual Note), it may most easily be read as the common use of ὅτι to introduce direct speech. In that case the following clause may be read either as a question ('Does he eat . . . ?') or as a statement or exclamation ('He is eating . . . !'); either way it is an outraged comment on what is assumed to be an unacceptable action. It is possible, however, to read ὅτι as itself part of the utterance, and interrogative in function, as in 9:11, 28; this is an unusual use of ὅτι, occasionally found also in the LXX, and perhaps to be understood as a contraction of τί ὅτι (see BAGD, 587a-b, 4.b; BDF, 300[2]). Whatever the syntax, the note of outrage is the same.

17 Jesus' reply consists of two parts, a 'proverb' in the third person, and a first-person statement of the purpose of his mission. Both focus on the same theme, the priority of those in need: the 'proverb' makes the point metaphori-

---

27. For an interesting justification of Mark's terminology see J. W. Bowker, *Pharisees*, 40-41. For the range of differing views on the relations between scribes and Pharisees see M. J. Cook, *Treatment*, 71-72; Cook himself believes (88-91) that scribes and Pharisees were identical, though Mark did not realise this.

cally using the language of physical illness, while the second clause speaks directly of the issue of 'sin', which has been the focus not only of this pericope (τελῶναι καὶ ἁμαρτωλοί) but also of the preceding one (ἐξουσία ἀφιέναι ἁμαρτίας). Jesus' mission, no less than John's baptism, is concerned with the ἄφεσις ἁμαρτιῶν. In the rest of the gospel this theme will not be explicit, but it has been laid down so clearly at the outset that the reader is expected to bear it in mind as the background against which to interpret the later statements of Jesus' purpose, in particular the λύτρον ἀντὶ πολλῶν of 10:45 and the words about the vicarious shedding of blood in 14:24.

Plutarch quotes the exiled Spartan king Pausanias as using a similar image to v. 17a when he was asked why he had left Sparta for Tegea despite his good opinion of Spartans: οὐδ' οἱ ἰατροὶ παρὰ τοῖς ὑγιαίνουσιν ὅπου δὲ οἱ νοσοῦντες διατρίβειν εἰώθασιν, 'It is not the custom of doctors to spend their time with the healthy, but where people are ill' (*Apophth. Lacon.* 230F); there are also Greek examples of the comparison of a philosopher with a doctor, such as Diogenes' saying that as a doctor must go among the sick, so a wise man must mix with fools (Dio Chrysostom, *Orat.* 8.5). It is a natural metaphor, and we have noted above (see on v. 5) how closely physical illness and sin are related also in biblical thought. Jesus' 'proverb' therefore defends the company he keeps on the ground of the spiritual need which it is his mission to meet. It is ridiculous to imagine a doctor who refuses to meet his patients; so any effective 'healer' must expect to get his hands dirty.

The following statement makes the same point. It is not clear who the δίκαιοι are. The term is often interpreted as ironical, referring to Jesus' critics as those who, in their own view, are δίκαιοι (and therefore do not need his ministry). It would certainly be difficult to support from the gospel traditions the idea that there is in reality a class of δίκαιοι to whom Jesus' call is irrelevant, so that there is a two-tier pattern of salvation, with some being saved by their own δικαιοσύνη while others need the εὐαγγέλιον proclaimed in 1:15. But to search for an identity for the δίκαιοι is to miss the point of the sentence, with its antithetical form. Taken literally, it appears to exclude the δίκαιοι from his concern, but similar antithetical statements such as Ho. 6:6 are properly interpreted as expressions of priority rather than of exclusion.[28] In expressing the priority of the ἁμαρτωλοί Jesus contrasts them with their hypothetical opposite, but the antithesis does not therefore invite us to identify actual δίκαιοι, either then or now, any more than the form of the other ἦλθον statement in 10:45 invites us to consider who is not included in the πολλοί.

The use of καλέω invites the question 'Call to what?' In the context of a meal, it could mean 'invite', and Mann therefore sees here a reference to the guest list for the messianic banquet; but as Jesus is not the host at this meal in Levi's house, the reference would be obscure in the narrative setting. The only previous

28. For the idiom see H. Kruse, *VT* 4 (1954) 385-400. Other examples include Gn. 45:8; Ex. 16:8; 1 Sa. 8:17; Je. 7:22-23; Mk. 9:37; Jn. 12:44.

use of the verb in the gospel (1:20) is of calling into full-time discipleship, but that can hardly be the sense here, since not all those in Levi's house were to join the itinerant group. In Paul καλέω is more of a technical term for God's initiative in bringing people to salvation, but no such usage has been prepared for in Mark, nor does it occur later in the gospel. The most obvious background is Jesus' κήρυγμα in 1:14-15, where people in general are 'called' to repent and believe in the good news, just as John has previously 'called' them to a baptism of repentance for the forgiveness of sins. Against this background, and with the emphasis on sin and forgiveness which we have noticed to be central to this and the preceding pericope, the most probable interpretation of καλέσαι is that which Luke at this point makes explicit, καλέσαι εἰς μετάνοιαν. In that case Mark gives no more encouragement than Luke to the bold argument of E. P. Sanders, *Jesus,* 174-211, that Jesus' offence in the eyes of the religious establishment was not that he called sinners *to repent* (to which surely no one could object), but that he summoned them to join his movement *without repentance* (and the appropriate restitution and/or sacrifice which repentance involved). Sanders is surely right that no one could object to the repentance of sinners; but what they found unacceptable was the breach of social and religious convention into which that mission led Jesus. To that extent they stood for the maintenance of the status quo, while Jesus' determination to proclaim the good news of forgiveness where it was needed, and thus to create a new community of the forgiven, led him into conflict with it.

Old and New in Religious Observance (2:18-22)

TEXTUAL NOTES

22. The various readings all express the same idea, of the loss (destruction) of both wine and wineskins. The majority reading looks like a stylistic improvement on the B reading, with its split subject, and its use (as also D OL) of ἀπόλλυμι rather than the more natural ἐκχέω for wine; it is at the same time a harmonisation with Matthew and Luke.

22. The absence of a verb in the final clause naturally led to corrective additions, harmonising either with Matthew (βάλλουσιν) or Luke (βλητέον). The omission of the whole clause in D OL is a more drastic form of correction, which serves also to produce a more symmetrical balance with the structure of v. 21. The unharmonised reading of ℵ* B is unlikely to have been added once the other Synoptic texts were in circulation.

This is a new story, not explicitly linked in time or place with the preceding incident, but there is nonetheless a significant continuity in Mark's placing of it here. The preceding story was about feasting; this is about fasting. A religious movement which was not prepared to allow scribal convention to get in the way of the welcoming of τελῶναι καὶ ἁμαρτωλοί is not likely to accept a discipline of fasting which went far beyond what normal Jews found necessary, and which would therefore further serve to exclude those for whose sake Jesus 'came'.

The issue is addressed by a further reference to joyful feasting, in the parable of the bridegroom. The Jesus movement was characterised by celebration rather than solemnity, and it was this which some observers found hard to accept.

The objection in this case is not to any act or saying of Jesus which is deemed improper, but to his disciples' failure to conform to the practice of certain Jewish groups (the disciples of John and the Pharisees) with regard to fasting. Their practice of fasting was not a matter of obedience to explicit directions in the OT, and presumably, from the fact that it is mentioned specifically as *their* practice, was not expected of all Jews. This is, then, a question of the relative merits of different (and competing?) renewal movements within Judaism, and the challenge conveys a covert claim to superior religious fervour on the part of these other groups. The Jesus movement is not taking its religious observance seriously enough.

While the failure noted is on the part of Jesus' μαθηταί (now perceived as a unit with a clear group identity), the question is addressed to Jesus himself. It is assumed, rightly, that their behaviour is governed by Jesus as their teacher, so that he is responsible for them. His response is to refuse to compete at the level of religious observance, and to declare instead that his disciples represent a vital new perspective which supersedes the traditional patterns of religion (even in their newly developed forms). The coming of the kingdom of God is a time of joy and celebration, and Jesus' disciples are living in the light of that, though a sombre footnote in v. 20 indicates that the note of celebration is not the whole truth about the Jesus movement.

Jesus' mission is therefore shown to be different in kind from other attempts to bring new life into Jewish religious commitment. Even the movement begun by John the Baptist, which has hitherto been presented in a positive light as beginning the work which Jesus will continue (and which will continue to be seen in the same way: 6:14-16; 8:28; 11:29-33) is not on its own in the same category as the Jesus movement which had now, as John himself predicted, taken its place and moved on to a new level of fulfilment.

There is nothing in the wording of vv. 21-22 to link them directly with the discussion of fasting.[29] Their epigrammatic style could have been applied to many aspects of the tension between old and new which Jesus' ministry provoked. But they are well placed here, both in that they underline the sense of radical newness which v. 19 has expressed, and in that, placed here in the middle of the sequence of conflict stories, they sum up graphically the essence of the contrast between the κήρυγμα of Jesus and the existing norms of Jewish religious life, even in their more progressive forms. The torn cloth and the burst wineskins display more effectively than many propositional arguments why it is that Jesus had to be perceived as a destructive force rather than simply a harmless enthusiast.

---

29. Sayings parallel to these occur, in reverse order, in *Gos. Thom.* 47, without any narrative context, and linked with other sayings about incompatibility.

18   While John's baptising movement had been located in the Jordan valley to the south, Jesus was apparently not the only Galilean to have been drawn to his preaching. While some of John's followers joined Jesus (Jn. 1:35-42), others continued to follow his teaching even after his imprisonment (cf. 6:29; Mt. 11:2-3), and remained a distinct religious group for many years (Acts 18:25; 19:1-7).[30] The 'disciples' referred to here have apparently returned to normal life in Galilee, rather than continuing in a wilderness community in the area of John's baptising ministry.[31] As a 'renewal' group it is not surprising that they, like the Pharisees, adopted a more demanding code of religious observance than was followed by most Jews at the time. The only regular fast prescribed in the OT law is that of the Day of Atonement, but Zc. 8:19 indicates that by the postexilic period four additional annual fasts had come to be observed, and Est. 9:31 adds another. Other references to fasting in the OT reflect individual choice rather than a set pattern (Lk. 2:37 shows an example of this voluntary fasting in the NT period). Pharisaic religion, however, had gone far beyond the OT requirements, and the twice-weekly fast referred to in Lk. 18:12 reflects the practice of at least some Pharisees at the time of Jesus (cf. *Did.* 8:1; *b. Ta'an.* 12a).[32] It is probable that some such regular fasting discipline is in view here, and that John's disciples, following their master's ascetic lifestyle (Mt. 11:18), had adopted the Pharisaic practice.[33] The fact that it was obvious that one group was fasting and the other not offers an interesting comment on Jesus' warnings against 'visible' fasting in Mt. 6:16-18; how did they know?

The objectors are not identified. From the fact that they refer to the disciples of John and of the Pharisees[34] in the third person, we must assume that the subjects of ἔρχονται καὶ λέγουσιν are an indefinite 'they', not the fasting group themselves. The question need not necessarily be read as deliberately hostile, but rather as expressing an outsider's interest in the varying practices of the different groups. But an element of challenge, perhaps of reproach, is probably to be read into the 'Why not?'

19   Jesus' reply is not a dismissal of fasting as such; indeed, v. 20 assumes that his disciples *will* fast (for the continuation of fasting in the Christian

---

30. See C. H. H. Scobie, *John,* 187-202, for the continuing 'baptist sect'.

31. See J. E. Taylor, *John,* 28, 209; cf. 102-6 for what it meant to be a μαθητής of John.

32. For the importance of fasting in Judaism after the OT period see J. Behm, *TDNT,* 4.929-31.

33. Belo assumes, however, that this was a special occasion: 'The disciples of John . . . have joined the Pharisees in a fast, probably to petition God that he would rescue John.' This then provides added point to the metaphor of the bridegroom: *their* 'bridegroom' has already been 'taken away'.

34. The mention of 'disciples of the Pharisees' is unusual (though cf. Mt. 22:16), as there is no evidence for such a body; one either was a Pharisee or not. But it is a natural expression for members of the Pharisaic group when mentioned in parallel with the disciples of John. J. E. Taylor, *John,* 208, takes it to refer to those who tried to live by Pharisaic rules 'while not necessarily counting themselves as Pharisees proper'. See further J. W. Bowker, *Pharisees,* 38-40; K. H. Rengstorf, *TDNT,* 4.443.

138

movement cf. Mt. 6:16-18; Acts 13:2-3; 14:23). It is rather an assertion that this is not an appropriate time for them to do so. As in v. 17 a situation from ordinary life is used to show up the inappropriateness of the (supposed) objection, and a question which allows only one answer (hence the opening μή), is reinforced by a direct statement of what everyone would take for granted in the case of a wedding party. Weddings are times for festivity, not fasting.

The effectiveness of the reply depends, of course, on whether the hearers concede that the current situation for Jesus' disciples is in fact analogous to that of wedding guests (or 'groomsmen', special friends of the bridegroom; the Semitic phrase οἱ υἱοὶ τοῦ νυμφῶνος could mean either, and the point of the analogy does not turn on their identification), and Jesus himself is analogous to a bridegroom. Entry into the kingdom of God is compared to admission to a wedding feast in Mt. 22:1-14; 25:1-13 (cf. Rev. 19:7-9), and the Fourth Gospel uses the imagery of the bridegroom and his friend to express John's joy at the coming of Jesus (Jn. 3:29).[35] The wedding imagery suggests a sense of new beginnings, and of a new relationship established with the people of God, and it especially conveys the joy and exhilaration of this new situation. But the focus here (as in Jn. 3:29) falls not on the wedding but on the bridegroom; it is Jesus himself (the only plausible identification of the 'present' bridegroom) who is the source of joy. This central place in the drama of the new beginning suggests a messianic role for Jesus, even though the bridegroom was not, as far as we know, a current image for the Messiah. This verse may therefore properly be read as a veiled messianic claim. Indeed, the choice of metaphor is perhaps even more bold in the light of the frequent OT portrayal of *Yahweh* as the bridegroom of Israel, and the use of marriage imagery for his eschatological relationship with his redeemed people (Is. 61:10; 62:4-5; Ho. 2:14-20).

It may be doubted how much of this symbolism Jesus' questioners might be expected to recognise and to accept. But at the simplest level that a wedding is a time of joy, and therefore not a time for fasting, they are asked to recognise something exceptional and exciting in Jesus' ministry, and the accounts so far of popular enthusiasm suggest that they would not have found this a difficult idea to grasp. But the phrases ἐν ᾧ and ὅσον χρόνον serve notice that this time of celebration is not to last forever.[36]

20 It is often assumed (following the older view that allegory is a mark of later church interpretation, and not part of Jesus' parabolic method) that this

35. B. Lindars, *NTS* 16 (1969/70) 324-29, understands Jn. 3:29 as originally a parable of Jesus, closely parallel to Mk. 2:18-19.

36. J. E. Taylor, *John* 206-7, dissents from this 'usual interpretation', on the grounds that Mt. 6:16-18 shows that Jesus' disciples *were* expected to fast during his ministry. She suggests that the bridegroom is not here a specifically messianic metaphor, and the feasting period not the whole of Jesus' ministry, but that the reference is to a specific visit of Jesus to a certain town, where his arrival is being celebrated with a feast at a time when one of the Pharisaic fasts should have been observed. Jesus' visit to the town justifies suspending the fast; after he has moved on, they will fast as usual.

verse (and usually v. 19b) is a later 'allegorising' addition to Jesus' simple bridegroom saying, intended perhaps to legitimise the practice of fasting in the post-Easter church, but also to give early warning of the theme of the cross which will become dominant from 8:31 onwards. But the wording of v. 19 (in both halves of the verse), as we have seen, already includes the note of warning, in that the celebration lasts only while the bridegroom is present. Verse 20 therefore follows naturally as part of the same saying, and from a literary point of view should be seen as authentic. The question of Jesus' ability to foresee his 'removal' (ἀπαρθῇ suggests force rather than natural causes, and is surely intended to refer to his violent death)[37] is of course far wider than this verse. If the passion predictions of 8:31ff. are accepted as an authentic part of the tradition, there is no reason to suspect this verse on dogmatic grounds. Its more veiled character is appropriate within the scheme of Mark's gospel to the period before Caesarea Philippi. In this verse, then, Jesus asserts that just as John the Baptist has already been violently 'taken away' (hence *his* disciples' willingness to fast), so also will he be.[38]

Just how and when the disciples will fast ἐν ἐκείνῃ τῇ ἡμέρᾳ is not indicated. Even if ἀπαρθῇ is understood specifically of the cross, it would be excessive literalism to take ἐκείνη ἡ ἡμέρα as referring to Good Friday alone, and thus as justifying fasting on Fridays.[39] The reference is more generally to a coming time when the immediate excitement of Jesus' ministry will give way to a more settled style of discipleship in which fasting will take its proper place. This note of continuity, looking beyond Jesus' ministry to a following 'church age', while often attributed to post-Easter rationalisation, is coherent with the measures Jesus will take throughout the gospel to prepare his disciples for continuing mission and communal existence. The idea that Jesus' vision for the future of the movement which he began was limited to an immediate consummation in the 'coming of the Son of Man' within the current generation will be discussed below (see on 9:1; 13; 14:62).

21 The two brief 'parables' of vv. 21 and 22 are closely parallel in structure (except for the slight expansion in v. 22c), and serve equally to illustrate the folly of trying to contain the new within the confines of the old.[40] Placed here in

37. *Gos. Thom.* 104 offers a version of this saying without the note of violent removal — 'When the bridegroom comes out of the bride-chamber, then let them fast and pray.'

38. Taylor, Cranfield, and Mann, following Lohmeyer, suggest that the enigmatic ἀπαρθῇ alludes to the double use of αἴρω in Is. 53:8, thus indicating the death of the servant of Yahweh. But the allusion is not obvious: the verb is a common one, and Is. 53:8 uses not the compound verb but the simple form; moreover, the subject of αἴρω there is not in fact the servant but his κρίσις and his ζωή.

39. So, e.g., Haenchen, Schweizer, Pesch, and especially H.-W. Kuhn, *Sammlungen*, 63-71. Guelich usefully discusses the issue.

40. J. B. Muddiman in J. Dupont (ed.), *Jésus aux Origines de la Christologie*, 271-81, suggests that they are not parallel, but rather contrasted: the first represents the ministry of John the Baptist, as the 'fuller', who attempts by a penitential régime to refurbish the old religion; the second represents the joyful renewal brought by Jesus, which leaves fasting behind. The first is a parable of shrinkage, the second of expansion.

Mark's gospel, they apply to the newness of Jesus' radical message of the kingdom of God, and its incompatibility with the existing forms of religion and society, as is already being shown in Mark's story by the conflicts with representatives of the status quo into which Jesus' ministry is increasingly leading him. Both parables speak not only of incompatibility, but of the destructive results of attempting a compromise with the old.[41]

ῥάκος ἄγναφον is cloth which has not been processed by the fuller, who cleaned and combed it to remove natural oil and gum, and bleached it ready for use in making garments. The cloth was thus preshrunk, but 'unfulled' cloth was still liable to shrink when washed; hence its disastrous effect when used as a patch on an old (and therefore already shrunk) garment.[42] εἰ δὲ μή, following a negative statement, has the effect of 'but if he does' or 'otherwise'. αἴρω is a transitive verb, so an object ('something') must be understood (BAGD 24b). τὸ καινὸν τοῦ παλαιοῦ follows awkwardly after αἴρει τὸ πλήρωμα ἀπ' αὐτοῦ; it is best seen as an explanatory addition, still dependent on the verb αἴρει, indicating the application of the parable by specifying the meaning of τὸ πλήρωμα and of αὐτόν (ἱμάτιον παλαιόν).[43] The whole clause thus runs, 'The patch takes something away from it, the new from the old', a rather clumsy way of saying that the shrinking patch pulls away from the old garment, leaving a worse tear than was there originally. The unusual use of πλήρωμα for 'patch', rather than to repeat ἐπίβλημα, may just possibly be intended to convey the sense of the 'fullness' of the gospel as compared with the preceding situation (so Belo), but is more likely merely a stylistic variation.

22 An ἀσκός was made of leather, which was at first soft and pliable, but which perished and became brittle with constant use. They were then liable to burst under the pressure of fermentation if used for οἶνος νέος[44] (the first stage of fermentation was carried out in a vat, but after straining out the lees the wine was placed in jars or skins to complete the process).[45] The final clause ἀλλὰ οἶνον νέον εἰς ἀσκοὺς καινούς, reads as obvious to the point of banality if

---

41. A. Kee, *NovT* 12 (1970) 13-21, objects to the term 'incompatibility': both the old coat and the old wineskins are regarded as worth preserving; 'old' does not mean 'bad' or 'obsolete'. The actual imagery is less important, on this view, than the warning against the danger of loss through inappropriate, thoughtless action, and the message is a call to repent, lest everything be lost. P. Trudinger, *BTB* 5 (1975) 311-15, agrees that the old is valued, and that 'incompatibility' is not the point, but rejects Kee's focus on repentance, and sees the moral in the appropriate combination of new with old in discipleship and church relations.

42. *Gos. Thom.* 47 interestingly reverses the imagery: 'No one sews an old patch on a new garment.'

43. N. Turner, *Grammar*, 209 n. 1, prefers the reading of A W, which puts ἀπ' αὐτοῦ before τὸ πλήρωμα; he translates the resultant sentence, 'The new fulness takes away some of it, namely, some of the old'.

44. P. Trudinger, *BTB* 5 (1975) 311-15, argues that wineskins would be reused many times; the danger was in reusing them without first preparing them by moistening the leather.

45. *Gos. Thom.* 47 adds the converse, 'and old wine is not put into a new wineskin, lest it spoil it'. Assuming that the first 'it' is the wine and the second the wineskin, this comment seems odd after the previous sentence which declares old wine preferable to new.

taken merely as an instruction to wine makers, but its epigrammatic form suggests that it is intended rather as a slogan to guide those who have understood the point of the parable in thinking through the implications of the gospel.

Clearly the new wine (and the new cloth) represents the teaching of Jesus and the new vitality which is coming into the religious experience of those who through him are encountering God's kingship. The old skins and the old garment are, in the narrative context, the structures of the existing religious tradition, as represented especially by the Pharisees and their scribal teaching, whether in theology (the forgiveness of sins) or practice (purity of table fellowship; fasting). Attempts to contain Jesus with these constraints have already proved futile, and his followers must be prepared to break free. It would be a mistake, however, to confine the relevance of these parables only to Jesus' confrontations with the scribes and to the specific issues raised in these chapters. The principle is a broader one, as applicable to the constricting influence of Christian traditions as it is to the context of first-century Judaism.

'Lord of the Sabbath' (2:23–3:6)

TEXTUAL NOTE

2:26. The omission of ἐπὶ Ἀβιαθὰρ (τοῦ) ἀρχιερέως in D W OL sy[s] is an obvious correction both to harmonise with Matthew and Luke and to remove the embarrassment of a historical error.

While 2:23-28 and 3:1-6 are clearly two separate pericopes, they are linked together in the synoptic tradition since both deal with the same issue, that of Jesus' attitude to the sabbath law, and it seems more appropriate therefore to deal with them together here. While the final verse (3:6) concludes the story of the healing in the synagogue, it also serves to underline the cumulative effect of Jesus' radical pronouncements in the two sabbath pericopes, and more generally of his controversial words and actions throughout this section of the gospel. What began as unspoken misgivings on the part of the scribes has become a formulated plan to eliminate Jesus as a threat to both religious (Pharisees) and political (Herodians) interests. Jesus and his followers are now clearly perceived by those in power as a new and subversive movement.

The observance of the sabbath was one of the principal distinguishing marks of the Jews as the people of God (sabbath and circumcision were the two most obvious such 'badges'), and as such was promoted and defended with more than merely pietistic zeal. It was a matter of national pride. The pious Jews who resisted the demands of Antiochus Epiphanes had at first been prepared to die rather than desecrate the sabbath by fighting in self-defence, though more pragmatic counsels soon prevailed (1 Macc. 2:29-41). The *Book of Jubilees,* written around the same period, enthusiastically promotes the sabbath (which even God and the angels observed in heaven before it was known on earth: *Jub.* 2:18, 30), and continues to insist on the death penalty for those who break it (*Jub.* 50:8, 13; cf. Ex. 31:14-15).

While the principle of sabbath observance was agreed upon by all Jews, problems arose over what this meant in practice. The OT offered the positive principles that the day was to be holy (with special prescribed sacrifices), and that it was to be a time of rest, together with the negative corollary that no work should be done on it. It was on this negative aspect that debate centred. What was 'work'? While the OT contains several illustrations of sabbath prohibitions (Ex. 16:22-30; 34:21; 35:2-3; Nu. 15:32-36; Ne. 10:31; 13:15-22; Je. 17:21-22), these did not add up to a comprehensive definition of 'work', and the need for a fuller definition was soon felt. The *Book of Jubilees* concludes with a more detailed list of sabbath prohibitions (*Jub.* 50:6-13), and a different list occurs in the *Damascus Document* of Qumran (CD 10:14–11:18). The process of definition continued within mainstream Judaism, and the Pharisees developed it into a luxuriant growth of halakhic case law, ultimately codified in the Mishnah; while the detailed codification belongs to the end of the second century, there is no reason to doubt that its material represents in principle the interpretations of sabbath law already accepted (at least by Pharisees) in the early first century. The intention is to leave nothing to chance, but by legislating for every circumstance to protect the faithful from ever breaking the prohibition on sabbath work. At its heart lies the list of thirty-nine prohibited acts in *m. Šab.* 7:2[46] (which include 'reaping', hence the objection in 2:24), but these in turn are then worked out in terms of specific situations and eventualities. The last of the thirty-nine proves a particularly comprehensive prohibition: 'taking anything from one place to another'. The result was the lengthy Mishnaic tractate *Šabbāt* (together with the almost equally lengthy *'Erubin,* offering elaborate ways to alleviate legally some of the more inconvenient sabbath restrictions). Intentional breaking of the sabbath remains a capital offence (*m. Sanh.* 7:4).[47]

It is against this background that we must understand the conflicts which arose between Jesus and the Pharisees over the sabbath. It is not that there was no room for debate and for development of the sabbath halakhah; debate was still continuing even within Pharisaism (not to mention the more stringent interpretations of Qumran). The problem appears to be that Jesus did not debate, but simply brushed aside the whole complex of sabbath prohibitions with sweeping generalisations which seemed to make the whole discussion unnecessary. There is no indication that Jesus either rejected the sabbath law as such, or questioned that the sabbath was intended as a day of cessation from work. But his understanding of what was and was not permissible did not coincide with current interpretation, and yet was asserted with a sovereign assurance which raised sharply the issue of halakhic authority.

46. There is a different list of fifteen prohibited acts in *m. Beṣah* 5:2.
47. For a convenient survey of the rules for sabbath observance see Schürer, 2.467-75.

In 2:23-28 that question is directly in focus: David's authority to override a legal prohibition is taken as the basis of Jesus' approval of the 'unorthodox' action of his disciples, and the concluding pronouncement that κύριός ἐστιν ὁ υἱὸς τοῦ ἀνθρώπου καὶ τοῦ σαββάτου deliberately makes the issue one of his personal authority. But each pericope also contains a general pronouncement in positive terms about the purpose of the sabbath which breathes a different atmosphere from that of halakhic regulation: τὸ σάββατον διὰ τὸν ἄνθρωπον ἐγένετο, καὶ οὐχ ὁ ἄνθρωπος διὰ τὸ σάββατον (2:27); ἔξεστιν τοῖς σάββασιν ἀγαθὸν ποιῆσαι ἢ κακοποιῆσαι; (3:4). While few could object in theory to the notion that the sabbath exists to benefit people (after all, it is repeatedly declared to be a day of joy) and is a time for 'doing good', to make such broad principles the basis for the decision on what is and is not permissible is to threaten to overturn the whole halakhic process.

23 For the construction καὶ ἐγένετο . . . παραπορεύεσθαι see on v. 15. The scene is probably still to be envisaged as close to Capernaum, to judge by the return to the synagogue (3:1) and the lakeshore (3:7). The σπόριμα would be fields probably of wheat or barley, the latter being ripe in April/May, the former a few weeks later. The season is thus early summer, but there is too little indication of a chronological arrangement in Mark's gospel to allow us to use this fact as the basis for a chronology of Jesus' ministry (cf. the use sometimes made of χλωρὸς χόρτος in 6:39 to indicate another springtime). The expression ὁδὸν ποιεῖν τίλλοντες is strange, since it is the plucking, not the travelling, which is usually thought to be the dominant idea. To read the participle as subordinate would suggest the ludicrous idea that they were clearing a path through the corn *by* plucking ears, which would be not only very ineffective, but also far in excess of the licence allowed in Dt. 23:25 to 'pluck the ears with your hand, but not put a sickle to your neighbour's standing grain' (for the *pe'ah* legislation which probably underlies this provision see Lv. 19:9-10; 23:22).[48] Presumably Mark means that, as the law allowed, they were plucking ears as they went, but he has expressed it awkwardly.[49]

24 The objection, as in v. 18, is not to what Jesus is doing but to his disciples' behaviour, which is assumed to have his approval.[50] There the objectors

48. See M. Casey, *Sources,* 140-43 for the *pe'ah* regulations and the way they may be reflected in this narrative.

49. It is sometimes suggested that ὁδὸν ποιεῖν is a Latinism, from *iter facere;* but this does not explain the odd reversal of the infinitive and participle. J. D. M. Derrett, *Studies,* 1.87-95, suggests that Mark intends us to envisage the disciples asserting Jesus' royal status by deliberately 'creating a road' for him through someone's field, as later Jewish law allowed the king to do (*m. Sanh.* 2:4); they did so on the sabbath so as to reach their destination by a shortcut, thus avoiding exceeding the limit for travel on the sabbath. If this is what Mark intended, he has left it very obscure, in that τίλλοντες τοὺς στάχυας, rather than breaking down the plants, would be an odd way to create a road! Equally imaginative is the suggestion of H. C. Waetjen, *Reordering,* 93, that while Jesus himself was 'scrupulously following a path', the disciples 'are trampling into the grain seemingly to do more extensive reaping'.

50. D. Daube, *NTS* 19 (1972/3) 1-15, offers some interesting reflections on 'Responsibilities of Master and Disciples'.

were not identified, but here, where it is a matter of sabbath observance, it is very properly the Pharisees who notice a breach of the agreed regulations. The objection is not to the plucking of someone else's corn in itself, for which the law made explicit provision, but that this falls within the classes of work prohibited on the sabbath, presumably as reaping (though Luke's addition of ψώχοντες ταῖς χερσίν also suggests another of the thirty-nine prohibited acts, viz., threshing); harvesting on the sabbath is expressly forbidden in Ex. 34:21. It is of course possible that Mark's odd expression ἤρξαντο ὁδὸν ποιεῖν τίλλοντες (see on v. 23) is intended to focus attention on the distance they were proposing to walk, rather than on the 'reaping', and that the objection is therefore to their exceeding the permitted limits of sabbath travel (just over one kilometre), but in that case one would expect Jesus himself to be included in the charge; it would also make the mention of the cornfields and the plucking of the grain otiose. The Pharisees do not specify in what way the sabbath regulations are being broken, nor does Jesus argue the point.

25 Jesus' reply consists rather of an appeal to Scripture for a precedent for doing, and authorising others to do, ὃ οὐκ ἔξεστιν. For a similar use of οὐκ ἀνέγνωτε (sc. Scripture) in controversy with religious leaders cf. 12:10, 26; whatever the rulings of subsequent halakhah, the authority of Scripture is assumed to be primary, and Jesus, in good rabbinic fashion,[51] poses a contrary scriptural text (1 Sa. 21:1-6).

The relevance of the text to the specific issue raised is not immediately obvious (other than that it relates a previous breach of the law, which is hardly in itself justification for a further infringement!). David acted as he did ὅτε χρείαν ἔσχεν καὶ ἐπείνασεν, but Mark (unlike Matthew) has not indicated any particular need on the part of Jesus and his disciples. Nor does either the account in 1 Sa. 21 or Jesus' summary of it mention that David did this on the sabbath, though this is a fair inference from the mention in 1 Sa. 21:6 of the removal and replacement of the bread, which was a sabbath duty (Lv. 24:8). The nature of the 'illegality' in David's case, using for himself and his men sacred food which was reserved to the use of priests, was not directly comparable to what Jesus' disciples were doing. The question is not in any case whether the specific action could or could not be declared legitimate; it was rather, as vv. 27-28 will make clear, whether Jesus had the right to override the agreed conventions, in his capacity as κύριος τοῦ σαββάτου. The focus of the scriptural allusion is not therefore so much on what David did, as on the fact that it was David who did it, and that Scripture records his act, illegal as it was, with apparent approval. The logic of Jesus' argument therefore implies a covert claim to a personal authority at least as great as that of David. Matthew has clearly under-

---

51. While the citing of contrary texts was normal rabbinic style, D. Cohn-Sherbok, *JSNT* 2 (1979) 31-41, has pointed out that Jesus' argument here is not valid according to rabbinic standards of proof; in particular, a haggadah such as 1 Sa. 21:1-6 cannot be used to establish halakhah (cf. D. Daube, *The NT*, 67-71). Cohn-Sherbok suggests that Jesus' misuse of the form of rabbinic argument served to provoke the hostility of the Pharisees.

stood the pericope in that way, and includes a parallel argument from the 'defilement of the sabbath' by the priests in pursuing their temple duties, on the grounds that τοῦ ἱεροῦ μεῖζόν ἐστιν ὧδε (Mt. 12:6; cf. the similar formula in 12:41, 42). The logic of the argument from David implies a parallel τοῦ Δαυὶδ μεῖζόν ἐστιν ὧδε, and the argument in Mark, with its climax in v. 28, is best understood on the same lines. The double mention of David's companions as also involved in his action (even though the story in 1 Sa. 21 leaves room for doubt whether David's companions are more than a convenient fiction on his part) is also relevant to the present context, since it provides a precedent for the principle that the disciples' action (to which objection has been made in the first place) is covered by the personal authority of their leader.

26   1 Sa. 21:1-9 does not say explicitly that David entered the οἶκος τοῦ θεοῦ (a sanctuary at Nob, perhaps the temporary location of the tabernacle), nor is there any indication that he went where he as a layman should not. But his arrival worried the priest, and the whole story reads as a rather cavalier overruling of the priest's scruples. Mark's inclusion of the clause εἰσῆλθεν εἰς τὸν οἶκον τοῦ θεοῦ therefore perhaps represents the irregularity of the situation portrayed in the OT account. The name of the priest, however, does not correspond; 1 Sa. 21:1-9 names him as Ahimelech, who was the father of the Ἀβιαθάρ who features prominently in David's subsequent story. There was apparently some confusion over these names, since Abiathar generally appears as David's priest along with Zadok, and yet the lists in 2 Sa. 8:17; 1 Ch. 24:6 give 'Ahimelech son of Abiathar' as priest along with Zadok. Mark seems to share that confusion; Abiathar was presumably there at the time (cf. 1 Sa. 22:20 for his subsequent escape from Nob), but he was not yet ἀρχιερεύς.[52] For the regulations for the showbread see Ex. 25:30; Lv. 24:5-9.

27   The absence of this verse from Matthew and Luke is intriguing. Did they find it too sweeping and radical in its implications for halakhic authority, an early adumbration of 'Situation Ethics'? It is certainly possible to read the phrase οὐχ ὁ ἄνθρωπος διὰ τὸ σάββατον as a literal rejection of all obligation to observe sabbath restrictions, and thus interpret it is an extremely radical pronouncement, in direct conflict with a central tenet of the law and of Jewish self-

---

52. Appeal is sometimes made in the interests of historical accuracy to alternative understandings of ἐπί with the genitive; it has been rendered 'in the lifetime of', thus offering the sense 'in the lifetime of Abiathar [who later became well known as] the High Priest', but this is unnatural when the holder of an office is mentioned (cf. Lk. 3:2; Acts 11:28, where the reference is to the tenure of office of the men mentioned, not to their lifetime; in Lk. 4:27 the reference is to the period of Elisha's prophetic activity, rather than to his lifetime); alternatively appeal has been made to the usage in 12:26, ἐπὶ τοῦ βάτου, 'in the passage about the bush', but it is not obvious in what sense 1 Sa. 21:1-9 could be regarded as belonging to a section of Scripture entitled 'Abiathar the High Priest'. It can be safely assumed that had it not been for the historical problem no one would have queried the obvious meaning, 'when Abiathar was High Priest'. M. Casey, *Sources*, 151, suggests that Mark's Greek derives from an Aramaic original which he reconstructs as 'in the days of Abiathar — a great/chief priest!' (139): the Aramaic referred to his lifetime, but Mark's Greek has mistakenly made it refer to his period of office ('a normal mistake in a bilingual').

consciousness. But here, as in the similar antithesis of v. 17, we see the danger of reading the negative as an absolute exclusion, whereas the pronouncement as a whole, with its two balancing components, is a statement of priority rather than of mutually exclusive options.

Or did Matthew and Luke disapprove of its anthropocentric tone, in the light of the OT view of the sabbath as deriving from the pattern of God's own activity (Ex. 20:11) and the later elaboration which made it an antecedent heavenly ordinance (*Jub.* 2:18, 30)? But if ἐγένετο is read not so much as a statement of historical origin as of purpose, v. 27a has good OT support, in that sabbath rest is for the benefit of workers (Dt. 5:14-15), and is presented not as a burden but as a blessing, a 'delight' (Is. 58:13), an emphasis which later Judaism preserved (*b. Šab.* 119a; *b. Pes.* 68b; cf. E. Lohse, *TDNT,* 7.15-16), as indeed it still does. When the negative element overwhelms the positive, as it has done repeatedly in the observance of the Christian Sunday as well as of the Jewish sabbath, something important has been lost. It is this sense of priority which Jesus' epigram as a whole is designed to promote. So understood, it is neither against the sabbath law nor out of keeping with at least one strand in Jewish thought, as represented by the rabbinic saying quoted in *Mek.* Ex. 31:14; *b. Yom.* 85b: 'The sabbath is delivered to you [Israel], and not you to the sabbath.'

28 For the meaning of ὁ υἱὸς τοῦ ἀνθρώπου see on v. 10. Here, even more strongly than there, a case has been made for a generic sense, since the preceding verse has not only been talking about ἄνθρωπος in general terms, but has also declared the priority of the interests of ἄνθρωπος in relation to sabbath observance. To declare ἄνθρωπος in general to be κύριος τοῦ σαββάτου would seem to be a logical conclusion, and might seem to cohere appropriately with the rabbinic view just quoted that 'The sabbath is delivered to you'. There is, however, a difference between that formulation or v. 27 and the implication of sovereignty in the term κύριος, and it is highly questionable whether either the rabbis or Jesus himself would have been prepared to declare humanity in general as κύριος of an institution which the OT describes as distinctively Yahweh's (see below). Moreover, the sabbath was given specifically to Israel, not to people in general.

But in any case the same problem arises here as in 2:10, that Mark and his readers lived in a Christian context where ὁ υἱὸς τοῦ ἀνθρώπου (singular; contrast 3:28) could have only one meaning, and that was as a title of Jesus; even if a generic sense might have been present in the original saying, it is inconceivable that Mark could have intended, or expected his readers to understand, a different sense for the phrase in this case. This is the more obvious when the saying is seen in the context of the whole pericope, which has been focused not on the rights of humanity in general, but on what *Jesus* is allowing his disciples to do, and the authority by which he does so. The argument from David's action, it has been suggested above, is not that what David could do anyone could do, but that what David could do because he was David was a valid precedent for the authority of someone greater than David. It is precisely as the Son of Man, therefore, that Jesus (and not just anybody else) is κύριος καὶ τοῦ σαββάτου.[53] Undoubtedly this is how both Matthew and Luke have understood the saying, since neither of them precedes it by τὸ σάββατον διὰ τὸν ἄνθρωπον ἐγένετο, and in Matthew the argument for the unique authority of the Son of Man arises directly out of the presence of one who is τοῦ ἱεροῦ μεῖζον. We can speculate on whether the saying originated in a context which allowed it to be understood generically; but its meaning in the text of Mark is clearly christological.

The phrase κύριος τοῦ σαββάτου is not presented as a stock phrase, still less a recognised title; if such a 'title' had been used, it would presumably have been with reference to Yahweh, who decreed the keeping of the sabbath, and in whose honour it was observed; note the OT phrases, 'a sabbath of/to Yahweh' (Ex. 16:25; 20:10; Dt. 5:14), '*my* sabbaths' (Ex. 31:13; Lv. 19:3, 30; Ezk. 20:12-13, etc.). Here, however, the concept represents yet another escalation in the unique ἐξουσία exercised by Jesus: he is being progressively revealed as κύριος in his teaching and action, in relation to spiritual powers and physical illness, in the declaration of the forgiveness of sins, and now even (καί) in relation to that most sacred of divine institutions, the sabbath. The christological stakes could hardly be pitched higher than this. Once again, the 'messianic secret' is strained to the limits.

This is the first use in Mark of κύριος (except representing the divine name when quoted from the LXX, 1:3). Its relatively few uses in Mark are usually with reference to God, and the only places where it may possibly be interpreted as a christological title are 11:3 (unlikely; see the commentary ad loc.) and 12:35-37, where it occurs in an 'academic' debate on Messiahship. Here its use is not titular, but in the normal lexical sense of the one who is in a position of superior authority.

3:1 The second sabbath incident is not inherently connected with the first, but the narrative sequence allows us to assume that Jesus and his disciples returned from their controversial walk through the cornfields outside the town to attend the synagogue service of that same sabbath. In that case, and assuming that the same Pharisees who had objected to the disciples' action are now also in the synagogue, the atmosphere is already charged, and the 'watching' of Jesus (παρετήρουν, v. 2) is not out of neutral interest, but, as the sequel shows clearly, marks a hostile search for further evidence of Jesus' unorthodox stance with regard to the sabbath. Jesus' annoyance (v. 5) is thus not the result of this incident alone, but cumulative.

---

53. Guelich stresses the ὥστε with which v. 28 begins, and insists that this verse must therefore derive its force from v. 27, and not from the earlier part of the pericope. It is questionable whether such a tight logical link need be sought. But it may perhaps be found in the use of ἄνθρωπος in the two sayings: if the sabbath exists for the benefit of ὁ ἄνθρωπος, its use may appropriately be regulated by the one who, as ὁ υἱὸς τοῦ ἀνθρώπου, represents and acts for humanity, and more particularly for Israel, to whom the sabbath law was given.

This is presumably again the synagogue at Capernaum: πάλιν suggests as much, and no indication has been given since 2:1 of a change in Jesus' centre of operations. That congregation has already witnessed a remarkable display of Jesus' ἐξουσία, not only in teaching but also in controlling a demon (1:21-28). That incident, together with the post-sabbath healings which had followed it (1:29-34) and the memorable incident with the lame man (2:1-12), has prepared the ground for the expectation of a further display of power — and of Jesus' lack of concern for sabbath regulations. The previous synagogue incident had, of course, also been on a sabbath (1:21), but the issue of sabbath law had not then been raised, perhaps because a command to a demon did not qualify as 'work' in the same way as a physical healing, but also because the question of Jesus' orthodoxy in this matter was not yet at issue. Now it is, and in this pericope the physical healing as such is overshadowed by the question of sabbath observance.

The potential patient is introduced in words similar to 1:23, but whereas in that case the demon took the initiative with a verbal challenge to Jesus, here it is Jesus who apparently takes the initiative by summoning the man in v. 3. Since a χεὶρ ἐξηραμμένη was presumably a long-term condition (paralysed as the result of polio or of a stroke? cf. 1 Ki. 13:4),[1] it is not clear why this man should be specially singled out on this occasion, or why it should be expected that Jesus should heal him on the sabbath, but in some way he is recognised by both Jesus and the Pharisees as a test case for Jesus' sabbath practice.

2 παρετήρουν has no expressed subject (as in 2:18), but the preceding pericope, and the specification that it was Φαρισαῖοι who went out to plot with Ἡρῳδιανοί (see on v. 6) against Jesus, indicates that the focus of the hostile attention was Pharisaic, even though no doubt the whole congregation was aware of the tension of the situation. It was the Pharisees who, after the confrontation in the cornfield, would be eager ἵνα κατηγορήσωσιν αὐτοῦ.

The assumption that to heal on the sabbath was culpable is clearly supported in rabbinic literature. While healing is not mentioned as such in the lists of prohibited acts in *m. Šab.* 7:2; *m. Beṣah* 5:2 (it is not, after all, part of normal work for most people), it is assumed rather than argued that healing is prohibited, the only exception being when there is reason to believe that life is in danger, so that to postpone healing until the next day would risk death. *M. Yom.* 8:6 sums up the principle: 'If a man has a pain in his throat they may drop medicine into his mouth on the sabbath, since there is doubt whether life is in danger, and whenever there is doubt whether life is in danger this overrides the sabbath.' Assistance in childbirth was also allowed, presumably because it could not wait (*m. Šab.* 18:3). See further E. Lohse, *TDNT,* 7.14-15; Str-B, 1.623-29. But a

---

1. See, however, M. Casey, *Sources,* 176-78, for the view that the complaint should not be understood as 'normally incurable', but as the sort of condition a traditional healer would be expected to cure, so that the incident does not focus on any miraculous power of Jesus, but only on whether he would heal on the sabbath.

paralysed hand could hardly be classed as an immediate threat to life. If any-thing like the Mishnaic understanding of sabbath law was already recognised (and v. 2 presupposes that it was), for Jesus to heal this man on the sabbath would be a deliberate violation of the accepted code.

3 In the command ἔγειρε εἰς τὸ μέσον we see again how partial the mo-tif of secrecy is in Mark's gospel. There is no attempt at privacy, no delay of the healing until a less public occasion when the issue of sabbath observance would not have been raised. Jesus is determined to force the issue by a public display both of his healing power and of his status as κύριος τοῦ σαββάτου.

4 In Matthew at this point (12:11-12) and in Luke on two other occa-sions when the issue of sabbath healing was raised (Lk. 13:15; 14:5) Jesus ar-gues from the principle accepted by the Pharisees (but not at Qumran, CD 11:13-14) that relief of animal suffering is permissible, within certain limits, on the sabbath; how much more then human suffering? In Mark this analogical ar-gument is not used, but simply the broad statement of principle, in the form of a rhetorical question (perhaps intended to echo the essential Deuteronomic choice, 'life and good, death and evil', Dt. 30:15), that ἀγαθὸν ποιῆσαι and ψυχὴν σῶσαι are permissible on the sabbath. There is, as often in Jesus' sayings, an element of exaggeration to make the point: to delay healing by one day would not be actually κακοποιῆσαι, still less ἀποκτεῖναι. As in 2:17, 27 the neg-ative functions as a foil to highlight the positive claim: the sabbath is a time for doing good, particularly for the relief of suffering. This positive aim is assumed to override the definitions of 'work' which scribal ingenuity had devised. To-gether with the principle enunciated in 2:27 (τὸ σάββατον διὰ τὸν ἄνθρωπον ἐγένετο), this verse establishes a positive approach to sabbath observance which is in principle so elastic that it will be hard to rule out any act which is not in itself unacceptable. Certainly, it leaves no scope for the rabbinic enter-prise of building a fence around the sabbath law.

The silence of Jesus' critics may be attributed simply to unwillingness to be drawn into an unprofitable argument, but also, as in 11:33, to the astute form of Jesus' question: to answer in the affirmative would be to undermine their whole approach to the sabbath and the basis of their objections to Jesus, but to answer in the negative would be not only impossible in itself (who could defend κακοποιῆσαι ἢ ἀποκτεῖναι, whether on the sabbath or on any day?), but also un-likely to win favour with the synagogue congregation as a whole. (It is ironical that the pericope will in fact finish with these same objectors plotting, presum-ably still on the sabbath, to take life, v. 6.)

5 For the double mention of Jesus' emotion cf. 1:41, 43. Here again it is Mark alone who includes this note in the story. This time, however, there is a discernible cause for Jesus' anger, so that no MSS give evidence of embarrass-ment by omitting or altering μετ' ὀργῆς, as happened with ὀργισθείς in 1:41. In-deed, Mark goes on to spell out the reason, in the πώρωσις τῆς καρδίας αὐτῶν. This phrase is almost a stock expression in the NT for those who cannot or will not perceive the truth, used most commonly with reference to Israel's failure to recognise Jesus as their Messiah (Rom. 11:7, 25; 2 Cor. 3:14; Jn. 12:40, citing Is. 6:10), but on two other occasions by Mark to describe the disciples' failure to appreciate the significance of Jesus' miracles (6:52; 8:17). If the καρδία, the seat of mental discernment and spiritual insight, is hardened (πωρόω derives from the concretion of minerals to form stone or of bone tissue to form a callus) it cannot function properly to accept new insight. Jesus' critics are 'set in their ways', and their insensitivity (or 'obdurate stupidity', Mann) both hurts (συλλυπούμενος) and angers him.[2]

The cure itself is so briefly narrated in the form of a command and response as to sound almost perfunctory. As a cure it was no more remarkable than others already narrated; it was the situation which made it worth special mention. It may be significant that no touch or other act is mentioned, only a word; if this was 'work', it was of a very nonphysical variety.

6 The Φαρισαῖοι have featured in each of the three preceding conflict stories (2:16, 18, 24), and the assumption that it was again they who were watching Jesus' actions in the synagogue ἵνα κατηγορήσωσιν αὐτοῦ (v. 2) is here confirmed by their going out (from the synagogue, presumably) to make plans against him. But their association with the Ἡρῳδιανοί is unexpected. The two groups will be associated again in 12:13, again with hostile intentions towards Jesus. The Greek term Ἡρῳδιανός follows a standard Latin form to denote the supporters or adherents of a leading figure (other examples of the form in Greek are Καισαριανός, Χριστιανός); Josephus uses similar terms, οἱ Ἡρῴδειοι (*War* 1.319), οἱ τὰ Ἡρῴδου φρονοῦντες (*Ant.* 14.451) to refer to those who supported Herod the Great, but in Galilee at this time they must have been supporters of Herod Antipas. The surprise sometimes occasioned by the combination of what appear to be religious (Φαρισαῖοι) and political (Ἡρῳδιανοί) interests depends on a very modern ideological separation of religion from politics. The Herod family controlled the appointment of High Priests before A.D. 6 and after A.D. 37; since most of those selected were from the house of Boethus (as opposed to the Sadducees who held the office under direct Roman patronage A.D. 6-37), it has been plausibly suggested that the Ἡρῳδιανοί were in fact the Boethusians.[3] If so, their religious interests were certainly not identical with those of the Pharisees, but their cooperation in order to silence a radical religious reformer is no more surprising than that of the various factions of the Sanhedrin in the arrest and trial of Jesus (see on 8:31). It

---

2. Schweizer, however, understands συλλυπέω here as 'to feel sympathy for', and thus translates 'Jesus was angry as he looked around at them, but at the same time he felt sorry for them, because they were so stubborn and wrong'. Stock similarly speaks of 'a godly sorrow for men who could no longer rejoice in the tokens of God's goodness to his creatures'.

3. For a full discussion, espousing this view, see H. Hoehner, *Herod*, 331-42. B. D. Chilton, *JSNT* 14 (1982) 104, identifies the Herodians with the Bene Bathyra, a group of rabbinic teachers whose 'prominent place in the Temple administration made them a power to be reckoned with in Jerusalem and beyond as chief partisans of the Herodian settlement'. See also N. Hillyer, *DNTT*, 3.441-43.

must be remembered, too, that it will be their leader Antipas who executes Jesus' predecessor John (6:17-28), an act in which Jesus sees an adumbration of his own fate (9:12-13).[4]

It is not likely that we should take συμβούλιον ἐδίδουν (a unique idiom, for which most MSS substitute the more familiar ποιέω) too strictly as 'adopting a plan' in the sense of a formulated strategy for bringing Jesus to trial and death; the succeeding narrative does not suggest anything so definite at this stage, but rather last-minute measures by the Jerusalem authorities at the final Passover (14:1-2, 10-11), following a further resolution to 'destroy' Jesus in 11:18. Here we have an agreement in principle that Jesus is to be opposed and, when the time is ripe, silenced. If the agreement is that he is wilfully breaking the sabbath, capital punishment properly follows (Ex. 31:14-15; *m. Sanh.* 7:4). The reader is thus enabled to put more substance into Jesus' enigmatic hint about the 'removal' of the bridegroom (2:20), and to envisage more concretely the two contrasting reactions to Jesus which will form the framework for the narrative and discourse of chapters 3–4, the rejoicing of the wedding guests and the plotting of those who are determined to 'destroy' the bridegroom.

WIDE RECOGNITION OF
JESUS' AUTHORITY TO HEAL (3:7-12)

TEXTUAL NOTE

7-8. This long and complex sentence has caused problems to copyists, and the readings listed represent a variety of ways of construing or simplifying it. The difficulties arise from the repetition of πολὺ πλῆθος in all but W, a few OL, and sy[s]; and from the two verbs describing the response, ἠκολούθησεν (-ησαν; -οῦν) (omitted by D *f*[13] OL) and ἦλθον πρὸς αὐτόν, leaving various options for grouping the six geographical locations listed as the place of origin of the crowds. The various permutations make little difference to the sense. One significant variation, however, is the omission of καὶ ἀπὸ τῆς Ἰδουμαίας in ℵ* W Θ *f*[1] etc., owing perhaps to the unfamiliarity of the location, or to disapproval of adherents from this source (see commentary ad loc.), but more likely either accidental in the course of a list of other locations beginning with I (thus Θ and *f*[1] omit Ἰουδαίας in v. 7 and have it instead in place of Ἰδουμαίας) or an assimilation to Matthew, who does not mention Idumaea.

This is the longest of Mark's summaries of the impact of Jesus' ministry. It does not arise directly out of its immediate context (unlike 1:32-34, 39) but is a relatively self-contained overview which could have been inserted at almost any point in the Galilean narrative. In this position it serves (1) to provide a contrast

4. In view of the lack of other references to Ἡρῳδιανοί, W. J. Bennett, *NovT* 17 (1975) 9-14, suggests that there was no group of this name, but that Mark has invented them to link the fate of Jesus with that of John the Baptist.

to the growing sense of opposition and conflict by reminding us that Jesus remains overwhelmingly popular; (2) to fill out the impression of the range of different reactions to Jesus' ministry which Mark is building up in preparation for the discussion of the issue in chapter 4; (3) to provide the context for the selection of twelve followers as Jesus' special companions in distinction from the larger crowd of enthusiasts.[5]

Here, as in the other lengthy summary still to come in 6:53-56, the focus is exclusively on Jesus' miraculous deeds (ὅσα ἐποίει, v. 8) as the basis of his popularity, rather than on his teaching, which we have seen to be from Mark's point of view an essential, if not the most important, component in Jesus' total ministry in Galilee. It is not that Jesus' ministry has changed: in 4:1-2 we will see him still teaching large and enthusiastic crowds. But Mark is enough of a realist to recognise that it was primarily the hope of physical and spiritual deliverance which motivated the crowds to gather from far afield. They have not come out of pure disinterested concern to hear the message of the kingdom of God, but to witness and to benefit from his power in healing (v. 10) and exorcism (vv. 11-12).

7-8 The lakeshore has been the scene of the calling of the first disciples (1:16; 2:13) and a favoured place for public teaching (2:13), as it will continue to be in 4:1-2. In contrast with the synagogue (3:1-6) it offers a neutral area, where Jesus can operate freely, unrestricted by either limits of space or official disapproval. Mark's verb ἀναχωρέω may convey this sense of 'tactical withdrawal', as it does in its more frequent use in Matthew (4:12; 12:15; 14:13; 15:21, each following indications of opposition and danger); thus Belo translates 'took refuge by the sea'. But as this is Mark's only use of the verb, it is hard to be sure; it would equally well convey the sense of getting away from the crowds, though if so the attempt was strikingly unsuccessful.

Mark uses πλῆθος only in these two verses; qualified by πολύ, it is a more dramatic term than the more common ὄχλος. Verbs following such collective nouns are normally singular in Mark, but sense sometimes triumphs over strict grammar, hence the plural ἀκούοντες . . . ἦλθον in v. 8. Many MSS have made ἠκολούθησεν into a plural in order to remove this anomaly, but the same phenomenon will occur in 4:1, where ὄχλος will govern both singular and plural verbs.[6] The use of two verbs, ἠκολούθησεν and ἦλθον πρὸς αὐτόν, has the effect of separating the Galilean crowd (who were already present to 'follow' him) from those from the more distant regions (who have first to 'come to him'). The difference of verb reflects their geographical location rather than any distinction in the degree of their commitment.

5. See L. E. Keck, *JBL* 84 (1965) 342-45, for an argument that this pericope is not, as often suggested, the introduction to a new section of the gospel, but rather the conclusion to the first main section, which Keck understands to begin at 1:16. It seems more satisfactory to regard it as a bridge passage.

6. ὄχλος takes a plural verb again in 9:15, and the verbs and pronouns in dependent clauses referring back to ὄχλος are always plural in Mark; see below pp. 165-66 and n. 34.

The geographical area indicated is surprisingly wide, since Mark has not hitherto given any indication of any impact outside Galilee (1:28). Judaea and Jerusalem would be a natural extension, especially in view of the interest aroused in those areas already by the preaching of John the Baptist (1:5), but the other regions are more surprising. Ἰδουμαία is mentioned nowhere else in the NT. While the name is used for Edom in the LXX, by the first century it applied to the area south of Judaea (the Negev), which had been settled by Edomites from across the Arabah, who were then forced by the Maccabees to accept Judaism. Politically it was by this time part of Judaea, but Jews regarded its population as at best part-Jewish (hence some of the unpopularity of the Herod family, descended from the Idumaean, Antipater). πέραν τοῦ Ἰορδάνου probably refers to Peraea (Josephus uses the same term for Peraea, *Ant.* 12.222), which together with Galilee made up Antipas's territory; Peraea was Jewish (as opposed to the Hellenistic Decapolis which occupied the more northerly part of Transjordan). περὶ Τύρον καὶ Σιδῶνα indicates the Phoenician area to the north of Galilee, to which Jesus will travel in 7:24; this was from the Jewish point of view pagan, Gentile territory, though it was closely linked with Galilee and probably had a significant Jewish population. Mark's geographical list is therefore a strange mixture. It conspicuously excludes, as we might expect, the areas of Samaria and Decapolis, which were regarded as off limits for patriotic Jews, but includes along with the recognised areas of Jewish population not only Idumaea (which was perhaps rather more acceptable than Samaria) but also the officially non-Jewish territory of Phoenicia. It indicates how far Jesus' reputation was spreading, but probably does not offer a firm basis for a demographic analysis of the early phases of the Jesus movement.

9 The use of ἵνα to introduce an indirect command is common in Mark (cf. v. 12; 5:18, 43; 6:8, 12, 25, 56, etc.). Crowd pressure has been a recurrent theme already (1:45; 2:2-4). The use of a boat as a mobile pulpit will be explained in 4:1-2 (there and elsewhere Mark will use πλοῖον, but his use of the diminutive πλοιάριον here apparently refers to the same small fishing boat; diminutives are common in Mark and often have no special force; see Taylor, 44-45). Here, where teaching has not been mentioned, the purpose of the πλοιάριον remains unexplained; it appears to be simply a means of temporary physical escape, ἵνα μὴ θλίβωσιν αὐτόν, since the healing in v. 10 presupposes physical contact. So the boat 'attends' (προσκαρτερῇ) Jesus, available when needed. While it is not stated that it is the disciples' own boat which is used, this would seem a natural assumption, and in that case we are offered an interesting insight into the call of Simon and the other fishermen: their 'abandonment' of their means of livelihood (1:18, 20) has not apparently left them without access to a boat, and the frequent mentions of the disciple group travelling by boat hereafter underline the point.[7] The

---

7. Chapters 4–8 contain six boat voyages across the lake (three return trips), with departure and arrival specifically noted each time, as well as the use of the boat as a pulpit in 4:1-2. For some comments on scholarly views on this Marcan theme see R. M. Fowler, *Loaves,* 57-68.

μαθηταί, hitherto seen merely as accompanying Jesus, here serve a practical purpose in looking after the master's physical needs.

10 To the picture of many physical healings (cf. 1:34) is now added the popular hope that by merely touching Jesus they will be cured. Mark does not here tell us whether such cures were in fact effected, but in 6:56 he does say so, and in 5:25-34 we will have a story of just such a cure, by a touch without the need being previously drawn to Jesus' attention. For a similarly 'magical' view of healing see Acts 5:15-16; 19:11-12, and for an OT precedent 2 Ki. 13:21. The result is vividly expressed in Mark's account of people 'falling over' Jesus to touch him, which gives added force to the fear of v. 9, μὴ θλίβωσιν αὐτόν. μάστιξ ('scourge') was probably originally used of physical complaints when they were understood to be divinely imposed afflictions or punishments, but by now has become a general term for ailments (cf. 5:29, 34; Lk. 7:21).

11 Demon possession is again treated separately from illness, and the encounter is between Jesus and the πνεύματα ἀκάθαρτα, with the 'hosts' passive except that their voices are used by the demons (hence λέγοντες rather than λέγοντα?) and their bodies to express submission (προσέπιπτον). Mark does not at this point actually mention that Jesus expelled the demons, but that is surely assumed. The focus, however, is on their recognition of him, both in their instinctive homage to a superior authority (προσπίπτω; is this a deliberate contrast with the less reverential behaviour of the physically sick, ἐπιπίπτω, v. 10 ?), and especially in their explicit declaration of him as ὁ υἱὸς τοῦ θεοῦ. This is a more christologically loaded term than ὁ ἅγιος τοῦ θεοῦ (1:24), and will be elaborated still further by the addition of τοῦ ὑψίστου in the remaining demonic confession in 5:7. This ultimate truth about Jesus, the highest christological confession of Mark's gospel, has already been declared by God himself in 1:11, and will be repeated to three chosen disciples in 9:7, but it remains hidden from people in general until it comes to the surface in the trial of Jesus (14:61-62), and is perceived by the centurion at the cross (15:39). But while human insight is not yet ready for this revelation, the demons are only too well aware of the status and identity of the one whom they instinctively recognise as their superior.

12 For ἐπιτιμάω see on 1:25; for the commands to silence addressed to demons see above on 1:25, 34, and for their place in the whole 'messianic secret' see below on 8:30. Here, as in 1:34, the motive for silencing the demons is not simply that they are undesirable witnesses, but that the truth they declare is not to be divulged (note that the phrase αὐτὸν φανερὸν ποιήσωσιν assumes that what they have said about him is true, so that to divulge it would be to 'blow his cover'). For now Jesus must remain, from the point of view of the general public, incognito.

VARYING RESPONSES TO JESUS:
SUPPORTERS AND OPPONENTS (3:13-35)

Jesus has already made a sensation, both by his teaching and by his miraculous activity. Mark has told us of the enthusiastic and widespread popular response, and of the large crowds following Jesus, but has also taken care to chart the beginning of suspicion and outright opposition, culminating in a decision to get rid of him. The remainder of the narrative which leads up to the first major discourse of the gospel (4:1-34) draws these threads together into a series of scenes which together represent the wide spectrum of response to Jesus. The discourse in chapter 4 will then explain the reasons for this wide divergence.

Mark's gospel contains many examples of the well-known storytelling technique variously described as 'interpolation', 'intercalation', 'dovetailing', or 'sandwiching', whereby a story is begun, then suspended while another (related) story is inserted, after which the original story is resumed and completed.[8] 3:20-35 is a classic example of this style, where Jesus' family are introduced in 3:20-21 as setting out to take control of him, and in vv. 31-35 they arrive but fail to achieve their purpose. In between in vv. 22-30 we hear of the hostile delegation of scribes from Jerusalem (a new and menacing development), and of Jesus' dialogue with them (filling in the interval while the family are on the way). The device enables the reader to compare and contrast two different levels of opposition to Jesus, with their parallel charges of madness (v. 21) and demon possession (vv. 22, 30).[9]

But there is more going on in this section than that. The final scene (vv. 31-35) contrasts two groups, the natural family (who remain 'outside') and Jesus' 'true family' consisting of 'those who do the will of God', who are around him in the house, forming an inner circle (literally, v. 34). So in contrast to the two groups who form the narrative sandwich in vv. 20-35, both of whom in their different ways represent opposition and rejection, we meet those who have responded positively to Jesus' message, and now form the true people of God. And the core members of this group have already been introduced to us in vv. 13-19, the chosen group whose role it is to 'be with Jesus' (v. 14) and to share his mission (though even within this group the shadow of betrayal is already cast, v. 19). Here then is a third group, bracketing the other two, and forming with them a more complete overview of the divided reactions which Jesus' ministry has provoked, the different types of soil into which the good seed has been sown (4:3-8).

Throughout this section the narrative draws attention to people's position

---

8. See Introduction, pp. 18-20.

9. S. C. Barton, *Discipleship,* 74-79, discusses how closely Mark intends the two groups of opponents to be linked, and in particular whether Jesus' solemn words about the scribes in vv. 28-29 are to be understood as applying to his family also. He concludes (77) with a 'qualified affirmative' on the latter point, but the qualification which follows (78) draws most of the sting of this conclusion, describing the family's unbelief as relative, not absolute like that of the scribes.

as either 'inside' (as part of the 'circle' around Jesus in the house) or 'outside'. This language will be picked up in a more clearly symbolic sense in 4:10-11, where οἱ περὶ αὐτὸν σὺν τοῖς δώδεκα are contrasted with οἱ ἔξω; but already the narrative structure of 3:13-35 has set up the contrast. Thus Jesus calls the Twelve ἵνα ὦσιν μετ' αὐτοῦ (v. 14); he comes (presumably with them) εἰς οἶκον (v. 20); his family ἐξῆλθον (v. 21), and in v. 31 are found ἔξω στήκοντες, while the crowd of insiders ἐκάθητο περὶ αὐτόν (v. 32); the family are again described as ἔξω in v. 32, while the true people of God are described as οἱ περὶ αὐτὸν κύκλῳ καθήμενοι (v. 34). We shall have more to say of this symbolism of inside/ outside with reference to 4:10-11, but it is clearly a significant element in Mark's telling of the story, presenting in visual form the contrast which will later be discussed theologically.[10]

The pericopes grouped in this section thus introduce the following groups:

vv. 13-19   Supporters ('insiders'): the Twelve
vv. 20-21   Opponents ('outsiders') 1: Jesus' family
vv. 22-30   Opponents ('outsiders') 2: scribes *from Jerusalem*
v. 31-35   Concluding tableau: insiders and outsiders.

Supporters: The Twelve (3:13-19)

TEXTUAL NOTES

14. The inclusion of μαθητάς after δώδεκα (W) is a natural harmonisation to Matthew and to common usage, whereas Mark consistently uses either οἱ δώδεκα or οἱ μαθηταί, but not both together, as a title for Jesus' close companions. More significant is the phrase οὓς καὶ ἀποστόλους ὠνόμασεν, which is included here by a number of important witnesses (ℵ B Θ *f*13 syh,mg and Coptic). It is suspect as a harmonisation to Luke, who uses the term ἀπόστολος as a title for the Twelve, and so includes this clause here, whereas Mark uses ἀπόστολος elsewhere only at 6:30, where its meaning is determined by the 'mission' context rather than as a known title of the Twelve. (Matthew's single use of ἀπόστολος is in this pericope, but is not parallel to the clause in question here.) The clause is therefore probably not original in Mark.

16. The clause καὶ ἐποίησεν τοὺς δώδεκα (ℵ B C* Δ) is understandably omitted by the majority of witnesses as a rather awkward repetition from v. 14, καὶ ἐποίησεν δώδεκα. But it may well be original, as it both resumes the sense after the long double ἵνα clause setting out the function of the Twelve, and now provides a titular heading (note τοὺς δώδεκα here, unlike v. 14) for the list which follows. The insertion of πρῶτον Σίμωνα (*f*13) is an obvious correction to provide an accusative to match the rest of the list (and to assimilate to Matthew).

10. W. E. Moore, *ExpTim* 98 (1986/7) 39-43, makes an interesting attempt to trace the theme of insiders and outsiders as a dominant motif through the whole of Mark's gospel. For a much more cautious estimate of its role see M. A. Beavis, *Audience,* 96-98.

17. Most witnesses read the plural ὀνόματα. Since only one name is mentioned, this is the more difficult reading, and should be preferred to the singular ὄνομα (B D, etc.), an obvious correction.

18. The problem of the identity of the obscure twelfth member of the group (see commentary) has led to the Western reading, Λεββαῖον (more widely represented in Matthew, where some MSS give Θαδδαῖος as a second name of Λεββαῖος, or vice versa), probably representing an alternative way of getting the Λευί of 2:14 into the apostolic list, if he was not identified with Μαθθαῖος (see B. Lindars, *NTS* 4 [1957/8] 220-22).

So far five individual followers of Jesus have been named (1:16-20; 2:14), and an indefinite group of μαθηταί have become familiar in the story as Jesus' regular companions (2:15-16, 18, 23; 3:7, 9). But they are not the only ones who have responded with enthusiasm to Jesus' ministry, and a distinction between μαθηταί and ὄχλος (-οι) will be maintained throughout the gospel. This pericope gives a clear basis for that distinction, in that an inner group of twelve is established; the implication of v. 13 is that the Twelve were deliberately selected from among a wider circle of Jesus' supporters. At several points in the gospel they will be referred to specifically as οἱ δώδεκα (4:10; 6:7; 9:35; 10:32; 11:11; 14:10, 17, 20, 43), and in 4:10 they are specifically distinguished as such from the wider group of οἱ περὶ αὐτόν. Where Mark uses the term οἱ μαθηταί after this point, the context suggests a small and close-knit group travelling together, and the term probably refers (like Luke's οἱ ἀπόστολοι, a term which Mark does not use in this sense; see Textual Note) specifically to the Twelve, who continue as Jesus' regular companions and are the object of his private teaching especially in 8:22–10:52. There is no use of οἱ μαθηταί in Mark which clearly has a wider circle in mind,[11] and on occasions where Mark wishes to include others beyond the Twelve he usually makes this clear (4:10; 8:34). We shall therefore assume hereafter that in Mark (unlike Luke) οἱ μαθηταί and οἱ δώδεκα are functionally equivalent, despite the odd fact that (*pace* W; see Textual Note) the term μαθητής is not actually used in this pericope where the Twelve are introduced.[12]

The fact that the Twelve were all male is attributable rather to the social climate of the time (and the nature of the group as an itinerant task force sharing basic resources and accommodation?) than to theological motives; for closely involved female followers and supporters outside the Twelve see comments below on 15:40-41, and cf. Lk. 8:2-3; 10:38-42.

The number twelve is presumably symbolic (as well as forming a practi-

11. See, however, on 4:34 below.
12. E. Best, *Disciples,* 157-58, suggests a number of passages where the μαθηταί may be seen as a larger group than the Twelve; in no case is the evidence decisive, and Best acknowledges that in general 'Mark makes little distinction in the way in which he uses the twelve and the disciples'. R. P. Meye, *SE* 2 (1964) 211-18, argues strongly for Mark's use of οἱ μαθηταί for the Twelve only. See also C. C. Black, *Disciples* 273-74 n. 5, summarising the debate.

cally manageable travelling group, able to fit into a small fishing boat). As the number of the tribes of Israel it suggests an ideology of the restoration of Israel, even though this implication is not brought out explicitly in Mark as it is in Mt. 19:28; Lk. 22:30.[13] The number was significant enough in itself to withstand any uncertainty as to just who constituted the group, and to necessitate the replacement of a lost member (Acts 1:15-26). NT lists of the Twelve (Mk. 3:16-19; Mt. 10:2-4; Lk. 6:14-16; Acts 1:13) vary not only in form of presentation but also in one of the names included, in that Luke's two lists offer Ἰούδας Ἰακώβου in place of the Θαδδαῖος of Mark and Matthew (textual variants complicate matters further by introducing Λεββαῖος; see Textual Note). Since nothing further is known of either Thaddaeus or 'Judas of James' (beyond the mention of Ἰούδας, οὐχ ὁ Ἰσκαριώτης in Jn. 14:22), there is little to be gained by speculation as to whether they are the same person. Indeed, several of the Twelve are quite unknown in the NT except as names on the list. Their number and their corporate identity were more important to tradition than any individual profile.

Their role is spelled out in vv. 14-15.[14] The two 'active' clauses, relating to preaching and exorcism (the absence of healing is surprising), indicate that they are to function as an extension of Jesus' own mission; indeed, they are to fulfil these functions only because they are 'sent out' by Jesus for this purpose. But they will not actually undertake these tasks until 6:7. Until then, they need to be prepared for them, and Mark indicates this by prefacing the two functional roles with a clause unique in the various accounts of discipleship in the NT, ἵνα ὦσιν μετ' αὐτοῦ, which might be no more than a recognition of their role as constant travelling companions during Jesus' itinerant ministry (as opposed to the 'crowds' of followers who come and go),[15] but should probably be read as a more theological reflection on the role of the disciple, in that their personal involvement with and training by the master is the essential prerequisite for the active ministry which follows (a similar point is made in narrative form in Luke's story of Mary and Martha, Lk. 10:38-42). Cf. Acts 1:21 for companionship with Jesus throughout his ministry as an essential qualification for membership of the Twelve.

13 While Mark does not mention Jesus' going εἰς τὸ ὄρος as often as Matthew, we shall see him making a similar 'retreat' into the hills to pray in 6:46 (cf. the ἔρημος τόπος in 1:35), and taking the disciples with him up a high

---

13. Hooker interestingly observes that the choice of twelve in addition to Jesus himself, rather than eleven with Jesus himself making up the number, 'represents an implicit claim regarding his own status'.

14. Myers' characterisation of the Twelve as 'a kind of vanguard "revolutionary committee", a "government in exile"', representing 'the community of resistance', finds no support in Mark's account of their call; Myers bases it on the unwarranted assumption that the ὄρος of 3:13 represents Sinai.

15. Cf. the request of the restored demoniac Legion ἵνα μετ' αὐτοῦ ᾖ (5:18), which is refused by telling him instead to return to his home and tell of his experiences there.

mountain κατ' ἰδίαν μόνους in 9:2 (cf. the retreat εἰς ἔρημον τόπον κατ' ἰδίαν in 6:32; also 7:24; 8:27). No specific mountain is in view, but rather a journey 'into the hills',[16] apparently to escape the crowds and thus to focus his attention on the chosen group of twelve. Both προσκαλεῖται and ἀπῆλθον πρὸς αὐτόν underline this sense of separation from the general mass of his followers,[17] and οὓς ἤθελεν αὐτός reinforces the point already made clear in 1:16-20; 2:14, that discipleship, at least in the sense of belonging to Jesus' closest entourage, is not a matter of the disciple's choice but of Jesus' (cf. Jn. 15:16).

14-15 ποιέω here has the sense of 'appoint', 'constitute', a Semitic idiom found in the LXX (1 Kgdms. 12:6; 3 Kgdms. 12:31; 13:33); cf. 1:17, though there the purpose was expressed by an infinitive, here by ἵνα. For ἵνα ὦσιν μετ' αὐτοῦ see introductory comments on this pericope above. The use of ἀποστέλλω provides a basis for the one Marcan use of ἀπόστολος in 6:30, where the sending out here envisaged has taken place (6:7); he does not use ἀπόστολος as a title for the Twelve as such (see Textual Note). Both κηρύσσειν and ἐκβάλλειν τὰ δαιμόνια have hitherto been the distinctive role of Jesus himself (note 1:38, 'Let *us* go . . . so that *I* may preach'), but the appointment of the Twelve prepares for the time when these roles will be shared (6:7-13). To fulfil them will require ἐξουσία, also a term which has hitherto been used exclusively of Jesus (1:22, 27; 2:10), but which will recur with a wider reference when the Twelve begin their mission (6:7). The summary in 6:13 indicates that the exorcistic ministry of the Twelve was broadly successful, but 9:14-29 offers a note of caution: there is nothing automatic about their ἐξουσία, and their 'success rate' cannot match that of Jesus himself, from whom their ἐξουσία is necessarily derived. The absence of healing (the most prominent activity of Jesus so far in the gospel) from their terms of reference is surprising (and is therefore remedied by many later MSS and versions, which add θεραπεύειν τὰς νόσους καί after ἐξουσίαν, under the influence of Mt. 10:1). The fact that in 6:12-13 healing will take its place along with preaching and exorcism as part of the normal mission of the Twelve suggests that its absence here is more a matter of summary reporting than of deliberate exclusion.

16 καὶ ἐποίησεν τοὺς δώδεκα (see Textual Note) resumes the introduction of the Twelve from v. 14a, but also, by the inclusion of the article, provides a titular heading ('The Twelve') to the list which follows. The list begins awkwardly, with the first member not introduced by name in the accusative, as the rest will be, but by a clause which assumes that his name is already present (see Textual Note). Mark agrees with Mt. 16:18 and Jn. 1:42 that the name Πέτρος

16. For this meaning of εἰς τὸ ὄρος see my *Matthew; Evangelist,* 313 and n. 82. On the slope of the Horns of Hattin, above Tiberias, a plaque inscribed with Mk. 3:13 has been erected by the Church of God of Prophecy of Cleveland, Tennessee; the location is speculative, but the lonely upland area, even today, gives a vivid impression of what εἰς τὸ ὄρος means.

17. P. S. Minear, in H. Baltensweiler and B. Reicke (ed.), *NT und Geschichte,* 79-89, provides a useful study of Mark's distinction between the μαθηταί (= the Twelve) and the ὄχλος, the wider group of those who supported Jesus, who are in turn contrasted with οἱ ἔξω.

(Rock) was given to Simon by Jesus himself, though he does not attempt to explain its significance as they do[18] (and as he will do with Βοανηργές); presumably this was already well known among Mark's readers. It was not a name in current use, either in its Aramaic form *kēpā'* or in Greek,[19] but deliberately coined by Jesus as a nickname[20] (ἐπιτίθημι is the root of our word 'epithet'). Having introduced Simon's better-known name, Mark will from this point consistently refer to him as Πέτρος; the only further use of Σίμων will be on the one occasion when Jesus is recorded as addressing him by name, 14:37.

17 James and John are already known to us; the details of their relationship and their father's name are given again in almost the same words as in 1:19, not only to remind us of their first introduction to the story, but also to distinguish this Ἰάκωβος from his namesake in v. 18. These two brothers also have a nickname given to them by Jesus (and mentioned only by Mark); the three most prominent disciples, who will in the future appear on a few occasions as a special 'inmost circle' (5:37; 9:2; 14:33; also, with Andrew, 13:3), are thus singled out for special attention at the beginning of the list.[21] Where additional names are given for other members of the group in order to distinguish them from namesakes, they are not introduced as 'epithets' given by Jesus. If ὀνόματα is the original reading (see Textual Note), it represents a clumsy way of noting that the one name Βοανηργές was given jointly to two people. Βοανηργές (or Βοανεργές; these are the most common among various spellings in the MSS) is usually explained as an attempt to put into Greek the Hebrew phrase *bᵉnê regeš* or *bᵉnê rōgez,* which would be roughly rendered by Mark's translation, υἱοὶ βροντῆς (*regeš* means 'a crowd' or 'commotion', and a related Arabic word means 'thunder'; *rōgez* means 'agitation' or 'anger', and in Job 37:2 *rōgez-qōlô* refers to 'the sound of thunder'), but a wide variety of other derivations and meanings have been proposed, all to various degrees speculative. Βοανη- is otherwise unknown as a transliteration of Hebrew *bᵉnê*, but

18. M. A. Tolbert, *Sowing,* 145-46, suggests that Mark understood the significance of the name differently from Matthew and the later church: it is to be explained from the πετρῶδες of 4:5, 16, in that Simon (and the other disciples) are 'rocky ground'; the name is thus a prediction of the disciples' hardness of heart which will become so prominent a feature of Mark's story. But 4:5, 16 do not occur sufficiently soon in the text to allow the reader easily to make this retrospective identification; nor does Tolbert's interpretation explain why Peter alone should bear the stigma of a name which so well suits the whole group.

19. The only known pre-Christian use in Aramaic is in Egypt in the fifth century B.C.; see J. A. Fitzmyer, in E. Best and R. McL. Wilson (ed.), *Text and Interpretation,* 127-30. There are no known pre-Christian examples of the Greek Πέτρος as a name (ibid., 131-32). For the idea, but not a name as such, cf. Is. 51:1-2, Abraham the 'Rock'.

20. What began probably as a nickname quickly became Simon's regular 'Christian' name (unlike Boanerges, which is never mentioned again). In decisively changing his name in this way, Jesus acted as God had done with OT figures (Gn. 17:5, 15; 32:28). Myers notes also the apocalyptic idea of a 'new name' (Rev. 3:12; 22:4).

21. The extensive textual surgery whereby W has made Βοανηργές into a title for the whole group of twelve rather than only for James and John cannot be accepted in the absence of any other support.

Mark's translation by the Semitic phrase υἱοί . . . virtually demands that he understands that to be its origin, perhaps representing some dialect pronunciation.[22] In the end we have nothing to guide us to the significance of the nickname other than Mark's υἱοὶ βροντῆς, which need not be a more exact etymological explanation than many of the 'etymologies' offered for names in the OT. The NT records do not give us enough information about James and John to enable us to judge how far this term might fit their character (if indeed that was its purpose),[23] but their hasty and violent reactions in 9:38; Lk. 9:54 give it some substance.

18-19 The remainder of the list is quickly presented. Even Ἀνδρέας, who has already appeared in the story (1:16, 29) as Simon's brother, receives no special mention. In 13:3 he will apparently join his brother in the inner circle, but otherwise he does not share the prominence of his three fellow fishermen. None of the remaining members of the group is mentioned again in Mark's story after this point, except of course Judas Iscariot, and the rest of the NT does not add much to our information about them. For Μαθθαῖος see above on 2:14; if he is the same person as Λευί Mark gives no hint of this. For Θαδδαῖος see the Textual Note above.[24]

Three of the remaining names receive a little expansion, in each case probably because they need to be distinguished from namesakes within the group: the names Ἰάκωβος and Σίμων have already appeared in vv. 16-17, and the existence of another Ἰούδας is clear from Lk. 6:16; Acts 1:13; Jn. 14:22, even though he does not appear in Mark's list of the Twelve (see introductory comments on this pericope above). For ὁ τοῦ Ἀλφαίου see on 2:14, where Levi is given the same patronymic. ὁ Καναναῖος corresponds to Luke's ὁ καλούμενος ζηλωτής, and is best explained as derived from the Aramaic *qan'ānā'*, 'enthusiast', 'patriot', for which Luke's ζηλωτής is the regular Greek equivalent.[25] This was not yet at the time of Jesus a party term, as it became at the time of the Jewish war; ζηλωτής is used in a religious rather than political sense in Acts 21:20; 22:3; Gal. 1:14, etc., and Simon may have gained his nickname for religious zeal.[26] But by the time Mark wrote his gospel the term probably had

22. R. Buth, *JSNT* 10 (1981) 29-33, suggests that Mark wrote Βονερεγεμ (which he derives from Hebrew *bᵉnê-ra'am*, literally 'sons of thunder') and that a Greek copyist produced Βοανηργές under the influence of βοάω and ἔργον: 'Thus: "shout-workers", "loud-voiced"'! M. Casey, *Sources,* 198, opts for a similar origin (though in Aramaic), but attributes the Greek form to a translator who misread the Aramaic letters.

23. Cf. J. R. Harris's suggestion (*Expositor,* 7th series, 3 [1907] 146-52) that the name refers to the Dioscuri, and was applied to the sons of Zebedee because they were twins.

24. The rabbinic list of Jesus' *five* disciples preserved in a baraita in *b. Sanh.* 43a is 'Matthai, Neqai, Netzer, Buni and Thodah'; whatever the source of these names (which may well be from wordplay rather than tradition), it is interesting that the closest parallels in the NT lists are Μαθθαῖος and the obscure Θαδδαῖος.

25. See, e.g., M. Hengel, *Zealots,* 69-70.

26. Hengel, *Zealots,* 392-94, is sceptical that the term could ever have been used in so innocuous a sense.

clear political connotations, so that, assuming that he understood the origin of the name, he would expect his readers to view Simon as a fervent nationalist (and thus an unlikely recruit for a movement which consorted with τελῶναι). The meaning 'Canaanite'[27] (which would make Simon a non-Jewish member of the Twelve, if the nickname is to be taken literally) is rendered very improbable by the fact that Matthew, who uses Καναναῖος here, uses the regular LXX form Χαναναῖος when referring to a Canaanite (Mt. 15:22).

'Ισκαριώθ has most frequently been understood as the Hebrew אִישׁ qᵉriyyôt, 'man of Kerioth' (this derivation goes back at least to the fourth century, as it is represented in the reading ἀπὸ Καρυώτου in א* Θ at Jn. 6:71, and in D at Jn. 12:4 etc.); other suggestions derive it from σικάριος ('bandit', 'freedom fighter'), or from the root šqr, 'lie' (in which case it would appear to be a retrospective title for the 'false disciple'), and several other conjectures have been offered.[28] If the meaning is 'man of Kerioth', and if this indicates his personal origin, Judas may be the only non-Galilean among the group, since the best-known towns of that name are in Judah (Kerioth-Hezron, Jos. 15:25) and Moab (Jer. 41:24); but since Hebrew qiryâ means 'town', and is the beginning of several place names, any such identification is rash. Unlike with Βοανηργές, Mark gives no indication that he knew its origin or meaning; it is simply a title which distinguishes this Judas from others. From the Christian point of view, however, his main distinguishing feature is ὃς καὶ παρέδωκεν αὐτόν. Mark's readers were no doubt already familiar with this aspect of the story, which is here alluded to without any explanation or background in the text so far. While παραδίδωμι has a wide range of meaning, when used with a personal object it usually has a hostile sense; it has already been used, equally without explanation, for the fate of John the Baptist (1:14), so that even a reader unfamiliar with the story should recognise an ominous note in this epithet (and might even connect it with the 'removal' of the bridegroom predicted in 2:20).[29]

27. Many later MSS, presumably unaware of the Aramaic root of Καναναῖος, read Κανανίτην.

28. Mann defends the meaning 'redhead', which lies behind the iconographic tradition of depicting Judas with red hair. For a full survey of suggested derivations and meanings see R. E. Brown, *Death*, 1410-16.

29. παραδίδωμι is the verb most generally used for Judas's act in the NT, and it has therefore been argued, notably by W. Klassen, *Judas*, that he was not originally depicted as a traitor, but as one who 'handed Jesus over' with friendly intention in order to promote a profitable dialogue with the priestly authorities. Luke, however, uses προδότης in parallel with his uses of παραδίδωμι elsewhere (Lk. 6:16) without any apparent awareness of a difference in meaning, and it may well be asked how 'handing over' a person to his enemies differs significantly from 'betrayal'.

Opponents 1: Jesus' Family (3:20-21)[30]

TEXTUAL NOTES

20. The plural reading ἔρχονται found in most later MSS and versions is a natural correction to an original ἔρχεται after a pericope which has introduced the Twelve, and before the enigmatic αὐτούς, which, if it refers to the Jesus circle, lacks an explicit plural antecedent.

21. It is not surprising that this enigmatic and uncomfortable statement (see comments below) has led to attempted improvements in D W OL by the elimination of the obscure οἱ παρ' αὐτοῦ and the introduction of οἱ γραμματεῖς καὶ οἱ λοιποί as a more acceptable source of the calumny ἐξέστη.

These twenty-eight words bristle with difficulties. It is hardly surprising that neither Matthew nor Luke contains this brief and potentially embarrassing notice. As traditionally understood (a tradition which I shall eventually support in this commentary, despite its considerable problems), these verses introduce the family of Jesus, whose approach to him will be concluded in the other half of the 'sandwich' in vv. 31-35 (see above on 3:13-35 as a whole). In that case, we have in the charge ἐξέστη a more explicit rejection of Jesus' ministry by his family than anywhere else in the gospels; this is not simply a failure to follow Jesus, but a positive and offensive repudiation. But the statement is so brief and imprecise that other interpretations can be offered. There is room for disagreement over the antecedent of αὐτούς, the identification of οἱ παρ' αὐτοῦ, the antecedent of αὐτόν, the subject of ἔλεγον, and the meaning and subject of ἐξέστη; the resulting permutations of exegetical possibilities are such that any understanding of these verses must be advanced with some diffidence.

There has been no previous mention of Jesus' family in this gospel, beyond the mere record that he came from Nazareth (1:9, 24). Apart from the completion of this story in vv. 31-35, they will reappear only at 6:3 in a passing reference by the people of Nazareth (Mark gives no hint that any of those at the cross were related to Jesus; see on 15:40-41). They thus remain for Mark completely outside the Jesus movement, as at best sceptical onlookers, and that 'outsideness' will be emphatically underlined in vv. 31-35. If it were not for 6:3 a reader of Mark would not even know the names of any of Jesus' natural family, and there is no suggestion that any of them will have a role in the later development of the movement. In view of the prominent role of James in the Jerusalem church through the middle years of the first century, Mark's historical restraint is remarkable.

20 The only οἶκος specifically identified so far (apart from a visit to Levi's house in 2:15) has been that of Simon and Andrew in Capernaum (1:29), and it is generally assumed that Mark intends us to understand that it was this

---

30. Following the UBS[4] verse division, whereby v. 20 begins with καὶ ἔρχεται; some versions begin v. 20 with the following καὶ συνέρχεται.

same house to which Jesus returned as his Capernaum base in 2:1.[31] It would naturally follow that the same house is intended here, and the experience of an inconveniently large crowd around it would not be a new one (2:1-4), as indeed πάλιν suggests. This time the crowd not only blocks access, but is so persistently intrusive as to interfere with the group's meals (cf. 6:31). This is assuming that the antecedent of αὐτούς is Jesus and the Twelve, who are assumed to be still with him in accordance with 3:14. Since Mark elsewhere uses a plural pronoun to refer to an ὄχλος (see on vv. 7-8, and further on v. 21 below), it is possible that αὐτούς refers to the crowd, giving here the same motif of the hungry crowd as in 6:35-36; 8:2; but here, unlike in those cases, there is no feeding miracle in view, and the recurrence of the same motif with reference to Jesus and his disciples in 6:31 suggests that it is they rather than the crowd who are being denied opportunity to eat.

21 This verse is traditionally interpreted as saying that Jesus' family went out from Nazareth to take Jesus under their control because of what they had heard about the scenes in distant Capernaum, having concluded that Jesus was out of his mind. This reading is so lacking in reverence both for Jesus and for his family that it is not surprising to see alternatives proposed. See the Textual Note above for one such attempt.

Another is represented by H. Wansbrough, who offers the translation, 'When they heard it, his followers went out to calm it [the crowd] down, for they said that it was out of control with enthusiasm.'[32] This proposal has not been generally accepted.[33] Some objections are as follows: Mark elsewhere

31. The anarthrous εἰς οἶκον (and ἐν οἴκῳ, 2:1) could, however, be read as 'at home', implying that Jesus returned to his *own* home. As there has been no change of location signaled since the focus on Capernaum in ch. 1, this would indicate either that Jesus had his own house in Capernaum separate from his family (so G. D. Kilpatrick, *JSNT* 15 [1982] 3-8), or that when Jesus took up his ministry down by the lake the family had moved to Capernaum with him (as the eldest male following the presumed death of Joseph; see on 6:3). This suggestion was attractively developed in an unpublished paper by my student P. R. Kirk, drawing on but going beyond Kilpatrick's proposal. (He notes, against Kilpatrick, that Jesus' mother and brothers are not stated in 6:3 to be still resident in Nazareth, only his sisters, who had presumably married local men and so did not move down to Capernaum with the rest of the family.) Kirk goes on to reconstruct the following scene in this way: Jesus' family and friends (οἱ παρ᾽ αὐτοῦ) were with him at home, but went out of the house (ἐξῆλθον) expecting him to follow to a less crowded place where they could take control of him; Jesus, however, stayed behind debating with the newly arrived scribes from Jerusalem, so that his family, (still) standing outside, were obliged to send in for him again (v. 31). As a historical reconstruction this is plausible, but it is questionable whether Mark could have expected his readers to work out so much from his undefined references to an οἶκος.

32. H. Wansbrough, *NTS* 18 (1971/2) 233-35; similarly, H.-H. Schroeder, *Eltern*, 111. This interpretation derives from G. Hartmann, *BZ* 11 (1913) 249-79; cf. also J. E. Steinmueller, *CBQ* 4 (1942) 355-59; P. J. Gannon, *CBQ* 15 (1953) 460-61. D. Wenham, *NTS* 21 (1974/5) 295-300, while pointing out several flaws in Wansbrough's exegesis, also adds points in its favour, and concludes that it is not to be ignored.

33. E. Best, *NTS* 22 (1975/6) 309-19, offers a typical example of its rejection, with detailed argument.

always uses a plural pronoun after ὄχλος;[34] 'to calm down' is not a natural meaning of κρατῆσαι; the 'amazement' of the crowd for which Mark uses ἐξίστημι or ἐξίσταμαι elsewhere is not something to be suppressed but is favourably reported;[35] and this interpretation destroys both the parallelism of the charges against Jesus in vv. 21 and 22 (with the parallel introductions ἔλεγον ὅτι), and the first part of the sandwich, which then explains the family's arrival in v. 31.

The main exegetical problem for the traditional interpretation is in the unusual phrase οἱ παρ' αὐτοῦ. The normal meaning would be 'his envoys' or 'his associates'. The context must decide just who are comprised under this phrase, and, as Wenham rightly points out, the context here would naturally suggest the disciples; there has been nothing to help the reader to refer it to Jesus' family, who have not yet been mentioned in the entire gospel. It must only be by a retrospective understanding in the light of v. 31, ἡ μήτηρ αὐτοῦ καὶ οἱ ἀδελφοὶ αὐτοῦ, that the reader, recognising the sandwich structure of the whole section, may realise just who it was who 'went out' in v. 21; but this would be a lot to expect of a first-time reader. It is possible that the phrase had a more specific meaning in colloquial use; there is evidence especially in papyri for the phrase being used to mean a person's 'kinsmen' or 'household' (MM, 479a; BAGD, 610a, I.4.b.β; cf. LXX Pr. 31:21; Sus. 33; Josephus, *Ant.* 1.193), though this could hardly be said to be its normal sense. But neither is it a normal Marcan term for the disciples or other associates of Jesus (note also the different phrase οἱ περὶ αὐτόν, 4:10).

While the preceding context might suggest that οἱ παρ' αὐτοῦ are the disciples, the sentence itself forbids this interpretation (assuming that the objections to Wansbrough's interpretation mentioned above are sufficient to rule out the identification of αὐτόν as the crowd). If the disciples are with Jesus in the house, they could not 'go out' to seize him, nor is the idea of the disciples manhandling Jesus one which easily fits into the Marcan account so far. Still less is it possible to imagine them thinking him insane (see below on the meaning of ἐξέστη), and even if this objection is turned by reading ἔλεγον as impersonal ('people were saying'), the other objections remain. If, then, οἱ παρ' αὐτοῦ cannot be the disciples, the identification as the family, in the proleptic light of v. 31, as 'coming out' from Nazareth to Capernaum in order to take control of Jesus seems the least unsatisfactory solution to an exegetical conundrum.

The reason for their action is expressed in the clause ἔλεγον γὰρ ὅτι ἐξέστη. Proposals to read ἔλεγον as impersonal, and therefore as having a dif-

---

34. Mk. 2:13; 4:1-2; 6:34, 45-46; 7:14; 8:2-3, 6-9; 9:15-16; 14:43-44; 15:8-9, 11-12, 15 (possibly also 3:32-33; see comments ad loc). While the verb immediately governed by ὄχλος is generally singular (as here; see, however, 4:1d; 9:15; and 3:8 with πλῆθος), subsequent verbs and pronouns developing the reference are always plural in Mark.

35. A singular verb in a subordinate clause referring to ὄχλος would also be unique in Mark; see the previous note.

ferent subject from the preceding clause, are the result rather of embarrassment over this view of Jesus' family than of any natural Marcan idiom. A close parallel in 14:1-2 tells strongly against an impersonal sense here, and in any case Mark's narrative has given us no cause to think that people in general thought Jesus insane; the parallel charge of demon possession in v. 22 comes not from people in general but from scribes 'from Jerusalem', who are thus differentiated from Galilean opinion.[36] Can the offence then be lessened by suggesting a weaker sense of ἐξίστημι? It is true that in its three other uses in Mark (5:42 is the only other active use; in 2:12 and 6:51 the middle is used) it refers to the (laudable) astonishment of those who witnessed Jesus' miracles (Matthew [once] and Luke-Acts also use it in the same sense), but three uses do not establish a presumption in favour of this meaning when (a) the verb is commonly used elsewhere to mean 'be mad' (A. Oepke, *TDNT,* 2.459-60; see especially 2 Cor. 5:13, where it is contrasted with σωφρονέω), and (b) the clause here is in parallel with an accusation of demon possession in v. 22. Nor is it easy to understand why a belief that Jesus was 'amazed' (about what?) should cause his people to want to seize him.[37]

In the end, then, in spite of all the difficulties, the traditional interpretation seems to make the best sense of Mark's admittedly obscure language, in the context of the whole structure of 3:13-35. Jesus' people back home have heard reports of the rowdy scenes in Capernaum, and decide that it is time to take Jesus in hand for his own sake and for the family's reputation, on the assumption that, to use a modern idiom, he has 'flipped'.[38] But before they can arrive to make their (unsuccessful) attempt to get hold of him, an even more damaging accusation comes from a different quarter, illustrating precisely the sort of unfavourable official notice which the family had perhaps been planning to avert.

Opponents 2: Scribes from Jerusalem (3:22-30)

TEXTUAL NOTE

29. The various nouns substituted for ἁμαρτήματος indicate both the unfamiliarity of this noun over against the normal ἁμαρτία, and the awkwardness of the expression ἔνοχος αἰωνίου ἁμαρτήματος, where a word for judgment or punishment might have been expected (see commentary).

---

36. See further E. Best, *Disciples,* 55, drawing on the fuller argument of H. Räisänen, *Mutter,* 30ff.

37. T. Dwyer, *Wonder,* 105-6, offers strong support for the traditional interpretation of ἐξίστημι here as 'to be out of one's senses'.

38. A. Y. Collins in C. M. Tuckett (ed.), *Scriptures,* 235-36, suggests that the family's attitude is understood as a fulfilment of Ps. 69:8, 'I have become a stranger to my kindred, an alien to my mother's children'.

While the concern of Jesus' family over his supposed 'insanity' was uncomplimentary, the parallel accusation in v. 22 is downright dangerous. In itself it is potentially extremely damaging to Jesus' popular reputation, as an attempt to brand him as a messenger not of God but of Satan, drawing not on divine power but on occult forces. But equally ominous is the source from which it comes, οἱ γραμματεῖς οἱ ἀπὸ Ἰεροσολύμων καταβάντες. Hitherto Jesus has met with local opposition in Galilee, in which γραμματεῖς have played their part (2:6, 16), and which has culminated in a plot against his life (3:6). But in Galilee Jesus remains so far a popular figure, so that whatever the schemes of the Pharisees and the Herodians, they are not going to find it easy to dispose of him. But Jerusalem is a different matter. People from Jerusalem have been drawn to Jesus' ministry (3:8), as they had been to that of John (1:5), and perhaps the reports they have taken back have resulted in this delegation from the capital to investigate, and as it turns out to oppose violently, this new movement in the northern province. A similar delegation of γραμματεῖς ἐλθόντες ἀπὸ Ἰεροσολύμων will come on the scene again in 7:1, leading to an equally bitter confrontation. In Jerusalem, it seems, Jesus has few friends, and those who are in positions of authority are rapidly forming an unfavourable impression of him. From 8:31 onwards Jesus will draw the obvious conclusion, that Jerusalem must be for him a place of repudiation and death, and so it will prove from chapter 11 onwards. For the time being Jerusalem remains a distant menace, but its emissaries give clear warning of the confrontation which lies ahead.

Exorcism has been so far, and will remain throughout the Galilean period, one of the most prominent aspects of Jesus' public activity. Much of Jesus' reputation as a man of ἐξουσία has derived from this source (note especially 1:27). Even if Jesus has been successful in his attempts to prevent the demons declaring his identity as Son of God (1:24-25, 34; 3:11-12), the mere fact of his instantly successful commands to the demons to leave is sufficient to mark him out as one who deploys undeniably supernatural power. The accusation of v. 22 is therefore an attempt to turn this perception against Jesus by attributing the source of that power to evil rather than to good. It is this deliberate perversion of the truth which provokes the unparalleled severity of Jesus' counterattack and the terrible saying about unforgivable sin.

At this point, more than anywhere in the gospel, exorcism becomes the subject of theological consideration. No new incident of exorcism is here narrated (contrast Matthew and Luke), but the significance of the whole exorcistic enterprise (in which Jesus' disciples as well as he himself are now involved, v. 15; cf. 6:7, 13) is opened up for discussion. Exorcism not only exhibits the power of Jesus (and of those who derive their ἐξουσία from him, 3:14-15). It also reveals something of what is happening at the level of the supernatural power struggle which underlies the earthly ministry of Jesus, of which 1:12-13 has already given notice. Jesus' control over demonic power speaks of the collapse of the βασιλεία τοῦ Σατανᾶ (vv. 24-26) in the face of the incoming of the βασιλεία τοῦ θεοῦ. The power of Satan, hitherto a real (though not unlimited) force in the world, has entered terminal decline (cf. τέλος ἔχει, v. 26). The strong man is now bound, and his possessions left vulnerable to the stronger one who now confronts him (v. 27). The ministry of Jesus thus represents the decisive turning point in the contest between good and evil for the control of the world and its people. All this is so clearly manifest to any unprejudiced observer that to attempt to explain it away by interpreting the ministry of Jesus as exercised in support of Satan's power rather than for its subversion is to commit the unforgivable sin of calling good evil and evil good, of confusing the Spirit of God with the spirit of darkness (vv. 28-30). Jesus is thus declared to be the one in and through whom the Spirit of God is now dramatically at work (as 1:8, 10, 12-13 have led us to expect). In Jesus and his ministry the lines are clearly drawn, and the question turns out to be not simply one of rival interpretations of miracles, but of who Jesus really is. The ultimate significance of the exorcisms is christological.

22 The inclusion of καταβάντες indicates that these are not just scribes who happen to be of Jerusalem origin but now live in Galilee, but rather a newly arrived delegation from the capital. Their immediately hostile accusation does not suggest a neutral fact-finding visit; they have come looking for a fight. The imperfect ἔλεγον here and in v. 30 suggests not a passing comment but a sustained campaign of vilification. ἔλεγον ὅτι Βεελζεβοὺλ ἔχει is formally parallel to the verdict of Jesus' family in v. 21, ἔλεγον ὅτι ἐξέστη. They are clearly also related in content, since madness and demon possession were related (though not identical)[39] ideas (cf Jn. 10:20; for other accusations of possession directed at Jesus, without madness being specified, see Jn. 7:20; 8:48, 52; for John the Baptist cf. Mt. 11:19). Allegations of madness, at various levels of seriousness, can, however, be made in the NT without mention of demonic possession (Acts 12:15; 26:24; 1 Cor. 14:23), and in the OT prophets, possessed by the Spirit of God, could sometimes be regarded as mad (2 Ki. 9:11; Je. 29:26; Ho. 9:7). There is thus at least an escalation in the seriousness, and the theological implications, of the two accusations, even if they are not totally distinct. However Jesus' family may have understood the cause of his 'madness', they are not recorded as attributing it openly to demonic influence. For the Jerusalem scribes, however, this is the essence of Jesus' problem, and Mark underlines the theological weight of this form of accusation by repeating it in v. 30. It is the charge of being possessed, rather than simply of drawing on demonic power as in Matthew and Luke, which Mark regards as making the scribes' allegation unforgivable.

For the use of ἔχω to describe demon-possession cf. 5:15; 7:25; 9:17, and

---

39. It is commonly asserted that madness and demon possession were virtually synonymous in Jewish thought. There is in fact surprisingly little evidence for this claim. It is possible that *Lives of the Prophets* 4:6, 10 (first century A.D.?) attributes Nebuchadnezzar's madness to demons (Beliar, Behemoth), though the text is not clear. W. Foerster, *TDNT* 2.15, offers no other instance, and the detailed study of E. Yamauchi, *GP*, 6.89-183, provides no other evidence of this connection among Jews (see pp. 119, 127 and cf. p. 102 for nondemonological understanding of psychological disorder in Mesopotamia).

see above on 1:23. The formula in v. 30 is normal Marcan language, but here the πνεῦμα ἀκάθαρτον is specified as no less than Βεελζεβούλ,[40] who is further defined as the ἄρχων τῶν δαιμονίων.[41] It seems clear from this identification, and from the sequel in vv. 23-26, that Mark understands Βεελζεβούλ as an alternative name for Satan. The name is not found in this sense in pre-Christian Jewish accounts of demons, or indeed in any previous literature,[42] the only previous occurrence of a similar name being that of the Philistine god, *Ba'al z^eb̂ub,* 'Baal of flies' (LXX Βααλ μυῖαν, 'Baal the fly'; cf. Josephus, *Ant.* 9.19) in 2 Ki. 1:2, 3, 6, and 16. It is conjectured that this was an abusive Hebrew corruption of an original *Ba'al z^eb̂ul* ('Baal of the height' or 'of the house'), but since as far as we know no such form was preserved in the OT versions, Mark can hardly have derived the form Βεελζεβούλ from there. In the end we simply do not know where Mark got it from or exactly what lexical meaning, if any, he would have understood it to carry.[43] It is, as he uses it, simply an alternative name for Satan.

The accusation ὅτι Βεελζεβοὺλ ἔχει occurs only in Mark. In Matthew and Luke the name Βεελζεβούλ occurs instead in what is in Mark a second charge, that Jesus' exorcisms depend on his using the power of the ἄρχων τῶν δαιμονίων, i.e., that he is a sorcerer, invoking occult power. (For the instrumental use of ἐν to denote a personal agent see BDF, 219[1] and cf. Mt. 12:28; Jn. 3:21.) The two charges are formally separate in Mark (καὶ ὅτι) and either could stand without the other. But by placing them together, followed by Jesus' reply to the second without any overt response to the first, Mark seems to regard them as two aspects of the same charge, that Jesus is possessed by a 'familiar spirit' whose power is the source of his success as an exorcist. That is why at the end of the pericope, which has focused on the second charge, Mark can still sum up the issue by a repetition of the first (v. 30).

The charge of sorcery, which recognises the supernatural character of Jesus' power but attributes it to demonic rather than divine origin, was one which continued to be levelled against Jesus in rabbinic polemic.[44] Its relevance to the

40. Spelling in the MSS varies between Βεελζεβούλ and Βεεζεβούλ. The form *Beelzebub* found in Latin and Syriac versions is a natural assimilation to the form in 2 Ki. 1:2-6.

41. It would be possible to read the two ὅτι causes of v. 22 as separate, in which case Βεελζεβούλ would not be formally identified as the ruler of the demons. But see below for the probability that Mark did not regard them as separate. Both Matthew and Luke make the identification, as does the Christian author of the *Testament of Solomon.*

42. Βεελζεβούλ features as the ruler of the demons in the *Test. Sol.* 3:1-6; 4:2; 6:1-11; 16:3-5, but this is generally agreed to be a Christian work, so that the name is derived from the NT.

43. L. Gaston, *TZ* 18 (1962) 247-55, shows that in both OT and later Hebrew *z^eb̂ul* is used for both heaven and the temple, each understood as God's dwelling place, and suggests that Βεελζεβούλ represents a Hebrew version of *b^e'el-š^emāyin,* the Aramaic name for the chief Greek god (and therefore from the Jewish point of view the chief demon), Ζεὺς Ὀλύμπιος. Gaston also notices the repeated conjecture that the name may have been intended to echo the late Hebrew *zebel* (compost heap), but dismisses this as its derivation, whatever popular usage may have made of it.

44. *B. Sanh.* 43a, 107b; *b. Šab.* 104b (taking Ben Stada as a pseudonym for Jesus). Early Christian writers refer to this as standard Jewish polemic: e.g. Justin, *Dial.* 69; Origen, *Contra Cels.* 1.6 and passim.

practice of exorcism depends on the status of Βεελζεβούλ as not just any demon, but the ἄρχων τῶν δαιμονίων, and therefore with authority over the lesser demons whom Jesus exorcises. Given such a hierarchical view of demons, the charge is not inherently ridiculous, though the purpose of such a campaign from the point of view of the chief demon is not easy to imagine, as Jesus' reply will show.

23a   Mark quite often uses προσκαλεσάμενος as a narrative device to introduce a significant statement or act of Jesus (7:14; 8:1, 34; 10:42; 12:43; cf. 6:7). Here it implies that while the scribes were speaking about Jesus rather than directly to him, he now initiates a direct confrontation. For the meaning of ἐν παραβολαῖς see on 4:2; it denotes enigmatic or figurative rather than explicit speech. It is worth noting that outside chapter 4 Mark uses παραβολή almost always in contexts of controversy with scribes (and in 12:1-12 a wider group of religious leaders); the παραβολαί here demolish the scribes' case against Jesus, that of 7:15 undercuts their whole understanding of purity, and that of 12:1-12 is immediately recognised as spoken πρὸς αὐτούς and fuels their determination to silence him. The parabolic sayings of 2:17, 19-22 (though not there described as παραβολαί) were also spoken in controversy with opponents. In each case the message is plain and provocative, but the language indirect. At the lowest level this pattern surely implies a prudential motive in using enigmatic language where straight speech might have been dangerous. More theologically, it graphically reinforces the teaching of chapter 4 on the different situation of insiders and outsiders, and the appropriateness of parables to the latter. In chapter 4 parables are, of course, spoken to a wider and less obviously hostile audience, but even there a clear line is drawn between those 'outside' to whom only parables are given and those to whom secrets are revealed. Here the scribes from Jerusalem are an extreme example of 'outsiders'.

23b-26   These parabolic sayings all develop the same basic theme, that since strength depends on unity, an attack on any part of Satan's domain is a sign not of collusion with him but of threat to his power. Jesus thus ridicules the strange notion expressed in v. 22b that the ruler of demons might allow his power to be used against his own forces. If that suggestion depended on a hierarchical concept of demonic power, Jesus will have none of it. He speaks entirely of Σατανᾶς himself (apparently understood as the same as Βεελζεβούλ), not of any lesser δαιμόνια; even the act of exorcism is spoken of as Σατανᾶν ἐκβάλλειν, on the assumption that in the presence and fate of a lesser demon the chief demon himself is involved. Even though each exorcism is presented in the narrative as a confrontation with a separate demon (or demons), from the theological point of view all are direct conflicts between Jesus and Satan; v. 27 will accordingly sum up the theological significance of Jesus' exorcisms as the binding not of this or that demon, but of the ἰσχυρός himself. This comprehensive view of demonic power under the personal figure of Satan marks a significant difference between the demonology of the NT and that of much contemporary Judaism (and subsequent Christianity, as represented in the *Testament of*

Solomon). The elaborate naming of demons and accounts of their relationships which we find, for instance, in the Enoch literature are in striking contrast to the NT, where the focus is on the single figure of Satan (by whatever name), and other demons remain shadowy figures clearly subservient to him.

The argument of vv. 23b-26 is on the surface a purely negative one, rebutting the accusation of the scribes, but making no positive contribution to the understanding of the exorcisms. The point is made hypothetically: *if* Satan acted in this way, it would be suicidal; therefore it may be concluded that he is not doing so, and that his kingdom will not thus be destroyed by civil war. In terms of the strict logic of the argument, therefore, the language about the fall of Satan's kingdom and house, and about his τέλος, remains hypothetical rather than predictive. But if this is not the right explanation of the exorcisms, another must be found, so that underlying the simple refutation of the scribes' charge is a more positive implication. The exorcisms show that Satan's kingdom *is* in fact under attack: if this is not from the inside, then he is facing an external enemy, and the successes of that enemy point to his downfall, not through civil strife but through conquest by a stronger power. While τέλος ἔχει is formally hypothetical, the wider context reveals that it in fact expresses the reality of the new situation introduced by Jesus' exorcistic ministry, which v. 27 will vividly, though still parabolically, describe.

Both βασιλεία and οἰκία occur as elements in the παραβολαί, providing illustrative images of a divided kingdom and a divided household. But the choice of imagery, at least in the case of βασιλεία, is significant. The object of Jesus' mission is the establishment of the βασιλεία τοῦ θεοῦ (1:14-15), and it will be the fate and progress of that βασιλεία which will be explicitly the subject of two of the parables in the next chapter (4:26, 30), while the opening parable of the soils will be interpreted in terms of knowing the secret of the βασιλεία τοῦ θεοῦ (4:11). In the explanation of that parable ὁ Σατανᾶς will reappear as the one who is intent on preventing that secret from being known (4:15). Mention of a βασιλεία τοῦ Σατανᾶ here therefore prepares for that theme. It is not a matter of a kingdom divided, but of two rival kingdoms in conflict. As proclaimer of the kingdom of God Jesus is necessarily engaged in the destruction of the kingdom of Satan. It is from that quarter, not from within, that Satan's τέλος is coming.

27 A further παραβολή (which occurs in a slightly different form and with no context in *Gos. Thom.* 35) gives a more positive model for understanding the significance of Jesus' exorcisms (the introductory ἀλλά indicates that this παραβολή offers a new perspective in contrast with what has preceded). No explanation is offered, but there can be little doubt from the context that the strong man represents Satan (who, as in vv. 23b-26, represents the whole oppressive force of evil within which individual demons operate), while his opponent and despoiler is Jesus.[45] The point of the parable, then, is that the fact that

45. The fact that ἰσχυρότερος has occurred in 1:7 leads many commentators to discern an echo in the use of ἰσχυρός (and therefore the implication that Jesus is ἰσχυρότερος) here. But the

Jesus is despoiling Satan (through his exorcisms) proves that he has subdued him; the implication is that Satan's power τέλος ἔχει, and that in the ministry of Jesus the kingdom of God is being established (as is spelled out at this point in the Q saying, Mt. 12:28).

The imagery recalls Is. 49:24-26,[46] and since the 'prey' taken from the strong man there represents God's people rescued from their oppressors, we should perhaps understand the strong man's σκεύη here as representing the people rescued (by exorcism) from Satan's oppression. We no longer live under the shadow of Jülicher, who decreed that any such interpretation of parabolic detail be automatically dismissed as illegitimate 'allegorisation', and it remains a matter of judgment how far the context suggests that the details of the imagery are meant to be noticed in this way. In a context where the issue is the significance of Jesus' exorcisms, this seems an entirely natural understanding of the σκεύη, which in no way distorts the point of the parable, but rather sharpens it.

It is more questionable, however, whether the same can be said of the use of the verb δέω, as the context supplies no such immediate equivalent for the act of binding, and the parable functions well enough if it is understood simply as a way of saying that the strong man has been subdued. In the light of the recent proliferation of language about 'binding Satan' in charismatic circles, sometimes to the point of developing it into a quasi-liturgical ritual more reminiscent of the pagan magical papyri than of the NT, we should be particularly wary of reading too much out of the use of δέω here. There are indeed several references to the 'binding' of demonic powers in Jewish literature; one passage refers to the 'binding' of an individual demon (though this follows rather than precedes its explusion, Tob. 8:3), but in most cases the reference is either to the antediluvian imprisonment of the fallen angels to await their final judgment (*1 Enoch* 10:4-5, 11-12; 21:1-6; *Jub.* 10:7-9) or to an eschatological disabling of the forces of evil (*Test. Levi* 18:12; *1 Enoch* 54:3-5; 69:28) perhaps deriving from the idea of the eschatological imprisonment of the 'host of heaven' in Is. 24:21-22.[47] Such ideas lie behind the thousand-year 'binding' of Satan in Rev. 20:1-3. Jewish eschatological hopes also included the themes of the release of Satan's captives (*Test. Dan* 5:11; *Test. Zeb.* 9:8; 11Q13 [*Melchizedek*] 11-13, 24-25) and the ability of the people of God to trample evil spirits under foot (*Test. Levi* 18:12; *Test. Sim.* 6:6). All this suggests that the imagery of 'binding the strong man' relates not to Jesus' exorcistic methods, but rather to the escha-

---

point of comparison is quite different (John the Baptist/Satan) and the adjective sufficiently common to make any intended allusion unlikely.

46. A link with Is. 53:12, τῶν ἰσχυρῶν μεριεῖ σκῦλα, is much less likely, as the thought there is probably not of robbing the strong, but of sharing with them. 'Strong man' imagery is used differently again in *Ps. Sol.* 5:3, where God is pictured as a strong man from whom no one can take anything, so that they must depend on him to give it.

47. There is also in *Jub.* 48:15-16 the idea of the demon prince Mastema being 'bound' temporarily at the time of the Exodus to prevent his intervention against Israel.

tological salvation which he now brings, as God's kingship renders Satan ultimately powerless to oppose God's will or to harm his people.[48]

We have considered above (on 1:12-13) the argument of E. Best that 3:27 assumes that Satan is already subdued, and that therefore we should understand 1:12-13 as portraying his decisive defeat. The logic of 3:27 is not necessarily as tight as that. Nothing may be seized from the strong man until he is bound, but this does not require that he be bound once for all, after which there is no further contest. Rather, each individual confrontation with Satan (in the person of one of the possessing demons who are under his control) will involve a 'power encounter', in which Jesus must assert his superior authority. There is no suggestion that the outcome will ever be in doubt (except in one case where Jesus' disciples attempt to draw on his authority without adequate spiritual preparation, 9:14-29) since the proclamation of God's kingship has brought about a new situation of eschatological victory over Satan; but, as in NT eschatology generally, that victory in principle must still be implemented in reality through real conflict. That is how Jesus' exorcisms are to be understood.

It is worth noting that it was the Spirit who initiated the confrontation with Satan in 1:12, and that v. 29 will include one of the very rare references to the Spirit outside the prologue — indeed, the only one which relates the Spirit to the ministry of Jesus. It is, v. 29 will imply, through the Spirit that Jesus is able to overcome demonic power. The 'binding' of the ἰσχυρός is being achieved not simply by a man, but by a man in whom the Spirit of God is working. The exorcisms thus reveal the essentially spiritual dimension of the ministry of Jesus. That is why it is so serious a matter to pervert their meaning into a Satanic conspiracy.[49]

28-30 The παραβολαί (v. 23) have finished with v. 27, and now give way to a direct warning. The saying of vv. 28-29, with its solemn opening ἀμὴν λέγω ὑμῖν, does not in itself have any direct reference to the controversy in which it is set, and may well have had an independent life in the tradition of Jesus' sayings; the partial parallel in Lk. 12:10 is part of a more general catena of sayings about support and opposition, and a variant form occurs independently in *Gos. Thom.* 44. It is, however, in this context that Mark and Matthew have recorded it for us, and Mark has made it clear that he intends it to be interpreted in the light of the Beelzebul controversy by bracketing it into the pericope with v. 30, which picks up the accusation of v. 22. In the setting in Mark's gospel, therefore, the βλασφημία referred to is the scribes' accusation of demonic collusion and possession.

This is the first occurrence in Mark of the formula ἀμὴν λέγω ὑμῖν, which

48. This is a more clearly relevant background to the ministry of Jesus in first-century Galilee than the pagan exorcistic incantations found in later Greek magical papyri which sometimes use the language of binding (καταδέω; also φιμόω; see on 1:25) along with or instead of the more usual (ἐξ)ὁρκίζω; see G. H. Twelftree, in *GP*, 6.375, 378; MM, 325b, 672b.

49. Cf. J. Camery-Hoggatt, *Irony*, 125-26, with reference to Jewish thinking about the contrasting spirits of holiness and of Beliar.

occurs regularly in all four gospels (though less frequently in Luke, and with a doubled ἀμήν in John) and is generally agreed to be a hallmark of Jesus' distinctive style of teaching. This bold assumption of authority (Jesus speaks in his own name, and his words, like the words of Yahweh in the OT, are 'truth') is unparalleled in Jewish literature. The Hebrew word *'āmēn* itself occurs twenty-three times (in six of which it is doubled) in the OT as an affirmative response or as the conclusion of a doxology, generally represented in the LXX by γένοιτο, but three times (and five times in noncanonical books) by ἀμήν. But there is no parallel to Jesus' introductory use of ἀμήν in pre-Christian Jewish literature.[50] Still less is there any instance of a Jewish teacher using the phrase ἀμὴν λέγω ὑμῖν.[51] The one nonresponsorial use of *'āmēn* in the OT adds a further and remarkable dimension to Jesus' usage: Is. 65:16 uses *'elōhê-'āmēn*, 'God of the Amen', as a divine title. A saying thus introduced is not to be taken lightly.

The focus of the saying is not on 'sin' in general but on βλασφημίαι: the αἰώνιον ἁμάρτημα of v. 29c is defined by the preceding relative clause as blasphemy against the Holy Spirit, and while v. 28 begins with a more general reference to ἁμαρτήματα, the concluding clause ὅσα ἐὰν βλασφημήσωσιν (not ὅσα ἐὰν ἁμαρτήσωσιν) indicates the sort of sin that is in mind. The basic pronouncement is therefore simply that all (other, understood) blasphemies may be forgiven, but not that against the Holy Spirit. The mere postulation of such a distinction between blasphemies suggests that βλασφημία is not here being used in the technical rabbinic sense (see above on 2:7); all such blasphemy was a capital offence, and if blasphemy is defined as uttering the divine name, it is not easy to see what 'blasphemy against the Holy Spirit' could mean. In more popular usage βλασφημία (-έω) had a wider range of meaning, including slanderous speech against other people (Rom. 3:8; 1 Cor. 10:30; in Mk. 7:22 βλασφημία forms part of a list of sins which generally focus on human relationships).

The balance of the saying places the emphasis on the second half: it could be paraphrased, 'Whatever may be the case with other slanderous speech, there is one sort which is unforgivable, that against the Holy Spirit'. It is therefore not appropriate to ask just what sort of blasphemies *may* be forgiven;[52] the point is

50. J. Jeremias's well-known argument to this effect, *Prayers,* 108-15, remains convincing despite the attempts of V. Hasler, *Amen,* and K. Berger, *Amen-Worte* and *ZNW* 63 (1972) 45-75, to overthrow it. See Jeremias's response in *ZNW* 64 (1973) 122-23. B. D. Chilton, *Rabbi,* 202, suggests a possible Aramaic precedent in the use of 'in truth' in the Targum of Is. 37:18; 45:14, 15, but, leaving aside the question of the date of this targum, while this use is not responsorial as in the OT, each occurs in the middle of a prayer or discourse, not as an introductory formula; they are in no way comparable to the formula ἀμὴν λέγω ὑμῖν.

51. There is an introductory ἀμὴν λέγω σοι in *Test. Abr.* 8:7 (probably late first century A.D., and possibly influenced by the NT use), but there the words so introduced are those of God himself. In *Test. Abr.* 20:2 the formula ἀμὴν ἀμὴν λέγω σοι is used by Death in speaking to Abraham.

52. The danger of this sort of question is illustrated by the version of this saying in *Gos. Thom.* 44, which preserves no narrative context, and so is able to offer the theologically absurd ruling that blasphemy against the Father or the Son is forgivable, while blasphemy against the Spirit is not (but cf. Mt. 12:32).

that one sort may *not*. πάντα ἀφεθήσεται τοῖς υἱοῖς τῶν ἀνθρώπων is not a free-standing saying with a validity of its own, but the foil to the negative statement which follows.

οἱ υἱοὶ τῶν ἀνθρώπων represents a common Semitic expression for humanity in general, and occurs as such in LXX Pss. 10:4; 11:2, 9; 13:3; 30:20. It is used in the same sense in Eph. 3:5, but nowhere else in the NT. It is hardly surprising that it does not occur elsewhere in the gospels, both because it is not idiomatic Greek and because the singular ὁ υἱὸς τοῦ ἀνθρώπου has become a title for Jesus, so that a Christian Greek reader would find it difficult to revert to the original Semitic sense. Its solitary occurrence here has therefore occasioned much discussion about the original form of Jesus' saying, particularly in view of the fact that both Matthew and Luke include a clause not found in Mark contrasting blasphemy against the Holy Spirit with blasphemy against ὁ υἱὸς τοῦ ἀνθρώπου, singular. The simple suggestion that Matthew has misread Mark's plural and thus created a Son of Man saying where none was intended faces the objections that (a) his parallel to Mk. 3:28 (Mt. 12:31a) correctly renders τοῖς υἱοῖς τῶν ἀνθρώπων by τοῖς ἀνθρώποις, (b) οἱ υἱοὶ τῶν ἀνθρώπων in Mark are the subject, not the object, of the act of blasphemy, and (c) Matthew's clause about blasphemy against ὁ υἱὸς τοῦ ἀνθρώπου is most closely parallel not to Mk. 3:28 but to Lk. 12:10, which probably represents an independent (Q) tradition. But in interpreting Mark we need not resolve this question, since in his text there is no trace of a reference to ὁ υἱὸς τοῦ ἀνθρώπου, unless it be supposed that he could not have used the plural in its regular Semitic sense. That it could be so used in the Christian church is proved by Eph. 3:5, and there is enough Semitic idiom in Mark to suggest that he would not have found this phrase uncomfortable.

The use of both εἰς τὸν αἰῶνα (a regular LXX phrase to translate *le*'*ôlām*, 'forever') and αἰώνιος (which primarily denotes endless time, though it can also carry the sense of 'belonging to the age to come') emphasises that Jesus is speaking of the ultimate fate of those concerned. The two clauses are probably to be understood as making the same point in negative and positive forms: he will never be forgiven, but will always carry his guilt. But the expression in the last clause is awkward (see Textual Note). ἔνοχος with genitive can mean either 'guilty' (of a sin or crime) or 'liable' (to punishment). Followed by ἁμαρτήματος it would be expected to have the former sense, but αἰώνιος would more naturally describe the punishment than the sin. The whole phrase therefore probably means 'guilty of a sin with eternal consequences', which in effect means the same as 'liable to eternal punishment'. The present tenses perhaps focus attention more directly on present guilt than on future punishment, but the inclusion of εἰς τὸν αἰῶνα and αἰωνίου ensures that the future consequence of that guilt is kept in view. Mark's words offer no help in the debate over whether that future punishment consists in annihilation or conscious suffering: either can be equally αἰώνιος. Nor does the text offer any answer to the question whether this eternal guilt is irrevocable, or whether there is an implied clause 'unless he repents'; it might be possible to draw a little comfort from the fact that this saying, unlike Heb. 6:4-6; 10:26-27, does not explicitly rule out the possibility of repentance, but the saying is designed to convey warning, not reassurance.

In the Marcan context the βλασφημία εἰς τὸ πνεῦμα τὸ ἅγιον consists in the allegation that Jesus is empowered in his exorcistic ministry not by the Spirit of God (as Mark's readers know well from 1:8, 10, 12-13) but by Βεελζεβούλ, the chief spirit of evil, and the juxtaposition of τὸ πνεῦμα τὸ ἅγιον with πνεῦμα ἀκάθαρτον (v. 30) suggests that this allegation involves a total perversion of the truth and a repudiation of the rule of God. While Jesus' words do not in themselves directly accuse the Jerusalem scribes of this ultimate spiritual defection, Mark's v. 30 does make them, and any who share their attitude to the ministry of Jesus, ἔνοχοι αἰωνίου ἁμαρτήματος.

The relevance of vv. 28-29 outside that particular situation depends on establishing how far a given situation is in principle comparable with the scribes' alleged perversion of the truth.[53] To confine the use of these verses only to considerations of exorcism would be pedantic, but on the other hand it may safely be asserted that the vast majority of pastoral cases involving those who fear that they have committed or might commit 'the unforgivable sin' have little or nothing to do with what this saying is talking about. It is a warning to those who adopt a position of deliberate rejection and antagonism, not an attempt to frighten those of tender conscience.

Concluding Tableau: Insiders and Outsiders (3:31-35)

TEXTUAL NOTE

32. καὶ αἱ ἀδελφαί σου (A D some OL and syr[h,mg]) might have been omitted from the majority of MSS and versions either by mistake (after the almost identical preceding clause) or in order to harmonise with Matthew and Luke, and to bring this verse into parallel with vv. 31, 33, 34, where only ἡ μήτηρ καὶ οἱ ἀδελφοί are mentioned. It could equally, however, have been added in order to provide a basis for the inclusion of ἀδελφή in v. 35, perhaps also influenced by the mention of Jesus' sisters in 6:3. The very wide attestation for its omission suggests the latter, though it is surprising that the insertion was not made already in v. 31 (and in vv. 33, 34).

The final pericope in Mark's portrayal of the varying attitudes to Jesus draws several threads together. At the narrative level it completes the account, begun

---

53. An interesting early interpretation occurs in *Did.* 11:7, where it is forbidden to test or to pass judgment on a prophet while he is speaking in the Spirit, on the grounds πᾶσα γὰρ ἁμαρτία ἀφεθήσεται, αὕτη δὲ ἡ ἁμαρτία οὐκ ἀφεθήσεται. The words seem clearly to be based on this saying, and the idea that Spirit-directed activity is inviolable is similar, but the testing of prophecy in the church is not in the same category as the scribes' accusation of collusion with Satan; indeed, the rest of *Did.* 11 expects prophecy to be tested, leaving 11:7 as an awkward intrusion.

in vv. 20-21, of the attempt by Jesus' family to control his embarrassing activity. In v. 21 they ἐξῆλθον, and now they arrive. These verses therefore complete the sandwich structure within which the controversy with the Jerusalem scribes is enclosed, comparing two different case studies of the repudiation of Jesus, at the family and the official level, the former offensive enough (ἐξέστη) but the latter (Βεελζεβοὺλ ἔχει) even more damaging in that it questions not only Jesus' sanity but also his spiritual allegiance. These verses also, however, bring back into view the 'Jesus circle' (literally κύκλῳ, v. 34), whose chosen representatives have been introduced in vv. 13-19, and who now surround Jesus in the house while the family stand outside. There is no actual event in this pericope; we are not even told what the family made of Jesus' strange words, and are merely left to assume (from the fact that they will not appear in the narrative again) that their attempt to lay hands on Jesus had to be abandoned and they returned to Nazareth. It is not so much a narrative as a tableau, enabling us to see graphically the contrast between insiders and outsiders. The focus is on Jesus' words in vv. 33-35, in which the element of dismissal of his natural family is balanced by the positive affirmation of a new 'family' of the true people of God.

Jesus' attitude to his mother and brothers has caused understandable difficulty. Taken as a model for family relationships, it suggests a repudiation of natural affection and family ties with which Christians are rightly uncomfortable, not least in the light of the fifth commandment. Mark's brief tableau presents Jesus as brusque to the point of rudeness, not only in what he says but in his not even welcoming his mother and brothers into the house after their journey. Even granted that their purpose in coming was not a friendly one, and that their aim was κρατῆσαι αὐτόν, a little more civility might have been expected. Nor does Mark's gospel redress the balance with the information provided elsewhere in the NT that both Mary and James were subsequently prominent in the Christian movement, and that Jesus did not abandon his filial duty (Jn. 19:25-27).

But Mark's interest is elsewhere. While he does not include the words of Jesus explicitly requiring a choice between loyalty to Jesus and to the family (Mt. 10:35-37 par.), 13:12 envisages persecution of disciples from members of their families, and in 10:28-30 it is assumed that discipleship may involve the abandonment of one's natural family for a new and larger 'family' circle. The latter passage relates closely to the present pericope, and suggests that the implication here is not so much that family relationships are in themselves unimportant, but rather that a higher priority (the call to discipleship in the light of the proclamation of the kingdom of God) may need to take precedence. The new family of the people of God into which the disciple is introduced is far more significant (ἑκατονταπλασίονα, 10:30) even than the natural family, and if 'doing the will of God' (v. 35) involves the incomprehension and even the hostility of one's own family, as it did for Jesus, this is a price worth paying. Mark's single-minded desire to stress the priority of the 'spiritual family' leaves him no scope in this pericope to offer a more balanced overall account of Jesus' relationship with his mother and brothers.[54]

The contrast between insiders and outsiders is vividly depicted by the spatial imagery of this scene. The members of Jesus' family are ἔξω στήκοντες (v. 31), and are again described as ἔξω in v. 32, while the crowd of supporters ἐκάθητο περὶ αὐτόν (v. 32) and are again depicted as περὶ αὐτὸν κύκλῳ καθημένους in v. 34. Each of these phrases will be picked up in the subsequent pericope in which the insider/outsider contrast is brought to the centre of attention, οἱ περὶ αὐτόν to denote the privileged recipients of revelation, and οἱ ἔξω those to whom it is not given (4:10-11).

31 In the light of v. 20 we are presumably meant to envisage the house as so crowded with Jesus' supporters that, as in 2:2-4, it was physically impossible to get near him. In 6:3 Mark will give us the names of Jesus' μήτηρ καὶ ἀδελφοί (see Textual Note for the reading which includes sisters as well), but beyond that he tells us nothing about them. Since Mark has given no hint of the tradition of Jesus' virgin conception, the existence of ἀδελφοί occasions no surprise, and there is no foothold in his text for the subsequent debate in the church as to whether they were half-brothers (sons of Joseph and Mary, and therefore sharing parentage with Jesus on the maternal side) or cousins (a device which owes nothing to exegesis but everything to apologetics in favour of an ever virgin mother). For the absence of a father (who might surely have been expected to take the lead in this delegation) see on 6:3.[55]

32 The ὄχλος is presumably the same as that in v. 20, and is to be distinguished from the Twelve,[56] whom Jesus called apart from the larger crowd of enthusiastic followers (3:7-9) in 3:14-19 before returning with them to the house where the ὄχλος could again find him. The Twelve were of course still with him in the house, but the κύκλος (v. 34) is much wider than only they. Thus the pronouncement of v. 35 about those who do the will of God applies not only to the chosen group of Jesus' travelling companions, but is more widely inclusive (ὃς ἄν). The subject of λέγουσιν (and therefore also the antecedent of αὐτοῖς in v. 33) is probably the ὄχλος, since in Mark whereas the main verb governed by ὄχλος is generally singular (in this case ἐκάθητο) subsequent verbs and pronouns referring back to it are always plural (see above on v. 21); alternatively, it could be an indefinite 'they' ('someone said'), but in the narrative context it makes little difference, since only members of the ὄχλος were within earshot.

33-35 There is no reason to think that Mark intended κύκλος to be taken in other than a purely literal sense; the dative is used as an adverb, meaning 'all

---

54. For the suggestion that Mark is here engaged in a polemic against Jesus' family, and in particular James the leader of the Jerusalem church, see J. D. Crossan, *NovT* 15 (1973) 81-113; É. Trocmé, *Formation,* 130-136. See contra S. C. Barton, *Discipleship,* 82-85.

55. It is questionable whether, as E. Best believes (*Disciples,* 62), the absence of 'father' would 'at once remind the Christian that the "father" of the new family was God'.

56. See Minear's article, referred to above, p. 160 n. 17.

round him'. But by picturing the crowd thus surrounding Jesus Mark gives a visual impression of the gathering of the 'circle' (in our metaphorical sense) of Jesus' followers. In declaring this group to be his true family, Jesus suggests a greater degree of coherence than merely an ad hoc gathering. Such coherence within the close-knit fellowship of the Twelve would be less surprising, but this is the wider, and in principle indefinitely extendable, family of ὃς ἂν ποιήσῃ τὸ θέλημα τοῦ θεοῦ.

This is a very broad expression, and one which in itself is not easily limited to a particular confessional group. It would express well the aim of most religious people, including especially the Pharisees. In this context no doubt the Jerusalem scribes of 3:22 thought that they were doing the will of God, and so surely did Jesus' family. For the phrase to be used, as it clearly is here, to distinguish one type of religious commitment from another, it must presuppose a particular understanding of what τὸ θέλημα τοῦ θεοῦ is. Mark does not use the phrase again, but in the context of his story so far it must surely relate to Jesus' proclamation of the coming of the kingdom of God, with its consequent call to repentance and belief of the εὐαγγέλιον (1:14-15), which is the only general injunction of Jesus which Mark has so far recorded. It is that call which both scribes and family have, in their different ways, rejected, and in so doing have put themselves outside τὸ θέλημα τοῦ θεοῦ.

The portrayal of the 'Jesus circle' as a family in which members are related to him as 'brother' is a remarkable concept in the light of the evidence that we have already seen that Mark wishes his readers to perceive Jesus as a person of unique status and authority, the Son of God, in whose ministry the OT promises of the eschatological coming of God himself are being fulfilled. E. Best is probably right to warn us against probing the imagery of this passage too literally: 'Mark does not work out the position of Jesus in this group. He certainly does not suggest that Jesus and Christians are all one big happy family with Jesus on the same plane as the others, or on a plane slightly higher.'[57] But it may not be illegitimate to recall the 'elder brother' imagery found elsewhere in the NT: Rom. 8:29; Heb. 2:11-13.

The inclusion of καὶ ἀδελφή in v. 35 is an interesting example of deliberately inclusive language. Only mother and brothers have been mentioned in the narrative and dialogue (see Textual Note), so that logical consistency required only ἀδελφός μου καὶ μήτηρ here, but Jesus' followers (and Mark's church) contained women as well as men, and their presence is appropriately recognised. (Contrast the more male-oriented version of this pericope in *Gos. Thom.* 99, which not only puts 'brothers' before 'mother' throughout, but omits 'sister' altogether.)

---

57. E. Best, *Disciples*, 62.

EXPLANATORY DISCOURSE:
THE PARADOX OF THE KINGDOM OF GOD (4:1-34)

TEXTUAL NOTES

8. αὐξάνω occurs in both active and passive with the intransitive meaning 'to grow', the former being the later form, and more common in the NT. Since most earlier MSS here have the passive form, the active is probably a later correction, perhaps influenced by the similar ending of the preceding ἀναβαίνοντα.

The vast majority of witnesses have an accusative singular masculine participle, which depends on ἀναβαίνοντα being understood as a masculine singular agreeing with καρπόν. This is mechanically the easier reading, since ἄλλα is a long way away to be recognised as the noun governing the participles; but it does not make good sense, as it is the plants rather than their καρπός which grow upwards. The reading of ℵ B etc., which takes the participles as neuter plural in agreement with ἄλλα is therefore to be preferred, the masculine readings being the result of a mechanical misconstruction of the text. The reading of ἄλλο (to match vv. 5, 7) in place of ἄλλα (ℵ* B C L W Θ) in many MSS (supported by the Latin and Syriac versions) would allow αὐξανόμενον to be read with ἄλλο rather than καρπόν, but as ἀναβαίνοντα would in that case have to be read as masculine singular the syntax would be even more confused. The plural ἄλλα is in any case required by the structure of the story (see on v. 4).

8 (and 20, where the data are almost the same). The confusion of εἰς and ἐν, in various combinations for the three numerical phrases, with the further option of ἕν in all three (D W f¹³, Latin and Coptic versions), and the lack of a breathing over εν in most uncials, leaves a tricky problem. It is probably best to assume that Mark intended ἕν in all three phrases (ἕν . . . ἕν . . . ἕν . . . following the plural ἄλλα is an intelligible if clumsy idiom), but that in the absence of a breathing this was misread as ἐν (this would be almost inevitable if ἄλλο was read instead of ἄλλα; see last note), leading to further modifications to try to produce sense. In a case where Greek MSS are disadvantaged by the lack of breathings, the versions carry extra weight as witness to early understandings of the text.

15. Both the readings ἐν ταῖς καρδίαις αὐτῶν (D Θ and most later MSS and versions) and ἀπὸ τῆς καρδίας αὐτῶν (A) are suspect as assimilations to Matthew and Luke respectively. The B reading εἰς αὐτούς and that of ℵ, ἐν αὐτοῖς, do not differ in meaning; the former is perhaps a more 'correct' idiom for sowing seed 'into' the recipient, but the latter reads more naturally with reference to people, and so is more likely to be a correction.

24. The omission of καὶ προστεθήσεται ὑμῖν in D W and some OL is perhaps due to assimilation to Mt. 7:2, but may be simply a mechanical error after a similar preceding phrase. τοῖς ἀκούουσιν (A Θ and most later MSS and Syriac and Coptic versions) is probably an early moralising addition: only those who listen will receive the bonus.

28. In later Greek πλήρης was sometimes used indeclinably ('from the first century A.D. on it is frequently found in colloq. H.Gk.'; BAGD, 670a). The phrase πλήρης σῖτον (Σ 28 etc.) might then have been original, but would naturally be corrected to the more classical masculine form πλήρη σῖτον found in most MSS. In addition, the fact that σῖτος (masc.) has a neuter plural form (τὰ σῖτα) might have led a scribe to 'invent' a corresponding singular neuter form πλῆρες σῖτον (so C*). Fortunately the exegesis is not affected by which grammatical form was original.

So far, despite Mark's emphasis on Jesus' teaching activity, little actual teaching has been recorded, other than in short epigrams. Now it is time for a substantial block of teaching. As our structural analysis of the gospel has shown, this discourse falls in the middle of the First Act of the drama, the Galilean ministry, just as the other main block of teaching (13:3-37) falls in the middle of the Final Act, the climactic events in Jerusalem. Each discourse provides an explanatory framework to help the reader gain a true perspective on the narrative which precedes and follows it.

The narrative so far has described the initial proclamation of the kingdom of God, and the response which that proclamation has evoked. That response has been surprisingly varied, ranging from the enthusiasm and commitment of the first followers who become the nucleus of the Twelve through to the plot of the Pharisees and Herodians to destroy Jesus and the ultimate blasphemy of the scribes from Jerusalem who attribute this new work of God to the devil. In between are other levels of response, the scepticism of Jesus' family, the puzzlement of those who find Jesus' practice out of keeping with existing religious norms (2:18), the superficial enthusiasm of those who crowd round in the hope of healing, the amazed recognition of Jesus' new kind of ἐξουσία by those who have witnessed his exorcisms and healings, and the large and growing crowd who follow Jesus around for whatever motive, but whose permanence as 'followers' still remains to be tested. Yet all these are responses to the same message and the same acts of Jesus. How can people respond so differently? If the proclamation of the kingdom of God is εὐαγγέλιον, why is it not being universally embraced? If the demons have been right in recognising Jesus as the Son of God (and they have, as 1:11 has already assured Mark's readers), how can those who hold positions of authority among the people of God not acknowledge him as such, and even worse write him off as Satanic (a question which will, of course, become more urgent as the story progresses)? It is such questions which the following discourse attempts to answer.

The βασιλεία τοῦ θεοῦ, which was announced with such fanfare in 1:14-15 but has not been mentioned directly since, now comes back into focus. The crucial words of explanation in vv. 11-12 focus on the μυστήριον τῆς βασιλείας τοῦ θεοῦ, and the setting of these verses between the parable of the sower and its explanation, as a response to the disciples' question about parables, indicates that that parable (which is, in terms of length, the main component of the discourse) is therefore also about God's kingship. The two 'story-parables' which occur later in the discourse are both introduced explicitly as models for understanding the kingdom of God. This is, therefore, a discourse about God's kingship, and it aims to explain the paradoxical fact that a proclamation of such ultimate importance can be ignored or even opposed by some who hear it. It reveals a fundamental clash between divine and human values, and the necessity of a more-than-human insight if the purpose of God is to be understood and welcomed.

The explanation is done by the medium of παραβολαί. This word, already introduced in 3:23, dominates chapter 4 (vv. 2, 10, 11, 13 [bis], 30, 33, and 34). The discourse both includes some examples of παραβολαί (vv. 3-8, 21-22, 24-25, 26-29, and 30-32) and discusses the nature and purpose of this form of teaching (explicitly in vv. 10-13, 33-34 and parabolically especially in vv. 21-25).

The extensive modern discussion of Jesus' parables has shown how inadequate is the Sunday School definition, 'an earthly story with a heavenly meaning'. Even those παραβολαί which take the form of a 'story' (and many, such as vv. 21-22, 24-25, do not) are often not simple illustrations of heavenly truth. They tend to puzzle as much as enlighten, and are designed to shock and challenge rather than to offer reassuring explanations or illustrations of moral platitudes. In the LXX παραβολή translates *māšāl,* which includes not only (or even primarily) illustrative stories, but epigrams, proverbs, pictorial sayings, even riddles (*māšāl* is placed in parallel with *ḥîdâ,* 'riddle', in, e.g., Pss. 49:5; 78:2; Pr. 1:6; Ezk. 17:2). The word has already occurred in 3:23 to introduce a group of figurative sayings (3:23-27); and similar sayings in 2:17, 19-22, while not described as παραβολαί, provide other examples of this kind of teaching. παραβολή is perhaps best defined negatively as the opposite of prosaic, propositional speech. It is speech whose meaning does not lie on the surface, but demands enquiry and insight, so that the degree of communication which it achieves will depend on the extent to which the hearer shares the background of thought and the values of the speaker. Parables are 'narratives that mean more and other than they seem to say, and mean different things to different people'.[1] And their meaning, when discovered, is not likely to lie at the purely cognitive level, but will include (indeed, may even simply be) a call to response at the level of attitude, will, and action. To understand a παραβολή is usually to be changed (or at least challenged to change), not just enlightened.

All this, which will be crucial to the understanding of the overall thrust of this discourse, is commonplace in modern discussion, and this is not the place to survey that discussion.[2] Much of its contribution is encapsulated, appropriately, in a visual image proposed some years ago by C. F. D. Moule, which still bears repetition:

> A parable is like a modern political cartoon. A good cartoon presents an interpretative analogy, and it is for the viewer to work out its meaning, first by understanding it, then by reacting to it critically and, finally, by taking action accordingly. If the viewer is half-witted or stupid or so shallow as to be virtually incapable of being educated, no doubt he will see nothing but the mere picture, and he will not get further than saying that he likes it or dislikes it. But anyone with a grain of intelligence will respond in one way or another.

1. F. Kermode, *Genesis,* 23.
2. The literature is vast. Useful surveys of modern discussion may be found in N. Perrin, *Language,* 89-193; R. H. Stein, *Parables,* especially 42-81; and most recently in the articles of K. R. Snodgrass and R. H. Stein in R. N. Longenecker (ed.), *Parables,* 3-50.

He will say "Yes, of course that is exactly what is happening. I hadn't seen it so clearly before, but now I know that I mustn't vote Conservative [or whatever it may be] again". Or perhaps he will say, "Yes, I see what the cartoonist is getting at, but I don't think his interpretation is fair. He is being cruel to X, who isn't really doing what the hog in the picture is doing." The moment the viewer is responding in one way or another, he and the cartoonist have entered into a partnership in creating something; education is proceeding.[3]

He might usefully have added that the degree of communication achieved depends on the viewer's awareness of the events or issues on which the cartoonist is commenting, and of the perspective from which the comment is made. How much you get out of it depends on how much you bring to it. So it is also with parables (see 4:24-25).

The elements of paradox and of challenge are built into Jesus' parables. Parables are therefore a preeminently appropriate means for conveying the message of the kingdom of God, which also, as Mark's gospel will increasingly show, overturns some of the most basic human attitudes and values, and challenges its hearers to a radically new programme of life and action. It is a message which some will find too uncomfortable and will therefore oppose, while others will simply fail to see the point at all. Even those who respond to it will find it constantly upsetting their fundamental assumptions and demanding a programme of re-education which will substitute τὰ τοῦ θεοῦ for τὰ τῶν ἀνθρώπων (8:33), as will be illustrated in the experience of the disciples throughout the central section of the gospel (8:22–10:52). Such a message is best conveyed by παραβολαί, and the present discourse will begin the process. Mark 4 is therefore neither simply a discourse about parables nor about the kingdom of God, but necessarily about both, since the two are inseparable.

Another key word of chapter 4 which underlines the same point is the verb ἀκούω. The opening parable is introduced by the call Ἀκούετε, which is not a normal introductory formula in Mark.[4] It is echoed in v. 9 with the parabolic formula ὃς ἔχει ὦτα ἀκούειν ἀκουέτω. We are thus introduced to what will in fact be a main theme of the discourse, the importance of 'hearing'. The problem of those outside is that their 'hearing' is ineffective (v. 12), and the interpretation of the parable of the sower will go on to explain the fate of each of the four types of seed in terms of what happens when the λόγος is 'heard' (vv. 15, 16, 18, 20); v. 23 will then again repeat the formula εἴ τις ἔχει ὦτα ἀκούειν ἀκουέτω, and v. 24 will add the warning βλέπετε τί ἀκούετε; finally, Mark will add the comment that Jesus' teaching in parables was καθὼς ἠδύναντο ἀκούειν. Such a concentration of attention on the verb ἀκούω throughout the discourse

3. C. F. D. Moule, in E. E. Ellis and M. Wilcox (ed.), *Neotestamentica et Semitica*, 96-97.

4. The nearest parallel is 7:14, ἀκούσατέ μου πάντες καὶ σύνετε, followed again by a saying concluded in many MSS by the formula εἴ τις ἔχει ὦτα ἀκούειν ἀκουέτω (7:16); there, as here, the saying so introduced is described as a παραβολή (v. 17), so that even if 7:16 is not part of the original text, the context is again a parabolic discourse.

not only draws the hearer's attention but tells us that this is a discourse about 'hearing', and that the division between insiders and outsiders is connected with how each group can 'hear the word'.

The term 'discourse' is used rather loosely, since this section of the gospel includes not only reported speech but also narrative description by the evangelist (vv. 1-2, 10, 33-34, plus the repeated narrative formula καὶ ἔλεγεν [αὐτοῖς], vv. 9, 11, 13, 21, 24, 26, 30). But the narrative is subservient to and comments on the reported speech. The whole complex is a collection of parable material (and is introduced as such in v. 2). It derives its coherence from its subject matter rather than from any clear structural pattern (contrast Matthew 13, with its carefully organised framework of balancing elements).[5] The parable of the sower dominates its first part, and by sandwiching the saying on the purpose of parables (vv. 10-12) between its two parts Mark makes it clear that he sees this as the key parable, by which the whole parabolic method is to be interpreted (the point is made explicitly in v. 13). Some independent proverbial sayings (παραβολαί) follow in vv. 21-25, which again relate to the question of Jesus' teaching method; they fall into two small paragraphs, vv. 21-23 on concealment and revelation, and vv. 24-25 on the effects of such teaching on the hearers. Two further agricultural similes depicting the surprising character of God's kingship (vv. 26-32) complete the collection, after which Mark adds his own editorial comment (vv. 33-34), picking up the theme of vv. 10-12 and turning it into a programmatic description of Jesus' overall method of teaching. The complex is clearly designed as a whole, and for that reason is being treated in this commentary as a single section, as surely Mark would have wished.

The minimal narrative elements within 4:1-34 complement the teaching, with its theme of divided response, of revelation granted to some but not to others. The chapter begins with Jesus surrounded by an ὄχλος πλεῖστος, to whom his teaching is clearly addressed, even though Jesus is himself physically separated from them in a boat (where, in the light of 3:9, we may reasonably assume he is accompanied by his disciples). To this large crowd Jesus gives a great deal of parabolic teaching (ἐν παραβολαῖς πολλά), much more, presumably, than merely the one parable recorded at this point. But in v. 10, when he is away from the crowd (κατὰ μόνας), he explains his teaching method to a more limited group, οἱ περὶ αὐτὸν σὺν τοῖς δώδεκα, and it is to them alone, not to the ὄχλος πλεῖστος, that he offers a detailed explanation of the parable of the sower. At this point ἐκεῖνοι οἱ ἔξω, to whom everything is given (only) in parables, appear to be the same as the crowd on the lakeshore with whom the scene began. From v. 21 onwards the audience is not specified. We might naturally assume that the repeated καὶ ἔλεγεν αὐτοῖς indicates the same audience as in vv. 10ff.

---

5. M. A. Beavis, *Audience,* 133-36, dismisses attempts to find a 'concentric' structure in the discourse, and argues instead that its structure reflects the rabbinic model of public teaching followed by private explanation and a 'prophetic/apocalyptic scheme of revelatory parable/interpretation', of which she gives several examples.

(οἱ περὶ αὐτὸν σὺν τοῖς δώδεκα), but since the content is now again exclusively parable, without explanation, this is hardly consistent with the pattern established previously. Moreover, the sequel in vv. 33-34 begins καὶ τοιαύταις παραβολαῖς πολλαῖς ἐλάλει αὐτοῖς τὸν λόγον, where it is hard to understand the αὐτοί as anyone other than the audience to whom the immediately preceding parables were addressed, and yet to these αὐτοί only parables are given, and they are contrasted with οἱ ἴδιοι μαθηταί to whom everything is explained. It seems, then, that the audience has changed (without Mark saying so), either at v. 26 or more probably at v. 21 (since vv. 21-25 are also pure παραβολή, and contain the parabolic formula εἴ τις ἔχει ὦτα ἀκούειν ἀκουέτω already used with the original crowd in v. 9). Certainly Mark's own comments in vv. 33-34 reinforce the message of the earlier narrative structure, that parables are for outsiders, explanations only for disciples.

Hitherto it has been possible to understand Mark's uses of ὄχλος as denoting the larger group of those who followed Jesus, from among whom the Twelve were selected, and in 3:31-35 we saw the ὄχλος who were with Jesus in the house (the true family of Jesus) contrasted with his natural family who remained ἔξω. Are the ὄχλος πλεῖστος of 4:1 (who are apparently characterised as οἱ ἔξω in 4:11) therefore different from the ὄχλος of 3:31? And are the latter to be identified with οἱ περὶ αὐτόν who form a wider circle of supporters in addition to the Twelve in 4:10? This would certainly offer a coherent theory of insiders and outsiders in these two chapters, but at the expense of concluding that Mark does not use ὄχλος consistently to refer to the same specific group. This is no great loss, since ὄχλος is in the nature of the case a nonspecific term, and there is no reason to attribute to Mark a more technical understanding of it than his usage in fact allows.[6] The desire to organise the various groups who appear in Mark's story into a neat and consistent pattern owes more to a concern for tidiness than to any indication that this was what he intended. No doubt there were, as indeed Mark's story assumes, people representing many different shades of response to Jesus, ranging from hostility or indifference to enthusiasm, and it should cause no surprise that the gathering on the lakeshore included some who were more responsive than others, with the Twelve at the upper end of the scale of enthusiasm and commitment.[7]

The language of vv. 11-12 (backed up by vv. 33-34) has caused great unease and voluminous scholarly discussion.[8] It appears to suggest a deliberate intention on the part of Jesus to conceal the μυστήριον τῆς βασιλείας τοῦ θεοῦ from the crowd of those who wanted to hear his teaching, so as to keep them ἔξω, segregated from the privileged group of disciples to whom alone he was

6. See the discussion of Mark's references to the ὄχλος in Best, *Disciples,* 116-19, concluding (119) that 'The very many and contrasting roles . . . show that the crowd possesses no unitary role in the gospel.'

7. For discussion of Mark's references to the crowd see further P. S. Minear in H. Baltensweiler and B. Reicke (ed.), *NT und Geschichte,* 79-89.

8. See the survey of scholarship relating to these verses in M. A. Beavis, *Audience,* 69-86.

prepared to explain himself. We shall consider these issues when commenting on those verses below, but it is important to realise that they do not stand alone, but are part of the whole discourse and are therefore to be interpreted in the light of its parables, particularly that of the sower. Even so, the wider theological issue of why some respond to the preaching of the εὐαγγέλιον while others do not will ultimately lie beyond the scope of a commentary on Mark 4. This chapter makes clear that such a division does exist, and in part explains *how* that may come to be, but it does not in itself tell us *why* some are inside and some outside. The ultimate theological question of the place of selection and division within the working of divine grace must be answered, if it be answered at all, from a broader scriptural perspective. The commentator on the present discourse may be able to suggest ways in which some of the more extreme conclusions drawn from these verses should be modified, but must in the end remain content to elucidate the meaning of Mark's words, however surprising and uncomfortable that may turn out to be.

While, as noted above, this discourse is designed by Mark to be read as a whole, for the purpose of commenting on it in detail it will be convenient to operate with some subdivisions, as follows:

1-2	The setting
3-9	Parable of the sower
10-12	The purpose of parables
13-20	Interpretation of the parable of the sower
21-25	Short parables on revelation and response
26-32	Two more parables about seed
33-34	Editorial comment — parables and explanations.

The Setting (4:1-2)

As in 2:13; 3:1, πάλιν directs the reader's attention towards a pattern which is developing in Jesus' ministry at this period. The lakeshore has become a regular location (1:16; 2:13; 3:7), which allows access to a larger audience than the synagogue, and the large crowd and the use of the boat have already been depicted in 3:7-9.[9] At that point, however, the purpose of the boat was not explained (other than simply as a place of refuge), since in that pericope the focus was on Jesus' healing rather than his teaching; now we see that it serves as a pulpit.[10] καθῆσθαι

9. Belo, 120, suggests that 3:7-12 and 4:1ff. 'form but a single sequence', with the intervening material (3:13-35) thus 'enshrined' (his term for what others call 'sandwiching'). This analysis adds yet further complexity to the 'double-sandwich' structure we have already noted in 3:13-35.

10. For a visual comment on this see Stanley Spencer's unfinished masterpiece, *Christ Preaching at Cookham Regatta*. The difference is that in Mark's story, unlike at Cookham, there is apparently only one boat, and the crowd is on the shore. Mark's picture suggests a more optimistic view of the impact of Jesus' preaching than Spencer's!

indicates the normal position for teaching (cf. 13:3; Mt. 5:1; Lk. 4:20). ἐν τῇ θαλάσσῃ looks strange if taken only with καθῆσθαι, but it serves to fill out the visual impression of the scene, by indicating that the boat from which Jesus taught was launched rather than on the beach, thus keeping him apart from πᾶς ὁ ὄχλος who remained on the beach.[11] On the identity of the ὄχλος see above; if we may assume that the boat was occupied by Jesus and the Twelve[12] (cf. 3:9, where it was the μαθηταί who manned it), the crowd on the shore would presumably include the ὄχλος of 3:32 (who probably reappear as οἱ περὶ αὐτόν in v. 10) as well as many more casual attenders. To Mark's characteristic emphasis on teaching as a central part of Jesus' mission (these verses include διδάσκω twice and διδαχή once, none of which is in Matthew's parallel) is added the comment which sets the tone for the whole discourse, that this teaching was given ἐν παραβολαῖς. For the meaning of παραβολή see above. In view of the element of enigma involved in its meaning, it is possible to translate ἐν παραβολαῖς with 'in riddles', 'enigmatically', with the emphasis not so much on the teaching method as on the idea of obscurity. In v. 11 this meaning of the phrase is highly appropriate, but at this point the issue of revelation and concealment has not yet come up, so that 'in parables' is probably what Mark means. This was the obvious sense in 3:23, where the sayings which followed, while figurative in form, were not at all obscure in their meaning. Nonetheless, an awareness that the English word 'parable' falls far short of the flexibility of meaning of παραβολή will enable the reader at this point to discern at least a hint of the ambiguity of the phrase ἐν παραβολαῖς, which Mark will exploit so effectively as the discourse continues.[13]

The Parable of the Sower (3-9)

This title, derived from Mt. 13:18, is too well entrenched in English usage to be supplanted, even though the sower himself is of little importance in the story (and is not identified in its interpretation in vv. 13-20), the focus being on the fate of the seed, and on the different soils into which it falls. The title commonly used in German, *Gleichnis vom viererlei Acker,* 'Parable of the Four Kinds of Soil', is more appropriate. But since the story is actually told in terms of six individual seeds, three of which fall into the same (good) ground but produce different levels of yield, it is probably best entitled 'The Parable of the Seeds'.

11. M. A. Tolbert, *Sowing,* 149-50, rightly observing that the focus of the following parable is on the earth (γῆ) rather than the seed, rather imaginatively finds significance in the fact that the crowds, unlike Jesus, are standing on γῆ: this is a lot to read out of the natural θάλασσα/γῆ terminology.

12. A first-century Galilean boat unearthed in 1986 and preserved in the Yigal Allon Centre at Ginosar is 8.20 metres long by 2.35 wide. If this is typical of boats in use on the lake of Galilee at that time, a group of thirteen would comfortably fill it.

13. See J. Jeremias, *Parables,* 16 and n. 22.

As long as NT scholarship was dominated by Jülicher's opinion that parables must be understood as making a single point, the careful depiction of the four types of soil and the individual fates of the seeds was dismissed as 'scenery', and the tendency was to regard the ultimate harvest as the main focus of attention. (Gnilka's title, 'The Parable of the Confident Sower', predisposes the reader in favour of this approach.) On that view, of course, the interpretation of the parable offered by all three synoptic evangelists misses the point, since it does not develop the harvest motif (indeed, it gives no interpretation of the harvest as such at all), but rather exploits the different effects of each type of soil in a way which has proved irresistible to preachers who wish to call their hearers to examine their own response to the Word of God.

The synoptic interpretation does not in fact apply the parable in that way, but is content to identify the symbolism in each of the four scenes and leave the application to the reader's own discretion, thus preserving something of the open-endedness which modern exegesis generally attributes to the parabolic method. If a reader/hearer wishes to apply the parable to his or her own spiritual condition and progress, the synoptic interpretation leaves that option open. But it is no less appropriate to what was more likely the concern of Jesus' followers when they first heard the parable, as an answer to the question 'Why is the message of the kingdom of God meeting with such a mixed reception?' It is that question (whether directed to the historical context of Jesus' ministry or, by a natural extension, transferred to their own experience in preaching the gospel) which should have become increasingly urgent for Mark's readers as they have observed the varying responses in the preceding chapters, and to that question the whole fourfold structure of the parable, not merely the contrast between lost seed and harvest, provides an appropriate answer.

In the context of the gospel narrative, therefore, the synoptic interpretation provides a guide to the symbolism of the parable which fits it 'as hand fits glove'.[14] The question whether the parable could have had originally a different purpose (such as the depiction of a bumper harvest against all odds, as an encouragement to despondent preachers), before being put to this use by the evangelists is necessarily speculative. There is no trace of a version of the parable which does not preserve the fourfold pattern.[15] Even the Gospel of Thomas, which sometimes presents more concentrated versions of the parables and other

---

14. B. Gerhardsson, *NTS* 14 (1967/8) 192, concluding a stimulating argument to this effect with respect to the Matthean version of the parable and its interpretation, 165-93; Gerhardsson suggests that the three types of unsuccessful seed in the parable are modelled on the clause in the *Šᵉmaʿ*, 'with all your heart and with all your soul and with all your might'.

15. *1 Clem.* 24:5, in illustrating the nature of the resurrection, speaks of a sower sowing 'dry and bare' seeds in the earth, out of which by the power of God a crop is produced, as ἐκ τοῦ ἑνὸς πλείονα αὔξει καὶ ἐκφέρει καρπόν. But this illustration is not presented as a parable of Jesus, and insofar as there is any intended echo of Jesus' teaching it is more likely to be of Jn. 12:24, where the theme of death and resurrection is explicit, than of the parable of the sower. The relationship of the *1 Clement* text to Mark's parable is discussed by B. W. Henaut, *Tradition,* 228-32.

sayings, preserves this one in the same structural form, despite differences of detail (*Gos. Thom.* 9); it does not include the synoptic interpretation, but the form of the parable itself encourages attention to the details.[16]

The parable of the sower is, as Moule argues, a 'multiple parable', so that to focus on the individual soil types and their effect is not to introduce an illegitimate 'allegorising' interpretation, but to 'make explicit what the multiple parable has already suggested'.[17]

Since Mark has himself provided us with a guide to the symbolism of the parable in vv. 13-20, we shall limit our attention at this point to the form of the 'story' itself.

3 For ἀκούετε see the comments above (pp. 184-85) on the importance of this verb in the discourse as a whole.[18] Coupled with the following ἰδού, and picked up in v. 9 by the formula Ὃς ἔχει ὦτα ἀκούειν ἀκουέτω, it compels the hearer's attention. The image of God as a sower occurs in Je. 31:27-28 (cf. Ho. 2:23), but as the sowing there ('with the seed of man and the seed of beast') represents the repopulation of Israel and Judah, there is no clear link with Jesus' imagery here.[19] In view of Jesus' frequent use of seed imagery in connection with the preaching of the kingdom of God (vv. 26-29, 30-32; Mt. 13:24-30; cf. Jn. 4:35-38) there is no need to seek any other source for this story than his own familiarity with farming methods.[20]

4 For καὶ ἐγένετο followed by a main verb see on 1:9. The first three scenes describe the seed in the singular, ὃ μὲν . . . ἄλλο . . . ἄλλο . . . (so that each scene describes the fate of a single [typical] seed), while in the fourth, where three individual seeds (hence the repeated use of ἕν) producing different

16. B. W. Henaut, *Tradition,* 222-28, discusses in detail the relationship between the Mark and Thomas versions of the parable, concluding (contra, e.g., J. D. Crossan) that Thomas does not provide independent evidence of the original form of Jesus' parable.

17. C. F. D. Moule, in E. E. Ellis and M. Wilcox (ed.), *Neotestamentica et Semitica,* 109. B. W. Henaut, *Tradition,* 195, regards Gerhardsson and Moule as two 'dissenting opinions' from the 'generally held' thesis that the interpretation given in the Synoptic Gospels does not represent Jesus' intention, and devotes a lengthy section (203-11) to a methodological critique of their approaches. For further comment on the authenticity of the interpretation, see below (introduction to vv. 13-20).

18. This opening summons reminds some readers of the *Šᵉmaʿ*, 'Hear, O Israel' (Dt. 6:4), and this reminiscence might then support B. Gerhardsson's suggestion, *NTS* (1967/8) 192, that the whole parable is modeled on the *Šᵉmaʿ*. In view of the prominence of the verb ἀκούω throughout the discourse, however, a specific allusion to Dt. 6:4 is not necessary to explain its use at the opening of the discourse.

19. *Pace* M. Sabin, *JSNT* 45 (1992) 14.

20. There is an interesting parallel in *4 Ezra* 8:41, a brief parable, not unlike that of Jesus, about the varied performance of seed which is sown. Another use of seed imagery in *4 Ezra* 4:28-32 differs from this parable in that two types of seed (bad and good) are distinguished, rather than different types of soil. Similar imagery occurs in *4 Ezra* 8:6; 9:30-37, the latter passage applying it to the failure of Israel to receive God's law, which he has 'sown' in them. This is certainly not the source of Jesus' imagery (*4 Ezra* is dated ca. A.D. 100). It may be an independent development, though it is not impossible that the author, who elsewhere displays a number of resemblances to NT language and ideas (J. H. Charlesworth, *Pseudepigrapha,* 1.522), was aware of Jesus' simile. For the common use of sowing and crops as a metaphor see B. W. Henaut, *Tradition,* 232-35.

yields are mentioned in a single sentence, the plural ἄλλα is used (see Textual Note). There are thus six individual seeds in view, three which failed and three which succeeded. Since seed was commonly ploughed in after sowing in ancient Palestine,[21] the seed which fell right at the edge of the field παρὰ τὴν ὁδόν (*Gos. Thom.* 9 makes it '*on* the road'), where it would not be ploughed in, remained available for the birds (cf. *Jub.* 11:11 for seed sown and eaten by birds before it could be ploughed in).

5-6 τὸ πετρῶδες ('rocky ground') is, as vv. 5b-6 make clear, ground where the underlying rock is close to the surface, not allowing sufficient depth of soil for successful growth. Verse 5b appears to suggest that the lack of soil actually causes seed sown in such a place to grow up more quickly, but this makes little agricultural sense. The focus is rather on the contrast between impressive upward growth and inadequate roots, resulting in initial success and subsequent failure; the interpretation in vv. 16-17 will pick up this contrast as a symbol of the enthusiastic but unstable convert. (*Gos. Thom.* 9 changes the symbolism to that of total failure from the beginning: 'did not send a root down into the earth and did not send an ear up to heaven'; echoing Is. 37:31). ὅτε ἀνέτειλεν ὁ ἥλιος is strange: unless the new plant lasted only one day, the sun must have risen many times; the reference is presumably to when the heat became intense.

7 In contrast with the plant in the rocky ground, which failed to survive at all, that which grew among thorns (the precise species is neither important nor discoverable) is not said to have died (συμπνίγω is to choke, but not necessarily to strangle; cf. Lk. 8:42), but to have been unable, owing to the competition for light and nourishment, to produce any grain; cf. the warning in Jer. 4:3 against sowing among thorns. (*Gos. Thom.* 9 adds a worm to the hazards in this case, but since worms could operate in any kind of soil this hardly fits the parable; perhaps it is a reminiscence of the destructive 'worm' in 9:48.)

There has thus been a progression in the three failed seeds, which is probably intended to be noticed in drawing out the symbolism: the first never started, the second started but died, the third survived but could not produce grain. But in the end none is of any value to the farmer, since he is looking for grain, not mere survival.

8 There is no indication of the proportion of the seed which fell in each type of soil, so that it is not legitimate to conclude that only one quarter proved fruitful.[22] Indeed, by carefully depicting the fate of *six* seeds Mark has effectively ruled out any notion that those that fail are in the majority. Rather here,

21. J. Jeremias, *Parables,* 11-12, states simply that 'sowing precedes ploughing'; it is more likely that the land was in fact ploughed up before sowing, but seed was subsequently ploughed in; see K. D. White, *JTS* 15 (1964) 303-5, criticising Jeremias's interpretation of the data; Jeremias replies in *NTS* 13 (1966/7) 48-53, accepting that ploughing could precede sowing; see further J. Drury, *JTS* 24 (1973) 368-70; P. B. Payne, *NTS* 25 (1978/9) 123-29.

22. Thus Myers, 176-77, draws sociological implications (based, unfortunately, on an uncritical acceptance of Jeremias's pronouncements) from the assumed 'focus on the majority of the seed, which went fruitless'.

by contrast with the three types of failure, are three further seeds which represent what should be the norm. The contrast is marked even by the way the sentence is constructed: the fate of each of the preceding seeds was described in the aorist, and in terms of what was done to it (eaten by birds, scorched by sun, choked by weeds) or of what it failed to achieve (καρπὸν οὐκ ἔδωκεν); but the seeds which fell in the good ground are the subject of an active sentence, with imperfect verbs (ἐδίδου, ἔφερεν) filled out by two present participles denoting continuous growth (ἀναβαίνοντα καὶ αὐξανόμενα; see Textual Note).

Several of Jesus' parables use groups of three[23] (as indeed do many folk tales and children's stories), so that the different levels of fruitfulness of the three seeds in v. 8 (for ἓν ... ἓν ... ἓν ... see Textual Note), contrasting with the three failed seeds which precede them, may be no more than a natural storyteller's device to produce a memorable sequence.[24] But the threefold climax may also have been intended to enrich the symbolism (all good disciples are fruitful, but their performance may not necessarily be uniform). Of the figures quoted ἑκατόν is clearly the dominant one (in Luke it is the only one), with τριάκοντα and ἑξήκοντα chosen as the natural figures to build up to it incrementally in three stages.[25] There has been much debate over the significance of the yield of a hundred. Those who see the parable as designed to focus on a remarkable harvest take it to be an abnormal, even miraculous, yield which 'symbolizes the eschatological overflowing of the divine goodness, surpassing all human measure',[26] while others regard it as good but by no means impossible. The difference arises in part from a difference of understanding as to what the figures denote. If ἑκατόν refers to the number of bushels harvested per bushel sown, then it would indeed be remarkable. But Mark's phraseology, ἓν τριάκοντα etc., and the way the whole story has been constructed in terms of the fate of individual seeds, suggests that he is speaking rather, as was common in the ancient world, of the number of grains per plant, and a hundred grains or more per plant is not at all abnormal, though certainly a good yield.[27] Gn. 26:12

23. Three passers-by (Lk. 10:31-34); three excuses (Lk. 14:18-20); three servants (Mt. 25:15ff.; Lk. 19:16-21); three requests for payment (Mt. 21:34-37).

24. Luke has, rather prosaically, cut it to a single figure of 100. *Gos. Thom.* 9 has also lost the threefold pattern: 'It bore 60-fold and 120-fold' (the latter figure is probably symbolic: it is described in another gnostic document as 'the perfect number that is highly exalted'; *Concept of Our Great Power* [Nag Hammadi Codices VI.4] 43:19-22).

25. J. G. Williams, *Gospel,* 110-12, explains the figures in terms of 'the repetition of ascending numbers' found in Hebrew poetry, as in Ps. 91:7; Am. 1:3, etc.

26. J. Jeremias, *Parables,* 150, basing his view on a partial reading of Dalman's statistics of Palestinian crop yields; Jeremias's interpretation, though since analysed and found wanting (see next note), continues to be repeated by commentators.

27. This conclusion, and the method of reckoning per plant, are convincingly argued by K. D. White, *JTS* 15 (1964) 301-3. White's argument (which goes on to criticise severely Jeremias's agricultural assumptions) is the more compelling as deriving from no theological presupposition, but from the observations of an ancient economic historian. Further evidence of ancient crop yields is collected by P. B. Payne in *GP,* 1.181-86; he, too, comments unfavourably on Jeremias's arguments.

reports the hundredfold yield of Isaac's fields as a sign of God's blessing, but does not suggest that it was miraculous. Mark's figures are extremely modest in comparison with what Jewish writers could produce in forecasting the miraculous harvest of the eschatological age.[28] The yield of the seeds in good ground represents what a farmer might reasonably hope for in a very good year.

9 This formula is not part of the parable itself, but a sort of refrain (echoing Je. 5:21; Ezk. 12:2) which is appropriate to the conclusion of any parabolic saying (cf v. 23; [7:16;] Mt. 11:15; 13:43; Lk. 14:35; Rev. 2:7, etc.; cf. also Mk. 8:18), which leaves its hearers with the responsibility of discerning and applying its meaning. It implies, as vv. 10-12 will explicitly state, that not everyone *has* ears to hear, so that not all who have listened to the parable will benefit from it.

The Purpose of Parables (10-12)

The sandwiching of these verses (which deal with parables in general) between the parable of the sower and its interpretation undoubtedly indicates Mark's belief that each throws light on the other. The change of focus from one specific parable to the parabolic method in general has been seen as a mark of artificial, even clumsy, editing by Mark, but against this view we should note (a) that v. 13 specifically links the understanding of the parable of the sower with the understanding of 'all parables', suggesting that the former is, at least in Mark's view, not just any parable, but the parable about parables, and (b) that v. 2 has already made it clear that the specific parable of the sower functions as an example of Jesus' wider parabolic teaching (ἐν παραβολαῖς πολλά). Whether or not vv. 10-12 were originally spoken in this context, there is nothing haphazard or unintelligent about their location here.

The content of these verses is apparently quite simple: a limited group, apart from the crowd, ask Jesus about parables, and he explains that while they are privileged to understand the secret of the kingdom of God, others have everything in parables, in order that they will not share that saving understanding. But few have been content to believe that Jesus really meant to say just that, and there are sufficient ambiguities or obscurities in the wording to allow wide scope for scholarly ingenuity to discover a more acceptable intent.[29] In particular the condensed quotation of Is. 6:9-10 in v. 12 provides ample room for debate, both as to the original sense of the Isaiah prophecy and as to the significance of its application to Jesus' parables. We can best find a way through the

---

28. See *b. Ket.* 111b-12a, where various amazing yields include 50,000 *kōr* from one *se'â* (which = 1,500,000-fold); cf. Papias (in Iren., *Haer.* 5.33.3-4): 'a grain of wheat shall bring forth 10,000 ears, and every ear shall have 10,000 grains, and every grain shall yield five double pounds of white, clean flour'.

29. For a full survey of scholarly discussion on these verses see M. A. Beavis, *Audience,* 69-86.

debate by looking at the terms used, as they appear in the text, while trying at all times to bear in mind the overall thrust of the pericope and its wider context in the discourse of chapter 4.

10 The tense of the verbs ἠρώτων and ἔλεγεν may be intended to indicate that vv. 10-12 relate to a more general pattern than merely the single occasion when Jesus preached from the boat. καὶ ἔλεγεν αὐτοῖς is of course too frequent a formula in Mark for its tense to carry any exegetical weight in a particular instance, but combined with the imperfect ἠρώτων it may reasonably be taken to suggest that these verses concern not simply a single enquiry, but a regular pattern of response to Jesus' parables on the part of οἱ περὶ αὐτὸν σὺν τοῖς δώδεκα. The related general summary in vv. 33-34 will also use imperfect tenses throughout.

This more general perspective is indicated also by the fact that the boat (v. 1) has apparently been forgotten (though it will reappear in v. 36).[30] While Jesus is in v. 10 κατὰ μόνας[31] (i.e., away from the ὄχλος πλεῖστος of v. 1), he is now surrounded by a group larger than the Twelve, presumably too large to be with him in the boat. The point is not trivial, because the unique phrase οἱ περὶ αὐτὸν σὺν τοῖς δώδεκα indicates a new and wider audience than the Twelve who were selected in 3:13-19, and whom we assume to have been with him in the boat.[32] The neat distinction between those in the boat and those on the shore is thus deliberately blurred, and the circle of privileged revelation (v. 11) is drawn more widely than the now closed group of the Twelve.[33]

Who then are οἱ περὶ αὐτόν? The question is important since it is to this group, with the Twelve, that the striking words of 4:11 are spoken. The phrase in itself is hardly a technical term with a defined reference of its own; it denotes simply those who at any time are accompanying or associated with the central figure of the story (cf. Acts 13:13). Here its obvious antecedent is the ὄχλος who were seated in a circle περὶ αὐτόν in 3:32, 34, and who were there identified by the broadly inclusive term ὃς ἂν ποιήσῃ τὸ θέλημα τοῦ θεοῦ.[34] Just as

---

30. The wording of 4:36 probably means that Jesus was still in the boat (in which case the location of vv. 10ff. remains awkward), but it could also be taken to mean that he re-embarked at that point; see ad loc.

31. The phrase occurs only here in Mark, but cf. the use of κατ' ἰδίαν in 4:34; 6:31-32; 9:2, 28; 13:3, in each case to denote periods of private teaching of the disciples away from the public arena.

32. See below on vv. 33-34 for the suggestion of R. P. Meye, *SE* 2 (1964) 211-18, that Mark here refers only to the Twelve: he understands the phrase to mean 'those with him who belonged to the Twelve'.

33. For a comparably awkward construction, designed to extend the audience beyond the Twelve, cf. 8:34: τὸν ὄχλον σὺν τοῖς μαθηταῖς αὐτοῦ. If, as has been suggested above, Mark uses οἱ μαθηταί to refer specifically to the Twelve (see on 3:13-19), there is a tension between the wider audience specified in v. 10 and the restriction of explanations to οἱ ἴδιοι μαθηταί in the related passage in vv. 33-34; see the comments there.

34. P. S. Minear, in H. Baltensweiler and B. Reicke (ed.), *NT und Geschichte*, 79-89, argues for this identification.

that group were contrasted with those who remained ἔξω (3:31, 32), so will this group be (v. 11). But if this is a group of adherents wider than the Twelve, but narrower than the ὄχλος πλεῖστος of v. 1, how is its membership made up? In 3:35 they are characterised as 'doing the will of God', and here they are those who ask about parables.

C. F. D. Moule[35] argues that it is in this latter characteristic that their identification (and thus the key to the understanding of vv. 11-12) lies. Among the large crowd there were some, and only some, who were sufficiently interested in what they had heard to join the Twelve in demanding further elucidation, while others went away having heard nothing but παραβολαί. On the priniciple to be enunciated in v. 25, to those who had this degree of curiosity, more would be given, but those who lacked it would lose any benefit they might have gained from hearing the παραβολαί. The gift of special revelation (v. 11) is thus not restricted to a predetermined circle of favoured followers into which no one else is allowed access, but is offered to those who ask for it. The group of those περὶ αὐτόν is self-selected, rather than predestined.

Moule's argument, developing the cartoon analogy noted above, is attractive, and fits well into the development of themes in the discourse, particularly the exhortations of vv. 9, 23, 24-25 on the importance of hearing rightly. It also goes some way towards defusing the apparently predestinarian language of vv. 11-12. It does not, however (and is not intended to), offer a complete solution to the theological problem of division and choice, since the issue is merely pushed one stage further back, and leaves unresolved the question as to why some are able to respond with interest while others remain indifferent (or, in terms of the parable of the sower, how the different kinds of soil come to be different in the first place). But that question, as we have already noted, is one to which the discourse of Mark 4 does not address itself, and which the exegete of this chapter would therefore be wise to regard as beyond his or her terms of reference.

But this is to anticipate the discussion of vv. 11-12. The enquiry which will give rise to that pronouncement is about αἱ παραβολαί (the plural reflects v. 2, and prepares for v. 33). While the parable of the sower is the specific trigger for this enquiry (and will from v. 13 be the object of Jesus' explanation), the scope of the question in Mark and Matthew (not Luke) is broader. To use parables as his principal method of public teaching (indeed, according to v. 34, his only method), makes Jesus highly distinctive as a teacher, and the variety of response which he is evoking raises not only the question of whether this is the most effective form of teaching, but also of whether there is something about his message which is particularly suited to this form of presentation, whether the medium is not in some way integral to the message. If the question of οἱ περὶ αὐτὸν σὺν τοῖς δώδεκα (the specific content of which is left unexpressed in Mark) was not yet formulated along quite such sophisticated lines, it was such

---

35. C. F. D. Moule in E. E. Ellis and M. Wilcox (ed.), *Neotestamentica et Semitica*, especially 97-103.

questions which were Mark's concern and to which this discourse as a whole offers an answer. That answer, however, is appropriately formulated not in prosaic propositions but itself ἐν παραβολαῖς — and as a result has presented commentators with rich scope for disagreement. That is the nature of parables!

11 The mention of a μυστήριον immediately sets the tone for Jesus' response, but can easily mislead English readers who naturally think of a 'mystery' as something which is inherently hard to understand, and which can be unravelled only by unusual cleverness — if it is not totally incomprehensible. But the true sense of μυστήριον is better captured by the English 'secret', which denotes not incomprehensibility but hiddenness. A secret is that which is not divulged — but once known it need not be hard to grasp. It is privileged information rather than a puzzle.

It was secrecy which was the most obvious character of the Greek 'mystery religions' and which gave them their name.[36] The esoteric knowledge and rites were to be guarded on pain of death from being divulged to those who were not initiates. μυστήριον, used only here in the gospels, occurs often in Paul's writings with a related sense of privileged knowledge, the difference from the mystery religions being that Christians were very keen to share the secret into which they had themselves been initiated through the preaching of the εὐαγγέλιον. Paul's point in using the word is that no human insight had devised or discovered the εὐαγγέλιον; it was the result of divine revelation. But now that the secret is revealed it is to be shared with others.

A more immediate background for the Christian use of μυστήριον, however, is probably to be found in the Aramaic word *rāz*, used in Dn. 2:18-19, 27-30, 47 (cf. 4:6) and consistently translated in both LXX and Thdt by μυστήριον.[37] The interpretation of Nebuchadnezzar's dream is a 'secret' which is hidden from the wise men of Babylon, but is 'revealed' to Daniel by God, 'not because of any wisdom that I have . . . but in order that the interpretation might be made known to the king'.[38] It is this sense of μυστήριον as something 'given' rather than deciphered, with a view to that revelation being shared with others, which is essential to all its uses in the NT, including here in relation to parables.

What is 'given' here is not merely a μυστήριον but the μυστήριον τῆς βασιλείας τοῦ θεοῦ. It will become increasingly clear as we go through the gos-

36. A. E. Harvey, *JTS* 31 (1980) 320-36 (responding particularly to R. E. Brown, *CBQ* 20 [1958] 417-43; *Bib* 39 [1958] 426-48; 40 [1959] 70-87; all brought together in *Background*), argues against the tendency to attribute NT uses of μυστήριον solely to the influence of Semitic usage, and makes a strong case for the Greek mystery-religion background as a major component in the metaphor.

37. Cf. Am. 3:7 for the idea of a divine 'secret', revealed to the prophets. The Hebrew *sôd*, however, is never rendered by μυστήριον in the LXX.

38. The term *rāz* is also important in Qumran thinking about the divine 'secrets' for which the community's teachers can provide the true 'interpretation' *(pešer)*. For other examples of the motif of secrecy and restricted revelation in apocalyptic literature see B. W. Henaut, *Tradition*, 178-81.

pel that the message of the βασιλεία τοῦ θεοῦ is something so paradoxical, so totally opposed to natural human insight, that it takes nothing less than divine revelation to enable people to grasp it. It is, after all, the kingdom *of God,* so that human thought alone is likely to be at a disadvantage in penetrating its secret. Even those to whom this μυστήριον has been given will continue to struggle with its surprising, and often unwelcome, implications, and especially in Act Two of the gospel we shall see the disciples continually failing to cope with its demands; indeed, in 8:17-18 the disciples themselves will be rebuked in language similar to that used here to describe the unresponsiveness of οἱ ἔξω. The parable of the mustard seed later in this discourse will point out that unaided human perception cannot comprehend the way in which God's kingship is being established; hence the necessity for divine revelation of the μυστήριον.

So the μυστήριον τῆς βασιλείας τοῦ θεοῦ has been given to 'you' — but not to others. The sense of privileged information is clearly present, but what about the idea of a μυστήριον as something to be shared with others, once it has been revealed (an idea which will be reinforced in vv. 21-22)? Verses 11b-12 seem rather to speak of concealment than of communication of the μυστήριον. The subjects of this second part of the saying, with its extension in the 'quotation' of Is. 6:9-10, are a contrasting group (ἐκείνοις δέ), who are further characterised as οἱ ἔξω. The echo of 3:31-35, already established by the phrase περὶ αὐτόν in v. 10, is unmistakable; the position of being ἔξω has already been portrayed in the situation of Jesus' mother and brothers who there remained ἔξω (vv. 31, 32) while the ὄχλος inside the house enjoyed direct access to Jesus. But while Jesus' natural family form a model for understanding the phrase, the language here is more general. Who then are οἱ ἔξω, and how are they to be differentiated from οἱ περὶ αὐτόν?

R. E. Watts[39] argues that the discourse of chapter 4, and this pericope in particular, is to be understood as a direct response to the challenge of the 'scribes from Jerusalem' in 3:22, and that in this context 'the appeal to Isaiah 6:9-10 suggests that the judicial blinding effected by Jesus' parables . . . concerns those who have steadfastly rejected Yahweh's delivering activity manifest in Jesus'. Watts therefore restricts the reference of οἱ ἔξω to this specific group, not to the ὄχλος πλεῖστος of v. 1 (whom he regards as still open to receive Jesus' message, and hence exhorted to hear carefully). This is a healthy reaction against the common assumption that οἱ ἔξω is a general term for all who fall outside the very restricted group which many believe to be depicted in v. 10, but it faces the objection that the uses of ἔξω in 3:31-32 relate not to the Jerusalem scribes but to Jesus' family, whose scepticism about Jesus is not at the same level of total repudiation as that of the scribes. Undoubtedly the Jerusalem scribes are included in οἱ ἔξω, and indeed represent the clearest form of that condition, but Watts' restriction of the term to them alone is more precise than the text allows. Just as οἱ περὶ αὐτόν allowed for a more inclusive reference than

---

39. R. E. Watts, *Exodus,* 194-210 (quotation from pp. 197-98).

is sometimes proposed, so does οἱ ἔξω. The distinction between insiders and outsiders is clear in principle, but the general tone of these verses does not encourage us to attempt specific identifications.

While insiders are given the secret of the kingdom of God, for the outsiders ἐν παραβολαῖς τὰ πάντα γίνεται. The verb γίνεται, occurring where a verb of speaking might have been expected, perhaps suggests that τὰ πάντα should be understood more broadly than merely as Jesus' *teaching;* his whole ministry, deeds as well as words, constitutes a revelation in parable to those outside. This might also explain why in the following quotation the order of the first two clauses is reversed, so that seeing precedes hearing: what they are failing to appreciate is not just a sequence of puzzling sayings, but the whole revelation, visible as well as audible, which is presented to them in the coming of Jesus. But in the wider context of the whole discourse the focus is clearly primarily on Jesus' teaching.

As long as παραβολή is understood as a (helpful) illustration, the clause ἐν παραβολαῖς τὰ πάντα γίνεται alone need have no threatening tone — parables are given to them in order to help them to understand and thus to become insiders. But the context does not allow this attractive notion, since their fate is *contrasted* with that of those to whom revelation is given, and the statement is followed by the ominous words of v. 12 which suggest precisely the opposite intention. Should we then go to the other extreme and, noting the sense of enigma which is often associated with the term παραβολή, translate the phrase ἐν παραβολαῖς as 'enigmatically', 'obscurely'? If vv. 11-12 stood alone that might be possible, but they are part of a chapter in which παραβολαί are collected not with a view to obscuring the truth, but rather to offer understanding of God's kingship, at least to those who are able to grasp it. The phrase ἐν παραβολαῖς must not be isolated from the general tenor of Jesus' parabolic teaching, both here and throughout the synoptic tradition, which is to convey truth (even if sometimes unwelcome truth, 12:12) rather than to conceal it. But in itself the phrase means simply 'in parables'.

It is probably misleading to pose the exegetical question of this verse in terms of the intention of parables either to reveal or to conceal, to attract or to repel potential adherents. The parable of the sower, which surrounds this brief pericope, suggests a different understanding. The intention of the sower is to produce a crop, but whether or not this is achieved depends not on a change in his intention, but on the condition of the soil into which the seed falls. The same seed produces contrasting results. So it is with parables. The same parable produces enlightenment in one and no response in another; the result is appropriate to the condition of the hearer (and that is why 'how you hear' is so central a theme of the chapter). The focus throughout is not on the aim of the teacher so much as on the receptivity of the hearers. And the appropriateness of the parabolic method to this situation is that the parable, like the cartoon, is by its very nature adapted to elicit the appropriate and contrasting responses from the different kinds of hearer. Its challenge to think through the significance of the image, and to respond appropriately to its demand, will inevitably show up the division which already exists between those who are open to new insight and those who are resistant to change. Thus the same parable which to some brings an understanding of the secret of God's kingship will leave others cold. They are the ones who remain ἔξω, and for them there is nothing but parable.

12 It is this second group who are described in the terrible words of Is. 6:9-10, quoted in abbreviated form (and with the first two clauses reversed; see above) in v. 12.[40] But the quotation is introduced by ἵνα, and it is this conjunction which more than anything else suggests a *purpose* of concealment in Jesus' pronouncement.

In order to evade this conclusion numerous suggestions have been made,[41] among which the following have been popular: (i) that ἵνα here (as in Mt. 18:16?) stands for a quotation formula, such as ἵνα πληρώθῃ (thus attributing the purpose to Scripture rather than to Jesus);[42] (ii) that ἵνα is a mistranslation for the Aramaic relative d^e-, which can have a final sense but in the Targum of Is. 6:9 has its regular meaning 'who';[43] (iii) that ἵνα may be used instead of ὥστε to express result rather than purpose (a use for which examples can be cited, but not among the sixty uses of ἵνα in Mark);[44] (iv) that while the lexical meaning indicates purpose, this is to be understood within the context of Semitic thought which tends to suppress second causes, so that human decisions are attributed to the overriding providence of God.

This last observation, while in no way removing the normal force of the conjunction, does help to set it in the appropriate theological context. The ultimate outcome falls within the overall purpose of God, and, as Is. 6:9-10 reminds us, this can embrace the rejection as well as the acceptance of the prophet's message.

While it may not be legitimate to claim that in Mark ἵνα can *mean* 'with the result that' ((iii) above), the force of the quotation cannot be far from that sense. The fate of those who hear parables and are not thereby enlightened is explained as being parallel to that of Isaiah's hearers, and as at that time this was part of the divinely envisaged and predicted scenario for Isaiah's ministry, so it is now for that of Jesus. This is not 'fulfilment' in the sense of a prediction coming true, but rather a typological correspondence between two phases in the ongoing history of God's appeals to his people. Such appeals have always met

---

40. For similar language about failure to grasp the prophetic message see Je. 5:21; Ezk. 12:2-3; Dn. 12:10; the latter, with its contrast of 'the wise' and 'the wicked', parallels the 'insiders/outsiders' contrast here (cf. Myers, 172).

41. The six main views are usefully listed and analysed in C. A. Evans, *To See,* 92-96.

42. So J. Jeremias, *Parables,* 17, and many others. There would be no other such usage in Mark; the ἵνα in 9:12 follows a quotation formula rather than introducing it.

43. So T. W. Manson, *Teaching,* 76-80; see, however, the cautionary comments of B. D. Chilton, *Rabbi,* 93.

44. See C. F. D. Moule, *Idiom-Book,* 142-46. Mark often uses ἵνα in an imperatival sense, generally in indirect speech (e.g., 3:9; 5:18, 43; 6:8) but sometimes also in direct (5:23; 10:51; 14:49), but this usage in no way reduces the sense of purpose.

with a divided response, and the situation is no different now (except that in Isaiah's case the prediction was of *total* rejection, with no alleviating promise of revelation given to those who hear in the right way). When Jesus teaches in parables this scriptural pattern repeats itself, as it must. Perhaps the closest Marcan parallel to the use of ἵνα to express this conviction is in its use (twice) in 4:22 to express not so much the *purpose* of the hiding, but rather what *must inevitably follow*.

But did Is. 6:9-10 really mean this? Was Isaiah really commanded to *cause* his hearers to disbelieve, as the first part of Is. 6:10 (which, significantly, Mark omits from his quotation) states so emphatically? Not surprisingly later Jewish interpretation found this idea too harsh; the LXX turns the causative verbs of the Hebrew in v. 10a into mere descriptions of the state of the people, and the Targum turns the whole of the first part of the pronouncement into a description of the antecedent state of the people (rather than the result of Isaiah's preaching), while the concluding clause (Mark's v. 12c) begins with *dîlemā'*, which, unlike the Hebrew *pen,* can mean not only 'lest' but also 'unless'. The latter sense would then allow the concluding clause to be read as an offer of future forgiveness if only they will 'turn', and in this sense the passage was quoted among the rabbis as a promise rather than a threat.[45] (Since Mark 4:12c uses ἀφεθῇ, corresponding to the targumic verb *šebaq* as against the 'healing' of the Hebrew and LXX, it has been suggested that this more optimistic tradition of interpretation is in his mind, but it must be said that his wording does little to encourage it, with the problematic ἵνα closely followed by μήποτε, which, unlike *dîlemā'*, allows little scope for hope of restoration.)[46]

These later modifications of Isaiah's language assume that he cannot have meant quite what he said. Another way to achieve the same interpretative end is to take the expression as ironical, since irony consists in using words to convey the opposite of their normal meaning. Irony, which depends so much on tone of voice or gestures, is notoriously difficult to convey in a written text, and therefore poses particular problems for a translator. A sensitive discussion of this passage for Bible translators by B. Hollenbach[47] concludes that both Is 6:9-10 and, derivatively, Mk 4:12 are to be understood as ironical, and proposes the following translation for the latter:

> . . . so that they may indeed see but not perceive,
>   and may indeed hear but not understand;
> because the last thing they want is to turn and have their sins forgiven!

45. J. Jeremias, *Parables,* 17.

46. The regular meaning of μήποτε is 'lest', 'in order that not', and there is no warrant for translating it 'unless'. In 2 Tim. 2:25 it has a more positive role, meaning 'with the hope that', but this results from the positive orientation of the preceding main clause, to which there is no corresponding element in this context.

47. B. Hollenbach, *BT* 34 (1983) 312-21.

In this rendering the exclamation mark is the crucial element; without it, the irony remains invisible on the printed page. Irony must therefore always be a slippery tool for the exegete, and can too easily be invoked as a counsel of despair.[48] But at least surely Moule is right to warn us against the 'pitiful literalism' which takes Is. 6:9-10 as 'an instruction to the prophet to make sure that his message was unintelligible'.[49]

If then it is right to understand Is. 6:9-10 as focusing more on the *fact* that God's message will meet with indifference or even hostility rather than on a divine *intention* to prevent its hearers from 'turning and being healed', the quotation fits very appropriately in the context of vv. 10-11 and of the parable of the sower. The only significant difference is that whereas the Isaiah passage gives no clear indication that there will be *any* response, the parable of the sower balances bad soil with good, and v. 11 envisages responsive 'insiders' as well as 'outsiders'. The difference depends on how they hear (or, in the terms of the parable, what sort of soil they are), and parables are a uniquely effective way to bring out that difference.

We noted above that a μυστήριον, once known, is to be shared with others. Isaiah's experience warns the disciple that not all will receive it with the same openness, and as the gospel progresses we shall see increasing emphasis on the need for the sharing of the μυστήριον to be limited by discretion at least for the time being (especially 8:30; 9:9); see on 8:30 for discussion of the 'Messianic Secret'. The present discourse has its element of secrecy too, in the invisible growth of the seed in v. 27 and the ludicrously small size of the mustard seed in v. 31; it is not yet time for God's kingship to be visible in power (9:1) for all to see. But vv. 21-22 dispel any idea of a long-term concealment of the message; what is now hidden must inevitably be brought to light. There is a sense, therefore, in which the terrible verdict of vv. 11b-12 may be regarded as only temporary, leaving hope that those categorised as ἔξω need not be permanently written off, that the division between insiders and outsiders is not a gulf without bridges. After all, οἱ περὶ αὐτὸν σὺν τοῖς δώδεκα had themselves not always been insiders, and the calling of the disciples to be ἁλιεῖς ἀνθρώπων suggests that Mark's gospel does not intend to promote a fatalistic resignation to the belief that those who are now outside can never be brought inside (at this point perhaps the imagery of the parable fails us, in that soil may be less easy to change than people). But these verses, with their allusion to the unhappy experience of Isaiah, do impart a note of sober realism to those charged with the proclamation of the εὐαγγέλιον, in the recognition that within the purpose of God there will always be bad soil as well as good.

48. J. Camery-Hoggatt, *Irony*, 127-30, disagrees with Hollenbach and others who claim that these words were intended to be ironical. This is, he suggests, merely 'an attempt to alleviate the rather vexing problem of the obduracy mentioned in v. 12. . . . In Mark's understanding the saying is straightforward.'

49. C. F. D. Moule in E. E. Ellis and M. Wilcox (ed.), *Neotestamentica et Semitica*, 99-100.

Interpretation of the Parable of the Sower (4:13-20)

The revelation of the secret of the kingdom of God now takes the form of an explanation of the parable which provoked the disciples' question. This pericope therefore gives us the most detailed example in Mark of what vv. 33-34 will describe as Jesus' regular practice, to offer to his disciples explanations of everything which was spoken only in parables to the larger crowd. Other such private explanations of striking pronouncements will occur in 7:17-23; 8:16-21; 10:10-12; and 13:3-37, and acts of Jesus will be similarly explained to the disciples alone in 9:28-29; 11:21-25.

The fact that none of these relates to a story-type parable has perhaps contributed to the widespread view that 4:13-20 is untypical, with the resultant suspicion of its authenticity as teaching of Jesus. Once παραβολή is understood in its broader biblical sense, however, that view cannot stand; indeed, 7:17-23 is explicitly introduced as the explanation of a παραβολή. E. E. Lemcio has also shown that the sequence of parable — question (sometimes implied) — explanation has a good OT pedigree (e.g., Ezk. 17:1-24; Zc. 4:2-10, 11-14).[50] Nor is it true to say that synoptic parables in general lack explanatory comment, even if not usually as extended as here: see 13:29; Mt. 13:36-43, 49-50; 18:14, 35; 20:16; 21:31-32, 43; 25:13; Lk. 7:43-47; 10:36-37; 12:21; 15:7, 10; 16:8-13; 18:6-8, 14.

Other traditional arguments against the authenticity of this pericope are discussed in detail by P. B. Payne.[51] Central among them has been the belief that the interpretation misses the original intention of the parable, a belief that we have already seen reason to question in discussing the parable above. The widespread reaction in more recent scholarship against the dogma that parables focus on a single moral point has led to a greater willingness to recognise the appropriateness of this interpretation to the actual 'multiple' form of the parable, and thus to a greater inclination to regard it as at least consonant with Jesus' original intention, whether or not he is actually credited with its formulation. The characteristically cautious discussion by Davies and Allison[52] well expresses this more positive evaluation of the synoptic interpretation: Davies and Allison incline to the view that 'even if the synoptic interpretation does not derive from Jesus himself, it rightly catches his intention' (375-76), and that 'it seems quite unreasonable to exclude dogmatically that Mk 4:13-20 rests upon an interpretation Jesus gave of the parable of the sower', even though the case for its dominical origin 'falls short of proof' (399).

One reason for doubting that the interpretation derives from Jesus has been the assumption that it represents an application of the parable to a particu-

50. E. E. Lemcio, *JTS* 29 (1978) 323-38. The familiarity of a similar pattern in rabbinic writings has been shown by D. Daube, *The NT,* 141-50.

51. In *GP,* 1.163-207.

52. W. D. Davies and D. C. Allison, *Matthew,* 2.375-77, 396-99.

lar situation in the growing church which would not have been relevant in the time of Jesus' ministry. It should be pointed out in this connection, however, that it is an 'interpretation' only in the sense of identifying the meaning of the symbolism of Jesus' story (or rather of *some* of it; there is no identification of the sower, nor even, remarkably, of the καρπός produced), not in the sense of applying that symbolism to a particular pastoral situation. It describes the types of people portrayed in the story, but does not identify them with any specific groups or individuals in the church or outside it.[53] People may be found to fit these descriptions at any stage in the church's history, and it has been the contention of this commentary that they could equally be discerned among the varied responses to the preaching of the kingdom of God during Jesus' earthly ministry, such as they have already been described in chapters 1–3. Nor do these verses prescribe the sort of use to which these descriptions are to be put, for instance, in terms of the evangelistic strategy of the church or of its members' spiritual self-examination; the parable, even as 'interpreted', remains open-ended in terms of its pastoral application.

The identification of those portrayed in the successive frames of the story presents some problems of expression. Whereas in the parable Mark has described each seed in the singular, the people so represented are, appropriately but slightly awkwardly, characterised in the plural. (Matthew's singular characterisations would in fact have fitted Mark's singular seeds better than Matthew's plural ones!) Still more awkwardly, whereas the difference in fact lies in the soil rather than in the seed, the people so differentiated are in the first scene correctly identified with the soil, but thereafter are introduced as if they were different types of seed (οἱ σπειρόμενοι/σπαρέντες).[54] But these are natural results of explaining a symbolic story, where like is not compared with like. For each scene of the story, with its description of the fate of the seed sown on that particular soil, the pedantic interpreter would need to say something like 'The fate of the seed sown in the rocky soil represents what happens to the word when it is preached among people who . . .'; and even then the focus would need to be on the particular character and circumstances of the people rather than on the 'word' as such. Mark's simpler form οὗτοί εἰσιν οἱ ἐπὶ τὰ πετρώδη σπειρόμενοι, οἵ . . . , if it is less logically tight, makes the point clearly enough for those who are not disposed to quibble. It is interesting that neither Matthew nor Luke, with their different ways of expressing the identifications, has achieved a perfectly logical structure either.

---

53. The unconventional attempts of M. A. Tolbert, *Sowing,* 153-59 (cf. 171), to identify the groups targeted within the structure of Mark's narrative offer thought-provoking examples of how these categorisations might work out, but it is not clear that Mark intended any such specific focus.

54. P. B. Payne, *NTS* 26 (1980) 564-68, is one of several who argue that Mark uses σπείρομαι in an Aramaic sense for the soil which 'is sown' rather than for the seed; but this proposal is hard to square with the use of ἐπί with accusative (vv. 16, 20) and εἰς (v. 18) to indicate the ground *into which* the sowing takes place, particularly in v. 20 where the soil can hardly be described as itself being ἐπὶ τὴν γῆν τὴν καλήν.

13 The first half of the answer does not exactly fit the question of v. 10, and assumes that an enquiry about the meaning of the parable of the sower was the basis of their more general question about parables, to which vv. 11-12 provided an answer. The second half, however, links the two themes, with the implication that to understand the parable of the sower *is* to understand πάσας τὰς παραβολάς. That is why ἡ παραβολὴ αὕτη needed to come at the beginning of the discourse: it is the key to all the rest, the parable about parables.[55]

The implied rebuke in Jesus' question reads strangely after v. 11. If they have been given the secret of the kingdom of God, how can they now fail to grasp this key parable? But worse rebukes will follow (e.g., 7:18; 8:17-18, 21). Clearly the 'giving' of the secret is not a simple act leading to immediate total enlightenment. The character of God's kingship is such that the whole period of Jesus' earthly ministry will not be enough for them to assimilate its paradoxical values, and a comprehensive programme of re-education of those very disciples to whom the secret 'has been given' will occupy the central act of Mark's drama. In any case, the point of this discourse is that enlightenment is 'given' by means of Jesus' patient private explanations of his parabolic teaching (vv. 33-34); it is because they have been given the capacity at least to begin to learn that they will receive the explanation which follows. Verses 13-20 are themselves part of that 'giving'.

14 The sower himself is not identified, and the seed only briefly; hereafter the focus will be on the effects of the different types of soil. In its historical context ὁ λόγος refers to the teaching which Jesus has been giving in Galilee (in the proclamation of which his disciples are themselves soon to share, 3:14), beginning with the εὐαγγέλιον of 1:15 and climaxing in the ἐν παραβολαῖς πολλά of v. 2. It is the varying response to this proclamation which has been the focus of interest in chapters 2–3, and of which this discourse offers an explanation. For the use of ὁ λόγος apparently as a technical term for the gospel throughout this pericope, as in later Christian usage, see comments on 2:2 and 4:33; by the time Mark wrote this would be familiar usage, but the fact that he uses so obvious a term from his own day does not in itself forbid us to believe that the tradition before him, and indeed Jesus himself, could have spoken of Jesus' own preaching, by whatever term it might then have been described, under the figure of the sowing of a seed.[56]

15 In identifying the first frame of the story Mark formulates his sentence more precisely than in the more shorthand form in vv. 16, 18, and 20 (see introductory comments to this section): the first group of people are not spoken

---

55. W. T. Shiner, *Follow,* 206-7 n. 14, dissents from this common opinion, arguing that it is not any special content in this parable which leads to Jesus' comment, but merely the fact that this parable happens to come first (and is the longest in the chapter), and so is taken as typical.

56. Is. 55:10-11 provides a significant precedent for describing the effect of the 'word' (of Yahweh) in the imagery of seed and fruitfulness, though the correspondence is not exact in that there the 'word' is apparently compared to the rain and snow rather than the seed.

of as if they were seed,[57] but are οἱ παρὰ τὴν ὁδόν, i.e., they correspond to the soil beside the road, so that the λόγος can be spoken of as sown εἰς αὐτούς (see Textual Note). Even these, the worst type of soil, are said to hear, just as each other type will (ἀκούω occurs in vv. 15, 16, 18, and 20). The difference lies not in the hearing, but in *how* you hear (vv. 9, 23, 24-25, and 33). In this case the failure is immediate (εὐθύς); the seed fails to penetrate and is lost, just as in Moule's analogy the 'half-witted or stupid' viewer of the cartoon sees nothing but a picture, or as in Ezk. 33:32 those who received Ezekiel's stern warnings heard nothing but 'one who sings love songs with a beautiful voice and plays well on an instrument'. Such ineffective hearing is attributed to the activity of ὁ Σατανᾶς, who, as the focus of opposition to the purpose of God and the ministry of Jesus (see on 3:22-27), is naturally determined to prevent the knowledge of God's kingship from being grasped. In 8:33 he will similarly be found promoting a concern for τὰ τῶν ἀνθρώπων in opposition to τὰ τοῦ θεοῦ.

16-17 The second type of response is initially much more promising, indeed enthusiastic (μετὰ χαρᾶς), but proves to be πρόσκαιρος. Such short-lived commitment was, of course, a recurrent feature of early church experience in the days of official persecution, but even in the time of Jesus' ministry most of the ὄχλοι who welcomed his Galilean début failed to stay the course, and no doubt a significant part of the reason for this was the growth of opposition, both official and unofficial, to this new movement, such as chapters 2–3 have already begun to illustrate. The threat to continued discipleship here represented by the heat of the sun is therefore interpreted in terms of pressure exerted upon the potential disciple from the social or religious environment, θλῖψις ἢ διωγμὸς διὰ τὸν λόγον, rather than, as in the next frame, from the disciple's own circumstances and priorities. There is no need to see διωγμὸς διὰ τὸν λόγον here as a concept appropriate only to later official persecution. Any social pressure arising out of the distinctive nature of the Jesus movement, with its implicit or explicit challenge to the norms of society, may be attributed to the effects of the λόγος which has brought about the change. Cf. 8:35; 10:29 for persecution and loss ἕνεκεν τοῦ εὐαγγελίου (and 10:30 for διωγμοί as an integral part of the disciples' experience).

σκανδαλίζω, which will occur prominently in 9:42-47, is often translated as 'cause to sin', but is in fact used more generally for anything which 'catches people out' or 'trips' them so as to render their discipleship ineffective. Here the focus is not on sin but on apostasy under pressure. The occurrence of σκανδαλίζομαι in 14:27, 29 for the disciples' desertion of Jesus under pressure

---

57. Many commentators (of whom J. Marcus, *Mystery,* 25-26 and n. 29, is typical) state that in this verse Mark identifies the people *both* as the soil (τὸν ἐσπαρμένον εἰς αὐτούς) *and* as the seed (οἱ παρὰ τὴν ὁδόν). But the opening clause does not have the participle (σπειρόμενοι, σπαρέντες) which in the other identifications (vv. 16, 18, and 20) shows that the seed is intended (Marcus appears not to have noticed this fact), and instead is immediately followed by ὅπου σπείρεται ὁ λόγος, indicating that it is the *soil* παρὰ τὴν ὁδόν which is in mind. The awkwardness is only, as noted above, in the need to use a plural expression to identify the (singular) soil as (plural) people.

well illustrates the point, though in their case the desertion was temporary; Mark does not suggest that he is thinking here of only temporary failure.[58]

18-19 The third soil-type represents discipleship which survives but is unproductive. Neither here nor in v. 20 is there any attempt to spell out what sort of καρπός is expected, or how it is to be recognised. Since, however, fruitful discipleship is contrasted with the material concerns listed at the beginning of v. 19, it may reasonably be assumed that fruitfulness involves conformity to the principles of the kingdom of God, with its opposition to such 'worldly' values.

ὁ αἰών on its own would not be a very clear expression, since NT thought, like Jewish thought generally, distinguishes two αἰῶνες, that which is present and that which is to come; but in combination with μέριμναι and followed by references to ἀπάτη, πλοῦτος, and ἐπιθυμίαι, there can be no doubt that it stands here for ὁ αἰὼν οὗτος, perceived in a negative light as the rival to God for the disciple's loyalty. Mt. 6:24-34 forms an appropriate commentary on the phrase αἱ μέριμναι τοῦ αἰῶνος and on the danger to effective discipleship which is posed when such concerns take priority over those of the kingdom of God. The danger of affluence is not so prominent an emphasis in Mark as in Luke or Paul, though it will be given stark expression in 10:17-27, where the story of the rich man provides an apt illustration of the point being made here.[59] What is at issue here is not so much the possession of wealth in itself, but rather the mental attitude which it engenders, hence the 'thought'-words μέριμνα, ἀπάτη, and ἐπιθυμία. ἀπάτη is a particularly powerful term, conveying here, as in its other NT uses, the sense of 'deception', even 'enticement', which threatens to seduce disciples from their true allegiance. (Is εἰσπορευόμεναι meant to depict these 'alien' concerns as unwelcome intruders into the disciple's life?)

αἱ περὶ τὰ λοιπὰ ἐπιθυμίαι seems a rather lame conclusion to the list, a sort of 'et cetera' to alert the reader that πλοῦτος as such is not the only object of worldly concern. It has therefore been suggested that τὰ λοιπά here represents the Hebrew/Aramaic *yeter*, which means not only 'remainder' but also 'superfluity', 'excess' (as in Ps. 17:14, Job 22:20), so that the whole phrase would aptly capture the essence of materialism as 'the constant desire for more'.[60] In this scene, therefore, in contrast with the preceding, the threat to effective discipleship comes not from external pressure but from the disciple's own divided loyalty.

20 The final frame (in which the three successful seeds of the parable

---

58. M. A. Tolbert, *Sowing,* 154-56 and passim thereafter, believes the reference here is intended to be to the disciples; see above, p. 161 n. 18, for her view that this was the significance of the name Πέτρος. But in terms of the narrative development there has been nothing so far to lead the reader to make this identification, and the privilege of the disciples expressed in v. 11 does not suggest that they are now intended to be seen in a bad light.

59. See T. E. Schmidt, *Hostility,* 103-18.

60. So T. E. Schmidt, *Hostility,* 106, following F. Zimmermann, *Origin,* 87-88.

are treated as a single group) receives only the minimal interpretation that these people 'hear the word and receive it'; the rest of the verse merely repeats the imagery of the parable and leaves to the reader to decide what sort of fruit may be in view, and what significance, if any, is to be given to the variety in the rates of yield. This is far removed from the 'allegorising' of which the synoptic interpretation of the sower has so often been accused; no respectable allegoriser could have ignored such an invitation. As was mentioned above on v. 8, it is possible that the three levels of fruitfulness are merely a narrative device to balance the three types of failure, and that therefore the versions in Mark and Matthew offer no further insight than that of Luke, which mentions only the hundredfold yield. But it is tempting to detect here also a recognition that the product of effective discipleship will not necessarily be uniform, a Marcan echo of the principle of Mt. 25:14-30, where equally faithful servants are given different degrees of responsibility, ἑκάστῳ κατὰ τὴν ἰδίαν δύναμιν, and produce proportionately different results.

Short Parables on Revelation and Response (4:21-25)

The four short epigrammatic sayings (or 'aphorisms') which make up vv. 21-22, 24b-25, have a complicated synoptic history. While most of them are similarly grouped following the parable of the sower in Lk. 8:16-18, they also have parallels at several points elsewhere in the synoptic tradition, often in contexts quite different from the present discourse, and with consequently different meanings; versions of the same saying may occur in more than one location in each of the other Synoptic Gospels.[1] Verses 21, 22, and 25 also have parallels in the *Gospel of Thomas*.[2] With the exception of v. 25 (cf. Mt 13:12) these sayings do not appear in Matthew's more extensive parable discourse. But the themes of revelation (vv. 21-22) and response (vv. 24-25) pick up important elements in the discourse so far, and the repetition in v. 23 of the parable formula from v. 9 further binds them into the discourse as a whole. If, as seems likely, these sayings existed independently at an earlier stage of tradition, Mark's collection of them for inclusion at this point is well considered.[3]

The sayings so collected are then arranged with care, as J. Lambrecht explains:

1. For v. 21 cf. Mt. 5:15; Lk. 8:16; 11:33; for v. 22, Mt. 10:26; Lk. 8:17; 12:2; for v. 24b, Mt. 7:2; Lk. 6:38; and for v. 25, Mt. 13:12; 25:29; Lk. 8:18; 19:26.

2. Respectively *Gos. Thom.* 33, 5 with 6b, 41; for v. 22 cf. also *Gos. Thom.* 108b.

3. Commentators continue to debate whether some at least of these sayings may had been already combined in the tradition as Mark received it. The diversity of views expressed and the lack of external controls make it unlikely that the matter could ever be finally resolved. Since the final form of the pericope comes to us from Mark, and represents the combination of sayings which he wished to include, whether or not it originated with him, we may circumvent the debate by speaking of it simply as Mark's collection.

It will be difficult to deny the neat and clever structural arrangement of vv. 21-25. The two short 'parables' of the Lamp (v. 21) and the Measure (v. 24b) both receive a brief, almost proverbial explanation and are *(sic)* introduced by γάρ (v. 22 and v. 25). These two thus formed small units are then linked together by means of a concluding (v. 23) and an introductory (v. 24a) exhortation to listen: this double appeal is the hinge of the whole small, yet remarkable, complex (vv. 21-25).[4]

Lambrecht's distinction between the '"parables"' (his quotation marks) of vv. 21, 24b and the 'almost proverbial explanations' of vv. 22, 25 suggests a more restricted definition of 'parable' than we have been assuming. The latter, even if less 'pictorial', are the sort of puzzling epigrams which fit well under the wider usage of παραβολή, so that the whole complex is entirely appropriate to a parable discourse, not only in its subject matter but also in its literary form.

21 The double question (which neatly illustrates the idiomatic use of μή(τι) and οὐ to introduce questions expecting the answers 'no' and 'yes' respectively) makes a simple point: lamps are meant to give as much light as possible. (The λύχνος is a clay lamp filled with oil, which is normally placed or hung on a λυχνία, a lampstand; the μόδιος is a grain measure holding nearly two gallons.) Like several of Jesus' images, this one is capable of a variety of applications: in Mt. 5:15 the context requires that the image be understood of the light shed in the world by the disciples' way of life; in Lk. 11:33 the intended application is less clear, since the saying is preceded by a passage about Jesus as the ultimate revelation (= 'light'?), but leads into other sayings about the 'light' within the disciples.[5] Here in Mark the context suggests that the light represents the parabolic revelation which is the subject of this chapter, and in particular the secret of the kingdom of God, the knowledge of which distinguishes insiders from outsiders.[6] If so, and if Mark has not been clumsily inconsistent in the construction of the discourse, this image tells strongly against any interpretation of vv. 11-12 which suggests that that knowledge is meant to be kept hidden rather than made as widely available as possible.

22 The point is now made more explicitly, even if still enigmatically, and the γάρ ensures that the two verses are taken together. There is, however, also a further development of the idea, in that while v. 21 spoke of the light which should not be hidden, this verse goes further in requiring things which

---

4. J. Lambrecht in M. Sabbe (ed.), *Marc,* 303.

5. In *Gos. Thom.* 33 it is linked with the odd injunction, 'What you shall hear in your ear proclaim in the other ear upon your housetops', a reminiscence of the saying which follows the Q parallel to Mark 4:22; this perhaps indicates a continuing awareness, independent of Mark, that the sayings brought together in Mk. 4:21-22 are related in theme.

6. The unexpected use (by Mark only) of the 'personal' verb ἔρχεται when the subject is an impersonal lamp suggests to some (e.g., Cranfield, Gnilka, Hooker, Lane) that Mark intends us to see the lamp as a figure for Jesus himself, whose light is to shine out despite his temporary hiddenness. The idea is not inappropriate, but the use of ἔρχομαι for 'to be brought' hardly seems so unnatural as to require it (see J. Schneider, *TDNT,* 2.666-67).

are already hidden to be uncovered. In Mt. 10:26 similar language is used to spur disciples to fearless witness even under persecution; in Lk. 12:2 it follows a warning about hypocrisy, with the implication that even if you keep things secret, they will be discovered; in *Gos. Thom.* 5 it is a promise to disciples that things they do not yet know will be revealed to them, but in *Gos. Thom.* 6 it seems to be (as in Lk. 12:2) a warning against hypocrisy.[7] Clearly the theme is capable of widely different applications. Here in Mark the wording of v. 22 does not in itself make explicit whether the uncovering of secrets is the role of God or of disciples (or of both?), nor to whom they are to be disclosed, but the fact that the issue of revelation and concealment has already been raised in vv. 11-12 provides a background against which it may be interpreted, and the hidden thing there was the secret of God's kingship.

The two halves of the couplet stand in 'synonymous parallelism'; i.e., they say the same thing in (slightly) different words.[8] ἀπόκρυφος is a synonym for κρυπτός, but one which carries extra connotations, as the word is typically used of secret wisdom or knowledge (cf Col. 2:3), both in pagan literature (especially in connection with magic) and increasingly in Jewish and Christian writing as the idea of esoteric knowledge gained currency. Hence the later use of the term to describe books of secret knowledge, such as the *Apocryphon of James* or the *Apocryphon of John* from Nag Hammadi.[9] There is no need to suppose such a technical sense here, but the saying as a whole probably serves to warn against the natural human tendency to treat God's revelation as a possession to be guarded from others. If vv. 11-12 could have been read as encouraging disciples to hide away the revelation they had received, this saying indicates that God's purpose is the opposite, that the hidden should become known. The double use of ἵνα may be intended to convey that the uncovering of that which is hidden is not only something which is bound to happen (see above on 4:12 for the suggestion that the ἵνα there may carry a similar meaning), but is to be understood as the purpose of God the revealer. Like the organiser of a treasure hunt, he hides things in order that they may be found.

Verses 21-22 therefore stand in tension with the implication usually read in vv. 11-12 that God does not want 'outsiders' to understand and be forgiven. Hidden things are to be made known, though we are not told when or by whom this is to be accomplished. (Perhaps there is a clue in 9:9, which introduces the idea of secrecy *until;* with regard to the disciples' own message, the resurrection will mark the turning point between hiddenness and open declaration.)[10] Ambrozic speaks of 'a surprising degree of unanimity among exegetes' to the effect that 'the secret which is, for a time, entrusted to a few . . . is destined to be

7. The varied uses of this image in Thomas are discussed by B. W. Henaut, *Tradition*, 279-281. Henaut also mentions some similar sayings from Jewish and Graeco-Roman sources (282).

8. *Pace* J. Marcus, *Mystery*, 150-51.

9. For the development of both the idea and the term see the interesting excursus by A. Oepke in *TDNT*, 3.987-1000.

10. J. Marcus, *Mystery*, 143-50, usefully develops this insight.

manifested to all very soon. There is thus a reference to the missionary activity of the community which takes place after Jesus' death and resurrection.' Vv. 21-22 are 'a supplement and a correction, as it were, of vss. 11-12.'[11] Secrecy is on any understanding a theme of Mark's gospel, and is presupposed in the wording of v. 22. But any comprehensive understanding of secrecy in Mark must find room for the declaration of these verses that secrets are meant to be revealed, and the theme will be further developed in the two seed parables of vv. 26-32.

23 This formula is already familiar to us from v. 9; see the comments there. Its inclusion at this point not only links this section of the discourse with the wider parable context but also alerts the hearer/reader of vv. 21-22 that these are also parabolic sayings, to be noted and interpreted with care. There may be more in them than meets the eye (or ear).

24 As we have noted above, the warning βλέπετε τί ἀκούετε stands apart from the rest of the verse; it is not linked with the 'measure' saying in its other synoptic occurrences, but it does occur, without the 'measure' saying, at the parallel point in Lk. 8:18a. These words pick up the recurrent theme of the discourse that it is not hearing alone which is important, but *how* you hear. They thus repeat the call of v. 23 to listen attentively, but whereas v. 23 rounded off the preceding teaching, the formula καὶ ἔλεγεν αὐτοῖς introducing this clause ensures that it relates rather to the teaching that follows. And that teaching is itself about effective hearing, in that it reinforces the message of the parable of the sower that there will be different degrees of response to what is heard, depending on what the hearer brings to the encounter.[12]

The context would lead us to expect βλέπετε πῶς (not τί) ἀκούετε, and that is what we find in Lk. 8:18. The whole discourse has been about the difference between effective and ineffective hearing. The same παραβολαί are heard by both insiders and outsiders; the difference lies in *how* they hear them, rather than in *what* they hear. Mark's sense is clear enough — a call to pay careful attention to what is heard — but his syntax is awkward.[13]

ἐν ᾧ μέτρῳ μετρεῖτε μετρηθήσεται ὑμῖν is another proverbial saying (using language typical of commercial grain contracts)[14] which can be applied to a variety of situations. Its theme is the principle of reciprocity. In Mt. 7:2 it is placed in parallel with ἐν ᾧ κρίματι κρίνετε κριθήσεσθε, the judgment in view

---

11. A. M. Ambrozic, *Kingdom,* 103.

12. Myers, 170, 177-79, suggests that βλέπετε τί ἀκούετε is intended not to call the hearers to agree with vv. 24b-25, but rather to warn them *against* the 'cynical realism' of the 'conventional wisdom' which Jesus quotes in vv. 24b-25 only to overturn it by means of the parables of vv. 26-32. βλέπετε τί ἀκούετε would thus mean '*Beware of* what you hear'. The problem with this exegesis, apart from the fact that it has eluded other readers of Mark for two millennia (including Matthew, as Myers recognises), is that the components of vv. 24b-25 occur quite frequently at other points in the synoptic tradition, with no indication at any other point that they are intended as targets for censure.

13. The interrogative τί, which should properly introduce an indirect question, 'Take care what you hear', is probably intended to function here as a relative, 'Pay careful attention to that which you hear'; see BDF, 298(4).

14. So B. Couroyer, *RB* 77 (1970) 366-70.

being probably (but not necessarily) that of God, while in Lk. 6:38 a slightly different form of the proverb is used apparently as an incentive to generosity in giving (with God again as the assumed source of the reciprocal measure). In Jewish literature it occurs frequently as a proverb for the appropriateness of divine judgment, in which the punishment fits the crime or the reward the deed (e.g., *m. Soṭah* 1:7; *b. Sanh.* 100a).[15] Mark's use of the proverb is rather more specialised than this general concept of 'measure for measure' in judgment. It serves here to encourage careful hearing, because the care expended in understanding and responding to Jesus' parables will be proportionately rewarded. What you get out of them depends on what you put in.

This principle could apply either positively or negatively (both aspects will be taken up in v. 25), but the addition of καὶ προστεθήσεται ὑμῖν (which does not occur in the synoptic parallels, nor, typically, in Jewish uses of the proverb; see Textual Note above) shows that it is the positive sense which is in mind. Parables, heard with proper understanding and response, will bring a rich reward; divine grace goes beyond the limits of mere reciprocity.

25 The γάρ again, as in v. 22, signals an extension of the same principle as is set out in the proverb of v. 24b. In fact, both aspects of that verse are taken up, the principle of reciprocity in the general outline of this saying, and that of God's generosity going beyond strict equality in the idea of more being given to those who already have[16] (though this time the threatening converse is also explicit). Similar sayings occur not only in the synoptic parallels to this passage but also in the conclusion of both synoptic versions of the parable of the talents/pounds (Mt. 25:29; Lk. 19:26), and, without context, in *Gos. Thom.* 41. This basic observation from the world of capitalist economics, that inequality tends to be compounded rather than rectified, is offered here not (*pace* Myers) as a basis for social or political action but as an illustration of the effect of teaching in parables (the repeated ἔχει being perhaps intended to echo the formula of vv. 9, 23, εἴ τις ἔχει ὦτα ἀκούειν ἀκουέτω).[17] As such it corresponds to the perspective already set out in the parable of the sower, that fruitful response depends on a pre-existing capacity to receive the word, and in vv. 11-12 with their contrast between 'you' (who correspond to ὃς ἔχει here) and those outside (who correspond to ὃς οὐκ ἔχει). The latter, unable to derive any spiritual insight from their

15. References are listed in W. D. Davies and D. C. Allison, *Matthew,* 1.670, and set out more fully by H. P. Rüger, *ZNW* 60 (1969) 174-82. See further Str-B, 1.444-46; B. D. Chilton, *Rabbi,* 123-25. For Jewish teaching about God's 'two measures', judgment and mercy, cf. J. Jeremias, *Parables,* 213-14. For similar sayings in early Christian literature see *1 Clem.* 13.2; *Pol.* 2.3.

16. This idea, implicit in Mark, is brought out further in both Matthean versions of the saying by the addition of the clause καὶ περισσευθήσεται, which corresponds to Mark's καὶ προστεθήσεται ὑμῖν in v. 24.

17. Hooker refers to later rabbinic passages (*b. Ber.* 40a; *b. Suk.* 46a-b) which declare that God puts more into a full vessel, not an empty one, again with reference to how people respond to his words. For a detailed argument that vv. 24b-25 'deal with epistemological questions', see J. Marcus, *Mystery,* 153-56. For Jewish parallels to the saying see B. W. Henaut, *Tradition,* 290-91.

hearing of parables, will lose any benefit which should have come to them through their encounter with divine revelation. (Luke's rewording of καὶ ὃ ἔχει as καὶ ὃ δοκεῖ ἔχειν recognises the paradoxical, even logically absurd, form of Jesus' saying, but in so doing rather pedantically blunts its edge).

There is a noticeable tension between the two parts of this complex of sayings. The 'optimism' of vv. 21-22, that all that is now secret will in due time be revealed, is balanced by the 'realism' of vv. 24b-25, that there will still be those who fail to benefit from divine revelation. These two insights together constitute the framework within which a coherent exegesis of this discourse as a whole, and therefore an understanding of Mark's 'theory of parables', must be found.

Two More Parables about Seed (4:26-32)

These two short similes are offered, true to the principle to be enunciated in v. 34, with no explicit explanation other than the opening clause of each, which tells us that each scene in some way illustrates the nature of the βασιλεία τοῦ θεοῦ. There may, however, be a further element of interpretation available for the hearer who is well versed in biblical language, in that each parable concludes with an echo of OT language, and thus suggests a context of thought within which the hearer should look for the meaning of the parable (though in the first parable this context is apparently not totally appropriate, as we shall see). But if, as v. 34 implies, Jesus did offer explicit interpretations of these similes to his disciples, Mark does not allow his readers to share them.

They do, however, come to us in a context in Mark which indicates how he expected them to be understood. The parable of the sower has already alerted us to the symbolism of seed as the 'word' which is being sown through Jesus' ministry, and that parable has been interpreted in terms of the revelation of the μυστήριον of the kingdom of God. The introduction to each of these parables picks up that theme. The whole chapter has focused attention on the differing degrees of perception and response which that 'seed' encounters. In particular vv. 21-22 have prepared the way for these two parables with the assertion that there is an inevitable, and divinely intended, progression from hiddenness to revelation. So when we read of the unnoticed growth of the seed leading in due time to a full harvest, and of the tiny mustard seed ultimately producing a plant of impressive dimensions, we are already predisposed to think of the paradox of the hidden, unrecognised status of God's kingship, as compared with its future consummation, when that which is hidden will be uncovered, and people will be able to 'see that the kingdom of God has come with power' (9:1). Within that overall framework of thought, however, each parable has its own distinctive message to contribute.

26-29 The first 'story' is introduced awkwardly, in that the βασιλεία τοῦ θεοῦ, which in vv. 30-31 will be compared to a seed, is here apparently compared to the man who sows it.[18] In fact, of course, the comparison is not to any one component in the story, but to the scene as a whole, as is indicated also by the frequent changes of subject (man, seed, ground, grain, man).[19] But the opening focus on the man fits the fact that the story is told with a special eye to how he experiences the results of his sowing.[20]

There is nothing extraordinary about the event narrated; it is a story of the normal experience of growth and harvest.[21] But it is a sound rule in parable interpretation to take as pointers to the parable's intended meaning any features of the story which are either improbable in themselves or are given unnecessary emphasis in the telling of the story, and in this case the reader is likely to notice particularly the fact that the man who is the beneficiary of the seed's growth contributes nothing towards it beyond the initial sowing of the seed and the eventual harvesting; in between he has nothing to do but wait.[22] Three 'unnecessary' expressions underline this aspect of the story: after the sowing all he does is καθεύδῃ καὶ ἐγείρηται νύκτα καὶ ἡμέραν; the seed grows ὡς οὐκ οἶδεν αὐτός; and the ground produces its crop αὐτομάτη (a striking and unusual word, more naturally applied to wild plants than to a cultivated crop: LXX Lv. 25:5, 11; 4 Kgdms. 19:29; Josephus, *Ant.* 12.317; *Life* 11).[23] Any farmer knows, of course, that this laid-back approach on the part of the farmer is not a true picture of agriculture in real life: a crop left to fend for itself after sowing in this way would probably be barely worth harvesting. So is the farmer's inaction and incomprehension a pointer to how this story illustrates the βασιλεία τοῦ θεοῦ?

One of the issues which we have assumed to underlie the parable of the sower is the problem of limited response to the initial preaching of the king-

---

18. The construction οὕτως . . . ὡς . . . βάλῃ is harsh ('gravely irregular', BAGD, 897b, II.4.c); a ὅταν or ἐάν following the ὡς would be expected, and is added in most later MSS. Cf. BDF, 380(4).

19. The change to ὁ καρπός as the subject in v. 29a produces the strange clause ὅταν παραδοῖ ὁ καρπός, which looks as if it should mean 'when the grain is ripe'; this apparently intransitive use of the verb παραδίδωμι (for the form of the subjunctive see BDF, 95[2]), in a sense for which there is no other warrant, has been explained as 'translation Greek' based on misreading an Aramaic term for 'be ripe' (M. Black, *Approach,* 163-64), though others suggest translating 'when the crop allows' (a rare use of παραδίδωμι, BAGD, 615b, 4).

20. For an interesting survey of varied interpretations of the parable see A. M. Ambrozic, *Kingdom,* 108-20.

21. For the sequence χόρτος, στάχυς, πλήρης σῖτος cf. the more elaborate account of the development of grapes in *1 Clem.* 23:4: βλαστός, φύλλον, ἄνθος, ὄμφαξ, σταφυλὴ παρεστηκυῖα, also designed to convey the sure accomplishment of God's purpose, ταχὺ καὶ ἐξαίφνης.

22. The initial aorist βάλῃ is followed by present tenses throughout the rest of the parable; this may be a way of indicating the routine round of agricultural life which follows the initial act of sowing, but in view of Mark's tendency to use historic presents need be no more than his natural style of telling a story.

23. For αὐτόματος to indicate that which happens by God's power without human intervention see LXX Jos. 6:5; cf. Wis. 17:6.

dom of God, and this parable may also be read in the light of that issue. At first there may be little to show for the sowing of seed, and a sceptical observer might think nothing was happening. But there is an inner dynamic in that message which will in due time produce its effect, even if human insight cannot fathom how the process works (ὡς οὐκ οἶδεν αὐτός). In the meantime the wise disciple will wait in confidence for God's work to be accomplished in God's way.[24]

The kingdom *of God,* then, does not depend on human effort to achieve it, and human insight will not be able to explain it. This aspect of the parable, focused in the farmer's inactivity, could suggest a quietistic theology which allows disciples to disclaim any responsibility in the establishment of God's kingdom.[25] Perhaps it was this danger which caused Matthew to exclude this story from his collection of parables of growth. But if the focus is on the dynamic of the kingdom of God, the farmer's inactivity functions merely as a foil to this main theme. Here, unlike the parable of the sower, the structure of the story does not suggest a multiple purpose which would require this subsidiary aspect of the imagery to be given a message of its own.

Belo, however, takes the sower to be Jesus, and therefore understands the parable as Jesus' assertion that 'even he does not know *in advance* the effects of his practice but is himself involved in the narrative at the point where the outcome is still undecided' (123); Marcus[26] similarly argues at length that the ἄνθρωπος represents Jesus, and goes on (180-85) to try to 'make sense of a sleeping and unknowing Jesus'. But this exegesis depends on the assumption that the ἄνθρωπος, who does not appear to be the main focus of the story, must be intended to have a specific identification. If the parable is primarily about the way the seed grows, and how the farmer experiences this, to insist on an 'identity' for the farmer, consistently applied throughout the story, is to require a degree of allegorical precision which even in these days of reaction against Jülicher hardly rings true. The following parable of the mustard seed, into which Matthew and Luke introduce an ἄνθρωπος while Mark and the *Gospel of Thomas* keep the seed as subject, illustrates the natural tendency to introduce a human subject even where the simile does not require it.

There is, however, one aspect of the wording of the story which might suggest a further dimension to its intended meaning. The concluding clauses, ἀποστέλλει τὸ δρέπανον, ὅτι παρέστηκεν ὁ θερισμός, are a fairly clear echo of LXX Jo. 4:13 (EVV 3:13), ἐξαποστείλατε δρέπανα, ὅτι παρέστηκεν τρύγητος.[27] The imagery in Joel is of the eschatological judgment, when Yahweh's

24. M. Sabin, *JSNT* 45 (1992) 16-17, suggests that this 'story of the unknowing, trustful sower' is a 'midrash' on Ec. 11:4-6.

25. This attitude could easily be read into Schweizer's interpretation of the parable as calling on us 'to wait with the carefree attitude which is becoming to the children of God, without any spiritual maneuvering or misguided efforts'.

26. J. Marcus, *Mystery,* 171-80.

27. The allusion is clearer in the Hebrew, where the final word is *qāṣîr,* '(grain) harvest';

enemies are gathered against Jerusalem, and will be cut down like the corn at harvest, while his people will enjoy security and prosperity in Zion. There is little difficulty in accommodating the implied eschatological note in Mark's parable, as God's kingdom reaches its ultimate fruition; but the negative imagery of Joel's harvest fits less naturally, when the seed in Mark's story has represented the growth of God's kingdom, not of opposition to it. This may be an example of echoing scriptural terminology without any intention to evoke the context from which it is drawn: the reference is to an eschatological harvest, and Joel's words provide a familiar way of expressing the idea, despite the more ominous note which they carry in his prophecy.[28] It is possible, though less likely, that the echo is deliberately designed to evoke, in the minds of those who knew Joel's prophecy well enough, the additional consideration that the eschatological fulfilment which is good news for some is bad news for others, but this would be a thought which has no other *point d'appui* in Jesus' story.

The first parable, then, is a message about rightly interpreting and responding to the period of the apparent inaction of the kingdom of God. Despite appearances to the contrary, it is growing, and the harvest will come. But it will come in God's time and in God's way, not by human effort or in accordance with human logic.

30-32 A more elaborate introductory clause,[29] with two deliberative subjunctive questions, alerts the reader to expect another parable in the form of a simile; the phrase ἐν παραβολῇ τίθημι uses the noun παραβολή in its more etymological sense of 'comparison', thus echoing the verb ὁμοιόω in the first question, and the following simile is expressed in the dative case (κόκκῳ σινάπεως) which naturally follows ὁμοιόω (cf. the fuller form in Lk. 13:18-19, 20-21, where τίνι ὁμοιώσω; is followed by ὁμοία ἐστίν + dative; cf. Mt. 11:16; Lk. 7:31). The description of the mustard seed and its growth then follows in the form of a relative clause, expanded by both subordinate and coordinate clauses.[30] It is not so much a 'story' as an observation of the normal course of

---

LXX τρύγητος has been influenced by the reference to vintage in the following clauses, even though a sickle is less appropriate to the harvesting of grapes (though see Rev. 14:17-19).

28. *Gos. Thom.* 21 includes the sentence 'After the fruit ripened he came quickly with his sickle in his hand and reaped it', at the conclusion to a complex of sayings which focus on eschatological readiness, again with no obvious negative connotation. But this looks like a reminiscence of Mk. 4:29a (even though the rest of the parable is absent), rather than a direct echo of Joel 4:13.

29. The form is similar to Is. 40:18, but that double question (addressed to the hearer, not deliberative) introduces a *futile* attempt at comparison, not an enlightening simile.

30. The syntax is broken in v. 32a by the resumptive clause καὶ ὅταν σπαρῇ, which is stylistically awkward (and is omitted by D), but serves to keep the sequence intact after the inserted participial clause. The participial clause itself also fits awkwardly since its neuter subject (μικρότερον ὄν) follows a masculine antecedent (κόκκῳ . . . ὅς), presumably influenced by the neuter σπερμάτων which follows (many later MSS correct to μικρότερος). The neuter is then continued in μεῖζον.

nature. It is a memorable observation which, like the parable of the sower, has been preserved in all three Synoptic Gospels as well as in *Gos. Thom.* 20.[31]

The plant concerned is probably the black mustard, *Brassica nigra,* which was grown for oil as well as as a condiment. In good conditions it may grow to a height of 3 metres or even more, but its seed is extremely small (over 700 to a gramme, C.-H. Hunzinger, *TDNT,* 7.289) and was proverbial for something tiny (Mt. 17:20; *m. Nid.* 5:2; *m. Ṭoh.* 8:8; *m. Naz.* 1:5, etc.), so that an annual growth of such height was remarkable. It is this contrast between an insignificant beginning and an impressive final size which is the point of the simile. While Matthew and Luke may exaggerate in calling the mustard a δένδρον (and Mark's κλάδοι μεγάλοι suggest a tree rather than a shrub), it would certainly stand out among the λάχανα (garden vegetables, which would mostly, like the mustard, be annuals), and would provide perches for birds.

The theme is a familiar one: 'Great oaks from little acorns grow'. Those who witnessed the initial proclamation of the kingdom of God must not despise small beginnings, nor should they be impatient for the full majesty of God's kingdom to be revealed (cf. perhaps the question of John the Baptist in Mt. 11:3). The message is clearly related to that of the previous parable, but presented here in a simpler form, with the focus on the contrast between beginning and end rather than on the process of growth.[32]

But again, as in the previous parable, the simile concludes with an OT echo. The birds nesting[33] in the branches are not strictly necessary to the description of the mustard, but serve to recall the imagery of Ezekiel's cedar-tree parables (Ezk. 17:23; 31:6) and of Nebuchadnezzar's dream, Dn. 4:9, 18 (EVV 4:12, 21), and the words are close enough to those of the LXX/Thdt in these passages to make the echo unmistakable for those who are familiar with them. Mark's rather inappropriate mention of the κλάδοι μεγάλοι of the mustard helps to strengthen the allusion, since the great branches are a part of the imagery in these OT figures. Ezekiel's two cedars and Nebuchadnezzar's tree represent the

---

31. The literary relationships between the 'Q', Mark, and Thomas versions of the parable are analysed by B. W. Henaut, *Tradition,* 252-61, concluding that Thomas does not represent an independent tradition: 'If Thomas is not dependent upon Mark, it is likely that he has used Mark's literary source.'

32. Some commentators suggest that there is deliberate irony in the plant chosen: not a noble tree like the cedar, but a mere garden vegetable. 'To the reader versed in all the great trees of Scripture, this surely comes as a jolt, even a joke. The birds of heaven are taking shelter here under a tree of about eight feet. The great tree of God's kingdom has gone domestic' (M. Sabin, *JSNT* 45 [1992] 21; so earlier R. W. Funk, *Int* 27 [1973] 3-9). This is a thought which fits well with Mark's emphasis on the paradoxical nature of the kingdom of God, and its affront to human standards of valuation, but it does not seem to be in focus in the way this parable is presented, which mentions specifically not only the proverbial smallness of the seed (which is sufficient reason for the selection of mustard specifically) but also the greatness, not mediocrity, of the plant which it produces.

33. κατασκηνόω, which echoes Thdt Dn. 4:12, 21, probably means not merely shelter but 'nest' (cf. κατασκήνωσις in this sense in Mt. 8:20). The imagery in the Ezekiel and Daniel passages is of birds nesting. *Gos. Thom.* 20, however, makes the branch (singular) a σκέπη (shelter) for birds.

growth of impressive empires, and the birds which nest in them are explicitly interpreted in Ezk. 31:6 as 'all great nations' who enjoyed the benefits of the Egyptian empire. The allusion here may therefore be intended to indicate the future wide scope of the kingdom of God, within which many nations (not only Israel) will find their place. Even if the nesting birds are no more than part of the imagery of growth and so should not be specifically identified, their OT background reinforces the 'imperial' pretensions of the kingdom of God, which will take the place of the human empires of OT times (cf. the use of imagery elsewhere in the synoptic tradition from Dn. 2 and 7, two memorable visions of a new kingdom to replace the pagan empires).[34]

The two parables of vv. 26-32 thus both warn against underestimating the significance of the proclamation of the kingdom of God, however unimpressive its initial impact may seem. What has begun in the Galilean ministry of Jesus will, by the power of God, one day prove to be of ultimate significance. If for the time being its power is hidden, it is not for that reason any less certain, and its growth will be spectacular.

Editorial Comment — Parables and Explanations (4:33-34)

Mark rounds off the discourse not now with words of Jesus but with his own summary of Jesus' teaching method; the use of imperfect tenses throughout indicates that what is here described is Jesus' normal practice, not just a temporary phase in his ministry.

33 τοιαύταις παραβολαῖς πολλαῖς reminds us of what v. 2 has already indicated, that the parables recorded in this discourse are only a selection. The phrase ἐλάλει αὐτοῖς τὸν λόγον could be understood as a typically Marcan pleonasm, meaning no more than 'he spoke to them' (it could be so construed also in 2:2; 8:32, though in the latter case the λόγος is surely the striking pronouncement of 8:31). But in Acts the phrase λαλέω τὸν λόγον (with or without τοῦ κυρίου etc.) is a frequent term for preaching the Christian message, and the use of ὁ λόγος to identify the seed in vv. 14-20 provides a similar background for understanding the phrase here (whereas in 2:2 there is no such clear background). While the content of that λόγος is not here specified, it is natural to understand it in the light of the focus of this whole discourse on the kingdom of God, particularly since that has been declared at the outset (1:15) to be the subject of Jesus' public preaching in Galilee.

The recurrent emphasis throughout the discourse on the importance of

34. Myers, 180, noting that the 'sheltering' role of the empires in Ezk. 31 and Dn. 4 is mentioned only to prepare for the overthrow of those empires, suggests that Jesus' parable has a similarly political intention: the tiny mustard seed will grow into a power which will overthrow the imperial might of Rome. Since, however, Jesus' parable gives no hint of a preceding empire, and the imagery of the nesting birds is applied to the mustard itself, not to its supposed rival, this seems a rather remote deduction.

rightly hearing the λόγος is picked up in the clause καθὼς ἠδύναντο ἀκούειν. If this verse stood alone, it might be possible to understand this simply as an assertion that Jesus used parables because these, unlike other forms of teaching, could be grasped by ordinary people. But it comes at the end of a discourse which has shown that there is no guarantee that even parables will be grasped by 'those outside', and has suggested that private explanations may be needed if even Jesus' committed followers, to whom the μυστήριον has been given, are to benefit from them. Moreover, the next verse repeats that scenario of public preaching and private explanation, with the clear implication that parables alone are not enough. Some commentators have therefore concluded that v. 33 is in contradiction with the discourse as a whole and with v. 34 in particular. If we are not to accuse Mark of such blatant inconsistency,[35] what can καθὼς ἠδύναντο ἀκούειν mean in relation to the public use of parables?

The parable of the sower has asserted that people's ability to 'hear' is quite varied, and is determined by factors in their own character and situation rather than by the form of teaching. But we have seen that parables, by their very nature, serve to bring out that variety. Because they need to be interpreted and applied, and call for a response which is likely to be more than intellectual, the same parables will leave some cold while others respond with enthusiasm — and by seeking further enlightenment. It is probably this variety in response that Mark here intends to remind us of. Among the crowds who hear the parables there are some who δύνανται ἀκούειν, and will therefore join those περὶ αὐτόν who seek and receive further explanation, but others will go no further. καθὼς ἠδύναντο ἀκούειν then alerts the reader to the fact that not all have that capacity (καθώς being used in the sense 'insofar as' or 'to the degree that'; see BAGD, 391b, 2); and it is the resultant polarisation which Mark again highlights in v. 34.

34 χωρὶς παραβολῆς οὐκ ἐλάλει αὐτοῖς sounds a remarkably broad generalisation. It is not easy to test its accuracy in Mark's gospel because so little *public* teaching is in fact recorded in this book. On the rare occasions when Mark does record the content of any public teaching before Jesus' arrival in Jerusalem, the focus of that teaching is indeed in epigrammatic sayings (παρα-βολαί [?]) which need subsequent elucidation for the disciples (7:14-15, 17-18; 10:5-9, 10-12). All the rest of the teaching recorded is directed to his disciples, and contains just the sort of explanatory material this verse suggests. The only exception is the series of public dialogues in chapter 12, and it may be questioned how far they constitute 'teaching' or 'speaking the word' as such. Mark has therefore been remarkably consistent in observing the parameters of this verse in the teaching actually recorded in the rest of his gospel. But there is a great deal that is not recorded. Does Mark really intend us to understand that

35. Or, as Lambrecht, in M. Sabbe (ed.), *Marc*, 276, argues, Mark, having expressed a 'spontaneous positive opinion' in v. 33, feels it necessary to 'correct himself' in v. 34 in order to maintain 'his own somewhat forced parable theory'.

when he speaks of Jesus διδάσκων in Nazareth (6:2) and other villages (6:6) or to the 5,000 (6:34) nothing at all was on offer but a string of uninterpreted παραβολαί (even in the broadest sense of that term)? Probably to ask such a question is to interpret Mark's general statement too pedantically; but we need not doubt that Jesus' reputation outside the circle of his own followers was as one who taught ἐν παραβολαῖς.

The pattern of explanation[36] to his disciples κατ' ἰδίαν picks up and generalises what we have seen in vv. 10-20, a method which will be repeated in 7:17-23; 10:10-12; 13:3-37 (cf. 9:28, 33), and the repeated ἰδίαν . . . ἰδίοις gives it emphasis. There is, however, a tension between this verse and v. 10, in that there the privileged audience contained not only the Twelve but also οἱ περὶ αὐτόν, a larger group which we saw reason to understand as those from among the crowd who wanted to know more. If, as we have suggested earlier (see above, p. 158), Mark typically uses οἱ μαθηταί to refer specifically to the Twelve, who were Jesus' companions on his travels, rather than to refer to a larger circle of supporters, this verse seems to be more restrictive than v. 10; indeed, the phrase οἱ ἴδιοι μαθηταί gives it an even more restrictive feel. It certainly stresses that the basis of the privileged situation of those who receive explanations is their personal relationship with Jesus: they 'belong' to him in a special way. But unless Mark has been deliberately or inadvertently inconsistent, they cannot here be only the Twelve.[37] In that case either we were wrong in concluding at 3:13-19 that there is a functional equivalence between οἱ μαθηταί and οἱ δώδεκα in Mark (and the evidence for that as a generalisation seems strong) or we must assume that here Mark is using the term οἱ μαθηταί more loosely than elsewhere. We have no right to demand consistency of language, and the phrase τοῖς ἰδίοις μαθηταῖς effectively conveys Mark's essential distinction between insiders and outsiders, even where the circle is less well defined than the specific number of the Twelve.

FURTHER REVELATIONS
OF JESUS' UNIQUE AUTHORITY (4:35–5:43)

The ἐξουσία of Jesus has already been vividly displayed, and commented on, in many incidents recorded in the first part of Act One. Now that the explanatory discourse is over Mark returns to further examples of Jesus acting in miracu-

---

36. See Räisänen, *Secret,* 105-6, for ἐπιλύω as a term for the interpretation of that which is otherwise unintelligible, used in that sense only here in the NT; cf., however, ἐπίλυσις, 2 Pet. 1:20.

37. This conclusion would be avoided if we could accept the argument of R. P. Meye, *SE* 2 (1964) 211-18, that σὺν τοῖς δώδεκα in 4:10 means 'belonging to the Twelve', and so further defines the same people denoted by οἱ περὶ αὐτόν rather than setting two different groups side by side. But others have not been convinced that this could be a natural meaning of σύν in such a context, nor that Mark could have constructed such a cumbersome phrase if all he meant was 'the Twelve' or even 'some of the Twelve'.

lous power. They will contain, as before, cases of physical healing and of exorcism, but now the stakes are raised by the inclusion of the first 'nature-miracle' recorded in this gospel, the calming of a storm on the lake by Jesus' mere word of command, which evokes from the disciples an appropriately awed christological question, 'Who then is this, that even wind and sea obey him?' But even that is not the climax, for in the story which concludes this sequence set around the lake the healing which Jesus performs is not just of physical illness, but of a girl already dead. There is thus in this section of the gospel a mounting sense of excitement, as the ἐξουσία of Jesus is tested by, and proves victorious over, ever more challenging situations of need.

There is a total of ten individual miracles recorded between 4:35 and 8:26 (four of them in this section), which are frequently seen as constituting two balancing groups, each of which begins with a lake miracle (4:35-41; 6:45-51) and contains a feeding miracle (6:34-44; 8:1-10). P. J. Achtemeier[38] has suggested that Mark found these two 'catenae' already grouped in the tradition; others believe that the parallel groupings are Mark's own construction. All five stories in Achtemeier's second 'catena' (6:45-51; 7:24-30; 7:32-37; 8:1-10; 8:22-26) take place outside Galilee, and it has been suggested that Mark thus deliberately shows the mission of Jesus to the Jewish community of Galilee (though 5:1-20 is already set on the Gentile side of the lake) being repeated for the benefit of the surrounding Gentile population. We shall return to this suggestion when we discuss 7:24–8:10.

The four incidents which make up this part of the gospel are linked together in a geographical sequence of which the lake is the focal point. 4:35 shows Jesus leaving the place of the lakeside teaching (on the west bank) to cross to the other side, and the first incident takes place during the crossing. On the other side they meet the demoniac Legion, and after his restoration they apparently return immediately to the Capernaum side (5:18, 21). Back on the west bank Jesus is approached παρὰ τὴν θάλασσαν (5:21) to go to the house of a leader of the (presumably Capernaum) synagogue, and it is while he is on the way that a further healing takes place. After the restoration of Jairus's daughter, Jesus finally leaves the lakeside area for his first return visit to Nazareth since his public ministry began (6:1). Mark thus achieves a satisfying and memorable narrative coherence in the setting of this whole complex of miracles around the lake, which will make the following visit to Nazareth, up in the hills, stand out still more starkly as a contrasting and disappointing experience.

---

38. P. J. Achtemeier, *JBL* 89 (1970) 265-91; *JBL* 91 (1972) 198-221.

Authority over Wind and Water (4:35-41)

TEXTUAL NOTE

40. The variants focus around the inclusion at different points of οὕτως, which does not occur at all in an impressive array of witnesses including א B D Θ, most Latin MSS, and the Coptic. It is simplest to suppose that οὕτως arose from a misreading of the less common οὔπω, and once inserted caused various expedients to accommodate it to the structure of the question.

Together with 6:45-52 (the other lake miracle), this pericope places Jesus in a more starkly 'supernatural' light even than the healing miracles. Control of the elements is even more extraordinary and inexplicable than the restoration of suffering human beings, and is in the OT a frequently noted attribute of God in distinction from human beings who find themselves helpless before the forces of nature[39] (Job 38:8-11; Pss. 65:5-8; 89:8-9; 107:23-32, etc.; the last of these must surely have been in Mark's mind as he narrated this story[40]). Here is divine power writ large, and it is appropriate that these two pericopes therefore conclude not only with the astonishment and fear of the disciples, but also with a note of their human inability to cope with the new dimension of understanding and faith which these events demanded (4:40-41; 6:52). The christological question, 'Who is this?' which has already been raised by previous miracles (1:27; 2:7-12; 3:11-12) becomes more insistent and more sharply defined in v. 41.

Since G. Bornkamm's famous 1948 study[41] of the parallel pericope in Matthew, some have felt it necessary to draw a distinction between the two evangelists' handling of this tradition, Mark reporting it simply as a miracle story (with typically Marcan touches of narrative interest), Matthew as a paradigm of discipleship. The main basis for this reading of the Matthew parallel is the context in which it is set, following the account of the two would-be disciples in 8:18-22, with the verb ἀκολουθέω picked up (unnecessarily from the narrative point of view) in 8:23. Otherwise Matthew tells the story in similar terms to Mark, though, as usual, with less narrative detail; the use of κύριε rather than διδάσκαλε for the disciples' address to Jesus is typical of Matthew's gospel generally, not special to this pericope. Bornkamm's case is well made, but should not be pressed to the point of suggesting that for Matthew the story is *no more than* an allegory of discipleship, and therefore fulfilling a quite different purpose from its use in Mark; it remains for Matthew primarily a miracle story, one of the collection in chapters 8–9 which serve to underline the ἐξουσία

39. P. J. Achtemeier, *Int* 16 (1962) 169-76, further suggests that this story should be set against the recurrent OT theme of God's battle against the sea, as a hostile primeval force.

40. R. P. Meye, in R. A. Guelich (ed.), *Unity and Diversity in NT Theology*, 1-13, argues that Ps. 107 forms the 'horizon' not only for this pericope but for the miracles in 4:35–8:26 as a whole.

41. *Wort und Dienst* (1948), 49-54.

of Jesus' messianic ministry. In this he is in agreement with Mark, whose more vivid narrative style gives added emphasis to the danger and panic of the disciples. Mark's wording does not allow us to say whether he also saw the symbolic potential of the story for disciples encountering the trials of life, but there can be little doubt that he would have welcomed such an application of his story, even if he did not deliberately promote it, as many commentators believe that he did.[42]

The variation in tenses throughout this pericope makes an interesting study in Mark's narrative style. Historical presents form the main framework of the first part of the story (λέγει . . . παραλαμβάνουσιν . . . γίνεται . . . ἐγείρουσιν . . . λέγουσιν), but they are interspersed with imperfects to indicate the continuing features of the situation (ἦν . . . ἐπέβαλλεν . . . ἦν). But when the climax is reached, the narrative goes consistently into the aorist, to indicate Jesus' decisive action (ἐπετίμησεν . . . εἶπεν . . . ἐκόπασεν . . . ἐγένετο . . . εἶπεν), after which the disciples' immediate reaction of fear is described in the aorist (ἐφοβήθησαν), followed by an imperfect to denote their continuing discussion of what it all meant (ἔλεγον). The tenses are far from haphazard; rather, they demonstrate the natural ability of the storyteller to focus his audience's attention appropriately on the different aspects of the story as it develops.

35 ἐν ἐκείνῃ τῇ ἡμέρᾳ suggests that Mark intends the reader to understand that all that he has reported in 4:1-34 represents a single day's teaching on the shore, from which Jesus now moves on to cross the lake that same evening. There have been clear indications in the preceding discourse that this is a somewhat artificial schema, particularly in the awkward change of audience (and of venue?) at v. 10 and in the generalising summary in vv. 33-34 which indicates that what precedes was not just a single 'sermon' but an anthology of Jesus' more extensive parabolic teaching. From the narrative point of view, however, the continuity works well, with the boat of v. 1 now pressed into service for a different purpose, and the ὄχλος πλεῖστος of v. 1 left behind while Jesus goes off alone with οἱ ἴδιοι μαθηταί (v. 34), who are the obvious antecedent to the αὐτοῖς of v. 35. εἰς τὸ πέραν, spoken in the neighbourhood of Capernaum, would mean to the east shore of the lake, which was outside Galilee and had a predominantly Gentile population. We are given no reason why Jesus wished to go there, though in the light of 1:45; 2:2; 3:9; 4:1 it may well be that this was intended to be a break from the pressure of too much popularity in lakeside Galilee. The beginning of v. 36 supports this suggestion.

36 The change of subject to the disciples ensures that the reader has the whole group in mind from the beginning of the story, though μετ' αὐτοῦ rather than μετ' αὐτῶν at the end of the verse keeps the focus firmly on Jesus as the key figure (unless αὐτοῦ refers back to τῷ πλοίῳ, which is the nearest

---

42. See, e.g., E. Best, 'The Church as Ship', *Following*, 230-34. He points out that the nature miracles are distinct from the healings and exorcisms in that the beneficiaries are members of the disciple community, not people from the crowd.

eligible noun; but the αὐτόν which precedes it is the more prominent antecedent).

παραλαμβάνουσιν αὐτὸν ὡς ἦν ἐν τῷ πλοίῳ is generally taken to mean that, despite the apparent change of venue in v. 10, Mark here depicts Jesus as still in the boat which he had entered in v. 1; ὡς ἦν ἐν τῷ πλοίῳ is then often read rather awkwardly as two separate descriptive phrases, 'just as he was, in the boat'. On this reading ὡς ἦν is a detached descriptive clause with no obvious meaning or purpose: what was it about Jesus' condition at the time which deserved this comment? (Swete paraphrased it, 'without going ashore to make preparations'; the idea may be appropriate, but ὡς ἦν is an odd way to say this.) It may be easier therefore to read ὡς ἦν ἐν τῷ πλοίῳ as a single idea, meaning something like 'since he was already in the boat' (hence REB, 'in the boat in which he had been sitting'; similarly, but more paraphrastically, GNB), though this, too, is hardly elegant style. An alternative possibility, in view of Mark's tendency not to distinguish very carefully between εἰς and ἐν (as we have seen in 1:21 where εἰς occurred where we should have expected ἐν; cf. 10:10; 13:9) might be to render it, 'they took him *into* the boat just as he was'. This rendering would give a more appropriate sense for παραλαμβάνουσιν (they were already in the boat and took him in with them) and would relieve Mark of the charge of narrative incoherence (in that Jesus is understood to have left the boat, as v. 10 suggests), but at the cost of accusing him of a fairly uncouth bit of grammar. Since it also leaves the awkward ὡς ἦν unattached and unexplained, this is perhaps the less attractive option.

The ἄλλα πλοῖα play no further part in the narrative, and leave the reader with the distracting question of how *they* fared in the storm, to which Mark offers no answer. There is no suggestion that their crews shared in the disciples' reaction in v. 41. It is hard, therefore, to see any other reason for their inclusion beyond the circumstantial reminiscence on the part of whoever told the story (Peter?) that as a matter of fact their boat was not alone on the lake that evening.

37 The lake of Galilee is subject to sudden storms, which can be quite violent. An open fishing boat with low sides such as that discovered in 1986 at Ginosar[43] would be vulnerable to high waves; ἤδη γεμίζεσθαι indicates that it 'was being filled' to the point that it was in imminent danger of sinking.

38 All three synoptic versions of the story mention that Jesus was asleep, a remarkable enough fact in the circumstances to form an essential part of the corporate memory of the event, but mentioned perhaps especially in order to contrast with the disciples' panic. Whether the sleep was due to physical exhaustion or to the untroubled serenity of divine omnipotence Mark does not say. Like Jonah's equally remarkable sleep in the storm (Jon. 1:5-6) it serves to highlight the crucial role of the key figure in the story where the other actors are helpless, though Jonah's role (as victim rather than victor) itself serves to emphasise Jesus' authority by contrast rather than by similarity ('something

43. See above p. 188 n. 12. The depth of the Ginosar boat is only 1.25 metres.

223

greater than Jonah is here', Mt. 12:41). Mark's mention of the προσκεφάλαιον ἐν τῇ πρύμνῃ (the Ginosar boat has a raised section at one end) is often mentioned as one of the marks of an eyewitness account underlying Mark's story, though it could equally be an insertion on the part of a storyteller who knew what Galilean fishing boats were like, and wished to give visual impact to his story.

Jesus, like Jonah, is awakened by the panic-stricken crew, but whereas Jonah was summoned to pray for divine intervention, Jesus is apparently expected to know what to do himself. The wording of the disciples' appeal is more down-to-earth than in the synoptic parallels: the address διδάσκαλε, which seems a trifle banal in contrast with Matthew's κύριε, σῶσον and Luke's ἐπιστάτα ἐπιστάτα, reflects the disciples' normal relationship with Jesus (cf. 9:38; 10:35; 13:1),[44] even though in this situation it is not Jesus' teaching ability which is needed. And the blunt οὐ μέλει σοι; is the language of panic rather than of respectful address. But clearly they have already been with Jesus long enough to take it for granted that he will have the solution to a problem beyond their control.

39 The greater realism in the disciples' rude rousing of Jesus according to Mark, in contrast with the more reverential 'prayer' in Matthew, is continued in the account of Jesus' response. Whereas in Matthew Jesus has time to rebuke their lack of faith before getting up to tackle the situation, in Mark he acts first and talks later. His authority is asserted in strikingly anthropomorphic commands, in that he 'rebukes' the wind as if it were an animate being, and addresses the lake as if it were an unruly heckler, 'Be quiet! Shut up!' For both the verb ἐπιτιμάω and the command πεφίμωσο (there φιμώθητι) see above on 1:25, where both were used in an account of exorcism, in which the demon was rebuked and silenced by Jesus. Both terms occur elsewhere, as we have seen, in connection with exorcism or magic, and the conjunction of the two verbs in 1:25 and here has led some commentators to suggest that Mark sees the calming of the storm as a sort of 'exorcism', in which the demonic forces which control wind and water are 'bound' and subdued. But that is a lot to build on two verbs, each of which has a much wider use than in specifically exorcistic contexts (as we noted at 1:25), in the absence of any other indication in this pericope (or elsewhere) that Mark understands the natural elements as under demonic control. This is natural anthropomorphism (cf. the 'rebuking'[45] of the sea in Pss. 18:15; 104:7; 106:9; Is. 50:2; Na. 1:4), despite the coincidence that the same verbs occur in 1:25, where an animate being is the object of Jesus' censure. Indeed, it may well be asked what words other than such anthropomorphisms Mark, as a graphic storyteller, could have used to express Jesus' words of command addressed to inanimate forces.

---

44. For Mark's use of διδάσκω/διδάσκαλος in contrast with that of Luke and especially Matthew, see my article in *GP*, 1.103-12.
45. Using the root *gā'ar;* see on 1:25.

The aorist tenses indicate an immediate result, and γαλήνη μεγάλη (replacing the λαῖλαψ μεγάλη of v. 37) emphasises the total transformation achieved by Jesus' intervention. While it may well be true, as some commentators have pointed out, that storms on the lake of Galilee can abate as quickly as they arise, Mark is not speaking of any natural change in the weather. Jesus' companions in the boat were experienced Galilean fishermen, and to them it was a matter not of natural causes but of authority and obedience (v. 41).

40 Those to whom the secret of the kingdom of God has been entrusted nonetheless apparently lack faith. Even as early as 4:13 we were warned that the insight of the 'insiders' has yet a long way to develop, and the theme of the fallibility and even obtuseness of the disciples will become stronger as the gospel progresses. What they lack here is not so much understanding as πίστις, which here as elsewhere in Mark (2:2; 5:34; 10:52; 11:22) is a practical confidence in supernatural power, the correlative to miracles.[46] So lack of faith makes disciples δειλοί, unable to respond to a crisis with the confidence in God (or, more pertinently, in Jesus) which is the mark of the true disciple. The οὔπω (see Textual Note) expresses the frustration which Jesus feels over their slowness in assimilating the divine perspective.

41 The disciples' response[47] (to the miracle rather than to the rebuke of v. 40) is φόβος μέγας ('a fear which is greater than any fear of a storm', Schweizer); such fear, unlike the 'cowardice' of v. 40a,[48] is the appropriate response of humans faced with a display of divine power or glory (5:15; 6:50; 9:6; 16:8); cf. the reaction of the crew in Jonah's ship when the storm suddenly ceased (Jon. 1:16). Presumably when the disciples woke Jesus, they were hoping for some sort of saving action, but the scale of it has overwhelmed them. The question τίς οὖτός ἐστιν; will remain unanswered within the narrative setting for some time (though Mark's readers already know the answer, 1:1-13); even when a formal answer is given in 8:29, the sequel will show that little real christological understanding underlies it. But already the disciples, by formulating the question in terms of the obedience of wind and water (see the introduction to this section for this as a divine prerogative in the OT), prepare the way for an answer which goes beyond a functional view of Jesus as the Messiah. Mark's readers, with the prologue in their minds, are well equipped to spell out that answer.

---

46. C. D. Marshall, *Faith,* 217-18, considers the view that their faithlessness lay in their failure to 'exercise miracle-working power themselves against the elements', but rightly concludes that this would hardly be consistent with the fact that Jesus' own use of such power is regarded in v. 41 as the basis for recognition of his 'unique identity'.

47. For the close formal parallel with the response of the crowd after Jesus' first miracle in 1:27 see W. T. Shiner, *Follow,* 216-17.

48. See T. Dwyer, *Wonder,* 111, for the contrast between the cowardice of v. 40 and the 'unavoidable [and therefore not blameworthy] reaction to uncanny power' in v. 41.

Authority over Demonic Power (5:1-20)

TEXTUAL NOTE

1. The complicated textual variants among the three synoptic versions are perhaps best accounted for by an original Γαδαρηνῶν in Matthew and an original Γερασηνῶν in Mark and Luke, with Γεργεσηνῶν and related variants as subsequent attempts (perhaps originating with Origen, *Comm. Joh.* 6.24 [41])[1] to provide a more suitable lakeside location (see commentary). The wide and early attestation of the geographically embarrassing Γερασηνῶν in Mark is in its favour, while the tendency for the Matthean text to dominate in the early centuries accounts for the early introduction of Γαδαρηνῶν into the textual tradition of Mark and Luke.

Following Jesus' astonishing control over the wild forces of wind and water, Mark tells of his equally remarkable control over the untamable force of a man possessed not just by one demon but by a whole army of them. To the question with which the previous pericope concluded, τίς ἄρα οὗτός ἐστιν; the sequel provides a more explicit answer, as even hostile demonic forces are obliged to recognize in Jesus the υἱὸς τοῦ θεοῦ τοῦ ὑψίστου.

Exorcism has already played a major role in Mark's account of Jesus' ministry in Galilee, with one specific narrative of an exorcism (1:21-28), two general summaries of Jesus' ministry of exorcism (1:32-34; 3:11-12) as well as that of the disciples (3:15), and a major controversy arising out of his exorcistic success (3:22-30). Further exorcisms will be recorded later (6:7, 13; 7:24-30; 9:14-29). But in this pericope we have Mark's most spectacular exorcism narrative; its distinctive features include the location in Gentile territory, the vivid depiction of the demoniac's condition (vv. 2-5), the concept of multiple possession, the naming of the demons, and the visible demonstration of success in the destruction of the pigs.

Mark's narrative enthusiasm is given full play, as may be seen by comparing the length of his story (330 words) with Matthew's (135 words). It is a story worth telling for its own inherent interest, but for Mark it serves in this context to underline more forcefully the unparalleled ἐξουσία of Jesus, which leaves the Gentile spectators afraid and uncomfortable with his presence, and which is summed up in the utterance by the demons themselves of the most striking christological title yet accorded to Jesus in Mark's narrative, υἱὸς τοῦ θεοῦ τοῦ ὑψίστου (v. 7). The conclusion to the story also extends Mark's account of the impact of Jesus' ministry, in that the news about him is now heard and received with amazement not only in the already impressive geographical area indicated in 3:7-8, but now also in the predominantly Gentile region of the Decapolis. This recognition that the Jewish Messiah has a ministry which must ultimately extend outside Jewish circles will become more central to Mark's plot towards the end of Act One (7:24 onward).

1. See T. Baarda in E. E. Ellis and M. Wilcox (ed.), *Neotestamentica et Semitica*, 183-88.

1 The location on the (Gentile) east shore of the lake is indicated by the term εἰς τὸ πέραν (cf. 4:35), by the name Γερασηνοί, and (later in the story) by the presence of a herd of pigs (unclean to Jews: Lv. 11:7; Dt. 14:8; cf. *m. B. Qam.* 7:7). The precise location is not clearly indicated in the tradition (see Textual Note). Matthew's Γαδαρηνῶν would locate it towards the southeast corner of the lake, where the city of Gadara (some six miles from the lake) may have controlled territory reaching the lakeshore. But Gerasa is in the hills of Transjordan, some thirty-five miles from the lake, and it seems impossible that its χώρα could extend to the lakeshore. In any case, the southeastern shore (the area nearest to both Gadara and Gerasa) offers no convincing site for the κρημνός of v. 13, whereas near El Kursi, further north on the east shore, there is a suitably steep bank. Hence the attraction of the later reading Γεργεσηνῶν, since 'Gergesa' is traditionally associated with El Kursi, and the existence there of an impressive Christian church of the fifth century suggests that it had some traditional association with the story of Jesus. It was there that Origen and Eusebius located the incident, and historically they may be right, if only because no other suitable site exists. Mark's Γερασηνῶν therefore represents probably either a loose use of the term generally for the whole of the Decapolis (for which see further on 7:31), of which Gerasa was a leading city, or simply a confusion of similar names, the better-known city substituting for the obscure Gergesa.

2 For ἐν πνεύματι ἀκαθάρτῳ see on 1:23. At this point the multiple possession is not in evidence, since it is only one man (*pace* Matthew) who is under demonic control. The presence of such a person in τὰ μνημεῖα, a place of uncleanness, has an obvious symbolic appropriateness, though it may also be noted that few more suitable places of shelter would be available to one ostracised from normal society than rock-cut tombs or burial caves.[2]

3-5 The intractable nature of this man's condition is described in a vivid parenthesis, which prepares the way for the revelation that he is possessed not just by one demon (as in all other NT accounts of exorcism except Lk. 8:2)[3] but by many. For the preternatural physical strength of the possessed, cf. Acts 19:16; it is sometimes a feature in accounts of demon possession today.[4] For the self-destructive behaviour, cf. 9:22, 26.

6 The encounter briefly introduced in v. 2 is now more fully described after the parenthetical description in vv. 3-5.[5] The man's voluntary approach to Je-

---

2. Mention of tombs might also have prompted a reader with a good knowledge of the LXX to think of Ps. 68:6, which in the LXX speaks of God settling in a home those who are solitary, fettered, rebellious, and living in graves (τάφοι). Another possible echo is of Is. 65:1-7 (so especially Pesch and Gnilka, following H. Sahlin, *ST* 18 [1964] 160-62).

3. The concept of multiple possession occurs also in Jesus' (tongue-in-cheek?) story of the refugee demon in Mt. 12:45; Lk. 11:26.

4. Some modern examples are collected in J. Richards, *Evil;* see, e.g., the cases cited on pp. 140-42. Cf. G. Dow, *Churchman* 94 (1980) 200.

5. Commentators routinely perceive a discrepancy with v. 2, in that in v. 2 the demoniac meets Jesus εὐθύς when he has left the boat, whereas here he comes running ἀπὸ μακρόθεν. Such an

sus is surprising in view of the attempt at disassociation in the next verse. Is it that there is something irresistible about Jesus' presence? Or is there an element of conflict within the man himself between his own desire to meet Jesus and the reluctance of the 'resident' demons? The verb προσκυνέω does not entirely resolve the uncertainty. In Matthew it occurs frequently to denote the positive homage of those who approach Jesus, with at least sometimes the implication of his more-than-human status (especially Mt. 2:11; 14:33; 28:8, 17), but its only other occurrence in Mark is of the mock homage of the Roman guards in 15:19. Here it is followed by an address which recognises Jesus' supernatural authority, but with reluctance rather than enthusiasm; the whole scene reminds us of the use of προσπίπτω in 3:11, where again the impression is of concession of Jesus' superior power rather than of 'worship'. Two spiritual powers are here in confrontation, and the nature of the man's approach makes it clear which is the superior.

7 The approach of the demoniac is similar to that in 1:23-24 (see there for the meaning of τί ἐμοὶ καὶ σοί; and the odd fact that the plural is used there and the singular here), but the stakes are now raised, in that Jesus is recognised as not just ὁ ἅγιος τοῦ θεοῦ but, even more grandiloquently, υἱὸς τοῦ θεοῦ τοῦ ὑψίστου, while in place of the simple question ἦλθες ἀπολέσαι ἡμᾶς; we find this time an attempt to bind Jesus by oath to leave the demons alone. The use of ὁρκίζω by the *demon* is surprising, since the term is more normally associated with the ex*orcist,* who binds the demon by oath to come out, as in Acts 19:13.[6] Is this a deliberate attempt by the demons to reverse the normal encounter, and to pre-empt Jesus' expected use of such an oath formula? It is certainly an attempt to establish control over Jesus, and in this connection it may be significant that it is preceded by a mention of Jesus' name and title (as in 1:24). There is plenty of evidence in the magical papyri that to know and declare the name of a person or spirit was believed to give power over them, and similar naming formulae are quite common.[7] In v. 9 Jesus will in turn elicit the name of the demon(s) before effecting the exorcism. But the title here given to Jesus is such that its use could hardly encourage the demons to expect to establish control over him. For the use of ὁ υἱὸς τοῦ θεοῦ in a similar context see 3:11. The addition of τοῦ ὑψίστου reinforces the point, and establishes Jesus as the spiritual superior.[8] The expectation on the part of the demons that Jesus' purpose must be to torment them assumes that his relation to them is one not only of superiority but also of hostility.[9]

observation surely derives from the pedantry of a scholar who has never told or listened to a well-told story. See further on v. 8 below.

6. See J. Schneider, *TDNT,* 5.462-65. Cf. G. H. Twelftree, *Christ,* 42-43.

7. See J. M. Hull, *Magic,* 67, 69.

8. See J. M. Hull, *Magic,* 67-68 for the frequent use of the title ὕψιστος in magical and related texts. Cf. G. H. Twelftree, *Christ,* 63. It corresponds to the Hebrew *'elyôn,* a title frequently used in the OT by non-Israelites referring to the God of Israel. See further for the wider religious use of ὕψιστος G. Bertram, *TDNT,* 8.614-20.

9. Matthew's addition of πρὸ καιροῦ suggests that he understood the expected 'torment' as an anticipation of the eschatological destruction of the forces of evil. Mark gives no such hint, and

8   Mark's aside[10] explains that this was not just an assumption: the imperfect tense indicates that Jesus had already taken the initiative, and that v. 7 represents one side of a protracted dialogue, with the demons trying to resist the exorcist's authority. If so, this parenthesis, together with the account of the healing of the blind man in 8:22-26, implies the intriguing possibility that Jesus' 'success' in both healing and exorcism, while never in doubt, was not always as instant as most of the narratives suggest.

9   The dialogue continues with Jesus' reciprocal demand for the demon's name (see on v. 7), a demand which apparently cannot be resisted. It is often assumed that this was a necessary part of Jesus' exorcistic 'technique', but Mark gives no hint that that was its purpose; neither here nor anywhere else in the gospels does Jesus use the name as part of a formula of exorcism. Rather the function of the name in this narrative is to provide a graphic indication of the multiple possession involved in this case, which in turn will explain the following incident with the pigs. The significance of the 'name' Λεγιών need not focus on the actual number of troops in a Roman legion (theoretically 6,000; contrast the number of pigs, specified as 2,000 in v. 13), so much as on the character of a legion as a large body of troops acting in concert;[11] Jesus is not confronted by one demon, but by an army of them.[12]

10   The dialogue up to this point has been ostensibly with the man rather than with the demons, and has been conducted exclusively in the singular. But with the clause ὅτι πολλοί ἐσμεν the man fades into the background, and the demons (plural) parley with Jesus. There is some variety in the gender by which they are designated (πολλοί, v. 9; λέγοντες, v. 12; but αὐτά, v. 10; ἐξελθόντα τὰ πνεύματα τὰ ἀκάθαρτα, v. 13), so that it is not clear whether the subject of

---

the threatened 'torment' of being evicted from their home and χώρα (v. 10) would be enough to explain the appeal.

10. Commentators seem to have an irresistible tendency to take any such 'aside' as an indication of an originally composite story, inelegantly stitched together (cf. on 2:10 above). In this pericope the 'parenthesis' of vv. 3-5 and the 'unnecessary' repetition in v. 16, together with this 'aside', are frequently invoked to justify such a conclusion. But it is not at all out of character for a storyteller to insert a piece of useful information to provide essential (or interesting) background, or to enable the hearer more easily to follow the development of the story, and repetition is a regular stock-in-trade of effective storytelling. The whole pericope reads well as a unity, provided that it is understood as a well-told story rather than the meticulous product of a scholar's desk.

11. H. C. Waetjen, *Reordering,* 115-17, suggests that the name represents not the number of soldiers but their function as the agents of 'colonialism', which 'creates an atmosphere of living death which fosters a systemic breakdown of the human personality'.

12. Myers, 190-94 (following J. Bowman, G. Theissen) sees a more direct significance in the name Λεγιών, in that he interprets the whole pericope as a symbolic account of Jesus' mission to liberate Palestine from Roman military occupation. Ingeniously constructed around certain graphic terms in the story, this theory suffers from the apparent inability of virtually all readers of the story until now to have grasped the point Mark allegedly intended to make. The location in Gentile Decapolis is also inconvenient, despite Myers' imaginative attempt to explain the mention of Gerasa on the basis of its violent capture by Lucius Annius in A.D. 68. For a similar allegorical reading of the pericope, apparently unaware of that of Myers, see D. W. Chapman, *Orphan,* 117-22.

παρεκάλει here is the demons (singular verb after neuter plural subject, understood) or the man. In view of the fact that Mark uses plural verbs for the demons in v. 12 (παρεκαλέσαν) and v. 13 (εἰσῆλθον), it may well be that the man remains the subject of παρεκάλει, as the voice necessarily used by the demons, but he is not speaking for himself but for them (αὐτά). The whole narrative therefore constitutes a striking example of the way the NT presents demon possession not as a psychological problem of the one afflicted, but as a matter of alien occupation. It is with the demons, not with the man, that Jesus must deal; only after the exorcism is complete will Jesus address the man in his own right (vv. 18-20).

By now the demons appear to have accepted that they must leave their 'host', but it is not clear why they should then be keen to remain in the χώρα.[13] It is often asserted that demons were believed to have specific geographical areas of operation, so that to relocate them was to render them powerless; there is little clear evidence for such a belief, though it may lie behind Tob. 8:3. More commonly, an exorcist might banish a demon to a remote area, away from human habitation, to keep it from further mischief (cf. Mt. 12:43-45). Luke, however, understands the alternative as much more drastic than a mere change of earthly location: εἰς τὴν ἄβυσσον ἀπελθεῖν (cf. Rev. 20:1-3).

11-12 The possibility of an alternative refuge in animals rather than in a man was apparently not a new one: a Babylonian exorcistic incantation offers a pig as an alternative host for the expelled demon.[14] The ritual uncleanness of pigs from a Jewish point of view would add further point to the transfer; from a man living among unclean tombs the unclean spirits transfer to unclean animals. The appeal πέμψον ἡμᾶς underlines further the total submission of the demons to Jesus' authority. There is no question that he will send them away; the only issue is where.

13 Jesus' acceptance of the appeal results in the destruction of a large herd of pigs. Neither Mark nor the other synoptic evangelists show any awareness of the moral questions which so naturally arise in a modern Western mind with regard to both the gratuitous and large-scale loss of animal life as well as the substantial economic loss inflicted on an innocent third party.[15] Perhaps Jesus' comment recorded by Matthew in another connection, πόσῳ διαφέρει ἄνθρωπος προβάτου; (Mt. 12:12) suggests the perspective in which the incident would have been understood.[16] What matters for Mark is the im-

---

13. G. Schwarz, *NTS* 22 (1975/6) 215-16, finds it so improbable that he suggests a misreading of an Aramaic original which is more correctly reproduced in Luke's ἄβυσσος.

14. R. C. Thompson, *The Devils and Evil Spirits of Babylonia* (London: Luzac, 1903/4), 2.10-15. See further J. M. Hull, *Magic,* 40-41.

15. H. C. Waetjen, *Reordering,* 118, supposes that so large a herd of pigs must have been intended to provide food for the Roman army, so that Jesus has (patriotically?) 'destroyed the food supply of the Roman legions stationed in the territory'.

16. Guelich goes further and suggests that from Mark's (Jewish) point of view the destruction of unclean animals was itself in fact a good thing, an act of 'the deliverance of a land', symbol-

pressive demonstration of the effectiveness of Jesus' command. Neither the onlookers nor the possessed man himself could be left in any doubt of the reality or of the scale of the deliverance effected. The point is underlined by the specific mention of the extraordinary size of the herd, ὡς δισχίλιοι, remarkable even in Gentile territory. Visible proof of the demon's relocation is a feature of some exorcism narratives, most famously in Josephus, *Ant.* 8.48 (overturning a bowl of water) and Philostratus, *VA* 4.20 (knocking over a statue). In both those instances the physical act was a demonstration previously agreed between exorcist and demon as a proof of departure, whereas here there is no suggestion that Jesus intended, or even expected, the demons to drive the pigs into the water; the real proof of the success of the exorcism is rather the change in the man himself (v. 15). But it would be natural for the stampede to be seen as a parallel confirmation that the forces which formerly drove him have now been removed.

The subject of ἐπνίγοντο is not the demons but the pigs,[17] described in the plural (χοίρους) earlier in the sentence, even though the most recent verb used of them is in the singular (ὥρμησεν ἡ ἀγέλη); the δισχίλιοι which immediately precedes the verb (and which refers to the pigs, not the demons) accounts for the change to a plural verb. Matthew's more compressed sentence is perhaps ambiguous, but Luke is quite clear (ἡ ἀγέλη . . . ἀπεπνίγη), and the reference in Mark's next verse to οἱ βόσκοντες <u>αὐτούς</u> makes Mark's subject unambiguous. Since demons were sometimes thought to inhabit water, it could in any case hardly be thought that the drowning of their 'hosts' would destroy them; it presumably merely left them 'homeless', as in Mt. 12:43-44.

14-17 The unusually long account of the 'crowd reaction' further testifies to the special character of this miracle, with a large gathering from the whole area (both πόλις and ἀγροί) assembled to witness τὸ γεγονός. The tense of τὸν δαιμονιζόμενον is, of course, now technically incorrect (as the following perfect ἐσχηκότα makes clear), but it was as ὁ δαιμονιζόμενος that his compatriots had hitherto known him, and the juxtaposition of that familiar title with his actual condition as ἱματισμένος καὶ σωφρονῶν vividly portrays the cause of their astonishment. Their expressed reaction, however, is one of fear, and the result is not, as on the Jewish side of the lake, a welcome to the miracle-worker but rather a request to leave the area. Even in the following verses we are not told that the amazement of the people of Decapolis (ἐθαύμαζον, v. 20) resulted as yet in any following for Jesus in that area; they feel better off without such a disturbing presence. Perhaps Mark's addition of καὶ περὶ τῶν χοίρων at the end

---

ising the removal of uncleanness from Gentile territory. This interpretation, which is more imaginative than rooted in any indication in Mark's telling of the story, would of course leave the moral questions unresolved.

17. It is remarkable that the pigs appear totally unable to swim: despite some popular beliefs — perhaps derived from this story — pigs are normally perfectly capable of swimming, even if not by choice. But, as in the case of the demolition of the roof in 2:4, verisimilitude gives way to memorable storytelling.

of v. 16 is a hint at the reason for their discomfort: no one can object to the δαιμονιζόμενος being restored to normality, but the loss of the pigs is another matter.

18 Jesus' meek acceptance of the local people's desire to be rid of him is assumed without comment. Whatever the original purpose of the trip across the lake (4:35 did not tell us), it appears to have been overtaken by events, and Jesus returns immediately to the Jewish shore, where again an enthusiastic crowd will welcome him (v. 21). There is, however, at least the opportunity to take back with them a new (and presumably non-Jewish) recruit to the disciple group, and the request of the δαιμονισθείς (note the 'correct' tense now that the man himself is in focus, rather than his compatriots' view of him) ἵνα μετ᾽ αὐτοῦ ᾖ echoes the phrase used to denote the special role of the Twelve in 3:14.

19 Jesus' refusal of an eager 'volunteer' is not said to be based (as in Mt. 8:18-22/Lk. 9:57-62) on any doubt as to the man's sincerity or commitment. The choice of the Twelve has already been made, and the addition of a Gentile member to Jesus' 'inner circle' would have been a radical departure for which there is no parallel during Jesus' ministry; but neither of these considerations is mentioned either. The reason for refusal is rather the positive one that this man has an opportunity, which is uniquely his, to spread the news of what God is doing through Jesus of Nazareth among those who have known what he was before, and who therefore cannot ignore the dramatic change which has resulted from his encounter with Jesus. In emphasising this motivation Mark no doubt expects his readers to understand that the same principle applies to others whose lives Jesus has changed, even in less dramatic circumstances.

In this narrative context ὁ κύριος, used in Jesus' words as a third-person designation of the one who is the source of ἔλεος, must surely refer to God rather than Jesus himself (Luke has explicitly ὁ θεός), however naturally later Christians might understand it to refer to ὁ κύριος Ἰησοῦς. (The only other place in Mark where ὁ κύριος could be read as a title of Jesus is 11:3, where that sense is equally improbable; see commentary there.)

The contrast with Jesus' command to silence in 1:44 (and subsequently in 5:43; 7:36; 8:26) is striking, and prompts the question why Jesus is so keen to avoid publicity among Jews but has no objection to Gentiles hearing about his miracles.[18] This is, of course, part of the whole enigma of the theme of secrecy in Mark. But if it is true that publicity among the Jews posed the risk not only of inconvenient popular enthusiasm (cf. 1:45–2:2) but also of a misguided popular assessment of his messianic role (see further on 8:30), in Gentile territory this risk did not exist, since it was far from the scene of Jesus' regular ministry, and

---

18. There is little to commend the suggestion of J. F. Williams, *Followers*, 111-12, that Jesus' command here is only 'somewhat different' from that in 1:44 and is to be interpreted as 'an indirect injunction to secrecy' in that v. 19 mentions only his immediate family, so that the general proclamation in v. 20 is as much an act of disobedience as that of the leper (see next note). This is to impose a uniformity of pattern of which Mark's text gives no indication.

there was no ready-made messianic expectation to contend with. Since this was not an area where Jesus himself would be preaching, it is appropriate that the news of God's new initiative in Jesus should be announced there by one of the local people who has himself experienced its power.

20 This man thus does with Jesus' encouragement what the leper (1:45) did in defiance of his instructions.[19] The use of κηρύσσειν suggests that here is a genuine Gentile equivalent to the proclamation which is being made both by Jesus (1:14, 38-39) and by his disciples (1:45; 3:14) among the Jews of Galilee. But whereas Jesus has told him to declare what ὁ κύριος (= God) has done for him, he attributes the agency to Jesus himself (Luke has the same discrepancy, even more marked since he has used ὁ θεός rather than ὁ κύριος in Jesus' instructions). In the narrative context this need betray no more than the man's rudimentary theological understanding, but Mark's readers might be expected to notice and appreciate the implied identification of the work of God with the work of Jesus. The man's proclamation produces amazement, but we are not told whether it had more lasting effect. The next time Jesus appears in Decapolis, however, he will be expected to heal, and the result will be further proclamation and further astonishment (7:31-37). Already the foundation has been laid for the extension to the Gentiles of the ministry and mission of the Jewish Messiah (13:10; 14:9).

Authority to Heal — Even the Dead! (5:21-43)

TEXTUAL NOTES

21. The absence of ἐν [τῷ] πλοίῳ in several early texts (and its location before τοῦ Ἰησοῦ in W), and the varying order and occasional absence of πάλιν and εἰς τὸ πέραν, produce a number of permutations none of which affects the sense of Jesus' return across the lake to the western shore. There seem to be no obvious reasons for the differences other than stylistic preference in the light of quite a heavy collocation of geographical indicators. Explicit mention of the πλοῖον is typical of Mark's narrative interest; cf. vv. 2, 18, the former of which is peculiar to Mark, the latter shared only with Luke.

22. The omission of ὀνόματι Ἰάϊρος in D and a few OL MSS is more likely to be accidental (or perhaps influenced by the absence of the name in Matthew) than a reflection of an original text omitting the name; if it is an insertion from Luke, it is odd that the form ὀνόματι Ἰ. is used rather than the more typically Marcan ᾧ ὄνομα Ἰ., which unusually occurs at this point in Luke (see further Metzger, *Textual Commentary*, 85-86).

36. ἀκούω is likely to have been substituted for παρακούω in the majority of MSS as the more familiar verb, which, while it misses the element of *over*hearing, is equally

19. Several interpreters, following Wrede, have also understood this as a case of disobedience: Jesus tells the man to speak only to his own family, but he proclaims it throughout Decapolis. But Mark suggests no such contrast: v. 19 is certainly not a command to silence, and v. 20 is introduced by καί, in contrast with the ὁ δέ of 1:45. See further H. Räisänen, *Secret*, 154.

appropriate to the context. The fact that παρακούω can also mean 'ignore' or even 'disobey' may have influenced the substitution.

41. Several variants have arisen owing to the unfamiliarity of the Aramaic words, and the chance similarity of ταλιθα to the name Ταβιθά in the raising formula in Acts 9:40. κουμ (ℵ B C etc.) represents the masculine form of the imperative, which could be used for male or female subjects; the strictly feminine form κουμι in most later MSS and versions is probably a deliberate correction.

The sequence of incidents around the lake (see on 4:35–5:43) reaches its climax with a narrative unit in which two miracles occur, in the second of which the revelation of Jesus' ἐξουσία reaches a new height with the raising of the dead. Following his control over wind and water and over the most intimidating of demonic power, this pericope leaves the reader with the impression that nothing can be impossible for Jesus, and the question Τίς ἄρα οὗτός ἐστιν; (4:41) becomes ever more insistent.

It is true that the narrative as Mark presents it leaves open at least the possibility that Jairus's daughter was not really dead, in that the report of her death in v. 35 is deliberately set aside by Jesus in v. 36, and explicitly denied in v. 39, after which the cure is related in terms of her 'getting up' rather than coming to life. But while Mark does not make her death explicit (except in the report of v. 35 which Jesus ignores), the crowd's scorn in v. 40 suggests that Mark, like Matthew and Luke, understood Jesus to be using figurative language which the crowd misunderstood as a literal denial of her death, a fact which was plain to all. There is no doubt that Matthew understood the girl to be dead, since he presents her father as stating the fact even on his first approach to Jesus; in Luke at that point she 'was dying', while in Mark she is in imminent danger of death. There is therefore some confusion as to just when she died, but to set the synoptists against one another on the crucial issue of whether this is merely the cure of a dangerously ill girl or an actual raising of the dead is surely to press the narrative differences too far.

This pericope is regularly cited as the classic example of Mark's 'sandwich' or 'interpolation' technique, whereby one episode is inserted within another. It may be so, but it is hardly the best example, since whereas in other cases the 'sandwich' structure is distinctive to Mark, here all three synoptists tell the story in the same form. Perhaps, on a standard view of Marcan priority, Mark set it up this way, and Matthew and Luke merely followed suit. It is equally possible, however, that the interrupted journey represents a well-remembered narrative sequence which derives from the tradition rather than from Marcan ingenuity. It is generally suggested that Mark's interpolations are designed to draw out some thematic connection between the linked items (most conspicuously in the association of the scribal accusation of demonic power with the family accusation of madness in 3:20-35, or the linking of the temple and the fig tree in 11:11-27, both of which are uniquely Marcan 'sandwiches'). Here, while the sequence certainly fulfils a valuable literary function in creating narrative suspense, it is not at all obvious what thematic connection is achieved by this particular 'sandwich', other than the rather obvious point that both victims are women.[20]

There is, however, one thematic connection which may be discerned both in the two parts of the 'sandwich' and in the preceding pericope, that of uncleanness.[21] In Decapolis Jesus confronted 'unclean spirits', located among tombs, and appropriately transferred into pigs, as unclean animals. Now back on the west bank he confronts the uncleanness of a menstrual disorder, and (assuming that she really was dead) of a corpse, and yet in both cases Mark records physical contact (vv. 27, 41). Since the issue of uncleanness, and of Jesus' apparently cavalier attitude to the laws of purity, will become a central feature of the story in chapter 7, it may be that Mark has deliberately prepared the way by this sequence of narratives. But it must be confessed that the issue is implicit rather than explicit in the account of the woman with the haemorrhage, and if anyone noticed the problem of potential defilement in the case of Jairus's daughter Mark gives no hint of it.

21 The essential scenery for the following narrative is put in place: the return to the west bank, the lakeside location, and the familiar crowds (in contrast with the one lonely and tormented man who met him on the other, Gentile, side of the lake, v. 2). The setting is presumably back in Capernaum, Jesus' regular lakeside base, from which he will set off in 6:1 for a visit to Nazareth, up in the hills.

22 The first suppliant is an important man. In the NT ἀρχισυνάγωγος is sometimes used in the singular to denote the individual who carried overall responsibility for and authority in the local synagogue. But Acts 13:15 speaks of a body of ἀρχισυνάγωγοι jointly responsible for the service in one synagogue; these are presumably the elders (cf. Lk. 7:3-5, and the ἄρχοντες of Jn. 12:42), who constituted the governing body of the synagogue, and from among whom the chief official (rō'š hakkᵉneset) was appointed. The fact that Jairus[22] is here described as εἷς τῶν ἀρχισυναγώγων suggests that he was an elder, but not himself the chief official; in that case the singular ὁ ἀρχισυνάγωγος in vv. 35, 36, and 38 simply reminds the reader of this opening identification, without implying that he was himself the chief official. But he is nonetheless a man of consequence in Capernaum society. His deferential approach to Jesus, a recent arrival in the town, is therefore meant to be noticed, though the self-abasement of falling at his feet may indicate as much his desperation as his recognition of Jesus as by now a respected teacher in the town, with a growing reputation for miraculous power.

23 Luke at this point tells us that the girl was twelve years old, and his

---

20. Some commentators find a further link in the fact that the woman has suffered for twelve years (v. 25) and Jairus' daughter is twelve years old (v. 42); this is surely a counsel of despair.

21. F. Kermode, *Genesis,* 131-35, imaginatively explores this theme throughout chapter 5.

22. See Textual Note. Several people called Jair appear in the OT: Nu. 32:41; Jdg. 10:3-5; Est. 2:5; 1 Ch. 20:5.

only daughter. Mark will reserve the mention of her age until v. 42, but by the use of the diminutive θυγάτριον (cf. παιδίον in vv. 39, 41 and κοράσιον in vv. 41, 42) conveys the same impression. ἐσχάτως ἔχει is a colloquial expression not (*pace* Matthew) for death, but rather for being *in extremis*. The appeal ἵνα ἐλθὼν ἐπιθῇς τὰς χεῖρας αὐτῇ[23] is therefore not yet the stupendous act of faith which we find in Matthew, where there is an explicit appeal for raising the dead; he is asking for miraculous healing before she dies, that she may be cured (σωθῇ) and thus continue to live (ζήσῃ). (Even if, with the Byzantine text, ζήσεται is read as in Matthew, it is the prior mention of death, not the form of the verb, which in Matthew gives it the sense of resuscitation.) For the laying on of hands as a natural gesture of healing cf. 6:5; 7:32; 8:23, 25; and cf. the mention of touch already in 1:31, 41.

24 A further mention of the crowd (cf. v. 21) prepares for the scene which follows. συνέθλιβον picks up the fear of physical pressure from the crowd already expressed in 3:9. To be jostled is, however, hardly an uncommon experience in an Eastern market; in this case it will offer the woman her chance to make physical contact unobtrusively.

25-27 The second suppliant, whose social standing is in marked contrast to that of Jairus, is introduced in a sentence which piles seven participial clauses on one another before reaching the main verb (ἥψατο) in v. 27. This interesting departure from Mark's more usual paratactic style allows the reader (or hearer) to build up a sympathetic mental portrait of the woman's situation before her story begins,[24] and predisposes us in her favour, despite the unappealing nature of her complaint, especially in the light of Jewish purity laws.[25] To be ἐν ῥύσει αἵματος for twelve years must surely describe some sort of menstrual disorder, even if the exact nature of the complaint cannot, and need not, be identified. Menstrual impurity is a prominent concern in the OT (especially Lv. 15:19-33) and was later to become the subject of a whole tractate of the Mishnah (*Niddah;* cf also *Zabim*); defilement through contact with even a normally menstruant woman must be scrupulously avoided. This woman's long and fruitless search for a cure was therefore motivated not only by physical distress but by her social and religious isolation. Mark's unflattering account of the medical profession provides a sharp (and perhaps deliberately humorous?) contrast with the completeness and immediacy of the cure she receives through

23. For ἵνα (not grammatically dependent on a preceding verb of command) as an oblique form of request cf. 10:51, where the preceding question, Τί θέλεις; provides the necessary antecedent; here the syntax presupposes an understood θέλω (as in 6:25; 10:35, θέλω ἵνα). Cf. BDF, 387(3); Turner, *Grammar,* 94-95.

24. C. D. Marshall, *Faith,* 104: 'The striking proliferation of participles in the opening sentence . . . conveys to the audience the relentless compounding of the woman's need over a twelve-year span.'

25. Myers, 201-2, points out that by attending to this 'statusless' woman, who is at 'the bottom of the honor scale', Jesus breaks his prior commitment to help the daughter of someone 'at the top of the honor scale'; this 'profound reversal of dignity' is meant to shock, and thus to liberate.

touching Jesus. Jesus was surely by now the talk of the town, and the incidents already recorded in Capernaum are more than enough to account for his reputation. But the woman's surreptitious approach is in strong contrast with the importunate crowds at the door in 1:32-34, the blatant bid for attention by the paralytic's friends (2:2-4), and Jairus's very public appeal.

27-28 We have noted (at v. 23) the frequent mention of touch in Jesus' healings, but in other individual cases in Mark's narrative it is Jesus who touches rather than who is touched. In a general summary in 6:56, however (and less explicitly in 3:10), Mark will also mention the popular expectation that to touch Jesus' clothes would ensure healing, and says that this expectation was fulfilled (cf. Mt. 14:36; Lk. 6:19). The woman's idea that to touch Jesus' clothes without his knowledge would convey the same effect as to be touched by him suggests a more 'primitive', even 'magical', understanding of miraculous healing (and one which will reach even more elaborate lengths in the expected effects of Peter's shadow, Acts 5:15, and of Paul's clothing, Acts 19:12). Modern readers often find it remarkable that Jesus does not repudiate her approach (and that of many more who sought to touch his clothes in 6:56), and indeed seems rather to accept it as not only practically effective but also an example of true πίστις (v. 34). Is there a foreshadowing here of his generous recognition of an independent exorcist, on the grounds that ὃς οὐκ ἔστιν καθ' ἡμῶν, ὑπὲρ ἡμῶν ἐστιν (9:38-41)? Mark's Jesus is less bound by correct procedure, and even correct theology, than some of his followers.

29-30 The narrative continues in a similarly 'primitive' vein, in that the effect of the cure[26] is immediately felt both by the patient and by the healer. ἔγνω τῷ σώματι presumably refers to the woman's physical sensation of well-being, while ἐπιγνοὺς ἐν ἑαυτῷ τὴν ἐξ αὐτοῦ δύναμιν ἐξελθοῦσαν suggests that this healing perceptibly 'took something out of' Jesus, in a way not paralleled in other gospel healing narratives. The sequence might suggest an almost mechanical sense of physical 'transfer' of δύναμις from one body to the other (cf. Lk. 6:19, where in response to a touch δύναμις παρ' αὐτοῦ ἐξήρχετο καὶ ἰᾶτο πάντας), though Mark is careful to counter this impression both by stressing that it was not mere physical contact that mattered (since many others were pressing against Jesus at the time) and that the basis of this healing, as in other synoptic miracles, is in fact πίστις (v. 34). Underlying the physical contact is a 'transaction' at a deeper level. It is this which takes the woman herself by surprise, when she finds that what she had planned as a secret one-way contact proves in fact to be two-way, and is thus brought into the open.

30-33 Jesus' sudden challenge takes everyone by surprise. The commonsense response of the disciples (to which Jesus does not even deign to reply) serves to heighten the peculiarity of his question; how can one 'touch' be singled out among a jostling crowd? The effect is again to set Jesus apart as one with supernatural insight, who can perceive the special situation

---

26. The vivid phrase ἡ πηγὴ τοῦ αἵματος derives from LXX Lv. 12:7.

of the one among the many. That supernatural insight does not, however, apparently extend to an instant recognition of the culprit, and the woman, who has already begun to make her escape, is obliged to return (ἦλθεν) and own up to her temerity. Her fear may derive not only from her awe in the presence of the miraculous healer and the general embarrassment of the situation, but also from the awareness that in touching Jesus without permission she has made him ritually unclean; if that is the case, however, neither Jesus nor Mark mentions the point.

34 No one else in the gospels is addressed by Jesus as θυγάτηρ; the nearest parallel is the use of τέκνον for the paralytic in 2:5. Here, as there, the effect is to offer reassurance (note Matthew's addition of θάρσει in both passages), which is particularly necessary in the light of Jesus' brusque challenge in v. 30, and the consequent 'fear and trembling' (v. 33) of the woman when she knows she has been discovered. For πίστις as the basis for healing cf. 10:52 (where the same formula is used) and 2:5; 5:36; 9:23-24; for the same condition for miracles generally see also 4:40; 11:22-24.[27] Such πίστις consists more of a practical conviction of Jesus' ἐξουσία than of a theologically developed understanding of who he is; even this woman's 'superstitious' belief in healing by physical contact is sufficient to count. The OT formula of reassurance and blessing, ὕπαγε εἰς εἰρήνην (cf. Jdg. 18:6; 1 Sa. 1:17; 2 Sa. 15:9), confirms that she may now enjoy at last the šālôm which she has long needed, and the further assurance ἴσθι ὑγιὴς ἀπὸ τῆς μάστιγός σου makes it clear that her cure is not a merely temporary remission. ὑγιής, despite its English derivatives, relates to physical health, not to 'cleanness'; the effect of the cure will be, however, to remove her impurity and restore her to a normal place in society.

35 The interrupted narrative is resumed with the news that the delay has proved to be fatal. There is no hint that the report is false, nor does anyone except Jesus (in v. 39) raise any question about the reality of the girl's death. Even though in Mark's narrative the original appeal was for healing before death (see on v. 23), the situation is now changed. It is therefore assumed that the appeal lapses, and Jesus has no more to contribute. Mark does not say whether Jairus shared this assumption — Jesus gives him no time to express his opinion.

36 παρακούω (see Textual Note) suggests that the report was made personally to Jairus, but that Jesus overheard it. The verb also carries the sense of 'ignore', and that is equally appropriate to the context, which presents Jesus as the one person who is not deflected by the report, and proposes to press on regardless. He takes charge of the situation, and expects faith, even in the face of death. They have just seen an example of the effect of faith (v. 34), but this is on quite a different level. We are not told whether anyone except Jesus himself could summon up such faith; v. 40a suggests that no one did. For πίστις/πιστεύω see further on 2:5; 5:34; 11:22-23.

---

27. See S. E. Dowd, *Prayer,* 96-117, for a full study of faith and miracles in Mark.

37 The limitation to three disciples may have been necessitated (as in 1:29-30?) by the size of the room in which the girl's body lay, but is in any case consistent with Jesus' tendency to allow only the three 'nicknamed' disciples (see on 3:17) to be with him at moments of special revelatory significance; cf. 9:2 (the transfiguration); 13:3 (the final discourse; with Andrew); 14:33 (Gethsemane). The supreme miracle of raising the dead is also for their eyes only.

38-39 The presence of noisy mourners is a clear indication that there was no doubt about the girl's death, and Jesus' response assumes that that is why they are there. See above (introductory comments on this section) for discussion as to whether Mark intends us to take Jesus' words literally, as a rejection of the diagnosis; it is certainly possible that a coma could have been misconstrued as death, and that Jesus (whether supernaturally or not) knew better. The words οὐκ ἀπέθανεν ἀλλὰ καθεύδει allow, indeed seem to require, that meaning. But the same words occur also in Matthew, who has already stated explicitly that the girl has died, and the derision which greets Jesus' words (presumably literally understood) in all three gospels suggests that Mark also believed that she was in fact dead. If, then, the saying is not meant to be a literal diagnosis, what did Jesus mean? Sleep as a metaphor for death is a common biblical usage, but the verb used in such cases both in the LXX and in the NT is always κοιμάομαι rather than καθεύδω (see 1 Thes. 5:10 for a possible exception, complicated by a different metaphorical sense in the preceding verses). In any case, the contrast 'not dead, but dead' would make no sense; καθεύδω must here have some other sense. It is used metaphorically in Eph. 5:14; 1 Thes. 5:6-7 to denote spiritual torpor (the opposite of living as 'children of light'), but this usage, too, seems irrelevant to the present story. The context here indicates that the girl's death is real, but temporary. There is, hardly surprisingly, no parallel for such a usage of καθεύδω, but the very fact that it is not the normal metaphorical term for death helps to make the point that there is something unique about this girl's situation. The finality which belongs to the concept of death (and therefore also to the verb κοιμάομαι as a metaphor for it) does not apply to her, since Jesus is about to reverse the verdict of death and raise her as if from sleep.[28] The use of καθεύδω rather than κοιμάομαι makes it possible, though still difficult, to appreciate this new perspective.

40-42 Such an unheard-of idea naturally evokes derision.[29] Mark does not specify the subject of κατεγέλων, leaving us to speculate as to whether the

---

28. J. Camery-Hoggatt, *Irony,* 139-40, describes Jesus' comment as 'a subtle peirastic irony. . . . Jesus is not rejecting that notion [that the girl is dead], but rather is superimposing upon it a secondary — or, as Mark sees it, a new primary — frame of reference. Death is not final, not ultimate.'

29. In later rabbinic literature it seems to be assumed that a rabbi could restore the dead to life. One such incident involving Rabbah is recorded in *b. Meg.* 7b, while another involving R. Ḥanina ben Hama in *b. 'Abod. Zar.* 10b evokes the comment from the Emperor Antoninus that he is 'well aware that the least among you can bring the dead to life'! Clearly this later literary motif does not represent popular belief in first-century Palestine.

girl's parents, or even Peter, James and John, joined in the laughter. These five, however, are the only ones allowed to witness the miracle. It is performed with a minimum of fuss (contrast the similar miracles of Elijah and Elisha, 1 Ki. 17:17-24; 2 Ki. 4:29-37), simply a grasp of the hand (cf. 1:31) and a word of command. Mark's preservation (and translation) of the Aramaic words (see Textual Note) is typical of his interest in vivid recreation of the scene (cf. 7:34), but the words themselves are so ordinary[30] that any idea that a 'magical' formula is thus offered is quite without foundation. (The similarity in sound to Peter's words in raising the dead in Acts 9:40, Ταβιθά ἀνάστηθι, where Ταβιθά is a name derived from the preceding narrative, is surely coincidental.) The resuscitation itself is also related in quite a matter-of-fact way (similar to the account of the healing of Peter's mother-in-law, 1:31), further emphasized by the trivial comment on the girl's age, which has no obvious function other than to add to the human interest of the story (unless it is intended to explain περιεπάτει: she is a twelve-year-old, not an infant). Even the reaction of the five witnesses, while powerfully expressed, is no more extravagant than after previous 'lesser' miracles; cf. 1:27; 2:12; 4:41; 5:15-17. The raising of the dead fits in appropriately with Jesus' other acts of power, rather than being singled out (as it is more clearly in John 11) as a miracle *sui generis*. It is possible that the use of the verbs ἔγειρε and ἀνέστη, both of which occur frequently in the NT to denote the resurrection both of Jesus and of believers, served to suggest to Mark's readers the idea that in this resuscitation of a dead girl there was a foreshadowing of the power over death which would be the basis of the Christian faith. But the verbs are common ones, and in this story could hardly have been avoided; Mark gives no overt indication that he wishes to suggest a resurrection typology. This was, after all, a return to earthly life (and subsequent death), not resurrection.

43 The command to secrecy is by now a familiar refrain in Mark, though 5:19-20 has provided a fascinating exception to the rule. This time the command stands even less chance of success, in a setting where the dead girl must soon be presented alive to the mourning neighbourhood. The story closes on a note of remarkable bathos — καὶ εἶπεν δοθῆναι αὐτῇ φαγεῖν. While the clause serves, no doubt, both to underline the reality of the girl's return to life and perhaps to reveal Jesus' practical concern for matters of physical as well as spiritual need, in the narrative context it looks like a deliberate move from the high drama of Jesus' conquest of death to the banality of ordinary life (cf. again 1:31), as the story line now moves to a much less dynamic phase in the visit to Nazareth.

---

30. The basic meaning of *ṭᵉlîṭā'* is 'lamb', but the term was used for children. The words might therefore appropriately be translated into English as 'Get up, kid'!

NOT EVERYONE IS IMPRESSED BY JESUS (6:1-6)

TEXTUAL NOTES

2. The range of stylistic variants recorded by UBS[4] for this verse do not affect the sense; all include both wisdom and acts of power as the basis for the response.

3. This is the only NT description of Jesus as himself a τέκτων. Origen's apologetic denial (*Contra Cels.* 6.34, 36) that Jesus is so described in the 'accepted' gospels, if it is not a slip of memory, presumably reflects the variant here which makes him τοῦ τέκτονος υἱός. The different forms of this variant are, however, probably due as much to assimilation with Mt. 13:55 as to scribal embarrassment. (But see also p. 242 n. 2 on the apologetic implications of the title 'son of Mary'.)

3. The name of the second brother is given by Matthew (where the names are nominative) probably as Ἰωσήφ, with significant MS support also for Ἰωσῆς and Ἰωάννης. It is remarkable that most Marcan MSS have resisted assimilation and preserved the name Ἰωσῆς, with the genitive represented either by Ἰωσῆτος or Ἰωσῆ. Where the same name occurs in 15:40, 47 (see commentary ad loc. on whether the same person is in view), there is a similar textual situation (not noted in UBS[4]), with Marcan MSS largely supporting Ἰωσῆς, and Matthean (where there is a parallel) Ἰωσήφ. Both Ἰωσῆς and Ἰωσήφ were probably Greek forms derived from the Hebrew Joseph (see *ABD*, 3.968); it seems that Mark preferred the less obviously Hebrew form.

Since Jesus' return to Galilee in 1:14 his teaching and activity have been concentrated around the lake, with Capernaum as his regular base. His original home, however, was up in the hills, at Nazareth (1:9), and it was as 'Jesus of Nazareth' that he was already known (1:24). A visit to Nazareth, some twenty-five miles from Capernaum, thus seems overdue, and that is what this pericope records, even though Mark declines to name the village which rejects its famous son.

The triumphal progress of Jesus through the recent part of the narrative (since the explanatory discourse of chapter 4) is in danger of leaving the reader with a false security. One after another the forces of wind and water, demonic possession, illness, and even death have yielded to his authority. Forgetting the picture of divided response in chapters 2–3, the reader may be beginning to feel there is something almost automatic about the 'success' of Jesus. This pericope therefore serves to redress the balance, and to remind us that the effect of his ἐξουσία cannot be taken for granted. If πίστις has been the key to at least some of the preceding miracles of deliverance (4:40; 5:34, 36), what is to be expected where it is absent?

1 Jesus and his disciples now make in reverse the journey made by his family in 3:21, 31. Their attempt to 'control' him then had proved fruitless, and they had returned to Nazareth while his mission continued down by the lake. Reports of that mission, however, have continued to reach Nazareth, so that the return of the local prodigy (with his followers from the lakeside towns) is a natural focus of interest.

2   The invitation to teach in the synagogue reveals at first a degree of goodwill, or at least the recognition that Jesus is now a person of significance.[1] Mark, unlike Luke, tells us nothing of what he taught; his interest is only in the response of the people. The use of ἤρξατο before διδάσκειν may suggest what Lk. 4:22, 28-30 spells out, that the teaching remained unfinished, being interrupted by the crowd reaction of vv. 2-3. But Mark frequently uses ἄρχομαι with the main verb in introducing a narrative development (cf. 1:45; 2:23; 4:1, etc.), with no such implication. As in the synagogue in Capernaum (1:22, 27), the congregation are astonished by both Jesus' words and his deeds. The σοφία which impresses them is presumably discerned from the teaching given at that time, but the δυνάμεις must be those of which they have heard at second hand (cf. Lk. 4:23), unless the healing of the ὀλίγοι ἄρρωστοι mentioned in v. 5 preceded the synagogue teaching. The primary cause of the astonishment is not, however, the wisdom and miracles in themselves, but the question Πόθεν τούτῳ ταῦτα; — as vv. 3-4 will go on to explain.

3   To the people of Nazareth Jesus is the local boy, and they know no reason why he should have turned out to be any different from the rest of his family. (Note the repeated οὗτος, which probably here, as in 2:7 and unlike 4:41, suggests a derogatory attitude — he is 'this fellow', not someone special.) There is no suggestion that local gossip had any inkling of anything unusual about his origin — and indeed if Mark knew of the tradition of Jesus' virgin conception he has kept it very quiet. The designation ὁ υἱὸς τῆς Μαρίας occurs nowhere else in the NT (whereas Jesus is described as υἱὸς (τοῦ) Ἰωσήφ in Lk. 4:22; Jn. 1:45; 6:42), and the unusual use of the mother's name has been read as Mark's cryptic way of indicating that he (and/or the villagers?) knew that Jesus was not actually the carpenter's son.[2] But Mark never mentions Joseph, and the absence of a father in 3:31-35 (see comments ad loc.) suggests that a simpler explanation is the traditional view that by the time of Jesus' ministry Joseph had died, and therefore featured nowhere in the story outside the infancy narratives of Matthew and Luke; in that case he was simply not a part of the tradition known to Mark. The absence of Joseph's name even in this verse, where members of the family are listed ex-

---

1. Note, however, that this is the last time Jesus will be depicted as welcome in a synagogue, and the only subsequent references to synagogues in Mark are as places of ostentation (12:39) and of the persecution of Jesus' disciples (13:9).

2. Jesus is given the title 'son of Mary' in the Qur'an in explicit recognition of his divine origin. But E. Stauffer, in E. E. Ellis and M. Wilcox (ed.), *Neotestamenta et Semitica,* 119-28, argues for a polemical background to this title in the Jewish accusation, which later gained wide currency, that Jesus' birth was illegitimate, a point sharply made by referring to him as 'son of Mary' rather than 'son of Joseph'. It is, he believes, as a result of this slander that the title was carefully avoided in all other NT references, and progressively eliminated in this verse by textual emendation. H. K. McArthur, *NovT* 15 (1973) 38-58, offers an exhaustive study of possible reasons for a Jew to be identified by his mother's name, and concludes that this is not a formal identification but an informal description — 'Oh yes! that's Mary's boy from down the street'. He therefore rejects any ulterior motive such as Stauffer suggests.

plicitly, supports this view. In that case Jesus, as the eldest son, would naturally have taken over the family business as ὁ τέκτων.

τέκτων is used predominantly of workers in wood, though it can be applied to craftsmen of other sorts, such as masons, sculptors, or smiths.[3] In a small village the τέκτων would need to be versatile, able to deal both with agricultural and other implements and also with the construction and repair of buildings. As such he was a significant figure in the village economy, probably also undertaking skilled work in the surrounding area. In this context, then, there is nothing derogatory in the term.[4] The point is rather in its familiarity; the τέκτων is (or rather was, until his fateful visit to John at the Jordan) a reassuring symbol of normality, not the sort of person from whom you expect σοφία and δυνάμεις.

The listing of the members of Jesus' family (see on 3:31 for the literal understanding of ἀδελφός) reminds us of how small a role most of them came to play in later Christianity. The names of all four brothers are common ones among Palestinian Jews of the time (as is that of Jesus, too), so that subsequent references to any of them are hard to identify. Ἰάκωβος is agreed to be the same man who later (as 'James the Just') became leader of the church in Jerusalem and was killed on the orders of the High Priest in A.D. 62 (Josephus, *Ant.* 20.200). Some believe that he was also the author of the Letter of James, and that the 'brother of James' who wrote the Letter of Jude was the Ἰούδας mentioned here, but the names are too common to allow certainty. Otherwise there are no clear references to them individually in the NT, but references to Jesus' brothers as meeting with the disciples in Acts 1:14, and to the ἀδελφοὶ τοῦ κυρίου alongside Paul, Peter, and the other apostles in 1 Cor. 9:5 suggest that the family as a whole eventually joined the church. Grandsons of Ἰούδας were reputedly still known to be members of the church at the end of the first century (Eusebius, *H.E.* 3.19-20). The ἀδελφαί are never named.[5]

4 Jesus explains the local refusal to take his mission seriously (ἐσκανδαλίζοντο, v. 3)[6] by a proverbial maxim, particularly applied to philosophers in the Greek world (cf. our 'Familiarity breeds contempt').[7] In addition to

---

3. See the classical study by C. C. McCown, in S. J. Case (ed.), *Studies in Early Christianity,* 173-89. Also P. H. Furfey, *CBQ* 17 (1955) 204-15: 'not a carpenter but a general wood-worker'; 'a highly skilled craft'.

4. On the other hand, G. W. Buchanan, *NovT* 7 (1964) 195-209, takes insufficient account of the social insignificance of Nazareth when he proposes that Jesus was from an upper-class background, and 'had once been a business-man but later joined a sect and became a scholar'. For a more realistic assessment of the social standing of the village τέκτων see D. E. Oakman, *Jesus,* 176-82.

5. See above on 3:20 for the suggestion of P. R. Kirk that the mention that the sisters are ὧδε πρὸς ἡμᾶς is meant to distinguish them from the rest of the family, who had moved down to Capernaum to live with Jesus, while the sisters, having married local men, stayed in Nazareth.

6. G. Stählin, *TDNT,* 7.350, argues that the verb expresses 'deep religious offence', and in this context indicates not merely a failure to appreciate Jesus, but denial and rejection.

7. Parallels from pagan literature have been frequently noted; for a convenient collection see W. D. Davies and D. C. Allison, *Matthew,* 2.459-60.

the synoptic parallels here (Mt. 13:57; Lk. 4:24) cf. also Jn. 4:44 (where the saying oddly precedes an account of Jesus being *welcomed* in Galilee),[8] and *Gos. Thom.* 31, where it is expanded by the comment (hardly self-evident) that no doctor cures those who know him. In Mark, however, the saying is given in a fuller and more emphatic form, listing rejection not only in the πατρίς (as in most versions) and in his own οἰκία (as in Matthew), but also among his συγγενεῖς, an addition which reflects the unhappy experience of 3:20-21, 31-35.[9] The specific use of προφήτης (in all the Christian versions of the saying) need not necessarily be more than proverbial; the rejection of prophets by their own people is a common theme of the OT. But we shall soon find that people were in fact already speaking of Jesus (and of John the Baptist before him) as a prophet (6:14-15; 8:28; 11:32), and Jesus is apparently not averse to that designation, even if it will prove to be less than the whole truth (8:27-30).

5 There is a delightful irony in the juxtaposition of the two clauses of this verse: for most people the healing of a few invalids by laying hands on them would hardly constitute οὐδεμία δύναμις. Matthew's statement that οὐκ ἐποίησεν ἐκεῖ δυνάμεις πολλάς avoids the paradox, but also loses the vividness of Mark's language. Both evangelists attribute Jesus' 'minimal' miraculous activity to the ἀπιστία of the people of Nazareth, but Mark's οὐκ ἐδύνατο is bolder, in suggesting that not even the ἐξουσία of Jesus is unlimited. Mark often highlights the importance of πίστις in healing and other miraculous contexts (2:5; 4:40; 5:34, 36; 9:23-24; 10:52; 11:22-24), so there is no surprise in seeing the opposite effect attributed to ἀπιστία, but the description of Jesus as *unable* to work miracles is christologically striking, and is not greatly alleviated by the mention of the ὀλίγοι ἄρρωστοι who were the exception to the rule.[10] For ἐπιθεὶς τὰς χεῖρας see on 5:23.

6 The mention of Jesus' surprise (only here in Mark; the verb is more normally associated with the crowds) further underlines the 'human' character of Mark's portrait of Jesus. It also highlights the contrast between Jesus' reception in Nazareth and the general popularity which he has come to enjoy in the lakeside towns. The immediate mention of teaching in other villages of the neighbourhood (κύκλῳ indicates that he remained in the hill country around Nazareth rather than returning yet to the lake) suggests that he did not stay long in Nazareth, but rather followed the principle which he is about to enunciate in v. 11. The specific mention that Jesus was διδάσκων is typical of Mark's summaries (1:21-22; 2:13; 4:1-2, etc.); it is not to be interpreted as exclusive (teaching *and not* performing miracles), since there is no indication that other villages shared Nazareth's hostile attitude, and the similar statement in 1:21-22 leads straight into miraculous activity (which is itself remarkably described as διδαχή).

---

8. This fact leads R. L. Sturch, *JTS* 28 (1977) 94-96, to conclude that the saying originated in a comparison with Jesus' warm reception in Samaria (to which, of course, Mark makes no reference).

9. See S. C. Barton, *Discipleship*, 90-91.

10. For the combined effect of the two clauses of v. 5 see C. D. Marshall, *Faith*, 193-94.

JESUS' MISSION EXTENDED
THROUGH THE DISCIPLES (6:7-30)

When Jesus called fishermen as his first disciples (1:16-20), he promised them that they would soon be fishing for people. When he selected the Twelve, it was in order that 'they might be with him and that he might send them out . . .' (3:14-15). The first part of that job description (being with him) has been amply fulfilled in the story since then; wherever Jesus has gone the disciples (or at least some of them, 5:37) have gone with him, their presence being noted even when they contribute nothing to the events recorded (as in 6:1). Even before 3:14-15 the presence of the disciples with Jesus has been regularly noted (1:21, 29, 36; 2:15, 18, 23; 3:7, 9). But all this time they have been companions and spectators, and sometimes a privileged private audience, rather than partners in his mission. They have offered practical help (3:9; 4:35-36), and their comments and questions have provided the focus for some of Jesus' teaching and action (1:36-37; 3:32; 4:10, 38; 5:31). But they have not yet been 'sent out' as fishers of men; they have been extras rather than actors in the proclamation of the kingdom of God.

This second aspect of the disciples' job description is the subject of the next section of the story. In 6:7-13 they are sent out, and in 6:30 they report back to Jesus. Yet the bulk of this section is not concerned with the disciples at all. Their activity raises the public profile of Jesus, and Mark takes the opportunity to record people's reaction to his mission, and in particular that of Herod Antipas; this in turn leads him into a digression about Antipas and John the Baptist, which apparently takes us far away from the disciples' mission, until the theme is suddenly reintroduced in 6:30, thus bracketing the vivid story of the death of John within the framework of the mission. This is a typical Marcan 'sandwich' or interpolation.[11] The intriguing question is what it is meant to achieve in the construction of the narrative. Is it simply a memorable little narrative inserted to add interest to the story and to provide a suitable 'filler' for the gap between the sending out of the disciples and their return?[12] Or is there some way in which this gruesome episode throws light on the developing situation of Jesus' ministry, and in particular on the mission of his disciples?

Jesus' ministry began in continuity with that of John (1:2-11), and in the context of the enforced closure of John's ministry through imprisonment (1:14). That imprisonment, barely alluded to in 1:14, is now explained, and its tragic sequel spelled out. And the man responsible for it may be assumed to be no more friendly to Jesus than to John; indeed, his supporters have already been

---

11. See above, pp. 18-20. For an interesting literary discussion of the role of this particular sandwich (or, as he puts it, 'heterodiegetic analepsis'!) see F. Kermode, *Genesis,* 128-31.

12. E. Best, *Following,* 192, suggests that Mark used the Antipas pericope to fill this particular gap while the disciples were away from Jesus in order to maintain his 'policy' of never depicting Jesus as working separately from his disciples (after 3:15), since in this pericope (unlike any other in the gospel after 1:9) neither Jesus nor his disciples appear.

seen in collusion with the Pharisees plotting Jesus' death (3:6), and will reappear in a similar role in 12:12-13. Jesus' cryptic words about the 'yeast of the Pharisees and of Herod' in 8:15 presuppose the same coalition against him. While Herod Antipas will not be an actor in Jesus' eventual destruction, which will take place in Jerusalem, far from his official jurisdiction, it is surely not unimportant for Mark's readers to know that the ruler of the area of Jesus' public mission is lined up on the side of the opposition. His wanton execution of Jesus' predecessor and associate (see 11:27-33 for the connection) is a sign of what the mission of the kingdom of God can expect from the kingdoms of this world, and in 9:12-13 Jesus will spell out more clearly that what 'they' (impersonal, but surely with reference to Antipas) have done to 'Elijah' (see on 1:6) will inevitably also be done to the 'Son of Man'.

That is the climate within which the disciples' mission is to take place, and the point is underlined by the similarity of their proclamation in 6:12 to that of John in 1:4. The possibility of a hostile reception has already been demonstrated in Nazareth (6:1-6), and is further envisaged in v. 11. There is a basic conflict of interests, even of ideologies, between the kingdom of God and the norms of human society. An ambassador of the kingdom of God is called not only to a mission of restoration and deliverance, but also to a conflict of which John's fate provides an extreme example.

The Mission of the Twelve (6:7-13, 30)

Having noted Mark's framework for the section as a whole, we may conveniently take both the outer parts of the 'sandwich' together. In the light of the considerable interest in the disciples and their function in Mark's gospel so far, the account of their mission is surprisingly brief, particularly when compared with Mt. 10, where a comparable account is expanded with a lot of other material on mission and persecution to form the second of Matthew's major discourse sections, and with Luke's two mission accounts, that in 9:1-6 being roughly parallel both in content and in narrative context to the present pericope, while 10:1-12 describes a further and similar mission of seventy(-two) disciples. This is in fact the only place in Mark's narrative where the Twelve are seen operating away from Jesus (except for his very temporary absences in 6:45-52 and, for some of them, 9:14-29). But perhaps in view of the emphasis on 'sending out' in 3:14 we are intended to read this pericope as typical of a repeated mission rather than recording one unique occasion. (The use of ἤρξατο in v. 7, and the imperfect verbs that follow it [ἐδίδου, παρήγγειλεν], may support such a reading, though see above on v. 2 for Mark's frequent use of ἄρχομαι as a narrative transition.)

The description of Jesus' mission charge in vv. 7-11 is remarkable in that the only specific function attributed to the Twelve is ἐξουσίαν τῶν πνευμάτων τῶν ἀκαθάρτων. The focus is on the manner of the mission rather than its con-

246

tent. It is only in the narrative account which follows in vv. 12-13 that we discover that their mission also involved preaching (as 3:14 has led us to expect); and even there preaching is only one of three activities, along with exorcism and healing (the latter also not mentioned in the charge). Verse 30 will confirm that it is more than just a teaching mission, as they report back on ὅσα ἐποίησαν καὶ ὅσα ἐδίδαξαν. Just as Jesus himself has become known as a healer and exorcist as well as a preacher, so, too, must his disciples.

The instructions given in vv. 8-11 focus on material provision for the journey, both in what the Twelve themselves should or should not take with them (vv. 8-9) and in the hospitality which they should expect instead (vv. 10-11). The emphasis is on travelling light and on mobility. In contrast with the fairly settled base which Jesus seems to have established for his own ministry in Capernaum (though that has proved to be in practice a base from which expeditions are launched to surrounding areas), they are to keep on the move, thus fulfilling by proxy Jesus' determination to reach the villages all over Galilee (1:38-39). Meanwhile, Jesus himself apparently remains at 'headquarters', presumably now back in Capernaum after the visit to the hill country in vv. 1-6, since when the Twelve report back to him in v. 30 he can immediately take them away across the lake in a boat.

7 Those sent out are, as in Mt. 10:1; Lk. 9:1, οἱ δώδεκα, a term which we have seen to be functionally equivalent in Mark to οἱ μαθηταί (see above on 3:13-19). Mark does not tell us of the existence of a wider group of μαθηταί such as could supply the seventy(-two) missioners of Lk. 10:1 (where they are described as ἕτεροι and are therefore presumably to be seen as additional to the Twelve). For Mark the pool of available missioners is apparently the Twelve alone. On their return in v. 30 they will be described, uniquely in Mark,[13] as οἱ ἀπόστολοι; the noun echoes the verb ἀποστέλλω here and in 3:14, and is used in its more etymological sense of 'those sent out'. There is nothing in Mark (assuming that the title is not part of the original text in 3:14) to suggest that ἀπόστολος designates an office, or even a member of a fixed group, though in practice the ἀπόστολοι are in fact οἱ δώδεκα. Its use in v. 30 denotes their function as missioners, a function fulfilled only here in Mark's narrative, though signalled in 3:14 as their more regular role. The practice of sending them out in pairs[14] (noted by Luke with reference to the seventy[-two] rather than the Twelve) will be repeated in the special 'missions' of disciples to deal with practical arrangements in 11:1; 14:13 (cf. also Lk. 7:19; Acts 9:38; 10:7). It is a sensible policy, providing mutual support and companionship, which was followed in the apostolic church (Acts 8:14; 11:30; 13:1-2; 15:39-40, etc.) and has been widely adopted since. J. Jeremias[15] has collected several examples of similar

---

13. See the textual note above on 3:14.

14. For the idiom δύο δύο in a distributive sense (where Greek normally used κατὰ δύο or ἀνὰ δύο), cf. vv. 39, 40. The same idiom occurs in both the Hebrew and LXX of Gn. 7:9. Cf. BDF, 248(1).

15. J. Jeremias in A. J. B. Higgins (ed.), *NT Essays,* 136-43. Jeremias also traces the frequent use of the 'paarweise' principle in the apostolic church.

commissions to pairs of disciples from rabbinic literature, even though there is no explicit OT precedent (Ec. 4:9-12 sets out its pragmatic basis); he suggests, however, that the OT requirement of at least two witnesses to establish legal testimony (Dt. 17:6 etc.) suggested the need for two messengers to support one another's message.

The ἐξουσία τῶν πνευμάτων τῶν ἀκαθάρτων which was envisaged in 3:15 as part of the purpose of their being sent out, but which they have not hitherto had the opportunity to use, is now actually given (and will be effectively deployed, v. 13), even though 9:18, 28-29 will remind us that there is no guarantee of 'success'. What has hitherto been a special mark of the ἐξουσία of Jesus (1:27; 3:11) is now to be shared with those who have been μετ' αὐτοῦ (3:14-15).

8 The travelling provisions which are forbidden, ἄρτος, πήρα (for carrying food?)[16] and even χαλκός, sound remarkably basic. Presumably the idea is not that they will not eat, but that food, and any other necessities for which money might have been needed, will be provided for them on the basis of the hospitality expected in v. 10.[17] But a ῥάβδος is exempted from the general prohibition of provision, presumably because travel without a staff was unthinkable (cf. Ex. 12:11).

It was not, however, unthinkable to Matthew and Luke, both of whom include the ῥάβδος among the *forbidden* items. This disagreement is so direct and simple that it has become a favourite test case in discussions about the detailed harmonisation of the gospels;[18] it is in fact more important as such than in its own exegetical significance, since the presence or absence of this one item of equipment makes little difference to the emphasis of these verses on avoiding excessive material provision. One apparently promising avenue of harmonisation is to note the different verbs used: Mark allows the *taking* (αἴρω) of a staff, whereas Matthew forbids the *acquiring* (κτάομαι) of one — i.e., perhaps the procuring of a new one rather than taking the one which the disciple is assumed to have already. Unfortunately, however, Luke forbids them to *take* (αἴρω) a staff; and in any case the use of κτάομαι rather than αἴρω in Matthew covers the whole list of prohibited items including money and πήρα, not just the staff. Various reasons for the difference may be conjectured, either in terms of the context of writing (differing sociological contexts for the gospels or different

16. The πήρα, a beggar's bag, was a known mark of the itinerant Cynic preacher (see BAGD, 656b). Despite attempts in recent years to characterise Jesus and his disciples as Cynics (notably by F. G. Downing, *Cynics*), it remains very questionable whether the Cynic was a familiar figure in first-century Galilee. (For an overview of recent discussion see R. F. Hock, *ABD*, 1.1221-26.) Any links between the present pericope and the known characteristics of Cynics are more likely the result of a similar concept of mission than of deliberate imitation or the adoption of a recognised public image; the πήρα is in any case here *forbidden*.

17. There is an illuminating parallel in Josephus, *War* 2.124-27, where Josephus describes the hospitality of Essenes to travellers who belong to their own sect; they can take for granted the hospitality of complete strangers, and therefore need carry nothing at all with them except weapons for protection against brigands.

18. See B. Ahern, *CBQ* 5 (1943) 332-37, for proposed harmonisations.

lengths of mission envisaged) or arising from the process of tradition (including the possibility of a common source other than Mark for Matthew and Luke — a 'Mark-Q overlap'), but the disagreement about the staff remains unresolved.

9 As the list of instructions continues the syntax becomes increasingly ragged. The third-person indirect command of v. 8 (using ἵνα), with its extended series of objects, is followed by two coordinate clauses (introduced by ἀλλά and καί) in the first of which a participle does duty for a main verb while the subjunctive verb of the second (presumably still governed by ἵνα, though it could equally be a change to direct speech) has gone over to the second person. The style is unliterary but quite intelligible as colloquial reported speech.

The σανδάλια pose a similar (though not identical) problem to the ῥάβδος; Mark allows them, while Matthew and Luke (in 10:4, not 9:3) do not. But the noun used by Matthew and Luke is ὑποδήματα, so it might be argued that different types of footwear are in view: ὑποδήματα are allowed, but σανδάλια are not. This convenient suggestion is, however, weakened by the fact that Mark uses not only the noun σανδάλια but also the participle ὑποδεδεμένοι, and also by the fact that no clear distinction between the two nouns seems to be justified by their usage: no type of footwear other than sandals is known to have been commonly worn by Galilean men, so that the nouns are effectively synonymous. Sandals, like the staff, are basic travelling equipment (cf. again Ex. 12:11);[19] it is possible that the prohibition in Matthew and Luke is of carrying spare pairs (while the permission in Mark is specifically for *wearing* sandals), but that is certainly not the natural reading of the text, especially in Lk. 10:4. With regard to the χιτών, however, all three evangelists are in agreement that it is *two* χιτῶνες that are forbidden — one will be worn, but no additional protection from cold (Mark's ἐνδύσησθε indicates this rather than carrying a change of clothes)[20] is needed.

The travelling religious teacher with staff, sandals, and a single χιτών but with no travelling pack or provision for the journey fits into a recognisable strand which extends from Elijah and John the Baptist through to the mendicant friars of the Middle Ages and several religious orders today. Outside the Judaeo-Christian tradition the Cynic preacher filled a similar role (see note on the πήρα, v. 8). Jesus' intention in sending them out in this way is not so much to encourage asceticism as such (they are after all to expect and accept hospitality),[21] but to em-

---

19. *M. Ber.* 9:5 forbids the visitor to the temple mount to take his 'staff, sandal and wallet' with him. These are clearly the normal equipment of a traveller. The suggestion of T. W. Manson, *Sayings,* 181, that the prohibition of these items on the disciples' mission is therefore intended to mark their mission as a 'sacred undertaking' is quite unnecessary even for Matthew and Luke; it could in any case not apply to Mark, where staff and sandals are permitted.

20. See Josephus, *Ant.* 17.136, for the possibility of two tunics being worn at the same time, and see further below on 14:63.

21. Schweizer, 130, says that Mark's reader should 'not fanatically regard asceticism as something worthwhile in itself. . . . One must not be so fanatical as to think that he is permitted to use only his faith in the miraculous against wild animals and snakes, and not to use a stick or a shoe.'

phasise that loyalty to the kingdom of God leaves no room for a prior attachment to material security.

10-11   In Middle Eastern society the expectation of hospitality for visiting teachers is no surprise; they ought to be able to take it for granted. A reasonably extended stay is apparently envisaged.[22] What is surprising is the clear expectation that there will be some τόποι (not just single households but whole communities?) where they and their message are not welcome. Even at Nazareth Jesus and his disciples had at first been welcomed, even to the extent of an invitation to teach in the synagogue. But the ἀπιστία which followed there is likely to be repeated elsewhere, and in such a case the disciples must be prepared to do what Jesus did at Nazareth, to move on and focus their ministry in places where they will be welcome. (Cf. Lk. 9:51-55 for another example of Jesus' acting by this principle himself.)

For ἐκτινάσσω τὸν χοῦν as a gesture of dissociation cf. Acts 13:51 (compare Acts 18:6). The gesture is more fully described in Lk. 10:10-11. The rabbis shook the dust off their feet when leaving Gentile territory, to avoid carrying its defilement with them.[23] Such a gesture serves εἰς μαρτύριον αὐτοῖς, a phrase which could suggest that it is intended to lead them to a change of heart, but which generally carries the negative overtone of a 'witness *against*' (see above on 1:44), a witness for the prosecution (this implication is explicit in Acts 18:6). A community 'marked' in this way as unrepentant (v. 12) will be liable to judgment (note how this gesture in Lk. 10:10-11 is followed immediately by the pronouncement of condemnation on unrepentant towns, vv. 12-16).

12   Even though not included explicitly in Jesus' charge in v. 7, proclamation (κηρύσσω) is an essential element in the disciples' commission (3:14), just as it is in Jesus' own ministry (1:14, 38-39). Mark's minimal account of the content of that proclamation, ἵνα μετανοῶσιν, echoes 1:15, but focuses on the expected response rather than on the kingship of God which was at the heart of Jesus' message. Summarised thus briefly, their message sounds like a simple continuation of the proclamation of John (1:4), and it is likely to have been so perceived by those who heard them. This echo gives added point to the reactions recorded in 6:14-16, and to the inclusion of an account of the fate of John in the middle of the narrative of the disciples' mission.

As in 1:32-34 etc. exorcism and healing are carefully distinguished. It was the former only which was specifically mentioned in the commission in v. 7, but the threefold ministry of preaching, exorcism, and healing which Jesus has already been exercising is now appropriately extended to the disciples. Anointing with (olive) oil is mentioned in association with healing only here in the gospels (and elsewhere in the NT only at Jas. 5:14); Jesus is never said to have done so. Oil was used medicinally in OT times (Is. 1:6; Jer. 8:22; 51:8) as

---

22. The danger of abuse of hospitality by travelling prophets and teachers which is envisaged in *Did.* 11–12 has apparently not yet arisen.

23. For the uncleanness of Gentile earth cf. *m. 'Ohol.* 2:3; *m. Ṭoh.* 4:5.

in other ancient societies, and the action of the Samaritan in pouring oil and wine on the wounds of the traveller in Jesus' parable (Lk. 10:34) was probably common practice. It may be, therefore, that the disciples' use of oil was purely a pragmatic, medical measure (which Jesus, with his more direct power, had no need to use?). But oil was also used in a more symbolic way, sometimes to express joy or honour (e.g., Ps. 45:7; Is. 61:3) or to symbolise the blessing of God, as when a healed leper was restored to society (Lv. 14:15-18); the anointing of priests and kings symbolised their divine commissioning. The anointing of the sick, both here and in Jas. 5:14, is therefore as likely to be a symbol of God's care for and restoration of the patient as that the oil itself contributed physically to the healing. Mark gives no indication that anointing was linked to specific forms of illness. His wording suggests a more general application in cases of physical healing, but clearly separates the use of oil from the practice of exorcism.

30 For the term οἱ ἀπόστολοι see above on v. 7. In keeping with the focus in Jesus' charge, the disciples' report back to Jesus is first on ὅσα ἐποίησαν and only secondly on ὅσα ἐδίδαξαν. The change of verb from κηρύσσω in v. 12 to διδάσκω here is a warning against positing too clear a distinction between the two verbs; both refer to the verbal communication of God's message.

The Reaction of Antipas (6:14-16)

TEXTUAL NOTE

14. The flow of the pericope is awkward whether we read ἔλεγεν (with reference to Antipas, whose conviction to this effect would then be restated in v. 16) or ἔλεγον (making this the first of three statements of the public perception, followed by ἄλλοι δέ . . . ἄλλοι δέ . . . , but without any expressed subject for the first ἔλεγον). The latter offers a rather more coherent sequence, assuming that the sentence is interrupted after Ἡρῴδης by a survey of popular opinions (parallel to that of 8:28) before being resumed in v. 16 with Antipas's endorsement of the first option; the change to ἔλεγεν (which is very widely supported) would be a natural 'correction' by a scribe who did not recognise the break in the sentence and therefore assimilated the verb to the preceding ἤκουσεν.

The mission of Jesus, now extended through his disciples, continues to cause comment and speculation, and now even Herod Antipas has heard about him, and comes to his own conclusion. This (with its sequel in vv. 17-29) is the first and only appearance of Antipas in person in Mark's story, though his 'party', the Ἡρῳδιανοί, have appeared in 3:6 (cf. 12:13), and Jesus will make a passing reference to him in 8:15. As ruler of Galilee and Peraea throughout the period of both John's and Jesus' ministry (in Peraea and Galilee respectively), he had cause to be concerned about any new religious movement which carried the potential for fostering a popular uprising. The large-scale popular enthusiasm for the preaching of both John and Jesus, and reports of the latter's politically sensitive language about an incoming 'kingdom of God', could hardly fail to arouse his suspicion. Josephus's account of his execution of John (*Ant.* 18.116-19) is explicitly in terms of John's potential as a leader of sedition (μὴ ἐπὶ στάσει τινὶ φέροι), on account of his persuasive preaching. To a man so concerned, it is hardly surprising that one successful 'revival' preacher looked very much like another, especially if he was aware of Jesus' original link with John before the latter's imprisonment.

This short pericope not only gives us information about Antipas's worries, but also provides an interesting insight into what Mark takes to be the popular response to Jesus outside the circle of the disciples. The options listed all fall within the category of 'prophet', thus endorsing Jesus' use of that term in v. 4; it was, apparently, the natural category to explore in assessing a religious teacher with conspicuous ἐξουσία and a penchant for miracles like those of Elijah and Elisha. The same range of opinions will be listed in 8:28, when Jesus will himself raise the question of his public image. But to identify him with John the Baptist, however appropriate, raises the problem that John is now dead, and therefore the concept of his being 'raised from the dead' in the person of Jesus is being canvassed.[24] It is a sufficiently plausible idea for even Antipas to take it seriously.[25]

14 See the Textual Note for the structure of the sentence: the first five words introduce the subject of the pericope, while from φανερὸν γάρ to the end of v. 15 Mark tells us parenthetically of the popular estimate of Jesus (the unexpressed subject of the first ἔλεγον being people in general).[26] The description of Antipas as βασιλεύς (contrast Matthew's and Luke's ὁ τετραάρχης) is not technically correct, since Augustus specifically refused to grant Antipas this title enjoyed by his father, so that he remained tetrarch only until he was deposed in A.D. 39 (and is consistently so described by Luke). Such constitutional niceties were, however, probably of little significance in Galilee, where Antipas acted, and was recognised, to all intents and purposes as 'king'; it was his active campaigning for that title which led to his eventual dismissal and exile. Even Matthew, who correctly records Antipas's title in 14:1, calls him βασιλεύς in 14:9. Mark calls him βασιλεύς throughout. He does not tell us explicitly what it was that Antipas 'heard' (Matthew adds τὴν ἀκοὴν Ἰησοῦ), but the whole pericope is expressed in terms of the reputation of *Jesus* rather than of his disciples, so that its setting within the account of the *disciples'* mission seems rather artificial.[27] Even if it was that mission which brought the issue to a head, it is Jesus'

24. See above on 5:40-42 for later rabbinic belief in the raising of the dead.

25. It was also taken so seriously by Enoch Powell that he built on this pericope his theory that in fact it was John the Baptist, not Jesus, who was raised from the dead, and that the gospel records of Jesus' ministry originated as accounts of the ministry of the risen John, subsequently appropriated for Jesus by the primitive church.

26. For the many 'impersonal verbs' in Mark see Taylor, 47-48; E. J. Pryke, *Style*, 107-15.

27. Hoehner, *Herod*, 192-97, argues that this pericope belongs to an earlier period in Jesus' ministry.

personal ὄνομα and δυνάμεις that are the focus of popular comment and therefore of Antipas's concern.

For the title Ἰωάννης ὁ βαπτίζων see on 1:4. The idea of the return of a great man after death is paralleled later in the myths about *Nero redivivus* (see *ABD*, 4.1080), though it is not easy to understand how John could be thought to be 'resurrected' in the person of someone who had already been known and active before John's death. Mark does not, of course, tell us when John was executed, and since he does not mention John as alive during Jesus' public ministry (contrast Mt. 11:2-6/Lk. 7:18-23), it is possible that he envisaged all of Jesus' public activity as subsequent to John's death (and possibly even intended the παραδοθῆναι of 1:14 to include death as well as imprisonment).[28] But Matthew and Luke also record the same identification of Jesus as the resurrected John, and in their gospels Jesus was certainly active while John was still alive. To call Jesus the 'resurrected John' is, therefore, better seen not as the articulation of a thought-out 'doctrine' of resurrection (still less involving any idea of reincarnation), but as a rather clumsy but vivid way of expressing a sense of continuity such as is better conveyed in the imagery of the transfer of the 'spirit of Elijah' to his companion Elisha (2 Ki. 2:15). The expression ἐνεργοῦσιν αἱ δυνάμεις ἐν αὐτῷ (rather than, e.g., αἱ δυνάμεις διὰ τῶν χειρῶν αὐτοῦ γίνονται; cf. v. 2) depends on a sense of δυνάμεις not as 'acts of power', but as 'miraculous powers' spoken of unusually in an almost personified way as active forces. The context does not, however, suggest the Pauline sense of δυνάμεις as quasi-angelic beings (Rom. 8:38; Eph. 1:21; cf. 1 Pet. 3:22), but rather the power of God, expressed in the plural perhaps in order to recognise the diversity and range of Jesus' acts of power. Such activity might be expected of one who has himself been miraculously raised from death, even though John was not known as a miracleworker during his life.

15 John the Baptist has himself already been described in language reminiscent of Elijah (1:6), and the link will be further strengthened in 9:11-13, even though Mark will not include, as Mt. 11:14 does, an explicit statement that John *is* Elijah. If Jesus is thought by some to be another John, then, it is not surprising that he is also seen as another Elijah. The expectation of an eschatological return of Elijah, based on Mal. 3:23-24 (EVV 4:5-6), is well documented, and underlies the account of the appearance of Elijah with Moses in 9:4 (see comments there and on 9:11). The phrase προφήτης ὡς εἷς τῶν προφητῶν as it stands need mean no more than someone who conforms to the prophetic category, but the fact that both previous identifications involve resurrection or return may possibly suggest that the third option also envisages the 'return' of another of the OT prophets (cf. Mt. 16:14, where Jesus is further identified with

---

28. Some commentators surmise that Mark, while himself aware of the overlap between John and Jesus, presents the crowds as unaware of Jesus' earlier ministry or of any association between the two men; see especially O. Cullmann, *Christology,* 31-34.

Jeremiah).[29] The consensus is clearly that Jesus is a prophet, but just how he fits into that ancient category is a matter of rather wild speculation.

16 The sentence begun in v. 14a is resumed, and the digression on popular views of Jesus now enables us to fit Antipas's own assessment into the popular speculation. He endorses the first view, but with the special nuance (emphasised by the word order and by the prominent inclusion of ἐγώ) that it was he himself who had been responsible for John's execution, so that John's 'reappearance' is a threat to him personally, coming back to haunt his guilty conscience. This observation provides the cue for Mark to tell the story of John's death, but the question of Antipas's view of Jesus fades from sight, except for the enigmatic warning to the disciples to beware of ἡ ζύμη Ἡρῴδου in 8:15. This suggests that Jesus had come to regard Antipas as his enemy, but Mark gives no hint of any action taken by Antipas against him (contrast Lk. 13:31-32; 23:7-12). If his identification of Jesus as a second John was meant seriously,[30] Mark does not tell us that he did anything about it (in contrast to his treatment of the first John). It is probably significant, however, that Mark records little public activity by Jesus within Antipas's territories after this point, and the narrative resumes with a 'retreat' to the other side of the lake.

Digression: The Death of John (6:17-29)

TEXTUAL NOTES

20. It is probably right to follow א B Θ etc. in reading ἠπόρει. Elsewhere in the NT ἀπορέω is used in the middle (hence W ἠπορεῖτο), and the unfamiliarity of the form may have led to the correction to ἐποίει in the majority of MSS (though see διηπόρει, Lk. 9:7, also with reference to Antipas). But πολλὰ ἐποίει is an awkward expression in context, and could have led to the introduction of ἠπόρει as a more appropriate verb for Antipas's reaction to John's teaching, perhaps under the influence of Lk. 9:7. See further D. A. Black, *NTS* 34 (1988) 141-45.

22. τῆς θυγατρὸς αὐτοῦ Ἡρῳδιάδος provides an obvious clash with v. 17, where Herodias is Antipas's (recent) wife, not his daughter. See the commentary below for reasons for believing that Mark cannot have intended this. In that case, however well attested αὐτοῦ is (א B D etc.), and however easily a change to αὐτῆς would be explained as both a solution to the discrepancy and an assimilation to Mt. 14:6 (unless, with D, Matthew's text is also made to refer to a daughter of Antipas called Herodias), we must assume that αὐτοῦ represents an early error. This might derive from a careless scribe

---

29. O. Cullmann, *Christology,* 34-35, prefers the Western reading which, by omitting προφήτης ὡς, more directly identifies Jesus as actually being one of the ancient prophets than merely being like them.

30. Hoehner, *Herod,* 190-91, suggests that the words are to be taken as 'irony or mockery'. He points out that Antipas is unlikely to have shared Pharisaic views of an afterlife (though he may well have been influenced by a superstitious Hellenistic belief in the dead returning to haunt their killers).

who was puzzled by the intrusive αὐτῆς and mechanically altered it to αὐτοῦ, thus producing a smoother text without realising what violence this did to the narrative in context. The majority reading, αὐτῆς (τῆς) Ἡρῳδιάδος, is therefore to be preferred.

23. The adverbial addition of πολλά here is not very elegant, but typical of Mark (cf. v. 20 and 3:12; 5:10, 23, 38, 43, etc.); its absence from the majority of MSS is an obvious stylistic improvement. A stylistic issue also governs the choice between ὅ τι (as the opening of direct speech) and ὅτι *recitativum* followed by ὅ; in this case it is not so easy to say which is the more Marcan expression, but the vivid inclusiveness of ὅ τι ἐάν fits the hyperbolical style of the story, and would easily be misread as ὅτι ὅ ἐάν by a scribe familiar with Mark's use of ὅτι *recitativum*. In both cases the more vivid if less elegant minority text printed by UBS[4] seems more likely to be what Mark wrote; in neither case is the sense significantly affected.

I have labelled the story of the death of John a 'digression', since this pericope (in contrast with vv. 14-16 which introduce it) stands out in Mark's gospel as having no overt link with Jesus or his disciples.[31] We have noted above that the 'sandwiching' of this story within the account of the disciples' mission, and following the discussion of Jesus' identity, is intended to tie the fate of John in with the Jesus story as a foretaste of what 'another John' must expect (note how the four references in Mark to Ἡρῴδης and to Ἡρῳδιανοί, 3:6; 6:14-29; 8:15, and 12:13 all imply hostility and threat to the work of God).[32] Jesus' mission has been seen as in continuity with that of John since 1:7-11, 14-15; and the link will be made clearer in 9:11-13 and especially in 11:27-33. So while the story has its own interest as providing the conclusion to the earlier account of John (left tantalisingly unfinished in 1:14), it also serves to set the scene within which Jesus will approach his own confrontation with authority.

As a story it well illustrates Mark's skill as a raconteur. Whereas Matthew contrives to tell it in a mere 136 words, Mark takes 249; he adds no additional elements to the story, but dwells more expansively on Antipas's indecision, the party, and the dance, so as to create a more memorable atmosphere of the sordid injustice of an oriental court. The hold of Herodias over Antipas reminds the reader of Ahab and Jezebel (1 Ki. 21), and John's role as the disapproving prophet reflects Elijah's in that story. The degenerate nature of Antipas's splendid banquet contrasts vividly with the wholesome simplicity of the very different feast which will follow next in Mark's narrative (6:39-43).

For the complex historical problems surrounding this story, particularly in relating it to the various statements by Josephus about the Herodian family, see the exhaustive study by H. W. Hoehner, *Herod,* 110-71. Its setting is Antipas's marriage to Herodias, of which John has openly expressed his disap-

31. See H. C. Kee, *Community* 55 (and 191, n. 20), following Lohmeyer, 117-18, for the view that this pericope, which is in more sophisticated style than is usual for Mark, may have an independent origin as 'a report from a previously existing document'. Cf. E. Trocmé, *Formation,* 54-55. To the contrary see Gundry, 312-13; Hoehner, *Herod,* 114.

32. See B. Van Iersel, *Reading,* 106-9, for a useful discussion of how this theme explains the place of the story of John's death in Mark's narrative.

proval. Josephus (*Ant.* 18.109-13) describes this marriage as the *casus belli* between Antipas and Aretas king of Petra, whose daughter had been married to Antipas but was displaced in favour of Herodias. Josephus further tells how people ascribed Antipas's defeat in this battle to divine retribution for his execution of John (*Ant.* 18.116, 119), though he makes no direct connection between John and the marriage with Herodias. Herodias was the wife of Antipas's half-brother, named by Josephus simply 'Herod' (son of Herod the Great and Mariamme), but by Mark (and by Matthew except in the Western text) as Philip. But Josephus (*Ant.* 18.136-37) says that Philip the tetrarch (son of Herod the Great and Cleopatra) was married to Salome, the daughter of Herodias. There is considerable obscurity surrounding both the relationships and the names of the Herod family (particularly since the name 'Herod' seems to have been used both as a personal name for certain members of the family and as a family name for all), and it is possible that the Herod who was Herodias's first husband also bore the personal name Philip, as did her son-in-law.[33]

17-18 Antipas's personal responsibility (and hence his sense of guilt; see on v. 16) is underlined by the emphatic αὐτός which opens the sentence. The mention of imprisonment picks up and gives substance to the enigmatic παραδοθῆναι of 1:14. The location of the prison is not mentioned; Josephus (*Ant.* 18.119) tells us that it was in Antipas's fortified palace at Machaerus (in Peraea, far from the scene of Jesus' Galilean ministry). The story envisages that it was in the same place where Antipas's birthday feast was held. For the identity of Φίλιππος see the comments above; ἀδελφός must mean half-brother (a normal relationship in Herod's complex family), as the only other known son of Herod the Great by Malthace (Antipas's mother) was Archelaus, who had been banished in A.D. 6. The scandal of Antipas's marriage to Herodias is not expressed in terms of his dismissal of his first wife, which under Jewish law he was entitled to do (though that was what provoked the war with Petra; see above); indeed, his father's polygamy might have justified him in simply adding a second wife. But this second wife was ἡ γυνὴ τοῦ ἀδελφοῦ σου, and therefore forbidden by the Levitical rules for marriage (Lv. 18:16; 20:21).[34] Even after a brother's death this would have been unacceptable (except in the specific case of a Levirate marriage), but the offence was compounded by the fact that her first husband was still alive (as Josephus emphasises; she flouted ancestral tradition τοῦ ἀνδρός . . . διαστᾶσα ζῶντος, *Ant.* 18.136); Jewish law did not allow a woman to divorce her husband, but Herodias apparently took advantage of her Roman citizenship to divorce her first husband under Roman law (a point which will be relevant when we come to Jesus' pronouncement in 10:12). The

---

33. So H. W. Hoehner, *Herod,* 131-36.

34. Herodias was also, as it happened, Antipas's niece, but that was acceptable in at least some Jewish circles (indeed, her first husband was also her uncle); see Hoehner, *Herod,* 137-39 n. 4.

marriage was thus doubly scandalous, and John could expect to have Jewish public opinion on his side in denouncing it. Mark's expression ἔλεγεν . . . τῷ Ἡρῴδῃ suggests that he did so repeatedly, and to Antipas's face, though it is not clear how easily, if at all, John might have gained personal access to Antipas before his arrest. It may be the narrator's licence, or possibly a preview of Antipas's interviews with John in v. 20. But whether to Antipas's face or not, John's denunciation was damaging to his régime, so that Mark's account may not be far distant from Josephus's statement that it was Antipas's fear of sedition which led to John's death.[35]

19-20 These verses set up the contrast, strongly reminiscent of the story of Ahab and Jezebel (whose 'target' was, of course, John's model Elijah), which the rest of the story will work out between a resolutely hostile Herodias and a wavering Antipas, who will eventually be tricked into pronouncing sentence against his better judgment. The parallel with Pilate's ineffectual resistance to the determined hostility of the priests in 15:1-15 is remarkable, yet another indication of Mark's desire to link together the fates of John and of Jesus (note how Pilate will in 15:14 by implication echo with regard to Jesus Antipas's view of John as δίκαιος καὶ ἅγιος). Herodias 'had it in for him' (the English idiom conveys remarkably exactly the sense of ἐνεῖχεν αὐτῷ), whereas Antipas's combination of fear[36] and respect for John led him not only to block Herodias's murderous intentions (συνετήρει indicates protection from Herodias rather than keeping in custody, though the latter was also, of course, true) but also to listen to him with close attention, and even with appreciation (ἡδέως). The implication is that, like Felix with another prisoner later (Acts 24:24-26), he was at least open to persuasion; but he remained confused and undecided (πολλὰ ἠπόρει; see Textual Note), as Luke tells us he also did about Jesus (Lk. 9:7, διηπόρει).

21 Antipas's birthday feast was a ἡμέρα εὔκαιρος from the point of view of Herodias, since it offered the opportunity to break through the resistance which Antipas had hitherto maintained to her plot against John. The mention that it was the important leaders τῆς Γαλιλαίας who were invited raises a problem, since Machaerus, where Josephus tells us that John was imprisoned and executed, was a long way away in Peraea, the other section of Antipas's tetrarchy. While it is possible that Galilean leaders were invited to make the journey to Peraea for the occasion (or were already there as part of Antipas's regular entourage), it is perhaps more likely that Mark was unaware (or that Josephus was misinformed) of the specific location of John's imprisonment.

---

35. Myers, 215-16 (following Horsley and Hanson), develops this point with regard to the delicate political situation resulting from Antipas's repudiation of his first (diplomatic) marriage. Cf. Hoehner, *Herod,* 142-46.

36. T. Dwyer, *Wonder,* 125-26, draws attention to a further parallel here between the passions of John and of Jesus, in that each is 'feared' by those who have earthly authority over them (cf. 11:18).

For the reputation of Antipas as a giver of extravagant parties see Josephus, *Ant.* 18.102.

22-23 The identity of the dancer is an intriguing problem.[37] If Matthew and most MSS of Mark are to be believed, she was Herodias's daughter by her former marriage, and while the gospels offer no name, tradition has identified her as Salome (the daughter of Herodias who married Philip the tetrarch, Antipas's half-brother); see above for the complex Herodian relationships. Salome was old enough to be married to Philip before he died in A.D. 34, and so may well have been a teenager at the time of John's death: the term κοράσιον (used for Jairus's daughter who was twelve, 5:41-42) is appropriate for a girl up to marriageable age.[38] According to the more difficult reading αὐτοῦ (see Textual Note), however, the girl would be Antipas's own daughter, herself named Herodias (NRSV, unusually among English versions, has adopted this reading). In the light of the confusion of names elsewhere in the family, it is of course not impossible that Antipas had a daughter with the same name as his second wife. Herodias could even have been a sort of dynastic name, the female equivalent of Herod, borne by several members of the family; but no other evidence exists of another Herodias, and the coincidence of names creates suspicion, which is further reinforced by the clear statement of Matthew that the dancer was Herodias's *daughter*. Moreover, Mark's story will go on to portray the dancer as acting under the direction of her mother (vv. 24, 28), and while that mother is not there named her desire to have John killed directly picks up the theme of Herodias's murderous intentions from v. 19. It seems, then, that Mark, like Matthew, assumed the dancer to be Herodias's daughter. It is for that reason that the Textual Note above has argued that αὐτοῦ, which should normally be preferred as the more difficult reading, must be an early error. The phrase τῆς θυγατρὸς αὐτῆς (τῆς) Ἡρῳδιάδος is unexpectedly emphatic (hence no doubt the scribal alteration); the αὐτῆς probably serves to remind the reader of Herodias's plotting (v. 19): 'it was the daughter of that very Herodias who came in . . .'.[39]

Some commentators suggest that for a princess to appear as a dancing girl before a male audience was culturally unthinkable (cf. Vashti's refusal in Est. 1:10-12); but Herodian culture was more influenced by that of Rome than by traditional Judaism, and Tacitus's accounts of far worse excesses in first-century Rome leave little reason to disbelieve this story. The nature of the dance is left entirely to our imagination, beyond the fact that it 'pleased' Antipas and his apparently male party. Extravagant gifts to successful entertainers are a favourite means of displaying wealth in many cultures, though Antipas's limit of τὸ ἥμισυ τῆς βασιλείας μου is more a traditional hyperbole (cf. Est. 5:3, 6; 7:2; cf. 1 Ki.

---

37. See Hoehner, *Herod,* 151-57, for a full discussion.

38. See Hoehner, *Herod,* 154-56.

39. J. E. Taylor, *John,* 242-43 n. 57, suggests that αὐτοῦ and Ἡρῳδιάδος refer to the girl's legal and natural parentage respectively, making her Herod's daughter 'of Herodias', but this seems an impossibly clumsy reading of the Greek without an intervening καί.

13:8) than a serious offer.[40] His repeated oath (πολλά; see Textual Note) suggests a drunken loss of control, as does the remorse of v. 26.

24-28 The remainder of the story needs little comment. The girl's mother is not named, but narrative continuity demands that she is Herodias (even if the reading τῆς θυγατρὸς αὐτῆς τῆς Ἡρῳδιάδος is not accepted in v. 22). Herodias's control over her daughter suggests that the girl was still quite young (unless, of course, the whole episode was a deliberate plan to catch Antipas off his guard, devised by mother and daughter together). For the alternation in the title ascribed to John (βαπτίζοντος, v. 24; βαπτιστοῦ, v. 25) see above on 1:4. Verse 26 describes a man in a trap, forced by social pressure and by his own thoughtless promise into doing what he knows to be wrong. Σπεκουλάτωρ is one of the more prominent Latinisms in Mark; Latin *speculator* originally meant a military scout, but came to be used of soldiers with a special commission, for instance, as bodyguards or when detailed to carry out an execution (for examples see Schürer, 1.371).

29 For John's disciples see above on 2:18, where they were clearly recognised as a distinct religious group continuing to operate as such after their master's imprisonment. The burial of John's body (with no suggestion of resurrection, despite vv. 14-16) appropriately signals the end of his ministry. But it also forms a suggestive counterpart to the burial of his 'successor' (15:42-46, again at the hands of a 'disciple' [see on 15:43] who came and took the πτῶμα, a word used nowhere else in Mark), which will prove to be anything but final.

A SEQUENCE OF MIRACLES AROUND THE LAKE; WHO *IS* JESUS? (6:31-56)

After the account of the disciples' mission, and the interlude concerning the death of John, we return to the main issue of who Jesus is (which was itself the theme which sparked off the digression in vv. 14-16). He remains the focus of growing public interest (vv. 33-44, 53-56), but interspersed with that public exposure is the more intimate and more christologically revealing experience of the disciples, now returned from their mission (vv. 31-32, 45-52). Yet even they remain unable to grasp the significance of what they are witnessing (v. 52).

As in 4:35–5:43, the medium of Jesus' gradual revelation is miracles, with healing as the constant backdrop (vv. 54-56, interestingly with no mention of exorcism this time), but with the focus now more specifically on 'nature miracles', the two stories which are directly related being those of the feeding of the crowd and the walking on the water. Following on the stilling of the storm, with its concluding christological question (4:41), these stories offer yet more evidence of the unique ἐξουσία of Jesus; the disciples may

---

40. Antipas was not, of course, βασιλεύς (see above), nor was it for him to dispose of the authority which he held only as a client of Rome.

have been given ἐξουσία to heal and to exorcise, but here is power on a different level altogether.

Also as in 4:35–5:43, the scene is set on and around the lake (vv. 32, 45, 47-51, 53-54). After the disappointing journey away from the lake into the hill country in 6:1-6, Jesus is now back in the area of his previous success and popularity, and that popularity is as yet showing no sign of waning, whatever may have been the case in Nazareth.

Feeding of Five Thousand Men (6:31-44)

TEXTUAL NOTES

33. The variation in the verb probably derives from the rather unusual use of προέρχομαι in the sense of 'arrive before', 'anticipate' (rather than 'go forward' or 'go in front of'), leading to the substitution of the more familiar προσέρχομαι or συνέρχομαι and to a variety of syntactical alterations. It may be also that some scribes found προέρχομαι difficult because they thought it improbable that foot travellers would be able to arrive earlier than those going by boat.

41. The presence or absence of αὐτοῦ does not affect the sense. Its absence in Matthew and Luke suggests that it may be original here (it is a typically Marcan locution), omitted in some MSS by assimilation.

44. It would be typical of Mark to be fuller than Matthew and for the additional words to be omitted by assimilation. τοὺς ἄρτους is probably therefore an original part of the text, though some doubt may be cast on this by the fact that Mark elsewhere generally makes a point of mentioning the fish as well.

In contrast to the unedifying banquet in Antipas's palace, the story goes on with a very different meal; the food is basic, but the circumstances and the reminiscences of OT events in the narrative mark out this simple meal as of more ultimate significance than the tetrarch's lavish birthday party.[41] For those with eyes to see it, this will be a foretaste of the messianic banquet, an introduction to the communal life of the kingdom of God.

The initial focus of the pericope is on the abortive attempt of Jesus to organise a 'retreat' for his disciples on their return from their mission (vv. 31-32), but the whole weight of the story falls on the feeding of the (unwanted) crowd who frustrated that plan. Apart from the periods in the boat (vv. 32, 45-52, the second of which at least was hardly a time of ἀνάπαυσις), the hope of a retreat seems not to have been fulfilled until Jesus' next trip away from the Capernaum area in 7:24.

The presence of large and insistent crowds has been a recurrent feature of Mark's account of Jesus' experiences around the northwest shore of the lake

41. R. M. Fowler, *Loaves*, 85-86, draws out Mark's deliberate linking of the two stories by contrast.

(1:37, 45; 2:2, 13; 3:7-12, 20; 4:2; 5:21, 24, 31). The deliberate expedition of five thousand men to a remote area to catch up with Jesus may therefore be no more than an extension of this same popular enthusiasm. But there are sufficient features in the story, particularly when the different gospel versions are compared, to lead some interpreters to the conclusion that on this occasion the motivation was different, that this was a purposeful gathering of men determined to persuade (or if necessary force) Jesus, now recognised as a man of undoubted charisma and leadership, to take up the role of military leader in a popular movement of insurrection.[42]

In Mark's own account we may note the striking specification, as in all four accounts, that the five thousand who were fed were ἄνδρες (reinforced by Matthew with the additional phrase χωρὶς γυναικῶν καὶ παιδίων), the OT image ὡς πρόβατα μὴ ἔχοντα ποιμένα (v. 34) which in 1 Ki. 22:17 denotes a leaderless army, the military-style organisation of the crowd into fifties and hundreds (though the terms συμπόσιον and πρασιά do not sound very military), and the strong language of v. 45 about Jesus' quick and firm action (εὐθὺς ἠνάγκασεν) to remove the disciples from the scene. But it is in John's account that we find the explicit statement that this crowd of men, having identified Jesus as the coming prophet, attempted to 'take him by force and make him king', an ambition frustrated only by Jesus' rapid escape into the hills (Jn. 6:14-15).

Two questions must be separated, that of the historical nature of the incident and that of how Mark intends it to be understood. In the light of the volatile political situation of Galilee under Roman rule, and of the undercurrent of Zealot sympathies which can be discerned from time to time behind the gospel narratives, culminating in the direct test of Jesus' attitude to Zealot philosophy in 12:13-17, and in the light also of the charge on which Jesus was eventually executed (15:2, 26), in the context of a στάσις involving Barabbas (15:7), a strong case can be made for a political and indeed military character to the gathering, not only in its outcome as recorded by John, but in the original intention of this large body of men in tracking Jesus down out in the wilderness (the traditional location for the launching of liberation movements; see above, pp. 56-58). If that was in fact the case, Jesus' rapid escape (Jn. 6:15) and his packing off of the disciples before they could be infected by the popular enthusiasm (Mk. 6:45) would be in keeping with the consistently anti-Zealot stance in which he is depicted in the gospels.

But whatever the historical reality of the situation, it is hard to believe that the military implications of the incident were a significant factor in Mark's telling of the story. None of the features of Mark's narrative listed above *demands* a military interpretation of the event; Jesus' response to the πρόβατα μὴ ἔχοντα ποιμένα is compassion and teaching, not military organisation, and the description of the seated companies as συμπόσια and πρασιαί would be curiously incongruous if they were understood as a martial parade. The whole story

42. The case is attractively presented by H. W. Montefiore, *NTS* 8 (1961/2) 135-41.

reads more like an ad hoc picnic than a military manoeuvre. Mark's interest is in the significance of the feeding miracle, not in whatever purpose the men may have had in mind in pursuing Jesus.

There is wide agreement that at least part of that significance is revealed by the verbs in v. 41 (λαβών, εὐλόγησεν, κατέκλασεν, ἐδίδου), which are those traditionally used to describe the eucharistic actions at the Last Supper, and which will appear again, in the same sequence, in 14:22. If, as 14:25 will indicate, that eucharistic meal is a foretaste of the messianic banquet in the kingdom of God, then what is offered to these men in the wilderness is a pointer to messianic fulfilment (and for Christian readers inevitably a pre-echo of the Last Supper itself). John will make the point more obviously by following his account of the incident with a discourse on eating the flesh and drinking the blood of the Son of Man; Mark leaves it to his readers to spot the connection.[43]

Another aspect to the symbolism of the event which an instructed reader could hardly miss (and which John also draws out in the same discourse, through the quotation of Ex. 16:4 etc. in Jn. 6:31) is the echo of Moses and the manna in the motif of bread miraculously provided in the wilderness.[44] The theme of Jesus as the new Moses is not prominent in Mark (see on 9:4), and this story is not told in such a way as to emphasise it, but Jewish readers would not be slow to pick up the comparison here.[45] More immediately obvious to those who knew the OT stories would be the similarity to Elisha's miracle in 2 Ki. 4:42-44, and they might have noted with appreciation the increase in the clientele from one hundred to five thousand while at the same time the number of loaves has decreased from twenty to five.[46] In this latter case there can be little doubt that Mark had the story in mind, since not only is the situation of a hungry crowd and lack of food similar, but the narrative focuses on the same motifs, the command to the servant/disciples to feed the crowd, their surprised question in response, the satisfying of hunger, and the food left over at the end.

43. In reaction against this almost universal understanding of the story in terms of its eucharistic echoes, R. M. Fowler, *Loaves*, 134-47, rightly points out that this interpretation is not necessarily available to a first-time reader of Mark who has not yet met with the Last Supper story, though Fowler accepts that readers already familiar with the eucharist would have read the story in that light, and that Mark may have so intended it.

44. The return of manna was part of the eschatological hope of *2 Bar.* 29:8; cf. Rev. 2:17. For rabbinic references to the provision of manna in the messianic age see Cranfield, 222.

45. See D. W. Chapman, *Orphan*, 55-67, for an extensive exploration of the 'messianic' significance of the feeding miracles in the light of the manna story; Chapman presents these stories (together with the explanatory dialogue in 8:14-21) as the principal basis of Peter's declaration that Jesus was the Messiah: it was through comparison of Jesus' acts with those of Moses that Peter 'worked out who Jesus was' (65).

46. A later rabbinic discussion (*b. Ket.* 106a) argued that Elisha must have had not 100 men but 2200, since 20 loaves among 100 was overgenerous for a time of famine; so the text must mean 100 men per loaf. Even this inflated figure, however, falls short of Jesus' ratio of 1:1,000.

Elijah also multiplied food for the widow of Zarephath (1 Ki. 17:8-16), though there is no echo of the wording of this story in Mark's narrative.[47]

So this narrative has echoes, for those hearers/readers who are equipped to recognise them, both of past miracles and of the future eucharistic feast. Mark clearly so intended it. But the patent symbolism should not lead us to miss what is surely the primary purpose in Mark's inclusion of this story, the sheer wonder of an 'impossible' act, and the testimony which this provides in answer to the growing christological question of this part of the gospel, 'Who is Jesus?' He is not merely the healer of afflicted individuals or the rescuer of endangered disciples; he is one who is not bound by the rules of normal experience of what is possible and impossible. In following him this representative group of Israelites, no less than those who followed Moses in the wilderness, will find all their need supernaturally supplied, for God is again at work among his people. (When we come to 8:1-10, however, any purely nationalistic satisfaction which this conclusion may arouse will be challenged.)

Both here and in the equally improbable story which follows it in 6:45-52, commentators are sometimes expected to explain what actually happened. It is an unprofitable question, and suggested answers are characterised by speculation rather than by evidence. Mark (and the other evangelists agree in this) has no interest in explaining how the 'laws of nature' were suspended. For him, and therefore for those of his readers who want to share his understanding of the story, it was simply a miracle.[48]

31-32 This setting of the scene, peculiar to Mark, serves both to link the story with the preceding account of the disciples' mission and to explain why the next episode will be located in an ἔρημος τόπος (an uninhabited area rather than desert as such; note the green grass, v. 39, and the surrounding ἀγροὶ καὶ κῶμαι, v. 36). At the same time it reinforces the repeated emphasis of Mark both on the uncomfortable popularity of Jesus (for οὐδὲ φαγεῖν εὐκαίρουν cf. 3:20) and on his habit of taking his disciples away from the crowd (for κατ' ἰδίαν cf. 4:34; 9:2, 28; 13:3, and κατὰ μόνας, 4:10) for periods of relief and of instruction. For δεῦτε see on 1:17. ὑμεῖς αὐτοί is unusually emphatic, and places the focus on the need of the disciples themselves: they have been serving others; now they themselves need to be cared for. Such 'retreats' are sometimes in the hills (3:13-19; 9:2; cf. 6:46), but any place which is away from other people

---

47. Cf also the story of the miraculous appearance of bread in Ḥanina ben Dosa's empty oven (b. Taʿan. 24b-25a). A search for parallels to this narrative outside the Jewish tradition has been unsuccessful: J.-M. Van Cangh in M. Sabbe (ed.), *Marc,* 314. For parallels generally see *Marc,* 309-21.

48. It is extraordinary to find Myers, 206, still saying, 'There is nothing "supernatural" reported to have transpired in this feeding of some five thousand men. . . . The only "miracle" here is the triumph of the economics of sharing within a community of consumption over against the economics of autonomous consumption in the anonymous marketplace.' Does he still hold what Taylor, 321, described as the 'facile' view that 'the incident was an idyllic expression of good comradeship'? And does he really think that that was what Mark meant to describe?

(which is the point of ἔρημος in this context; cf. 1:45) will serve. Here it is reached by crossing the lake, and is therefore presumably not far from the shore; v. 33 apparently pictures the crowd as already waiting for them when they disembarked, so that the site of the miracle appears in that case to be near the landing place.

Mark does not tell us where this particular ἔρημος τόπος was, but Luke locates the incident at Bethsaida (or rather presumably in its neighbourhood, since he, too, calls it an ἔρημος τόπος). Bethsaida Julias was on the northeast side of the lake, the other side of the Jordan inflow from Capernaum and the territory of Antipas. This location would suit Mark's narrative at this point, and the return by boat to Gennesaret (v. 53), back on the west shore, would be a natural sequel. The problem is that in v. 45, immediately after the feeding miracle, Mark (alone) has Jesus sending the disciples off by boat *towards* Bethsaida, a journey which he further describes as εἰς τὸ πέραν (see Textual Note at v. 45), but which apparently finishes at Gennesaret, some two or three miles southwest of Capernaum. Mark's geography cannot easily be harmonised with Luke's, except by deleting πρὸς Βηθσαϊδάν from v. 45, but surprisingly there is no MSS evidence for this convenient emendation.

A solution has been found by postulating a second settlement called Bethsaida on the west side of the Jordan inflow, which it is suggested would better suit the description of the Bethsaida of Jn. 1:44; 12:21 as τῆς Γαλιλαίας and the linking of Bethsaida with Chorazin and Capernaum in Mt. 11:20-24, whereas the better-known Bethsaida Julias, on the east of the river, was in Philip's tetrarchy (and, as an essentially pagan city, is less likely to be the hometown of three of Jesus' Jewish disciples). To have two settlements of the same name on either side of the river, distinguished by different titles, Julias and some other, would be possible (especially since Bethsaida means simply 'fishing village'), but there is no evidence for a second Bethsaida other than by inference from the above gospel texts. It would also be strange to find Mark and Luke referring to different Bethsaidas each without any indication that there was another town of the same name, especially as on this view the disciples' crossing proposed in Mark 6:45 would be from one Bethsaida to the other.

An alternative and probably better solution is to discount Luke's placing of the incident and to assume that Mark has in view a place on the northwestern shore (such as the traditional site at Tabgha) not too far from Capernaum and on the same side of the Jordan inflow (which would make the pursuit by the crowd on foot in v. 33 easier to imagine), with Jesus' disciples then sent in v. 45 eastwards towards Bethsaida on the other side of the Jordan inflow, but beaten back by a northeast wind and hence finishing up in the opposite direction at Gennesaret.[49]

33 The description of the gathering of the crowd seems rather artificial:

49. For a brief survey of these and other solutions offered to the geographical problem see J.-M. Van Cangh in M. Sabbe (ed.), *Marc*, 327-30.

the opening part of the verse suggests that chance onlookers decided to follow on the spur of the moment, but the gathering of so large a group as five thousand men ἀπὸ πασῶν τῶν πόλεων (see below, p. 268 and n. 62 there), their knowledge of the intended destination of the boat or their ability to follow its route while themselves travelling on foot (and with the Jordan River to cross on the way, if Luke's placing of the incident is accepted), and their achievement in apparently getting there first (προῆλθον; see Textual Note) so as to be waiting for Jesus and his disciples on the shore — all these factors suggest that Mark has oversimplified the process by which so large a crowd came to be in the ἔρημος τόπος looking for Jesus. The 'military' interpretation mentioned above might provide a more plausible basis for the gathering.

34 The description of the crowd as ὡς πρόβατα μὴ ἔχοντα ποιμένα is an obvious metaphor for lack of care and leadership, and one used in the OT for Israel in the wilderness after Moses (Nu. 27:17, where the problem is solved by the appointment of Joshua), for Ahab's army after his death in battle (1 Ki. 22:17), for the people of God when their appointed leaders have failed in their trust (Ezk. 34:5-6), and for their helplessness when their (messianic) leader is taken away (Zc. 13:7). While the metaphor in itself would suit a military context (see above), it clearly has also a wider application (cf. its use in a different context in Mt. 9:36, where it forms the basis for the disciples' mission of teaching and healing). Here it denotes the 'untended' state of the ordinary people of Galilee (perhaps a reflection on the inadequacy of their current leadership; cf. 7:1-23; 12:38-40), which arouses Jesus' compassion and to which he responds as in 4:1-2 by an extended period of teaching.[50] The only subject of whom the verb σπλαγχνίζομαι is used in the NT is Jesus (apart from parable characters who represent Jesus or God). It is not a common verb in Mark (especially if we are right in not reading it in 1:41), but it occurs in the accounts of both feeding miracles (8:2); combined with the simile of sheep without a shepherd it presents Jesus above all as 'the one who cares'.[51]

35-36 ὥρα πολλή is a phrase used occasionally in Greek literature (not elsewhere in the NT) for a 'late hour'; here it must mean towards the end of the afternoon, when Jews would normally have their main meal.[52] The disciples' appeal to Jesus to send the people away reveals an interesting balance in their relationship: Jesus is clearly in charge, and yet this is not the only time when they feel the need to remind him of his responsibilities (cf. 1:36-37; 4:38; 10:13). The inclusion of ἑαυτοῖς makes clear that the disciples have no thought

---

50. E. Best, *Temptation,* 76-78, suggests that the reference to teaching here sets the tone for Mark's whole understanding of the miracle which follows: 'Mark sets out Jesus as the shepherd who feeds his people with true teaching; from his supply there is more than enough to feed all their needs.'

51. This is the title of ch. 10 of E. Best, *Story.*

52. It surely goes beyond the bounds of exegesis to argue, as S. Masuda, *NTS* 28 (1982) 193, does, that because elsewhere in Mark ὥρα is used only in connection with Jesus' passion and parousia (even in 11:11; 14:37?), its use here must link this pericope with the Last Supper.

of catering to the crowd themselves — they have barely enough food for their own use.

37-38 The response is unexpected, and unwelcome. To have the responsibility of feeding the crowd put upon themselves serves only to reveal their inability to cope with the situation. In any case, the disciples cannot see why they should accept this responsibility, and their question is surely ironical. Even if they had the money, and enough bread was available for sale in the neighbourhood,[53] why should they spend so large a sum as two hundred denarii (more than half a year's wages)[54] on food for a crowd of strangers? (Cf. 2 Ki. 4:42-43 for a similar exchange.) But Jesus refuses to be put off, and insists on an inventory of food available (in the boat?). The small amount of basic Galilean rations which they find (the ἄρτοι were probably round, flat loaves, large enough at most for one person for a day) is remarkable, since Jesus and his disciples had set out for a period in an ἔρημος τόπος, and might have been expected to take food with them for the length of their stay, but Mark does not notice the problem. At any rate, from the disciples' point of view the disappointing result of their search puts an end to any thought of their providing food for the crowd.

The figures are an essential part of the story. Five loaves, two fish, five thousand men, and twelve baskets occur in all four gospel accounts (and seven loaves, four thousand men, and seven baskets in both versions of the parallel story, Mk. 8:1-10; Mt. 15:32-39). In addition, it is interesting to see the figure of two hundred denarii appearing in both Mark's and John's accounts of the story. The careful preservation of all these numbers leads some to suppose that they are recorded for their symbolic value (five for the books of the law, twelve for the tribes of Israel, etc.), but Mark gives no hint that this was his intention. The point of the numbers is rather to emphasise the magnitude of the miracle (the more so when the numbers are contrasted with those in Elisha's feeding miracle, 2 Ki. 4:42-44); as such they would naturally become fixed in the oral repetition of the story. The mention of twelve baskets probably owes more to the number of disciples who were serving than to any Israel symbolism.[55]

39-40 Although he has given no hint to the disciples of what he intends to do about the 'crisis', Jesus nonetheless instructs them (assuming that αὐτοῖς refers to the disciples; ἀνακλίνω is a transitive verb, with πάντας as its object) to organise the crowd into groups, ready for the meal to be served. Their reaction can only be imagined. The vivid description suggests the eyewitness ac-

---

53. According to Gundry, 330, two hundred denarii would buy 2,400 loaves, roughly half a day's ration each for the five thousand men present. It is not obvious, however, where 2,400 loaves would be found for sale.

54. For the δηνάριον as an expected day's wage see Mt 20:1-15. In Tacitus, *Ann.* 1.17 (set in the reign of Tiberius, but written nearly a century later), it is held out to disgruntled soldiers as a good daily wage to be negotiated for.

55. Guelich, 343-44, mentions some of the symbolic possibilities, and is cautiously open to an Israel symbolism here in contrast to 8:1-10. For more general discussion of number symbolism in the feeding miracles see S. Masuda, *NTS* 28 (1982) 203-6.

count of someone who was present at this extraordinary picnic. The χλωρὸς χόρτος probably fixes the time of the incident as spring, before the grass dries up and goes brown, though Mark's motive in mentioning it after the shepherd metaphor of v. 34 may be rather to allude to the shepherd's role in leading his flock to 'green pastures' in Ps. 23:2.[56] A συμπόσιον is a group of people eating or (more commonly) drinking together, and suggests a relaxed, even convivial atmosphere; συμπόσια συμπόσια is distributive, 'in parties'. πρασιά is literally a garden plot or flower bed and is not elsewhere used to describe people, so that πρασιαὶ πρασιαί (similarly distributive, 'in rows') offers a remarkably visual impression of the scene, with men lined up in groups like plots of vegetables on the green grass. The organisation κατὰ ἑκατὸν καὶ κατὰ πεντήκοντα, while it could in the right context have a military flavour (cf. also Ex. 18:21),[57] here serves for ease of distribution (and also as the basis for the count recorded in v. 44). All this careful disposition of the crowd is introduced by the verbs ἀνακλῖναι and ἀνέπεσαν. These terms are especially associated with the Graeco-Roman style of reclining at table. In a Jewish context, where meals were generally taken seated, these terms would normally indicate a more formal 'banquet' setting, following the Graeco-Roman style, rather than an ordinary meal.[58] While at an open-air picnic sitting at table was in any case out of the question, it is possible that by using such terms Mark intends to hint that, while it was hardly a formal occasion and the fare was basic, there was an air of festivity about it which made it, at least with hindsight, a foreshadowing of the messianic banquet.

41 None of the four 'eucharistic' verbs (see above, p. 262) is in itself at all surprising. These are the normal actions of the Jewish head of the family at a meal, taking bread, pronouncing the blessing, breaking it, and distributing it.[59] The addition of ἀναβλέπω is a natural accompaniment to the pronouncing of the formula of blessing,[60] which for bread took the traditional form 'Blessed art thou, Lord our God, King of the world, who bringest forth bread from the earth' (*m. Ber.* 6:1). We are told specifically that the food over which the blessing was spoken was still the five loaves and two fish; at what point, and how, they became multiplied is left to our imagination. The repeated mention of the δύο ἰχθύες followed by πᾶσιν at the end of v. 41 emphasises yet more clearly the ludicrously inadequate amount of food supplied.

56. Gundry, 328, discusses the possibility of links with Ps. 23 in the pericope as a whole.

57. On this OT basis the Qumran community organised itself into groups of 1000, 100, 50, and 10 for ordinary community life (1QS 2:21-22; CD 13:1-2) and for the final battle (1QM 4:1-5).

58. See J. Jeremias, *Words,* 48-49.

59. See J. Jeremias, *Words,* 108-9, 174-77. G. H. Boobyer, *JTS* 3 (1952) 161-71, argues that the normal Jewish pattern of blessing is sufficient to explain Mark's wording, without any specifically eucharistic allusion; similarly, in a modified form, Guelich, 342-43, and more strongly Gundry, 331-32.

60. The motif recurs in 7:34, where again it is natural to understand it as a gesture of prayer, as in, e.g., Job 22:26-27; Lk. 18:13; Jn. 11:41; 17:1.

42-43 No room is left for doubt over the scale of the miracle: *all* ate, all were *full* (χορτάζομαι indicates far more than a token meal), and even the leftovers were vastly more than the original supply of food.[61] The κόφινος, described by BAGD, 447b, as 'a large, heavy basket for carrying things', was mocked by the Roman satirist Juvenal (3:14; 6:542) as the typical equipment of the poor Jew. To have twelve of them available out in the countryside is surprising. The words δώδεκα κοφίνων πληρώματα might merely indicate the quantity of leftovers (enough to fill twelve κόφινοι) rather than refer to actual receptacles used, but 8:19 suggests that they actually had twelve baskets there; perhaps they were kept in the boat (as containers for the catch?).

44 All four evangelists agree that the five thousand were ἄνδρες. Matthew, here and in the feeding of the four thousand, adds χωρὶς γυναικῶν καὶ παιδίων, which is normally understood (as in the use of the same phrase in Ex. 12:37 [not LXX]) to mean that there were women and children additional to the five thousand, thus making the number fed even greater. In view of the consistent use of ἄνδρες in all the gospel accounts, however, it is possible that Matthew's phrase means 'and there were no women and children', and that all four accounts therefore present this deliberately as an all-male gathering, the women and children having been left at home. If we entertain the possibility outlined above that this was a gathering of patriots with an insurrectionary motive, the exclusion of women and children would be the more probable. At any rate, for whatever reason, Mark tells us that the five thousand were *men*.[62]

Mark's accounts of miracles often end with a mention of the amazement of the crowd; in this case, where the crowd were themselves the beneficiaries of the miracle, this might seem even more appropriate, and Mark's silence both here and at the end of the second feeding miracle in 8:9 is surprising. Perhaps he means us to assume that they were unaware of the miraculous origin of the food, and simply took it for granted. What matters for Mark is rather the response of the disciples, or rather their failure to respond in the right way (v. 52; 8:17-21).

Walking on the Water (6:45-52)

TEXTUAL NOTES

45. See pp. 453-454 above on the geographical problems surrounding this verse. Surprisingly no MS omits the most troublesome phrase πρὸς Βηθσαϊδάν even though it

---

61. The purpose of collecting the leftovers (which could not be expected to keep fresh for long) is not mentioned; Gundry, 326, 348, 357-58, believes that it was this bread that the disciples were eating in 7:2.

62. To put this large gathering into perspective, the total population of Capernaum at this time, including women and children, was probably about ten thousand. This throws light on the statement in v. 33 that the five thousand came ἀπὸ πασῶν τῶν πόλεων, since the total adult male population of Capernaum would be well under five thousand.

is absent from Matthew. The omission of εἰς τὸ πέραν by P45 (probably) W ƒ¹ sysᵉ is probably an attempt to ease the problem; the alternative that it was not part of Mark's text and was added by assimilation to Matthew seems less likely in view of the very wide textual attestation for the phrase.

47. The inclusion of πάλαι in a significant group of MSS (P45 D etc.) may well be original. πάλαι normally means 'long ago', which is clearly inappropriate here; elsewhere, however, Mark (15:44) uses it in parallel with ἤδη ('already'), which Matthew in fact uses at this point. Scribes confronted by this less familiar usage may have preferred to omit an apparently redundant and inappropriate word, the more so since it is not found in the Matthew parallel.

51. There is some variation in how the disciples' astonishment is expressed. The double phrase λίαν ἐκ περισσοῦ would be typical of Mark, and we may best explain the readings which offer either λίαν alone or (ἐκ) περισσοῦ(-ῶς) alone as 'improvements' of Mark's prolix style. The intrusion of περιέσωσεν in Θ and Φ looks like a misreading of the 'redundant' περισσῶς. The widely attested addition of καὶ ἐθαύμαζον after ἐξίσταντο further increases the emphasis without affecting the sense; in other such expressions of amazement, Mark uses only one such verb, so this may be a later expansion (modelled on Acts 2:7).

The expedition on the lake which began in 6:32 now continues, and the revelation of the supernatural power of Jesus is further underlined as one 'nature miracle' is closely followed by another. The two pericopes are directly linked by the geographical movements mentioned and were apparently preserved as a continuous narrative in the tradition, since in both Matthew and John the same two incidents are equally firmly linked (though Matthew expands this pericope with the account of Peter's abortive attempt to walk on the water, Mt 14:28-32).[63] Luke, however, does not record this incident on the lake, and his narrative continues immediately after the feeding miracle with Peter's confession, from which the story moves quickly into the journey to Jerusalem. Mark 6:45 thus marks the beginning of Luke's 'Great Omission' (he has none of the contents of Mk. 6:45–8:26). Whatever the reason for the absence from Luke of this large block of Marcan material as a whole, as far as this pericope is concerned it is possible that, if Luke knew it, he felt it to be unnecessary after having already recorded one lake miracle in 8:22-25 (= Mk. 4:35-41). (A similar consideration would apply to the feeding of the four thousand, another part of Luke's Great Omission.)

This pericope has in common with 4:35-41 a late crossing (ὀψίας γενομένης, 4:35; 6:47), a storm or strong wind (4:37; 6:48), the disciples' fear (4:38, 40; 6:49-50), the calming of the storm by Jesus (with the same phrase ἐκόπασεν ὁ ἄνεμος, 4:39; 6:51), and the disciples' reaction of fear or astonishment (4:41; 6:51). When allowance is made for the regular features of a miracle story, however, the differences are more impressive than the similarities, in that

63. This apparently traditional link is to be contrasted with P. J. Achtemeier's proposal (see p. 220 above) that the feeding of the five thousand concludes one pre-Marcan miracle catena, while the walking on the water begins a second.

this time the disciples are alone in the boat and Jesus comes to them walking on the water (it is this rather than the calming of the wind which is the memorable feature of this story). He comes to them as a figure of mystery and terror, not a familar companion to be awakened in a crisis. While the earlier incident was sufficiently astonishing to provoke a christological question (4:41), its more down-to-earth atmosphere contrasts with the numinous appearance and 'impossible' behaviour of Jesus in this pericope, after which the disciples are left not so much impressed (as in 4:41) as bewildered and (metaphorically) out of their depth. This response by the disciples leads to a surprisingly negative conclusion to the pericope in 6:52.

Thus two themes run through this pericope. The first is clearly the supernatural power of Jesus, as Mark continues to build his picture of a Jesus who, though he could walk, eat, and sleep with his disciples as master with pupils, is nonetheless more than an ordinary human being (compare OT descriptions of God walking on or through the sea: Job 9:8; Ps. 77:19; Is. 43:16). But corresponding to the increasingly supernatural character of the portrait of Jesus is the increasing inability of his disciples to cope with it. The incomprehension of the disciples is well known as a theme emphasised more in Mark's gospel than in the other accounts, but it is not evenly distributed through the narrative. Up to this point the disciples have been portrayed more as the privileged recipients of special revelation, in contrast with the uncomprehending crowds (4:11-12, 34; cf. 3:31-35), but 6:52 introduces a new and ominous note (perhaps already hinted at in 4:13) which will be further developed in 8:14-21, and will become a central feature of the second main section of the narrative after Caesarea Philippi.

With regard to the question 'What actually happened?' see the remarks made in introducing the preceding pericope. The suggestion that Jesus may have walked on a submerged sandbank which happened to be conveniently located (or was 'wading through the surf near the hidden shore', V. Taylor) takes no account of the actual nature of the lake of Galilee, nor of the fact that fishermen who knew the lake well would not be likely to be impressed.[64] Mark tells us that Jesus walked on the lake, and we have no way of getting behind his account to suggest any other explanation for what he clearly understood to be a supernatural feat.

45-46 We noted in introducing the previous pericope the possibility that the five thousand men may have come together with an insurrectionary aim, together with John's explicit statement that they tried to force Jesus into taking such a course (Jn. 6:14-15). The surprisingly strong verb ἠνάγκασεν would fit this scenario: Jesus packs the disciples off in a hurry to get them away from the

---

64. J. D. M. Derrett, *NovT* 23 (1981) 330-48, offers a detailed presentation of the 'sandbank' theory, including (333-35) interesting details of the presence and movement of sandbanks around the Jordan inflow. Such a location takes no account of Mark's ἐν μέσῳ τῆς θαλάσσης, nor of the fact that local fishermen might have been expected to know the characteristics of the delta area at least as well as modern scholars.

contagious atmosphere, while he himself retreats (the alternative reading φεύγει in Jn. 6:15 would make the point even more vividly) into the hills alone (for εἰς τὸ ὄρος see on 3:13). But Mark's narrative has not given us specific warrant for discerning such evasive action in these verses, and perhaps we should see in ἠνάγκασεν no more than his characteristically vivid turn of phrase. In Mark Jesus is able to dismiss the crowd (ἀπολύω conveys a sense of authority; contrast the hasty flight of Jn. 6:15), and his walk up into the hills is stated to be for prayer (as in 1:35) rather than merely to escape. He thus remains in control of the situation, however volatile the mood of the crowd may have been.

The phrase ἀποταξάμενος αὐτοῖς is assumed by most commentators to be a second statement of Jesus' dismissal of the crowd, but ἀποτάσσομαι, a quite neutral verb of leave taking, would be something of an anticlimax after ἀπολύω, and the plural αὐτοῖς would most naturally refer back to the disciples, who were the object of the preceding sentence, even though the ὄχλος (singular) has been mentioned in an intervening subordinate clause. (The disciples, being the main focus of the narrative, are again referred to simply as αὐτούς in v. 48, without further need to identify the referent.) Mark mentions Jesus' farewell to the disciples so as to prepare for their astonishment at finding him nevertheless beside them on the lake sometime later.

For the problem created by the disciples' destination, εἰς τὸ πέραν πρὸς Βηθσαϊδάν, and for some suggested solutions, see on v. 32 above.

47-48 The feeding of the five thousand began in the late afternoon (ὥρας πολλῆς γενομένης, v. 35). Since then considerable time has elapsed in the organisation of the crowd, the feeding, the clearing up, and the dismissal of the crowd, so that ὀψίας γενομένης must represent a time well into the night, rather than the conventional translation 'when evening came'. This is confirmed by the mention of the fourth watch (the last part of the night, before dawn, roughly 3–6 a.m.) in v. 48; indeed, the double mention of 'seeing' (ἰδών, v. 48; ἰδόντες, v. 49) suggests that pre-dawn light already allowed faint visibility. However strong the wind, a rowing boat is not likely to have taken ten hours or more to cross the northern part of the lake of Galilee, as would be required if ὀψίας γενομένης is understood only of the evening. The disciples' situation is not, in contrast with 4:37-38, presented as one of danger, but rather of inability to make progress, together with extreme physical effort and discomfort (βασανιζομένους, 'tortured', will ring true for those who have experience of rowing a heavy boat against strong wind).

Since Mark specifically mentions that Jesus' coming to the disciples followed from his seeing their difficulties, and that his walking on the water was πρὸς αὐτούς, the clause καὶ ἤθελεν παρελθεῖν αὐτούς is surprising.[65] While

65. Some commentators follow Lohmeyer in suggesting that παρελθεῖν here echoes the revelatory 'passing by' of God in Ex. 33:19-23; 34:6; 1 Ki. 19:11. But whereas in those OT passages the context makes the revelatory purpose plain, here, in the absence of any such contextual indication, this is too much to read into the very ordinary verb παρέρχομαι, when its literal sense is obviously applicable, however surprising; in addition, the fact that the disciples did not recognise Jesus

ἤθελεν in itself does of course denote intention,[66] in the narrative context the clause is best seen not as a statement of what was in Jesus' mind but of how his approach appeared from the disciples' point of view:[67] this mysterious figure on the water seemed at first to be making his way past the boat (and thus to be making better progress than they, with all their muscle power, could achieve).[68] The normal meaning of ἐπὶ τῆς θαλάσσης, especially with a verb of walking (and following ἐπὶ τῆς γῆς in the preceding verse), is 'on the lake', indicating the supernatural act of walking on water.[69] An alternative from a purely lexical point of view might be suggested in another, less common, use of ἐπί with the genitive to mean 'at' or 'near';[70] the post-resurrection appearance of Jesus in Jn. 21:1 was ἐπὶ τῆς θαλάσσης τῆς Τιβεριάδος, and the subsequent narrative shows that while his disciples were out on the lake in a boat, Jesus himself was on the shore. This cannot, however, have been Mark's meaning here, since he has emphasised that the boat was ἐν μέσῳ τῆς θαλάσσης and that Jesus came to them there, subsequently joining them in the boat. Moreover, their frightened impression that he was a ghost suggests something more numinous than seeing a man walking on the shore. Matthew, of course, with his addition of Peter's attempt to follow suit, makes the supernatural character of Jesus' walking on the water even more explicit, but in Mark it is quite clearly intended.

49-50 Luke tells us that the disciples' immediate response to the appearance of the risen Jesus was to assume that they were seeing a πνεῦμα, and that Jesus had to assure them that he was in fact a being of flesh and bones, capable of eating solid food (Lk. 24:37-43). Such a disembodied spirit must have seemed an obvious explanation also for the physically impossible action they now saw on the lake, and φάντασμα (not used elsewhere in the NT, except in the Matthew parallel) denotes such a ghost in both Jewish and pagan literature. In this case, however, they are not thinking of *Jesus'* ghost (having no reason to suppose him dead); there is as yet no recognition. As soon as he is able to assure them of his

---

conflicts with the theme of those passages. Even more remote from any natural interpretation of the verb in its Marcan context is the proposal of H. Fleddermann, *CBQ* 45 (1983) 389-95, that παρελθεῖν here should be understood, on the basis of Am. 7:8; 8:2, to mean 'to save'.

66. Liddell and Scott offer a few classical uses of ἐθέλω used in the sense of μέλλω, which would suggest a meaning here 'was about to' rather than 'intended to'. The usage is rare, however, and finds no clear parallel in the Greek of the NT period.

67. The exhaustive discussion of this clause by T. Snoy in M. Sabbe (ed.), *Marc*, 347-63, recognises this as a widely held interpretation, though he himself believes that 'le texte ne permet pas cette explication' (352). His own preference is for a double change of mind on the part of Jesus: having first intended the disciples to see him walking on the water, he then decided (as part of the 'messianic secret') to go past unrecognised, but then relented in view of the disciples' terror and identified himself to them.

68. Perhaps the clause is best understood in relation to Lk. 24:28, where Jesus' apparent intention to go further is seen from the point of view of the disciples with him. Note, too, the combination in Job 9:8-11 of the ideas of God's walking on the sea and 'passing by' unrecognised; Mark may have had this text in mind in framing these verses.

69. For numerous examples see BAGD, 286a, I.1.a.α.

70. BAGD, 286a, I.1.a.γ.

identity (ἐγώ εἰμι),[71] the ghost theory vanishes, and the fear which it inspired will be replaced by amazement at the supernatural power of Jesus. Mark emphasises the reassuring character of Jesus' words, both by the double introduction (εὐθὺς ἐλάλησεν μετ' αὐτῶν, καὶ λέγει αὐτοῖς) and by the two exhortations θαρσεῖτε and μὴ φοβεῖσθε which support the essential information ἐγώ εἰμι. Their alarm in such an unprecedented and 'spooky' situation was natural, and Jesus takes it seriously and responds with appropriate reassurance.

51-52   The resolution of both the adverse circumstances and the fear of the disciples is related in few words. Mark's interest now is more in their reaction and in what it reveals of the extent of their spiritual perception at this point. Amazement or fear on the part of people in general has been a recurrent feature of Mark's narrative (1:22, 27; 2:12; 5:15, 20, 42), and one which serves the positive purpose of highlighting the unique authority of Jesus. In 4:41 the disciples, too, have been overawed by what they have seen, and there, too, the question 'Who then is this?' serves to enhance the impression of the uniqueness of Jesus. Here, too, they are duly astonished at what they have seen (see Textual Note), but now their very natural fear and awe is apparently[72] taken by Mark as an indication of their lack of understanding and, still worse, their καρδία πεπωρωμένη (the two expressions do not differ substantially in meaning, since in Jewish thought the 'heart' is the seat of thought and understanding, but καρδία πεπωρωμένη, with its echo of Is. 6:10, has a more ominous ring). By this time, apparently, the disciples, if not the crowd, should have got beyond the stage of instinctive astonishment to one of understanding who Jesus is. In particular it seems that it is the loaves (i.e., the preceding miracle story) which should have caused them to see things in a new light. In 8:14-21 Jesus will himself directly rebuke the disciples for their failure to grasp the significance of the feeding of the five thousand and of the four thousand (cf. Jn. 6:26-34 for a similar failure, this time on the part of the crowd, to draw the appropriate christological conclusions from the feeding of the five thousand). It is not immediately clear why among so many other remarkable acts of power the feeding miracles should be singled out as having such special evidential value.[73]

71. The temptation to see this common Greek phrase as a deliberate use of the divine name of Ex. 3:14 or an echo of the Isaian formula *'ªnî hû'* should probably be resisted, despite the numinous character of the occasion. A declaration of divinity does not seem appropriate at this point in the narrative where the focus is on the initial failure to recognise Jesus and his consequent self-identification, for which ἐγώ εἰμι is normal colloquial Greek (cf. Mt. 26:22, 25; Jn. 4:26; 9:9; 18:5); see further below, p. 610 n. 34. Certainly v. 52 makes it clear that the disciples did not understand Jesus to have just revealed himself as God.

72. It is possible, however, to take the γάρ as relating not to the immediately preceding clause but to the lack of faith shown in the pericope as a whole. So T. Dwyer, *Wonder,* 132-33, following the studies of C. H. Bird and K. Tagawa. While this understanding of γάρ seems less natural, it coheres with Dwyer's general understanding of the amazement motif as not in itself negative.

73. Hooker, 169, suggests that the two miracles are linked by their relation to the two main miracles of the Exodus period, the crossing of the sea and the provision of manna; having seen Jesus 'reenact' the latter, they should not have been surprised to see him now emulating the former.

This, as we have noted above, is the beginning of Mark's 'polemic' against the disciples' failure to grasp the significance of Jesus' person and mission, and to assimilate adequately the new perspectives of the kingdom of God which, according to 4:11-12, have been specially revealed to them (though 4:13 has suggested that their understanding is still limited). Both the terms used in 6:52 will recur as the theme develops in the rest of the gospel. The charge of failing to 'understand' (συνίημι), which in 4:12 (in the quotation of Is. 6:9-10) was the mark of 'those outside' in sharp distinction from the disciples, will be repeated twice against the disciples in 8:17, 21, and in the former of those verses it will again be linked with the accusation of a καρδία πεπωρωμένη (for the echo of Is. 6:10 also in this phrase see the version quoted in Jn. 12:40). This latter phrase has also been used previously of the condition of those who opposed Jesus' ministry (3:5); now the disciples are falling into the same condition. This is remarkably strong language to use for what appears to be the natural slowness of ordinary people to adjust to the presence of the extraordinary in their midst, particularly in a gospel which has already used just these terms, and this same OT model, to describe outsiders and opponents of Jesus.[74] Mark thus prepares us for a changing, and less flattering, perception of the disciples in the rest of the gospel.[75]

Many Healings (6:53-56)

The sequence of miracles around the lake which began in 6:31 now concludes with a return to the familiar area of the western shore, where Jesus remains the focus of attention and of popular enthusiasm, at least for his miraculous healing power. Teaching is not mentioned in this brief summary (contrast 1:14-15, 39; 2:2, 13; 4:1-2, 33; 6:2, 6). In 6:34 teaching was merely mentioned in passing, all the emphasis in Mark's narrative falling on the miracle which followed. Throughout this section of Mark's story it is Jesus the miracle worker who is being portrayed, and it was in this capacity that the crowds sought him out. More surprising is the lack of any mention of exorcism in this summary (contrast 1:32-34, 39; 3:7-12, 14-15; 6:7, 13), but Mark has already placed great emphasis on that aspect of Jesus' ministry, and perhaps need not be expected to repeat it on every occasion.

74. See M. A. Beavis, *Audience,* 89-91, for the significance of 'the hardening theory' in Mark, and its foundation in Is. 6:9-10. Q. Quesnell, *Mind,* has taken 6:52 as the basis for his wide-ranging analysis of Mark's theology in this connection.

75. The proposal of J. O'Callaghan, *Bib* 53 (1972) 91-100, that a small papyrus fragment from Qumran (7Q5) came from a Greek text of the Gospel of Mark (and therefore was much earlier than any other known manuscript of the NT) depends on identifying the dozen or so clearly recognisable letters on the fragment with parts of Mk. 6:52-53. A case for O'Callaghan's identification of the fragment is presented in detail by C. P. Thiede, *Manuscript.* Few textual scholars have been convinced; see the cautionary comments of Gundry, 343-44, and Mann 307-8.

For the arrival in Gennesaret in the context of the rather obscure geography of this part of the narrative, see on v. 32. Gennesaret is in the same area of the northwest shore of the lake where the other summaries of Jesus' healing activity have been located (1:32-34; 3:7-12); here, in contrast to Nazareth up in the hills (6:1-6), he is already well known as a healer. People are thus naturally keen to take advantage of his presence (v. 55). The result (v. 56) sounds like quite a spectacular progress around the settlements of this well-populated lake-side area, and the apparently total medical 'success rate' in this region contrasts vividly with the situation in Nazareth (v. 5), though perhaps it is unwise to press the naturally comprehensive language of a summary into a literal 100 percent result. In this region, unlike Nazareth, it seems that 'faith' in Jesus is the norm.

In the whole summary Jesus is the focus of attention but not the subject of the verbs: Jesus does not go out looking for patients; it is the people who take the initiative. For the idea that merely touching Jesus' clothes would produce healing see above on 5:28 (and cf. 3:10). The specific mention of the κράσπε-δον (the fringe or tassel which the Jewish man was required by the law to wear; Nu. 15:38-39; Dt. 22:12) might suggest to those familiar with the story of the woman with the haemorrhage in its Matthean and Lucan form (Mt. 9:20; Lk. 8:44) that Mark uses the term to recall that incident, and perhaps that he therefore understood that woman's healing as a precedent which now encouraged others to expect the same result. But Mark did not mention the κράσπεδον in that incident. The hope of healing through touch may well have been stimulated by that woman's experience, but the κράσπεδον is probably mentioned merely as the most easily accessible part of Jesus' clothing.

A FORETASTE OF CONFRONTATION IN JERUSALEM: THE ISSUE OF PURITY (7:1-23)

TEXTUAL NOTES

3. The difficulty of making sense of πυγμῇ, together with its wide attestation, leaves little room for doubt that it is the original reading. Its omission (Δ sy^s cop^{sa}) or the substitution of πυκνά (א W etc.) are obvious devices to deal with a troublesome word.

4. The addition of ὅταν ἔλθωσιν after ἀπ' ἀγορᾶς in Western witnesses is apparently an attempt to provide a suitable verb for the awkward prepositional phrase to relate to; it is hard to imagine its being deliberately omitted if original.

4. ῥαντίσωνται is probably a correction, since a Christian scribe confronted by βαπτίζομαι as a term for Jewish ritual washing might well have wished to substitute a less 'Christian' word. It is also possible that the awkward syntax of the sentence caused some to read ἀπ' ἀγορᾶς as the object of the verb ('[things] from the market'), for which the middle voice βαπτίζομαι would not be appropriate (the active of ῥαντίζω would also seem more natural, but for the middle meaning 'purify for oneself' see BAGD, 734a, 2.b).

4. The evidence is strong both for and against the inclusion of καὶ κλινῶν. It is perhaps a little more likely that scribes omitted the phrase (referring to the legislation on unclean beds in Lv. 15) because it seemed inappropriate with a list of food vessels than that it was added subsequently in order to provide a fuller list of Jewish purification rituals (the washing of the bed is not explicitly mentioned in Lv. 15).

7-8. The inclusion either immediately before (D Θ most OL) or immediately after (A K ƒ¹³ etc.) v. 8 of a list of traditional rituals echoing v. 4, together with the last words of v. 13, is probably due to the desire to specify how the scribes merited the charge of v. 8. When a clause comes in different places in the manuscript tradition, this is often a sign of secondary addition, and the unadorned text of the earlier Greek MSS seems the most probable.

9. The choice between στήσητε and τηρήσητε on grounds of external evidence is not obvious, and either makes appropriate sense in context. It may be slightly in favour of στήσητε that to 'establish' the tradition might make a more powerful foil to rejecting the word of God, while in a context concerning correct legal behaviour τηρέω may have seemed a more natural word to expect.

15. The inclusion of v. 16, εἴ τις ἔχει ὦτα ἀκούειν, ἀκουέτω in most of the later manuscript tradition fits well in this parabolic context, where the opening formula of v. 14b and the use of παραβολή in v. 17 both echo the language of chapter 4, where this same formula occurs in vv. 9, 23. But in view of its omission in the earlier Alexandrian tradition (א B L Δ* etc.) its very appropriateness probably marks it out as a secondary addition suggested by the parabolic context.

19. καθαρίζον and the indicative versions καὶ καθαρίζει (-εται) are best understood as attempts to 'correct' the syntax by scribes who did not recognise the parenthetical nature of the clause. That they produce no appropriate sense is not in their favour (as 'lectio difficilior') when there is so obvious an explanation for their invention.

While this long section of the gospel divides clearly into two sections (vv. 1-13 and 14-23), and the former of those may less satisfactorily be divided into vv. 1-8 and 9-13, the continuity of subject matter is such that, as in the case of the sabbath controversy pericopes in 2:23–3:6, it is better treated here as a single unit in order to emphasise the continuation of the theme of purity throughout the section, even though the focus is significantly widened in vv. 14-23. The narrative which follows in 7:24-30 is also closely linked to this theme, but its formally distinct character requires separate treatment.

In relation to what precedes, however, the beginning of chapter 7 marks an ominous change. In the sequence of miracle stories around the lake in 6:31-56 Jesus has appeared as a figure of powerful action rather than a teacher, and has met with popular acclaim. With the beginning of chapter 7 we return to a situation of controversy and of teaching, the two closely woven together. Opposition and rejection have of course been recurrent themes in the Galilean ministry so far, but with this new pericope the tension between Jesus and the religious leadership rises to a new level of mutual repudiation, and Jesus deliberately fuels the fire with a more radical pronouncement even than his controversial comments on the sabbath (vv. 15, 19).

The sinister significance of this incident with regard to the future development of the story is seen in the fact that the source of opposition to Jesus is now not the local scribal leadership but, as in 3:22, a delegation ἀπὸ Ἰεροσολύμων. It was from such a group that the accusation of involvement with Beelzebul came. The charge this time (allowing his disciples to eat without washing) seems much less serious, but leads, and perhaps was intended to lead, to a stark polarisation of views which must pit Jesus' new teaching irrevocably against current religious orthodoxy, and which will, in the fulness of time, lead the community of his followers outside the confines of traditional Judaism altogether. It is hardly a coincidence that in the narrative which follows Jesus himself moves outside Jewish territory and begins to exercise his ministry among non-Jews. The controversy over ritual purity, with its radical implications for the status of the food laws which divide Jew from Gentile, thus appropriately acts as the narrative hinge between the Jewish and Gentile phases of Jesus' ministry in the north, and at the same time points forward to what awaits him in the subsequent phase of the drama when he makes his way to Jerusalem, the place from which this hostile delegation has come.

While the whole section is focused on the theme of purity, there is a remarkable difference of approach between its two main components. Put simply, whereas in vv. 1-13 Jesus berates the scribes for undermining the authority of the OT law, in vv. 14-23 he apparently undermines one of its key provisions himself. While in vv. 1-13 Jesus' attack is directed only against scribal tradition, in vv. 14-23 the scribes are no longer mentioned and Jesus' criticism is directed instead against a fundamental principle of the OT law itself. This surprising change of direction, and the apparently inconsistent standards which it implies, must be kept in mind as we study the text of each part of the section.[1]

The food laws of Lv. 11 and 17, and the whole concept of ritual purity which underlies them, were of central importance to Jewish culture and identity. Together with the rite of circumcision and their observance of the sabbath, the literal adherence to these dietary laws served to mark out the Jews as the distinctive people of God, and to separate them socially from other people.[2] The sharing of meals is one of the most basic forms of social integration, and these laws effectively made it impossible for Jews to share in meals prepared by non-Jews. While the issue raised by the scribes in v. 2 is at the relatively inoffensive level of ritual washing before meals (a matter on which Jews themselves held different views), by his pronouncement in v. 15 Jesus deliberately

---

1. A stimulating and provocative study of the pericope by J. Marcus in C. M. Tuckett (ed.), *The Scriptures in the Gospels,* 177-95, notes the apparent inconsistency of the arguments used, and especially how some of the points made by Jesus might with more obvious justice have been made by the Pharisees! Marcus attempts to reconstruct the first-century polemical situation out of which the pericope arose, and offers on pp. 190-91 his own 'reconstruction' of the Pharisaic attack on the Christian attitude towards Scripture and tradition.

2. On the 'boundary markers which distinguished Jew from Gentile' see, e.g., J. D. G. Dunn, *Partings,* 28-31.

widens the discussion to include this ritual separation which constituted one of the 'badges' of Jewish national identity.

Once the Christian movement came to include significant numbers of non-Jews, it was inevitable that the food laws would become a matter of existential importance, as their literal persistence would make table fellowship between Jewish and Gentile Christians impossible. Both in Acts and in the Pauline letters we see the sensitivity of the issue. It was one of the most burning areas of controversy in first-century Christianity, as we see especially in Peter's vision at Joppa and its outcome (Acts 10:9-16, and the rest of Acts 10–11), in the Council of Jerusalem and its famous 'compromise' decree (Acts 15:1-29), and in the 'Antioch incident' of Gal. 2:11-14. Paul's discussion of the dietary disputes in the Roman church in Rom. 14 focuses in part on the same issues, and his pronouncements in Rom. 14:14, 20, with their authority formula πέπεισμαι ἐν κυρίῳ Ἰησοῦ, echo the words of Mk. 7:15, 19;[3] the tradition of Jesus' teaching on this issue (and perhaps the substance of Mark's comment on it in v. 19c) was thus already known to Paul in the fifties.[4]

But if Jesus had made as clear a statement directly on this issue as Mark indicates (v. 19c), how is it that it remained so much a matter of debate among his followers? Surely this pericope should have sufficed to settle the issue once for all on the highest authority (as indeed Paul appears to use it in Rom. 14)? Some commentators therefore propose either to understand Mk. 7:19c in a less definitive sense or to regard it as a personal contribution by Mark which goes beyond any implication which might properly be drawn from Jesus' recorded epigram, and indeed as Mark's deliberate contribution to what remained an area of controversy within the church for which he was writing. It is certainly true that v. 19c is more explicit in its application to the food law issue as such than anything in the actual tradition of Jesus' words as we have it recorded in Mark or Matthew, but it is hard to imagine that any Christian reader of either of the two different forms in which the key pronouncement is recorded (Mk. 7:15; Mt. 15:11) could have failed to recognise the relevance of the principle to the issue of the dietary laws and their effect on Jew-Gentile social relations once this issue had become a focus of debate within the church. If Mark is making that application more explicit, he is doing no more than any other intelligent reader of Jesus' epigram might have done.[5]

The explanation for the church's remarkable slowness in drawing out the implications of what Jesus had said is not to be found by questioning the valid-

---

3. See Van Iersel, 53-54, for the relevance of Mark 7:19 to the situation presupposed in Rom. 14.

4. Cf. S. Westerholm, *Jesus*, 81-82; D. Wenham, *Paul*, 92-97. Wenham suggests echoes of this pericope also in 1 Cor. 6:12-13; Col. 2:21-22.

5. On this debate, and on the central significance of Mk. 7:15 for understanding the origin of Christian abandonment of the food laws, see J. D. G. Dunn, *Jesus, Paul and the Law*, 37-60. Dunn understands Mk. 7:15 as a 'sharpened' but faithful representation of an original saying of Jesus more like Mt. 15:11.

ity of Mark's interpretation, but rather in the instinctive conservatism of almost all religious communities, which tends to resist any change to fundamental traditional values until there is no other option. Once one recognises the radical implications for Jewish communal identity (and indeed for the authority of Torah) of any abandonment of the food laws, it is hardly surprising that the full significance of Jesus' uncomfortable epigram took some time to penetrate, and that there were some groups within first-century Christianity for whom the process took longer than others. Mark clearly represents the more 'progressive' (Pauline) wing in that debate.

It is often suggested that at this point there is a significant, and deliberate, difference between the perspectives of Mark and of Matthew.[6] (There is no Lucan parallel; the purity debate falls within Luke's 'Great Omission'; see above, p. 269.) Matthew's failure to make any comment comparable to Mark's καθαρίζων πάντα τὰ βρώματα suggests to many that he was unwilling to raise the issue of the food laws directly, and his inclusion in 15:20 of the comment that τὸ ἀνίπτοις χερσὶν φαγεῖν οὐ κοινοῖ τὸν ἄνθρωπον brings the discussion safely back at the end to the less controversial issue of hand washing, a matter of scribal tradition, not of OT law, thus keeping Jesus clear of the charge of doing precisely what he had claimed in Mt. 5:17 not to be doing, 'abolishing the law'. This commonplace of comment on Matthew certainly reveals a difference of presentation from Mark, but it is surely incredible that an evangelist (of Matthew's acute sensitivity to matters of Jewish law) who retained the crucial epigram of 15:11 could have been unaware, or expected his Jewish readers to be unaware, of its implications for the food laws. It is permissible to find in Matthew a more apologetically careful record of Jesus' views on purity, but to regard his version as totally innocuous from the point of view of the continued validity of the food laws is naive.

1-5 The structure of vv. 1-5 is complex, and different methods of punctuation have been proposed. It is generally recognised that vv. 3-4 function as a parenthetical comment, after which v. 5 picks up again from v. 2, but editors vary as to whether they see v. 5 as the continuation of an interrupted sentence or as syntactically a new beginning resuming the theme of the earlier sentence in vv. 1-2. On the latter view, vv. 1-2 form a complete sentence, with v. 2 as a further participial clause coordinate with ἐλθόντες ἀπὸ Ἱεροσολύμων and governed by συνάγονται as its main verb — they 'came together . . . having arrived from Jerusalem and having seen . . .'. On the whole this provides the more satisfactory flow of thought, since if a full stop is placed at the end of v. 1 (as in UBS[4], NA[27]) v. 2 has to be treated as an unfinished sentence awkwardly picked up at the beginning of v. 5 with a καί which is out of place following a particip-

---

6. One prominent difference between the two accounts is the different ordering of the material in the first half of the pericope, but this difference, while it may affect the rhetorical force of the attack, does not seem to betray any difference of perspective on the issue of defilement. It will be discussed below under v. 6.

ial introduction. If vv. 1-2 are read as a complete sentence, there is then no need for dashes to set off vv. 3-4, though to put them in parentheses helps the reader to recognise their explanatory character.

1 Matthew's phrase ἀπὸ Ἱεροσολύμων Φαρισαῖοι καὶ γραμματεῖς suggests a single group coming from Jerusalem to Galilee. Mark's wording, however, divides the group into the (presumably local) Φαρισαῖοι and τινες τῶν γραμματέων ἐλθόντες ἀπὸ Ἱεροσολύμων. Judging from the area of their concern, these scribes from Jerusalem were themselves also Pharisees, and no distinction between the two groups is discernible in the pericope. The local Pharisees are already established in the narrative as the focus of opposition to Jesus in Galilee (2:16, 24; 3:6). Local scribes have also been mentioned in 2:6, 16, but the reappearance here of *Jerusalem* scribes (first encountered in 3:22), indicates a reinforcement of the local opposition by a delegation from the capital. The fact that in both instances they are described as having arrived (κατα-βάντες, 3:22; ἐλθόντες here) from Jerusalem probably indicates that they have come specially to investigate and/or to dispute with Jesus.

2 As in 2:18, 23-24, it is the behaviour of Jesus' disciples rather than his own actions which provides the point of dispute (see on 2:24). The issue this time (as in 2:18) is not one of obedience to the OT laws, but of rules subsequently developed in Pharisaic circles.[7] While no doubt it could normally be expected that hands would be washed before a meal for hygienic reasons (since food was often taken from a common dish),[8] the only hand washing required in the OT for purposes of ritual purity[9] is that of priests before offering sacrifice (Ex. 30:18-21; 40:30-32). The extension of this principle to the eating of ordinary food,[10] and to Jewish people other than priests, was a matter of scribal development, and it is uncertain how far it had progressed by the time of Jesus.[11]

---

7. Even when the hand-washing regulations were firmly established, the rabbis defended them only as 'words of the scribes', not as having the authority of Torah (*b.'Erub.* 21b; *b. Ḥul.* 106a).

8. R. P. Booth, *Purity,* 118-19, discusses and dismisses the possibility that the Pharisees' objection here was on merely hygienic grounds.

9. The hands were regarded as a source of ritual impurity since they are 'ever busy' (*m. Ṭoh.* 7:8), and therefore liable to be in contact with unclean things. The principle is developed in detail in the mishnaic tractate *Yadayim* ('Hands').

10. One passage in the Mishnah states that whereas washing is required in certain cases before eating sacred food, for 'common food' it is not (*m. Para* 11:5).

11. The historical development of purity laws with special reference to hand washing is exhaustively discussed by R. P. Booth, *Purity,* 117-87, with a useful summary of conclusions on 186-87. A good case can be made from (admittedly ambiguous) rabbinic references that as early as Hillel and Shammai (i.e., by the time of Jesus) the ritual uncleanness of the hands was a matter of discussion (*Purity,* 169-73). But Booth argues that the sort of impurity conveyed by the hands in the likely circumstances of Jesus' disciples would not be removed by washing merely the hands but would require complete immersion; he therefore suggests that the Pharisees concerned were *ḥaberim* who practised a supererogatory hand washing not required by Pharisaic law as such, and who were trying to influence Jesus and his disciples to adopt it, and thus to become also *ḥaberim* (189-203).

It is unlikely that ritual hand washing was yet the norm among ordinary people, and it may well be that what the Pharisees were here expecting of Jesus and his disciples was their own distinctive practice. Surely a self-proclaimed religious teacher might be expected to require of his followers at least as rigorous a ritual practice as the Pharisees expected of theirs, and not to let them behave like the *'am hā-'āreṣ*. For the use of κοινός and κοινόω to denote ritual impurity (a specifically Jewish usage, found in the gospels only in the present pericope in Mark and Matthew) cf. Acts 10:14-15, 28; 11:8-9; 21:28; Rom. 14:14; Heb. 9:13; 10:29. Mark adds the explanatory clause τοῦτ' ἔστιν ἀνίπτοις for the sake of his Gentile readers.[12]

The plural τοὺς ἄρτους is unexpected; the singular would normally be used to refer to bread, or more widely to food, in general. Some commentators therefore see here a reference back to the five loaves of 6:38-44, again referred to in the plural in 6:52; 8:19. Bread is certainly a recurring theme of this part of the narrative, soon to be reinforced with a second feeding miracle and specific mention again of seven ἄρτοι in 8:5-6, 20, and by the concept of the 'children's bread' in 7:27. The whole Galilean phase of the narrative will conclude with a discussion focused on the meaning of 'the loaves' (8:11-21). But no explicit link is made between the ἄρτοι of this verse and the other references to bread in chapters 6–8, and it is not easy to infer any connection in principle. Moreover, from the narrative point of view, scribes recently arrived from Jerusalem are highly unlikely to have been present to witness the feeding miracle so as to comment on any supposed ritual irregularity in which it may have involved the disciples.[13] There is therefore probably no significant difference between the plural of this verse and the singular of v. 5.

3-4 Mark's explanatory account of Jewish rituals of purity is apparently directed to Gentile readers of the gospel. It is a broad-brush, unsophisticated account, which conveys a general sense of meticulous concern to avoid defilement rather than a nuanced presentation of the purity laws of the OT and of scribal tradition. The inclusion of πάντες οἱ Ἰουδαῖοι in this description along with the Pharisees is more impressionistic than historically exact, since there is no evidence that the sort of precautions described were yet observed by Jews in general, if indeed they ever were.[14] It was precisely the observance of such rules which marked out the members of the Pharisaic party from the general

---

12. For the development of this meaning of κοινός see R. P. Booth, *Purity,* 120-21.

13. Gundry, 348-49, suggests that Mark envisages the disciples, having finally found an opportunity to eat, now eating the leftovers (6:43) from 'the loaves' of the miracle; the scribes are witnesses not to the miracle but to this subsequent meal.

14. According to the *Letter of Aristeas,* a (probably) second-century-B.C. work describing the translation of the Septuagint in the third century B.C., the translators washed their hands in the course of their prayers ὡς ἔθος ἐστὶ πᾶσι τοῖς Ἰουδαίοις (*Aristeas,* 305). This seems as exaggerated a generalisation as Mark's, but again serves to alert the Gentile reader to a specifically Jewish concern. But for an unusually positive account of the early origin and wide dissemination of hand-washing rituals see Gundry, 358-60.

populace.[15] Even among the Pharisees the practice may not have been as rigorous or as uniform as Mark indicates.[16]

πυγμῇ (see Textual Note) means literally 'with the fist'. We have no other evidence for what the expression might mean in connection with hand washing, and the various quasi-literal meanings proposed by translators and commentators[17] ('up to the wrist'; 'up to the elbow'; 'their hands and their wrists'; 'with cupped hands'; 'with a handful of water')[18] are merely guesses; others, perhaps more wisely, opt for a less literal paraphrase (not necessarily presupposing the variant reading πυκνά) such as 'thoroughly' or 'ceremonially'.[19] Whatever the exact form it took, what Mark describes is ritual purification rather than hygienic washing.

For τὴν παράδοσιν τῶν πρεσβυτέρων see on v. 5.

ἀπ' ἀγορᾶς stands awkwardly outside the syntax, and requires something else to be supplied for it to relate to. This might be a verb ('when they come in from the marketplace', as in the Western textual tradition) or a noun ('things bought from the marketplace'). The choice between these options is in turn dependent on whether the verb is read as βαπτίσωνται or ῥαντίσωνται (see Textual Note), the former fitting better with the verb, the latter with the noun. Since the rest of the comment is on the washing of hands and of vessels rather than the purification of the food itself, the Western reading seems more likely to represent Mark's intention (even if not his text). The reference then is to the need for those who have been in the marketplace, and thus exposed to various possible sources of ritual impurity, to purify themselves before eating. The washing in this case is not merely of the hands, but apparently involves immersion of the whole person[20] (cf. Tob. 7:8 for bathing as well as hand washing before eating, though this one instance does not prove that immersion was the norm before all meals).[21]

15. For a useful survey of Pharisaic purity laws in the first century see E. P. Sanders, *Judaism*, 431-40. The Pharisees, he concludes, 'aspired to a level of purity above the ordinary, but below that of priests and their families, and also well below that of the Qumran sect'. The situation is further complicated by uncertainty as to the relation between the terms 'Pharisee' and *ḥaber*. The two are not identical, and the *ḥaberim* were apparently a smaller group, devoted to a more rigorous code of purity such as this passage assumes, to which some (perhaps most?) Pharisees belonged. Sanders discusses the question in his *Paul*, 61-62, 154-56; *Jesus*, 187-88. For the purposes of this commentary, however, the term 'Pharisee' must suffice.

16. E. P. Sanders, *Judaism*, 437-38. Cf. R. P. Booth, *Purity*, 189-203.

17. Among many articles, that by M. Hengel, *ZNW* 60 (1969) 182-98, offers a useful overview of suggestions before presenting his own argument that it is a Latinism meaning 'a handful' *(pugillus)*.

18. The last suggestion perhaps finds some support in the rules of *m. Yad.* 1:1 for the amount of water needed for hand washing.

19. A note by J. M. Ross, *ExpTim* 87 (1975/6) 374-75, interestingly suggests an idiom 'to clean with the fist' which was meant no more literally than our use of 'elbow grease'.

20. For this connotation of βαπτίζομαι in relation to OT and Jewish ritual see *DNTT*, 1.144-45. Full immersion (in a *miqwâ*) as a preliminary to worship is well attested both in literary sources and by the discovery of *miqwā'ōt*, but is less probable before an ordinary meal (see above, p. 280 n. 11).

21. For Jewish ablution rituals in general see R. L. Webb, *John*, 95-162, and for the practice within mainstream Judaism in the first century especially 108-12.

The 'catch-all' formula καὶ ἄλλα πολλά ἐστιν ἃ παρέλαβον κρατεῖν broadens the scope of Mark's comment to the regulations for ritual purity in general, and the remainder of v. 4 then illustrates the point by moving beyond the washing of the person to the washing of food vessels, attested as a Pharisaic concern also in Mt. 23:25; Lk. 11:39. The inclusion also of beds (if original; see Textual Note) is incongruous, but presumably represents a desire to offer an even more comprehensive account of Jewish purification rites by including also the theme of Lv. 15.

5 The charge for which vv. 1-4 have prepared the ground is now recorded. It assumes that to omit ritual hand washing is against τὴν παράδοσιν τῶν πρεσβυτέρων. Jesus will pick up the term παράδοσις in his response, but will describe it pointedly not as τῶν πρεσβυτέρων but as τῶν ἀνθρώπων (as opposed to the word *of God,* v. 8) and as ὑμῶν (vv. 9, 13), thus questioning the automatic assumption by the Pharisees and scribes that there is authority inherent in tradition as such. It would in fact, as we have seen, have been a valid debating point to question how ancient and how widely accepted this particular tradition really was: who were the πρεσβύτεροι from whom it had been received? The term is not specific, and refers merely to 'received wisdom', and that wisdom may not have been of very long standing, nor have been shared by all groups within Judaism at that time.[22] But for the scribes, as for religious groups generally, there is an assumption that what has once been established by usage is normative; for them this practice is now self-evidently right.[23] Jesus' response will therefore focus on this more fundamental issue of the relative authority of tradition as such as a guide to the will of God, rather than on the provenance of the particular tradition in question.

6-7 Mark and Matthew present Jesus' response to the charge in different sequence. In Matthew Jesus replies immediately with the countercharge of contravening the commandment of God through their tradition, followed by the illustration from the *qorbān* legislation, after which the attack is rounded off with the quotation from Is. 29:13. In Mark the Isaiah quotation comes first. Matthew's order is smoother, in that there is an easily intelligible progression in the sequence charge — illustration — supporting quotation; and the words of Mt. 15:3, καὶ ὑμεῖς παραβαίνετε . . . διὰ τὴν παράδοσιν ὑμῶν, form a powerful immediate rejoinder to the charge διὰ τί οἱ μαθηταί σου παραβαίνουσιν τὴν παράδοσιν τῶν πρεσβυτέρων; But perhaps Mark's rougher order, which presents the condemnatory quotation from Isaiah, introduced by the sarcastic καλῶς, without having yet explained in what way it applies to these particular 'hypocrites', gains in rhetorical effect, in that the apparently unprovoked scriptural onslaught makes a more powerful impact on the readers, leaving them ea-

---

22. See above, p. 280 n. 11 and p. 282 n. 15.

23. By the time of the Mishnah the traditions on hand washing had become sufficiently authoritative for a rabbi who questioned them (Eleazar b. Enoch) to be 'put under a ban' (*m. 'Eduy.* 5:6).

ger to know the basis of the charge, and thus preparing the way for vv. 8-13. This order also has the effect that the charge in v. 8 can be worded so as to pick up the theme of the Isaiah quotation in the phrase τὴν παράδοσιν τῶν ἀνθρώπων.

The introductory formula (containing the only use in Mark of the 'Matthean' term ὑποκριτής)[24] assumes that Isaiah's words, which originally described the superficial religious devotion of his eighth-century contemporaries rather than predicting a future situation, can be directly applied to, indeed were written about, ὑμεῖς. This 'contemporising' use of OT texts is typical of much NT interpretation, and presupposes a typological understanding of continuity in the relationship between God and his people such that earlier events and situations appropriately serve as models for a later era of fulfilment, even though in themselves they had no predictive force.[25]

The quotation is from LXX Is. 29:13, with the wording slightly adapted in the first and last lines in a way which does not affect the sense. But the LXX of the second half of the verse differs from the Hebrew by the inclusion of μάτην, for which there is no Hebrew equivalent (unless it is found by reading *wᵉtōhû* instead of *watᵉhî;* such a reading of the Hebrew consonants may well have produced the LXX text), and by the inclusion of διδάσκοντες (implied but not stated in the Hebrew *mᵉlummādâ*) so that those condemned are seen as teaching, not merely following, human commands. The suggestion that the relevance of the quotation in this context depends on the LXX wording, and therefore cannot derive from Jesus, depends on three questionable assumptions: that Jesus could not have known and used the LXX;[26] that the Masoretic text must represent the Hebrew text known in Palestine in the first century; and that the inclusion of μάτην and of διδάσκοντες materially affects the sense. The specific statement that the worship described is 'vain' undoubtedly sharpens the application, and the inclusion of διδάσκοντες fits well with the specific application of the charge to scribes rather than to the people in general, but the text even in its Hebrew form describes a worship which is based on externals and is of purely human origin, which is just the point which Jesus goes on to make about the scribal traditions, whereas the specifically LXX point that their worship is 'in vain' is nowhere drawn into Jesus' comments. To recognise that the LXX version sharpens the point is by no means to show that Jesus could not have used Is. 29:13 even in its Hebrew form as the basis for his attack on scribal religion.[27]

The contrast in Isaiah between lips (words) and heart is not taken up as a

24. Mann, 310, delightfully translates the term by 'you pettifogging lawyers' — the translation is explained in W. F. Albright and C. S. Mann, *Matthew,* CXV-CXXIII, though in the Matthew parallel to this verse they in fact preferred the American term 'shysters'.

25. For comments on this 'typological' approach more generally see my *Jesus and the OT,* 38-43, 75-80, and for this passage 68-69.

26. See Gundry, 351.

27. See my *Jesus and the OT,* 248-50.

regular form of expression in the gospels, but reflects an important prophetic theme (cf. Is. 1:12-17; Hos. 6:6; Am. 5:21-24; Mic. 6:6-8, etc.) and corresponds to the charge elsewhere in the gospels that scribal religion is more concerned with external correctness than with fundamental attitudes and relationship to God (Mt. 23:23-28; Lk. 11:37-44). The priority of the internal over the external will be picked up as the focus of the alternative approach commended by Jesus in vv. 14-23, where the word καρδία will recur prominently in vv. 19 and 21. But before we come to that, Jesus' immediate concern will be with the theme of the second half of the Isaiah quotation, that rules and regulations based on merely human authority do not provide the sort of response which God requires of his people.[28]

8 The basic charge is economically expressed by means of three contrasting pairs of words: ἀφέντες . . . κρατεῖτε; ἐντολὴν . . . παράδοσιν; θεοῦ . . . ἀνθρώπων. The fundamental contrast is the last — true religion is focused on God, not a merely human activity. What comes from God has the authoritative character of ἐντολή, which requires obedience; what comes from human authority is merely παράδοσις, which may or may not be of value in itself, but cannot have the same mandatory character. Yet they have held fast to the latter, while allowing the former to go by default. ἀφίημι perhaps does not yet denote deliberate rejection, but rather a wrong sense of priorities, resulting in *de facto* neglect of God's law, but in vv. 9 and 13 the charge will be of more deliberate evasion of the divine demands. The charge would be indignantly denied by the scribes, whose developing traditions were intended, in a later rabbinic phrase, to be 'a fence around the Torah' (*m. 'Abot* 1:1; 3:14), which remained the primary authority. But Jesus will go on to demonstrate that, whatever the theory, in practice the OT law was taking second place.

9 This verse repeats much of the form and wording of v. 8, and the introductory clause καὶ ἔλεγεν αὐτοῖς, normally taken to mark the opening of a separate tradition, perhaps indicates that Mark has here combined two independent sayings to the same effect (where only one appears in Mt. 15:3). That may well be so, but both clearly relate to the same context of controversy over scribal tradition. In combining the two Mark has in fact not merely repeated the point but produced an escalating argument, in three respects: ἀφίημι is replaced by the more deliberate ἀθετέω; the παράδοσις τῶν ἀνθρώπων becomes more pointedly τὴν παράδοσιν ὑμῶν; and the sense of perverse intention is heightened by the ἵνα clause, which implies that the law of God was a hindrance which had to be removed in order to establish their tradition. The introductory καλῶς, echoing the same word which introduced the Isaiah quotation, also adds an appropriate note of sarcasm. This second charge thus sharpens the attack,

---

28. The quotation of Is. 29:13, in almost the same words, together with the same introductory formula, is picked up in the fragment of an otherwise unknown early Christian gospel known as *Papyrus Egerton* 2 (text in Aland ad loc.). There, however, the context is less clearly appropriate: in response to the question about Roman taxation, Jesus asks angrily, 'Why do you call me Teacher with your mouth and yet not [do] what I say?' after which the quotation follows.

and sets the scene for an example of just such deliberate suppression of the divine purpose in favour of a more convenient scribal tradition.

10-12   The ἐντολὴ τοῦ θεοῦ is represented by two direct quotations from the Torah (with Moses specifically mentioned as the author to differentiate this from later elaborations of the law). The fundamental text is the fifth commandment from Ex. 20:12; Dt. 5:16; the addition of Ex. 21:17 (LXX 21:16) serves to illustrate the seriousness of the basic commandment by specifying an extreme case of *dis*honouring father or mother and the consequent death penalty. This is not a matter to be trifled with. Yet scribal tradition had found a way of relieving a son of the responsibility of 'honouring' father or mother, not in the area of disrespectful speech but at the more practical level of financial support (which was assumed to be inherent in the 'honour' required by the commandment), by means of the *qorbān* provision. No doubt this provision, once introduced, would then be justified by the scriptural principle of not breaking an oath or vow (Nu. 30:2; Dt. 23:21-23), without enquiring whether the vow had been an appropriate one in the first place.

Just how this convenient device worked is not entirely clear. It appears that it was possible for the son's resources from which the parents might reasonably expect to receive support to be declared Κορβᾶν with the result that they became technically 'divine property' and so were no longer accessible to the parents. But it is not clear on what basis the son could himself retain the benefit of the funds so secured while denying them to the parents (which was presumably the intention, rather than a merely spiteful attempt to deprive his parents while at the same time losing the use of the funds himself). Rabbinic discussion, as we shall see below, does presuppose that this was possible.

Josephus, like Mark, offers δῶρον as a translation of the Hebrew *qorbān* in *Ant.* 4.73, where it refers to the Nazirites who regarded themselves as a 'gift' to God, and in *Ap.* 1.167, where it is an unspecified oath formula. The term occurs frequently in Leviticus and Numbers to denote a (sacrificial) 'offering', and is in all cases translated in LXX by δῶρον. So Κορβᾶν means something offered, dedicated to God (cf. Matthew's use of κορβανᾶς for the temple treasury, where such offerings were stored, 27:6).[29]

In rabbinic literature the term recurs frequently as a formula used when making an offering (whether of food, money, or property), as a result of which the thing dedicated becomes unavailable for normal use; in practice the formula seems to have been used primarily for the negative purpose of excluding a particular person from the use of the property (cf. the formula here Κορβᾶν . . . ὃ ἐὰν ἐξ ἐμοῦ ὠφεληθῇς; the same form of words occurs in *m. Ned.* 8:7),[30] rather than positively to transfer it to divine use. The mere utterance of the word

29. Cf. Josephus, *War* 2.175 for the use of κορβωνᾶς for the temple treasury, and for the public outrage when Pilate appropriated its funds for secular use.

30. The same intention seems to lie behind an ossuary inscription of the early first century A.D. from near Jerusalem which reads, 'All that a man may find to his profit in this ossuary is *qorbān* to God from him who is within it'; see J. A. Fitzmyer, *JBL* 78 (1959) 60-65.

qorbān (or its equivalent *qōnām*) makes the vow binding. These two words recur frequently throughout the text of the Mishnah tractate *Nedarim,* illustrating the extent to which rabbinic discussion of such dedicatory vows had already developed by the second century, with special reference to alleviating the hardship caused by ill-considered or wrongly motivated vows. Among issues discussed was the possible conflict between the obligation of a vow and the duty owed to father or mother under the fifth commandment. In such a case the rabbis whose views are reflected in the Mishnah inclined to give priority to the commandment, and so to allow a man to be released from his vow (*m. Ned.* 9:1); Jesus was apparently aware of a more rigorous scribal view which refused any such remission.[31] οὐκέτι ἀφίετε αὐτὸν οὐδὲν ποιῆσαι suggests that such cases were brought before a scribal 'court' to decide whether or not remission was allowed, and that the scribes might refuse to release a man from his vow even where he himself now wished to be released.

There is an interesting case in the Mishnah (*m. Ned.* 5:6) where a man who had excluded his father under such a vow from any enjoyment of his property now wished to evade the force of his oath so as to enable the father to join in his grandson's wedding feast; he therefore made a gift of his courtyard and the feast to a friend, so that his father could be admitted (to what was now the friend's property), but the friend in turn made a similar vow with regard to his newly acquired property, thus frustrating the donor's intention! This case illustrates two points relevant to our passage: (i) the original *qorbān* vow was regarded as unalterable, even though the son himself now wished to repeal it; (ii) the property so 'dedicated' remained still at the son's disposal, even though out of his father's reach. It is such a situation which is apparently presupposed by Jesus' comments here.[32]

The subject matter of vv. 10-12 is not of course directly linked to the theme of purity in the pericope as a whole. A mechanical application of tradition criticism therefore naturally labels these verses as an alien intrusion into the context of a discussion of purity, but this is hardly a necessary conclusion if it is recognised that the *qorbān* issue is introduced here not because the subject matter is related but in order to illustrate the basic difference of approach between Jesus and the Pharisees. This example drawn from a quite distinct area of law and ethics serves merely to illustrate and to hold up to criticism the disproportionate concern for the authority of scribal tradition out of which the accusation in v. 5 has sprung.

13 Jesus' charge against the scribes is now summed up in a formula similar to the escalating statements of vv. 8 and 9, but since the specific case discussed has been concerned with scribal legislation the already strong verb

31. See S. Westerholm, *Jesus,* 76-78, for a discussion of the development in rabbinic attitudes to release from vows, with special reference to *m. Ned.* 9:1.

32. For a useful presentation of the rabbinic data on κορβᾶν see K. H. Rengstorf, *TDNT,* 3.861-66.

ἀθετέω (v. 9) is here replaced by the more formally legal term ἀκυρόω, 'to annul' or 'repeal' (cf. Gal. 3:17). They have actually dared to rule τὸν λόγον τοῦ θεοῦ to be unlawful! The phrase ὁ λόγος τοῦ θεοῦ is not, as modern usage might suggest, an accepted synonym for 'the Bible'. This and its parallel in Matthew 15:6 are the only occurrences of the phrase in those two gospels. In the rest of the NT its main use, especially in Luke-Acts, is to denote the Christian message and its proclamation, though there are a few instances where it is used of a specific divine utterance in the past (known to us from the OT, of course) rather than of Scripture as such (Jn. 10:35; Rom. 9:6; 2 Pet. 3:5). The only NT passage which may anticipate the later Christian habit of referring to Scripture as 'the Word of God' is Heb. 4:12, though there it is debatable whether the reference is to Scripture as a whole or only to the divine pronouncement of judgment in Ps. 95 which is there being discussed. Here, therefore, it is unlikely that the scribes' fault is to be understood specifically as contravening *Scripture,* but rather as undermining a specific divine pronouncement (the fifth commandment) in favour of their own human tradition. ὁ λόγος τοῦ θεοῦ is thus functionally equivalent to ἡ ἐντολὴ τοῦ θεοῦ in vv. 8 and 9.

The generalising clause καὶ παρόμοια τοιαῦτα πολλὰ ποιεῖτε has the same function as καὶ ἄλλα πολλά ἐστιν ἃ παρέλαβον κρατεῖν in v. 4 (and a similar clause added in many MSS before or after v. 8; see Textual Note) in that it extrapolates from the specific case(s) mentioned to a general tendency of scribal religion to put the emphasis in the wrong place. If the legislation recorded in the Mishnah may fairly be taken as evidence of what was already at least an incipient trend in the time of Jesus, there is some justification for the generalisation.

14 What has hitherto been a private discussion between Jesus and the scribal delegation is now deliberately opened up to include ὁ ὄχλος (the recipients of Jesus' public teaching in 2:13; 4:1; 6:34, etc.). Indeed, the Pharisees and scribes are not mentioned again; their accusation has been rebutted, and now Jesus takes the initiative in raising publicly a much more fundamental issue of purity which goes far beyond the limited question of the validity of the scribal rules for hand washing. No specific regulation is now in view, but rather the basic principle of defilement by means of external contacts which underlies all the purity laws of the OT and of scribal tradition.

But this principle will be discussed not by a scribal-type ruling, but, following the teaching philosophy declared in 4:33-34, by means of a παραβολή (v. 17), an epigrammatic saying whose potentially wide application is balanced by its enigmatic form, so that it is for the hearers to work out its significance for themselves (see the discussion of the nature and purpose of parables in the introductory comments on chapter 4).[33] Like the parables of chapter 4, such a

---

33. For the parallels between chs. 4 and 7 see M. A. Beavis, *Audience,* 91-93. See further E. E. Lemcio, *JTS* 29 (1978) 323-38, for the wider background to the dialogue form represented in these two chapters of Mark.

saying is likely to leave some within the ὄχλος merely puzzled, while others will, perhaps gradually, come to realise the radical implications which Mark himself will spell out for his readers in his editorial comment in v. 19. The 'parabolic' introduction to the epigram, ἀκούσατε . . . καὶ σύνετε, appropriately echoes the language of chapter 4: it will demand not only 'hearing' (4:3, 9, 15, 16, 18, 20, 23, and 24), but also 'understanding', and if Isaiah's prophecy quoted in 4:12 is to be believed, there will be many who will hear without understanding. Even the disciples themselves are in danger of failing to understand, according to v. 18 (cf. their failure to 'understand' the wider significance of Jesus' ministry: 6:52; 8:17, 21), and so, as in chapter 4, will be given a private explanation (vv. 17-23).

15   The form of this pronouncement, which is very widely accepted as an authentic saying of Jesus (whatever its original wording — see below),[34] is an antithetic parallelism typical of Jesus' epigrammatic pronouncements; for the οὐ . . . ἀλλά . . . form cf. 2:17 (bis), 22; 10:43; 12:25, and for a wide range of similarly antithetical sayings in all strata of the gospel tradition see J. Jeremias, *Theology,* 14-20. Such οὐ . . . ἀλλά . . . constructions in a Semitic context can sometimes be understood in a more relative than absolute sense ('not so much . . . as . . .' rather than 'not at all . . . but only . . .'; cf., e.g., Ho. 6:6; Je. 7:22-23), and such a sense is sometimes claimed here to avoid the implication that Jesus was actually abrogating the principle of unclean food.[35] But Mark's inclusion of v. 19c shows that he did not so interpret Jesus' words, and the other Marcan examples of the form listed above do not encourage a relative sense.

Not all Jewish purity laws were concerned with things 'going into' a person. Defilement was contracted also by touching unclean things (particularly corpses), by the person's own state of health (particularly skin disease), and by the various bodily emissions detailed in Lv. 15; all of these rendered a person 'unclean' and therefore excluded from public worship or social intercourse until the required purification ritual had been completed (Lv. 7:19-21 etc.). The wording of Jesus' pronouncement is not therefore directly applicable to all aspects of purity law, only to that which concerned food. Taken literally its reference to what 'comes out from' a person as a genuine source of impurity might even be taken as suggesting that while unclean food could not defile, bodily discharges could, and thus as championing the laws of Lv. 15 over against those of Lv. 11.[36] But that is precisely the sort of literal interpretation which this pericope rejects. Jesus' pronouncement is concerned with basic principles, not with casuistry, and at that level any distinction in principle between different types of ritual defilement would be hard to sustain.

The force of this pronouncement cannot easily be confined to the issue of

---

34. Cf. R. P. Booth, *Purity,* 205-15, for the authenticity of this saying in a modified form.

35. See, e.g., R. P. Booth, *Purity,* 69-71.

36. R. P. Booth, *Purity,* 205-13, argues persuasively against this 'cultic' sense in favour of an 'ethical' sense.

hand washing with which the pericope began. While the washing ritual (where recognised) did indeed involve the impurity of food eaten without due preparation, this was only a very minor aspect of the concept of defilement by 'what goes in'. Far more prominent were the very detailed regulations of Lv. 11 specifying which animals could and could not be eaten by the people of God, spelled out in terms of 'clean' and 'unclean' foods, and the prohibition of eating blood first declared in Gn. 9:4 and developed in Lv. 17. It was such laws, firmly rooted in the Torah, that would more naturally come to a Jewish mind on hearing Jesus' words.

The wording of this saying in Matthew and in *Gos. Thom.* 14, while differently phrased, focuses equally clearly on the question of 'what goes in' and 'what goes out' (and by specifying 'out of *the mouth*' rules out more clearly than the Marcan form the remote possibility of understanding Jesus' words with reference to bodily discharges). It has, however, been regarded by some commentators as less 'sharp' than that of Mark, and thus as drawing back from the radical implications which Mark will make explicit in v. 19. Thus J. D. G. Dunn states that the inclusion of the three distinctive features of the Marcan saying (οὐδὲν . . . ἔξωθεν . . . δύναται . . .) 'makes the *rejection* of the Jewish food laws an inevitable corollary for the person who holds this view', while Jesus' saying in its original form was 'less radical and more ambiguous than Mark has it, a saying which could be most straightforwardly rendered as Matthew has in fact rendered it'.[37] While it may be granted that οὐδέν, ἔξωθεν, and δύναται add to the rhetorical force of the pronouncement, it is not clear that the Matthean form is any more 'ambiguous': the principle that defilement comes from inside and not from outside is equally clear, and indeed Matthew's specific mention of what goes into and comes out of *the mouth* might rather be said to make the application to the food laws even more 'inevitable'. Mark has certainly made a more explicit comment on the implications of Jesus' παραβολή in v. 19, but in the basic saying itself neither evangelist leaves any room for ambiguity.

17 Following the pattern established in 4:10-12, 33-34, after the public proclamation of the παραβολή comes the private explanation to his disciples, and the double phrase εἰς οἶκον, ἀπὸ τοῦ ὄχλου emphasises the change of audience, just as κατὰ μόνας did in 4:10 and κατ' ἰδίαν in 4:34. Also as in 4:10, the initiative for the explanation comes from a question by the disciples — indeed, Jesus' response in v. 18 suggests that he felt that the point was too obvious to need any explanation. For the meaning of παραβολή, and its appropriateness especially in this polemical context, see above on 3:23; 4:1-34 (introduction); 4:1-2.

18a καὶ ὑμεῖς indicates that the disciples at least should have been able to understand the παραβολή. But their failure to grasp the significance of Jesus'

---

37. J. D. G. Dunn, *Jesus, Paul and the Law,* 37-60; quotations from pp. 41, 51. It is intriguing that S. Westerholm, *Jesus,* 147 (n. 109), comes to precisely the opposite conclusion: 'Mt. has restated the logion in a less ambiguous manner'.

ministry is now, in contrast with 3:31-35; 4:11-12, an increasingly prominent theme of the narrative, highlighted in 6:52 and further developed in 8:17-21, and one which threatens to put them on a level with the uncomprehending crowds with whom they were so sharply contrasted in 4:11-12. What differentiates them is not an inherent ability to grasp spiritual truth, but the fact that they are privileged to receive special instruction from Jesus.

18b-19 The first part of the 'explanation' virtually repeats the words of the first half of the original pronouncement in v. 15. Verse 19 goes on to provide an earthy account of what happens to external things (food) when they go inside the body: their temporary stay is only in the κοιλία (the stomach, representing the digestive system as a whole), from which they are discarded into the ἀφεδρών ('latrine', a rare word). The implication is that they make no contact with the part of the person which really matters, and this is described as the καρδία, as opposed to the κοιλία. Many languages use the names of physical organs to denote aspects of personality, but there is some flexibility as to what metaphorical force each organ carries, not only between different languages but even within the same language. In Greek even the κοιλία can occasionally be used for a person's 'inner being' in a way not dissimilar to καρδία (see especially Jn. 7:38; cf. LXX Ps. 39[40]:9; Pr. 20:27; Hab. 3:16), but more normally the κοιλία represents the less spiritual aspect of a person (Rom. 16:18; 1 Cor. 6:13; Phil. 3:19). 'Heart' is the term most commonly used in biblical literature for the essential personality. Whereas in English 'heart' tends to connote emotion, in both Hebrew and Greek it conveys equally, and perhaps more strongly, the spiritual and intellectual processes, including the will. It refers to what makes people what they really are, their individuality. It is thus particularly with the heart that a person relates to God, and a purported relationship with God which bypasses the heart is a mockery. It is then the heart, in this sense, which Jesus declares to be unaffected by what comes in from outside. Food is of merely nutritional significance, and has in itself no bearing on a person's relationship with God.[38]

19c The syntax clearly marks out καθαρίζων πάντα τὰ βρώματα as a parenthetical editorial comment, since there is no masculine singular subject within the reported speech to which it can relate (hence the emendations found in some MSS, representing attempts to 'correct' the syntax by those who failed to recognise the nature of the clause; see Textual Note). The subject therefore is Jesus (the subject of λέγει, v. 18a), whom Mark thus interprets as 'cleansing all food' in the sense of declaring that it is no longer to be regarded as ritually 'unclean'. This is, as we noted above, a natural, indeed inevitable, deduction both from the principle stated by Jesus in v. 15 and from its further elaboration in vv. 18b-19b where the

---

38. For a comparable and more dramatically expressed contrast between outward and inward purity see the intriguing (and possibly authentic?) account in *P.Oxy.* 840 of an encounter in the temple between Jesus and his disciples and 'a certain Pharisee, a chief priest called Levi'. Text in Henn.-Schn., 1.93-94; cf. my *Evidence,* 69-70.

progress of the food is shown to have no effect on the καρδία. The revolutionary significance of this declaration, and its relevance to the relations between Jews and Gentiles in the early years of the Christian movement, have been considered in the introduction to this pericope as a whole.

20-23 A new introductory formula, ἔλεγεν δὲ ὅτι, further confirms the parenthetical nature of v. 19c, after which the discourse needs to be reintroduced. But while there has been a literary break, the thought flows on continuously since vv. 18-19 have completed the 'exposition' of only the first half of Jesus' παραβολή, the rejection of the concept of defilement by 'what goes in'; vv. 20-23 now develop the more positive message of the second half, concerning the importance of 'what comes out'. Unlike the things which do not defile because they do not make contact with the καρδία, the really defiling things are those which actually originate *in* the καρδία. They are described first by the broad term οἱ διαλογισμοὶ οἱ κακοί, which directly governs the verb ἐκπορεύονται, after which a long list of nouns follow in apposition, spelling out what form the διαλογισμοὶ κακοί might take. 'Bad thoughts' (διαλογισμός can carry a more purposive sense than merely 'thinking'; cf. BAGD, 186a, 'evil machinations') therefore serves as an umbrella term for all the more specific vices which follow, some of which are expressed as actions rather than thoughts or words, but all of which originate in the καρδία, the seat of thought and will. All these vices are therefore ἔσωθεν, and thus represent the real character of the person from whom they issue. It is such moral qualities and their practical outworking which destroy a person's relationship with God, not the 'external' matter of which is eaten. 'Defilement', then, is seen exclusively in moral terms.[39]

The vice list is presented with gusto. Where Matthew has six items, Mark has twelve. Matthew's more restrained list approximates quite closely to the second table of the decalogue, but Mark's, while including most of the same items (but not the echo of the ninth commandment in Matthew's ψευδομαρτυρίαι), ranges far and wide. The effect is in the cumulative impression of so many 'bad thoughts' rather than in each taken individually, and detailed comment seriatim is scarcely necessary, though a few comments will be added below.

One curious feature of the list is that while all Matthew's nouns are plural, in Mark the first six are plural and the other six are singular. It may help to account for this feature if we note that some of the nouns in the first half of the list (and arguably all those in Matthew's shorter list) represent specific, and therefore repeatable, acts — κλοπαί, φόνοι, μοιχεῖαι — , while those in the second half (none of which except βλασφημία appears in Matthew) denote vices in the abstract — δόλος, ἀσέλγεια, etc. But in fact the distribution is not so simple, since the first half also includes πορνεῖαι, πλεονεξίαι, and πονηρίαι, all of which

---

39. Belo, 143-44, rightly warns against the 'bourgeois' tendency to express the contrast too simply in terms of 'a religion of the heart, of interiority', since that which is 'inside' is revealed by 'coming out' in moral choices and actions. The message is rather, he suggests, that 'we must not *cut off* the inside from the outside'.

would more naturally occur in the singular as denoting vices of character, like the nouns which follow. It is true that πορνεῖαι occurs also in the parallel list in Matthew (where all the nouns are plural), where the plural may be understood unusually (as also perhaps in 1 Cor. 7:2) of individual acts of sexual misconduct rather than of the concept in the abstract; πονηρίαι also occurs in Acts 3:26, where the plural refers probably to the various ways in which 'wickedness' may be manifested.[40] But both these plural uses are exceptional, and for πλεονεξία the plural seems even more unnatural. Mark's division of the list into equal halves of plural and singular nouns seems more a matter of rhetoric, artificially imposed, than a response to the natural meaning of the individual nouns. Singular and plural are similarly combined in the vice lists in Gal. 5:19-21 and 2 Cor. 12:20.

The first part of the list reflects (though less clearly than that of Matthew) some of the commandments of the decalogue: κλοπαί, φόνοι, and μοιχεῖαι represent the eighth, sixth, and seventh commandments respectively, πορνεῖαι may be seen as a further extension of the seventh, and πλεονεξίαι relates loosely to the tenth. Beyond that point the list does not seem to reflect a particular source, but is simply a gathering up of some of the more obvious ways in which διαλογισμοὶ κακοί are manifested in human conduct. Many other such lists of vices (and virtues) occur in Jewish and pagan ethical literature, as well as elsewhere in the NT (notably Gal. 5:19-21; cf. also, among others, Rom. 1:29-31; 1 Cor. 6:9-10; Col. 3:5, 8; 1 Tim. 1:9-10; 2 Tim. 3:2-5; Tit. 3:3; 1 Pet. 4:3);[41] the technique is familiar, but there is no reason to see any one or more of these lists as providing a specific model for Mark.

Most of the terms occur in other lists of vices in the NT, and cause no surprise in this list. An unusual feature is ὀφθαλμὸς πονηρός, an idiomatic expression for envy or lack of generosity (Mt. 20:15; cf. Dt. 15:9; Pr. 22:9 [Heb.], etc.; the play on words in Mt. 6:22-23 depends on this sense of the phrase, together with the connotation of generosity in ἁπλοῦς). The final term, ἀφροσύνη, is rather unexpected, as 'foolishness' may not seem to us to be a *moral* failure in the same category as the rest. In OT wisdom literature, however, the 'fool' is regularly bracketed with the 'wicked', and his foolishness consists in his wrong attitude to God which prevents him from knowing how to behave properly; there is a similarly moral/spiritual connotation in the use of ἄφρων in, e.g., Lk. 12:20; Eph. 5:17-18.

As they stand, these verses appear to assume that all that comes out of every person is evil, and thus to set out a very radical view of the 'total depravity' of humanity. But that is to read them out of context. The discussion is of what does and does not defile, and so only those things are mentioned. One might paraphrase, 'Insofar as a person is defiled, it is not by what goes in, but by the

40. See BDF, 142: 'The plural of abstract expressions frequently serves in poetry and in (elevated?) prose in a way foreign to us as a designation of concrete phenomena.'
41. See further *DNTT,* 3.928-29.

things that come out, such as . . .'. That good things may also come out of the heart is neither affirmed nor denied by these verses; that is a different subject.

THE MISSION EXTENDED
TO NEIGHBOURING PEOPLES (7:24–8:10)

The debate about purity has raised the question of how far, if at all, the mission of Jesus has a relevance beyond the community of Israel, whose observance of the Mosaic food laws was an effective practical barrier to social contact with those who did not observe them. Mark's specific deduction that Jesus' teaching has 'made all food clean' signals a radically new approach which will in due time make possible the integration of Jews and Gentiles into a single community of discipleship. This new perspective is now reflected in the narrative, which sees Jesus move deliberately outside Jewish territory. His initial intention is apparently not to engage in a 'Gentile mission' as such but simply to remain incognito (7:24), but events soon dictate otherwise and he responds, even if at first reluctantly, to Gentile needs. The first pericope in particular highlights the racial issue, as Jesus 'debates' with the Syrophoenician woman the basis on which the 'children's bread' can properly be enjoyed also by the 'dogs', and shortly afterwards a second feeding miracle, in all essentials repeating the pattern of the first, quite literally makes that bread available to a wider, Gentile, community. Thus the Jewish messianic banquet is enjoyed also, if on a slightly diminished scale, by the neighbouring Gentiles.

The widely held view that there is a deliberate focus on the Gentiles in this section, as presented both by Mark and by Matthew (it is part of Luke's 'Great Omission'), depends on the cumulative effect of a number of features of the narrative. First, there are the geographical movements recorded. Jesus 'gets up and goes away from there' (ἐκεῖθεν ἀναστὰς ἀπῆλθεν; cf. 1:35, where a similar phrase again indicates a widening of the sphere of mission), i.e., from the house mentioned in 7:17, the Galilean location of which was indicated by the arrival at Gennesaret in 6:53, and moves north into Phoenicia (τὰ ὅρια Τύρου, 7:24). When he returns southwards from there it is διὰ Σιδῶνος and ἀνὰ μέσον τῶν ὁρίων Δεκαπόλεως, a distinctively Gentile area to the east of the lake (7:31), and the remaining action is apparently located there until the eventual return in 8:10 to the unfortunately unidentifiable Δαλμανουθά (see on 8:10). There they are back in Jewish territory, to judge by the presence of Pharisees (8:11), but soon they are back on the lake en route first for Bethsaida (just across the river from Galilee) and then for the thoroughly pagan area of Caesarea Philippi. The first (Galilean) act of the drama thus in fact ends with a deliberate extension of Jesus' area of activity outside the Jewish sphere.[42]

---

42. See P. J. Achtemeier, *JBL* 89 (1970) 265-91 and *JBL* 91 (1972) 198-221, for the suggestion that 6:45–8:26 contains a pre-Marcan grouping of five miracles all set outside Jewish territory,

To these geographical indications we may add the specific identification of the woman in 7:24-30 as Ἑλληνίς, Συροφοινίκισσα τῷ γένει (cf. Matthew's even more racially loaded Χαναναία), with the consequent discussion of the rights of Gentile 'dogs'. Another incidental indication may be found in the reference in 8:8 to σπυρίδες, a more general term for baskets as opposed to the more specifically Jewish κόφινοι of 6:43. Matthew makes the context of a Jewish healer in a Gentile setting even clearer by having the crowds glorify 'the God of Israel' (Mt. 15:31).

Mark has, of course, depicted Jesus in Gentile territory before, in his visit to the land of the Gerasenes (5:1-20), and he has told us that the crowd following Jesus in Galilee included people from Idumaea and from around Tyre and Sidon (3:8). But those were Gentile touches in an essentially Jewish story. Now the Gentile focus is more pronounced and deliberate, and the issue of the boundaries of the people of God is coming more explicitly to the surface. It is an issue which by Mark's time had become one of the most burning questions in the development of the early Christian movement. Granted that Jesus was the Messiah of Israel, what did this mean for his relevance to the rest of the world?

A Gentile Woman (7:24-30)

TEXTUAL NOTES

24. The inclusion of καὶ Σιδῶνος after Τύρου, while very widely attested, is best understood as an assimilation to the familiar joint designation in Mt. 15:21, possibly also influenced by the mention of Sidon along with Tyre in 7:31 (where again the reading of the majority offers a simple Τύρου καὶ Σιδῶνος against the reading Τύρου alone [better supported there than here] followed by διὰ Σιδῶνος).

28. The inclusion of ναί in the majority of MSS is generally accounted for as a further assimilation to Matthew. But its strong attestation suggests the alternative possibility that it was omitted from the tradition represented by P[45] D W etc. because it was misunderstood as turning the woman's reply into a meek acceptance of Jesus' words (which it certainly is not) rather than, as it should be read, a firm repudiation of his οὐκ ἔστιν καλόν. The substitution of ἀλλά after κύριε in D suggests such a misunderstanding. I therefore think it more likely that ναί belongs to the original text in Mark, as in Matthew.

This remarkable story of another abortive attempt to 'retreat' from the scene of action and conflict (cf. 6:31-34) leaves many readers uncomfortable, since it suggests that Jesus was genuinely reluctant to help the woman, and was only

designed to balance five Jewish miracles in 4:35–6:44, each group beginning with a sea-crossing miracle and including a feeding miracle. See above, p. 220. The theory leaves certain loose ends, but is based on a sound observation of the changed focus in this part of Mark's narrative.

persuaded to do so by her persistence and debating skill, as a grudging concession rather than as a matter of principle. In Matthew's version, with its more marked tone of reluctance and even rejection, and its apparently even more 'racist' language, the problem becomes more acute. But it is hard to believe that Mark would have recorded the story at this point in his gospel if he saw it as anything less than a strong affirmation of Jesus' openness to the Gentiles; he has after all already recorded Jesus' positive response to an even more severe case of demon possession in a Gentile in 5:1-20. This pericope follows the liberating principle of 7:15, 19, and leads on to further acts of healing and relief apparently among Gentile people. Within that sequence this pericope marks the further opening of the door rather than an attempt to swing it shut again.

Misunderstandings of the pericope spring largely from the failure to read it as a whole. It is a dialogue within which the individual sayings function only as parts of the whole, and are not intended to carry the weight of independent exegesis on their own. The whole encounter builds up to the totally positive conclusion of vv. 29-30, while the preceding dialogue serves to underline the radical nature of this new stage in Jesus' ministry into which he has allowed himself to be 'persuaded' by the woman's realism and wit. He appears like the wise teacher who allows, and indeed incites, his pupil to mount a victorious argument against the foil of his own reluctance. He functions as what in a different context might be called 'devil's advocate', and is not disappointed to be 'defeated' in argument. As a result the reader is left more vividly aware of the reality of the problem of Jew-Gentile relations, and of the importance of the step Jesus here takes to overcome it. The woman's 'victory' in the debate is a decisive watershed as a result of which the whole future course of the Christian movement is set not on the basis of Jewish exclusivism but of sharing the 'children's bread'.

The mention of 'bread' again (cf 6:35-44, 52), shortly to be taken up in a further feeding story, this time for the benefit of Gentiles (8:1-10), and then made the subject of Jesus' rebuke of his disciples' lack of understanding in 8:14-21, suggests that this pericope forms part of a developing 'bread' motif. Bread here is an image for the blessings of the Messiah's ministry to his own people and, following on from this incident, among the Gentiles. In that connection the reader may well be led to ponder on the contrast between the disciples' failure to understand about 'bread' (6:52, to be picked up again in 8:14-21) and this Gentile woman's ability to understand and turn to her advantage Jesus' bread metaphor. If so, this pericope serves to undergird the developing Marcan theme of the disciples' lack of insight which we noted at 6:52, and which has just been repeated in 7:18.

The incident is, formally speaking, an exorcism, though the dialogue and its implications are ultimately more important than the specific problem solved. Whereas previous exorcism stories have focused on the unique authority of Jesus in direct confrontation with the resident demon(s), in this one the cure is effected at a distance and without any personal contact between Jesus and either the demon or the possessed person. This unusual feature may be connected with the Gentile context, since the only other examples of healing at a distance in the gospels (Mt. 8:5-13/Lk. 7:1-10; Jn. 4:46-54) probably also involve a Gentile subject or subjects. The inappropriateness of the Jewish Messiah entering a Gentile house (so most obviously Mt. 8:7-8, punctuating v. 7 as a question as I am sure it must be) thus further underscores the racial element. The distant cure also, of course, serves to emphasise in a new way the authority of Jesus, whose word alone, without his physical presence, has power to dismiss the demon.

24 Apart from the Gentile location, this pericope starts in a way already familiar in Mark's narrative: Jesus wishes to get away from public attention (cf. 1:35; 3:13; 4:10; 6:31-32), uses a 'house' for the purpose (cf. 1:29; 2:1; 3:20; 7:17), but is unable to escape those in need (cf. 1:32-33, 36-37, 45; 2:2; 3:7-12, 20; 6:33-34). And after 3:8 we cannot be surprised that even in τὰ ὅρια Τύρου his fame has preceded him. Mark does not tell us that Jesus visited Tyre itself, merely its ὅρια, the administrative district for which it was responsible. Mark's Jesus is not generally a frequenter of cities, still less pagan ones, but remains out in the countryside (cf. 8:27). Tyre, whose territory adjoined northern Galilee, had long been an important trading city. It had close links with Palestine, particularly under Herod the Great, and its coinage was widely circulated there; indeed, it exercised considerable economic dominance over the neighbouring area of Galilee (Stock, 210-13). But it was clearly foreign territory, and Josephus, *Ap.* 1.70, describes the Tyrians as 'notoriously our bitterest enemies'.

25-26 Few of those who approached Jesus had so much against them, from an orthodox Jewish point of view. She was, first of all, a woman, and therefore one with whom a respectable Jewish teacher should not associate. She was a Gentile, as the double designation Ἑλληνίς, Συροφοινίκισσα emphasises. And her daughter's condition might be expected to inspire fear and/or disgust, while the 'uncleanness' of the demon suggests ritual impurity. That Jesus ultimately responded to a request from such a suppliant, and even that he was prepared to engage her in serious dialogue, is typical of his unconcern for convention when it stood in the way of his mission.

Following the discussion of purity in vv. 1-23 Mark's regular term for a demon, πνεῦμα ἀκάθαρτον, here has special force — it was not only her racial origin which made her 'unclean'. While Ἕλλην, like Ἑλληνιστής, might in a different context refer to language and culture rather than strictly to racial origin, there is no doubt that here it carries its normal biblical connotation of Gentile (as opposed to Jewish), and the term Συροφοινίκισσα (the prefix Συρο- distinguishes the Phoenicians of the Levant from those of North Africa around Carthage) reinforces the point. That such a woman chose to approach a Jewish healer, and even fell at his feet, indicates either desperation or a remarkable insight into the wider significance of Jesus' ministry (and into the biblical pattern of salvation history). The subsequent dialogue suggests at least an element of the latter.

27 Jesus' response, though nowhere near as brutal as in Matthew, is certainly not diplomatic. It takes the form of a παραβολή, the form of teaching we have been taught to associate with οἱ ἔξω (4:11). The whole tone of the sentence is negative to the point of offensiveness, and suggests that Jesus has no intention of helping the woman. The use of κυνάρια seems to add gratuitously to the offence, since dogs were regarded by the Jews, and probably equally by their Semitic neighbours, as unclean animals. Biblical references to dogs (except in the story of Tobit) are always hostile. To refer to a human being as a 'dog' is deliberately offensive or dismissive (cf. 2 Sa. 16:9; Ps. 22:16; Phil. 3:2); Jews typically referred to Gentiles as dogs. The diminutive form (used in biblical literature only in this pericope), perhaps indicates the status of the dogs in Jesus' image as dogs of the house rather than of the yard, but it does not remove the harshness of picturing Gentiles en masse as 'dogs' as opposed to 'children'.[43] It is the sort of language a Gentile might expect from a Jew, but to find it in a saying of Jesus is shocking.

The inclusion of πρῶτον softens the blow a little, in that it suggests that there may still be a legitimate place for the dogs after the children have been satisfied (χορτάζομαι [see 6:42] indicates to eat one's fill, not just have a taste), but the Gentiles remain at the end of the queue. πρῶτον thus suggests the same salvation history which Paul declares in Rom. 1:16, Ἰουδαίῳ τε πρῶτον καὶ Ἕλληνι. This was, of course, the actual sequence of the Christian mission in the apostolic period, and indeed as a salvation-historical programme it recapitulates the biblical concept of mission based on the special choice of Israel as the centre from which God's blessings will spread out to other nations, as it is expressed from Gn. 12:2-3 onwards (cf. Is. 2:2-4; 49:6, etc.). But as a response to the Gentile woman's request it is very harsh, and does not encourage her to expect help at the present time. At best it is 'a challenge to the woman to justify her request' (Hooker). Fortunately she is equal to the challenge, and persists where many would have capitulated.[44]

28 Jesus' image (and his inclusion of πρῶτον) have given the woman the cue she needs, and enable her, on the basis of his own saying, to refute his οὐκ ἔστιν καλόν and replace it with a defiant Ναί, κύριε (see Textual Note) — 'Yes, it *is* right'. By using the vocative κύριε (its only appearance in Mark, in striking contrast with Matthew) the woman recognises Jesus' authority and her

---

43. Note the presence of several diminutives in this pericope: θυγάτριον (v. 25), δαιμόνιον (vv. 26, 29, 30), κυνάριον (vv. 27, 28), ψιχίον (v. 28), παιδίον (v. 28). This feature probably reflects the style of popular storytelling, and suggests that it would be inappropriate to find any significant difference of meaning in any one of the diminutive forms used (contra Gundry, 374-75).

44. Gundry, 373-74, suggests that Jesus' image is not, in this context, to be understood racially, but as his objection to being diverted from his plan to spend time teaching his disciples (which Gundry finds implied in the desire to remain unnoticed, v. 24) to attend to a demon-possessed child. This imaginative reconstruction seems to do little justice to the wider Gentile context noted above and to the specifically geographical and racial terms used in vv. 24 and 26, and unnecessarily pits Matthew against Mark in their understanding of the story.

dependence on his help, but need not convey any more specific theological insight; it is an appropriate address to a distinguished stranger. The following words, even though not introduced by a γάρ as in Matthew, express the foundation for her confidence. Granted that the children have priority, the dogs, too (καί), have a legitimate share in the food available. Jesus' own image is thus pressed to its full extent, and provides the basis for her request to be granted, not refused. It is a remarkable twist to the argument, and one which displays as much humility on the woman's part as it does shrewdness. She does not dispute the lower place which Jesus' saying assumes for the Gentiles, and even accepts without protest the offensive epithet 'dog', but insists that the dogs, too, must have their day. Putting it more theologically, the mission of the Messiah of Israel, while it must of course begin with Israel, cannot be confined there. The Gentiles may have to wait, but they are not excluded from the benefits which the Messiah brings. On this basis, she is bold enough to pursue her request; even the crumbs will be enough.

29-30 Διὰ τοῦτον τὸν λόγον makes it clear that the woman's response, and the attitude which it reveals, has changed Jesus' apparent intention. It is of course impossible now to be sure on the basis of the printed text alone whether his words were designed to provoke such a response, or whether he genuinely did intend to refuse her request and was persuaded by her argument. Much may have been conveyed by tone of voice and gesture.[45] But Mark, by placing the incident in the setting of the opening up of Jesus' ministry to the Gentiles (see pp. 294-95), suggests that his initial reluctance should be taken with a pinch of salt (see introductory comments on this pericope). It is, however, the woman's remarkable saying, whether deliberately evoked by Jesus or not, which has secured her request. The dialogue, rather than the exorcism, remains the focus of interest in the pericope. No account of the exorcism is offered, and no word of command recorded; the removal of the demon is simply spoken of as already a past event (ἐξελήλυθεν).

A Healing in Decapolis (7:31-37)

TEXTUAL NOTES

31. See the textual note on 7:24 above. Here the reading Τύρου καὶ Σιδῶνος is less well supported, and is best seen as a further reversion to the familiar biblical pair of names. The difficult geography of a journey from the region of Tyre to Decapolis via Sidon (which is in almost the opposite direction) would be another reason for 'correction' by a scribe who knew something of the geography of the area.

---

45. The point is well brought out by J. Camery-Hoggatt, *Irony*, 150-51, commenting on v. 27: 'To read only what lies "on the surface of it" is to misread it. It is instead to be read as a bit of tongue-in-cheek. . . . It is peirastic irony, . . . a form of verbal challenge intended to test the other's response. It may in fact declare the opposite of the speaker's actual intention.'

35. The presence or absence of εὐθέως makes little difference to the sense, since with the striking exception of the healing at Bethsaida in 8:22-26 Mark leaves us to assume that all Jesus' healings were immediate. Εὐθύς (-έως) is such a common feature of Mark's style that it could well be original before ἠνοίγησαν. But since there is no likely reason for its deliberate omission, perhaps it is better to treat it as an addition to the text in order to magnify the miracle. Εὐθύς (-έως) occurs instead before ἐλύθη in ℵ and a few other MSS, and is printed by Aland there and not before ἠνοίγησαν; this variation in position makes it the more likely that it is an addition to the original text.

Jesus' journey outside Galilee now leads him apparently (see on v. 31 for the obscure geography) back to the Decapolis, the largely non-Jewish region to the east of the lake of Galilee, which was also the scene of the spectacular exorcism in 5:1-20. This time, however, it is a physical abnormality that is cured. The incident, recorded only by Mark, is notable not only for its non-Jewish location, but also for the use of saliva for healing (cf. also 8:23), for the recording of Jesus' Aramaic word of healing (cf. the formula remembered in 5:41), and for the addition of a further complaint (deaf and dumb) to the list of those he has already healed. In the light of the vision of Is. 35:5-6, 'Then the ears of the deaf shall be unstopped . . . and the tongue of the speechless sing for joy', such a healing is loaded with eschatological significance. The actual method of healing is described in more detail than usual, and the crowd reaction in v. 37 suggests that this was a particularly impressive form of healing. In 9:17, 25 another case of deafness and dumbness (along with other more spectacular symptoms) is attributed to demon possession, but here there is no hint of the language of exorcism; the healing is effected by touch (which is not mentioned in any of Jesus' exorcisms, except after the exorcism has been completed, 9:27) and by a word of command addressed not to a demon but to the patient himself.[46]

Another prominent feature of this story is the already familiar theme of Jesus' aim to avoid public notice, and his failure to do so. He not only demands silence (v. 36), but also takes the patient away from the crowd before healing him (v. 33), yet the result is again yet more public announcement and admiration (vv. 36-37). These have been repeated themes already in Mark's story (for the 'secrecy' see 1:34, 44; 3:12; 5:37, 43 and for its failure 1:45; 2:1-2; 3:7ff.; 6:33). But there is in this respect a curious tension between this incident and the previous visit to Decapolis, when Jesus unusually instructed the cured demoniac to tell his own (Gentile) people about what had happened (5:19-20). Perhaps the difference is to be explained by the further development of Jesus' mission since the Gerasene incident, so that now even in Gentile territory there is danger in too much publicity; or perhaps the part of Decapolis in which this incident is set is to be understood as having a more significant Jewish population. Mark does not explain, or apparently even notice, the tension, so that we can only speculate as to its basis.

46. J. M. Hull, *Magic*, 78-82, argues that this case does involve demon possession, but his arguments depend on quite imaginatively 'reading between the lines' of the Marcan account.

This story is in a number of ways closely parallel to that in 8:22-26.[47] Both are set outside Galilee; in both the crowd asks for Jesus' help but he takes the patient away to heal him in private; in both he is recorded unusually as touching specifically the organs affected, and in both there is mention of the use of saliva. That both these stories, with their more detailed account of Jesus' healing method, are among the very few pericopes of Mark which do not appear in either Matthew or Luke, indicates perhaps either Mark's special interest in Jesus' healing technique or the discomfort of the other synoptists with the more 'earthy' (some would say 'magical') nature of the accounts (and their non-Jewish location?).

It is generally agreed (see ad loc.) that the story of the healing of the blind man at Bethsaida is intended by Mark to function as a symbolic introduction to the following account of the gradual enlightenment of the disciples, whereby their 'blindness' (8:17-18) is removed. It is therefore possible that this closely similar and equally elaborate story of the cure of deafness and dumbness has a similar function, symbolising the enabling of Jesus' disciples to hear and speak the word of God properly (see further below on v. 33). Many commentators adopt this interpretation, but it must be noted that there is far less direct encouragement for such an interpretation of this miracle than for the Bethsaida miracle, either in the surrounding wording or in the placing of this story within Mark's narrative.[48] It must be rather a matter of inference from the 'parallel' pericope.

31 If we accept the reading διὰ Σιδῶνος, the text describes a round-about journey which takes Jesus first northwards from the district of Tyre to that of Sidon, then back south to the Lake of Galilee, 'in the middle of the region of Decapolis'. Since the Decapolis reached up to the lake only at its south-east quarter, a route from the region of Sidon to the lake in the region of the Decapolis would involve a considerable detour to the east and south. All of this route would be through non-Jewish territory, but there is no obvious reason why Jesus should go on such a long journey through this largely desert region in order to regain the lake.[49] Mark's geographical terms may not be used with precision. It is possible that while Hippos (halfway along the east shore of the lake) was the most northerly city of the Decapolis adjoining the lake, popular language used the term for the whole largely Gentile area to the east of the Jordan inflow, around and south

---

47. The similarities are analysed by R. M. Fowler, *Loaves,* 105-8. See also M. A. Beavis, *Audience,* 122-24, for a structural comparison of the two incidents, and 114-26, 161-63 for a proposal as to a broader structural pattern embracing also the trial scenes and the Caesarea Philippi episode, which she suggests indicates a symbolic function in the two healing narratives. For the proposed symbolism see further, e.g., Cranfield, 254-55.

48. J. F. Williams, *Followers,* 129, sees the two healing narratives as together illustrating the rebuke of the disciples for being both blind and deaf in 8:17-18, but whereas the narrative sequence makes this highly likely for 8:22-26, the fact that this pericope precedes the rebuke makes it less easy for the reader to connect the two.

49. J. Sergeant, *Lion,* 61-62, suggests that 'if Jesus is being portrayed as an exile, giving Herod's Galilee as wide a berth as possible, the geography at 7:31 is exactly right'.

of Bethsaida, which was properly in the tetrarchy of Philip. The Decapolis was in any case more a league of cities than a defined geographical area, and surviving lists of the cities which composed it do not agree. Mark's terms may leave us geographically confused, but they convey clearly enough that Jesus, on his return to the lake from his journey into Phoenicia, remains outside properly Jewish territory rather than taking the more direct route to the Capernaum area. However and whyever he got there, Jesus is back in the Decapolis.[50]

32 This healing, like the preceding exorcism, is the result of an apparently unsolicited approach to Jesus by the local people, which suggests that his reputation as a healer was now strong in the Decapolis as well (as 5:20 might have led us to expect). κωφός is used in both secular and biblical Greek to mean either 'deaf' or 'dumb', or where appropriate both (the two conditions being not infrequently linked, on account of the difficulty of the congenitally deaf in learning to speak). Mark presumably uses κωφός here primarily in the sense of 'deaf', since he adds as a further complaint the term μογιλάλος, which is used either for complete inability to speak or for a serious speech impediment (μόγις means 'hardly', 'with difficulty').[51] The story makes it clear that the man was both deaf and dumb, since both treatment (v. 33) and cure (v. 35) are explicitly described in terms of both hearing and speech, and the crowd reaction focuses on both elements of the cure (v. 37). μογιλάλος is not used elsewhere in the NT, and in the LXX occurs only in Is. 35:6; in view of the likely influence of that passage of Isaiah in v. 37, it is probable that Mark's use of it here is also a deliberate allusion. The request for a cure is expressed simply as ἵνα ἐπιθῇ αὐτῷ τὴν χεῖρα, since this has been a standard feature of Jesus' healing method (but not of his exorcisms); see 1:31, 41; 5:23; 6:5; 8:25. As it turns out, Jesus' healing method in this case will prove to be more complex.

33 In the similar story of the healing of the blind man at Bethsaida (8:22-26) the same pattern occurs of a request from the crowd, after which Jesus takes the patient away and effects the cure in private. (Previously he has taken the disciples away on their own for instruction, 4:10; 6:31; 7:17; does the similar action in these two healings suggest a symbolic dimension, the restoration of physical hearing and sight representing the opening of the disciples' spiritual ears and eyes?) In each case also there follows a command not to divulge what has happened. Since both these events take place outside Galilee, this desire for secrecy is the more remarkable (see introductory comments on

50. H. Räisänen, *Secret,* 153-54, following D. A. Koch, *NTS* 29 (1983) 145-66, argues that to interpret the specific mention of the Decapolis as indicating a Gentile location is 'completely overinterpreting Mark's geography'. But Mark's use of so specific a term, following the equally specific Gentile location of vv. 24-30, suggests otherwise. Cf. its use in an equally clearly Gentile context in 5:20.

51. A variant μογγιλάλος occurs in a good number of (mostly later) MSS. It represents an even rarer term, referring to the quality of the voice as 'harsh' or 'hollow' rather than to unclear speech and is unlikely to be the true text in view of the echo of Is. 35:6 (unless, of course, the same reading is adopted there), and of the following narrative which speaks of the cure of dumbness.

this pericope). Bethsaida (the home of three of Jesus' inner circle of disciples, Jn 1:44) clearly had a significant Jewish population, and the same may have been true in this part of the Decapolis; in that case the secrecy here, as earlier in the gospel, may result from the danger of misdirected messianic enthusiasm. But in any case Jesus does not seem to have set out to be known primarily as a healer, and the desire to remain unnoticed (7:24) presumably still applies.[52] The next phase of Mark's story will see Jesus increasingly focusing his attention on the instruction of his disciples, with a corresponding reduction in public exposure and in healing miracles.

In previous healings Jesus' touch has been described only in general terms. Here (and again in 8:23, 25) he touches specifically the affected organs, and in each case saliva is used (as it is also in Jn. 9:6). This would not have been as surprising in the ancient Mediterranean world as it is to us; there are several ancient accounts of the use of saliva especially in curing blindness.[53] To debate whether this practice should be classed as magical or as purely medical is probably to draw too sharp a distinction, since folk medicine and magic ran close together. There are clearly magical stories where saliva is used as a curative agent,[54] but there are also mentions of its use in more normal medical practice (e.g., Galen, *On Natural Faculties* 3.7). The famous story told by Tacitus (*Hist.* 4.81) of how a blind man in Alexandria was cured by the saliva of the emperor Vespasian (to Vespasian's own surprise) implies that it was not saliva as such, but specifically the emperor's saliva, which was effective. Similarly here it is *Jesus'* saliva which cures; it is effective not in itself as a medical agent, but, like the touch of the hand, as it identifies with the powerful person of the healer. πτύσας ἥψατο probably means (as in Jn. 9:6) that Jesus applied the saliva with his hand, rather than that he spat directly onto the tongue. How far these specific contacts with the ears and tongue were the physical 'means' of healing, and how far a psychological assurance to the patient of Jesus' ability to heal, is a question which is probably both inappropriate and unanswerable. But physical contact is clearly more appropriate in the case of a man who would be unable to hear spoken words.

34 The story conveys the impression that it was rather Jesus' word of command which effected the cure. For looking up to heaven in a healing context cf. John 11:41. Like the upward look at the feeding of the five thousand, specifically mentioned in all four accounts (6:41 and parallels), it emphasises the divine dimension in Jesus' miraculous power. στενάζω, used only here in the gospels, is more surprising; it is sometimes seen as part of a magical healing routine, but probably for Mark serves, like the use of ὀργισθείς and ἐμβριμησάμενος in the healing of the leper (1:41, 43), to suggest Jesus' deep emotional

---

52. The general theme of secrecy offers a better explanation of Jesus' action here and in 8:23 than to attribute it to the healer's desire to prevent people from discovering his healing technique (especially the use of saliva, only in these two pericopes); so, e.g., Gnilka, 1.314.

53. Gundry, 389, offers a full list of primary sources and modern discussion on the subject.

54. See J. M. Hull, *Magic,* 76-78.

involvement. But the focal element in the cure is the word of command, recorded both in its Aramaic form and in translation (as in 5:41). Εφφαθα probably represents the Aramaic[55] ethpeel imperative, *'etpᵉtaḥ,* which has a reflexive sense: 'Open up!' If, as Mark's translation indicates, the form is singular, it is formally addressed to the man (who ought not to be able to hear it!) rather than to his ears, but in effect it is the ears which are commanded to function again. The use of Aramaic in a probably non-Jewish context is not particularly significant, since the language was widely spoken outside Jewish circles, but Mark's recording of the Aramaic form suggests a memory of an impressive command on the part of someone who was there, perhaps the patient himself, for whom this may have been the first word he had ever heard.

35 The effect is immediate (whether or not εὐθέως is included — see Textual Note), and both deafness and dumbness are cured at once.[56] Mark employs vivid language, both in using ἀκοαί where we might have expected ὦτα (presumably to emphasise the function of the ears rather than the physical organs as such) and in the image of the untying of the tongue (cf. our 'tongue-tied'). The addition of ἐλάλει ὀρθῶς suggests that the problem had been that the man's speech was unintelligible (as μογιλάλος, v. 32, probably also indicated).

36-37 For the direct disobedience to Jesus' call for silence cf. 1:44-45. This time the command is addressed not only to the patient but to the crowd who had brought him to Jesus for healing (v. 32), and who therefore, despite the privacy of the event itself (v. 33), would be well aware of what had happened. To expect to keep such a clearly miraculous event quiet was in any case a forlorn hope. The imperfects διεστέλλετο and ἐκήρυσσον suggest a protracted appeal for silence, and equally protracted disobedience.[57] The astonishment of the crowd (a regular feature of miracle stories; cf. 1:27-28; 2:12; 4:41; 5:15, 20, 42; 6:51) is here more dramatically expressed (including the hapax legomenon ὑπερπερισσῶς), and suggests that the healing of the deaf and dumb was a matter of particular amazement, for these are two of the elements in Isaiah's vision of the blessing which will result from God's own eschatological coming (Is. 35:5-6). The more general verdict καλῶς πάντα πεποίηκεν, pronounced by a presumably largely Gentile crowd, indicates that the Jewish Messiah is now meeting with wider approbation, and paves the way for a crowd of four thousand, some of them from a distance away, to follow him out into a deserted area in the next pericope.

---

55. The word has generally been understood as Aramaic, though some have argued that it is Hebrew (notably I. Rabinowitz, *ZNW* 53 [1962] 229-38; *JSS* 16 [1971] 151-56). The issue is apparently not capable of definitive resolution; see S. Morag, *JSS* 17 (1972) 198-202.

56. Cranfield, 253, argues from the upward look, groan, and use of physical manipulation and saliva that this story, like 8:22-26, describes a cure 'accomplished with difficulty and not instantaneously'. This is, to say the least, not obvious from Mark's text.

57. J. F. Williams, *Followers,* 122-23, takes the imperfects as generalising beyond this specific incident: 'Mark leaves the impression that Jesus repeatedly commanded silence concerning his healing miracles and that the command was repeatedly disobeyed.'

Feeding of Four Thousand (8:1-10)

TEXTUAL NOTES

7. The various readings (αὐτά or ταῦτα; order of participle and pronoun; omission of pronoun) do not affect the sense. εὐλογήσας αὐτά is probably the best attested. The omission of the pronoun may have been caused by discomfort over the inclusion of a direct object (the fish) rather than leaving it to be assumed that God is 'blessed', though the same idiom occurs clearly in Lk. 9:16; 1 Cor. 10:16. εὐχαριστήσας in D is probably an assimilation to v. 6, aided by an assumed eucharistic interpretation.

10. The various forms of the name Δαλμανουθά, the different ways of designating it as a destination (τὰ μέρη, τὸ ὄρος, τὰ ὅρια), and the substitution of different forms of a more familiar name (Μαγεδάν, Μαγδαλά, both found in the textual tradition of the parallel Mt. 15:39) all result naturally from the presence in the text of an otherwise unknown name. τὰ μέρη Δαλμανουθά is the reading which best explains the rest.

The geography has been discussed above, p. 294. The last-named location in the narrative is the Decapolis (v. 31), and Mark leaves us to assume the same scene until the next geographical note in v. 10. It is thus a reasonable assumption that this narrative takes place on the eastern side of the lake, after which they return in 8:10 by boat to the Jewish territory on the western shore (where Pharisees are again in evidence), and then in 8:13 return in the opposite direction, duly arriving at Bethsaida (at the north end of the eastern shore) in 8:22. Apart from the obscurity of Δαλμανουθά (see on v. 10), this makes a coherent sequence of journeys. It is on this basis that the present pericope has been understood by most commentators as recording an incident in the primarily non-Jewish territory of the eastern shore, and thus as continuing the theme of Jesus' ministry among Gentiles. The wording of the pericope does not in itself demand a Gentile setting (the use in v. 8 of a different term for baskets from that used in 6:43 is at best a hint in this direction); it is its place in the developing plot of the gospel which leads to that conclusion, together with the question why else Mark should have chosen to include a second feeding miracle (on a reduced scale) which so closely duplicates the pattern of the feeding of the five thousand (6:31-44).

Given a Gentile location, however, the second feeding miracle fits well into Mark's plan, as the third of a set of miracles (an exorcism, a healing, and a nature miracle) which extend the mission of the Messiah of Israel for the benefit also of neighbouring peoples. The narrative thus fills out Jesus' discussion with the Syrophoenician woman about allowing the dogs a share in the children's bread, and in this incident the 'bread' is quite literally shared. That discussion accepted that the Gentiles' share might be only 'scraps', and perhaps it is for this reason that Mark so carefully records a different set of statistics for this feeding: fewer people (four thousand instead of five thousand) fed with more loaves (seven instead of five) and 'a few small fish' but with less food left over (seven baskets instead of twelve). The numbers are meant to be noticed (see vv. 19-21).[1]

In 6:44 Mark stated specifically that the five thousand were ἄνδρες. Here (unlike Matthew, 15:38) he is not specific, and we are left to assume a mixed crowd. If there was at least a potentially militaristic tone to the feeding of the five thousand (see introductory comments on 6:31-44), we are given no encouragement to see such a dimension here, where a Gentile crowd could not have had the same nationalistic motivation.

In other ways, however, the stories run closely parallel, with the motifs of the hungry crowd, Jesus' compassion, the incredulity of the disciples at the thought of feeding such a crowd in the wilderness, the question πόσους ἔχετε ἄρτους;, the command to the crowd to recline on the ground, the 'eucharistic' sequence of verbs (λαβών, εὐχαριστήσας/εὐλογήσεν, [κατ-]ἔκλασεν, ἐδίδου . . . ἵνα παρατιθῶσιν), the crowd's eating and being filled (ἐχορτάσθησαν), the baskets of fragments, and the recording of the number in the crowd. Both in their content and in their narration the two accounts are clearly twins.

Many commentators have therefore assumed that the two pericopes are variant accounts of a single original event. Most suggest that two versions of the story (differing completely over the numbers of people, loaves, and baskets) had already developed before Mark wrote his gospel. But this would be an unusual way for oral tradition to operate, since its normal tendency is to preserve specific details like numbers unchanged while varying the 'scenery'; the two feeding accounts in Mark show precisely the opposite phenomenon, a closely similar story-line but with all the numbers changed. Since the numbers are emphasised in each account, it is hard to believe that tradition would have treated them with such negligence. Furthermore, it is not easy to envisage a situation within the mid-first-century church which would allow Mark to remain unaware that only one such incident had in fact occurred.

An alternative view is that Mark received only a single account, and, presumably in order to make the point that the blessings of Israel were available also to the Gentiles, created a second story, retaining the essential framework but changing all the numbers. But this too hardly rings true to Mark's method. Whereas Matthew does sometimes present what appear to be doublets of the same story (Mt. 9:27-31 with 20:29-34; 9:32-34 with 12:22-24; 12:38-39 with 16:1-4), this is not character-

---

1. It has been suggested that there is a more direct significance in the numbers, in that five (books of the law) and twelve (tribes of Israel) are clearly 'Jewish' numbers, while four (corners of the earth) and seven (completeness) point to a worldwide dimension to the Messiah's mission. Such suggestions are hard to prove or disprove, and the question which (if any) of Mark's readers would have been in a position to pick up the symbolism is equally unanswerable. Another ulterior motive behind the numbers is suggested by É. Trocmé, *Formation*, 181, following earlier commentators, who wonders whether the numbers of baskets in the two feedings represent the twelve apostles and the seven deacons of Acts 6, so that Mark is thus 'pleading for the rights of the Seven'. Trocmé claims, 'There would seem to be nothing against this conclusion.' Perhaps, but is there anything *for* it? For other imaginative interpretations of the number seven here see Guelich, 405; Gundry, 396-97.

istic of Mark elsewhere. Moreover, in 8:19-21 the two feeding miracles are commented on as separate events, carefully distinguished in detail, which does not look like the work of a man who was aware of only one such event.

It thus seems more economical to accept that there were two such incidents, separately remembered and passed down in tradition, but, naturally enough, told in increasingly similar terms as time went on, except only that the different sets of numbers were faithfully preserved. This would accord with the form-critical observation of the tendency of stories of the same type (most notably healing and exorcism stories) to assimilate to a standard narrative form while retaining their distinctive features in detail. The two feeding stories are perhaps more closely similar to one another than any other pair of miracles in any one gospel, but the combination of similarity of form with distinctiveness in detail rings true to the oral tradition process as we see it elsewhere in the gospels.[2]

The following detailed comments will focus on areas of difference from the feeding of the five thousand; for other details and more general issues see comments on 6:31-44 above.

1-3 πάλιν underlines Mark's belief that this was a sequel to an earlier and similar event, and alerts the reader to compare and contrast the two stories. There is no explicit mention of who the crowd consists of, nor (in contrast with 6:33-34) of how they have come to be with Jesus in an uninhabited area for a period of three days.[3] But preceding pericopes have given hints of Jesus' growing reputation as a healer even in non-Jewish areas (7:24, 32), and the wide dissemination of the story of the healing of the deaf and dumb man (7:36-37) must have had its effect. Mark does not say whether the three-day period has been spent in teaching or in healing, or in both, but to remain so long away from home and food supplies suggests a remarkable enthusiasm and persistence among this presumably largely Gentile crowd. The personal nature of their attachment to Jesus is emphasised by the phrase προσμένουσίν μοι, while ἀπολύσω αὐτούς assumes Jesus' control over their movements. ἀπὸ μακρόθεν does not necessarily indicate that the crowd includes people from other provinces;[4] even a day's journey within the Decapolis region would be too far after three days without food.[5]

---

2. A full discussion of the question whether there was one feeding miracle or two by J. Knackstedt, *NTS* 10 (1963/4) 309-35, concludes in favour of two. For a more recent and independent argument to the same effect see Gundry, 398-401. J.-M. Van Cangh in M. Sabbe (ed.), *Marc*, 337-41, argues, as do many others, for a pre-Marcan literary doublet.

3. The nominative ἡμέραι τρεῖς to denote duration (here and in Mt. 15:32) is strange. BDF, 144, label it a 'parenthetical nominative'. They offer a few parallels in expressions of time in the LXX as well as in papyri, but it remains an awkward and inelegant piece of Greek.

4. F. W. Danker, *JBL* 82 (1963) 215-16, argues that the phrase echoes the Jewish tendency to speak of Gentiles as those 'far off' (he instances Jos. 9:6, 9 and Is. 60:4), thus designating *some* of the crowd as Gentile. (See contra Gundry, 396.) This is a possible nuance, but the literal meaning of the phrase is entirely appropriate and adequate to the context.

5. The phrase ἐν τῇ ὁδῷ suggests to E. Best, *Disciples*, 192-93, that the feeding is to be understood as a metaphor for teaching, the essential provision needed for continuing on the 'way' of

4 The disciples' incredulity at the suggestion (not here, as in 6:37, a direct instruction) that food should be found for the crowd was natural enough in 6:37, but one might expect them to have learned from that experience.[6] Perhaps Mark simply uses the effective literary motif again without reflecting on how inappropriately it fits the second time.[7] But the failure of the disciples to learn from the events they witness and to recognise the new dimensions which Jesus' ministry involves will become an increasingly prominent theme in the next act of Mark's story, and it will be precisely the point of Jesus' rebuke to his disciples in 8:17-21 that they have failed to learn from repeated experience.[8] The sarcastic wording of their reaction, with χορτάσαι ἄρτων sharply juxtaposed to ἐπ' ἐρημίας, will be dramatically recalled when the same verb χορτάζω appears again in v. 8 to describe what has in fact been achieved there in the ἐρημία.

5-6 The exact repetition of the question πόσους ἔχετε ἄρτους; from 6:38 suggests a tone of almost humorous resignation: 'Here we go again!' The answer, though larger than last time, is no less ludicrously out of proportion to the size of the crowd. From this point on the story unfolds along just the same lines as last time, though without the vivid description of the picnicking crowd in neat divisions on the green grass. The use of εὐχαριστήσας rather than εὐλογήσας (which will, however, be used of the fish in the next verse) may indicate a desire to draw out the eucharistic significance of the feeding, but since the two verbs were virtually interchangeable in Jewish Greek usage, it may be no more than a stylistic variation.

7 In the previous story the fish were repeatedly mentioned at each stage. Here they occur only once, almost as an afterthought after the feeding with bread has already been recorded. They thus have their own separate 'blessing', and the story reads as if they formed a second course to the meal. Surprisingly no number is given for the fish this time; they are simply mentioned dis-

discipleship. But whereas later uses of the phrase in 8:27; 9:33; 10:32, 52 clearly refer to the 'way' of travelling with Jesus towards Jerusalem, here the ὁδός leads away from Jesus. The phrase is too weak a peg for such a metaphor, and the narrative does not require it. Similarly, to read the 'three days' of v. 2 as a pointer to the resurrection (so, e.g., W. H. Kelber, *Kingdom*, 61) is to hang too much weight on a simple, everyday phrase.

6. Gundry, 393-94, suggests that the situation is different, in that 6:36-37 indicated at least some possibility of buying food in the neighbourhood, whereas this time they are in a true ἐρημία, far from any habitation, and the need is more acute after three days without food.

7. W. T. Shiner, *Follow,* 222-26, suggests that what we find improbable because of our 'linear' style of reading a narrative would not have seemed out of place to Mark, whose narrative approach was 'cumulative'. The repetition of the motif of incredulity thus creates 'coherence at the discourse or rhetorical level of the Gospel at the expense of coherence at the narrative level'.

8. R. M. Fowler, *Loaves,* 93-99, explains the disciples' comment as deliberate irony on Mark's part, designed to cast the disciples in a negative light. Since Fowler believes that 8:1-10 was the traditional story, out of which Mark created the feeding of the five thousand, the disciples' response would have been entirely natural in the traditional story taken by itself, but by setting it in his gospel after he has already told his enhanced version, Mark has made them appear to be fools. 'What was once an innocent rhetorical question has been transformed by virtue of the backdrop against which it is now read' (*Loaves,* 154).

missively as ἰχθύδια ὀλίγα, 'a few little fish', or perhaps 'a few scraps of fish'. After the series of diminutives in 7:24-30 it is tempting to read ἰχθύδια as a deliberate contrast with the full-scale ἰχθύες of 6:31-44, and thus as indicating that the Gentiles get only the less valuable food (cf. the ψιχία of 7:28 in contrast with the children's bread), but this is probably overinterpretation. More likely Mark uses the term merely to indicate the inadequate quantity of the supply for the crowd.

8-9 The scale of the miracle may be slightly reduced this time, but the crowd are no less fully satisfied (ἐχορτάσθησαν), and there is plenty to spare. σπυρίς is a general term for basket (contrast the more specifically Jewish term κόφινος in 6:43). The term is used for a food basket or hamper, but it could be large enough to carry a person (Acts 9:25). The use of ἀπολύω, as in v. 3 and in 6:45, indicates Jesus' control over the crowd.

10 This time the disciples are not left to fend for themselves on the lake; Jesus embarks with them. The availability of τὸ πλοῖον at the end of what appears to have been a long overland journey is not explained: the question is irrelevant to Mark's purpose, which is to get them back to the western shore in preparation for a further crossing to the northeast in 8:13-22. Their destination is therefore now presumably somewhere on the northwest side of the lake, around Capernaum or Gennesaret (Matthew at this point mentions Magadan or Magdala), but Mark uses a name, Δαλμανουθά (see Textual Note) which is found nowhere else, and which cannot safely be identified with any known settlement. We cannot be surprised that there were small fishing villages along the lake which are not otherwise recorded and which have left no trace in later place names, but it is surprising that Mark should use a term which must surely have been as obscure to most of his readers as it is to us. But we do not know where it was, and there is no value in mere speculation.

SUMMARY SO FAR: BOTH OPPONENTS AND SUPPORTERS STILL HAVE A LOT TO LEARN (8:11-21)

This bridge passage moves Jesus and his disciples decisively away from Galilee, and so signals the end of the first act of Mark's drama. There is no clean break between Acts One and Two, but rather a gradual progression, in which 8:22-26 as well as the present section will play a part. As the group cross the lake and make their way towards their most northerly scene in the area of Caesarea Philippi, the reader is gradually prepared for the decisive new turn which the story will take from that point. The varied activity and response of the Galilean period is now to give way to the new direction introduced by the christological question and answer of 8:27-29, and by the focus on the cross which will result from them and will dominate the second act. But before Mark takes us to that decisive turning point, he concludes his first act with two enigmatic scenes which look both back over the preceding chapters and forward to the re-education of the disciples on the way to Jerusalem. These two short scenes invite us to consider how much (or rather how little) both Jesus' enemies and his followers have yet been able to grasp of the true significance of his ministry. Both groups still have much to learn, and in Act Two the disciples at least will be given the opportunity to learn it.

This section consists of two pericopes, linked together in the geographical sequence of movements around the northern part of the lake but otherwise independent. The first shows the incomprehension and growing hostility to Jesus on the part of his now traditional opponents, the Pharisees, and signals an end to significant dialogue with them on his part (though they will reappear briefy in 10:2 and 12:13). The second shows the apparently equal incomprehension of the disciples, leading not to hostility but to bewilderment. But their 'blindness' (vv. 17-18), unlike that of the Pharisees, is curable, as vv. 22-26 will symbolically demonstrate; that will be Jesus' task in Act Two.

Jesus Abandons the Pharisees (8:11-13)

After the first feeding miracle Jesus had crossed the lake and immediately come into conflict with Pharisees in Galilee (7:1-23); now after the second feeding miracle he returns again across the lake from Gentile territory, and again his arrival in Galilee brings him face to face with Pharisaic opposition. While Pharisees have not occurred in Mark's story as often as in Matthew or Luke, the reader is by now familiar with them as an expected source of criticism and opposition to Jesus' ministry. Either alone (2:24) or with scribes (2:16; 7:1) or Herodians (3:6) their name has repeatedly signalled official displeasure in contrast with the popular enthusiasm which has marked Jesus' Galilean ministry. This brief cameo underlines their negative role. Not only do they demand a σημεῖον to authenticate Jesus' ministry, but Mark adds that their motive in doing so was not an openness to be convinced, but πειράζοντες αὐτόν, presumably with the hope of discrediting him also in the eyes of the people at large. Jesus' refusal of a σημεῖον thus represents a conscious decision to terminate both his dialogue with the religious leadership and his public ministry in Galilee. Those who have not yet been convinced of his message will not now be offered any further incentive to believe. The pregnant phrase ἀφεὶς αὐτούς marks a decisive abandonment of the Pharisees, rather than any further attempt to win them, just as later Jesus will 'go out from' the temple, uttering his dramatic prediction of its destruction, to mark the end of his appeal to the hierarchy in Jerusalem (13:1-2).

In the parallel passage in Matthew and Luke (and in the second such incident narrated by Matthew, Mt. 16:1-4) Jesus' refusal of a σημεῖον is modified by a reference to the 'sign of Jonah'. This enigmatic comment, differently developed by Matthew and Luke, was presumably not in the tradition as Mark knew it, but belongs to a 'Q' version of the demand for a sign. In Mark the refusal is absolute, even if oddly phrased, and indicates that ἡ γενεὰ αὕτη (the phrase is emphatically repeated) has had all it is going to get. If they cannot accept what they have already seen and heard, there is no point in any further demonstration of the coming of the kingdom of God. They have missed their opportunity. The reader may well think back to chapter 4, with its chilling distinction between those to whom the secret of the kingdom of God has been revealed and 'those outside' to whom all is in parables (enigmas) without explanation. ἡ γενεὰ αὕτη seems to function here as a general term for 'those outside', as opposed to the disciples who will continue with Jesus in the boat and will be the recipients of still more privileged teaching in the chapters that follow. The division which chapter 4 presented is thus here dramatically enacted as Jesus turns away from the Pharisees, the spokesmen of 'this generation', and goes off in the boat with his disciples.

11 Whereas in 3:22; 7:1 opposition has come from Jerusalem scribes, Mark here gives the impression that the source of the demand is the local (Galilean) Pharisees, who, on his arrival at Dalmanutha, ἐξῆλθον (from their homes, presumably) to confront him. Conscious of their (self-imposed?) role as guardians of religious orthodoxy and practice in the area, and perhaps feeling threatened by the wide popularity and influence of this unorthodox teacher, they aim to put him in his place by demanding to see his credentials. While συζητέω can have a neutral sense, 'discuss' (as in 1:27; 9:10), more often it has a negative connotation, 'dispute (with)'. Mark mentions no other subject of debate, so that the effect of συζητεῖν αὐτῷ is, like the following πειράζοντες αὐτόν, to indicate their hostility. They do not come for dialogue, nor do they expect any σημεῖον to be given; their aim is simply to discredit Jesus.

σημεῖον is not used in the Synoptic Gospels (as it is in John) as a general term for a 'miracle'. Here the term does not therefore mean that they merely wanted to see a miracle, but rather focuses on the question of authentication (though the evidence requested is expected to be of a supernatural character, ἀπὸ τοῦ οὐρανοῦ).[9] Given the number of remarkable events already recorded in Mark's gospel, some at least of which should have been known to these Pharisees, it is not easy to see what more they required, but perhaps they had not yet personally witnessed any of the miracles, and were not prepared to trust to hearsay. It must be remembered, too, that the scribes in 3:22 did not doubt the occurrence of Jesus' exorcisms, but attributed them to demonic rather than to

9. Gundry, 402, argues that they were not asking for a miracle but 'a different kind of display, one that resists attribution to satanic power, magic or any other source besides God himself. . . . Exactly what kind they leave open'. It is not clear what would be more convincing than clearly miraculous activity, though Gundry draws on the argument of J. Gibson, *JSNT* 38 (1990) 37-66, that what was in mind was 'apocalyptic phenomena'. Gibson in fact is much more specific, and argues that what was in view was 'a phenomenon whose content is apocalyptic in tone, triumphalistic in character, and the embodiment of one of the "mighty deeds of deliverance" that God had worked on Israel's behalf in rescuing it from slavery', and that Jesus refused such a sign because he repudiated 'triumphalistic, imperious activities'.

divine power. For them, even admitted miracles needed some authenticating sign to show that they were 'from heaven'.

The concept of a (usually miraculous) sign to authenticate a prophet or other person claiming divine authorisation is a thoroughly biblical and Jewish one (cf. Paul's comment on the Jewish demand for σημεῖα in 1 Cor. 1:22).[10] Such signs are a prominent feature in the story of Moses (Ex. 4:1-9, 29-31; 7:8-22, etc.), and are clearly intended to be accepted as proof of his divine mission, though it should be noted that not all miraculous 'signs' are to be trusted (Ex. 7:11-12, 22; 8:7; Dt. 13:1-3). Elijah's calling down fire from heaven (1 Ki. 18:38) was a further spectacular example of the sort of authentication the Pharisees may have had in mind; cf. also Is. 7:10-17; 38:7-8. In the NT both Luke (in Acts) and John frequently use σημεῖον in a totally positive sense to denote the miracles of Jesus and of his followers, understood as visible indications of the power of God at work through his chosen servants (though again, as in the OT, 'signs' can also be performed by the opposition: Mk. 13:22; 2 Thes. 2:9; Rev. 13:11-15).

So the desire for a σημεῖον is not in itself self-evidently wrong. By adding πειράζοντες αὐτόν, however, Mark indicates that the request was disingenuous, and thus prepares the way for Jesus' refusal of what might seem, on the face of it, a reasonable request. Coming from the Pharisees, the request denotes not a readiness to be convinced, but an excuse for refusing to respond to the clear evidence already available in Jesus' teaching and ministry.

12 In 7:34 Mark has mentioned Jesus' sighing or groaning (στενάζω) while healing the deaf and dumb man, and other terms describing Jesus' strong emotions occurred in the story of the leper in 1:41, 43. Here an intensified form of the same verb (ἀναστενάζω, to sigh or groan deeply)[11] indicates his distress not over a physical complaint but over the unresponsiveness of 'this generation', revealed in the demand for a σημεῖον when so many miracles have already testified to his unique authority.[12] The use twice over of the phrase ἡ γενεὰ αὕτη suggests that the unbelief which demands an authenticating sign is not confined to the Pharisees alone. Certainly there is no indication that the γενεὰ μοιχαλὶς καὶ ἁμαρτωλός of 8:38 is limited to the Pharisees or any other specific group, while Jesus' exclamation Ὦ γενεὰ ἄπιστος in 9:19 appears to include even the disciples along with the surrounding crowd. Such accusations directed against the present γενεά as a whole (more characteristic of Matthew than of Mark) suggest that now that Jesus' public ministry in Galilee is over the eager response of the earlier chapters has not been generally sustained, and the people

10. O. Linton, *ST* 19 (1965) 112-29, usefully discusses the meaning of signs in Judaism, and argues that the focus is on the authentication of surprising teaching; see, e.g., *b. Sanh.* 98a; *b. B. Meṣ* 59b.

11. In classical usage the prefix ἀνα- would more likely indicate to groan *aloud*, but τῷ πνεύματι here suggests rather an internal emotional upheaval.

12. See J. Gibson, *JSNT* 38 (1990) 38-42, for the suggestion that Mark has already given us in 2:1-12 an example of Jesus performing a miracle as an authenticating sign.

as a whole share the scepticism of the Pharisees.[13] It is against this background that Jesus will now focus his attention more directly on the limited group of his committed disciples.

For ἀμὴν λέγω ὑμῖν see on 3:28. This is only its second occurrence in Mark, but in the remainder of the gospel it will occur more prominently. Here, as in 3:28, it introduces a solemn statement of judgment in a context of opposition to Jesus. The judgment this time is the refusal of the sign they want, leaving their scepticism unrelieved. The phrasing of the warning is Semitic, with a conditional clause (without main clause) serving the function of an emphatic negative statement. For the idiom (which implies a suppressed self-execration: 'May God do so-and-so to me, if . . .', as in 2 Ki. 6:31) cf. LXX Ps. 94[95]:11, εἰ εἰσελεύσονται εἰς τὴν κατάπαυσίν μου, cited in Heb. 3:11; 4:3, 5. See BDF, 372(4).[14]

13   The use of ἀφίημι with a personal object may be no more than a narrative device to move the story on from one location and group of people to another, as in 4:36. In other contexts, however, it implies a more definite dissociation, as in 12:12 and particularly 14:50. After the strongly dismissive tone of v. 12, and in view of the change of focus in Jesus' ministry which now follows, it seems better to take the phrase ἀφεὶς αὐτούς here as more strongly marked. This is Jesus' deliberate disengagement from discussion with the Pharisees and the γενεά they represent. He gets into the boat to leave Galilee and its crowds, in order to concentrate on the instruction of the disciples who now go with him εἰς τὸ πέραν.

The Disciples' Blindness (8:14-21)

TEXTUAL NOTE

15. The unexpected juxtaposition of the singular Ἡρῴδου with the plural Φαρισαίων, and the fact that Ἡρῳδιανοί are associated with Φαρισαῖοι in 3:6 and 12:13, explains the substitution of τῶν Ἡρῳδιανῶν for Ἡρῴδου in P[45] and other MSS.

This enigmatic pericope combines the motifs of bread (literal) and yeast (metaphorical) with that of the disciples' blindness or incomprehension, and the latter theme is then developed with reference to their failure to grasp the significance of the two 'bread' miracles. These themes are closely interwoven, but in a way which defies easy analysis of the flow of thought.[15] It is not clear whether we

---

13. Gundry, 406, argues, however, that the term γενεά is used here in a more restricted sense, and refers only to the Pharisees.

14. For further comment on why the demand for a sign must be rejected within the overall flow of Mark's narrative, see C. D. Marshall, *Faith,* 66-70.

15. F. Kermode, *Genesis,* 47, comments: 'Although this passage has been subjected to the intense scrutiny of the commentators, no one, so far as I know, has improved on the disciples' performance. The riddle remains dark.'

are to understand Jesus' use of the yeast metaphor as a deliberate exploitation of the disciples' concern over the lack of bread, or whether Mark wants us to see the lack of bread as an unfortunate coincidence which causes the disciples to miss the point of his warning about yeast by thinking too literally. But it is in thus missing the point that they reveal their failure to grasp the significance of Jesus' ministry and teaching, and Jesus goes on to drive the point home by taking up their concern over literal bread and showing how recent events have proved even that to be out of place. There can be no excuse for those who have participated in those two miracles to fail to grasp the significance of the one who performed them. No σημεῖον was given in response to the Pharisees' demand, but the disciples have had two σημεῖα already, and it has left them no wiser.[16] The disciples are thus comprehensively wrongfooted, and the way is prepared for the major focus on their re-education which will dominate Act Two.

This elusive dialogue contains a striking (and rather shocking) echo of the language of chapter 4.[17] In 8:11-13 the Pharisees have been left in the position of the unenlightened 'outsiders' of 4:11. But the language of Is. 6:9-10, which in 4:12 was used to describe those 'outsiders', is now applied in vv. 17-18 no less starkly to the disciples themselves, despite the fact that in 4:11 it was they who were described as the privileged possessors of the 'secret' hidden from the outsiders. Act One thus comes to an end on a sombre note; even where divine enlightenment has been given, it has not yet produced true understanding (note the repeated use of συνίημι in vv. 17, 21, as well as other ways of expressing the same idea in vv. 17, 18). This paradoxical note, already sounded clearly in 6:52 where very similar language has been used about the disciples' lack of understanding, will be maintained throughout the gospel: the patient re-education of the disciples during chapters 8–10 will leave them still bewildered by the turn of events in Jerusalem, running away in Gethsemane and leaving the women to watch the end at Golgotha, while even the women, privileged to receive a special announcement that Jesus is risen, bring the gospel to a dismal end by saying nothing to anyone, 'for they were afraid'. This pericope is thus not an incongruous note in the course of a steady upward progress, but rather sets the tone for a dénouement for which the enthusiasms and enlightenment of the earlier chapters have left the reader hitherto largely unprepared.

14 The connecting motif of the pericope, bread, is introduced by a

16. See, however, D. W. Chapman, *Orphan*, 58-61, for the view that this dialogue is the trigger for Peter's recognition in 8:29 that Jesus was the Messiah; in terms of the following story of the healing of the blind man, it was this dialogue which provided the 'second touch' that enabled Peter to see clearly.

17. W. T. Shiner, *Follow*, 226-33, explains this passage as 'explicitly bring[ing] together the two threads of parable and miracle' that have run through chapters 4–8, with a recurrent pattern of 'parable, incomprehension, rebuke, and explanation'. He appropriately describes Jesus' enigmatic saying in v. 15 as a παραβολή.

statement of the problem in two parts: they have forgotten[18] to bring bread (or more literally 'loaves'), and all that is there already in the boat is a single loaf. On two previous occasions they have been caught out with inadequate provisions, though the five ἄρτοι of 6:38 and the seven ἄρτοι of 8:5 might have provided at least a modest snack for the disciple group alone — it was the addition of a large crowd of 'guests' which in each case had precipitated a crisis. This time, with only a single ἄρτος, even the group in the boat by themselves will not have enough to share (see on 6:38 for the size of an ἄρτος). The rather heavy construction εἰ μὴ ἕνα . . . οὐκ εἶχον underlines the embarrassment of the situation.[19]

15 The imperfect tense of διεστέλλετο suggests that Jesus' warning against the Pharisees and Herod is not an isolated and unprovoked exclamation, as might at first appear, but rather a summary of a more extended discourse (Mark elsewhere generally uses the aorist of διαστέλλομαι for Jesus' commands to secrecy, except in 7:36b, where the reference is to repeated instructions after the initial command). For the imperative of ὁράω introducing a command or prohibition see 1:44; Mt. 9:30; 18:10, etc.; for βλέπετε as a warning ('look out') cf. 4:24; 13:5, 9, 23, 33, and with ἀπό ('beware of') 12:38. In context the warning against the Pharisees follows on from vv. 11-12, as a reflection on the breach which has now so clearly opened up between them and Jesus. The inclusion of Herod (Antipas) is more surprising, since Mark has not presented Antipas hitherto as a direct enemy of Jesus, though Antipas's interest in Jesus and linking of him with John the Baptist (whom he has already executed) has alerted the reader to him as a potential threat (6:14-29), and in 9:12-13 Jesus will imply that John's fate at the hands of Antipas is a foreshadowing of his own. More directly relevant is the equally unexpected mention of the Ἡρῳδιανοί (see Textual Note) as colluding with the Pharisees to plot Jesus' removal as far back as 3:6, and their reappearance in the same alliance in 12:13. See on 3:6 for the significance of this alliance. To link Antipas with the Pharisees is thus to focus not so much on ideological opponents alone as on those who, for different reasons, constitute a real threat to Jesus' life. His disciples

---

18. J. B. Gibson, *JSNT* 27 (1986) 31-47, improbably suggests that ἐπελάθοντο should not be translated 'had forgotten', but 'had (deliberately) neglected'. In their desire to prevent their Master from carrying out another feeding miracle for Gentiles, these Jewish disciples had made sure that no spare bread would be available for him to use. Jesus therefore rebukes them not for lack of faith but for thus revealing their fundamental lack of sympathy with his universalist agenda.

19. The specific mention of *one* ἄρτος has been taken by some commentators to indicate a symbolic meaning: Jesus himself is the 'one bread' who is sufficient for all their needs; see, for instance, J. Manek, *NovT* 7 (1964) 10-14; Q. Quesnell, *Mind*, 242-43, etc. Myers, 225-26 (following N. A. Beck, *CBQ* 43 [1981] 49-56), sees the whole point of the ensuing dialogue in the distinction between the plural ἄρτοι with their symbolic numbers (taken as representing the separate development of Jewish and Gentile 'circles') and the single ἄρτος, which represents the one eucharist which suffices for all Jesus' followers. See also Stock, 224-26, for an even more confident exegesis along the same lines. If Mark had any such esoteric symbolism in mind, he has given no indication of it clear enough for most ordinary readers to notice.

are to be alert to the danger in which he (and therefore they) now stand as a result of the opposition he has aroused in Galilee.

Both the brief, enigmatic nature of the saying and the following incomprehension of the disciples mark v. 15 out as a παραβολή in the same sense as the term was used in 7:17. And as in chapter 4 the failure to understand the παραβολή is expressed in terms drawn from Is. 6:9-10. But here, unlike in chapters 4 and 7, no direct explanation is offered to the disciples, but rather a series of teasing questions in vv. 18-21 which remain, as Mark has presented them, as enigmatic as the original παραβολή itself.

Yeast is used metaphorically in a number of ways. While it can directly symbolise evil (1 Cor. 5:8), it can also be used positively as a picture of the growth of the kingdom of God (Mt. 13:33). Its main metaphorical force in the NT seems to be in the powerful growth and influence of yeast (1 Cor. 5:6; Gal. 5:9), and in its association with Jewish Passover observance, which demanded the removal of yeast (1 Cor. 5:7-8). In Jewish use there is a similarly wide range of metaphorical connections. The significance of the metaphor here is thus not immediately self-evident. In Mt. 16:12 it is interpreted as the διδαχή of the Pharisees and Sadducees,[20] and in Lk. 12:1 as the ὑπόκρισις of the Pharisees, but the metaphor in itself does not demand either meaning. In Mark it remains elusive, and Jesus' warning is focused more on the Pharisees and Herod themselves as Jesus' enemies than on any specific connotation of their ζύμη. The introduction of the term serves more to link Jesus' warning with the problem of lack of bread than to add any specific content to the warning.

After this verse neither the specific metaphor of yeast nor the warning against the Pharisees and Herod plays any further part in the pericope. The subject will be rather the disciples' concern over bread, which, whether by accident or design, has been triggered by the mention of yeast. It is not clear whether Mark intends us to see Jesus as dropping the subject, diverted by the disciples' misunderstanding, or whether he regards v. 15 as having sufficiently made its point to the disciples. To us, its point remains largely obscure, or at least undeveloped.[21]

16-17a The disciples' response relates only to the mention of ζύμη, and ignores the Pharisees and Herod. Verse 16 is awkwardly expressed but is best understood as 'They were discussing with one another [the fact] that they had

20. According to A. Negoita and C. Daniel, *NovT* 9 (1967) 306-14, Matthew has the right interpretation, because what Jesus actually said in Aramaic was *'ᵃmîrāh* ('teaching'), but the disciples thought he said *ḥᵃmîrā'* ('yeast'), which would have sounded the same. They believe that Mark expected his readers to be sufficiently familiar with Aramaic to pick up the double entendre. Even if that were possible, what Mark says Jesus said is ζύμη, not διδαχή.

21. M. A. Beavis, *Audience*, 105-14, suggests a more coherent development, based on the contention that 'the warning against the "leaven" of the Jewish leaders reflects back on the Pharisees' request for a sign in vv. 11-13, which in turn must be read in the light of the feeding miracle in 8.1-10'. Her interpretation is grounded in important observations on parallel structures in several parts of Mark's gospel, but it is perhaps too subtle for most readers (or hearers) to grasp, particularly in view of the clear disjunction (in location) between 8:1-10 and 8:11-13.

no bread', taking the ὅτι as introducing indirect speech (in contrast with the parallel in Mt. 16:7, where it is ὅτι *recitativum* followed by a first-person verb). The imperfect διελογίζοντο probably indicates that they 'went on discussing', this having been the problem already raised in v. 14, before Jesus' warning about the Pharisees and Herod, which is thus brushed aside by their more immediate concern. (To understand their concern as a direct response to Jesus' saying about the yeast would necessitate translating the imperfect less naturally as 'They began to discuss', despite the fact that the lack of bread has already been signaled in v. 14.) Jesus' rebuke in v. 17 is thus caused not only by the fact that their material concern is in itself inappropriate (as vv. 19-21 will go on to explain), but also by their ignoring of the more important issue which he has raised in v. 15.

17b-18   Jesus' rebuke continues with a series of rhetorical questions all expressing in different ways the failure of the disciples to understand what is happening.[22] Cf. the use of the same terms in 7:18: ἀσύνετοί ἐστε; οὐ νοεῖτε; The final words of v. 18 (καὶ οὐ μνημονεύετε) can be construed (as by UBS[4], GNB, etc.) as the main clause introducing the ὅτε clause that follows, but are probably better construed (as in most English versions) as a further staccato question. (Its function in leading into the reminder of past events in vv. 19-20 is of course unaffected by the decision whether to punctuate with a question mark or a comma at the end of v. 18.) 'Remembering', together with perceiving, understanding, seeing, and hearing, is an essential part of the process of enlightenment in which they have been so conspicuously unsuccessful.

The question ὀφθαλμοὺς ἔχοντες οὐ βλέπετε καὶ ὦτα ἔχοντες οὐκ ἀκούετε; echoes the thought of Is. 6:9, though the wording differs from other allusions to that text, and is in fact more closely parallel to Je. 5:21; Ezk. 12:2; Ps. 115:5-6. The idea of sense organs which do not function is a natural way of describing people's lack of spiritual awareness (or in Ps. 115 the impotence of idols), and Jesus' rebuke draws on that recurrent theme of the OT. But it seems likely that Is. 6:9-10 is the passage primarily in mind,[23] since other echoes of its language are found in the preceding questions οὐδὲ συνίετε; (cf. LXX Is. 6:9: οὐ μὴ συνῆτε) and πεπωρωμένην ἔχετε τὴν καρδίαν ὑμῶν; (cf. LXX Is. 6:10 ἐπαχύνθη ἡ καρδία τοῦ λαοῦ τούτου; in the version quoted in Jn. 12:40 the verb used is πωρόω). Both συνίημι and καρδία πεπωρωμένη have already occurred in Mark's editorial comment on the disciples in 6:52, which in turn recalled the reference to Is. 6:9-10 in 4:12. Jesus thus charges his disciples with being no better off than the 'outsiders' to whom that text has already been applied. Their privileged insight into the secret of the kingdom of God seems for now to have deserted them. There is, however, the saving addition of οὔπω in vv. 17 and 21,

22. Myers, 225, points to a similar sequence of rebukes relating to heart, eyes, and ears in Moses' comment in Dt. 29:2-4 on Israel's failure to learn the lessons of the 'signs and great wonders' of the Exodus.

23. A primary reference to Is. 6:9-10 rather than to the Jeremiah or Ezekiel texts is argued by M. A. Beavis, *Audience,* 90-91, 109-10.

with the implication that their incomprehension, unlike that of the outsiders in chapter 4, is only temporary.

The specific use of the metaphor of blindness prepares the way for the next pericope, where the healing of a blind man will be used to symbolise the enlightenment which the disciples so obviously need. Jesus' attempt to provide that enlightenment, set over against the continued obtuseness of the disciples, will be a major theme of Act Two of Mark's gospel, now about to begin. At the same time the metaphor of deafness recalls the recently narrated healing of the deaf man, a miracle which is in many ways closely parallel to that of the blind man at Bethsaida. The present pericope, with its focus on spiritual obtuseness, is thus framed between two literal miracles of perception.[24]

19-20 As in 6:52, it is the significance of οἱ ἄρτοι that they should particularly have been able to grasp. At that stage only one such miracle had occurred; now they have participated in a second, but still the penny has not dropped. The detailed reminder in these verses of the facts and figures of the two feeding miracles thus serves to underline their obtuseness in general, and the inappropriateness of their concern about lack of bread for this lake crossing in particular. In this context it might seem that Jesus' rebuke relates only to the specific issue of food: having been involved recently in two such miracles they can surely not now worry again about lack of food as long as they are with Jesus, whose power to provide food from meagre resources has been amply demonstrated. But in 6:52 there was no such practical issue in view: what they should have grasped from οἱ ἄρτοι is not merely that they have a ready supply of food available, but something more fundamental about Jesus himself. In view of the question which he will put to them in v. 29, ὑμεῖς τίνα με λέγετε εἶναι;, it appears that he has been hoping for a more adequate grasp of his authority and mission as the Messiah, and that their inappropriate concern about food for the journey has highlighted this deeper inadequacy in their understanding.[25]

The questions and answers focus on the baskets of leftovers, presumably because the collection of these, for which the disciples had been personally responsible, and their amazement at the amount left over, is likely to have been their most abiding memory of these two extraordinary events. There is no need to search for any specific symbolism in the leftovers as such, still less in the

24. See T. J. Geddert, *Watchwords,* 70-81, for an elaborate argument to the effect that this whole section of Mark is focused on the issue of 'epistemology'.

25. A number of interpreters have found eucharistic significance in the references to bread in this passage. While it is very probable, as we have seen, that Mark intended his readers to read the feeding stories in the light of their knowledge of the eucharist, it is another matter to suggest that he envisaged Jesus as rebuking his disciples for failing to connect these miracles with the still future symbolic use of bread at the last supper. The wording of this pericope (in contrast with the clear eucharistic language of the feeding accounts) does not suggest such an idea (unless it be in the use of ἔκλασα in v. 19, and 'breaking bread' is a common enough phrase), and the specific focus in vv. 19-20 on the leftovers rather than the feedings themselves tells strongly against it.

numbers twelve and seven.[26] The reminder of the facts of the case serves simply to reinforce the disciples' awareness of the magnitude of the two miracles.[27]

21 What then should the disciples by now have understood? Mark does not tell us directly, and perhaps he does not need to, as this pericope serves to lead us into Act Two, where their lack of understanding will be repeatedly illustrated. It will become clear as Act Two unfolds that they are living through the dawning of the kingdom of God in the person of Jesus the Messiah, but that they have as yet only dimly grasped what this might mean. They have seen and benefited from the multiplication of food, but have so far appreciated even such striking miracles only at a superficial level. To them, unlike the Pharisees of 8:11-13, σημεῖα have been given in abundance, but they have not yet profited from them.

26. For a brief summary of some of the symbolic interpretations suggested see M. A. Beavis, *Audience,* 111-13. One of the most common is that twelve represents Israel and seven represents Gentiles, for which see above, p. 306, n. 1. We noted there that, while Mark does seem to emphasise a Jewish and Gentile setting for the two feedings respectively, the suggested numerical symbolism is less probable. In this dialogue there is even less to suggest it.

27. J. Sergeant, *Lion,* 56-57, suggests that the comparison of the numbers is important, the second miracle being on a much reduced scale compared with the first (more food available, fewer people fed, fewer leftovers). The reducing scale indicates that 'The sands are running out. The daylight is fading. Hence the urgency of Jesus' plea for sight before the day ends.' M. A. Tolbert, *Sowing,* 183, speaks of a 'decline in Jesus' ability', which 'has not to do with Jesus but with the increasing faithlessness he encounters'. L. W. Countryman, *CBQ* 43 (1981) 643-55, similarly associates this diminishing scale of the feeding miracles with a general decline in the ease and efficacy of miracles when those of the 'first cycle' (4:35–6:44) are compared with those of the second (6:45–8:9). This is Mark's way of showing that miracles are not signs, and that they are an inadequate basis of faith. The rebuke to the disciples is because they (along with most interpreters, we might add) have not yet grasped this theology of miracles.

ACT TWO: ON THE WAY
TO JERUSALEM (8:22–10:52)

The central section of Mark's narrative is focused geographically on Jesus' movement from north to south, leading up to his arrival in Jerusalem, for the only time in Mark's story, in 11:1. It thus stands between two quite distinct phases in the story of Jesus the Galilean, the first in and around his home territory, the second in the 'foreign' territory of Judaea. But this second act of the drama is more than just a bridge passage. The cumulative effect of the following observations indicates that in addition to having a different geographical location it also has an integrity and a distinctive focus of its own.

1. The passage is 'framed' by two accounts of the healing of a blind man (8:22-26; 10:45-52). As we shall see, these are frequently regarded as playing a symbolic role for Mark, in relation to the 'blindness' of the disciples (6:52; 8:17-18, 21).

2. The incomprehension of the disciples, already a noticeable theme of the gospel, now becomes central. Each of the three passion predictions which function as a sort of framework for this section of the gospel (8:31; 9:31; 10:33-34) is immediately followed by an example of the disciples' failure to grasp the values of the kingdom of God, leading to careful explanation by Jesus of where their perspective was at fault. The re-education of the disciples to the revolutionary viewpoint of the kingdom of God, in which the first will be last and the last first, takes up much of this part of the gospel, most notably in chapter 10.

3. The style of Jesus' ministry undergoes a significant change after 8:21. Apart from the healings of the two blind men (see above) the only miracle recorded in these chapters is the exorcism in 9:14-29, and even that functions as much as a basis for teaching the disciples as a miracle in its own right; otherwise there are no further miracles on the way to Jerusalem. Nor does Jesus spend time any longer teaching the crowds: ὁ ὄχλος is strangely present during what appears to be a private retreat at 8:34, and certain incidents involve a crowd as spectators (9:14; 10:1, 13, 46), but the focus throughout is now on Jesus' private instruction of his disciples. The point is made explicitly in 9:30-31.

4. Recurrent uses of the phrase ἐν τῇ ὁδῷ and related language (8:27; 9:33-34; 10:17, 32, 52) emphasise not only the geographical movement of the story but also the sense of discipleship as a journey. The tendency of early

Christians to refer to their movement as ἡ ὁδός (Acts 9:2; 16:17; 18:25-26; 19:9, 23; 22:4; 24:14, 22) suggests that the term has more than merely literal significance for Mark, and that this 'journey' section of the gospel is also a study of discipleship.

5. Hitherto Jesus' sayings have contained only an isolated hint of his coming death (2:20). From 8:31 onwards, as soon as his identity as Messiah is explicitly acknowledged, he speaks repeatedly of what that messianic mission will involve when they get to Jerusalem (8:31; 9:12, 31; 10:33-34, 38, 45), not only for himself but also for those who follow him (8:34–9:1; 10:30, 39). The cross is explicitly set before the disciples, and its shadow now falls over all the journey to the capital city where Jesus is to be rejected and executed. There is a sense of time running out.

For these reasons this part of the gospel is to be understood as a coherent subsection in the story, the second act of Mark's three-act drama.[28] Its content justifies the frequent tendency to describe this as the 'discipleship section' of the gospel, but its place within Mark's total dramatic structure requires us also to note not only its geographical function as the link between the northern and southern phases of Jesus' ministry, but also more importantly its role in preparing both disciples and readers for the rejection and death of Jesus which will bring the story to its climax in Jerusalem, and which now begins to dominate the horizon.

FIRST HEALING OF A BLIND MAN (8:22-26)

TEXTUAL NOTE

26. The wide range of expanded readings appear to be attempts to spell out the purpose of Jesus' instruction not to return to the village, by making the 'secrecy' theme explicit. It is more likely that such explanation was added than that an originally more explicit instruction was made more enigmatic.

Structural analyses of Mark differ as to whether this pericope belongs with the preceding section or with what follows. It is a bridge passage, moving Jesus

---

28. Thus E. Best's study of discipleship in Mark *(Following Jesus)* is in effect an exposition of Mark 8:27–10:45, with supplementary data added from the rest of the gospel. See especially pp. 15-16, 146 for the integrity of this section. See further Best, *Disciples,* 1-16. Those who recognise this as a distinct section of the gospel do, however, vary as to just where it should be understood to begin. The two healing stories with which it begins and ends are generally recognised as 'bridge passages' which could with equal validity be grouped either with what precedes or with what follows. Otherwise, the end of the section is clear, with the arrival at Jerusalem, but a case could be made on different grounds for its beginning at 8:14 with the departure from Galilee, at 8:22 with the first story of a blind man, at 8:27 with the watershed declaration of Jesus' Messiahship, or at 8:31 with the first passion prediction. Mark's work is not divided into clear sections, and the lack of agreement on exactly which new theme marks the decisive change testifies to its narrative coherence.

and his followers on their way to Caesarea Philippi, picking up the theme of blindness from 8:18, and leading into the extended attempt to cure the disciples' blindness which will conclude with another healing of a blind man in 10:45-52. Because these two healings form a framework around Mark's second act I will here treat them as belonging to it as introduction and conclusion.

We have noted in discussing 7:31-37 how similar that narrative is to this healing story, in its non-Galilean location, its attention to the detail of Jesus' healing method, its mention of his touching the affected parts of the body and his use of saliva, and the attempt to avoid publicity by taking the patient away from the crowd who had asked for the healing.[29] In discussing 7:31-37 we noticed the significance of the healing of a deaf and dumb man in the light of Is. 35:5-6. That prophecy begins with the opening of the eyes of the blind, a work which is attributed to God also in Ps. 146:8; Is. 29:18. In the light of such OT passages these two pericopes together add up to a very impressive claim with regard to who Jesus is.

Neither story is paralleled in Matthew or Luke. The detailed and apparently almost 'magical' nature of the cures may not have appealed to them (neither Matthew nor Luke ever mentions the use of saliva in healing), and in this case another factor may have been the delay in the full restoration of sight. While in Mark's scheme this delay is likely to have symbolic significance (see below), the story taken on its own may have been felt to detract from the otherwise instantaneous nature of Jesus' recorded cures. Since each of them had other stories of the healing of the blind, the Bethsaida story may have seemed to add little. It is only in its place in Mark's plot that it gains a special value of its own.

The very widespread tendency among commentators to attribute symbolic value to this narrative in Mark is in part attributable to its location as the bridge passage into Act Two, balanced by the healing of Bartimaeus as the conclusion to this act before Jesus arrives in Jerusalem. The metaphorical use of the language of blindness, drawn from Is. 6:9-10, has occurred already in 4:12 where it applies to the crowds in deliberate contrast to the 'enlightened' disciples, and in 6:52 and 8:17-18 where the disciples themselves are also found wanting in spiritual perception. The Bethsaida incident follows immediately after the accusation of blindness during the crossing of the lake, and it is the progressive attempt to cure that spiritual blindness which will be the main focus of the narrative of the journey to Jerusalem. The process will begin immediately with the dialogue at Caesarea Philippi.

The argument for a symbolic intention is strengthened by the peculiar character of this healing, as one accomplished in two stages. The 'blindness' of the disciples is similarly dispelled only gradually. Already in 4:11 they are declared to have received special revelation concerning τὸ μυστήριον τῆς

---

29. See above p. 301, especially n. 47, for the work of R. M. Fowler and M. A. Beavis on the parallel structures of the two passages.

βασιλείας τοῦ θεοῦ, and yet that revelation has left them with much still to learn (6:52; 7:18; 8:17-18, 21). The new phase of the narrative which is now beginning will focus on their further enlightenment, but it will not be completed in a single 'cure'. Successive examples of their failure to understand will each be followed by further re-education, but even when the journey is complete and the narrative reaches its climax in Jerusalem the disciples will be characterised more by dullness and failure than by the dynamic new perspectives of the kingdom of God. Even Peter, the spokesman, whose ringing declaration of Jesus' messianic status is the foundation of the disciples' new perspective, will a few verses later be rebuked for viewing Jesus' mission from the human, not the divine angle (8:29-33). He has 'seen', but not yet clearly. Of all this the two-stage healing of the blind man at Bethsaida offers an apt illustration.[30]

The by now familiar theme of Jesus' desire to avoid publicity for his healing powers recurs in this narrative both in his taking the man away from the village to heal him, and in his instruction afterwards not to return into the village (cf. 7:33, 36). What may have been understood at first as merely a pragmatic desire to escape overenthusiastic crowds will in the following pericopes take on the added dimension of a specifically theological 'secrecy', as Jesus forbids his disciples to talk publicly about their new insights into his mission (8:30; 9:9). In this way, too, the story of the blind man at Bethsaida can be read as symbolic of a deeper level of 'cure'.

There are, then, good reasons for believing that Mark included this story at this point in his narrative because for him it illustrated a fundamental theme of the journey to Jerusalem, the curing of the disciples' blindness. But the symbolic does not exclude the literal. In this story, as in the cure of the deaf-mute in Decapolis, Mark offers also a carefully observed account of another miracle of healing, unusual in its detail, but equally a testimony to the unique authority of Jesus at the physical as well as the spiritual level.

22 In 6:45 Jesus sent his disciples across the lake πρὸς Βηθσαϊδάν, but that journey in fact finished at Γεννησαρέτ (6:53) on the western shore (see on 6:31-32 for the geographical problems). Further journeys in Phoenicia and the

---

30. Various commentators have attempted a more precise identification of the 'two stages' in removing the disciples' blindness. R. H. Lightfoot, *History,* 90-91 (followed by several other interpreters), found the parallel specifically in 8:27-30, with the disciples' partial understanding in v. 28 corresponding to the first laying of hands on the blind man, and Peter's clear messianic confession in v. 29 corresponding to the second; the command to silence in v. 30 then parallels Jesus' sending the man home in v. 26. (Cf. A. Richardson, *Miracle-Stories,* 86: 'The Blind Man of Bethsaida is none other than St. Peter, whose eyes were opened near Caesarea Philippi.') The problem with any such specific identification is that we soon find that Peter's vision after 8:29 is anything but full and clear, and incomprehension remains a feature of all the disciples right to the end of the gospel. E. S. Johnson, *NTS* 25 (1978/9) 380-83, therefore proposes more plausibly to find the counterpart to the second laying on of hands in Jesus' resurrection and the coming of the Holy Spirit. It may be questioned, however, whether Mark had any such specific focus in mind. See further E. Best, *Following,* 134-39; J. F. Williams, *Followers,* 130-32, the latter arguing against a symbolism of the enlightenment of the disciples altogether.

Decapolis brought them back to Δαλμανουθά (8:10), presumably again on the northwestern shore, and from there they have now crossed to the northeastern corner of the lake, the area where Luke locates the feeding of the five thousand.[31] The Bethsaida healing, like that in the Decapolis (7:32), results from an unidentified group of people bringing one of their number to be healed. Mark has not specifically mentioned a previous visit by Jesus to Bethsaida, but he has repeatedly told us of the wide extent of Jesus' reputation as a healer, and Bethsaida was not very far from Capernaum. No instance of the healing of blindness has yet been recorded, but Mark's general summaries of Jesus' healing ministry in 1:34 (ποικίλαι νόσοι) and 3:10 (ὅσοι εἶχον μάστιγας; cf. 6:56) have prepared the reader for such a request. They expect Jesus to heal by a touch, as he has regularly done (1:31, 41; 5:23; 6:5; 7:33); cf. the desire of those seeking healing to touch Jesus (3:10; 5:27-28; 6:56).

23 The mention of a κώμη here and in v. 26 is surprising, since the former village of Bethsaida had recently been raised to the status of a fortified city (and given the name Julias) by Herod Philip (Josephus, *Ant.* 18.28).[32] Perhaps we are to envisage Jesus here (as later near Caesarea Philippi, v. 27) avoiding the city itself and visiting an outlying settlement.[33] See on 7:33 both for the removal of the patient from the public arena and for the physical means of healing, especially the use of saliva. The two stories and their settings are sufficiently similar for the same considerations to apply. In this case, however, Jesus is described as spitting directly into the blind man's eyes and then touching with his hand. The physical contact would be especially important for a blind man. The use of the less common poetic term ὄμματα here may indicate no more than a search for variety of expression as the more normal term ὀφθαλμοί will occur in v. 25, but it is possible that the more archaic language, together with the use of saliva, is intended to suggest a more formal ritual of healing.

While εἰ is commonly used to introduce an indirect question (cf. 3:2; 10:2; 15:36, 44), it can also introduce a direct question in biblical (not classical) Greek, in both the LXX and the NT; the usage is thought to derive from the Hebrew use of *hᵃ*- and *'im* in the same way. This is the only such use in Mark, but cf. Mt. 12:10; 19:3; Lk. 13:23; Acts 1:6; 7:1. The exploratory question appro-

---

31. Myers, 110, 240, sees this arrival in Bethsaida as 'completing an intention introduced in 6:45 — the unfinished voyage to Bethsaida'. Quite apart from the geographical problems surrounding 6:45, there has been too much geographical movement in the intervening chapters to make it likely that Mark intended his readers at this point to recall 6:45.

32. But see Lane, 283 n. 42, for the possibility that despite its new status Bethsaida remained organisationally a large κώμη, and thus that Mark is quite correct in his terminology. More fully, A. N. Sherwin-White, *Society,* 127-31.

33. Myers, 240, speaks of 'Mark's ideological antipathy toward urban Hellenism', leading to a '"narrative avoidance" of the city' (cf. pp. 150-51), but locates that trait in this pericope only in Jesus' taking the man out of Bethsaida (which he believes Mark designates a κώμη because he 'refuses to recognize its new Hellenistic identity'). A 'narrative avoidance' of the city might better be served by having Jesus visit a dependent κώμη *rather than* Bethsaida itself.

priately introduces the uniquely 'tentative' nature of this healing story; normally Jesus has no need to ask any question, as the healing is immediate and obvious.

24 The dual sense of ἀναβλέπω, to 'look up' and to 'see again' (after blindness),[34] is effectively exploited: the man 'looked up', and reported on the result of his attempt, which was that already he could 'see again', even though not yet perfectly. His report is intriguing. Note that περιπατοῦντας agrees with ἀνθρώπους, not with δένδρα: not 'I see people who look like walking trees', but 'I see people, and I see them walking like trees'. The contrast with seeing τηλαυγῶς in v. 25 makes it clear that this is intended as a description of indistinct sight; he sees moving shapes, which because they are walking about ought to be people, but he cannot yet see them clearly enough to identify them — they might as well be trees! The sense would have been clearer (but less vividly bizarre) if περιπατοῦντας had been more directly linked with τοὺς ἀνθρώπους ('I see people walking, but they look like trees'). The awkwardness of the sentence is produced by the unnecessary introduction after the ὅτι of a second verb of seeing (βλέπω, ὁρῶ), perhaps to emphasise that the formerly blind man can now see again.

25 The 'second attempt' by Jesus is unique to this story. It results in a full healing which is emphasised by the use of three parallel expressions for the complete restoration of sight: διαβλέπω, as opposed to merely βλέπω, denotes unimpeded clarity of vision (cf. Mt. 7:5); ἀποκαθίστημι denotes restoration to full health and the proper function of the eyes (cf 3:5); ἐνέβλεπεν τηλαυγῶς ἅπαντα leaves no room for uncertainty over the completeness of the cure.[35] The imperfect is perhaps used in the latter clause to indicate the beginning of a new situation: from this point on he will be able to see everything clearly.

26 Jesus has deliberately taken the man away from the village before healing him, and now forbids him to return that way. The various expansions of the text (see Textual Note) show that this instruction has been understood as parallel to the injunctions to silence following other healing miracles. In this case, where the man has been brought to Jesus by the villagers specifically in order to be cured, it seems particularly unrealistic; no one will have any doubt how his sight came to be restored. Are we to understand that Jesus is simply 'buying time' to allow himself and his disciples to leave the area before the news gets around, or has Mark simply repeated the standard formula of secrecy without regard to its appropriateness in this case?[36] At any rate, there is no strong focus on the theme of secrecy, nor are we told this time about the reac-

34. See E. S. Johnson, *NTS* 25 (1978-9) 376-77, concluding that the normal meaning in relation to blindness is 'see again'.

35. See E. S. Johnson, *NTS* 25 (1978-9) 377-79, for the meanings of the verbs.

36. Gundry, 419-20, suggests that the man's going home rather than returning to the village to resume begging (the inevitable occupation of a blind man) is a public demonstration of the reality of the cure. V. 26 on this view has nothing to do with secrecy, but rather the opposite, public testimony.

tion of the crowd as was the case in 7:36-37 (where the injunction to silence was to the whole crowd, not just to the patient).[37]

LEARNING TO RECOGNISE JESUS (8:27–9:13)

The journey begins in the far north of Palestine, more than a hundred miles north of Jerusalem. There will be several weeks in which to work through the questions which must now occupy the disciples' minds. The process begins with a sequence of events and discussions which together pose inescapably the central issue of who Jesus really is, the issue on which the whole of the rest of the teaching and learning in these chapters must depend. Mark's narrative is deliberately constructed as a continous sequence,[38] in order to bracket together the different (indeed contrasting) insights which these opening pericopes contribute to the disciples' growing awareness of whom it is that they have been called to follow, and of what that following must mean for them. In particular, there is a strong counterpoint between the exaltation of Peter's confession and the immediate deflation which follows in 8:31-33, and again between the grim language of taking up the cross and losing one's life and the glory on the high mountain. The alternate highs and lows forbid a simplistic understanding of the Messiah's mission and force the disciples into a radical rethinking of their conventional values. Slowly and painfully they are learning to recognise Jesus.

Jesus Is the Messiah (8:27-30)

Ever since the disciples first left their nets to follow Jesus the question of Jesus' identity has been pressing upon them, and perhaps with rather less urgency upon all those with whom Jesus has come into contact. Their instinctive recognition of his authority when he called them to follow him and to become ἁλιεῖς ἀνθρώπων calls for an explanation, and every subsequent demonstration of authority and miraculous power has made the question more pressing. Mark's readers have been given a privileged insight into who Jesus is in the revelations of the prologue (1:1-13), but the disciples have no such inside information, and have been left to work out for themselves what the events they have witnessed and the teaching they have heard imply about the person they recognise as their διδάσκαλος. Their special insight into the secret of the kingdom of God (4:11)

37. J. F. Williams, *Followers,* 132-36, inferring from Mark's silence that this time the command to secrecy was obeyed, argues that whereas previous failures to obey the command inhibited Jesus' teaching ministry, Mark here by implying obedience to the command 'sets up a change of scene in which Jesus interacts with his disciples' away from public pressure.

38. The only narrative break is between 9:1 and 9:2, and this is conspicuously bridged by the unusually precise time-indication μετὰ ἡμέρας ἕξ; see below on 9:2 for the close connection between the two pericopes.

has not yet led them to formulate, or at any rate to articulate, a settled answer to the question of Jesus' identity. The crowds who have remained 'outside' have been even further from fully grasping the significance of what is happening.

Mark has frequently recorded people's amazement at Jesus' authority in word and deed (1:22, 27; 2:12; 5:20, 42; 6:14-16; 7:37) and his celebrity as a healer and teacher (1:45; 2:2, 13; 3:7-8; 4:1; 6:54-56). He has recorded the disciples' awe-struck question 'Who is this?' (4:41; cf. 6:51). But that question does not seem yet to have met with a satisfactory answer, and the emphasis more recently has been on their failure to make the necessary connections (6:52; 8:17-21). The only 'title' they have yet used to address him is διδάσκαλε (4:38); even κύριε has occurred so far only on the lips of a Gentile woman (7:28). Twice Jesus has dropped the enigmatic title ὁ υἱὸς τοῦ ἀνθρώπου into his comments on his own authority (2:10; 2:28), but it has not been picked up and has played no further part in the narrative. The most unconventional evaluation of Jesus has been that of Antipas, that he is John the Baptist raised from the dead (6:14-16). Clearly it is time for the christological question to be brought into the open.

8:27-30 (or, better, the fuller complex 8:27-33) is conventionally said to be the watershed in Mark's narrative. Up to this point the tension has been building up towards its climax in the eventual recognition of who Jesus is, while from this point on, the christological question having been explicitly posed and answered, the plot sets off downhill again towards the fulfilment of Jesus' messianic mission on the cross and in his resurrection, with 8:31 and its subsequent echoes in 9:31 and 10:33-34 providing the agenda for this second part of the story. That watershed is symbolised by the geographical movement of the narrative, which begins at the most northerly point of Jesus' travels high among the mountains in 8:27, and from there moves relentlessly southward towards the dénouement in Jerusalem. The second act of the drama, heralded by 8:22-26, effectively begins here.

This 'watershed' analysis is qualified by the recognition that the title ὁ Χριστός which is so powerfully introduced in 8:29 immediately disappears from the story, apart from an enigmatic and unmarked use in 9:41, until it comes dramatically back into focus, as if a new revelation, in 14:61-62. But of course that is to a different audience who were not privy to the declaration at Caesarea Philippi. And the 'loss' of the title in Jesus' conversations with his disciples after 8:29 is not an accident, as is shown by the 'gagging order' of 8:30 and the deliberate substitution of ὁ υἱὸς τοῦ ἀνθρώπου from 8:31 on. Even if the title ὁ Χριστός is not used, the concept which underlies it remains the focus of Jesus' teaching about his mission from this point on, in a way which was impossible before the christological issue had been clarified.

27 The former city of Paneas or Panion, in a well-watered area in the foothills of Mount Hermon within the tetrarchy of Trachonitis, had recently been enlarged by the local ruler Herod Philip and renamed Caesarea in honour of Augustus, by whose gift it had passed into the control of his father, Herod the

Great. Its original name derived from the local worship of Pan (which succeeded an earlier Canaanite Baal cult), and the little we know of its history suggests that, despite the 'Jewish' identity of its ruler, it was essentially a Hellenistic and pagan city.

As previously with reference to Tyre (7:24), another pagan city, Mark does not suggest that Jesus and his disciples went to the city itself, but rather to its κῶμαι. See on 8:23 for the meaning of this term. Here the plural together with the name of the city in the genitive clearly indicates small settlements associated with the city rather than the city itself; as a regional capital, Caesarea Philippi controlled a wide area which would contain many smaller settlements. So this is not a 'mission' to Caesarea Philippi, but a retreat with his disciples in the countryside, and in an area where the population was probably not predominantly Jewish. In 9:30-31 Mark will depict Jesus deliberately avoiding public exposure in order to concentrate on teaching the disciples, and the same impression is probably intended here.

The christological issue is approached by asking first the more comfortably 'objective' question. The disciples, as they have mingled with the crowd, have been in a better position than Jesus himself to tune in to popular reactions to his ministry, and he asks for a report on what people are saying about him. His question assumes that people will have been obliged to find an explanation for what they have observed by identifying Jesus in some category out of the ordinary. They must have a pigeon hole to put him in, but which have they chosen?

28 The disciples' answer is awkwardly abbreviated: there is no subject for the first proposal to correspond to the ἄλλοι which introduces the second and third; and the first two opinions are expressed in the accusative (picking up the case of με in v. 27), while the third is in the nominative preceded by ὅτι, thus offering an incomplete clause ('that [you are] one of the prophets'). The addition of a ὅτι before Ἰωάννην in several MSS (‮א‬* B C*) is presumably an attempt to alleviate the abruptness of the accusative with which the reply begins, though a ὅτι *recitativum* merely repeats the function of λέγοντες.

The three options offered all fall into the category of 'prophet', and clearly that is how many people did classify Jesus. But John the Baptist and Elijah are figures of the past, and the term εἷς τῶν προφητῶν most naturally has the same implication. Jesus is not just 'a prophet', but one of *the* prophets, and thus a reappearance of a past and well-known prophetic figure (cf. Luke's version προφήτης τις τῶν ἀρχαίων ἀνέστη, while Matthew offers the specific suggestion of Jeremiah). Antipas's wild surmise that Jesus was John the Baptist *redivivus* (6:14-16) is thus found to be not so eccentric after all: other people were offering similar suggestions. It is of course a matter of debate how literally they would have expected such language to be taken; it may have been intended to convey a continuity of ministry and even an uncanny resemblance without postulating literal reincarnation. We do not know enough about popular Jewish thought at the time to be sure, and in any case we are dealing at best with a secondhand report, even if Mark has provided a verbatim record of what the disciples said.

If it is true that Jews in the first century believed that prophecy had become extinct with Malachi, the reincarnation of one of the old prophets would perhaps be the most natural way of explaining the presence once again of a prophetic figure in Israel. But there is good reason to doubt whether the cessation of prophecy during the Second Temple period was as widespread a dogma as has been traditionally supposed;[39] it seems to have been possible to think in prophetic terms about John the Baptist without invoking reincarnation (11:32; Mt. 11:9).

From the point of view of Mark's narrative, however, the precise form of popular belief is not important. What matters is that Jesus is popularly perceived as a prophet. This is undoubtedly a positive, indeed a highly laudatory, assessment. But the sequel will show that it falls short of the truth about Jesus. Like many today who express their appreciation of Jesus (often alongside other religious leaders) as a great teacher, the people of his own day, as reported by the disciples, have not yet grasped the full significance of his ministry.

29 Jesus' ὑμεῖς δέ indicates that a better answer is still needed, and that it is the responsibility of the disciples to supply it. If they have been entrusted with τὸ μυστήριον τῆς βασιλείας τοῦ θεοῦ (4:11), surely by now they are in a position to evaluate the significance of the one through whom it has come into being. Their spokesman is Πέτρος, whom Mark consistently calls by this name after introducing the nickname in 3:16 (up to that point he equally consistently used Σίμων). Mark does not say explicitly how far Peter's declaration represents his own personal conclusion, and how far it represents the joint thinking of the disciples. But he gives no indication that Peter is in a special position (in contrast with Mt. 16:17-19), and Jesus' response in vv. 30-31 is addressed to the disciples corporately. When Peter again responds in v. 32, Mark makes a point of noting that Jesus' counterrebuke is issued ἰδὼν τοὺς μαθητὰς αὐτοῦ, indicating that they, too, were party to the misunderstanding which Peter has voiced. It seems likely, therefore, that we are to understand Peter to be more a spokesman for the group than the originator of a purely personal insight which would have taken the other disciples by surprise. He will appear in the role of representative for the group again in 9:5; 10:28; 11:21; 14:37.

ὁ Χριστός occurred in Mark's 'title page' in 1:1, but has not been heard since. Its appearance in many MSS of 1:34 testifies to the awareness among early readers of the gospel that the christological question was an important undercurrent of the narrative, and that the supernatural insight of the demons, deliberately suppressed by Jesus, would focus on his messianic role. But Mark has reserved the open use of the title until this moment. Now at last the truth about Jesus is recognised and acknowledged.

39. D. E. Aune, *Prophecy*, 103-6, together with his study of prophecy in early Judaism, 106-52.

30 In view of the climactic significance of the declaration in v. 29, the sequel is all the more remarkable. This central truth, which alone makes sense of the story so far, is nevertheless to be kept secret. See on 1:25 for Mark's use of ἐπιτιμάω; here, as in 3:12, it is followed by ἵνα, and here, as there, the issue is the open declaration of who Jesus is. The strength of the verb (used previously for silencing demons) is remarkable. There is no suggestion, of course, that Peter's declaration was wrong: the phrase λέγωσιν περὶ αὐτοῦ presupposes that there is something which might be said, and therefore that there is something to be kept secret. That Jesus is ὁ Χριστός is a truth, but not one for open proclamation. The incongruity of this demand is pointed up by the contrast with the use of παρρησίᾳ in v. 32: Jesus has no inhibitions in speaking about the suffering and death awaiting the υἱὸς τοῦ ἀνθρώπου, but his identity as ὁ Χριστός may not be revealed.

So much has been written about the 'Messianic Secret' in Mark that it is sometimes forgotten that this is the only place in the gospel where a specifically *messianic* secret is mentioned. The theme of secrecy has been prominent throughout, and it has included the silencing of the demons ὅτι ᾔδεισαν αὐτόν, which indicates a christological dimension to the theme. But 8:30 is the only place where Jesus' identity as ὁ Χριστός is the explicit subject of the call for secrecy. In 9:9 a similar command will be given with regard to the christological revelation received on the mountain of transfiguration, but again without an explicitly messianic focus (and again using instead the title ὁ υἱὸς τοῦ ἀνθρώπου, as in v. 31).

What is here forbidden is not christological speculation, or even the expression of such ideas within the privacy of the disciple group, but their public declaration — ἵνα μηδενὶ λέγωσιν. The time for such public declaration will come in 14:61-62, but for now it is inappropriate. When that time comes, it will be Jesus himself, not the disciples, who breaks the secrecy.

Decades of discussion as to the basis of this secrecy have still not displaced the rather obvious explanation in terms of the climate of thought among those who had witnessed and been impressed by Jesus' Galilean ministry. The popular enthusiasm for Jesus, and the hope that he might be persuaded to take a more political role as the leader of a Jewish uprising (see on 6:31-44 and 6:45-46), would mean that messianic language could be seriously misunderstood on the part of both friends and enemies. In view of what Jesus is about to reveal concerning his real mission in v. 31 there could hardly be a more unfortunate misunderstanding, or one more calculated to derail his enterprise as it approaches its decisive phase in the journey towards Jerusalem.[40] So language about Jesus as ὁ Χριστός is forbidden.

The problem lies in the wide range of content which could be found in that title, depending on what background you brought to it. It will become clear

---

40. Gundry, 427, adds that such publicity might again generate the sort of crowds that would infringe the privacy Jesus is now seeking for the instruction of his disciples.

immediately that what Peter (and presumably the other disciples) read into the term was quite different from how Jesus himself understood it. With a wider public, who have not had the benefit either of the special insight granted to the disciples according to 4:11 or of Jesus' private teaching, the potential for misunderstanding is clearly greater still. It is precisely because Jesus' concept of Messiahship is so new (one might almost say perverse) that it was dangerous to use publicly a title which had, for most Jews of the time, its own ready-made connotations, which were very different from Jesus' sense of mission.

ὁ Χριστός was a particularly hazardous title from this point of view. In the OT *hammāšîaḥ* is not a technical term for a coming deliverer (though *māšîaḥ* in Dn. 9:26 perhaps approaches this sense), and in the LXX there is no clear use of ὁ Χριστός in the absolute as a term for a coming deliverer. But in the later pre-Christian centuries 'the anointed one' and related terms, while still not occurring very frequently in anything like a technical sense, were apparently becoming a convenient repository for a range of eschatological hopes and concepts derived from or developed out of the OT. The targums give evidence of the wide currency of the term 'the Messiah' to sum up the hopes engendered by the OT.[41] In such a situation the meaning which ὁ Χριστός would convey depended on the background of thought and community of the person using it. But given the strong popular hope of national liberation mingled with a recognition of the need for spiritual restoration of the people of God (as expressed, for instance, in *Pss. Sol.* 17), there is little doubt that in unsophisticated circles it would be a term with a strongly political flavour, and therefore one which was likely to be a hindrance rather than a help in communicating Jesus' distinctive understanding of his mission.[42]

Such a 'historicist' approach to the messianic secret has been widely undervalued in scholarly discussion,[43] but it remains at the very least a significant element in explaining the use (and non-use) of the title in Mark's story. The fact that by the time Mark wrote the title 'Christ' had become standard church terminology, and had developed a very specifically Christian range of connotation, makes it the more remarkable that Mark recognises and draws such sharp attention to the ambivalence which the term enjoyed at an earlier stage of its linguistic evolution.

41. Among many other treatments of messianic terminology in later Judaism, see especially M. de Jonge and A. S. van der Woude in *TDNT*, 9.509-27. There is an attractive brief summary of the evidence in N. T. Wright, *Victory*, 481-86.

42. G. Vermes, *Jew*, 129-56, remains a useful discussion of this issue. See especially p. 134, 'If in the inter-Testamental period a man claimed, or was proclaimed, to be "the Messiah", his listeners would as a matter of course have assumed that he was referring to the Davidic Redeemer and would have expected to find before them a person endowed with the combined talents of soldierly prowess, righteousness and holiness.'

43. The longevity of Wrede's speculation, which has set (and perhaps skewed) the agenda for subsequent discussion, that the theme of secrecy is a Marcan apologetic invention, is one of the more remarkable phenomena of biblical scholarship. N. T. Wright, *Victory*, 529 n. 181, suitably comments that it 'has long outlived its sell-by date'.

The Messiah (and His Followers) Must Suffer (8:31–9:1)

TEXTUAL NOTES

35. ἐμοῦ καί is missing in P45 D and several OL MSS. It is not easy to see why an original mention of loyalty to Jesus should have been deliberately removed, though it could have been lost accidentally. But on the other hand the presence of ἐμοῦ both in the comparable texts in 10:29 (with τοῦ εὐαγγελίου) and 13:9 (without τοῦ εὐαγγελίου) and in both the Matthean and Lucan parallels at this point suggests that it could be a harmonising addition here, which would mean that Mark here originally read simply ἕνεκεν τοῦ εὐαγγελίου.

38. The omission of λόγους by a small number of MSS leaves an intelligible though different sense (Jesus' *people* rather than his words), but the overwhelming weight of evidence for the longer reading, and the fact that in the parallel in Luke 9:26 λόγους is omitted by a quite different though equally small group, suggests that it may have been an accidental omission owing to homoioteleuton. The presence of καί rather than μετά in the final phrase in P45 W is probably due to assimilation to Luke 9:26.

Any division within this continuous section of narrative is artificial. Verse 31 follows on closely from v. 30, as it sets the real and unexpected mission of the Messiah over against Peter's more conventional viewpoint. Many commentators make a break instead after v. 33, between Jesus' dialogue with his disciples and the unexpected inclusion of an ὄχλος in the audience for the monologue which follows. Another break might be discerned in the connective formula καὶ ἔλεγεν αὐτοῖς in 9:1, though most are agreed that the traditional chapter division at this point was unfortunate. But I have chosen to treat 8:31–9:1 as a single unit, and to set it off from 8:27-30, because these verses are all bound together by the theme of suffering and death, starkly introduced in 8:31, and explored in its implications both for Jesus and for his disciples up to and including 9:1.

Despite the prevalence of rejection and death in this passage, the tone is neither gloomy nor fatalistic. The death of which these verses speak is not a meaningless or tragic fate, but is freely accepted and purposeful. The suffering and death of the Son of Man is necessary (δεῖ), the means of fulfilling his messianic mission. It is the prelude to resurrection, and can be spoken of with assurance (παρρησία, v. 32). Peter's attempt to deflect him from it merits the sternest rebuke. The death of those who follow him is the result of their deliberately choosing to follow him on the way of the cross, and is paradoxically the way to life. It is embraced for the sake of the gospel, while to evade it would be to forfeit one's 'life'. Those who endure rejection from other people will be welcomed by the Son of Man in heavenly glory. For some there will be the vision of the powerful presence of the kingdom of God even before they face death; for the rest, we may assume, that vision will be the reward which follows from their martyrdom.

All this represents a powerful new theme in Mark's story, and one which

332

will be vital for his readers as they approach the events with which the story will come to its climax in Jerusalem. There have indeed been plenty of indications already of the growth of hostility towards Jesus and his followers, and occasional hints that that hostility will end in death (2:20; 3:6). But what is new here is the conviction that his death will come not as the triumph of the opposition but as the fulfilment of the divine purpose, to be welcomed rather than bewailed. The Son of Man who will be rejected and killed is the same who will then come in his Father's glory with the holy angels. The death is the means to the glory, and the outcome will be the powerful coming of the kingdom of God. Mark does not yet offer any formulated theology of atonement or of the divine plan of salvation; it is enough that the disciples begin to grasp this broad new perspective on death and life.

It is not only Jesus' destiny that they must begin to see in a new light, but their own. They too, to whom he is speaking, must in their turn follow him on the road to death, and through that death be taken up into his glory and triumph. Here is a whole new scenario for the disciples to absorb. Their natural human repugnance in the face of what appears to be defeat and disaster must give way to the divine logic which turns human valuation upside down. The road to Jerusalem will be the classroom in which they begin to learn this radical new ideology of the kingdom of God. It is no surprise that they are slow learners, and that even by the end of the road they are not yet prepared for what is to come. But the theme has been loudly trumpeted at the outset, and discipleship will never be the same again.

31 Mark quite frequently uses ἄρχομαι to focus his reader's attention on development in the story (like his use of εὐθύς) rather than to indicate a marked change of theme. He has already used it in this way with διδώσκειν in 4:1; 6:2; 6:34, and perhaps no more is intended by καὶ ἤρξατο διδάσκειν αὐτοὺς ὅτι here. But the novel content of the pronouncement that follows, and the fact that its theme will be repeated prominently from now on, suggests that we should read it as signaling a new and central theme in Jesus' teaching to his disciples.[44]

For ὁ υἱὸς τοῦ ἀνθρώπου see on 2:10. Its use here, following so closely on the first open use of ὁ Χριστός in v. 29 and the command to silence, marks a deliberate substitution of a less-known and more enigmatic title for the more familiar Χριστός (as also in 14:61-62). What Jesus is going to say about his fate is in sharp contrast to what ὁ Χριστός would naturally convey, and so this more elusive title is more suitable to his purpose. To speak of rejection, suffering, and death as the necessary destiny of the υἱὸς τοῦ ἀνθρώπου is indeed shocking enough, for the vision in Dn. 7:13-14 from which the phrase derives is of a con-

---

44. The clause does not, however, seem to have the same structural significance here that it does in Mt. 16:21: Matthew uses ἄρχομαι much less freely, but here produces the more emphatic introductory formula ἀπὸ τότε ἤρξατο Ἰησοῦς Χριστός δεικνύειν . . . , which J. D. Kingsbury (and others following him) takes to mark the opening of the third and last main section of Matthew's gospel (following a similar formula in 4:17).

quering, majestic figure in heavenly authority. Verse 38 will use the same title in a context which echoes that more natural connotation. But because the phrase ὁ υἱὸς τοῦ ἀνθρώπου would not yet be understood to refer to a recognised messianic figure, there was no popular 'blueprint' for the mission of such a figure which would make it psychologically impossible to grasp the concept of suffering and death as his role, however unexpected such an idea might be.

The basis for this 'necessity' (δεῖ)[45] is not spelled out here, but in 9:12; 14:21, 49 it is traced explicitly to what 'is written', and the same thought surely underlies this and Jesus' other predictions of his passion. It is in the divine purpose revealed in Scripture, rather than in the inevitabilities of Palestinian politics, that Jesus finds the pattern for what is to happen to him. It is only with difficulty that any basis for this conviction can be found in Dn. 7, the source of the title which Jesus uses in his passion predictions. It is true, of course, that the human figure of v. 13 is revealed later in the chapter to represent the holy people of God (vv. 18, 22, etc.), and that those holy people have been subjected to the violence of the fourth beast before the divine judgment is given in their favour and the beast is destroyed (vv. 21, 25). But it is not in their suffering and defeat but in their victory that they are represented in Daniel's dream by the human figure, and in Jewish exegesis of Dn. 7 the 'one like a son of man' is regularly represented as a victorious, not a suffering figure.[46]

There is no need, however, to seek the source of Jesus' δεῖ specifically in Dn. 7, even though this is the source of the title ὁ υἱὸς τοῦ ἀνθρώπου. While several of the sayings in the gospels which use this title do contain elements which echo Dn. 7, many of them do not. The title, once coined, was clearly used by Jesus much more broadly than merely to draw on that one OT passage. It derives its content from Jesus' total view of his mission, to which Dn. 7 supplies only a part. The element of suffering and death is much more plausibly derived from the OT theme of 'the persecution of God's prophets and ambassadors by an impenitent people' (Anderson), and more specifically from those OT passages which do point, however cryptically, to the idea of messianic suffering. Psalms 22 and 69 will be echoed in Mark's passion narrative on the assumption that their depiction of the persecution of the righteous can appropriately be referred to the fate of the Messiah;[47] Zc. 9–14 contains the recurring theme of an apparently messianic figure who is rejected by his people, pierced and smitten (Zc. 11:4-14; 12:10-14; 13:7-9; cf. Mk. 14:27); and most obviously Is. 53 speaks of a servant of God who suffers and dies and whose fate is in some way linked to the restoration of his people. I argued many years ago, in the light of attempts to minimise the influence of Is. 53 and related passages on the NT

45. Cf. the 'necessity' of the divine purpose in some apocalyptic writings: Dn. 2:28, 29, 45 — ἃ δεῖ γενέσθαι; cf. Rev. 1:1; 4:1.

46. See my *Jesus and the OT,* 179-83, 185-88, for a survey of Jewish interpretation of Dn. 7.

47. Another psalm which was influential in this area was apparently Ps. 118, with its image of the 'rejected stone' in v. 22. See F. J. Matera, *Kingship,* 116-19, for an argument that this was the principal scriptural source of the passion predictions. See further on 9:12 below.

understanding of the death of Jesus, that this was after all by far the most probable source of Jesus' conviction that he must suffer and die,[48] and subsequent discussion has not caused me to change that assessment. Verbal echoes of the vicarious suffering of God's servant in Is. 53 will be found later in this gospel in 10:45 and 14:24, both sayings attributed to Jesus, which interpret the saving significance of his own death. In the light of those allusions, it seems most probable that in 8:31; 9:31; 10:33-34, even though there is no verbal echo of Is. 53, Mark expects his readers to be aware that Jesus understood his mission as the Son of Man in terms derived from these OT pointers towards messianic suffering, with Is. 53 as probably the most influential.

Each of the three passion predictions in 8:31, 9:31, and 10:33-34 is differently worded, though all agree on the concluding elements, ἀποκτανθῆναι καὶ μετὰ τρεῖς ἡμέρας ἀναστῆναι. πολλὰ παθεῖν occurs only here, and is a relatively colourless summary which will be filled out in more specific detail in 10:33-34. The following clause is more specific. ἀποδοκιμασθῆναι picks up a term familiar from LXX Ps. 117[118]:22, where Christians recognised in the rejected stone an image of Jesus' fate at the hands of his people's leaders, and of his subsequent vindication by God (12:10; Mt. 21:42; Lk. 20:17; 1 Pet. 2:4, 7).[49] For the Messiah to be dishonoured and spurned was bad enough, but far worse is the specific identification of those who will treat him so: ὑπὸ τῶν πρεσβυτέρων καὶ τῶν ἀρχιερέων καὶ τῶν γραμματέων. This formidable list comprises the three main power groups who made up the Sanhedrin (the 'elders' being leading representatives of the lay nobility),[50] and thus represents the most influential political/religious authority in Israel subject to the Roman provincial authorities.[51] Their listing together here makes it clear that this is a comprehensive rejection of Jesus by all the leading representatives of God's people Israel, and thus raises as acutely as possible the paradox of the unrecognised Messiah. By repeating this impressive list later in his gospel, Mark will ensure that at the crucial points of the subsequent confrontation and condemnation in Jerusalem the reader is reminded that the authorities of Israel are united in their rejection of their Messiah (11:27; 14:43, 53; 15:1; in 15:1 the addition of ὅλον τὸ συνέδριον underlines the point).[52] We know from Josephus and other records

48. 'The Servant of the Lord in the Teaching of Jesus', *TynB* 19 (1968) 26-52, reprinted in a slightly abbreviated form in my *Jesus and the OT,* 110-32.

49. See further on 12:10-11 below, and for the importance of the rejection/vindication theme here and in Mark's passion theology generally see D. Juel, *Messiah,* 52-55.

50. See, for instance, J. Jeremias, *Jerusalem,* 222-32. Josephus, *War,* 2.411, refers to what appear to be the same three elements as forming the official leadership in Jerusalem, using the term οἱ δυνατοί for the 'elders'.

51. While ἀρχιερεύς is properly used in the singular to denote the High Priest, the plural, both in the NT and in Josephus, also includes former holders of the office who still sat in the Sanhedrin, and probably members of the high-ranking priestly families from among whom the High Priest was selected. See Schürer, 2.232-36.

52. This is the only place where the elders appear first in such a list. In all other cases the ἀρχιερεῖς come first, whether mentioned with γραμματεῖς alone (10:33; 11:18; 14:1; 15:31) or with

that there was both disagreement and rivalry between the different parties which were represented in the Sanhedrin (see also Acts 23:6-10), but their opposition to Jesus and his teaching would be sufficient to bring them together on this issue (see on 3:6).

Each of Jesus' passion predictions in 8:31, 9:31, and 10:33-34 ends with the resurrection, and it will be assumed already in 9:9 that the disciples are familiar with the idea (though wrongly, as 9:10 reveals). It will again be assumed in 14:28 (cf., cryptically, 14:58). But even Mark's brief account of the events in Jerusalem indicates that the disciples were not in fact expecting Jesus to rise, and the other gospels underline the point more strongly. Mark offers no explanation of their failure to grasp such a striking idea, emphatically repeated. Perhaps we are to assume (and 9:10 suggests this) that the idea was so totally foreign to their thinking that they could not absorb its meaning, and perhaps imagined that Jesus was using some sort of metaphorical imagery for ultimate vindication (though the very specific μετὰ τρεῖς ἡμέρας would not sit comfortably with such a sense). At any rate it seems clear that it was the more easily intelligible theme of suffering and death which stayed in the disciples' minds.

Mark's wording of the resurrection prediction differs from that of Matthew and Luke in two ways. In all three predictions he uses the active verb ἀνίστημι rather than the passive of ἐγείρω which is more commonly used of the resurrection of Jesus in the NT, particularly in Paul, and occurs in all three predictions in Matthew (probably; inevitably there are textual variants); Luke has ἐγερθῆναι in 9:22 but ἀναστήσεται in 18:33. Attempts to draw a clear distinction in principle between the active and passive ways of speaking of Jesus' resurrection have not been very impressive;[53] at most it may be suggested that Mark's active form, in contrast with the inevitably passive character of the verbs which lead up to it, emphasises that despite whatever people can do to him the Son of Man will have the last word. But it is reading too much into a stylistic preference to suggest that Mark's choice of verb indicates any disagreement with the general NT perception of the resurrection as *God's* act of power, vindicating his obedient Son.

The other distinctive feature of Mark's wording is the phrase μετὰ τρεῖς ἡμέρας, which he uses in all three passion predictions, whereas Matthew and Luke consistently use τῇ τρίτῃ ἡμέρᾳ. (In Mt. 27:63-64, however, the Jewish authorities appeal for the tomb to be guarded ἕως τῆς τρίτης ἡμέρας on the basis that Jesus had predicted his resurrection μετὰ τρεῖς ἡμέρας, a surprising survival of the Marcan formula.) Mark's phrase reflects Jewish usage,

---

both the other groups (in which case the order of the latter two groups varies: scribes before elders in 11:27; 14:43 and elders before scribes in 14:53; 15:1). Gundry, 429, takes the first position of the elders here, against Mark's editorial tendency, to indicate that Mark is here quoting the tradition of Jesus' words. For comments on the reasons for the order and the titles included in each passage see Gundry, 431-32.

53. The issue is usefully summarised in *DNTT*, 3.276.

whereby 'after three days' would mean 'the day after tomorrow',[54] but in a broader cultural context this idiom might not be understood, resulting in the embarrassment of a discrepancy between prediction and fact, in that all the gospels agree on a period of only some thirty-six hours between Jesus' burial and resurrection.[55] The phrase used by Matthew and Luke is therefore apologetically safer, even if in a Jewish context its meaning was not significantly different.[56]

Resurrection after three days is part of the sequence governed by δεῖ, and therefore might be expected also to be derived from the OT. In Is. 52:13; 53:10-12 the servant's death is to issue in vindication, 'raising up' and length of days, but this key passage offers no explicit basis for the three days. One possible source is the 'three days and three nights' of Jon. 2:1 (EVV 1:17), after which Jonah was 'restored to life', and which is explicitly alluded to in connection with Jesus' resurrection in Mt. 12:40. Another possible allusion is to Ho. 6:2, where the hope of being 'raised up after three days' refers not to physical resurrection but to national restoration; an echo of that passage in this context must either be with scant regard to its original meaning,[57] or on the basis of a typological view of Jesus' death and resurrection experience as in some way 'fulfilling' the more limited hopes of eighth-century Israel.[58] But it is not necessary to press the scriptural basis of the δεῖ to the point of requiring a direct OT source for each clause of the prediction.

32-33 For τὸν λόγον ἐλάλει see on 4:33. The λόγος here is not just teaching in general, but the ground-breaking pronouncement of v. 31. παρρησίᾳ indicates the emphasis with which this new perspective is presented (contrast the secrecy of v. 30), and shows that the 'disgrace' involved in rejection and execution is not a matter for embarrassment or concealment. This παρρησία makes the force of Jesus' unwelcome words in v. 31 all the more uncomfortable for the disciples, and goads Peter into remedial action.[59] Like Priscilla and

---

54. Cf. Josephus, *Ant.* 7.280 with 281; 8.214 with 218: in each case an event promised μετὰ τρεῖς ἡμέρας is expected to occur τῇ τρίτῃ τῶν ἡμερῶν.

55. R. McKinnis, *NovT* 18 (1976) 97-98, suggests that Mark uses μετὰ τρεῖς ἡμέρας rather than τῇ τρίτῃ ἡμέρᾳ because for him the phrase denotes the period from Jesus' rejection and 'handing over', the beginning of the events predicted, rather than from the last of them, his death.

56. Matthew does not, however, avoid in 12:40 the apparently even more embarrassing phrase τρεῖς ἡμέρας καὶ τρεῖς νύκτας, which is supplied by LXX Jon. 2:1 (EVV 1:17), and which he does not feel it necessary to gloss. For evidence that even this phrase need mean no more than 'the day after tomorrow/before yesterday' see 1 Sa. 30:12 with 13; cf. Est. 4:16 with 5:1).

57. See, however, H. K. McArthur, *NTS* 18 (1971-2) 81-86, for the rabbinic use of Ho. 6:2 in association with the resurrection of the dead, though this cannot be dated certainly before the third century. McArthur believes that this is the primary background to the NT 'third day' tradition.

58. See my *Jesus and the OT,* 53-55, for further thoughts on these possibilities.

59. For some interesting parallels of negative reactions of disciples and friends to their master's risking death (Socrates, Apollonius of Tyana, Paul) see W. T. Shiner, *Follow,* 255-60. Shiner goes on (261-64, with further analysis on 265-76) to show how the rebuke functions from a literary point of view to underline the shocking nature of Jesus' statement, and to provide a transition to the following teaching.

Aquila in Acts 18:26, who felt it necessary to correct the misguided παρρησία of Apollos, he προσλαμβάνεται Jesus to correct his bizarre view of the messianic role. προσλαμβάνομαι suggests a confidential approach, taking the misguided zealot on one side to prevent any more embarrassing outbursts. We are not told the content of Peter's protest, but ἐπιτιμάω suggests that it was firm and none too gentle (cf. the same verb in 1:25; 3:12; 10:13, 48, and comments on 1:25). The repetition of this same verb in 8:30 (Jesus to disciples), 32 (Peter to Jesus), 33 (Jesus to Peter) marks a serious confrontation of incompatible ideologies. That the confrontation is not merely between Jesus and Peter, but involves the whole disciple group for whom Peter acts as spokesman, is made clear by ἐπιστραφεὶς καὶ ἰδὼν τοὺς μαθητὰς αὐτοῦ, which neatly picks up the narrative element of Peter's taking Jesus aside — he is not going to be 'taken aside', and deliberately involves the whole group by implication in his reply, even though it is addressed, as it must be, specifically to Peter.

ὀπίσω μου is not in itself a term of dissociation; in the gospels it more normally refers to 'following' in a good sense (see on 1:7 and 1:17), and it will be used in that way in the very next verse. But with ὕπαγε rather than δεῦτε it is not a summons but a dismissal, and the addition of the epithet Σατανᾶ completes the fiercely negative tone of Jesus' counterrebuke.[60] The name Σατανᾶς has occurred already in 1:13; 3:23, 26; 4:15 as the familiar Jewish term for the devil (also called Βεελζεβούλ in 3:22), but its use for a human being, however antagonistic, is unparalleled. It functions here as more than just an extravagant term of abuse (a use for which there is in any case no other evidence),[61] and implies that Peter's protest, even though properly described as 'human' thoughts (φρονεῖς τὰ τῶν ἀνθρώπων), is so much at odds with the thoughts of God as to be attributed to a more supernatural source. By opposing the will of God (δεῖ) for his Messiah, Peter and those who agree with him are acting as spokesmen of God's ultimate enemy (cf. Satan's role in 'taking away the word' [of God] in 4:15).[62]

60. Belo, 158, translates ὕπαγε ὀπίσω μου as 'get *from* behind me', a deliberate rescinding of δεῦτε ὀπίσω μου in 1:17: 'Jesus is telling Peter here: Stop being my disciple'. He claims that 'the Greek text authorizes both translations', but does not explain how. ὀπίσω μου is not so technical a term for discipleship as to demand this unnatural reading of the Greek. Gundry, 433, also reads it in this 'technical' sense, but finds exactly the opposite meaning in Jesus' words: 'Jesus tells Peter to go back to his position among the disciples, where he belongs, following after Jesus, not taking him aside by walking ahead of him or at least beside him.' This, too, is probably reading too much into a simple preposition.

61. It is sometimes suggested that, in view of the root meaning of the Semitic term, 'the Adversary', it might be used here in that weaker sense, 'my adversary', rather than with overt reference to the devil himself. Not only is there no parallel to such a use, but the retention of the Aramaic form rather than the use of a Greek equivalent such as ἀντίδικος surely indicates that it was recognised and remembered as a proper name, applied, however incongruously, to a human spokesman of Satan.

62. S. R. Garrett, *Temptations*, 76-82, argues that Mark here deliberately presents Peter as acting as Satan's proxy, similarly to Job's wife, Siti[do]s, in *Test. Job* 26-27, so that Satan continues his testing of Jesus through Peter's agency.

The characterisation of Peter's ideas as τὰ τῶν ἀνθρώπων as opposed to τὰ τοῦ θεοῦ sums up the problem which we have seen in considering the call to secrecy in v. 30. The divine purpose revealed in v. 31 makes no sense in human terms. If even the privileged disciples are unable to get beyond their 'human' understanding of the Messiah's role, what hope is there for people in general to get it right? The problem lies not at the level of competing loyalties (as is suggested by the RSV translation 'on the side of'), but at that of incompatible ideologies, of a human perspective which cannot grasp the divine purpose.

34 Mark uses προσκαλέομαι to alert the reader to expect something new or emphatic to be revealed, or some new instruction to be delivered to the disciples (cf. 3:13, 23; 6:7; 7:14; 10:42; 12:43). What is surprising here is that the object of the verb is not just the disciples, whom one would expect, but τὸν ὄχλον σὺν τοῖς μαθηταῖς αὐτοῦ. We have gained from vv. 27-33 the impression that the setting is a private retreat in the countryside in the far north of Palestine, where Jesus was presumably little known and the population probably largely non-Jewish. A crowd of people in this area who were at least potentially followers of Jesus seems incongruous, and they will play no further part in the narrative. From the narrator's point of view, however, the introduction of the ὄχλος serves here, rather like οἱ περὶ αὐτὸν σὺν τοῖς δώδεκα in 4:10, to widen the audience for a key pronouncement; their inclusion in the audience asserts that the harsh demands of the following verses apply not only to the Twelve but to anyone else who may wish to join the movement. The introductory phrases εἴ τις θέλει and ὃς γὰρ ἐάν (vv. 35, 38) further generalise the scope of the paragraph; this is not a special formula for the elite, but an essential element in discipleship.

ὀπίσω μου is used here not as in v. 33 but in its more normal NT sense (see 1:17, 20 etc.), and the double use alongside it of ἀκολουθέω (cf. 1:18; 2:14) confirms that we have here a basic condition of discipleship.[63] It is to join Jesus on the way to execution. This is the first use of σταυρός by Mark, and neither noun nor verb will occur again before chapter 15. Jesus' predictions of his death in 8:31; 9:31; 10:33-34 do not spell out the means of death, and this specifically Roman form of execution would not be the first to come to a Jewish mind when hearing of death at the behest of the Jewish authorities. By the time Mark wrote his gospel, of course, Jesus' crucifixion was well known, and his readers would need no explanation for the σταυρός here. But at the beginning of the journey to Jerusalem such language is calculated to shock, and evokes a vivid and horrifying image of the death march with all its shameful publicity. The preservation of so specific an image at more than one point in the gospel tradition (see also the Q saying Mt. 10:38; Lk. 14:27) may suggest that it originates from Jesus' own awareness of how he would die rather than from Mark's reading back the later event.

63. For the background to the call to follow see E. Best, *Following*, 33-34, and for its meaning in relation to Jesus, 36-39.

The metaphor of taking up one's own cross is not to be domesticated into an exhortation merely to endure hardship patiently. In this context, following 8:31, it is an extension of Jesus' readiness for death to those who follow him, and the following verses will fill it out still in terms of the loss of life, not merely the acceptance of discomfort. While it may no doubt be legitimately applied to other and lesser aspects of the suffering involved in following Jesus,[64] the primary reference in context must be to the possibility of literal death.

The call to take up the cross is preceded by ἀπαρνησάσθω ἑαυτόν, a phrase not paralleled in the gospel tradition. The verb ἀπαρνέομαι is particularly associated with Peter's eventual denial not of himself but of his master; in that context it means to dissociate oneself completely from someone, to sever the relationship. So the reflexive use implies perhaps to refuse to be guided by one's own interests, to surrender control of one's own destiny. In 2 Tim. 2:13 ἀρνήσασθαι ἑαυτόν (of God as subject) means to act contrary to his own nature, to cease to be God. What Jesus calls for here is thus a radical abandonment of one's own identity and self-determination, and a call to join the march to the place of execution follows appropriately from this. Such 'self-denial' is on a different level altogether from giving up chocolates for Lent. 'It is not the denial of something to the self, but the denial of the self itself.'[65]

35-37 The talk of losing and gaining the ψυχή in these verses depends on the range of meaning of ψυχή, and poses problems for the translator. The same noun denotes both the 'being alive' (as opposed to dead; cf. 3:4; 10:45) which one might seek to preserve by escaping persecution and martyrdom, and the 'real life' which may be the outcome of such martyrdom, and therefore is to be found beyond earthly life. It is in this latter sense that the English word 'soul' is traditionally used here, but the wordplay is better preserved by retaining 'life' but where necessary qualifying it with 'true/eternal' or 'earthly'.[66]

The immediate subject of these verses, following as they do the imagery of taking up one's cross in v. 34, is surely the literal loss of (earthly) life which the disciple is called to accept as a potential result of following Jesus. Only that sense fully does justice to the wordplay. To extend this sense to the loss of privilege, advantage, reputation, comfort, and the like may be legitimate in principle, but only so long as this primary and more radical sense is not set aside. To cling to the things of this life, the things which humanity naturally values most,

---

64. This is well argued by E. Best, *Following,* 38-39, though perhaps to the extent of weakening the literal sense too much.

65. E. Best, *Following,* 37. See 37-38 for a fuller examination of 'self-denial' here.

66. See, however, E. Best, *Following,* 41-42, for the proposal that ψυχή should be understood as 'the real or essential person' throughout these verses. In that case the paradox will be found not in a play on different senses of the noun, but in the juxtaposition of opposite verbs in relation to it. The overall effect is perhaps not significantly affected by this interpretation, but insofar as it reduces the focus on the possibility of literal martyrdom, I find it less appropriate to the context. The same problem arises with Mann's use of 'self' to translate most (not all) of the occurrences of ψυχή in these verses.

is the way to forfeit *true* life; clinging to life itself is the ultimate example of this concern, and is set in contrast with the acceptance of death (for the right reason) as the way to real life. Jesus himself, in his death and resurrection, will be the supreme example of this new perspective.

The promise of true life is not attached to death in itself, but to the loss of life ἕνεκεν [ἐμοῦ καὶ] τοῦ εὐαγγελίου (see Textual Note). The possibility of literal martyrdom as the outcome of Christian discipleship is clearly envisaged here; cf. 13:9 (ἕνεκεν ἐμοῦ). Jesus' expectation of his own death must have raised this possibility, and the experiences of the early church from Acts 7 onwards would add weight to it. The specific mention of the εὐαγγέλιον as the cause of loss of life indicates that the disciples are to play an active role in mission rather than merely privately following the teaching of Jesus, and that it is in this missionary work that they are likely to meet with persecution and death. Best rightly emphasises that the addition of this phrase indicates the inadequacy of a view of discipleship as merely the *imitation* of Jesus.[67]

In the Synoptic Gospels κόσμος does not carry the negative connotation it has elsewhere in the NT, and especially in John; it denotes the created world in a neutral sense. κερδῆσαι τὸν κόσμον ὅλον therefore simply expresses the height of human ambition and achievement, measured in terms of earthly life. While ζημιόω sometimes carries a juridical sense of penalty or punishment, the context here does not require that nuance. Its more normal sense is simply loss or disadvantage. ζημιωθῆναι in v. 36 therefore denotes the opposite of κερδῆσαι; this is a profit and loss account, and it is clearly understood that the loss of the ψυχή (here '*true* life') far outweighs any gain in terms of earthly advantage.

The same idea is differently expressed in the rhetorical question[68] of v. 37, where again the assumption is made that the ψυχή is all that ultimately matters, and that nothing else can compensate for its loss.[69] The ἀντάλλαγμα (cf. LXX Job 28:15) is the 'exchange rate' at which the ψυχή is valued; it is beyond price. The language of exchange echoes Ps. 49:7-9 (though LXX there uses λυτρόω/λύτρωσις, not ἀνταλλάσσομαι/ἀντάλλαγμα), but whereas the psalm speaks of a payment to avoid physical death, here the focus has moved to '*true* life', which is even more beyond the reach of human valuation. There is no reason in this context to read into the question any developed theology of redemption; it is simply a statement of comparative value.

38 The contrast in values between this earthly life and true life is developed now in terms of shame and honour. The honour in human society which might be preserved by concealing one's allegiance to Jesus and his teaching is

---

67. E. Best, *Following*, 40-41.

68. The aorist subjunctive δοῖ indicates a 'doubtful or deliberative question' (BDF, 366[1]), 'doubtful' here in the sense that it is assumed that no answer can or will be given.

69. Cf. *2 Bar.* 51:15, where the fate of the unrighteous is described as having 'exchanged their souls (presumably ψυχή in the Greek original)' for a life of affliction, lamentation, and evil.

to be set against the shame (repudiation) which would result in the eternal sphere. Shame here and now is a small price to pay for acknowledgement and honour then.

The two theatres are vividly described. The present context is γενεὰ μοιχαλὶς καὶ ἁμαρτωλός, a concept expressed only here in Mark, but reappearing in Matthew's γενεὰ πονηρὰ καὶ μοιχαλίς (Mt. 12:39; 16:4), and in his frequent denunciations of 'this generation' as set against God and ripe for judgment (Mt. 11:16; 12:41, 42, 45; 17:17; 23:29-36). μοιχαλίς expresses the frequent charge in OT prophecy that Israel is committing adultery againt God, her true husband; 'this generation' is thus characterised as a whole as in rebellion against God and therefore also against his Messiah. The polarisation assumed in these verses marks a more pessimistic assessment than was found in most of the Galilean phase of the story, and points forward rather to the confrontation in Jerusalem.

The second theatre is expressed as the coming of the Son of Man in glory. Christian interpretation traditionally understands these words as referring to a specific future *event,* the parousia, but the balance of the saying is better preserved by understanding it of a new *situation,* contrasted with 'this generation'. As similar expressions will recur in climactic pronouncements in 13:26 and 14:62, it is important to clarify what language about 'the coming of the Son of Man' implies, since in Christian tradition such language has come to have an almost automatic reference to the parousia or 'second coming'. I shall argue more fully at 13:26 and 14:62 that this interpretation, which seems so 'natural' to us, would not have been at all natural for Jewish readers/hearers of this gospel in the first century to whom the imagery of Dn. 7:13-14 would have been very familiar. That passage describes Daniel's vision of a υἱὸς ἀνθρώπου who is seen 'coming' (LXX ἤρχετο; Thdt ἐρχόμενος) to be presented before the throne of God where he is given universal and eternal sovereignty over all nations; the themes here of glory and of the presence of the angels are also derived from the context of that vision in Dn. 7:9-10 (though a further OT echo may also be seen in the coming of God καὶ πάντες οἱ ἅγιοι μετ᾽ αὐτοῦ in Zc. 14:5). The scene is thus set in heaven where God is on his throne surrounded by the angelic court, and its focus is on the enthronement of the υἱὸς ἀνθρώπου to rule over the earth. Such a scene makes an entirely appropriate contrast with 'this generation' in its rebellion against God's sovereignty; it is before the heavenly authority of the Son of Man that the disciples must answer for their loyalty or cowardice.

There is thus no reason in this context to take the verb ἔλθῃ as referring to a 'descent' to earth at the parousia.[70] It is an allusion to the wording of Dn.

70. See further on 13:26 and 14:62 for allusions to Dn. 7:13 in other sayings of Jesus in Mark, and for the question of what relevance, if any, they may have to the parousia. Myers, 248, argues persuasively that a parousia reference would be irrelevant at this point.

7:13, where the 'coming' is the entry of the υἱὸς ἀνθρώπου into his kingship, exercised over the earth indeed, but located in the heavenly throne room. This language refers not to a specific event, but to the state of sovereign authority to which Jesus looks forward as the proper destiny of the Son of Man. His rejection on earth will lead to vindication and glory in heaven, and his followers must be prepared for a parallel experience. The same Son of Man who is soon to be the victim of human 'justice' will then be revealed as the true and ultimate authority; disciples must realise that it is recognition before that court that will matter in the end, whatever the reactions of 'this generation'.

One feature of this saying which is not derived from Dn. 7 is the designation of God as the πατήρ of the Son of Man. This is a new element in the gospel, though in the light of God's declaration in 1:11 that Jesus is his beloved son, the title can cause no surprise to Mark's readers. For the disciples at the time it would not necessarily seem strange, if they shared the Jewish tendency to think of the Messiah, the title by which they have now come to recognise Jesus, as God's Son in the light of 2 Sa. 7:14 and Ps. 2:7. Jesus will refer to God as his πατήρ again only in 13:32 (linked with ὁ υἱός) and in 14:36 (as a direct address to God in prayer).

9:1 The form of this enigmatic saying varies among the Synoptic Gospels, but in all of them it is associated directly with Jesus' words about the Son of Man coming in his Father's glory with the angels. The connecting formula varies: in Matthew it follows on directly with an ἀμὴν λέγω ὑμῖν ὅτι, and in Luke with λέγω δὲ ὑμῖν ἀληθῶς, but in Mark the insertion of καὶ ἔλεγεν αὐτοῖς suggests that it may have been an independent saying which Mark has attached here. If so, he made the link because he felt that it followed on appropriately from 8:38, and expected the one saying to be interpreted in the light of the other. The obvious links are twofold: this saying picks up from vv. 34-38 the theme of death as a possible fate for disciples, and it looks forward to a future and glorious situation which, while it is expressed quite differently from 8:38, has a similar atmosphere of divine glory and authority.

The saying is marked out by the formula ἀμὴν λέγω ὑμῖν ὅτι as an authoritative pronouncement (see on 3:28). The wording that follows is formal and even clumsy, not only in the odd placing of ὧδε before τῶν and in the heavy phrase οὐ μὴ γεύσωνται θανάτου where οὐκ ἀποθανοῦνται would have sufficed, but also in that the whole clause εἰσίν τινες ὧδε τῶν ἑστηκότων οἵτινες οὐ μὴ γεύσωνται θανάτου ἕως ἂν ἴδωσιν seems a remarkably cumbersome way of saying 'some of you will see'. The introduction of the idea of 'not dying until' serves to remind us, however, that Jesus has just been talking about dying for the sake of the gospel (and the periphrasis γεύομαι θανάτου is perhaps appropriate to a violent rather than a natural death); that is the destiny which they have embraced in following Jesus, but for some of them there will be something to look forward to before that death comes. They are a privileged few, only τινες ὧδε τῶν ἑστηκότων; the others need not expect any such revelation before their death. Who they are, and how and why they are chosen out from the rest of the group, is left unexplained.[1] We shall return to the question when we have considered what it is that they are to see.

The perfect tense of ἐληλυθυῖαν indicates that they are not to see the 'coming' of the βασιλεία τοῦ θεοῦ, but rather to witness the fact that it *has* come. The prediction thus focuses not on its arrival, but on the point at which its presence, already a reality, is (a) visible and (b) displayed ἐν δυνάμει. Here the link with the language of 8:38 about the coming of the υἱὸς τοῦ ἀνθρώπου becomes significant, since both these elements of 'seeing' and of 'power' will be present also in the two other sayings which will be based on Dn. 7:13-14 (13:26: ὄψονται . . . μετὰ δυνάμεως πολλῆς; 14:62: ὄψεσθε . . . τῆς δυνάμεως). There is thus a continuity of motifs between these three key sayings (treating 8:38 and 9:1 together as one 'saying') which can hardly be accidental, and suggests that their subject matter is related. This will be important when we come to the exegesis of those later sayings.

The idea that God's kingship is already present was declared already in 1:15, and is implied in the present conflict between the βασιλεία of Satan and that of God in 3:23-27. But it remains a μυστήριον (4:11) visible to some and not to others; it comes unrecognised, in its own time (4:26-29); at present it remains as inconspicuous as a mustard seed, but one day its growth will be obvious to all (4:30-32). Thus the contrast implied here is between its secret presence in the time of Jesus' ministry, and its future open and powerful manifestation. It is the latter which will be seen by some of those standing there.

How and when it will be thus visible is not spelled out here, beyond the promise that it will be within the lifetime of some of those present. This time limit is another theme which links the three sayings based on Dn. 7:13-14: the prediction of 13:26 is followed by the declaration that this generation will not be over before these things have happened (13:30), and the pronouncement in 14:62 is of what 'you', Jesus' judges in the Sanhedrin, will see. These sayings are not predictions of some event in the indefinite and probably distant future. All relate to the contemporary generation. There is nothing here to suggest the parousia.

Many suggestions have been made as to how some of the disciples might have been expected to perceive the powerful presence of God's kingship within their lifetime.[2] They include Jesus' death on the cross and the symbolic tearing

1. B. D. Chilton, *God in Strength,* 267-74, suggests, on the basis of his own reconstruction of the 'original' form of the saying, that 'those standing here' are Elijah and Moses, the 'deathless ones', who will stand with Jesus on the mountain in v. 4. Apart from the uncertainty of Chilton's reconstructed text, the obvious difficulties with this view are (a) that Elijah and Moses have not yet appeared in the text, and will not be 'here' until six days later (though Chilton eliminates ὧδε from his 'original' text), and (b) the fact that they are 'deathless' makes it strange to talk about their 'not tasting death *until* . . .'. Moreover, it is not clear what reassurance the disciples might be expected to draw from the predicted experience of Elijah and Moses.

2. See K. E. Brower, *JSNT* 6 (1980) 17-41, for a useful listing of suggestions, including documentation for all those mentioned above; his own preference is for the cross. On pp. 21-23 he cites me

of the temple curtain; his victory over death in the resurrection; his ascension and the heavenly enthronement which it implies; the powerful coming of the Spirit at Pentecost; the dynamic growth of the church despite opposition; the fall of Jerusalem in A.D. 70, understood as the point at which the authority of the Son of Man supplanted that of the earthly city. No doubt the list could be extended, but all these events may be understood as in some sense a manifestation of the powerful establishment of God's kingship, and all would be within the lifetime of at least some of those standing there.

In the case of the earlier events (cross, resurrection, ascension, and Pentecost) the reference to τινες is less appropriate, since we have no reason to believe that *any* of the audience of 9:1 would be dead before they had taken place. The fall of Jerusalem by itself would not obviously demonstrate the powerful presence of God's kingship, unless on the basis of a rather esoteric understanding of salvation history. But in any case, there is no need to be so specific. In any or all of these ways, and no doubt in others too, those with eyes to see could have perceived before they died that God had powerfully taken control of events and was working out his purpose in history. Even if some of them were to die before this was clearly visible, the process had begun, and the mustard seed was growing. That is all that the wording of 9:1 requires. To classify this, as is sometimes done, as a failed prediction of an immediate parousia and end of the world is surely perverse: if that was what Mark intended, he has chosen a very obscure way to express it.

Another line of interpretation is to notice the setting of this saying immediately before the account of the transfiguration (9:2-13), and linked to it by an unusually precise time interval ('after six days'). The transfiguration is described as something which the three disciples *saw,* and the heavenly glory surely implies power. In reply to the standard objection that 'some standing here will by no means taste death until' is a ludicrously pompous way to describe an event which is to take place only a week later, it must be noted that this objection ignores the significance of τινες; it was only *some* of the disciples (three) who were with Jesus on the mountain, and the rest of them would indeed 'taste death' without seeing anything comparable. It is a more serious objection that a temporary vision on the mountain seems to fall some way short of ἡ βασιλεία τοῦ θεοῦ ἐληλυθυῖα ἐν δυνάμει; it was at best a heavenly preview of what was still to be achieved in earthly reality. But the link between 9:1 and 9:2-13 is too explicit to be overlooked, and we may well conclude that Mark understood the event on the mountain to be at least a partial and proleptic fulfilment of Jesus' words, even though the historical reality remained to be made visible perhaps in the ways suggested above.[3]

as locating the fulfilment of Mk. 9:1 specifically in the fall of Jerusalem in A.D. 70, an interpretation which I in fact described as 'tempting' (*Jesus and the OT,* 140) without committing myself firmly and exclusively to it. I would not now wish to be as definite on this as Brower understood me to be. For a much fuller survey of interpretation through the Christian era see M. Künzi, *Naherwartungslogion.*

3. The exegesis of 9:1 offered above is more fully developed in my *Divine Government,* 66-73.

Whatever the precise fulfilment envisaged, 9:1 functions in its context as a needed reassurance to the disciples after the pessimistic projection for their likely fate in 8:34-38.[4] The ultimate power is with God, not with those who will threaten their life, and the time will soon come when they will see that to follow Jesus is not to be on a 'hiding to nothing', but to share in God's assured victory.

Jesus Revealed Again as Son of God (9:2-13)

Even if it is doubted whether Mark intended this incident to be read as *the* fulfilment of Jesus' words in 9:1 about seeing the kingdom of God having come with power, it is generally agreed that the sequence is not accidental. These verses record an experience shared by only *some* of those who in 9:1 were 'standing here', and they date it specifically just six days after Jesus' pronouncement, a precision in temporal connection which is unique in Mark. Moreover, Jesus has spoken of what 'some of those standing here' will *see,* and vv. 2-8 describe what the disciples *saw* (Matthew calls it a ὅραμα). So the incident on the mountain is narrated from the point of view of the disciples' experience rather than that of Jesus: ἔμπροσθεν αὐτῶν, v. 2; ὤφθη αὐτοῖς, v. 4; Peter's reaction, v. 5; the disciples' fear, v. 6; ἐπισκιάζουσα αὐτοῖς, v. 7; a voice addressed to them, describing Jesus in the third person, and calling on them to listen to him, v. 7; περιβλεψάμενοι . . . εἶδον, v. 8; μεθ' ἑαυτῶν, v. 8.

The 'otherworldly' character of the scene on the mountain points to the βασιλεία τοῦ θεοῦ. The dialogue which follows in vv. 9-13 shows that the disciples' understanding of what they had witnessed was also in eschatological terms (the scribal teaching on the coming of Elijah), such as Jesus' pronouncement about the kingdom of God having come in power might be expected to evoke.

In some sense, then, Mark seems to have intended his readers to see 9:1 as pointing forward to the transfiguration narrative. There is no need for us to go further and pronounce whether or not this incident is to be seen exclusively as *the* fulfilment of that prediction. As we have seen on 9:1, the words are not specific enough to require such precision. Undoubtedly Peter, James, and John were caught up into an incident which enabled them to see God's sovereignty affirmed and his purpose working out in the coming of his Messiah. No one else is recorded as having had this same visual experience. But in other ways as weeks and years passed the growth of the mustard seed from insignificance to power would be increasingly obvious to those with eyes to see it, and so 9:1 would be progressively fulfilled in the lifetime of those who heard Jesus'

---

4. E. Trocmé, *Formation,* 123 n. 1, based on his article in *SE* 2 (1964) 259-65, suggests that Mark intends the saying to offer not reassurance but warning: 'Among those here present there are cowards who would never be willing to die before the end of the world, who avoid taking risks so that they may be alive to see the great Day come!'

words. What is distinctive about the experience of the three disciples on the mountain is that their vision of divine power and glory *preceded* the apparent defeat of the cross, to which v. 12 deliberately points forward. The paradox of the mission of the rejected Messiah is at the heart of the powerful coming of the kingdom of God. The whole pericope thus adds up to a mind-stretching combination of themes which will leave even the privileged three disciples bewildered, and certainly undermines any simplistic triumphalism which 9:1 might have triggered.[5]

While the visual experience on the mountain is unique in the gospel records, the voice from heaven echoes the voice after Jesus' baptism in 1:11, and the two pronouncements together offer the most direct testimony to Jesus' identity as the Son of God, declared on the authority of God himself. From the narrative point of view there is a progression, in that the earlier declaration was apparently to Jesus alone (hence the second-person address), whereas here it is a third-person pronouncement to the three disciples; the secret is being shared, even if still to only a handful of chosen disciples. But from the point of view of the reader, the two pronouncements have the same theological force. What was definitively declared at the outset is here reinforced at a crucial point in the story, just after the recognition of Jesus' Messiahship and in the light of his first clear prediction of his coming rejection, death, and resurrection. So at the fundamental level nothing has changed. It is as Son of God that the υἱός τοῦ ἀνθρώπου will go as it is written of him. It is in this light that we the readers, no less than Peter, James, and John, must interpret the coming events in Jerusalem. However improbable it may appear, it is the Son of God who will suffer and die. Jesus' public declaration of his identity in 14:61-62 will not take us by surprise, and we will be able to recognise who it is who is on the cross even before the centurion blurts it out (15:39).

The heavenly glory of vv. 2-8 is in striking contrast to the humiliation just predicted in 8:31. This pericope thus serves as a counterbalance to the 'gloom' of the preceding verses. But the contrast is not total, once we also take vv. 9-13 into account. The suffering of the Son of Man returns to our attention in v. 12, and the secrecy enjoined in 8:30 with reference to Jesus' messianic role is reinforced in v. 9 with regard also to the vision the disciples have just experienced. The light and dark elements are not set up as a contradiction but blended into a total messianic agenda in which Mark's love of paradox finds its fullest expression.

The significance of this incident as a christological revelation is focused in three aspects of the disciples' experience: (1) the visible alteration of Jesus before their eyes demonstrates him to be more than a merely human teacher;

---

5. H. C. Kee, in J. Reumann (ed.), *Understanding the Sacred Text*, 137-52, argues that the primary focus of the pericope is 'not a theophany *to*, nor an epiphany *of*, Jesus, but a proleptic vision of the exaltation of Jesus as kingly Son of man granted to the disciples as eschatological witnesses'; for the theme of kingship see especially ibid., 147-49.

(2) his association with Elijah and Moses demonstrates his messianic role; (3) the voice from heaven declares his identity as the Son of God. These factors, set in the context of the new understanding of Jesus and his mission which they have gained at Caesarea Philippi and through Jesus' subsequent teaching, mark a gigantic step forward in the disciples' developing appreciation of the scale of the divine plan they have become caught up in.[6]

Underlying Mark's telling of the story are clear echoes of the OT. This is explicit in the naming of Elijah and Moses as Jesus' companions in the vision. The 'transformation' of Jesus and the shining of his clothes may recall the shining of Moses' face in Ex. 34:29-35, though Mark offers no verbal echoes or direct parallels to that account. More explicit are the repeated reminders of Moses' experiences at Sinai in Ex. 24. Moses took three named companions (though also seventy others) up onto the high mountain to meet with God (Ex. 24:1, 9), and there they had a vision of divine glory (24:10); subsequently Moses went higher with only Joshua as companion (24:13-14); cloud covered the mountain (24:15), and after 'six days' Moses went up into it (24:16); there God spoke to Moses (Ex. 25ff.); when Moses relayed God's words to the people, they promised to obey (24:3, 7). Mark's narrative does not reproduce exactly the Exodus story, but there are enough verbal and conceptual echoes to trigger thoughts of a new Sinai experience, and perhaps of Jesus as a new Moses (see on v. 4).[7] The fact that Elijah also met with God on the same mountain (1 Ki. 19:8-18) reinforces the link.

We have no access to 'what actually happened' in physical terms (i.e., what a cine-camera would have recorded) beyond the gospel narratives themselves. Mark, as we have seen, narrates the whole scene in terms of what the disciples saw and experienced, but the language is of actual changes (μετεμορφώθη, ἐγένετο, ἐγένετο, ἐγένετο), and Peter's suggestion of building τρεῖς σκηνάς suggests that he did not regard Elijah and Moses, any more than Jesus, as merely figures in a 'vision'. Mt. 17:9 characterises the whole experience as a ὅραμα, but this term, while it can be used (like English 'vision') of an experience which is 'all in the mind', does not necessarily suggest anything less substantial than Mark's parallel phrase ἃ εἶδον; it means simply 'that which is seen'. The story is unique, and speculation as to the physicality of the experience must remain unsatisfied. Even the resurrection appearances of Jesus recorded in the other three gospels do not offer a useful parallel, for while they describe a body which was not bound by the normal rules of time and space, their atmosphere is remarkably down-to-earth (Jesus is mistaken for a gardener, an unknown fellow traveller or a stranger on the shore) in contrast with the visi-

6. E. Best, *Following*, 57-58; *Disciples*, 220-22, argues that Mark has deliberately added a focus on discipleship to a story which in the tradition was of a christological revelation.

7. J. A. Ziesler, *ExpTim* 81 (1969-70) 263-68, attractively argues for the importance of the Exodus background in this pericope. F. R. McCurley, *JBL* 93 (1974) 67-81, agrees with the Exodus background, and argues that μετὰ ἡμέρας ἕξ reflects a standard Semitic literary pattern of a six-day period followed by a climactic event on the seventh.

ble, unearthly glory of the transfiguration and the reappearance of long-dead men of God to speak with Jesus.[8]

2 Apart from the connected sequence of events through chapters 14–16, Mark generally offers no indication of time when introducing a new pericope. If he does, it is usually through a colourless phrase like δι' ἡμερῶν (2:1) or ἐν ἐκείναις ταῖς ἡμέραις (8:1). In chapter 11 he is more specific in linking the events in the temple with the story of the fig tree (ὀψίας οὔσης τῆς ὥρας, τῇ ἐπαύριον, ὅταν ὀψὲ ἐγένετο, πρωΐ), and we shall argue that this is a deliberate attempt to link the two scenes in the reader's mind. But μετὰ ἡμέρας ἕξ is even more specific, and unlike any other such linkage in the gospel. Its effect is to link the ensuing story closely with the saying of 9:1, and to invite the reader to interpret the one in the light of the other. There may well also be a deliberate echo of the six days leading up to the divine discourse on the mountain in Ex. 24:16 (see above), but if this had been Mark's primary purpose in including the phrase he could have created a tighter correspondence (six days *on* the mountain rather than six days' journey to it). Luke's ὡσεὶ ἡμέραι ὀκτώ loses any echo of Exodus, but maintains the close link with the preceding pronouncement.

For the special position of Peter, James, and John see above on 5:37. But whereas there the restriction to three disciples may have been explicable by the limited space available in the room, here (and in 14:33) there is no such pragmatic motive. These three are singled out for special revelation, and taken up the mountain apparently for the specific purpose of witnessing Jesus' glory. Only 'some' of those who heard 9:1 are to receive the vision. In the light of such special privilege it is hardly surprising that these three were to assume positions of leadership in the disciple group, and, less creditably, to feel that they deserved it (10:35-37).

The purpose of going up the mountain was apparently at least in part to find solitude (κατ' ἰδίαν μόνους), just as Jesus had taken the whole disciple group away into a deserted area for a rest in 6:31, and away to the remote region around Caesarea Philippi in 8:27. We cannot know whether he was aware of what was about to happen and so chose a mountain as a suitable place for such a vision,[9] especially given the association of both Moses and

---

8. The frequently repeated assertion of Bultmann that 'It has long since been recognized that this legend was originally a resurrection story' (*History,* 259) is now widely discounted. At almost every point it differs in form from the resurrection appearances of the other gospels; see G. H. Boobyer, *Transfiguration,* 11-16; R. H. Stein, *JBL* 95 (1976) 79-96; Gundry, 471-73, etc. The 'striking links' which Mann, 356, finds between this pericope and Mark's resurrection narrative (16:1-8) turn out on inspection to be tenuous, the most impressive being the fear which causes Peter not to know what to say (but in fact to say the wrong thing) and the women to say nothing at all to anyone in 16:8; hardly a compelling basis for postulating a deliberate echo. There is, however, more to be said for the view that, rather than being a misplaced resurrection narrative, it is a 'prefigurement of the Resurrection' (M. E. Thrall, *NTS* 16 [1969/70] 310-12).

9. Gundry, 457, understands the high mountain as a 'suburb of heaven'. Cf. M. E. Thrall, *NTS* 16 (1969/70) 312: 'The Transfiguration is a scene which takes place on the outskirts of heaven.'

Elijah with mountains, or whether it was merely a suitable place for a retreat with the disciples, as in 3:13, or alone, as in 6:46. But this time he chose not just τὸ ὄρος, the hill country in general, but a specific but unnamed ὄρος ὑψηλόν. Its identity can only be guessed, and Mark's geographical sequences are not exact enough to allow us to locate it from the flow of the surrounding narrative. We are not told that the six days since Caesarea Philippi have been spent in travelling, and if they are still in that area some part of the Hermon massif would be an obvious guess, since it rises far higher (2826 m.) than any other mountain in or near the area of Jesus' known travels. But the presence at the foot of the mountain of a Jewish crowd (including scribes) who are well aware of the reputation of Jesus and his disciples for exorcism (9:14-18) casts doubt on a location so far north. Walking at a steady rate, it would have been possible to reach the traditional site of the transfiguration, Mount Tabor,[10] in six days from Caesarea Philippi, though if Mark's geographical notices are taken to reflect an actual itinerary it seems strange to move determinedly so far southwards only to return northwards for nearly half that distance to Capernaum in 9:33. An alternative suggestion is Mount Meron,[11] the highest point in Palestine west of the Jordan valley, much closer to Caesarea Philippi and more nearly en route to Capernaum. At 1208 m. Meron is much higher than Tabor (588 m.), though the surrounding hills rob it of the distinctive eminence of Tabor, which rises as a single steep mound from the plain. The impression from the top of Tabor is of a very respectable height, especially if one has climbed it on foot! But, apart from the demands of the tourist industry, it seems neither important nor possible to determine just where the 'high mountain' was.

The traditional term 'transfiguration' has lent a special aura to Mark's relatively broad term μεταμορφόομαι, which by derivation means to be changed in 'form', but it can be used in a less literal sense as in Rom. 12:2, μεταμορφοῦσθε τῇ ἀνακαινώσει τοῦ νοός (cf. 2 Cor. 3:18). The following clauses will describe a change in the appearance of Jesus' *clothes,* and it could be argued that these clauses are epexegetic of the main verb μετεμορφώθη, so that no change to Jesus' own physical appearance is intended. But that is not, on the face of it, what Mark says: it is Jesus, not his clothes, who is said to be 'changed'. Both Matthew and Luke describe a change in Jesus' physical appearance (ἔλαμψεν τὸ πρόσωπον αὐτοῦ ὡς ὁ ἥλιος; ἐγένετο τὸ εἶδος τοῦ προσώπου αὐτοῦ ἕτερον), and this is the more natural interpretation of Mark's

10. There is evidence of settlements on Mount Tabor since the Iron Age, and it was held as a strategically important site by Antiochus III and by Alexander Jannaeus, but it is unlikely that the whole extensive summit area was occupied until Josephus fortified it at the beginning of the Jewish War (*War* 2.573), with a wall surrounding the whole summit (*War* 4.54-56). It is thus probably not correct, as many do, to dismiss Tabor as a site for the transfiguration on the grounds that its top was occupied at the time (e.g., Cranfield).

11. See W. L. Liefeld in R. N. Longenecker and M. C. Tenney (ed.), *New Dimensions in NT Study,* 167 n. 27.

wording too, with the description of his clothes following on from a personal 'transformation'.[12] There is, however, no verbal echo of the account in Ex. 34:29-35 of Moses' face shining when he came down from the mountain (though see on 9:15 below); that was a reflected and transient glory, but Jesus', though only briefly visible, was intrinsic to himself.

3 Shining white clothing is a feature of accounts of the appearance of heavenly beings, not only in the resurrection narratives (16:5; Mt. 28:3; Lk. 24:4; Jn. 20:12; cf. Acts 1:10) but also in Dn. 7:9 and in other apocalyptic texts (*1 Enoch* 14:20; *2 Enoch* 22:8-9; *3 Enoch* 12:1; *Test. Job* 46:7-9); cf. Ps. 104:1-2, where God wears light like a garment. στίλβω is used especially of the glittering of brightly polished metal or the shining of stars. Mark's attempt to underline the unique glory of Jesus' clothing is in danger of descending to bathos: 'whiter than any earthly laundry can make them'. The point is presumably that no naturalistic explanation can account for what the disciples witnessed.

4 The unhistorical order in which Elijah and Moses are first mentioned (reversed in v. 5) is surprising and is found only in Mark. It is probably best accounted for by the fact that the dialogue with the disciples which follows in vv. 11-13 will focus on Elijah rather than Moses. The phrasing Ἠλίας σὺν Μωϋσεῖ is also surprising, and could be taken to indicate that Moses is the chief visitor, whose presence one might expect, but that Elijah also accompanies him;[13] most commentators, however, find precisely the opposite nuance, that 'Moses is playing a subsidiary role' (Hooker). In view of the changed order in the next verse it is unlikely that Mark chose the phrase to indicate precedence either way; it means 'Elijah and Moses'.

Of the many suggestions as to the significance of these two figures in Mark's narrative, probably the least valid is the traditional idea that they represent the law and the prophets. The fact that Elijah's name precedes Moses' would be very odd on this view; besides Elijah was not a writing prophet, and it is not in that capacity that he is discussed in vv. 11-13. What his presence triggers in the disciples' minds is the promise of his eschatological return (for which see below on vv. 11-13), and it is this which would probably have been uppermost in Jewish minds at that time (hence the popular tendency to identify Jesus as a new Elijah, 6:15; 8:28). Moses, too, featured in eschatological hopes, at least in the form of the promised 'prophet like Moses' of Dt. 18:15-19 who

---

12. See further J. A. Ziesler, *ExpTim* 81 (1969-70) 265-66. Commentators frequently assume that Matthew and Luke 'agree against Mark in having Jesus' face as well as his clothes shine' (Marcus, *Way,* 83). Mark's καί at the beginning of v. 3 is, however, more naturally interpreted as adding new information than as explaining the nature of the previously mentioned change of appearance. It is therefore not necessary to propose, with Belo, 162, that 'The garments stand, by metonymy, for the body, so that the body of Jesus is the real object of the vision, a body "touched" by heaven.'

13. Cf the use of σύν in 4:10 and 8:34, in each case to link a less predictable group, mentioned first, with the Twelve, whose presence is taken for granted.

was the central figure in Samaritan messianic hope. The reappearance of these two great figures of the past thus symbolises the coming of the long-expected messianic age.[14]

The eschatological roles of Moses and Elijah were fostered by the fact that in some Jewish thought they, together with Enoch, were the 'deathless ones'[15] of the OT, Elijah because of his translation to heaven (2 Ki. 2:11) and Moses because of his mysterious disappearance on Mount Nebo and the lack of a known grave (Dt. 34:5-6).[16] Mark may have hoped that his readers would find in this fact a pointer towards Jesus' coming victory over death.[17]

Both Elijah and Moses also prefigured in their experience the coming rejection and suffering of the Messiah. Elijah (as v. 13 will indicate) was a model for the suffering of God's spokesman at the hands of the ungodly, and his despair in the wilderness (1 Ki. 19:14) was to be echoed in Jesus' emotion (περίλυπος ἕως θανάτου, 14:34) in Gethsemane. Moses, for all his qualities of leadership, found himself repeatedly rejected by his people.

Both were men of Sinai. When the visitor to Mount Sinai today begins the descent from the traditional cave of Moses on the summit, the next building reached is the chapel of Elijah on a lower plateau. It was on the mountain that each of them met with God and heard his voice, and now Jesus on another high mountain meets with them before God again speaks from the cloud. The subject of Jesus' transfiguration, with Moses and Elijah, for the sixth-century mosaic in the apse of the church in St. Catherine's Monastery at Sinai was well chosen.

How many of these, or indeed other, motifs would occur to the minds of Peter, James, and John, or of Mark and his readers, is uncertain. But however exactly it might be formulated, the reappearance of two such great men of God from the past, and their conversation with Jesus, would evoke a sense of Jesus' climactic place in the ongoing purpose of God, and of the coming of the long-awaited age of fulfilment in his person. Schweizer, 183, summarises: 'This story has united two expectations which were alive in Judaism: the coming of the prophet of the end-time who is like Moses and the appearing of Elijah at the dawning of the end-time. It has declared to every Jew that the fulfilment of the

14. See H. C. Kee, art. cit. (p. 347 n. 5) 144-46, for the eschatological importance of Elijah in first-century Judaism. Kee explains the order Ἠλίας σὺν Μωϋσεῖ from the greater prominence of Elijah as an eschatological figure.

15. See above p. 344 n. 1 for Chilton's suggestion that these 'deathless ones' are referred to in the phrase τινες ὧδε τῶν ἑστηκότων οἵτινες οὐ μὴ γεύσωνται θανάτου.

16. There are several patristic references to a lost apocryphal work called the *Assumption of Moses*, which apparently spoke of Moses' removal to heaven (cf. Jude 9). This work may have been the concluding part of (or a revised edition of) the *Testament of Moses*, the extant text of which breaks off before the end of Moses' farewell speech. For Jewish belief that Moses did not die see J. Jeremias, *TDNT*, 2.939 n. 92.

17. For M. E. Thrall, *NTS* 16 (1969/70) 314-15, this is the main purpose of the inclusion of Elijah and Moses, but the emphasis is more on contrast than on similarity, in that 'Elijah and Moses did not die, but were translated. Jesus died, and was raised from the dead.'

history of Israel and of every hope for the glorious end-time have already begun with the coming of Jesus.'[18]

The relevance of Elijah to an understanding of Jesus will be picked up in vv. 11-13, but it may be appropriate here to say a little more about Moses. The extensive echoes in Mark's story of the Sinai account of Ex. 24 (see introductory comments to this pericope) suggest a deliberate linking of Jesus with Moses which goes beyond the actual appearance of Moses in the narrative,[19] and the reader might well also recall Ex. 34:29-35, though with no direct help from Mark. The voice from heaven will also imply that Jesus fulfils the eschatological role of the 'prophet like Moses' in Dt. 18. We have noted elsewhere that the idea of Jesus as a new Moses may be detected in his account of the feeding of the Jewish crowd (see on 6:31-44 above). For those who saw Jesus as the fulfilment of God's age-long purpose, and so were disposed to trace connections of continuity and of climax between the words, events, and characters of the OT and the stories of Jesus (as many of the writers of the NT were), a 'new Moses typology' was one of the most obvious links. We meet it in various forms in other parts of the NT. But while Mark was clearly aware of this typology, it is not a dominant theme in his gospel. Even in this pericope, where Moses appears in person and the narrative structure recalls his Sinai experience, the theme is not developed as might be expected, and it is Elijah rather than Moses whose presence is commented on by the disciples. New Moses typology is more a part of Mark's inherited pattern of thought than a theme which he is particularly concerned to press on his readers, however gladly he takes the opportunities which this incident affords to make the connection.[20]

5-6 If ἀποκρίνομαι is understood only of a response to a previous utterance, its double use here is inappropriate. But it frequently represents the Hebraic idiom *waya'an* which serves to continue, or even begin, a discourse (BAGD, 93b, 2: 'speak up'). Peter's words are a response not to any words already spoken, but to the whole bewildering situation in which the disciples find themelves. The vocative 'Ραββί, occurring here for the first time, means the same as διδάσκαλε (see on 4:38), but in this context, where Jesus has been revealed to be so much more than merely a human 'teacher', it seems even more inadequate. It appropriately conveys Peter's total failure to grasp the significance of the occasion, and fits well with his bizarre proposal to erect shelters on

18. Cf. M. D. Hooker in L. D. Hurst and N. T. Wright (ed.), *The Glory of Christ in the NT,* 59-70, for the role of Elijah and Moses as witnesses to Jesus, Jesus' 'sponsors' (68).

19. See, however, also the points of contrast listed by Gundry, 475-76.

20. E. Best, *Disciples,* 218-19 (cf. *Following,* 57), argues (against J. A. Ziesler, *ExpTim* 81 [1969/70] 263-68) that Moses typology is more obvious in the Matthean and Lucan accounts than in Mark, and that since 'elsewhere in Mark there is no clear Moses typology', this was not part of Mark's redactional intention here. In view of the several echoes of Exodus and of Dt. 18:15-19 noted above, this goes too far. Quite opposite is J. Marcus, *Way,* 80-92, who offers an extended analysis of Mosaic elements in this pericope and their significance for Mark's christology, drawing particularly on postbiblical developments of the Moses story.

the mountain for each of the august 'teachers'. Mark's use of the Hebrew term here rather than his normal Greek equivalent (used ten times, as against three uses of Ῥαββί and one of Ῥαββουνί) fits the strongly OT feeling of the moment, particularly the presence of Moses, the prototype teacher of the law.

Peter's sense of privilege (καλόν ἐστιν ἡμᾶς ὧδε εἶναι) is not matched by discretion. The καί which introduces his proposal suggests that the emphasis falls on ἡμᾶς: we three disciples (for whom Peter, as often, acts as spokesman) might seem to be mere spectators, irrelevant to the sensational event which is occurring, but it is a good thing we are here because we can set up the three shelters which you and your respected visitors deserve. The hortatory subjunctive ποιήσωμεν conveys a definite proposal, 'let us make', which is virtually a declaration of intent. The σκηναί would presumably be shelters of branches and leaves such as were made at the Feast of Tabernacles (LXX translates *sukkâ* by σκηνή, σκήνωμα, σκηνοπηγία); they would offer shelter from the sun and a more dignified place for these important people than merely standing in the open. There is no suggestion in the narrative that this event took place at Tabernacles,[21] however, and if that had been the case presumably all six persons present would have needed σκηναί, not just the three mentioned. The proposal is simply a clumsy way for a practical man to express his sense of occasion, on the assumption that the event was to last longer than in fact proved to be the case. There is no need to read into Peter's words a deliberate attempt to 'tie down' or 'institutionalise' the elusive presence of Elijah and Moses; at this stage he had no reason to expect them to leave.[22] Nor do the proposed σκηναί correspond to Moses' 'tent of meeting' (Ex. 33:7-11 etc.; Heb. *'ōhel,* but also σκηνή in the LXX), which was for meeting with *God* outside the camp. Peter is simply doing the best he can to rise to the occasion, caught up in a unique and incomprehensible situation. But Mark, with hindsight, reminds us of how inappropriate the idea really was: οὐκ ᾔδει τί ἀπικριθῇ. And lest we blame Peter for a unique lack of perception, he includes the other two disciples in the same bewilderment: ἔκφοβοι γὰρ ἐγένοντο.[23] We can hardly be surprised.

7   The cloud is probably to be understood as covering the whole mountaintop, enveloping all six persons. Oepke (*TDNT,* 4.908) suggests that αὐτοῖς should be understood only of Jesus, Moses, and Elijah, the disciples being left outside the cloud, but the natural antecedent is the whole group, since in the preceding sentences it has been Peter and the other disciples who have been the focus of attention. The fact that the voice is described as coming to them ἐκ τῆς νεφέλης does not require that they were outside it.

While a cloud is a frequent theophanic motif in the OT (Ex. 13:21-22;

21. So especially H. Riesenfeld, *Jésus.*

22. Belo, 162, offers the remarkable suggestion, '*Perhaps* the tents were to be for the three, while they, strengthened by the support of Heaven, would go and gather an army of Zealots.' It is not clear who 'they' refers to.

23. For the rare 'intensive' term ἔκφοβος see T. Dwyer, *Wonder,* 141. He quotes from Aristotle a use of the term for a 'fright enough to make one's hair stand up on end'.

33:9-10; 40:34-38; 1 Ki. 8:10-11, etc.), the echoes here are more specifically of the Sinai narratives, in the coming of a cloud on the mountain (Ex. 19:16; 24:15-16) and the voice of God speaking from the cloud (Ex. 19:9; 24:16; 24:18–25:1; 34:5). Ex. 19:9 offers a particularly interesting parallel, in that God's speaking out of the cloud to Moses was intended to ensure that the Israelites would thereafter heed his words; here, too, the voice is not so much a pronouncement to Jesus but is addressed to the disciples, and calls on them as a result to 'listen to him'. The manifestly divine means of communication authenticates the messenger.

In Jewish tradition the *bat qōl* (see above p. 79, n. 71) was an inferior substitute for the direct communication of God's voice. Here we have no *bat qōl*, but God himself is heard to speak. This, together with the return of the glory of the Shekinah cloud, constitutes a new level of divine revelation. 'God is communicating in two ways, both of which were long since despaired of in Judaism.'[24]

The command ἀκούετε αὐτοῦ also echoes Dt. 18:15, where the promised 'prophet like Moses' is to be accorded the same authority as Moses himself at Sinai. Thus while the divine pronouncement conveys the same OT nuances as the parallel words at Jesus' baptism (see on 1:11), a further messianic element is added in the motif of the Mosaic prophet. But no messianic expectation of the OT prepares the reader completely for the explicit christology of these words, addressed this time not only to Jesus himself but deliberately to his three chosen disciples: Jesus is the beloved Son of God. The royal uses of the language of divine sonship in 2 Sa. 7:14 and Ps. 2:7 point this way, but fall far short of this direct identification by the voice of God himself in a context where Jesus' supernatural splendour has just been dramatically revealed. In the light of these words, Peter's proposal to put Elijah and Moses on a par with Jesus is seen to be even more out of place.[25]

8 Again it is the disciples' impressions that are described. ἐξάπινα περιβλεψάμενοι suggests that they have hidden their faces while the voice spoke. Now that all is quiet again, they look up, and the scene has changed. (Mark's use of the rare word ἐξάπινα rather than his usual εὐθύς emphasises the dramatic change.) We are not told explicitly just when and how Jesus' appearance returned to normal, but it seems that already the 'vision' is over: Elijah, Moses, and the cloud are gone and the voice does not speak again. The phrase Ἰησοῦν μόνον μεθ' ἑαυτῶν suggests the return of normality, and in the dialogue that follows and the eventual return to the crowd there is no suggestion that the 'numinous' atmosphere of the mountaintop is maintained. Unlike Moses, whose face continued to shine when he came down and caused consternation among those who saw him (Ex. 34:29-35), Jesus is himself again. The continuing effect is in the disciples' minds, not in physical appearances.

24. W. L. Liefeld, art. cit. (see above, p. 350 n. 11) 170.
25. This point is emphasised by M. E. Thrall, *NTS* 16 (1969/70) 308-9: Peter's fault is that he fails to place Jesus on a different level from Elijah and Moses.

9 So now as the scene of the transfiguration is left behind, it is time for reflection on what it meant. But first Jesus issues a command to silence like that which followed Peter's declaration in 8:29. (Luke mentions their silence as a fact, but does not attribute it to a direct command of Jesus.) The verb this time is not ἐπιτιμάω (which serves in that context to prepare for the double use of the same verb in vv. 32, 33) but διαστέλλομαι, used several times by Mark in similar 'secrecy' contexts (5:43; 7:36; cf. 8:15) for a stern injunction. This time, however, in contrast with all the other commands to secrecy in Mark, a time limit is set for their silence. There is a similar time limit in Dn. 12:4, 9, though there the secrecy is to be maintained until 'the time of the end'. Here the limit is much shorter: by the time Mark's readers come to the story, the time limit has already expired, and the secret may be freely divulged.

The subject of the disciples' secrecy is not this time a verbal formula but, as when such injunctions have followed miracles in earlier chapters, the scene they have witnessed (which includes, of course, the words of God from the cloud). Indeed, they have no formula (such as ὁ Χριστός in 8:29) which can sum up the several christological nuances of the revelation on the mountain, still less do justice to the majesty and awe of the experience. But the experience was for them alone, not even for the other nine close disciples. We can only guess what the other nine (and still more the wider circle of followers and the general public) would have made of the (probably incoherent) account that Peter, James, and John might have given. But it is likely that the messianic and eschatological connotations of the vision would have sparked off the same sort of triumphalism and misdirected hopes which made the term ὁ Χριστός itself so hazardous. There is triumph to come, but before that there is to be rejection and death in Jerusalem. Only after that, and after ὁ υἱὸς τοῦ ἀνθρώπου ἐκ νεκρῶν ἀναστῇ, would it be possible for the vision to be shared without provoking the wrong sort of messianic enthusiasm. By that time, the open secret of Jesus' resurrection would already have made public something of what this private vision had told them about Jesus.

Jesus' use of the title ὁ υἱὸς τοῦ ἀνθρώπου with reference to his future resurrection is consistent with 8:31, where the resurrection is the last in the sequence of events predicted for ὁ υἱὸς τοῦ ἀνθρώπου. It also fits the background to the title in Dn. 7 where the imagery is of vindication and enthronement, a background already reflected in the use of the same title in 8:38.

10 The word order allows the option of construing πρὸς ἑαυτούς either with τὸν λόγον ἐκράτησαν or with συζητοῦντες. The former would offer an idiom not closely paralleled elsewhere in Mark, meaning 'they kept the word to themselves'; the latter is much more typical of Marcan usage, since he uses πρὸς ἑαυτούς several times for discussions within a defined group (1:27; 10:26; 11:31; 12:7; 14:4; 16:3), in each case with a strongly deliberative connotation. 1:27 offers a close parallel in that the governing verb is again συζητέω. If then πρὸς ἑαυτούς belongs with συζητοῦντες, the previous clause uses κρατέω metaphorically on its own to mean 'to guard' or 'hold on

356

to';[26] compare Luke's use of συντηρέω in 2:19 and διατηρέω in 2:51 for Mary's pondering the ῥήματα of Jesus' birth and childhood. A similar metaphorical use is found in 7:3, 4, 8, κρατεῖν τὴν παράδοσιν.[27] In this case, therefore, Jesus' command to silence was taken seriously: his λόγος was carefully remembered and apparently his injunction was obeyed.

No doubt the disciples' bewilderment is partly due to the fact that talk of rising ἐκ νεκρῶν seems strangely out of place after Jesus' association with the two 'deathless ones' on the mountain. But Mark's wording suggests that it was the whole concept of resurrection, not just its appropriateness for Jesus, which they could not grasp. For a valuable survey of Jewish thought about resurrection see C. Brown in *DNTT*, 3.261-75. While any generalisation from such varied writings is dangerous, from time to time a hope of continued fellowship with God beyond death found expression in various ways. Often it was a corporate hope for the people of God rather than concerning an individual, and generally it seems to have been associated with an eschatological age rather than seen as an event within history. If the disciples understood Jesus to be talking of his own individual restoration to life after death within the normal course of history, they had good reason to be bewildered, as no clear precedent for such an idea can be found in extant literature of the period. They would more easily have understood 'resurrection' language less literally, probably as part of a more general eschatological hope rather than of his individual destiny.

The concept should not be new to them, since it was incorporated in Jesus' prediction in 8:31. But the radical newness of the whole concept of messianic suffering dominated that pronouncement, and it is that rather than the prediction of resurrection which is picked up in the following dialogue; the resurrection clause seems to have passed unnoticed, perhaps because, as here, they did not know what to make of it, whereas the prediction of rejection and death was only too plain.

11 For the interrogative use of ὅτι (which BDF, 300[2], regard as 'especially Markan') see on 2:16. That verse allowed other constructions, but here and in 9:28, in each case following ἐπηρώτων, the interrogative use (perhaps an abbreviation from τί ὅτι) seems clear; if so it does not differ in meaning from τί. The disciples' question arises naturally out of the appearance of Elijah on the mountain, and confirms the essentially eschatological implications of the incident; a reappearance of Elijah could mean only one thing, the coming of the 'great and terrible day of the LORD' (Mal. 4:5). But Elijah's coming is to be 'before' that day comes; he is to come πρῶτον. (Note that neither Malachi nor the disciples' question here suggests that Elijah is to precede the *Messiah;* he is the herald of the 'day of the LORD'.) How then does his presence on the mountain

---

26. Hooker suggests 'they seized on this saying'; Mann, 'they fastened on this saying'.

27. This seems preferable to Cranfield's rendering 'they obeyed the injunction to silence', since the following participial clause focuses on their thoughts about resurrection, not on their obedience.

fit in with the eschatological dimension of Jesus' ministry and the coming of the kingdom of God?

The disciples' question relates not to the ancient text of Malachi, but to current scribal teaching (λέγουσιν). For the development of the hope of the return of Elijah see especially Ben Sira 48:10. It is implicit in several apocalyptic texts, and features in a number of rabbinic texts which, however varied in date, attest to a continuing expectation of Elijah's eschatological return. For details see J. Jeremias, *TDNT*, 2.931-34.[28] The disciples' awareness of such a scribal doctrine is thus not surprising, and the experience on the mountain would naturally bring it to mind.

12-13 Jesus' reply is cryptic. The first clause is clear enough; it simply accepts that the scribal teaching is correct and fills it out with a summary of the purpose of Elijah's coming (Mal. 4:6; Ben Sira 48:10b) in the words ἀποκαθιστάνει πάντα. But the μέν in the first clause alerts us that Jesus will not simply repeat what the scribes are saying, but will add his own distinctive angle to the teaching about Elijah. Instead of a further statement with δέ, however, the following clause takes the form of a rhetorical question, challenging the disciples to expand their mental horizon beyond what the scribes have taught.[29] Surprisingly this question relates not, on the surface, to Elijah at all, but to the Son of Man,[30] and not to an eschatological work of restoration but to suffering and death. Yet this question too, like the teaching about Elijah, relates to what 'is written'. What then is the logical connection between the two clauses of v. 12?

Verse 13 resolves this puzzle by establishing two important connections: first, that the prophecy of Elijah's return has already been fulfilled, so that the experiences of Jesus as Son of Man are part of the same sequence of events as the return of Elijah; second that (in contrast with the language of Mal. 4:5-6) the experience of 'Elijah' has been of rejection and ill-treatment (ἐποίησαν αὐτῷ ὅσα ἤθελον), which thus foreshadows what is to happen to the Son of Man. Mark does not, like Matthew, make it easier for the reader by explicitly identifying John the Baptist as the returning Elijah, but he could reasonably expect his readers to make the connection, remembering that Jesus has been popularly linked with both Elijah and John the Baptist (6:14-15; 8:28), that it was in the context of John's imprisonment that Jesus' public ministry began (1:14), and that John's martyrdom (6:16-29) has been a prominent feature of Mark's account of the buildup to the recognition of Jesus' messianic identity and the revelation of his coming passion.[31]

28. Cf. J. E. Taylor, *John,* 283-87, including Qumran material not available to Jeremias in the *TDNT* article.

29. See J. Marcus, *Way,* 98 (and n. 24), for this construction following μέν.

30. The suggestion of W. Wink, *John,* 14, that the saying originally had 'that son of man' (meaning Elijah) and has been mistranslated does not help us with understanding the text in Mark, where there can be no doubt whom ὁ υἱὸς τοῦ ἀνθρώπου refers to.

31. W. Wink, *John,* 15-16, believes that it was on the mountain, as he talked with Elijah, that Jesus discovered the identity of John as Elijah. 'The secret of Jesus' messiahship (8:28–9:10) thus

Thus the raw materials are in place to allow the reader to establish the dual links first between Elijah and John the Baptist and then between Elijah/ John and Jesus' own suffering as the Son of Man. But the sequence of clauses is clumsy, and the effect much more cryptic than in Matthew's 'tidied-up' parallel. If v. 12b had *followed* v. 13, the whole train of thought would have been much easier to follow.[32]

To return to some details of the wording, ἀποκαθιστάνει πάντα summarises the account in Mal. 4:6 of Elijah's mission of restoring (LXX ἀποκαταστήσει) family relationships, a mission which is further developed in Ben Sira 48:10 in the clause καταστῆσαι φυλὰς Ιακωβ. He was to prepare the people for the eschatological coming of God by removing sinful division from among them. The NT accounts of John the Baptist do not emphasise this theme, but at this point Jesus is not recounting the experiences of the new Elijah, but spelling out the content of the scribal expectation.

The double use of γέγραπται makes explicit what was implicit in the passion prediction of 8:31, that these things are 'necessary' (δεῖ) because they are part of the pattern already established in the OT. This scriptural imperative applies not only to Jesus' own future suffering but also to that of his forerunner. The reader already knows what has in fact proved to be John's fate, but we have not hitherto been told that this aspect of his story was already 'written'; the scriptural authentication which Mark has provided for John's mission in 1:2-3 focuses on his positive role of preparation, not on his suffering and death. The prophecy of Mal. 4:5-6 gives no hint of martyrdom, nor is this a part of the developing Jewish Elijah-expectation. The scriptural basis claimed in v. 13 is found not in any explicit prediction, but by a typological reading of the Elijah stories of 1 Ki. 17-19, 21 as a model for what was to happen on his return. There we see Elijah as the typical martyr figure, driven by his faithfulness to God's commission into potentially fatal conflict with the royal house (1 Ki. 19:2-3, 10, 14). His bold confrontations with Ahab and Jezebel prefigure John's open challenge to Antipas and Herodias; the difference is that Herodias will succeed where Jezebel failed.[33]

The summary of the fate of the Son of Man in v. 12 picks up the phrase πολλὰ παθεῖν from 8:31; see comments there on its likely OT background.[34] In

issues directly in the secret of John's Elijahship.' Mark does not make the identity explicit because he wants to maintain an 'Elijianic secret' alongside his messianic secret.

32. See M. D. Hooker, *Son of Man*, 129-31, for an attempt to defend Mark's order.

33. J Marcus, *Way*, 97-107, sets out a complicated and rather speculative argument to the effect that Mark is not claiming that the suffering of the returning Elijah is itself predicted, but rather that this is the conclusion of a rabbinic-type argument intended to reconcile a scriptural contradiction by means of the syllogism 'Since Jesus is a suffering Messiah, his forerunner must be a suffering Elijah'. His argument depends on a questionable interpretation of Ἠλίας μὲν ἐλθὼν πρῶτον ἀποκαθιστάνει πάντα as interrogative; see Gundry, 484-85.

34. See also J. Marcus, *Way*, 94-97, for a useful discussion, in relation to Mk. 9:12, of the Jewish tendency to use a formula such as γέγραπται to introduce 'an exegetical conclusion rather than a quotation'.

this case, however, instead of repeating the following verb ἀποδοκιμασθῆναι Mark uses ἐξουδενέομαι. The meaning is much the same, but if ἀποδοκι-μάζομαι was intended to echo LXX Ps. 117[118]:22, that echo is lost. In Acts 4:11, however, Ps. 118:22 is quoted with the verb ἐξουθενέομαι in place of the LXX ἀποδοκιμάζομαι, so it is possible that Mk. 8:31 and 9:12 are echoing different but equally recognisable Greek versions of the psalm text (cf. also ἐξουδένημα in LXX Ps. 21:7 [EVV 22:6]).[35] On the other hand, it has also been suggested that ἐξουδενηθῇ is meant to recall the double use of *bāzāh* in Is. 53:3, translated by ἐξουδενωμένος in Aquila, Symmachus, and Thdt, though not in the LXX.[36] Whether or not a direct verbal echo is established, the thought of rejection is clearly present in both Ps. 118:22 and Is. 53:3, and few more probable sources can be suggested for the conviction that Scripture predicts the rejection of the Son of Man.

The disciples' question concerned the scribal teaching about Elijah's return πρῶτον. Jesus has not only endorsed that teaching, but added that the expectation has already been fulfilled, and has linked the suffering and rejection of the returning Elijah with his own. As πρῶτον indicated, the coming of 'Elijah' prepares the way for the imminent fate of the Son of Man. What then was the significance of Elijah's appearance on the mountain, if Malachi's prophecy has already been fulfilled in John the Baptist? No direct connection is made, but the perfect tense of Ἠλίας ἐλήλυθεν directs the disciples' minds away from their natural assumption that what they had just witnessed was the fulfilment of the prophecy. That has already happened, and the vision on the mountain stands apart. Its significance is not in the coming of Elijah as such, but in the person of Jesus as himself the focus of the fulfilment of OT hopes. The brief appearance of Moses and Elijah on the mountain testifies to *his* eschatological role, rather than giving to either of them a role of their own in the messianic events now unfolding.

SUCCESS AND FAILURE IN EXORCISM (9:14-29)

TEXTUAL NOTES

14. It seems likely that Mark wrote the plural ἐλθόντες . . . εἶδον, continuing the account of the four men who went up the mountain, and that the verbs were altered to the singulars found in most MSS and versions in order to focus attention on Jesus, thus providing an antecedent for αὐτόν (v. 15) and the singular verbs which follow.

23. The abrupt and probably unfamiliar idiom Τὸ εἰ δύνῃ (see notes ad loc.) has

---

35. A. Y. Collins, in C. M. Tuckett (ed.), *Scriptures,* 232-35, regards Ps. 22 as the principal OT source of this verse: 'Psalm 22 is re-read in such a way that it becomes a prophecy of the rejection of the person and message of Jesus as the Messiah'.

36. See my *Jesus and the OT,* 123-24. More fully, and with reference to wider discussion of the significance of ἐξουδενέω, see D. J. Moo, *The OT,* 89-91.

been 'improved' in the alternative readings (and by the correctors of ℵ), which offer a smoother but redundant clause by taking δύναμαι to refer to the father's ability to believe rather than as an echo of his apparent questioning of Jesus' ability to help in the preceding sentence.

24. MSS evidence strongly supports the omission of μετὰ δακρύων, which appears to be an early Western storytelling embellishment.

29. The words καὶ νηστείᾳ are found in the vast majority of witnesses, both MS and versional (and accordingly also included in this verse where it occurs in MSS of Mt. 17:21). Their omission in ℵ* B has persuaded most critics to omit them, influenced by the fact that in 1 Cor. 7:5 the same addition to προσευχῇ, though in a far less impressive range of witnesses, is generally agreed to be secondary, and to reflect early church devotional practice (cf. Acts 10:30 for a similar variant). In this context, however, where the issue is not general devotion but exorcistic practice, there is less reason to detect the influence of later conventional terminology. While the words might have been added to promote a current ascetic spirituality, they might equally have been omitted to discourage a current overemphasis on fasting, or perhaps because a scribe felt them to be incompatible with the dismissal of fasting in 2:19. In the light of the massive external evidence for the inclusion of καὶ νηστείᾳ, they should perhaps be retained, despite the confident A-rating in UBS[4] (unless it is believed that ℵ and B together can never be wrong!). Huck-Greeven retains.

Mark's narrative, which in Act One was full of miracles, has changed in its emphasis. Apart from the two healings of the blind which 'frame' the journey to Jerusalem, this is the only other 'normal' miracle recorded in the gospel after Act One. There is of course also the cursing of the fig tree in chapter 11, but that is, as we shall see, a symbolic act of power quite unlike the miracles of Act One, in which Jesus' special ἐξουσία is deployed to meet human need. Here we are on more familiar ground, and the pericope is in broad terms similar to Mark's other specific accounts of exorcism: a serious case of demon possession is graphically described, and a preliminary dialogue (with the demon, 1:23-25, 5:7-10; with the parent of the possessed, 7:25-29 and here) leads to a word of command resulting in the immediate expulsion of the demon and the restoration to normality of the possessed person. What distinguishes this narrative from the others is the previous failure of the disciples (vv. 14-18) and their subsequent question about why they had failed (vv. 28-29). It is this feature which gives this story a special appropriateness for Act Two. While Jesus' power is again clearly displayed, as in Act One, the focus now is not on the impression made on the crowd but on the lesson which the experience taught the disciples. It thus belongs appropriately with the verbal teaching which predominates in Act Two, as an object lesson on discipleship and faith. It is an element in the gradual reorientation which the disciples are undergoing as they discover what it means to follow Jesus, and this lesson, like so many others in this part of the gospel, derives from the display of their own inadequacy.[37]

37. It is this different orientation which accounts for some of the peculiarities of this pericope as compared with other miracle stories. D. W. Chapman, *Orphan*, 110-17, rightly notes

This pericope thus takes its place in the sequence of events and teaching which were set in motion at Caesarea Philippi. The high point reached in the declaration of Jesus' Messiahship has led immediately into bewildering and discouraging words about suffering and death, not only for Jesus but for those who follow him. This anticlimax has then been counterbalanced both by the promise of 9:1 and by the privilege of Peter, James, and John on the mountain. Already, however, that experience has led to further talk about suffering and death, and now the mountain is left behind and we re-enter the real world below where the other disciples have proved unable to rise to the demand made of them. They still have a lot to learn, and the rest of chapters 9 and 10 will be devoted to their instruction and preparation for responsibilities ahead.

The lesson here, then, derives from a spectacular failure to fulfil the commission to cast out demons which has been given to the Twelve in 3:15 and 6:7, and which they have already begun to undertake successfully (6:13). In the light of that earlier success, this failure has come as an unwelcome surprise to them, as well as to the watching crowd. Was that earlier commission to exorcise only temporary? What had they done wrong? Was it because they had been left on their own without Jesus (but surely the exorcisms of 6:13 were also performed in his absence)? Such reflections no doubt lie behind the question which they pose to Jesus in v. 28, 'Why could we not cast it out?' It is with Jesus' answer to that question that Mark's pericope closes, showing his reason for including this story at this point in his gospel.

But for all that it remains a dramatic account of an exorcism by Jesus, and Mark tells it with gusto. It is one of the more impressive examples of Mark's tendency to tell at greater length and with fuller circumstantial detail a story which Matthew and Luke can deal with much more concisely.[38] Mk. 9:14-29 consists of 272 words, whereas Lk. 9:37-43a tells the same story in 144 words, and Mt. 17:14-20a in a mere 110 (to which he appends in v. 20b one of two parallel sayings about faith which correspond to Mark 11:22-23 rather than belonging to this story as Mark records it).

The symptoms described are in many ways similar to those of an epileptic fit, and many versions and commentators have simply labelled the story as that of the 'Epileptic Boy'. All three evangelists, however, narrate it unambiguously as an exorcism, and Mark and Luke offer no term comparable to our 'epilepsy'. Matthew includes the verb σεληνιάζεται which is often understood to correspond to our 'epilepsy', and is sometimes even simply translated as such. But the term is not so specific; it denotes a condition connected with the moon (hence AV, 'lunatick'), but it can be connected with epilepsy only by the prior assumption that Mt. 17:14-20 describes an epileptic. In the ancient world

---

these differences, but accounts for them instead by the theory that Mark has written this story as an allegory of the salvation Jesus brings to Israel by casting out the 'rebellious spirit' which has been the root of the nation's problems from the beginning.

38. J. F. Williams, *Followers,* 138-39 n. 1, shows how the apparently repetitive nature of the narration serves 'to enrich Mark's characterization of the people in the story'.

knowledge of brain function was limited, and we know that the symptoms of epilepsy could be attributed to a supernatural force (it was known among pagans as the 'sacred disease'). There are ancient texts which link it with the moon,[39] but σεληνιάζομαι does not in itself denote epilepsy.[40]

Ancient accounts of medical conditions are seldom precise, and the terminology used differs from ours. It seems not unlikely that the personality disorder associated with demon possession could result in violent symptoms similar to those produced by the electrical disturbance in the brain which we call epilepsy,[41] but that is by no means to equate the two. In the circumstances it seems wiser to avoid the word 'epilepsy' here, and to interpret the story, as all three evangelists tell it, as one of exorcism.[42] This may help to avoid two opposite and unhelpful extremes, on the one hand the reductionist assumption that all biblical accounts of demon possessions are merely primitive ways of describing malfunction of the brain, and on the other hand the simplistic attribution of epilepsy as we know it to demonic causes.

14-15 Neither the crowd nor the scribes play any further part in the story, beyond a brief crowd reaction in v. 26b. But their mention, in a section of the gospel which focuses primarily on the private conversations of Jesus and his disciples, serves to heighten the drama of the occasion and the embarrassingly public nature of the disciples' failure. συζητέω (especially when followed by πρός) sometimes carries a hostile sense, 'dispute with', and here, where the grammatical subject of συζητοῦντας is specifically the γραμματεῖς, we are reminded of other occasions when hostile criticism has come not from the crowd but from a group of scribes (2:6, 16; 3:22; 7:1). The disciples' failure has given them further grounds for scepticism. The crowd, on the other hand, appears to be well disposed, at least in the welcome they give to Jesus, perhaps already hoping for a more successful treatment of the boy's condition. Their leaving the disciples and running up to greet Jesus emphasises the distinction between the Master and his followers.

But ἐξεθαμβήθησαν is unexpected. Normally verbs of astonishment (see

---

39. Galen 9.903 is the most explicit: (ἡ σελήνη) τὰς τῶν ἐπιλήπτων τηρεῖ περιόδους. Lucian, *Toxaris* 24, mentions a deformed woman of whom it was said that she used to 'fall down' (καταπίπτειν) when the moon was waxing, though the complaint is not otherwise identified as epilepsy. In *Philopseudes* 16 Lucian refers to demon-possessed people who 'fall down in the light of the moon, and roll their eyes and fill their mouths with foam', though again without a specific mention of epilepsy (these are the only two references given in LSJ for καταπίπτω as meaning 'to have the falling sickness').

40. An interesting account of the treatment of epilepsy by Rufus of Ephesus in the second century A.D. in H. C. Kee, *Medicine,* 48-50, indicates a purely physical understanding of both cause and treatment.

41. Cf. the careful discussion from a medical perspective by J. Wilkinson, *ExpTim* 79 (1967/8) 39-42. Wilkinson concludes that the symptoms are those of 'the major form of epilepsy' but goes on to argue that such symptoms might be caused by demon possession.

42. P. J. Achtemeier, *CBQ* 37 (1975) 481 n. 35, gives reasons for not identifying this as a case of epilepsy.

on 1:22) denote the crowd's reaction to a miracle or to some striking teaching, but they have seen and heard nothing yet, nor has the narrative given us reason to believe that they had any inkling of what has happened on the mountain. It is tempting to detect an echo of the Israelites' awe before Moses when he came down from the mountain with his face shining (Ex. 34:29-35),[43] but we have noted that Mark has avoided any clear allusion to that narrative. Verse 8 suggests an immediate return to normality, and the secrecy demanded in v. 9 would be strange if the 'transfiguration' of Jesus remained visible for all to see. More likely Mark uses the verb rather extravagantly to denote the powerful impression which Jesus' personal presence by now created; 'this authority emanates from him even before he speaks or acts' (Schweizer).[44]

16-18 In view of the subject of the participle in v. 14, and the repetition here of the same verb, the αὐτούς to whom Jesus addresses his question must be the scribes, even though the crowd are the nearer antecedent. Τί συζητεῖτε πρὸς αὐτούς echoes συζητοῦντας πρὸς αὐτούς in v. 14, and refers to the scribes' dispute with the disciples, not to their (or the crowd's) questioning among themselves (cf. 1:27; 9:10 for this sense of συζητέω).[45] The answer, however, comes not from the scribes but from the man whose request has precipitated the problem. The address διδάσκαλε is used in Mark both by disciples (see on 4:38) and by those outside the group who seek Jesus' help or opinion (cf. 5:35; 10:17; 12:14, 19, 32); 5:35 and 14:14 suggest that he was popularly known as ὁ διδάσκαλος. The man's aim had been to enlist Jesus' help in person (πρὸς σέ), but in Jesus' absence he has had to be content with the 'second team'. Nonetheless he expected the disciples to be able to effect a complete deliverance of his son (ἵνα αὐτὸ ἐκβάλωσιν), and has been disappointed at their failure. The use of οὐκ ἴσχυσαν rather than merely οὐκ ἐδύναντο increases their discomfiture: they proved too weak, and have been defeated in a power struggle (cf. the use of ἰσχύω in 5:4 in another exorcism narrative: no one had the strength to tame him).

The boy's condition is consistently described as demon possession rather than a medical complaint (ἔχοντα πνεῦμα, καταλάβῃ, ῥήσσει αὐτόν, αὐτὸ ἐκβάλωσιν), and the rest of the pericope will maintain this perspective. But the symptoms described (and further developed in vv. 20, 22, and 26) are similar to those of an epileptic seizure. See the introduction to this pericope for the prob-

43. J. Marcus, *Way,* 82-83; Hooker, 222-23. Gundry, 487-88, does not suggest a reference to Ex. 34, but explains the crowd's astonishment by the supposition that Jesus' clothes were still glistening.

44. T. Dwyer, *Wonder,* 147, lists a wide range of different explanations of the use of ἐκθαμβέομαι here, noting that the verb (which occurs in Mark also in 14:33; 16:5, 6) is unusual and intensive. He explains the function of the verb here in terms of Mark's desire to prepare the reader for the approaching passion, but offers no explanation for it in this narrative setting other than simply that 'it is Jesus himself who is amazing' (149).

45. Metzger, *Textual Commentary,* 100 (with 616), apparently assumes a reflexive sense here.

lem of diagnosis. ῥήσσω is usually understood to be a less common 'by-form' of ῥήγνυμι, which normally means to 'tear' or 'break', a suitably violent word in this context, but not easy to visualise in physical terms; there is evidence, however, that ῥήσσω also occurs as a poetic word for 'throw down', 'dash to the ground' (see BAGD, 735b), and in the light of v. 20 this seems a more likely sense here. The symptoms described in ἀφρίζω (foam [at the mouth]) and τρίζω τοὺς ὀδόντας (gnash the teeth) are clear enough, and ξηραίνομαι (to harden, grow stiff) probably denotes a seizure of the whole body which has a paralysing effect (cf. the use of the same verb for a paralysed arm in 3:1). These terms, and the behaviour described in vv. 20, 26, indicate a temporary physical seizure caused sporadically by the 'resident' demon rather than a permanent condition (note v. 18, ὅπου ἐὰν αὐτὸν καταλάβῃ).

It is surprising, therefore, to find that the demon is described as πνεῦμα ἄλαλον. The same characteristic is picked up by Jesus' address to the demon in v. 25, τὸ ἄλαλον καὶ κωφὸν πνεῦμα. While there is nothing improbable in this combination of problems, it is interesting that neither Matthew nor Luke mentions a speech defect, and Mark's narrative focuses on the 'epileptic' symptoms rather than on the restoration of speech. The fact that the boy was also dumb seems to be one of those 'irrelevant' narrative details which Mark so often preserves even though it is not where his interest is centred.

19 The antecedent of αὐτοῖς (and therefore the identity of the γενεὰ ἄπιστος) is not clear. Is it the last speaker (the father, with his son), the disciples (whose failure is the last element in the preceding speech), the crowd in general, or the scribes whose dispute with the disciples had been the subject of Jesus' previous question? Or is Jesus' exclamation a more general expression of exasperation, addressed not to a specific αὐτοῖς but to his whole human environment? It is not possible, and probably it is unnecessary, to answer these questions with confidence. If anyone has displayed a lack of faith so far in this pericope, it is presumably the disciples in their failure to exorcise; Matthew certainly so understood it (διὰ τὴν ὀλιγοπιστίαν ὑμῶν, Mt. 17:20). So they are at least included in the rebuke (see on 8:12), even if it is not aimed at them alone.[46] But the nine disciples who were left behind hardly constitute a whole γενεά. Their faithlessness is symptomatic of the wider human condition, as Jesus in his ministry so often encountered it, an unwillingness to take God at his word and a horizon limited to merely human possibilities. As in 8:12 (and more frequently in Matthew), Jesus' frustration with human 'tunnel vision' erupts into a rare diatribe (echoing Dt. 32:5) against the whole contemporary γενεά to whom his ministry was addressed (see on 8:12).[47] The rhetorical questions, ἕως

---

46. Gundry, 489 (cf. 497), argues that the disciples are not included, and that 'Jesus is condemning the crowd, including the father and the scribes in it, for making the disciples' failure a reason to dispute the power of Jesus himself'; this seems rather abstruse.

47. This exclamation, with its echo of Moses' characterisation of Israel as a rebellious generation, is perhaps the strongest element in the argument of D. W. Chapman (see above, p. 361 n. 37) that the whole pericope is intended to be an allegory of Israel's 'rebellious spirit'.

πότε πρὸς ὑμᾶς ἔσομαι; ἕως πότε ἀνέξομαι ὑμῶν; need be no more than idiomatic expressions of frustration. In the light of a developed incarnational theology they might be understood to express the concept of a temporary period on earth which was to be ended by an anticipated return to Jesus' true home in heaven, but even at the time of Mark's writing this would be to press more specific content out of the terms used than the idiom requires. πρὸς ὑμᾶς denotes merely association or involvement with (cf. 6:3; 14:49), while ἀνέχομαι (to put up with) shows that that association was not a happy one for the speaker. Jesus has had enough of unbelief.

But the remedy is not at this point further teaching for the crowd or even for the disciples, but a visible demonstration of his own ἐξουσία and of the liberating power of God. With the command φέρετε αὐτὸν πρός με (which is just what the father had originally tried to do, v. 17) the reader is put on the alert to see the disciples' failure overturned.

20 As usual in describing demon possession and exorcism, Mark speaks of the agency of the demon rather than of the victim (though the latter part of the sentence describes the resultant behaviour of the boy: πεσὼν . . . ἐκυλίετο). It is the demon which 'sees' Jesus and reacts to him immediately by convulsing its 'host'.[48] On this occasion, however, as in 7:24-30, no dialogue with the demon is recorded, merely a word of command. The demon expresses its response to Jesus not verbally (which was presumably impossible for a πνεῦμα ἄλαλον) but physically through the behaviour of the 'host'. συσπαράσσω (cf. σπαράσσω in v. 26 and in 1:26) roughly corresponds to ῥήσσει in the father's description in v. 18 (Lk. 9:42 combines the two verbs). The simple form of the verb, while originally used for such violent action as a dog tearing up a carcass (and thus closer to the meaning of ῥήγνυμι; see on v. 18), came to be used medically for retching or convulsion, and this seems the most likely sense here. The description of the boy rolling around on the ground foaming at the mouth is more dramatic than ξηραίνεται in v. 18, but it is not difficult to understand both the convulsions and the paralytic seizure as parts of the same 'epileptic' condition.

21-22 For Jesus' (or the evangelists') interest in the duration of a condition cf. 5:25; Lk. 13:11, 16; Jn. 5:5; 9:1.[49] To mention it serves to heighten the impressiveness of an immediate deliverance, but in this case the enquiry may also be part of Jesus' 'diagnosis' of the problem to be confronted. This was no recent or temporary condition. The father's reply adds further cause for concern in that the seizures brought about by the demonic presence rendered the boy helpless and thus vulnerable to injury or death through fire or water. The personal verb ἔβαλεν (with the πνεῦμα as the unexpressed subject) followed by ἵνα suggests that such injury or death is not just a collateral hazard, but the malevo-

48. The masculine participle ἰδών with the neuter subject (τὸ πνεῦμα) is presumably a *constructio ad sensum,* in that it was through the boy's eyes that the demon 'saw'. See further on 5:10, where the host and the demons are interwoven as subjects and objects of the verbs, and cf. 1:24, where the demon's speech is reported as that of the host.

49. The use of ὡς is strange: it is possibly a variant of ἕως. See BDF, 455(2, 3).

lent intention of the demon (though in 5:13 the drowning of the new 'hosts' of the expelled demons does not seem to have been to their advantage).

In 1:40 the leper had apparently expressed uncertainty over Jesus' willingness to help (ἐὰν θέλῃς); this man seems to doubt his ability (εἴ τι δύνῃ). If, as we suggested in 1:40, the leper's ἐὰν θέλῃς was no more than polite diffidence, the same cannot be said here. In the light of the disciples' recent failure the father is understandably cautious in asking for deliverance even by Jesus. This is clearly a difficult case, and not even Jesus may have the power to tackle it. But even a little help is better than none: εἴ τι δύνῃ. If that is the implication, it is hardly surprising that the man's words draw a sharp reaction from Jesus in v. 23. For σπλαγχνίζομαι see on 6:34.

23-24 These verses highlight the significance of faith for the reception of divine power.[50] The disciples' failure has already been implicitly attributed to unbelief (γενεὰ ἄπιστος, v. 19), and though the explicit answer to their question in v. 29 is about prayer, the two concepts are closely related: the effectiveness of prayer depends on the faith of the one praying (11:22-24). Here, however, it is the faith of the father rather than that of the exorcist which is in question; faith is not a mechanical aid to the exorcist, but rather the attitude, or better the relationship with God, required of all concerned if the force of evil is to be defeated.[51]

The neuter of the article is sometimes used to introduce a quoted word or phrase (e.g., Mt. 19:18; Rom. 13:9; 1 Cor. 4:6?; Gal. 5:14), sometimes as here picking up a word or phrase from the preceding sentence (Gal. 4:25; Eph. 4:9; Heb. 12:27). In all other such NT uses, however, the phrase so formed takes its place in a full sentence (except in Mt. 19:18, where it stands as the reply to the question Ποίας;). Here a complete sentence can be found only by the rather cumbersome expedient of postulating an elliptical sense, 'So far as the εἰ δύνῃ is concerned [I tell you]' (BDF, 267[1]).[52] The phrase is better taken here as syntactically independent, and read as an idiomatic exclamation, Τὸ εἰ δύνῃ!, echoing the man's tentative request in a tone of ironical rebuke: '"If you can" indeed!' How dare he express any doubt on the matter? Grammatically it is rough but effective, but scribal attempts to smooth it out into a proper sentence (see Textual Note) suggest that the idiom was not readily recognised as acceptable syntax.[53]

A new sentence then begins with πάντα, affirming the contrary to the man's presumed scepticism (for God's ability to do the impossible see further on 11:22-23). It is debated whether τῷ πιστεύοντι here refers to the father or to Jesus the

---

50. See above on 2:5; 5:34, and more fully S. E. Dowd, *Prayer,* 96-117.

51. C. D. Marshall, *Faith,* 116-18, argues that the father of the patient is specifically included in the general faithlessness of which Jesus complained in v. 19, so that in vv. 21-24 we see 'an initial coming to faith by the suppliant'.

52. Cf. Cranfield, 'As to your "If you can", . . .'

53. See Schweizer, 186, for a translation reflecting such a 'smoother' flow to the dialogue, apparently ignoring the τό: '"Have pity on us and help us, if you possibly can!" "Yes," said Jesus, "if *you* can! Everything is possible for the person who has faith."'

healer, but in the context both meanings are probably in view: Jesus has the ability to heal because of his faith, and the healing may be expected to be granted in response to the faith of the petitioner (as in 2:5; 5:34, 36).[54] It is the latter sense that is picked up in the father's reply. The apparent *carte blanche* offered by πάντα δυνατὰ τῷ πιστεύοντι, as of many other NT assurances about prayer, may need to be tempered by pastoral advice,[55] but it puts the emphasis where it should be, on the unlimited power of God in whom faith is placed; it rules out the suggestion that any force, certainly not the present demonic opponent, can be too much for God. But such assurances naturally promote an introspective concern as to how real the petitioner's faith is, and the father's famously paradoxical reply captures the tortured self-doubt of many sincere pray-ers. Belief and unbelief are mixed in most of us, and perhaps Mark would encourage us to notice that this common condition proved in the event to be no obstacle to his request being granted. At least he put his ἀπιστία in the right perspective by not dwelling on it but asking Jesus to help with it.[56] His belief, however uncertain, was all that was needed, and from this point he plays no further part in the narrative, so that all the attention falls where it should, on the power of Jesus.[57]

25 There is no need to assume that a different ὄχλος is introduced here. Either the crowd of v. 14 is still growing as new spectators arrive, or perhaps Jesus' consultation with the father and his son has been aside from the crowd, and now people are closing in on them again, so that it is time to act. For ἐπιτιμάω in a context of exorcism see on 1:25 (cf. 3:12). The demon, previously described as πνεῦμα ἄλαλον or just τὸ πνεῦμα, is now described by Mark's regular term τὸ πνεῦμα τὸ ἀκάθαρτον (used in every account of exorcism in this gospel), clearly marking the boy's condition, for all its distinctive traits of dumbness and 'epilepsy', as one of demon possession.

The word of command to the demon is fuller in this case than in other exorcisms, including a description of the nature of the spirit, a statement of the identity of the exorcist, and a specific command not only to leave the boy but also not to return. The use of κωφόν with ἄλαλον (v. 17) probably adds little, since the two words can be virtually synonymous, though κωφός is a broader term, and may indicate that the boy was deaf as well as dumb (see on 7:32); the doubling of adjectives is typical of Mark's prolix style of storytelling. The inclusion of the pronoun ἐγώ suggests that ἐγὼ ἐπιτάσσω σοι (unparalleled in the gospels in such a context) is not a redundant piece of 'padding', but draws at-

54. C. D. Marshall, *Faith,* 118-20.

55. S. E. Dowd, *Prayer* 133-62, discusses the problem of theodicy in the context of unanswered prayer, with special reference to Jesus' 'unanswered' prayer in Gethsemane.

56. J. F. Williams, *Followers,* 139-41, helpfully analyses Mark's account of the father as included in the faithlessness to which Jesus referred in v. 19, but progressing from there through doubt (v. 22) to 'believing and unbelieving at the same time'. Williams emphasises that the father, though weak in faith, was at least, unlike the disciples, aware of his problem.

57. For fuller discussion of the 'ambiguity' of the father's faith/unbelief see S. E. Dowd, *Prayer,* 110-14.

tention to the person issuing the order: 'It is *I* who command it'. The demon may have been able to resist the lesser authority of the disciples, but has now met its match (cf. the recognition of Jesus and of his authority by demons in 1:24; 3:11; 5:7, 10). The command to come out is normal, but the addition of καὶ μηκέτι εἰσέλθῃς εἰς αὐτόν is unique in the gospels. Josephus (*Ant.* 8.47), however, tells how Eleazar, after expelling a demon, adjured it μηκέτ' εἰς αὐτὸν ἐπανήξειν, and Philostratus (*VA* 4.20) records the command of Apollonius of Tyana to 'leave the young boy and never possess anyone else'. Mt. 12:43-45 envisages the possibility of the return of an expelled demon, and the request of Legion's demons for an alternative home (5:12) indicates the problem of homelessness for an evicted demon, a problem which an exorcist had to take into account, hence this specific command not to return. For the father it is a much-needed reassurance that a condition which has persisted ἐκ παιδιόθεν is now at an end.

26-27 For the cry of the expelled demon cf. 1:26 and notes on 1:23; the verb σπαράσσω (cf. on v. 20 above) also occurs in 1:26. The departure of the demon, which has been responsible for the boy's violent movements, leaves him inert. The account of Jesus' taking his hand and raising him up echoes the language used of the raising of Jairus's daughter (5:41-42), but here we are left in no doubt that the impression of death was temporary and mistaken. This is not another resuscitation, but the restoration of the boy to normality after a traumatic experience of exorcism.

28-29 For the οἶκος as the place of private questioning and instruction after a public event or pronouncement see also 7:17; 10:10 (cf. 4:10). For the same connotation in κατ' ἰδίαν cf. 4:34 and the similar κατὰ μόνας in 4:10. Still smarting, no doubt, from their public humiliation, the disciples are genuinely puzzled as to the reason for their failure, after their initial successes in exorcism (6:13). For ὅτι as an interrogative 'Why?' see on 2:16; 9:11.

Jesus' reply is surprising, both in that it appears to differentiate demons into categories of 'difficulty', and also (particularly if καὶ νηστείᾳ is not part of the text; see Textual Note) in that it implies that the disciples did not pray.

To take the latter point first, were the disciples so confident in their own authority that they had attempted an exorcism without turning to God for help? The situation presumably did not allow them the luxury of an extended time of prayer before making the attempt, but the simple phrase ἐν προσευχῇ does not specify the duration or quality of the prayer, and an immediate and instinctive appeal for divine power might be expected to be the natural response of those who have been with Jesus.[58] If, however, καὶ νηστείᾳ is part of the text (see Textual Note), the situation is rather different, since fasting is not achieved in a moment: 'prayer and fasting' suggests a régime rather than the immediate response to a crisis. While Jesus has ruled out obligatory fasting for the disciples while

---

58. For the link between faith and prayer in this context see C. D. Marshall, *Faith,* 222-23; S. E. Dowd, *Prayer,* 116-21.

369

he is still with them (2:19), this reading would suggest (as does Mt. 6:16-18) that they were still permitted, and even encouraged, to fast and pray on occasion, and that this would have been an appropriate preparation for the spiritual conflict involved in exorcism.

To return to the other surprising element in Jesus' reply, τοῦτο τὸ γένος apparently classifies the πνεῦμα ἄλαλον as making exceptional demands on the exorcist (and therefore perhaps as more difficult to expel than those they have previously encountered, 6:13). The NT does not elsewhere differentiate demons in this way, though Mark has gone out of his way in 5:3-5 to depict the demons which possessed Legion as particularly intractable. In Jesus' encounters with demons, however threatening, a simple word of command has sufficed in every case, and the present narrative has not depicted Jesus himself as engaging in a special régime of prayer (and fasting). But the disciples' authority was always derivative, and prayer is an appropriate recognition of that fact in any encounter with spiritual evil. Perhaps, then, τοῦτο τὸ γένος is not after all intended to place this particular demon into a special class, but denotes demons in general as a γένος which can never be tackled in merely human strength. The disciples' problem, on this understanding, has been a loss of the sense of dependence on Jesus' unique ἐξουσία which had undergirded their earlier exorcistic success. They have become blasé and thought of themselves as now the natural experts in such a case, and they must learn that in spiritual conflict there is no such automatic power. Their public humiliation has been a necessary part of their re-education to the principles of the kingdom of God.

MORE LESSONS ABOUT THE WAY OF THE CROSS (9:30-50)

The process of re-educating the disciples which began in 8:31 with the first announcement of Jesus' coming rejection and death is now resumed with a second such announcement (9:30-32). As in 8:32-33, the disciples again respond by revealing how completely they have misunderstood the values of the kingdom of God, and Jesus offers a further lesson in the reversal of natural expectations (9:33-37). Mark follows this basic lesson with some further teaching on the unexpected dynamics of discipleship, first through correcting a further 'gaffe' by a well-meaning disciple, John (9:38-41), and then by means of a series of apparently independent short sayings, linked by catchwords (9:42-50).

This section of the gospel lacks the obvious coherence of the earlier part of the journey material (8:27–9:13), and looks more like a collection of Jesus' teaching which Mark wanted to include and has put in for convenience here after the second passion prediction.[59] All of it relates in different ways to disci-

---

59. E. Best, *Following*, 75, arguing that vv. 33-50 came to Mark as already a unit of tradition, comments: 'We have here an instance of Mark's tendency to use a sequence of sayings, whose beginning related to his subject even if its end did not.'

pleship, and all of it challenges the natural human assumptions of the disciples as a close-knit community of men with a shared mission. It thus belongs appropriately in this part of the gospel, even if the links between the individual sayings included are sometimes less than compelling.

Geographical notices in vv. 30 and 33 maintain the journey setting, though as yet we have not moved beyond the scenes of the Galilean ministry in Act One. After this short collection, a further (and rather obscure) geographical notice in 10:1 will move us on to a later phase of the journey, closer to Jerusalem, and the sense of urgency will increase. But for now the process of reorientation continues patiently.

Second Prediction of the Passion (9:30-32)

30 The location of the previous pericope was apparently at the foot of the Mount of Transfiguration, but since the mountain cannot be identified with any confidence (see on v. 2) it is not possible to specify what is intended by ἐκεῖθεν. The journey, which began northeast of Galilee (8:27), now continues through the familiar territory of Act One. In this area Jesus is well known, and we might expect to hear again of the gathering of enthusiastic crowds. But that is not now Jesus' purpose, and he escapes recognition, presumably by avoiding areas of population as he had to do in 1:45. If παραπορεύομαι here carries the sense of 'pass by' (cf. 11:20; 15:29) rather than 'pass through', the construction with διά would underline the idea of going through incognito (though the same combination in 2:23 hardly carries this sense).

In 6:31 Jesus attempted to escape public attention in order to secure rest for himself and his disciples. In 7:24 we are not told why he sought privacy. But here the new focus of the gospel is revealed by a more positive statement of purpose in the γάρ that follows. Jesus' mission is now to teach his disciples, and that takes priority over any public activity.

31 The imperfect tenses, as well as the fact that this is the second of a series of three such predictions, indicate that what is stated in this verse is the continuing theme of his teaching at this stage. It is thus a reminder rather than adding anything new to what we already know from 8:31. Indeed, this is a relatively brief summary of the theme of the coming rejection, death, and resurrection of the Son of Man, stark and clear in its content, but not going into so much detail as the other two predictions.

The one clause which occurs here for the first time is παραδίδοται εἰς χεῖρας ἀνθρώπων. The present tense, followed by futures (ἀποκτενοῦσιν, ἀναστήσεται), emphasises that the future course of events is already decided, and the process has begun as they go towards Jerusalem. The verb παραδίδωμι has occurred already, both of the fate of John the Baptist (1:14) and to sum up the role of Judas Iscariot in 3:19 (see notes there). It will recur frequently with specific reference to Judas (14:10-11, 18, 21, etc.) but also more generally of what is to happen to Jesus (10:33). Judas is not its only subject: the 'handing over' by the Sanhedrin (10:33; 15:1, 10) and by Pilate (15:15) mark the further stages of Jesus' passion. In such usage παραδίδωμι indicates that the object of the verb is in the power of the subject, and implies that the outcome is one which the object would not have chosen. There is thus an implication of hostility, even though the verb does not in itself mean to 'betray' (see note on 3:19). Here it takes the place of πολλὰ παθεῖν καὶ ἀποδοκιμασθῆναι in 8:31: that is what the 'handing over' will lead to.[60] It is probable that Mark and his readers would also have been familiar with the Pauline use of παραδίδωμι with God as the subject (Rom. 8:32; cf. 4:25), and this may have been a secondary connotation of the use of the verb in this context.[61] εἰς χεῖρας ἀνθρώπων is surprisingly unspecific, and ἄνθρωπος does not by itself suggest either enmity or wickedness. Does the use of ἄνθρωποι reflect Mark's conviction that Jesus is more than ἄνθρωπος, the divine figure paradoxically surrendered to human power? Or does it depend on seeing God as the subject of the verb, voluntarily handing over his Messiah into human control? Probably the choice of the word is mainly dictated by the play on words — ὁ υἱὸς τοῦ ἀνθρώπου in the hands of ἄνθρωποι — a turn of phrase which is deeply ironical in the light of the sovereignty over all humanity which was predicted for the υἱὸς ἀνθρώπου in Dn. 7:14.

32 After the pronouncement of 8:31 the disciples' incomprehension was implied by Peter's shocked response (8:32) in which the rest of the disciples were implicated in 8:33. Now it is stated openly. ἀγνοέω normally means to be ignorant, but in relation to a saying the meaning shades easily into incomprehension ('not to know the meaning of'). Luke spells it out: ἠγνόουν . . . καὶ ἦν παρακεκαλυμμένον ἀπ' αὐτῶν ἵνα μὴ αἴσθωνται αὐτό (Lk. 9:45). Mark seldom uses ῥῆμα, and its use probably characterises the saying as one of special importance, a more formal pronouncement (cf. 14:72). The disciples are not usually reluctant to ask Jesus to explain difficult sayings (4:10; 7:17; 9:11, 28; 10:10; 13:3); is their reluctance on this occasion because they could guess that the answer would be one they would not want to hear, especially after the alarming response which followed Peter's questioning of the previous such pronouncement (8:33-38)? ἐφοβοῦντο suggests as much. 'They understand enough to be afraid to ask to understand more'.[62]

---

60. The suggestion that uses of παραδίδωμι in relation to Jesus' passion are intended to recall its use in LXX Is. 53:6, 12 probably reads too much into a common verb with a wide range of uses. Marcus, *Way*, 188-89, explores this tentatively, but confesses, 'We would feel better about this conclusion if the word were combined with other language drawn from Isaiah 53, which is not the case in any of the Markan texts' (n. 136).

61. Against this see Gundry, 506-7.

62. E. Best, *Following*, 73. This psychological explanation of the disciples' fear seems to me more appropriate in context than the view of T. Dwyer, *Wonder*, 150 (following Gnilka), that it is a 'holy terror', an 'uncanny sense of the numinous'.

A Radical Lesson on Status (9:33-37)

Jesus' second announcement of his passion has been met by incomprehension and fear, but now the disciples go even further and reveal that their thoughts are moving along quite different lines. While Jesus' eyes are fixed on martyrdom, they are preoccupied with the question of status. While Jesus is talking of rejection and death, they are apparently thinking of a continuing movement in which leadership will be an issue. But God's kingship will come about through defeat, not victory, and within it the world's values are turned upside down; the first are last, and the last first (10:31). So the process of reorientation continues through the lowly example of a child.

33-34 The arrival in Capernaum is surprising after v. 30; surely there of all places Jesus could not avoid being recognised. Mark appears not to have noticed the problem. But in Capernaum there is no more public ministry, but only a private dialogue ἐν τῇ οἰκίᾳ (symbolic of privacy, but in narrative terms presumably we are to think again of the house of Peter and Andrew). The disciples have been reluctant to question Jesus (v. 32), so he instead questions them, in order to bring out how little they have yet understood. Τί ἐν τῇ ὁδῷ διελογίζεσθε; is not an attempt to gain new information, for Jesus is clearly aware (through supernatural insight or from having overheard the argument?) of what has been going on. It is a challenge to bring into the open a debate of which they are apparently ashamed, aware that Jesus will not approve. Hence their silence. There is an almost comical incongruity in the picture of these grown men acting like guilty schoolboys before the teacher, an impression which is only heightened when Jesus goes on to use a child as an example to them.

The question τίς μείζων may have been sparked by the selection of Peter, James, and John for the trip up the mountain, leaving the others feeling aggrieved — and the more so after their humiliation over the failed exorcism. Perhaps also they have already grasped sufficient of what Jesus has been saying to realise that his death is a real possibility, which then leaves the pressing question of who is to take the lead after he is gone.[63] The issue will surface more powerfully in the bid for leadership by James and John and in Jesus' response to it in 10:35-45.

35 Καθίσας is unusual in Mark's narrative to introduce teaching (but cf. Mt. 5:1, and the sitting in the boat to teach in Mk. 4:1-2), but given the location inside the house and followed by ἐφώνησεν τοὺς δώδεκα it conveys the sense of a deliberate, even formal, piece of instruction. This is an issue which must be addressed, and the teacher sits and summons his disciples to gather round and listen. The teaching given is paralleled many times in the synoptic tradition, not only in 10:43-44 and parallels but also in Mt. 23:11-12 and in other passages which speak of high and low status (Lk. 14:11; 18:14) and of the reversal of roles (10:31 par.; Mt. 20:16; Lk. 13:30); in John it is memorably symbolised in

---

63. Cf. *Gos. Thom.* 12: 'The disciples said to Jesus, 'We know that you will go away from us. Who is it that will then be great over us?''

the footwashing (Jn. 13:12-17). This is such a radical challenge to natural human valuation that it needs constant repetition. The preeminent status in the kingdom of God is characterised by the twin elements of lowliness (ἔσχατος) and service (διάκονος, a term which should not be read in the light of later ideas of 'office' in the church, but simply as one whose job it is to provide for the needs of others, a domestic; in 10:43-44 it will be used in parallel with δοῦλος). The question τίς μείζων; could hardly be more inappropriate.

36-37   The use of a child as a teaching aid, both here and with a slightly different introduction in Mt. 18:1-5, has explicitly (in terms of its context) to do with status, not with any character traits supposedly typical of children. The child represents the lowest order in the social scale, the one who is under the authority and care of others and who has not yet achieved the right of self-determination.[64] To 'become like a child' (Mt. 18:3) is to forgo status and to accept the lowest place, to be a 'little one' (Mt. 18:6, 10, 14; 10:42). Mark does not use the same terms as Matthew, but the latter's fuller version rightly draws out the implications of Mark's child analogy. In this pericope there is no call (as in Matthew) to become like a child (that will follow in 10:15), but rather the injunction to 'receive' the child, to reverse the conventional value-scale by according importance to the unimportant.[65]

If the οἰκία is again that of Peter and Andrew, the child is presumably a younger member of the family, who would properly have been staying in the background but is now suddenly placed ἐν μέσῳ αὐτῶν. Only Mark adds here and in 10:16 the homely picture of Jesus ἐναγκαλισάμενος the child, which makes the message visual as well as verbal; ἀγκάλη is the bent arm, and the verb means to take in the arms, to embrace (cf. 10:16). The phrase ἕν τῶν τοιούτων παιδίων rather than simply ἕν παιδίον probably widens the scope of this pronouncement beyond children as such to those who are like children in their littleness and unimportance. δέχομαι is a general term for receiving, for example, as a guest (6:11), but in this context it carries the nuance of welcome, of treating as significant rather than ignoring or suppressing. Such a welcome is given ἐπὶ τῷ ὀνόματί μου, a phrase not hitherto used in this gospel, but which now becomes the focus for the teaching that follows in vv. 38-41. In those verses it conveys acting on the authority of Jesus, and that might be an appropriate sense here too, inasmuch as it is he who is calling on his disciples to act in this way, though perhaps the sense is more broadly of 'doing as I would do'. In 13:6 people who come ἐπὶ τῷ ὀνόματί μου are claiming to represent (or to be?) Jesus, and the phrase may be intended here also to depict the child as *representing* Jesus, so that to receive the child is in effect to receive him (an idea memorably developed in Mt. 25:40, 45). Certainly the same idea of representa-

---

64. E. Best, *Story,* 88, rightly emphasises this ancient attitude, in contrast with modern Western views of children.

65. See, for example, Hooker 228 for the suggestion that 9:37 and 10:15 have become exchanged in transmission, since each fits better the context of the other.

tion governs the following clause: Jesus represents the one who sent him, so that to receive him is to receive God.[66]

The idea of Jesus as one 'sent' is more typical of John than of Mark, and occurs only here in this gospel (except parabolically in 12:6). Jesus ἀποστέλλει his disciples on their mission (3:14; 6:7; cf. 11:1; 14:13), but here he himself is the one sent. While the terminology is new, the idea of a mission which he 'must' fulfil has already appeared in 8:31; 9:12 and will become stronger in 10:33-34, 38 and particularly in the language of 'coming to' in 10:45. This sense of mission and representation does not in itself imply the divinity of Jesus, any more than the representative role of the παιδίον identifies the child with Jesus. The messenger can represent the sender without personal identity. But in Mark's church it is likely that already the concept of receiving God through receiving Jesus would have carried some of the christological weight which it achieves in Jn. 14:6-11, 20-24.

A Warning against Cliquishness (9:38-41)

TEXTUAL NOTES

38. The complex variants do not significantly affect the sense. They concern (1) the tenses of the verbs (imperfect or aorist for κωλύω; imperfect or present for ἀκολουθέω); (2) whether or not οὐκ (ἡ)ἀκολουθεῖ ἡμῖν occurs twice (both as a description of the man and as a reason for the prevention); (3) if it occurs only once, the order of the two remaining clauses. The ℵB reading adopted by UBS⁴ (καὶ ἐκωλύομεν αὐτόν, ὅτι οὐκ ἠκολούθει ἡμῖν) is well supported, but may be suspect as an assimilation to the text in Lk. 9:49 (except for the tense of ἀκολουθέω and ἡμῖν for μεθ' ἡμῶν). The repetition of the clause οὐκ (ἡ)ἀκολουθεῖ ἡμῖν, while not so well supported, would be typical of Mark's style, especially here to emphasise the man's dubious allegiance, and would be a prime candidate for scribal tidying up by assimilation to the Lucan text.

41. It is not surprising that scribes, with the phrase ἐπὶ (ἐν) τῷ ὀνόματί μου (σου) already before them three times in vv. 37-39 should introduce it again here, especially if they found the idiom ἐν ὀνόματι ὅτι less familiar.

This little didactic story follows very appropriately from the lesson of vv. 33-37, the call to disciples to be ready to receive those whom they might naturally reject, and the connection is reinforced by the repetition three times in these verses of the phrase ἐπὶ/ἐν τῷ ὀνόματί μου/σου (or equivalent, v. 41) which was the reason given for receiving the child in v. 37. Where the name of Jesus (i.e., a relationship with him) is concerned, natural human considerations of who is in and who is out will be subverted.

---

66. The change of tense from the aorist δέξηται for receiving the child to the present δέχηται for receiving Jesus is probably no more than natural linguistic variation. To argue from it that receiving the child is a single act while receiving Jesus is a lifelong relationship would be overexegesis.

375

The effect of the pericope is to encourage a welcoming openness on the part of Jesus' disciples which is in stark contrast to the protective exclusiveness more often associated with religious groups, not least within the Christian tradition. The story occurs in Mark and Luke but not in Matthew, and it is possible that its inclusive tone did not appeal so much to Matthew and his church (see on v. 40 for the contrasting formulae of Mark and Matthew). The man concerned is not a recognised member of the group of disciples, but he does profess to operate in the name of Jesus, and the results of his activity are beneficent. It is this criterion rather than a narrower group identity which the pericope accepts.

There is a clear resemblance to the story of Eldad and Medad in Nu. 11:26-29, with John taking up the preventative role of Joshua in that story, and Jesus echoing Moses' open-minded attitude and repudiation of the 'jealousy' of his loyal follower.

Exorcism has been a prominent feature of the ministry both of Jesus and of his disciples, and from 3:14-15; 6:7, 13 it would seem that it is a special feature of the authority given to the Twelve. To find the practice carried out in the name of Jesus by someone unknown to them is therefore a severe blow to the disciples' sense of identity, and undermines their special status. The issue of status, which underlay the teaching of vv. 33-37, is therefore still in focus. To make matters worse, this pericope follows hard on the story of the disciples' failure in exorcism in 9:14-29. To see an 'outsider' apparently succeeding where they, the chosen agents of Jesus, have failed is doubly distressing.

38 This is the only pericope in the gospel where John plays a solo role, and it is not a creditable one. He and his brother James will feature together in an even more unfortunate episode in 10:35-45. As members of the 'inner circle' (1:16-20, 29; 5:37; 9:2; 13:3; 14:33) they not only share the failure of the other disciples to embrace the values of the kingdom of God, but even take the lead in demonstrating their unresponsiveness and in earning Jesus' rebuke. The impulsive hostility to an outsider revealed in this incident (cf. Lk. 9:54) perhaps gives some basis for the otherwise puzzling epithet Βοανηργές (see on 3:17). If the imperfect tense of ἐκωλύομεν is correct (see Textual Note), it probably indicates an unsuccessful attempt rather than the repeated prohibition of a persistent 'offender'.

There is some other evidence in the gospels for exorcists outside the immediate circle of Jesus and his disciples (Mt. 12:27, 43-45), and there are a number of mentions of exorcism, Jewish and pagan, in roughly contemporary sources (though apparently not on the scale of Jesus' exorcisms).[67] The mention of περιερχόμενοι Ἰουδαῖοι ἐξορκισταί in Acts 19:13 indicates that it was a practice with recognised (professional?) practitioners. Some of them invoked the name of Jesus (after his death and resurrection), not always with satisfactory re-

---

67. See E. F. Kirschner, *Place,* ch. 2, especially the summary on pp. 28-29. Cf. above, pp. 100-101.

sults (Acts 19:13-16). This is the only mention of a similar practice during Jesus' lifetime.

This pericope, in contrast with Acts 19:13-16, assumes that the exorcisms were successful. The ground of John's objection was not lack of success, but the use of Jesus' name outside the group of disciples. The man's offence is that οὐκ ἀκολουθεῖ ἡμῖν. Mark uses ἀκολουθέω quite frequently as a term for discipleship, but elsewhere its object is always Jesus himself. The expectation that someone should follow *us* (presumably the group associated with Jesus) is new and revealing. 'Never was a "royal we" less appropriate!' (Myers, 261). What John is looking for is not so much personal allegiance and obedience to Jesus, but membership in the 'authorised' circle of his followers. We should perhaps understand ἡμεῖς here as specifically the Twelve, regarded as having an exclusive link with and commission from Jesus, so that other people's association with him must be through their mediation. Even if such a possessive doctrine is not explicit, it fits John's restrictive action and explains the terms of Jesus' response.

39 Three γάρ clauses follow Jesus' instruction to leave the exorcist alone, offering three grounds for a more tolerant attitude. First, the fact that the man is able to work a miracle in Jesus' name shows that he cannot be an enemy. Mark has used δύναμις as a generic term for Jesus' own miraculous acts in 6:2, 5, and this man's exorcisms are in the same class, carried out on Jesus' authority. There is no suggestion that the man is personally known to Jesus; rather, he has associated himself with him by using his name, and his choice of that authority, together with the fact of his success, marks him as being on the right side. Such a person cannot in consistency go on to speak as his enemy, and so there is no justification for Jesus' disciples to oppose him.

40 This broad maxim invites comparison with Matthew's formula ὁ μὴ ὢν μετ' ἐμοῦ κατ' ἐμοῦ ἐστιν (Mt. 12:30). Each excludes any middle ground, but the Matthean formula sounds exclusive and dismissive, the Marcan inclusive and welcoming.[68] Luke has both formulae (9:50; 11:23), and so presumably did not regard them as contradictory. While both formulae occur in a dispute over exorcism, the difference in context is significant, the Matthean formula being aimed at those who attributed Jesus' own exorcistic activity to Beelzebul, the Marcan acknowledging the *bona fides* of an exorcist using the name of Jesus. Where there is no middle ground, a declared enemy is not to be put in the same category as an unaffiliated sympathiser. (The difference between the 'me' of Matthew and the 'us' of Mark is probably not significant: in the Matthew context the issue is how people evaluate Jesus himself, while here it is more a matter of belonging to the group.) But while there is thus no formal incompatibility between the two formulae, the fact that it is Mark who has preserved for us the

---

68. Both are paralleled in Cicero's words to Caesar (*Pro Ligario* 11 [32]): 'We have often heard you say that while we reckon everyone as enemies except those who are with us, you yourself count all those who are not against you as on your side.'

more inclusive formulation probably tells us something about his attitude to 'outsiders'. Its optimistic implications are drawn out in an apocryphal saying of Jesus (*P.Oxy.* 1224): ὁ γὰρ μὴ ὢν καθ' ὑμῶν ὑπὲρ ὑμῶν ἐστιν. ὁ σήμερον ὢν μακρὰν αὔριον ἐγγὺς ὑμῶν γενήσεται. The cliquishness which too easily affects a defined group of people with a sense of mission is among the 'worldly' values which must be challenged in the name of the kingdom of God.

41 The third γάρ clause envisages a kind act towards a disciple ἐν ὀνόματι ὅτι Χριστοῦ ἐστε, performed by someone outside the group, and the ἄν generalises it to include potentially a very wide category of sympathisers. For the drink of water, a basic courtesy in Eastern society, cf. Mt. 10:42, a close parallel to this saying, but set in the more specific context of mission and persecution. For ἐν ὀνόματι ὅτι see BDF, 397(3), 'on the claim, on the basis that'. The choice of this idiom is, however, deliberate, as it both echoes the threefold use of ἐπὶ (ἐν) τῷ ὀνόματι in vv. 37-39 and prepares for the introduction of the actual *name* Χριστός in the subordinate clause. This phrase thus brings the series of 'name' formulae to a climax where the actual name is spelled out: ὅτι Χριστοῦ ἐστε. It is *that* name which gives this kind act its specific significance and justifies the reward. This is not mere benevolence, but the demonstration that a person is ὑπὲρ ἡμῶν by means of practical help given specifically to those who belong to Jesus.

This is the only use of the title Χριστός attributed to Jesus himself in the gospel, except for 12:35 and 13:21 where it is used 'objectively' rather than overtly as a title for Jesus himself. It is the more surprising in that Peter's use of this title in 8:29 has been the subject of a strict command to silence, while both there and in 14:62 Jesus responds to the 'offer' of the title by others by substituting for it ὁ υἱὸς τοῦ ἀνθρώπου. Why then do we not find ὁ υἱὸς τοῦ ἀνθρώπου (or more simply μου) here? Probably because here the explicit focus is on the 'name' itself, with ὄνομα used repeatedly. While Mark wants his readers to understand that during his earthly ministry Jesus did not freely use the title Χριστός even in private among his disciples, he is also aware that it is this title, rather than the enigmatic ὁ υἱὸς τοῦ ἀνθρώπου, which will be the basis of people's treatment of Jesus' disciples after his death. For Mark's readers it is the title Χριστός which is the touchstone of a person's allegiance.

The language of reward, which is so prominent in Matthew, appears explicitly only here in Mark (though see 10:28-30 for the idea). It is a paradoxical term to use in connection with a gift of water, which is so basic a feature of Eastern hospitality as to require no reward. But even so small an act betokens a person's response to Jesus in the person of his disciples (cf. Mt. 25:31-46), and as such will not be unnoticed.

The three sayings collected in vv. 39-41 thus illustrate in different ways the open boundaries of the kingdom of God, where both committed disciple and sympathetic fellow traveller find their place. The unknown exorcist represents this outer circle, and is to be welcomed as such. There are indeed opponents and 'outsiders', as we see repeatedly in the rest of the gospel, but disciples are called on to be cautious in drawing lines of demarcation. They are to be a church, not a sect.

Further Sayings on Discipleship (9:42-50)

TEXTUAL NOTES

42. The absolute use of οἱ πιστεύοντες as a synonym for disciples (as in Acts 2:44; 4:32, etc.) would be unique in Mark, though 9:23 partially prepares for it. The addition of εἰς ἐμέ would thus be a natural 'improvement' as well as an assimilation to Mt. 18:6, and the range of authorities which omit it is sufficiently broad (ℵ D Δ and some OL MSS) to favour the shorter reading.

43, 45. The phrase εἰς τὴν γέενναν seems a firmly established part of the text in both verses (its omission in W *f*¹ *f*¹³ etc. in v. 43 [noted in UBS³, not in UBS⁴] probably reflecting a desire to drop the unfamiliar Semitic term in favour of something more universally recognised; assimilation to Mt. 18:8 is another factor). The presence of εἰς τὸ πῦρ τὸ ἄσβεστον (which parallels but is not identical to the Matthean phrase εἰς τὸ πῦρ τὸ αἰώνιον) at some point in the tradition seems necessary to account for the presence of this or a variant in many witnesses of both verses, and the decision of UBS⁴ to retain it in v. 43 but not in v. 45 (where its support is rather less, and it would naturally have been repeated from v. 43) seems appropriate.

44, 46. These verses repeat what is firmly in the text at v. 48. It is more likely that the omission of vv. 44 and 46 in a wide range of witnesses represents the original text than that an original threefold repetition was eliminated.

49. This enigmatic verse was apparently as impenetrable to ancient scribes as to modern commentators. The insertion of a reference to the salting of sacrifices is an attempt to render it meaningful, but in D and some OL MSS the original saying has then dropped out, leaving an even more obscure saying than that which it was introduced to explain. The reading which explains the existence of the others is simply πᾶς γὰρ πυρὶ ἁλισθήσεται, a classic example of a *lectio difficilior.*

Verses 42-47 parallel Mt. 18:6-9, and there is a further parallel to vv. 43-47 in Mt. 5:29-30 and to v. 42 in Lk. 17:2. Each of these contexts differs from the immediate context here (though Mt. 18:6-9 follows a partial parallel to Mk. 9:33-37). Verse 50 also has partial parallels in differing contexts in Mt. 5:13; Lk. 14:34-35. We are therefore apparently dealing here with a little complex of sayings which lacked a fixed narrative context, and which occur together in this form only in Mark. They are linked together by repeated key words (σκανδαλίζω, vv. 42 and 43-47; πῦρ, vv. 43-48 and 49; ἅλας, vv. 49 and 50). It is generally agreed that the complex was collected together on this catchword basis, for easier memorisation, before coming to Mark.

The link between this complex and the preceding pericopes is less clearcut. On the one hand, τῶν μικρῶν τούτων in v. 42 picks up the terminology of Mt. 10:42, which is closely parallel to Mk. 9:41, but since the Marcan version omits that phrase the link is not visible in the Marcan text. On the other hand, τῶν μικρῶν τούτων also recalls τῶν τοιούτων παιδίων in v. 37, but that saying is separated from the present verse by the pericope about the unknown exorcist. Verse 42 would follow more naturally immediately after v. 37, and vv. 38-41 seem to have been intruded into a previously existing sequence, though if Mark had known the saying of v. 41 in its Matthean form it would have offered a more direct link with v. 42. The tradition process which led to this linkage is obscure, but Mark (or whoever brought these sayings together) clearly felt that there was a congruity of subject matter. Verse 42 (the danger of hindering the faith of a 'little one') follows as the negative counterpart to v. 41 (the reward for taking care of a disciple).

The whole little complex of sayings, like the preceding pericopes, focuses on the demands of discipleship, both negatively and positively. The sayings thus fit into the overall thrust of this part of the gospel, however artificially they may be linked with one another.

42 The verb σκανδαλίζω (Mark does not use the noun σκάνδαλον), which is the key to vv. 42-47, has occurred in the passive in 4:17 for those who under pressure cease to be effective disciples, and a similar passive use in 14:27, 29 will refer to the apostasy of the disciples when Jesus is arrested. The active use in the present context is best understood of one who causes such a failure on the part of others, who 'trips' or 'disables' another's discipleship. How this may be done is not spelled out; it is the result rather than the means that the verb describes. The NIV translation 'cause to sin' is therefore too narrow; there are many other ways in which another's faith and discipleship may be wrecked. NJB and REB, 'is/causes the downfall of' (similarly in vv. 43, 45, and 47), better captures the metaphor, while GNB's 'causes to lose his faith in me' rather prosaically spells out its likely reference.

To be the cause of another's spiritual shipwreck is so serious an offence that a quick drowning would be preferable to the fate it deserves; the μύλος ὀνικός, the stone from a mill ground by donkey power, far heavier than that of a hand mill, ensures an immediate death. The stone is rather grotesquely pictured as 'placed round' (περίκειται) the neck like a collar, rather than hung from it (Mt. 18:6, κρεμασθῇ). καλόν ἐστιν μᾶλλον indicates a comparison: the drowning is not itself the appropriate fate of such a person (the perfect tenses following εἰ introduce an 'unreal' or hypothetical supposition), but rather serves as a foil to set off the greater severity of the actual punishment merited; cf. Jesus' words about Judas in 14:21. What that punishment is will be indicated in the language of γέεννα and πῦρ ἄσβεστον which dominates the following verses.

This is Mark's only use of μικροί to denote disciples, a use which Matthew has developed more fully (Mt. 10:42; 18:6, 10, 14; cf. 25:40, 45). The description of them as πιστεύοντες (see Textual Note) makes it clear that Mark is using the term in a similar sense, even though the lack of a clear narrative context makes it difficult to identify the immediate referent of τούτων. Should we think of the unknown exorcist of vv. 38-41 as an example of such a 'believing little one', or does the thought go back to the child of v. 36 and those repre-

380

sented by him (see above for the possibility that v. 42 was originally more closely linked with vv. 33-37)? As Mark's text stands the question cannot be answered with confidence,[69] but the context as a whole makes it unlikely that the μικροί should be understood only, or even mainly, of children. Disciples of any age are potentially vulnerable to such 'tripping'. After the disciples' abortive discussion of τίς μείζων (v. 34) it is very appropriate that μικροί be used to denote disciples in general. And it is the μικροί who matter so much to Jesus that to trip even one of them up is more than a capital offence.

43, 45, 47-48 See the Textual Notes for the omission of vv. 44 and 46. For the poetical tracing of sins to different parts of the body cf. Pr. 6:16-19; Job 31:1, 5, and 7. The formulation of vv. 43, 45, and 47 is almost parallel, given the change in the part of the body mentioned (ἡ χείρ, ὁ πούς, ὁ ὀφθαλμός) and the resultant change in the description of the consequent disablement (κυλλόν, χωλόν, μονόφθαλμον); but there are a few differences. The change from ἀπόκοψον (vv. 43, 45) to ἔκβαλε (v. 47) is of course required by the different organ involved. Apart from insignificant variations in word order, we may note also the escalation from the relatively colourless ἀπελθεῖν to the more vivid βληθῆναι (which in v. 47 suggestively echoes the ἔκβαλε of the protasis: one type of 'throwing' is preferable to the other; cf. also βέβληται εἰς τὴν θάλασσαν in v. 42, again preferable to being thrown into γέεννα), the change from ἡ ζωή in vv. 43, 45 to ἡ βασιλεία τοῦ θεοῦ in v. 47, and the expansions of τὴν γέενναν in vv. 43 and 48 (see Textual Note).

Mark's uses of ἡ βασιλεία τοῦ θεοῦ hitherto have related more to the nature and outcome of the ministry of Jesus, and thus more to earthly developments than to the eternal state, so that the parallel here with ἡ ζωή (set over against ἡ γέεννα) introduces a new and more otherworldly use of the phrase. But again in 10:15, 23-25 there will be talk of 'entering' the βασιλεία τοῦ θεοῦ, and there the phrase will stand in relation to the fuller expression ζωὴ αἰώνιος (10:17, 30), while the use of σωθῆναι in 10:26 as an apparent synonym with εἰς τὴν βασιλείαν τοῦ θεοῦ εἰσελθεῖν indicates a similar meaning to this passage. In 14:25 there is a clearly futuristic use, where Jesus looks forward to drinking new wine in the βασιλεία τοῦ θεοῦ. There is thus no discernible difference in meaning here between ἡ ζωή and ἡ βασιλεία τοῦ θεοῦ; both refer to the ζωὴ αἰώνιος which is the ultimate state of the faithful disciple.

This is Mark's only reference to ἡ γέεννα, a term used in apocalyptic literature for the ultimate place of punishment of the ungodly (see J. Jeremias, *TDNT,* 1.657-58). Its more frequent use by Matthew (5:22; 10:28; 23:15, 33 in addition to the two parallels to this passage) indicates that it had a clear and

---

69. C. D. Marshall, *Faith,* 155-58, argues that '"these believing little ones" acts as a summary designation for all the characters depicted in the preceding interchange between Jesus and the Twelve', including the 'children' of vv. 36-37 (who are not only literal children but insignificant disciples), the unknown evangelist and those he represents, and those who offer a cup of water to disciples.

well-known meaning, so that its use alone in v. 45 (see Textual Note) would communicate adequately. But the concept is filled out in vv. 43 and 48.

τὸ πῦρ τὸ ἄσβεστον (v. 43) picks up the common imagery of fire as the agent of judgment and destruction, perhaps exploiting the origin of the word γέεννα in the Valley of Hinnom (Heb. *gē-hinnōm*) where the fires of Jerusalem's refuse dumps burned continuously. It remains a matter of doctrinal debate whether the unquenchable fire (an echo of Is. 66:24; see below) refers to the unending conscious torment of those committed to it or to a fire which destroys but which never goes out because new fuel is continually added. The wording of this pericope does not in itself settle the question either way,[70] quite apart from the danger of using vivid traditional imagery to establish formal doctrine.

In v. 48 (which is not found in either Matthean parallel) the same theme is picked up (τὸ πῦρ οὐ σβέννυται), but the addition of the undying worm extends the metaphor in a graphic but puzzling way. Are worms also derived from the imagery of the rubbish dump, as an alternative method of destruction to the fire? If so, why need the worm be undying? But of course Mark has not created this mixed image; it is derived from Is. 66:24, itself the basis for later Jewish concepts of Gehenna,[71] where the LXX wording is very close to Mk. 9:48, even to the gruesome inclusion of the possessive αὐτῶν with ὁ σκώληξ (LXX Is. 66:24 also has αὐτῶν with τὸ πῦρ, an idiom which Mark does not reproduce). In Isaiah the clause describes the state in which the dead bodies of God's enemies will be seen, presumably envisaged as decomposing and burning on the battlefield. The combination of fire and worms as the fate of the wicked is echoed in Jdt. 16:17; Ben Sira 7:17. It is evocative language, which is better appreciated in its awful deterrence than analysed as to precisely how the two methods of destruction relate to each other, or just what is the function of the worm.

The extended warning of vv. 43-48 picks up the theme of 'tripping' from v. 42, but the victim is not now someone else (a 'little one') but oneself, 'tripped' by one's own hand, foot, or eye. Danger comes to the disciple not only from outside but from within. The metaphor is not explained;[72] it is for the

---

70. Jdt. 16:17, which like this verse derives from Is. 66:24, clearly understands the victims of worm and fire to remain conscious, as κλαύσονται ἐν αἰσθήσει ἕως αἰῶνος.

71. See B. D. Chilton, *Rabbi*, 101-7. Chilton also argues from the targumic background that the threefold repetition of the formula in vv. 44, 46, and 48 (see Textual Note) may have been original.

72. J. D. M. Derrett, *Audience*, 201-4, berates 'the theologians' for assuming that the language is metaphorical when in fact there is evidence for actual amputations as punishment in ancient Judaism (though no provision for it in Jewish law apart from the specialised case of Dt. 25:12), but he does not go on to explain how literal punitive amputation might fit this passage (where it would be self-inflicted). In any case, his two instances of the amputation of hands from Josephus (*Life* 171-77) hardly add up to a way of life. (His further evidence in *Theology* 76 [1973] 365-66 sets the issue in a wider context, but provides no further contemporary Jewish evidence.) But the fact that such things *could* happen literally certainly helps to make the metaphor effective. Gundry, 514, following Derrett, takes the exhortations as literal calls to self-mutilation, not as metaphorical, despite Jewish prohibitions of self-mutilation (Dt. 14:1), and regards Pesch's metaphorical interpretation as 'timid'. Fortunately most other commentators are equally timid.

reader individually (the sayings are expressed in the singular throughout, except for the αὐτῶν derived from the LXX in v. 48) to determine what aspect of one's own behaviour, tastes, or interests is a potential cause of spiritual downfall, and to take action accordingly. The metaphor of amputation could hardly be more shocking; this is a matter of ultimate seriousness. Nothing less than eternal life or death is at stake. Christians who disparage 'hell-fire preaching' must face the awkward fact that Mark's Jesus (and still more Matthew's and Luke's) envisaged an ultimate separation between life and γέεννα which demanded the most drastic renunciation in order to avoid the unquenchable fire, and that he did not regard even his disciples as immune from the need to examine themselves and take appropriate action.[73]

49   These four words (see Textual Note) offer a vividly mixed metaphor, left without explanation. If their inclusion here derives from any more substantial factor than that vv. 48 and 49 both mention fire, it is presumably to be attributed to a coherence of theme with the preceding verses.[74] The extreme seriousness of the demands of discipleship and the call for renunciation in vv. 42-48 prepare the reader to consider the cost of following Jesus, and the universal scope of this saying (a simple future tense following πᾶς) reminds us of the conviction with which Jesus has predicted his own suffering (δεῖ, 8:31; γέγραπται, 9:12; the simple present tense of παραδίδοται and the futures which follow it in 9:31). These enigmatic words,[75] we may reasonably assume from their context, relate to the cost of taking up the cross to follow Jesus.

Apart from general considerations on the metaphorical use of both fire and salt in biblical literature (each of which yields a variety of possible lines of interpretation, but it is the use of the two together which is unusual and arresting), the most promising line of approach is via Lv. 2:13, the requirement that grain offerings (which were burned) must be accompanied by salt, together with the more sweeping generalisation, 'With all your offerings you shall offer salt'. Salt is not mentioned elsewhere in the Levitical regulations for sacrifice, but Ezra 6:9; 7:22 include salt among the provisions required for restoring temple ritual, and Ezk. 43:24 mentions salt added to animal burnt offerings in the restored temple. To be 'salted with fire' seems then to evoke the imagery of temple sacrifice, but the victims who are 'salted' are now the worshippers themselves. Their dedication to the service of their suffering Messiah is like

73. Myers, 263, interprets the sayings corporately: the 'whole body' is the community of believers, and the members who must be removed are informers or apostates within that 'body'. He does not address the problem which the singular pronouns of vv. 43, 45, and 47 present for this proposal.

74. J. D. M. Derrett, *Theology* 76 (1973) 364-68, imaginatively also suggests a link in the imagery, in that amputated limbs would be cauterised by a process using both salt and fire.

75. It is hardly surprising that textual emendations and alleged mistranslations have been suggested. One of the more interesting is the proposal of T. J. Baarda, *NTS* 5 (1958/9) 318-21, that ἁλισθήσεται derives from a confusion of two Aramaic verbs *tbl* ('season') and *ṭbl* ('baptise'), so that the original saying was 'Everyone will be baptised with fire'.

that of a burnt offering, total and irrevocable. Fire occurs frequently as an image for eschatological suffering. The inclusion of the imagery of salt surprises the modern reader, since fire alone would have made this point. But anyone familiar with sacrificial ritual would not find it out of place. And once introduced, it contributes further nuances. The salt of Lv. 2:13 is described as 'salt of the covenant with your God' (cf. 'covenant of salt', Nu. 18:19; 2 Ch. 13:5), while in Ex. 30:35 salt, as an ingredient of the sacred incense, is linked with the qualities 'pure and holy'. These are among the resonances which the striking image of salting with fire might evoke from someone familiar with OT sacrificial language, and indeed with the ritual as it actually continued in Jerusalem up to A.D. 70.[76] In this context it speaks of one who follows Jesus as totally dedicated to God's service, and warns that such dedication will inevitably be costly in terms of personal suffering.[77]

50 Salt remains the connecting theme of these two apparently independent sayings. The first is well known from elsewhere in the synoptic tradition (Lk. 14:34; Mt. 5:13), but it uses the metaphor of salt in a way which does not relate directly to the sacrificial imagery which apparently underlies v. 49, since the salt seems now to represent not an experience undergone by the disciple, but a good quality to be preserved (a usage continued in the separate saying of v. 50b). The sequence may not be entirely arbitrary, however, since the disciple's character may be understood to derive from the sacrificial dedication symbolised in v. 49: the process of 'salting with fire' produces a 'salty' disciple.

Among the various uses for salt in the ancient world the most prominent are as a preservative or cleansing agent or as flavouring.[78] In either case it symbolises the beneficial (καλόν) influence of the disciple on society, most obviously in Mt. 5:13 with the declaration ὑμεῖς ἐστε τὸ ἅλας τῆς γῆς.[79] Salt was a necessity of life: 'The world cannot endure without salt' (*Sop.* 15:8; cf. Ben Sira 39:26). But its function is lost if it ἄναλον γένηται. Strictly speaking sodium chloride is a stable compound which cannot lose its quality. But the 'salt'

---

76. For salt in connection with temple sacrifices see Josephus, *Ant.* 12.140; *m. Mid.* 5:3.

77. Mann, 384, offers a suggestive interpretation along these lines: 'There is a reference to the purging and purifying effects of the eschatological situation in which the disciples stood, and out of which they would emerge as "seasoned" protagonists.'

78. For a full account of the background, together with some imaginative exegesis, see N. Hillyer, *DNTT,* 3.443-49.

79. The belief that salt, lightly applied to the ground, acted as a fertiliser is attested in a few Latin authors (Hillyer mentions Cato, Virgil, and Pliny, but without references), and this has led some commentators (e.g., Gundry) to the view that ἡ γῆ in Mt. 5:13 is 'the soil'. Luke's suggestion that salt might be εὔθετον εἰς γῆν (14:35) may support this idea, but it does not occur elsewhere in biblical literature: salt renders ground barren rather than fertile (Dt. 29:23; Jdg. 9:45; Je. 17:6). Davies and Allison, *Matthew,* 1.472-73, list no fewer than eleven possible uses/significances of salt without mentioning its use as fertiliser. The fact that the restoration of the value of salt in Mk. 9:50 and Lk. 14:34 is denoted by ἀρτύω (a term used especially in a culinary context) indicates that they understood salt here as a seasoning (cf. Col. 4:6).

used in Palestine, derived either from the deposits around the Dead Sea or from salt pans in which its water was evaporated, was not pure sodium chloride, and the salt could leach out leaving other minerals like gypsum.[80] Once that has happened, it is ludicrous to think of trying to season (ἀρτύω) that which should itself have been seasoning. So disciples who have lost the 'salting' (v. 49) that makes them καλόν are no longer effective. The threat of being 'thrown out' which follows this saying in Matthew and Luke is absent in Mark, but the thought may nevertheless be inferred from the threat of γέεννα and unquenchable fire in vv. 43-48. Instead of the negative result, however, Mark prefers to follow up the image of unsalty salt with a more positive exhortation, in a second 'salt' saying which has no parallel in the other gospels.

Salt has so far pointed to the sacrificial character of discipleship (v. 49) and to a generally beneficent quality of life (v. 50a). Verse 50b offers a rather more specific application of the metaphor. The good salt which should characterise disciples consists in (καί used epexegetically) or results in (καί of consequence) peaceful relationships. While salt as a metaphor for peacefulness is in itself an unusual use, in the OT salt symbolises a covenant (Lv. 2:13; Nu. 18:19; 2 Ch. 13:5) while in some rabbinic writings salt stands for wisdom or pleasing speech (cf. Col. 4:6), which is a sound basis for good relationships.[81]

There is no single, fixed metaphorical meaning of salt, and it is probably unwise to be too specific in decoding its significance in this little sequence of sayings. Broadly they convey the message that discipleship is a serious matter, that it carries the potential for 'coming unstuck', and that it is important to work at it in such a way that the disciple group retains its integrity and distinctiveness as a community of peace.

THE REVOLUTIONARY VALUES
OF THE KINGDOM OF GOD (10:1-31)

In one sense there is no break at the end of chapter 9: the teaching of Jesus' disciples on the way to Jerusalem and in the shadow of the cross continues. But Mark's puzzling geographical notice in 10:1 indicates at least a change of scene, together with a resumption of public teaching, and the introduction in 10:2-9 of a discussion with outsiders rather than private dialogue with disciples also shifts the scene for a time, even though from 10:10 onwards the disciples become again the focus of attention.

---

80. N. Hillyer, *DNTT*, 3.446, gives interesting examples of how salt could deteriorate in Palestine.

81. Cf. the use of μωραίνω in Mt. 5:13 and Lk. 14:34, where Mark has ἄναλον γίνομαι. This idiom, usually explained on the basis of the ambiguity of Aramaic *tāpēl* (to be foolish or to be insipid), suggests that the connection of salt with wisdom was well understood.

The dominant emphasis of this next phase of teaching, leading up to the third passion prediction in 10:33-34, is the radical difference between the conventional values hitherto espoused by the disciples (and by the society to which they belong) and the new perspective of the kingdom of God. The phrase ἡ βασιλεία τοῦ θεοῦ occurs prominently in vv. 14, 15, 23, 24, and 25, a greater concentration than in any other part of the gospel, and the idea is never far away as human values and attitudes are challenged and indeed turned upside down from the standpoint of a kingdom in which the first are last and the last first (10:31).

This revolutionary perspective has already been emerging since 8:31 as Jesus has called his disciples to accept the paradoxical concept of a messianic mission accomplished through rejection and suffering, to lose their life in order to find it, to choose between the approval of other people and the claims of the Son of Man, to become the least and the servant in order to be the first, to welcome those whom they would naturally reject, and to envisage the possibility of drastic renunciation in this world in order to gain 'life'. In the following pericopes these already bewildering demands are reinforced in ways which leave the disciples increasingly uncomfortable and reveal how far their re-education has still to go in order for God's kingship to be established among them. And the demands are pressed home in relation to some of the most basic ingredients of life, marriage and divorce, children, possessions, and affluence. The whole complex of teaching will then come to its climax in the third passion prediction and in the most searching 'bouleversement'[1] of all as a result of the crass attempt of James and John to reassert a more conventional view of status and authority in vv. 35-45.

Marriage and Divorce (10:1-12)

TEXTUAL NOTES

1. The variants are due to the puzzling geography of v. 1 (see commentary). The simple πέραν read by a wide variety of mainly Western and Caesarean MSS and versions has a claim to originality as the most difficult reading (since no part of Judaea was πέραν τοῦ Ἰορδάνου from the perspective of Palestine), but might equally be the result of assimilation to Mt. 19:1. διὰ τοῦ πέραν gives the most easily intelligible route, and is therefore suspect as a deliberate correction. καὶ πέραν apparently implies a surprising route via Judaea to Peraea, and might therefore have been a candidate for correction by a scribe aware of the geographical setting, though since the omission of καὶ only seems to make matters worse this would not be a natural correction to make. In choosing, therefore, between two improbable readings (πέραν or καὶ πέραν) it is perhaps marginally better to opt for the latter since it differs from Matthew.

---

1. A suggestive term used in this connection by Helmut Gollwitzer (or rather his translator) in an article 'Liberation in History', *Int* 28 (1974) 411: Jesus demanded 'a bouleversement of the value scale'.

2. Most of the variants make little difference to the sense, but the reading of D etc. omits Pharisees altogether. Since it would be very natural for a scribe to specify unidentified interlocutors as Pharisees, the 'expected' opponents of Jesus (especially in a matter of halakhah), the shorter reading seems more probable, and the more so since Pharisees would naturally be inserted to assimilate to Mt. 19:3.

6. The shorter reading might be attributed to assimilation to Mt. 19:4. But Mark, unlike Matthew, lacks an expressed subject for the sentence quoted from Gn. 1:27, and the last expressed subject is Moses, not God, so the addition of ὁ θεός is best explained as an obvious scribal clarification.

7. The clause καὶ προσκολληθήσεται πρὸς τὴν γυναῖκα αὐτοῦ omitted by א B etc. seems so central to the argument that it is hard to imagine the quotation from Gn. 2:24 being made without it. But by the same token it is hard to explain its deliberate omission if it were once in the text. It is therefore probably safer to assume that the clause dropped out accidentally (as the first of two lines both beginning with καί). Within the line, the construction πρὸς τὴν γυναῖκα, which corresponds to the better-supported text of the LXX, is more likely, since τῇ γυναικί is both stylistically more elegant and assimilates to Mt. 19:5.

This, the only teaching about divorce in Mark's gospel, is given a deliberately public setting (v. 1) and consists primarily of a halakhic debate comparable to that in 7:1-15, leading up to a blunt and undeveloped pronouncement by Jesus which undercuts current scribal orthodoxy. Then, as in chapter 7, the disciples demand an explanation, and receive it in private. The crowd and the scribal interlocutors are left merely with the radical pronouncement, according to the pattern established in 4:34: for the outsiders merely παραβολαί, but explanation for the disciples.

The comparison with chapter 7 goes further. In each case the debate stems from a challenge to Jesus by questioners, and in each case Jesus replies by widening the discussion to include scriptural material which they would not have thought directly relevant. The result of this comparative study of Scripture is that Jesus can denounce the scribal approach as superficial and call for a more radical obedience to the essential purpose of God than their regulations envisaged. On that basis he contradicts their 'orthodox' view. The direction of the challenge differs: in chapter 7 the call for inward rather than outward purity seems to justify a less rigorous approach to the halakhic issue raised, whereas here the effect is to rule out their more 'liberal' stance. But in both controversies, Jesus' aim is to uncover what is fundamental to living as God requires, to move from mere regulations to ethical principles.

While the permitted grounds of divorce were debated in the rabbinic world, the admissibility of divorce (of a wife by her husband, not vice versa: Josephus, *Ant.* 15.259) as such was not questioned: Dt. 24:1-4 (the only legislation relating specifically to divorce in the Torah) was understood to have settled the issue. The more restrictive interpretation of the school of Shammai (only on the basis of 'unchastity', *m. Giṭ.* 9:10) was almost certainly a minority view. More typical, probably, is Ben Sira 25:26: 'If she does not accept your control, divorce her and send her away', or Josephus's laconic comment (*Life* 426): 'At this time I divorced my wife, not liking her behaviour.' Josephus paraphrases Dt. 24:1, 'He who wants to be divorced from the wife who shares his home for whatever cause — and among people many such may arise — . . .' (*Ant.* 4.253), and the school of Hillel allowed this to cover a spoiled meal, or even, so R. Akiba, 'if he found another fairer than she' (*m. Giṭ.* 9:10).

In such a culture Jesus' absolute prohibition of divorce must have been stunning, for his disciples as much as for his interlocutors. Hence their request for an explanation, but the explanation which follows does not at all weaken the simple force of his pronouncement but rather spells out its implications even more uncompromisingly. Such explanation as they were offered had already been given in the dialogue preceding the pronouncement, in which Jesus both questioned the appropriateness of the use of Dt. 24:1-4 as an ethical basis, and offered an alternative and more fundamental consideration drawn not from the Sinai law code but from the original order of creation before the Fall. If marriage was instituted as a permanent 'one-flesh' union of man and woman, then it must always be against the will of God for it to be broken. The legal provision of Moses in Dt. 24 was not intended as a statement of God's purpose for marriage, but as a regrettable but necessary means of limiting the damage when that purpose has already been abandoned. It is a provision to deal with human σκληροκαρδία, not a pointer to the way things ought to be. The marriage ethics of the kingdom of God must be based not on a concession to human failure, but on the pattern set out in God's original creation of man and woman. What *God* has joined together must not be separated by *human* initiative.

The argument depends on pitting one strand of Torah against another, and declaring the understanding of marriage set forth in the creation story to be a firmer basis for discovering the will of God than a later 'trouble-shooting' legal provision. But could such a simple ethic work out in the complexities of the real world and of human weakness? Hence the long history of modifications, beginning with the minimal extenuation implied in Matthew's repeated 'exceptive clause' (Mt. 5:32; 19:9) and continuing in the attempts of commentators through the ages to make Jesus mean something less inconvenient than his words mean at face value. It is of course a fact that in the real world marriages do break down and divorces happen and that even the most idealistic upholder of the permanence of marriage must find ways to deal with the tragic products of a society gone wrong, as Moses had to. But if we are to do justice to Mark's understanding of Jesus, we will do so not by attempting to weaken his bold statement of God's purpose for marriage but by recognising any broken marriage for what it is, a breach of God's standard, and by regarding any resultant provision for divorce not as good, but as, like the Mosaic legislation in Dt. 24:1-4, a regrettable concession to σκληροκαρδία. Modern society shows us what can happen when a provision for damage limitation comes to be regarded as a right or even a norm. In such a context Jesus' clear-sighted return to 'the way it was meant to be' has a refreshing and compelling simplicity, and must not be relegated to the category of an 'ideal' which we all admire but do not seriously expect to be implemented. God's design for unbroken, lifelong marriage is not an 'ideal' in that sense, but the realistic standard to which we are expected to conform and on which the health of human society depends. Mark's Jesus allows us no lower aim.

If we find this an uncompromising demand, so did Jesus' disciples then, in the light of their society's expectations. The enquiry of v. 10 was no doubt one of shocked incredulity (cf. Mt. 19:10, 'In that case it's better not to marry at all!'). What society takes for granted, Jesus challenges. Thus this pericope, which as a piece of halakhic discussion may seem rather out of place in the middle of a sequence of private teaching on discipleship, serves no less than those which follow to highlight the radical and subversive demands of the kingdom of God, and thus contributes to the discomfort and reorientation of the disciples.

1 ἐκεῖθεν presumably refers back to the last specific location mentioned, Capernaum in 9:33; the next will be Jericho in 10:46. The route followed between those points is a matter of conjecture, and is not an obvious concern of Mark. A Galilean pilgrim to Jerusalem would commonly go down the east side of the Jordan, avoiding Samaria, and then cross to Jericho for the ascent to Jerusalem. But this verse, on either of the two likely readings (see Textual Note), does not easily fit that pattern. If καί is not read it speaks of 'the regions of Judaea beyond the Jordan', a puzzling phrase since Judaea was on the west side of Jordan, the same side from which Jesus has come in Galilee. πέραν τοῦ Ἰορδάνου frequently in biblical literature (and once in Josephus, who normally uses the more technical Περαία) refers to the east bank,[2] and in the gospels generally seems to mean Peraea, the territory governed at this time by Antipas on the east side of the Jordan and the Dead Sea and south of the Decapolis. Politically this was not Judaea, but it is possible that from the Galilean perspective these two parts of 'the south' were lumped together under the term Judaea despite their different government.[3] If, on the other hand, καί is read, Judaea and Peraea are properly kept apart, but the order would then suggest going via Judaea to Peraea, the opposite of Jesus' likely route (though compare the order in 11:1, where the destination, Jerusalem, is mentioned before the places en route). As in 7:31, Mark's description of the itinerary is not clear, but in his narrative context the two terms Ἰουδαία and πέραν τοῦ Ἰορδάνου serve to indicate progress towards Jerusalem, and bring Jesus into what is unfamiliar and potentially hostile territory (remembering the ominous

2. Mt. 19:1, which poses the same problem as this verse, has been taken by H. D. Slingerland, *JSNT* 3 (1979) 18-28, as the basis for an argument that Matthew was written in Transjordan, and therefore saw Judaea as πέραν τοῦ Ἰορδάνου. The same can hardly be argued for Mark, since in 3:8 the same phrase is used for an area additional to Galilee and Judaea (see on 3:8).

3. D. W. Chapman, *Orphan*, 167-68, issues an important warning against assuming that Mark and his readers belonged to a 'map culture', and suggests with regard to this verse (171) that people in those days probably had little awareness of when they crossed 'boundary lines'.

implications of the two mentions of Jerusalem in 3:22 and 7:1, and the goal of Jesus' journey).

As in 8:34, a crowd (or rather 'crowds'; this is the only time Mark uses the plural ὄχλοι) appears unexpectedly, though 3:7-8 has informed us of the spread of news about Jesus beyond Galilee: the arrival of the prophet whose reputation they have heard before would naturally draw a crowd. While both the crowd and Jesus' 'habitual' teaching to them represent a change of focus within Act Two with its concentration on private teaching of the disciples, they are typical of Mark's editorial introductions or summaries in Act One. From his narrative point of view the crowd serves here to ensure a suitably wide audience for the halakhic debate and for the key pronouncement to be made in v. 9, as well as a source from which the questioners of v. 2 may be drawn.

2 If Φαρισαῖοι is not part of the original text (see Textual Note), this is one of several occasions when Mark introduces actors or speakers without identifying them; cf. 2:3, 18; 3:2; 5:35; 10:13. But even so the nature of the question and the discussion that follows make it likely that we should understand these unspecified 'people' as scribes or Pharisees (as Matthew explicitly makes them), particularly since Mark portrays the question as a test (πειράζοντες αὐτόν), a role in which we have become accustomed to seeing scribes and Pharisees. The intention of the question itself is not necessarily hostile since it would be appropriate to seek the views of a visiting 'rabbi' on matters of current debate, but Mark's use of πειράζω in similar contexts in 8:11 and 12:15 suggests that it was not so innocent (see on 8:11). Moreover, the phrasing of the question in Mark (contrast Matthew) focuses not on the allowable grounds of divorce, which was a legitimate matter of current debate, but on whether divorce itself is permissible, on which as far as we know mainstream Jewish teachers of the time were agreed.[4] Probably, then, they already had some indication that Jesus' views on the subject were extreme, not likely to endear him to people (or at least men) in general, and leaving him open to the charge of contradicting the Mosaic law. In view of the fate of John the Baptist (6:17-29) an injudicious reply concerning divorce might well also land Jesus (the 'second Baptist') in trouble with Antipas and his wife, especially as Jesus has now moved into the area both of John's activity and of his death at Machaerus in Peraea. The question of course envisages only a man's right to divorce his wife; Jewish law and practice had no concept of a woman divorcing her husband, though Jesus will raise (and dismiss) that possibility also in v. 12.

3-4 The verbs in this opening exchange are interesting. Jesus asks about commands (ἐντέλλομαι), but they reply in terms of permission (ἐπιτρέπω). This reflects the equivocal nature of the legal basis of divorce in Dt. 24:1-4. That passage does not specifically 'command', or even 'permit', divorce but rather

---

4. It is, however, likely from the evidence of CD 4:21; 11Q19 *(Temple)* 57:17-19 that the Qumran sect disallowed divorce.

regulates (in v. 4) the situation which results after a divorce has taken place and been duly certified: vv. 1-3 consist only of conditional clauses setting up the scenario for which v. 4 provides a legal ruling (that the husband who divorced his wife may not remarry her). The divorce which created that situation is presupposed but is not itself the subject of the legislation. βιβλίον ἀποστασίου γράψαι καὶ ἀπολῦσαι is thus not a quotation from Dt. 24, but a summary of what is assumed to be its 'permission'. To interpret this even as permission for divorce is a matter of inference from the fact that divorce is envisaged without expressed disapproval. It certainly falls far short of a 'command' (as Matthew's Pharisees boldly make it, Mt. 19:7). Jesus' interlocutors here, therefore, show some sensitivity towards the rather ambivalent sanction which Dt. 24:1-4 provides for divorce. But since there is no other relevant legislation in the Pentateuch, it had to serve.

Jesus' question was about what 'Moses' commanded, and they have tried to answer him, naturally enough, from the legal material of the books of Moses. But the Pentateuch contains more than the law codes themselves, and Jesus will now go on to show how 'Moses' (in that wider sense) offers a very different perspective, which fits the category of 'command' better than the traditional legal text they have quoted.

5 Moses' ἐντολή must refer to the whole long sentence Dt. 24:1-4, which does indeed conclude with an injunction (that the divorced and remarried wife may not subsequently return to her original husband), rather than to the words βιβλίον ἀποστασίου γράψαι καὶ ἀπολῦσαι, which are not in fact what Moses 'wrote', nor do they represent what that law actually 'commands'. It is the whole complex sentence, with its recognition of the reality of divorce and remarriage, which Jesus now declares to be directed towards[5] τὴν σκληροκαρδίαν ὑμῶν, where the ὑμεῖς represent presumably the people of Israel in general rather than the specific group whom he is addressing.

σκληροκαρδία, though not in itself frequent in the LXX (Dt. 10:16; Je. 4:4; Ben Sira 16:10; cf. Pr. 17:20; Ezk. 3:7), picks up a frequent OT accusation, often mentioning a 'stiff neck', that the people of God are hardened against him and impervious to his demands. (A similar accusation is expressed in different words in 4:12, drawing on Is. 6:9-10; cf. the καρδία πεπωρωμένη of 8:17.) Such language (and σκληροκαρδία in particular) is used primarily of people's attitude towards God rather than of the way they treat each other. It thus refers here not to men's cruelty towards their wives, but to their rebellion against God's will for them. It is such σκληροκαρδία which has led them into divorce in the first place, and made it necessary for Moses to legislate for a situation which was never envisaged in the divine purpose.

---

5. Gundry, 538, strangely reads πρός here in a telic sense: Moses wrote this 'to *incite* hardheartedness'. He offers no clear explanation of how and why Dt. 24:1-4 should have been so intended. Given the wide range of usage of πρός, this paradoxical reading is both unnecessary and inappropriate to the context.

6-8 Over against this later legal provision, Jesus sets God's original intention as it appears in a pair of quotations from Gn. 1:27 and 2:24. These come from the ἀρχὴ κτίσεως, the period before the Fall. Jesus' argument is expressed in terms of the temporal primacy of this provision for marriage rather than specifically in terms of the subsequent effect of sin, though it may be that ἡ σκληροκαρδία ὑμῶν is intended to remind us of what has gone wrong since God first designed human sexuality. But the main point is that this is how it was meant to be from the beginning, and first principles must take primacy over subsequent remedial provisions.

Gn. 1:27 does not in itself directly relate to the issue of marriage and divorce (though it is interesting that it is quoted in this connection also in CD 4:21, where, as here, it is apparently scribal acceptance of divorce which is under attack), but is included as the necessary basis for the second quotation. When God designed humanity as ἄρσεν καὶ θῆλυ it was with a view to the sexual union which Gn. 2:24 spells out. The threefold pattern of Gn. 2:24 (see Textual Note), leaving parents, union with wife, and man and woman becoming μία σάρξ, provides the essential basis for marriage, and its relevance to divorce is that the imagery of a single 'flesh' could hardly be more clearly designed to express that which is permanent and indivisible. It lifts marriage from being a mere contract of mutual convenience to an 'ontological' status. It is not merely that 'one flesh' *should* not be separated; it *cannot*. Jesus' comment that οὐκέτι εἰσὶν δύο underlines this concept: they are no longer two independent beings who may choose to go their own way, but a single indivisible unit.

There is room for debate over just when and how this union takes place, whether it is primarily a matter of sexual intercourse (as in 1 Cor. 6:16, again quoting Gn. 2:24), or of a ceremony performed in private or in public. Such considerations do not, however, affect the simple logic of Jesus' quotation, or in any way modify the principle of lifelong union between man and woman as the way God intended it to be.

9 The antithesis between ὁ θεός and ἄνθρωπος highlights the basis of Jesus' rejection of divorce: it is a human decision (that of the husband, who had the right to make such a decision on his own, rather than that of a legal officer) attempting to undo the union which God has created. God's act is expressed as a fait accompli by means of the simple aorist συνέζευξεν:[6] once the sequence set forth in Gn. 2:24 has been undertaken, the 'one flesh' is a fact, not a matter of provisionality or choice. Given the recognition of Gn. 2:24 as the authoritative basis for marriage, the argument is simple and complete, and Jesus sees no need to qualify the uncompromising conclusion: marriage is for life.

10 For the οἰκία as the place of private questioning and instruction see on 7:17 and cf. 9:28, 33. The position of πάλιν links it more naturally to the return to the house (assuming a verb of entry εἰς τὴν οἰκίαν) rather than to the expressed verb of the sentence, ἐπηρώτων, from which it is separated not only by

---

6. For συζεύγνυμι as a metaphor for marriage cf. Josephus, *Ant.* 6.309.

the subject but also by περὶ τούτου; the disciples have not previously asked him περὶ τούτου, for the very obvious reason that they have just heard Jesus' verdict on divorce for the first time.[7] Like his pronouncement in 7:15, it is sufficiently unexpected and far-reaching to demand further explanation.

11-12   Jesus' reply consists of two balancing statements. The first, concerning a man who divorces his wife, is shared, with variations, with Matthew (5:32a; 19:9) and Luke (16:18a). The second, concerning a woman who divorces her husband, is peculiar to Mark, whereas Matthew (5:32b) and Luke (16:18b) have a different balancing clause concerning a man who marries a divorced woman. All these statements share the same basic understanding, that divorce followed by remarriage results in adultery; the different versions especially of the second statement presumably reflect the need to apply this principle to different circumstances faced in the churches in which the gospels were compiled. Mark's second statement is perhaps the most surprising, as it presupposes the possibility of the wife initiating a divorce, which was not envisaged in Jewish law, though it was in Roman.

The pericope so far has concentrated on divorce, without mention of remarriage, even though it was remarriage which was the point at issue in Dt. 24:1-4 from which the discussion began. Jewish divorce was specifically with a view to remarriage: the certificate given to the divorced wife read, 'You are free to marry any man' (*m. Giṭ.* 9:3). Jesus' pronouncements here therefore assume that remarriage will follow divorce, and it is the combined divorce-and-remarriage which he brands as adultery. The question sometimes raised today whether Jesus would have approved divorce without remarriage, or whether he at least regarded the divorce as less serious a sin than the remarriage, is one which would not have arisen in the Jewish world; a separation without at least the right to remarry would not be 'divorce'. In any case, the prohibition of divorce in v. 9 was expressed without any mention of subsequent remarriage. What is happening in these verses is a further spelling out of the implications of that pronouncement, not a change of subject.[8]

The basis for declaring divorce-and-remarriage to be adultery is that the original one-flesh union was inseparable, and that the purported divorce has not changed that. It is as much adultery as if the husband had had intercourse with another woman during the marriage. The words ἐπ' αὐτήν might conceivably be understood with reference to the new wife ('with her', literally

---

7. P. Ellingworth, *JSNT* 5 (1979) 63-66, explains πάλιν . . . ἐπηρώτων by assuming that the unnamed questioners of v. 2 (assuming the shorter reading) were the disciples. The context is against that, as the disciples are not mentioned in v. 1, but rather a crowd whom Jesus was teaching, and out of whom we may assume the question came.

8. It is hard to see how H. C. Kee, *Community,* 155, arrives at his unsupported assertion that vv. 11-12 'allows for divorce, but not for remarriage'. Nor is it clear how Hooker discovers 'a basic contradiction between v. 9, where divorce itself is inconceivable, and vv. 10-12, where it is remarriage *after* divorce which is forbidden'; if divorce is 'inconceivable', it is hardly surprising that when the inconceivable happens the resultant divorce-and-remarriage is condemned.

'upon her'),[9] but are more naturally taken of the original wife ('against her'; cf. the uses of ἐπί with the accusative in 3:24-26; 13:8, 12). In that case Jesus here recognises that the wife has rights over her husband's behaviour as well as vice versa. The divorce and remarriage is an offence not only against God's purpose for marriage but against the wife who is thereby wronged. In the Jewish world a man could be said to commit adultery against the husband of the woman concerned, or a woman against her own husband, but the idea of adultery *against the wife* is a remarkable development towards equality of the sexes.

The balancing statement about the wife who divorces her husband may reflect an origin for Mark's gospel, or at least for this tradition, in Rome, where the law recognised a wife's right to divorce.[10] In the Jewish world this was not permitted,[11] and the famous case of Herodias (see on 6:17) is the exception which proves the rule;[12] it was not only the fact of her close relationship to Antipas but also her 'divorce' from her first husband (perhaps informal, but more likely invoking Roman law) which provoked John the Baptist's condemnation of her second marriage. Josephus reflects the Jewish sense of scandal: τοῦ ἀνδρὸς διαστᾶσα ζῶντος (*Ant.* 18.136). It was because she was a woman that her 'divorce' was disapproved, but for Mark's Jesus there is no difference at this point between men and women: if either initiates a divorce and then remarries, the result is the same, adultery.

The practical application of this teaching in a society in which both adultery and divorce are common and legally permissible cannot be straightforward. But Mark's Jesus offers no direct guidance on the problem, simply a clear, unequivocal, and utterly uncompromising principle that marriage is permanent and divorce (together with the resultant remarriage) is wrong. Whatever the other considerations which pastoral concern may bring to bear, some of them no doubt based on values drawn from Jesus' teaching on other subjects, no approach can claim his support which does not take as its guiding principle the understanding of marriage set forth in vv. 9 and 11-12.

9. N. Turner, *BT* 7 (1956) 151-52, suggests on the basis of a not very exact parallel with Je. 5:9 that it means 'going after' her (the second wife). An attempt by B. Schaller, *ExpTim* 83 (1971/2) 107-8, to support the sense 'with her' on the basis of Aramaic and Syriac idiom also operates at some distance from Greek usage.

10. Note, however, the argument of D. R. Catchpole, *BJRL* 57 (1974/5) 111-12, for a *Sitz im Leben* in Palestine.

11. A Western variant in v. 12 has ἐξέλθη ἀπὸ τοῦ ἀνδρός καὶ ἄλλον γαμήσῃ, which would more accurately reflect the option open to a Jewish wife. This, rather than a formal divorce sanctioned by Roman law, may in fact be what Herodias did. But this reading reduces the impact of Jesus' final saying, since there is no novelty in describing a woman's leaving her husband for another man as adultery if there was no question of divorce.

12. In the comparable case of Salome, who sent her husband Costobarus a document dissolving their marriage, Josephus comments simply that this was οὐ κατὰ τοὺς Ἰουδαίων νόμους (*Ant.* 15.259). For evidence of other such exceptional cases, on the fringes of Judaism, cf. E. Bammel, *ZNW* 61 (1970) 95-101.

Children (10:13-16)

TEXTUAL NOTE

13. A large number of MSS and versions read τοῖς (προσ)φέρουσιν instead of αὐτοῖς, and most of the same witnesses have the imperfect ἐπετίμων rather than aorist ἐπετίμησαν. These readings differ from Matthew and the former also from Luke, and on this basis they would normally be preferred, but the former (and perhaps the latter?) is very likely to be explained as a scribal clarification to avoid the impression that it was the children themselves who were the object of the rebuke — though it is remarkable that a similar correction does not appear in the textual traditions of Matthew and Luke.

While this little pericope does speak of Jesus' attitude to children, especially in its concluding verse, its role in this context is primarily to illustrate again the failure of the disciples to see things as Jesus sees them. The story is told from the point of view of their attitude and Jesus' rebuke of it, and the key saying in v. 15 uses children as an illustration of discipleship rather than focusing on them in themselves. The twofold mention of the βασιλεία τοῦ θεοῦ makes the perspective clear.

In 9:36-37 the child was introduced by Jesus to illustrate the issue of status in the kingdom of God, and the specific issue raised was that of 'receiving' such a child in Jesus' name. Here it is other people (the parents?) who take the initiative rather than Jesus. The disciples thus have the opportunity to 'receive' little children and reject it, but Jesus lives up to his previous exhortation by receiving and blessing them. But this time the lesson drawn from the disciples' discomfiture is summed up not in terms of receiving children as such but in the enigmatic language of receiving the kingdom of God ὡς παιδίον.

Underlying the disciples' attitude and the resultant teaching is the same concept of the child as the least important member of society which we noted at 9:36-37. Jesus repudiates this valuation both by word and by example. The pericope thus has an important role to play in guiding the church's attitude to children and the priority given to their spiritual welfare, τῶν γὰρ τοιούτων ἐστὶν ἡ βασιλεία τοῦ θεοῦ, even if to use it as a prooftext specifically for infant baptism is to go beyond its original focus.[13]

13 The unspecified subject of προσέφερον may reasonably be assumed to be the parents of the children. Their very anonymity helps to make the point about status: they, and their children, are not anybody special. The imperfect tense suggests that they were trying unsuccessfully, because of the disciples' obstruction. The use of παιδίον (as in 9:36-37) probably suggests quite young children, though since Mark never uses παῖς, the force of the diminutive should not be pressed. παιδίον is used of a twelve-year-old in 5:39-42, and in 9:24 of a boy whose condition has persisted ἐκ παιδιόθεν. A better indication of the age

---

13. For arguments against a baptismal meaning in this pericope see E. Best, *Disciples*, 80-97, especially 83-86, 92-94.

of these children may be found in the fact that Jesus could take them in his arms (v. 16).[14]

There is no need to suppose any formal ceremony in the requested touch, and in the blessing by laying his hands on them in v. 16. To request such blessing from a distinguished visitor and 'holy man', especially one who already enjoyed a reputation as a healer in the area (3:7-8), need be no more than natural 'folk religion'; indeed, it need not necessarily be particularly religious. The later evidence for a custom of bringing children to rabbis for blessing and prayer on the Day of Atonement (*Sop.* 18:5) is an example of this natural tendency, but there is no reason to suppose, with J. Jeremias,[15] that it could happen on no other occasion and that therefore this incident must have taken place on the Day of Atonement. For the importance of touch in Jesus' healing ministry see 1:41; 8:22, and for people touching Jesus see 3:10; 5:27-31; 6:56.

We cannot know whether any particular circumstances prompted the disciples' unwelcoming attitude, or whether they felt that in principle children should not be allowed to bother the teacher. They have already forgotten the lesson of 9:37. It makes little difference whether αὐτοῖς (see Textual Note) refers to the children themselves (the nearest antecedent) or (more probably) to the subject of the preceding clause, the parents (in that case the masculine means it was not only the mothers); the effect is the same.

14 Among Mark's variety of terms for Jesus' emotions this is the only use of ἀγανακτέω, though ὀργή has been mentioned in 3:5 and (probably) 1:41, and there is little difference in meaning. It covers both irritation at their failure to learn and repugnance at their attitude in itself. Only a few verses earlier they have been found hindering someone whom Jesus approved (9:38-39), and the repetition of κωλύω here brands them as obstructionists who stand in the way of the generous intentions of Jesus.

The possessive[16] genitive τῶν τοιούτων may be compared with Mt. 5:3, 10, αὐτῶν ἐστιν ἡ βασιλεία τῶν οὐρανῶν. It indicates not so much exclusive ownership, but having a rightful share in. These are the people in whose lives God's rule is established, and who consequently share in its blessings. But who are they? Does this refer to children as such, and thus imply the automatic participation of all children in God's kingdom (a participation which may then be forfeited in later life)? In terms of church doctrine, does this pronouncement then justify the contention that all children must be presumed saved until they come to years of discretion and can decide for themselves? And is it therefore a sound basis for baptising infants? Even to ask such questions is to indicate an agenda which is not, on the surface at least, that of this pericope, and inferences drawn from it for such an agenda must be treated with caution. It is important,

14. Luke 18:15 makes them βρέφη (infants), and *Gos. Thom.* 22 in an apparent parallel has babies being suckled.

15. J. Jeremias, *Baptism,* 49.

16. F. A. Schilling, *ExpTim* 77 (1965/6) 56-58, takes it as 'qualitative genitive', and interprets 'the Kingdom of God is of the nature of a child'. See below, p. 397 n. 18.

too, to notice that the genitive is not τούτων but, as in 9:37, τῶν τοιούτων. If in 9:37 the focus was, as we have argued, not on children as such but on those whom the child in that pericope represents, the 'little ones' of the kingdom of God, the meaning here is likely to be the same. In that case the pronouncement τῶν τοιούτων ἐστιν ἡ βασιλεία τοῦ θεοῦ is not only or even mainly about children, but about those who share the child's status. It is to such people, the insignificant ones who are important to Jesus (who will of course include, but not be confined to, children) that God's kingdom belongs. It is the literal children whom Jesus tells the disciples to allow to come to him, but the reason is that they belong to and represent a wider category of οἱ τοιοῦτοι, who are the ones who matter to God.

15 The fourteen ἀμήν sayings in Mark are generally understood to mark out particularly important pronouncements, and several of them convey promises or warnings about spiritual rewards and penalties (see 3:28; 9:1; 9:41; 10:29). Here, too, there is a warning against failing to enter the kingdom of God; cf. 9:43, 45, 47 concerning entry into either ζωή or ἡ βασιλεία τοῦ θεοῦ, and see there for this usage of ἡ βασιλεία τοῦ θεοῦ as a virtual equivalent to ζωὴ αἰώνιος. Here that βασιλεία is spoken of as both 'received' and 'entered', which well illustrates the impossibility of tying it down to a single univocal concept. While 'entering' it apparently refers to eternal destiny, 'receiving' it relates more to a person's attitude and response towards God's demands in this life. To 'receive the kingdom of God' means to be God's willing subject, gladly embracing the radical values which Jesus has come to inculcate.[17] It is such 'reception' now which is the key to 'entry' hereafter.

The nature of that reception depends on how we translate ὡς παιδίον. If παιδίον is taken as nominative, it means 'as a child receives it'; if accusative, it means 'as one receives a child'. There seems no basis for preferring either on syntactical or stylistic grounds. The fact that 9:37 has spoken specifically about 'receiving a child' perhaps favours the accusative interpretation, but it is not easy to see how 'receiving' a concrete person relates to 'receiving' an abstract idea such as the kingdom of God.[18] The nominative interpretation, on the other hand, would offer a Marcan equivalent to Matthew's language about 'becoming like children' (Mt. 18:3), a note which is otherwise surprisingly not explicit in either Mk. 9:36-37 or the present pericope, though it is probably implied by the fact that Jesus' choice of the child as a model in 9:36 is in the context of a dispute about greatness. The context must decide between the two options, and the

---

17. See A. M. Ambrozic, *Kingdom,* 143-48, for the use of δέχομαι in wisdom literature as 'a technical term which describes a willing and understanding acceptance of wisdom in its various manifestations'.

18. The accusative interpretation is argued by F. A. Schilling, *ExpTim* 77 (1965/6) 56-58. He believes that the kingdom of God is here compared to a child (as it is elsewhere to a sower, seed, net, etc.), 'a being fresh, at the beginning of life, in need of affection', and 'must be accepted as a child is taken into loving embrace'. Against the accusative interpretation see J. I. H. McDonald, *SE* 6 (1973) 329.

sequence from v. 14b supports the nominative: there is a parallel between God's kingdom belonging to people like children, and entry to it being reserved for those who receive it as children do.[19] Taking the pericope as a whole, the reason the disciples were unable to appreciate the significance of children in relation to the kingdom of God is that they themselves have not yet learned to 'receive' it like children. Their 'grown-up' sense of values prevents them from being in tune with God's value scale.

16 For ἐναγκαλισάμενος see on 9:36. κατευλογέω (used only here in the NT) does not seem to differ in meaning from εὐλογέω. It would be overexegesis to see in the compound verb a foil to the disciples' churlishness: Jesus by contrast gave the children a *thorough* blessing! The participle τιθείς spells out how the blessing was given, and the laying on of hands fulfils the original request for a touch in v. 13. There is no special 'liturgical' significance in the laying on of hands: it is a natural sign of association, used often in healing (1:41; 5:23; 6:5; 7:32; 8:23, 25), but also as a traditional symbol of blessing (Gn. 48:14-18).

Affluence (10:17-27)

TEXTUAL NOTES

19. Since μὴ ἀποστερήσῃς is an unexpected intrusion into the well-known clauses of the decalogue, its omission in some significant witnesses is best explained as deliberate, either because it was not recognised as one of the commandments (and could be seen as merely repeating the theme of μὴ κλέψῃς), or by assimilation to Matthew and Luke, who also omit it.

21. The addition of ἄρας τὸν σταυρόν (σου) in A W and many later MSS, even though not in conformity to Matthew and Luke, looks very much like a 'moralising' expansion.

24. The shorter reading has the effect of universalising the difficulty of entering the kingdom of God, though the specification of οἱ τὰ χρήματα ἔχοντες in v. 23 and πλούσιος in v. 25 restricts it contextually. It is possible that τοὺς πεποιθότας ἐπὶ χρήμασιν was a later addition from the context to avoid this universal sense, but the fact that the wording is different from that in vv. 23 and 25 is in its favour, and the shorter reading might then be attributed to a scribal desire to avoid redundancy. But the substitution of *trust* in wealth for wealth itself looks suspiciously like a convenient softening of Jesus' harsh verdict on the affluent, hence the preference for the shorter reading.

25. The substitution of κάμιλον for κάμηλον in a few minuscules is an obvious attempt to 'improve' Jesus' bizarre comparison; see the commentary below.

26. πρὸς ἑαυτούς is very widely supported, and represents a natural sense, yet one

---

19. See further E. Best, *Disciples,* 94-96. Best comments: 'A child trusts adults; he has confidence in them; he receives from them what they offer. So the disciple is to trust God and receive the Kingdom.' Schweizer, 207, speaks of 'the empty hand of a beggar'. J. I. H. McDonald, *SE* 6 (1973) 330-32, compares rabbinic language about 'taking the kingdom upon' oneself when reciting the $\check{S}^e$*ma*, and tentatively links this saying with the child's experience of Bar Mitzvah.

which might easily be 'corrected' to πρὸς αὐτόν in order to preserve the interchange between the disciples and Jesus.

The issue of status is carried further in this next pericope, which concerns a man who because of his wealth could expect to be in the front rank, and would surely have been seen as a most desirable recruit to the kingdom of God. While vv. 17-22 focus on the man himself, in vv. 23-27 we share the disciples' amazement at the undiplomatic way in which Jesus has responded to his apparently sincere approach, and Jesus takes the opportunity to disorientate them still more by restricting further the criteria not merely for importance in the kingdom of God, but for belonging to it at all. The repeated depiction of the disciples' astonished incomprehension leads up to a key pronouncement on the difference of perspective between human beings and God (v. 27). The threefold repetition of the phrase εἰς τὴν βασιλείαν τοῦ θεοῦ εἰσελθεῖν, following hard on the words about sharing, receiving, and entering that same βασιλεία in vv. 14-15, provides an unmistakable guide to where Mark wishes his readers to find the relevance of the story of the rich man. It is, again, all about the 'upside down' values of God's kingdom. Verses 28-31, treated here as a separate pericope, nonetheless follow on closely and explore further the priorities involved in the commitment to discipleship, concluding with the formula which sums up all that this section of the gospel has been saying: in God's kingdom πρῶτοι become ἔσχατοι and ἔσχατοι πρῶτοι.

Seen in that wider perspective, the story of the rich man is more than simply an expression of Jesus' attitude to wealth; it is part of a broader critique of conventional human values. But that does not mean that it is not to be interpreted as a statement on affluence. Like each of the preceding pericopes, it both contributes to the overall re-education of the disciples and carries its own specific and uncomfortable message. In Jewish society it was generally taken for granted that wealth was to be welcomed as a mark of God's blessing; rabbis like Hillel and Akiba who rose from obscurity and poverty to wealth and influence are commended without embarrassment.[20] But this quite natural valuation is turned on its head by Jesus.[21]

This pericope is in fact the major contribution of Mark's gospel to the distinctive Christian teaching about possessions which is more fully developed in the other Synoptic Gospels, especially Luke. We read of a man whose way to 'life' was blocked by his unwillingness to surrender his possessions and follow Jesus, a classic example of the warning of 4:19: 'the cares of the world and the lure of wealth and the desire for other things come in and choke the word, and it yields nothing'. All readers of the gospel must face the uncomfortable question

20. M. Hengel, *Property*, 19-22.
21. There was also, however, a strand of hostility towards the rich in some Jewish thinking, exemplified by some of the prophets, and developed especially in *1 Enoch*. See A. M. Ambrozic, *Kingdom* 165-69, for examples of riches viewed as 'a typical instrument of alienation from God and oppression of the poor'.

whether the call to renunciation was for this man alone, or whether it can be universalised. A careful reading between the lines of the gospel narratives reveals that those who had 'left everything' to follow Jesus (v. 28; cf. 1:18, 20; 2:14) seem nonetheless to have retained the use of some possessions (Peter's house at Capernaum, 1:29 etc.; his fishing boat and tackle, Jn. 21:3; Levi's party, 2:15) and that the itinerant group of Jesus and his disciples depended on the hospitality and material provision of supporters such as Mary, Martha, and Lazarus at Bethany (Lk. 10:38-42; Jn. 11; 12:2) or the women of Lk. 8:2-3. On such grounds many have gratefully concluded either that Jesus did not really mean 'all', or that there were (and are?) two levels of discipleship, only the more rigorous of which (to which, as we shall see below, Jesus was calling this individual) demands full renunciation. Gundry's comment is perhaps apposite: 'That Jesus did not command all his followers to sell all their possessions gives comfort only to the kind of people to whom he *would* issue that command.'[22]

But the story does not end at v. 22. The following dialogue with the disciples leaves little room for concluding that this particular rich man was exceptional; Jesus' words are starkly universal, hence the disciples' dismay. Wealth as such, not just this man's wealth, is an insuperable barrier to the kingdom of God (and the vivid image of v. 25 is designed precisely to underline the *impossibility,* not just difficulty, of the salvation of the rich). The disciples' inference in v. 26 is quite correct, from a human perspective. It is only in v. 27 that a ray of light comes in to alleviate the bleakness of the picture, but it remains enigmatic, leaving the resolution of the problem to the inscrutability of the divine purpose rather than offering a humanly comprehensible solution. And vv. 28-31 do not make matters any easier, as they speak of compensation for those who *have* left everything, but say nothing to comfort those who have not.

Here, then, as in vv. 2-12, Mark leaves us with a totally uncompromising ethic which seems impossible to apply in the real world, where some degree of 'wealth' seems essential to survival and indeed to effective discipleship and the ability to do good. 'Wealth' is relative: even those who would consider themselves poor in modern Western society live at a level which would have been unimaginable to most of Jesus' hearers, and remains so to many in other parts of the world today. The carefree life of the total dependence on God exemplified by the birds and the flowers which is commended in Mt. 6:25-33 can be adopted, if at all, only by a radical opting out of modern society which is hard to square with the gospel call to be the salt of the earth and the light of the world. So does this mean that the present pericope is of no practical value to us, merely an interesting historical glimpse into an extreme asceticism which the Christian church quickly and necessarily left behind? As with the teaching on divorce, that is a dangerously comfortable conclusion. The nature and degree of renunciation of wealth which the gospel requires may be something which will be worked out differently in different times and circumstances, but if we lose

22. R. H. Gundry, *Matthew,* 388.

sight of the principle that affluence is a barrier to the kingdom of God we are parting company from Jesus at a point which seems to have been fundamental to his teaching as all three synoptic writers understood it.

17 After the return to the house in 10:10 and the unlocated incident with the children, we now find Jesus on the road again: the repetition of ὁδός does not allow us to forget what lies ahead, and puts the call to follow him (v. 21) in a sombre context. The key figure in this story is introduced simply as εἷς; all the information we need about him will be supplied by the story itself, but it will not be until the very end of the story that the vital point will be stated: ἦν ἔχων κτήματα πολλά. Mark mentions neither his youth (Mt. 19:22) nor his political status (Lk. 18:18). The combination of προσδραμών and γονυπετήσας (see on 1:40) suggests a degree of seriousness, even of urgency, which is well borne out by his opening words. His address to Jesus as διδάσκαλε is not surprising: it has been used already by well-disposed outsiders (5:35; 9:17) as well as disciples (4:38; 9:38). But the addition of ἀγαθέ is remarkable: Mark nowhere else uses ἀγαθός of a person, and its combination with διδάσκαλε (producing a form of address for which no contemporary Jewish parallel is known) suggests either flattery or an outsider with an unusually positive view of Jesus (one who in terms of 9:40 must surely be regarded as ὑπὲρ ἡμῶν). It is the unusual character of the address which gives the cue for Jesus' probing response in v. 18.

The question seems sincere and indicates a serious spiritual quest, the search for ζωὴ αἰώνιος. For ζωή see on 9:43, 45, and for αἰώνιος on 3:29. In the light of those usages we must suppose that the two terms together, here and in 10:30 (the only other occurrence in Mark), refer as they do commonly in the NT to ultimate salvation, seen as beyond this present life. The man therefore believes in life after death, but also that it cannot be taken for granted. He must do something in order to be entitled to it. κληρονομέω is used widely in the LXX for being entitled to and gaining possession of something (especially the promised land), without the specific concept of inheritance being central, and there is no need therefore to read into the choice of this word a 'Pauline' theology of inheritance.[23] The man simply wants to know how he can be entitled to ζωὴ αἰώνιος. It is sometimes suggested that τί ποιήσω; is meant to betray a 'Pelagian' concept of salvation by works, but the narrative does not support this, as Jesus' reply is also in terms of things to 'do' (v. 19), and the 'one thing lacking' in v. 21 is equally framed in terms of 'doing' (selling and following). Mark is untroubled by any controversy over faith and works.

18 This tantalising verse apparently raises an objection to the way the man has addressed Jesus, but the point is not followed up, and we are left to guess what the objection was. Perhaps Jesus suspects flattery in the fulsome ad-

---

23. The ideas of eternal life and inheritance are differently associated in *Pss. Sol.* 14:1-5, where eternal life is the destiny of God's faithful people, who are themselves the κληρονομία of God.

dress, and by stretching the meaning of ἀγαθός to the point of perfection que-
ries its appropriateness to any man. As a formal definition this would be pedantic, since in normal speech there was no objection to referring to people as
ἀγαθός, but *ad hominem* it might serve to probe the man's sincerity. If, on the
other hand, Jesus does accept his sincerity, the response asks him to re-examine
his idea of 'goodness' (and therefore perhaps of the sort of 'doing' that might
make him eligible for eternal life) in the light of God's absolute goodness, beside which that of any human being is merely relative.[24] That Jesus does so by
seizing on the man's address to him as ἀγαθέ, and thus implicates himself in the
relative goodness of humanity, is a problem only in the context of a formal dogmatic assertion of the sinlessness and divinity of Jesus. At the time of Jesus'
ministry this could hardly have been an issue, and the fact that Mark and Luke
record the exchange in this form suggests that they, too, did not see it as a problem. Matthew's rephrasing of both question and answer is apparently designed
to deflect the possible inference that Jesus is asserting that he is not (in the absolute sense) good and therefore is not God, but it may be questioned whether
any original reader of Mark would naturally have seen any such implication
here — still less that by drawing attention to the use of ἀγαθός for himself Jesus is in fact inviting the questioner to confess him as divine. That would be a
monumental non sequitur.

19 Jesus assumes that this total stranger is familiar with the decalogue
— a significant pointer to its place in Jewish society at that time. The ἐντολαί
quoted represent the second part of the decalogue, those injunctions which govern behaviour towards other people, and which therefore admit of relatively objective assessment. The only one that is missing is 'You shall not covet', which
is concerned with thought rather than behaviour, and so does not so easily form
part of a moral checklist. In its place is μὴ ἀποστερήσῃς (see Textual Note), otherwise unknown in this connection (and missing here from Matthew and Luke).
It is hard to see any practical difference between κλέπτω and ἀποστερέω. It has
been suggested on the basis of Pliny's report to Trajan (*Ep.* 10.96.7) about
Christian morals that it relates specifically to the withholding of goods left on
deposit (which was a common sense of ἀποστερέω in classical Greek), but the
word is not in itself so specific. It is better seen simply as an attempt to draw out
in more behavioural terms the implications of the tenth commandment: appro-
priating someone else's possessions is likely to be a practical result of coveting.
The commandments are given in the Hebrew order (which differs from that of
the LXX; the μή + subj. form also differs from LXX οὐ + indic.), except for the
postponement of the fifth, the only one positively formulated, until the end.

20 Mark's middle ἐφυλαξάμην (Matthew and Luke have active) should
strictly mean 'I have avoided, kept myself from'; unless this is sloppy grammar,

---

24. J. F. Williams, *Followers,* 143-45, finds the point of Jesus' retort in 'a challenge to the
man's concept of goodness, because . . . the man considers himself to be good on the basis of his
own adherence to the law. . . . However, although he is obedient, he is not good.'

it would indicate that ταῦτα πάντα here means not the commandments them-selves, but the acts which they prohibit (so Gundry). Either way, the meaning is clear: the man is claiming a clear conscience with regard to these command-ments. There is no indication that the claim was insincere. He was presumably unaware of the more far-reaching interpretation of some of these command-ments by Jesus (Mt. 5:21-28). Taken as rules of conduct, they could be kept to the letter (except perhaps the positive requirement of honouring parents, which is less easily quantified), and the man was, and knew himself to be, correct in his behaviour on all these points. He is proving to be altogether a most attrac-tive recruit for the kingdom of God.

21 The comment (by Mark only) that Jesus ἠγάπησεν αὐτόν eliminates any suggestion that the man's profession is insincere and that Jesus has been engaged in unmasking hypocrisy. ἐμβλέπω denotes a searching look (see 14:67): so far he has passed Jesus' careful scrutiny, and Jesus is duly impressed. The final demand is not meant to be a means of putting him off: Jesus wants him on board.

ὑστερέω takes the genitive of that which something falls short of, but the accusative to denote the one affected by the lack is unusual (hence the reading σοί in many MSS; see Legg), but see LXX Ps 22[23]:1, οὐδέν με ὑστερήσει (see BDF, 180[5]). 'Fails you', 'lets you down' is as close as English comes to the idiom. The 'one thing' is expressed in unequivocal terms: two aorist impera-tives (πώλησον, δός) prescribe a single, complete disinvestment and donation, while the following present imperative δεῦρο ἀκολούθει μοι (cf. 1:17, δεῦτε ὀπίσω μου; 2:14, ἀκολούθει μοι) sets a new course for the future. Jesus is asking not only for renunciation of possessions but also for a total change in his life-style: he is to join the itinerant group of Jesus' closest disciples, with their com-munal resources and dependence on the material support of others.[25]

In return, he will receive θησαυρὸν ἐν οὐρανῷ. Mark does not have the Q passage which contrasts the transient treasures of earth with incorruptible θησαυρὸς ἐν οὐρανῷ (Mt. 6:19-21), but this saying conveys the same message, which will be further reinforced in vv. 29-30. The renunciation is presented not as something simply good in itself, but as the means to a far better end. It is all a matter of perspective.

22 The rare verb στυγνάζω (στυγνός in LXX Dn. 2:12 denotes anger; στυγνάζω in Ezk. 27:35; 28:19; 32:10 denotes people 'appalled' at the fate of Tyre and Egypt) perhaps suggests physical appearance which betrays emo-tion; in Mt. 16:3 it refers to an 'overcast' sky (cf. LXX Wis. 17:5, the 'angry' darkness of Egypt). His face clouded. The *Gospel according to the Hebrews,* as quoted by Origen, adds the homely touch: 'He began to scratch his head and it displeased him'. His sorrowful decision illustrates the Q saying, οὐ

---

25. Contrast the rabbinic provision (*m. ʾArak.* 8:4; *b. Ket.* 50a) that only a part of one's goods (not more than one fifth) may be dedicated to God. See further M. Hengel, *Property,* 20-21, for re-strictions on charity, to prevent people impoverishing themselves.

δύνασθε θεῷ δουλεύειν καὶ μαμωνᾷ. Peter will be quick to point out the contrast with the decision he and his colleagues had made when they first met Jesus (v. 28).

23 We might have expected an immediate protest from the disciples over Jesus' intransigent and unrealistic attitude which has led to the loss of this very desirable recruit, but Jesus himself seizes the initiative and articulates their unspoken shock. Mark has used περιβλεψάμενος before to indicate that Jesus is responding to unspoken thoughts (3:5 and perhaps 3:34; cf. ἰδὼν τοὺς μαθητάς in 8:33). The problem relates not only to the practical issue of following Jesus in his itinerant ministry, but more basically to entry into the kingdom of God (see above on 10:15 and on 9:43, 45, 47); it is assumed that in rejecting the one the rich man has forfeited the other. This first comment still apparently allows the *possibility* of the affluent entering the kingdom of God; even that will be put in question in vv. 25-27. But their entry will be δυσκόλως, with difficulty or discomfort (a word which classically referred to someone hard to please, used only in this pericope in the NT). There seems no significant difference between the various terms used for affluence: ἔχων κτήματα πολλά (v. 22), τὰ χρήματα ἔχοντες (v. 23), πλούσιος (v. 25). Possessions, far from being the advantage which the world assumes, are in themselves an obstacle to entering God's kingdom.

24-25 The disciples, already dismayed by the experience of the rich man, are even more taken aback by Jesus' generalisation from it. His further comment only makes matters worse, first by repeating the same declaration, but then by adding to it an epigram which makes the entry of the rich into God's kingdom not only difficult but impossible. His address to the disciples as τέκνα is unique in Mark, but may be paralleled with the address to the cripple in 2:5 and by Abraham's address to the rich man in Lk. 16:25. It is unlikely to recall specifically the teaching about children in 9:36-37; 10:13-16, since παιδίον has been used consistently in those passages, and is best understood as a colloquial and affectionate epithet for his close companions, 'lads'. The omission of a specific mention of the rich in v. 24 (see Textual Note) gives the repetition of the saying a more universal sound (hence, no doubt, the textual variant), but the reader naturally carries over the full saying of v. 23 into its abbreviated repetition, and the use of πλούσιος in v. 25 leaves no room for misunderstanding in context.

For the form εὐκοπώτερόν ἐστιν . . . ἤ . . . in a proverbial-type saying cf. Lk. 16:17; also the question asked before the healing of the paralytic in 2:9 and parallels. Ben Sira 22:15 uses εὔκοπον . . . ἤ . . . in a similar way, but the comparative form is apparently a distinctive idiom of Jesus. When, as in this case, the 'easier' event is manifestly impossible, the harder is even more so. The grotesque idea of a camel going through the eye of a needle is a proverbial way of stating the impossible: a rabbinic saying (*b. Ber.* 55b; cf. also *b. B. Meṣ.* 38b; *b. 'Erub.* 53a) uses an elephant going through the eye of a needle (along with a date palm made of gold) as an image of the impossible, and LSJ (s.v. κάμιλος) refer to an Arab proverb to the same effect. The camel, as the largest animal in Palestine, was the natural local choice for the same image.[26]

The manifest impossibility of this feat which so scandalised the disciples has worried biblical interpreters ever since. One attempt to 'improve' the saying (see Textual Note) is the reading κάμιλον (rope) for κάμηλον found in a few minuscules and translated in the Georgian version, though the sort of ship's hawser apparently denoted by this very rare and late word is no more likely than a camel to go through the eye of a needle. Another modification, repeated by preachers until it has popularly acquired the status of an established datum, is the suggestion popularised in the nineteenth century[27] that 'the eye of the needle' was a term for a small gate within the large double gate in the city wall, through which pedestrians could enter without opening the large gates as would be necessary for a camel train. The resultant image of a camel stripped of its load and bending its knees and neck to get through the pedestrian gate offers rich homiletical possibilities, but sadly it remains an unsupported guess. 'There is not the slightest shred of evidence for this identification. This door has not in any language been called the needle's eye, and is not so called today.'[28] But worse than the lack of evidence for this conjecture is its effect in actually undermining the point of the proverb. That which Jesus presented as ludicrously impossible is turned into a remote possibility: the rich person, given sufficient unloading and humility, might just possibly be able to squeeze in. That was not what Jesus' proverb meant, and it was not how the disciples understood it (v. 26).

26-27 The escalation from δυσκόλως to impossibility is matched by a corresponding increase in the disciples' astonishment, from ἐθαμβοῦντο (v. 24) to περισσῶς ἐξεπλήσσοντο. In a culture which interpreted wealth as a sign of God's blessing, if the rich cannot be saved, who can be?[29] Their discussion among themselves (see Textual Note) focuses on salvation (σωθῆναι), taken as equivalent to εἰς τὴν βασιλείαν τοῦ θεοῦ εἰσελθεῖν (see on 9:43, 45, 47). This 'theological' use of σῴζω is found in Mark only here and probably in 13:13: normally σῴζω refers to restoration of physical health, and sometimes to preserving earthly life. In 8:35 the play on words involves a more spiritual sense

---

26. S. E. Dowd, *Prayer,* 75-77, discusses this saying (together with 2:9) as an example of the widely used literary device of the ἀδύνατον (for which see 70-72).

27. Lagrange cites this view as early as the fifteenth century (Poloner), while Gundry traces it back to Theophylact in the eleventh, and Schweizer to an unnamed commentator in the ninth.

28. G. N. Scherer, writing in the nineteenth century, quoted by K. E. Bailey, *Peasant Eyes,* 166; Bailey's own lengthy Middle Eastern experience and study of Eastern commentaries confirms Scherer's observation.

29. T. Dwyer, *Wonder,* 153-57, explains the disciples' astonishment not by anything 'scandalous' in Jesus' pronouncements, but by the authority with which they are given. This is partly on the ground that the disciples who have themselves left their earthly goods (v. 28) should not find this teaching surprising. But that is to take the narrative out of sequence. Peter's claim in v. 28 *follows* their uncomfortable reaction to Jesus' teaching, as an attempt to salvage something out of the general dismay.

for saving the ψυχή, but this verse and 13:13 are the only absolute occurrences of the verb in something like the 'Pauline' sense. But its close link here with ζωὴ αἰώνιος (v. 17), θησαυρὸς ἐν οὐρανῷ (v. 21), and εἰς τὴν βασιλείαν τοῦ θεοῦ εἰσελθεῖν (vv. 23, 24, 25) leaves no doubt of its meaning.

ἐμβλέψας (cf. v. 21), like περιβλεψάμενος in v. 23, suggests Jesus' awareness of their thoughts, spoken to one another but not perhaps to him. His reply accepts the logic of their deduction: it *is* impossible. But that impossibility is then placed on the debit side of the human/divine balance. What human beings cannot do, God can.[30] They have considered the criteria for entering God's kingdom from a human perspective, and from that perspective those criteria, as Jesus has now set them out, cannot be met. But if it is *God's* kingdom, we are not limited to human calculation. The salvation of the rich is always a miracle, but miracles are God's speciality.

This climactic statement certainly helps to resolve the tension which has built up through the pericope, and allows hope in what had seemed a hopeless situation. But by removing the solution into the divine sphere it leaves human comprehension still unsatisfied: *how* are the rich to be saved,[31] and does v. 27 effectively put rich and poor back on the same footing? Does the fact that God can override the problem of affluence mean that we are therefore entitled to ignore the warnings of vv. 23-25? As so often Jesus' sovereign pronouncement provides deep food for thought, but not a cut-and-dried answer. It reminds us that it is only from the divine perspective that the divine kingdom can be understood, but it does not offer us a tidy theology. The following verses will offer further challenging lessons in perspective and priorities rather than intellectual satisfaction on the matter of salvation.

Losses and Gains (10:28-31)

TEXTUAL NOTE

31. The presence or absence of the article before the second ἔσχατοι is a matter of stylistic preference which does not affect the force of the epigram. Its omission in ℵ A D etc. is probably to be explained as assimilation to Matthew.

We have already noted the continuity of this pericope with the last. The same themes recur: the radical demands of following Jesus, the contrast between the true disciples and the one who failed to make the grade, the giving up of possessions, treasure in heaven, eternal life. But there is a change of focus, too. Peter once again takes the centre of the stage (we have not heard from him since the

30. Cf. Zc. 8:6, where the LXX uses ἀδυνατέω for *yippālēʾ* (to be difficult or extraordinary).
31. T. E. Schmidt, *Hostility,* 114, comments: 'To the implied question "How?" v. 28 supplies the answer, and vv. 29-31 the confirmation: obedience.' But since vv. 28-31 are not about the rich but the disciples, this is at best a partial answer.

transfiguration), and as so often his intervention leads to a mixed response. Praise for his whole-hearted discipleship and the promise of a hundredfold reward are balanced by the threat of persecutions to come and by a double-edged saying about priorities in the kingdom of God which could be understood, and may well have been meant, as a warning about his assumption of the role of leading disciple. We treat this as a separate pericope, therefore, while aware of the importance of reading it in relation to the story of the rich man and its aftermath, with which it is linked in all three synoptic accounts.

28 Peter again takes the initiative (ἤρξατο λέγειν), though speaking in the name of the whole itinerant disciple group. There is perhaps a touch of smugness in his observation that where the rich man has fallen short they have come up to Jesus' stringent expectations. It is simply an observation, not as in Matthew a question (τί ἄρα ἔσται ἡμῖν;), but it implies that the warnings which the rich man's example has led Jesus to utter against affluence cannot apply to them — and thus perhaps that their place in the kingdom of God is assured.

29-30 The list of losses in v. 29 is linked by ἤ, but the list of gains in v. 30 by καί. This is probably no more than stylistic variation, so that it is overexegesis to conclude that the abandonment of any *one* of the items in the list will be rewarded by the gain of *all* of them (though of course it is true that not everyone will have every item in the list to begin with). Certainly 'what is gained will far outweigh what is lost' (Cranfield), but this is conveyed more by ἑκατονταπλασίονα than by the change of conjunction. The appearance of ἀγρούς at the end of the list after the members of the family (rather than with οἰκίαν at the beginning) is surprising, but may perhaps be explained by the fact that while almost everyone has a house and family to leave, only a few would possess land, so that this is a special addition for the affluent. The list in v. 30 corresponds to that in v. 29 except for the omission of fathers; this may reflect the theological scruple that the disciple has only one heavenly Father (Mt. 23:9; cf. the omission of 'father' in the family list at 3:35). It is significant in the light of Jesus' teaching in vv. 2-12 that there is no suggestion of leaving a wife behind (and cf. 1 Cor. 9:5 for Peter's later practice); contrast Lk. 18:29.

This is another ἀμήν saying, and again it speaks of ultimate rewards (see on v. 15). It is not a commendation of poverty for its own sake, but of the renunciation of family ties and of the security of possessions ἕνεκεν ἐμοῦ καὶ ἕνεκεν τοῦ εὐαγγελίου (see on 8:35), deprivation as a result of discipleship. The degree of renunciation should not be overstated: after Peter and his colleagues had left their nets to follow Jesus (1:16-20) the home of Peter and Andrew remained available to them (1:29), and is generally assumed to have been the house used by Jesus as his base in Capernaum. It was not for the time being so private as it might have been, but it remained theirs. And in that house lived Peter's mother-in-law, and presumably other members of the family. The boat of 3:9; 4:1, 36, etc. may well have belonged to Peter or one of the other fishermen-disciples. We should then understand ἀφίημι here not of a disposal of property (such as Jesus had asked of the rich man, v. 21) and of a total renunciation of family ties, but of the leaving behind of both family and possessions for the period of their itinerant ministry. This is not monastic poverty so much as pragmatically sitting light to possessions and family ἕνεκεν τοῦ εὐαγγελίου.

Such renunciation finds a hundredfold recompense even νῦν ἐν τῷ καιρῷ τούτῳ. Set in contrast with ἐν τῷ αἰῶνι τῷ ἐρχομένῳ, this can only mean an earthly recompense, but it is open to question what form that recompense is to take. Quite apart from the dubious desirability of a hundred mothers or children, there is little in the story of the early church or in subsequent history to suggest that Mark could have taken this promise literally; disciples and missionaries have not generally been conspicuous for their material gain. We should think of the less tangible rewards of discipleship, and of the extended family of the followers of Jesus (see 3:34-35).[32] These far outweigh the security and enjoyment of possessions and family to which the rich man had returned. But there is an addition to the list which draws attention because of its different form (μετὰ διωγμῶν rather than καὶ διωγμούς); this is the sting in the tail. The disciples' experience νῦν ἐν τῷ καιρῷ τούτῳ is characterised not only by gain but by persecution (a further indication that material prosperity is not the issue here). What they have already witnessed of people's response to Jesus gives weight to this warning, and they cannot have forgotten his sombre words in 8:34-38. More such warnings will follow (10:39; 13:9-13).

But if discipleship here and now remains a mixed blessing, from the perspective of the kingdom of God it is not to be compared with the coming αἰών. The language of two αἰῶνες is not typical of Mark, though see 4:19 for the present αἰών implicitly contrasted with the kingdom of God. But the contrast between earth and heaven, between present and future, runs through his gospel in other words, and here we are particularly reminded of the treasure in heaven promised to the rich man as a result of giving up his earthly possessions (v. 21). This treasure is now spelled out again as ζωὴ αἰώνιος, the very goal which the rich man sought but failed to find (v. 17).

31 This epigram functions as a sort of slogan for the revolutionary values of the kingdom of God as Jesus has been presenting them. Apart from parallels to this verse, similar words recur in other contexts in Mt. 20:16 and Lk. 13:30, and 9:35 has already expressed a similar reversal. At this point in the gospel, after a series of increasingly bewildering challenges to the values and priorities hitherto taken for granted by the disciples, it serves as a fitting summary of the teaching which Jesus has given since the second prediction of the

32. S. C. Barton, *Discipleship*, 103-7, finds in this pericope the view that early Christianity was 'a social world in the making', and suggests that it brings to a culmination the perspective implied throughout 10:1-27, that Jesus 'gives instruction in three areas crucial for constructing and maintaining an alternative social world: marriage rules, the place of children and the control of property'. He adds, however, the important qualification that 'What is proposed is not an alternative social pattern to replace the household . . . , but alternative households to compensate (and more so) for those left behind' (107).

passion in 9:31. It will be followed by a further prediction of the cross, which in turn will lead to a yet more searching subversion of conventional attitudes in vv. 35-45.

Following on from vv. 28-30, these words could be understood as entirely positive from the disciples' point of view, as a reinforcement of the promise of vv. 29-30 that those who by following Jesus have made themselves 'last' in worldly terms will prove in the end to be 'first', and that those, like the rich man, whose comfortable situation in life might make them seem first will in fact be the last. But in that case it is perhaps surprising that the conjunction is δέ. While little can be based on so common and so flexible a conjunction alone, its presence suggests that we should not forget that the pericope began with words of Peter which at the least assert the 'superiority' of the disciple group to the rich man and those he represents. The fact that it is again *Peter* who makes this observation and thus takes the lead among his colleagues suggests a more personal application of these words. It is not long since the disciples have been occupied with question of τίς μείζων (9:34), and Peter's initiative in v. 28 may suggest that he has his own answer to that question. But even he, exemplary though his commitment has been, cannot assume that he has a right to be 'first'; the kingdom of God is not so predictable. Such a gentle rebuke to Peter implied in these words would give a suitable launching pad to the attempt of James and John to establish their own rival claim to primacy in v. 37.

FOLLOWING JESUS IN THE WAY OF THE CROSS (10:32-45)

The journey towards Jerusalem and the cross comes to its climax with the third and most detailed passion prediction, followed by the most emphatic of all Jesus' reversals of accepted values in the call to serve rather than be served. This searching challenge culminates in v. 45 with the first and clearest statement of the purpose of his own coming death. Hitherto Jesus has spoken of its necessity, but now he offers a new perspective on the concept of messianic suffering which sets what might otherwise have been seen as a meaningless tragedy in the context of the redemptive purpose of God. This is not a setback to Jesus' mission, a victory for his opponents; it is what he came for.

But as has been made clear since 8:31, what is to happen to Jesus will also have its implications for those who follow him on the road to Jerusalem. The unforgettable cameo of v. 32 focuses this theme, and the misguided hope of messianic glory which motivates James and John in their request in v. 37 enables us to see the gulf which separates Jesus' sense of mission from the natural aspirations of his all-too-human followers. For them, as for him, the fulfilment of God's redemptive plan will involve leaving behind the world's scale of achievement and accepting that the first will be last and the last first. With that lesson yet again reinforced, both he and they will be as ready as they can be for the fateful arrival in Jerusalem.

Third Prediction of the Passion (10:32-34)

TEXTUAL NOTE

34. A 'correction' of μετὰ τρεῖς ἡμέρας to τῇ τρίτῃ ἡμέρᾳ was almost inevitable, both to assimilate to the phrase consistently used by Matthew and Luke and to avoid the embarrassment of a phrase which appears to predict a longer period in the tomb than was in fact the case. In 8:31 comparatively few MSS make the change, but in 9:31 and here the majority do so. Nonetheless it is so hard to imagine any scribe substituting μετὰ τρεῖς ἡμέρας for an original τῇ τρίτῃ ἡμέρᾳ that editors have no hesitation in accepting μετὰ τρεῖς ἡμέρας in all three passages.

This little section contains no incident as such, but rather serves to set the scene for what is to come, first by a graphic depiction of the mood of the characters as they come towards the goal of their journey, and then by the most detailed of Jesus' statements about what is now so soon to happen. The themes are already familiar, but are now presented with greater force as Jerusalem comes closer.

It is at the end of v. 34 that the major additional section quoted by Clement of Alexandria from the 'Secret Gospel of Mark' was located. The only evidence for this supposedly more extensive version of Mark, intended for restricted circulation among an esoteric group ('a more spiritual gospel for the use of those who were being perfected'), is the quotation of two passages from it in an eighteenth-century copy of a letter of Clement first discovered by Morton Smith in 1958.[33] If we may accept, as many patristic scholars have done, that the Clement letter is genuine, the question remains what was the origin of the additional material which Clement believes came from Mark himself. Clement was fond of secrecy, esoteric teaching, and mystical experiences, and was more open than most patristic writers to accept the authenticity of purportedly apostolic writings, which are now understood to be of second-century origin. There is no good reason to regard this expanded version of Mark as any less 'apocryphal' than the other gospels to which he accorded similar recognition.[34]

The 'Secret Gospel' text as quoted by Clement continues as follows after 10:34 (in my literal translation):

And they come into Bethany; and there was there a certain woman whose brother had died. And she came and knelt before Jesus and says to him, 'Son of David, have mercy on me'. But the disciples rebuked her. And Jesus was angry, and went away with her into the garden where the tomb was. And im-

33. For full details see M. Smith, *Clement.* More popularly, M. Smith, *Secret Gospel.* This discovery formed the basis for Smith's own reconstruction of an 'alternative' Jesus, *Magician.*

34. For a very brief assessment see my *Evidence,* 80-83. More fully, e.g., F. F. Bruce, *'Secret' Gospel.* A more recent discussion by Gundry, 603-23, focuses especially on the attempts of H. Koester and J. D. Crossan to establish the 'Secret Gospel' as the original gospel of Mark, our canonical Mark being therefore a second-century revision; Gundry is not persuaded.

mediately a loud voice was heard from the tomb. And Jesus came near and rolled away the stone from the door of the tomb; and he went in immediately where the young man was, and stretched out his hand and raised him up, taking hold of his hand. But the young man, looking at him, loved him, and began to entreat that he might be with him. And they came out of the tomb, and came to the young man's house, for he was rich. And after six days Jesus gave him instructions, and in the evening the young man comes to him, wearing a linen cloth over his naked body. And he stayed with him that night, for Jesus was teaching him the mystery of the kingdom of God. And he arose from there and returned to the other side of the Jordan.

A further very short extract is said to come after the words καὶ ἔρχονται εἰς Ἰεριχώ in 10:46. It reads as follows:

And the sister of the young man whom Jesus loved and his mother and Salome were there, and Jesus did not receive them.

The longer extract looks like a version of the story of Lazarus (Jn. 11), woven together with the young man in the garden (Mk. 14:51-52), with probable echoes also of the 'beloved disciple' of John and the rich man whom Jesus loved (Mk. 10:21). There are a number of stylistic features which resemble Mark's writing, but the influence of the Fourth Gospel is much stronger. It is the sort of pastiche of gospel data with additional second-century features (the loud voice from the tomb; the hint of initiation rites with a sexual dimension)[35] such as we find in other apocryphal gospels. As evidence for second-century developments it is interesting and important, but it is unlikely to contribute anything to our understanding of Mark.

32 A further mention of the ὁδός (cf. 9:33, 34; 10:17) brings us back to the journey motif which undergirds Act Two of the gospel, but now that motif is heavily underscored. First the destination is now explicitly spelled out for the first time: ἀναβαίνοντες εἰς Ἰεροσόλυμα. The mention of the Sanhedrin in 8:31 has already given a clear indication of where it is that Jesus is to be rejected and die, but now the city, which has previously been mentioned as the source of scribal opposition (3:22; 7:1), is identified by name in v. 32, and then again in v. 33. ἀναβαίνω is partly literal (from the east the road to Jerusalem is a steep climb), but also echoes the OT language of pilgrimage: 'thither the tribes go up' (Ps. 122:4; cf. Ps. 24:3; Is. 2:2-3, etc.). The arrival in Jerusalem will be in time for the Passover festival, and Jesus and his group would not be the only pilgrims on the way to the festival. Now as the climax approaches, Mark offers us a vivid cameo of the attitudes of this unusual pilgrim group on the road.

First comes Jesus himself leading the way, striding ahead purposefully as if anxious to get on with it (cf. Lk. 9:51: τὸ πρόσωπον ἐστήρισεν τοῦ πορεύε-

---

35. This aspect clearly worried Clement, who points out that the text does not contain the words γυμνὸς γυμνῷ and other dubious material about which his correspondent had consulted him.

σθαι εἰς Ἰερουσαλήμ). Then, following their teacher as rabbinic disciples were expected to, come the disciples, astonished (ἐθαμβοῦντο, the same verb as in v. 24); the subject of the verb is not specified, but the flow of the narrative demands that the disciples, with whom we have just seen Jesus in dialogue in vv. 23-31, are the subject of ἦσαν, and thus also of the next plural verb linked simply by καί.[36] Usually the cause of astonishment is either specifically mentioned (ἐπὶ τοῖς λόγοις αὐτοῦ, v. 24) or supplied by the immediately preceding context (as in 1:27). Here it can hardly be Jesus' words arising out of the last incident, since their astonishment over those has already been mentioned twice over (vv. 24, 26). Rather, it is found in the preceding clause, ἦν προάγων αὐτοὺς ὁ Ἰησοῦς: his determination to reach Jerusalem with all that he has foretold there leaves them bewildered, coming along behind Jesus in amazement. But then a third group is mentioned, οἱ δὲ ἀκολουθοῦντες being distinguished by δέ from the immediate group of disciples.[37] This wider group of fellow travellers (taking ἀκολουθέω here in the literal sense, rather than as a technical term for discipleship) are also affected by the ominous atmosphere, and are quite simply afraid. In a few simple clauses Mark has managed to provide a vivid sense of the urgency and, for all but Jesus, the incomprehensibility of the death march to Jerusalem.

Even though there is now a wider company on the road, it is specifically to οἱ δώδεκα that Jesus again spells out what is coming; παραλαμβάνω (as in 5:40; 9:2; 14:33) indicates a private audience with a small group apart from the rest. In 8:31 Jesus' passion was presented as a necessity (δεῖ), and here too it is not merely a possibility but a future certainty, τὰ μέλλοντα συμβαίνειν.

33-34 Elements from the preceding two passion predictions (8:31; 9:31) are combined into this climactic statement about the fate awaiting the υἱὸς τοῦ ἀνθρώπου, and more detail is added.[38] First there is the specific mention of Ἱεροσόλυμα (see on previous verse). Then the 'handing over' (see on 9:31) is specifically linked with the ἀρχιερεῖς καὶ γραμματεῖς of 8:31 (the omission of the πρεσβύτεροι this time is surprising, but probably not significant). Thereafter

36. This sequence makes improbable the alternative view (e.g., M. D. Hooker, *Son of Man*, 138-39) that the subject of ἐθαμβοῦντο is indefinite, while the definite οἱ δὲ ἀκολουθοῦντες denotes only the disciples who have left everything to follow him, and therefore are afraid for themselves. Gundry reads ἦσαν somewhat unnaturally as people in general, thus making this a general pilgrimage setting, with Jesus (and the Twelve and others who are following him closely) going ahead of the larger crowd.

37. See the previous note. The following παραλαβὼν πάλιν τοὺς δώδεκα more naturally returns our attention to the Twelve after a wider group has been mentioned. Others (e.g., Best, *Following*, 120-21; Lane, 373; T. Dwyer, *Wonder*, 159-60) suggest that the δέ before ἀκολουθοῦντες is not meant to introduce a separate group, but merely adds a further comment about the disciples; but Mark usually uses δέ to provide contrast rather than continuity (Gundry, 570, 573), and it is unnatural to read the total phrase οἱ δὲ ἀκολουθοῦντες as anything other than a change of subject.

38. R. McKinnis, *NovT* 18 (1976) 89-95, 98-100, suggests that the six verbs of vv. 33b-34 (beginning with κατακρίνουσιν) fall into three pairs linked by sound as well as sense, and traces this to the use of a 'pre-Markan hymn'.

the passion events are presented in two phases, first the actions taken by the ἀρχιερεῖς καὶ γραμματεῖς (in v. 33), then those taken by the ἔθνη (in v. 34). Each phase follows from a 'handing over' to the respective body. This sequence corresponds closely to what will be described at the end of the gospel, where Jesus will first be handed over (14:10 etc.) by Judas to the Jewish authorities, and then handed over (15:1) by them to the Romans.[39] It is interesting especially that whereas in 8:31 the death of the Son of Man was mentioned in the passive, with no subject directly expressed, and in 9:31 it was attributed generally to οἱ ἄνθρωποι, here it is specifically the ἔθνη who will kill him, though it is the ἀρχιερεῖς καὶ γραμματεῖς who will condemn him to death.

The Jewish phase of the passion is thus presented by two verbs, first κατακρινοῦσιν, then παραδώσουσιν. This corresponds to what we know of the competence of the Jewish authorities at that time: condemnation could not lead directly to death, but must be implemented by handing over to the Romans who had that power. The description of the Roman governing authorities as τὰ ἔθνη makes the point clearly: this final phase of the passion will be taken out of Jewish hands. This is not a matter of apportioning blame (after all, the condemnation is clearly attributed to the Jewish leaders), but of historical reality. But it carries the humiliating irony that the Jewish Messiah, while condemned by his own people, will in fact meet his death at the hands of Gentiles.

Four verbs (ἐμπαίξουσιν, ἐμπτύσουσιν, μαστιγώσουσιν, ἀποκτενοῦσιν) then describe the Roman actions against Jesus, each of which will be specifically included in the events which will be recorded in 15:15-25, though there the scourging (using a different verb, φραγελλόω) will precede the mocking and spitting. While no doubt Mark's wording is designed to reflect the story as he is going to tell it, it is worth noting that, even though the terms do not correspond directly to the LXX, each of these four elements is included in the 'blueprint' for the suffering of the Isaianic servant (mockery and spitting, Is. 50:6; 53:3; cf. also Ps. 22:7; scourging, Is. 50:6; 53:5; death, 53:8-9, 12).[40] If, as we shall see in v. 45, Jesus' understanding of what was to happen to him was in part based on the sufferings of the servant, it may be that we should not attribute the wording of this prediction wholly to Marcan hindsight.[41]

While the rest of this third prediction is significantly expanded, the final four words about resurrection remain the same as in 8:31 and 9:31. While the ultimate outcome of Jesus' mission remains an essential element, the detailed focus at this stage is firmly on the more immediate prospect of suffering and death.

---

39. F. J. Matera, *Kingship*, 94-97, sets out in detail the agreements and disagreements between the wording of this prediction and the passion narratives.

40. See J. Marcus, *Way*, 188-90.

41. Gundry, 575, argues also that hindsight would have been more likely to produce a specific reference to crucifixion rather than the more general verb ἀποκτείνω.

Greatness in Service (10:35-45)

TEXTUAL NOTES

36. There is some confusion in the MSS between a construction with subjunctive ποιήσω or with infinitive ποιήσαι. The syntactically impossible reading of ℵ¹ B, τί θέλετέ με ποιήσω, must result from a conflation of the two constructions. The reading which best explains the variants is τί θέλετε ποιήσω (with ἵνα understood), the abruptness of which led to correcting the subjunctive to an infinitive, with the consequent addition of με.

40. ἄλλοις is an easy misreading of ἀλλ' οἷς in the absence of word divisions, and indeed in most early MSS it is impossible to say which reading was intended. The preceding οὐκ requires a following ἀλλά (sy\ˢ, having read ἄλλοις, found it necessary to add a 'but'). The addition of ὑπὸ τοῦ πατρός μου in ℵ* etc. is an assimilation to Matthew, made more attractive by the lack of an explicit balance in the text to οὐκ ἐμόν.

43. ἔσται may be explained as an assimilation to the following clauses, and possibly also to Matthew, where, however, the same variant occurs. In Mark the external evidence for ἐστιν is significantly stronger than in Matthew.

The previous passion predictions have each been followed by an example of the disciples' failure to grasp Jesus' new scale of values and by consequent remedial teaching. Here the pattern is repeated even more strongly, as James and John display a remarkable lack of awareness of what Jesus has just been saying about the mission of the Son of Man coupled with a personal ambition which is totally out of keeping with all that has been said since 9:33; moreover, the other disciples seem to share their perspective, and Jesus responds with the most thoroughgoing statement yet of the revolutionary values of the kingdom of God. The passage divides naturally into two sections. The first (vv. 35-40) focuses specifically on the request of James and John together with Jesus' response. Following the implied rebuke to Peter in v. 31, the other two members of the 'inner circle' of Jesus' disciples think the time opportune for a bid to establish their own position, and in a way which excludes Peter. The issue of status is thus yet again brought to our attention, with James and John as the negative examples. The setting of their request, with its presumption that Jesus is on the way to 'glory', is remarkable, following immediately after the most ominous and detailed of Jesus' passion predictions. Does Mark wish us to suppose that they have simply not heard what he has said, or that they have picked up the royal connotations of ὁ υἱὸς τοῦ ἀνθρώπου when understood in the light of Dn. 7:13-14, and have filtered out all the less desirable aspects of his statement? Jesus' response accepts their desire to share his destiny, but offers a more realistic view of what that will mean. But in the end v. 40 undermines the whole premise on which their request was based, that status in the kingdom of God can be bestowed as a favour, or even earned by loyalty and self-sacrifice.

The second section (vv. 41-45) picks up the theme of 9:35 and again subverts the whole notion of leadership and importance which human society takes for granted. If v. 31 served as a summary of Jesus' teaching about status up to that point, v. 43a now offers a further 'slogan' which encapsulates the revolutionary effect of his teaching about the kingdom of God: οὐχ οὕτως ἐστιν ἐν ὑμῖν. The 'natural' assumptions and valuations by which people operate no longer apply in the kingdom of God. It is a genuinely alternative society. His own loss of his life for the sake of others not only embodies this new scale of values but also offers the disciples a model to follow. And because his death will be not a meaningless loss but the means to a God-given end (λύτρον ἀντὶ πολλῶν), this final pronouncement of Act Two gives at least the beginning of an answer to the question which must have been growing in the mind of any reader who has felt the full force of the three passion predictions: *Why* must he die? The ransom saying thus brings the central section of the gospel to an appropriate conclusion, and one which prepares the reader for the arrival in Jerusalem and the beginning of the fulfilment of Jesus' warnings.

35-36 προσπορεύονται suggests perhaps that the brothers attempted to 'corner' Jesus, though v. 41 makes it clear that their request was made in the hearing of the other disciples. This is the only time the two feature together in the gospel without Peter as the other member of the inner circle (1:16-20, 29; 5:37; 9:2; 13:3; 14:33), though cf. 9:38 for John alone. Peter, on the other hand, has taken the lead in 8:29-33, and has acted as spokesman for the three in 9:5. His recent discomfiture in 10:31 perhaps suggests to them that his leading position is not unassailable. Their roundabout approach (ὃ ἐὰν αἰτήσωμέν σε), however, suggests some delicacy in broaching such a self-centred request. The requested *carte blanche* draws from Jesus a suitably cautious reply. The syntax is compressed (see Textual Note): ἵνα before ποιήσω would have mirrored their wording and should probably be understood here (cf. v. 51 for the same construction).

37 The request, precipitated perhaps by the excitement of coming near Jerusalem, the 'royal' city, assumes that Jesus, as 'king', has positions of honour and influence in his gift: δὸς ἡμῖν will be picked up by οὐκ ἔστιν ἐμὸν δοῦναι in v. 40, showing that this assumption was false. For δίδωμι with ἵνα ('grant that') cf. Rev. 9:5; 19:8. To speak of sitting (rather than reclining, as at a banquet) on the right (or left) of someone implies a royal throne with the places of highest honour on either side;[42] there are of course only two such places, leaving no room for Peter.

That they envisage Jesus as king is confirmed by mentioning his δόξα. This is a term he has used only once, in 8:38, and there with reference to the δόξα of his Father rather than his own, though the role of judgment there envisaged for the Son of Man suggests that he shares the royal authority, and there-

---

42. The seat on the right is the most prestigious. The left (Latin *sinister*) was often, by contrast, thought of as the side of ill omen (hence the less common euphemism εὐώνυμος, 'of good name, propitious', which replaces ἀριστερός in v. 40; there is no difference in meaning). But where the king is flanked by courtiers on both sides, there is no dishonour in being on the left (see, e.g., 1 Ki. 22:19; Ne. 8:4). See *DNTT*, 2.148.

fore the δόξα, of God. The vision of Dn. 7:14 is of dominion, glory, and kingship given to the υἱὸς ἀνθρώπου, and while δόξα does not occur in either LXX or Thdt to describe that status, it sums up the vision well enough; Mann translates 'in your triumph'. As Jesus has used the title ὁ υἱὸς τοῦ ἀνθρώπου for himself, his disciples have grasped its royal connotations and can envisage a time when it will be fulfilled for Jesus (as they have already seen it briefly in the transfiguration), and therefore also for his faithful followers. Nor does Jesus disabuse them of this notion in his reply in v. 40. But all the emphasis in the preceding chapters has been on the cross rather than the kingship, and it is probably asking too much of James and John to expect them yet to have worked out a theology of victory through the cross. More likely they have seized on that part of Jesus' language which is congenial to them, and ignored the rest. Perhaps they still hope, as Peter did in 8:32, that all the talk about rejection and death in Jerusalem is a mistake, and that as Jesus now approaches 'his' capital he may yet be coaxed back to take the more sensible way.

38 For Jesus the route to glory is clear; it is by way of the ποτήριον and the βάπτισμα which await him (taking the present tenses of πίνω and βαπτίζομαι as referring to a future fate already decided, as in 9:31 παραδίδοται), and anyone who wishes to share the glory must first also share those experiences. The cup as an image for Jesus' destined suffering will recur in 14:36 (cf Jn. 18:11). In the OT the cup is sometimes an image of blessing (Pss. 16:5; 23:5; 116:13) but more often of judgment (Ps. 75:8; Je. 25:15-29; 49:12; Ezk. 23:31-34; Hab. 2:16; cf. Rev. 14:10; 16:19). Normally it denotes the punishment of the wicked, but in Is. 51:17-23 and La. 4:21 it is used of the suffering of God's people, which will now be passed from them to their oppressors. It is therefore perhaps pressing the image too far in this context to suggest that Jesus uses it specifically to draw out the idea of vicarious suffering, as he drinks the 'cup' which is deserved by the wicked, though the vicarious implications of the cup saying in 14:24 would be familiar to Mark's readers. The 'cup' offered here to James and John, however, is not vicarious, but simply an image for destined suffering. The similar metaphorical use of βάπτισμα (cf. Lk. 12:50) has no such clear precedent. Secular Greek offers examples of βαπτίζομαι as a metaphor for being 'overwhelmed, or 'swamped' by misfortune, sorrow, etc. (see BAGD, 132, 3.c), and LXX Is. 21:4 has ἡ ἀνομία με βαπτίζει. This is not, however, like the cup, a use which would be likely to be immediately familiar in a Jewish context, and in Mark there is a much more obvious antecedent in the baptism of John. That did not in itself suggest suffering, though Christian theology soon developed baptism into Christ as a symbol of death leading to new life, as the baptised believer shares in Christ's death and resurrection (Rom. 6:3-4). It is unlikely that Jesus used the term in that Pauline sense, despite the gallant attempt of A. Oepke, *TDNT,* 1.538: 'It is not impossible that in a bold and profound image, hardly understandable to the men of his day, he anticipates the results of the religious developments of decades.' It may, however, have been a factor in Mark's preservation of this striking image. But in the narrative context we must suppose that Jesus has coined a remarkable new metaphor, drawing on his disciples' familiarity with the dramatic physical act of John's baptism, but using it (somewhat along the lines of the secular usage mentioned above) to depict the suffering and death into which he was soon to be 'plunged'.[43] For the construction τὸ βάπτισμα βαπτίζομαι, where the cognate accusative is one of 'inner content after the passive verb' (Taylor), see BDF, 153(2), and cf. Lk. 12:50; Acts 19:4.

39-40 With Christian hindsight we may assume that Jesus' question in v. 38 was intended to be rhetorical: of course no one else could share his unique role of redemptive suffering. But at the time the cup and the baptism would not appear in that light. For James and John they represent a regrettable but necessary hurdle on the way to δόξα, and as such the suffering must be faced: δυνάμεθα. They may lack understanding, but not loyalty or courage.

Jesus' response is surprising and seems to undermine the point of his previous question: even if they fulfil the 'conditions' he has set down, their request still cannot be granted. The cup and the baptism thus prove not to be qualifying conditions at all, but rather a way of indicating that their whole conception of δόξα and of the way it is to be achieved is misguided. It cannot be earned even by the extreme suffering which he must undergo and which they in their turn will indeed share. He has already warned his disciples in 8:34-38 of the cost of following him, even to the extent of martyrdom, and James and John must reckon with that. See Acts 12:2 for James's fulfilment of this prediction; John's is more obscure, though Christian tradition identifies him with the political prisoner on Patmos whose visions of faithful witness and martyrdom fill the last book of the NT.[44] But that is not the basis on which the places of honour are to be allocated.

Verse 40 surprisingly does not deny that there will be such places of honour, but refuses to reserve them for even the most ambitious or the most loyal disciple. ἀλλ' οἷς ἡτοίμασται (see Textual Note) is a compressed expression in which the relative stands in for the main clause; we must assume a main verb such as 'it will be given', contrasting with the preceding statement that it is not for Jesus to give it.[45] Those to whom it will be given are those οἷς ἡτοίμασται, where the passive without expressed agent must in this context, as often in Jewish writings, indicate God as the one who has prepared it (see Textual Note).

43. For extensive bibliography on the metaphor see BAGD, 132a-b. For studies of the background to both cup and baptism see G. Delling, *NovT* 2 (1957) 92-115; A. Feuillet, *RB* 74 (1967) 356-91; S. Légasse, *NTS* 20 (1974) 163-70.

44. A tradition which cannot be traced earlier than the fifth century, that John died along with his brother, most probably derives from the need to find a fulfilment for Jesus' words here. The more common and earlier tradition is that he died in old age in Ephesus. See L. Morris, *Studies*, 280-83.

45. See Gundry, 578, for a suggested alternative translation, with ἀλλά meaning 'except': 'is not mine to give except [that it is mine to give] to those for whom it has been prepared'. This would make little ultimate difference to the meaning in context, but eases the implied limitation on Jesus' authority.

For God's 'preparing a place' for his people cf. LXX Ex. 23:20; Mt. 25:34; 1 Cor. 2:9; Heb. 11:16. But we are left no wiser as to who these favoured people are, and that is surely deliberate. In the light of the preceding pericopes, we may be fairly certain that it will not be those who would have been expected, or who would expect themselves, to take precedence, but rather those who are like the child, the little ones. The effect of the whole exchange is in the end, even after James and John have accepted the necessity of the cup and the baptism, to rule out of court their request and the concern for status which underlies it. The well-informed reader might reflect that those who were soon to be on Jesus' right and left were to be not honoured disciples but ληϲταί, and the setting not a throne but a gibbet (15:27).

41 The reaction of the other disciples is expressed by the same verb, ἀγανακτέω, which was used for Jesus' response to their churlish treatment of the children (10:14). Is theirs then also a righteous indignation, repudiating the self-centred attitude of their two colleagues? Have they now learned the lessons about the kingdom of God sufficiently to be able to take Jesus' side against the very status-seeking they had previously been guilty of (9:34)? Mark's consistently critical presentation of the disciples in this part of the gospel is against such an interpretation, as is the fact that the rebuke which follows in vv. 42-44 is apparently addressed not to James and John but to them all. This suggests that their annoyance is not over the ambition of the two brothers as such, but over the fact that they have got in first and tried to gain an unfair advantage over their colleagues in the competition for the highest places. On this issue they are all equally at fault.

42 If in v. 35 we were right to see James and John as 'cornering' Jesus, προσκαλεσάμενος indicates the reintegration of the group of twelve as Jesus summons the grumbling ten (αὐτούς) back together with them. For προσκαλε- σάμενος as a Marcan introduction to a key and usually surprising pronounce- ment cf. 3:23; 7:14; 8:34; 12:43. οἴδατε introduces a matter of common knowl- edge, a truism; it is its very obviousness which will make the οὐχ οὕτως of v. 43a the more arresting. Jesus takes up the idea of royal privilege from the brothers' request and universalises it with regard to the ἔθνη. While ἔθνη *could* be used here in its widest sense (this is how authority is exercised in any nation or political unit), the plural far more often in the NT denotes the Gentiles. It is not so much, however, that Jesus wishes to acquit Jewish leaders of the sort of attitude to authority which Gentiles display (the Herod dynasty would have of- fered clear enough examples), but rather that if you wanted to see absolute power in the first-century world it was necessary to look outside politically sub- ject Israel to those who held real power. οἱ δοκοῦντες ἄρχειν, rather than simply οἱ ἄρχοντες, does not question the reality of their rule, but rather draws atten- tion to the fact that they are *seen* to rule, and that their status is publicly recog- nised. Cf. οἱ δοκοῦντες for influential people in Gal. 2:2, 6, and with infinitive 2:9; see further G. Kittel, *TDNT* 2.233. Neither ἄρχειν nor οἱ μεγάλοι denotes a specific office: they are general terms for those who are in a position to impose their authority on others. The two κατα- compounds (κατεξουσιάζω is a coinage, 'scarcely to be found in secular Greek'; BAGD, 421b) are clearly pejorative; cf. Acts 19:16 for a vivid illustration of this connotation in κατακυριεύω, and the clearly pejorative use (echoing this passage) in 1 Pet. 5:3. They convey the oppressive and uncontrolled exploitation of power, the flaunting of authority rather than its benevolent exercise.

43-44 οὐχ οὕτως ἐστιν ἐν ὑμῖν (see Textual Note) sums up the revolutionary ethics of the kingdom of God. The natural expectations of society are reversed, and leadership is characterised by service, by being under the authority of others, like a διάκονος[46] or δοῦλος. Nor is this just a matter of recognising a higher rank within a recognised hierarchy: it is to *everyone* (πάντων) that precedence must be given. The terms used echo previous dialogues: μέγας recalls the discussion τίς μείζων in 9:34, and πρῶτος recalls the formulae of 9:35 and 10:31; πάντων διάκονος has already occurred in 9:35 in parallel to πάντων ἔσχατος. The only new term introduced here is δοῦλος, a further extension of the idea of subjection, since a δοῦλος had far less self-determination even than a διάκονος. But the incremental repetition, through the corresponding pronouncements of v. 43b and v. 44 which echo 9:35, together with the contrasting statement of the values of the ἔθνη in v. 42, renders this the most powerful statement yet of the alternative value scale of the kingdom of God. The sequel in v. 45 renders it unforgettable.

45 The conjunction καὶ γάρ and the repetition of the theme of service link this declaration closely with what precedes. The υἱὸς τοῦ ἀνθρώπου provides the supreme model of status reversal in that he whose destiny it was διακονηθῆναι (Dn. 7:14 LXX: πάντα τὰ ἔθνη τῆς γῆς κατὰ γένη καὶ πᾶσα δόξα αὐτῷ λατρεύουσα; Thdt: πάντες οἱ λαοί, φυλαί, γλῶσσαι αὐτῷ δουλεύσουσιν) was instead to become πάντων διάκονος. The term διακονέω is not used with Jesus as subject elsewhere in the gospel tradition, except in the roughly parallel Lk. 22:27 (and parabolically in Lk. 12:37), though the idea is graphically presented in the footwashing and following teaching in Jn. 13:1-17. It does not denote a particular role, but rather the paradoxically subordinate status of the one who should have enjoyed the service of others. The following καὶ δοῦναι does not so much specify the form of service, but rather adds a further and yet more shocking example of the self-sacrificing attitude which he in turn enjoins on his followers.

The LXX never uses the διακον- root for the *'ebed-YHWH* in Is. 42–53, but rather παῖς or δοῦλος. διακονέω here is not, then, a verbal echo of the LXX

---

46. Myers, 280-81, argues that since the two literal uses of διακονέω in Mark (1:31; 15:41) have women as their subject, the term is chosen here to indicate to the male disciple group that 'women alone are fit to act as servant-leaders'. Here, then, is an even more radical reversal of social convention; patriarchy is condemned and women should lead. This is a bold inference from two uses of the verb in quite separate contexts. Myers might also have noted that Mark has another literal (or at least quasi-literal) use of the verb where the subjects are angels (1:13); what does this imply about leadership in the church?

of those passages, especially as the 'service' there rendered is to Yahweh, not, as here, to other people. In view of the echo of the language of Is. 53 in the following clause, however, Mark's readers may well have found, and been intended to find, a portrait of Jesus 'the Servant' also in the paradoxical notion of the Son of Man as a διάκονος.

This (with its Matthew parallel) is the only use of λύτρον in the NT, though λύτρον ἀντὶ πολλῶν is echoed by ἀντίλυτρον ὑπὲρ πάντων in 1 Tim. 2:6. Various cognates occur, particularly the Pauline term ἀπολύτρωσις for 'redemption' from sin through the death of Christ. In secular Greek λύτρον was used mainly for a payment to secure release, whether from slavery or from capture. The verb λυτρόω occurs frequently in the LXX for God's 'redemption' of his people, not only from slavery in Egypt but also from spiritual oppression, and λύτρον (normally in the plural) is used for payments to preserve a life which is legally forfeit (including the firstborn) or subject to divine punishment. For a full survey of the uses of this word group see C. Brown, *DNTT*, 3.189-200. The essential meaning is deliverance by the payment of an 'equivalent'.

There has been intense debate over the scriptural background of the clause δοῦναι τὴν ψυχὴν αὐτοῦ λύτρον ἀντὶ πολλῶν, and in particular over whether these words are intended to recall the language of Is. 53, and thus to delineate Jesus in terms of the figure of the *'ebed-YHWH*.[47] I have contributed to that debate[48] and do not wish to repeat here all that I have published earlier. A brief summary must suffice. δοῦναι τὴν ψυχὴν αὐτοῦ is close to Is. 53:12 *he'râ lammāwet napšô* ('poured out his soul to death'; LXX, παρεδόθη εἰς θάνατον ἡ ψυχὴ αὐτοῦ), and there is a further echo of the phrase *śîm napšô* in Is. 53:10, though the subject there is God rather than the servant himself. Apart from verbal echoes, the concept of voluntarily giving up life is of course central to Is. 53. The object of the giving of life *(śîm napšô)* in 53:10 is as an *'āšām* ('sin offering'; LXX, περὶ ἁμαρτίας), a sacrifice offered in place of a guilty person to remove guilt (Lv. 5:17-19 etc.), and the idea of ransom (λύτρον ἀντί) is close to this, even though the LXX does not use λύτρον to translate *'āšām*. πολλῶν recalls the repeated 'many' of Is. 53:11, 12 (*rabbîm* twice; LXX, πολλοί three times), where it is the 'many' who will be the beneficiaries of the servant's self-offering, as he bears their sins and so makes them righteous. This accumulation of verbal echoes of Is. 53:10-12 is compelling in itself, and it is the more so when it is recognised that the whole thrust of Is. 53 is to present the servant as one who suffers and dies for the redemption of his people, whose life is offered as a substitute for their guilt. It would be hard to construct a more ad-

---

47. In addition to commentaries, see among more recent studies W. J. Moulder, *NTS* 24 (1977) 120-27; D. J. Moo, *The OT,* 122-27; G. R. Beasley-Murray, *Kingdom,* 278-83; R. E. Watts, *Exodus,* 258-87; for earlier bibliography see my article in next note.

48. *TynB* 19 (1968) 26-52, especially 32-37; largely repeated in *Jesus and the OT,* 110-32, especially 116-21. This study was primarily in response to the well-known arguments of C. K. Barrett and M. D. Hooker against a background in Is. 53.

equate short summary of this concept than the clause δοῦναι τὴν ψυχὴν αὐτοῦ λύτρον ἀντὶ πολλῶν, quite apart from the obvious verbal echoes. 'It is as if Jesus said, "The Son of Man came to fulfil the task of the *'ebed Yahweh*".'[49]

But Jesus is not just quoting the OT. He is making a statement about his own mission. This is the purpose for which he came (ἦλθεν). Such ἦλθον-sayings occur in various strands of the gospel tradition (e.g., Mt. 5:17; 10:34-35; Lk. 12:49; 19:10; Jn. 9:39; 10:10, etc.). In Mark we have seen such a statement of purpose in 2:17 (and cf. 1:39). There the emphasis was on the calling of sinners, in the context of the ἄφεσις ἁμαρτιῶν which John had preached and which Jesus had exemplified in 2:1-12 (see on 2:17). The mission of the Isaianic servant was also concerned with the people's sins (Is. 53:5, 6, 8, 10-12), and this ransom saying makes explicit the vicarious nature of that mission. It will be picked up again in a further allusion to Is. 53 in 14:24. Even though sin is not specifically mentioned here, seen against its Isaianic background this verse fills out what the calling of sinners in 2:17 implied. This, then, is the stated purpose of Jesus' mission. His many acts of mercy, healing, teaching, challenging the norms of society, and all the other elements of Mark's story must be seen in the light of this one purpose, δοῦναι τὴν ψυχὴν αὐτοῦ λύτρον ἀντὶ πολλῶν. Mark does not offer a lot of soteriological discussion, but what he does give is simple, clear, and far-reaching. Here is his answer to the puzzle of why Jesus had to die.

But we must not forget that this crucial verse, however great its soteriological implications, occurs in context as a model for Jesus' disciples to follow. It is not the λύτρον ἀντὶ πολλῶν that they are expected to reproduce: that was Jesus' unique mission. But the spirit of service and self-sacrifice, the priority given to the needs of the πολλοί, are for all disciples. They, too, must serve rather than be served, and it may be that some of them will be called upon, like James and John, to give up their lives. There is no room for quarrels about τίς μείζων.

SECOND HEALING OF A BLIND MAN (10:46-52)

See on 8:22-26 for the 'framing' function of the two healings of blind men at the beginning and end of Act Two, and the symbolic role of the story in relation to the disciples' spiritual blindness. In the narrative context this story, like that of the blind man at Bethsaida, functions also as a bridge passage, leading us now from the journey (Act Two) into the Jerusalem phase of the story (Act Three). The preparation of the disciples for Jerusalem has already reached its climax in v. 45, but this final incident on the way moves the plot on from the rather vague geographical information of 10:1 to a specific location, Jericho, the last town before the traveller reaches the environs of Jerusalem, a mere

49. O. Cullmann, *Christology,* 65.

day's walk away. So we see Jesus and his disciples, with a growing crowd of fellow pilgrims, leaving this last town for the strenuous climb up from the Jordan valley to the city more than 1,000 metres above. But as they set out, the company is augmented by a further and unexpected recruit.

The last potential recruit we met was an admirable, respectable, and wealthy man (10:17-22), but to the disciples' consternation he has not been welcomed into Jesus' entourage. Now we meet a man at quite the other end of the scale of social acceptability, a blind beggar. And it is he, rather than the rich man, who will end up following Jesus ἐν τῇ ὁδῷ, with his sight restored, whereas the rich man has gone away 'blind'. This man has nothing to lose, nothing to sell, and so his commitment can be immediate and complete. While we hear nothing of his subsequent discipleship, the fact that Mark records his name and his father's name suggests that he became a familiar character in the disciple group.

So just as Jesus' teaching on purity in 7:1-23 was followed by a story illustrating Jesus' openness to the 'unclean' (7:24-30), so now his extended teaching on the reversal of values in the kingdom of God is summed up in the recruitment of the least likely disciple, the 'little one' who is welcomed, the last who becomes first. As Bartimaeus joins Jesus ἐν τῇ ὁδῷ he functions as an example of discipleship, with whom 'Mark encourages the reader to identify'.[50]

This is Mark's last healing story; once Jesus arrives in Jerusalem other concerns will have to take priority. It is also the only one where the person healed is named; relatives are named in 1:30 (Simon) and 5:22 (Jairus), but the patients remain anonymous (the 'naming' of the demons as Legion is in a different category). As far as we know, none of the others joined the disciple group, so that they remained simply 'cases', whereas Bartimaeus apparently became well known, at least in Mark's church (neither Matthew nor Luke records the name).

46 Mark is quite specific about the location of Bartimaeus' healing, mentioning both the arrival in Jericho and the fact that the healing took place on the way out. Luke, on the other hand, locates it on the approach to Jericho, perhaps knowing from tradition that it was on the outskirts, and assuming that it would be on the way in. The discrepancy is not significant, and scarcely justifies the suggestion[51] that Bartimaeus was conveniently situated somewhere between the two contemporary sites of 'Jericho'.[52] The ὄχλος ἱκανός (ἱκανός is used slightly colloquially for a 'good crowd'; cf. Lk. 7:12; Acts 11:24, 26; 19:26) are not bystanders but fellow pilgrims; this is no longer a small private party. Cf. 10:1, 32 for indications of a larger pilgrim group than the Twelve as

50. J. F. Williams, *Followers*, 151. Williams devotes a lengthy section to Mark's presentation of Bartimaeus as 'an exemplary character' (151-71).

51. P. Ketter, *Bib* 15 (1934) 411-18.

52. Herodian Jericho was in fact located on the Wadi Qelt, about a mile from the site of the OT city, which was probably also still occupied (*ABD*, 3.737), but it is perhaps unlikely that at this period 'Jericho' *tout court* would be used to denote the latter as well as the 'modern' town.

the journey nears its end, and for further comment see on 15:40-41, where a group of accompanying women are introduced. This wider company will feature in this pericope as first the discouragers and then the encouragers of Bartimaeus, and will then furnish the supporters needed for the crowd scene in 11:8-9. ὁ υἱὸς Τιμαίου (which is no more than a translation of the Aramaic name Βαρτιμαῖος) is surprising: even if some of Mark's readers would not have known Aramaic, the meaning of the name can hardly be important to them. Unless there was some interest in Timaeus himself (did he as well as his son become known among the disciples?), this must be put down simply to Mark's prolixity. Τίμαιος is familiar as a Greek name, and it is possible that in the mixed culture of first-century Palestine it was borne by this Jewish beggar's father (cf. Ἀνδρέας and Φίλιππος among Jesus' Jewish disciples), though it could represent a Semitic name such as Ṭim'ay.

47-48 'Jesus' was one of the commonest names in first-century Palestine, so that the identification ὁ Ναζαρηνός (cf. 1:24) is natural in this foreign territory. Jericho is a long way from Nazareth, but we have heard already how Jesus' reputation as a healer has spread far beyond Galilee (3:7-8). If, as Mark's narrative suggests, this is his first visit to the area, it would be natural for a blind man to try to take advantage of the occasion. Unable to see where Jesus is, he shouts hopefully into the crowd.

This is the only time in Mark when Jesus is addressed as υἱὲ Δαυίδ, and nothing in this gospel (unlike Mt. 1:1-17, 20) has prepared us for this specific title.[53] For Jewish people it would be functionally equivalent to Χριστός, but the voicing of David's name increases the loading of royal and nationalistic ideology which it carries. Peter's recognition of Jesus as ὁ Χριστός in 8:29 would have given a sufficient basis for the disciples to use such language, if Jesus had not banned it (8:30). But they have observed the ban, and so its first use now by an outsider is remarkable. No other onlooker has interpreted Jesus in messianic (as opposed to merely prophetic) terms in this gospel. Whether we should think of Bartimaeus as having unusual spiritual insight or as simply aiming to gain attention by the most flattering address he can think of, his words open up a new phase in the gradual disclosure of Jesus in Mark. For it is now time, as Jesus approaches Jerusalem,[54] for the messianic aspect of his ministry to become more public, and in the next pericope this language will be on everybody's lips (11:9, ἡ ἐρχομένη βασιλεία τοῦ πατρὸς ἡμῶν Δαυίδ). Jesus' own attitude to it then will

---

53. The suggestion of B. D. Chilton, *JSNT* 14 (1982) 92-97, drawing on the work of D. C. Duling, *HTR* 68 (1975) 235-52, that there was a concept of the Son of David as a *healer* leans rather too heavily on the assumption that 'Son of David' would point to Solomon, and on the Jewish tradition that Solomon was an exorcist. But exorcism and healing are not the same thing, and there is no clear contemporary evidence for this connotation, rather than royal Messiahship, in the title Son of David; see my *Matthew, Evangelist,* 285 n. 13. For the messianic significance of υἱὸς Δαυίδ cf. *Pss. Sol.* 17:21.

54. See J. Marcus, *Way,* 137-39, for the connection between the title 'Son of David' and Jerusalem and the temple.

be left unclear, but later (12:35-37) he will place a question mark against it. Here, however, he makes no comment, still less a rebuke, in response to this double salutation in such openly messianic language. The secrecy enjoined at Caesarea Philippi is beginning to weaken, and the way is being prepared for Jesus' eventual open declaration of his Messiahship in 14:62.

The blind beggar at the roadside was no doubt a familiar figure to the people of Jericho and around. Like the disciples in 10:13, they (πολλοί, not just the disciples this time) rebuke someone of no status who wants to gain access to Jesus — and like the disciples they are overruled. For ἐπιτιμάω ἵνα cf. 3:12; 8:30; but whereas in those instances it was Jesus who thus prevented disclosure of his identity, here it is the crowd who try to silence the 'messianic confessor', and Jesus who takes his part against them. The effect of their attempt to silence Bartimaeus is of course that the title υἱὲ Δαυίδ is further emphasised by repetition in the narrative. Marcus refers to 'the literary boomerang effect of the attempt to silence Bartimaeus'.[55]

49-50 Given Jesus' urgency in 10:32, his stopping (and presumably bringing the whole crowd to a halt) for a beggar is remarkable. The crowd's sudden and complete change of heart indicates the authority of Jesus: they are now as enthusiastic as before they were dismissive, and become the medium for Jesus' call to Bartimaeus.[56] For θάρσει as a rallying cry to those in distress cf. 6:50 and still more Mt. 9:2, 22. The throwing off of the ἱμάτιον serves no purpose in the story except to make it more vivid,[57] and ἀναπηδήσας (springing up) is another graphic touch, contrasting the man's purposeful activity now with his previous pathetic 'sitting by the roadside'.

51-52 For the compressed syntax of τί σοι θέλεις ποιήσω; cf. v. 36. For Ῥαββουνί cf. Ῥαββί in 9:5; 11:21; 14:45; but in each of those cases the speaker is a disciple. The 'privileged' status which Mark has given to Bartimaeus allows him not only to call on Jesus as υἱὲ Δαυίδ but now also allows him to address him already as we might expect a disciple to do. There seems no difference in effect between Ῥαββί and the 'heightened form' (BAGD) Ῥαββουνί. The request is expressed simply and boldly; the aorist subjunctive ἀναβλέψω looks for an instantaneous and complete recovery of sight (as in fact happens in v. 52), rather than the more protracted process we have seen in 8:23-25. Jesus' reply uses terms already familiar from other healing stories; for ὕπαγε cf. 1:44; 2:11;

---

55. J. Marcus, *Way*, 138 n. 31.

56. The threefold repetition of φωνέω in v. 49 suggests to some (C. D. Marshall, *Faith*, 125, 141; J. F. Williams, *Followers*, 156) that Mark is presenting this as a 'call story' like those of 1:16-20 and 2:14, but the absence of φωνέω from those stories does not encourage us to find an echo here.

57. *Pace* C. D. Marshall (see below, p. 425 n. 59). J. F. Williams, *Followers*, 156-57, lists a number of suggested implications and concludes that 'Bartimaeus left behind what he possessed in order to be with Jesus, so that the beggar does what the rich man refused to do', thus promoting his view of this as a 'call story'. Gnilka, 2.110, compares 2 Ki. 7:15 for the discarding of clothes when in a hurry. A variant in 565 and syr[s] has ἐπιβαλών, a more decorous action when going to meet an important person, but less vivid.

5:19, 34; 7:29, and for the formula ἡ πίστις σου σέσωκέν σε cf. 5:34; Lk. 7:50; 17:19. In 5:19 ὕπαγε marked a refusal to allow the healed person to become a disciple, but in other cases it is simply a recognition that the person is now cured and may go, so that there is no need to see a conflict here between ὕπαγε and Bartimaeus's deciding to follow Jesus. For the centrality of faith in healing see on 5:34.

ἠκολούθει αὐτῷ ἐν τῇ ὁδῷ occupies such a prominent place at the end of the pericope and of the whole section of the gospel which leads up to the arrival in Jerusalem that it seems clear that Mark intended more than a mere circumstantial note.[58] The two terms ἀκολουθέω and ἡ ὁδός both speak of discipleship,[59] and the prominence of the latter phrase in Act Two ensures that its occurrence at the end of that Act reminds us of this central theme. Bartimaeus, now set free from his blindness, represents all those who have found enlightenment and follow the Master. So as the pilgrim group sets off again up the Jerusalem road, with one additional member, the reader is prepared to witness the coming of the Son of David to 'his' city, and challenged to join him on the road.

---

58. See J. F. Williams, *Followers*, 160-63, though Williams also stresses that while Bartimaeus is presented as 'an exemplary follower' he remains separate from the disciples, thus representing the wider category of followers drawn from the crowd whom Jesus has invited in 8:34 to join him.

59. The same implication has been found in the threefold use of φωνέω in v. 49 (see note ad loc.) and in Bartimaeus's discarding of his cloak (his only possession) in v. 50 (so C. D. Marshall, *Faith*, 141-42), but we have noted above that ἀποβαλὼν τὸ ἱμάτιον needs no symbolic explanation in context.

ACT THREE: JERUSALEM (11:1–16:8)

The geographical structure of Mark's story now brings Jesus for the first time to Jerusalem, to an area which for a Galilean was essentially foreign, and where Galileans could expect at best to be tolerated as fellow Jews rather than welcomed as fellow citizens. Explicit mentions of Jerusalem in the Galilean phase of Mark's story are limited to two accounts of scribes from Jerusalem arriving in Galilee with hostile intent (3:22; 7:1), and even in Act Two, while the city has been clearly indicated by the mention of the members of the Sanhedrin in 8:31, its name has occurred only in 10:32, 33 as the journey nears its end. It has been portrayed as a place to be afraid of, the place where Israel's Messiah will be rejected by the leaders of Israel and will be killed, and the strong portrayal in 10:32 of the amazement and fear of Jesus' followers as they approach the city has left the reader in no doubt of what is to be expected. Now as Act Three begins the pilgrim group makes its way up the last stage of the journey from Jericho towards the city.

With the geographical movement comes a corresponding change in the nature of Jesus' activity. Private teaching gives way to public confrontation, and the miracles which have been so central to Jesus' popular appeal in the north virtually disappear. Even on the way southward, apart from the two symbolic healings of blind men which frame Act Two, only one miracle of deliverance has been recorded (9:14-29). That phase has now been left behind, and in the whole of Act Three the only miraculous action recorded is the strongly negative 'sign' of the withering of the fig tree (11:12-14, 20-21). 'No healing miracles occur during the days in Jerusalem, for the faith upon which such miracles depend is absent in those people now surrounding Jesus.'[1]

But while Mark's portrayal of the city in Acts One and Two has been consistently negative, there is another aspect to Jerusalem. It remains the city of David, the chosen capital of the nation which God has chosen to be a light to the nations, and to which even a Galilean Jew belongs. It is the site of the temple, the visible focus of the worship of Israel's God. That is why, if Peter's declaration in 8:29 was correct, Jesus could not stay in Galilee. The Messiah must come to 'his' capital and present himself to his people. And he comes with a significant boost to his credibility, in that he has been hailed as 'Son of David'

---

1. M. A. Tolbert, *Sowing*, 231.

at Jericho not by one of his own Galilean followers but by a Judaean (albeit one of no social standing) in the hearing of a large crowd. Whatever may be the expectations of the chief priests, the scribes, and the elders, there is ground to hope that among the ordinary people of Jerusalem Jesus may find a response to his mission.

The first part of Act Three (chs. 11–12) will trace the interweaving of these two subplots, the official hostility of the authorities and the response of the people. In these chapters both Jesus and the religious authorities issue challenges and manoeuvre for position, while the crowd remains an interested onlooker, impressed by Jesus but not yet committed like his disciples. But in the end the crowd is left largely to one side, as the religious authorities make their move in chapter 14. From that point on, though there will be a brief but significant crowd scene before the governor's palace in 15:6-15, the initiative lies with the chief priests, and the fulfilment of Jesus' passion predictions unfolds with a sense of inevitability, culminating in the cross. The passion predictions did not end with the cross, however, but added a resurrection after three days, and with tantalising brevity Mark will close his story with the fulfilment also of that clause, and a pregnant pointer to a return to Galilee where it all began.

There are thus two clear phases in the story of Act Three, first the period of public confrontation in Jerusalem (chs. 11–12), then the passion narrative and resurrection account (chs. 14–16). Between these two phases comes a lengthy discourse which serves, like the parable discourse in the middle of Act One, to give the reader an opportunity to pause and think about the significance of what is being narrated. Focused on Jesus' prediction of the destruction of the temple, that discourse will invite us to think about the end of the old order and to recognise the ultimate authority of the Son of Man. Thus when in chapters 14–15 we see Jesus as the apparently helpless victim, the loser in a local power struggle, chapter 13 reminds us to set these events against the broader canvas of God's purpose for Israel. Within that broader perspective Jesus is not victim but victor, and the ringing declaration and challenge of 14:62 will set the record straight. So when eventually we find the executed Jesus alive again and summoning his disciples to meet him in Galilee, the whole gospel, for all the mystery of its 'unsatisfying' ending, comes full circle, and the opening announcement of the coming of God's kingship remains on course.

THROWING DOWN THE GAUNTLET (11:1-25)

Jesus' arrival in Jerusalem, for the first and only time in Mark's narrative, and at the end of a lengthy account of the journey from the north, marks a climactic moment in the story. In the period leading up to the Passover festival, when large numbers of other pilgrims would have been making their way into the city, it might have been possible for Jesus and his disciples to arrive quite inconspicuously if they had so wished. Instead, by means of two dramatic actions

427

(the royal procession outside the city walls and the demonstration in the temple) Jesus makes sure that his arrival is noticed. Both actions claim a unique status and authority for Jesus, and neither is calculated to win the goodwill of the religious authorities; a direct challenge to Jesus' credentials will quickly follow (11:27-33). In introducing his third act in this way, Mark allows his readers no doubt that this is the beginning of a decisive confrontation, in which neither side will be in a mood to compromise.

The procession towards Jerusalem and the attack on the temple traders are blatantly public acts which effectively throw down the gauntlet to the Jerusalem authorities and force them to respond. Mark also interweaves with the second of these events a curious incident, the withering of the fig tree, which takes place away from the crowd and the authorities, but which conveys in pictorial form an equally vehement repudiation of the status quo. For those who can appreciate its symbolism, it points forward to the radical teaching of chapter 13 on the terminal decline and replacement of the Jerusalem régime, focused in the failure and the coming dissolution of the temple worship. The drastic implications of Jesus' public actions are thus reinforced for Mark's readers by this more private gesture, and the whole complex of three symbolic actions sets the scene for the bitter and ultimately fatal conflict which will follow.

The Royal Procession (11:1-10)

TEXTUAL NOTE

3. The variety of readings is partly due to uncertainty whether the subject of ἀποστέλ(λ)ει is (1) ὁ Κύριος (understood as Jesus) or (2) the τις of the preceding clause. The presence of πάλιν, if original, would require (1), whereas the Matthew parallel supports (2). The future ἀποστελεῖ is on either construction the easier reading since the sense is clearly future, and is also more likely to be a correction to agree with the more probable reading in Matthew. In a church where Jesus was routinely known as ὁ Κύριος it is more likely that πάλιν would be added to the text to support reading (1) than that it would drop out. The most likely original reading therefore is that of A C² etc., αὐτὸν ἀποστέλλει (without πάλιν). The variations in word order may be due to the more awkward syntax created by the introduction of πάλιν.

Nowhere else in the gospels do we read of Jesus riding. The special attention which is given in this pericope to the provision of a mount and the way Jesus, once mounted, becomes the centre of attention for more than just his immediate disciples indicate that this was a deliberate departure from his normal practice of travelling by foot. At Passover season[2] this may have been a particularly con-

---

2. Mark's narrative sequence demands that he understood this incident to have happened a few days before Passover (14:1, 12). The suggestion (most famously by T. W. Manson, *BJRL* 33 [1951] 271-82; further bibliography in B. A. Mastin, *NTS* 16 [1969/70] 76-82) that Jesus' 'trium-

spicuous decision, since there is some evidence that it was expected that Passover pilgrims who were physically able to do so should walk into the city.[3] If, then, Jesus chose, on this one occasion in his public life, to ride into the city, he was aiming to be noticed. The great outburst of praise and of nationalistic sentiment which Mark records in vv. 8-10 did not take him by surprise, and indeed he could be said to have engineered it, with his own disciples very likely acting as cheerleaders.[4]

The royal and nationalistic tenor of v. 10 suggests also that Mark presupposes what Matthew and John make explicit, that the choice of a donkey as Jesus' means of transport was intended, and was understood by the crowd, to be a deliberate allusion to Zechariah's prophecy of the king who comes into Jerusalem riding on a donkey (Zc. 9:9-10). This is a clearly messianic passage in Zechariah, and the shouts of the crowd about the coming kingdom of David take it as such. Even without an explicit quotation of the Zechariah text, it can hardly be doubted that Mark so understood Jesus' intention. Further messianic associations likely to be evoked by the use of a donkey are the oracle of Judah in Gn. 49:10-11, and perhaps the mule which Solomon rode to his enthronement in 1 Ki. 1:38-40.[5]

Even though no words of Jesus on the subject are recorded, this, following so closely on Bartimaeus' unchecked use of υἱὲ Δαυίδ, amounts to a clear messianic declaration by Jesus, and the end of any secrecy on the subject except in the purely formal sense that the declaration is by actions (and the unrebuked words of the crowd) rather than by explicit words of Jesus. Such words will follow in 14:62, but by then they should occasion no surprise to those who have read the implications of all that Jesus has done and said since his arrival at Jerusalem, beginning with this blatant messianic self-advertisement.[6]

In the narrative context it is important to note the identity of the crowd who shout Hosanna. We have noted in the previous pericope the deliberate

---

phal entry' was originally set at the Feast of Tabernacles is supported from John's mention of palm branches (recalling the *lûlab* of Tabernacles celebrations) and the cries of Hosanna, which according to *m. Suk.* 4:5 were used at that festival, accompanied by the waving of the *lûlab* (*m. Suk.* 3:9). The 'branches' in Mark, however, are not the *lûlab,* but rather vegetation spread on the road (see on v. 8); and Hosanna was not used *only* at Tabernacles. Psalm 118 from which it originated and which provides the greeting of v. 9 was not specifically a Tabernacles psalm, but the last of the Hallel psalms which were sung at all the main festivals, especially at Passover as the greatest of the annual pilgrimages.

3. *M. Ḥag.* 1:1 exempts from the OT requirement for festival pilgrimage 'one who cannot go up [to Jerusalem] on his feet'. The point is emphasised by A. E. Harvey, *Jesus,* 121.

4. Myers, 294, compares the event with 'carefully choreographed street theater' with a political aim.

5. The proclamation of Jehu as king in 2 Ki. 9:13 is sometimes cited as a parallel, but there there is no donkey and the setting is not in Jerusalem. The use of cloaks as a 'red carpet' is the only significant link, and this appears to be more a matter of cultural similarity than of direct echo.

6. For the wider background of royal procession, and especially the coronation procession of Solomon, 'son of David', in 1 Ki. 1:32-40, see D. R. Catchpole in E. Bammel and C. F. D. Moule (ed.), *Politics,* 319-21.

mention of an ὄχλος ἱκανός accompanying Jesus and his disciples as they leave Jericho for Jerusalem (see also on 15:40-41), and we must assume that the same crowd are now completing the journey together. The location is still outside Jerusalem (v. 1), and Jesus will not in fact enter the city until v. 11. The traditional description of this scene as the 'Triumphal *Entry*' is therefore inaccurate: it describes Jesus' approach to the city, not his entry. The shouting crowd are therefore the pilgrim group to whom we have already been introduced, and Mark puts their identity beyond doubt by using the phrase οἱ προάγοντες καὶ οἱ ἀκολουθοῦντες (v. 9). This is not yet, then, the Jerusalem crowd, but the pilgrims, probably mostly like Jesus Galileans, who are accompanying him and his disciples to the city for the festival. (See on 15:40-41 for some comments on the composition of this crowd.) They are already predisposed, after the event at Jericho, to favour Jesus and to echo Bartimaeus' evaluation of him as υἱὸς Δαυίδ. Those who react with enthusiasm to the arrival of the Galilean Messiah are thus Jesus' Galilean supporters rather than the potentially more sceptical Jerusalem crowd whom he has not yet encountered. Matthew adds a note to make this contrast explicit in 21:10-11, but even in Mark the point is clear. There is no warrant here for the preacher's favourite comment on the fickleness of a crowd which could shout 'Hosanna' one day and 'Crucify him' a few days later. They are not the same crowd. The Galilean pilgrims shouted 'Hosanna' as they approached the city; the Jerusalem crowd shouted, 'Crucify him'.

1 The subject of ἐγγίζουσιν is left to be supplied from the context. After the role of the crowd in the previous pericope, and with an even more prominent role for the crowd in this pericope, we should assume that 'they' are not only Jesus and his disciples, but also the accompanying ὄχλος ἱκανός of 10:46. The final stage of the journey, begun in 10:46, now approaches its end. The double εἰς is a little awkward: the destination Ἱεροσόλυμα is mentioned first, then the point in its outskirts which has been reached when this incident begins. That point is indicated by the pair of names Βηθφαγὴ καὶ Βηθανία treated as a single unit. Bethany is mentioned several times in the gospels, a village some two miles out of Jerusalem on the Jericho road, where Jesus and his disciples would spend the night during the coming week (vv. 11-12; 14:3). Bethphage is presumably a smaller hamlet associated with Bethany. Its traditional site is just before the crest of the hill on the way from Bethany to Jerusalem; it is mentioned in the Talmud as a suburb outside the walls of Jerusalem. Both places were therefore on the slopes of the Ὄρος τῶν Ἐλαιῶν, so that if πρός has its normal sense of motion towards, it might indicate that in reaching Bethphage and Bethany they were coming to (the crest of) the Mount of Olives; but πρός may indicate proximity rather than motion towards (cf. 2:2; 4:1b; 6:3; 9:19a; 11:4). This apparently unnecessary mention of the Mount of Olives may arise from Mark's awareness of its messianic connotations (Zc. 14:4; cf. Ezk. 11:23; 43:1-5).

2 We do not know whether the κώμη κατέναντι ὑμῶν was Bethphage, Bethany, or some other neighbouring settlement. The commission of the two disciples is given with such precision and certainty of what they would find that Mark must intend us to think either of Jesus' supernatural knowledge or of a carefully prepared plan. Since this is, from Mark's narrative point of view, new territory for Jesus, the presence of supporters just outside Jerusalem with whom he could have made such an arrangement is surprising (though from the historical point of view this is no problem, since the Fourth Gospel gives clear witness to Jesus' earlier connections in the Bethany area, and while Lk. 10:38-42 is not explicitly located in Bethany there seems no reason to doubt that the same family was involved). Did Mark perhaps take to be supernatural knowledge what was in fact the result of a well-laid plan, using contacts of which Mark was unaware? The ready response of the bystanders in v. 6 after the 'password' has been spoken might suggest as much.

Interesting light on the background for this story comes from the proposal of J. D. M. Derrett[7] that Jesus was here exercising the right of a king (or even sometimes of a rabbi) to requisition an animal, even if not all the details of Derrett's case are equally compelling. The animal that is requisitioned is described by Mark and Luke only as a πῶλος. Matthew and John call it specifically an ὄνος or ὀνάριον, and both quote Zc. 9:9 which, in their Greek versions, speaks of a πῶλος ὄνου (John) or an ὄνος . . . πῶλος υἱὸς ὑποζυγίου (Matthew). But the LXX of that passage does not have ὄνος. W. Bauer argued that in Greek literature where no species is mentioned in the context πῶλος must mean a young *horse*,[8] but his conclusion does not hold for specifically Egyptian and Palestinian literature;[9] five of the six uses of πῶλος in the LXX translate Hebrew *'ayir* ('male ass'), usually without any neighbouring use of ὄνος to define it. In the Hebrew of Zc. 9:9 the animal is explicitly a donkey, but the LXX has only the terms ὑποζύγιον and πῶλον νέον. Mark's πῶλος together with the statement that no one had yet ridden on it is therefore a clearer echo of LXX Zc. 9:9 — πῶλον νέον — than if he had specified that it was a donkey. His readers, aware of the gospel tradition, would have no difficulty in recognising the traditional donkey in Mark's πῶλος. The note that the πῶλος had not been ridden not only reflects the LXX νέον but also echoes the special value placed in the OT on a hitherto unused animal for religious purposes (Nu. 19:2; Dt. 21:3; 1 Sa. 6:7), and perhaps, too, the convention that no one else may ride the king's mount (*m. Sanh.* 2:5). The specific mention that the donkey was tied up (repeated in v. 4) might trigger in the mind of a well-informed reader an echo of the messianic text Gn. 49:10-11, where the coming ruler is described as tying his donkey's colt to a vine.[10]

3 It makes no difference whether τί; is read as interrogative adverb ('Why are you doing this?') or pronoun ('What is this that you are doing?'); the

7. J. D. M. Derrett, *NovT* 13 (1971) 241-58.

8. See BAGD, 731b, summarising Bauer's article in *JBL* 72 (1953) 220-29.

9. See H.-W. Kuhn, *ZNW* 50 (1959) 82-91; O. Michel, *NTS* 6 (1959) 81-82.

10. So especially J. Blenkinsopp, *JBL* 80 (1961) 55-64; F. J. Matera, *Kingship,* 71-72; also Lane, 395-96; Pesch, 2.179.

resumption of this clause in v. 5 favours the latter. The sight of strangers untying a donkey in the village street would certainly provoke a protest, and the
cryptic answer which Jesus provides would not by itself persuade any but the
very gullible. It is much more likely that this was a prearranged 'password' than
that ὁ κύριος αὐτοῦ χρείαν ἔχει was intended to be a convincing explanation to
anyone not already 'in the know'. The κύριος has been variously interpreted as
God ('it is needed on divine service'), Jesus (here uniquely in Mark described
as ὁ κύριος), or the donkey's owner (assumed to be with Jesus on the journey).[11]
αὐτοῦ must be construed with χρείαν ἔχει (otherwise the sentence would mean
simply and irrelevantly 'Its owner is in need'), leaving ὁ κύριος as a title by itself, and it is unlikely in a Jewish context that this could be taken without further specification to mean 'its owner' or even 'the boss', meaning the owner of
the donkey. We have noted on 5:19 that it is improbable that Mark would use ὁ
κύριος in dialogue to refer to Jesus (as opposed to the vocative κύριε). Even
Luke, who unlike Mark uses the title editorially for Jesus, does not use it in dialogue until after the resurrection (24:34) unless it is so understood in his parallel to this passage. It is not impossible that this usage, which became natural to
Christians after the resurrection, was coined by Jesus for the purpose of this
password, but the formula is much more likely to reflect the regular Jewish use
of the phrase as a divine title. In that case the password asserts that the donkey
is needed for God's service, a bold claim by Jesus for the significance of his
own arrival in Jerusalem, but one which is no surprise to those who have
learned from Mark that Jesus is bringing in God's kingdom.

The uncertainty over who is the subject of ἀποστέλλει (see Textual
Note) is resolved if we accept that ὁ κύριος is God. In that case the password
ends at ἔχει, and the following clause (without πάλιν; see Textual Note) is, as
in Matthew, Jesus' prediction of the questioner's response to it: 'he will immediately send it here' (ὧδε being the place from which Jesus is sending the
disciples on their errand). The same sequence of password and response will
recur at v. 6, confirming that that was Mark's intention here too. The reading
of these words as an extension of the password (with ὁ κύριος understood to
be the subject of ἀποστέλλει), giving the promise that Jesus would return the
donkey straight after use, would be a natural misreading for Christians familiar with ὁ κύριος as a title of Jesus; the addition of πάλιν would follow. The
present tense of ἀποστέλλει (see Textual Note) is surprising (on either interpretation), but Mark has already used present tenses for predictions of future
events in 9:12, 31.

4-7 The scenario envisaged in Jesus' instructions in vv. 2-3 is now narrated with no significant alteration but with some typically Marcan additional

---

11. Gundry's view (following Derrett) that ὁ κύριος is Jesus, deliberately presenting himself
as the donkey's 'master', 'exercising a lordly prerogative by requisitioning the colt', seems unnecessarily abstruse. R. G. Bratcher, *ExpTim* 64 (1952/3) 93, thinks Jesus really was the owner, having
acquired the donkey in preparation for his arrival.

detail: the position of the donkey πρὸς θύραν ἔξω ἐπὶ τοῦ ἀμφόδου,[12] the specification of the source of the question as τινες τῶν ἐκεῖ ἑστηκότων, and the filling out of the question itself with λύοντες τὸν πῶλον for τοῦτο. The donkey being hitherto unridden and not prepared for use had no saddle cloths, and so the two disciples (there is no sign of a change of subject) used their own outer garments.

8 While the use of the disciples' clothes as saddle cloths met a normal need for riding, the actions of the wider group (πολλοί and ἄλλοι together involve the whole crowd) are unnecessary and extravagant. For clothes laid on the road as a 'red carpet' for a dignitary cf. 2 Ki. 9:13. The στιβάδες are simply unspecified vegetation, the word being used classically for straw, rushes, leaves, and other materials used for bedding (it is John who makes them βαΐα τῶν φοινίκων, palm branches), and provide further festive floor covering.[13] Since there is no main verb in the second clause we must assume that the vegetation, once cut, was (as Matthew says explicitly) spread on the road like the clothes, rather than held in the hand like the *lûlab* (wands made of palm, myrtle, and willow) which formed part of the ceremonial at the Feast of Tabernacles (2 Macc. 10:7; *m. Suk.* 3–4).[14]

9-10 The shouts which interpret the celebratory actions are attributed to οἱ προάγοντες καὶ οἱ ἀκολουθοῦντες, the members of the crowd which has accompanied Jesus from Jericho (see the introductory comments on this pericope). The balancing structure of the shouts based on Ps. 118:25-26

A Ὡσαννά

   B Εὐλογημένος ὁ ἐρχόμενος . . .

   B Εὐλογημένη ἡ ἐρχομένη . . .

A Ὡσαννά . . .

perhaps derives from the antiphonal chanting of that Hallel psalm. Ὡσαννά represents the 'save us now' (Hebrew *hôšî'â-nā')*[15] of Ps. 118:25, the last of the Hallel psalms recited at all major festivals in Jerusalem. As an exclamation in a pilgrimage psalm Hosanna apparently passed into more general use as a cultic

---

12. The mention of the street seems strangely redundant, and Justin (*Apol.* 1.32.6) and Clement of Alexandria (*Paed.* 1.5.15) apparently read ἀμπέλου for ἀμφόδου, thus producing an echo of Gn. 49:11 (see above on v. 2). There is, however, no MS evidence for this reading.

13. This seems more probable than Mann's proposal (435-36, following A. E. Harvey, *Jesus,* 125) that 'This was apparently a purely utilitarian gesture, since the thin mattresses *(sic)* would help the donkey on the steep slope'.

14. Lv. 23:40 does not specify whether the branches were used in this way or for building the shelters. Cf. 1 Macc. 13:51; Rev. 7:9 for use of palm branches for celebration irrespective of Tabernacles.

15. Gundry, 630, suggests that Ὡσαννά deliberately echoes the Hebrew form of Jesus' name, *Y^ehôšûa'*. Mark's Greek text does not allow his readers to detect such an echo, and in view of the known use of Hosanna and its appropriateness at festival time (see next note) this seems an unnecessary subtlety.

shout of praise, like Hallelujah, with the element of entreaty largely forgotten;[16] see especially Mt. 21:9, 15 where the following dative τῷ υἱῷ Δαυίδ shows it to be an ascription of praise. The addition of ἐν τοῖς ὑψίστοις in v. 10 points to the same usage here, the phrase ἐν τοῖς ὑψίστοις acting as a reverential periphrasis for the name of God (cf. Lk. 2:14).[17]

The clause which follows the first ὡσαννά is taken from the verse which immediately follows its occurence in Ps. 118. In the psalm εὐλογημένος ὁ ἐρχόμενος ἐν ὀνόματι κυρίου is a greeting addressed to an individual arriving at the temple, followed by a general blessing to the crowd, 'We bless you [plural] from the house of the Lord'. While the festival context made this psalm generally appropriate to express the crowd's religious enthusiasm, the singular form of this particular greeting made it specially appropriate for greeting Jesus, the individual rider at the centre of the demonstration. The phrase ὁ ἐρχόμενος ἐν ὀνόματι κυρίου was not in its original context specifically messianic,[18] and neither does ὁ ἐρχόμενος (with or without ἐν ὀνόματι κυρίου) seem to have been in use subsequently as a messianic title. But the person addressed in the singular in v. 26 of the psalm may well have been the king celebrating a national victory, so that the formula was well suited to express the crowd's perception (on the basis of Zc. 9:9-10) of the royal and victorious arrival of Jesus in Jerusalem.

The greeting is expanded in v. 10 with words no longer drawn from Ps. 118. The first three words are repeated (with the necessary gender change), but now in place of a person it is a kingdom whose arrival is greeted. The concept of a kingdom 'coming' is familiar from 1:15 and 9:1, but that was the kingdom of God announced by Jesus. The kingdom of David has an altogether more political and nationalistic ring. The title υἱὸς Δαυίδ which the crowd heard at Jericho has been remembered, and it is hardly surprising if now the king riding into the city of David is expected to reestablish Israel's national sovereignty, the βασιλεία τοῦ πατρὸς ἡμῶν Δαυίδ.[19] In deliberately enacting Zc. 9:9-10 Jesus can have expected no less; David is not mentioned at that point in Zechariah (but see 12:7–13:1), but the king riding in triumph into Jerusalem as 'your king' is clearly modelled on David.[20] It may be, as we

16. M. Suk. 4:5 says that hôšî'â-nā' was ritually repeated during the procession round the altar at Tabernacles, when the lûlab was also held. In that context the term (in its Hebrew form) probably retained its use as a prayer. 'Hosanna' as a shout of praise was already fixed in Christian liturgical use by the time of the Didache (10:6, ὡσαννὰ τῷ θεῷ Δαυίδ). Mann, 436, offers as modern parallels 'Sieg Heil!' and baseball chants.

17. By translating the phrase back into Hebrew and then altering one consonant of the putative Hebrew, Belo produces an alternative 'translation': 'Save us from the Roman'.

18. The Targum, which heavily rewrites the psalm in a messianic and specifically Davidic direction, attributes these words to 'the builders' (cf. v. 22), presumably speaking of David, since the following words, 'They will bless you from the sanctuary of the LORD', are attributed to David, apparently replying to the builders.

19. Jews commonly used 'father' of the patriarchs rather than of David, but cf. Acts 4:25.

20. For the echoes in Zc. 9:9-10 of David's return after Absalom's rebellion see D. R. Jones, VT 12 (1962) 256-58.

shall see at 12:35-37, that Jesus would wish to challenge a *purely* Davidic understanding of his royal claim, but he could not claim that the crowd's Davidic interpretation of his ride into the city was unjustified, however limited their perception of its significance.[21]

This first dramatic public gesture, therefore, has placed the Galilean preacher firmly in contention for the title 'King of the Jews', and that title will be at the centre of his Roman trial (15:2, 9, 12, 18, 26, 32). For the Jewish leaders it would not have the same connotations as for the Roman governor, and 'Son of David' had an honourable place in their messianic ideology. But that does not mean that they would be pleased to hear it shouted outside the walls of Jerusalem by an excited Galilean crowd escorting a Galilean pretender, particularly one whose teaching and activity in Galilee have already given cause for scribal concern.[22]

The Barren Temple and the Withered Tree (11:11-25)

TEXTUAL NOTES

19. Variation between singular (Jesus) and plural (Jesus and disciples) in verbs of motion linking pericopes has been a feature both of Marcan style and of the MSS tradition. Here both readings are strongly supported, but the plural seems the more natural since a plural follows in v. 20; the singular would then be due to the fact that in vv. 15-19 the focus has been on Jesus alone.

22. The addition of εἰ looks like a correction to ease a rather abrupt imperative by echoing the more familiar construction of Mt. 21:21; Lk. 17:6, without recognising that the opening clause of the long sentence thus created becomes redundant before the later condition of faith (see further S. E. Dowd, *Prayer,* 59).

24. The aorist ἐλάβετε is the bolder and more striking expression, and λαμβάνετε looks like a softening correction, assimilating the tense to the preceding γίνεται. λήμψεσθε is even less demanding, and may also have been introduced from the different construction in Mt. 21:22.

25. Verse 25 has shifted the focus by introducing a further condition of effective prayer, and one which conveys in different words the thought of Mt. 6:14. The MSS which have added v. 26 supplement v. 25 with a more exact echo of the converse statement in Mt 6:15 (with considerable variations reflecting its catechetical use). In view of the obvious usefulness of this additional verse in churches, its absence from a wide range of witnesses is convincing.

21. For current Davidic hopes see, in addition to *Pss. Sol.* 17, the Palestinian version of the fourteenth of the Eighteen Benedictions used in the synagogue (text in Schürer, 2.460-61), which looks for 'the kingship of the house of David, thy righteous Messiah' and addresses God as 'Lord, God of David, who buildest Jerusalem'.

22. On the historical question why, if events took place as Mark records, the Jewish and Roman authorities took no immediate action to counteract this popular demonstration, see the sensible comments of Gundry, 632.

The title given to this section, 'The Barren Temple and the Withered Tree', is borrowed from the important study by W. R. Telford.[23] It recognises the significance of Mark's distinctive way of interweaving the two stories, which Mt. 21:12-22 simply places side by side. This is one of the more elaborate examples of Mark's tendency to weave separate incidents together by shifting the spotlight to and fro between two narrative scenes, so as to enable the reader to interpret each incident in the light of the other. The resultant enhancement of both episodes is impressive, and in particular a clear theological raison d'être is provided for the otherwise pointless and embarrassing account of the cursing of the fig tree.

The narrative sequence may be set out as follows:

A First visit to the *temple* (11:11)
   B Cursing of the *fig tree* (11:12-14)
A Jesus takes action in the *temple* (11:15-19)
   B The *fig tree* is found to be dead (11:20-25)
A Jesus returns to the *temple* (11:27),

where his authority will be challenged and the controversy with the chief priests, the scribes, and the elders will begin; the temple remains the scene of that controversy until 12:44, to be followed by Jesus' decisive abandonment of the temple and prophecy of its destruction in 13:1-2.

To recognise this structure offers an answer to the puzzlement of some commentators over the function of Mark's unique v. 11, often described as an anticlimax after the royal procession, in that when Jesus eventually reaches the temple, the heart of 'his' city, nothing happens: Jesus simply 'looks at the temple as a tourist might and then leaves' (Schweizer, 227). But his 'looking around' is not without purpose, and he leaves, in Mark's telling of the story, in order to return and take decisive action the next day. In the meantime an incident will occur which gives to the reader (and to the disciples?) some food for thought on what that action is all about.

While it is appropriate, therefore, to treat vv. 11-25 as a single unit, it will nonetheless be convenient to make some comment on each of the two incidents separately before we turn to more detailed notes.

1. The Temple Incident

The temple was not only the heart of Israel's religious life but also the symbol of its national identity. The rededication and purification of the temple in 164 B.C. after Antiochus Epiphanes had defiled it with the worship and altar of Zeus and the restoration of temple worship were the high points of the Maccabean

---

23. W. R. Telford, *Temple.*

victory, and were commemorated annually thereafter in the Feast of Dedication in December. The patriotic as well as religious symbolism of the temple was thus enormous, and the magnificence of Herod's rebuilding matched its symbolic significance.

It is likely that among the many factors leading to Jesus' death the one which most united all elements of the Jewish people against him was that he was perceived (like another Jesus a generation later; Josephus, *War* 6.300-305) as an opponent of the temple.[24] This is a theme which will develop through the rest of Mark's story,[25] reaching its climax in the bystanders' jibe at Jesus on the cross in 15:29-30, followed by the tearing of the temple curtain in 15:38. This first incident in the temple might seem on the surface to be in favour of the temple rather than against it, protecting it from misuse and restoring it to its intended role as a 'house of prayer for all nations'. But with hindsight it could be seen (as Mark records the temple authorities as recognising already in v. 18) as the beginning of an increasingly explicit campaign against what the temple now stood for, the first demonstration of a judgment which must ultimately lead to the total dissolution of the building itself.[26] Mark, by associating Jesus' action with the cursing of the fig tree, ensures that his readers see it in this wider and more ominous perspective.

Mark records the event as the individual action of Jesus, unlike the involvement of the crowd in the royal procession. His attack on the traders and money changers, who were there in the Court of the Gentiles with the permission of the temple authorities and who provided a convenient and probably essential service to worshippers visiting the temple from outside Jerusalem, was not simply (if it was at all) a protest against exploitation by unscrupulous traders. It extended also to their customers (τοὺς ἀγοράζοντας) and even to anyone who was carrying things through the area. It was a repudiation of the way the temple's affairs were being conducted (and therefore of those under whose authority this took place), not simply an attempt to correct abuse of the system.[27] What Antiochus had done by blatant idolatry, the Jewish leaders themselves have allowed to happen under the pressure of commercial interests. Temple worship has lost its true focus, and must again be purified.[28]

As apparently a one-man demonstration it is unlikely to have had any

24. This point is developed prominently by E. P. Sanders, *Jesus,* especially pp. 61-90, 301-5.

25. See D. Juel, *Messiah,* 127-39, for a useful survey of 'the temple theme in Mark'.

26. Even within this pericope alone H. C. Waetjen, *Reordering,* 182, finds sufficient evidence for the verdict, 'Jesus is not "cleansing the temple". As "the one who comes in the name of the Lord," he is closing it down.' He speaks of Jesus' action as symbolising 'the negation of this central systemic structure of Judaism', which 'marks the termination of its power and privilege but especially its oppression and dispossession of the Jewish masses' (183).

27. See C. A. Evans, *CBQ* 51 (1989) 257-63, for evidence of widespread criticism of the temple establishment and for corruption among the high-priestly families.

28. N. Q. Hamilton, *JBL* 83 (1964) 365-72, provides interesting information on the role of the temple as the national 'bank' and the focus of economic activity.

long-term practical effect, and we may well assume that the tables were back in place the next day.[29] But it has marked Jesus out as more than an idealistic teacher. He is a radical reformer, and he has thrown down the gauntlet to the temple authorities in a way they cannot ignore, and to which they will respond in vv. 27-28 by questioning his authority.

The ride into the city has already raised this question. In presenting himself as Jerusalem's messianic 'king', Jesus has in effect already placed himself above the Sanhedrin as the ultimate authority in the holy city. Among the actions expected of the Messiah was the purification of the temple's worship (Ezk. 37:26-28; *Pss. Sol.* 17:30-32)[30] and even the replacement of the temple itself (following Ezekiel's vision of the new eschatological temple, Ezk. 40-48, and drawing on Zc. 6:12-13; cf. Tob. 14:5; *Jub.* 1:27-29; *1 Enoch* 1:28-29).[31] In addition, other OT texts spoke of 'the Lord' visiting his temple and purifying its worship (Mal. 3:1-4), and predicted that in the eschatological holiness of Jerusalem 'There shall no longer be traders in the house of the LORD' (Zc. 14:21). None of these texts is directly alluded to in Mark's wording, but they would be likely to occur to an observer with a reasonable knowledge of the OT and of current messianic expectation. Indeed, it would not be inappropriate to describe Jesus' action as deliberately re-enacting Zc. 14:21.[32] Following on the royal procession to the city, this action looks like a further deliberate claim to messianic authority.[33] Seen in that light, this was not an attempt at short-term reform of the system but a symbolic declaration of eschatological judgment.[34]

---

29. See, e.g., A. E. Harvey, *Jesus* 129-31, for a good example of the common view that what Jesus carried out was merely a symbolic gesture, along the lines of OT 'acted prophecies', rather than a real attempt to change things. D. R. Catchpole, in E. Bammel and C. F. D. Moule (ed.), *Politics,* 332-33, usefully fills out the historical context and the likelihood of official intervention if any large-scale disturbance had taken place.

30. This expectation reflected the historical importance of the restoration/purification of the temple in association with bids for national independence, under Hezekiah, Josiah, and Judas Maccabaeus. C. A. Evans, *CBQ* 51 (1989) 250-56, provides a useful survey of scriptural and later Jewish expectations of temple-cleansing.

31. See the full discussion in E. P. Sanders, *Jesus,* 77-90. For the Qumran theology of the 'new temple', see B. Gärtner, *Temple,* 16-46.

32. 'If "on that day" there was no longer to be "any merchant in the house of the Lord of hosts" (Zech. 14:21), "that day" had come because the Messiah was there' (B. F. Meyer, *Aims,* 200). The relevance of Zc. 14:21 is further explored by C. Roth, *NovT* 4 (1960) 174-81.

33. This aspect of the incident is strongly emphasised by B. F. Meyer, *Aims,* 197-202; cf. B. Gärtner, *Temple,* 105-11.

34. If this understanding of the significance of the event is correct, it supports the general consensus that the incident took place on Jesus' final visit to Jerusalem, rather than at the outset of his ministry where John has placed it. Such a climactic challenge to the temple and its authorities could not have been ignored, leaving Jesus to continue his activity as if nothing had happened. The suggestion, still sometimes met as an attempt to 'harmonise' Mark and John, that it happened twice is about as probable as that the Normandy landings took place both at the beginning and the end of the Second World War.

2. The Fig Tree

The last miraculous action performed by Jesus in Mark's gospel has always been a problem for commentators and preachers.[35] Unlike the other 'nature miracles' (miraculous feedings, calming the storm, and walking on the lake) it is a purely destructive act, which achieves no useful purpose. Even worse, Jesus' curse on the tree appears to be a spontaneous and spiteful reaction to his personal disappointment at finding no figs, and when in addition Mark goes out of his way to tell us that it was in any case not the time of year when figs might be expected, the whole story seems quite discreditable. It reminds one of the vindictive behaviour of the holy child narrated in the second-century *Infancy Gospel of Thomas*.[36] It is hard to imagine why Jesus should have misused his miraculous power in this petty way, and still harder to understand why anyone should record it. It should have been possible to find a more wholesome narrative basis for the lessons on the power of faith which both Matthew and Mark have seen fit to draw from the story.

In view of this embarrassment over the story, it is not surprising that commentators have seized eagerly on the possibility that it not only lends itself to a symbolic interpretation but also was so intended by Jesus, offering an acted parable (comparable to the spoken parable of Lk. 13:6-9) of God's judgment on 'unfruitful' Israel and in particular on its temple. Mark's structuring of this section suggests such an interpretation, as we have seen, and it is supported by the prophetic use of fig trees and their fruit (especially the 'early' or 'first-ripe' figs) to symbolise the people of God and their obedience.[37] See most obviously Je. 8:13; 24:1-10; Ho. 9:10, 16-17; Mi. 7:1, and in the NT Lk. 13:6-9. Mi. 7:1-6 provides a particularly illuminating parallel. Similar symbolic use is found frequently in postbiblical Judaism.[38] This evidence suggests that Mark and his readers would have had no difficulty in recognising the symbolism of the unsuccessful search for figs. Moreover, when the fig tree occurs again later in this gospel in a parabolic use in 13:28, it will again be in connection with the fate of the temple; while the symbolism is not the same as here, it will again focus on the close connection between the fig tree's leaves and the promise of fruit.

The story is told with special emphasis on the leaves: it was the leaves, visible from a distance, which promised fruit, and it was the finding of no fruit *but only leaves* that triggered Jesus' violent reaction. Yet fig leaves appear in advance of the normal fruiting season (which is the point in 13:28). At Passover time in Palestine the leaves are already opening, though not yet thick, but the first fig harvest (the 'early' or 'first-ripe' figs) would not normally be expected

---

35. For a fascinating if rather bewildering survey of interpretations see Telford, *Temple*, chapter 1. Much more briefly, C.-H. Hunzinger, *TDNT*, 7.756-57.

36. *Infancy Gospel of Thomas* 3, 4, 5, 14 (Henn.-Schn., 1.393-97).

37. For a full study of the symbolic use of the fig tree in the OT see Telford, *Temple*, 132-63.

38. Telford, *Temple*, 179-96.

until May/June. At Passover, as Mark rightly comments, it is not the time for figs. Why then did Jesus hope to find fruit on a fig tree in leaf at that time?

One possible explanation (among several proposed over the years) is as follows. As the leaves appear on the tree about Passover time, there are already small green figs forming, known at that stage as *paggîm*. They are not very palatable and certainly not ripe for harvest, but they can be eaten *faute de mieux* (I have tried!), and some have claimed (I am not sure on what evidence) that they are actually preferred to the summer fruit by 'the natives'.[39] It may be then that those were what Jesus was hoping for (Gundry, 636, points out that v. 13 says only τι, not specifically 'figs'), especially if the tree had, as Mark's emphasis suggests, a particularly well-developed show of leaves, which might have encouraged the hope of the fruit being further advanced than normal at that time of year. But there were not even these undeveloped figs, οὐδὲν εἰ μὴ φύλλα. It was an empty show.

For such theories we are in the hands of the horticultural experts, and it may be questioned how far most commentators, for all their technical language, actually understand the ways of figs. I do not claim to do so, and the 'expert evidence' offered by commentators varies so considerably, even to the point of contradiction, that, while the above theory appeals to me, I do not feel able to offer a confident explanation.

The one point on which all seem to be agreed, however, is that Mark has significantly focused the problem by the comment, ὁ γὰρ καιρὸς οὐκ ἦν σύκων.[40] There is, surprisingly, unanimous textual support for this parenthesis: despite various differences in wording, the οὐκ remains constant.[41] Without this clause, if Jesus might reasonably have expected to find ripe figs and was disappointed, his action, even if still unusual, might seem more justified. Hence the attraction of the view that it is the Passover setting that is the problem, and that the incident actually happened in the summer or autumn. We have noted the view that Jesus' arrival in Jerusalem might originally have related to Tabernacles,[42] and if the two stories were originally connected this

39. So A. H. McNeile, *Matthew*, 302. *M. Šebi.* 4:7 speaks of eating young figs out in the field before they are ripe enough to bring into the house.

40. J. N. Birdsall, *ExpTim* 73 (1961/2) 191, noting that Jesus' action is related to Mi. 7:1, suggests that we 'explain the γάρ-clause in v. 13 as a pointer of the Evangelist calling attention to the portion of Scripture which elucidates the event in the gospel history'. Mi. 7:1 certainly describes the situation after fig harvest, but whether a reader could perceive in this clause the equivalent of 'see Micah 7:1' is questionable.

41. K. Romaniuk, *ZNW* 66 (1975) 275-78, attempts to remove the force of the negative by turning the whole clause into a question, 'For was it not the season of figs?' If so, the question with γάρ comes in the wrong place: it should precede, not follow, the clause about not finding anything but leaves. The proposal also assumes an original non-Passover setting for the story; but since Mark clearly does have a Passover setting in mind, it is incredible that he should leave such a misleading question unaltered if he recognised it as a question — and if he did not the proposal offers us no help with understanding *Mark's* text: Passover time is *not* the time for figs.

42. See above, p. 428 n. 2. See further C. W. F. Smith, *JBL* 79 (1960) 315-27.

would offer a time in the autumn when some late figs might not yet have been harvested. Attractive as this suggestion might be from the historical point of view, however, it does not help at all to understand Mark, whose ὁ γὰρ καιρὸς οὐκ ἦν σύκων does not allow us to believe that he so understood the story, and further confirms that in his view the whole complex of events in chapters 11–16 belongs to the Passover week. For Mark, Jesus' frustration *was* horticulturally unreasonable.[43] He tells the story not because it offers a model for reasonable behaviour, but because of its symbolic value. A tree in full leaf at Passover season is making a promise it cannot fulfil; so, too, is Israel. And just as Micah, speaking for God, described his disappointed search (equally unreasonably at the other end of the growing season) for the 'first-ripe fig for which I hunger' (Mi. 7:1), so Jesus on his initial visit to the temple has found all leaves, but no fruit. His summary verdict on the 'braggart' fig tree (Plummer) is a verdict on the failure of God's people and is of a piece with his developing polemic against the 'barren' temple.[44]

The conclusion of the fig-tree story in v. 21 is followed in vv. 22-25 by a sequence of sayings, probably originally independent, which begin by taking the destruction of the tree as a model for disciples as well to expect to be able to achieve the impossible through faith in God (vv. 22-23), then go on to the necessity of faith in prayer generally (v. 24), and finally add the need for those who pray to forgive others (v. 25). This is Mark's only collection of Jesus' teaching on prayer.[45] Following on from the charge that the temple is no longer able to function as an οἶκος προσευχῆς, this portrait of disciples as a praying community might lead Mark's readers to some fruitful reflection on where the true focus of God's people was now to be found.[46]

---

43. Gundry suggests that the γάρ clause does not relate to Jesus' not finding anything but leaves, but 'takes two steps backward to explain why Jesus went to find "something" instead of "figs" or "fruit"'. Apart from the awkwardness of the 'two steps back', which has eluded other readers, this is to place too much weight on a very unemphatic τι.

44. R. H. Hiers (*JBL* 87 [1968] 394-400) and J. D. M. Derrett (*HeyJ* 14 [1973] 249-65) propose that ὁ γὰρ καιρὸς οὐκ ἦν σύκων deliberately draws attention to the unseasonable nature of Jesus' hope because fruit *out of season* was a mark of the New Age which he was hoping to see. But not only does Mark's story give no hint of such an eschatological dimension, but the proposal also places an artificial weight on the γάρ which most naturally gives the explanation for the preceding statement. The Hiers/Derrett interpretation requires something more like 'and you will not see the point of this unless you realise that it was not the season for figs', which is a lot of weight for γάρ to carry without further help from the context.

45. S. E. Dowd, *Prayer*, 2-5, justifiably complains of 'the neglect of 11:22-25 by Markan scholarship', a neglect which her book as a whole is designed to remedy. The fact that these verses fit into Mark's narrative as the conclusion to the temple–and–fig-tree section means, she asserts, that they have tended to be passed over too quickly by commentators and not given an adequate treatment in their own right.

46. S. E. Dowd, *Prayer*, 43-55, explores at length the theological link between the loss of the temple and the prayer of the Christian community, and on this basis argues for the integral place of vv. 22-25 in the pericope, rather than their being an awkward addition of material on another subject.

11 This verse is often bracketed with vv. 1-10 rather than with what follows. But by bringing Jesus inside the city (in contrast with the scene outside the walls in vv. 1-10), and specifically into the ἱερόν, it points forward rather than back, forming the first member in the alternate focus on the two narrative scenes as set out above. Jesus' first visit to the temple gives him the opportunity to see for himself what is going on there, and to plan his action for the next day. What happens in the morning will not be a spontaneous act of outrage, but a planned demonstration. 'Planned for prime time and maximum exposure, it was a "demonstration" calculated to interrupt business as usual and bring the imminence of God's reign abruptly, forcefully, to the attention of all.'[47]

It is only when this verse is taken as the conclusion to vv. 1-10 that it seems an anticlimax (see Schweizer's comment quoted above).[48] The crowd's role has concluded at v. 10, still outside the city, and Mark does not suggest that the royal procession actually entered the gates. Jesus' entry to the city and the temple is at this stage incognito; it is the next day that he will claim attention. Meanwhile he 'looks around', not (*pace* Schweizer) as a tourist, but by way of reconnaissance for the next day.

The ἱερόν (mentioned for the first time) here and in all that follows means not the ναός or sacred building itself containing the Holy Place and the Holy of Holies (which Jesus, not being a priest, could not enter) but the whole complex of buildings and courtyards which now covered the temple mount, a total area of some fifteen hectares. The huge outer court, the Court of the Gentiles, in which the traders' stalls were set up, is the scene for all the public activities and teaching of chapters 11–12 until 12:41, where the specific mention of the γαζοφυλάκιον shifts the scene into the Court of the Women.

Because Jerusalem itself was not big enough to hold the many thousands of Passover pilgrims, people camped on the hillsides around and stayed in neighbouring villages. Jesus and the Twelve stayed in Bethany, technically outside even the extended limits of the city allowed at Passover time (Bethphage being the outer limit; see on v. 1), but convenient enough; it was only on Passover night itself that pilgrims were obliged to sleep within the boundaries, hence the later move to Gethsemane (14:32), closer to the city walls.[49] Jn. 11:1–12:11 with Lk. 10:38-42 indicates that they had hospitable supporters in Bethany, and the otherwise unknown Simon the Leper (see on 14:3) seems to have been another. Jesus and the Twelve continue to live communally as a limited group, despite the considerably wider circle of supporters we have seen in vv. 1-10.

47. B. F. Meyer, *Aims,* 197.

48. An interestingly different perspective is offered by Myers, 297: 'Many have puzzled over this verse, complaining that it adds nothing to the narrative; but that is precisely its power — *nothing happens.* Mark has drawn the reader into traditional messianic symbolics, only to suddenly abort them. This prepares us for the shock when Jesus *does* "intervene" in the temple — not to restore, but to disrupt, its operations.'

49. For the limits of Jerusalem and Passover arrangements see J. Jeremias, *Jerusalem,* 60-62.

12-13   See on 9:2 for the infrequency of specific temporal links between episodes in Mark before the passion narrative. This makes the temporal sequence set out in vv. 11-20 the more significant:

v. 11   ὀψίας ἤδη οὔσης τῆς ὥρας
v. 12   καὶ τῇ ἐπαύριον
v. 19   καὶ ὅταν ὀψὲ ἐγένετο
v. 20   πρωΐ.

The effect is to tie the two narrative scenes of the temple and the fig tree closely together by means of evening and morning journeys linking the two, enabling the reader to see the sequence as a connected whole and thus reinforcing the effect already achieved by the interweaving of the two stories.

See the introduction to this section for the problems associated with the fig tree and its lack of fruit, the season of the year, and the symbolic associations of fig trees in the OT and later Judaism. A further problem raised by some commentators is that Jesus could hardly be hungry after a good breakfast with Lazarus, Martha, and Mary.[50] This assumes that we know more about the eating habits of Jews in general and of this household in particular than is the case; nor is the desire for fruit dependent on being near starvation.[51]

14   Here is a classic case of ἀποκριθείς used, as often in Mark, to mean not a reply to anything said, but a response to a situation. Jesus is 'replying' to the tree's failure to provide what he wanted. The address to an inanimate object is necessary so that the cause of the tree's death will be obvious to the disciples, and Mark adds the otherwise redundant καὶ ἤκουον οἱ μαθηταὶ αὐτοῦ in order to establish this point. Jesus' words are usually described as a 'curse', and Peter will so interpret them in v. 21. They are more strictly a negative wish, but when that wish extends εἰς τὸν αἰῶνα[52] the effect is not much different, especially in the light of the dramatically quick and destructive result which his words will produce (v. 20).

15   The trade in animals which had passed the criteria for sacrifice was necessary for visiting worshippers, as was the changing of money into the special Tyrian coinage required by the temple treasury for payment of the so-called 'temple tax' of half a shekel (Ex. 30:11-16). The money changers (for the late

50. So, e.g., K. Romaniuk, *ZNW* 66 (1975) 276, who uses this to show that the story is not in its proper setting.

51. A. de Q. Robin, *NTS* 8 (1961/2) 276-81, suggests that Jesus' supposed hunger derives from a mistake: Jesus, commenting on the state of the nation, quoted Mi. 7:1, 'My soul desires the first-ripe fig', and his disciples thought he really wanted and expected fruit. ὁ γὰρ καιρὸς οὐκ ἦν σύκων is then the puzzled comment of a disciple at the time.

52. The suggestion (e.g., Mann, 440-41) that εἰς τὸν αἰῶνα here means 'until the end of the present era', implying that it would bear fruit again when the New Age began, introduces a concept of eschatological fruitfulness which (*pace* Hiers; see above, p. 441 n. 44) is not hinted at in Mark's telling of the story, and in any case is hard to square with the total death of the tree following Jesus' words (v. 20).

443

Greek term κολλυβιστής see MM) set up their stalls during the period when the 'tax' was due to be paid, a couple of weeks before Passover (*m. Šeq.* 1:1, 3).[53] All this seems quite unexceptionable. What was questionable, however, was whether these facilities needed to be provided within the temple precincts themselves rather than somewhere in the vicinity. There is evidence that sacrificial animals were sold on the Mount of Olives,[54] and that it was only within recent years that traders had been allowed to move across the valley into the Court of the Gentiles,[55] so that Jesus' protest might have met with a positive response from those who resented the change. Be that as it may, Mark tells the story in such a way as to suggest that Jesus' protest was not against the trade in itself, nor against any supposed exploitation by the traders (for in that case why should he expel buyers as well as sellers?), but rather against its being in the wrong place. This is not what the temple courts were for.

All four gospels use ἐκβάλλειν to describe Jesus' action.[56] Given the huge extent of the Court of the Gentiles, this is remarkable, especially when it is described as a one-man act. John's vivid picture of Jesus driving the traders out with a whip suggests the dramatic impact of his action, and we can imagine something of a stampede to get out of the way of this unpredictable zealot, but perhaps Mark's ἤρξατο excuses us from envisaging the whole huge courtyard area left literally empty of both buyers and sellers. Mark and Matthew mention the sale only of περιστεραί (the sacrificial offerings especially of the poor, Lv. 5:7, 11; 12:8), and it is perhaps easier to envisage these in the temple courts than the sheep and cattle of John's account.

16 Only Mark adds this much more far-reaching demand by Jesus. It confirms his view that Jesus' objection was not so much to the trade as such, but to its location, since there is no trading activity mentioned in this verse, but merely the use of the temple court as a thoroughfare by those carrying loads. It is again a matter of an inappropriate use of the temple area. Cf. *m. Ber.* 9:5: conduct which is regarded as unseemly in the temple area includes its use as a 'short bypath'.[57] σκεῦος, where no more specific sense is indicated by accom-

---

53. If the money-changers' stalls were removed immediately after the due date for payment (Nisan 1), this incident would have to be dated a full two weeks before the Passover; but *m. Šeq.* 6:5 suggests that late payment was common, so that the stalls may well have remained in place much closer to Passover.

54. J. Jeremias, *Jerusalem,* 48-49.

55. See V. Eppstein, *ZNW* 55 (1964) 42-58, for Caiaphas's introduction of traders into the Court of the Gentiles about A.D. 30, in opposition to the wishes of the Sanhedrin. His thesis is discussed by C. A. Evans, *CBQ* 51 (1989) 265-67.

56. The suggestion of Belo, 180, that the verb is intended to equate those expelled with unclean spirits, which are also 'thrown out', reads far too much into a common verb. A more likely echo would be of LXX Ho. 9:15, ἐκ τοῦ οἴκου μου ἐκβαλῶ αὐτούς, in the same context in which Hosea has used the image of the fig tree (v. 10), and will go on to mention withered roots (v. 16; see below on v. 20).

57. A. E. Harvey, *Jesus,* 129, compares the rules in *m. Meg.* 3:3 even for the (less holy) site of a ruined synagogue: no ordinary work is allowed there, nor its use as a 'short bypath'.

panying words or context, is a very general term for any *'thing, object* used for any purpose at all' (BAGD, 754a, 1.a).[58] There seems no basis in the context for restricting its meaning here to the paraphernalia required for sacrificial worship (as in Heb. 9:21, where τῆς λειτουργίας specifies the meaning), which in any case would have to be carried through the temple courts for use in the ναός, if they were not already in situ.[59] As with the traders, it is hard to envisage Jesus single-handedly imposing an effective ban on all carrying of goods in any part of the Court of the Gentiles, and we should probably think more of a symbolic protest.

17 The misuse of the temple area which Jesus' action has highlighted is spelled out by means of two OT quotations. While all three Synoptic writers have the quotation from Is. 56:7, only Mark completes the sentence with the phrase πᾶσιν τοῖς ἔθνεσιν. In Isaiah it is this phrase which is the point of the sentence, which forms part of a series of promises that in the coming age foreigners and other outsiders will enjoy full rights in the worship of God in Jerusalem, and Mark's inclusion of the phrase as part of a quotation defending Jesus' reform of the use of the Court of the *Gentiles* is likely to be deliberate. The Court of the Gentiles was as far as non-Jews were allowed to go into the temple precincts, and any who wished to pray there might not find it easy to discover a quiet area away from the trade and 'carrying through'. While most people in the Court of the Gentiles would be Jews,[60] and it would be going too far to suggest that the primary object of Jesus' protest was the interests of Gentile worshippers as such, it is not inappropriate that Mark, with an eye to his Gentile readers, has included this part of the Isaiah quotation. But it does not seem to be here, as in Isaiah, the main point of the quotation, since Mark nowhere specifies that this was the Court of the Gentiles, and his non-Jewish readers in areas away from Palestine could not be expected to know that when they read simply of τὸ ἱερόν. But for anyone, Jew or Gentile, this was a *temple* court, a sacred place. While other activities might take place there (after all, Jesus himself

---

58. The attempt by J. M. Ford, *Bib* 57 (1976) 249-53, to restrict its meaning here to 'money bags' is not lexically convincing, even though it suits the theme of the suspension of economic activity in the temple courts.

59. Reference is sometimes made to Josephus, *Ap.* 2.106, 'No vessel whatever might be carried into the temple', but this refers not to the Court of the Gentiles but to the ναός itself. C. Roth, *NovT* 4 (1960) 177-78, links this verse with the prophecy in Zc. 14:20-21 (the last clause of which we have seen to be significant for Jesus' action) that in the last day every pot in the temple would be holy; so any utensil brought casually into the temple would become holy, and must not be taken out again (hence the prohibition of carrying the σκεύη *through* the temple). But Zechariah's prophecy applies to the whole of Jerusalem and Judah, not just the temple, and the LXX here uses λέβης not σκεῦος.

60. It is surprising how often the title 'Court of the Gentiles' is taken to mean that it was designated specifically for the use of Gentiles. See, e.g., R. H. Lightfoot, *Message,* 64, who regards it as remarkable that the Jewish temple included 'a court *for* the Gentiles' (my italics). Cf. Lane, 406: 'an area consecrated for the use of Gentiles who had not yet become full proselytes to Judaism'. It was in fact simply the outer court of the temple complex, its name being due to the fact that Gentiles were allowed no further in.

would soon be teaching and arguing in that same court), it must be available for prayer. It was because the commercial activities had crowded out worship as the main purpose of the temple[61] that Jesus protested, and sought to bring about Isaiah's vision of the eschatological role of the temple.

The other quotation, however, introduces a more negative note. What is going on in the temple is not just a distraction from true worship, but turns it from an οἶκος προσευχῆς into a σπήλαιον λῃστῶν. It is on this phrase from Je. 7:11 that the popular view of Jesus' action as a protest against *unfair* trading has been based. It is of course quite possible that both traders and money changers were profiting disproportionately from their services, but nothing in Mark's account suggests that that was Jesus' concern. λῃστής does not mean a swindler but rather a robber or bandit, and particularly by Mark's time an insurrectionist (see on 15:27). Its use here is not necessarily because the term was in itself specifically appropriate,[62] but because the memorable LXX phrase, especially when read in its context, vividly recalled the prophet's denunciation in his great Temple Sermon of the misplaced confidence of those whose behaviour belied their profession of respect for the temple.[63] They went out to 'steal, murder, commit adultery, swear falsely and make offerings to Baal', only to return to the temple ('my house, which is called by my name') as to a place of safety; they had made it like the 'robbers' cave' to which villains resort after their criminal forays. Jesus' use of the phrase does not necessarily accuse the Jews of his day of the same crimes as Jeremiah's contemporaries (including robbery), but highlights their lack of respect for God's house by comparing it with that earlier flagrant abuse of the sanctuary. Those who heard might have reflected that Jeremiah's sermon went on to predict the destruction of the temple (7:12-15), and that that prediction was fulfilled soon after; Jesus will soon be making the same prediction (13:2).

18 In 8:31 Jesus predicted that he would be rejected by the πρεσβύτεροι καὶ ἀρχιερεῖς καὶ γραμματεῖς. Now for the first time since his arrival in Jerusalem two of these groups appear in the narrative, so far only as spectators, but already with an explicit statement of their determination to destroy him, which recalls the similar resolution of the Φαρισαῖοι καὶ Ἡρῳδιανοί in 3:6. The omission of the πρεσβύτεροι as in 10:33 (they will reappear in 11:27 and in subsequent lists in 14:43, 53; 15:1) is probably a stylistic avoidance of too much repetition; they are the least 'colourful' of the three groups. For the ἀρχιερεῖς Jesus' high-handed action in 'their' temple, with its implication that it was not

---

61. Lane, 405-6, draws attention to *m. Šeq.* 4:7-8; 5:3-5 and to Josephus, *War* 6.423-24, for some indications of the scale of trading, turning the Court of the Gentiles into what he calls 'an oriental bazaar and a cattle mart'.

62. C. K. Barrett, in E. E. Ellis and E. Grässer (ed.), *Jesus und Paulus,* 15-16, argues that the 'Zealot' (and therefore nationalist) connotations of λῃστής are here deliberately placed over against the internationalist agenda of πᾶσιν τοῖς ἔθνεσιν.

63. D. Juel, *Messiah,* 132-34, draws out the significance in context of this allusion to Jeremiah's sermon.

being run as God required, was a clear challenge to their authority. The scribes appear here as part of the same power group, but the narrative of Jesus' activities and teaching in Galilee has provided plenty of material for specifically scribal concern (especially 3:22; 7:1 regarding scribes from Jerusalem). Even if they were unaware of what had happened outside the walls of Jerusalem the previous day, they could already see that he was dangerous.

The clear differentiation between the authorities and the crowd is important (see above, pp. 426-27). While no doubt some of Jesus' supporters from the previous day may have been present, this is now essentially a Jerusalem crowd, and at this stage they, too, are on Jesus' side. ἐξεπλήσσετο ἐπὶ τῇ διδαχῇ αὐτοῦ may seem premature, as Jesus has not yet begun his public teaching in the temple, but even the minimal amount of διδαχή involved in his temple protest (especially v. 17; see, too, 1:27 for διδαχή used to include actions) would be enough to mark him as a man with a distinctive message. At this stage they are attracted rather than repelled by his radicalism.

19 The departure from the city (stated in the imperfect tense, indicating that this was a regular pattern), presumably again to Bethany since they will return in the morning by the same route, serves not only to draw a line under this incident, giving a pause before the official challenge in vv. 27-33, but also allows Mark to return us to the story of the fig tree (see on v. 12), so that its lesson in relation to what Jesus has just done in the temple may be learned.

20-21 In Matthew the death of the fig tree is instantaneous (παραχρῆμα twice). In Mark its destruction is complete (ἐκ ῥιζῶν),[64] but is visible only on their next visit. Either is of course equally miraculous — healthy full-grown trees (unlike Jonah's plant) do not wither up in a mere twenty-four hours. For ξηραίνω of vegetation cf. 4:6, and of the human body 3:1; 9:18. It is not easy, and perhaps not important, to decide whether Matthew has telescoped an originally more extended event, and has capitalised on this foreshortening by then introducing παραχρῆμα, or whether Mark has stretched out a previously single incident in order to fold it around the protest in the temple. For Ῥαββί see on 9:5. Here it is perhaps less inappropriate than on the mountain, but even so there is some paradox in its use: such raw power was not looked for in most rabbis' pronouncements. For the use of καταράομαι to describe Jesus' negative wish see on v. 14; Mark gives no hint that the term, however distasteful to some modern readers, is inappropriate to describe what Jesus has done.[65] It is Jesus' powerful word, not coincidence, which has destroyed the tree, and the following verses will take up the theme of God's power operating dramatically through a human word.

22-23 While the structure of Mark's narrative indicates that the fig-tree

---

64. Is there a deliberate echo here of LXX Ho. 9:16, τὰς ῥίζας αὐτοῦ ἐξηράνθη, following on the imagery of the previously fruitful fig tree in v. 10?

65. *Pace* S. E. Dowd, *Prayer,* 58, who finds it significant that the word is attributed to Peter and not used directly by the narrator, and concludes that 'the evangelist interprets Jesus' words in 11:14 as a prayer'.

episode is to be read as a symbol of God's judgment on Jerusalem and its temple, the explicit lesson which is drawn from the event by the addition of this saying is, as in Matthew, on what may appear to be a different subject altogether. What Jesus has just done is a model for how true believers may also draw on the power of God. For those who have faith the impossible is achievable, and the lesson is illustrated by an example every bit as physical as the withering of the tree, throwing a mountain into the sea. If, as seems quite likely, this saying (as well as those that follow in vv. 24-25[26]) was originally independent of the fig-tree story, it would easily be linked with it by this similarly dramatic illustration. But even if originally independent, vv. 22-25 are not an alien intrusion in this context, for the imminent loss of the 'house of prayer' in Jerusalem (v. 17) poses the urgent question of where the tradition of prayer is then to continue. The implication of these verses thus appears to be that 'the Jerusalem temple is condemned and replaced by the praying community'.[66]

The communal aspect of prayer is evident from the fact that vv. 22 and 24-25 are expressed in the plural (and the singular form of v. 23 derives from a ὃς ἄν which generalises the statement); prayer is here presented as something which the community of disciples undertakes together, not a private transaction between the individual believer and God.

Ἔχετε πίστιν θεοῦ (see Textual Note) is a more arresting expression for πιστεύετε θεῷ, but does not differ in meaning. (The suggestion that πίστις θεοῦ means God's faithfulness, which the disciples are either exhorted to 'take hold of' or assured that they already 'have', is surely forced. For a genitive following πίστις to indicate the object of faith cf. Acts 3:16; Rom. 3:22, 26; Gal. 2:16, etc.)[67] It stands syntactically alone as a simple exhortation, but the ἀμήν- pronouncement which follows in v. 23 fills out its implications: Jesus is not talking about faith in a general sense, but about the faith which successfully invokes God's miraculous power, and the inclusion of πιστεύῃ ὅτι ὃ λαλεῖ γίνεται among the conditions for such success confirms the connection. For πίστις/πιστεύω in connection with miracles see above on 2:5; 5:34; 9:23-24, and the full discussion by S. E. Dowd, *Prayer,* 96-117.

The throwing of a mountain into the sea is as useless and destructive an act as causing the death of a fig tree, and is best seen as merely a proverbial-type saying (like the camel going through the eye of a needle; see on 10:25) for the impossible.[68] There is a similar Q-saying in Mt. 17:20, the Lucan parallel to which interestingly has a συκάμινος tree in place of the mountain (Lk. 17:6).

66. S. E. Dowd, *Prayer,* 45, introducing a valuable and wide-ranging discussion of 'the relationship between prayer and temple', 45-55. Similarly (and independently) C. D. Marshall, *Faith,* 163-72.

67. On this and other alternative translations see S. E. Dowd, *Prayer,* 60-63. Dowd concludes in favour of 'Have faith in God!'

68. For a range of similar ἀδύνατον sayings in ancient literature see S. E. Dowd, *Prayer,* 69-72. Dowd discusses at length (78-94) the various views in Graeco-Roman philosophy and in Hellenistic Judaism on divine omnipotence and miraculous intervention.

Paul's use of the image πίστις ὥστε ὄρη μεθιστάναι in 1 Cor. 13:2 may reflect knowledge of these sayings of Jesus,[69] since no contemporary literary parallel is known elsewhere, though it is a relatively obvious way of stating the impossible and so could be independent. In later rabbinic writings there are several references to those who accomplish 'feats of an exceptional, extraordinary or impossible nature'[70] as those who move mountains.

The very obviousness of the image casts suspicion on Telford's contention[71] that τὸ ὄρος τοῦτο is not just any old mountain, but specifically the temple mount, visible across the valley as Jesus spoke, and that therefore this saying is still concerned with judgment on the temple, whose 'removal' Jesus will shortly predict (13:2). ὄρος is not used elsewhere in the gospel tradition to refer to the temple, even with a qualifier to make the reference explicit; on its own it is unlikely to have been so understood (though memories of Is. 2:2-3 might make such a use intelligible). If it is felt necessary to find an identification for τοῦτο, the geographical situation of the narrative would suggest not the temple mount but the Mount of Olives (with the Dead Sea, visible from its summit, as the 'sea' into which it is thrown), particularly in view of Zechariah's prophecy of the splitting and movement of the Mount of Olives (Zc. 14:4). But Zechariah does not envisage its being thrown into the sea, so that even if the imagery, used on the slopes of the Mount of Olives, might well have triggered memories of Zechariah's vision, Jesus' words hardly amount to a prescription for its fulfilment by the disciples. All that is required to make sense of the passage is a proverbial statement of the impossible, and any more specific allusion must be regarded as not proven.

The condition for achieving the impossible is stated both negatively (μὴ διακριθῇ ἐν τῇ καρδίᾳ αὐτοῦ) and positively (πιστεύῃ ὅτι ὃ λαλεῖ γίνεται). Both will be echoed by Jas. 1:6, using διακρίνομαι in the distinctively Christian sense of 'doubt' or 'hesitate' (so BAGD, 185a, 2.b).[72] The present tense of γίνεται, in contrast with the ἔσται which follows, adds yet more to the demanding nature of the faith portrayed: the one who utters the command must believe that the event is already happening.

24 A further and more general saying about faith and prayer (though vv. 22-23 have not specifically mentioned 'prayer' as such) picks up the same idea of unwavering belief, but now without any reference to the impossibility of what is sought; indeed, this verse applies not just to spectacular 'commands' but to all requests in prayer (πάντα ὅσα προσεύχεσθε καὶ αἰτεῖσθε). The fig-tree episode thus progressively fades from view through vv. 22-23, 24, and 25, and

---

69. So D. Wenham, *Paul,* 81-83. Note the occurrence of similar but less-developed sayings reflecting the synoptic tradition in *Gos. Thom.* 48, 106.

70. Telford, *Temple,* 115. He sets out and discusses the relevant texts in pp. 110-17. None of them talks of throwing mountains into the sea; the most common elaboration is of 'uprooting mountains and grinding them together'.

71. Telford, *Temple,* 56-59, 95-127. See contra S. E. Dowd, *Prayer,* 72-75.

72. See S. E. Dowd, *Prayer,* 103-5.

the teaching is generalised. Very likely these were all originally independent sayings, brought together on the end of the fig-tree pericope seen as a model of effective prayer (and linked, like the sayings of 9:37-50, by key words: πιστεύω . . . ἔσται αὐτῷ/ὑμῖν in vv. 23 and 24; προσεύχομαι in vv. 24 and 25). Verse 26, if authentic (see Textual Note on v. 25), would represent a further accretion. The aorist tense of ἐλάβετε (see Textual Note) takes still further the demand made on faith in the γίνεται of v. 23: you must believe not only that it is happening, but that you *have* received it already (cf. Is. 65:24; Mt. 6:8).

This saying, together with the concept of God doing the impossible in answer to prayer in v. 23, raises sharply the problem of unanswered prayer which we have noted already at 9:24. The simplistic reading of this passage which attributes all 'unanswered' prayer to inadequate faith on the part of the one praying can be pastorally disastrous, and must be set against the fact that the will of God is not necessarily to be equated with that of the person praying. A valuable discussion of the issue of theodicy in relation to unanswered prayer is to be found in S. E. Dowd, *Prayer*, 133-62, with special reference to Jesus' 'unanswered' prayer in Gethsemane.

25   This additional saying on prayer extends the conditions of effective prayer:[73] not only faith is required, but also forgiveness.[74] The importance of avoiding broken relationships within the disciple community is noted in Mt. 5:23-24; 18:21-35, and the Lord's Prayer itself ensured that everyone in the Christian community was aware that forgiveness (the forgiveness of other people so that one's own sins may be forgiven) was a prerequisite for effective prayer.[75] The wording here is similar to that of Mt. 6:14-15, even to the extent of the very 'Matthean' phrase ὁ πατὴρ ὑμῶν ὁ ἐν τοῖς οὐρανοῖς. Indeed, not only is this the only appearance in Mark of the idea of a 'heavenly Father'; it is the only place in this gospel where God is spoken of as the father of disciples at all. The use of παράπτωμα for sin is also unique in Mark, and echoes Mt. 6:14-15. The saying which Matthew has attached to the end of the Lord's Prayer as a very appropriate comment on its fifth petition seems to have come to Mark independently as an important catechetical guideline, and since, unlike Matthew, he has no other section of teaching on prayer this was the most appropriate place to include it.

---

73. S. E. Dowd, *Prayer*, 124, rightly discounts the idea that the verse was added to counteract the example of Jesus' cursing of the fig tree: Mark does not seem to regard it as a bad example.

74. C. D. Marshall, *Faith*, 172-74, discusses arguments against the authenticity of v. 25 as a Matthean gloss (though there is no textual authority for its omission), but concludes that it is authentically Marcan. S. E. Dowd, *Prayer*, 40-43, rebuts more specifically the arguments of W. R. Telford, *Temple*, 50-54, against the authenticity of v. 25, and rejects roundly his more tentative suggestion, *Temple*, 54-56, that v. 24 might also be a scribal gloss.

75. S. E. Dowd, *Prayer*, 126-29, illustrates the widespread understanding that unrepented and unforgiven sin would render prayer unacceptable to God.

CONFRONTATION WITH
THE JERUSALEM ESTABLISHMENT (11:27–13:2)

The two dramatic public acts of Jesus on the approach to the city and in the Court of the Gentiles (the latter reinforced for Mark's readers by the symbolism of the destruction of the fig tree, witnessed only by the disciples) have made him a marked man, as Mark has pointed out in 11:18. He has thrown down the gauntlet, and now it will be taken up, first by the full 'panel' of Sanhedrin authorities, the ἀρχιερεῖς καὶ γραμματεῖς καὶ πρεσβύτεροι (11:27), then by two more specific groups, the Φαρισαῖοι καὶ Ἡρῳδιανοί (12:13) and the Σαδδουκαῖοι (12:18) and by an individual γραμματεύς (12:28), before Jesus, having silenced his opponents (12:34), takes the initiative with a question of his own (12:35) and follows it up with a general condemnation of γραμματεῖς (12:38-40), made all the sharper by the contrast with a poor widow whose simple devotion outweighs that of all the rich and influential visitors to the temple (12:41-44). Fitted into this sequence is a parable told by Jesus specifically (according to Mark) in order to discredit the authorities who have challenged him (12:12).

The cumulative effect of this sequence of controversy is to leave the reader with the impression of Jesus locked in combat with a wide coalition of the most influential people in Jerusalem, but holding his own and ultimately having the last word. And in the process the messianic claims acted out in 11:1-25 are further developed as Jesus links his authority with that of John the Baptist, locates himself in the sequence of God's prophetic messengers as the last and most important, and indeed as the 'son', and poses a query about the adequacy of the messianic title 'Son of David' which leaves open the pregnant question of what title then *is* adequate.

Over against the Jerusalem authorities stands the Jerusalem crowd, silent spectators of the duel, but contributing to the dynamics of the conflict by their tacit support for Jesus which makes it impossible for his enemies to move openly against him (11:32; 12:12, 17, 37). They may not indulge in the exuberant acclamations of the pilgrims outside the city, but they are so far to be numbered among those who are ὑπὲρ ἡμῶν (9:40), and it is to them that Jesus is able to address his strictures against the scribes.

All of this takes place in the ἱερόν, the holy space where Jesus' second and more daring demonstration has just taken place, and which he has just attempted to 'purify'. In that symbolic arena he is now engaged in dialogue over various matters of religious and political interest, but particularly with reference to his own role and authority. The sense of alienation between Jesus and those who now control the temple and the religious life of Israel grows stronger through this section, until Jesus issues an open denunciation of the scribes' insincerity and perverted values. The climax is reached when Jesus finally leaves the temple in 13:1, never to return, and in response to the disciples' admiration of its outward magnificence declares openly what he has already hinted at in his allusion to Jeremiah's temple sermon, that its time is finished, and 'not one stone will be left on another'. The coming physical destruction of the temple is an event of such epoch-making significance that the disciples naturally want to know what he means, and so Mark's narrative will be suspended for a time in chapter 13 as Jesus spells out the implications of the end of the old order and the ultimate authority of the Son of Man.

In contrast with 11:11-20, this section gives no further indications of time. The next such note will be in 14:1. All the contents of 11:27–12:44 could easily be fitted into a single frenetic morning, and it may be that that is how Mark expects his readers to envisage it, with Jesus leaving the temple and going out to give his private teaching to the disciples on the Mount of Olives (13:3-35) later that same day. But he does not say so, and it is equally possible that he is aware that the period of confrontation was more extended than that, and has deliberately offered only a selection of incidents to give the flavour of it. Our appreciation of the significance of this powerful sequence of controversies does not in any case depend on our ability to find an answer to that question.

'By What Authority?' (11:27-33)

TEXTUAL NOTE

31. The Western inclusion of the deliberative question τί εἴπωμεν; (noted in UBS[3], not UBS[4]) is not necessary for the sense. Since such redundancy is typical not only of Western readings but also of Mark's style, it may well be original (see the commentary for the speech as a whole), its omission by the majority of witnesses being explicable either as a simplifying assimilation to Matthew and Luke or as haplography, with another εἴπωμεν following.

Jesus' words and deeds in Galilee have created an impression of ἐξουσία to which the people in general have responded with admiration (1:22, 27; 2:10, 12). But this 'charismatic' authority is a different matter from the official authorisation required to claim a decisive voice in the affairs of Jerusalem and its temple. What Jesus has done since his arrival at Jerusalem, and the way people have responded to it, has constituted a claim to authority which cannot be ignored by those who have the official responsibility for the religious and communal life of the city, and the challenge of v. 28 comes as no surprise.

Mark's telling of the incident suggests a hostile approach rather than an open-minded request for information. But the messianic flavour of Jesus' actions in vv. 1-17 means that it is a question which he intended to provoke, and to which he has a clear answer to give, and might lead us to expect an open declaration now of his messianic claim. That this does not occur may be attributed to two factors. First of all, at the level of Mark's construction of his plot, while the earlier secrecy has begun to be breached not only by Jesus' actions but also by Bartimaeus's unrebuked use of υἱὲ Δαυίδ and the taking up of this theme by the pilgrims in 11:10, Jesus' open declaration of his Messiahship will be reserved for the climactic moment of 14:62, in a far more formal setting than this encounter in the Court of the Gentiles. In the meantime, Jesus himself has issued his declaration only by means of symbolic actions which, however obvious their intention, fall short of an open verbal claim. In the dialogues which follow there will still be an element of concealment, as Jesus states his claim only by means of a character in a parable (12:6), an oblique quotation from a psalm (12:10-11), and a teasing question without an answer (12:35-37). Secondly, at the level of the narrative situation, there is little doubt that an open declaration of Jesus' messianic claim at this point would have offered, as it will do in 14:62, the ammunition which his opponents will need to denounce him to the Roman authorities.

So here, too, Jesus' reply is apparently evasive, a counterquestion which leaves his interlocutors with no response that they can safely make, ending the whole encounter in stalemate. But, effective as it may be as a debating ploy, the effect of Jesus' response is not purely evasive but, like the dialogues which follow, contributes an important element to the developing christology of this part of the gospel.[76] By comparing his own ἐξουσία with that of John the Baptist, Jesus invites two conclusions: first that his authorisation, like John's, was ἐξ οὐρανοῦ, and second that he himself is at least not inferior in importance to the eschatological prophet whose significance Mark has highlighted in the great combined quotation in 1:2-3. Those who have interpreted Jesus as a second John (6:14-16; 8:28) have not been on the wrong lines, even if their estimate falls short of the full truth. Those who have listened carefully to John's proclamation must go further and identify Jesus as the 'stronger one' whose mission supersedes that of John (1:7-8). These implications are left unspoken, but the veiled claim to divine authorisation and to a role which is at least prophetic and eschatological is left for the reader to ponder.

Thus while at the level of explicit reply this request for authorisation has received no more response from Jesus than the previous one in Galilee in 8:11-12, for those who will look below the surface there is a clear enough answer.

27-28 This is the third entry of Jesus and his disciples to Jerusalem in Mark's scheme (see vv. 11, 15), hence the πάλιν. The repetition at each entry of the name Ἰεροσόλυμα insistently reminds the reader that we have now reached the place where Jesus' predicted rejection and suffering is to take place. In 14:49 we shall hear of Jesus teaching daily in the temple during this period, and vv. 17-18 have already mentioned Jesus' teaching there and the crowd's response (though that particular reference focuses more specifically on Jesus' comments on temple commerce than on more general teaching). The colonnades of the Court of the Gentiles offered ample shaded space for groups to gather around a teacher, and with the festival crowds now gathering it would be surprising if the Galilean preacher did not have a regular audience. So when

---

76. *Pace* Gundry, 667: 'The whole dialogue has to do with nothing deeper than saving and losing face.'

Mark speaks of Jesus ἐν τῷ ἱερῷ περιπατῶν he is referring not to a passing 'touristic' visit but to Jesus' regular place of activity now that he has reached Jerusalem. For the full listing of ἀρχιερεῖς καὶ γραμματεῖς καὶ πρεσβύτεροι see on 8:31: Jesus' prediction of rejection by the whole official leadership of Israel is now beginning to be fulfilled, and we should think of this as a quasi-official delegation. It is they who initiate the dialogue (ἔρχονται πρὸς αὐτόν . . . καὶ ἔλεγον αὐτῷ). Cf. 8:11 for a similar challenge earlier by Pharisees in Galilee.

In Mark's narrative scheme the question follows on the day after Jesus' disruptive demonstration in this same courtyard, so that ταῦτα must refer primarily to that event. We may suppose that they have also heard something about the way Jesus had approached the city and the welcome given him by the pilgrim crowd. But the events of the previous day alone are quite enough to provoke their concern and to demand an explanation. ποῖος here probably does not differ from τίς (cf. 12:28); Gundry's suggestion that we think of different types of authority which might have been claimed ('prophetic, priestly, royal and messianic possibilities') is probably too subtly theological for this context. BAGD, 684b, 2.a.γ, suggest that ποῖος should be read as the equivalent of τίνος: by *whose* authority? If so, the addition of a second question, τίς σοι ἔδωκεν τὴν ἐξουσίαν ταύτην;, draws out the implication of the first question more pointedly by its implied accusation — 'We did not give it to you.' The Galilean preacher has no official status here in Jerusalem.

29-30 The sequence of tenses and moods (future indicative — aorist imperative — future indicative) connected by καί, while not very elegant, is entirely clear in its meaning. The second clause has the effect of a condition: I will ask . . . , and *if* you answer I will tell you. . . . They could properly have disputed Jesus' right to set this condition for responding to their question, but the counterquestion was a recognised move in both Hellenistic and rabbinic debate (cf. 10:3), and they do not challenge it. Perhaps Mark wants us to believe that they recognised that the counterquestion was not an irrelevant change of subject, but that the correct answer to his question would by itself provide, or at least suggest, the answer to theirs, and their refusal to answer his question would signal their unwillingness to accept his implied answer to theirs.

To mention John's baptism, the most distinctive and memorable feature of his public activity and the one from which his popular title derived, is to point to his whole ministry. For the impact of that ministry on Judaea and Jerusalem see 1:5. As the prophetic forerunner, whose role it was to 'prepare the way of the Lord', John had begun the reformation movement among the Jewish people to which Jesus was the obvious heir. There was a direct line of continuity, obvious to all observers, between them, and after all John had spoken of a 'stronger one' who was to come after him. Even John's baptism was, by his own account, an anticipation of the more effective baptism to be brought by the 'stronger one' (1:8). So their verdict on John's message must be linked to their view of Jesus: if they accept John's authority, they must also accept his as the greater. Mark has not told us of any disapproval of John on the part of the Jerusalem authorities (contrast Mt.

3:7-10; 11:16-19; 21:32, none of which is paralleled in Mark), but only of the hostility of Antipas and Herodias which led to his death. But the response to Jesus' question in vv. 31-32 assumes that they had not shared the popular enthusiasm for John, and had not 'believed him'. ἐξ οὐρανοῦ is a Jewish reverential periphrasis for 'from God' (cf. the use of οὐρανός in 1:11; 8:11; 11:25). For the contrast between divine and human valuation cf. 8:33.

31-33 The dilemma[77] into which Jesus' counterquestion puts them arises not from any uncertainty in their own minds about John. Their answer, if they could have spoken freely, would apparently have been unequivocal: ἐξ ἀνθρώπων. The effectiveness of Jesus' ploy depends on his being aware of popular feeling on the subject, which it would be unwise of them to flout in this public place. We have noted in the introduction to 11:27–13:2 the significant though silent role of the crowd as the spectators of this series of confrontations. Already the distance between the leaders and the crowd is working in Jesus' favour. It will play an increasingly important part in the drama in 12:12 and 14:2, and only in 15:11-15 will the balance be decisively shifted to allow Jesus to be destroyed. For the moment, Jesus is on safe ground, and they know it.

The phrasing and syntax of their deliberation is rough. See the Textual Note for the likelihood that Mark started it with the deliberative question τί εἴπωμεν; from which the following clauses then flow as two alternative answers with their projected consequences. The first option is expressed clearly enough, but the second is broken off as Mark expresses in his own words the cause of their dilemma instead of allowing them to complete their sentence with an apodosis making the same point (as they do, more elegantly but perhaps less forcefully, in Matthew and Luke). The four words that remain, ἀλλὰ εἴπωμεν ἐξ ἀνθρώπων, can be construed either as the beginning of a second conditional clause matching ἐὰν εἴπωμεν ἐξ οὐρανοῦ in v. 31, but with the ἐάν left unexpressed, or as a further deliberative question, 'But shall we say "From men"?', or even as a tentative decision on their part, 'But let us say "From men"', which is then aborted by their recognition of the diplomatic gaffe that would involve. While the general sense is clear, the syntax is awkward, and the decision on how to punctuate the aposiopesis after ἀνθρώπων is a matter of taste.

For ἔχω meaning to consider or reckon cf. Mt. 14:5; 21:46; Lk. 14:18-19; Phil. 2:29. ὄντως contrasts what is really the case with a previously expressed or assumed statement of the opposite — 'it really is true after all that . . .'; see, for example, Lk. 23:47; 23:34; 1 Cor. 14:25. Here the opposite is found in the presumed view of the officials that John's authority was merely human, so that he was not a true prophet at all. To be ὄντως προφήτης is, on the contrary, to have your authority ἐξ οὐρανοῦ. The word order is strange, but perhaps by putting ὄντως before the ὅτι Mark wishes to emphasise that the people, as opposed to their leaders, have it right.

---

77. Myers, 307, helpfully translates διαλογίζομαι by 'equivocate', pointing out that Mark always uses the word to describe 'ideological confusion' (2:6, 8; 8:16-17; 9:33).

The Parable of the Vineyard (12:1-12)

This parable seems to interrupt the sequence of the controversy stories, in that it is not a dialogue but a monologue by Jesus (though with an editorial note of the response, v. 12), and as such arises from his initiative, not from a challenge or question put to him by the leaders. But the threat implied in v. 9 contributes strongly to the development of the confrontation, and the christological implications of the figure of the 'son' and of the quotation of Ps. 118:22-23 further develop the challenge which Jesus has been issuing both dramatically through his arrival at Jerusalem and his demonstration in the temple and in the unspoken implications of his counterquestion about John the Baptist. There is no change of location or of audience at 12:1, and both Gundry and Mann therefore treat 11:27-33 and 12:1-12 together as a single section: 'The pericope . . . falls into two halves, a dialogue between the Sanhedrin and Jesus (11:27-33) and a parable spoken by him to and about them (12:1-12)' (Gundry, 656).

In Matthew this parable is the middle member of a trilogy of polemical parables placed between the challenge to Jesus' authority and the other controversy stories, in each of which there is a message of displacement: the religious authorities displaced in favour of the tax collectors and prostitutes who responded to John's preaching (21:31-32), the defaulting tenants displaced in favour of those who will produce the fruit (21:41; another 'nation', 21:43), the first-invited guests displaced in favour of those brought in from the streets, 'both bad and good' (22:10). Matthew's expansion shows well how the vineyard parable functions in its Jerusalem context. Those who are watching the confrontation between the religious authorities and Jesus are faced with a choice; there is no room for both. The theological question posed by this parable is therefore where the true people of God is now to be found. In speaking it 'against them' (v. 12) Jesus is implicitly claiming that it is in him, not in the old régime which they represent, that God's designs for his people will find their fulfilment.

The choice of a vineyard as the setting for the story already suggests that it is about the long saga of God's dealings with Israel. The vine or vineyard as an image for Israel in its relation to Yahweh is well known from the OT (e.g., Ps. 80:8-18; Is. 27:2-6; Je. 2:21; 12:10; Ezk. 19:10-14; Ho. 10:1). But the wording of v. 1 is more specific, in that it echoes in detail the introduction to Isaiah's song of the vineyard (Is. 5:1-2), an allegory, explicitly drawn out, of God's disappointment with his people. Jesus' parable does not develop the image in the same way: in Isaiah it is the vineyard which has failed, here it is the tenants; in Isaiah the vineyard is to be abandoned and devastated, here it will be entrusted to new tenants. Isaiah's message is thus one of unrelieved disaster, whereas Jesus' parable offers hope for a new beginning. But the new beginning will come only after judgment on the existing régime.

The different ways in which the parable is told in the three Synoptics and in *Gos. Thom.* 65 have led to speculation about its original form. The *Thomas* version is simpler and contains several independent elements which are not obviously the result of theological elaboration ('a *good* man'; only two servants; the first beaten so that 'a little more and they would have killed him'; the servant's report back to the owner; the owner's speculation 'Perhaps he did not know them [*sic*]'). It lacks the details which echo Is. 5:1-2 and the throwing of the son out of the vineyard, and finishes with the killing of the son with no further comment or application other than 'He who has ears, let him hear' (though the following logion is a saying based on Ps. 118:22). The *Thomas* version is therefore often regarded as closer to the original parable,[1] ending with the murder and lacking the quotation of Ps. 118:22-23,[2] with Luke's (which also lacks the details from Is. 5:1-2, and has only three servants, against the larger numbers in Mark and Matthew) as a relatively modest elaboration and Mark and Matthew as further developments along the same trajectory of more explicit development of the allegory and its application to the Jerusalem confrontation. Underlying the debate on this question are of course a number of broader issues, especially the overall view of synoptic relationships held by the interpreter, the general estimate of the *Thomas* tradition and the possibility of its preserving earlier material, and the place of allegory in Jesus' parables. The latter is particularly important, and more recent scholarship is increasingly unwilling to take it for granted that the simpler and less 'allegorical' version is necessarily the earlier. The days are long gone when it was axiomatic that Jesus never used allegory and that his parables were simple moral lessons.[3]

But it is not essential to our interpretation of Mark to be able to agree on the relative originality of the different versions of the parable.[4] As it stands in Mark's gospel it is clearly designed to be read as a pictorial account of God's dealings with Israel through the prophets culminating in the sending of his 'son', and the rejection and death of that son at the hands of those to whom Is-

1. See, however, the argument of B. Dehandschutter in M. Sabbe (ed.), *Marc*, 203-19, that the *Thomas* version is an adaptation from that of Luke, and that therefore we must start from Mark in seeking the original form. Cf. also K. R. Snodgrass, *NTS* 21 (1974/5) 142-44.

2. It is commonly thought that the parable and the psalm quotation did not originally belong together, since the former is essentially pessimistic, the latter optimistic (so, e.g., J. Marcus, *Way*, 111-12). But unless v. 9 is also removed from the parable, this contrast is overdrawn, since the new tenants indicate a hopeful new beginning. Rejection and its reversal are thus essential to both parable and quotation.

3. J. D. M. Derrett, *JTS* 25 (1974) 426-32, cites an interestingly similar rabbinic parable (*Sipre* Deut. 312) concerning a king who leased a field to successive tenants, who stole from him and had to be ejected; after three such ejections, the king had a son and so terminated the tenancy. The parable is followed by an allegorical interpretation in terms of Israel's history.

4. There have been many suggestions as to the purpose of the parable in its allegedly original form, such as a vindication of the offer of the gospel to the poor (Jeremias, *Parables*, 70-77); a vindication of the ministry of John the Baptist (Mann, 462-63); an attack on the strong-arm tactics of the Zealots (J. E. and R. R. Newell, *NovT* 14 [1972] 226-37); a commendation of resolute opportunism (J. D. Crossan, *JBL* 90[1971] 451-65); a manifesto for Palestinian land rights against aristocratic expropriation (J. D. Hester, *JSNT* 45 [1992] 27-57), etc. Interesting as these hypothetical reconstructions may be, they do not help us with interpreting *Mark*.

rael has been entrusted, together with a clear threat of the displacement and destruction of the failed tenants (v. 9) and a psalm quotation which neatly sums up this eventual turning of the tables. Even without the editorial comment in v. 12, it would have been obvious from the context in which Mark has set the parable that its target was the ἀρχιερεῖς καὶ γραμματεῖς καὶ πρεσβύτεροι with whom Jesus has been in dialogue in 11:27-33 and who constitute the antecedent to the αὐτοῖς of v. 1, and therefore also the αὐτούς of v. 12. It is to them, as the current representatives of Israel's leadership through the centuries, that the vineyard has been entrusted, and it is they who face dispossession and punishment. As for the identity of the υἱὸς ἀγαπητός, Jesus is silent, but after 1:11 and 9:7 (the only other occurrences of υἱὸς ἀγαπητός in the gospel) Mark's readers will be in no doubt, quite apart from the clear symbolism of the murder and throwing out of the vineyard; and the expectation of the rejected stone becoming the κεφαλὴ γωνίας, following on from the death of the son, must for them have symbolised Jesus' vindication through resurrection.

In the narrative context much of this had to be obscure at least to the Jewish leaders. Even for Jesus' disciples it would have required a firmer grasp of the significance of his passion-and-resurrection predictions than we have seen reason to think they had yet achieved. As with all parables, the degree to which it communicates depends on the extent of the background knowledge and the theological alertness which each hearer brings to it. To those who have, more will be given — and Mark's readers are privileged to be in that category. But even for the Jewish leaders at the time Mark's comment in v. 12 seems appropriate. Given the clear Israel symbolism of the vineyard, the failure of the tenants to produce the crop and their resultant dismissal was transparently πρὸς αὐτούς, and the killing of the son was surely intended to remind them of their designs against Jesus (11:18). If so, they must have realised, however dimly, that the imagery of the one υἱὸς ἀγαπητός involved an outrageous claim on Jesus' part, even if they could have had no idea of how he could expect to be vindicated after death and become κεφαλὴ γωνίας.[5]

1 αὐτοῖς (see comments above) means the group who have challenged Jesus in vv. 27-28. As members of the three constituent parts of the Sanhedrin they represent Israel's current official leadership. For the meaning of παραβολή see above, pp. 183-84. The phrase ἐν παραβολαῖς functions as an adverb (cf. 3:23; 4:2, 11, and see on 4:2); the plural is not significant. This is the most elaborate story-parable in Mark's gospel, and the one with the most obviously allegorical intention. See above for the symbolic associations of the vineyard in the OT. The details of the preparation of the vineyard from ἐφύτευσεν to ᾠκοδόμησεν πύργον echo directly LXX Is. 5:2, though the items are not in the same order.[6] The allu-

---

5. For a full account of interpretation of the parable up to 1975 see M. Hubaut, *Parabole*.

6. LXX φραγμὸν περιέθηκα represents two Hebrew verbs, wayᵉʿazzᵉqēhû wayᵉsaqqᵉlēhû. The first, *ʿāzaq,* is a hapax legomenon in the OT, usually translated 'dig about', but in New Hebrew it means 'surround', 'enclose', and the Aramaic equivalent means 'ring' (BDB); the second, *sāqal,*

sion is unmistakable to anyone with a knowledge of Isaiah: the vineyard is Israel.[7] For ἐκδίδομαι (for the aorist middle form ἐξέδετο for classical ἐξέδοτο see BDF, 94[1]) as a commercial term for leasing see MM, who render the middle 'let out for my advantage'; this is not benevolence but a commercial transaction involving a large capital investment and expecting a return.[8] The relationship of absentee landowner to tenant farmer is one which would be familiar in first-century Palestine, where much of the land was now held in large estates rather than farmed as previously by owner-occupiers.[9] This development had escalated during the Herodian period, leading to a great increase in landless Jewish peasantry, and therefore to widespread popular resentment and unrest.[10]

2-5 The normal method of payment for the tenancy was for an agreed proportion of the crop to be surrendered to the owner. In the case of a new vineyard it would be at least four years before a crop would be harvested,[11] so that there is a long interval between the beginning of the tenancy and the καιρός for the sending of the collector; the tenants have had time to feel securely entrenched. The fact that those sent to collect the rent are δοῦλοι does not mean that they can easily be ignored. The slave of a rich landowner was himself a person of consequence. In not only refusing the rent but also assaulting and insulting the collectors the tenants are in the plainest terms repudiating the owner's claim to the vineyard and challenging him to enforce payment if he can. For κενὸν ἀποστέλλω for

---

means to 'stone', which in this context is understood to mean to clear of stones. The enclosing fence or wall of the LXX thus represents a different but related way of describing the agricultural preparation of the vineyard (using the cleared stones to 'enclose' it? so Gundry, *Use* 44, citing also the Peshitta and the Vulgate for the same rendering). This is hardly a strong basis for Jeremias's claim (*Parables,* 70-71) that the use of the LXX phrase demonstrates 'secondary editorial activity', since the words Mark records, whether spoken in Hebrew, Aramaic, or Greek, would clearly recall the careful preparation of the vineyard described in Is. 5:2. See my *Jesus and the OT,* 247.

7. A further point of relevance to the Marcan context is suggested by B. D. Chilton, *Rabbi,* 111-14, in that the Targum interpreted the tower in Is. 5:2 as the temple; anyone aware of that interpretation might then link the parable with Jesus' recent action in the temple and with the role of the Jewish leaders as its guardians. Cf also D. Juel, *Messiah,* 136-37. This association is developed further by C. A. Evans, *BZ* 28 (1984) 82-86; J. Marcus, *Way,* 119-24.

8. For the historical verisimilitude of the story in the socio-economic context of first-century Palestine see especially J. Jeremias, *Parables,* 74-76; J. D. M. Derrett, *Law,* 286-312, each with a wealth of interesting detail. The fact that the story is designed as an allegory does not mean that its setting is not true to life, even though its details, as we shall see, may stretch that verisimilitude in order to accommodate the allegorical intention.

9. See J. Jeremias, *Parables,* 74-75, though Mark's ἀπεδήμησεν need not indicate a *foreign* landlord. Myers, 308, contributes the interesting suggestion that the religious leaders in Jerusalem to whom Jesus is speaking might themselves be absentee landowners, and that 'Mark's listeners . . . could revel in the role-reversal that demoted the ruling class to the lowly status of unruly tenants'.

10. See J. D. Hester, *JSNT* 45 (1992) 34-36. Hester's article goes on to argue that the popular response to Jesus' story in its original form would therefore have been one of warm approval for the tenants as popular heroes, re-establishing Israel's ancestral land rights over against the aristocratic and plutocratic expropriation of the Herodian era (so that originally the vindicated stone represented the tenants, not the son), but that subsequent reinterpretation has turned them into villains.

11. So J. D. M. Derrett, *Law,* 289-90.

to send away empty-handed cf. LXX Gn. 31:42; Dt. 15:13; Lk. 1:53. The description of the ill-treatment of the slaves is incremental: δέρω (classically to 'flay') in the NT is a more general term for physical abuse; κεφαλιόω (see BDF, 108[1] for the form) occurs nowhere else, and is assumed to mean 'hit on the head' (though it could mean 'decapitate': is there an allusion here to John the Baptist?), while ἀτιμάω adds insult to injury. The killing of the third slave brings the sequence to a climax, though the versions of Thomas and Luke, which reserve death for the son alone, might seem more dramatically effective. But Mark, followed by Matthew, goes on to mention πολλοὺς ἄλλους,[12] not just the two (Thomas) or three (Luke), and includes death[13] as the fate of several, not just the one. Assuming that the reader has recognised the OT prophets behind the figure of the slaves, the story is being filled out beyond the bounds of the likely behaviour of either landlord or tenants in order to reflect history. Many prophets, not just two or three, came to Israel with Yahweh's claims, and while many of them were rejected and ill-treated, some of them also were killed (Je. 26:20-23; 2 Ch. 24:20-22; Mt. 23:34, 37; cf. the traditions of the martyrdoms of Isaiah, Jeremiah, Ezekiel, Micah, and Amos in the 'Lives of the Prophets' [first century A.D.]). The most recent had been John the Baptist, whose divine mission Jesus has just implicitly defended in 11:29-33.

6 In real life it is even more improbable that the landlord would risk his son after such clear evidence that the tenants mean mischief, and would expect any different response, than that he would have gone on sending so many slaves before reaching this point. The allegory is increasingly stretching the verisimilitude of the story. But Mark is telling the story for its message, and the sense of climax is carefully developed: ἔτι ἕνα εἶχεν . . . υἱόν . . . ἔσχατον . . . and the owner's assumption that his son, unlike the slaves, would at last command respect. This is not just another attempt, but one last throw, God's last appeal to his people, and he is taking an incredible risk. The position of ἕνα before the verb and separated from υἱὸν ἀγαπητόν adds emphasis both to the finality of this expedient (there is only one person left to send) and, theologically, to the uniqueness of the son over against the numerous slaves. The further addition of ἀγαπητόν not only heightens the drama but also recalls the language of the voice from heaven in 1:11 and 9:7 (with its echo of Abraham's sacrifice of τὸν υἱόν σου τὸν ἀγαπητόν, ὅν ἠγάπησας in Gn. 22:2) so that the reader is in no doubt who the 'son' represents.[14] In Mark's narrative context, while those to whom the parable was directed had not had the benefit of the voice from heaven, they, too, must naturally understand this single climactic figure as Je-

---

12. The verb governing πολλοὺς ἄλλους cannot be ἀπέκτειναν, since the following participles specify that only some of them were killed, the rest beaten. We must assume an understood verb such as 'they treated in the same way'.

13. For the form ἀποκτέννω as opposed to Mark's usual ἀποκτείνω see BDF, 73.

14. It is interesting to note that in Is. 5:1-2, which has been so clearly alluded to in v. 1, the owner of the vineyard is twice described as ὁ ἠγαπημένος and the song itself as ᾆσμα τοῦ ἀγαπητοῦ. Might a well-informed and subtly inclined reader also have picked up the nuance that the son not only represented the owner but that it was really *his* vineyard?

sus, following on so closely after their question as to the source of his authority and his implication that it was ἐξ οὐρανοῦ. Without directly using 'Son of God' as a title for himself, Jesus has by this parable already given sufficient grounds for the question asked in 14:61 by the chairman of the Sanhedrin (whose representatives he is here addressing), Σὺ εἶ . . . ὁ υἱὸς τοῦ εὐλογητοῦ;

7-8 Much has been made of the oddity of the tenants' assumption that if the son is killed they will take over the vineyard. Did they assume that the son had come to take over because his father was dead?[15] Or that the owner, who has so far failed to put in a personal appearance, was too old or too far away to bother or be able to resist their takeover? There is nothing in the story to say so. J. D. M. Derrett has argued alternatively that under Jewish law possession of a property without payment of rent for four years (see on v. 2 above) constituted a title to ownership, and the killing of the son gave them time to seize the crucial fourth year's harvest; the legal basis of his argument has, however, been disputed.[16] But in any case it is probably not appropriate to read Jesus' story in terms of formal legal claims; this is instinctive piracy rather than reasoned policy. In the development of the story the tenants' hope of ownership of the vineyard serves as a foil to their eventual expulsion from it.

The throwing of the son out of the vineyard has obvious symbolic significance in relation to the rejection of Jesus, but in that case the order of death followed by throwing out is surprising (and is reversed by Matthew and Luke, reflecting the death of Jesus outside Jerusalem). At the level of the story proper the murder followed by the throwing out of the body (not even a decent burial) provides a vivid climax, and perhaps Mark intends no more. Nor does he exploit the verb ἐξέβαλον by using it again in v. 9 to speak of the owner ejecting the tenants in their turn.

9 As in Is. 5:3-4, a question invites the hearers to adjudicate the case. Matthew produces an ironical effect by having Jesus' interlocutors answer the question themselves and in so doing pronounce their own fate. But in Mark, as in Is. 5:5-6, the narrator answers his own question. At the story level the owner must at last come back on the scene himself in order to carry out the sentence, and there is probably no further symbolism intended in ἐλεύσεται (such as God's 'coming' to destroy the temple, or the 'coming' of the Son of Man). ἀπολέσει, too, might perhaps fit the story (capital punishment for the murder of the slaves and the son), but the choice of that verb rather than, for example, ἀποκτείνω or [κατα]κρίνω conveys a more ominous message: this is not just the penalty for murder in the story, but the destruction of all that the old régime has stood for. It also echoes 3:6 and 11:18, where the aim of the authorities is to eliminate (ἀπόλλυμι) Jesus: the tables will be turned. But the destruction of the tenants does not mean the end of the vineyard (contrast Is. 5:5-6); new tenants will be installed. The language remains that of the story, and so the new tenants

---

15. J. Jeremias' reconstruction of the scene (*Parables*, 75-76) depends on this assumption.
16. See K. Snodgrass, *Parable*, 38.

are not specified.[17] Mark's readers would have had no difficulty in identifying the ἄλλοι as the church, but Jesus' words remain uninterpreted to those who heard him in the temple. Such interpretation as vv. 10-11 may offer remains cryptic, the more so since the one who eventually 'comes out on top' in that quotation is not a plural group to correspond to the ἄλλοι but a singular 'stone'.

While the details of the story have been strained to accommodate the allegory intended, we have so far been offered no explicit guide to interpretation. The Isaianic language of the introduction and the odd features of the story as it has developed have invited the reader/hearer to look beyond the storyline and to recognise the presence of παραβολή (as indeed Mark has explicitly warned us in v. 1), and the allusion to Israel, the prophets, and Jesus has become increasingly transparent as the story has developed, but even if it should have been possible for those who first heard the story to identify the likely meaning of everything up to the fate of the son, the destruction and replacement of the tenants remains enigmatic.

10-11 For the question οὐδὲ τὴν γραφὴν ταύτην ἀνέγνωτε; introducing a quotation from the OT to illuminate a point, cf. 2:25; 12:26. In none of these three cases is the quotation one which would naturally spring to mind in the context, as the form of the question might suggest. All three involve a creative transfer of a biblical text to a different setting. Ps. 118:22-23 (quoted here exactly according to the LXX)[18] celebrates a divine deliverance and reversal of fortunes, expressed in v. 21 in the singular though celebrated by 'us' (plural) in vv. 23-24.[19] It is usually understood as referring to a national event, but the singular stone lends itself to a more individual application,[20] and as such it became a favourite Christian text for Jesus' vindication after his rejection and death: in

17. Many commentators state without argument that they represent *Gentiles* replacing Jews. This is not only not in Mark's text, but is also in conflict with the fact that Jesus has conspicuously avoided the language of Is. 5 about the *vineyard* being abandoned, and speaks instead only of a change of tenants.

18. The fact that it is a verbatim quotation renders unlikely Gundry's idea (663) that Mark takes the feminine αὕτη in the third line to refer back to κεφαλή in the second line. αὕτη was an unidiomatically literal LXX rendering of Hebrew zōʾt, and Mark has simply reproduced it.

19. See J. D. M. Derrett, *SE* 4 (1968) 180-86, for a messianic understanding of the psalm, with David as the original rejected stone. See especially the Targum which reads in v. 22: 'The *boy* which the builders abandoned was among *the sons of Jesse* and he is worthy to be appointed *king and ruler.*' J. Marcus, *Way,* 114-15, discusses the eschatological understanding of the psalm in post-biblical Judaism as a prophecy of national vindication for Israel. Marcus goes on to suggest that Mark has deliberately inverted this hope by using the psalm quotation to predict the supremacy of the predominantly Gentile church *over* Israel; he speaks of 'the upside-down holy war against Israel and on behalf of the Gentiles depicted in Mark 12:9'. But in v. 9 the vineyard (which represents Israel) is not abandoned (as in Isaiah) and still less made the target of 'holy war', but is given a new lease of life under new tenants.

20. F. J. Matera, *Kingship,* 79-84, argues for a 'royal' understanding of the psalm both in its original setting and in Jewish interpretation in the NT period, with the stone of v. 22 representing the king. See, however, B. Gärtner, *Temple,* 133-36, for a corporate understanding of OT 'stone' language at Qumran as referring to the community.

addition to the parallel passages here see also Acts 4:11; 1 Pet. 2:4, 7, and the further development of 'stone' imagery through different texts in Rom. 9:32-33; see on 8:31 above for another echo of Ps. 118:22.[21] Here the themes of rejection, reversal, supremacy, the work of God, and amazement all contribute to the understanding of the preceding parable of the rejected son and the subsequent turning of the tables by the intervention of his father. What the parable did not contain was any concept of the rejected son himself being vindicated and taking the supreme place; indeed, the imagery of the parable did not allow it without moving outside the story situation to include the possibility of resurrection after death. It is that crucial move which this quotation allows, thus completing the total scenario by weaving in the final and hitherto neglected element of Jesus' three passion predictions. This is a creative use of Scripture which Jesus' hearers at the time could certainly not have been expected to work out for themselves, despite the rebuke implied in the opening question.

It is often suggested that the linking of this quotation with the parable derives from the assonance of the Hebrew words *bēn* (son) and *'eben* (stone). This could work only in a Semitic context,[22] and so would be lost on many of Mark's readers. While the word-play would have been enjoyed by anyone in a position to grasp it, it is not at all essential to the relevance of Ps. 118:22-23 to the parable. In rabbinic literature scribes and scholars are sometimes referred to as 'builders',[23] and this may have helped some hearers to see the relevance of the quotation to Jesus' situation, increasingly rejected by the scribal establishment.

The imagery of the quotation requires that the κεφαλὴ γωνίας (cf. the ἀκρογωνιαῖος of Eph. 2:20; 1 Pet. 2:6) be the most important stone in the building. Many interpreters see the term here as referring to the cornerstone at the base,[24] which would be the first to be laid, the metaphor of 'head' being used for its importance rather than for its being on top. But that seems a most unnatural use of κεφαλή (and the Hebrew *rō'š*), which suggests (as does ἀκρογωνιαῖος) a stone at the top of the building; Symmachus uses ἀκρογωνιαῖον in 2 Ki. 25:17 for the capital of a pillar as well as here in Ps. 118:22.[25] We should perhaps think of the large stone at the corner of the top course, which is fitted last to complete the building, and which is likely to be decorated and to draw the eye. Our ignorance of Hebrew architectural terminology at this point does not, however, affect the sense of the quotation: the one rejected has become the most important of all.

---

21. On the development of stone imagery in the NT see B. Lindars, *Apologetic*, 169-86.

22. The Targum actually reads 'boy' in place of 'stone', as part of its messianic rewriting of the psalm, presumably on the basis of this wordplay.

23. See J. Marcus, *Way*, 124-25.

24. This view is supported in 1 Pet. 2:6-8 where the stone which is described as ἀκρογωνιαῖος and κεφαλὴ γωνίας is also one over which people can stumble and therefore is presumably at ground level. But Peter is not averse to mixing his metaphors, as v. 5 of the same chapter vividly shows.

25. Hence the arguments of J. Jeremias, summed up in *TDNT*, 1.791-93, 4.274-75, drawing on *Test. Sol.* 22:7 which uses both terms, for the meaning 'keystone', or the final stone of the building. See further M. Barth, *Ephesians 1-3*, 317-19; J. D. M. Derrett, *SE* 4 (1968) 181.

The second verse of the quotation might serve as a motto for the whole of Mark's gospel. It is the gospel of paradox, of human amazement at the unexpected work of God. The kingdom of God has been shown especially in chapter 10 to demand the reversal of human values and expectations. In it the first are last and the last first, the rejected stone becomes the most important of all, and 'we' are left gazing in wonder at the inscrutable ways of God as they are being revealed not only in the teaching but also in the experience of his Messiah.

12 The inhibition of the authorities because the crowd took the other side has already been mentioned in 11:32 in relation to their opposing estimates of John the Baptist. Here the crowd's support for Jesus is more explicit, and the same inhibition will underlie the need for the chief priests to gain the help of Judas in order to effect a secret arrest (14:1-2). The subject of ἔγνωσαν is ambiguous. If, as we would normally expect, it is the same as that of the preceding verb, i.e., the authorities, it is not immediately obvious how it explains their fear of the crowd (assuming that the γάρ clause relates to what has gone immediately before). But if it is the crowd (the last-mentioned antecedent), why should the crowd's awareness of the target of the parable make the authorities afraid of them?[26] The sentence is compressed, and may perhaps best be teased out as follows: 'They were trying to arrest him (but could not yet because) they were afraid of the crowd since they knew (and were aware that the crowd also knew) that he had spoken this parable against them (so that the crowd was now more likely to take his side against them).' So for the time being they can take no action, and they leave him in possession of the field. But while this full grouping of ἀρχιερεῖς καὶ γραμματεῖς καὶ πρεσβύτεροι will not appear again until 14:43, the fact that no new subject is announced for the next verb, ἀποστέλλουσιν, indicates that they remain active in the background.

The Roman Poll Tax (12:13-17)

The sequence of approaches to Jesus by the authorities, suspended in 12:1-12 by Jesus' polemical monologue, now resumes with a question from the Pharisees and the Herodians which Mark explicitly designates as hostile, ἵνα αὐτὸν ἀγρεύσωσιν λόγῳ. Moreover, the questioners do not come on their own initiative, but have been 'sent', and the sequence of plural verbs without expressed change of subject since 11:27 leaves little doubt that the subject of ἀποστέλλουσιν is still the ἀρχιερεῖς καὶ γραμματεῖς καὶ πρεσβύτεροι. This is an official delegation with the aim of discrediting Jesus.[27]

All Roman taxes (customs, tolls, etc.) were unpopular, but the poll tax

26. Most recent translations have avoided the problem by rearranging the order of Mark's clauses.

27. For a valuable study of the whole incident in its historical context see F. F. Bruce in E. Bammel and C. F. D. Moule (ed.), *Politics,* 249-63.

(κῆνσος)[28] was a particularly offensive demand for Jewish patriots. First imposed less than a generation earlier by means of Quirinius's census when Judaea became a Roman province under direct rule in A.D. 6, it was the immediate cause of the revolt led by Judas of Galilee in that year (Josephus, *War* 2.118; *Ant.* 18.4-10, 23-25). That revolt had been quickly stamped out, but it remained the inspiration for subsequent patriotic leaders, culminating in the Zealot movement which precipitated the climactic revolt of A.D. 66 and the consequent siege leading to the destruction of Jerusalem in A.D. 70. This question was therefore an essentially political one, aimed to elicit Jesus' stance with regard to 'Zealot' ideology. As a Galilean he was not liable to pay the κῆνσος, which applied only to provinces such as Judaea which were under direct Roman rule. They approach him as a 'foreign' visitor who might be expected to offer a more 'objective' judgment, but his response may be expected to be of interest to the political authorities of Judaea.

But for Judas the issue had been as much theological as political. Josephus describes his call to revolt in these terms: 'He called his fellow countrymen cowards for being willing to pay tribute to the Romans and for putting up with mortal masters in place of God [literally 'after God', μετὰ τὸν θεόν]' (*War* 2.118); 'They have an unconquerable love of freedom, since they have accepted God as their only leader and master' (*Ant.* 18.23). The theology underlying such language is that allegiance to God and to Rome as a pagan occupying power are fundamentally incompatible. It is in the light of this ideology that Jesus' formula Τὰ Καίσαρος ἀπόδοτε Καίσαρι καὶ τὰ τοῦ θεοῦ τῷ θεῷ must be understood.[29]

The 'trap' (ἀγρεύσωσιν) is generally understood to consist in the impossibility of answering the question to everyone's satisfaction. 'Yes' would alienate Jewish patriots, who would see it as a pro-Roman answer; 'No' would provide a basis for denouncing Jesus to the provincial authorities as a rebel (Lk. 20:20 makes this last point explicit). The 'amazement' of those who heard his answer suggests that he has succeeded in escaping this dilemma, and interpreters have disagreed ever since as to which side, if either, his pronouncement actually favours. But its cleverness is to be found not only, or even mainly, in a studied compromise, but rather in that he has undermined the questioners' position in two important ways, one essentially theological, the other more *ad hominem*.

The *ad hominem* element in Jesus' response relates to why Jesus asked to be shown a denarius and drew attention to its εἰκὼν καὶ ἐπιγραφή. The silver denarius was the required coinage for tax payment, and it carried a portrait of

---

28. The term 'poll tax' generally used for the Latin loanword κῆνσος is in fact an oversimplification. The direct taxes levied by the Romans in the provinces included both a *tributum soli* (tax on agricultural produce) and a *tributum capitis,* which literally means 'poll tax', but included both a flat-rate capitation charge and a property tax. It was the assessment of the province for the latter which was the specific purpose of Quirinius's census in A.D. 6 (Josephus, *Ant.* 18.1-3). See Schürer, 1.401-4.

29. *Gos. Thom.* 100 interestingly adds, 'and give to me what is mine'.

the emperor together with his official title, which at this time under Tiberius would include the words DIVI AUG. FILIUS, 'Son of the divine Augustus'. For a strict Jew this was not only politically but also religiously offensive, involving both a 'graven image' and also words which should not be applied to any human being, certainly not to a pagan Roman. But for everyday commerce the Jews were able to avoid 'idolatry' by using copper coins, locally minted, which bore no image.[30] By asking his questioners to show him a denarius Jesus wrong-footed them. He himself apparently did not have a denarius, but his questioners were able to produce one. They were therefore in no position to criticise Jesus for lack of patriotism or of religious scruples, if they themselves were already carrying the 'idolatrous' imperial money.[31]

The theological basis of Jesus' response is more far-reaching. It is that the Zealot ideology underlying the supposed dilemma is false. Instead of setting loyalty to God and to Caesar in opposition to each other, the straightforward meaning of Jesus' words is that both may be maintained at the same time. He gives no specific guidance as to what is one's obligation to each party, though the implication of his ἀπόδοτε Καίσαρι following on the recognition that the denarius bears Caesar's name surely implies that the use of the denarius to pay the poll tax falls clearly within the category of Caesar's dues. His pronouncement assumes that there is no clash between the legitimate claims of Caesar and of God. It is therefore an answer no Zealot could have given. But neither is it simply pro-Roman: God also has his rights.[32]

Jesus' response to this question thus provides a basis for the more developed teaching of Rom. 13:1-7 and 1 Pet. 2:13-17, each of which similarly assumes that it is possible to be loyal to the Roman government and to God at the same time and indeed goes further in grounding this instruction (which in Rom. 13:6-7 includes specifically the payment of taxes) in the belief that the (pagan) civil authorities are a God-given institution. None of these passages envisages a conflict of loyalties, and therefore they offer no guidance for those situations, with which the church soon found itself only too familiar, where God and Caesar appear to be pulling in opposite directions. But it is an important starting point for debating such conflicts to recognise that for Jesus, as well as for Paul and Peter, the *normal* situation is one of compatible loyalties rather than, as the Zealots would have insisted, one of conflict between Caesar and God.

In this pericope, therefore, as in each episode of the temple dialogues, Jesus has done more than evade a trick question. He has confronted the 'Zealot' assumption which underlay the Pharisees' and Herodians' question with a more positive assessment of the political responsibility of the people of God, even

30. For coins in use in first-century Palestine see Schürer, 2.62-66, and specifically on the issue of nonidolatrous coins, Schürer, 1.379-81.

31. J. D. M. Derrett, *Law,* 313-37, provides much useful background to the confrontation.

32. On the interpretation of, e.g., S. G. F. Brandon, *Zealots,* 345ff., which sees 'God's rights' as including the land of Israel and its produce and therefore as in conflict with paying tribute to a foreign government, see F. F. Bruce, art. cit. (p. 464 n. 27) 259-60.

under foreign domination. A theocracy is not the only valid form of government. To be loyal to God does not necessarily demand civil disobedience.

13 For the subject of ἀποστέλλουσιν see on v. 10. The composition of the 'delegation' is interesting. The Φαρισαῖοι are not surprising: they were an important component in the Sanhedrin (cf. Acts 23:6-7) and have already featured prominently as critics of Jesus' activity in Galilee (2:16, 24; 7:1-5; 8:11) and perhaps further south (10:2; but see Textual Note there). We have already heard of their association with Ἡρῳδιανοί in a plot against Jesus in 3:6 (see notes there),[33] but whereas the Herodian interest was more natural in Galilee, it is perhaps surprising to find this group singled out here in Jerusalem (where they may have come to accompany Antipas on his Passover visit, Lk. 23:7), and in connection with a political question which applied specifically to Judaea, not to the provinces under Herodian jurisdiction. Our very limited information about the Ἡρῳδιανοί does not allow us, however, to reconstruct their specific interests with any confidence.[34] ἀγρεύω, 'to hunt, catch', normally of animals for food, forms a vivid metaphor for their hostile purpose (contrast the benign metaphorical use of the derivative verb ζωγρέω in Lk. 5:10).

14 For διδάσκαλε as an address to Jesus see on 9:17. Its use in these dialogues (cf. vv. 19, 32) need reflect no more than Jesus' popular reputation, possibly an established way of speaking of him as ὁ διδάσκαλος, though after Mark's note of the hostility of his questioners we should perhaps detect in it here and in v. 19 also the insincerity of the flatterer. Certainly the following clauses suggest blatant flattery, and v. 15 describes their attitude as ὑπόκρισις.

For ἀληθής of a person, 'truthful', 'genuine', cf. Jn. 7:18. The opposite of ἀλήθεια is not so much falsehood as partiality; a truthful and unprejudiced presentation of the ὁδὸς τοῦ θεοῦ depends on not being swayed by any special interest. μέλει τινι περί has the positive sense of 'to care about' in Jn. 10:13; 12:6; 1 Pet. 5:7, but here its less creditable sense, 'to show partiality towards', is required by the following clause. For βλέπω εἰς πρόσωπόν τινος as an idiom for partiality cf. λαμβάνω πρόσωπον, Gal. 2:6; θαυμάζω πρόσωπον, Jude 16, and the use of προσωπολημψία and cognates in Acts 10:34; Rom. 2:11; Eph. 6:9; Col. 3:25; Jas. 2:1, 9; Luke here uses λαμβάνω πρόσωπον. The idiom is familiar from the OT: Lv. 19:15; Dt. 10:17; Ps. 82:2; Pr. 18:5 all use *nāśā' pānîm*, trans-

---

33. M. J. Cook, *Treatment,* chapter 3, especially pp. 40-48, argues that the present pericope originally belonged to a pre-Marcan collection of controversy stories, in which it followed immediately after 3:1-5 and before 3:6; hence the mention of Pharisees and Herodians together in only these two places. He goes on to argue (81-83) that the Herodians therefore appear only in a Galilean context, but does not explain why a question about the Judaean poll tax should be posed in Galilee.

34. E. Trocmé, *Formation,* 91 n. 4, suggests that the Pharisees and Herodians 'were two groups of antagonists between whom Jesus was obliged to weave his way carefully in order not to attract the hostility of either'. This imaginative reconstruction seems to depend on the view that the Pharisees favoured individual 'conscientious objection' to paying taxes (p. 90), while the Herodians are 'representatives of political opportunism or even, one might say, of the secret police' (p. 93 n. 2). Neither characterisation seems well established.

lated in the LXX by either λαμβάνω πρόσωπον or θαυμάζω πρόσωπον.[35] The essential contrast is between the interests of ἄνθρωποι and the 'way of God', God's revealed will; Jesus' questioners claim to recognise him as God's unprejudiced spokesman. This is flattery no doubt, but Mark would nevertheless surely expect his readers to recognise in these words a true assessment of Jesus the διδάσκαλος.

The question, when it comes, is in terms of what is 'permitted' (ἔξεστιν). All Mark's previous uses of ἔξεστιν (2:24, 26; 3:4; 6:18; 10:2) have referred to what is permitted under *divine* law, whether that of the OT directly or that of current scribal interpretation of the OT. When the matter under discussion is one which is not only permitted but mandatory under the law of the Roman occupation, to phrase the question in terms of what is 'permitted' is to suggest the possibility of a conflict between divine and human law. It invites Jesus to claim divine sanction for opposing the human government. The question thus already presupposes the 'Zealot' ideology of a fundamental opposition between Caesar and God. Καῖσαρ, originally the family name of Julius, was by now the regular title of the Roman emperor in common speech. The question relates in principle to the office rather than specifically to its current holder, Tiberius.

15-16 For Jesus' knowledge of people's thoughts cf. 2:8; 5:30. ὑπό-κρισις is a word more typical of Matthew than of Mark, and in Mark's only use of the noun ὑποκριτής (7:6) the idea is not so much of conscious insincerity as of a distorted perspective. Here, however, it is closer to our English sense of 'hypocrisy'. For πειράζω see on 1:13, and for parallel uses with regard to hostile questioners 8:11 and 10:2.[36] On the request for a denarius see the introductory comments on this section. As the recognised day wage of a labourer (Mt. 20:2), it represented a considerable sum, probably more than Jesus' itinerant group would have to hand in whatever currency. The full inscription around the garlanded head of Tiberius would be TI[BERIUS] CAESAR DIVI AUG[USTI] F[ILIUS] AUGUSTUS. On the reverse there would be the title PONTIF[EX] MAXIM[US], 'High Priest', a further provocation to Jewish sensibilities.[37]

17 The logic of Jesus' pronouncement is indicated by the verb ἀπόδοτε. The question had been about 'giving' (δίδωμι, v. 14) the tax to Caesar, but Jesus speaks instead of 'giving back', i.e., giving that which already belongs to the receiver, especially paying a debt; for this sense of ἀποδίδωμι see, for instance, Mt. 5:26; 18:25-34; Lk. 7:42; 10:35. The use of Caesar's coin symbolises the dependence of the subject people on the benefits of Roman rule, and to use that

35. In view of the familiarity of the idiom it is most unlikely that Mark intended a double entendre with 'looking at the face' on the coin (so Gundry, 693), an issue which does not in any case enter the text until v. 16.

36. In all these accounts of Jesus 'tested by his enemies', but especially in this passage with its language also of trying to 'catch' Jesus, S. R. Garrett, *Temptations,* 66-69, believes that Mark is consciously echoing the passage in Wis. 2:12-24 which speaks of the attempts of the ungodly to test and discredit God's true servant.

37. For the coin see H. St.J. Hart in E. Bammel and C. F. D. Moule (ed.), *Politics,* 241-48.

coin to pay the poll tax is to recognise and discharge that indebtedness. The verb thus suggests that the payment is not only 'permitted', but is in fact right in itself, so that to withhold it would be to defraud.[38]

What 'belongs to Caesar' is in this context primarily the monetary obligation of the poll tax, though Jesus' words are broad enough to permit a more expansive understanding of civic responsibility as well. But the second member of the pronouncement (καὶ τὰ τοῦ θεοῦ τῷ θεῷ) is entirely open-ended, and must be filled out by the reader's understanding of God's claim on his people.[39] It will be that understanding which determines whether the claims of Caesar and of God come into conflict, but the way the pronouncement is formulated suggests that such conflict should be expected to be exceptional rather than normal.[40]

The compound form ἐκθαυμάζω (cf. ἐκθαμβέομαι in 9:15) intensifies the astonishment.[41] The subject of the verb is unexpressed, but since the dialogue is set in the public arena of the Court of the Gentiles we may assume that both the crowd and the questioners are included, so that this note advances the buildup to the conclusion in v. 34 that as a result of Jesus' answers no one dared ask any more questions.

The Sadducees and Resurrection (12:18-27)

TEXTUAL NOTES

23. There are two main issues raised by the variant readings (other than insignificant changes of word order): (1) the presence or absence of οὖν, (2) the presence or absence of the clause ὅταν ἀναστῶσιν. The οὖν may be an assimilation to Matthew and Luke, but it is in any case implicit in the conclusion to the rambling question. The clause ὅταν ἀναστῶσιν is widely attested in the versions even though missing from most early MSS, and was likely to be omitted either as apparently redundant (but see notes below) or by assimilation to Matthew and Luke; there is no obvious motive for its insertion.

---

38. Belo, 187, apparently reads Τὰ Καίσαρος ἀπόδοτε Καίσαρι as a negative verdict: 'This coin, with its image and inscription, does not belong to God or to Israel; on the contrary, it is the mark of the uncleanness inflicted on the country by the occupying power; what Jesus is rejecting is the occupation.' Even if this were a valid interpretation, it is not clear how this reading leads to the conclusion that Jesus' words do not allow the payment of the tax. How else is Caesar's 'unclean' money to be 'given back' to him?

39. The thought that as the coin bears Caesar's image so a person bears God's image, and that therefore what is owed to God is ourselves (so, e.g., C. H. Giblin, *CBQ* 33 [1971] 521-25), attractive as it may be, is certainly not explicit in the text and is not required to make sense of Jesus' pronouncement.

40. Myers, 312, asserts that the obligations to Caesar and to God are 'stated clearly as *opposites*', and on this ground rejects the 'bourgeois' exegesis which has Jesus approving the payment of the tax. While this conclusion suits Myers' ideological position, he offers no explanation as to why he sees the two halves of Jesus' exhortation (joined by καί) as 'opposites'.

41. The verb occurs only here in the NT. For its wider usage and intensive force see T. Dwyer, *Wonder,* 171-72.

26. In LXX Ex. 3:6 the phrase θεὸς Αβρααμ καὶ θεὸς Ισαακ καὶ θεὸς Ιακωβ, without articles (except that LXX A has an article before the first θεός only), follows an introductory ὁ θεὸς τοῦ πατρός σου which is omitted in all the synoptic quotations. All three synoptic quotations show textual variations here, but it seems probable that Matthew included articles before all uses of θεός, and Luke only before the first. It is perhaps more likely that Mark agreed with Luke (and substantially with the LXX) in omitting the last two articles (and possibly the first; so D W) and that they were added by assimilation to Matthew; but the matter is of stylistic rather than exegetical interest.

The question from the Pharisees and Herodians was political, with a theological nuance. The Sadducees now pose a purely theological question, earthed in a specific test case. Jesus' response to this question will be a matter of complete indifference to the Roman government, but because it focuses on an area of current controversy on which the dominant 'parties' in Jerusalem were sharply divided, it carries the potential for alienating one or other faction among the listeners. In addition, since the questioners seem to assume that Jesus supports the 'Pharisaic' notion of an afterlife, it offers the opportunity to discredit him as a wise teacher by presenting him with a reductio ad absurdum of that position which any Pharisaic teacher might be expected to find equally embarrassing, and so making him look ridiculous before the crowd.

'Sadducee', a name used only here in Mark, seems from Josephus and rabbinic sources to denote a theological and legal viewpoint, associated with the more 'aristocratic' elements in Jewish society, rather than a tightly organised 'party'.[42] Sadducean views were espoused by most of the prominent priestly families, so that this viewpoint held a dominant position in the Sanhedrin (the polarisation of views within the Sanhedrin, illustrated in Acts 23:6-8, is strongly emphasised by Josephus). This delegation therefore probably represents the ἀρχιερεῖς to whom Mark frequently refers from 11:18 onwards, and who were at the heart of the coalition against Jesus (8:31; 10:33, etc.), the specific name Σαδδουκαῖος being used here because the point at issue was one distinctive of that theological position. At the heart of their distinctive views was a conservative view of religious authority which rejected more recent oral tradition and gave primacy to the written scriptures, with the five books of the Torah as the supreme canonical authority.[43] They therefore rejected the relatively recently developed belief in an afterlife.

Probably only two passages in the OT clearly express a belief in resurrection and life after death (Is. 26:19; Dn. 12:2), though several poetic texts (notably Pss. 16:9-11; 49:15; 73:23-26; Job 19:25-26) may be seen with hindsight to be pointing in that direction.[44] From the second century B.C. onwards such a be-

42. For a useful recent discussion of the historical evidence for Sadducees see G. G. Porton, *ABD*, 5.892-95. More fully, Schürer, 2.404-14.

43. See further Schürer, 2.407-9.

44. For OT and later Jewish beliefs about resurrection see C. Brown, *DNTT*, 3.261-75. More fully G. W. E. Nickelsburg, *Resurrection;* H. C. C. Cavallin, *Life after Death.*

lief becomes increasingly frequent and explicit especially in apocalyptic works and in the traditions concerning the martyrs of the Maccabean period. For the Pharisees, with their openness to new developments in religious thought, it was therefore an attractive idea, and one which, according to Josephus, they enthusiastically adopted. But the Sadducees could find no basis for such a belief in the Pentateuch, and the minimal pointers towards an afterlife in the rest of the OT were not sufficient for them to embrace the idea. For them, as for most of the OT writers, Sheol was a final resting place, and any continuity was to be understood in terms of reputation and posterity, not in terms of personal survival.

The question assumes that Jesus shares the Pharisaic belief. In the rest of the synoptic traditions there is not very much to support this assumption, but on a few occasions a life after death is presupposed (Lk. 14:14; 16:19-31; 23:43); Jesus' predictions of his own resurrection (8:31; 9:9, 31; 10:34) are of course a special case. It is only in this pericope, however, that Jesus directly deals with the issue, and here his support for the 'Pharisaic' view is unequivocal. He repudiates in strong terms the Sadducean presuppositions of his questioners as erroneous (πλανάομαι, vv. 24, 27), and as based on ignorance both of the implications of the scriptures they claimed as their authority and of the character of the God to whom they testify (v. 24). Verse 25 then offers a description of the after-life, and vv. 26-27 provide a scriptural argument to support belief in the resurrection of the people of God. This scriptural argument is drawn, significantly, not from a later poetic passage of the OT, but from the account of Moses' meeting with God in Ex. 3, a passage whose authority the Sadducees could not dispute.[45]

The subtlety of the argument is such that it is hard to blame the Sadducees for not having drawn this inference from the Moses story. It has sometimes been understood as a simplistic argument from the tense of the verb 'I am' in Ex. 3:6, but there is no verb either in the Hebrew text or in Mark's quotation (contrast Matthew, who follows the LXX), and an argument based on the tense of an *unexpressed* verb would be not subtle but simply invalid. The argument is better understood as a reflection on the character of the covenant God whom Moses encountered, a God who through his new name 'I AM' is revealed as the living God, the ever-present helper and deliverer of his people. If such a God chooses to be identified by the names of his long-dead servants Abraham, Isaac, and Jacob, with whom his covenant was made, and whom he committed himself to protect, they cannot be simply dead and forgotten: οὐκ ἔστιν θεὸς νεκρῶν ἀλλὰ ζώντων.[46] It is a cryptic, allusive argument worthy of a rabbinic

---

45. In *b. Sanh.* 90b a number of rabbinic attempts to derive the doctrine of resurrection from the Torah are listed. While generally more imaginative than persuasive, they include one which bears comparison with Jesus' argument as interpreted here: 'R. Simai [c. A.D. 210] said: Whence do we learn resurrection from the Torah? — From the verse "And I also have established my covenant with them [the patriarchs] to give them the land of Canaan": it does not say "to give you", but "to give them"; thus resurrection is proved from the Torah.'

46. This approach, now widely accepted, was persuasively presented by F. Dreyfus, *RB* 66 (1959) 213-24.

teacher,[47] but its basis, far from being merely the tense of a verb, is in the fundamental theological understanding of Yahweh, the living God, and of the implications of his establishing an 'everlasting covenant' with his mortal worshippers.

All that, however, was the second stage of the argument, where Jesus takes the initiative and challenges the theological assumption underlying the question. As far as the question itself is concerned, τίνος αὐτῶν ἔσται γυνή;, while for the Sadducees it was apparently no more than a debating ploy, based on a totally improbable scenario of multiple remarriage under the levirate law, it must be recognised that, given a belief in an afterlife, it is in fact a very real question of considerable pastoral significance. Even without a levirate law, people do remarry, whether as a result of death or divorce, and the prospect of encountering more than one former spouse in the afterlife is a real one. What then becomes of the monogamous marriage bond, when it must be shared in eternity with more than one partner? While this is a more pressing question in our society with its culture of 'serial polygamy' with or without formal divorce and remarriage, already in Jesus' time, and even given his strict ethic of the indissolubility of marriage, the issue was raised by remarriage after bereavement.

In response to this concern Jesus offers in v. 25 a view of eternal life in which marriage is apparently irrelevant. For those for whom marriage is the basis of the deepest joy and love on earth, this is a hard saying. It may be mitigated by the fact that what Jesus excludes from the afterlife is the *process* of 'marrying and being given in marriage' rather than the resultant *state* of being married; but if that state is carried over into the next life, the problem of 'competing' relationships remains. Instead Jesus suggests that the earthly perspective, within which the exclusiveness of the marriage bond has a central place, is inappropriate to a new quality of life which is not like that of human beings on earth but of 'angels in heaven'.[48] Earthly life is temporary, and therefore requires the procreation of further life, in the context of marriage, for its continuance, but heavenly life is eternal, and there is no place in it for procreation. Marriage and reproduction belong only to the earthly sphere (note that it is marriage, not love, which Jesus declares to be inappropriate in heaven). Angels, as eternal beings, have no need to reproduce. And in such a context the exclusiveness and jealousy which belong to marriage are no longer appropriate.

---

47. This is not to say that it follows the rules of rabbinic hermeneutics; D. M. Cohn-Sherbok (*JSNT* 11 [1981] 64-73) argues that it does not, and that it therefore shows that Jesus was 'not skilled in the argumentative style of the Pharisees and Sadducees'. The point is rather that its 'scripturally artistic' approach (Gundry, 703) is closer to the ingenuity of rabbinic exegesis than to modern convention. F. G. Downing (*JSNT* 15 [1982] 42-50) suggests that Philo's use of the same text in *Abr.* 50–55 is more parallel to Jesus' argument, but quite apart from the vastly different scale of the arguments Philo's treatment is not interested in Abraham, Isaac, and Jacob as real men, but in their allegorical potential as representing the virtues of φύσις, μάθησις and ἄσκησις. As men they are merely θνητοί; ἀφθαρσία is attributed not to them, but to the virtues they represent.

48. Cf 2 *Bar.* 51:10 for the view that the departed become 'like the angels'.

Something like that seems to be the logic of Jesus' very compressed argument. It is based on a theology of angels and of heaven which is for us a matter of faith rather than experience, and as such may leave many readers less than satisfied. But its purpose is to challenge the assumption of the Sadducees that an afterlife, if it exists, must be just like this one, and can therefore be evaluated in terms of life on earth (cf. 1 Cor. 15:50). That is to fail to appreciate τὴν δύναμιν τοῦ θεοῦ.

As in previous dialogues, therefore, Mark presents Jesus as responding to a trick question not only with a clever answer but also with one which offers positive theological (and in this case pastoral) content which is appropriate not only to the immediate situation of the controversy in the temple but also to the ongoing life of the church. Brief and frustratingly cryptic as it is, it provides a basis for theological teaching.

18-19 The present tense of the clause οἵτινες λέγουσιν ἀνάστασιν μὴ εἶναι indicates that it is not a specific description of this particular group but characterises the Sadducean position in general. By singling out this aspect of Sadducean belief Mark both sets the theological context for the dialogue and suggests the cynical nature of a question based on a belief which they themselves do not hold. The address διδάσκαλε (cf. v. 14) is particularly appropriate for what purports to be a serious theological question such as a rabbi might be expected to pronounce on. And like many a rabbinic question, it starts from the common ground of a legal text in the Pentateuch. For specific attribution of a pentateuchal regulation to Μωϋσῆς cf. 1:44; 7:10; 10:3-4. What follows is a paraphrase of the basic levirate law in Dt. 25:5-6, which incorporates also an echo of the clause ἀνάστησον σπέρμα τῷ ἀδελφῷ σου in LXX Gn. 38:8, a famous example of that law in practice. The levirate law is based in the assumption that a man's 'survival' is through the continuation of the family line, and for those who could see no other form of 'resurrection' this remained an important issue. The use of the verb ἐξαναστήσῃ in the echo of Gn. 38:8 (LXX ἀνάστησον), following so soon after the reminder that the Sadducees do not believe in ἀνάστασις, neatly emphasises that this is the only sort of 'resurrection' they can envisage. While there is little evidence of the observance of this law in the OT (and in the two instances recorded there is resistance on the part of the survivor: Gn. 38:9-10; Ru. 4:6-8), the existence of a large body of rabbinic law on the subject (Mishnah, tractate *Yebamot*) indicates that it was still in force in the time of Jesus.

20-23 The test case is probably to be regarded as fictitious (though Matthew's addition of παρ' ἡμῖν, echoed in some Western MSS of Mark, suggests that in his view they intended it to be taken as factual), designed to discredit a doctrine of resurrection which could lead to such an embarrassing outcome. The story of Sarah, the survivor of seven unconsummated marriages (Tob. 3:8), may have suggested the scenario to them, though there is no levirate principle involved in that story, merely repeated widowhood and remarriage, with a happy ending. The clause ὅταν ἀναστῶσιν in v. 23 (see Textual Note), while it may seem redundant after ἐν τῇ ἀναστάσει, perhaps serves to draw out the point of the story: 'when *all eight of them* rise'.

24 As with the poll tax, Jesus' response is not a simple answer to the question, but a repudiation of the assumptions on which it was based. But this time he does not simply set aside their 'error' (πλανάομαι; cf. also v. 27), but analyses it. διὰ τοῦτο normally, as in Mark's other two uses of the phrase (6:14; 11:24), refers back to the immediately preceding words as the reason,[49] but here there are no preceding words of Jesus, and it is more naturally understood (as in the phrases διὰ τοῦτο ὅτι and διὰ τοῦτο ἵνα) as introducing a reason which is then spelled out in the participial clause μὴ εἰδότες. . . . The basis of their error is twofold. First of all, they do not know τὰς γραφάς; for the plural cf. 14:49. For the Sadducees, who saw their position as based on Scripture and not on later ideas, that was a particularly wounding accusation, and one which Jesus will need to justify in vv. 26-27. Whether they would accept that his interpretation of Scripture there was legitimate may well be doubted. But more fundamentally they have also missed τὴν δύναμιν τοῦ θεοῦ. Resurrection is not a matter of human potential but of divine power; their rejection of it is the product of a secular perspective. It is this charge which is developed in v. 25.

25 γαμέω normally denotes the bridegroom's action, 'take a wife', γαμίζω the father's 'give in marriage', and the verbs are similarly combined in Mt. 24:38; Lk. 17:27, though the uses of both may be flexible, and there is disagreement over which sense is intended in the other NT use of γαμίζω in 1 Cor. 7:38. The two verbs together speak of marriage as a social institution, appropriate to earthly life but not to the life to come. The argument does not require that angels be sexless beings,[50] but merely that they have no need to reproduce and therefore to marry.[51] The argument from the nature of angels would carry little weight with the Sadducees if, as Luke asserts, they did not believe in them (Acts 23:8-10), but Luke's assertion (which is not echoed in Josephus's accounts of the Sadducees) is surprising in that there is no shortage of angels in the Pentateuch on which Sadducean beliefs were supposedly based.

26-27 For περὶ δέ as an indication of change of subject see on 13:32. Here it marks the shift from the specific question asked by the Sadducees to the fundamental rejection of belief in resurrection which underlies it, and which Jesus is now challenging on the basis of the γραφαί which he has just accused them of failing to grasp. The change from the active ἀναστῶσιν in vv. 23, 25 to

---

49. Gundry, 702, 705-6, argues for the same use here, the reason referred to being the Sadducees' question and what it reveals of their beliefs; but as he then has to construe the following μὴ εἰδότες as a *second* reason the result is unnecessarily complicated.

50. For Jewish beliefs on the sexuality of angels see W. D. Davies and D. C. Allison, *Matthew*, 3.229-30. Belo, 189, protests against the Greek ideology which leads to the belief that 'the eschatological narrative will be the affair of eunuchs', and concludes that 'while procreation and marriage are excluded, we do not see why sexual love, which is a power, should be a priori excluded'.

51. Cf. *1 Enoch* 15:7 for the idea that marriage is not appropriate for 'the spiritual beings of heaven'.

the passive ἐγείρονται here may be intended to draw attention to the fact that resurrection is not automatic but is the result of God's active concern (as the argument of vv. 26-27 will assume), a demonstration of the δύναμις τοῦ θεοῦ (v. 24). For οὐκ ἀνέγνωτε; cf. 2:25; 12:10, in each case introducing an argument from Scripture which, as in this case, is not obvious on the surface of the OT text, but which derives its force from the context into which that text is introduced. Jesus now refers them to that same Μωϋσῆς whom they have quoted in v. 19. The source of the quoted text is, unusually, specifically identified, not only by book (ἐν τῇ βίβλῳ Μωϋσέως, denoting probably the Pentateuch as a whole rather than merely the Book of Exodus in which Moses' story is primarily told)[52] but also by section, ἐπὶ τοῦ βάτου. In the absence of chapter and verse numbers, the use of a striking feature of the text, in this case Moses' encounter with God at the burning bush, formed an appropriate means of reference. Such references by keywords indicating the content of a passage are found in rabbinic literature and in Philo,[53] and there is a NT parallel in Rom. 11:2, ἐν Ἠλίᾳ, 'in the story of Elijah'. The ἐπί followed by the genitive is best understood not as a means of reference to a passage called 'the Bush' but as part of the phrase ἐπὶ τοῦ βάτου, 'at the bush', which denotes Ex. 3:1ff (BAGD, 286a, I.a.γ).[54]

The variation in MSS with regard to the presence or absence of articles with each occurrence of θεός in the quotation of Ex. 3:6 (see Textual Note) is not exegetically significant. The absence of the LXX verb εἰμι (though the Latin and other versions have of course had to supply it) corresponds to the Hebrew syntax, and shows that the argument is not based on its tense.[55] For the logic of Jesus' conclusion see the introductory comments on this pericope. It depends on a belief in the living God and in his covenant commitment to his people, which is firmly founded not just on Ex. 3:6 but on the whole story and theology of the Pentateuch, so that even if the Sadducees may have found his inference from that particular text too subtle, they ought to recognise the scriptural foundation of the conclusion he draws. 'God of the dead' is not a term which is appropriate to Yahweh as he is revealed in the books of Moses.[56]

The pericope concludes with Jesus' comprehensive verdict on Saducean error rather than with an indication of people's reaction as in vv. 12, 17, 34, and 37, but that element is supplied in v. 28 by the scribe's recognition that Jesus has answered well.

---

52. See G. Schrenk, *TDNT,* 1.616, for the use of the singular βίβλος for the whole Pentateuch.

53. For examples see W. Sanday and A. C. Headlam, *Romans,* 310-11.

54. Another possible translation would be 'in the book of Moses at the bush', taking 'Moses at the bush' as a 'title'. But the use of βίβλος is against this, and suggests rather the 'Book(s) of Moses'.

55. *Pace,* e.g., R. N. Longenecker, *Exegesis,* 68-69; Anderson, 279.

56. That Jesus was not the only one to hold this belief is indicated by *m. Sanh.* 10:1, which includes among those who have no share in the world to come 'he that says that there is no resurrection of the dead prescribed in the Torah' (a Pharisaic attack on Sadducean belief?).

The Greatest Commandment (12:28-34)

TEXTUAL NOTE

34. The omission of αὐτόν by ℵ D W Θ and many other MSS is an obvious correction to the redundancy of Mark's grammar; its omission in most OL and some other versions is naturally explained as a matter of idiomatic translation rather than of textual difference.

Two hostile questions are followed by one which, while it deals with a subject of keen rabbinic debate and therefore offers the possibility of an undiplomatic or unpopular answer, is presented by Mark (unlike Matthew and Luke,[57] who regard this questioner too as [ἐκ]πειράζων αὐτόν) in a positive light, both in his introductory comment that the questioner has been impressed by Jesus' previous answer, and even more by depicting the questioner as satisfied by Jesus' answer to his own question. Moreover, the scribe's pleased response leads into a lengthy supplementary statement of his own, to which in turn Jesus replies with a remarkably positive verdict on him as 'not far from the kingdom of God', all of this final section being peculiar to Mark.[58]

This mutual congratulation lends a quite new atmosphere to this latest encounter. Together with the information that thereafter no one dared ask any more questions and the fact that the next question is posed not to Jesus but by him (and is left unanswered), Mark's way of narrating this episode suggests that in the contest which has been taking place since 11:27 it is Jesus who is now emerging as the clear winner. He will then follow up his advantage with some caustic comments on the scribes (who have been part of the group opposing him since his arrival in Jerusalem) and on other influential people in the temple.

This pericope then marks a significant turning point in the Jerusalem confrontation. And yet it is remarkable that the questioner who introduces it and who responds so warmly to Jesus' teaching is εἷς τῶν γραμματέων, a member of the group who have been some of Jesus' chief opponents in Galilee, who have been implicated in the challenge to Jesus since his arrival in the city, and who will soon be singled out for attack in vv. 38-40. Perhaps it is significant that he is only εἷς, so that his positive attitude and spiritual perception stand in significant contrast to the γραμματεῖς taken as a whole, who will continue to recur in the passion narrative as partners in the coalition against Jesus. One open-minded scribe symbolises what might have been, but he stands alone.[59]

---

57. While the setting of the double quotation of Dt. 6:5 and Lv. 19:18b in Luke is quite different, and it is the νομικός rather than Jesus who combines them, the passages are parallel in a literary sense, with Matthew sharing Luke's term νομικός rather than Mark's γραμματεύς.

58. See, however, Gundry's argument (710) that Mark intends us to see this questioner as equally hostile initially, but then 'capitulating'.

59. There is an interesting discussion of Mark's attitude to the scribes in E. Trocmé, *Formation,* 94-99. In contrast to Mark's overall hostility to the scribes, this man is 'the exception

The question of v. 14 was primarily political with theological overtones, and that of v. 23 essentially theological. Here, as is appropriate to a question from a scribe, we move onto more legal ground. The question is familiar from scribal debates about the law.[60] Given that there are, according to scribal reckoning, 613 separate commandments in the five Books of Moses (R. Simlai [c. 250] in *b. Mak.* 23b), the question of priority could not be avoided. The rabbis discussed which commandments were 'heavy' and which 'light', and sometimes ranked certain categories of law as more essential than others.[61] There was a natural desire for a convenient summary of the law's requirements, a single principle from which all the rest of the Torah was derived (the rabbis used the term $k^e l\bar{a}l$ for such a summarising principle).[62] See *b. Šab.* 31a for the famous request to Shammai and Hillel to 'teach me the whole Torah while I am standing on one leg', and Hillel's reply, 'Do not do to your neighbour what is hateful to you; this is the whole Torah: the rest is commentary.' Jesus' own summary in Mt. 7:12 is strikingly similar, and again carries the rider, 'This is the law and the prophets'.

The use of Lv. 19:18b in this connection is paralleled by R. Akiba's statement that this text is 'a great principle ($k^e l\bar{a}l$) in the Torah' (*Sipra* Lv. 19:18). Dt. 6:4-5 was also familiar as a summary of true religion, through its twice-daily repetition as the opening clause of the *Š^ema'*. A few Jewish writings bring together love for God with love for other people (*Test. Dan* 5:3; *Test. Iss.* 5:2; 7:6), though not by means of actual OT quotations.[63] Philo on a number of occasions states a similar double duty, and in *Spec. Leg.* 2.63 asserts that the two ἀνωτάτω κεφάλαια are piety and holiness towards God and φιλανθρωπία and justice towards men.[64] So, while these sources vary in date and do not all represent Palestinian thought, it seems likely that the gist of Jesus' response to the question would have caused no surprise. But for his ex-

---

that proved the rule'. He is presented as 'an appeal to the honest scribes to leave their authorities and organized parties in order to recognize the superiority of Jesus as an interpreter of Scripture and a representative of the best rabbinic tradition' (p. 97). See also J. F. Williams, *Followers,* 172-74.

60. For many examples see Str-B, 1.900-908.

61. For example, *t. Pe'ah* 4:19, 'Charity and deeds of loving-kindness outweigh all other commandments in the Torah'. *M. Ḥag.* 1:8 singles out certain categories of law (concerning property, temple service, and purity) as 'the essentials of the Torah'.

62. In *b. Ber.* 63a Pr. 3:6 is offered as a 'short text upon which all the essential principles of the Torah depend'. *B. Mak.* 24a finds the law reduced to eleven principles in Ps. 15, to six in Is. 33:15-16, to three in Mi. 6:8, to two in Is. 56:1, and to one in Am. 5:4b and in Hab. 2:4b.

63. Cf *Jub.* 36:7-8, which links the duty of fearing and worshipping God with that of loving one's brother.

64. By ἀνωτάτω κεφάλαια Philo may well mean the 'superscriptions for the two tables of the decalogue' (C. Burchard) and in *Decal.* 108–10 he describes those who keep the first table as φιλόθεοι and those who keep the second table as φιλάνθρωποι. Since Philo understood the decalogue to be the summary of the Torah (*Decal.* 20.154), he is close in principle to Jesus' use of the double love commandment here as a summary of the law. Cf also Philo, *Abr.* 208, for a briefer twofold summary.

plicit linking together of these two very familiar OT texts we have no Jewish precedent.[65]

His summarising of the demands of the law in terms of love was clearly influential, for not only does love feature prominently both in the NT accounts of Jesus' teaching and in the exhortations of the writers of the NT letters, but Paul explicitly teaches that πλήρωμα νόμου ἡ ἀγάπη (Rom. 13:10, following an explicit quotation of Lv. 19:18b as the demand in which all other commandments are summarised, ἀνακεφαλαιοῦται; similarly Gal. 5:14), and Jas. 2:8 gives pride of place to Lv. 19:18b as the νόμος βασιλικός.

Jesus is asked which commandment is πρώτη, and he responds by listing the two love commandments as πρώτη and δευτέρα, but then goes on to speak of these two commandments as 'greater' than all others (cf. Mt. 22:38, where πρώτη is apparently equated with μεγάλη). His questioner, in agreeing with him, declares such love to be περισσότερον than the ritual commandments of sacrifice. This evaluative language is not typical of the rabbis, who spoke of 'light' and 'heavy' commandments, but on the understanding that all are equally valid,[66] and who, while they might look for summarising principles, do not seem to have ranked individual commandments as 'first' or 'more important'.[67] The difference may not have seemed great at the time, but the sort of language Mark uses here lends itself to later Christian discrimination between elements in the law, particularly with regard to the continuance of animal sacrifice. The scribe's 'demotion' of the sacrificial laws below the obligation to love, and Jesus' warm reception of this view as indicating closeness to the kingdom of God, could not but hasten the Christian abandonment of the ritual elements of the Torah.

28 As with each of the previous questions Mark specifically mentions the questioner's approach to Jesus (cf. 11:27; 12:13-14, 18); Jesus, the teacher in the temple, is the fixed point while others come and go. But whereas other questions have been posed by groups, giving the impression of official delegations, this comes from an individual, and it soon becomes clear that his attitude is not that of the majority of the γραμματεῖς. He comes already favourably disposed towards Jesus, and leaves even more so. Such an open-minded enquirer prefigures the minority support which Jesus and his followers will find even in the Sanhedrin (15:43; Acts 5:33-39; cf. Jn. 7:50-51; 19:38-40). His favourable impression derives from listening to the previous dialogues (see on 8:11; 9:14

---

65. See J. Piper, *Love,* 92-94, for both the originality and the authenticity of this combination by Jesus, in response to the arguments to the contrary by C. Burchard in E. Lohse (ed.), *Das Ruf Jesu und die Antwort der Gemeinde,* 39-62.

66. So especially *m. 'Abot* 2:1: 'Obey a light commandment as carefully as a heavy one, for you do not know how each will be rewarded.' 4 Macc. 5:20 recognises a distinction between μικρά and μεγάλα in the observance of the law, but insists that both are of equal validity (ἰσοδύναμον). See further W. Grundmann, *TDNT,* 4.535-36.

67. For some examples of rabbinic ways of avoiding the force of unpalatable laws without denying their validity see E. P. Sanders, *Jesus,* 248-49.

for the sense of hostile confrontation in συζητέω). καλῶς in this context means not just 'cleverly' (so as to escape the intended trap or even to win the argument), but that Jesus' answers have been good, wholesome, satisfying, leading the scribe to hope for an equally enlightening (not just clever) answer to his own more fundamental question; cf. the combination of καλῶς with ἐπ' ἀληθείας in v. 32.

If ποῖος here carried its classical sense 'what kind of', the question would relate to a category of commandment rather than expecting one specific text to be quoted. But by NT times this sense had been eroded, and ποῖος is commonly used as an alternative to τίς. Jesus' reply takes it in that sense, as surely the feminine singular πρώτη requires. After ἐντολή the masculine/neuter form πάντων is surprising, and has led to the suggestion that it does not mean 'all (other) commandments' but simply means 'everything', which would then result in 'a widening of the boundary of the question from that of the Law to that of morality in general'.[68] But while the idea of one commandment being the 'first' in a ranking of commandments is natural enough, πρώτη πάντων is not a natural way to say 'more important than anything else'. BDF, 164(1), describe πάντων here as 'a frozen masc.-neut. form', by which they presumably mean that it derives its gender from the use of a stereotyped idiom πρώτη πάντων rather than from the gender of the noun ἐντολή. At any rate it seems clear that Jesus is being asked to identify a 'first commandment'.

29-30 Only Mark records Jesus' use of Dt. 6:4 (the theological preamble) along with the ethical demand of Dt. 6:5. It is the latter, of course, which is the point of the quotation: Dt. 6:4 is not in itself a 'command'. But by including it Mark not only makes the text more instantly recognisable as the opening part of the Šᵉmaʽ, but also grounds the 'first commandment' in the essential tenet of Jewish belief, monotheism, and so establishes Jesus' theological orthodoxy.[69] The quotation is in LXX form, but with two variations. In place of δυνάμεως in the final phrase Mark has ἰσχύος; there is no great difference in meaning, and ἰσχύος (Luke uses the same noun) may well reflect an alternative Greek version which was in common use.[70] It represents the Hebrew mᵉʼōd, delightfully rendered by BDB 'muchness, force, abundance, exceedingly', which was rendered in the targums by māmônāʼ, 'possessions', and clearly allows a range of possible Greek renderings. The other difference from the LXX is that Mark has added the phrase καὶ ἐξ ὅλης τῆς διανοίας σου, thus giving four phrases where Deuteronomy had only three. There is some variation in the three nouns in the LXX versions of Dt. 6:5 and of the related text 2 Ki. 23:25, all four of Mark's nouns being represented among the variants, but with the exception of the

68. R. J. Banks, *Law,* 165-66.
69. See J. Marcus, *Way,* 145-46, for the suggestion that this orthodox statement is placed here deliberately to counterbalance the suggestion of 12:36-37 that as 'David's Lord' Jesus will be enthroned beside God, thus promoting a suspect 'two powers' theology.
70. In the related text 2 Ki. 23:25 LXX uses ἰσχύς instead of δύναμις. The same phenomenon in some texts of LXX Dt. 6:5 is probably due to NT influence.

Lucianic revision (presumably influenced by NT texts) no LXX version has more than the three nouns of the Hebrew. Mark and Luke, however (according to the best represented text), each have four nouns, though Mark reverts to only three in the scribe's résumé in v. 33. Matthew, like Dt. 6:5, has only three nouns, but by retaining Mark's additional διάνοια and omitting ἰσχύς he has left himself without an equivalent to the third Hebrew noun, m^e'ōd.[71] These variations indicate a text in regular liturgical or catechetical use. They do not greatly affect the overall sense of the pronouncement, but the NT expansion from three nouns to four seems to be a distinctive feature of Jesus' use of it. It is difficult to differentiate clearly between the force of καρδία, ψυχή and διάνοια in the context of Hebrew thought, but the addition of διάνοια (BAGD 187a: 'understanding, intelligence, mind, thought') *may* suggest a deliberate extension of the familiar text to emphasise the intellectual faculty as a key element in God's service.

31 Jesus was asked for one 'first commandment', but responds with two, which together hold the preeminent position. The two are linked both by the key verb ἀγαπήσεις[72] and by the fact that they represent respectively the first and second parts of the decalogue.[73] In 10:19 Jesus has quoted only the commandments of the 'second table', as being the most appropriate for the rich man's ethical self-examination, but here, where what is requested is a general statement of priorities, both 'tables' are represented, and with a clear priority between them, πρώτη and δευτέρα: love of other people finds its true place only on the basis of a prior love of God. See the introduction to this section for the widespread perception, Jewish and Christian, of the appropriateness of Lv. 19:18b as an ethical summary, and cf. its use in Mt. 19:18-19 in conjunction with the commandments of the 'second table'. In its realistic assumption that it is normal to love oneself it may seem in conflict with Jesus' demand for self-denial (8:34-37), but that passage calls not for a low view of self as such, but rather for a higher loyalty to the claims of Jesus.

There is, however, the question of how far τὸν πλησίον σου extends. There is little doubt that in the OT context (note that the first half of the verse forbids vengeance against 'the sons of your own people') it denoted a fellow member of the covenant community (though Lv. 19:34 extends it also to the 'resident alien'); even if the 'corollary' καὶ μισήσεις τὸν ἐχθρόν σου which Jesus quotes in Mt. 5:43 is an addition to the text, it is one which draws on the likely meaning of 'neighbour' in its original setting. The term πλησίον at least potentially restricts the scope of the love required. That is why when Luke records Jesus' approval of Lv. 19:18b as an ethical guide the dialogue continues (Lk. 10:29) with the question

71. The different versions and main textual variants are displayed in a table on p. 22 of R. H. Gundry, *Use,* to which should be added the range of patristic citations shown by Legg ad loc.

72. The link may have been helped by the fact that the Hebrew verb-form (the jussive w^e'āhabtā) occurs in the OT only in these two places and in the texts which 'echo' them in Dt. 11:1 and Lv. 19:34.

73. See above, p. 477 n. 64.

καὶ τίς ἐστίν μου πλησίον; with the parable of the Good Samaritan as its shockingly inclusivist answer. Here the point is not explored, and it may be that the scribe's enthusiasm for Jesus' answer was based on a more limited (and exegetically correct) understanding of the 'neighbour' than Jesus intended or than subsequent Christian interpretation has given to this passage.

32-33 For καλῶς as an exclamation in response to someone else's statement ('Well said', 'Hear, hear!') cf. Rom. 11:20 (BAGD, 401b, 4.c). The scribe's approving paraphrase of Jesus' pronouncement picks up and develops both its theology and its ethics. The clause εἷς ἐστιν derives directly from Dt. 6:4, but οὐκ ἔστιν ἄλλος πλὴν αὐτοῦ is a more explicitly monotheistic formula which echoes Dt. 4:35 and the language of Deutero-Isaiah (e.g., Is. 45:21), and links the thought back again to the decalogue, οὐκ ἔσονταί σοι θεοὶ ἕτεροι πλὴν ἐμοῦ (Ex. 20:3). The scribe's quotation of Dt. 6:5 brings yet more variation to that flexible text, though again without any significant change in the sense, in that though the scribe properly returns to only three nouns, the second of them is now σύνεσις, which has no place elsewhere in the textual tradition. Its meaning is not far from that of διάνοια and has a similarly 'intellectual' tone.

But while the alteration to the form of the quoted text makes little difference to the sense, the words that follow are striking. Jesus' general concluding formula μείζων τούτων ἄλλη ἐντολὴ οὐκ ἔστιν is now given a more specific focus by setting his double love commandment against the foil of πάντα τὰ ὁλοκαυτώματα καὶ θυσίαι. Compared with them the double love command is περισσότερον, 'much more' (the comparative form being more emphatic than just περισσόν), affirming the greater importance or priority implied by the πρώτη of both question and answer. This sweeping 'demotion' of the whole system of temple sacrifice on the part of a scribe (much of whose professional concern focused around sacrificial regulations) is remarkable,[74] though it may be paralleled by the summaries of the law attributed to both Hillel and Akiba (see above, p. 477). Its terms strongly recall Ho. 6:6, where in the LXX the same two nouns, θυσία and ὁλοκαυτώματα are subordinated to ἔλεος (towards other people?) and ἐπίγνωσις θεοῦ. It does not of course, any more than did Ho. 6:6 (and cf. e.g., 1 Sa. 15:22; Is. 1:10-17; Je. 7:22-23), imply any doubt as to the validity of the sacrificial system; the point is its relative importance.[75] But Jesus' commendation of the scribe's sense of perspective will not have been lost on Mark's readers who, even before the temple system was forcibly brought to an end in A.D. 70, were facing (or had already decided) the question whether Christians should continue to be associated with the ritual aspects of the law in the light of Jesus' 'fulfilment' of it.

---

74. Contrast the famous saying of R. Simeon the Just: 'By three things is the world sustained: by the Torah, by the temple worship, and by deeds of love' (*m. 'Abot* 1:2).

75. A similar perception is attributed to R. Johanan ben Zakkai in *'Abot R. Nat.* 4:5 (20a): seeing the temple in ruins, he said, 'My son, be not grieved, for we have another means of atonement which is as effective, and that is the practice of lovingkindness, as it is stated, For I desire lovingkindness and not sacrifice.'

34 It is probably too subtle to see in the rare adverb νουνεχῶς (with good sense, discretion, *nous*) a deliberate echo of the phrases ἐξ ὅλης τῆς διανοίας (v. 30), ἐξ ὅλης τῆς συνέσεως (v. 33), but the scribe's reply has assured Jesus that his mind is well attuned to the divine perspective. This places him οὐ μακρὰν ἀπὸ τῆς βασιλείας τοῦ θεοῦ, not yet a part of it apparently, but unlike the rich who will find it so hard to enter the kingdom of God (10:23, 24, 25) this man is a promising potential recruit.[76] It is a pity that we hear no more of his further progress. In Mark's previous mentions of the kingdom of God we have repeatedly noted a contrast between the divine and human perspective, and a sense of surprise, even of shock, as the unfamiliar values of God's kingship are recognised. It is a secret given only to those who follow Jesus and hear his teaching (4:11). But here is a man who is already a good part of the way through the readjustment of values which the kingdom of God demands and which the disciples have been so painfully confronting on the way to Jerusalem.

After such an encouraging comment it is surprising to read that no one dared ask any more questions. Does Mark intend us to think back to the discomfiture experienced by the earlier questioners, or are we to assume that the 'good sense' displayed by this man is so exceptional, and the implications of his statement so radical, that others are wary of associating with him? But perhaps it is more likely that Mark intends no such direct link with the immediately preceding pericope, and that the final clause of v. 34 is simply a bridge passage to prepare for the new pattern from v. 35 where it is Jesus himself who poses the question or speaks on his own initiative.[77]

The Status of the Messiah (12:35-37)

TEXTUAL NOTE

36. ὑποπόδιον, the LXX term, is found in most NT citations of or allusions to Ps. 110:1 (Lk. 20:43; Acts 2:34; Heb. 1:13; 10:13). In 1 Cor. 15:25 there is a simple ὑπό, and in Mt. 22:44 (probably) ὑποκάτω, which may have been derived from reminiscence of LXX Ps. 8:7. In view of the LXX form of the rest of the quotation, it is perhaps more likely that Mark followed the LXX at this point too (as in a wide range of MSS and versions), and the text was later assimilated to Matthew. But the authorities for ὑποκάτω, though not numerous, are also impressive.

---

76. J. F. Williams, *Followers,* 175, draws out the links between this pericope and that concerning the rich man, to whom he argues that Mark has deliberately set the scribe up as a contrast.

77. This understanding of the final sentence of v. 34 is reasonable in its own right, without invoking the theory of D. Daube that the four 'dialogues' of chapter 12 are modelled on the questions and answers of the Passover haggadah, where the fourth explanation is given to the one who 'knows not how to ask' (Stock, 15).

The only question posed by Jesus in the sequence of temple dialogues[78] is remarkably enigmatic, the more so since it is unanswered and is left hanging tantalisingly in the air.[79] It raises an apparently academic question about 'the Messiah', without any overt indication that Jesus is that Messiah, though in the context of Mark's gospel, coming between Peter's declaration in 8:29 and Jesus' own open messianic claim in 14:61-62 (which again uses words from Ps. 110:1 concerning his coming glory), there is no doubt that the reader is expected to apply it to him. In the narrative context, too, it is hardly likely that those who were aware of Jesus' ostentatiously royal ride to the city, with the shouts of Hosanna and the invocation of the coming kingdom of David, could have seen this question as having no relevance to Jesus' own identity and status, even though its 'academic' presentation prevents it from being used against him as a messianic claim.

The title 'Son of David', first heard explicitly in 10:47, 48, has been brought into sharper focus by the shouts of the crowd in 11:10. As a popular equivalent for 'Messiah' it has served to express the hopes of many that Jesus is the long-awaited 'King of the Jews', and Jesus' failure to suppress it when uttered by Bartimaeus or to curb the messianic language of the crowd outside Jerusalem seems to indicate that he did not find it unacceptable. Indeed, the manner of his approach to the city seems to have actively encouraged it. Yet the thrust of this pericope seems to be at least to devalue this title, if not to disavow it altogether, and 'Son of David' will not occur again in Mark's story. When we add the extremely compressed and enigmatic nature of Jesus' rhetorical question, it is hardly surprising that this pericope has led to quite divergent interpretations.

Its main point, however, is clear enough: the Messiah is to be understood as David's 'lord' rather than as his 'son'.[80] Discussion focusses on the means by which this conclusion is drawn from Ps. 110:1 and the christological implications it may be expected to carry.

Given the assumptions made by Jesus (that the psalm is by David, that the 'lord' it speaks of is the Messiah, and that one addressed as 'lord' is superior to the one using the title), which we shall discuss in the notes below, the inference is properly drawn that the Messiah is superior to David, and it is in this light

---

78. There has been discussion as to whether this pericope represents an actual dialogue during Jesus' final week or whether it reflects a debate in the post-Easter church. As we shall see, the argument would have been potentially embarrassing for a church which had come to take it for granted that Jesus, as Messiah, was the Son of David. For a brief but cogent discussion of the authenticity of the pericope see D. L. Bock, *Blasphemy*, 220-22.

79. D. M. Hay, *Glory*, 114, suggests that 'Mark's dominant motive for including this saying about David's son was probably a literary one, that of creating a tension in the gospel not to be resolved before Jesus' trial'.

80. This understanding is supported as early as the late first or early second century in *Barn.* 12:10-11, which paraphrases this pericope, concluding 'See how David calls him "lord" and does not say "son".' Preceding the reference to Ps. 110 is the statement that Jesus is 'not the son of a man but the Son of God'.

that the title 'Son of David' is queried. But what is the point of setting up such an argument?

It can hardly be, in Mark's intention or in his readers' interpretation, that Bartimaeus and the crowd were wrong and that Jesus is not the Son of David. It seems to have been an unquestioned conviction in first-century Christianity that the title 'Son of David', even though not much emphasised especially in the Gentile church, was appropriate for Jesus. His Davidic descent was a credal 'given' for Paul (Rom. 1:3-4; cf. 2 Tim. 2:8); it was the subject of a careful demonstration in Matthew's genealogy, leading up to the formal adoption of Jesus by Joseph, 'son of David' (Mt. 1:20), and 'Son of David' recurs as a title seven times in his gospel; it plays a prominent role in Luke's infancy narrative (Lk. 1:27, 32, 69; 2:4, 11); it remains an essential part of Jesus' credentials in Rev. 5:5; 22:16. It is inconceivable that there were Christians, even Gentile Christians, after the middle of the first century who would not have taken it for granted that Jesus was the Son of David. If it had been Mark's intention to supplant this belief he would have needed a far more direct approach than these three verses offer, and he would have had to rewrite 10:47-48 and 11:10.[81]

There are two more likely lines of interpretation, which are not necessarily mutually exclusive. Negatively, the title 'Son of David', while too firmly fixed in the tradition to be supplanted, might have been felt to encourage too nationalistic and political an understanding of Jesus' mission,[82] and therefore this pericope may be designed to consign it to the category of 'true but inadequate', or 'true but liable to misunderstanding'. After the enthusiastic shouts of the pilgrim crowd about the 'coming kingdom of our father David' (11:10) there was the real possibility of 'Son of David' language being interpreted, by friends as well as enemies, in a way Jesus would not have wished to associate himself with.[83]

More positively, the unanswered question leaves open the possibility of filling the gap left by 'Son of David' with a more christologically adequate title. In Matthew's version the original question is open-ended, Τίνος υἱός ἐστιν; and the dismissal of the answer τοῦ Δαυίδ leaves the question still open; there can be little doubt that Matthew and his readers would have supplied the answer

81. B. D. Chilton, *JSNT* 14 (1982) 88-112, offers the novel proposal that, far from denying his Davidic connections, Jesus is here asserting that he is Son of David but 'intended to deflect the growing suspicion that he claimed to be messiah'. Chilton argues that whatever 'Son of David' may have meant to other Jews, for Jesus it was not a messianic title, but indicated (a) his actual descent and (b) his healing and exorcistic activity: see above, p. 423 n. 53, for this interpretation of 'Son of David'. For a brief but cogent response see J. Marcus, *Way,* 151-52.

82. So especially J. Marcus, *Way,* 146-49, and Lane's commentary. Cf. J. Jeremias, *Theology,* 259; E. Lohse, *TDNT,* 8.484-85.

83. On this understanding Jesus' treatment of 'Son of David' here would be closely parallel to his treatment of ὁ Χριστός in 8:29-33 (cf. 14:61-62); it is not incorrect but inadequate, and potentially misleading in the light of popular expectation. D. M. Hay, *Glory,* 111, speaks of 'a deliberate rejection of the mundane interpretation of Ps 110 perhaps favored by Hasmoneans and other post-exilic Jews'.

'the Son of God', and Mark may well have expected his readers to do the same, though his formulation of the dialogue does not prompt them so blatantly.[84]

Mark, unlike Matthew and Luke, identifies the belief that the Messiah is the Son of David as the teaching of the γραμματεῖς. This identification gives a specific 'sparring partner' as in the previous dialogues, and links this pericope with the scribe who asked the previous question (v. 28) and with the blanket condemnation of scribes which will follow in vv. 38-40. The final stages of the public confrontation in Jerusalem, therefore, are focused particularly on the difference of perspective between Jesus and the scribes. Since the scribes have also been prominent in the earlier controversies in and around Galilee, and will be one of the main partners in Jesus' condemnation in chapters 14–15, this focus increases the coherence of Mark's story. Any hope of a rapprochement between Jesus and the scribes which may have been raised by the story of the one open-minded scribe of vv. 28-34 is therefore firmly quenched.[85]

35 The location of the dialogues was fixed by the mention in 11:27 that it was as he was walking in the temple that the members of the Sanhedrin approached Jesus with their challenge to his authority. Since then no change of scene has been indicated, and now we are reminded again that Jesus is teaching ἐν τῷ ἱερῷ, where he will remain (as 12:41 will confirm) until he makes his dramatic exit in 13:1. As a Passover visitor, with no place of his own in Jerusalem, he has made the public arena of the Court of the Gentiles his base of operations since his arrival, and is by now presumably becoming a familar figure there.[86]

The question Jesus poses is a theological one, and therefore it is appropriate that he traces the designation of the Messiah as the 'Son of David' to the teaching of the scribes (whose view he accepts as a starting point, as he did in 9:11-13), even though it was by now a widely held belief. ὁ Χριστός represents the Hebrew/Aramaic term Messiah, 'anointed', which, though a post-OT development as a recognised title for the eschatological deliverer, was by now a familiar part of theological thought and of popular hope. Many different eschatological strands could be subsumed under this title, depending on who used it,

---

84. Much light is thrown on this puzzling pericope by the argument of J. Marcus, *NovT* 31 (1989) 125-41, concerning 14:61, where he concludes that the combined title ὁ Χριστὸς ὁ υἱὸς τοῦ εὐλογητοῦ is a case not of 'non-restrictive apposition' ('the Messiah, i.e., the Son of God') but of 'restrictive apposition' ('the Messiah–Son-of-God' as opposed to any other Messiah). In particular Marcus contrasts this alleged claim to be 'Messiah–Son-of-God' with the lesser office of 'Messiah–Son-of-David'. On pp. 135-37 Marcus interprets 12:35-37 in this light: Jesus replaces the merely 'restorative' role of a Son of David with the more far-reaching ('utopian') role of a Messiah who sits at God's right hand. He concludes, 'Although the title "Son of God" is not explicitly used in any of the Synoptic versions of this pericope, it is probably implicit in all three Synoptic passages that Jesus is not just the Son of David because he is the Son of God.'

85. J. Marcus, *Way*, 133-37, argues that the citation of Ps. 110:1 in the middle of a series of pericopes focusing on scribes invites the reader to see the scribes as among those 'enemies' over whom, according to Ps. 110:1-2, the Messiah at God's right hand is summoned to rule.

86. For possible christological significance in the location in the temple see J. Marcus, *Way*, 137-39.

but among them the dominant view, deriving from the oracle of 2 Sa. 7:12-16, was that God would raise up a new king of the line of David to be the focus of his people's eventual liberation and restoration. υἱὸς Δαυίδ was a convenient title to encapsulate this hope, and its use in this sense is first attested in the first-century-B.C. *Pss. Sol.* 17:21.[87] Since this is generally understood to represent the views of a pious group in Jerusalem, quite likely the Pharisees, it seems reasonable to conclude that it represents what 'scribes' (the majority of whom were associated with the Pharisaic party) would have been teaching well before the time of Jesus. The first premise of Jesus' argument is therefore not controversial: this was indeed scribal teaching.[88]

36 The argument now depends on the view that the words of Ps. 110:1 are those of αὐτὸς Δαυίδ, and that he is speaking about the Messiah, ὁ κύριός μου. Both assumptions would be rejected by the large majority of OT scholars today. Psalm 110, while no longer thought of as belonging to the Hasmonean period, is assumed to be a typical royal psalm, in which the anonymous psalmist envisages God's summons to the current king, ὁ κύριός μου (probably at the time of his enthronement), to sit at his right hand in triumph. If any connection with David at all is allowed (and most would not date the psalm so early), it would be not as author but as the one addressed by God in the psalm.[89] And on that understanding of the psalm Jesus' argument has no basis.

Thirty years ago I argued, on the basis of some then current views among OT scholars and of the unique character and language of this psalm, that it was not a typical royal psalm, and that the premises of Jesus' argument should be upheld against the consensus of modern scholarship.[90] Looking back at that argument, I still feel that it had value. Ps. 110 *is* different from other royal psalms, at least in its association of kingship with priesthood in the same person, and subsequent scholarship has identified a significant strand in Jewish interpretation which understands the κύριος addressed by God to be the Messiah.[91] Moreover, this understanding of the psalm will be presupposed again in 14:62. In terms of first-century views at least, therefore, Jesus' reported argument has validity, since no one at that time would have doubted that a psalm which begins

---

87. Cf. the earlier 'branch of David' (Je. 23:5; 33:15). For a useful survey of Davidic tradition in the OT and in later Judaism see J. A. Fitzmyer, *Essays,* 115-21.

88. See E. Lohse, *TDNT,* 8.480-82.

89. For a representative survey of modern views of the psalm see L. C. Allen, *Psalms 101–150,* 83-85. The consensus is that it is Davidic only in that it celebrates the monarchy which began with David, and messianic not in its original intention but as with other royal psalms by transfer from the historical monarchy to an idealised future king.

90. *Jesus and the OT,* 163-69.

91. See D. M. Hay, *Glory,* 26-33; D. Juel, *Exegesis,* 137-39. In other words, the arguments of Billerbeck with regard to the rabbinic understanding of the psalm which I followed in *Jesus and the OT,* 164-65, are still worthy of consideration. See further J. Marcus, *Way,* 133-34, for 'a stream of [eschatological] interpretation of the psalm that can be traced from the Old Testament through intertestamental Judaism and into the New Testament'; Marcus relies particularly on the links between Ps. 110 and 11Q13 *(Melchizedek).*

with the formula *l^eDāvid mizmôr* was written by David; nor would Mark or the other evangelists be likely to preserve the record of an argument whose premises were manifestly unacceptable. Given the way Jesus and his contemporaries read Ps. 110, the argument is convincing enough: David, the author, referred to the Messiah, the addressee, as κύριος, and thus as his superior rather than his son. Where I would not be so confident as thirty years ago is in the further contention that the interpretation which was agreed in the first century is necessarily a better guide to the historical origin and exegetical sense of the psalm than the views of most modern scholarship. It may be so, but the argument was not mounted for the sake of twentieth-century critics and does not have to pass their scrutiny to be effective. As a rhetorical question launched by Jesus in the temple it achieves its purpose.

For David's speaking ἐν τῷ πνεύματι τῷ ἁγίῳ cf. 2 Sa. 23:2; Acts 1:16, and for the Holy Spirit as the medium of prophetic inspiration cf. Acts 28:25; 2 Pet. 1:21. David is described as a prophet in Acts 2:30-31 and by Josephus, *Ant.* 6.166, but in any case the psalms, too, were regarded as the product of divine inspiration. It is sometimes suggested that Jesus' argument depends on the LXX text, with its double use of κύριος, and could not have been derived from the same text in Hebrew or Aramaic. This is a curious assertion since the basis of the argument (given that David is the author and the Messiah the addressee) is that the one addressed is superior to the author (and therefore is not his son), and that inference is as validly made from the Hebrew *'^adōnî* or the Aramaic *mārî*, each of which equally denotes superiority.[92] The fact that the regular LXX translation of the divine name by ὁ Κύριος produces the wordplay κύριος τῷ κυρίῳ μου gives the Greek text a special wordplay, but in no way affects the essential point of the superiority implied by 'lord'. In spoken Hebrew, with *'^adōnay* pronounced in place of the divine name, a very similar wordplay would be achieved: *n^e'um '^adōnay la'dōnî*.

37 Given the premises discussed in the notes on v. 36, the conclusion implied by Jesus' rhetorical question is clear.[93] People do not call their sons 'my lord'; the Messiah is David's lord rather than David's son. While in itself this conclusion is christologically unsatisfying, it leaves the way open for a more adequate christology to be put in the place of 'Son of David'.[94] Mark (unlike Matthew) does not guide the reader as to what that christology should be, but probably by the time his gospel was written he hardly needed to. It is most

92. See my *Jesus and the OT,* 163-64. F. J. Matera, *Kingship,* 88-89, argues that κύριος serves here as a 'surrogate for king', so that 'by addressing the Messiah as his Lord, David also salutes him as his king'.

93. See R. E. Watts, *Exodus,* 287 and n. 277, for πόθεν as marking not a negation, but 'an unsettling or surprising fact that requires explanation'.

94. The suggestion of N. T. Wright, *Victory,* 509, that the priestly character of the king in Ps. 110:4 is in view, indicating that 'the king [Jesus] will supersede the present high-priestly régime', is derived not from this pericope in itself but from his general interpretation of the Jerusalem confrontation as focused on Jesus' 'authority over the temple'.

likely, both in the light of the christological emphases of the rest of the gospel, and perhaps also because the discarded title has introduced the idea of sonship, that readers would think of the title 'Son of God'.[95] While the word κύριος has played a prominent part in the argument, it does not follow that κύριος as a christological title per se would naturally come to mind,[96] still less that the reader would identify the second κύριος of the psalm quotation with the first.[97]

The approval of the Jerusalem ὄχλος for Jesus' teaching has been mentioned already in 11:18 and is implied in 11:32; 12:12, 14:2. When we next hear of the crowd in the trial scene in chapter 15 their attitude will be very different, and Mark will explain the change by the influence of the ἀρχιερεῖς (15:11). For now, however, there is no sign of any such influence. A large and favourable crowd provides a receptive audience for Jesus' next words, which are now no longer in dialogue with specific questioners, but are a warning against the scribes addressed to the general public present in the Court of the Gentiles (as with many transitional formulae, v. 37b could be attached either to vv. 35-37a or to vv. 38-40).

Of Scribes and Widows (12:38-44)

TEXTUAL NOTE

41. There is no difference in meaning between κατέναντι and ἀπέναντι, and both are adequately represented in the NT. Since Mark uses the former in 11:2 and 13:3, it is more likely his stylistic preference. The inclusion of the name of Jesus in order to clarify the subject (which is clear from the context but not specified in this pericope) is probably a later addition.

Verses 38-40 are linked to the two preceding pericopes by the mention of scribes and to vv. 41-44 by the mention of the widow. Any grouping of these concluding sections of chapter 12 is therefore a little arbitrary. Some commentators link vv. 35-37 with vv. 38-40 as a single section ('Jesus' Exposé of the Scribes', Gundry; cf. Anderson). I prefer to link vv. 38-40 with vv. 41-44, on the grounds of the reversal of status which they display: in vv. 38-40 the ostentatious scribes are the exploiters and the widows the victims, whereas in vv. 41-44 a poor widow is used to show up the ostentation of the wealthy. While the wealthy in v. 41 are not identified as scribes, the theme of ostentation links the two scenes, and the double mention of widow(s) is surely intended to suggest a

95. See J. Marcus, *Way*, 141-45, for the probability that Mark intended his readers to draw this conclusion. In *Barn.* 12:10 the argument from Ps. 110:1 (see p. 483 n. 80 above) is introduced by the assertion that Jesus is οὐχὶ υἱὸς ἀνθρώπου ἀλλὰ υἱὸς τοῦ θεοῦ.

96. See J. D. Kingsbury, *Christology*, 110-11.

97. Note the suggestion of J. Marcus, *Way*, 145-46, that Mk. 12:35-37 is deliberately preceded by the quotation of Dt. 6:4 in 12:29 in order to avert any suggestion that Jesus is here being equated with God, resulting in a 'two powers' theology. See above, p. 479 n. 69.

comparison which will be very much to the disadvantage of the scribes and those like them. But Mark had no subheadings, and the scenes of Jesus' searching teaching in the temple flow on without any real break towards their powerful climax in 13:1-2.

After the encounter with the perceptive scribe in 12:28-34, the blanket attack on scribes as a class in vv. 38-40 is surprising. While very much shorter than the extended diatribe against scribes and Pharisees in Mt. 23 (cf. Lk. 11:37-54), it is no less violent and indiscriminate. Apart from vv. 28-34, it is true, all the scribes we have met in this gospel have been critics, if not openly enemies, of Jesus, and here in Jerusalem their hostility has come to a head as Jesus had predicted (8:31; 10:33). But there is no comparable denunciation of the priests or elders. The phrase βλέπετε ἀπό does, however, recall an equally sweeping though less specific warning against the Pharisees and Herod in 8:15, similarly understood as enemies of Jesus and his mission. But the warning here is not related to what they may have in mind to do to Jesus, but to their general character as ostentatious, exploitative, and hypocritical (Lane, 439, uses the term 'self-intoxication'). In this context the effect is to offer the crowd a choice as to the sort of leader they will follow, and Jesus pulls no punches in exposing the shortcomings of scribes in general. How far this constitutes a valid and 'objective' assessment of first-century scribes may be debated; certainly 12:28-34 together with Jesus' recognition of some tenets of scribal teaching (9:11-13; 12:35) points in another direction. But this is polemics in the context of a highly charged and potentially fatal confrontation,[98] and a suitably broad brush is applied.

The ostentation of the scribes described in vv. 38-39 appropriately prepares for Jesus' comments on the highly visible generosity of affluent visitors to the temple treasury. The scene is in the Court of the Women, so-called not because it was specifically for women but because it was the nearest point to the temple building proper which was open to women. Here stood a range of thirteen 'trumpet chests' (*m. Šeq.* 2:1; 6:5; so-called presumably from their shape) designed to receive monetary offerings, including not only the half-shekel temple tax but also 'freewill offerings'. The half-shekel was obligatory for men, but any contribution to the other chests was voluntary, and would be noticed by anyone who, like Jesus and his disciples, was watching (ἐθεώρει). Perhaps it was a recognised tourist attraction.

Jesus' comment on the widow's offering is not an attack on wealth or the wealthy as such, but rather on the scale of values which takes more account of the amount of a gift than of the dedication of the giver.[99] It develops further the new

---

98. Belo, 192: 'The Messiah is occupying the temple and holding a protest meeting against the dominant ideology.'

99. For some similar sayings and stories in Jewish and other literature see Pesch, 2.263; G. Stählin, *TDNT*, 9.449. A close parallel is in *Lv. Rab.* 3.5, where a priest who despises a woman's offering of a handful of flour is told in a dream that it is as if she had sacrificed her own life. Cf. the exhortation in Tob. 4:8 not to be ashamed to give even if you have little.

perspective of the kingdom of God which Jesus has been so assiduously teaching his disciples on the way to Jerusalem, especially his comments responding to their astonishment at his treatment of the rich man in 10:23-27. These remarks, too, are addressed specifically to the disciples (note προσκαλεσάμενος in v. 43; cf. 8:34; 10:42) and do not form part of the public denunciation of the scribes. Jesus again calls those who follow him to abandon the world's conventions of importance: the first are to be last and the last first. As he will do again in 14:3-9, Jesus honours an anonymous woman whose practical expression of her devotion is not appreciated by his male disciples.[100] But this private teaching agrees closely with the tenor of his public rebuke of the scribes, whose desire for public honour typifies the superficial values of conventional society.[101]

38-39 Yet another mention of Jesus' διδαχή (cf. 11:18; διδάσκω, 11:17; 12:14, 35; 14:49; διδάσκαλος, 12:14, 19, 32) underlines how Mark understood the focus of Jesus' activity in the temple since he came to Jerusalem. Here the term appropriately contrasts Jesus with the scribes, the regular religious 'teachers', whom he is about to attack. ἐν τῇ διδαχῇ αὐτοῦ (cf. 4:2) suggests that the few words actually recorded are merely a selection from the much more extensive teaching programme to which Jesus himself will refer back in 14:49. What is now recorded, however, is not so much teaching as polemic. θέλω, often a rather colourless word, here has a strong meaning (BAGD, 355b, 4.a, 'take pleasure in'): these are the ambitions of the scribes. The four objects of their desire, all aspects of social prominence, are expressed slightly awkwardly in that the first is an infinitive and the rest nouns, since there is no convenient noun for 'walking about'. A στολή is not an everyday garment, but a festive or celebratory robe (cf. Lk. 15:22; Rev. 6:11; 7:9)[102] and suggests 'dressing up'.[103] Deferential ἀσπασμοί are a mark of social standing (Mt. 23:7-12 expands the point). For the social significance of the front seats in the synagogue (i.e., those

100. Note the parallel ὃ ἔσχεν ἐποίησεν (14:8), πάντα ὅσα εἶχεν ἔβαλεν (12:44). The scale of giving is of course vastly different, but not the reckless abandon involved. The link between these two pericopes is explored by Stock, 319-21, who characterises the two women as 'two unforgettable *anawim*', who form a 'frame' around the farewell discourse of chapter 13.

101. A. G. Wright, *CBQ* 44 (1982) 256-65 (followed by Mann, 494-95; Myers, 320-21), proposes that Jesus is not commending the widow's gift, but rather deploring the fact that, under pressure from the religious establishment, she has given more than she could afford. While this interpretation might accord well with the 'eating up of widows' houses' in v. 40, it has little to commend it in the way vv. 41-44 are expressed. As with many attempts to overturn accepted exegesis, one wonders why no one thought of reading the text this way before! See in response E. S. Malbon, *CBQ* 53 (1991) 593-604. Malbon's article offers an interesting range of different 'narrative contexts' against which the pericope may be interpreted. See also J. F. Williams, *Followers,* 177-78 n. 3.

102. Several commentators (e.g., Anderson, Cranfield, Hooker) assume that the *ṭallît* (prayer shawl) is here referred to, thus adding an element of *religious* ostentation, but this is not required by the context and is not a known use of στολή. Gundry, 727, suggests that 'Jesus is referring to regular robes decorated for religious show with longer-than-usual tassels (Matt. 23:5)'. See further Mann, 489-90; H. Fleddermann *CBQ* 44 (1982) 54-57.

103. The word is used for priestly robes in Josephus, *Ant.* 3.151; 11.80; LXX Ex. 28:2, and for royal robes in LXX 2 Ch. 18:9; Est. 6:8.

in front of the ark, facing the congregation) cf. the comments of Jas. 2:2-4 concerning the Christian συναγωγῇ, and for the best couch at a dinner cf. Lk. 14:7-10; see Josephus, *Ant.* 15.21 for flattery by means of the best seats and greetings.[104] Cf. Jn. 13:1-17 for a graphic repudiation of a similar preoccupation with status and reputation among Jesus' own disciples.

40 The nominatives οἱ κατεσθίοντες . . . καὶ . . . προσευχόμενοι do not relate syntactically with the preceding sentence, where the scribes appeared in the genitive, but since no main verb appears before λήμψονται, which has its own subject οὗτοι, they are probably to be taken as a *constructio ad sensum* after the lengthy description of the scribes' ambitions has left the genitive noun and participle on which they depended so far behind.[105] In that case the subjects of these participles are not a new group, or even a subgroup of the scribes, but must still be the scribes in general.

The vulnerability of widows is a recurrent theme in biblical literature,[106] so that to defraud them is particularly despicable. κατεσθίοντες τὰς οἰκίας is a vivid phrase for taking material advantage of them (like our 'eat someone out of house and home'); cf. καταφαγών σου τὸν βίον (Lk. 15:30).[107] How the scribes were alleged to do this can be only a matter of speculation. It could be through excessive legal fees, through mismanaging to their own advantage an estate of which they were made trustees,[108] through taking their houses as pledges for unpayable debts, through promoting the temple cult which 'eats up' the resources of the pious poor,[109] or more generally through exploiting their hospitality and trust.[110] The following clause καὶ προφάσει μακρὰ προσευχόμενοι is

104. Lane, 439-40, gives a graphic account of the social standing and respect accorded to scribes.

105. N. Turner, *Grammar,* 317, includes this in his list of 'excusable solecisms'! The alternative construction, taking the nominative participles as beginning a new sentence with 'a *casus pendens* followed by resumptive οὗτοι' (Cranfield; similarly Gundry, 720, 727; several commentators assume this construction, but not most versions, except REB) results in a very awkward sentence, and one which reads as a *non sequitur* if the subject intended is not the same as in vv. 38-39; this sense would in any case need some indication of change of subject such as δέ. If, on the other hand, the subject is the same, the choice of explanation as to the grammatical construction makes no difference to the sense.

106. See S. Solle, *DNTT,* 3.1073-75.

107. Similar language is used in *Test. Mos.* 7:6-10 of unnamed officials (perhaps scribes?) who 'eat up the goods of the poor, claiming that they are acting according to justice'. Cf *Ps. Sol.* 4, especially v. 11.

108. So J. D. M. Derrett, *NovT* 14 (1972) 1-9; critical comment by H. Fleddermann, *CBQ* 44 (1982) 61.

109. A. G. Wright (see above, p. 490 n. 101); H. Fleddermann, *CBQ* 44 (1982) 61-66; Myers, 321-22. Fleddermann recognises that μακρὰ προσευχόμενοι is an unnatural way to say 'promoting the temple cult'.

110. J. Jeremias, *Jerusalem,* 111-16, provides a fascinating study of the economic circumstances of scribes, and concludes that many were poor and that while some were in paid employment 'in the main the scribes lived on subsidies'. He concludes that this passage refers to 'the scribes' habit of sponging on the hospitality of people of limited means' (114). For more general information on Jerusalem scribes see J. Jeremias, *Jerusalem,* 233-45.

closely linked with the 'eating up' of their houses, and προφάσει would naturally describe the fraudulent means by which it is achieved. In that case the reference could be to the sort of payment for the prayers of a religious professional which became common in medieval Christianity. It is true that πρόφασις can mean a (valid) reason, as in Jn. 15:22, but its more usual sense is 'pretext' and this is its meaning in other NT uses (note Phil. 1:18, where it is contrasted with ἀλήθεια). Mann's translation 'for appearances' sake' is perhaps too gentle. The suggestion that it means something like 'with such an end in view', implying an ulterior motive,[111] makes little difference to its pejorative force in this context where the 'end' is eating up widows' houses. For insincere prayer cf. Mt. 6:5, though there the emphasis is on the public performance rather than the length of the prayers.

Similarly, while κρίμα sometimes means the act of judging, its normal meaning of 'condemnation', 'punishment' is demanded by the context here. The reference cannot be to an earthly or human judgment (which would hardly take cognisance of ostentation as a punishable offence), but must be to God's eschatological judgment, of which Jesus has spoken so vividly in 9:42-48. Such a judgment does not leave room for the gradation of punishments which seems to be envisaged in the comparative περισσότερον (though this could be understood simply as 'very severe'), but probably it is better in context to take the comparative not of varying levels of condemnation or punishment, but rather of the more obvious guilt of these people than of other less blatant sinners. If the nominative participles of v. 40 could be interpreted of a specially wicked group of scribes, the comparative might then contrast them with the general run of scribes whose ostentation (described in vv. 38-39) is a less serious crime, but the syntax scarcely allows this, as we have noted above.

41 As in v. 38, the subject does not need to be expressed (see Textual Note) since there has been a continuous sequence of Jesus' speaking, without response, since v. 35. γαζοφυλάκιον ('treasury') is used in the LXX and Josephus (sometimes in the plural) of the treasure stores in the temple buildings, but its reference here to the collecting chests in the Court of the Women is demanded by the context, which has an ὄχλος, including a woman, 'throwing in' donations. (In Jn. 8:20 the same sense seems required, as Jesus and the crowd to whom he was speaking could hardly have been inside the 'strong room'.) χαλκός is strictly 'copper' or 'bronze', and the widow's two coins would be of copper. But the large sums donated by the rich would presumably be in silver or gold coins (as were the half-shekels for the temple tax, which had to be paid in Tyrian silver coins), so that χαλκός is here used in its more general sense of 'money'. The objects for which the money was given (apart from two chests for the temple tax) are listed in the Mishnah as 'Bird offerings', 'Young birds for whole-offerings', 'Wood', 'Incense', 'Gold for the *kappōret* [perhaps sacred vessels?]', and 'Freewill offerings' (six chests being devoted to the last).

---

111. So Derrett, art. cit. (p. 491 n. 108), 7-8.

All contributions were therefore for the work of the temple; charitable donations for the poor were made separately. For the huge amounts of money contributed see Schürer, 2.270-74.

42 There is a marked contrast between the πολλοὶ πλούσιοι . . . πολλά of
v. 41 and the μία χήρα πτωχή of this verse.[112] There is no reason to think that
she was the only such person present, but Jesus singles her out as an object lesson. The λεπτόν (Hebrew $p^e r\hat{u}t\hat{a}$) was the smallest denomination of currency in
use, a copper coin less than a centimetre in diameter and worth less than one
hundredth of a denarius (which was itself half the value of the half-shekel temple tax).[113] Mark identifies its value by reference to the Roman κοδράντης (a
transliteration of *quadrans,* which was the smallest Roman coin, a quarter of an
as). The use of the Latin term is not necessarily due to a Roman origin for the
gospel, since 'Roman designations of coins were already in the first century
A.D. more common in Palestine than the Greek and Hebrew designations still
also in use';[114] Matthew also uses the term (5:26).

43-44 Both προσκαλεσάμενος (see the introduction to this section)
and the formula ἀμὴν λέγω ὑμῖν (see on 3:28) mark this out as a saying to be
noted. It both commends the widow's self-sacrificing generosity as an example for all God's people (*pace* Gundry, 730) and (and probably more significantly for its context in Mark) turns upside down the normal human valuation
of people. What matters in God's sight is not what a person has (and therefore
is able to give without pain) but the devotion which causes her to give even at
great personal cost, even though the amount of the gift may be completely
negligible in comparison with the enormous wealth of the temple. The gift
does not matter to God so much as the giver. And, it is implied, this should
also be the basis of his people's valuation. By such a criterion the first will often be last, and the last first. The two $p^e r\hat{u}t\bar{o}t$ are πλεῖον than all the silver and
gold put together.

The point is laboured in the wording of v. 44: her ὑστέρησις (destitution)
is compared with their περίσσευον, the spare change which will never be
missed (cf. περίσσευμα, 8:8); she has given πάντα ὅσα εἶχεν (cf. the example of
the disciples, 10:28, and the failure of the rich man to do likewise, 10:21); it is
ὅλος ὁ βίος αὐτῆς, and yet she voluntarily gave both coins, rather than just one!
While Jesus was not averse to exaggeration to make a point, it is quite possible
that in first-century Palestine the donation of two $p^e r\hat{u}t\bar{o}t$ would have left a poor
widow without the means for her next meal (cf. the widow of Zarephath, 1 Ki.
17:12).

---

112. Gundry asserts that 'The poverty of the widow will naturally be taken as due to a scribal devouring of her estate (v. 40)'. I wonder! Many have not noticed this 'natural' reading. Widows
are frequently depicted as poor with no such reason adduced.

113. For the coins of Roman Palestine see, e.g., Schürer, 2.62-66.

114. Schürer, 2.64.

No Future for the Temple (13:1-2)

TEXTUAL NOTE

2. In NT Greek either λίθος ἐπὶ λίθον (as in Matthew) or λίθος ἐπὶ λίθῳ (as in Luke) would be idiomatically acceptable, but the strong predominance of the former in MSS of Mark suggests that the latter is a scribal correction to Luke's more 'classical' use; the sense is not affected. ὧδε is also strongly represented, but would be a natural 'clarification' of a sense which is otherwise indicated (as in Luke) only by the context, so it may well be due to assimilation to Matthew.

Here is another misleading chapter division. While 13:1-2 is the setting for the question (13:3-4) which in turn provokes the discourse of 13:5-37, it functions also, and no less importantly, as the culmination of the lengthy section on Jesus' confrontation with the authorities in the temple which began in 11:27, following from his provocative acts in 11:11-25. Without 13:1-2 the sequence of dialogues in chapters 11–12 is left without a conclusion.

In the earlier part of the confrontation Jesus was, from the narrative point of view, primarily on the defensive, responding to awkward questions posed by those who represented the power structure of the Jewish capital and of the temple as an institution — though his responses have been far from defensive in tone and content. But already in 12:1-12 and increasingly since 12:34 (οὐδεὶς οὐκέτι ἐτόλμα αὐτὸν ἐπερωτῆσαι) Jesus has taken the initiative, posing the next question himself (without receiving a reply) and going on to denounce the representatives of religious power and to overturn conventional values of importance and status. It is thus appropriate that the whole episode ends not with the authorities taking action against Jesus (that will come later), but with Jesus, now the unquestioned winner in the contest, himself severing the connection by leaving the temple and pronouncing its downfall.

The unnamed disciple's superficial admiration for the magnificence of the buildings, contrasted with Jesus' declaration of their ultimate bankruptcy, furnishes yet another example of the reorientation to the new perspective of the kingdom of God to which the disciples are committed but which they remain slow to grasp, and which Mark expects his readers to embrace. The old structure of authority in which God's relationship with his people has hitherto been focused, is due for replacement. The language of a ναὸς ἀχειροποίητος to replace the existing man-made structure (14:58), while it is not explicit at this point, is clearly implied. As Mt. 12:6 has it, 'Something greater than the temple is here'. The discourse which will follow in vv. 5-37 will fill out the nature of that 'something greater'.

This, the only place in Mark where Jesus explicitly predicts the destruction of the temple (it has been threatened symbolically in the fate of the fig tree; see the introductory comments on 11:11-25), is the only basis recorded by Mark for the charge which was to be brought against Jesus at his trial (14:57-

494

58) and would remain in the minds of those who mocked him on the cross (15:29-30). While Mark (unlike Matthew) brands the charge as false (14:57) — and no doubt in formal terms it was, since 13:2 does not say that *Jesus* will destroy the temple — there is no doubt that these words of Jesus played a significant role in his eventual rejection and condemnation, and may well have been in large measure responsible for his loss of the popular goodwill which we have noted hitherto. (While Mark presents v. 2 as a reply to an individual comment rather than as part of Jesus' public teaching, it was uttered in a public place [contrast the private setting of vv. 3-37] where others could hear; and it is not unlikely that so far-reaching a pronouncement was made, or at least hinted at, more than just this once.) See the introductory comments on 11:11-25 for the importance of the temple in the mind of the people of Jerusalem and for the argument of E. P. Sanders that it was Jesus' attitude to the temple which ultimately united all of them against him. See Acts 6:13-14 for this theme as a focus of continuing hostility to the Christian movement.

Jesus was not the first to predict the temple's destruction. God's declaration to Solomon at the temple's dedication envisaged such a possibility if Israel proved disobedient (1 Ki. 9:6-8), and the threat was taken up by Micah (3:12), and repeatedly by Jeremiah (7:12-15; 12:7; 22:5; 26:6). It was only the memory of Micah's prophecy which saved Jeremiah from execution for treason on this basis (Je. 26:10-19), and another prophet with the same message, Uriah, was not so fortunate (Je. 26:20-23). A generation after the death of Jesus another Jesus, son of Hananiah, was put on trial for threats against the city and its temple (Josephus, *War* 6.300-309).[1] Jesus was embarking on a dangerous course.

While ἐκπορευομένου αὐτοῦ ἐκ τοῦ ἱεροῦ is not in itself a highly coloured phrase, its wider context suggests that Mark intended it to be noticed. Jesus has been in the temple continuously since 11:27; now he leaves it, and will not return again in Mark's narrative. The only other thing we hear of the temple (apart from the charge at Jesus' trial and on the cross) will be the tearing of its curtain as Jesus dies. Moreover, he goes from the temple onto the Mount of Olives (v. 3), presumably leaving by the east gate. It does not take a very profound knowledge of the Book of Ezekiel to recall the dramatic description of God's abandonment of his temple as the chariot throne of God's glory rises up from inside the temple, pauses at the east gate, and comes to rest on 'the mountain east of the city' (Ezk. 10:18-19; 11:22-23). So now again the divine presence is withdrawn from the temple, and it is left to its destruction.

1 While most of Jesus' teaching in the temple area will have been in the Court of the Gentiles, in 12:41-44 he has been in the more restricted area of the Court of the Women. Now he returns through the Court of the Gentiles presumably to the east gate of the temple area, from which a steep path crossed the

---

1. Cf. *b. Yoma* 39b for a prediction of the temple's destruction attributed to Jesus' contemporary, Johanan ben Zakkai. In *1 Enoch* 90:28-29 the temple is to be destroyed in order to be rebuilt on a grander scale.

Kidron valley to the Mount of Olives. The unnamed disciple's admiration of the temple buildings would be typical of a Galilean visitor to Jerusalem. Even Josephus, who knew Jerusalem well, speaks in superlative terms of the magnificence of the temple (*War* 5.184-226; note especially the visual impact of the combination of gold and white marble described in 5.222-23); a later rabbi records that 'It used to be said: He who has not seen the temple in its full splendour has never seen a beautiful building' (*b. Suk.* 51b; *b. B.Bat.* 4a).[2] ποταπός means 'of what kind', but in such an exclamation it implies 'how magnificent!' The οἰκοδομαί might be any part of the temple complex, such as Solomon's portico through which the east entrance passed, but the main focus is most probably on the sanctuary itself. The specific mention of λίθοι, while it serves in Mark's context to prepare for the saying λίθος ἐπὶ λίθον in v. 2, corresponds to Josephus's specific mention of the enormous blocks of stone used in the building (though a single block of forty-five cubits in length, *War* 5.224, is hard to believe). The disciple's amazement is shared even by modern visitors who see the huge ashlar blocks in the remaining Herodian walls, and these were only the substructure, not the temple proper.

2 It makes little difference whether βλέπεις ταύτας τὰς μεγάλας οἰκοδομάς is read as a statement or a question, and whether βλέπεις is understood as unmarked, the equivalent of the act of pointing, or as an implied rebuke ('You can't take your eyes off . . .'). For the disciple's touristic awe Jesus substitutes a cruel realism. Splendid as the structure may be, its time is over. 'Jesus' reply is to dismiss the magnificent display as — in the context of his ministry and mission — a massive irrelevance' (Mann, 495). For λίθος ἐπὶ λίθον cf. Lk. 19:44, where the reference is apparently to Jerusalem as a whole, not only the temple. In view of the immense size of the stones of the temple (see on v. 1), the language is particularly vivid. The two aorist passive subjunctives (ἀφεθῇ; καταλυθῇ) with οὐ μή convey a very 'emphatic denial'.[3] Jesus does not specify the time or the agent of the temple's destruction (contrast the charge in 14:58), but already before A.D. 70 it must have been obvious that the literal fulfilment of this prediction might be only a matter of time. It was to be remarkably literal: Josephus (*War* 7.1-3) records the temple's being leveled to the ground, after previously being burned (*War* 6.249-66). Even the now-sacred Western Wall was not part of the temple but only the supporting structure for the platform on which it was built. At this point there is no evaluative comment, merely a factual prediction, but the discourse that follows will spell out what it all means.[4]

2. For details of the temple buildings see J. Jeremias, *Jerusalem*, 21-25.

3. N. Turner, *Grammar*, 95-96.

4. M. A. Tolbert, *Sowing*, 259-60, suggests that the repeated occurrence in these two verses of the terms λίθος and οἰκοδομή is meant to remind the reader of the λίθος and the οἰκοδομοῦντες of Ps. 118:22, as quoted in 12:10, and thus to indicate that the destruction of the temple is the necessary preliminary to the elevation of the previously rejected λίθος. The theology fits well with the discourse that follows, even if one may doubt that the allusion would be readily detected.

EXPLANATORY DISCOURSE:
THE END OF THE OLD ORDER (13:3-37)

TEXTUAL NOTES

8. The addition of καί before ἔσονται (or in some witnesses its substitution for ἔσονται) is a natural 'improvement' to the awkward asyndeton of ἔσονται λιμοί, as a second and shorter ἔσονται clause. The addition of λοιμοί in a few texts may be accounted for both by assimilation to Luke and by the similarity in sound and appearance to λιμοί, and both that addition and the more common insertion of καὶ ταραχαί would help to fill out the very meagre clause ἔσονται λιμοί. The inclusion of ταραχαί is widely attested, and is not due to assimilation to another version, and so has more claim to be original than λοιμοί; but it might also be the result of a careless scribe misreading the following ἀρχή. The text seems to have been subject to imaginative expansion.

33. Prayer is more likely to have been added than omitted, as a conventional extension of the exhortation to watch, especially in the light of 14:38 (cf. with ἀγρυπνέω, Lk. 21:36; Eph. 6:18), but is less appropriate here, especially as it produces an awkward series of three unconnected imperatives.

In my structural analysis of the gospel I have pointed out the similar function of the two main discourses of Mark in relation to the first and third 'acts' of the drama. Each comes roughly in the middle of its 'act', and, following a packed sequence of events and encounters, provides the reader with an opportunity to reflect on the significance of what has been happening in the story so far. After each discourse the narrative resumes with no less pace, but now we have had the opportunity to gain a true perspective on the underlying drama and, unlike those who are actors in it, we can see the individual episodes as parts of the larger whole of the unfolding purpose of God through the ministry, life, death, and resurrection of the Messiah.[5]

The discourse in chapter 4 was preceded by stories illustrating the deep divisions which Jesus' ministry was beginning to provoke among those who witnessed his teaching and his actions, and offered an understanding of those divisions on the basis of the μυστήριον τῆς βασιλείας τοῦ θεοῦ. In chapters 11–12 we have witnessed a similar division between disciples, crowd, and officialdom, but now the more ominous buildup of opposition to Jesus and his mission indicates that events are quickly moving to the climax of rejection and death which Jesus has been predicting since 8:31. The mutual hostility between Jesus and the Jerusalem establishment has now reached its culmination in Jesus' open prediction of the destruction of the temple, with its powerful symbolism of the end of the existing order and the implication that something new is to take its place. This is to be a time of unprecedented upheaval in the life and leadership of the people of God. Jerusalem, and the temple which is the focus of its author-

5. See M. A. Beavis, *Audience*, 94, 127-29, for further comment on similarities between the functions of the two discourses within the gospel.

ity, is about to lose its central role in God's economy. The divine government, the βασιλεία τοῦ θεοῦ, is to find a new focus.

All this will be set forth in the discourse which follows.[6] The prediction of the destruction of the temple from which it takes its cue is plain enough, but as the discourse develops its language becomes increasingly allusive, drawing on themes of OT apocalyptic and political prophecy which are not as familiar to most modern readers as they would have been to at least a proportion of Mark's original readers.[7] As a result, widely divergent interpretations of the discourse have been proposed, and it remains the most disputed area in the study of Mark's gospel. In the account which follows I intend to keep clearly in view the context in which it is set, and the questions to which therefore it may be expected to provide answers. The disciples' question with which it begins seeks elucidation of Jesus' pronouncement about the destruction of the temple, and it is this question which must set the agenda for our interpretation of the discourse which follows. It is about 'the end of the old order'.

It has been increasingly recognised in recent study that to describe Mark 13 as 'apocalyptic' is misleading. At the literary level a brief discourse set like this in the course of a historical narrative bears little resemblance to the type of 'apocalypse' which Jewish writers were producing around the first century A.D. or even that which has become the last book of the NT. Nor does it include many of the familiar features of apocalyptic such as the attribution to an ancient prophetic figure, the heavenly journeys and angelic revelations, the symbolism of numbers or of animals, or the systematisation of world history past, present, and future into a coherent scheme.[8] What it shares with some apocalyptic writings is a focus on what is soon to happen, a sense of climactic events and impending judgment, and a call to faithfulness and alertness in a time of disintegration of the status quo. To that extent it has apocalyptic characteristics in content, even if not in literary form, and its use of familiar language from prophetic and apocalyptic parts of the OT is appropriate to that orientation. But it is not 'an apocalypse',[9] and to label it as such is to risk seriously distorting the focus of a discourse which is concerned more to damp down premature eschato-

---

6. It is often suggested that chapter 13 is modeled on the 'farewell discourses' familiar from the OT and from the later Jewish 'Testaments'. But the setting is wrong for such a discourse, with the speech offered in response to a question with only a handful of disciples present. Nor is this Jesus' last speech in the gospel. His words at the last supper (when all the disciples were present) might better be seen as his 'farewell'. See further Gundry, 751. This is not the place for a farewell discourse, but for a challenging reflection on the significance of the events about to take place in Jerusalem.

7. Mann, 500-504, sets forth in tabular form a wide range of OT quotations and allusions in the discourse (drawing on all three synoptic versions).

8. K. Grayston, *BJRL* 56 (1973/4) 379-80, tests Mark 13 against eight apocalyptic motifs isolated by K. Koch, and concludes that 'marks of apocalyptic are scarce'.

9. M. D. Hooker's comment, *BJRL* 65 (1982/3) 80-81, about the danger of attaching labels is apposite: 'I doubt very much whether Mark said to himself: "I am going to write an apocalypse". . . . We should beware of ready-made stick-on labels.'

logical excitement than to encourage it,[10] and whose focus is as much on the pastoral need to prepare disciples for difficult times ahead as it is to explain the future course of events.[11] A discourse which is constructed primarily around second-person imperatives addressed to the disciples[12] does not look like what is normally understood by 'apocalyptic'.[13]

It would be inappropriate to attempt here the task (impossible in the compass of a commentary on the whole gospel) of providing an adequate summary and critique of scholarly views on Mark 13 even within the twentieth century. Fortunately, the task is in any case unnecessary, owing to the labours over many years of G. R. Beasley-Murray, whose earlier definitive work, *Jesus and the Future* (London: Macmillan, 1954) has now been abbreviated and combined with an abbreviated version of his *A Commentary on Mark Thirteen* (London: Macmillan, 1962), both works being comprehensively updated[14] in *Jesus and the Last Days: The Interpretation of the Olivet Discourse* (Peabody, MA: Hendrickson, 1993). While, as will be obvious to anyone reading Beasley-Murray's brief comments on my own earlier publication on the subject,[15] I do not agree with the view of Mark 13 which he has consistently espoused, nor do I think he has done justice to the hermeneutical considerations which have caused me and others to adopt a radically different approach to the discourse, I am glad to salute the valuable work of systematisation and exposition of a wide variety of views which he has accomplished, and gratefully refer the reader to his latest work for a massive and widely researched account of some 150 years of scholarship on Mark 13.

While earlier study of Mark 13 was primarily concerned with how the chapter came to be in the form it is[16] and with the origin of the materials it

10. M. D. Hooker, *BJRL* 65 (1982/3) 95, comments, 'It seems to me that it urges inaction rather than action.'

11. E. Trocmé, *Formation,* 208, significantly describes the aim of Mk. 13 as 'seeking to arm Christians against the manifold temptations of apocalyptic'.

12. βλέπετε in vv. 5, 9, 23, 33; μὴ θροεῖσθε in v. 7; μὴ προμεριμνᾶτε in v. 11; προσεύχεσθε in v. 18; μὴ πιστεύετε in v. 21; μάθετε in v. 28; γινώσκετε in vv. 28 and 29; βλέπετε and ἀγρυπνεῖτε in v. 33; γρηγορεῖτε in vv. 35 and 37. Note also the third-person imperatives in vv. 14-16. K. Grayston, *BJRL* 56 (1973/4) 383-87, uses these imperatives as a basis for isolating a supposed 'original nucleus' of the discourse, giving instructions directly related to current crises in the church; he suggests that this nucleus was subsequently expanded by third-person comments which had the effect of transforming it into 'a matter of final importance'.

13. Cf. the verdict of C. Rowland, *Heaven,* 43-48; L. Gaston, *No Stone,* 47-51.

14. More than half of the survey of scholarship consists of a chapter covering 'Contributions Since the Rise of Redaction Criticism' (162-349), which are subsequent to his 1954 study.

15. *Jesus and the OT,* 227-39, discussed in Beasley-Murray, *Last Days,* 247-49.

16. Among many important studies we should note especially L. Hartman, *Prophecy,* an attempt to trace the development of the materials which make up Mk. 13 with special reference to their background in Daniel and other OT and later apocalyptic texts. The study is carried out in parallel with a study of how a number of Jewish apocalyptic works were composed, and is based on the identification of Mk. 13 as 'apocalyptic', which we have seen reason to question. Hartman cautiously describes Mk. 13:5-27 as essentially a 'midrash' on Daniel, originating in the teaching of Jesus, to which other mainly parenetical material was then added, and the whole then related to the destruction of the temple.

contains[17] (a concern exemplified by the extraordinarily long period during which scholarship was dominated by T. Colani's 1864 theory of a Jewish-Christian 'Little Apocalypse' underlying the gospel discourse), in the latter part of the twentieth century, in accordance with the perspective of redaction criticism and of subsequent trends in literary criticism, attention has focussed more especially (and surely rightly) on what the text as it stands actually means, and why Mark included it in this form at this point in his gospel.[18]

While it is clear that as it stands in Mark the discourse takes its cue from Jesus' prediction of the destruction of the temple, opinions are divided over whether it remains focused on that context or embraces also a longer eschatological perspective to include Jesus' second coming, and if so at what point the transition is made, and what is the nature of the relationship between the destruction of the temple and the parousia.[19]

The view that the whole discourse is to be understood as relating to the temple's destruction and contains no parousia reference at all has the merit of simplicity and of respecting the narrative context in which it is set, but remains a minority view. It is now perhaps best exemplified in the work of N. T. Wright,[20] published too late to be included in Beasley-Murray's survey. Wright's interpretation agrees for the majority of the discourse with the view adopted in this commentary, but differs from it primarily in not recognising a clear break and change of subject matter at v. 32. For the crucial verses 24-27 this view corresponds with my own conviction that the apocalyptic language of these verses, drawn almost entirely from identifiable OT texts, relates, as did those texts in their own contexts, not to the collapse of the physical universe and the end of the world but to imminent and far-reaching political change, in the context of the predicted destruction of Jerusalem. On this view

17. For a recent (and self-consciously 'old-fashioned', p. 2), detailed source-critical and tradition-critical analysis of the synoptic versions of the discourse and of related NT material see D. Wenham, *Rediscovery*. Wenham concludes quite boldly that it is possible to discern behind the various NT material a single and quite extensive 'pre-synoptic' discourse deriving from Jesus. The rediscovered discourse is reconstructed in *Rediscovery*, 359-64.

18. Chapter 5 of Beasley-Murray's *Last Days* provides convenient if brief summaries and critiques of the major (and some minor) studies and commentaries between 1952 and 1989. The most recently published of these, T. J. Geddert, *Watchwords*, is an independent and sometimes iconoclastic study of 'Mark 13 in Markan Eschatology', aiming to relate the contents of the discourse to themes characteristic of the gospel as a whole, in order to demonstrate that 'Mark really did know what he was doing' (18). Geddert's work is idiosyncratic and often controversial. He offers some fresh perspectives on the study of Mk. 13, but his insistence on Mark's principle of deliberate ambiguity, refusing to answer the sort of questions which readers both ancient and modern want to pose, makes his book hard to engage with in terms of exegetical options.

19. It is the contention of T. J. Geddert, *Watchwords*, that this issue has remained controversial because it was Mark's purpose precisely 'to produce the very uncertainty which has troubled scholars, and that he deliberately incorporated the very ambiguity which scholars want to eliminate' (257).

20. N. T. Wright, *Victory*, 339-66.

the 'coming of the Son of Man' is language not about an eschatological descent of Jesus to the earth but, as in the vision of Daniel from which it derives, about the vindication and enthronement of the Son of Man at the right hand of God, to receive and exercise supreme authority. In other words, what is being described in vv. 24-27, as in the OT passages from which their language is drawn, is a change of government: the temple and all that it stood for is out, and the Son of Man is in. The same theme will be picked up, in similar language, in the climactic declaration of Jesus' sovereignty in 14:61-62. I shall defend this exegesis below. For now it is necessary only to note that its effect is to remove at a stroke the single most embarrassing feature of chapter 13 for traditional Christian interpretation, the quite unequivocal and very emphatic statement in v. 30 that the events just described will take place before this generation has passed. They did!

Why then am I not content, with Wright, to remove the parousia altogether from Mark 13? First of all, there is a marked change of subject in v. 32. It is not merely that περὶ δέ frequently has this function elsewhere in the NT, but also that whereas in the discourse up to that point Jesus has spoken of 'days' which are coming and of events summarised as ταῦτα (πάντα), v. 32 speaks instead of ἡ ἡμέρα ἐκείνη. No such (singular) day has been mentioned so far, and there is a marked contrast between the certainty of the temporal prediction with regard to the date at which ταῦτα πάντα will occur (v. 30) and the ignorance of even the Son concerning the 'day and hour' now envisaged.[21]

Even so, taking Mark alone it might be possible to argue that this is merely a distinction between the certainty of the general period (within the generation) and the uncertainty of the specific time within that period. But Matthew, too, has an equally marked change of subject at his v. 36, and his use of the actual term παρουσία twice in 24:37-39 to denote the event spoken of in v. 36 (and in v. 27 to differentiate that event from those associated with the fall of Jerusalem), as well as his introduction of it into the initial question (24:3), leaves little room for doubt that from v. 36 onward he understood Jesus to be speaking of the parousia and not, as up to that point, of the fate of the city and temple.[22] His further extension of the discourse through to the end of chapter 25 confirms that after 24:36 he has moved on to speak of the time of final and universal judgment rather than of the destruction of Jerusalem. In Matthew, then, even if the language of Mk. 13:24-

---

21. Hooker, 300, writing from within the traditional parousia interpretation of vv. 24-27, describes well the change which occurs at v. 32 when she characterizes vv. 32-37 as 'a passage which apparently contradicts everything preceding it by urging the need to watch constantly, since the time of the parousia is unknown to anyone. Here is the real tension of this chapter.'

22. Wright's argument in *Victory*, 341-42, that παρουσία means no more than the opposite of ἀπουσία, and so is appropriate to the royal 'arrival' of the Son of Man into his heavenly authority, is unconvincing in view of the fact that by the time Matthew (who alone among the evangelists uses the word in this connection) wrote his gospel the word had become a recognised technical term for Jesus' second coming.

27/Mt. 24:29-31 is understood of the events of A.D. 70, Jesus' discourse goes on to embrace a more ultimate eschatological perspective, and the adaptation of the disciples' question in 24:3 to include the παρουσία and the συντελεία τοῦ αἰῶνος confirms that this was his view.[23] That Matthew so understood the discourse does not of course prove that Mark did also, but it does show both that the change of subject which I find at Mk. 13:32 corresponds to another first-century reading of the same tradition and that it made sense in the context of first-century Christianity to think of Jesus combining a prediction of the fall of Jerusalem with teaching about his own parousia conceived as a separate event. So while the language of Mk. 13:32-37 relates far less clearly to the parousia than does Mt. 24:36–25:46, it seems likely that that is its subject, and that this represents a change of focus from the language about the 'coming of the Son of Man' (*not* παρουσία) in v. 26, which is a theologically loaded way of describing the significance of what happened in A.D. 70.

But while I part company from Wright with regard to vv. 32-37, I remain as convinced as I was in 1971 that the subject of the discourse up to v. 31 is for Mark, as it was for Jesus, the destruction of the temple. The basis of this interpretation in the wording of the key section vv. 24-27 will be spelled out below, but at this point it is as well to recognise that it meets with instinctive resistance on the part of almost all Christian readers simply because we have been brought up to believe that the sort of apocalyptic language used in vv. 24-27, and in particular the vision of 'the Son of Man coming in clouds' belongs exclusively to the parousia and related events of the 'last days' (the title of Beasley-Murray's recent work illustrates this assumption). Even those who accept that the prophets used language about the sun and moon being darkened and the stars falling as symbolic of catastrophic political events of their own times, and that Daniel's vision of a son of man coming with clouds is of a heavenly enthronement, not of a 'coming to earth', continue to insist that in the discourse of first-century Christianity this is 'parousia language'. So deeply ingrained is this instinctive interpretation that it is hard for those brought up on the traditional view to appreciate the force of an exegesis which starts from the OT sense of such language rather than from its subsequent Christian development.

But where the same Dn. 7 language (τὸν υἱὸν τοῦ ἀνθρώπου . . . ἐρχόμενον μετὰ τῶν νεφελῶν τοῦ οὐρανοῦ) is used in 14:62 there has been in recent years, as we shall see when we come to that passage, 'a considerable shift of opinion'[24] towards the view that this is an enthronement text rather than a parousia prediction. That 'shift' has not yet, however, been matched with regard to 13:26, presumably because to read the words in their Danielic sense here challenges the traditional interpretation of the whole discourse,

23. This interpretation is set out in my *Matthew* (1985), 333ff.
24. G. R. Beasley-Murray, *Kingdom*, 300.

not just of an individual saying, however pivotal, and perhaps also because the 'cosmic imagery' of the two verses immediately preceding continues to exert an irresistible influence in favour of an 'end of the world' interpretation. But once it has been accepted that in 14:62 Jesus could use the language of Dn. 7:13-14 to speak of his imminent vindication at the right hand of God, there is no basis for continuing to insist that in 13:26 the same language must refer to the parousia.

In *Jesus and the Old Testament* I attempted to show that within the synoptic tradition of the sayings of Jesus Dn. 7:13-14 was variously applied to periods from the immediate post-resurrection authority of Jesus (Mt. 28:18) to the last judgment (Mt. 25:31-34), but that nowhere was the 'coming' understood as a coming to earth at the parousia.[25] The earliest use of Daniel's language in this latter sense is probably Rev. 1:7, and thereafter it quickly became established in patristic exegesis.[26] But for our exegesis of Mark it is necessary to get behind this later Christian development and to try to read the vision of Daniel as Jesus and his apostles would have understood it.[27] In other words, if you come to Mk. 13 with the assumption that traditional Christian exegesis is right, it is hard to see how it could mean anything else; but if you read it in the context of first-century understanding of prophetic and apocalyptic language, the traditional exegesis is not at all so obvious.[28]

The following outline (adapted from my *Divine Government,* p. 128) may help to clarify my understanding of the development of the discourse, and of how it answers the question posed in v. 4, a question relating specifically to the fulfilment of Jesus' prediction in v. 2. The different levels of indentation are intended to display the gradual approach to the answer by way of negative answers ('not yet') and a preliminary stage of fulfilment ('but when . . .') until the answer eventually comes in vv. 24-27 ('but in those days'; 'and then'; 'and then'), after which v. 32 introduces a new (though related) subject, which was not included in the original question.

25. *Jesus and the OT,* 139-48.

26. For the NT see *Jesus and the OT,* 202-4, for patristic exegesis 210-12, and for a summary and conclusions 214-17, 219-22.

27. For a brief account of this with special reference to Mark see my *Divine Government,* 73-82.

28. I have discussed some responses to my 1971 study of Mark 13 (by D. Wenham and M. Casey) in my *Divine Government,* 121 n. 20, where I conclude: 'Both Wenham and Casey in their different ways show how my approach to Mark 13 will not work *given the traditional Christian understanding of language about the coming of the Son of Man;* but it is precisely that traditional understanding that I wish to question, and neither seems to me to have been able to detach themselves from that presupposition.' The same may perhaps be said of Beasley-Murray's brief comments (248-49).

Indicators of Time and Sequence in Mark 13

v. 2 *(No time indicator in prediction)*

v. 4 *WHEN?* (and what will be the sign?)

> v. 5 *Watch out* — it is NOT YET (v. 7b)
>
> v. 8 all this is only THE BEGINNING
>
> v. 9 *Watch out* — it is NOT YET
>
> v. 10 good news to all nations FIRST
>
> v. 13 the 'end' still in the future

v. 14 *But when* . . . i.e., as opposed to the NOT YET of vv. 5-13, here the sequence begins (in 'those days', v. 19)

> v. 21 *At that time* this is not yet the end
>
> v. 23 *Watch out*   you have been forewarned

v. 24 *But in those days, following that distress* (reference back to v. 19)

> so an unbroken sequence from the *when* of v. 14

v. 26 *And then* ⎫
v. 27 *And then* ⎭ so here at last is the answer to 'When?' (v. 4)

> v. 28f. The fig tree (a parable of necessary chronological sequence) shows that *these things* indicate that 'it is near'
>
> v. 30f. And therefore *all these things* must inevitably occur within *this generation.*

---

v. 32 *BUT about THAT day or hour* . . .

> which 'day or hour'? — no (singular) 'day' or 'hour' so far mentioned

v. 33 *Watch out* — it may be ANY time

> So vv. 32-37 speak throughout of an UNKNOWN time, which comes without announcement, in contrast to the
>
> > NOT YET ⎫
> > BUT WHEN ⎪
> >   ⎬ of vv. 5-31
> > THEN   ⎪
> > WITHIN GENERATION ⎭

It is this understanding of the discourse which will be presupposed in the exegesis which follows. There will be opportunity to explain and defend various specific aspects of it in the exegesis of individual sections and verses, but a grasp of the interpretation as a whole will enable the reader to understand how I see each part as fitting into the whole.

This discourse, like that of chapter 4, should be treated as a whole. But for convenience of discussion we shall, as in chapter 4, operate with subdivisions, as follows:

3-4	The disciples' question
5-8	The end is not yet
9-13	The prospect of persecution
14-23	The beginning of the end
24-31	The coming of the Son of Man within 'this generation'
32-37	An unknown day and hour: be ready.

The Disciples' Question (13:3-4)

The geographical sequence from the genitive absolute of v. 1 to that of v. 3, with Jesus going out from the temple and then sitting on the Mount of Olives opposite the temple, ensures that these verses are closely linked with vv. 1-2, as does the fact that without Jesus' prediction in v. 2 there is no antecedent for the ταῦτα of the disciples' question. The subject of the question is therefore clearly determined both by the context and by the location specifically identified as κατέναντι τοῦ ἱεροῦ. It is about the destruction of the temple.

The pattern is by now familiar: Jesus makes a striking or puzzling pronouncement in public (the parable of the sower, 4:3-9; the declaration that defilement is not external but internal, 7:15; the prohibition of divorce, 10:9) and the disciples, in private (κατὰ μόνας, 4:10; εἰς οἶκον ἀπὸ τοῦ ὄχλου, 7:17; εἰς τὴν οἰκίαν, 10:10; cf. 9:28), demand an explanation. In this case it is not all the disciples who receive the explanation, but only the original four of 1:16-20.

The question has two parts, joined by καί, each of which concerns ταῦτα. It is only an exegetical prejudgment, together with familiarity with the Matthean form of the question, that can suggest that the two parts of the question have a different reference. Mark's wording gives no hint of a second subject, and to take the second ταῦτα as referring to a different subject from the first, when no other subject has been mentioned, is surely an exegetical tour de force.[29] Even more remarkable is the suggestion that ταῦτα πάντα refers specifically to the contents of vv. 5ff., thus making Mark credit the disciples with precognition of what Jesus is about to say.[30] If Mark intended to introduce a sec-

29. The point is well established by Gundry, 736-37.
30. So, e.g., Anderson, Hooker, Mann.

ond subject into the question, he could have found ways of saying so, as Matthew did; but he has not.

The twofold form of the question does not introduce a new subject, but gives a double angle to the disciples' concern over Jesus' words about the temple. They want to know not only when it will be destroyed, but what σημεῖον will enable them to be prepared for it.

The first part of the question will eventually, after a few false starts, receive quite a specific answer, introduced by ὅταν (v. 14), and developed through ἐν ἐκείναις ταῖς ἡμέραις (v. 24) to the climax of καὶ τότε (v. 26), καὶ τότε (v. 27); the answer is then summed up in the quite definite though not exact time setting of v. 30: it will take place within this generation.

The response to the second part of the question is, however, apparently less forthcoming. What might appear to be σημεῖα in vv. 5-8 turn out to be at best inconclusive: the end is not yet (v. 7); this is only the beginning of the birth pangs (v. 8). It is with v. 14 that we begin to get something more like σημεῖα, sufficient at least to require immediate flight. But it is in that very context that we find the only occurrence of σημεῖον in the discourse, and it is a strongly negative one, warning against the spurious σημεῖα produced by the ψευδόχριστοι. It would be easy to conclude from this, as does Geddert on the basis of the only other reference to σημεῖα in Mark (8:11-13),[31] that Mark is totally opposed to the concept of σημεῖα, and that we are intended to read the second part of the disciples' question as mistaken, with Jesus' discourse designed to undermine their misconceived desire for a sign. Yet in vv. 28-29, without using the word σημεῖον, Jesus will speak clearly of one event (the budding of the fig tree) which is the harbinger of another (summer), and will draw the conclusion that the appearance of ταῦτα will enable them to know that ἐγγύς ἐστιν. It is hard to draw any meaningful distinction between such language and that of a σημεῖον, and when we add the function of the βδέλυγμα τῆς ἐρημώσεως in v. 14 as a warning to flee before it is too late, it does not seem that, despite its failure to use σημεῖον in a positive sense, Jesus' discourse is designed to dismiss the second half of the disciples' question as inappropriate.[32] It is, rather, a natural expansion of the first half: 'When will it happen, and how will we know that it is due?'[33]

31. T. J. Geddert, *Watchwords,* 29-58, 203-6.

32. Hooker, 301-2, may be nearer the mark with her distinction between three warnings against being misled by false signs (vv. 5-8, 9-13, 21-23) and three 'true signs' in vv. 14, 24, and 28. But she goes on to suggest that these 'true signs' are so close to the events that, like the nuclear four-minute warning, they 'provide no real warning at all' since it is now too late to prepare; the point of vv. 14-23, however, seems to be that this is the last chance to escape — it is not yet too late.

33. It is a mark of the awkwardness of the traditional understanding of the discourse as focussing on the parousia that Gundry, 738, has to speak of Jesus 'ignoring the four disciples' question' and using it 'as a platform from which to speak on a variety of topics dealing with the future'. An exegesis which takes the answer as responding to the question rather than ignoring it is surely to be preferred.

3 As in v. 1, the genitive absolute is grammatically inappropriate since its subject is part of the main clause, but this is not uncommon in Mark, and the two genitive absolutes serve here to mark out the successive phases of Jesus' temple prophecy, first the simple prediction as he leaves the area, then the more extended reflection on it as he sits on the hillside opposite. See on 11:1 for the possibility that the Mount of Olives is mentioned not only because it was the natural route back to Bethany (see on 11:11) but also because of its messianic connections.[34] But here the more obvious effect is to recall the place where according to Ezk. 11:23 God stopped after abandoning the temple (see on vv. 1-2). κατέναντι need be no more than a note of location, giving a viewpoint over the temple just as in 12:41 Jesus had a viewpoint over the treasury; as such it is a narrative prompt to the reader to recognise that the following discourse refers to the fate of the temple, which dominates the view as Jesus speaks. But following on his abandonment of the temple and prediction of its destruction κατέναντι τοῦ ἱεροῦ may also be intended to underline that Jesus is 'over against' the temple in a more profound sense as well (ἐναντίος means 'opponent').[35] For κατ' ἰδίαν cf. 4:34 (and 4:10 κατὰ μόνας); 6:31-32; 7:33; 9:2, 28. This is the only place after 1:16-20 where Andrew joins the 'inner circle' (cf. 5:37; 9:2; 14:33), though he is listed next after them in 3:18. His presence here with his brother and former colleagues (perhaps relatives) is neither surprising nor specially significant. The subject of the singular verb ἐπηρώτα must be Peter, presumably as usual acting as spokesman, the other three disciples being appended as being also present to hear the reply (cf. the singular κατεδίωξεν with the same plural subject in 1:36).

4 The persistent view that the second half of the question has a more 'eschatological' reference than the first half, while it is primarily due to a prior judgment about the subject matter of the discourse which follows, is also sometimes supported by Mark's use of the verb συντελεῖσθαι, which for us recalls Matthew's extension of the question to cover also the συντέλεια τοῦ αἰῶνος. But unless we are to assume that when Mark wrote his readers were already familiar with Matthew's version of the question (and that would still be a minority view), Matthew's phrase is not a good guide to the intended sense of Mark's verb. ταῦτα πάντα are the same ταῦτα as in the first half of the question, the things predicted by Jesus in v. 2, the plural presumably due to the recognition that the single 'event' of the temple's destruction would not be accomplished in an instant but must be an extended process. The completion of this process, the stage by which every last stone had been dislodged, is appropriately expressed by συντελέω, to bring to completion. While the verb could appropriately be

34. See also S. C. Barton, *Discipleship*, 114-15.

35. Myers, 321, regards κατέναντι in both 12:41 and 13:3 as a 'stage direction . . . proleptic of judgment'. It is interesting that the Egyptian who led a rising against Rome a few years later gathered his followers on the Mount of Olives, promising that from there they would see Jerusalem's walls fall down at his command (Josephus, *Ant.* 20.169-70).

used to describe an eschatological consummation, its normal use (as in Lk. 4:2, 13; Acts 21:27) is of the 'carrying out', 'accomplishing', 'completing' of a process. It is the technical term ἡ συντέλεια τοῦ αἰῶνος in Matthew (cf. the use of συντέλεια for the Hebrew *qēṣ* in LXX Dn. 8:19; 11:27) which brings in a specifically eschatological reference (cf. Mt. 13:39, 40, 49; Heb. 9:26) which does not belong to the verb on its own.

The End Is Not Yet (13:5-8)

The discourse begins on a note which is one of its most persistent characteristics, the warning against premature expectation. It begins with an imperative, βλέπετε, which will be repeated in vv. 9, 23, and 33. The disciples, and those who following them will read these words, are called to discernment and warned against the sort of superficial impressions of 'fulfilment' which have been the bane of students of apocalyptic and eschatological literature ever since. Sometimes false impressions are self-inflicted, as people naively read off from world events the 'signs of the end' (vv. 7-8). Sometimes, however, they are deliberately fostered by those who have something to gain by working on the credulity of the faithful (vv. 5-6). Jesus' disciples will be liable to both kinds of misinformation as they look for the fulfilment of his words about the destruction of the temple. They must be on their guard.

What we know from Josephus of the forty years or so between Jesus' ministry and the destruction of the temple amply illustrates these warnings. While the rise of ψευδόχριστοι καὶ ψευδοπροφῆται would be a particularly prominent feature of the years of the war against Rome and the siege of Jerusalem (vv. 21-23), long before that there would be self-styled messiahs (ἐπὶ τῷ ὀνόματί μου) only too ready to lead those who would follow them into disastrous conflict with Rome, giving a foretaste of the confrontation which eventually would lead to the fall of the temple (see below on v. 6 for details). In such an atmosphere there would be ample opportunity for 'misleading many', particularly if the pretenders could offer persuasive σημεῖα.

The wars and natural disasters of vv. 7-8 (see Textual Note) could have a similar effect, as they often have, on those looking for a time of upheaval. Such events feature frequently in eschatological prophecies.[36] But there can have been few times in human history when such things could not be observed at the level of sober history. For examples from the mid-first century A.D. see below on vv. 7-8.

All these things were to be expected, and were not signs of the event Jesus has predicted: οὔπω τὸ τέλος. Here is another word which seems to some to suggest a reference to the end of the world, but τέλος is a very general

---

36. For numerous examples see Davies and Allison, *Matthew*, 3.339-41. Also L. Hartman, *Prophecy*, ch. III, especially pp. 71-77 on earthquakes.

word for 'end', the completion of a process (e.g., 3:26; Mt. 26:58; Lk. 1:33), and the nature of that 'end' depends on the context.[37] Here there has been no word of any 'end' other than that of the temple's destruction, for which in this context τὸ τέλος is the obvious term to use. The disciples have asked when the catastrophic event predicted by Jesus will be accomplished (συντελέω), and he replies by speaking first of when that completion (τέλος) is *not* to take place.

The listing of dramatic events in vv. 7-8 was not a complete red herring, however. They do not mark the time of the τέλος, but they are at least the ἀρχὴ ὠδίνων. Here is a term which apparently has a more eschatological connotation, since Jewish eschatology came to think of a time of suffering preceding the coming of the Messiah, which was sometimes described in terms of 'labour-pains' (see G. Bertram, *TDNT,* 9.671-72). This rabbinic language, however, is later than the NT period. In this context, as generally in the NT (see below on v. 8), it is a live and very powerful metaphor for a period of great suffering, with the probable note also of looking forward to what lies beyond the suffering. ὠδῖνες alone would say 'not yet' (the pains precede the birth), and when ἀρχή is added the sense of postponement becomes dominant. There is a birth to be looked forward to, but the wars, earthquakes, and famines of vv. 7-8 show only that it is coming, not when it will come. Even to speak of a birth at all is perhaps to press the metaphor too far, in that such an expression as ὠδῖνες τοῦ θανάτου does not seem to envisage a birth, only pain; but as the discourse proceeds we shall see that the coming destruction of the temple will bring with it a new beginning.

The answer given to the disciples' question in the first four verses of the discourse is thus a negative one, clearing away the natural tendency to look for signs of the temple's destruction in the stirring and ominous events of the coming years, in the areas both of politics and of natural disaster. The disciples must not allow themselves to be misled. They will have enough to do to maintain their own witness to the truth through these difficult days, as vv. 9-13 will show, without being distracted by premature excitement.

5 As in 4:1 ἤρξατο λέγειν alerts the reader to expect a substantial discourse. His words are addressed specifically to the four disciples, but v. 37 will extend their scope to 'all'.[38] For the imperative focus of the whole discourse, signalled at the outset by βλέπετε, see above, p. 499, n. 12. The repetition of βλέπετε in vv. 9, 23, and 33, together with the related imperatives ἀγρυπνεῖτε (v. 33) and γρηγορεῖτε (vv. 35, 37) in the latter part of the discourse, sets the tone as one of warning, requiring of the disciples not so much an intellectual

37. It is perhaps significant that in the LXX τέλος often translates *qēṣ* and cognates in the general sense of 'end, border, boundary', but when *qēṣ* is used eschatologically it is translated instead by συντέλεια (see on v. 4).

38. K. E. Brower, in K. E. Brower and M. W. Elliott (ed.), *Reader,* 140, describes vv. 5 and 37 as an *inclusio.* The term may suggest too technical a literary intention, but he is surely right that according to v. 37 'Mark has his implied readers in view'.

grasp of the future timetable (as their question might imply) as an attitude of careful preparedness.[39]

6 See on 9:37 for ἐπὶ τῷ ὀνόματί μου in the sense of acting on the authority of Jesus, or claiming to represent him (hence the warning in v. 5 not to be misled: their language is such as a disciple would naturally respond to).[40] All we are told specifically about the danger posed by these impostors, however, is that they will say Ἐγώ εἰμι (ironically the very words which Jesus will use himself to establish his role in 14:62). There is no plausible context in first-century Judaism in which we can envisage anyone making a simple claim to divinity by adopting the divine name from Ex. 3:14, and in any case such a claim would be so blatantly false as to need no warning. So we must assume some predicate with the verb, and probably the best way to take it in the light of the meagre contextual guidance is that they were not so much claiming to act on Jesus' authority as in fact aiming to usurp his place,[41] not by claiming to be Jesus *redivivus* (surely too far-fetched a concept in this context) but by arrogating to themselves the role which was rightly his, that of Messiah (note that Matthew so interprets it, by adding ὁ Χριστός).[42] In that case they will come into the same category as those described in v. 22 as ψευδόχριστοι καὶ ψευδοπροφῆται, who will be hailed by someone saying Ἴδε ὧδε ὁ Χριστός. If the same sort of people are in view in both parts of the discourse, the reason for the repetition will be that here the focus is on the pre-war situation, but in vv. 21-22 on the time of the siege itself.

For such 'messianic' leaders in the years between Jesus' ministry and the Jewish war see, for instance, Josephus, *Ant.* 20. 97-99 (Theudas), 102 (sons of Judas of Galilee), 169-72 (the Egyptian), 167-68, 188 (various unnamed 'impostors'). Some of the rebel leaders are recorded merely as political nationalists, but in first-century Judaea politics and religion were never far apart. Theudas and the Egyptian both claimed to be prophets, and Josephus speaks of other rebel leaders whom he distinguishes from the *sicarii* as having 'purer

39. T. J. Geddert, *Watchwords,* ch. 3, rightly describes the discourse as offering a 'Markan perspective on discernment', but by subsuming the use of βλέπετε under the heading of 'epistemology' and by postulating a consistent and deliberate intention behind all Mark's uses of this common verb, he runs the risk of overspecifying a 'quite ordinary term' (his words). The overall thrust of the discourse is less 'intellectual' than Geddert's language of 'epistemology' suggests.

40. E. Trocmé, *Formation,* 209, relying on ἐπὶ τῷ ὀνόματί μου, insists that those described must be within the Christian community. They are 'the heads of the Church, who boast of being Jesus' successors and of having assumed after his death his role of Davidic Messiah. . . . It is James and his group who are attacked here.' Gundry, 761-62, also argues against the deceivers being non-Christian Jews, but he does not identify who within the Christian community they may be. Schweizer, 268, suggests Simon Magus as a possible model, associated with the Christian community but a threat to it (so also M. Hengel, *Studies,* 21).

41. Hence the suggestions that ἐπὶ τῷ ὀνόματί μου should here be translated not 'in my name' but 'with my name' or 'under my name'; see G. R. Beasley-Murray, *Last Days,* 391 n. 49. Cf. Mann, 'using my name'.

42. See further J. Gibson, *JSNT* 38 (1990) 48-49; Gundry, 737. E. Stauffer, *TDNT,* 2.353 refers to ἐγώ εἰμι in this context as 'a technical formula for the self-revelation of Christ'.

hands but more impious intentions . . . deceivers and impostors, under the pretence of divine inspiration' who promised the people they led into the wilderness that God would give them σημεῖα ἐλευθερίας (*War* 2.258-59). We are not told that any of these insurgents before Bar Kochba (c. A.D. 132) actually claimed the title Messiah, but 'prophet' and 'king'[43] point in that direction. We should remember, too, that almost all our information comes from Josephus, who so consistently avoided using the term Χριστός that it occurs in the whole of his writings only in the two places where he (or his reviser) uses it as a title for Jesus (*Ant.* 18.63; 20.200). So if any of these people did make specifically messianic claims, we would not expect Josephus to have recorded them as such. Self-proclaimed prophets who promise miraculous signs are as near as he gets to 'messianic' language. All these incidents took place well before the war broke out in A.D. 66, and Josephus gives the impression that they are only a selection.[44] For πολλοὺς πλανήσουσιν (note that these πολλοί are not said to be from among Jesus' disciples) cf. the πλεῖστος ὄχλος who followed Theudas (400 according to Acts 5:36) and the four thousand *sicarii* who followed the Egyptian according to Acts 21:38 (30,000 according to Josephus, *War* 2.261).

7 After ἀκούσητε πολέμους the additional ἀκοὰς πολέμων is formally redundant, but the rounded and memorable prophetic phrase which results is typical of Mark's style.[45] Cf. Je. 51:46 for the call not to be perturbed by 'rumours of violence'. For θροέομαι cf. 2 Thes. 2:2, where it is parallel with being 'shaken from your mind' by reports that the Day of the Lord has already come. The disciples are to be calm and not to jump to hasty conclusions. δεῖ γένεσθαι is not specifically eschatological language;[46] wars are sure to happen, and their occurrence is *not* to be seen as having any eschatological significance. For οὔπω τὸ τέλος see pp. 508-9 above; this is why they are not to panic: history will continue to take its regular course.

The years between Tiberius and Nero were relatively peaceful in the Roman empire as a whole, but an inhabitant of Palestine might have heard, for instance, of the wars in Parthia in A.D. 36 and sporadically thereafter, or the war between Antipas and the Nabataean king Aretas, in which Rome also became involved in A.D. 36-37, long before Judaea itself was engulfed in war, not to mention the series of local uprisings which were ruthlessly put down by the Romans in the years before the war (see on v. 6).

43. After the death of Herod the Great both Simon and Athronges proclaimed themselves king (Josephus, *Ant.* 17.273-84). Josephus goes on to comment that at that time anyone with a following of brigands might 'make himself king' (*Ant.* 17.285).

44. Cf. also the Samaritan who in A.D. 35 promised to uncover Moses' sacred vessels on Mount Gerizim (Josephus, *Ant.* 18.85-87). Note also the otherwise unknown 'insurrection' involving Barabbas which had apparently happened only just before these words were spoken (15:7).

45. Gundry's distinction (763) between wars 'heard' because they were within earshot and 'reports of battles' taking place at a distance is pedantic overexegesis of a sonorous phrase.

46. See my *Jesus and the OT*, 254, against T. F. Glasson. In classing the proposed allusion in these words to Dn. 2:28-29 as 'at the most, possible' I was too generous. The apocalyptic formula 'what is to happen' is not the same as Jesus' simple statement '[These things] must happen'.

8 The γάρ indicates that these clauses are further amplification of the warning about wars in v. 7, and the future tenses have the same effect as the preceding δεῖ: these things are bound to go on happening. The conflicts described are international, involving different nations and kingdoms, rather than civil wars such as divided the Roman empire after the death of Nero in A.D. 68. κατὰ τόπους means 'from place to place'; BAGD, 406a, II.1.a, quote a Greek astrological text: λιμὸς καὶ λοιμὸς καὶ σφαγαὶ κατὰ τόπους (cf. Textual Note above).

First-century earthquakes[47] might include one experienced at Jerusalem in A.D. 67 (Josephus, *War* 4.286-87; cf. 1.370 for an earlier severe earthquake in Palestine), and further afield Acts 16:26 mentions an earthquake in Philippi, while news of the partial destruction of Pompeii by an earthquake in A.D. 62 or of a major earthquake in Asia Minor in A.D. 61[48] would probably have reached Palestine. There was a major famine in the reign of Claudius, c. A.D. 46 (Acts 11:28; Josephus, *Ant.* 3.320; 20.101; Schürer, 1.457 n. 8).

As noted above (introductory comments on vv. 5-8), evidence for anything like a technical term 'birth pang of the Messiah' (always singular in the rabbis) comes from after the NT period.[49] Before that labour pains were used as a metaphor for great suffering in a wide variety of contexts. In the LXX ὠδῖνες used metaphorically sometimes refers to death (2 Sa. 22:6; Ps. 18:4) but more often depicts the suffering of nations and cities in crisis (Is. 13:8, Babylon; Je. 6:24, Jerusalem; 22:23, Lebanon; Mi. 4:9-10, Zion). While history and eschatology are often hard to disentangle in the prophets, these passages seem to relate primarily to current history; Is. 26:17-18 is closer to the later rabbinic eschatological imagery.[50] In the NT outside this passage and the Matthew parallel the metaphor is used only of the 'pains of death' (Acts 2:24, echoing Ps. 18:4-5), of Paul's pains in bringing his converts to birth (Gal. 4:19), of the world's agonised anticipation of the time of salvation throughout history until now (Rom. 8:22), and to describe the *sudden* onset of the Day of the Lord (not a period of preparation for it) in 1 Thes. 5:3 (cf. *1 Enoch* 62:4, of the agony of those

47. Pesch, 2.280, proposes to read σεισμοί not of literal earthquakes, but as in LXX Je. 10:22; 47:3; Na. 3:2 of the rumble of the wheels of war chariots, but not only is this a very obscure use to expect readers to pick up when the normal literal meaning is so appropriate, but it also ignores the frequency of earthquakes as items in a prophetic list of disasters.

48. Pliny, *Nat. Hist.* 2.84; see further Gnilka, 2.188 and n. 14; B. Reicke, in D. E. Aune (ed.), *Studies in NT and Early Christian Literature,* 131.

49. Cf. the conclusion of Gundry, 763: 'Jesus either revises rabbinic usage, disregards it, or does not know it. Or it had yet to appear.' For Jewish usage generally see G. Bertram, *TDNT,* 9.668-72 and texts cited by Str-B, 1.950.

50. The texts quoted by D. S. Russell, *Method,* 272, to establish an OT origin for the rabbinic concept either do not speak of childbirth at all or are among those listed above. He makes much of 1QH 3[11]:7-10 as a sectarian anticipation of the same idea; this is certainly a striking metaphorical use of the language of labour, but Russell's interpretation of it as referring to 'the emergence of God's redeemed people through great toil and suffering' is only a suggestion. In Rev. 12:1-6 the birth of a child is part of the apocalyptic vision, but the reference to labour pains in v. 2 is merely as part of the 'story', not as a term in itself for preliminary eschatological suffering.

facing final judgment, not of a preliminary suffering); cf. the imagery of labour in Jn. 16:21 for the disciples' temporary suffering. This range of usage suggests a 'live' metaphor, capable of being adapted to a wide variety of uses, not a technical term in the later rabbinic sense which would therefore carry its own ready-made eschatological application.[51]

The Prospect of Persecution (13:9-13)

In the unsettling period described in vv. 6-8, which is to be expected before the fulfilment of Jesus' prediction, the disciples will not be merely spectators. Indeed, those who follow Jesus can expect to be singled out for hatred and ill-treatment by those in power, just as he himself has been. This is not a theme peculiar to this discourse: Jesus has warned them before of difficult times ahead for those who follow him (6:11; 8:15, 34-38; 10:30; cf. 4:17). Indeed, it is significant that much of the content of this part of the discourse has been felt by Matthew and Luke to fit appropriately at an earlier point in the story (Mt. 10:17-22; Lk. 12:11-12) relating to events during the time of Jesus' ministry rather than in the interval between his death and the destruction of the temple. In that sense, nothing will have changed. But in these verses there is a mood of escalating tension, and the specific mention in v. 10 that within this context of persecution the universal preaching of the good news must take place πρῶτον shows that the disciples' question has not been forgotten. Here then is another element of what must happen before the τέλος arrives. The interim period is not to be a time of passive waiting but of proclamation, of the experience of persecution, and of faithful endurance εἰς τέλος.

The previous section began with an imperative, βλέπετε, and went on to speak in the second person of what the disciples were to hear and how they must respond to it (μὴ θροεῖσθε), but otherwise consisted mainly of third-person description. Now a second βλέπετε leads into a more predominantly second-person section of the discourse, appropriately introduced by βλέπετε ὑμεῖς ἑαυτούς and concluding with an exhortation, ὁ ὑπομείνας εἰς τέλος οὗτος σωθήσεται, which functions as both command and reassurance to disciples under pressure. Even the two third-person 'predictions' in this section (vv. 10 and 12) serve to underline the disciples' calling, as witnesses to the εὐαγγέλιον (vv. 9 and 11) and as the objects of universal hatred because they follow Jesus (v. 13a).

This is, then, the most 'personalised' part of a discourse which as a whole is, as we have noticed already, characterised more by exhortation and pastoral preparation than by abstract prediction. As a result, even with the inclusion of

51. This discussion is not intended to question the later Jewish use of language about the 'birth pangs of the Messiah', nor to deny that the idea of preliminary eschatological suffering for which they used such language may already have been current in Judaism before the Christian era, but simply to assert that we have no evidence that the metaphor of labour pains was a recognised way of expressing that belief as early as the time of Jesus (or Mark).

the necessary proclamation of the good news πρῶτον, the movement of Jesus' response to the disciples' question seems to have slowed down almost to the point of digression. Jesus is in no hurry to move from the 'non-signs' of vv. 5-8 to the beginning of real signs in v. 14. The disciples must first be prepared for what may prove to be a longer time of waiting for the τέλος than they may have imagined, a time which will put their faithfulness to a severe test.

The sayings which make up vv. 9-13 do not read as an organic whole so much as a collection of sayings brought together around the themes of persecution, proclamation, and endurance, linked by the threefold repetition of the verb παραδίδωμι (vv. 9, 11, 12). The present verse-divisions represent quite adequately the natural breakdown of the passage into separate units, though we shall note some thought connections which link them together even where they do not follow smoothly in form or expression.[52]

9 The other uses of βλέπετε in this chapter are a more general call to alertness, without any direct object (though the μή-clause following βλέπετε in v. 5 gets closer to it); cf. the βλέπετε ἀπό of 8:15; 12:38 and βλέπετε τί ἀκούετε in 4:24. The direct object here, ἑαυτούς, makes the warning more personal: they themselves are in danger. The warning is not so that they should try to escape persecution, but to prepare them to endure it faithfully. The lack of expressed subject for παραδώσουσιν has the effect of generalising the threat: it is people in general who will be against them. And the choice of this verb, with its echoes of 9:31; 10:33, suggests a link between their treatment and that of Jesus himself.[53] For Mark's use of παραδίδωμι to mark the successive stages in Jesus' passion, as well as the related suffering of John the Baptist and of Jesus' disciples, see 1:14; 9:31; 10:33; 13:9, 11, 12; 14:10-11, 18, 21, 41-42; 15:1, 15.

The sentence with its three verbs (παραδώσουσιν, δαρήσεσθε, σταθήσεσθε) and three prepositional phrases (εἰς συνέδρια, εἰς συναγωγάς, ἐπὶ ἡγεμόνων καὶ βασιλέων) is probably best construed as a series of three clauses each consisting of a verb and a prepositional phrase, separated by two καίς, with the verb coming first in the first clause and last in the other two. It may be objected first that εἰς συνέδρια καὶ εἰς συναγωγάς forms a natural pair following παραδώσουσιν (or, on yet another interpretation, preceding and qualifying δαρήσεσθε) and secondly that εἰς συναγωγὰς δαρήσεσθε is an awkward idiom (apparently meaning something like 'you will be taken into synagogues for a beating'; or perhaps εἰς is used simply as equivalent to ἐν), but these considerations are outweighed by the awkwardness of taking δαρήσεσθε as a clause on its own and the unbalanced sequence of clauses which results.[54]

---

52. B. Reicke, in D. E. Aune (ed.), *Studies in NT and Early Christian Literature,* 131-33, surveys ways in which the predictions of these verses were in fact fulfilled in the years leading up to the Jewish War.

53. R. H. Lightfoot's attempt to link the whole discourse with the passion narrative (*Message,* ch. 4) is particularly successful with regard to vv. 9-13.

54. Gundry, 739, 765, opts for this alternative reading, supporting it from the more consistent use of εἰς which it allows and making a virtue of the 'emphasis' (I have called it 'awkward-

On that understanding the first two clauses have a Jewish tone (συνέδρια, συναγωγαί), while the last relates to the authorities of the Roman empire (ἡγεμόνες, βασιλεῖς: βασιλεύς could be applied [albeit incorrectly in the case of Antipas] to the Herodian rulers as 'Jewish' rulers under the Roman aegis, but would apply particularly to the Roman emperor; ἡγεμῶν normally refers to a Roman provincial governor). συνέδριον is regularly used in the NT in the singular of the Sanhedrin in Jerusalem, but there were also local Jewish law courts known by the same name (see *m. Sanh.* 1:6 for the constitution of these courts of twenty-three members, distinguished from the 'greater Sanhedrin' of seventy-one members; cf. Schürer, 2.184-88, 225-26), and it is more likely that disciples would find themselves arraigned before these. For synagogues as places of corporal punishment (δέρω is a general term for 'beat'; cf. 12:3, 5; but the synagogue setting, following on the mention of συνέδρια, suggests official punishment) cf. Mt. 23:34; Acts 22:19; the thirty-nine stripes repeatedly inflicted on Paul by 'the Jews' (2 Cor. 11:24) were a synagogue punishment, administered by the 'minister of the synagogue' (*m. Mak.* 3:10-12; cf. Dt. 25:1-3 for the basis of the practice).[55] The legal atmosphere of the first two clauses is continued in the third: for ἐπί with the genitive of appearing before a court see BAGD, 286, I.1.a.δ; indeed, it is hard to imagine in what other capacity disciples might expect to appear before governors and kings. The disciples must therefore be prepared for official opposition in both Jewish and Roman courts (as the Book of Acts well illustrates). Both could be found in Palestine, though the next verse suggests also a wider perspective.

Two important phrases qualify this bleak picture. First, their trial is to be ἕνεκεν ἐμοῦ; see on 8:35 (and cf. 10:29). It is by following Jesus, who is himself about to stand before both Sanhedrin and governor, and proclaiming the good news about him that they will get into trouble, and in that cause even to lose your life is gain (8:35), how much more a mere flogging. Secondly, their very appearance in court will be itself an act of witness. For εἰς μαρτύριον αὐτοῖς see on 1:44. If the same negative tone is to be found in the phrase here as in 6:11 and (probably) 1:44, it is on the assumption that the officials will not embrace the εὐαγγέλιον; but it will have been presented to them.[56]

10 This declaration may seem a non sequitur in the middle of a section dealing with persecution and legal trial, and may well have been inserted by

---

ness'; later Gundry himself calls it 'orphanage') produced by the asyndeton of δαρήσεσθε on this view. Mann, 512, translates in the same way, though his comment (516) oddly seems to ignore the majority interpretation, followed in this commentary, and considers only the alternative (adopted, e.g., by Pesch) of linking εἰς συνέδρια καὶ εἰς συναγωγάς with δαρήσεσθε, thus leaving παραδώσουσιν ὑμᾶς on its own as an introductory clause.

55. Further details in C. Schneider, *TDNT,* 4.516; more briefly, Lane, 461 n. 60.

56. D. Wenham, *Rediscovery,* 278, comments: 'Whether this testimony is a blessing or curse to those who hear will depend on their response.' Many commentators believe that the phrase has a primarily positive tone here, in the light of the proclamation of *good* news in the next verse; their trial will be an opportunity for evangelism.

Mark between vv. 9 and 11, which seem to belong together. But if so he has done so with good reason, since the occasion for the trial is the disciples' faithful witness to Jesus, which will bring them to present their μαρτύριον even before Gentile rulers. By this uncomfortable means (as well as by more conventional methods, one hopes) the εὐαγγέλιον will make its way εἰς πάντα τὰ ἔθνη.[57] The link between proclamation of the good news and persecution is well established already by 6:11 and 8:35-38 (and more fully in the 'mission discourse' of Mt. 10 which in fact contains more material on persecution than on mission). Cf. 14:9 for the expectation that the εὐαγγέλιον will continue to be proclaimed widely after Jesus' death. The εὐαγγέλιον which began as the message *of* Jesus (1:14-15) is well on the way to becoming the good news *about* Jesus (1:1).

And this good news is destined for πάντα τὰ ἔθνη. Jesus' excursions into Gentile territory (5:1-20; 7:24–8:10) and his Gentile following in 3:8 have begun to prepare us for this vision, and we have seen in 7:24–8:10 a deliberate extension of the blessings of Israel's Messiah to the surrounding peoples. It is possible that the specific inclusion of πάντα τὰ ἔθνη in the Isaiah quotation in 11:17 is a further pointer in this direction, even if that is not the main thrust in context. Later the confession of Jesus as Son of God by a Gentile officer will be a foretaste of the universal church (15:39). But this verse (and by implication 14:9) is the most explicit indication in Mark's gospel of the universal scope of the good news and therefore of the Christian mission, as it will be spelled out in Matthew's final commission (28:19-20) and in the whole narrative of Luke's second volume. In v. 27, as we shall see, that vision will be further developed.

In this context of answering the disciples' question 'When . . . and what sign?' interest focuses especially on πρῶτον. 'First' implies that there is something else to follow, but the sentence finishes without supplying it. Nor is it obviously supplied within vv. 9-13 as a whole: the persecution expected is not a sequel to the universal proclamation of the good news, but rather the context within which it will be achieved. It is only when we go to the wider context of the discourse and the question which gave rise to it that an explanation for the πρῶτον is found. The proclamation of the gospel to all nations is the precursor to the event which the disciples have asked about, and that, we have argued, is the destruction of the temple. In that case, here is another 'sign'. The temple will not be destroyed (and with it the central role of Israel in God's purposes come to an end) until the good news has already gone out beyond Israel to πάντα τὰ ἔθνη, and so the new 'temple' which replaces the physical building will not be a solely Jewish institution. We shall see this vision expressed in v. 27 in the gathering of the elect from all over the world into the newly estab-

---

57. G. D. Kilpatrick's argument (in D. E. Nineham [ed.], *Studies in the Gospels,* 145-58; *JTS* 9 [1958] 81-86) that καὶ εἰς πάντα τὰ ἔθνη should be read (following W Θ and several ancient versions) as part of the previous sentence has not been favourably received, though Trocmé, *Formation,* 210-11 n. 2, finds it 'very attractive'. Hooker, 310-11, is also unusually positive towards it.

lished sovereignty of the Son of Man. The proclamation of the εὐαγγέλιον is the means by which this ingathering will be accomplished, and the scope of that proclamation must therefore be universal. Moreover, it must be carried out πρῶτον, so as to be the basis for that new beginning which follows from the end of the old order (and of the temple which symbolises it). So before the temple is destroyed, the good news must be proclaimed to all nations.

How useful a 'sign' might this declaration be? Mission enthusiasts, assuming that the reference here is to the parousia rather than to the destruction of the temple, have sometimes taken this text very literally and have inferred that the parousia is and must be delayed until the last nation on earth has received the good news. Even given the parousia reference such a use of this verse raises many problems, such as just what constitutes an ἔθνος, how literally 'all' must be taken, and at what stage the good news can be said to have been proclaimed to a given ἔθνος (the infiltration of a single gospel tract or radio broadcast, the establishment of a viable church, or what?). Fortunately such questions are irrelevant to the stance taken in this commentary, in that the event before which it must have happened has already taken place more than nineteen centuries ago.

Is v. 10 then an unfulfilled prediction? It is perhaps not technically a prediction so much as a declaration of intent (δεῖ), but in any case its focus is not on the total number of ἔθνη evangelised, but on the fact that the good news for the Jews has become the good news for the Gentiles. Too careful a calculation of mission objectives achieved is also put in question by the perspective of Paul, who in the mid-fifties could already claim to have 'fully preached' (? — the meaning of πεπληρωκέναι is debatable) the gospel of Christ all the way round from Jerusalem to Illyricum so that he has nowhere else to go in that area (Rom. 15:19, 23; cf. Rom. 16:26; Col. 1:6, 23). From that point of view Mark, writing in Rome sometime later, would have found no difficulty in perceiving that the good news had indeed been proclaimed to πάντα τὰ ἔθνη while the temple was still standing. There was already in existence an international people of God even if not every nation on earth had yet heard the good news (or indeed was even known to exist at that time).

11 We are back now with the trial scenes of v. 9 (note the resumptive use of παραδιδόντες) but with the element of proclamation (v. 10) now dominating the disciple's concern when on trial. For the absolute use of παραδίδωμι cf. 1:14, there referring to arrest and imprisonment; here the focus is apparently on committal to trial. προμεριμνάω is first found in this passage; it is a fairly obvious coinage from the common μεριμνάω (see especially Mt. 6:25-34) when the object of concern lies in the future. The promise that words will be supplied is for hard-pressed disciples on trial, not for lazy preachers! Given the low social status of most of Jesus' early disciples, the prospect of an appearance even before a local συνέδριον would be daunting enough, much more before ἡγεμόνες καὶ βασιλεῖς, but their inadequacy will be supplied by divine aid, so that the opportunity for effective μαρτύριον will not be lost. This is one of only three mentions of the Holy Spirit in Mark after the prologue, and the only one which envisages the Holy Spirit as active in relation to disciples. The assurance given is reminiscent of the Johannine concept of the παράκλητος: see especially Jn. 14:26; 15:26-27; 16:8-11 for the Spirit's role as 'prompter' for the disciples' witness. Luke enthusiastically records the fulfilment of this promise (Lk. 12:11-12; 21:12-15; in the latter it is Jesus himself rather than the Spirit who will supply the words) in the narratives of Acts 4:8, 31; 5:32; 6:10; 13:9, etc.

12 This saying, reminiscent of Mi. 7:6,[58] sets the official persecution envisaged in vv. 9 and 11 into the wider context of conflict even within the family. It is the general idea rather than the specific words that recalls Micah's prophecy: the family members mentioned are different, and among the verbs used only ἐπαναστήσονται echoes the LXX text. Contrast Mt. 10:35, where the Micah text is closely followed, though not in LXX form. Micah's warning was of a general breakdown of society in Judah, so that 'your enemies are members of your own household', but this saying is more focused, both in that the context indicates that the family hostility is specifically directed against those who have chosen to follow Jesus, and also in that it twice mentions not only hatred but killing, an almost unthinkable violation of such close family ties as between brothers or between parents and children. This is a level of persecution against Christians for which we have little direct evidence in the first century at least until Nero's anti-Christian purge following the fire of Rome in A.D. 64, though the deaths of Stephen and of the two Jameses (Acts 12:1-3; Josephus, *Ant.* 20.200) and the persecution headed by Saul show what might happen even within a Jewish context. παραδώσει εἰς θάνατον suggests the role of informers: already in the Neronian persecution being a Christian was a sufficient cause for execution, and people were convicted on the testimony of others (Tacitus, *Ann.* 15.44); by the time of Pliny's governorship in Bithynia c. 112 such informing on Christians was normal (Pliny, *Ep.* 10.96.5-6).

13 The general situation outlined in v. 12 is personalised to the disciples.[59] The hatred they must expect is διὰ τὸ ὄνομά μου, specifically as followers of Jesus (cf. ἕνεκεν ἐμοῦ, v. 9). For the name as an idiom for association with Jesus cf. ἐν/ἐπὶ τῷ ὀνόματί μου in 9:37, 38, 39, and 41. The expectation of general hostility and ostracism is a particularly strong Johannine theme (Jn. 15:18-21; 16:1-4; 17:14-16; 1 Jn. 3:13; 4:4-6), but was a feature of much early Christian self-consciousness, and is echoed probably in Tacitus's famously ambiguous description of the reason for persecution of Christians, *odium humani*

---

58. N. T. Wright, *Victory,* 347-48, sees this as 'a classic example of an entire passage [Mi. 7:2-10] being evoked by a single reference'. The Targum Jonathan version of Mi. 7 provides even closer links with this passage, particularly a reference specifically to brother giving up brother to death: see L. Hartman, *Prophecy,* 168-69.

59. There may be continuing influence from Mi. 7, in that the first sentence of v. 13 again echoes the thought of Mi. 7:6, while the second sentence may draw on the language of Mi. 7:7, 'As for me, I will look to the Lord, I will wait for the God of my salvation' (LXX, ὑπομενῶ ἐπὶ τῷ θεῷ τῷ σωτῆρί μου).

generis (Tacitus, *Ann.* 15.44). There is no expectation that this hostility will be overcome, only that it must be endured. After the use of τέλος in v. 7 for the horizon of the immediate discussion, the destruction of the temple, it might seem natural to take it in the same sense here, but here there is no article, and εἰς τέλος is a standard expression (often reflecting the Hebrew *lāneṣaḥ*, 'forever'; for NT examples see Lk. 18:5; Jn. 13:1) with the general meaning of 'right through', 'forever', without any specific τέλος being in focus (cf. our idiom 'for as long as it takes'), and it is probably better taken in that sense here. It is the disciple who endures whatever may come without giving up who will ultimately come out alright. For σῴζω in this more 'spiritual' sense (as opposed to its normal meaning in Mark of physical restoration) see on 10:26. It would make nonsense of the sequence from v. 12 to take σωθήσεται here as meaning 'will not be killed'; the sense is closer to that of 8:35,[60] of the true life which is assured for those who remain faithful even to the extent of losing their physical life in the cause of Jesus and his good news. This last sentence of the section is therefore not so much a prediction about the 'end' (and thus does not directly contribute to answering the disciples' question) as a call to endurance and the assurance that those who suffer for Jesus will not be ultimately the losers.

The Beginning of the End (13:14-23)

Jesus has begun his answer to the question about when the temple will be destroyed by speaking of unsettling events which must happen, but 'the end is not yet', and he has gone on to focus on the disciples' experience of persecution during that time and to exhort them to faithful endurance. During this time also the good news about Jesus must be taken beyond Israel to πάντα τὰ ἔθνη. It is a time of uncomfortable readjustment, as the new situation resulting from the coming of Jesus causes the familiar lines to be redrawn, in preparation for the drastic dénouement which he has predicted. But now it is time for him to begin to answer their question more directly. ὅταν δὲ ἴδητε introduces a 'sign' more specific and visible than anything which has emerged from vv. 5-13, which indicates that we have moved from the period of delay towards that of fulfilment.

The mention of a βδέλυγμα τῆς ἐρημώσεως focuses our attention again on the temple, in which Daniel had originally spoken of the unwelcome presence of such a βδέλυγμα (Dn. 9:27; 11:31; 12:11), and the response to its appearance there is to be that people in Judaea must escape to the mountains (vv. 14-16). The time of distress which will then set in (vv. 17-20) is generally recognised, as its context surely demands, as referring to the period of Roman conquest of Judaea and of Jewish infighting in the capital which culminated in the siege of Jerusalem and would be brought to its climax in A.D. 70 with the capture and devastation of the city and the destruction of the temple. During this period, as

---

60. Luke's parallel (21:19) is even closer: ἐν τῇ ὑπομονῇ ὑμῶν κτήσεσθε τὰς ψυχὰς ὑμῶν.

in the preliminary period (v. 6), there will again be pseudo-messiahs and a real danger of being 'led astray' (vv. 21-22). But disciples are to be on their guard; they have been forewarned (v. 23).

This section thus presents an account of the situation preceding the fall of the city, from the appearance of the βδέλυγμα τῆς ἐρημώσεως, the last chance to escape, into the horrors of the siege. But it still does not provide a full answer to the disciples' question: it offers a σημεῖον indeed, but does not yet include the actual destruction of the temple within its scope. The following section, however, will begin ἀλλα ἐν ἐκείναις ταῖς ἡμέραις. . . . So at v. 23 we have not yet reached the end of the events which must follow the appearance of the βδέλυγμα τῆς ἐρημώσεως: the climax is still to come. How it comes we shall see in the next section of the discourse. For now, we remain in the period of build-up to the climax, though getting agonisingly close to it.

But if it is generally agreed that the content of this part of the discourse refers to the period of the Jewish war, there is no such agreement about the event which introduces it. The context imposes certain constraints on our understanding of the βδέλυγμα τῆς ἐρημώσεως. (1) It must be in some way recognisable in terms of its meaning in Daniel, which was of a profanation of the temple involving the setting up of the βδέλυγμα τῆς ἐρημώσεως and the cessation of regular sacrifices. The setting in Daniel makes it clear that this refers to the abolition of the temple cult ordered by Antiochus Epiphanes in 167 B.C., and 1 Macc. 1:54, 59 confirms that the βδέλυγμα ἐρημώσεως itself represents the altar of Zeus which was then built over the altar of burnt offering in the temple. There is no evidence that the phrase was used in any other connection, so that those who heard it must have understood it, if they understood it at all, in terms of the Daniel prophecies. Since the specific events of the Maccabean period were now far in the past, its use in the first century could be understood only of an event or object which in some recognisable way corresponded to what Antiochus had done. How close that correspondence needs to be is a matter of judgment; the aside ὁ ἀναγινώσκων νοείτω may suggest that it requires some subtlety of interpretation. (2) It is an event sufficiently recognisable to provide a clear prompt to those living in Judaea that it is now time for urgent flight. (3) It is at a time shortly before the Roman advance and the siege, while escape is still possible but close enough to make it necessary to act immediately.

Some such sacrilege will mark the beginning of the process which leads to the temple's destruction. To discern the fulfilment of this warning in a particular known historical event belongs not so much to exegesis of the text as to historical curiosity and to the theological apologetics which faces the question 'Did Jesus get it right?' Several such historical identifications have been proposed, and will be discussed in the notes below. There is no agreement on any of them, and in any case we must bear in mind that, even with the help of Josephus, we do not know everything that happened in Jerusalem in those years.

The date of Mark's writing is of course a significant factor in understanding his text at this point. If he was already looking back on the events of the siege and the fall of the city, the enigmatic nature of his language is surprising (contrast the 'parallel' in Lk. 21:20), as is also our inability to find a reasonably certain identification of the event in which he believed Jesus' prediction had been fulfilled. Couldn't he have made a more convincing case than this in the light of what actually happened? It is thus more probable that he was recording a known prediction of Jesus before the event, and so had no control over how words might be fitted to events.[61] There is, however, also the intermediate view that he was writing between the appearance of the βδέλυγμα and the fall of the city, and that the call to escape before it was too late was an immediate one for his first readers, that the gospel, or at least this part of it, was a tract for the times, a political pamphlet urging precipitate action in the light of a very recent and well-known event which meant that the end could not be far away. The reader must not just understand, but act immediately on that understanding. Such a reconstruction, with variations, has a long history, from Colani onwards. But it shares the same problem with the more generally *post eventum* view, that such a call to immediate action surely requires a more clearly recognisable sign than the enigmatic words of v. 14. To avoid this problem by the supposition that Mark's use of Daniel's language is a cryptic device in case his writing fell into the wrong hands, intelligible only to those who knew the code (ὁ ἀναγινώσκων νοείτω), has the air of an exegetical counsel of despair, and leaves the puzzling question what Mark might have to fear and from whom if he had been more explicit.[62] All in all, a *vaticinium ante eventum* makes better exegetical sense.

The description of the crisis in vv. 17-20, as a time of unprecedented suffering and one which no-one could hope to survive without divine intervention, does not outrun the detailed and lurid description of the siege in Josephus, *War,* e.g., 5.424-38, 512-18, 567-72; 6.193-213. But who is it for?

This section is introduced, like the two previous sections, by a second-person address (ὅταν ἴδητε) and concludes with another βλέπετε in v. 23, backed up by the solemn reminder that προείρηκα ὑμῖν πάντα. The disciples are therefore expected to heed these warnings and predictions and, presumably, to recognise in these events the precursors of the destruction of the temple. In between these second-person addresses, however, the discourse does not seem to focus on the disciples' personal situation very directly. The imperatives of vv. 14-16 are in the third person, directed at 'people in Judaea' rather than the disciples specifically. If they are involved in these events at all, it is as part of the

---

61. Verse 14 forms the basis for the argument of D. W. Chapman, *Orphan,* 142-57, that Mark wrote before A.D. 68; Chapman proposes A.D. 50 as the most likely date.

62. The explanation by Myers, 335, 'He simply cannot speak directly about Roman military operations, for to do so would be to betray his resistance community', not only assumes a questionable interpretation of the βδέλυγμα τῆς ἐρημώσεως but also presupposes a life-setting for Mark which is not self-evident. To whom would he be betraying what?

general populace of Judaea, not with a special role in their own right. The description of the suffering associated with the flight and siege in vv. 17-20 is also mainly in the third person, including a specific focus on the problems of women, though within it there is a second-person exhortation to pray that it may not happen in the winter. Are the disciples being urged to pray for others affected by the war, especially women, or are they themselves affected? Or is this imperative not addressed specifically to the disciples but to anyone involved in the crisis? Similarly when the issue of pseudo-messiahs recurs in vv. 21-22, it is introduced, as it was in vv. 5-6, by a second-person imperative not to be misled, yet the description of the impostors is in general terms, with their target not specifically the disciples but more generally the ἐκλεκτοί. The double occurrence of this term in vv. 20-21, repeated again in v. 27, but occurring nowhere else in Mark, introduces a further complication into the question of the scope of this section of the discourse.

All this adds up to a baffling variety of address and of reference. It may well point to a composite origin for this section from a number of independent sayings, but that does not help with the exegesis of these verses as they stand in Mark. Mark, if it is he who has put this little collection together, has achieved a suitable flow of subject matter (from the sign to the evasive action, the sufferings of the crisis period, and the danger of impostors), but has left quite obscure the way it is all meant to apply to the disciples. Does Jesus expect them to be present in Judaea when the crisis comes? Is it they themselves who are to flee, and if so will they get away in time or will they be among those undergoing this unprecedented suffering and praying for themselves along with others that it may not be winter? Will they meet the pseudo-messiahs in Jerusalem as the end approaches, or will these be operating more widely? And who are the ἐκλεκτοί: are they the disciples, or a wider group of followers of Jesus, or are they not a specifically Christian category?

This is therefore a puzzling section of the discourse, allowing much scope for exegetical variation both in detail and with regard to its overall perspective. We shall pick up the above questions in the notes that follow, but not always with great confidence in the answers suggested. It is therefore the more important first to remind ourselves that the uncertainties about just how the disciples themselves are to fit into the events described do not affect the main function of these verses within the flow of the discourse as a whole. That function is to carry us on from the time of 'not yet' and endurance into the time when the end game begins, and to leave us by the time we reach v. 24 ready for the final answer to the disciples' question. In terms of the structure of the discourse as a whole vv. 14-23 represent the beginning of the end.

14 τὸ βδέλυγμα τῆς ἐρημώσεως occurs in LXX Dn. 12:11, and βδέλυγμα ἐρημώσεως in Thdt Dn. 12:11 and in LXX Dn. 11:31 (where Thdt has βδέλυγμα ἠφανισμένον). In the related text Dn. 9:27 both versions have βδέλυγμα τῶν ἐρημώσεων, and in Dn. 8:13 both have ἡ ἁμαρτία ἐρημώσεως. In all these passages except the last the Hebrew phrase is šiqqûṣ (mᵉ)šômēm ('a detested thing [normally used of idols] which desolates', or perhaps 'appals'),[63] and in all cases the reference is clearly to the same event of the desecration of the temple sanctuary and the cessation of the regular burnt offering. No other use of this phraseology has been preserved except for 1 Macc. 1:54, where the same phrase is used in the account of the abolition of the temple cult in 167 B.C. (to which the Daniel passages also clearly referred), and is specifically identified as referring to an altar erected on top of the altar of burnt offering (cf. 1 Macc. 1:59). The historical reference is therefore unmistakable, and the additional note that this object stands ὅπου οὐ δεῖ fits the placing of the heathen altar on top of the altar of burnt offering in the temple. What the disciples should be on the lookout for, then, seems to be a repetition in some way of the sacrilege of 167 B.C.

Mark's masculine participle ἑστηκότα[64] is unexpected. βδέλυγμα is neuter, and the masculine could hardly be taken as a *constructio ad sensum* when the subject is an altar. There is nothing in the Daniel passages or in 1 Maccabees to suggest giving a personal meaning to the βδέλυγμα τῆς ἐρημώσεως. Is Mark then transferring the language to speak of a personal violator of the temple? That has been the conclusion of many who have then associated this passage with the prophecy in 2 Thes. 2:3-4 of the ἄνθρωπος τῆς ἀνομίας who will take his seat in the ναὸς τοῦ θεοῦ proclaiming himself to be God, and have taken it as referring not to the events preceding the destruction of the temple but to the eschatological conflict. That is not the only explanation of Mark's masculine, however, and the fact that Mark's βδέλυγμα is standing, not sitting like the man of lawlessness, while not in itself a crucial difference, may point us in a different direction. When Antiochus's emissaries desecrated the temple by setting up a pagan altar, they also designated it the temple of Ζεὺς Ὀλύμπιος (2 Macc. 6:2) and installed a statue of its new god; if Mark had in mind a counterpart to such a statue of the (male) god Zeus, he might well have spoken of 'him' standing (masculine) in the temple.[65]

Matthew refers explicitly to Daniel's prophecy, so that in his version of the discourse the aside ὁ ἀναγινώσκων νοείτω could be understood as part of the reported speech, calling on the reader *of Daniel* to take note. Mark has not left us that option, since he refers to no written text. The clause must therefore be an aside by the author (for similar asides see 2:10; 3:30; 7:3-4, 19), calling on the reader of his discourse to take note of the preceding clause. That is all that νοέω

---

63. On the suggestion that the LXX version is not an exact translation of the Hebrew and that the NT use of the phrase depends on the difference see my *Jesus and the OT,* 254-55, especially n. 43.

64. Gundry, 772, considers and rejects the possibility that it is a neuter plural.

65. See G. R. Beasley-Murray, *Last Days,* 409-10, for literature on the statue and for this explanation of Mark's masculine. Str-B, 1.951, gives some rabbinic references for the statue. L. Gaston, *No Stone,* 24, while convinced that there was no statue historically, notes that 'in the entire Jewish tradition, and in many of the church fathers, Daniel's *šiqqûṣ* was interpreted as an idol, i.e., a statue set up in the temple'.

need imply: the aside is an N.B.[66] But in view of the cryptic nature of the reference to a βδέλυγμα standing where he should not it is probably also a warning that the meaning is not on the surface and will need to be thought out if the reader is to be in a position to take appropriate note of this 'sign' (cf. Rev. 13:18; 17:9 for the need for νοῦς in order to profit from cryptic symbolism). To perceive the relation of coming events to the desecration of the temple by Antiochus may need some lateral thinking.

Once the presence of the βδέλυγμα is perceived, action must not be delayed (τότε). The summons is not to people in Jerusalem but to those ἐν τῇ Ἰουδαίᾳ. Mark mentions Judaea as such only three times elsewhere, in two of which Jerusalem is also mentioned as a separate item in the geographical list (1:5; 3:7), while in the third (10:1) it denotes Jesus' arrival in the province on the way to Jerusalem, where he will not arrive until the next chapter. It seems unlikely, therefore, that he used the term carelessly here as a synonym for Jerusalem (which it is not). It is Judaea as a province which is in danger, and from which people are exhorted to escape εἰς τὰ ὄρη. Since much of Judaea, including Jerusalem and many of the main cities, is in 'the mountains', this may be a call not so much to emigrate to another province (Marxsen's theory that Mark is writing to urge the church to go north to Galilee to await the coming of the Son of Man lacks any basis in the text) as to abandon the towns and hide away in the hills. See on 3:13 for the meaning of εἰς τὰ ὄρη. Cf. Ezk. 7:16 for the hills as a place of survival when Judah was overrun by the Babylonians, and for other OT references to refuge in the hills see, for instance, Gn. 14:10; Je. 16:16. There is a nearer precedent in 1 Macc. 2:28 where we are told that in 167 B.C. Mattathias, as soon as he had declared his opposition to Antiochus's new religious policy, ἔφυγεν εἰς τὰ ὄρη with his sons, leaving all their possessions in the town (cf. also 2 Macc. 5:27).

Such a call could fit into what we know of the war in Judaea at a number of points. In Josephus's account the actual siege of Jerusalem does not begin until the early part of A.D. 70, by which time the war in Judaea had already lasted on and off for three and a half years. After the initial abortive campaign of Cestius Gallus in Judaea in late 66, Vespasian concentrated first on Galilee and Peraea, but then brought most of Judaea under control in the early part of 68. Operations were then suspended owing to the Roman civil war, until a further campaign in mid-69 subjugated the rest of the province except Jerusalem and the fortresses of Herodium and Masada. It was not until Passover of A.D. 70, after Vespasian had again suspended the war to become emperor, that Titus's army arrived before the walls of Jerusalem. At what point in this sequence of events in Judaea it might have been appropriate to escape to the hills is a matter of speculation, but our understanding of Mark's text, if he wrote before

---

66. Gundry, 742-43, rightly notes that the 'reader' would normally have been the one reading the text aloud to an audience. In that case, is it possible that Mark is instructing him not only to grasp the meaning for himself, but also to explain it to those listening?

524

any of these events occurred, is not affected. Judaea is facing a time of great suffering, and ordinary people must be prepared for hard times.

Among suggested historical identifications of the βδέλυγμα τῆς ἐρημώ-σεως, which was to trigger this flight, three merit mention here. (a) The instruction by the emperor Gaius (Caligula) that a statue of himself should be installed in the temple at Jerusalem has the obvious attraction that a male statue might explain the masculine ἑστηκότα, and it is hard to imagine a more horrifying profanation of the temple or one more comparable to that of Antiochus. Two obvious problems, however, outweigh the attraction: the instruction was never carried out, and in any case the date (A.D. 40) is so far in advance of the war in Judaea as to make it a poor 'sign', as Mark must have known.[67]

(b) The Roman legions carried standards which were regarded with religious awe by the soldiers, but as idolatrous by Jews; they were therefore never carried into Jerusalem, to avoid provoking Jewish hostility (cf. Pilate's abortive attempt to do so; Josephus, *Ant.* 18.55-59). To see such standards in the temple area would be as grave a profanation as Antiochus had perpetrated; Josephus even records that the Roman soldiers offered sacrifices to the standards in the temple courts while the sanctuary was burning (*War* 6.316). The obvious advantage of this identification is that it links Mark's βδέλυγμα τῆς ἐρημώσεως with Luke's 'parallel', 'Jerusalem surrounded by armies', but again it has no value as a sign to escape: by the time the Roman standards were standing where they ought not escape was impossible, and Judaea's war was over.

(c) Josephus (*War* 4.150-57) records than in the winter of 67/8 the Zealots under John of Gischala took over the temple itself as their headquarters and μεμιασμένοις τοῖς ποσὶ παρῄεσαν εἰς τὸ ἅγιον, appointing their own mock high priest to carry out a travesty of temple ritual; popular outrage led to fighting within the temple itself (4.196-207) with Zealot blood defiling the sanctuary (201). Cf. also *War* 4.388 for an 'ancient prophecy' that the city would be taken and the temple burned when 'native hands' had first defiled it; Josephus sees this prophecy fulfilled in the Zealots' actions. Even allowing for the extravagance of Josephus's language, this outrage might have reminded some of the desecration under Antiochus, and it took place just before the first major campaign of Vespasian in Judaea, when it was still possible to escape into the hills. Might Mark's reader have recognised in these events the βδέλυγμα τῆς ἐρημώσεως, and possibly even have referred the masculine ἑστηκότα to John of Gischala? Perhaps, but whether that is what either Mark or Jesus had in mind we cannot say.

As mentioned above, the wording of vv. 14-16 does not directly suggest that the disciples (who were Galileans) would themselves be involved in the

---

67. See L. Gaston, *No Stone,* 25-27, for the view that this part of the discourse originated as a prophetic oracle in the winter of A.D. 40-41, before Gaius's death removed the threat. If so, it is hard to account for Mark's reproduction of such an oracle decades later. The argument of D. W. Chapman (see p. 521 n. 61 above) for a date for Mark about A.D. 50 includes the suggestion that Jesus' words about the βδέλυγμα 'moved to the fore in the Palestinian church when Caligula threatened to set up a statue of himself in the temple' (155).

troubles of Judaea. The third-person imperatives are addressed 'to whom it may concern'. Eusebius, *H.E.* 3.5.3, records a tradition that πρὸ τοῦ πολέμου[68] the Christian community of Jerusalem emigrated from the city to Pella in the Decapolis (which, as a Gentile city, was not involved), and that they were prompted to do so by 'a certain oracle given by revelation to the approved people there'. The common suggestion[69] that that oracle was Mk. 13:14 is doubtful in view of the fact that Pella is not in τὰ ὄρη; it is in fact below sea level, some 3,000 feet lower than Jerusalem. A significant number of scholars, following Brandon, doubt the historicity of Eusebius's report.[70]

15-16 Luke's equivalent to these verses is found not in chapter 21 but at 17:31 where it refers not to the war in Judaea but to the 'days of the Son of Man'. It is perhaps standard language for an emergency (cf. Gn. 19:17; εἰς τὰ ὀπίσω may be meant to recall Lot's wife, LXX Gn. 19:26; cf. Lk. 17:31-32), but insofar as it is to be taken literally it shows that the situation envisaged is not of the siege in Jerusalem, but of people living out in the countryside of Judaea and still able to run away (though how one could run away from a rooftop without coming down is a mystery;[71] perhaps μὴ καταβάτω μηδὲ εἰσελθάτω represents a compound action of descending-and-going-in; cf. Mann, 'come down into the house'). Gundry's distinction between the man on the rooftop as a 'man of leisure' and the one in the field as a 'field hand' reads too much social stratification into everyday locations.

17-18 ἐν ἐκείναις ταῖς ἡμέραις must refer back either to the time when the βδέλυγμα τῆς ἐρημώσεως is seen or to the period of flight for those in Judaea. Since the latter is to follow immediately on the former, it makes little difference. The flight to the hills will be particularly hard for pregnant women and nursing mothers, and winter weather conditions can only add to the hardship and the difficulty of quick movement. This last comment increases the impression that what is being described here is not the siege itself, since winter weather would be the least of the problems inside the city (though in fact the siege was over before winter); it is the plight of the refugees in or on the way to the hills. The call to pray is issued without a clear indication of subject: are the disciples to whom Jesus is talking to pray about the timing of the flight, and if so is this altruistically for the sake of those who will be affected, or are they themselves expected to be among the refugees? Or has the οὐαί construction in effect made the women the addressees at this point, so that they are called to

---

68. Epiphanius, *De Mens.* 15, records the same tradition, dating it 'when the city was about to be conquered by the Romans', but ascribes the warning to an angel.

69. For instance, Pesch, 2.292, 295; Lane, 468.

70. See G. R. Beasley-Murray, *Last Days,* 412-13 and n. 106. S. Sowers, *TZ* 26 (1970) 305-20, provides a detailed response to Brandon's arguments; further support for a modified form of the Pella tradition is offered by J. J. Gunther, *TZ* 29 (1973) 81-84.

71. Beasley-Murray's explanation is imaginative, but speculative: 'to go down the stairs of the courtyard to enter the house, select goods to take with him, climb up the stairs, and then go down the outer stairway' (*Last Days,* 417). Some such idea may lie behind the addition of εἰς τὴν οἰκίαν after καταβάτω in an impressive variety of MSS and versions. Gundry, however, cites Josephus, *Ant.* 13.140, for the possibility of jumping from roof to roof.

pray about their own problems? The second-person address is not continued (until v. 21), and does not seem to be strongly marked here, so perhaps προσεύχεσθε is better taken as a generalised exhortation to prayer addressed to anyone whom it may concern.

19 Not only the γάρ but especially the phrase αἱ ἡμέραι ἐκεῖναι (cf. v. 17, and repeated in v. 24) links this statement firmly to the setting of the previous verses, the war in Judaea. But now there is no more talk of flight to the hills and the reference seems to include more specifically the siege in Jerusalem, whose horrors Josephus so graphically describes (for references see the introduction to this section); the 'shortening of the time' in v. 20 is more easily understood of the siege proper than of the general distress of Judaea.

The expression ἔσονται αἱ ἡμέραι θλῖψις is inelegant but effective: the unremitting horror of the situation will be such that the days will *be*, not just be the setting for, a θλῖψις. The language recalls Thdt Dn. 12:1, θλῖψις οἵα οὐ γέγονεν ἀφ' οὗ γεγένηται ἔθνος ἐπὶ τῆς γῆς ἕως τοῦ καιροῦ ἐκείνου (LXX similar). In Daniel the reference is to the eschatological conflict which will bring to a climax the wars of the 'time of the end', but will issue in the deliverance of 'your people, everyone who is found written in the book'. The protection of the ἐκλεκτοί in v. 20 may thus be a further reflection on this text. But since this is the sort of language which is used frequently of a great disaster (cf Ex. 9:18; 10:14; 11:6; Joel 2:2; 1 Macc. 9:27; 1QM 1:11-12; *Test. Mos.* 8:1; Rev. 16:18), it is probably unwise to press too closely any specific link with the Daniel text here. Of the passages just listed, Ex. 10:14; 11:6; Joel 2:2 also include the future dimension represented in our text by καὶ οὐ μὴ γένηται. These are, apparently, stock expressions for unparalleled suffering, and are not to be pressed literally (e.g., by asking whether the Holocaust was not worse than the Jewish War). It should be noted, however, that καὶ οὐ μὴ γένηται sits very uncomfortably with any interpretation which understands these words to be describing the end of history. ἀπ' ἀρχῆς κτίσεως ἣν ἔκτισεν ὁ θεός is a good example of Mark's expansive phraseology (less politely, 'redundancy') and does not necessarily require a special emphasis on the divine role in creation.[72]

20 See on the previous verse for the possibility that this verse also draws on the thought of Dn. 12:1, though here there is no direct verbal echo. The idea of the shortening of the time for the deliverance of God's people (later picked up in *Barn.* 4:3) is found occasionally in apocalyptic writings; see 2 Esdr. 2:13; 4Q385 frag. 3, and more generally for God's 'hastening the time' Ben Sira 36:10; 2 Bar. 20:1-2; 54:1; 83:1. For the idea, if not the language, cf. Is. 65:8, where the threatened judgment is held back for the sake of God's 'servants' (and cf. Gn. 18:23-33, where the presence of even ten 'righteous' would have rescued Sodom). The aorist tenses of ἐκολόβωσεν represent a future act of God which is already decided and may therefore be spoken of as already done.

---

72. It is not obvious how 'the tautological second reference to creation increases emphasis on unprecedentedness of severity' (Gundry, 777).

Apart from OT quotations Mark has used ὁ κύριος for God in 5:19 and (probably) 11:3; κύριος must have the same meaning here, but the lack of an article is unexpected (though see the OT quotations in 1:3; 12:11, 29, 36). Whereas in v. 13 σῴζω was applied to disciples and signified their ultimate 'salvation' in spite of persecution, here where it is applied to πᾶσα σάρξ (presumably meaning specifically those caught up in the θλῖψις of v. 19) it is closer to its more normal sense in Mark, and means physical survival.

The siege of Jerusalem, though terrible, lasted only five months, and that relatively short period is attributed to God's concern for his ἐκλεκτοί (though πᾶσα σάρξ would benefit). The concept of God's ἐκλεκτοί, reinforced here by οὓς ἐξελέξατο (another example of 'redundancy', but here surely the repetition is intended to place a strong emphasis on God's new initiative) and repeated in vv. 22 and 27, has no parallel elsewhere in Mark, though it is found in the NT letters as a recognised term for the members of the Christian community as the special objects of God's saving grace (Rom. 8:33; Col. 3:12; 2 Tim. 2:10; cf. Rev. 17:14). Here, following the echo of Dn. 12:1 in v. 19, it perhaps picks up the phrases 'your people, everyone who is found written in the book' in that text. The concept of Israel as a chosen people is familiar from the OT, and 1 Peter significantly applies the term ἐκλεκτοί together with other standard Jewish self-descriptions (παρεπίδημοι διασπορᾶς) to his Gentile readers (1 Pet. 1:1; cf. 2:9). Here in Mark there is as yet no question of Gentile ἐκλεκτοί (though see v. 10 for their future inclusion and v. 27 for ἐκλεκτοί in this wider sense), but if, in accordance with other Christian usage, he is using the term for Jesus' disciples as a chosen subgroup *within* Israel, this is a bold claim, reminiscent of the prophetic 'remnant' theology. There is no other obvious reference for the term in this context, and other NT usage suggests that by Mark's time it would have been familiar as a self-description of the Christian community.[73] In that case, the presence of the disciple community among suffering Israel is the reason for God's merciful shortening of the time of distress. Cf. Lk. 18:7-8 for God's speedy action to vindicate his ἐκλεκτοί, but there they seem to be the sole beneficiaries.

21-22 If there was scope for messianic pretenders in the decades between Jesus' ministry and the outbreak of war (see on v. 6), the years of war and siege offer more. Assuming that these are the same sort of impostors as we have encountered at v. 6, we may note the royal pretensions of Menahem, son of Judas of Galilee, who (according to Josephus, *War* 2.433-48) around A.D. 66 came into Jerusalem 'as if he were really a king' (434) and worshipped in the temple 'arrayed in royal robes' (444); similarly Simon Bar-Giora (*War* 4.503-44, etc.) about A.D. 69 gained the obedience of his fellow citizens 'as to a king' (510).[74] Such language in a Jewish context suggests messianic pretensions. As for false

---

73. J. Jeremias, *Theology*, 131, describes it as 'a fixed technical term for the messianic community of salvation'. It is so used of other Jewish subgroups also in *1 Enoch*, e.g., 1:1; 38:2-4; 62:7-8, and at Qumran, e.g., 1QS 8:6; 1QH 2[10]:13.

74. Simon was eventually paraded and executed in Titus's Roman triumph, which suggests that the Romans, too, saw him as the 'king' of the Jews (Josephus, *War* 7.154).

prophets, Josephus supplies us with examples in *War* 6.285-300 with reference to the later stages of the siege, complete with a variety of σημεῖα καὶ τέρατα preceding the fall of the city. (For ἐναργῆ τέρατα καὶ σημεῖα as the stock-in-trade of 'impostors and deceivers' cf. Josephus, *Ant.* 20.167-68; the idea goes back to Dt. 13:1-3, where the phrase δίδωμι σημεῖον ἢ τέρας occurs in the LXX.)[75]

Verse 22, however, suggests that the attention of the ψευδόχριστοι καὶ ψευδοπροφῆται will be directed particularly towards the ἐκλεκτοί rather than towards the people as a whole. In the nature of the case Josephus, who manages to avoid mentioning Christians altogether,[76] offers us no help in identifying such people. The claims of v. 21, too, differ from that of v. 6 in that this is not a self-proclamation, but a claim to be able to show them ὁ Χριστός. It is possible that we have here evidence of a Christian preoccupation with the parousia hope, and that the Χριστός who is claimed is the returning Jesus; this would then be a 'realised eschatology' similar to that of which Paul warns in 2 Thes. 2:1-2 — and the evidence of 2 Thessalonians is that the ἐκλεκτοί proved only too ready to be led astray, particularly when σημεῖα καὶ τέρατα were in evidence (2 Thes. 2:9-10).[77] For the compound ἀποπλανάω cf. 1 Tim. 6:1, which makes explicit the implication probably to be read in any case from the ἀπο-, that this is a deception which would lead the ἐκλεκτοί away from their Christian discipleship. The addition of εἰ δυνατόν, however, conveys an optimistic expectation that their faith will prove equal to the test.[78]

23 The emphatic position of ὑμεῖς brings us back to the immediate addressees of the discourse, to whom the previous two occurrences of βλέπετε (vv. 5, 9) were also directed. The situation of Judaea in the sixties and of the siege of Jerusalem is one in which they may not be personally involved, hence the more impersonal wording of the warnings of vv. 14-22. But they will be aware, as any Jew must be, that these terrible things are going on, and they are to draw the appropriate conclusions. Jesus' predictions of these events

75. J. Gibson, *JSNT* 38 (1990) 49-53, discusses the 'signs' of false prophets in relation to the Jewish pretenders of the pre-war years, and notes a close link with the Exodus miracles, concluding (following S. V. McCasland, *JBL* 76 [1957] 149-52) that σημεῖα καὶ τέρατα was in effect a technical term for the miracles of the Exodus and conquest period.

76. The only occurrence of Χριστιανός in the whole of his works is in the disputed text of the *Testimonium Flavianum* (*Ant.* 18.64), which may well be a Christian rewriting of what Josephus wrote; the only mention of what we can recognise as a Christian group is in the account of the murder of James (*Ant.* 20.200), and even there Josephus avoids either the name Χριστιανός or any indication that this was the reason for James's death.

77. M. D. Hooker, *BJRL* 65 (1982/3), understands the primary focus of Mk. 13 to be on a situation similar to that reflected in 2 Thessalonians. L. Hartman, *Prophecy*, devotes a lengthy chapter (178-205) to links between Mk. 13 and the Thessalonian correspondence, and concludes that Paul used an early form of the eschatological discourse.

78. S. R. Garrett, *Temptations*, 151-59, argues that Mark wrote specifically for those whom he understood to be 'ones destined to be put to the test' through 'not only trials of affliction, but also trials of seduction'.

(προείρηκα ὑμῖν πάντα) mean that when they do happen the disciples will be prepared for what is to follow, and will not be caught unawares. And what is to follow must surely, by this stage of the discourse, be the answer to their question about when the temple was to be destroyed. The events of vv. 14-22 now constitute a clearer and more immediate σημεῖον of the predicted devastation than the more long-term prerequisite of the universal proclamation of the good news (v. 10). The end has begun.

The Coming of the Son of Man within 'This Generation' (13:24-31)

It is especially in these verses that the interpretation of the discourse adopted in this commentary differs from the majority view. It will be as well at the outset, therefore, to outline the flow of thought as I understand it (see the chart of 'Indicators of Time and Sequence in Mark 13', above, p. 504).

The disciples' question (vv. 3-4) concerned the destruction of the temple which Jesus predicted in v. 2. They wanted to know when it would be and what sign would herald it. In vv. 5-8 Jesus has spoken of 'signs' which are *not* signs of that event: the end is not yet. In vv. 9-13 he has 'digressed' to speak of the difficulties of this intervening period for his disciples, but has also indicated that during this period the good news must πρῶτον be comunicated outside Israel — a 'sign' of a sort, but a very broad one. Then in vv. 14-22 he has spoken of a more specific sign, and one which calls for immediate response: the βδέλυγμα τῆς ἐρημώσεως will usher in a time of unprecedented and almost unendurable suffering, but that time will be cut short for the sake of the ἐκλεκτοί. But he does not say in v. 20 how it will be cut short, and by v. 22 he has still not come to the destruction of the temple but only hinted at its profanation by the βδέλυγμα τῆς ἐρημώσεως. So by the time Jesus sums up the discourse so far with προείρηκα ὑμῖν πάντα, there is an irresistible sense that the preliminaries are over, and that the answer to the question is now coming to its climax.

So far everything has fallen short of the full answer, but ἀλλά at the beginning of v. 24 alerts us to a new stage of fulfilment. The setting remains ἐν ἐκείναις ταῖς ἡμέραις, but now we are moving beyond the θλῖψις of v. 19 to what must immediately follow it. And so we reach at last the destruction of the temple, described not in the prosaic terms of v. 2 but in the richly coloured and evocative language of OT prophecy. Almost every word of vv. 24b-27 is drawn from the prophets, and we shall examine the specific echoes in the notes below. The passages cited in vv. 24b-25 use the language of cosmic disintegration to denote, as often in prophecy, climactic (*not* climatic!) changes to the existing world order. The lights are going out in the centres of power, and the way is being prepared for a new world order. And in vv. 26-27 it comes: Daniel's vision of the enthronement of the Son of Man will be seen to be fulfilled, and that Son of Man will send out his angels from his heavenly throne to collect into his kingdom the ἐκλεκτοί not now of Israel only but of all nations.

With that, the question is answered. The word 'temple' has not appeared, but the imagery has powerfully conveyed to those who are familiar with OT prophecy the fundamental 'change of government' which is symbolised by the destruction of that now discredited building in Jerusalem and all that it represented. From now on it will not be the national shrine which will be the focus of the people of God, but the Son of Man to whom has now been given, as Dn. 7:14 predicted, an everlasting and universal dominion which embraces all nations and languages.

And yet the question is still not fully answered. The disciples wanted to know about the time and the sign, and so vv. 28-31 finally sum up the implications of what Jesus has said from this point of view. The little parable of the fig tree reinforces the need for readiness when the disciples see ταῦτα taking place. We shall return to what is meant by ταῦτα in the notes below, but they are clearly an immediate 'sign' of the approaching dénouement. And in v. 30 the time is finally and emphatically (ἀμὴν λέγω ὑμῖν) spelled out not now in prophetic symbolism but in plain words: it will all take place within 'this generation'. And lest there be any room left for uncertainty, Jesus caps the whole predictive oracle with the assurance that his words are as sure and eternal as the word of God himself. With that, his answer to the question of v. 4 is complete. What follows in v. 32, introduced by περὶ δέ, will be on another subject.

The key to this understanding in particular of vv. 24-27 lies in our willingness and ability to hear the prophetic imagery as it would have been heard by those in Jesus' day who were at home in OT prophetic language, rather than as it is 'naturally' heard by Christian readers for whom the 'coming of the Son of Man' has since gained a different connotation through its association with the idea of παρουσία (a word which is conspicuously absent from this discourse in Mark). In the introduction to the discourse as a whole I have commented on this issue (above, pp. 502-3), and on the built-in resistance which this 'contextual' exegesis meets when traditional interpretations are simply and often unconsciously assumed. I hope the sceptical reader may be prepared to grant me at least a temporary 'suspension of disbelief' as I work through the details of the imagery and its background. And if the resultant exegesis helps to make more coherent sense of the flow of the discourse as a whole, as outlined above, perhaps that suspension may become permanent.[1]

24-25 It is sometimes suggested that the 'strongly adversative ἀλλά'[2] indicates a change of subject,[3] and alerts the reader that the spotlight is at this point moving away from the time of the Jewish War to a more ultimate perspec-

---

1. For a different treatment of this section of the discourse which strongly reinforces the same basic interpretative approach see N. T. Wright, *Victory,* 354-65.

2. Gundry, who uses this phrase (745), finds the contrast, however, not in time but between 'the deceptive, private way in which false christs will come and the overpowering, open way in which the Son of man will come'. Cf. Lane, 473 n. 87.

3. Gnilka, 2.200: 'Mit "aber" (ἀλλά) wird die grosse Wende eingeleitet.' Pesch, 2.302: 'Der Neueinsatz mit ἀλλά deutet an, dass der "Übergang zu etwas Neuem" intendiert ist.'

tive of the parousia and the end of the world (a subject allegedly included in the second half of the disciples' question — but see above on v. 4). That is a lot to derive from an ἀλλά! It does indeed indicate a contrast between what has just been described and what is to follow, but that contrast does not need to be in time, but in the scale of events, as we move from the preliminaries, horrible as they may be, to the climax of Jesus' vision of what is to come. Indeed, the following words firmly rule out any suggestion that the discourse has now moved to a different time or place: ἐν ἐκείναις ταῖς ἡμέραις could not be more explicit. What is to be described in these verses will take place at the same period as the events of vv. 14-22. This is the immediate sequel, following directly from (μετά) the θλῖψις described in v. 19. To suppose that v. 24a allows, let alone requires, a change of scene from the Jewish War to the parousia flies in the face of what it actually says.[4] If vv. 24b-27 are going to be about the parousia, then v. 24a requires that the parousia must be understood to happen at the time of the Jewish War — and not many interpreters are comfortable with that view, either as that of Mark or as a matter of history.[5]

The language of v. 24b is paralleled at several points in the prophetic literature (Ezk. 32:7; Jo. 2:10, 31; 3:15; Am. 8:9) but is verbally most closely related to LXX Is. 13:10, part of the oracle against Babylon, σκοτισθήσεται τοῦ ἡλίου ἀνατέλλοντος, καὶ ἡ σελήνη οὐ δώσει τὸ φῶς αὐτῆς. In v. 25 the closest verbal link is with LXX Is. 34:4,[6] part of the oracle against 'all nations' but with special reference to Edom, καὶ τακήσονται πᾶσαι αἱ δυνάμεις τῶν οὐρανῶν . . . καὶ πάντα τὰ ἄστρα πεσεῖται . . . ,[7] where the 'powers of the heavens' are probably to be understood as a poetic synonym for the stars. In most of these passages the immediate reference is to the imminent downfall of specific nations

---

4. It is noteworthy that in order to avoid the obvious sense of the passage Beasley-Murray, *Last Days,* 422-23, finds it necessary to suppose that these verses originally had a different context, in which ἐν ἐκείναις ταῖς ἡμέραις referred to the 'last days', and that it was only when Mark put the paragraph into this context that it 'gained a narrower meaning than that which was intended', so that he then inserted μετὰ τὴν θλῖψιν ἐκείνην in order to create a space ('after', not 'during'). Such an unnatural expedient ought surely to lead us to question the exegetical assumptions which necessitate it.

5. The view that the discourse does locate the parousia at the time of the destruction of the temple and that as a matter of fact it did take place in A.D. 70 was presented by J. S. Russell, *The Parousia* (published anonymously, London, 1878; 2d ed. under the author's name, London, 1887). It is followed in essence by A. Feuillet, in W. D. Davies and D. Daube (ed.), *The Background of the NT and Its Eschatology,* 261-80 (see my *Jesus and the OT,* 230 n. 12, for a critique of Feuillet). L. Gaston, *No Stone,* 483-87, suggests that Matthew interpreted Mark in this sense, and so believed that the parousia had occurred in A.D. 70.

6. A further suggestive political allusion, though not verbally so close, is found by N. T. Wright, *Victory,* 354-55, in the oracle of Is. 14 against the king of Babylon, the 'day star, fallen from heaven'. So also B. M. F. Van Iersel, *Bib* 77 (1996) 88-89.

7. This is the text of LXX B and Lucian, read also by Origen under an obelus. The first clause is not found in other LXX versions, though it is in the Hebrew text. For comments on the textual issue and the LXX translation see my *Jesus and the OT,* 255-56. For fuller detail see J. Verheyden in C. M. Tuckett (ed.), *Scriptures,* 536-38.

(Egypt, Babylon, Edom, Israel, and Judah), though in Jo. 3:15 there is a more universal perspective (all the nations gathered for judgment before Jerusalem).[8] In the original prophetic context, therefore, such 'cosmic' language conveys a powerful symbolism of political changes within world history, and is not naturally to be understood of a literal collapse of the universe at the end of the world. It is, in the words of Wright, 'typical Jewish imagery for events within the present order that are felt and perceived as "cosmic" or, as we should say, "earth-shattering".'[9] The events so described are catastrophic for the nations concerned, and to use such language adds a heavy ideological loading of divine judgment. God is redrawing the map of world politics, and the familiar structures of international affairs will never be the same again. But the dramatic collapse of the power structures is not the end of world history, but the beginning of a new and better phase, in which God's purpose will be worked out.[10]

The natural sense of such language, used in a Jewish context, is surely clear. Mk. 13:24b-27 is not about the collapse of the universe,[11] but about drastic events on the world scene, interpreted in the light of the divine judgment and purpose.[12] What is startling about the use of such language by Jesus in this context is not that he uses the same imagery as the prophets, but that he uses it with regard to the fate of *Jerusalem* and its temple. In most uses of such language in the prophets the target was a Gentile nation which posed a threat to Israel or Judah. But now the target is Jerusalem itself, and more specifically God's house in Jerusalem. This is not entirely new: the darkening of the sun in Am. 8:9 referred to the fate of Israel, and that in Jo. 2:10 to the locust-plague in Judah. The OT prophets knew of God's judgment on his own people as well as on foreign nations, and we have noted in commenting on v. 2 the prophetic precedent for Jesus' prediction of the destruction of the temple itself. But there is nonetheless a savage irony in the use of words taken from Isaiah's patriotic denunciation of Babylon and Edom to pronounce now the downfall of the temple which for him had been the symbol of

8. In later apocalyptic, while such language is relatively uncommon, it has apparently a more 'end of the world' reference appropriate to the focus of those works, e.g., *Test. Mos.* 10:5; *Sib. Or.* 3:796-803; 4 Ezra 5:4-5.

9. N. T. Wright, *Victory,* 362.

10. Cf. G. R. Beasley-Murray, *Last Days,* 424-27, on the nature of the imagery: 'there is no suggestion that the Son of Man comes to destroy the world; the function of this ancient mythological language is purely to highlight the glory of that event and set it in its proper category: it represents the divine intervention for judgment and salvation' (425). By 'that event' he means, of course, the parousia; shorn of that assumption his words would be even more appropriate to the way the OT prophets used such language.

11. Cf. D. Lamont, *Christ and the World of Thought* (Edinburgh, 1934), 266: 'Only a pitiful prosiness could imagine that Jesus meant an actual dropping of the stars upon the earth.'

12. B. M. F. Van Iersel, *Bib* 77 (1996) 84-92, argues that many of Mark's readers would have understood the sun, moon, and stars as referring not to political entities but to the pagan gods and goddesses of Rome. Even if a Roman origin for the gospel is agreed, it is unlikely that Mark, with his strongly Jewish background, would have envisaged such an interpretation, especially since his terms are so clearly drawn from the Jewish scriptures.

God's triumphant presence among his own people.[13] In the following statement the same irony will be even more sharply deployed.

26 If vv. 24b-25 have portrayed the negative side of Jesus' prediction, the
end of the old order, in vv. 26-27 we turn to the positive, the new order which is to
take its place. See above on 8:38 for the significance of Jesus' use of the language
of Dn. 7:13-14. Here the echo is even more explicit, the words τὸν υἱὸν τοῦ
ἀνθρώπου ἐρχόμενον ἐν νεφέλαις[14] all echoing directly the imagery of v. 13. Daniel's vision, as we have seen at 8:38, is one of enthronement, of the 'one like a son
of man' coming before the throne of God to be given universal and everlasting dominion. It is the imagery of setting up a new kingship to replace the failed régimes
of previous empires, and it is located not on the earthly scene but in the presence
of God in heaven.[15] Here then is the ultimate divinely sanctioned authority,
to which 'all peoples, nations and languages' must now be subject.[16]

In Daniel's vision the 'one like a son of man' was a symbolic figure representing the 'saints of the Most High'. But Jesus has already used his own special title ὁ υἱὸς τοῦ ἀνθρώπου, drawn from that verse, sufficiently consistently
to leave no doubt that in his interpretation of Daniel's vision it is he himself
who is to receive that ultimate authority. As Israel's Messiah he receives the
kingship on behalf of the people of God. And yet the context, the destruction of
the temple, seems to embody not the triumph but rather the defeat of Israel.
Here is an even more telling counterpart to the irony of vv. 24-25. There prophetic visions of the downfall of Israel's enemies were drawn on to depict
God's judgment on Israel herself as represented in the temple. Here a vision of
Israel's triumph is transferred to a 'Son of Man' whose authority is to supersede
that which Jerusalem's temple has hitherto represented. Here, for those who appreciate the nuances of the OT language, is a startling statement of the idea that
Jesus himself, and derivatively the church, that international body of people

13. See contra J. Verheyden in C. M. Tuckett (ed.), *Scriptures*, 540-46, who discusses the
significance of the imagery of vv. 24-25 on the assumption that the passage is about the parousia,
and concludes that the emphasis in the theme of the shaking of the heavens falls less on judgment
than on 'a theophany of the Son of man in glory' (546). He concedes that the original sense of the
OT passages on which these verses draw is of judgment, but must conclude that 'when these motifs
are taken out of that context, as in Mark 13:24-27, the connotation is lost' (550).

14. Ἐν νεφέλαις is not significantly different from either the *'im* of the Aramaic or the ἐπί of
LXX or the μετά of Thdt. See Beasley-Murray, *Last Days*, 429.

15. Mann, 528, supporting J. A. T. Robinson's insistence that the 'coming' is to God, not to
earth, comments, 'Search as we will, we can find no tradition in the Judaism of Jesus' time of a
Messiah coming *from* God.'

16. This interpretation of Dn. 7:13-14, and therefore also of Jesus' sayings dependent on it,
as relating to enthronement rather than to 'parousia', has already been set out at 8:38, and will be
further developed at 14:62, where it is now accepted by probably the majority of interpreters. That
most of them do not follow the logic of that recognition through to the interpretation of this verse,
with its closely similar language, is presumably due to a prior judgment as to what Mk. 13:24-27 is
about. A good example is L. Gaston, *No Stone*, 384-92, who demonstrates that other allusions to
Dn. 7 do not refer to the parousia, but assumes that 13:26 is the one exception. Not the least merit of
the interpretation adopted here is that of consistency.

who acknowledge his sovereignty, is now to be understood as the true Israel, the people of God through whom God's earthly agenda, hitherto focused on Jerusalem and its temple, is now to be carried forward. This is an idea familiar enough from the rest of the NT, particularly the letters of Paul, 1 Peter, and Hebrews, but it is clearly anticipated in Jesus' pregnant use of the language of Daniel's vision to mark the radically new phase in God's dealings with his world which will be seen when Israel's temple is no more and he, the Son of Man, is seated at God's right hand as the universal sovereign (cf. 14:62 for further development of this imagery).[17]

How will this be 'seen' (ὄψονται), and by whom? If this is not the prediction of a visible 'descent' of the Son of Man to the earth (and nothing in the language of either Dn. 7:13-14 or this passage suggests that), what is being 'seen' is a heavenly authority. It is interesting that each of the other Marcan passages based on Dn. 7:13-14 is also closely linked to 'seeing' (8:38–9:1, ἕως ἂν ἴδωσιν; 14:62, ὄψεσθε): the heavenly enthronement is expected to have 'visible' consequences, which in each case are expected to appear within the living generation. See on 9:1 for some of the suggestions which have been made for when and how such 'seeing' might be possible. The immediate context here offers at least two possibilities for earthly evidence that the Son of Man is on his throne: the destruction of the temple (expressed in the strongly 'visual' imagery of vv. 24b-25) and the gathering of the international people of God (v. 27). These are the negative and positive sides of the transfer of authority from the temple to the Son of Man, from the national people of God to an international people of God. The powerful growth of the church will provide evidence within the living generation that the Son of Man is now the supreme authority.[18]

The close links between the three sayings based on Dn. 7:13-14 include not only the element of 'seeing' and the limitation to the living generation, but also the language of 'power' (9:1, ἐν δυνάμει; 13:26, μετὰ δυνάμεως πολλῆς καὶ δόξης; 14:62, ἐκ δεξιῶν τῆς δυνάμεως; note, too, the theme of glory in 8:38). This is what Daniel's vision is all about, the transcendent power of God which has put an end to usurping human 'powers' and has established the final, universal sovereignty of the Son of Man. So also when the temple is destroyed the existing δυνάμεις σαλευθήσονται (v. 25), while by contrast the newly established 'power and glory' of the Son of Man will be there for all to see.

17. G. B. Caird, a consistent advocate of the sort of exegesis followed in this commentary, deserves to be quoted here: in the teaching of Jesus 'the coming of the Son of Man on the clouds of heaven was never conceived as a primitive form of space travel, but as a symbol for the mighty reversal of furtunes within history and at the national level' (*Jesus,* 20).

18. The subject of ὄψονται is not specified, and as with Mark's other references to an unspecified 'they' it is natural to take this of people in general, equivalent to a passive 'It will be seen that. . . .' See, however, O. J. F. Seitz, *SE* 6 (1973) 489-90, for the suggestion that the subject is αἱ δυνάμεις αἱ ἐν τοῖς οὐρανοῖς (v. 25), understood not as the stars but as 'astral or cosmic spirits'. B. M. F. Van Iersel, *Bib* 77 (1996) 84-92, similarly suggests that 'a Greco-Roman reader' would 'recognize in these witnesses the defeated gods who see the enthronement of the son of man take place before their eyes'.

27 The sovereignty bestowed on the Son of Man (Dn. 7:14)[19] is to be exercised in the gathering of his[20] ἐκλεκτοί from all over the world. See on v. 20 for the identity of the ἐκλεκτοί as the growing community of Jesus' disciples. Their 'gathering' (ἐπισυνάξει), echoes OT predictions of the 'gathering' of the Jewish exiles back to their land, primarily Dt. 30:4 (LXX συνάξει) and Zc. 2:10 (EVV 2:6; LXX συνάξω),[21] both of which also speak of gathering from the ends of the earth (Dt. 30:4, ἀπ' ἄκρου τοῦ οὐρανοῦ ἕως ἄκρου τοῦ οὐρανοῦ; Zc. 2:10, ἐκ τῶν τεσσάρων ἀνέμων τοῦ οὐρανοῦ); the main part of v. 27 looks like a combined allusion to these two texts.[22] Cf. also Ps. 147:2 (τὰς διασπορὰς Ἰσραὴλ ἐπισυνάξει). Here again is an ironical reversal of the sense of the OT language used:[23] the gathering of the ἐκλεκτοί of the Son of Man will be from the whole world not by extracting Jewish exiles from their places of captivity, but by including people of all nations in what had been hitherto the Jewish community of the people of God. This is the fulfilment of the vision of v. 10, that the εὐαγγέλιον will be proclaimed to all nations.

If the 'gathering' refers to the growing membership of the people of God, what is the role of the ἄγγελοι? I once argued that, since the basic meaning of ἄγγελος is 'messenger' (even though its NT uses are predominantly in the secondary sense of 'angel'), here 'the context favours strongly the primary meaning'.[24] In that case v. 27 would be describing the work of Christian missionaries, sent out by the enthroned Son of Man to bring in the true people of God from all nations. I now regard that interpretation as possible, but not necessary to my understanding of the passage. In view of the association of angels with the enthroned Son of Man in 8:38, and in the absence of any clear indication that the normal NT meaning of ἄγγελος is inappropriate here, I now think it more likely that angels are here credited with a 'missionary' role in the ingathering of God's people;[25] cf. the description of angels in Heb. 1:14 as λειτουρ-

---

19. 'The present verse is the equivalent in the synoptic apocalypse of the gathering of the "peoples, languages and nations" of Dan 7:14' (Mann, 533).

20. The ἐκλεκτοί are not linked with a possessive pronoun in vv. 20 and 22, though οὓς ἐξελέξατο in v. 20 serves the same function even more strongly by identifying them as *God's* chosen. The omission of αὐτοῦ here by D L W Ψ f¹ etc. is probably to be attributed to assimilation to the apparently absolute use in the previous verses, or even to the desire to avoid attributing the ἐκλεκτοί to different persons, God in v. 20 and the Son of Man here. The text with αὐτοῦ is generally agreed to be original.

21. LXX here mistranslates the Hebrew *pēraśtî*, which has the opposite meaning, 'I scattered'. The passage is a call to the exiles to return, but this clause states parenthetically the extent of the previous dispersion from which they are to return; the LXX, perhaps under the influence of Dt. 30:4, has missed its parenthetical nature and so substituted future gathering for past scattering.

22. For comments on this 'combined quotation' see my *Jesus and the OT*, 256-57.

23. The consistency of this sort of ironical reversal through the various scriptural allusions of vv. 24-27 is another argument in favour of the exegetical approach adopted here.

24. *Jesus and the OT*, 238, with references to others such as R. A. Knox and P. Carrington who have adopted the same interpretation.

25. L. Gaston, *No Stone*, 33-34, suggests an OT basis for this role of the angels in Zc. 14:5, where the wider context speaks of a gathering of the dispersed not only of Israel but of other nations

γικὰ πνεύματα εἰς διακονίαν ἀποστελλόμενα διὰ τοὺς μέλλοντας κληρονομεῖν σωτηρίαν.

For the geographical expressions ἐκ τῶν τεσσάρων ἀνέμων ἀπ' ἄκρου γῆς ἕως ἄκρου οὐρανοῦ, see the comments above on the combined allusion to Dt. 30:4 and Zc. 2:10 (EVV 2:6). Those two texts between them account for most of the specific words used, and the idea of the worldwide scope of the ingathering is based on them.[26] Compare the references to gathering in from east and west, north and south in Ps. 107:3; Is. 43:5-6; 49:12, again with reference to the Jewish return from exile, but likewise echoed by Jesus when speaking of the gathering of an international people of God (Mt. 8:11; Lk. 13:29).

28-29 The disciples' question about a σημεῖον has still not been forgotten. The fig tree provides a παραβολή, this word being used now in a sense closer to the common conception of an illustrative example.[27] Verses 28-29 are in effect an extended simile: just as you learn of the approach of summer by observing the behaviour of the fig tree, so you may learn of the coming of 'it' by seeing ταῦτα γινόμενα. In each case the appearance of the one is an infallible σημεῖον of the arrival of the other.

In Palestine the fig tree comes into leaf[28] in March/April (see above, pp. 439-40). The early harvest (the 'first-ripe' figs) can be expected in May/June. While τὸ θέρος can mean simply the season of summer, summer is the time of fruit and other crops,[29] and θέρος may have a particular connotation of harvesttime (ὁ θερισμός). The leaves give sure promise that fruit will follow (and if that promise is not fulfilled, woe betide the tree, 11:12-14).

The choice of the fig tree for this simile is probably due merely to the fact that, as one of the few deciduous trees in Palestine, it is an obvious example (perhaps prompted by one nearby on the Mount of Olives; Gundry, 746; Lane, 479). But we should not forget that in chapter 11 we have seen the fig tree used as a symbol of the temple and its failure. Here the imagery is of normal growth and fruiting, not of barrenness, but in this context of the destruction of the temple the reader may well recollect that other fig tree which failed and which symbolised not the *time* of the temple's fall but the completeness of its destruction.

In the second part of the simile the counterpart of the budding leaves is

---

(14:16). Gundry, 784, declares, without giving any evidence, that 'Angels gather the elect, whereas human beings evangelize the nations'; he does not explain how the two activities differ.

26. The resultant expression as a whole is not directly paralleled in the OT, though it is in Philo, where it likewise means 'the farthest reaches of earth and heaven'; cf also *1 Enoch* 57:2 (see G. R. Beasley-Murray, *Last Days,* 433).

27. See Beasley-Murray, *Last Days,* 438-40, for similarities between this parable and the parables of growth in chapter 4.

28. The subject of ἐκφύῃ (present subjunctive active) is strictly the κλάδος rather than the tree itself; the accentuation ἐκφυῇ, making it an aorist subjunctive passive, would involve an unnecessary change of subject — 'the branch grows tender and the leaves are produced' — but in either case the image is the same.

29. θέρος sometimes has that meaning in classical Greek (see LSJ) and in the papyri (see MM).

ταῦτα γινόμενα, that of the summer is the fact that ἐγγύς ἐστιν ἐπὶ θύραις (ἐπὶ θύραις, described by Turner, 27, as a 'fixed idiom',[30] is a graphic synonym for ἐγγύς, like our 'on the threshold'; cf. the juxtaposition of ἤγγικεν and πρὸ τῶν θυρῶν in Jas. 5:8-9). Neither expression is as specific as we might wish. The latter is made even less clear by the quite unjustified tendency of some to translate it as 'he is near' (RV, RSV, NRSV, JB, NJB). ἐγγύς is an adverb, not a masculine adjective, so that the phrase means 'he/she/it is near', leaving the identification of the 'he/she/it' to be determined by the context. And here the context leaves little room for doubt. The disciples had asked when the temple would be destroyed and how they would know the time. Jesus' reply, with the focus shifting emphatically back to the disciples again (καὶ ὑμεῖς . . . γινώσκετε), now homes in directly on the latter part of their question: *this* is how you will know that it (the destruction of the temple, the subject of your question and of the whole discourse so far) is near; this is the σημεῖον you asked for.

If, as the context demands, ἐγγύς ἐστιν refers to the destruction of the temple, what are the ταῦτα which will point to its coming as clearly as the fig leaves point to summer? Again the context must decide, and again the context gives us a suitable antecedent. The sign that it was time to escape was the βδέλυγμα τῆς ἐρημώσεως, and the events which are described in vv. 14-22 are a description of the period of distress which will lead up to the fall of the city; the repetition of ὅταν ἴδητε here from v. 14 also points to that as the antecedent. ταῦτα must therefore refer to the matters set forth in vv. 14-22, after which the destruction of the temple will follow quickly and inevitably; there will be little time to get away. It is therefore quite inappropriate to the flow of the discourse to understand v. 29 as referring to anything subsequent to the destruction of the temple. That would make it useless as a sign in response to the disciples' question, as well as introducing a quite unnecessary tension with the clear temporal limit set in v. 30. Verse 29 thus sums up all that Jesus has just spelled out in vv. 14-27, the preliminaries in vv. 14-22 (ταῦτα γινόμενα) and the climax itself in vv. 24-27 (ἐγγύς ἐστιν ἐπὶ θύραις).

30 If it were not for the embarrassment which it causes to those who think Jesus is here talking about the parousia (and so got it wrong),[31] this verse would have posed no great problems. Its language is clear and definite, not now in symbols but in a straightforward statement of a time limit. It is, moreover, emphatic and authoritative (see on 3:28 for ἀμὴν λέγω ὑμῖν, used here for the only time in this discourse; the οὐ μή construction adds to its decisiveness); it is not to be sidelined.

The time limit is the passing away of this generation (cf. 9:1, οὐ μὴ γεύσωνται θανάτου ἕως . . .) While Mark's other uses of γενεά are not temporally marked, simply referring to Jesus' contemporaries as a γενεὰ ἄπιστος etc.

30. Cf *TDNT*, 3.173-74. To recognise this is to invalidate Gundry's argument (788) that the phrase demands a personal subject for ἐγγύς ἐστιν since 'events do not come through doors, persons do'.

31. Gundry speaks of the desire to 'wiggle out of the non-fulfilment of v 30' (788), and of 'seeking an out' (791).

(8:12, 38; 9:19), here the whole construction of the sentence, as well as the disciples' question 'When?' in v. 4, demands the regular temporal sense: people alive as Jesus is speaking will still be there to see the fulfilment of his words.

Attempts to evade this obvious sense (on the part of those who care about Jesus' reliability — not all commentators do) have followed one (or both) of two lines, the reinterpretation of ἡ γενεὰ αὕτη to mean something other than people then living, or the identification of ταῦτα πάντα as something other than the events Jesus has just been describing. While this commentary is in the happy position of having no embarrassment to avoid because it takes Jesus' words at their face value as a prediction of the destruction of the temple within that generation, a few comments on each of these tactics may be appropriate.

The proposal to read ἡ γενεὰ αὕτη as the Jewish race goes back at least as far as Jerome, but has little to be said for it lexically or contextually. While BAGD, 154a, 1, offers the meaning 'clan', 'race', 'kind' in a single instance (Lk. 16:8), and regards it as 'possible, for instance, in Mt. 23:36', the vast majority of uses relate to time, and in particular to 'contemporaries'. Mt. 23:36 (also introduced by ἀμὴν λέγω ὑμῖν) is in fact quite close in wording to the present saying: ἥξει ταῦτα πάντα ἐπὶ τὴν γενεὰν ταύτην. Far from supporting Jerome's interpretation, it strengthens the case against it, since it follows Jesus' words about the murder of the prophets and the challenge to his contemporaries to 'fill up the measure of your ancestors', and leads immediately into his prediction of the devastation of Jerusalem and the destruction of the temple. Of course, the γενεά there referred to are Jewish, but the focus is on the contemporary generation of Jews, and the fact that it is they, not some future generation, who will bear the divine judgment through the destruction of the temple. And even if the lexicon might allow it, in the present context in Mark to predict the continued existence of the Jewish race until some future and unspecified ταῦτα πάντα γένηται would be a curious irrelevance when the disciples want to know when the temple will be destroyed.

Another suggestion is that ἡ γενεὰ αὕτη does not mean 'this generation' but 'that generation', namely, the people who will be alive at the time when the ταῦτα of v. 29 (interpreted of some future age unconnected with the fall of Jerusalem) begin to happen. Even if our interpretation of v. 29 is wrong, and it is talking about the age of the parousia, this would be an odd interpretation of ἡ γενεὰ αὕτη: ought it not to be ἡ γενεὰ ἐκείνη? Given our understanding of v. 29, of course, the attempt to find in the phrase any generation other than that of Jesus has no reference point in the text. Still less plausible is the suggestion that ἡ γενεὰ αὕτη could mean the human race in general, a sense for which there is no relevant parallel, and which would surely have needed to be expressed in a less misleading way.[32]

---

32. Gundry's words (791) about any such attempt to 'extend' the generation are apposite: 'The emphatic negation, "will by no means pass away", turns vapid. *Of course* this generation would not pass away if by definition it could extend out indefinitely!'

As for the identification of ταῦτα πάντα as something other than the events described in the preceding verses up to v. 27, this depends also on a whole interpretative approach to the discourse which we have seen reason to reject. It betrays its weakness at this point in that insofar as there is in the text any clear antecedent by which ταῦτα πάντα may be identified it is the use of those same words in the disciples' question in v. 4. There is a clear continuity between the question when μέλλῃ ταῦτα συντελεῖσθαι πάντα and the answer that this generation will not pass away until ταῦτα πάντα γένηται. If the former phrase referred to the destruction of the temple (and, as we have seen, nothing in its context suggests any other reference), then so must the latter. ταῦτα πάντα in this context must therefore refer to the whole complex of events Jesus has just been predicting in vv. 14-27.[33] The answer to the disciples' question is thus comprehensively rounded off by as plain and definite a time scale as they could have wished for.

31 This emphatic assertion of the permanent validity of Jesus' words heavily underlines the implications of the introduction ἀμὴν λέγω ὑμῖν to the preceding pronouncement. You may rely on him. The words are remarkable, in that they echo the declaration of Is. 40:7-8, that while grass and flowers may wither, God's word stands forever. The reliability of the word of Jesus is no less than that of the word of God himself. For the fixed order of the created universe as a guarantee of permanence cf. Is. 51:6; 54:9-10; Je. 31:35-36; 33:20-21. This verse is not therefore speaking of a future passing away of heaven and earth as something which may be contemplated, still less as part of what Jesus is predicting,[34] but rather, as in Isaiah and Jeremiah, using the unthinkableness of such an event as a guarantee for the truth of what Jesus has declared. In Mt. 5:18; Lk. 16:17 the same imagery is used for the permanent validity of the law; Jesus' λόγοι are thus put on a par with the Torah in terms of authority and permanence.

---

33. It is of course possible to claim that Jesus has temporarily forgotten about vv. 24-27, and has now reverted only to the events of vv. 14-22, despite the very emphatic temporal link which has been made between those events and vv. 24b-27 by the connecting formulae in v. 24a. This interpretation, which I have elsewhere called the 'leapfrog' exegesis (the discourse leaping from temple to parousia to temple and back to parousia), is probably the most common in popular attempts to escape the embarrassment of an unfulfilled prophecy in v. 30, but is not often seen in a clear-cut form in academic studies. One of the clearest is Lane, 478. See further my *Jesus and the OT*, 228, and mention of some older commentaries there in n. 5.

34. C. Fletcher-Louis, in K. E. Brower and M. W. Elliott (ed.), *Reader*, 145-69, argues that the passing away of heaven and earth is further symbolic imagery for the destruction of the temple, and that this verse is therefore again predicting that event. The second half of the verse then presumably declares that Jesus' words will outlast the temple. But this is to miss the rhetorical force of the use of the (impossible) ending of heaven and earth as a foil for the still more improbable failure of Jesus' words, as in the Isaiah and Jeremiah passages cited above. Fletcher-Louis (148) comments that 'Mark 13:31 is conspicuously absent' from my 1971 discussion of Mark 13. The reason for its absence is not, as he supposes, that I found its content incompatible with my exegesis, but that I do not think it adds *any* 'content' to the future agenda set out in Mk. 13, but rather serves merely to underline what has already been said.

An Unknown Day and Hour: Be Ready (13:32-37)

Περὶ δέ . . . as the opening phrase of a paragraph signals a change of subject. It is used several times in this way in 1 Corinthians as Paul moves from answering one question to the next,[35] and we have seen it used in this way by Mark already in 12:26, where Jesus turns from the specific issue of the place of marriage in the resurrection life to the more general issue of the validity of resurrection belief itself. Here it naturally suggests a similar shift to a new topic, and the more so because the dependent genitive consists of a pair of phrases (τῆς ἡμέρας ἐκείνης ἢ τῆς ὥρας) which are here introduced into the discourse for the first time. While the plural αἱ ἡμέραι (ἐκεῖναι) has been used several times to describe the period of the siege of Jerusalem (vv. 17, 19, 20, 24), no singular day has been mentioned which provides a suitable antecedent to ἡ ἡμέρα ἐκείνη in v. 32. Moreover, the statement of ignorance concerning this 'day or hour' contrasts strongly with the resounding certainty (ἀμὴν λέγω ὑμῖν) of Jesus' pronouncement of the time within which the ταῦτα described in the previous verses will occur (v. 30). We have moved emphatically from the known to the unknown.[36]

In terms of the flow of the discourse, then, v. 32 seems to require to be read as the beginning of a new subject,[37] as I have argued above (pp. 501-2) in opposition to those like N. T. Wright who believe the whole discourse refers only to the destruction of the temple. What that new subject is depends upon what meaning can be given to ἡ ἡμέρα ἐκείνη ἢ ἡ ὥρα. In the Matthean version of the discourse this poses no problem, since the disciples' question which introduces it in Mt. 24:3 refers *both* to the destruction of the temple *and* to Jesus' παρουσία and the συντελεία τοῦ αἰῶνος. At Mt. 24:36, therefore, the discourse moves from answering the first part of the question to the second, so that the ἡμέρα referred to must be that of Jesus' παρουσία, and this interpretation is immediately confirmed by the occurrence of the term παρουσία in 24:37, 39,[38] and by the nature of the parables which make up the bulk of the rest of the discourse in the remainder of chapter 24 and throughout chapter 25. In Mark we have none of this explicit guidance, though the themes of vv. 33-37 are such as we find elsewhere in parousia contexts, the unexpected arrival, the call to be ready, and the parable of the porter which is like a brief summary of the first of

35. 1 Cor. 7:1, 25; 8:1; 12:1; 16:1. Cf also 1 Thes. 4:9; 5:1; Acts 21:25.

36. The sharp opposition between the fall of Jerusalem and the 'unknown day and hour' is well brought out by J. Winandy, *RB* 75 (1968) 63-79, with special emphasis on the importance of the new terminology introduced in v. 32.

37. Cf. P. Carrington, *According to Mark* (Cambridge: Cambridge University Press, 1960), 293-94, 298, who, having interpreted 13:24-27 of the destruction of the temple, marks off 13:32-37 as a new and separate section, headed 'The Advent Parables'.

38. Note that the one use of the term παρουσία in the Matthean discourse prior to v. 36 is to deny emphatically that the events of the siege are the setting for the parousia: when the parousia happens it will not be a matter of speculation and dubious claims, but will be obvious to all (Mt. 24:27).

the Matthean parousia parables in Mt. 24:45-51. These features suggest that despite the absence of an expressed antecedent for the ἡμέρα ἢ ὥρα in Mark the reference is the same as in Mt. 24:36ff. The phrase ἡ ἡμέρα ἐκείνη has this sense in a number of places in the NT where an explicit antecedent is equally lacking. In Mt. 7:22 and Lk. 10:12 the context requires that it refer to the day of judgment, but the identity of the 'day' is no more explicit in those passages than here. The same reference to the day of judgment is clearly intended in 2 Tim. 1:12, 18; 4:8, though again no antecedent is expressed in these contexts. In 1 Cor. 3:13 ἡ ἡμέρα alone suffices to convey the same reference. It seems, then, that in early Christian parlance 'that day' or even just 'the day' was in itself a recognised eschatological term where the context allowed it to be so understood.[39] Mark could thus expect his readers to detect in the use of this phrase a shift from the historical events of the Jewish War to a more ultimate perspective, without having to spell this out. Any readers/hearers who managed to miss the idiom would quickly realise the change of subject when they heard in vv. 33-37 what the coming of ἡ ἡμέρα ἐκείνη was to be like.

But even if Mark's language signals a clear shift of subject, it remains to ask why this new theme should be introduced into the discourse at all when (unlike in Matthew) the question to which the discourse offers an answer concerns only the fate of the temple. Why then does Mark record Jesus as adding an apparently irrelevant appendix concerning his parousia? It should be noted that if these verses do introduce the subject of the parousia, this is the only treatment of the subject in Mark's gospel. Matthew's extensive expansion of the discourse (and its introductory question) to include the parousia parables indicates, however, that he and his readers found a natural link between the coming judgment on Jerusalem and the more ultimate judgment associated with the parousia of the Son of Man, and it is unlikely that this thinking was confined to the circles for which Matthew wrote. If such a link was present in the minds of Mark's potential readers (and indeed in that of Mark himself), the parousia is by no means an irrelevant subject to add on to the discourse, particularly when there is such a clear and important temporal distinction to be drawn between the two events, the one a historical judgment to take place within the generation, the other an unknown day for which one must always be ready but for which one can never set a date. Whatever the theological links between the two times of judgment, they must not suppose that the two are also chronologically joined.

This 'appendix' is linked to the earlier part of the discourse by the recurrence of the key word βλέπετε (vv. 5, 9, 23, and 33), which is now, however, strengthened by the addition of ἀγρυπνεῖτε (v. 33) and γρηγορεῖτε (twice, in vv. 35 and 37, picking up the verb from the parable of the porter in v. 34). But the

---

39. For similar use of language in the OT see Beasley-Murray, *Last Days,* 457-58; Lane, 481 — though in most of the passages cited the surrounding context offers a more suitable antecedent than appears here.

use of the imperative also reflects the changed perspective of the discourse after v. 32. In two of its earlier occurrences (vv. 5, 23) βλέπετε has conveyed a warning against being misled into premature expectation, especially by people falsely claiming to be the Messiah. Here it expresses an almost opposite warning, against failing to be ready for the parousia of the real Messiah. While the period preceding the fulfilment of Jesus' prediction of the destruction of the temple will call for a cool, level-headed refusal to become excited too soon, the expectation of the unknown day and hour of the parousia demands constant alertness. The language of keeping awake derives from the parable of vv. 34-35: it is the appropriate attitude of those who know their master might come at any time.[40]

32 For the identification of the ἡμέρα ἢ ὥρα as the time of the parousia see the preceding introductory comments. The list of those who might be expected to know the secret is apparently in an ascending order which places ὁ υἱός above the angels, and second only to ὁ πατήρ. Such a high christology reflects the divine declarations in 1:11 and 9:7, but here the statement is attributed to Jesus himself. The focus of the saying is not of course on christology but on the time of the parousia, so that the use of the title ὁ υἱός occurs almost in passing. But that makes it all the more striking: it does not have to be argued for, but is taken as read. We are not even told explicitly that ὁ υἱός is Jesus, though the reader of Mark's gospel can have no doubt about this. It is an appropriate title for the person who can address God naturally as Ἀββὰ ὁ πατήρ (14:36). We have been prepared to some extent for this remarkable usage by Jesus' parable of the υἱὸς ἀγαπητός in 12:6, where the identification of Jesus as the υἱός, the one who is closest to God and thus can represent him, is clear even though not explicit. His claim to be ὁ υἱὸς τοῦ εὐλογητοῦ will eventually be made publicly and definitively in 14:61-62. But here Mark indicates that his closest disciples should already have been able to recognise him as the Son[41] who stands in the divine hierarchy above the angels and next to God himself.

It is ironic that a saying which has such far-reaching christological implications has in fact become more familiar in theological discussion as a

---

40. M. D. Hooker, *BJRL* 65 (1982/3) 94-95, finds vv. 34-36 a 'real problem', in that the need to keep watch depends on the expectation of an imminent arrival. 'This suggests that he is already at hand, and the urgency of this command is at odds with the earlier part of the discourse, which emphasized that the end could not be expected yet. . . . The final section . . . apparently contradicts *all* (her italics) the previous six paragraphs by urging the need to watch constantly, since the time of the parousia is unknown to anyone.' Hooker offers no solution to this supposed inconsistency, which illustrates the awkwardness of the traditional exegesis of the chapter. If, on the other hand, as I have argued, there is a marked change of subject and perspective at v. 32, so that only in this final section of the discourse is the parousia in view, Hooker's 'problem' becomes a natural and necessary feature of the discourse.

41. Gundry, 794-95, rightly points out that the use of 'the Son' rather than the fuller form 'the Son of God' is to be accounted for by the occurrence of 'the Father' immediately afterwards. He shows that where the two titles are collocated in similar ways elsewhere it is normal for 'the Son' alone to be used.

christological embarrassment. The assertion of Jesus' ignorance on a subject of such importance as the time of his own parousia seems to many incompatible with his status as Son of God.[42] If this title implies that he is himself divine, and God is omniscient, how can the Son of God be ignorant? More specifically, if this is a matter which the Father does know and the Son does not, must we conclude that to be Son of God means something less than full participation in the divine attributes?

Even to express these questions directly is to be aware immediately of a change of context. This is the language of later Christian theological debate, not of the gospel of Mark. Whatever later readers may have made of it, Jesus' 'confession of ignorance' seems to pose no embarrassment or even surprise for Mark. Perhaps he had not as yet made as tight a link between the title 'Son of God' and the claim to full divinity as was developed in later incarnational theology. Or perhaps he would have felt comfortable with what many centuries later was to be formulated as kenotic christology, the belief that when God becomes incarnate it is inappropriate to expect such divine attributes as omniscience to be evident within the temporary confines of an authentically human existence. We cannot know how he would have responded to these later questions, and it is likely that this issue, and the embarrassment which it brings to his text at 13:32, would not yet have occurred either to him or to his readers. To debate it in a commentary on Mark's gospel would be anachronistic.

The focus of v. 32 is not on christology, but on eschatology. Unlike the thoroughly predictable end of the temple, the time of Jesus' parousia is known only to God. Even the Son himself, who might most have been expected to share the secret, does not know.[43] The situation calls, therefore, not for calculation of dates or careful observation of signs, but for constant readiness.

33　For the phrase ἡ ἡμέρα ἢ ἡ ὥρα this verse appropriately substitutes ὁ καιρός; the reference is the same, to the unknown time of the parousia. The moral is drawn out in a striking pair of imperatives. Whereas as βλέπετε in vv. 5 and 23 was a call to the cooling of expectation, and in v. 9 a call to prepare for hard times ahead, here it has a more positive note. Linked with ἀγρυπνεῖτε (see Textual Note), it is a summons to vigilance, literally staying awake, a metaphor which is continued in the double exhortation γρηγορεῖτε in vv. 35 and 37; the converse is the danger of being caught asleep (v. 36). The metaphor is vivid, but apparently impractical. No one can stay awake all the time, not even a porter (v. 34), and the awareness that the parousia may happen at any time does not relieve us of the ordinary business of living. Matthew's parable of the bridesmaids (Mt. 25:1-12) intriguingly addresses this issue, with its concept of a pre-

42. Hence the tendency in many MSS of the more-used Gospel of Matthew to omit the phrase οὐδὲ ὁ υἱός (so, in Mt. 24:36, ℵ[a] K L W sy[s] and the majority of minuscules and later versions, as well as patristic citations as early as the third century). Mark, being less used, escaped this apologetic emendation.

43. For a similar restriction see 10:40: it is God alone, not Jesus, who assigns the places of honour.

paredness for the bridegroom's coming which is nevertheless compatible with falling asleep in the meantime (though the coda attached to the parable in 25:13 seems to take away all that has just been offered). Mark has no such concession to reality: both the exhortation and the parable which illustrates it focus single-mindedly on the danger of being caught unprepared. How we can remain prepared while maintaining the ordinary responsibilities of life (yes, and its relaxations) we are left to work out for ourselves.

34-36 Verse 34 is a grammatically incomplete sentence. ὡς introduces a simile or parable which illustrates the exhortation to watchfulness in v. 33, and leads on to a similar exhortation at the beginning of v. 35, after which simile and exhortation are woven together by the use of a second-person address within the framework of the parable. The sense is clear enough: the absent householder who may return unexpectedly is the Son of Man, and the slaves left on duty are his followers in the interval between his going away and his return. The sense is best expressed by adding a phrase to introduce v. 34, such as 'It is as if . . .' or 'The situation is like that of . . .' The motif of the absentee householder is familiar in the gospel tradition, not only in Matthew's parousia parables (24:45-51; 25:14-30) and Luke's related parables of the watching slaves (12:35-38; cf. 12:42-48) and the pounds (Lk. 19:11-27), but also already in Mark with a different setting in the parable of the tenants of the vineyard (12:1-12).[44]

The description of the situation in v. 34 is awkwardly expressed, without a main verb. The householder's departure is signalled simply by the adjective ἀπόδημος, and the commissioning of the slaves by the participles ἀφείς and δούς. The clauses which follow τὴν ἐξουσίαν function in apposition to it, the first having no verb (ἑκάστῳ τὸ ἔργον αὐτοῦ), but the second expanded into a coordinate clause by the addition of ἐνετείλατο ἵνα γρηγορῇ. The sense is clear, however inelegant the form of expression, and the effect of the introduction of the main verb and ἵνα clause into the last member is to focus attention on the specific responsibility of the porter rather than on the various tasks allocated to the other slaves. It is thus the porter whom we are to take as our model, as vv. 35-36 will spell out.

The porter's verb, γρηγορέω, is then turned into a direct exhortation to the readers, γρηγορεῖτε οὖν . . . μὴ ἐλθὼν ἐξαίφνης εὕρῃ ὑμᾶς καθεύδοντας, within which is inserted an explanatory clause, οὐκ οἴδατε γάρ. . . . This explanatory clause is expressed still in terms of the situation of the parable, as if the readers were themselves in the position of the porter. It is a striking and effective way of drawing us directly into the application of the parable.[45]

It is often observed that the parable assumes a return at night, which in

44. The complex relationship between the various synoptic parousia parables is helpfully discussed by R. J. Bauckham, *NTS* 23 (1976/7) 165-70.

45. R. J. Bauckham, *NTS* 23 (1976/7) 167-69, discusses this literary technique under the title 'deparabolization'.

real life would be most improbable (especially after a lengthy absence such as ἀπόδημος suggests), since people in the ancient world tried to avoid travelling at night (though see Lk. 11:5-6 for an exception). As often, the improbable elements in the story serve as pointers to the parable's intention: the nighttime is the most difficult and improbable time to be on the watch, and the parousia will be equally unexpected. It will be very easy to be caught napping. The four time words (ὀψὲ and πρωΐ are adverbs, and the nouns μεσονύκτιον [accusative of time][46] and ἀλεκτροφωνίας [genitive of time, see BDF, 186(2)] function adverbially as well) represent the conventional Roman division of the twelve hours of the night into four quarters or 'watches' of three hours each. (Mark is thus more comprehensive than Lk. 12:38, who mentions only the two middle watches, the most difficult to keep.)[47] The unfortunate porter is expected to maintain his post through all four watches. The Christian disciple, it seems, is never off duty (see comments on v. 33). For καθεύδω as a metaphor for spiritual insensitivity cf. Eph. 5:14; 1 Thes. 5:6-7.[48]

37 The conclusion of the discourse explicitly widens its application beyond the original audience of four (v. 3) to 'all' (cf. Peter's question in Lk. 12:41, whether the parable of the burglar, and perhaps also the preceding parable of the watching slaves, applies πρὸς ἡμᾶς ἢ καὶ πρὸς πάντας). While the question of the date of the destruction of the temple was directly relevant only to a limited audience, the changed perspective of the concluding verses has widened the relevance of the discourse to all disciples, all of whom must live with the prospect of an unexpected parousia. The discourse thus concludes with a rousing imperative, γρηγορεῖτε.

---

46. The accusative of time, which is normally understood as denoting an *extent* of time (BDF, 161 [2]), may seem inappropriate to the single point of midnight (or of the householder's arrival), though if μεσονύκτιον denotes the whole midnight watch rather than the specific time of twenty-four hours, the difficulty is less. Alternative readings (μεσονυκτίου, A D Θ and the 'majority text'; μεσονυκτίῳ, Σ and a few minuscules) reflect this grammatical uncertainty.

47. This seems more likely than the common assumption that Luke is following the Jewish tendency to speak of three four-hour watches, and so mentions the last two of them.

48. T. J. Geddert, *Watchwords,* 89-103, offers an imaginative interpretation of the parable (based on a suggestion by R. H. Lightfoot, *Message,* 53, which is also developed independently by Stock, 346-47) as directly linked to the following passion narrative, with the four watches of the night corresponding to the stages from the last supper to the conclusion of the Sanhedrin trial, with a special focus on the Gethsemane story as the supreme call to watchfulness, in which the disciples were to fail but Jesus himself was to prove the 'model doorkeeper'. While it is true that the verb γρηγορέω occurs in Mark only in 13:34-37 and 14:34-37, in both of which passages it is a prominent motif, and that both passages include the sequence 'watching-coming-finding-sleeping' (following W. H. Kelber, *Passion* 48), this is a slender base on which to build such a complex theory of deliberate literary linking, especially as the context here in chapter 13 concerns not the imminent passion but watching for the parousia. Geddert's assertion that the link is 'too meticulously crafted to be only a figment of the readers' imaginations' (96) is not self-evident. See further, Gundry, 799-800.

SETTING THE SCENE FOR THE PASSION (14:1-11)

The first part of Act Three (before the explanatory discourse in ch. 13) has described the developing confrontation between Jesus and the Jerusalem authorities, up to the point where it has resulted in a decisive break. On the one hand the authorities have ceased to initiate any further dialogue with Jesus, and on the other hand Jesus has abandoned the temple area where his teaching and debates have been located, pronouncing the coming devastation of the temple as he did so.

Chapter 13 has given the reader the opportunity to think about the implications of this breakdown. The coming destruction of the temple symbolises the end of the old order, and the loss of Jerusalem's significance as the focus of God's presence and activity on earth. In its place is to be set up the authority of Jesus, the vindicated and enthroned Son of Man, who will gather the true people of God from all corners of the earth into a new community of grace. All this is now inevitable. It is guaranteed by the indestructible word of Jesus. Within the generation it will all have taken place.

So now the time for talking is over, and it is time for the events to unfold which Jesus has insistently predicted since Caesarea Philippi, and which will set in train the scenario so vividly sketched out in chapter 13. The confrontation between the rival authorities is now to reach its tremendous climax in the final scenes of Mark's drama, as the paradox of the rejected and executed King of the Jews is played out in deadly earnest. And it is symbolically appropriate that it should be played out at Passover, the festival which marked the original establishment of Israel as the covenant people of God rescued from slavery in Egypt. There will be a new Passover, and a new covenant, for the new people of God.

This symbolism will be a central aspect of the story of Jesus' last meal with his disciples, with which the sequence of the events of the passion will shortly begin. But first Mark has constructed a careful setting of the scene, in the form of a 'double sandwich', as follows:

14:1a   The Passover is coming
    14:1b-2   The chief priests plot the removal of Jesus
        14:3-9   A woman anoints Jesus in advance for his burial
    14:10-11   Judas provides the answer for the chief priests
14:12ff   Preparing the Passover

The outer layer of the sandwich sets the events in their symbolic context, the Passover festival with its sacrificial meal. Within this framework is a further sandwich which contrasts the hostility of the religious leaders and the treachery of one of Jesus' leading disciples with the extravagant love and loyalty of one of the least of his followers. Those who ought to know better are now determined to stop at nothing to get rid of a troublesome rival, while an unnamed woman is held up as a model of true devotion which even Jesus' closest disciples are not able yet to appreciate. As so often in Mark, the first prove to be last and the last first, when it comes to the values of the kingdom of God.

The Passover and the Priests (14:1-2)

The Passover proper (τὸ πάσχα) refers to the events of a roughly twelve-hour period which spanned two Jewish days — the Jewish day began at sunset, not at midnight as we (and the Romans) reckon. On Nisan 14, during the afternoon, the lambs for the Passover meal were slaughtered in the temple. After sunset (and therefore on the next Jewish day, Nisan 15) the Passover meal was held. The Passover proper therefore spanned Nisan 14 and 15. The festival of Unleavened Bread (τὰ ἄζυμα), originally a separate festival, followed on directly from the Passover and lasted seven days, Nisan 15-21 (Nu. 28:15-16). In practice the two festivals were treated together as a single period of celebration; either τὸ πάσχα or τὰ ἄζυμα could be used for the whole eight-day period, but the use of the two together here is more precise. The date indicated in v. 1 is probably Nisan 13 (μετὰ δύο ἡμέρας being understood inclusively; see on 8:31), but nothing hangs on the identification of the date here: it is with v. 12 that the chronological debate begins. Mark is simply signalling here the close approach of the festival for which Jesus and many other pilgrims from Galilee and all over the Jewish world have come to Jerusalem to prepare.

Estimates of the number of people in and around Jerusalem at Passover time in the first century are necessarily speculative. Josephus's figure of around three million (War 2.280; 6.423-27) is generally agreed to be a vast exaggeration, though modest compared with the rabbinic account of 1,200,000 lambs, implying some 12 million participants (b. Pes. 64b). J. Jeremias's calculations based on the numbers of lambs and the space available in the temple for killing them produced a more realistic figure of 180,000.[1] But even this is several times the normal population of the city (perhaps 30,000, according to Jeremias),[2] and many pilgrims had to stay outside the city, many in temporary camps (see on 11:11).

The festival period was therefore potentially a volatile one, and the concern of the religious authorities is understandable. The report of Jesus' tumultuous arrival outside the city, and the degree of popular support which he had received during the days of debate in the temple precincts (11:18, 32; 12:12, 37), made a θόρυβος a serious possibility if they took action against Jesus openly. That was why Judas' offer to hand Jesus over (privately) was so welcome; this was just the sort of δόλος they were looking for.[3] The ἑορτή during which they

1. J. Jeremias, Jerusalem, 77-84.
2. J. Jeremias, Jerusalem, 84. E. M. Meyers and J. F. Strange, Archaeology, 52, drawing on the work of M. Broshi and J. Wilkinson, suggest 37,000 to 44,000.
3. The Passover situation and Judas's subsequent action are in themselves sufficient to explain the need for δόλος in Mark's account; an intended allusion to the treatment of the righteous sufferer in Ps. 10:7-8, as suggested by Marcus, Way, 172, is possible but not necessary.

are unwilling to act is presumably the whole eight-day period (rather than the Passover proper) since that is the period during which the large crowd, including the Galilean pilgrims, might be expected to be in Jerusalem. According to the chronological scheme followed in this commentary (see on v. 12) they stuck to this plan, in that the arrest of Jesus took place during the night which began Nisan 14 (i.e., before the Passover ceremonies began the next day), though of course the city was already crowded by that time, so that without Judas's help an arrest before the festival would have been impossible.[4]

In the passion narrative the religious authorities who take action against Jesus are variously described, the one constant factor being the ἀρχιερεῖς. The full listing of ἀρχιερεῖς, γραμματεῖς, and πρεσβύτεροι (see on 8:31) will recur in 14:43, 53; 15:1, but Mark does not find it necessary to produce the full list every time, and increasingly from v. 10 onwards the ἀρχιερεῖς are made to stand for the whole group of opponents. The inclusion of γραμματεῖς but not πρεσβύτεροι here is probably not significant, except in echoing the same pairing in 11:18 where the plot was first mentioned, so reminding us that there is a 'coalition' involved, not merely a specific group of ἀρχιερεῖς.[5]

The Anointing of Jesus (14:3-9)

TEXTUAL NOTE

5. The omission of ἐπάνω in a few texts assimilates to the specific figure given in Jn. 12:5; it may also be due to dislike of Mark's idiom (BDF, 185[4], describe ἐπάνω as 'a vulgar substitute for πλείων').

The events of the passion narrative proper begin with a scene which, but for its close link with Jesus' impending death in vv. 6-8, might well have been part of the sequence of episodes in Act Two where the disciples reveal their lack of understanding about the values of the kingdom of God. Just as in 10:13-16, we find here also a sequence of rebuke and counterrebuke, of churlish disapproval which provokes Jesus to another subversive declaration that it is the last who are in fact first. It is not the self-righteous charity of the (presumably male) on-

---

4. J. Jeremias, *Words*, 71-73 (cf. Gundry, 807-8), supports the theory that the arrest was on Nisan 15 by translating μὴ ἐν τῇ ἑορτῇ not as 'not during the festival' but as 'not in the presence of the festival crowd', a version for which he can find some lexical support, but which is hardly the natural sense when it is precisely the date of the festival, not the crowd, which has just been noted in v. 1. Quite apart from the fact that the priests may not in fact have stuck to this policy because of the course of events (particularly the offer of Judas), the supposed inconsistency which Jeremias's suggestion is designed to avoid depends on his dating of the passion events, with which this commentary does not agree.

5. Mark's specific mention of the three main elements of the Sanhedrin in 8:31; 11:27, etc. militates against the unsupported assertion of Mann, 553, that 'We are not dealing with an official policy of the Sanhedrin, but rather with a plan set in motion by some of its principal members'.

lookers which will be remembered, but the rash extravagance of an unnamed woman whose devotion to Jesus leaves no room for pious calculation.

Of the four anointing stories in the gospels, Matthew, Mark, and John set the scene in Bethany at Passover time, just before Jesus' arrest, while Lk. 7:36-50 is set in Galilee earlier in Jesus' ministry and differs substantially in content. In particular the connection with anointing for Jesus' burial, which forms the theological focus of the story for Matthew, Mark, and John, is absent from Luke. Apart from the basic theme of a woman anointing Jesus and being defended by him against criticism for so doing (and the basis of criticism also varies: extravagance in Matthew, Mark, and John; moral character in Luke), Luke agrees with Matthew and Mark only in the name of the host (but not his status: 'leper' in Matthew and Mark, 'Pharisee' in Luke), and Simon is so common a name that this is not likely to be a significant coincidence. None of the synoptic writers names the woman: only John identifies her as Mary the sister of Martha (and locates the incident in their house). It was Ephraem in the fourth century who first suggested that she was Mary of Magdala. Luke agrees with John in having Jesus' feet anointed and wiped with the woman's hair (in Matthew and Mark the ointment is poured on his head). This complex pattern of relationships probably indicates a separate tradition in Luke, perhaps of a different incident, though there is likely to have been some assimilation of the stories in transmission.[6]

John's version, set somewhat earlier in the week (six days before Passover) and in the house of Martha, Mary, and Lazarus rather than that of Simon, is essentially close in content to Mark's, but his tendency to provide names (Mary and Judas) has rather weakened the telling contrast in Mark between the unnamed woman and her critics whom we should probably identify as including at least some of Jesus' disciples (as Matthew makes explicit), and not merely the untypical Judas. For John, as for Mark and Matthew, anointing suggests burial, and the story thus forms an appropriate prologue to the passion narrative by showing Jesus as already virtually having 'one foot in the grave'. Not that any of the evangelists say that this was what the woman had in mind; it is rather an additional level of significance which Jesus perceives in what was apparently intended simply as an extravagant expression of love. By making this connection Jesus reminds the disciples yet again of the predicted outcome of his coming to Jerusalem, and warns them that his death and burial are now very close. The end game has begun.

But Mark sees more in this incident than a further passion prediction. The woman's καλὸν ἔργον provides a telling contrast with the limited outlook of the other guests in Simon's house. Their concern for the routine responsibility of

---

6. J. D. M. Derrett, *Law*, 266-75 (= *SE* 2 [1964] 174-82), offers an imaginative reconstruction of the Marcan scene on the assumption that the woman was, as Luke says, an ex-prostitute, so that the valuable ointment represented the proceeds of her immoral earnings. Mark's narration of the story offers little encouragement to such an assimilation.

providing for the poor, worthy as it is in itself, betrays the lack of an appropriate sense of occasion. This is Jesus' hour, the time when his predictions about his own destiny are coming to fulfilment, and his ministry is reaching its tragic yet essential climax. The poor can wait; something more vital is taking place, and the woman has proved more sensitive to it than even Jesus' closest companions. And that is why, when the story of these pivotal days comes to be told, she will have an honoured place in it. Anonymous as she is, she will be part of the good news which will soon be spread around the world, and her καλὸν ἔργον, even if not her name, will be remembered.

3 Two genitive absolutes (ὄντος αὐτοῦ . . . , κατακειμένου αὐτοῦ) set the scene; technically they should not be absolute, as the αὐτοῦ in both cases is the same subject as the αὐτοῦ in the main clause (unless a separate sentence begins with συντρίψασα; see below), but to coordinate the first two clauses with this later αὐτοῦ would have made an intolerably clumsy sentence. In 11:11-12 Mark has told us that Jesus and his disciples spent the first night at Bethany, and since in 11:19 they again left the city for the second night we may reasonably assume that they slept in Bethany throughout the days of preparation for the Passover (Lk. 21:37 says they spent the nights on the Mount of Olives, on the further slope of which Bethany was located). The occasion for this incident is presumably therefore an evening meal before the festival began: κατάκειμαι, while it need mean no more than lying down in the case of those who are ill (1:30; 2:4), when used of a healthy person normally denotes reclining at a meal (see on 2:15; Jn. 12:2 makes this explicit). The host, Simon, is otherwise unknown, presumably a local supporter of Jesus like Martha, Mary, and Lazarus. The fact that he could host a meal in his house indicates that his title ὁ λεπρός did not literally denote his present condition. He may have been a former leper, now cured (by Jesus?), or may have acquired his nickname by some other association which we cannot now know; the name Simon was so common that some distinguishing title was needed.

The woman was apparently not a fellow guest, as she is described as arriving (ἦλθεν) while Jesus is already at the meal; this tallies with Luke's description of the scene (7:37-38, 45) rather than with John, where Mary is one of the hostesses. ἡ ἀλάβαστρος (often neuter: see BDF, 49[1] for the variations in form and gender) denotes a perfume vase, commonly though not necessarily made from what we now call alabaster. The four genitives which Mark uses to describe its contents form a deliberately weighty phrase, emphasising that this was no ordinary perfume. μύρον is a general term for perfume or fragrant ointment. νάρδος specifies that this is the highly prized perfume made of spikenard, whose oil was imported from India and therefore expensive. πιστικῆς (agreeing with νάρδου, which is feminine) occurs in relation to ointment only here and in the parallel in John, and is variously interpreted: the adjective is occasionally used in nonbiblical Greek as a derivative of πίστις, meaning 'faithful', 'reliable', and so it is suggested that it might mean that the spikenard is 'genuine', 'pure'; Liddell and Scott derived it from πίνω, and so translate 'liquid'; others suggest a more technical meaning reflecting a botanical name (for several such suggestions see BAGD, 662a). In the end it must be confessed that we do not know what πιστικός means as applied to perfume, but it seems to have the effect of increasing the sense of special value. Monetary value is explicitly the sense of the last term, πολυτελής, and that value is further specified in v. 5: this single jar of perfume could be sold for a whole year's wages.

The syntax seems clumsy: either there is a sentence with two uncoordinated main verbs (ἦλθεν and κατέχεεν), or, more likely, a full stop should be placed after πολυτελοῦς, producing an awkward asyndeton in the second sentence beginning with συντρίψασα where Mark's normal style would be a coordinating καί. συντρίβω when used literally of objects means to break or shatter. Only Mark mentions this detail, which seems an unnecessarily wasteful and inefficient means of getting the perfume out of the flask. There seems to be no basis for the common suggestion that breaking the neck of the flask was the only way to get the perfume out — as Gundry rightly points out, it must initially have been put into the flask somehow! Gundry (802, 813), following Cranfield, believes rather that by breaking the flask she 'makes it henceforth unusable', thus demonstrating the completeness of the sacrifice, but this is perhaps too cerebral an account of a rash and instinctive action. It was a dramatic and impulsive gesture rather than a planned visual aid.[7]

Anointing the head with fragant oil (or at least with the cheaper olive oil, Lk. 7:46) was a familiar mark of festivity and of fellowship (Ps. 23:5; Am. 6:6); Ps. 133:2 suggests that the amount involved could be quite lavish, though a whole jar poured over one person's head goes well beyond normal courtesy. Jesus is not so much anointed as drenched in fragrant oil, and the comparison with the anointing of a whole body in v. 8 emphasises the point. Commentators commonly see the anointing as messianic[8] (hence the anointing of the head rather than the feet as in Luke and John, 'a sign of royal and priestly dignity' according to Mann, 555), in Mark's understanding if not in the woman's intention, but this is not explicit in the text, which does not use χρίω or its derivatives, and goes on to interpret the festal gesture in terms of death and burial rather than of messianic commissioning (see further Gundry, 813-14).

4-5 While objection to the woman's action is a feature of all the anointing stories, the objectors vary. In Luke it is Simon, the host (silently), in Matthew Jesus' disciples corporately, in John Judas alone. Mark's τινες is less specific. Such indefinite subjects are a characteristic feature of Mark's style (cf. 14:57, 65; 15:36 for similar use of τις, and, without τις, 1:32; 2:3; 3:32; 6:55;

---

7. Hooker, 329, suggests a further symbolism, in that 'ointment jars used in anointing the dead were often broken and left in the tomb'.

8. J. K. Elliott, *ExpTim* 85 (1973/4) 105-6, claims that anointing the head was specifically a mark of kingship, so that in the original event 'Jesus is hailed as King-Messiah', even though Mark has seen fit to overlay this original significance with the motif of the preparation of Jesus' body for burial (as an apologetic device to escape the embarrassment of the lack of proper burial rites for Jesus).

7:32, etc.). Often the context gives a clue to their identity, and here they are presumably fellow guests at the meal. Since Jesus is accompanied by his disciples during these days, including their visits to Bethany for the night (11:11-12, 19-20), it is likely that they would have made up a substantial part if not the whole of the gathering in Simon's house. In that case Mark's τινες would not differ in fact from Matthew's οἱ μαθηταί, but the identification is not expressed, so that Mark seems unusually to have missed an opportunity to underline explicitly the disciples' failure to grasp the values of the kingdom of God.

The critics' attitude is expressed strongly. ἀγανακτέω (used of Jesus' response to the disciples in 10:14 and of that of the remaining disciples to James and John in 10:41) expresses strong indignation over an offensive action or attitude, while ἐμβριμάομαι is even more vivid (see on 1:43). Mann translates 'They turned upon her in anger'; Gundry uses 'growling'. Jesus' response in v. 6 suggests that the woman found her critics intimidating. The phrase ἀγανακτοῦντες πρὸς ἑαυτούς suggests not so much silent (internalised) indignation as the expression of that indignation to one another within the group; cf. the other uses of πρὸς ἑαυτούς for shared emotions or deliberative consultations in 1:27; 10:26; 11:31; 12:7; 16:3. And the dative following ἐμβριμάομαι indicates (as in 1:43) that their hostility was openly directed against the woman.

The basis of their anger is the alleged waste of a valuable resource.[9] It is not that the perfume should have been kept, but that it would have achieved much more good by being sold for the benefit of the poor (as Jesus had earlier demanded, 10:21) than by being poured over Jesus. Their social concern is admirable (unlike the unworthy motive which Jn. 12:6 imputes to Judas) and would be echoed by many today. It must be a quite exceptional cause which justifies such lavish expenditure in preference to the undoubted benefit to many which the sale of the perfume might have achieved. And the onlookers, unlike the woman, cannot perceive such a cause in the presence of Jesus. It is on this lack of insight that Jesus will have to correct them, and in so doing vindicate the woman's intuitive action.

The genitive δηναρίων τριακοσίων does double duty both as the genitive of price (BDF, 179) and as the genitive governed by the adverb ἐπάνω used as an improper preposition ('a vulgar substitute for πλείων'; BDF, 185[4]). The compressed syntax continues in that the subject of δοθῆναι should be the money raised by the sale rather than the perfume itself as the grammar strictly requires. But, compressed as it is, Mark's sentence is idiomatically clear and effective.

6-7 The phrase κόπους παρέχω τινί is an idiom roughly equivalent to our 'give someone a hard time', though less good-natured (cf. Lk. 11:7; 18:5; Gal. 6:17). The superiority of the woman's καλὸν ἔργον does not mean that to

9. For the δηνάριον as a daily wage, see Mt. 20:1-15; by that reckoning ἐπάνω δηναρίων τριακοσίων is roughly a year's wages. In 6:37 the smaller sum of two hundred denarii was reckoned as appropriate to provide food for five thousand.

care for Jesus[10] is intrinsically better than to care for the poor, since that also is
εὖ ποιῆσαι, but lies rather in her sense of occasion. Care for the poor is a regular
obligation (and one which received particular emphasis at Passover time;
Gundry, 811), but in this historic moment that proper routine concern takes second place.[11] In the indignant response of the guests, the good has become the
enemy of the best.

ὅταν θέλητε might suggest that giving to the poor was merely an optional
extra. But in first-century Judaism it was more than that. The concern for the
poor expressed in Dt. 15:1-11 (which includes the recognition, echoed here by
Jesus, that 'the poor will never cease out of the land') had become the basis of
an extensive and carefully regulated system of donation to poor relief, which
included the mandatory 'tithe for the poor' as well as numerous opportunities
for personal charity.[12] The point is not that you may neglect the needs of the
poor, but that they can be catered for at any time: the opportunity will not go
away.

8 ὃ ἔσχεν ἐποίησεν is a compressed expression, with ἔχω used probably
in the sense of 'be able'; for such uses with the infinitive see BAGD, 333, I.6.a,
proposing that here the infinitive ποιῆσαι is to be understood. The use of ἔχω
rather than δύναμαι may be due to the thought of the perfume which the woman
already possessed, and therefore was now able to put to this special use. Others
would have their own forms of service to offer; this was the contribution which
she was uniquely in a position to make. προέλαβεν μυρίσαι is also a compressed
and rather awkward construction; for comparable infinitive constructions cf.
BDF, 392(2). The meaning is clear: she has acted in advance to anoint Jesus'
body for its still future burial.[13] We need not assume that the woman consciously intended this funereal symbolism (still less that she could know that
when in fact Jesus' body was buried his resurrection would anticipate and make
unnecessary the normal process of anointing, 16:1).[14] Rather, it is Jesus' special
knowledge of what is now about to happen which has focused his mind on the

10. For ἐν ἐμοί as a Semitic idiom (where εἰς would be more normal in Greek) see Gundry,
810. For the occasional use of ἐν + dative as equivalent to a dative alone, see BAGD, 261a, IV.4.a,
though Mk. 14:6 is in fact listed, perhaps less appropriately, under I.2 (p. 258b).

11. Compare the relegation of the equally proper religious observance of fasting for the
temporary period that Jesus 'the bridegroom' is present (2:19-20). Schweizer, 289, comments: 'It is
the time of the "bridegroom" (2:19), in which the religious duties of fasting (2:19) and giving to
charity (14:5 . . .) can no longer be given primary importance, because the presence of Jesus calls
for a kind of conduct which surpasses the standards of everyday life.'

12. See J. Jeremias, *Jerusalem,* 126-34.

13. D. Daube, *The NT,* 313, finds here the equivalent of the rabbinic terms *qadham* or
hiqdîm used for services rendered in advance.

14. J. Jeremias, *Theology,* 284, finds the significance especially in Jesus' expectation of being executed as a criminal, and therefore being denied the anointing which goes with a proper
burial. D. Daube, *The NT,* 312-24, discusses the anointing stories in the light of the Jewish concept
of *niwwul* ('disgrace'): it was an apologetic embarrassment that the body of Jesus had been buried
without proper rites including the customary anointing, and this pericope serves to deflect the criticism.

prospect of death and burial, and so leads him to find this added meaning in her act of devotion.

9 The formula ἀμὴν λέγω ὑμῖν signals a pronouncement to be noted. The woman's deed is to be remembered with honour, and that commemoration is to be specifically εἰς μνημόσυνον αὐτῆς. And yet she remains anonymous! Presumably it is the act and its symbolism (ὅ ἐποίησεν) which are to be remembered, rather than the identity of the person who performed it,[15] but the final phrase in that case remains curiously personal.[16] This phrase is sometimes compared with the eucharistic formula of 1 Cor. 11:24, 25; Lk. 22:19, but any suggestion that the woman's deed is somehow put on a par with Jesus' self-offering is rendered unlikely by the fact that Mark has avoided the eucharistic term ἀνάμνησις (probably already familiar in that context by the time he wrote) in favour of the more neutral term μνημόσυνον.

As in 13:10, the εὐαγγέλιον, which earlier in the gospel denoted the message preached by Jesus, has now become a message *about* Jesus, and here includes specifically the narrative of his last days. Moreover, it is now not merely a call to the people of Galilee, but a proclamation to be made εἰς ὅλον τὸν κόσμον (cf. 13:10, εἰς πάντα τὰ ἔθνη).[17] That Mark should have such a view of the future worldwide proclamation of the gospel is not surprising, but that he should attribute such an expectation to Jesus in the days immediately before his death (and in a context where that death has been the focus of the immediately preceding comment) is more remarkable. He wants his readers to understand that Jesus does not view the death which he has been so insistently predicting as the end of his life's work. Already he is looking beyond it, and while there is no explicit mention of the resurrection at this point, it is hard to see what εὐαγγέλιον there might be to proclaim if Jesus was to remain dead and buried. Not only is Jesus' death transcended by this pronouncement, but it is apparently taken up to be itself part of the εὐαγγέλιον, which is to include his pre-burial anointing. How much of this the disciples (or even the unnamed woman) might be expected to grasp at the time may be open to question, but Mark wants us to have no doubt that Jesus knows where he is going, and already views his approaching passion in the framework of God's redemptive purpose, the εὐαγγέλιον.

---

15. Myers, 359, suggests that she remains anonymous because 'she represents the female paradigm, which in Mark embodies both "service" and an ability to "endure" the cross'.

16. Gundry, 818 (following J. Jeremias, *ZNW* 44 [1952/3] 103-7), argues on the basis of OT language about remembering that the remembering is done not by people on earth but by God and the angels. The passage gives no hint of this interpretation, and the specific mention of the proclamation of the gospel *on earth* militates strongly against it. A further alternative, 'as her memorial *to me*' (J. H. Greenlee, *ExpTim* 71 [1959/60] 245, taking up the suggestion in J. B. Phillips's translation) seems even more remote from Mark's Greek.

17. Against the suggestion of J. Jeremias, *ZNW* 44 (1952/3) 103-7, that the reference is not to human preaching but to a single worldwide angelic proclamation of the gospel in the end times, see Gundry, 817-18.

The Priests and Judas (14:10-11)

Judas Iscariot is not a major player in Mark's drama. Apart from his listing with the Twelve in 3:19, he is mentioned by name only here and in the account of the arrest in 14:43-45, while in 14:18-21 the prospect of betrayal by one of the Twelve is raised without identification. Mark shows no interest in his motivation, and the money he received is mentioned only in passing as an indication of the priests' eager acceptance of his offer, not as the reason for his action. Judas is a minor but essential element in the history Mark records, but (unlike in the other gospels and Acts) does not seem to be the object of interest for his own sake.

A commentary on Mark may therefore be excused the routine speculation about Judas's motives. (His possibly non-Galilean origin, for which see on 3:19, provides a suggestive additional dimension, but hardly by itself a motive for betrayal.) But even to record the mere fact that one of Jesus' closest followers turned violently against him surely invites comment. By the time Mark wrote the betrayal had become an accepted fact of history, to be included in the story but apparently not requiring explanation, still less the lurid accounts of Judas's subsequent death which Matthew and Luke supply. The paradox of a traitor disciple is one which fits appropriately into Mark's robust and uncomfortable account of Jesus, the unrecognised and rejected Messiah. But unlike Peter, the other most spectacular failure among the Twelve, Judas merits no further attention once he has done what he had to do.

Judas' role is described as one of 'handing Jesus over' to the ἀρχιερεῖς. The verb παραδίδωμι is the one regularly used in the gospels to describe his action. προδίδωμι ('betray') is never so used, and only Lk. 6:16 uses the noun προδότης to describe Judas. In the light of the later Christian portrayal of Judas as the traitor, this choice of vocabulary is unexpected, and on that basis it has been argued that the original understanding of Judas's action was not as one of treachery, but rather as that of an 'honest broker' arranging a meeting between Jesus and the authorities with a view to promoting a constructive dialogue — a move which in the event went badly wrong, to Judas's dismay.[18] Such a revisionist view has not convinced many. It runs counter to the strongly negative tone of all the gospel accounts of Judas (the earliest evidence we have), especially of his role in the arrest of Jesus, which hardly reads like the arrangement of an innocuous conference; nor does it fit with Luke's use of προδότης as a functional equivalent for παραδίδωμι in his other references to Judas. While παραδίδωμι may not be the word we would have expected, it is hard to read it as other than a hostile act when the authorities to whom Jesus is to be 'handed over' are those who have been portrayed consistently throughout the gospel as his mortal enemies. See further on 3:19 and 9:31 for the connotations of the verb. By the time Mark wrote it had clearly become the accepted term to de-

18. So W. Klassen, *Judas*. See above, p. 163 n. 29.

scribe not only what Judas did but also more generally what happened to Jesus as well as to John the Baptist. Judas's role was only one part of the more comprehensive 'handing over' which Jesus had predicted for himself.

Why did the priests need Judas? After several days of public exposure in the temple area they could hardly have any problem in identifying Jesus even in a crowd (though apparently the men sent to arrest Jesus in the garden at night did need such identification, v. 44). A more likely reason has been indicated in vv. 1-2: in order to avoid popular resistance they needed to secure Jesus in a less public location than the temple area, and for that they needed someone who could inform them of his movements, in particular of where he might be found at night.[19] Only a member of the group who lived with Jesus could provide such information, hence the delight of the priests at Judas' offer. It is as guide to the arresting party that Judas will reappear in 14:43-44.

When Jesus is brought to trial in 14:53-65, we shall find the High Priest well informed about the supposed claims of Jesus (14:61). According to Mark's record Jesus has not publicly claimed to be the Messiah (indeed, he has specifically prohibited public use of such language, 8:30), though his actions have at several points implied such a claim; and his one public statement implying that he is the Son of God takes the veiled form of a character in a parable (12:6-8). It is within the disciple group that such language has been more openly used, and another part of Judas's service to the priests may have been to fill out a dossier of Jesus' words and actions which could be used against him at his trial, to prove that the incautious words of his followers (11:9-10) had not been unfounded.

10 For εἷς in the sense of τις, as in 10:17, 14:47, see BDF, 247(2) with the suggestion that it 'forms the contrast with the rest of the group'; the addition of the article (though it is absent in many MSS) removes εἷς still further from its numerical sense, leaving it as simply an indefinite descriptive pronoun; cf. the idiom, ὁ εἷς . . . ὁ ἕτερος (Mt. 6:24 etc.). It serves also to remind the reader of Judas's previous appearance in the list of the Twelve, 3:19. In vv. 1-2 we left the priests plotting Jesus' removal, and now the phrase ἀπῆλθεν πρός underlines the sense of an opposing camp, so that by this physical move Judas has also changed sides.

11 The brief account of Judas's move is phrased throughout in terms of his own initiative, to which the priests respond with surprised pleasure, rather than as his being 'recruited' by them. The hostility of the Jerusalem authorities has become obvious enough during the preceding confrontations in the temple to make it clear to Judas where his offer would meet with a ready response; Jn. 11:57 even indicates that Jesus had been officially declared a 'wanted man'. The unspecified amount of ἀργύριον (only Matthew mentions the sum) will not

---

19. The unpredictable reaction of the crowd is a sufficient reason for this need; the text offers no basis for Myers' suggestion (360) that 'the community has gone underground', and 14:49 weighs heavily against it.

be mentioned again, but its inclusion here reduces Judas, whatever his motive may have been, to the indignity of a paid informer. εὐκαίρως focuses on the problem of timing which the priests have already discussed in vv. 1-2, and which had made it necessary for them to find an informer who could help them to avoid a public arrest.

LAST HOURS WITH THE DISCIPLES (14:12-42)

With v. 12 we return to the outer layer of the 'sandwich' corresponding to v. 1a, as we are reminded that the festival of Passover, the immensely significant setting within which the final drama of Jesus' life is to be played out, has now arrived. The trap is ready to be sprung, and Jesus' repeated predictions of the rejection and death which await him in Jerusalem are about to be fulfilled.

But first there is important business to transact. Jesus has come to Jerusalem for the Passover, and he is determined that it will be celebrated, even if not in the normal circumstances. And the Passover is a corporate experience, observed as a group of family or friends come together to share the meal which recalls the basis of Israel's existence as the people of God. So the final phase of the drama, which will eventually become the story of Jesus alone against the authorities, begins with Jesus and his closest disciples together as they have been throughout the gospel. Ever since the first calling of the Galilean fishermen in 1:16-20, this has been not simply the story of Jesus, but the story of Jesus and his disciples, a close-knit task force who have travelled, lived, slept, and shared resources together. So now they come together for a farewell meal, but much more than that, a last Passover together, and one at which things will be said and done which will have a vital impact on the future effectiveness of the group when Jesus is no longer with them.

There is a continuity in the narrative from the preparation of the meal through its occurrence and the dialogue to which it gives rise and on into the garden to which they go from the guest room; here it is still the same group (with the exception of Judas, whose departure from the supper is assumed, not mentioned) who remain together until the violent interruption of Judas and his helpers breaks them up and leaves Jesus abandoned in the hands of his enemies, thereafter to stand alone. So these short paragraphs between vv. 12 and 42 belong together, as a record of the last hours Jesus was to spend with his chosen task force. It is typical of the paradoxical style of Mark's story that they finish not with a triumphant launch into mission but with utter confusion and defeat, and with the task force disbanded and demoralised while their leader is marched off to mockery and death.

While there is a coherence to the section 14:12-42 as outlined above, this section is thus still only the first phase of the passion story. In particular, there are three pieces of unfinished business in the the three predictions of betrayal and desertion which Mark has included in this section (vv. 18-21, 27-28, 29-

31), each of which will find its fulfilment in the events to be recorded in the rest of chapter 14. See the introductory comments on 14:26-31 for the way Mark has bound his narrative together with the theme of betrayal, predicted and fulfilled.

The Last Supper (14:12-25)

TEXTUAL NOTES

24. In a 'liturgical' text where assimilation on the basis of familiar eucharistic usage is likely, the shorter text, which is also the more likely text in Matthew, has a better claim to originality. In particular the theologically suggestive echo of Je. 31:31 in the adjective καινῆς which occurs in a different grammatical construction in Lk. 22:20 and 1 Cor. 11:25 would be a natural insertion, while there would be no good reason for its exclusion once in the text.

25. The οὐκέτι of A B and the majority text may have been an explanatory gloss (similar in effect to the προσθῶ/προσθῶμεν of D Θ), but it is perhaps more likely that the shorter reading without οὐκέτι (א C W etc.) was an assimilation to Matthew.

To refer to the last supper as a 'farewell meal', while it is correct as far as it goes, misses the main significance of the event for Mark. Here we have none of the lengthy parting instructions of Jn. 13–16 but a basic account of a Passover meal (with a surprisingly detailed account of its preparation) within which Mark records just two memorable statements by Jesus, the prediction of betrayal by one of the Twelve, and a symbolic interpretation of the bread and the cup which transforms the traditional symbolism of the Passover into something altogether new.

But in what sense was this a Passover meal? The debate occasioned by the differing statements of John and the Synoptics has been extremely complex, and the issue remains unresolved. At its simplest, it involves the apparently clear statement of Mk. 14:12, 14, 16 (with which Matthew and Luke agree, and which Lk. 22:15 reinforces) that this meal was τὸ πάσχα, contrasted with the implications of Jn. 13:1; 18:28; 19:14 that the Passover meal had not yet taken place at the time of Jesus' trial. On this basis it is generally concluded that the last supper of the Synoptics was the regular Passover meal held on the evening which began Nisan 15 (see notes on the dates on p. 548), while John's is a meal held on the night before the killing of the Passover lambs, the beginning of Nisan 14. Attempts to account for this divergence have traditionally taken one of four approaches: (a) to argue on the basis of calendrical differences that different groups in Jerusalem might be observing Passover on different days; (b) to reinterpret the statements of John so as to allow his last supper also to fall on Nisan 15; (c) to argue that despite appearances the meal described in the Synoptics was not in fact the Passover proper; (d) to postulate that Jesus deliberately and irregularly held his Passover meal a day early on Nisan 14, and that the Synoptic accounts, misled by the Passover nature of the meal, have assumed that the date was Nisan 15. Within each of these approaches (especially the first)[20] there are many variations which it would be beyond the scope of this commentary to detail. I have attempted such a survey in a 1986 article[21] which, while not covering more recent nuances, still gives a reasonable overview of the main theories on offer. Here I shall confine myself to outlining the view which I myself find most persuasive, though well aware that it is a minority opinion. The detailed notes on vv. 12 and 17 will explain how it relates to the text of Mark.

1. Evidence outside the gospel accounts points towards the 'Johannine' dating. The rabbinic tradition that Jesus died 'on the eve of Passover' (b. Sanh. 43a; cf. 67a) is echoed in the Gos. Pet. 2(5), 'the day before the unleavened bread, their feast', and 1 Cor. 5:7 ('Christ, our Passover sacrificed') would fit well with, though it does not absolutely demand, the Johannine chronology. Astronomical evidence strongly suggests that whereas Nisan 14 probably fell on a Friday (as the Johannine chronology requires) in A.D. 30 and 33, there was no date between 27 and 34 when Nisan 15 was a Friday.[22]

2. If, then, we accept that the last supper took place on the Thursday evening which began Nisan 14, it was a day in advance of the official Passover. Yet the case for its being nonetheless a Passover meal in intention, based on the Synoptic accounts, seems overwhelming.[23] It therefore seems most likely that Jesus deliberately anticipated the official date in his anxiety to hold a Passover with his disciples while it was still possible (cf. Lk. 22:15), aware that by the official date he would not be there to do so. The failure to mention a Passover lamb as part of the last supper[24] might then suggest that Jesus and his group, in common with Jews who had to celebrate the feast away from Jerusalem (and with those who continued to celebrate it after the destruction of the tem-

20. They include not only the well-known theory of A. Jaubert based on the evidence for a divergent calendar at Qumran, but also arguments from calendrical divergence (generally speculative rather than clearly evidenced) between Pharisees and Sadducees (D. Chwolson, P. Billerbeck), between Palestine and the Diaspora (M. H. Shepherd), and between Galilee and Judaea (J. Pickl, S. Dockx, H. W. Hoehner).

21. R. T. France, Vox Evangelica 16 (1986) 43-54. For a more recent survey see R. E. Brown, Death, 1361-69.

22. J. Finegan, Chronology, 292-96; G. Ogg in D. E. Nineham et al., History and Chronology in the NT, 92-96.

23. To the classic argument of J. Jeremias, Words, 41-62, may now be added a fresh examination in M. Casey, Sources, chapter 6, which confirms that Mark's account bears many of the marks of a regular Passover meal, and argues that the features not mentioned would have been taken for granted by Mark's readers, familiar with the regular Passover ritual, once he has signalled in vv. 12-16 that it is indeed a Passover meal.

24. The absence of a lamb at the last supper is of course merely an argument from silence, and M. Casey, Sources, 222-24, takes it for granted that φαγεῖν τὸ πάσχα can only mean 'to eat the Passover lamb', so that the lamb, while not mentioned as such, is presupposed. See further below on v. 12 for Casey's understanding of ὅτε τὸ πάσχα ἔθυον as 'while Jesus and his disciples were sacrificing the lamb'.

ple),[25] held the meal without a lamb, since the lamb must be slaughtered in the temple and the official date for the sacrifice there had not yet come.[26]

3. A similar 'Johannine' conclusion has been reached by many, who have then assumed that therefore the Synoptic writers were wrong in their dating. I would suggest, however, that the time indications in Mark which have been taken to indicate that he thought the supper was held on Nisan 15 (the 'official' time) do not necessarily do so. The point at issue is the Jewish way of reckoning days. Western commentators instinctively assume that the evening which *followed* the slaughter of the lambs in the afternoon belongs to the same 'day', but since the Jewish day was normally understood to begin at sunset it is in fact part of the *following* 'day'.[27] Thus when Mk. 14:12, which is the key text for the supposed 'synoptic chronology', sets the time of preparation for the supper on the 'day' when the lambs were sacrificed, this would, on the normal Jewish method of reckoning days, only be on the evening *following* the sacrifice if the preparations were made before sunset. If, however, the meal was prepared (as it was certainly eaten) *after* sunset, it would only be on the same 'day' as the sacrifice if it took place on the *previous* evening. On that understanding, Mark's careful note of time in fact places the last supper, as John does, on the evening which *began* Nisan 14, not on that which followed it.[28] In other words, he was as clearly aware as John was that Jesus held his Passover meal not on the official day, but deliberately one day early.

4. It should be noted that Mark himself adds weight to this 'Johannine' dating of the last supper by his comment in 14:2 that the chief priests planned to arrest Jesus μὴ ἐν τῇ ἑορτῇ. Unless they changed their mind, this rules out the view that Jesus was arrested on the evening when everyone else was eating the Passover meal, whereas the previous evening was still clear of the Passover celebrations.[29]

5. This understanding of Mark's text requires that not only the meal but also the preparations described in vv. 12-16 took place in the early hours (after

25. For the celebration of Passover without a lamb when the required sacrifice in the temple was not possible, see G. F. Moore, *Judaism,* 1.40-41. Cf. Schürer, 1.522-23.

26. It may not, however, be inevitable that a Passover meal held on Nisan 14 must be without a lamb. M. Casey, assuming that a Passover meal without a lamb is unthinkable (see n. 24 above), argues from the ruling of R. Joshua recorded in *m. Zeb.* 1:3 that 'premature' sacrifices of Passover victims in the temple on Nisan 13 did in fact take place in Jerusalem before A.D. 70, 'when there were so many pilgrims in Jerusalem that the victims could not possibly all have been sacrificed on the afternoon of 14th Nisan. It follows that everyone knew that many victims were sacrificed on 13th Nisan, and that this was accepted practice' (*Sources,* 224; cf. *TynB* 48 [1997] 245-47). D. I. Brewer, *TynB* 50 (1999) 295 (cf. 296-97) supports Casey's argument.

27. Gundry, 824, refers to a number of studies arguing that by this period Jews used a sunrise-to-sunrise method of reckoning days alongside the traditional sunset-to-sunset method. It is not, however, argued that this was the normal method, and in default of any indication to the contrary we should assume that the traditional method was used.

28. A similar view is outlined by L. C. Boughton, *TynB* 48 (1997) 257-59.

29. For Jeremias's attempt to evade this conclusion by translating μὴ ἐν τῇ ἑορτῇ 'not in the presence of the festival crowd' see above, p. 549 n. 4.

sunset) of Nisan 14, the 'day' when the official sacrifice was to take place. The meal itself is described in v. 17 as beginning ὀψίας γενομένης, a term sufficiently flexible (see below on v. 17) to allow for considerable prior activity after sunset. While a Passover meal was a very special occasion, to prepare such a meal for a relatively small group of people need not take more than an hour or two, at least if there was no lamb to be roasted, and when the room had already been 'prepared' in advance (14:15). Ex. 12:8 requires that the Passover meal be eaten 'during the night' (in contrast to a normal evening meal, eaten in the late afternoon).[30] The sequence envisaged for the events of that Nisan 14 (Thursday evening to Friday sunset) would then be as follows:

After sunset:	disciples ask about and make preparations
During the night:	Passover meal held; walk out to Gethsemane; arrest and preliminary hearing of Jesus
At daybreak:	transfer to Pilate; formal trial and conviction
Morning/noon:[31]	crucifixion
Afternoon:	official date for sacrifice of lambs.

This is, as mentioned above, what is generally regarded as the 'Johannine' chronology, but it is my contention that if Mark is understood to be using the Jewish method of reckoning a 'day' it also corresponds to his statement in 14:12, provided that the preparations for the meal took place in the early evening when Nisan 14 had already begun. In 15:46 (see notes there) he will presuppose this chronology in his account of Joseph of Arimathaea undertaking actions late on the day of Jesus' crucifixion which would have been inappropriate and probably impossible if that day had been Nisan 15, when the same restrictions would apply as on the sabbath.[32] It is on this chronological scheme that the following commentary will be based.[33]

Interpreters have generally assumed (and Christian art has taken for granted) that there were only thirteen persons present for this Passover meal, Jesus and the Twelve. This would have been a normal size of 'household' for a Passover meal (a minimum of ten were required for one lamb; b. Pes. 64b). But Casey[34] argues from the fact that the chosen room was μέγα (v. 15) that there must have been more, and that Jesus would not have excluded his other faithful followers, including women and, perhaps, children, from such an important

---

30. See J. Jeremias, *Words,* 44-46.

31. See below on 15:25 for the problem of the time of crucifixion.

32. J. Jeremias, *Words,* 74-79, lists and discusses a variety of other aspects of the Synoptic accounts of the events following the meal which seem incompatible with the Nisan 15 dating which he favours. While Jeremias suggests ways of deflecting most of these objections individually, their cumulative effect is more powerful than he allows.

33. This position is more fully set out and defended in my article in *Vox Evangelica* 16 (1986) 50-54.

34. M. Casey, *Sources,* 227-28.

'family' occasion; he estimates about thirty. It is by no means clear, however, as Casey suggests, that the δύο τῶν μαθητῶν sent to prepare the room (v. 13) are not themselves part of the Twelve (indeed, Luke tells us that they were Peter and John); μετὰ τῶν δώδεκα (v. 17) would then naturally be read as using the familiar designation ('a conventional technicality', Mann) to indicate the total group gathered for the meal when the rest of the disciples joined the two who had gone ahead.[35] And the fact that the betrayer is first said to be εἷς ἐξ ὑμῶν addressing the whole company (v. 18) and then εἷς τῶν δώδεκα (v 20) more naturally means that only the Twelve were present with him than that the focus is narrowed in the second statement. Mark's specific statement that οἱ δώδεκα came with Jesus to the meal strongly supports the traditional view.

A Passover was a symbolic meal with explicit interpretation. *M. Pes.* 10:1-7 details the traditional blessings over the cups and recitation of the Hallel and the answers given by the head of the family to the child's question (arising from the requirement in Ex. 12:26-27 that the significance of the meal should be explained to children), and something like this ritual was probably already normal in Jesus' day. It includes specific explanation of the elements of food eaten. It was not therefore surprising that Jesus, as head of the 'household', should offer explanatory comments and blessing over bread and wine, and it may be that Jesus did indeed first offer the traditional explanations before adding his own new pronouncements. But if so, Mark has not seen fit to remind his readers of what was already familiar. What he does record is not the traditional words but something radically new. The form of words varies in the three Synoptic accounts and 1 Cor. 11:23-26, presumably reflecting developments in liturgical use even by the time those texts were written,[36] but the content is impressively consistent: the bread represents Jesus' body and the wine his blood, and their reception of these elements symbolises the beneficial effects of his imminent death. The tortuous progress of subsequent debate about eucharistic theology should not be allowed to obscure this stark but profound symbolism. In the context of the Passover meal, the memorial of the rescue of God's covenant people from slavery and of the lamb whose death was a necessary part of that deliverance, these words gave the disciples a whole new dimension against which to set Jesus' insistent prediction that he had come to Jerusalem to die.

12 See above on 14:1-2 for the chronological terms used. ἡ πρώτη ἡμέρα τῶν ἀζύμων, while strictly it ought to mean Nisan 15, the first of the seven days of unleavened bread which followed the Passover itself, could also be used of Nisan 14, the first day of the total feast of Passover-with-unleavened-bread (Josephus, *War* 5.99 calls Nisan 14 ἡ τῶν ἀζύμων ἡμέρα; the

---

35. Gundry, 835, suggests that the two had returned after making the preparations to rejoin the group and to show them the way, so that it was in fact literally οἱ δώδεκα who arrived with Jesus.

36. I. H. Marshall, *Supper,* 43-51, discusses whether the Marcan or the Lucan/Pauline form of the words over the bread and cup represents the earlier form, and favours 'the greater originality of the Lucan/Pauline wording', though noting that 'the basic elements incorporated in the various forms of the sayings are primitive'.

removal of leaven from houses began on the evening which began Nisan 14, *m. Pes.* 1:1-3; for the designation of Passover as ἄζυμα cf. Josephus, *Ant.* 17.213; 18.29; 20.106).[37] Here it must surely be so used, since it is tied down by the specific reference to the sacrifice of the πάσχα, which took place on the afternoon which concluded Nisan 14.

The subject of ἔθυον is not specified. M. Casey[38] links it directly with the following clause so that the question is asked while *Jesus and his disciples* are killing their lamb in the temple. More commonly the clause is linked with the note of time which precedes it, and the imperfect verb taken as impersonal, providing a note to specify the day indicated, 'the day of the Passover sacrifice'. In that case, the clause does not determine whether the time of the regular sacrifice was past, present, or future at the time of the narrative, but merely that it was on that same day. On the chronological understanding outlined above it would in fact be still in the future, on the afternoon which concluded Nisan 14 (which modern time-reckoning would call the *next* 'day'). Luke's clause ᾗ ἔδει θύεσθαι τὸ πάσχα (Lk. 22:7) also suggests a ritual still to be carried out.

Was the disciples' question then premature? Not necessarily, because even if they expected to eat the Passover meal at the regular time the next evening, it might be prudent to make preparations in advance, especially since they were as yet unaware that the room was already ἐστρωμένον ἕτοιμον (v. 15). But if Jesus was deliberately intending to anticipate the regular date for the Passover, there is no reason why he should not have already taken the disciples into his confidence, thus provoking this question. The question 'Where?' was necessary as the Passover meal must be eaten within the city, so that their normal venue at Bethany would not do. Visitors to the city would thus normally have to arrange to use someone's room for the occasion. The reference to Jesus in the singular (ἵνα φάγῃς) rather than to 'us' is remarkable, and makes it clear that, even though shared with the Twelve, this is to be very much *Jesus'* meal.

13-16 For sending disciples in pairs for specific purposes cf. 6:7; 11:1. Even more clearly than in 11:1-3, the instructions given to the disciples are so detailed and confident as to indicate a prearranged plan: Jesus has a contact in Jerusalem whose premises he has arranged to use for this special meal. Indeed, it is not very likely, given the pressure on space in Jerusalem at Passover time, that a suitable room could have been made available without prior arrangement. We are not told where the question was asked, though the need to first go away εἰς τὴν πόλιν (and the description of the disciples' action in v. 16) is hard to square with Casey's suggestion that they were already in the temple (see on v. 12); more likely they were still in Bethany (the last narrative location, vv. 3-9) or somewhere on the way between.

ἀπαντήσει ὑμῖν (rather than 'you will meet') suggests that the man is on the lookout for them, rather than a chance encounter. He will be easily identi-

37. See further M. Casey, *Sources*, 221.
38. M. Casey, *Sources*, 222-23.

fied, since water jars, to supply domestic needs, were normally carried only by women (men who needed to carry water would use a skin rather than a jar) — apparently this is a prearranged means of recognition, to get them to the house of the οἰκοδεσπότης with whom Jesus had made prior arrangements. It is intriguing to wonder who this οἰκοδεσπότης was on whom Jesus could so confidently rely, since in Mark's narrative we have had no basis to suppose that Jesus had any supporters or even acquaintances in Jerusalem. This is one of several indications of the artificiality of Mark's narrative structure, and of the probability that, as John indicates, Jesus had in fact been in Jerusalem, perhaps several times, earlier in his ministry. At any rate, the οἰκοδεσπότης is someone who will have no difficulty in recognising Jesus under the title ὁ διδάσκαλος, and who will not take offence at Jesus' description of his own best room as τὸ κατάλυμά μου! Moreover, he will be found already to have made the basic preparations by the provision of carpets (ἐστρωμένον)[39] and presumably couches for the guests to recline on. It is only the meal itself which is left for the disciples to arrange.

κατάλυμα designates a place to rest or stay the night, sometimes a tent but also a guest room,[40] though in LXX 1 Sa. 9:22 it is a dining room accommodating over thirty people. The further description of the room as an ἀνάγαιον μέγα, a 'large upstairs room' indicates a relatively wealthy household rather than a single-storey peasant house, but any attempt to guess its location from Mark's text is futile.

17 The Passover meal must be eaten at night (Ex. 12:8; *m. Pes.* 10:1). If, as argued above, the two disciples prepared the meal after sunset on the evening which began Nisan 14, Jesus and the other ten would have joined them some two hours or more after sunset. ὀψίας γενομένης is a fairly elastic term, used in 15:42 for a time clearly before sunset, elsewhere for a time after the day's work (or sabbath rest) was finished at sunset (1:32; Mt. 20:8), but in 6:47 for a time which was well into the night, apparently not long before dawn since a specific mention of the fourth watch of the night follows (see on 6:47-48). The term thus allows us to envisage the supper beginning at some time between sunset and midnight (to allow time for the subsequent events which will be narrated before the approach to Pilate in the early morning, 15:1; the Passover meal could continue until midnight, but not beyond, *m. Pes.* 10:9).

18 Passover was a special meal, and the room provided was more luxurious and formal than would have been normal for the communal meals of the disciple group with Jesus. In such a setting it is appropriate that they reclined (ἀνακεῖμαι) for the meal, in the style favoured by the wealthier classes and for

---

39. See Josephus, *Ant.* 8.134 for the use of ἐστρωμένος for rooms 'floored' with cedar boards; with no other specification, however, the normal usage of στρώννυμι and cognates would suggest soft furnishings, particularly in speaking of preparing a room for a festive meal.

40. Its conventional translation as 'inn' in Lk. 2:7, in defiance of Luke's use of πανδοχεῖον in 10:34 where he *does* mean 'inn' and κατάλυμα in 22:11 where he doesn't, owes more to developed Western tradition than to ancient usage.

more festive occasions, though we need not necessarily envisage a full Roman *triclinium* arrangement. For the Passover meal, as opposed to ordinary meals, this was the accepted convention.[41]

Jesus has already talked of being 'handed over' to his enemies (9:31; 10:33), but no agent has been mentioned. The reader, of course, now knows what to expect (vv. 10-11), but for the disciples this is the first hint of treachery within their own ranks. The formal ἀμὴν λέγω ὑμῖν ὅτι emphasises the enormity of the idea, and the wording of the prediction with the phrase ὁ ἐσθίων μετ' ἐμοῦ echoes Ps. 41 with its complaint that 'Even my bosom friend in whom I trusted, who ate of my bread, has lifted his heel against me' (Ps. 41:9). The unnatural treachery experienced by the psalmist is a prefiguration of what was to happen to another righteous sufferer, as 'the Son of Man goes as it is written of him' (v. 21).[42]

19-20 For the easily understood but grammatically crude 'vulgarism' εἷς κατὰ εἷς see BDF, 305. All the disciples other than Judas apparently share equally in the combined incredulity and self-doubt[43] which prompt the question Μήτι ἐγώ; There is no specific focus on Judas in Mark's account of the supper, either by recording his question separately (Mt. 26:25) or by means of the Beloved Disciple's question and the offer of the 'sop' leading to Judas's departure from the meal (Jn. 13:23-30). Jesus' answer in Mark is quite unspecific beyond that it will be one of the Twelve, all of whom would have been dipping bread in the common dish with Jesus at the meal. Nor are we told at what point Judas left the group in order to gather his posse and bring them to Gethsemane. But apparently he left unhindered, so that presumably the other disciples remained in ignorance as to which of them it would be. In the absence of any mention of his leaving after v. 21 (as John says he did, Jn. 13:30), we are left to assume that he remained present throughout the meal, and was thus among those who received the bread and wine in vv. 22-24; the statement ἔπιον ἐξ αὐτοῦ <u>πάντες</u> in v. 24 strongly suggests as much.

---

41. J. Jeremias, *Words,* 48-49. The Fourth Gospel's description of the Beloved Disciple ἀνακείμενος ἐν τῷ κόλπῳ τοῦ Ἰησοῦ/ἀναπεσὼν ἐπὶ τὸ στῆθος τοῦ Ἰησοῦ (Jn. 13:23, 25; 21:20) presupposes this arrangement.

42. So J. Marcus, *Way,* 172-73. For the suggestion that Ps. 41 was understood as referring to the treachery of Ahitophel, which foreshadowed that of Judas, see, e.g., T. F. Glasson, *ExpTim* 85 (1973/4) 118-19. M. Casey, *Sources* 229-30, suggests that Ps. 41 has influenced the wording of Mark's account of Judas's betrayal throughout, and even contributed to the disciples' understanding of Jesus' resurrection. F. W. Danker, *JBL* 85 (1966) 467-72, suggests that this psalm 'has offered the ingredients in terms of which Mark 14:1-25 is narrated', finding echoes of it also in the anointing of Jesus and in the motif of 'hope of ultimate triumph of the sufferer'.

43. Gundry, 836, argues persuasively that the Μήτι form of question should here be understood as having its usual connotation that the expected (or hoped for) answer is No. But the fact that the question is asked at all justifies the term 'self-doubt'. M. Casey suggests an Aramaic original *'n 'nh* which was a negative protest, 'Certainly not me!' rather than a question (*Sources,* 230-31), but even if that were so we must interpret the text in the light of Mark's choice of a question form to translate it.

21 We have already been reminded that the rejection and death of the Son of Man is in accordance with Scripture (9:12; cf. the δεῖ of 8:31: see comments there). That may be all that is intended by the clause καθὼς γέγραπται περὶ αὐτοῦ here, but since the focus in this context is more specifically on his betrayal and the following clause goes on to predict the fate of the betrayer, there may be a more specific scriptural focus in mind, most likely that already alluded to in v. 18, the typology of the treacherous friend in Ps. 41.[44] M. Casey suggests that another text in mind may have been a verse from the Hallel which would be sung at this Passover meal, 'Precious in the sight of the LORD is the death of his faithful ones' (Ps. 116:15).[45] ὑπάγω, in itself a fairly neutral word for 'going away',[46] is used here as a functional equivalent to the following παραδίδοται, summarising the fate which has been outlined in the earlier passion predictions (and perhaps intended to remind us of Jesus' prediction in v. 7, ἐμὲ οὐ πάντοτε ἔχετε). The fate of the betrayer is not spelled out, but the impact of οὐαί together with the clause καλὸν αὐτῷ εἰ οὐκ ἐγεννήθη, is vivid enough. Even though Mark will tell us nothing later of Judas's subsequent fate (contrast Mt. 27:3-5; Acts 1:18-19), there is no suggestion that his treachery, even though 'according to Scripture', was anything but a culpable[47] and irrevocable decision. The use of διά rather than ὑπό for Judas's agency may be intended to indicate that his action was not simply his own, but part of a divine plan; but that does not lessen his responsibility for it. The double use of ὁ ἄνθρωπος ἐκεῖνος strikingly maintains the anonymity of Jesus' prediction.

22 Mark's account of Jesus' actions and words over the bread and the cup, from which the Christian rite of the Lord's Supper is derived, is the shortest and most basic of the four in the NT (the Synoptic Gospels and 1 Cor. 11:23-26), assuming the authenticity of the longer text in Lk. 22:19-20. It is thus the more noticeable that it nonetheless contains all the key 'eucharistic' verbs (λαμβάνω, εὐλογέω/εὐχαριστέω, κλάω, δίδωμι), on which see on 6:31-44 above, together with the interpretative words identifying the symbolism of both bread and cup. There is no explicit command to 'eat' and 'drink' in Mark as there is in Matthew, but both may reasonably be understood to be subsumed under the λάβετε which follows the giving of the bread and the statement that they all drank from the cup. Nor does Mark include the command τοῦτο ποιεῖτε εἰς τὴν ἐμὴν ἀνάμνησιν which occurs in both Luke and Paul, but by the time his gospel was written this would have been taken for granted on the basis of regular liturgical experience. The focus of the ac-

---

44. So J. Marcus, *Way,* 173.

45. M. Casey, *Sources,* 233.

46. In the Fourth Gospel it occurs several times of Jesus 'going' to his death in accordance with God's will, but this is the only such use in the Synoptic Gospels. M. Casey, *Sources,* 233-36, derives it from the Aramaic and Hebrew 'zl (go away, disappear), which is sometimes used of dying.

47. See above on vv. 10-11 for W. Klassen's theory that Judas acted in good faith and for the best. It seems that Mark does not share this view.

count as Mark presents it, however, falls not on liturgical prescription nor on 'memory' as such but rather on the symbolism of Jesus' death ὑπὲρ πολλῶν (vv. 22-24) and on the eschatological dimension (v. 25). It would have been these aspects of Jesus' words which most immediately affected the disciples at the time, and it is that immediate relevance in the original Passover context that Mark has chosen to emphasise as he tells the story of Jesus' last meal with his disciples, rather than its role as the basis for Christian eucharistic worship.

The ἄρτος is the unleavened bread of the Passover meal.[48] Jesus, as host, naturally took it, blessed it, and broke it, these being the normal actions of the father at a family meal. The 'blessing' (εὐλογέω) is not a special act of consecration (note that the parallel verb in v. 23 is εὐχαριστέω, which could not have that connotation), but was presumably the regular 'grace', 'Blessed are you, Lord our God, king of the world, who bring forth bread from the earth'. The 'giving thanks' for the cup in v. 24 would then take a similar form, referring to God's 'creation of the fruit of the vine'.[49] But further words followed.

The unleavened bread, together with the Passover lamb and the bitter herbs, was one of the items over which interpretative words must be spoken as part of the Passover ceremony, the specific point of the symbolism being 'because our fathers were redeemed from Egypt' (*m. Pes.* 10:5). But the interpretative words spoken by Jesus are very different. While the symbolism of past redemption may be implicit, it is not included in the formula Mark records. In the fuller versions of Luke and Paul the phrase τὸ ὑπὲρ ὑμῶν [διδόμενον] points towards a redemptive significance, though in the present rather than the past, but in Mark this is left unsaid. The simple, stark words τοῦτό ἐστιν τὸ σῶμά μου leave the disciples to think it out, until the words over the cup in v. 24 supply the note of vicarious death.

The most obvious symbolism when broken bread is interpreted as the body of Jesus is the simple fact of death.[50] He has several times predicted his death, and now he is symbolically enacting it for them, to leave them in no doubt that he has meant what he said. That in itself was a symbolism powerful enough for them at the time. But they must inevitably take the thought further, since Jesus has said λάβετε: the broken bread was being shared and

48. ἄρτος is not in itself determinative of the type of bread, but the Passover context leaves no room for doubt. For unleavened bread described as ἄρτος rather than specifically ἄζυμος cf. Josephus, *Ant.* 3.143, 256 (cf. 3.142 for its being unleavened); the LXX also uses ἄρτος for the (un-leavened) showbread. The fact that Mark does not specifically mention the unleavened character of the bread renders unlikely the view of V. K. Robbins (in W. H. Kelber [ed.], *Passion*, 26-28) that there is a polemical use of the imagery of leaven underlying Mark's account here.

49. For the equivalence of εὐλογέω and εὐχαριστέω in this context see I. H. Marshall, *Supper*, 41.

50. Gundry, 831, rightly argues that the use of σῶμα is a deliberate reference not so much to the *person* of Jesus as to his *death*. He suggests the translation, 'This is my corpse'. Cf the parallel use of σῶμα just before this narrative for the dead body of Jesus (14:8).

eaten, so that in some as yet undefined sense they were to participate in what his death meant. And the Passover context, with its normal redemptive symbolism of the unleavened bread, might already have started them thinking along the lines which later became the basis of eucharistic theology, without Mark's needing to record any further explanatory words at this point. Much theological reflection was to come later, but for the moment Jesus' words over the bread, even in the rudimentary form in which Mark presents them, speak symbolically but clearly of an inevitable death from which in some sense they were to benefit.[51]

I have used the language of 'symbolism' deliberately, without attempting any more precise definition of the force of ἐστιν. Since it is generally agreed that in Aramaic the statement of Jesus would not have had an expressed verb, the elaborate attempts in later eucharistic debate to determine the nature of Jesus' 'eucharistic presence' from the Greek verb are built on a shaky foundation. 'Symbolism' is as much as the words allow us to discover with confidence, and no more is needed to make sense of Jesus' words in their original Passover context.[52]

23-24 Rabbinic accounts of the Passover meal mention individual cups, but Mark's wording makes it clear that on this occasion a common cup was used, either because Jesus deliberately chose to do so or because the later rabbinic custom was not yet widely observed.[53] The specific mention that πάντες drank from the cup must include Judas. According to the later Mishnaic rules at least four cups of wine were drunk at a Passover meal. It was when the second cup was drunk (before the main meal began) that the full account of the Passover event was recited in answer to the child's question (*m. Pes.* 10:4), and it may be that it was this opportunity which Jesus took to speak of a new act of redemption now about to happen (cf. Luke's two cups, with the words of vicarious death spoken over the second, Lk. 22:17-20); or he may have added his special interpretation after the traditional blessing which was said over the third cup, the 'cup of blessing' which followed the main course. Mark simply does not spell out how Jesus' remembered words fitted into the normal structure of the meal.[54] The formula τοῦτό ἐστιν τὸ αἷμά μου alone would directly parallel the words over the bread, conveying the same sense of an inevitable death from which they were to benefit. But this time the nature of that benefit is not left to

51. I. H. Marshall, *Supper,* 87-89, discusses attempts to make the sacrificial imagery more precise by appealing to the Passover itself, to a covenant sacrifice, to the deaths of martyrs, and to the Isaianic Servant.

52. The following words of I. H. Marshall, *Supper,* 86, appropriately illustrate the danger of reading too much into the Greek ἐστιν: 'One might compare how a person showing a photograph of himself to a group of friends could say, as he points to it, "This is me".'

53. The evidence for Jewish custom on this matter is discussed briefly by I. H. Marshall, *Supper,* 63, who concludes that we cannot be sure of first-century practice.

54. G. J. Bahr, *NovT* 12 (1970) 181-202, gives a full account of the traditional structure of the meal, but concludes that Mark's account, unlike Luke's, does not allow us to locate Jesus' words at any particular point in it.

the imagination, but drawn out in the richly allusive words τῆς διαθήκης[55] and τὸ ἐκχυννόμενον ὑπὲρ πολλῶν.[56]

A number of biblical allusions suggest themselves.[57] τὸ αἷμα τῆς διαθήκης echoes Ex. 24:8, Moses' words at the original covenant ceremony at Sinai, which of course followed soon after the Passover and Exodus events, and consummated the process of the formation of God's people Israel after their rescue from Egypt. As the original covenant was sealed with a blood sacrifice, with the blood sprinkled over the people who were to be members of the covenant community, so a new covenant is also to be inaugurated by a sacrifice, and the blood shared among the people of the new covenant. While Mark's text probably avoids explicit mention of a *new* covenant as is found in Luke and Paul (see Textual Note), it is impossible to draw out the symbolism implied by the echo of Ex. 24:8 without using such language and thus bringing to mind the prophecy of a new covenant in Je. 31:31-34, and it seems likely that both Jesus and Mark would have understood Jesus' covenant language in that light. The phrase ἐν αἵματι διαθήκης in LXX Zc. 9:11 offers a further possible echo, again in a context which speaks of redemption in the return of Israel's captives after the exile.[58] But it is the words of Ex. 24:8 which most naturally spring to mind, especially in the context of a Passover meal. As God first rescued his people from Egypt and made his covenant with them at Sinai, so now there is a new beginning for the people of God, and it finds its focus not in the ritual of animal sacrifice but through the imminent death of Jesus. Here is the basis for a thoroughgoing Christian ecclesiology in relation to the people of God in the OT, but for the moment it remains at the level of allusion.

But that is not all the symbolism drawn out by Jesus' words over the cup. The 'pouring out' of blood is again the language of sacrifice (cf. ἐνέχεεν, προσέχεεν in Ex. 24:6), but the addition of ὑπὲρ πολλῶν brings in another suggestive textual echo, of the repeated πολλοῖς, πολλούς, πολλῶν of LXX Is. 53:11-12, again in the context of shedding blood and of redemption through vicarious death, as a term for those who will benefit from the death of God's servant. In Is. 53:12 his death is described in terms of 'pouring out his life/soul' (Hebrew *heʿrâ;* LXX παρεδόθη prosaically eliminates the metaphor). The phrase τὸ ἐκχυννόμενον ὑπὲρ πολλῶν therefore vividly recalls the language of the final section of the prophecy of the suffering Servant of Yahweh in Is. 53,

55. Against the common assertion that τὸ αἷμά μου τῆς διαθήκης represents a construction which would be impossible in Aramaic, see the sensible comments of M. Casey, *Sources,* 241, and more fully his article in *JTS* 41 (1990) 1-12.

56. L. C. Boughton, *TynB* 48 (1997) 249-70, presents linguistic evidence for what is in any case a fairly obvious implication of Mark's phraseology, that the participle ἐκχυννόμενον is future in reference, referring not to the pouring out of the wine at the supper but to the shedding of Jesus' blood on the cross on the following day.

57. For a detailed analysis of the OT background to this saying see R. E. Watts, *Exodus,* 351-62.

58. So, e.g., J. Marcus, *Way,* 157.

the point at which the redemptive significance of the Servant's death becomes most explicit.[59] Jesus' words over the cup thus pick up the concept of vicarious death which he has already presented in 10:45, with a deliberate further echo of that same remarkable passage in Isaiah; see further the discussion of the Is. 53 allusion at 10:45 above.[60]

Nor should we forget the Passover context of these words; the shedding of the blood of the Passover lambs commemorated the Exodus event when the death of the lambs was part of the divine provision for the rescue of the Israelites from slavery in Egypt, as a result of which they came to Sinai to be taken into a covenant relationship with Yahweh as his special people.[61]

How much of this tissue of OT allusion may have come to the mind of the disciples at the time may be left to the imagination; it is likely that the profoundly shocking idea, for a Jew, of 'drinking blood', and even more that of drinking the blood of their Lord, was so overwhelming that it left little room as yet for theological analysis. But even if they did not catch the specific echoes, they could hardly fail to recognise the language of sacrifice and to understand that Jesus was speaking of his imminent death as the basis of the redemption of 'many'. And the fact that they are invited to drink the wine which bears this symbolism makes it clear that they are among those 'many'. How much more widely the term might come to apply is a question which they could safely leave unanswered for the moment.

25 The second element in Jesus' words over the bread and wine is the eschatological dimension.[62] Introduced by ἀμὴν λέγω ὑμῖν, this is a pronouncement meant to be noticed. Like the preceding symbolism of the broken body and poured out blood, this verse also emphasises that Jesus' life on earth is coming to an end: there is to be no more drinking of wine here.[63] But this verse also now looks beyond the imminent death to a 'day' when Jesus will drink τὸ γένημα τῆς ἀμπέλου (the phrase used in the traditional thanksgiving for wine) again. And this will be not merely a restoration of the status quo; rather, the

---

59. See my *Jesus and the OT,* 120-23, for a fuller analysis of the allusion and its significance. Also my *Jesus and the OT,* 244 n. 18, against the suggestion that *he‘râ* in Is. 53:12 means 'laid bare' rather than 'poured out'.

60. J. Jeremias, *Theology,* 291, concludes: 'Without Isa. 53 the eucharistic words remain incomprehensible.' The full discussion by R. E. Watts, *Exodus,* 354-62, strongly supports this verdict.

61. This aspect of the symbolism is rightly emphasised by Mann, 575.

62. 'The word "until" . . . is indelibly inscribed on the banner that stands over every Lord's Supper' (Anderson, 315).

63. J. Jeremias (followed by numerous commentators) describes this saying as an 'avowal of abstinence' (*Words,* 207-18). But the emphasis in context is surely on the positive theme of a future feasting rather than on the negative element of 'abstaining'. Against the idea of a 'vow' here see J. A. Ziesler, *Colloquium* 5/1 (1972) 12-14 (response by D. Palmer, *Colloquium* 5/2 [1973] 38-41, and reply by Ziesler, *Colloquium* 6/1 [1973] 49-50). The οὐκέτι with future tense also renders Jeremias's conclusion that Jesus did not drink the wine at the last supper improbable (see Gundry, 833). That he abstained in order to 'intercede for his deluded people' is an unsupported speculation. For a general survey of the debate over Jeremias's view see A. M. Ambrozic, *Kingdom,* 191-95.

571

wine will be καινός, and the situation will be that of the βασιλεία τοῦ θεοῦ. Previous references to the βασιλεία τοῦ θεοῦ have envisaged a state of affairs already coming into existence through Jesus' earthly ministry (see discussion on 1:15, and the references to entering or receiving the βασιλεία τοῦ θεοῦ in 10:15, 23-25), but here the perspective is still clearly future, 'when God has established his reign'.[64] The kingship of God whose arrival Jesus has already announced is not yet fully in operation; cf. the expectation in 9:1 that people were yet to see that it had come ἐν δυνάμει, and the expectation fostered in 4:30-32 that its full development was to be a gradual process. When Jesus drinks wine again it will be in a situation where God's kingship is more fully realised than was yet in evidence at that Passover meal before Jesus' death.

The words of this verse are not specific with regard to the time envisaged. The reference to 'new wine' may indicate the expectation of the 'messianic banquet' when God will have made all things new (see, e.g., Is. 25:6-9; *1 Enoch* 62:13-16; *2 Bar.* 29:5-8; 1QSa[28a] 2:11-22; Mt. 8:11-12; Rev. 19:9). While one classic vision of the future banquet promises that the wine will be well aged and mature (Is. 25:6), the frequent references to 'new wine' *(tîrôš)* in the OT show that it was understood to be a mark of prosperity and good living (Gn. 27:28; Dt. 33:28; Jo. 3:18; Zc. 9:17, etc.); 1QSa[28a] 2:17-19 specifically mentions the drinking of *tîrôš* in the presence of the Messiah. 'New' was a key term for all that God was expected to do in the time of ultimate salvation.[65] So Jesus is looking forward to a good time coming, after (and, as vv. 22-24 suggest, because of) his imminent death. But the time and place are left unspecified. It is unlikely that Jesus' vision here extends, as Karl Barth suggested,[66] no further than the forty days after the resurrection when he would continue to appear on earth with his disciples, for in that case it is not clear why the wine drunk at that time (Acts 10:41 specifically mentions eating and drinking with the disciples) should be described as καινός. Most commentators have therefore assumed that ἐν τῇ βασιλείᾳ τοῦ θεοῦ looks rather to that heavenly authority into which Jesus is so soon to enter, 'sitting at the right hand of Power' (14:62).

Verses 22-24 and 25 thus present two contrasting and yet suggestively linked aspects of what is now to happen. The 'cup of death' (v. 24) and the 'cup of future glory' (v. 25) not only continue the Marcan contrast between the present aspect of the coming of God's kingdom, hidden in rejection and suffering, and its future glory,[67] but also link the two as part of a single purpose: it is through Jesus' imminent death ὑπὲρ πολλῶν that the salvation will be achieved which represents the consummation of God's kingship.

---

64. J. Jeremias, *Theology,* 98 n. 2. J. Marcus, *Way,* 156-57, finds in this verse an echo of Zc. 14:9 where the theme of Yahweh's future kingship is expressed using the phrase 'on that day'.

65. See J. Behm, *TDNT,* 3.449; A. M. Ambrozic, *Kingdom,* 189-91.

66. Cranfield, 428.

67. So A. M. Ambrozic, *Kingdom,* 200-201.

Prediction of the Disciples' Failure (14:26-31)

TEXTUAL NOTES

28. The UBS[4] text rightly omits mention of the so-called Fayyum Fragment (text in Aland, 444), a third-century papyrus which includes a version of these verses with v. 28 omitted. The fragment is in other ways a fairly free and radically abbreviated citation of the narrative rather than a copy of the gospel text as such, and the omission is more likely to be due to abbreviation than to a shorter text tradition. See further Gundry, 852-53.

30. The variations in the position of δίς in the MSS where it occurs indicate considerable uncertainty in the textual tradition, and the omission of δίς has significant support (ℵ D W and several Old Latin MSS), the more so since B, which has δίς here, nonetheless omits the first cockcrow in v. 68. But the omission of δίς is so obvious a harmonistic device to eliminate the double cockcrow (which occurs only in Mark) that it should nevertheless be rejected, since it is hard to see why the embarrassment of a second cockcrow should be added into the tradition if it was not represented originally.[68]

In terms of narrative sequence these verses form a bridge between the last supper narrative and the events in Gethsemane where Jesus' predictions of his fate begin to be fulfilled. But in the overall structure of Mark's passion narrative they have a more significant role. In vv. 10-11 and 18-21 we have learned of the treachery of one of the Twelve, but now that dire prospect is balanced by the even more far-reaching tragedy of the failure of the whole group to support Jesus when the time comes. The Passover meal is thus 'framed' by two predictions of betrayal.[69] Moreover, Jesus' prediction of the failure of the Twelve provokes Peter's ill-judged protestation of loyalty which in turn elicits a personal warning of his own imminent denial of his master. Both predictions will duly be fulfilled, that with regard to the Twelve at 14:50-52 and that with regard to Peter at 14:66-72. The whole narrative buildup to Jesus' trial and death is thus interspersed with the theme of betrayal and desertion on the part of his followers, predicted and fulfilled, as follows:

68. See, however, an interesting suggestion by J. W. Wenham, *NTS* 25 (1978/9) 523-25, that the whole textual confusion on this issue here and in vv. 68 and 72 is best accounted for by an original single cockcrow in Mark, as in the other gospels; the early interpolation of καὶ ἀλέκτωρ ἐφώνησεν in v. 68 then set in train all the other variations in order to make Mark internally consistent, eventually affecting even a text like B which had resisted the insertion. Wenham's solution has, as he says, 'an Occam-like simplicity', but fails to explain why an accidental insertion (itself rather weakly explained by 'the scribe's eye [having] fallen on the phrase καὶ ἀλέκτωρ ἐφώνησεν at verse 72', four verses later) should have been accepted into so much of the textual tradition when it created such an obvious harmonistic problem. (See D. Brady, *JSNT* 4 [1979] 43, for Wenham's second thoughts on his proposed interpolation.) Wenham is right to emphasise the remarkable confusion in the textual witnesses on this point, but perhaps his suggestion is a useful warning against assuming that textual corruption always followed a simply charted course.

69. So, rightly, Myers, 355.

A. 14:18-21   *Prediction* of betrayal by one disciple
      14:22-25   The Passover meal
B. 14:26-28   *Prediction* of desertion by all the Twelve, leading to
C. 14:29-31   *Prediction* of denial by Peter
      14:32-42   The prayer in Gethsemane
A^1. 14:43-49   *Fulfilment* of predicted betrayal by Judas
B^1. 14:50-52   *Fulfilment* of predicted desertion by the Twelve
      14:53-65   The Sanhedrin 'trial'
C^1. 14:66-72   *Fulfilment* of predicted denial by Peter.

The effect of this heavily weighted structure is to emphasise two themes which are of central importance for Mark's overall presentation of the story of Jesus, first the weakness and failure of the disciples (which has been so prominently displayed in Act Two, but now comes to its ignominious climax) and secondly the overall control of events by Jesus, the apparent victim. He has demonstrated by his repeated passion predictions that what is to happen in Jerusalem is neither accident nor defeat, but the fulfilment of the divine purpose, and now as each stage of the tragedy unfolds he shows by his accurate predictions that he is not being taken by surprise. What appears to be victory for the forces arrayed against him is in fact all contained within the pattern of his foreknowledge and purpose in carrying out what is 'written of the Son of Man'.

And just as Judas' betrayal was to be καθὼς γέγραπται περὶ αὐτοῦ (v. 21), so also is the desertion by the other disciples (v. 27). The basis of Jesus' predictions is not just his own personal foreknowledge, but the pattern already found in Scripture. The disciples of the Son of Man are bound up with him in the fulfilment of what has been written.

26   The singing of the 'Egyptian Hallel' (Pss. 113–118) was an established part of the ritual of the Passover meal. According to the Mishnah Pss. 113–114 would be sung before the meal and Pss. 115–118 after it (*m. Pes.* 10:5-7). Mark does not specify what the group sang before they left the κατάλυμα, but we may reasonably assume that it was Pss. 115–118, or at least a part of them.[70] If the verb ὑμνέω suggests to us something like the hymns sung at our Sunday services, we should take note of Casey's comment on the singing of the Hallel in the temple: 'This did not sound like Handel's *Messiah*. To our ears, it would be a strange, loud and raucous noise'.[71]

Unlike on previous evenings, the group did not return to Bethany, but went only as far as the nearer slope of the Mount of Olives, which for the purposes of the Passover festival was counted as within the boundary of the city even though it was outside the walls and overlooked the city across the Kidron valley. Judas knew where to find them, so this intention must have been agreed before he left the group (perhaps at the end of the meal). The Ὄρος τῶν Ἐλαιῶν

---

70. R. E. Brown, *Death,* 122-23, is sceptical of attempts to identify what they sang.
71. M. Casey, *Sources,* 222.

has already been mentioned as the place from which Jesus began his dramatic approach to Jerusalem as its king (11:1), and to which he returned to pronounce judgment on its temple after his claim had been rejected (13:3; see on 13:1-2 for the possible echo of Ezekiel's vision); it is thus an appropriate place for him now to spend his last free moments as he faces up to the reality of the rejection and death which he has been predicting.

27 The verb σκανδαλίζομαι is not in itself very specific, but the διασκορπισθήσονται of the following quotation gives it a sharper focus, and the event will fill it out (v. 50). In 4:17 σκανδαλίζομαι denoted what was apparently a terminal loss of effectiveness as a disciple, and a similarly drastic implication probably lies behind the use of σκανδαλίζω in 9:42-47 (see on 9:42). Here the 'stumbling' is serious indeed, but not terminal. They will fall to rise again. But that is what we and Mark's readers know with hindsight; for the disciples on the way to Gethsemane there was as yet no such reassurance (but see the next verse). As scattered sheep with their shepherd struck down, they faced a dire prospect. If the prediction in v. 18 that *one* of them was going to betray Jesus was enough to cause all of them to doubt their own ability to remain faithful, this pronouncement reinforced the message and left them no room for hope that Jesus was talking about someone else. The prediction this time is not of betrayal but of 'scattering', but the implication is that their loyalty will not be able to stand the strain of coming events, as Peter's indignant response makes plain.

This is at least the second time that the second part of the Book of Zechariah has been drawn on as a pattern for Jesus' passion — the third, if there is an intentional echo of Zc. 9:11 along with that to Ex. 24:8 in v. 24.[72] The same prophetic book which portrays the Messiah as a king riding into Jerusalem on a donkey (see on 11:1-10) also presents the rejected shepherd, described as Yahweh's 'associate' but yet apparently struck down by the sword of God himself (Zc. 13:7-9).[73] If these are two aspects of the same prophetic perspective,[74]

72. For the further suggestion by J. Marcus of an allusion to Zc. 14:9 in 14:25 see above. Marcus, *Way,* 154-58, finds echoes of Zc. 9–14 in every verse of Mk. 14:24-28, but several of them are at a very general level (Mount of Olives, shepherd, resurrection) rather than involving allusion to specific texts.

73. For Mark's πατάξω the Hebrew text and the ancient versions read an imperative, Yahweh's instruction to the sword to strike the shepherd. Mark's indicative is best explained not as a variant text but as a grammatical adaptation necessitated by the abbreviated quotation, which does not include the explicit mention of the 'sword' in the opening line of the oracle, to which the command is addressed. Since the imperative is addressed by Yahweh to his sword, to present it as a simple indicative 'I will strike' conveys the same sense in the most economical way. See my *Jesus and the OT,* 107-8, 241, 246. But see also J. Marcus, *Way,* 161-63, for the suggestion that Mark's use of the first-person indicative is intended as a deliberate counter to the military connotations which shepherd/sheep imagery often has in the OT by emphasising that the suffering of the shepherd comes from God himself, as in Is. 53. Gundry, 845, 847, however, asserts that the subject of πατάξω remains deliberately unidentified so as to 'keep God from blame', but does not explain how a reader who knew the Zechariah text should fail to recognise God as the subject. See further Van Iersel, 429-30.

74. I have argued this, drawing on P. Lamarche, *Zacharie IX–XIV* (Paris: Gabalda, 1961), in my *Jesus and the OT,* 103-5.

the passage forms a uniquely appropriate source for Jesus' interpretation of his own messianic suffering, and Matthew takes further the lead offered here in Mark by including also not only an explicit citation of Zc. 9:9-10, but also allusions to Zc. 12:10 and 11:12-13 (Mt. 21:4-5; 24:30; 27:9-10), all in connection with aspects of Jesus' passion as the 'Shepherd-King' rejected by his own people ('flock'). The importance of this motif in Zc. 9–14 for the developing Christian passion tradition has often been noted,[75] and it is already present in a less developed state in Mark. There is no reason to doubt that what was so obvious to later Christian interpreters would also have been clear to Jesus himself as he faced up to the reality of his mission as the rejected Messiah.

Zc. 13:7-9 is an enigmatic little passage within this wider prophetic complex, which envisages the partial destruction of God's people following the striking down of their leader, who is described by Yahweh as 'my shepherd, the man who is my associate'. The outcome, however, is not to be total disaster, as one-third of the 'flock' will be preserved and, refined through suffering, will again be recognised as God's own people. If the disciples knew the Book of Zechariah well enough, they might have recalled this happy ending to the prophetic oracle, but there is no such hope in the words Jesus here quotes, and in the foreboding atmosphere they are unlikely to have found any room for comfort in Jesus' stark prediction of their 'stumbling'.

28 But it is not all gloom. Just as Jesus' passion predictions in 8:31; 9:31; 10:33-34 have all concluded with resurrection after three days, and the cup of death at the Passover meal has been balanced by the future new wine of the kingdom of God, so now there is hope beyond the disaster.[76] Jesus' own resurrection has been mentioned sufficiently already to need no further explanation, but is simply taken for granted in the phrase μετὰ τὸ ἐγερθῆναί με. The change of verb from the active ἀνίστημι of the passion predictions (the future middle in 9:31; 10:34 is active in sense) to the passive of ἐγείρω is probably not significant. Both locutions occur freely in the NT, with no clear difference in sense, ἐγείρω being the more common, both in the passive and in the active with God as subject. To interpret the uses of ἐγείρω as emphasising the initiative of God while ἀνίστημι focuses on Jesus' own power over death is overexegesis, and there is no clear reason why Mark should at this point have wished to shift from the latter focus to the former. In connection with the resurrection of Jesus the two verbs are to all intents and purposes synonyms.[77]

75. C. F. Evans, *JTS* 5 (1954) 5-8; F. F. Bruce, *BJRL* 43 (1960/61) 336-53; idem, *This Is That,* 101-14; B. Lindars, *Apologetic,* 110-34; R. T. France, *Jesus and the OT,* 103-10 and ch. 5 passim; H. Cunliffe-Jones, *Word;* D. J. Moo, *The OT,* 173-224; J. Marcus, *Way,* 154-64; I. Duguid in P. E. Satterthwaite (ed.), *Anointed,* 265-80.

76. 'This first augury of the end of the story is arguably the single most important narrative signal in the second half of the Gospel, a kind of "literary lifeline" that Mark throws to the reader' (Myers, 365).

77. The passive form of ἐγείρω is sometimes used in an intransitive sense, as if it were a middle; see, e.g., 2:12; 13:8, 22; 14:42. In such uses it can be virtually indistinguishable from

The new note this time is the inclusion of the disciples together with Jesus in this future hope. After the damning prediction of v. 27 this is what they needed to hear. Even their 'stumbling' and the scattering of the flock is not to be terminal (in contrast with the fate of Judas, v. 21). There is a satisfying symmetry in vv. 27 and 28: the 'striking' of the shepherd results in the scattering of the flock, but his resurrection will result in their regathering.[78] Apart from the parallel passage to come in 16:7, the only other transitive use of προάγω in Mark is in 10:32, where it conveys the striking picture of Jesus striding ahead towards Jerusalem and death while his bewildered flock follow fearfully behind. After the imagery of shepherd and flock in v. 27 the verb (which could mean simply 'to precede'; cf. its intransitive use in 6:45) most naturally conjures up the picture of the Palestinian shepherd walking ahead of his flock into new pasture (cf. Jn. 10:3-4),[79] and this verse taken alone would lead us to expect a later account of the risen Jesus taking his disciples with him from Jerusalem to Galilee.[80] But in fact we find in 16:7 that it is not until they get to Galilee that they will see him. If there was ever an account of a resurrection appearance in Mark (see introduction to 16:1-8), it is likely that it was similar to that of Mt. 28:16-20, where (as 16:7 suggests) the disciples went to Galilee and met Jesus.[81] So the shepherd imagery of προάγω here is probably not to be pressed into a literal postresurrection journey.[82]

In the scheme of Mark's gospel the specific mention of Galilee is important. The province which was the home territory of Jesus and his disciples, and

---

ἀνίστημι. But with reference to the raising of the dead the regular passive meaning of ἐγείρω is more probable, especially since in many cases the active is used with God as the subject.

78. Against the suggestion of E. Lohmeyer that this verse looks forward not to a post-resurrection meeting but to the parousia see, briefly, W. R. Telford, *Theology,* 147-49; more fully R. H. Stein, *NTS* 20 (1973/4) 445-52.

79. This is so obvious an image that it hardly seems necessary, with J. Marcus, *Way,* 155, to derive it specifically from the shepherd imagery which recurs throughout Zc. 9–14.

80. C. F. Evans, *JTS* 5 (1954) 9-11, shows that both classically and biblically προάγω normally means to 'lead' rather than to precede, though Matthew is a notable exception to this rule. See on 16:7 for Evans's view that this saying is not concerned with a literal postresurrection journey but with the future mission to Gentiles (symbolised by 'Galilee').

81. On the basis of the prominence of Peter in this passage and his explicit mention in 16:7 O. Cullmann, *Peter,* 61, suggested that Mark originally included the appearance to Peter which is mentioned but not narrated in 1 Cor. 15:5: Lk. 24:34.

82. E. Best, *Following,* 199-203, accepting that προάγω here more naturally means 'go at the head of' rather than 'precede', concludes that the focus is not on a literal resurrection appearance as such but on the continuing life of Jesus at the head of his community ('Galilee' being used in a non-literal symbolic sense). But to recognise the symbolic significance of Galilee is not to exclude a literal return there. Van Iersel, 497-500, 505-6 (taking up his argument in *ETL* 58 [1982] 365-70), further evaporates any literal meaning by translating εἰς τὴν Γαλιλαίαν as 'in Galilee' and reading the verse as speaking not of a journey but of a continuing situation in the future when 'Jesus will go ahead wherever it is that people are willing to follow him'. While Van Iersel is correct in saying that by NT times εἰς can mean 'in' rather than 'into', he does not demonstrate that this meaning is required here, and if it comes down to a matter of preference, the priority must surely go to what was still the nomal meaning of the preposition.

in which all the stirring events and hopes of Act One have been located, remains the natural place for a future hope to be located. Jerusalem is for Jesus the place of rejection and death, and for the disciples the place of ignominious failure, but Galilee is the place of resurrection and restoration. It is perhaps not entirely by coincidence that Jerusalem is mentioned twice in Act One (3:22; 7:1), in both cases as the source of the official opposition which is ultimately to lead to Jesus' death, while in Act Three Galilee is likewise mentioned twice (14:28; 16:7) as the place where hope is to be restored after the disaster of Jerusalem.

29-31 The singling out of Peter as spokesman is in keeping with his role throughout the gospel, but here serves the specific purpose of preparing the reader for the story of his failure in vv. 66-72. Verse 31 shows that he did speak for the rest of the group, though his own protestation is specifically for himself even if the others are not prepared to back him.[83] This brash self-confidence contrasts remarkably with the self-doubt of v. 19, but two factors have changed the situation. First, the announcement of betrayal by a member of the Twelve took them by surprise at the meal, but now they have had time to reflect on it and to reach a settled determination to remain loyal. Secondly, the issue there was of active betrayal; here it is of the more passive experience of 'stumbling' and being scattered, and they think they are willing to face up to that.

The focus, however, is firmly on Peter himself, and Jesus' prediction in v. 30 is of his own special experience. Peter's self-confident promise is met by a solemn ἀμὴν λέγω σοι followed by a very specific time scale, σήμερον ταύτη τῆ νυκτί: Peter's bravado is to be as short-lived as that. ταύτη τῆ νυκτί is made even more specific by the mention of the cockcrow which is to be such a poignant feature of the story of Peter's denial. The crowing of the cock is traditionally the sign that dawn is approaching, and despite some remarkable claims for the regular nocturnal timekeeping of cocks in Jerusalem[84] the gospel texts do not require us to be any more specific than that. Attempts to make it more specific by finding a reference not to a literal cockcrow but to the trumpet call from the Roman barracks which signalled the end of the third watch of the night (the

---

83. Gundry, 845, asserts that the indicative σκανδαλισθήσονται 'suggests that Peter thinks the tripping up of his fellow-disciples quite possible', in contrast with his own self-confidence. Mann, 585, draws the same implication from εἰ καί.

84. Especially H. Kosmala, *ASTI* 2 (1963) 118-20; 6 (1968) 132-34, arguing from the habits of twentieth-century cocks in Jerusalem for regular and distinct times of crowing at about 12:30 a.m., 1:30 a.m., and 2:30 a.m.; on this understanding the second cockcrow to which Mark's text refers would be that at 1:30 a.m. D. Brady, *JSNT* 4 (1979) 46-52, compares Kosmala's observations with other claims and finds considerable variation, but a general agreement that as well as welcoming the dawn cocks are liable to crow several times between midnight and 3 a.m. He does not, however, find any evidence for the use of 'second cockcrow' as a recognised time indication (though see Juvenal, *Sat.* 9.107-8 for 'second cockcrow' denoting a time before daybreak), and thinks it likely that Mark, in referring to the cock crowing twice, is referring merely to the repeated crowing which could be expected about dawn. This would then lead naturally into the succeeding narrative at 15:1, where the meeting takes place πρωΐ.

watch known as ἀλεκτοροφωνία, see 13:35) have rightly been criticised as not doing justice to Mark's phraseology.[85] Jesus' prediction is that Peter will deny him three times before the night is over.

The point could have been made, as it is in the other gospels, by mentioning simply the crowing of a cock. Why then does Mark have the cock crowing *twice,* and later make a point of mentioning both crowings in his narrative at vv. 68, 72 (see Textual Note)? The simplest explanation, particularly for those who take seriously the tradition that Peter was himself the source of much of the material in Mark's gospel, is that Mark preserves the account in its fullest and most detailed form (as Peter himself would have remembered and repeated it), but that the vivid personal memory of the double cockcrow was omitted as an unnecessary additional detail in the other accounts. There is after all nothing improbable in a repeated crowing: even a single cock would be unlikely to crow once and then stop, and if there were others in the neighbourhood they would take it up.

This seems a more straightforward explanation than to search for some reason why Mark alone should have wished to insert a second cockcrow. One suggestion is that Mark is attracted by the δίς — τρίς echo, and finds significance in the comparison. D. Brady draws out this suggestion by the following paraphrase: 'This very night, before a cock has raised its voice twice to witness to its wakefulness to approaching dawn, you Peter will raise your voice not merely twice but three times, and not to witness to your wakefulness, but to witness to the wakelessness of your allegiance to me.' So understood 'the incident belongs . . . to a common biblical theme: man's rebuke by the lower creation.'[86]

What Jesus now predicts for Peter is worse even than the 'stumbling' and desertion in v. 27 which Peter has already so strongly repudiated. A threefold denial is not simply a momentary succumbing to pressure, but a deliberate dissociation. This is not merely weakness but apostasy, and no wonder the suggestion evoked an even more vehement (ἐκπερισσῶς)[87] repudiation of the idea. If desertion was unthinkable, denial must be more so. See on 8:34 for the only other use of ἀπαρνέομαι in Mark, and cf. Lk. 12:9 where the person who denies Jesus before others will be 'disowned' in the presence of the angels.

Peter's remonstration in v. 31 shows clearly that at last he (and presumably the other disciples) has grasped the seriousness of Jesus' insistent passion predictions. Jesus is going to die, and the alternative to dissociation may prove to be to be willing to die with him. Peter is realistic about the prospect, even if not about his own ability to go through with it.

---

85. See D. Brady, *JSNT* 4 (1979) 44-46; R. E. Brown, *Death,* 606.

86. *JSNT* 4 (1979) 54-55.

87. This seems to be Mark's own coinage (though cf. the even more superlative ὑπερεκπερισσοῦ/-ῶς in 1 Thes. 3:10; 5:13; Eph. 3:20). 'It is comparable in some ways to the fairly recent coinage in American English of "humongous"' (Mann, 585).

Jesus' Prayer in Gethsemane (14:32-42)

TEXTUAL NOTES

39. It would be easy to explain the addition of these words by a desire to express the content of Jesus' second prayer (as Matthew does more explicitly), the words themselves being derived from Matthew's account of the third prayer (26:44). But the phrase is very strongly attested here, and it is equally possible that it was omitted in D and some Old Latin MSS either accidentally or because Matthew does not have the phrase at this point.

41. The insertion of τὸ τέλος (and the subsequent change of ἦλθεν to καί in D etc.) are probably to be explained by the wish to fill out the stark and unfamiliar idiom of ἀπέχει as a sentence by itself. The omission of ἀπέχει (Ψ etc.) is an alternative solution to the same difficulty.

After the disturbing predictions of betrayal and desertion in vv. 18-21, 27-31 the reader is prepared for violent action. But first there is a pause, a period of quiet out on the hillside which allows time for prayer, and even for sleep. The time is not long, for there is a considerable sequence of events during that same night still to unfold before we reach the morning in 15:1. But for now there is a brief chance for the reader to take stock of what has been said at and after the Passover meal, and for us to observe how both Jesus and his disciples prepare for the ordeal which is shortly to come. The contrast is striking: Jesus, who has hitherto spoken in a more detached, third-person way about the coming suffering of the Son of Man, is now deeply moved by his awareness of the fate which has caught up with him, and engages in repeated and earnest prayer, while his three closest disciples as persistently fall asleep and are unable to share their master's vigil, just as they will soon prove unable to stand by him in the face of his enemies. Jesus' three times of prayer are balanced by their three periods of sleep, despite Jesus' explicit instruction to them to stay awake (v. 34).

So the Gethsemane scene is a study in human weakness, even in the weakness of the most trusted of Jesus' disciples. But that is only a subplot. The main focus is on Jesus himself, and more particularly on Jesus as he relates to his Father. We have heard occasionally of Jesus at prayer (1:35; 6:46), but without being privy to the content of his prayer, and we have twice been privileged to hear God himself speak about his Son (1:11; 9:7), but here we penetrate as closely as Mark will allow us to the heart of that mysterious relationship. It is summed up in the filial address Ἀββὰ ὁ πατήρ, the more striking because given to us in both Aramaic and Greek, and it is revealed as a blending of two wills, which pull in different directions but are brought together by the Son's willing submission to the Father's purpose. Here is the raw material for much later christological debate, but in the narrative context it serves to set Jesus before us clearly as the obedient Son, strong in his submission to suffering and death,[1] in

---

1. For all Mark's stress in this pericope on the reality of Jesus' emotional distress, it is his resolution to go through with the Father's will which is the dominant note; contrast the view of

contrast to the disciples who for all Peter's bluster will fall at the first hurdle. It is this extraordinary scene which probably lies behind the vivid account in Heb. 5:7-10 of Jesus' 'prayers and supplications, with loud cries and tears, to the one who was able to save him from death'.[2]

Mark's version of this scene, while very close to Matthew's, is a little more economical, in that he records Jesus' words in prayer only once (though with the addition of an introductory summary before the direct speech), uses the summary formula τὸν αὐτὸν λόγον εἰπών for the second prayer instead of the third where Matthew has it, and omits any specific mention of the third prayer. Luke is less expansive (unless Lk. 22:43-44 is authentic), and eliminates the threefold prayer and return as well as the special role of Peter, James, and John, so that the result is a simple absence of Jesus from the whole disciple group, who are all found asleep on his return. The essential prayer, however, is the same in all three synoptic accounts.

32 We know from v. 26 that their destination was the Mount of Olives, and there is no reason to doubt the tradition that Γεθσημανί (the name is otherwise unknown) was on its western slope, just across the Kidron valley from Jerusalem. This would fall within the extended boundary which on account of the overcrowding of Jerusalem at festival time was recognised as 'greater Jerusalem' for the purpose of Passover celebration (see on 11:11), whereas Bethany, their normal lodging, was outside it. On Passover night those observing the festival were required to stay within this boundary. On the chronological scheme followed in this commentary Jesus would not have been so restricted since this was still the night *before* Passover, but for him nevertheless to observe this convention would be consistent with his treating their last meal together as a real Passover meal even though held a day early.

χωρίον does not in itself tell us much about the nature of the place, though it implies an area of ground without housing; John's description of it as a 'garden' (κῆπος; the fact that he speaks of Jesus and the disciples 'entering' it implies a walled garden) is therefore plausible, and its name Γεθσημανί, reflecting the Hebrew and Aramaic for 'oil press', suggests an olive orchard, of which there were no doubt many on the Mount of Olives then as there still are all around the area today; oil presses were commonly located in the orchards where the olives grew. Any more specific identification of the location is a matter of tradition rather than of information given in the gospel accounts. Both Luke (21:37; 22:39) and John (18:2), neither of whom uses the name Γεθσημανί, indicate that the place was a regular rendezvous for Jesus and the disciples, which would explain Judas's knowledge of where Jesus could be found, though Mark's focus on Bethany has left no room for him to mention it before this point.

W. H. Kelber, *Passion*, 44, that in this scene Jesus is 'on the verge of retracting his passion predictions and close upon disavowing his vocation as the suffering Son of Man'.

2. For the relationship between the Gethsemane scene and Heb. 5:7-10 see R. E. Brown, *Death*, 227-34.

On both the previous occasions when Mark has depicted Jesus at prayer (1:35; 6:46) he was praying alone, having taken specific measures to get away even from his closest disciples. So now again he goes away from the disciples in order to pray. Prayer for Jesus (unlike some others, 12:40) was not a public performance.

33-34 It is thus the more noticeable that on this occasion, while the rest of the disciple group are left at a distance, the 'inner circle' of Peter, James, and John are allowed to share this intimate experience, as they alone have previously witnessed the special moments when Jesus' unique relationship with God has been revealed through his raising the dead and through the transfiguration (5:37; 9:2). It may also be significant that it is these three disciples specifically who have already declared their willingness to share Jesus' suffering (10:38-39; 14:29, 31); now they have their opportunity to live up to their brave words. On the Mount of Olives, as on the Mount of Tranfiguration,[3] these three will prove inadequate to share fully in the experience, but they will be able to register enough to ensure that this significant moment will be remembered in Christian tradition.

Jesus' words indicate, however, that it is not only as witnesses that he has brought them with him away from the others. The Son of God is human enough to need support at this testing time, for there is now a new note in Jesus' approach towards his death.[4] Elsewhere Mark uses ἐκθαμβέομαι as a particularly strong term for people's surprise or shock on seeing something remarkable and unexpected (9:15; 16:5; cf. also ἔκθαμβος in Acts 3:11, the only other NT use of this compound; but see the notes on 9:15 above); the verb contains an element of fear.[5] Jesus' 'shock' here, however, is not caused by an event already witnessed, but by the prospect of what is to follow. ἀδημονεῖν is more explicitly a strong term for distress: Jesus is perturbed as the fulfilment of his predictions approaches. A third strongly emotional term, περίλυπος, adds further to the impression that Jesus is being stretched to the limit. The LXX uses περίλυπος for Cain's state of mind before he killed Abel (Gn. 4:6) and Mark has used it in 6:26 for Antipas's remorse over his fatal oath. Its use here, however, together with ἡ ψυχή μου, is due particularly to its echo of the refrain in Ps. 42:5, 11; 43:5, ἵνα τί περίλυπος εἶ, ψυχή;[6] It may be that Jesus' eventual acceptance of the will of his Father in Gethsemane owed something to his acquaintance with that psalm, where a mood of despair eventually gives way to a calm trust in God:

---

3. For links between the transfiguration and Gethsemane pericopes in Mark see Lane, 521 n. 91, drawing on A. Kenny, *CBQ* 19 (1957) 444-52.

4. Mann, 588-89, rightly draws attention to Mark's use of ἤρξατο here to indicate a new element.

5. In LXX Ben Sira 30:9 it is used of the effect of a spoiled child on its parent: NEB translates it there 'shock', NRSV 'terrorize'. J. D. G. Dunn, *Spirit*, 19, summarises the sense as 'shuddering horror' (so also Cranfield, Lane, and Stock). See further T. Dwyer, *Wonder,* 178-79: 'a shuddering awe at an encounter with the holy'.

6. For the allusion see my *Jesus and the OT,* 57-58. See further R. E. Brown, *Death,* 154-55.

'Hope in God; for I shall again praise him, my help and my God.' At this point in the narrative, however, that acceptance is still in the future, and the emotional turmoil expressed in this powerful sequence of words is unrelieved. Indeed, it is a distress ἕως θανάτου, which could be either a strong term for a 'deadly' emotional upheaval[7] (cf. Jonah's being 'angry enough to die': LXX λελύπημαι ἕως θανάτου, Jon. 4:9) or, probably more likely in this context, refers explicitly to the cause of that emotion (distress 'at the approach of death'), as the death which Jesus has long been predicting now fills the horizon.[8] Under this dark shadow of apprehension Jesus appeals for his disciples' support in staying close by and keeping awake while he prays.[9]

35 προελθὼν μικρόν suggests that he remained within earshot,[10] so that Peter, James, and John, unlike the other disciples, were witnesses to the prayer, though how much they saw and heard before they fell asleep can only be guessed. The fact that the contents of the prayer found their way into Christian tradition may suggest that they did not go to sleep immediately, though it is also possible that Jesus himself talked about the Gethsemane experience in his post-resurrection meetings with his disciples.[11] Bowing with one's face to the ground (Matthew specifies that Jesus ἔπεσεν ἐπὶ πρόσωπον, and Mark's ἔπιπτεν ἐπὶ τῆς γῆς probably suggests the same posture) was a recognised attitude of supplication (Lk. 5:12; 17:16) or of worship on the part of those witnessing a supernatural event or experiencing the presence of God (Mt. 17:6; Lk. 24:5; 1 Cor. 14:25; Rev. 7:11; 11:16). It was not, as far as we know, a normal attitude for ordinary prayer, and serves here further to underline the depth of Jesus' emotion (though 'panic' [Gundry, 855] seems wide of the mark).

Mark's summary of the prayer in indirect speech uses different language from the direct speech of v. 36, in that the condition which is implied in πάντα δυνατά σοι is here made explicit in εἰ δυνατόν ἐστιν (which Mt. 26:39 includes within the prayer itself), and the imagery of the removal of the cup is rephrased less pictorially as the passing of ἡ ὥρα. The repetition of the term ἡ ὥρα in 14:41 will thus make it clear that this request has not been granted. This use of

---

7. REB, 'My heart is ready to break with grief', conveys this sense well.

8. J. W. Holleran, *Gethsemane,* 14-16 (following J. Héring in W. C. Van Unnik (ed.), *Neotestamentica et Patristica,* 65-69), discusses a number of interpretations of ἕως θανάτου, and accepts Héring's preference for the sense 'so sad I want to die'; Héring justifies this in the light of Jesus' subsequent prayer to be spared death by arguing that it is the cross which Jesus wants to avoid, so that a peaceful death now in Gethsemane would be far better. See also R. E. Brown, *Death,* 155-56.

9. R. E. Brown, *Death,* 156-57, discusses various other views of why Jesus wanted them to stay awake. Brown favours an eschatological note similar to the call to watch in the parable of the porter (13:33-37).

10. It was normal to pray aloud, even when alone; see Gundry, 864. For the distance involved cf. Lk. 22:41, ὡσεὶ λίθου βολήν.

11. For some sensible comments on what he calls the '"village atheist" objection' that disciples who were both asleep and at a distance could not have known what Jesus said, see R. E. Brown, *Death,* 174.

ἡ ὥρα to refer to Jesus' passion has a Johannine ring (the term is used similarly in the 'Johannine Gethsemane' account, Jn. 12:27), but to speak of deliverance from 'the hour' is not unnatural in this context where the predicted event is imminent.[12] εἰ δυνατόν ἐστιν further underlines the impression created by Jesus' predictions and the references to the fulfilment of Scripture (especially 14:21, to be repeated in v. 49) that Jesus' willing submission is nonetheless to be seen in the context of an already declared divine purpose.

36 There is general agreement that to address God as 'Father' was both Jesus' normal practice in prayer (the only exception in the gospel tradition is Mk. 15:34; see the comments there) and was distinctive of him, not a matter of general Jewish piety at the time.[13] Here we have, uniquely in the gospels, the Aramaic term Ἀββά (an emphatic vocative)[14] recorded as well as its Greek equivalent.[15] The much-discussed contention of J. Jeremias that an address to God as Ἀββά is unparalleled in Jewish literature, and marks a unique sense of intimacy with God, remains valid, even if the issue has been clouded by the frequent assertion by preachers that this familiar term equates to the English 'Daddy'. J. Barr's argument that 'Abba is not Daddy'[16] is well taken, in that there is nothing childish about the special relationship implied (it was also used, for example, by disciples addressing their rabbi), but that was not Jeremias's point. The term conveys the respectful intimacy of a son in a patriarchal family. And in that sense Jesus' use of this form of address to God is striking and unparalleled,[17] until it was taken over from him by his followers: Paul introduces Ἀββά as the sign of an amazing and hitherto inadmissible relationship of the individual believer with God (Rom. 8:15; Gal. 4:6).

12. See Gundry, 868, for cautions against taking ὥρα here as an eschatological technical term. Contra R. E. Brown, *Death*, 167-68.

13. J. Jeremias, *Abba*, 15-67 (published in English as *Prayers*, 11-65; see especially 54-62); idem, *Theology*, 61-68; J. D. G. Dunn, *Spirit*, 21-26.

14. So R. E. Brown, *Death*, 172, summarising the findings of J. A. Fitzmyer.

15. For the use of the Greek nominative with article in place of the more normal vocative πάτερ see BDF, 147. J. W. Holleran, *Gethsemane*, 24-26, discusses whether we should envisage Jesus himself using both the Aramaic and the Greek together, but concludes that Jesus is likely to have used Aramaic alone and that the dual expression Ἀββά ὁ πατήρ, which occurs as a prayer formula in the identical form in Rom. 8:15 and Gal. 4:6, is more likely to have originated in the early Christian communities.

16. J. Barr, *JTS* 39 (1988) 28-47.

17. Jews did, of course, speak about certain people as 'sons of God', usually in the plural but occasionally in the singular, including a few special rabbis: the evidence is conveniently summarised in G. Vermes, *Jew*, 194-200, 206-10. But Vermes' further attempt to find parallels for Jesus' use of Ἀββά as a form of address in prayer (210-11) is singularly unproductive. Vermes has taken the argument further in *Judaism*, 39-43, but the examples he offers are of the plural 'Our Father' or of statements about God, not of the vocative used by an individual. There is a vocative address to God as πάτερ in Ben Sira 23:1, 4, as part of a collection of titles, not as an address on its own, and a single instance in Wis. 14:3, but these, as Jeremias points out, represent Diaspora usage, under 'the influence of the Greek world' (*Theology*, 63). The debate over Jeremias's claim is well summarised by R. E. Brown, *Death*, 172-75.

Jesus' appeal to his Father is based on the twin assumptions that on the one hand πάντα δυνατά σοι, but on the other hand God has a will which is to be accepted rather than altered by prayer. It is the blending of these two convictions which gives all prayer its mysterious dynamic, and frustrates any 'quick-fix' approach. The reader who remembers 11:22-25 will be aware that all the conditions for effective prayer have been met, so that Jesus' deliverance *is* possible.[18] But it is not for us, or even for Jesus as God's Son, to assume that the God who 'can' answer every request will necessarily be willing to do so. Prayer, so understood, consists not in changing God's mind but in finding our own alignment with God's will. Where our desire is not in line with God's purpose, it is the former which must give way: οὐ τί ἐγὼ θέλω ἀλλὰ τί σύ.[19] If that is true for ὁ υἱός μου ὁ ἀγαπητός (1:11; 9:7), how much more for the rest of us.[20] It is in Jesus' instinctive acceptance of this sense of priority that he will find his strength to go through the next twenty-four hours. To that extent, though not in the way he would have wished, his prayer was answered.

The specific (and ultimately unsuccessful) request is expressed as the removal of τὸ ποτήριον τοῦτο, and its removal is not now the impersonal παρέρχομαι ἀπό of v. 35, but the direct action of the Father in taking it away (παραφέρω ἀπό).[21] The image of the cup of suffering and judgment is familiar from 10:38-39 (see notes there).[22] It is that metaphorical usage which provides the background for Jesus' prayer rather than the ποτήριον of v. 23, which was a literal cup, however symbolic its contents became, and was offered to the disciples to drink, not given to Jesus. The fact that the cup of suffering is pictured as being given to Jesus by his Father (who is thus able also to take it away) strikingly expresses the conviction which underlies Mark's narrative of the passion, that God controls the whole process culminating in Jesus' death. At the same time the fact that Jesus, who in 10:38-39 could speak with apparent calm of the cup in store for him, is now so appalled at the prospect that he begs to be rid of it vividly conveys the reality and human cost of that passion.[23] This is in strong

18. S. E. Dowd, *Prayer,* 151-58, discusses the Gethsemane scene in the light of the teaching on prayer in 11:22-25, emphasising the problem of theodicy that 'the God who wills to move the mountain does not always will to take away the cup'.

19. For τί used as a relative see BDF, 298(4); Mann, 591, speaks of Mark's 'near impatience with grammar' here. The use of οὐ rather than μή means that the elliptical clauses should be read as indicative rather than imperative, 'I seek' or 'it will be' rather than 'let it be'; but the sense of acceptance is much the same as if it had been imperative. Cf. S. E. Dowd, *Prayer,* 133 n. 1 and 156: 'The issue is not what I will but what you will'.

20. R. E. Brown, *Death,* 175-78, discusses this clause in the light of the Lord's Prayer.

21. Cf. Is. 51:22 where God himself takes away from Jerusalem 'the cup of staggering, . . . the bowl of my wrath'.

22. R. E. Brown, *Death,* 168-70, wishes to separate the ideas of suffering and of judgment, and sees the former as the primary focus here. See further S. R. Garrett, *Temptations,* 93, who finds in the cup an image of eschatological judgment.

23. For some sensible comments on the apparent conflict between Jesus' awareness of God's purpose and his prayer to be spared it see R. E. Brown, *Death,* 166-67.

contrast with idealised portrayals of martyrs who go gladly to their death.[24] The Jesus who accepts his Father's will does not do so with a 'docetic' indifference but with a mental as well as physical agony which will reach its horrifying climax in the cry from the cross in 15:34.[25]

37-38 That all three disciples could so quickly have gone to sleep despite Jesus' specific request to stay awake (v. 34) — and could within a short time go to sleep twice more after being awakened — may perhaps be explained by the late hour (and a good meal?) and by the extreme tension under which they have been living, but probably we should not be looking so much for verisimilitude as for the literary function of the repeated sleep of the disciples as a contrast to Jesus' repeated prayer and wakefulness. The situation thus gives rise to words of rebuke and warning which no doubt Mark expected his readers to take as applicable to themselves as well as to the first disciples. (Cf. 13:35, 37 for the call γρηγορεῖτε so as not to be found sleeping, 13:36, though the reference there is to an eschatological coming and the sleep is part of a parabolic image.)[26]

The rebuke specifically to Peter[27] reminds us of his recent protestation of loyalty to death (vv. 29-31): he has not begun well. The use of ἰσχύω rather than δύναμαι implies a lack of strength or stamina, a particularly wounding charge for the self-confident Peter. But the other disciples, too, are clearly implicated, and the warnings that follow in v. 38 are all in the plural. Editors differ over the punctuation of v. 38: if a comma is placed after γρηγορεῖτε but not after προσεύχεσθε the following ἵνα clause becomes the subject of the prayer (so Gundry, 872), whereas if a comma is placed only after προσεύχεσθε the ἵνα clause becomes the purpose of the combined command γρηγορεῖτε καὶ προσεύχεσθε. But since the wakefulness and the prayer are in any case closely linked, the different ways of construing the syntax make little difference to the sense. It was in both wakefulness and prayer that the disciples had failed.

This is Mark's only use of the noun πειρασμός, but for the verb see on 1:13; the range of meaning discussed there applies to the noun, too. The issue

---

24. 'There is no romance in martyrdom, only in martyrologies' (Myers, 366).

25. S. R. Garrett, *Temptations,* 104-15, argues against R. E. Brown that the ποτήριον is to be understood as a 'cup of wrath', not in the sense that Jesus is himself the object of God's wrath, but that he will experience on the cross what that wrath is like.

26. The use of similar language does not mean, *pace* Kelber, *Passion,* 48-49, that the disciples' sleeping in Gethsemane must necessarily be seen to have 'eschatological repercussions'. The eschatological connections of this language are, however, emphasised by S. R. Garrett, *Temptations,* 91-94.

27. It is sometimes suggested (e.g., by W. H. Kelber, *Passion,* 54, following H. B. Swete) that Jesus' use of the name Σίμων rather than Πέτρος is itself a rebuke, indicating that he has failed to live up to the strength implied in his 'apostolic name'. But the nickname has not been explained in Mark (as it is in Mt. 16:18), and as this is the only time in Mark's gospel when Jesus addresses him by name, the choice of Σίμων rather than Πέτρος is hardly significant (in Mt. 17:25, after the nickname Πέτρος has been given and explained, the vocative Σίμων is still used with no pejorative purpose).

of whether 'temptation' or 'testing/trial' best conveys the sense in English is very much the same here as in the ongoing discussion with regard to the translation of the Lord's Prayer, whose terminology of being 'led into' πειρασμός is similar to the locution ἔρχομαι εἰς πειρασμόν here.[28] What confronts the disciples at this point is both 'testing' in the sense of an ordeal which they will prove unable to cope with and 'temptation' in that the urge to run away will put their own safety before loyalty to God and his Son. It is interesting, however, that the object of their wakefulness and prayer is expressed not as finding the strength to withstand πειρασμός but (as in the Lord's Prayer) as keeping out of it altogether. With our English distinction between the two senses of πειρασμός we might have wished to be more nuanced: 'that when the test comes you may not be tempted to disloyalty'. But the breadth of the Greek πειρασμός allows a more concise if less specific expression.

The reason for wishing to be kept out of πειρασμός is expressed in the saying τὸ μὲν πνεῦμα πρόθυμον, ἡ δὲ σὰρξ ἀσθενής, which no doubt applies particularly to the disciples in their inability to stay awake, but is expressed in the more general terms of a gnomic verdict on human nature. The classical μὲν . . . δὲ . . . construction is uncommon in Mark, and gives a proverbial-type balance to the two halves of the statement. The πνεῦμα/σάρξ contrast which is so typical of Paul occurs only here in Mark, and does not carry the same theological weight. The σάρξ here is not evil, merely weak. But it may be too simple to interpret it as merely a Cartesian contrast between the material and immaterial 'parts' of a person; rather, the πνεῦμα represents the 'higher' aspirations of humanity at its best (for πνεῦμα denoting a person's 'inner self' cf. 2:8; 8:12) while the σάρξ is the 'lower' nature which is content to take the easy way of comfort and self-interest rather than pursue those aspirations.[29] So understood Jesus' warning certainly includes the physical weakness which has prevented the disciples from remaining awake, but also extends beyond purely physical limitations. R. E. Brown[30] argues that Jesus' words apply to himself as well as to the disciples: the purpose of his prayer has been to overcome his human weakness which shrinks from fulfilling the Father's will.

39-40 Having given an account both of Jesus' prayer and of his rebuke to the disciples, Mark (unlike Matthew) sees no need to repeat the details,[31] but uses the summary formula τὸν αὐτὸν λόγον εἰπών (see Textual Note). But the disciples' repeated failure to stay awake draws a further note both of explana-

---

28. See Mann, 592, for the view that both here and in the Lord's Prayer the πειρασμός has a specifically eschatological sense; this is not just any time of testing, but *the* Trial when 'all the conflicts of the ministry . . . were now coming to a single, inexorable point'.

29. For a survey of interpretation of the flesh/spirit contrast here see J. W. Holleran, *Gethsemane*, 39-45. See also R. E. Brown, *Death*, 198-99, with special reference to the use of this terminology at Qumran; S. R. Garrett, *Temptations*, 94-95.

30. R. E. Brown, *Death*, 199-200.

31. Gundry, 854, suggests that the imperfect tenses of ἔπιπτεν, προσηύχετο, and ἔλεγεν (vv. 35-36) are intended to cover the threefold repetition of the posture and the words of the prayer.

tion and of comment on their discomfiture (which assumes that Jesus has uttered a similar rebuke to that in vv. 37-38). The 'explanation' ἦσαν γὰρ αὐτῶν οἱ ὀφθαλμοὶ καταβαρυνόμενοι really only underlines their sleepiness rather than explaining it, but perhaps it is intended to remind us of the lateness of the hour. It is clearly not an adequate explanation, as the disciples are portrayed as feeling ashamed of not being able to stay awake. Their embarrassed silence recalls that of 9:34; once again the disciples are put in the wrong (cf. also 9:6, where they are silenced not so much by embarrassment as by bewilderment).

41-42 The third sequence of prayer and return is not narrated at all, but is taken for granted in the reference to Jesus coming to the disciples τὸ τρίτον. From his words we understand that the disciples have again gone to sleep. Jesus' words which run through from Καθεύδετε to the end of v. 42 are not easy to follow as a connected discourse. They read rather as a staccato series of utterances which seem to presuppose a lapse of time, or at least a change of situation, between the apparent permission to sleep and the call to get up.[32] The difficulty is commonly resolved by interpreting Καθεύδετε τὸ λοιπὸν καὶ ἀναπαύεσθε not as a command giving them permission to sleep this time but as either a heavily ironical comment or an indignant question; the majority of recent versions take this option.[33] On this interpretation τὸ λοιπόν is a surprising expression: we might expect 'yet again' or 'still', but τὸ λοιπόν more naturally means 'from now on' or 'for the remaining time'.[34] Hence the New Jerusalem Bible version, 'You can sleep on now and have your rest. It is all over.' This version indicates that Jesus' third return to his disciples is different from the first two, in that he has now finished praying and no longer needs them to stay awake with him. This interpretation gives a more natural sense for τὸ λοιπόν, but leaves unresolved the awkwardness of the almost immediate transition to 'Get up! Let us go!' Perhaps we are to assume that after Jesus' first words sounds were heard which indicated the approach of the arresting party and led him to countermand his permission to sleep.

The staccato syntax continues with ἀπέχει as a one-word sentence standing alone (see Textual Note).[35] Most interpreters derive its meaning here from

---

32. The OL MS k (Codex Bobbiensis) has restructured vv. 41-42, inserting 'And after a little while he aroused them saying' before 'the hour has come'; see Metzger, *Textual Commentary*, 114-15.

33. Gundry's suggestion (857) that it is an 'exasperated command' falls somewhere between these options.

34. The suggestion in BAGD, 480a, 3.a.α, 'Do you intend to sleep on and on?' is an attempt to fit the context rather than a recognised use of τὸ λοιπόν. Their alternative suggestion 'meanwhile', supported by a use in Josephus, *Ant.* 18.272, does not fit easily in context after two similar rebukes have already been given. In the suggestion of BDF, 451(6), 'So you are still sleeping!' τὸ λοιπόν is apparently represented by the 'so' rather than by the 'still'. J. W. Holleran, *Gethsemane*, 51, argues that 'so' can be an adequate translation for τὸ λοιπόν in the NT; so also R. E. Brown, *Death*, 208.

35. J. W. Holleran, *Gethsemane*, 52-56, surveys some of the many attempts to find a suitable sense in this verb in this context.

the common usage of ἀπέχω in the papyri for a financial 'receipt in full', and take it as roughly synonymous with the following ἦλθεν ἡ ὥρα, meaning something like 'It is enough',[36] or 'It is all over'.[37] This would then be Jesus' acceptance that the 'cup' is now about to be presented to him. Such a metaphorical use of ἀπέχω, with no expressed object, is unusual,[38] and a more literal sense has been suggested here with Judas as the subject: 'he has been paid' (and so is now ready to act).[39] But that seems too much to assume in a context where Judas has not been directly in view (he is not mentioned until the next verse). The same objection applies to Gundry's view that it means 'He [Judas] is distant', to be followed by the announcement in the next verse that he has arrived.[40] In the end all interpretations of this obscure interjection are guesses, and in the context either 'Enough' or 'It is settled' seems as good a guess as any.[41]

ἦλθεν ἡ ὥρα picks up not only the ὥρα of v. 35 but the whole sequence of Jesus' passion predictions culminating in the twin announcements of betrayal and of death at the Passover meal: the time of fulfilment has now arrived. And the first act in that sequence is to be the betrayal. παραδίδοται in v. 21 could on its own be understood either as a 'divine passive' (God as the one 'handing over') or quite impersonally (the Son of Man is to fall into the hands of sinners, without any indication of the agency involved). But the repetition of the verb in v. 42 with specific reference to Judas makes it clear that Jesus is speaking of the act of betrayal which he has so recently predicted (vv. 18-21).[42] In place of the

36. This is the Vulgate rendering, but Greek evidence for this meaning is virtually nonexistent.

37. M. A. Tolbert, *Sowing,* 216-17, opts for a similar meaning but with a different referent, the disciples. Drawing on her view that Mark presents the disciples as 'rocky ground', she interprets Jesus' threefold appeal to them to stay awake as their last chance, which they have failed to take. 'All has failed; their bill is paid in full; the account book on them is now closed; their fate is sealed'.

38. BDF, 129, list a few remote parallels for an 'impersonal' use meaning 'properly "it is receipted in full, the account is settled"'.' H. Hanse, *TDNT,* 2.828, frankly admits that 'there are no parallels and we have to decide as best we can', and suggests 'It is not in place', presumably drawing on another sense of ἀπέχω, 'to be distant'. He does not say *what* is 'not in place' — presumably sleep?

39. J. de Zwaan, *Expositor* 6 xii (1905) 452ff. His proposal is regularly noted but not followed. G. H. Boobyer, *NTS* 2 (1955/6) 44-48, agrees that Judas is the subject, but suggests that in the light of what follows Jesus is the object: 'He is taking possession of (me)' (or, as we might say, 'He's got me!').

40. Gundry, 857, 874-75. Hooker, 350, considers this possibility but reads ἀπέχει as a question, thus: 'Far off? No! Already here!' Gundry, taking it as a statement, must assume that in v. 41 Jesus has seen Judas and his party at a distance, thus allowing the disciples a short time for further sleep before he wakes them in the next verse on Judas's arrival.

41. Cf. the comment of W. H. Kelber, *Passion,* 55: 'Perhaps one should let the term speak in its suggested ambiguity. A moment pregnant with meaning has arrived. The fate of both Jesus and the disciples is sealed. "The account is settled."' For a fuller account of suggested renderings, see R. E. Brown, *Death,* 1379-83.

42. The attempt by R. E. Brown, *Death,* 211-13, to relate this usage to the wider setting of 'handing over' language loses the specific focus in this context where Judas's action is about to be related.

handing over εἰς χεῖρας ἀνθρώπων which Jesus has earlier predicted (9:31) we now have the more loaded phrase εἰς τὰς χεῖρας τῶν ἁμαρτωλῶν. Judas himself is certainly a ἁμαρτωλός in turning against the Son of God, but the description of those to whom he will hand Jesus over as also ἁμαρτωλοί is less immediately obvious. If the reference is to the arresting party, it is a question whether they were doing more than their official duty; if to the religious authorities who had sent them, their status as ἁμαρτωλοί (in anything more than the general sense which applies to everyone) depends on the perspective of the speaker. From the point of view of Mark and his church the Jerusalem authorities were now known to have committed the greatest sin in rejecting the Son of God, but in the narrative context it seems that their guilt is already presupposed.[43]

Judas' arrival on the scene (for ἤγγικεν as an indication of arrival see on 1:15)[44] is the spur for action. ἐγείρεσθε ἄγωμεν in another context might sound like a call to run away, but that cannot be its meaning here, where we have been repeatedly shown that Jesus intends to go through with the events he has predicted, and where the prayer just concluded has led to his acceptance of the Father's will. This is a call to advance rather than to retreat. They are probably simply going to rejoin the other disciples close by, ready to meet the arrival of the expected posse.

THE ARREST AND TRIALS OF JESUS (14:43–15:15)

So far in Mark's account of this fateful Passover we have heard the story of Jesus and his disciples. They have been together, and the dialogue has focused on the group as a whole, their attitudes to Jesus and what he is to do for them, their vulnerability and unpreparedness for what is to follow. From the moment of Judas's arrival at Gethsemane the disciples fade out of the picture and before long are physically separated from Jesus for the rest of the story. The only exception is Peter, and his presence will be an embarrassment rather than a help to Jesus. From now on Jesus will be in the company not of his supporters, however unreliable, but of his enemies. And whereas hitherto it has been he who has taken the initiative in all that has been done and said, he becomes now the passive victim, his spoken words are few (though important), and his fate in the hands of

---

43. Since Jews often referred to Gentiles as ἁμαρτωλοί, it is sometimes suggested that Jesus' ultimate death at the hands of the Romans (as predicted in 10:33) is here in view rather than the events of the next few hours when he remains in Jewish hands. Gundry, 876, suggests that since the term was used by Jews both of Gentiles and of 'impious Jews', it is here deliberately turned against those (Jews) who would have so used it. S. R. Garrett, *Temptations*, 100-104, argues that the 'handing over into the hands of sinners' also carries the connotations of being handed over into Satan's power for testing (as was Job according to Job 2:6).

44. The suggestion of W. H. Kelber, *Passion*, 45, that the use of the same 'crucial' verb here gives an eschatological dimension to Jesus' passion by linking it with the 'coming' of the kingdom of God builds far too much on the fact that the same verb form occurs twice in the space of fourteen chapters.

others. This, then, is the time for all that he has predicted throughout Acts Two and Three of Mark's drama to become reality: the Son of Man is delivered into the hands of sinners (v. 41).

The sequence of events is familiar enough and is similar in all four gospels: arrest in Gethsemane, hearing at night before the Jewish leadership (John notes the time spent in Caiaphas' house, 18:24, 28, but tells us nothing of the hearing there, and instead gives a brief account of a preliminary hearing before Annas, 18:13-14, 19-23), decision early in the morning to bring him before the Roman prefect, and the formal trial before Pilate (which John relates in much fuller detail, and into which Luke inserts a brief appearance before Herod Antipas, 23:7-12) leading to the imposition of the penalty of crucifixion. We shall consider later the question of the nature and legal status of the Jewish hearing, but there is now general agreement that, whatever its status in Jewish eyes, the 'real' trial, and the only one which could reach a verdict leading to the death penalty, was that before the Roman prefect. There is thus an appropriate and indeed necessary sequence in the events which make up this section of the passion narrative, so that the pericopes we are here considering form a coherent whole.

The Arrest (14:43-52)

The rationale given above for treating 14:43–15:15 as a connected whole and thus 14:43 as a point of transition is valid in terms of the contents of the pericopes concerned, but of course Mark was not writing his passion narrative in self-contained units, and there is no narrative break between 14:42 (the announcement of Judas's arrival) and 14:43 (that arrival narrated); the location remains Gethsemane. Indeed, so close is the connection that Van Iersel, 432, argues that the events in Gethsemane recorded in 14:32-52 should be treated from the literary point of view as 'one single episode' (Gundry, without explicit argument, does the same). Such a difference of division of the text illustrates the artificiality of the subdivisions to which commentators must resort in order to impose a structure on their treatment of what was in Mark's intention a single flowing narrative. Both Van Iersel's division and the one followed here are, in their different ways, based on valid observations of what is in the text, and the choice as to which areas of continuity and of development in the plot should take precedence in the structuring of a commentary is a matter of taste and convenience. I find it more illuminating to highlight the transition in the narrative when the predicted events begin to unfold than to focus on the undoubted literary continuity of the two parts of the Gethsemane story, hence the divisions adopted here.

The first part of the account of Jesus' arrest focuses on the treachery of Judas. The prediction of Jesus has been clear and specific (one of the Twelve), and now it is fulfilled to the letter. But once he has played his part Judas fades into the background, and from v. 46 it is with the arresting party as a whole that the narrative is concerned. Throughout the pericope Jesus is portrayed as fully aware of and prepared for what is coming. His only words (vv. 48-49; contrast the accounts of Matthew and John where Jesus has much more to say) are a rebuke for resorting to armed force, the implication being that they should have realised that he was not going to offer any resistance. Everything is happening ἵνα πληρωθῶσιν αἱ γραφαί, and Jesus is content that it should be so. He who is physically the victim and captive gives the impression of being in a deeper sense in charge of the situation. The disciples, on the other hand, fall to pieces. A desultory attempt at armed resistance by a supporter (v. 47) is followed by the disciples' ignominious flight, and the odd little story of the young man who ran away naked underlines the complete capitulation of Jesus' supporters, leaving him alone in the hands of his enemies. But then this, too, is what Jesus has specifically predicted, because this, too, was according to the Scriptures (14:27).

It is then only in vv. 43-45 that Judas briefly takes centre stage. He has an essential role in the story, both as the link between Jesus' group and the Jewish authorities and as the one whose treachery was the subject of such a striking scene at the Passover meal. But once this necessary part has been played, Mark has no further interest in Judas, and he will not be mentioned again. It is as if Christian tradition has left Mark no option but to include Judas in his story, and he has been happy to develop the theme of scriptural fulfilment and of the fulfilment of Jesus' own prediction through Judas's action, but that is as far as Mark's interest in Judas goes. Whatever may have been the case for the other gospel writers (Mt. 27:3-10; Acts 1:15-26; Jn. 12:4-6; 13:26-30), and for later Christian tradition with its progressive demonisation of Judas, for Mark Judas is only a minor detail in the story. It is Jesus, not Judas, who is the centre of interest as the Gethsemane story concludes.

43 Judas's arrival ἔτι αὐτοῦ λαλοῦντος serves not only to tie the events which follow closely with the scene of Jesus' prayer and the disciples' weakness, but also to show Jesus as on top of the situation, not taken by surprise. The description of Judas (again) as εἷς τῶν δώδεκα is not by now necessary for the reader to identify him, but underlines once more the depth of his treachery. The full listing of the constituent groups of the Sanhedrin (see on 8:31, and cf. 11:27; 14:53; 15:1) emphasises that this is not a random mob[45] but an officially sanctioned (παρά) arresting party (which includes 'the slave of the High Priest'). Mark does not specify who made up the posse, but the fact that they come from the temple authorities and that Jesus speaks in v. 49 of their opportunity to arrest him in the temple where he was πρὸς ὑμᾶς leads the reader to think naturally of the Jewish temple guards rather than of a Roman force (as

45. Several commentators think that the term ὄχλος and the mention of clubs (ξύλα) suggest a 'rabble' (Hooker) or 'hastily gathered mob' (Anderson) rather than an official force, but neither term requires this connotation, and Mark's 'official' language is marked.

John apparently has, with a σπεῖρα under a χιλίαρχος distinguished from the servants of the priests, Jn. 18:3, 12). There is, as yet, no reason for the Romans to be involved. For the temple guards see Schürer, 2.284-87; by NT times they were a substantial force, organised in military fashion with officers known by military titles under a στρατηγός (Acts 4:1; 5:24-26).[46] A detachment of these guards had been detailed to go with Judas to make the arrest.[47]

44-46 After the last week's events in the temple one would think that Jesus was by now a sufficiently well-known figure, especially to the temple guards, to make any identification signal unnecessary; but Gethsemane would be dark, and Jesus was just one among a crowd of Galilean visitors to the city who would be there. The notorious signal of the kiss is therefore narrated, but Mark does not dwell on it as Luke does (Lk. 22:48). A kiss was a normal social greeting (Lk. 7:45; Acts 20:37; Rom. 16:16, etc.) particularly between rabbis and their disciples, which in itself would cause no surprise;[48] it therefore conveniently identifies the person to be arrested without rousing suspicion.[49] The use of ῾Ραββί also occasions no surprise in Mark, where (unlike in Matthew) it has already occurred as an address to Jesus by disciples (9:5; 11:21; cf. 10:51 for ῾Ραββουνί used by a suppliant), corresponding in Hebrew to their normal Greek address διδάσκαλε. Judas's instruction to the guards, κρατήσατε αὐτὸν καὶ ἀπάγετε ἀσφαλῶς, suggests that he expected resistance, whether from Jesus or from the other disciples, and the guards duly grab Jesus physically to prevent escape.

47 All four gospels record the memorable event of the cutting off of the ear of the High Priest's slave, though only John supplies a name for both the assailant (Peter) and the victim. ὁ δοῦλος τοῦ ἀρχιερέως (not just *a* slave) may suggest a person of some consequence, perhaps singled out for attack because he was in charge of the arresting party.[50] In Luke the assailant is one of the dis-

---

46. For the appropriateness of swords and clubs for such a force see Lane, 524.

47. J. Blinzler, *Trial*, 61-70, discusses the composition of the arresting party drawing on all four gospels. He concludes that all (including John) are describing Jewish, not Roman, personnel, and suggests that the ὄχλος described by Mark is more likely to have been 'police or court servants' at the disposal of the Sanhedrin rather than the Levites who formed the temple guard itself, while John's more military language indicates the presence also of 'the Temple guard, commanded by the Temple colonel'.

48. See R. E. Brown, *Death*, 254-55. Mann, 596, contends, however, that a disciple was not permitted to take the initiative in greeting his teacher; on that understanding Judas's kiss was also a 'calculated insult'.

49. Some commentators take the use of καταφιλέω in v. 45, as opposed to simply φιλέω in v. 44, to indicate an unusually prolonged or fervent embrace, but it is doubtful whether usage supports this distinction. See BAGD, 420a: the references there to Josephus, *Ant.* 7.284 and 8.387 do not refer to anything more than a normal greeting. MM, 334b, are doubtful about such a distinction as proposed in the RV mg. at Mt. 26:49, 'kissed him much'.

50. So Gnilka, 2.270. G. W. H. Lampe in E. Bammel and C. F. D. Moule (ed.), *Politics*, 343-45, noting that this incident does not seem to connect directly with either what precedes or what follows, and comes rather inappropriately after the arrest rather than attempting to prevent it, argues that Mark records it for its symbolic significance. The victim, described as ὁ δοῦλος τοῦ ἀρχιερέως,

ciples (εἷς τις ἐξ αὐτῶν, 22:50 — and they have only recently been discussing the need for swords, 22:35-38), and Matthew's phrase εἷς τῶν μετὰ Ἰησοῦ implies the same, but Mark's εἷς τις τῶν παρεστηκότων is unexpected and would most naturally mean a bystander who was not connected with Jesus (as in Mark's other uses of this verb: 14:69, 70; 15:35, 39). If he had meant a disciple he could have said so, or used εἷς τῶν δώδεκα. We have not been told of anyone else present on the hillside (though we will meet one in vv. 51-52), and Jesus' prayer has been understood to be a private occasion shared only by Peter, James, and John, but in the crowded state of the Jerusalem area at Passover time there may well have been others around, perhaps attracted by the very obvious passage of the detachment of temple guards and following them to see what was afoot. That one such bystander, particularly if another Galilean pilgrim, should get caught up in the incident and strike a blow for Jesus would not be surprising, and that may be what Mark meant by his unexpected reference to a 'bystander'.[51] How likely it is that a 'civilian' bystander would be carrying a sword at night on a hillside within greater Jerusalem at Passover time is hard to judge, but the fact that the guard came armed to tackle possible resistance (see v. 48) renders it not improbable. Neither that fact nor the strange dialogue in Lk. 22:35-38 is a sufficient basis on which to build a theory that the Jesus movement was linked with a Zealot-type insurrectionist force: weapons were carried for protection, then as now.

48-49 In Mark, unlike the other gospels, Jesus makes no response directly to the person who attacked the slave. Is this perhaps a further indication that he did not think it was one of Jesus' disciples? Instead he pours scorn on the whole military character of the expedition (and by implication on the armed resistance it has provoked) as appropriate to the arrest of a λῃστής. The implication is that Jesus is not like that, and they should have known as much. λῃστής is a pejorative word which no one would be likely to use of himself: its use by Josephus as virtually a technical term for members of the Zealot and related movements is conditioned by his desire to distance himself from such people. The way Jesus uses the word here adds to the irony that he will himself end up crucified between two λῃσταί (15:27), as if he were one of them. Thus from the beginning of the passion events to their end Jesus finds himself unwillingly associated with the λῃσταί, from whose ideol-

---

is a person of importance, representing his master. In the deliberate insult of cutting off his ear, a gesture of contempt is being made against the High Priest himself; indeed, had the High Priest himself suffered this injury it would have disqualified him from the High Priesthood. It is thus a symbol of the deconsecration of Caiaphas as unfit for his office. The suggestion is backed up by interesting evidence about the significance of cutting off ears in the ancient world, but it suffers from the fact that the servant is not himself the High Priest, and that Mark betrays no sign of this symbolic insult either in the way he tells this story or in any subsequent reference back to it. It plays no part in Jesus' trial.

51. Gundry, 860, following Pesch, 2.400, suggests that it was one of the arresting party (who alone would have swords) who injured one of his companions by accident.

ogy he had so deliberately distanced himself in 12:13-17. But in this context the term need not have its later political connotation. It may be enough to understand it here simply of a bandit (as in the Jeremiah quotation in 11:17). If so, Jesus' complaint is the more telling: they have watched him discussing theological issues with the priests in the temple, and now they come for him as if he were a common thief! His reference to his temple teaching in v. 49 thus not only reminds them of the opportunity they have failed to take (for good reasons, no doubt, in view of the popularity of Jesus with at least some of the crowd in the temple) but also underlines the inappropriateness of the role they have cast him in by coming for him with swords and clubs. The terse ἀλλ' ἵνα πληρωθῶσιν αἱ γραφαί presupposes a main clause to the effect 'This is happening . . .' (as Mt. 26:56 spells it out; see BDF, 448[7]); no OT text is cited specifically to justify the manner of Jesus' arrest, and Mark's thought may be more general (see on 8:31; 9:12 for the scriptural basis of the passion predictions), but he may have had in mind the passage which Luke cites to justify the need for a sword at this juncture, καὶ μετὰ ἀνόμων ἐλογίσθη (Lk. 22:37 citing Is. 53:12).

50   Jesus' protest does not have, and probably was not expected to have, any effect on the guard. Jesus knows what is to happen, and is prepared for the Scriptures to be fulfilled. The effect is rather on his disciples who now can have no doubt that Jesus does not intend to resist arrest, and is prepared to go to his death. The increasing fears of recent days have been proved valid, and their resolution crumbles. The five words of this verse say all there is to be said. It is a factual statement rather than one of blame, and in the circumstances it is hard to see what other option the disciples had once Jesus had made it clear that he would not sanction violent resistance. They could hardly volunteer to go with him: it was only Jesus the guards had come to arrest. And to follow surreptitiously behind the guards as Peter did (v. 54) could not be expected to achieve anything; for Peter it was the way to even deeper disgrace. They ran away because there was nothing else for them to do.

51-52   After that tragic climax the mysterious story of the young man with the linen cloth seems to us like an anticlimax, almost as light relief. But there is no sign that Mark intended it in that way. It adds yet more to the sense of Jesus' abandonment, in that not only the Eleven but even this anonymous sympathiser can only run away.[52] We do not know who he was, but it is a reasonable guess that he was someone who might be known to Mark's readers and could corroborate the story of his undignified escape through the olive groves (cf. the mention of the otherwise irrelevant Alexander and Rufus, 15:21). Beyond that all is conjecture, including the suggestion, hallowed by frequent repetition, that it was Mark writing himself anonymously into his own story in a mi-

---

52. Anderson, 324, suggests that the tenses of κρατέω in vv. 46 and 51 are intended to convey a contrast in that Jesus was arrested (aorist) without resistance while the attempt to arrest (present) this man was thwarted by his escape.

nor role in the manner of Alfred Hitchcock.[53] It may be quite a good conjecture, in that it does at least offer some reason for the inclusion of what otherwise appears a very inconsequential coda to the Gethsemane story.[54]

Many commentators find this episode too trivial to deserve its place in the narrative at a purely factual level, and so seek a symbolic purpose.[55] Not many have been convinced by the attempt to derive it from the OT.[56] More frequently it is noted that σινδών occurs also in 15:46 for Jesus' burial shroud, and on this basis some suggest that this story in some way prefigures the resurrection account, which will also include a νεανίσκος who was περιβεβλημένος στολὴν λευκήν (16:5) as well as the motif of running away (16:8).[57] Myers, 368-69, asserts that nonsymbolic interpretations of the incident 'insult the literary integrity of the gospel', and finds a link with the resurrection pericope in that the young man, who represents the disciples, is there 'rehabilitated' in a white robe, symbolising the ultimate rehabilitation of the disciple community. Many suggest also a baptismal motif underlying the young man's abandoning of his σινδών, when this is linked with the στολὴ λευκή of 16:5.[58] But the verbal links which are used to support any association of this νεανίσκος with the one introduced in 16:5 are altogether too slender to support the supposed connection (see below on 16:5); nor does the range of competing and sometimes conflicting interpretations based on this supposed link inspire confidence.[59]

Taking this cameo then at its face value within the narrative context, we are introduced here to someone additional to the Eleven, who are all included

53. Gundry, 882, usefully summarises some of the ways this conjecture has been developed, including the explanation of the young man's inadequate clothing as due to his having got out of bed in a hurry. E. Best, *Story,* 26, traces its popularity to the second half of the nineteenth century.

54. It is interesting and a little ironical that one of the most elaborate attempts to link the νεανίσκος here with other figures in Mark (not only the νεανίσκος at the tomb [see next paragraph] but also the Gerasene demoniac, as well as a tangential link with Jairus's daughter), ends up with something close to the nineteenth-century view that the νεανίσκος is the author himself 'anonymously placing himself in the narrative, with the clear intention of establishing the authority of the text by means of an eyewitness report': S. R. Johnson, *Forum* 8 (1992) 123-39.

55. For a survey of a variety of symbolic interpretations of 14:51-52 see E. Best, *Story,* 26-27; R. E. Brown, *Death,* 299-304.

56. The suggestion that the passage is intended to recall Am. 2:16, 'Those who are stout of heart among the mighty shall flee away naked in that day', is most improbable. Not only is there nothing in the context of Am. 2:16 to suggest its relevance to the story of Jesus' arrest, but also νεανίσκος τις would be a strange figure to recall the 'stout of heart among the mighty'. (Lane, 527, is unusually sympathetic to this supposed allusion.) Still less is there any similarity with Joseph's flight from Potiphar's wife, leaving his cloak behind (Gn. 39:12).

57. So, e.g., Gundry, 862-63, suggesting that the young man's escape is meant to create a 'parallel that will anticipate Jesus' resurrection'; similarly earlier A. Vanhoye, *Bib* 52 (1971) 401-6.

58. So especially R. Scroggs and K. I. Groff, *JBL* 92 (1973) 531-48; see also Stock, 373-75.

59. Mann, 599-601, surveys a variety of attempts to link the two pericopes, but is himself reluctant to adopt any proposed explanation of the verbal links which he nonetheless regards as 'altogether too much to ascribe to chance'. In the absence of any more plausible explanation than those above, I find 'chance' a more compelling alternative. For some sane comments on the lack of connection between the two νεανίσκοι see H. Fleddermann, *CBQ* 41 (1979) 414-15, 418.

in v. 50. νεανίσκος τις suggests someone of no special importance; moreover, someone who had come directly to Gethsemane from the Passover meal would not have been dressed as this young man was. But he is sufficiently identified with the Jesus party to be seized by the guards. Here then is a sympathetic bystander (note συνηκολούθει αὐτῷ, a phrase which could denote a sort of 'associate disciple', though it need mean no more than someone following through curiosity).[60] We have considered at v. 47 the possibility of such bystanders at Jesus' arrest, though this one, far from being armed, was apparently very inadequately clothed, the σινδών being presumably a cloth worn as a loose ἱμάτιον, easily discarded, rather than a χιτών with sleeves. The ignominious flight of this anonymous sympathiser serves in the narrative context to underline the complete failure of Jesus' friends to support him when the moment came. Apart from his captors, Jesus leaves Gethsemane alone. (See on 10:32-34 for this mysterious young man's dubious role in the 'Secret Gospel'.)

The Jewish Trial (14:53-65)

TEXTUAL NOTES

62. The 'Caesarean' reading of Θ f[13] and a number of minuscules σὺ εἶπας ὅτι ἐγώ εἰμι in place of the simple ἐγώ εἰμι is not included in the apparatus of UBS[4], but should be mentioned because of its exegetical importance if genuine, and because a number of critics and interpreters, notably Streeter and Taylor, have argued in its favour. The vast majority regard it as an assimilation to the equivocal replies in Matthew and Luke (and to Pilate in Mark). For a detailed and cautious analysis of the issue see R. Kempthorne, *NovT* 19 (1977) 197-208.

65. The substitution of τῷ προσώπῳ αὐτοῦ for αὐτῷ in D and some OL, while omitting the covering of the face, is clearly an assimilation to Matthew. Θ has made the substitution without omitting the second clause, resulting in an awkward double mention of the face.

65. The various longer texts are best explained as expansions of an original simple Προφήτευσον which was felt to be too obscure; they reflect various aspects of the fuller versions in Mt. 26:68 and Lk. 22:64 (see further P. Benoit in W. C. Van Unnik [ed.], *Neotestamentica et Patristica,* 97-100).

Mark continues to weave the threads of the passion narrative together into a continuous whole within which the scene shifts between the key players. Verse 53 carries us with the arresting party from Gethsemane to the venue for the next

---

60. For H. Fleddermann, *CBQ* 41 (1979) 415-18, the story of the νεανίσκος is 'a dramatization of the universal flight of the disciples'. He rightly points out the close verbal connection with the preceding account of the events in Gethsemane through the repetition of the terms κρατέω and φεύγω, and goes on to suggest that the involuntary nakedness of the young man contrasts with Jesus' nakedness on the cross, voluntarily accepted.

main scene, the High Priest's house. But within that venue there are two separate scenes to accommodate a subplot along with the main plot, and the spotlight will shift from the one scene to the other. The main scene is the gathering of members of the Sanhedrin, presumably in the main hall of the house (apparently on a higher level than the courtyard; see κάτω in v. 66), and here it is Jesus who is under the spotlight. But in the courtyard outside is another group centred around Peter. Now that the rest of the disciples are off the scene, the spotlight will fall on Peter, the only one who has dared to follow Jesus (so far proving true to his boasted loyalty in 14:29, 31), though secretly. So in the remainder of chapter 14 Mark will move the spotlight to and fro, first to the main hall (v. 53), then outside to the courtyard (v. 54), then back to the hall for the main event (vv. 55-65), and then back out into the courtyard for Peter's ordeal (vv. 66-72), before returning for a last time to the hall in 15:1 in time to pick up the story as the protagonists move on to a new location and a new and very different trial.

The effect of this way of telling the story (in contrast with Luke, who records Peter's denial before Jesus' hearing) is to throw Jesus and Peter into sharp contrast. Each will be under pressure, but whereas Jesus both in his silence and in his final dramatic utterance will stand firm, Peter will crumble. Jesus will go to his death, but with his witness to his mission undimmed; Peter will escape, but at the cost of his integrity as a disciple of Jesus. It is a study in witnessing under pressure, in how to do it and how not to do it. As such, it could be expected to offer serious food for thought to Mark's readers as they assessed their own faithfulness and built up their strength for witness in a potentially hostile world.

But of course there is far more to this account than a paradigm for discipleship. This is the climactic point to which the whole gospel narrative, particularly since Caesarea Philippi, has been building up. Jesus has repeatedly predicted his rejection by οἱ ἀρχιερεῖς καὶ οἱ πρεσβύτεροι καὶ οἱ γραμματεῖς, and now here he is face to face with them, not in the more neutral arena of a Court of the Gentiles filled with a potentially winnable crowd, but in a private gathering in the High Priest's house. Since his arrival in Jerusalem there has been a developing conflict focused on the question of authority (11:27-33). Jesus has chosen to challenge their leadership on their own ground, and now it is time to find out who really is in charge. They have reached the point where, to borrow the language of the Westerns, 'This town isn't big enough for both of us'.

But this is more than a leadership contest. Notwithstanding his messianic gesture in riding towards the city on the donkey, Jesus has not come to take over the running of Jerusalem. He has hinted, and sometimes more than hinted, at a higher authority and a mission on a different level from that. It is this issue which must now be brought to the fore, and the issues raised in the High Priest's hall go to the heart of the matter, first the alleged threat to replace the temple, and then, following closely from that, the key question, Σὺ εἶ ὁ Χριστὸς ὁ υἱὸς τοῦ εὐλογητοῦ; That is the issue to which everything else has been leading, and it is only at that point that Jesus will break his irritating silence with the ringing declaration of v. 62, words not of apology but of defiant authority. After that there is no room for compromise, and the predicted rejection is complete, summed up in a quasi-judicial verdict of guilty and in violent mockery.

That is to say, in this pericope, and particularly in v. 62, we have reached the christological climax of the gospel. And in that climax we reach the heart of Mark's paradoxical presentation of Jesus: at the narrative level he is overpowered and cannot save himself; at the theological level he reigns supreme.

Many important issues raised by these much-debated verses are best treated as we work through the successive phases of the trial verse by verse. But two more general issues are better treated first, the issue of how Mark presents the charge against Jesus, and that of the formal character and legality of this 'trial'.[1]

1. The Charge against Jesus

Official opposition to Jesus can be traced back almost to the start of Mark's account of his ministry in Galilee. The local scribes and others have objected to his claim to forgive sins, his mixing with 'sinners', his free attitude towards fasting, and his readiness to override their understanding of the proper observance of the sabbath (2:7, 16, 18, 24; 3:2). On these bases there was already by 3:6 an agreement in Galilee that Jesus must be eliminated. As the story has developed, Jerusalem scribes have joined their Galilean counterparts in denouncing Jesus as in league with the devil and as sitting loose to the laws of purity (3:22; 7:1). The Galilean ministry finished with a mutual dissociation of Jesus and the local Pharisees (8:11-13). All this was potent enough ammunition to use against a dangerously 'free-thinking' northern preacher, but it was still from the point of view of the Jerusalem authorities a problem at a distance.

With his arrival in Jerusalem not only did the problem arrive on their doorstep, but Jesus seemed to go out of his way to provoke them by his symbolic actions in riding conspicuously up to the city as leader of a crowd of enthusiastic Galileans and in disrupting the business of the Court of the Gentiles, leading naturally to their challenge as to the basis of his authority for such actions. His answer implied that he claimed the same authority as John the Baptist, the authority of God himself, and the polemical parable of the vineyard pointedly cast them in the role of defaulting tenants and himself in that of the only son of the owner, God. Their attempts to incriminate him by asking awkward questions proved unsuccessful, and left him in possession of the field of debate, with the crowd listening to him with approval.

---

1. On the further issue of how a report of the actual proceedings may have found its way into Christian tradition see the sensible comments of D. L. Bock, *Blasphemy*, 195-97. For a more wide-ranging critique of many of the literary-critical objections raised against the validity of Mark's record of the hearing see K. Schubert in E. Bammel and C. F. D. Moule (ed.), *Politics*, 385-402.

All this was enough to mark Jesus out as a troublemaker and to provoke them to seek his removal. But he went on to make matters worse by first denouncing the scribes as pompous parasites and then predicting the imminent demise even of the temple itself, the very foundation of the Jewish power structure headed by the chief priests. Such a man was dangerous not only to their leading position in society but to public order and morale.

There is within this developing confrontation plenty of incentive for action against Jesus, and plenty of material which could be used as evidence against him. Perhaps Mark wishes us to assume that several of the matters just listed may have been raised among the various allegations which are dismissed collectively in v. 56 as ψευδομαρτυρία on the grounds that the necessary agreement of two or three witnesses (Dt. 19:15) could not be secured.

But what they had decided on was the death penalty (14:1), and for that a very serious offence must be proved. In Mark's account of the hearing two specific charges are mentioned. The first is not at all unexpected in the light of what we have read, the charge that Jesus plans to destroy the temple (vv. 57-59). Mark insists that even on this charge they could not produce the required agreement of witnesses (though Mt. 26:60-61 disagrees with him on this), but it clearly played a central part in the hearing, and remained the basis of the public rejection of Jesus in Jerusalem (15:29), as indeed it did in the attempt to suppress the Christian movement after his death (Acts 6:13-14; 7:44-50). It was not on this charge specifically that Jesus was convicted, but it clearly played a significant role in his rejection not only by the Sanhedrin but also by the wider population of Jerusalem.

The second charge appears at first sight to be a quite different one, almost a non sequitur after vv. 57-59. It takes the form of a question, Σὺ εἶ ὁ Χριστὸς ὁ υἱὸς τοῦ εὐλογητοῦ; and it is Jesus' positive answer to this question which leads to his conviction for βλασφημία, the offence for which, from the Jewish point of view, he was to be executed. We shall deal in the notes on v. 64 with the definition of βλασφημία and the question of just how Jesus' response in v. 62 constituted blasphemy, but here we need to note that it was in some way connected with his alleged claim to be the Messiah. Not that Mark has portrayed Jesus as claiming openly to be the Messiah; rather, the opposite (8:29-30). But the authority which his actions and teaching have implicitly claimed certainly did not arise from any human authorisation. Moreover, even if not explicit in words, his ride towards the city and his demonstration in the temple were both, as we have noted above, implicitly messianic actions. His words about the coming destruction of the temple and the universal authority of the enthroned Son of Man which takes its place, while recorded in Mark only as a discourse to four chosen disciples (though there is no reason why others should not have heard the crucial prediction of 13:2, uttered still in the temple area), has evidently in some form leaked out to a wider public, and constitutes a claim of breathtaking proportions for those who are able to recognise Jesus' reference to himself in the veiled language about the Son of Man.

The sequence within this pericope from the temple charge to the question about Messiahship is thus not at all a non sequitur. It is rather an attempt by the High Priest to draw out more directly the claim to a unique, God-given authority which is implied in the alleged threat to the temple, an allegation on which Jesus has refused to comment. By bringing together this apparent claim to messianic authority with the even more outrageous status as Son of God which Jesus has implicitly claimed in the parable of the vineyard, the High Priest aims to bring into the open the basis on which Jesus has apparently been setting himself above the properly constituted authority of the appointed leaders of Israel. The answer is not only as positive as the High Priest could have wished, but also goes on to assert that unique authority in a defiant pronouncement which at last takes the wraps off Jesus' view of who he is. After this climactic challenge the verdict is easily reached, and Jesus is condemned to death as a blasphemer. That blasphemy, however, is to be found not in any narrowly defined misuse of language, but in a total claim to which the whole of Jesus' public life and teaching has been building up, and which sets him irrevocably in conflict with the Jerusalem authorities. See further on v. 64 below.

2. Was This a Legal Trial?

This question has been exhaustively discussed, generally on the assumption that the rules set out in the Mishnah tractate *Sanhedrin* for capital trials are the appropriate legal yardstick against which to set Mark's narrative. A number of discrepancies have been noted, chiefly that according to the Mishnah capital trials were to take place during the daytime, must not be held on the eve of a festival, must be held in one of three specified courtrooms which did not include the High Priest's house,[2] must begin by hearing the case for the defence, and must not reach a conviction on the same day the trial began.[3] The fact that none of these provisions appears to be observed in Mark's account of what happened in the High Priest's house has then led many commentators to the conclusion that this was a trial which broke the rules. There are two problems with this assumption.

First, it is impossible to be sure how far the provisions codified in the Mishnah c. A.D. 200 represent accepted practice nearly two hundred years earlier, especially in view of the far-reaching changes which were forced upon Jewish institutions by the destruction of the temple in A.D. 70 and the subsequent reorganisation of the rabbinic establishment at Javneh with the Pharisees now the dominant party. Moreover, the mishnaic rules do not reflect the conditions of the Roman occupation and assume that the Jewish court had the right to pass a capital sentence with the execution carried out by stoning, burning, beheading, or strangling. It is therefore at least questionable whether in Jerusalem

---

2. J. Blinzler, *Trial,* 112-14, discusses the official locations for meetings of the Sanhedrin.
3. For a fuller listing and discussion of alleged illegalities see R. E. Brown, *Death,* 357-63.

in the days of Tiberius the rules as we now have them in the Mishnah were already there to be broken.[4]

Secondly, it is by no means clear that what went on in the High Priest's house that night was meant to be a formal 'trial' to which such rules would be applicable. The fact that so many of the mishnaic rules were not observed (if they were yet in operation) may lead us more appropriately to question the supposedly formal nature of the proceedings than to accuse the Sanhedrin authorities of ignoring their own rules. The issue has been carefully assessed in a recent work by D. L. Bock, who comes to the conclusion that 'this gathering was never seen or intended as a formal Jewish capital case, but a kind of preliminary hearing to determine if Jesus was as dangerous as the leadership sensed and whether he could be credibly sent to Rome'. In view of the fact that the Jewish authorities had no right to execute,[5] it was a Roman verdict which was in view from the beginning. What took place as soon as Jesus was brought to the High Priest's house was a hasty 'attempt to gather charges, so that a case could be made before Rome and Pilate'.[6] This description fits Mark's account, which reads not as a trial on an already formulated charge, but as a search for a charge which could be made to stick.[7]

If that is so, and I think it best fits the evidence, the issue of correct legal procedure is beside the point. This was a gathering of such members of the Sanhedrin as could be gathered at an unsociable hour of the night, perhaps with new members arriving as the hearing continued, until early in the morning a sufficient quorum was present to draw up and agree on a charge to be placed before Pilate (15:1). From the Roman point of view that was all it could be, since

4. Gundry, 893, adds the further consideration that since there was later rabbinic provision for 'irregularities for emergencies and protection of the Torah', it would probably also have been permissible at the time of Jesus for the Sanhedrin to have proceeded irregularly in a case which they treated as 'an emergency fraught with grave danger to the Torah'.

5. The statement to this effect in Jn. 18:31 (supported by the statement in the Jerusalem Talmud that the Jews lost the right to execute 'forty years before the temple was destroyed') has been widely (but not universally) agreed in recent scholarship to represent the historical situation, especially following the study of A. N. Sherwin-White, *Society,* 32-47. The recorded exceptions of the stoning of Stephen (Acts 7:58-60) and of James the Just (Josephus, *Ant.* 20.200) are best understood as lynchings *ultra vires,* the latter being recorded specifically as having been carried out when there was no procurator in office to prevent it. The permission to execute Gentiles who crossed the barrier in the temple is specifically said to be a special concession (Josephus, *War* 6.126) — the exception which proves the rule. For a fuller discussion of the competence of the Sanhedrin, with details of the arguments for and against the accuracy of Jn. 18:31, see Schürer, 2.218-23. See also R. E. Brown, *Death,* 363-72, for a recent survey of the debate.

6. D. L. Bock, *Blasphemy,* 189-95 (quotations from pp. 191 and 194). It is in line with this conclusion that Bock has deliberately avoided using the familiar term 'Trial' in the title of his book. Mann, 613, concludes a lengthy discussion of the nature of the Sanhedrin hearing by asserting that it 'was not a trial at all and not even what might be described as a "grand jury" enquiry'.

7. In this respect Mark's account corresponds interestingly with the quite independent account of the preliminary hearing before Annas which in the Fourth Gospel takes the place of a hearing before Caiaphas, in which Annas 'asked about Jesus' disciples and his teaching', but no specific accusation is made (Jn. 18:19).

a capital 'trial' as such was beyond the jurisdiction of the Sanhedrin. From the Jewish point of view, perhaps, the formal position was less important, and it was the agreement of the Sanhedrin that Jesus was dangerous and must be eliminated which would count for more than the formality of a Roman sentence. In Jewish eyes, then, what happened in the High Priest's house might be regarded as the 'real' trial of Jesus, and I have retained the familiar term 'trial' in my heading in recognition of this perception; but formally speaking that is too grand a word to describe this preliminary hearing.

53 After the brief account of the escape of the disciples and the young man, we return to the arresting party (v. 46), who now complete their role by delivering Jesus safely to those who had sent them to arrest him. The full phrase οἱ ἀρχιερεῖς καὶ οἱ πρεσβύτεροι καὶ οἱ γραμματεῖς (cf. 8:31; 11:27; 14:43) underlines the solemnity and official nature of the occasion, and the addition this time of πάντες further increases the tension by contrasting the lone figure of Jesus with the assembled representatives of official Judaism.[8] The comments above on the less-than-formal nature of the proceedings have suggested that perhaps not all seventy-one members of the Sanhedrin might have been assembled at this time of night, or that members may have continued to arrive during the proceedings (though, of course, it is possible that the High Priest, having planned to have Jesus in custody at this time, had issued a 'three-line whip' in advance). In that case Mark's πάντες achieves literary effect rather than numerical exactitude.[9]

The ἀρχιερεύς is never named in Mark's gospel (and so will not be named in this commentary); it is Matthew and John who tell us that it was Caiaphas, High Priest from 18 to 37; his period of office, like that of Pilate, includes all the dates that can plausibly be suggested on other grounds for the date of Jesus' trial and death.[10] Given the ambiguous situation reflected in Luke's mention of two High Priests (Luke 3:2), with Caiaphas's predecessor and father-in-law Annas still retaining the dignity if not the formal role of High Priesthood (and still referred to simply as ὁ ἀρχιερεύς in Jn. 18:19-23, even though John spells out his status quite explicitly in 18:13), it could be suggested that Mark here had Annas rather than Caiaphas in mind, but there is nothing to say so, and in the absence of any evidence to the contrary we should assume that he is using the term in its official sense. The location is not specified, but πρὸς τὸν ἀρχιερέα, together with the following mention of ἡ αὐλὴ τοῦ ἀρχιερέως, is normally and probably rightly taken to indicate the High Priest's house rather than one of the formal meeting chambers in which, according to *m. Sanh.* 11:2, the Sanhedrin met for capital trials.

8. J. Blinzler, *Trial,* 93-97, supplies details of the groups and individuals who made up the Sanhedrin at this time. Mark's explicit listing of the constituent groups renders unlikely the suggestion of J. D. M. Derrett, *Law,* 407 n. 1, that Jesus' case was heard not by the Sanhedrin itself but by 'the priestly committee', a separate and smaller body for which there is some mishnaic evidence.

9. Gundry, 896-97, argues, however, that a full attendance of seventy-one members is intended.

10. For details of Caiaphas and of his extraordinarily long tenure of office see J. Blinzler, *Trial,* 91-93.

54 Mark now prepares us for the event to be recorded in vv. 66-72 by shifting the spotlight away to the αὐλή, the enclosed but unroofed area around which a more affluent house was constructed (and in this case at a lower level than the main rooms; see κάτω [v. 66]). Here the servants and various less distinguished visitors could gather, and on this occasion probably some or all of the arresting party were still there after completing their mission. That Peter was apparently able to join the crowd unnoticed (contrast Jn. 18:15-16) suggests a semipublic and crowded area. His following ἀπὸ μακρόθεν suggests secrecy, an unwillingness already to be publicly identified with the prisoner, but ἕως ἔσω shows that he has followed as far as he is able. So at least Peter, unlike all the other disciples, has not yet abandoned Jesus; his boast of vv. 29 and 31 was not entirely empty. θερμαινόμενος makes it clear that τὸ φῶς is here used to mean a fire (which would also, of course, cast light on his face; see v. 67): BAGD, 871b-872a, 1.b.α, mentions a few parallels to the usage (cf. MM, 680); Lk. 22:55-56 uses πῦρ and φῶς as synonyms.[11] A fire in the courtyard is not surprising: I can testify from personal experience that it can be *very* cold in Jerusalem at night at Passover time.

55-56 For ὅλον τὸ συνέδριον see on πάντες in v. 53. In Jewish trials there was no official prosecutor; prosecution was conducted on the basis of the testimony of witnesses. But the expression ἐζήτουν μαρτυρίαν εἰς τὸ θανατῶσαι αὐτόν conveys two significant impressions of the nature of this hearing. Firstly, it was, as we have noted above, a hearing in search of a charge, not a trial based on an already formulated accusation. Secondly, while the charge was not yet decided, the verdict was! In putting the matter in this way Mark has already declared the 'trial' to be more a kangaroo court than an impartial judicial hearing. The objective of killing Jesus already declared in 14:1 rules this gathering, so that whatever procedure is followed will be designed to produce the required capital charge to bring before the Roman prefect.[12]

If this view of the hearing is right, it is the more remarkable that Mark records an attempt to observe proper legal procedure, in that charges on which witnesses could not agree were not pursued.[13] The disagreement was presumably the result of cross-questioning the witnesses as laid down in *m. Sanh.* 4:5–5:4. There was, therefore, a concern on the part of the authorities that justice should be seen to have been done in that the charge on which Jesus was to be brought before the

---

11. H. C. Waetjen, *Reordering,* 219, argues that Mark must have had some special reason to use so unusual a term, and offers the following remarkable explanation: 'Peter is deriving warmth from some kind of light, and the most reasonable assumption seems to be that its source is Jesus. . . . The light emanating from Jesus is so strong that he, Peter, is able to draw warmth from it for himself.'

12. Myers, 371, puts it in his typical style: 'The powers railroad Jesus because they know he is committed to their overthrow; in political trials, justice is subordinate to the need for conviction.' D. Juel, *Messiah,* 62-64, sets out the evidence for Mark's view of a 'court committed to a guilty verdict'.

13. There is little to support the suggestion that Mark's emphasis on false witnesses is designed to recall Pss. 27:12; 35:11; see D. J. Moo, *The OT,* 247-48; D. Juel, *Messiah,* 121-22.

prefect was to be one which conformed to the normal Jewish requirement of the agreement of two or three witnesses (Nu. 35:30; Dt. 17:6; 19:15). The Jewish leadership could not be seen to be guilty of condoning ψευδομαρτυρία, one of the basic prohibitions of the decalogue (Ex. 20:16; Dt. 5:20); nor, convinced of the rightness of their cause, would they themselves wish it.

57-59 Mark is quite clear that even the charge concerning the temple could not be established by this criterion: it was also ψευδομαρτυρία (v. 57), and the witnesses failed to agree on it (v. 59). Matthew pointedly disagrees, in that he records this charge separately from the ψευδομαρτυρία, introducing it by ὕστερον δέ and as the united testimony of two witnesses (Mt. 26:60). There is no way of discovering whether Mark or Matthew is historically right on this point, but it seems clear that the charge, whatever its legal status, was an important element in the cumulative case against Jesus, and it was this rather than his alleged blasphemy which was remembered by the bystanders at the cross (15:29).[14] The seriousness of such a charge may be judged by remembering the experience of Jeremiah, who barely escaped with his life when accused of predicting the temple's destruction, and of Uriah, who did not escape (Je. 26:7-24).

It seems, however, that Mark, even though he stigmatises the charge as ψευδομαρτυρία, regards it nonetheless as theologically significant.[15] He has not recorded a threat by Jesus that he himself will destroy the temple, nor a promise to rebuild it, but the words of Jesus in 13:2 provide a memorable starting point for the first part of such a charge even if they do not supply the alleged saying in so many words. Jesus' prediction of the fate of the temple was, Mark tells us, spoken in response to a disciple's admiring comments, apparently while still in the temple area; following Jesus' recent demonstration in the temple such words, heard by people outside the disciple group, would provide the basis for a damaging public perception of Jesus' prophetic objective.[16] As for the restoration διὰ τριῶν ἡμερῶν, the only remotely relevant sayings hitherto in Mark have been uttered only in private to the disciples, and have concerned Jesus' own resurrection μετὰ τρεῖς ἡμέρας (8:31; 9:31; 10:34); they bear no relation to the temple. It is John who connects the two ideas (Jn. 2:19-22), and nothing in Mark prepares us for such a symbolic connection. Yet in the words of the charge as Mark records them there is a clear pointer to something more than a physical demolition and rebuilding of the Jerusalem temple. Four aspects of its wording call for attention.

14. E. P. Sanders, *Jesus,* has particularly stressed the importance of Jesus' perceived hostility to the temple as perhaps the main reason for his loss of popular as well as official support. He discusses the sayings relating to the destruction and rebuilding of the temple on pp. 71-76 and concludes that even on his remarkably stringent criteria of authenticity some such sayings must be derived from what Jesus actually said and did. Cf. Myers, 375 (following G. Theissen): 'A platform based upon rejecting the role of the temple would not have been popular among those economically dependent on it — which was the better part of the Jerusalem populace!'

15. See D. Juel, *Messiah,* 118.

16. Gundry, 905-6, discusses the possible trajectory from Jesus' words in 13:2 to this charge via information given to the authorities by Judas. In the process, he believes, the prediction of 13:2 has become 'mingle-mangled' with Jesus' predictions of his own resurrection.

First, we find here (and in 15:29) ναός, the term generally understood to designate the sanctuary building proper, rather than ἱερόν, the broader term for the whole temple complex including even the vast Court of the Gentiles. It is the latter term which Mark has used consistently hitherto to indicate the site of Jesus' teaching and activity in Jerusalem, and it was the disciple's admiration of the ἱερόν which evoked Jesus' prediction of destruction with special reference to αὗται αἱ μεγάλαι οἰκοδομαί, apparently extending more widely than just the ναός. The introduction of a new term, 'sanctuary' rather than 'temple', thus indicates that something different is afoot here, and in particular distances this alleged threat from what Jesus had in fact predicted about the fate of the ἱερόν.[17]

Secondly, only in Mark do we find the two adjectives χειροποίητος and ἀχειροποίητος used to contrast the threatened ναός with its replacement. χειροποίητος is used in the LXX for 'man-made' idols as opposed to the living God, and the negative form ἀχειροποίητος is an obvious coinage for its opposite. The sanctuary to be destroyed is then a physical, human construction, but its three-day replacement will be of a quite different type, and its workmanship will not be human. The use of χειροποίητος in Acts 7:48 (cf. Acts 17:24) to dispute God's dwelling in a physical temple echoes the same idea, in a context where Stephen's rhetoric is deliberately picking up Jesus' thought in response to the charge that the Christian movement is against the temple (Acts 6:13-14).[18] Compare Heb. 9:11, 24, where Christ's true sanctuary is contrasted with the earthly sanctuary in that it is οὐ χειροποίητος, τοῦτ' ἔστιν οὐ ταύτης τῆς κτίσεως.[19]

Thirdly, only in this version of the temple saying (contrast Mt. 26:61; Jn. 2:19, and even Mark's own subsequent reference to the issue in 15:29) is the future sanctuary referred to as ἄλλον, not a rebuilding of the present structure but of another, as indeed the χειροποίητον/ἀχειροποίητον contrast also indicates.

Fourthly, the physically absurd concept of rebuilding διὰ τριῶν ἡμερῶν (in itself an expression for a short space of time, as in Ho. 6:2, but with other resonances for the Christian reader) lifts this pronouncement above the level of a literal rebuilding.

Presumably the gravamen of the charge as presented before the High Priest was Jesus' alleged threat to destroy the temple, literally. But by wording it in this way Mark has gone much further than a hostile witness is likely to

17. For Mark's use of the two terms see D. Juel, *Messiah,* 127-28.

18. Mann, 623-24, quotes from a letter of A. Spiro arguing that the attack on the Jerusalem temple as 'hand-made' reflects Samaritan polemic and suggesting that Mark has Samaritan sympathies.

19. For the same terminology used to distinguish the earthly from the heavenly or spiritual in other contexts, see 2 Cor. 5:1 ('house' = body); Eph. 2:11; Col. 2:11 (circumcision). These latter uses together with the Hebrews uses noted above are the basis of the conclusion of D. Juel, *Messiah,* 156, that the terms indicate 'a contrast between what is natural and unnatural, between man-made and miraculous, between something of this order and something of another order'. Juel discusses the interpretation of (ἀ)χειροποίητος at length on pp. 144-57.

have wanted or indeed been able to go, and has woven into the (false) charge a (true) statement[20] of what was by his time a significant theme in Christian preaching and apologetics, the theme of a new sanctuary. The topic recurs frequently in the NT (notably Mt. 12:6; 1 Cor. 3:16-17; 6:19; 1 Pet. 2:4-5), with the implication that God's presence is no longer located in a building but in his people both individually and, more often, corporately.[21] This is the ναὸς ἀχειροποίητος to which this verse alludes, and a Christian reader, even without knowing Jn. 2:19-22, could hardly fail to recognise in the idea of its being raised up διὰ τριῶν ἡμερῶν a reference to Jesus' resurrection, through which this new relationship with God becomes possible.[22] All this is good Christian theology, but hardly likely to form part of the ψευδομαρτυρία offered to the High Priest. Mark, while dismissing the charge as false, is taking the opportunity to remind his readers that the prediction on which it was based (13:2) had more far-reaching implications than merely the destruction of a building.[23]

Within the context of the hearing, even if technically false, the charge contributes to the development of the case against Jesus. The destruction and rebuilding of the temple are clearly not within the province of an ordinary preacher, and there is evidence that some Jews in the first century believed that the existing temple was to be replaced with a new one in the last days.[24] And while this was normally regarded as the work of God himself, there were some who thought that the work of rebuilding would be the task of the Messiah.[25] In

20. E. Best, *Following,* 214, develops the theme of truth spoken by 'false' witnesses in Mark. For a careful attempt to trace the development in Christian understanding of the mission of Jesus which led to this 'true/false' formulation see R. E. Brown, *Death,* 448-53.

21. For a full study of this theme see B. Gärtner, *Temple;* R. J. McKelvey, *Temple.* D. Juel, *Messiah,* 159-68 (following G. Klinzing, *Umdeutung*), summarises the evidence that the Qumran community also understood themselves under the imagery of a 'temple'.

22. Cf. B. Gärtner, *Temple,* 112-13. E. E. Ellis in J. B. Green and M. M. B. Turner (ed.), *Jesus of Nazareth: Lord and Christ,* 201-2, understands the allusion to Jesus' resurrection here as part of a developing 'deity-christology' which he traces through several other Marcan texts (192-203). Cf. also Gundry, 899-900, for the view that the charge here implied is that Jesus 'arrogated to himself divine roles'.

23. Contrast the version of this saying in *Gos. Thom.* 71, which reads simply: 'I shall destroy this house and no one will be able to rebuild it.'

24. Ezk. 40-48 provides the starting point for hopes of a new temple. See also, e.g., *1 Enoch* 90:28-29; 91:13; *Jub.* 1:17, 27. See further R. E. Brown, *Death,* 441-43. The repudiation of the Jerusalem temple by the people of Qumran did not indicate that no temple was needed, but that a new one was awaited; see 4Q174 *(Florilegium)* 1:1-7; 11Q19 *(Temple)* 29:8-10.

25. This belief derives from 2 Sa. 7:13 and from Zc. 6:12, and is clearly found in rabbinic literature. Evidence clearly reflecting this belief for the first century A.D. is not extensive (more frequently God himself is spoken of as the builder), but see the targums on Is. 53:5 and Zc. 6:12-13; 4 Ezra 13:36. In 4Q174 *(Florilegium)* the building of the new temple is linked with the coming of the Messiah, though he is not said to be the builder, an omission which Gundry, 899, considers to be significant as 'passing over a golden opportunity'. On the *Florilegium* text see further D. Juel, *Messiah,* 172-81, and on the evidence from targums Juel, *Messiah,* 182-196. For a useful recent summary of discussion on this issue see D. L. Bock, *Blasphemy,* 213 n. 69. Note the importance of 2 Sa. 7:12-14 as a starting point for this belief; see J. D. G. Dunn, *Partings,* 52.

that case the next issue raised in v. 61 is, as argued in the introduction to this section, a logical extension of the idea implied in the temple charge that Jesus is making claims which are appropriate only to the Messiah.

60 By standing up and taking centre stage the High Priest signals that the hearing has reached its decisive phase. Instead of facing unconvincing allegations from a variety of people Jesus now confronts direct questioning from the High Priest himself. The first question, however, does not introduce a new subject, but challenges Jesus to respond to what has already been alleged. In one sense there was nothing to respond to, since no agreed testimony had yet been offered. But Jesus' silence in the face of a growing list of allegations may have seemed contemptuous, and certainly did not make it any easier for the hearing to reach its desired end. The High Priest's words are best construed as two questions, with a question mark after οὐδέν as well as after καταμαρτυροῦσιν. The first is then a rhetorical challenge to Jesus' silence, the second a direct invitation to respond. But to take it as a single question, with the τί doing duty for a relative (BDF, 298[4], 299[1]), while grammatically awkward, would achieve the same sense.

61 The High Priest's direct intervention meets with the same response of silence. In v. 60 Mark left Jesus' silence to be assumed, but now he states it emphatically and formally with a typical dual expression.[26] The silence is impressive in itself, placing Jesus above the unedifying succession of ψευδομαρτυρία, but to a Christian reader familiar with the prophecy of the suffering servant in Is. 53 it no doubt also reinforced Jesus' assumption of that role (Is. 53:7), though Mark does not directly echo the wording of that passage.[27] The High Priest is therefore obliged to take the initiative again, this time with a question which goes to the heart of the reason Jesus has been brought before him.

Lohmeyer, 328, commented that Σὺ εἶ was an emphatic way to introduce the question, and described it as 'spöttisch oder ingrimmig' (sarcastic or furious). It thus indicates the High Priest's annoyance and implies how ludicrous it is for someone in Jesus' helpless position to make such grandiose claims. This suggestion may well reconstruct the High Priest's likely mood, but it can hardly be drawn from the phrase Σὺ εἶ itself since it is hard to see how else such a question could be asked; the expressed pronoun which in a statement would draw attention by its redundancy is a necessary part of the question about someone's identity. I have discussed the terms in which the question is formulated in the introduction to this section, and have suggested there that they draw out the basis of the authority implicit in Jesus' public words and actions since coming to Jerusalem (and indeed before), together

---

26. Elsewhere Mark always expresses the aorist of ἀποκρίνομαι in the passive form. Here he uses the middle, a classical usage which in the papyri (as in the LXX) was employed specifically in formal legal situations for responding to a charge (MM, 64b-65a).

27. The allusion is helpfully discussed by D. J. Moo, *The OT,* 148-51; R. E. Watts, *Exodus,* 363-64.

with the special status which he hinted at by casting himself in the role of the only son of the owner of the vineyard. While Mark has recorded no open claim by Jesus to be Messiah or Son of God, in these public deeds and words there is enough fuel for such a charge. It is also possible that part of Judas's offer to the chief priests had been to brief them also on Jesus' more private teaching to his disciples.

Both terms are ones which Jesus himself has hitherto in Mark used with caution, if at all. Not only has he only once been recorded as referring to himself, untypically, as ὁ Χριστός (see on 9:41), but he has instructed his disciples not to speak about him in such terms (8:30) and has conspicuously substituted the term ὁ υἱὸς τοῦ ἀνθρώπου to refer to himself and his mission (8:31 etc.).[28] The 'messianic' implications of what he has said and done (notably the ride to Jerusalem) have not been expressed in the title itself. As for 'Son of God', while it has been used by God and by demons (1:11; 9:7; 3:11; 5:7), Jesus has directly referred to himself as ὁ υἱός only once, to a private audience of four disciples (13:32), and in public has contented himself with the veiled hint of a parable character who is not explicitly identified.[29] The High Priest's question is therefore well framed to draw into the open what has hitherto been a matter of indirect implications.[30]

It has sometimes been suggested that no Jewish High Priest in the early first century would have thought of coupling the two titles ὁ Χριστός and ὁ υἱὸς τοῦ θεοῦ (εὐλογητοῦ). It is now clear, however, from a few references at Qumran that the thought of the Messiah as 'Son of God' was not foreign to the Judaism of this period,[31] though not in the metaphysical sense of later Christian theology. In any case, what brings the two titles together in Mark's narrative context is not any preexisting connection between them but the fact that Jesus is understood to have been presenting himself in both these capacities, not necessarily together, but as two aspects of his alleged claims to a special authority. In bringing the two ideas together in a single loaded ques-

28. The connection of this passage with 8:29-31 is clear in that both concern the declaration of Jesus' Messiahship, and the secrecy of the one is contrasted with the open declaration of the other. It is not so obvious that the two passages are deliberately constucted in a parallel and yet contrasting manner as is suggested by M. A. Beavis, *Audience,* 116-19.

29. For the importance of 12:1-12 as background to the present text see J. D. Kingsbury, *Christology,* 117-19.

30. An interesting discussion of 'The Silence of Jesus' by J. C. O'Neill, *NTS* 15 (1968/9) 153-67, argues that while Jesus thought himself to be the Messiah, and acted in a way which showed this, he refrained from declaring his own Messiahship because it was a Jewish understanding at that time 'that the Messiah would not be able to claim Messiahship for himself, but must wait for God to enthrone him' (165). Unfortunately, Jesus' ἐγώ εἰμι in 14:62 does not fit in with this pattern, and O'Neill finds it necessary to defend the reading of Θ etc. there (see Textual Note on v. 62) which assimilates Mark to Matthew and Luke with an apparently equivocal answer.

31. See 4Q174 *(Florilegium);* 4Q246 *(ps. Dan.)* 2:1; perhaps 1QSa[28a] 2:11-12. As 4Q174 makes clear, this was not an innovative Qumran usage since it was based on 2 Sa. 7:14, which, together with Ps. 2:7, had long been understood to refer to the Messiah. See further M. Hengel, *Son of God,* 43-45; D. Juel, *Messiah,* 108-14.

tion the High Priest is neatly summarising what Jesus is understood to have been implying about himself.[32]

The use of εὐλογητός in place of θεός reflects the Jewish avoidance of direct use of the name of God. In this context where 'blasphemy' is at issue, the usage is important, as the later formal definition of blasphemy involves 'pronouncing the name itself' (*m. Sanh.* 7:5). It is therefore the more noticeable that in Jesus' response in v. 62 the same delicacy is observed, where he uses ἡ δύναμις in place of 'God'. ὁ εὐλογητός alone as a title for God (as opposed to the frequent adjectival use, 'Blessed be God . . .', Lk. 1:68; Eph. 1:3; 1 Pet. 1:3, etc.) does not occur elsewhere in biblical literature, but its appropriateness in a Jewish context is attested by such formulae as 'Bless the Lord who is to be blessed *(hammᵉbārûk)'* (*m. Ber.* 7:3); in *1 Enoch* 77:1 God is described as 'the Eternally Blessed'.[33]

62 With this verse we come to the christological climax of the gospel. In view of the persistent theme of secrecy which has run through this gospel, including specifically secrecy concerning Jesus' messianic status (8:29-30), it is the more remarkable that it is only in Mark that Jesus replies to the High Priest's question with a simple and emphatic affirmative, Ἐγώ εἰμι.[34] In Matthew and Luke the answer, while affirmative in substance, is guarded and circumlocutory (σὺ εἶπας in Matthew; in Luke the question comes in two parts, the first [Messiah] answered by 'If I tell you you will not believe' and the second [Son of God] by ὑμεῖς λέγετε ὅτι ἐγώ εἰμι). Mark will have the same circumlocution when Jesus responds to Pilate's question, 'Are you the King of the Jews?' (15:2), but here, before the highest authority of Israel, he depicts Jesus as having no hesitation.[35] The time for concealment is

32. J. Marcus, *NovT* 31 (1989) 125-41, raises the significant question whether the two titles in the phrase ὁ Χριστὸς ὁ υἱὸς τοῦ εὐλογητοῦ are to be understood as in 'non-restrictive apposition' (so that they are effectively synonyms) or in 'restrictive apposition', whereby the second qualifies and restricts the first, thus indicating which *type* of Messiah Jesus claims to be. In view of the known variety of messianic models in first-century Jewish thought, Marcus argues for the latter: Jesus is asked not simply whether he is a 'Messiah–Son-of-David' (a claim which, however questionable, is hardly blasphemous) but whether he is 'Messiah–Son-of-God', a new and disturbing concept which 'introduces an idea of quasi-divinity that is the basis of Jesus' condemnation'.

33. See further D. L. Bock, *Blasphemy,* 215-17, with additional later Jewish references. Bock effectively refutes the claim by D. Juel, *Messiah,* 79, that ὁ υἱὸς τοῦ εὐλογητοῦ is a 'pseudo-Jewish expression created by the author'.

34. E. Stauffer, *Jesus,* 102 (and cf. 142-59), argued that Jesus' words deliberately echo the *ᵃnî hû'* of Is. 43:10, 13 etc, and others have similarly suggested that Jesus' Ἐγώ εἰμι was in effect a pronouncing of the divine name (cf. Ex. 3:14); Hooker, 362, considers this a 'possibility', and Stock, 381, finds in the ἐγώ εἰμι an 'affirmation of parity' (with God). But, quite apart from the fact that an uttering of the divine name hardly answers the High Priest's question, this is to build far too much on a natural Greek expression. In answer to the question Σὺ εἶ . . . ; the correct and only idiomatic way to give an affirmative answer is Ἐγώ εἰμι. See above on 6:50 (p. 273 n. 71) and on 13:6. In *TDNT,* 2.352 Stauffer himself lists Mk. 14:62 as an 'ordinary use' of ἐγώ εἰμι as opposed to the 'full emphatic sense' of a divine self-revelation. See further D. Juel, *Messiah,* 99.

35. Myers, 376, following Vincent Taylor, favours the Θ reading σὺ εἶπας ὅτι ἐγώ εἰμι (see Textual Note), and suggests in that light a bold and, as far as I know, unparalleled 'alternative translation': 'Jesus returns the High Priest's mockery: "Am I?"'

over,[36] and the truth must be declared firmly and openly to those who presume to set themselves as judges over him.

Indeed, in contrast with Jesus' previous silence, he now seems eager to explain how he understands his status and mission. The ἐγώ εἰμι is followed by a καί, whereas Matthew in view of the more guarded σὺ εἶπας needs to set the following positive statement off with a πλήν (cf. Luke's δέ). Jesus is going on to unpack what the titles he has just acknowledged imply, though it is significant that here, just as in 8:29-31, having received the title ὁ Χριστός from the High Priest, he discards it in favour of his own chosen title, ὁ υἱὸς τοῦ ἀνθρώπου. In 8:31, however, he used the title to speak of his future rejection and death; here he uses it to speak of glory and power. The pronouncement is made up almost entirely of words from two OT passages, Ps. 110:1 and Dn. 7:13.[37] The two texts are woven together in that the Daniel introduction about 'seeing the Son of Man' precedes the imagery from Ps. 110, which is then filled out with the substance of the Daniel vision. But while the words (except for the 'euphemism' τῆς δυναμέως noted above) are drawn from these two passages, the total effect is greater than the sum of the parts, and puts both texts in a new light.

In the first place, whereas the 'seeing' of Dn. 7:13 denoted the prophet's own vision, now it is Jesus' judges who 'will see the Son of Man'. Unlike Matthew and Luke, Mark does not specify *when* they will see, but in the comments that follow I shall argue that he has in mind the same immediacy which is expressed in Matthew's ἀπ' ἄρτι and Luke's ἀπὸ τοῦ νῦν. That is, after all, what the second-person address would naturally imply: the vision will be that of those who hear Jesus speaking, not of some future generation.[38] It is only the mistaken presupposition that these words have to do with the parousia which has led anyone to think otherwise (and to try to evade the force of the very clear time indications in Matthew and Luke with indefensible 'translations' such as NIV's 'in the future'). In introducing the discussion of 13:3-37 I have already mentioned[39] the increasing recognition among interpreters that the language of 'coming with clouds' here has no more reference to a coming *to earth* (at the

---

36. Belo, 219, explains why there is no longer a danger of his 'Messiahship' being misunderstood in Zealot-type terms: 'Not simply the fact that he was a Nazarean, a Galilean, a carpenter, a rabbi to sinners and tax collectors, for all this was already legible in the past. . . . The new thing here is his situation as a prisoner, the *powerlessness* of his body, the stopping of his practice by the forces of the SOC [Belo's abbreviation for the 'social code', i.e., the status quo].'

37. C. F. D. Moule, *Origin,* 24-26, considers sympathetically the suggestion made independently by C. H. Dodd and O. J. F. Seitz that the two passages were brought together by way of Ps. 80:16, 18, where a 'son of man' is described also as 'the man of [God's] right hand', but concludes that the two passages are already so closely linked in content as to need no such catalyst to bring them together. Seitz's arguments are set out in *SE* 6 (1973) 481-88.

38. N. Perrin in W. H. Kelber (ed.), *Passion,* 91-92, attempts to evade this rather obvious point by the speculation that Mark intends his readers to understand the 'you' here as referring to themselves. As he rightly comments on this bold reinterpretation, 'By the very nature of the case nothing can be proven.'

39. Above, pp. 502-3.

parousia) than it had in its original context in Dn. 7:13. While relatively few commentators have yet accepted that 13:26 refers to a 'coming' within history to receive authority from God, in 14:62 that interpretation has now become firmly (though by no means universally) established.[40]

The combination of Ps. 110:1 and Dn. 7:13 produces a mixture of metaphors which some have found troubling, in that they cannot envisage anyone both 'sitting' and 'coming', at least in that order.[41] (The problem is compounded if the 'coming' is interpreted as a coming *to earth,* but since that is not what either Daniel or Mark says we need not pursue that red herring.) It has therefore sometimes been assumed that the simple καί with which Mark links the two metaphors conceals a time break: first sitting and then subsequently coming. But this again is not what Mark says, and the whole problem arises from a failure to interpret familiar OT metaphors as such, metaphors. Both passages in fact express in their distinctive ways the same concept of a sovereign authority. This is obvious in the case of the psalm, 'sitting at the right hand of [God]', but if Dn. 7:13 is read in context it conveys the same message, in that the one who comes before God in the clouds of heaven is immediately given 'dominion and glory and kingship' which are both universal and unending (on the interpretation of Jesus' references to Dn. 7:13 see above on 8:38 and further comments at 13:26). Dn. 7:13-14 is, in other words, no less than Ps. 110:1 an enthronement oracle,[42] and it is that universal and unending dominion which Jesus here declares that he himself will now receive — and they will see it.[43]

How they will see it is not spelled out. But when the prisoner about to be

40. Commentators who favour the non-parousia interpretation here include Gnilka, Hooker, and Mann. G. R. Beasley-Murray, *Kingdom,* 300, speaks of 'a considerable shift of opinion' in this direction in recent years, deriving especially from the work of T. F. Glasson and J. A. T. Robinson. M. D. Hooker, *Son of Man,* 167-71, was an early harbinger of this change. Beasley-Murray describes the non-parousia interpretation rather exaggeratedly as now 'a major consensus', though his following comments suggest that he himself is not yet fully persuaded. A parousia reference is still maintained by Lane and Gundry, while a surprising number of commentators manage to avoid making their view on this issue clear at all.

41. In a Cambridge seminar G. M. Styler once memorably illustrated the fact that the order in which items are mentioned is not necessarily meant to be chronological by reference to a notice displayed at the entrance to St Catherine's College fellows' car park: 'These gates may be closed at any time and unauthorised cars removed'.

42. 'Although the phrase "sitting at the right hand" . . . is most directly an allusion to Ps. 110:1, it is also consonant with the picture in Dan. 7:13-14 of the humanlike figure being presented to the Ancient of Days and made his co-regent.' (J. Marcus, *Way,* 165). See also O. J. F. Seitz, *SE* 6 (1973) 484-88.

43. For the theme of 'seeing' in Jewish martyrdom texts see D. L. Bock, *Blasphemy,* 207; J. Marcus, *Way,* 165-67. Both emphasise especially *1 Enoch* 62:3-5, which speaks of the high officials seeing the Son of Man enthroned in glory and being terrified. (The connection was made earlier, e.g., by F. H. Borsch, *NTS* 14 [1967/8] 565-67.) If we could be sure that the *Similitudes of Enoch* were earlier than the time of Jesus and Mark, we might regard this as a likely influence on the wording of Jesus' pronouncement here, but the date of that part of *1 Enoch* remains too uncertain to allow any confident claim. It is in any case testimony to a parallel development of the theme of vindication drawing on the imagery of Dn. 7.

condemned and executed declares that his judges will see his God-given authority, we are clearly in the realm of vindication, a vindication which was to begin with Jesus' resurrection and according to Luke to be more visibly confirmed by his ascension (seen, however, like his resurrection not by the Sanhedrin but by his disciples). The language about 'sitting at God's right hand' soon became established in Christian tradition to denote the universal sovereignty of the risen Jesus, 'waiting till his enemies be made his footstool' (Heb. 10:12-13, and numerous allusions to Ps. 110:1 in Hebrews). That sovereignty began to become visible outside the group of disciples with the powerful growth of the NT church, and in a negative sense in the demise of Jerusalem and its temple as the focus of God's rule on earth (in connection with which we have already seen Dn. 7:13 deployed in 13:26; see notes there). All this offers a similar range of interpretation to what we found for the 'seeing' in 9:1, and again here it is in connection with 'power'. We need not be more specific, since Mark is not, but within this complex of events it would certainly be possible for Jesus' judges within their lifetime to see that the 'Messiah' they thought they had destroyed had in fact been vindicated and exalted to the place of supreme authority.

We have already considered the 'messianic' significance of both Ps. 110:1 (see on 12:35-37) and Dn. 7:13 (see on 8:38; 13:26) and need not go over the same ground again. In view of their multiple appearance in the gospel tradition and, in the case of Ps. 110, in later Christian interpretation of Jesus, it is reasonable to conclude that each individually, but more still the two in combination as here, provided an essential basis for Jesus' own understanding of where his mission was leading. This is further underlined by the fact that it is from the latter of these two passages that Jesus took his own chosen term to express his mission, ὁ υἱὸς τοῦ ἀνθρώπου. His use of that title here in place of the High Priest's ὁ Χριστός serves to emphasise the contrast between this vision and the connotations which the term Χριστός might have evoked for most Jews at the time. He *is* the Messiah (ἐγώ εἰμι), but his messianic vision is on a different level altogether from what the High Priest may have been implying. Any concept of the Messiah as a nationalistic deliverer at a political level has been left far behind: Jesus' 'triumph' is to be at the right hand of God. Even though the charge brought before Pilate will resuscitate the more political connotations of the term Χριστός, Jesus has in this climactic declaration again distanced himself decisively from any such understanding of his mission.

For Jesus' use of ἡ δύναμις rather than directly pronouncing the name of God,[44] parallel to the High Priest's use of ὁ εὐλογητός, see the comments on v. 61 above. There are several rabbinic parallels to this substitution, using the Hebrew *hagge bûrâ*.[45]

---

44. O. J. F. Seitz, *SE* 6 (1973) 494, offers OT evidence for the naturalness of 'the Power' as 'a metonym or reverential surrogate for the divine name'.

45. D. L. Bock, *Blasphemy*, 217-19. Several of the passages cited refer to Moses' unique privilege of hearing the voice of 'the Almighty', though none go so far as to speak of sitting beside

63 According to mishnaic rules, when blasphemy has been proven using euphemisms in open court, the chief witness is asked to repeat the offending words verbatim in a closed session so that the people as a whole do not hear them, and then 'the judges stand up on their feet and rend their garments, and they may not mend them again' (*m. Sanh.* 7:5; for tearing clothes as an expression of grief see Gn. 37:34; Jos. 7:6; 2 Sa. 1:11 and in response to blasphemy 2 Ki. 18:37; 19:1). In this case no witnesses are needed, as the judges themselves have heard the offending words, and the dramatic gesture by the High Priest (who was already standing, v. 60) speaks for them all. It is possible that the whole group also tore their clothes as the later rules required, but Mark's silence on this matter suggests that the procedure had not yet been formalised to that extent. The plural χιτῶνες is surprising, as normally a single χιτών was worn, though see Josephus, *Ant.* 17.136, for the possibility of two tunics being worn at the same time. As the High Priest's robes, even when not officiating in the temple, were no doubt more elaborate than normal everyday wear,[46] he may have had more than one garment which could be described loosely by the common term χιτών, or perhaps, unusually, χιτῶνες here does duty for clothes in general (so BAGD, 882a) as ἱμάτια does here in Matthew and more generally.[47]

64 The unclassical use after ἀκούω of the genitive τῆς βλασφημίας (contrast Matthew's τὴν βλασφημίαν) for the thing heard (rather than the person) is probably not significant, as the NT has several examples of this usage (BAGD, 32a, 1.b.γ). The question of what constituted the βλασφημία has been much discussed. It is generally agreed that a claim to be the Messiah by itself, even if false, could not properly be regarded as blasphemous.[48] But Mark's account offers no basis for believing that Jesus had committed blasphemy in the sense of the later formal definition of blasphemy as 'pronouncing the Name itself' (*m. Sanh.* 7:5); indeed Jesus, like the High Priest, has conspicuously avoided doing so by his use of the acceptable substitute ἡ δύναμις.[49] While it is always possible to argue[50] that Jesus in fact did pronounce the name of God

---

him. For a more detailed study of Jewish usage see A. M. Goldberg, *BZ* 8 (1964) 284-93, arguing that ἡ δύναμις is not so much a general 'substitute' for the name of God as a more specific term for God acting as judge ('die zum Gericht herrlich erscheinende Gottheit').

46. We should not understand Mark to be speaking of the formal High-Priestly vestments, which were kept locked up in the fort of Antonia and taken out only for liturgical use on feast days (Josephus, *Ant.* 18.91-94; cf. 15.403-4).

47. It is probably taking Mark's choice of term too literally to suggest that he specifically envisages 'tearing down to the bare skin' (Gundry, 887; cf. 914).

48. In the light of the discussion by J. Marcus (see above, p. 610 n. 32), this frequent observation should be qualified: it was not blasphemous to claim to be 'Messiah–Son-of-David', but Jesus' alleged new category of 'Messiah–Son-of-God' would be a different matter.

49. For the suggestion that the Name was pronounced in Jesus' reply Ἐγώ εἰμι see above, p. 610 n. 34.

50. As Gundry, 915-18; C. A. Evans, *Jesus,* 412-13. See the response by D. L. Bock, *Blasphemy,* 197-200.

(which in his quotation from Ps. 110:1 would have been reproduced in Greek by the LXX term ὁ κύριος), and that the substitute name has been imported subsequently into the traditional account to avoid offence, this seems an unnecessarily complicated explanation, particularly in view of the fact that elsewhere in Mark there seems to be no embarrassment in having Jesus refer to God as either θεός or κύριος, including his other quotation of Ps. 110:1 in 12:36. The suggestion arises from the assumption that in the time of Jesus 'blasphemy' meant specifically (and only) what is defined later in the Mishnah, but this is a very questionable assumption.[51]

Fortunately, we have a recent exhaustive and careful study of the matter by D. L. Bock,[52] and his conclusions will be the basis of these comments. Bock surveys references to blasphemy in a very wide range of Jewish literature from the OT to the NT period and beyond, and concludes that the mishnaic definition is narrower than general usage. Arrogant speech and even action against God and his people (and even the temple) could in some mainstream Jewish circles be construed as 'blasphemous' and punished as such. There is thus much more scope in the alleged words and deeds of Jesus to support a charge of blasphemy than merely an explicit use of the name of God.

Bock then goes on to discuss another related topic, how far in the Judaism of this period it was considered legitimate to speak of anyone 'sitting at the right hand' of God.[53] An equally full survey of this less commonly traversed ground concludes that whereas it was conceivable that a few very special people in the past (notably Moses and Enoch) might in some Jewish circles be considered worthy of the honour of sitting beside God, for anyone to make such a claim for himself was unthinkable, and 'to equate anyone else with God is to risk thinking blasphemously'.[54]

In the results of Bock's surveys we have ample material to enable us to explain the High Priest's verdict of βλασφημία. Given this climate of thought, it was not merely any particular words which Jesus had used that led to his conviction, but the whole nature of the claim to a special relationship with God which was rightly understood to underlie those words. To say such things of anyone else among one's contemporaries would be bad enough; for a Galilean preacher to make such claims for himself was outrageous.

Further, Jesus has spoken of those who hear him 'seeing' him in his role

51. R. E. Brown, *Death,* 522-23, points out that much of the discussion on this issue is beside the point, since the mishnaic definition is in Hebrew, while as far as Greek usage is concerned, 'one is hard pressed to find even a single example of a word of the stem "blasphem-" used precisely and specifically for naming the divine Name'.

52. D. L. Bock, *Blasphemy.* The discussion of blasphemy proper takes up pp. 30-112, and is usefully summarised on pp. 110-12.

53. D. Juel, *Messiah,* 104, following O. Linton, draws attention to the parallel with the 'condemnation' of Stephen, which Juel argues was also for blasphemy, when he spoke of seeing the Son of Man standing at the right hand of God (Acts 7:56).

54. D. L. Bock, *Blasphemy,* 183, summarising the fascinating and ground-breaking discussion of pp. 113-83.

as ruler and judge at God's right hand.[55] This is a breathtaking reversal of roles, and casts the Galilean preacher in the role of judge over them, the appointed leadership of God's people. Here was another basis for the charge of blasphemy, for Ex. 22:27 (EVV 22:28) places 'cursing a leader of your people' alongside 'reviling God', and Jesus' words have in effect demoted them from their God-given role of leadership. Such threatening language was unforgivable.[56]

So what Jesus has said in v. 62 supplies more than enough evidence for a verdict that he was guilty of blasphemy (unless, of course, what he said was true, and that appears not surprisingly not to have been entertained as a possible explanation). Cranfield, 445, suggests that the rather clumsy expression[57] αὐτὸν ἔνοχον εἶναι θανάτου reveals Mark's awareness that this was not a formal trial, so that 'they were not pronouncing a sentence but rather giving a legal opinion'; Mann, 615, goes further: 'There was no judicial or even semi-judicial proceeding before the Sanhedrin. . . . Mark can only — at most — say that there was an agreement that Jesus "deserved" to die.' As far as the legal standing of this hearing is concerned, that is probably correct, but by using the verb κατακρίνω Mark makes it plain that the Sanhedrin members were in intention condemning Jesus to death, even though they did not have the formal capacity to execute him.

The penalty for blasphemy was death by stoning (Lv. 24:10-16; m. Sanh. 7:4-5). Had they had the right to do so, this is presumably what the Sanhedrin would have wished to do, but under the Roman occupation they lacked that power[58] (though it was occasionally carried out *ultra vires,* Acts 7:58-60; Josephus, *Ant.* 20.200; the latter significantly took place when no Roman procurator was in office) and so must find a way to have the execution carried out under Roman law, and by Roman means.[59] In a Roman court βλασφημία, as un-

55. See J. Marcus, *Way,* 165-67, for the element of 'judgment' implicit in the imagery of Dn. 7 and its ironic implications for this scene where Jesus is officially the one on trial. The dismissal of this element by Gundry, 914, depends on too rigid a separation between the roles of the Ancient of Days and the Son of Man in Dn. 7.

56. This aspect of the blasphemy charge is well drawn out by D. L. Bock, *Blasphemy,* 206-9.

57. R. E. Brown, *Death,* 529, tries to convey the double sense of ἔνοχος ('guilty of' and 'liable to') by the phrase 'guilty, to be punished by death'.

58. See above, p. 602 n. 5.

59. Crucifixion as such is generally thought of as a distinctively Roman form of punishment (though already famously copied by the Jewish ruler Alexander Jannaeus over a century earlier), but something much like it was also apparently envisaged in the strictly Jewish context of Qumran for a similar offence: 11Q19 *(Temple)* 64:6-13 speaks of 'hanging on the wood (or tree)' as the appropriate penalty for someone who has 'done evil to his people' by passing on information about them and betraying them to a foreign power. While this may be taken as simply treason, D. L. Bock, *Blasphemy,* 208, suggests a connection also with blasphemy in that the people are also *God's* people. Even before the 11Q19 text was published, E. Bammel, in E. Bammel (ed.), *Trial,* 162-65, was able to construct an argument for Jewish use of crucifixion since the second century BC. See further M. Hengel, *Crucifixion,* 84-85, arguing that no Jewish crucifixions took place after Herod the Great.

derstood by the Jews, would not count as a capital offence, but Jesus' open acknowledgement of his status as ὁ Χριστός has provided the basis for a charge which can be made to sound like political treason. We shall reach this next stage of the proceedings in 15:1-2.

65 But first Mark has to record some remarkable behaviour on the part of the leading citizens of Jerusalem. Luke, perhaps feeling that such undignified conduct is inappropriate for the members of the Sanhedrin themselves, attributes this ill-treatment of Jesus to 'the men who were holding him', but Mark rules out that option by mentioning οἱ ὑπηρέται separately and subsequently. His τινες can then only be members of the Sanhedrin. The explanation may lie in the fact that in Mark, unlike in Luke, this action takes place immediately after the verdict of blasphemy has been reached; like the tearing of the clothes the physical abuse of the convicted man may be part of the accepted ritual, a way of visibly dissociating themselves from his blasphemy. This is the contention of J. D. M. Derrett,[60] who goes on to claim that the demand for the blindfolded Jesus to 'Prophesy' is similarly to be explained as the sequel to the conviction, in that (on the basis of Is. 11:3) one who claimed to be Messiah was popularly expected to be able to identify his assailant by smell without seeing him. In any case, once we get rid of the idea that this was a formal trial, there seems less reason to doubt that some of the Sanhedrin might wish to express their hatred and disdain for the 'blasphemer' in such a direct way. The reader is not likely to miss the irony of their sarcastic demand that Jesus 'prophesy' when the way they are treating him is in fact itself a direct fulfilment of what he has earlier predicted as his own fate in Jerusalem (just as the incident immediately following in vv. 66-72 will fulfil exactly another more recent prediction).

Jesus' last passion prediction (10:33-34) has included spitting, but there as part of what the Gentiles will do (as indeed they will at 15:19). Spitting is a universal way of expressing contempt and insult (Job 30:9-10; cf. its formal judicial use in Dt. 25:9), and as such was part of the fate to be endured by the Servant of Yahweh in Is. 50:6, so it fits appropriately in this Jewish context. The blindfolding and beating, while they could be simply further ill-treatment for its own sake, may be more specifically linked with the call Προφήτευσον, as Derrett suggests. Mark does not spell out just how Jesus is expected to 'prophesy'[61] (see Textual Note), but the expansion in both Matthew and Luke with τίς ἐστιν ὁ παίσας σε; indicates a much more specific focus, the ability of this alleged Messiah to identify those who hit him; Matthew's further addition of Χριστέ reinforces Derrett's suggestion, which on the basis of Mark's text alone remains insecurely founded, even though Mark explicitly mentions the

---

60. J. D. M. Derrett, *Law,* 407-8.

61. J. Jeremias, *Theology,* 77-78, argues that this 'kind of blind man's buff' shows that the essence of Jesus' alleged fault was that he was a false prophet. D. J. Moo, *The OT,* 346-47, discusses the possibility that it derives from the idea that he claimed to be 'the prophet like Moses'.

blindfolding which Matthew simply assumes (see Textual Note).[62] In the light of Mt. 5:39 ῥαπίσμασιν ἔλαβον[63] (ῥαπίζω elsewhere often means to hit with a stick or whip) may not here differ significantly in meaning from κολαφίζειν, to strike with the hand or fist (though Mt. 26:67 perhaps treats the two actions as different); but ῥαπίσματα adds a further echo of LXX Is. 50:6.[64] The involvement of οἱ ὑπηρέται broadens the sense of the rejection of Jesus by his own people, and also prepares us for the change of scene in v. 66 to the contrasting experience of Peter among the servants out in the courtyard. (Gundry, 888, 919-20, thinks that the last clause of v. 65 implies that after the members of the Sanhedrin have abused Jesus he has been brought out and put into the hands of the ὑπηρέται in the courtyard, where Peter is also sitting.)

Peter's Repudiation of Jesus (14:66-72)

TEXTUAL NOTES

68 and 72. Most of the textual variants in these verses derive from the two crowings of the cock which (if authentic) are a distinctive feature of Mark's narrative over against the three other gospels, and represent means of harmonising Mark to the more familiar single-crowing tradition. See the textual note on 14:30 above, and the further discussion (p. 573 n. 68) of the arguments of Wenham and Brady. On the view there adopted, we may best regard the omission of καὶ ἀλέκτωρ ἐφώνησεν in v. 68 and of ἐκ δευτέρου and of δίς in v. 72 as part of the same harmonistic tendency. The fact that MSS are far from consistent in the degree of their harmonisation suggests a continuing tension between the desire to harmonise and respect for the received text. The omission of καὶ ἀλέκτωρ ἐφώνησεν by B W and a number of versions in v. 68 while retaining ἐκ δευτέρου in v. 72 may be explained either as careless editing or by the assumption that ἐκ δευτέρου made specific mention of the first cockcrow unnecessary. Other variants in the latter part of v. 72 appear to be attempts either to harmonise along the same lines as in v. 30 or to avoid the awkward collocation of δίς and τρίς. Both vv. 30 and 72 display a remarkable variety in word order and construction.

72. ἔκλαυσεν (ℵ* A* C) looks like simple harmonisation to the tense in Matthew and Luke (which is in any case more natural in context). ἤρξατο (D Θ) is probably an attempt to put into better Greek the assumed meaning of the odd participle ἐπιβαλών (on which see below), in the same way that most of the versions have rendered it.

---

62. P. Benoit, in W. C. Van Unnik (ed.), *Neotestamentica et Patristica,* 92-97, analyses the relation between the different gospel accounts, and discusses a variety of alleged parallels to the incident in ancient literature, none of which (except Is. 50:4-6) is sufficiently close to the dynamics of the Sanhedrin's condemnation of Jesus to contribute significantly to our understanding of this verse. For further details on ancient games of mockery involving blindfolding see D. L. Miller, *JBL* 90 (1971) 309-13.

63. For the unusual idiom (a 'crude colloquialism'; Mann, 628) as a 'vulgar' Latinism see BDF, 5(3b), 198(3). R. E. Brown, *Death,* 576-77, suggests the translation 'got him with slaps'.

64. For the likelihood that this verse intentionally alludes to Is. 50:6 see D. J. Moo, *The OT,* 139-44; R. E. Watts, *Exodus,* 363.

We have noted at v. 54 the narrative preparation for the following scene located in the courtyard outside the High Priest's hall where the hearing concerning Jesus has been held, and in v. 65 the indication of the shift back to that secondary scene in the mention of the ὑπηρέται. We thus come now to the second of Mark's contrasting accounts of men under pressure. Indeed, a section break after v. 65 is more a matter of convenience than of a really new beginning, and Gundry (883) has good reason for treating the whole of vv. 53-72 as a single unit of narrative in that Peter's denials stand in deliberate contrast alongside Jesus' bold affirmation and are not merely a 'sidelight to Jesus' trial'.

This is the point where Jesus' very specific prediction of v. 30 will be equally specifically fulfilled, just as the more general prediction of v. 27 has already been fulfilled at Gethsemane. Peter's determination to be loyal to Jesus (vv. 29, 31) has brought him much further than the other disciples, but he, too, will now find the truth of Jesus' declaration that the spirit may be willing but the flesh is weak (v. 38). His willingness to come so much further into danger has raised the stakes, and accordingly his fall is dramatically more serious, even apparently to the extent of publicly cursing his master. After such flagrant disloyalty Mark's narrative can only leave Peter weeping, and he, like Judas, disappears from the rest of the narrative, leaving Jesus alone, betrayed and unsupported.

But there is one vital difference between Peter and Judas. While Peter will not again feature in Mark's narrative, he *will* be singled out for specific mention in the message of hope from the young man at the tomb in 16:7. Peter remains not only a member but the leading member of the disciple group, and as such he is summoned to the triumphant relaunch of Jesus' mission in Galilee. Mark does not directly explain the reason why Judas's defection is terminal but Peter's only temporary, but perhaps the answer is to be found in part in the last word of which Peter is the narrative subject, ἔκλαιεν. His remorse, contrasted with Judas's apparently settled disloyalty, points to failure under pressure rather than a deliberate change of allegiance, and for that, Mark's readers will have noted with relief, there remains the prospect of forgiveness and rehabilitation.

The threefold denial forms a memorable narrative sequence. As Mark relates it, the three challenges and the denials they provoke follow an incremental scale. The first challenge comes from a single slave girl apparently speaking to Peter privately, the second from the same girl but now appealing to a group of bystanders, and the third from the whole group of bystanders. In answer to the first Peter need only contradict one person's allegation, with the second he is forced into a public denial, and with the third he goes far beyond mere contradiction to an oath which must make any Christian reader flinch. The progress of his trial is also marked by a change of scene after the first denial, when he moves away from his more exposed position near the fire into a probably less-well-lighted area, the προαύλιον, and of course by the repeated crowing of the cock after the first and third denials, to remind the reader of what Jesus had predicted.

66-67   See on v. 54 for Peter's position near the fire (and therefore visible in its light; see the use there of φῶς rather than πῦρ); θερμαινόμενον reminds us of that scene. The household of someone as socially prominent as the High Priest would have contained a good number of slaves, male and female, who when not on duty would naturally gather in the αὐλή. The first challenge comes from just one of these.[65] The female diminutive form παιδίσκη may have the effect of emphasising her social insignificance — hardly a person for Peter to be afraid of. But in the NT (where the masculine παιδίσκος is not used) παιδίσκη does not generally have clear diminutive force, and can serve merely as the feminine form of παῖς (see Lk. 12:45). ἐμβλέψασα (which, following ἰδοῦσα, suggests a more searching look) presumes that she recognises Peter because she has seen him with Jesus[66] before, perhaps in Gethsemane, but more likely as one of the Galilean group who have been a prominent feature in the temple precincts during the days leading up to the Passover. In describing Jesus as ὁ Ναζαρηνός, the title by which he has already been publicly described outside the circle of his own followers (1:24; 10:47), she emphasises the foreign distinctiveness of this northern group, as the bystanders will repeat in v. 70. There may also be an element of sarcasm in the use of a term which elsewhere in the NT has 'essential undertones of dissociation and at the same time contempt'.[67]

68   The simple verb ἀρνέομαι need mean no more than to say that the preceding statement is false (as in Lk. 8:45; Jn. 1:20, etc.). But after the use of με/σε ἀπαρνέομαι in vv. 30 and 31 the reader is likely to detect also the fuller sense of 'disowning' Jesus (see above on 8:34 for this sense of the compound form; and cf. Mt. 10:33; Lk. 12:9 for a similar use of the simple verb); while (ἀπ)αρνέομαι was not used in 8:38, the reader may well recall Jesus' ominous words about the consequences of 'being ashamed' of him in this generation. The typically Marcan pleonastic expression οὔτε οἶδα οὔτε ἐπίσταμαι[68] is virtually tautologous, a rhetorical device to strengthen the force of the denial.[69] σὺ τί λέγεις is best understood as an indirect question expressing the content of Peter's professed ignorance,[70] rather than punctuated as a separate question as in the very clumsy RV mg.: 'I neither know, nor understand: thou, what sayest thou?'

---

65. Gundry, 920, suggests that the use of μία rather than τις may be designed to emphasise 'the narrowing down of the narrative from the whole Sanhedrin (vv. 53, 55) to some of them and their servants (v. 65) and now to a maid'.

66. It would be a remarkably alert reader who would detect in this use of μετά an echo of the original calling of the disciples to be μετ' αὐτοῦ in 3:14; so Gnilka, 2.292.

67. K. H. Rengstorf, *DNTT*, 2.334. Mann, 630, finds 'the note of scorn' here 'emphatic'.

68. BDF, 445(2), regard this use of οὔτε . . . οὔτε . . . as 'inadmissible', and the reading οὐκ . . . οὐδὲ . . . found in a few MSS as 'correct'. Most early Greek copyists, however, seem to have found Mark's idiom both clear and acceptable.

69. Mann, 629, suggests a differentiation of the two verbs as follows: '"I know nothing," he answered. "I do not understand what you mean."'

70. For a similar formula of disavowal see *m. Šebu.* 8:3, 6: 'I do not know of what you speak'.

Peter's move to the προαύλιον (probably the gateway or vestibule leading into the αὐλή from the street outside) was presumably an attempt to escape from an embarrassing encounter, and at the same time to get into a less-well-lighted place away from the fire. But he has not left altogether, but still seems to cling to his boast that he alone would stay with Jesus (14:31). For the first crowing of the cock see the Textual Note on 14:30 and on v. 68 above, and the notes on 14:29-31 for the likelihood of repeated crowings during the hours before dawn. The mention of the cockcrow here serves to increase the tension for the reader who remembers Jesus' prediction; it apparently has no effect on Peter.

69 The article indicates (and πάλιν confirms) that ἡ παιδίσκη is the same person as in v. 66; she has followed Peter out into the vestibule (or perhaps can see him out there as she talks about him to those near her)[71] and insists on her identification of him as a follower of Jesus. But this time she appeals to others to corroborate her assertion. The bystanders in the High Priest's courtyard would be likely to include some of the group who had arrested Jesus, who would therefore be in a better position to identify Peter as one of the men they had confronted there. The identification of Peter this time as ἐξ αὐτῶν, not simply as having been with Jesus, suggests that while it was only Jesus whom they had been sent to arrest, his followers were perceived as a coherent group of troublemakers.[72] Their rapid flight from Gethsemane, and the subsequent account by John of their meeting behind closed doors 'for fear of the Jews', confirm that they felt themselves to be a suspect group.

70 Peter's second denial, like Jesus' second prayer in Gethsemane, is reported without further detail, though the change in tense is surprising. Does the imperfect indicate a continuing or repeated denial rather than a single statement, or might it have a conative force: he tried to deny it? The difference from the first denial is not in its content but in the audience, now a group of bystanders who have heard the girl's allegation. But this more public denial also fails to convince, and a further challenge follows μετὰ μικρόν (allowing time for them to listen further to Peter's accent?). This time it is the group of bystanders as a whole who repeat the charge, using the girl's identifying phrase ἐξ αὐτῶν, but now confirming it by the observation that Peter is Γαλιλαῖος. Even at Passover time, when the city was full of pilgrims from other areas, a Galilean in Jerusalem (and particularly within the High Priest's courtyard) was sufficiently distinctive to draw attention, and Jesus and his disciples had come to public notice from the start as a Galilean group (see the introductory comments on 11:1-10). In view of the generally low view which Judaeans held of Galileans there is probably a note of contempt, possibly also

---

71. So R. E. Brown, *Death*, 602.

72. G. W. H. Lampe, *BJRL* 55 (1972/3) 346-68, considers the relevance of the story of Peter's denial to Christians who later faced official persecution, at a time when to be 'one of them' was dangerous, and traces aspects of its use by patristic writers.

of menace, in the phrase Γαλιλαῖος εἶ. Mark, unlike Matthew, does not say how Peter was identified as a Galilean, but Matthew's explanation that his northern accent gave him away rings true, especially if we are right to understand the imperfect ἠρνεῖτο as indicating that Peter continued trying to bluster his way out of trouble.

71 ἤρξατο indicates a new element in Peter's third denial. His recorded words, οὐκ οἶδα τὸν ἄνθρωπον τοῦτον ὅν λέγετε, are more explicitly a disavowal of Jesus than those in v. 68, and τὸν ἄνθρωπον τοῦτον is a strikingly dismissive way for Peter to speak of the person whom he has previously hailed as ὁ Χριστός. But the most telling new factor is the double mention of an oath. The second term, ὀμνύναι ὅτι, is the natural way to say that Peter underscored his statement by swearing that it was true, using some such formula as 'May God do . . . to me if . . .'. If the preceding ἀναθεματίζειν means 'to invoke a curse on himself' as some versions suggest (RSV, NIV) and as many commentators have assumed, it would then express the same sense. Mark is certainly capable of using two roughly synonymous expressions to emphasise a point, but it is questionable whether that is what he is doing here, since ἀναθεματίζω standing alone does not mean to swear in the sense of 'to invoke a curse on oneself'. It is a transitive verb,[73] essentially meaning to dedicate something to God (LXX Nu. 18:14), but almost always used in the LXX in the negative sense of 'devote to destruction', hence 'curse'. This usage lies behind the Pauline use of ἀνάθεμα as a curse formula (1 Cor. 12:3; 16:22; Gal. 1:8, 9). In the only other NT uses of the verb in Acts 23:12, 14, 21 the reflexive sense is achieved by adding ἑαυτούς; without that addition its meaning is to curse someone or something other than oneself. (Matthew here uses the rare καταθεματίζω, which is not discernibly different in meaning.) In this context the natural object to be understood is Jesus, so that Mark portrays Peter as voluntarily doing what Pliny was later informed that 'real Christians' could not be compelled to do (Pliny, *Ep.* 10.96.5), cursing Jesus.[74] This understanding of the text, which Christian interpreters naturally find unwelcome (hence translations such as RSV, NIV), is the most probable sense of Mark's words, though he has avoided too blatant offence by leaving the object of the verb unstated.[75]

72 Mark's characteristic narrative connection καὶ εὐθύς links Peter's third denial directly with the event which Jesus has said will follow it. See the Textual Notes above and at 14:30 for the harmonistic problems arising from the second cockcrow. Within Mark taken alone there is no problem: the second cockcrow is precisely the signal Jesus has mentioned in his prediction at 14:30,

73. BAGD, 54b, offer no justification for designating this one use 'intransitive'.
74. This interpretation was classically argued by H. Merkel in E. Bammel (ed.), *Trial*, 66-71, and independently by G. W. H. Lampe in *BJRL* 55 (1972/3) 354.
75. J. Behm, *TDNT*, 1.355, and K. E. Dewey in W. H. Kelber (ed.), *Passion*, 101, both believe that Mark deliberately leaves the object of the verb ambiguous, though they differ as to the nature of the ambiguity. E. Best, *Disciples*, 168 n. 31, disagrees, claiming that 'such ambiguities are not a Markan characteristic'.

and the repetition of those words rounds off the pattern of prediction and fulfilment. The point is emphasised by Mark's rather involved wording: 'the saying (ῥῆμα, used by Mark only here and in 9:32 of an equally emphatic and unwelcome prediction by Jesus), how Jesus had said to him . . .'[76] The slight variation in word order in the quoted prediction, if the text printed by UBS[4] is correct (see Textual Notes here and at 14:30), has the effect of placing δίς and τρίς side by side, an awkward but memorable play on words. We can only speculate on why Peter should apparently have failed to take warning from the first cockcrow, but break down at the second.

The three words which express his response, καὶ ἐπιβαλὼν ἔκλαιεν, are puzzling. An aorist tense, as in Matthew and Luke, would have seemed more natural for his 'bursting into tears', and it is loading the imperfect very heavily to take it as 'wept uncontrollably' or the like.[77] But ἐπιβαλών is even less natural. BAGD, 290a, 2.b, cannot fit this use under any of their attested meanings of ἐπιβάλλω (a 'wide-ranging, but oddly intransigent, verb'; Mann, 632), and offer a variety of suggestions including 'covering his head', 'thinking about it', and 'beginning [to weep]' or 'setting to [and weeping]', the latter being supported by one papyrus and a third-century use in Diogenes Laertius as well as by the variant texts (see Textual Note) which are probably themselves attempts to make sense of ἐπιβαλών.[78] A new suggestion by M. Casey[79] is that the verb means 'throwing [more abuse]', reflecting a Syriac/Aramaic idiom, but he rather undermines his proposal by going on to suggest that this might have resulted from a Greek translator mistaking Aramaic *sr'* ('begin') for *sd'* ('throw'); he thus supports 'beginning' as the original meaning, even if it is not what Mark thought it meant.

Mark's choice of idiom must remain obscure, but the essential sense is not in doubt: Peter's bold denials give way to remorse as he realises that he has fallen into precisely the trap of which Jesus had warned him. With that Mark's account is complete, and we are left to guess how the bystanders reacted to this apparent confession of guilt and how Peter escaped from his compromising situation in the προαύλιον of the High Priest's house.

---

76. See J. N. Birdsall, *NovT* 2 (1958) 272-75, for the effect of this use of ὡς to refer 'not to a simple recollection on Peter's part of the words of a prediction made by Jesus so shortly before, but the flooding back into his mind at the cockcrow of the whole situation described for us in Mk. xiv.17-31'.

77. Cf. F. Hauck, *TDNT,* 1.529: 'he began to weep bitterly'. Mann, 632, finds in the tense of the verb 'a long-continued grief, following upon shattering self-discovery'.

78. For a fuller range of classical and Hellenistic Greek uses of ἐπιβάλλω see F. Hauck, *TDNT,* 1.528-29; he also supports the meaning 'beginning'. So also BDF, 308. R. E. Brown, *Death,* 609-10, lists nine suggested meanings here.

79. M. Casey, *Sources,* 85-86.

The Roman Trial (15:1-15)

TEXTUAL NOTES

1. The reading ἐποίησαν (D Θ and many versions) simply 'improves' the syntax with its two participial clauses preceding the main verb. The choice between ποιήσαντες and ἑτοιμάσαντες for the first participle depends on whether συμβούλιον is taken to mean 'plan' or 'consultation/council meeting'. The ℵ C L reading ἑτοιμάσαντες assumes the former, whereas the ποιήσαντες of the majority of MSS (supported also by most of the versions) could go with either. Its fuller attestation and the fact that the D Θ reading also derives from it suggest that it is original, and that ἑτοιμάσαντες was an attempt to fix the former meaning (which is also found in Matthew, though with ἔλαβον) and thus avoid a repetition of the convening of the Sanhedrin in 14:53.

8. The sudden arrival (ἀναβάς) of the crowd is surprising, and the verb ἀναβαίνω less natural than Matthew's συνάγομαι. ἀναβοήσας (a verb Mark does not use elsewhere) therefore looks like an 'improved' reading, substituting the crowd's vocal activity, which is the subject of the rest of the sentence, for its physical movement.

12. θέλετε ποιήσω is a sufficiently inelegant phrase (hence the addition of ἵνα in some later MSS) to prompt emendation, and the fact that Matthew does not have θέλετε in this verse strengthens the probability that it was omitted in ℵ B C W etc. in order to harmonise as well as to improve the style. The θέλετε in Mt. 27:21 is different in sense and syntax, and would not be likely to suggest a harmonising addition here. The parallel construction θέλετε ἀπολύσω in v. 9 supports the originality of θέλετε here too.

12. It is more likely that ὃν λέγετε would be omitted by a scribe anxious to maintain the dignity of Jesus' title (and to conform to Pilate's unqualified use of the title in v. 9; cf. Jn. 18:39) than that it would be added (here but not in v. 9) out of a sense of the historical improbability (or theological inappropriateness?) of Pilate's unqualified use of the title. The omission of ὅν in B produces a meaningless sentence and is therefore probably accidental; if so, B is added to the weighty attestation for the longer reading.

We have noted above that the Jewish hearing, however important for the formal repudiation of Jesus by the Jerusalem leadership, was not an official 'trial', in that there was no formulated charge and the Sanhedrin did not have the power to execute a capital sentence. It was rather a search for a plausible charge to bring against Jesus at an official trial which, on a capital charge, must be held before the Roman prefect, who alone could pronounce a death sentence. The 'blasphemy' which confirmed the Jewish leaders' view that Jesus must be executed must therefore be adapted into a charge with a more political tone which a Roman governor could understand and would be obliged to take seriously. The task was not difficult, since the central issue at Jesus' hearing had been the claim to a special authority overriding even that of the properly constituted Jewish leadership, and in that connection Jesus had not only willingly accepted the title Χριστός but had gone on to arrogate to himself an even higher authority. True, the terms of his claim had been theological rather than overtly political, but they provided ample basis for a charge that he was claiming royal authority among his own people, and such a claim under the Roman occupation would naturally be seen as treasonable, placing Jesus within the category of nationalist leaders who, following Judas of Galilee, rejected Roman rule as incompatible with the status of the people of God. Such an interpretation underlies the title ὁ βασιλεὺς τῶν Ἰουδαίων which is at the centre of the Roman trial and its verdict (vv. 2, 9, 12, 18, 26, 32), and the placing of Jesus on a par with the admitted στασιαστής Barabbas. While Mark does not directly tell us who introduced the royal title into the proceedings, his phrase ὃν λέγετε in v. 12 confirms what was in any case probable, that it was this title which the Sanhedrin had chosen to encapsulate the charge against Jesus before the prefect.

Before the Sanhedrin Jesus had remained irritatingly silent, but had eventually been provoked into a clear declaration of who he was. Before Pilate he has even less to say. A single apparently evasive answer in v. 2 is his last word before the cross, and Mark draws attention to the fact (vv. 4-5). Jesus has, it seems, said all there is to say, and he now lets events take their predictable course. The only issue now is whether Pilate can be persuaded to cooperate, and that issue is soon resolved. Pilate's attempts to thwart the Jewish leaders' plan (whether from a real perception of injustice or more likely a basic unwillingness to be dictated to by the subjects he despised) appear more half-hearted in Mark than in Luke or (especially) John, and once the sympathies of the gathered crowd are clear he sees no point in continued resistance.

Apart from his necessary involvement in giving permission for Jesus' burial in vv. 43-44, this is the first and only appearance in Mark's story of Pontius Pilatus, prefect of Judaea A.D. 26-36. The prefect was directly appointed from Rome, but governed the minor province of Judaea under the supervision of the legate of the imperial province of Syria. He was normally resident in Caesarea, but at Passover time, when Jerusalem was crowded with pilgrims, he took up residence in his 'praetorium' (official residence) in Jerusalem, probably Herod's former palace on the western hill, in what is now known as the Citadel south of the Jaffa Gate.[1] But as Mark makes nothing of the location of Jesus' trial, the identification of Pilate's official residence is not important for exegesis.

Pilate cannot have enjoyed being in Jerusalem, for it was there that several of his violent confrontations with Jewish sentiment had taken place or would do so (Lk. 13:1; Josephus, *Ant.* 18.55-59, 60-62; Philo, *Leg. Gai.* 299-305). Philo (*Leg. Gai.* 301) describes Pilate as 'naturally inflexible, a blend of

---

1. The debate over whether in Jerusalem Pilate would normally reside in Herod's former palace (as he did when he was in Caesarea) or in the Fort of Antonia (on the north side of the temple precincts) continues, but in my view the arguments for Herod's palace (which Philo, *Leg. Gai.* 299, describes as 'the residence of the prefects') have the better of it (see the detailed argument of P. Benoit, *RB* 59 (1952) 531-50, published in English in Benoit's *Jesus,* 1.167-88; more briefly, J. Blinzler, *Trial,* 173-76; J. Wilkinson, *Jerusalem,* 137-40; R. E. Brown, *Death,* 705-10; Schürer, 1.361, especially n. 38). A recent discussion by B. Pixner, *ABD,* 5.447-49, offers a third option, arguing on the basis of early Christian tradition that the site was just across the Tyropoeon Valley from the temple, a former Hasmonean royal palace in what is now the Jewish Quarter; Pixner roundly dismisses the possibility of Antonia as the location.

self-will and relentlessness', and the incidents recorded of his career outside the gospels reinforce the picture of a man who could not or would not understand Jewish (or Samaritan) religious and patriotic sensitivity, and to whom confrontation and brutal suppression of dissent came more naturally than diplomacy.[2] The Sanhedrin would be aware that such a governor would not easily be persuaded to accede to their demand, and Mark's account of their approach to him indicates careful planning. In the end it was apparently not the insistence of the Sanhedrin leaders which forced his hand, but the prospect of another popular uprising in favour of Barabbas and against Jesus; but Mark ensures that we see the hand of the Sanhedrin behind the 'popular' demonstration (v. 11).

Mark's account of the day of crucifixion is carefully set forth in an explicit time frame in terms of three-hour intervals:

Verse 1:	πρωΐ (= daybreak; see below)	Delivery to Pilate
Verse 25:	ὥρα τρίτη	Crucifixion
Verse 33:	ὥρα ἕκτη	Darkness begins
Verse 34:	ὥρα ἐνάτη	Cry and death of Jesus
Verse 42:	ὀψίας γενομένης	Burial

See below on the respective verses for comment; while problems are raised especially by v. 25, the outline is clearly designed to be memorable.

1 Another καὶ εὐθύς (see on 14:72) carries the narrative rapidly on to its next phase. Mark wants us to see the morning decision not as a separate event after an interval, but as the direct continuation of the Sanhedrin hearing narrated in 14:53-65[3] (compare Luke's narrative which details the Sanhedrin proceedings in the morning, ὡς ἐγένετο ἡμέρα, after Peter's denial and the cockcrow, whereas Mark and Matthew give the details at night and merely a summary in the morning). The second cockcrow has brought us close to dawn (see on 14:29-31), and πρωΐ picks up from that point. The move to the praetorium, the trial, mockery, and journey to Golgotha must all be fitted in before the third hour (9 a.m.), 15:25, so πρωΐ here must mean at or even before daybreak.[4] The actors are the same three groups we have become familiar with in 8:31; 11:27; 14:43, 53, but the fact that this time a μετά subordinates the πρεσβύτεροι καὶ γραμματεῖς to the ἀρχιερεῖς makes it clear who are making the running, and from 15:3 onwards the ἀρχιερεῖς alone are named as Jesus' accusers.[5] It has after all been the leader of the priestly

---

2. For brief accounts of Pilate and his period of office see J. Blinzler, *Trial,* 177-84; R. E. Brown, *Death,* 693-705. The latter argues that Pilate was a better governor than Philo suggests, and that his handling of the case of Jesus of Nazareth was very much in character.

3. See J. Blinzler, *Trial,* 145-48.

4. See A. N. Sherwin-White, *Society,* 45-46, for comments on the timing of a Roman official's day, in support of the likelihood that the approach to Pilate was made 'as soon as it was morning'. Cf. J. Blinzler, *Trial,* 172-73.

5. E. Trocmé, *Formation,* 100-101, comments: 'In the Evangelist's eyes, the ἀρχιερεῖς are a sort of executive college forming the core of the Sanhedrin without being identical with it (14:55), and enforcing its decisions.'

group who has acted as spokesman during the hearing. This time, however, there is the further addition of the phrase καὶ ὅλον τὸ συνέδριον. Since the three groups just mentioned made up the membership of the Sanhedrin, this phrase cannot designate an additional group. It serves rather to emphasise (more strongly than the πάντες of 14:53) that this is now a full gathering of the Sanhedrin, competent to draw up a case to present to Pilate. It is likely that members have been arriving through the night hearing, so that by now they are a sufficient quorum (and Mark's phrase suggests more than a mere quorum) to ratify formally the result of the night's proceedings.

In this setting συμβούλιον ποιήσαντες (see Textual Note) could mean either 'held a consultation/council meeting' (i.e., were formally constituted into a decision-making body) or 'made a plan' (i.e., agreed on the charge and the tactics for the imminent visit to the prefect; cf. 3:6, Mark's only other use of συμβούλιον). Matthew (ἔλαβον) and the ℵ C L texts of Mark (ἑτοιμάσαντες) presuppose the latter meaning for συμβούλιον, but if we have been right to understand the proceedings of 14:53-65 as relatively informal and unofficial, both senses would be appropriate here in Mark, and it does not much matter which is chosen:[6] this was the point of formal decision on which the approach to Pilate must be based.

This is the first mention of Jesus being bound, though the forcible arrest in 14:46 might have included binding (so Jn. 18:12). Now that he is a prisoner on a formal charge he is treated as such.[7] The verb παραδίδωμι is used in its natural sense without any special theological nuance, but the alert reader may remember Jesus' words in 10:33, παραδώσουσιν αὐτὸν τοῖς ἔθνεσιν. The verb παραδίδωμι which came to our attention in the passion predictions of 9:31 and 10:33-34 recurs several times in Mark's narrative, not only for Judas's action (14:10, 11, 18, 21, 41, 42, 44) but also for the subsequent stages of Jesus' progress towards the cross here and in vv. 10 and 15 which mark the progressive fulfilment of those predictions.

2 Mark's account of Jesus' examination by Pilate is very concise, consisting of a couple of questions and one ambivalent answer, followed by Pilate's bargaining with the priests and the crowd, during which Jesus takes no further part. Mark provides no legal details, not even a formal verdict, so that any reconstruction of the actual proceedings in the light of known Roman judicial procedures is necessarily speculative.[8]

Pilate's opening question (which takes the same form as that of the High Priest in 14:61; see comments there on the danger of reading too much

---

6. F. J. Matera, *Kingship,* 8-10, suggests that the participle should be understood as referring not to a part of the action reported in v. 1 but as a recapitulation of the preceding scene: 'the chief priests, having already held a council (during the night), now bound Jesus and took him. . . .' This is a possible but less idiomatically natural reading of the participle. Neither reading requires this verse to be read as the report of a separate meeting.

7. See E. Bammel in E. Bammel and C. F. D. Moule (ed.), *Politics,* 415.

8. R. E. Brown, *Death,* 710-22, surveys such attempts.

into σὺ εἶ;) can only have been based on the information supplied by the Sanhedrin. The phrase ὁ βασιλεὺς τῶν Ἰουδαίων has not occurred in the gospel so far. Jesus has been among Jews, for whom the title ὁ Χριστός (or υἱὸς Δαυίδ, 10:47-48; 12:35-37) would be more natural. ὁ βασιλεὺς τῶν Ἰουδαίων is more likely to be used by a non-Jew, and is so used throughout this chapter (in 15:32 the Jewish leaders use the more Jewish form ὁ βασιλεὺς Ἰσραήλ in deliberate allusion to the [Gentile] inscription on the cross). As such it was an appropriate 'translation' of Jesus' messianic claim into language which a Roman governor would understand and which he would immediately recognise as potentially treasonable.[9] But it is also a title which clearly has a strongly positive implication for Mark. The kingship of Jesus, now newly introduced (since the kingship previously mentioned has been that of God), becomes the focal theme for the rest of Mark's account of the passion, occurring explicitly six times (vv. 2, 9, 12, 18, 26 and 32) and underlying especially the account of the soldiers' mockery in vv. 16-20. The reader is expected to recognise that, however inappropriate the charge at the trial and on the placard on the cross may have been in terms of popular understanding at the time, and however much mocked by the uncomprehending Roman soldiers and even the Jewish leaders themselves, Jesus does enter into his true kingship, paradoxically enthroned on the cross.[10]

Jesus' reply contrasts remarkably with the bold affirmation of 14:62. While σὺ λέγεις could be understood as a denial, 'You say that; I do not',[11] the consensus among recent interpreters is to take it as a 'Yes, but . . .', which is 'affirmative in content, and reluctant or circumlocutory in formulation'.[12] Inasmuch as ὁ βασιλεὺς τῶν Ἰουδαίων is another way of saying ὁ Χριστός, it is a correct statement of who Jesus has declared himself to be in 14:62, but the political connotations of such a title as spoken by a suspicious Roman governor do not correspond to Jesus' perception of his role, or to the record of his ministry which Mark has given us. There is evidently sufficient equivocation about the form of Jesus' brief reply to leave Pilate unconvinced of the political implications of the charge, though his continued use of the title ὁ βασιλεὺς τῶν Ἰουδαίων suggests that he did not take it as a negative answer as such.

3-5 As in the hearing before the Sanhedrin, we are told of numerous unspecified accusations against Jesus (πολλά and πόσα together suggest several

9. Josephus, *Ant.* 17.285, mentions that would-be rebel leaders commonly called themselves βασιλεύς. For some specific examples see *Ant.* 17.271-72 (Judas), 273-74 (Simon); *War* 2.60-62 (Athronges). Josephus also records that the actual title ὁ τῶν Ἰουδαίων βασιλεύς had been adopted by Alexander Jannaeus (or Aristobulus?; *Ant.* 14.36) and was the title of Herod the Great (*Ant.* 16.311; cf. 15.373), so that its political implications would be obvious.

10. For a sustained exposition of the centrality of this theme for Mk. 15 see F. J. Matera, *Kingship.*

11. Gundry, 932-33, argues for a negative sense. Van Iersel, 459, goes even further: 'Jesus has given an answer that sounds more negative than an outright denial.'

12. D. R. Catchpole, *NTS* 17 (1970/1) 226, summing up a careful study of the idiom in Jewish sources and in its various NT appearances.

different accusations rather than merely repetition of the one main charge).[13] Some may have been the same as those raised at the earlier hearing (including the charge of aiming to destroy and replace the temple), but dressed in such a way as to make their revolutionary implications clear. For Jesus' silence see on 14:60-61. This time his silence will remain unbroken.[14] In view of Pilate's suspicion of the priests' motives (v. 10) it is quite possible that a protestation of innocence on Jesus' part would have swung Pilate more definitely onto his side, but not for the first time Jesus fails to take an opportunity to influence the outcome of the trial and so to avoid the fate which he has accepted at Gethsemane as the Father's will. θαυμάζω often carries a note of admiration, and Pilate's subsequent attempts to secure Jesus' release suggest that he was impressed by the contrast between the priests' vehemence and Jesus' silence.[15]

6 While political amnesties and release of prisoners have often been used as gestures of goodwill and to mark times of celebration, the specific custom presupposed here and in the other three gospels is not attested by any independent evidence.[16] Jn. 18:39 specifies that it was a Passover custom; Matthew and Mark use the more general phrase κατὰ ἑορτήν which, lacking the article, might mean that this was a custom at all festivals (a possibility envisaged by BAGD, 280a), but more likely in this context it refers also to Passover.[17] Blinzler offers evidence for similar amnesties elsewhere in the Roman world.[18] In Judaea there was a precedent in Archelaus's release of prisoners on request (Josephus, *War* 2.4, 28), and Albinus later did so more than once (Josephus, *Ant.* 20.208-10, 215), though neither of these amounts to an annual custom. Thus, while there is no exact parallel to the custom reported in the gospels, it is not improbable that Pilate found a similar concession politically expedient; the annual release of a single prisoner is a very modest concession compared with many political amnesties. If there was no such custom, it is not easy to see

13. Taking πολλά and πόσα as accusative of object (using the classical construction [BAGD 423a, 1.a] of κατηγορέω with the genitive of the person and the accusative of the accusation; cf. Acts 28:19) rather than adverbially, as Gundry, 924-25, 933, prefers.

14. E. Bammel comments: 'The silence is the conclusion drawn and posture adopted by the one who has already invoked divine justice against the Sanhedrin and who is now not any longer willing to defend himself' (Bammel and Moule [ed.], *Politics*, 422).

15. For the possibility of an echo of Is. 52:15 in Pilate's amazement see J. Marcus, *Way*, 187-88.

16. The reference in *m. Pes.* 8:6 in a Passover context to 'one whom they have promised to bring out of prison' could be based on such a custom (so J. Blinzler, *Trial*, 218-21; C. B. Chavel, *JBL* 60 [1941] 273-78) but does not in itself require it, and it cannot be assumed that a mishnaic ruling would reflect the specific conditions of Pilate's period as prefect nearly two hundred years before the Mishnah was compiled.

17. R. E. Brown, *Death*, 795.

18. J. Blinzler, *Trial*, 205-8. See further R. E. Brown, *Death*, 814-19, and especially R. L. Merritt, *JBL* 104 (1985) 57-68, for related Assyrian, Babylonian, Greek, and Roman customs, on the basis of which Merritt proposes that Mark's story (which he does not believe to be historically based) deliberately 'echoed the known customs of prisoner releases at festivals in the ancient world'.

where such a well-established part of the Christian passion tradition might have been derived from.[19] For the people's right to choose, cf. the custom at gladiatorial contests of asking the people whether a given contestant should live or die.

7 ὁ λεγόμενος does not here have the pejorative sense 'the so-called . . .' (as in 1 Cor. 8:5; Eph. 2:11), but introduces a new character into the story: 'There was a man called Barabbas. . . '. (Cf. Lk. 22:47 for a similar use, though in that case the character introduced is not new to the narrative.) Βαραββᾶς is an Aramaic patronymic;[20] his personal name Ἰησοῦς is recorded only by Matthew.[21] In the gospel traditions he appears only in the minor role of foil to Jesus of Nazareth in the people's choice, but that is enough to indicate that he was not a common criminal but a well-known man with a popular following.[22] Jn. 18:40 describes him as a λῃστής, the term which Josephus uses for anti-Roman insurrectionists; while John did not necessarily use the term in that special sense, it does correspond to Mark's information that Barabbas was imprisoned μετὰ τῶν στασιαστῶν. We have no other information about this specific στάσις during the governorship of Pilate,[23] but such events occurred sporadically from A.D. 6 onwards until the Jewish War of A.D. 66-73,[24] and Barabbas as a member (and presumably a leading member, since he was singled out for amnesty) of such a

19. The authenticity of the account is defended by E. Bammel in Bammel and Moule (ed.), *Politics*, 427-28.

20. The name seems to have been quite common (so BAGD, 133a), and is usually explained either as 'son of a teacher (Rabban)' or 'son of Abba', Abba being a well-attested personal name (R. E. Brown, *Death*, 799-800; cf. Schürer, 1.385 n. 138).

21. It is sometimes suggested (e.g., by Cranfield, 450, following Deissmann) that the name Ἰησοῦς stood originally also in Mk. 15:7 (which would give a more normal sense to ὁ λεγόμενος as introducing his surname to distinguish him from Jesus of Nazareth), and that it was expunged from the textual tradition through the same Christian squeamishness (well represented by Origen) which removed it from the majority of texts in Matthew. While this is entirely possible, in the absence of any trace of the name in the Marcan textual tradition it remains mere speculation. See further Mann, 637. (Mann apparently states on p. 637 that the name Jesus for Barabbas 'is found in some manuscripts of Mark'; he does not say which, and Legg's exhaustive listing offers no example.)

22. S. L. Davies, *NTS* 27 [1980/1] 260-62, summarises and takes further the earlier arguments of H. A. Rigg and H. Z. Maccoby that 'Bar-abba' ('Son of the Father') was originally a title for Jesus of Nazareth, and that there was no historical Barabbas. See contra Mann, 638-39; R. E. Brown, *Death*, 811-12.

23. The suggestion of Belo, 224, that the reference is to 'the messianic sequences relating to the entry of Jesus into Jerusalem and into the temple' depends on his 'hypothesis' (as far as I know unsupported) that on that occasion 'various *sicarii,* in keeping with their usual practice, profited by the movement Jesus had roused' (330 n. 194). P. W. Barnett, *NTS* 21 (1974/5) 568, speculates whether this στάσις may be the same event that is alluded to in Lk. 13:1 and also that resulting from Pilate's appropriation of temple funds for his aqueduct (Josephus, *War* 2.175-77; *Ant.* 18.60-62).

24. Tacitus's laconic statement that in Judaea *sub Tiberio quies* need not be pressed to exclude the possibility of any local uprising: the accounts of Pilate's prefecture in Josephus and Philo hardly support total *quies*. See further Gundry, 934-35. For an accessible summary of the evidence for 'revolutionary' figures in first-century Palestine and the titles used for them, emphasising the more volatile political atmosphere after the restoration of direct rule in A.D. 44, see R. E. Brown, *Death*, 679-93.

dissident group would naturally be a popular hero. Mark does not say in so many words either that Barabbas was a στασιαστής or that he had himself committed murder, but the fact that he was imprisoned with such a group speaks for itself. The two other λῃσταί who were subsequently crucified along with Jesus (v. 27) probably belonged to the same group, left behind when Barabbas alone was released. Thus Jesus found himself in compromising company; the occurrence of a στάσις recently enough for its perpetrators to be still in prison awaiting execution means that this was a dangerous time for anyone to be charged in Jerusalem with claiming to be ὁ βασιλεὺς τῶν Ἰουδαίων; no doubt the priests had reckoned with that.

The dynamics of the situation are powerfully brought out by G. Theissen in his 'historical novel', *The Shadow of the Galilean*. He pictures his fictional hero Andreas as a long-standing friend and admirer of Jesus Barabbas, who is presented as a high-minded patriot who has decided that the way of armed resistance is the only honourable option. Alongside that ideology Andreas comes to hear of another Jesus, from Nazareth, who is preaching instead an otherworldly but attractive ideology of loving one's enemies. Andreas is torn between these contrasting but equally demanding programmes, and watches helplessly as Pilate offers the people a choice between these two leaders; the result is no surprise, and the pacifist dies in place of the freedom fighter. In a letter to Andreas the released Barabbas confesses the superiority of Jesus' way, but insists that neither ideology can flourish in the absence of the other. Here is food for thought.[25]

8 The ὄχλος appears suddenly in the narrative. Perhaps we are to understand that on this Passover morning it was known that Pilate was to exercise his amnesty, and a crowd of Jerusalem citizens (supporters of Barabbas?; so Cranfield) came together as at any other Passover to witness and if possible to influence his choice. But v. 11 suggests that this year other factors may have been at work: the chief priests who guided the crowd's choice may also have been responsible for recruiting and briefing a crowd to support their case against Jesus, even if at this stage they could not have anticipated Pilate's move in proposing their prisoner for the Passover amnesty. A 'crowd' gathered outside the governor's residence very early in the morning need not have been very large, nor necessarily representative of all the people in Jerusalem at Passover time. It is highly improbable that this city crowd contained many, or indeed any, of the 'crowd' of Passover visitors who had accompanied Jesus on his approach to the city (see the introductory comments on 11:1-10, where we noted that it was the Galilean pilgrims who shouted 'Hosanna' but the Jerusalem crowd who shouted 'Crucify him').

ἀναβάς is literally appropriate since Herod's palace was built on a high point overlooking the lower part of the city and the temple area, but it need mean no more than 'coming up' in the sense of arriving; we are probably to

---

25. G. Theissen, *Shadow*. The 'Barabbas letter' is on p. 177.

envisage the crowd gathering outside the residence as the official delegation from the Sanhedrin went in with their prisoner. Their request at this stage is not for a specific person to be released (it is the priests who will promote the name of Barabbas in v. 11), though with a popular leader like Barabbas in custody it would not be difficult for both them and Pilate to anticipate the likely outcome. In Mark's compressed syntax the imperfect ἐποίει of the subordinate clause does duty also for the object of the request: 'to do as he always did for them'.

9   Mark usually follows θέλω with an infinitive, or occasionally with ἵνα (see Textual Note on v. 12), but the less elegant construction with a simple aorist subjunctive (with ἵνα presumably understood; cf. BDF, 366[3]) has occurred also in 10:36, 51, in the former of which it has provoked a variety of textual emendations to improve the style (see Textual Note there).

Pilate's surprise move was not very perceptive (unless it was based on a mistake: 'Had he heard them asking for Jesus [i.e., Barabbas] and thought they meant Jesus of Nazareth?' Cranfield, 451). Perhaps to him one would-be βασιλεὺς τῶν Ἰουδαίων was much like another, and his suspicion that the charge against Jesus was ill founded led him to favour the less obviously guilty man. Politically Jesus must have seemed less of a threat to him than Barabbas. But the essence of amnesty is to gain popular approval, and there is little to suggest that the average inhabitant of Jerusalem would have given serious consideration to this recently arrived Galilean as their representative. The favourable response to his challenge to the authorities in the temple precincts (11:18; 12:12, 37) did not put him in the category of a potential leader to compare with Barabbas; indeed, his response to the political challenge concerning the poll tax (12:13-17) would have left many unsatisfied with his patriotic stance, and his attitude to the temple (see on 14:58, especially p. 605 n. 14) would not endear him to the people of Jerusalem. Perhaps Pilate was misled by the charge against Jesus into imagining that he was a more popular and significant figure in Jerusalem than was really the case. In terms of popular support in relation to Barabbas there was no contest. Thus the only time Pilate takes the initiative in this scene, he is unsuccessful. It is others who are calling the tune.

10   Pilate's suspicion of the chief priests'[26] motives presumably derives from his observation of their attitude compared with that of Jesus during the interrogation in vv. 2-5, perhaps also from his general awareness of the religious politics of his subjects. From the point of view of Mark's readers φθόνος suitably encapsulates the note of rival claims to authority which has run through the preceding hearing. It perhaps also reflects Jesus' previous popularity with

---

26. οἱ ἀρχιερεῖς is omitted in a few MSS and versions, perhaps accidentally because the same phrase occurs immediately afterwards, or possibly because Matthew does not have it here. But it is clear from the preceding context that Mark understood the chief priests to be the subject, whether expressed or not.

the crowd over against the authorities (11:18; 12:12, 37), which had made them cautious about arresting him (14:1-2).[27]

11 We have been informed in v. 6 that the choice of the prisoner to be released lay not with Pilate but with the people (the indefinite 'they' there leaves open the channel by which this choice was normally decided and communicated to him). His proposal in v. 9 was therefore only a suggestion which it would be unwise for him to enforce, and left the field open for a counter-proposal. As noted above, Barabbas may already have been the people's obvious choice, in which case the priests wisely backed it (the only other NT occurrence of ἀνασείω in the sense of to 'stir up' or 'incite' is, significantly, in the parallel passage in Lk. 23:5, as the priests' version of what *Jesus* has been doing with the people). Barabbas, even though deprived of his followers, may still have been a political embarrassment to their *modus vivendi* with Rome, but his challenge to their authority was less direct than Jesus' had proved to be.

12 See the Textual Notes, and for the syntax of θέλετε ποιήσω see on v. 9. It is not clear whether αὐτοῖς refers to the priests (technically the subjects of the previous sentence) or the crowd, to whose demand (under the priests' direction) Pilate is responding; see on vv. 13-14 for reasons for thinking it is the crowd, but since they are responding to the incitement of the priests the issue is not important. If ὃν λέγετε is authentic here, Pilate is raising the question of how the title under which Jesus has been brought before him is to be understood. In offering an amnesty for ὁ βασιλεὺς τῶν Ἰουδαίων in v. 9 Pilate must have thought that some at least of the crowd would welcome Jesus under that title. Now that his offer has been rejected he reminds the crowd that it was their priests who had introduced the title; so if they do not want their 'king' released, what do they want?

13-14 The ambiguity concerning the reference of αὐτοῖς in v. 12 continues with the repeated οἱ δέ of these verses. Inasmuch as ἔκραξαν is more appropriate to a shouting crowd, and only the crowd's outcry in vv. 8 and 11 offers the necessary antecedent to πάλιν, and in the light of the fact that v. 15 says that it was the ὄχλος that Pilate was trying to please, we should probably understand the subject here (and therefore also the antecedent of αὐτοῖς in v. 12) as the crowd, but the question is academic since Mark has made it clear in v. 11 that the crowd and the priests are acting in unison. Crucifixion was the normal Roman penalty for provincial political rebels (otherwise it was normally reserved for slaves except in very extreme cases),[28] and so the form of execution demanded is consistent with the accusation that Jesus was claiming to be a βασιλεύς, and indeed was the only realistic option if Pilate were to declare him guilty on this charge. It is disconcerting to find it requested by a Jewish crowd (the approved Jewish methods of execution being stoning, burning, beheading,

---

27. R. E. Brown, *Death*, 802-3, couples the normal sense of φθόνος as 'envy' with the more positive sense of 'jealous zeal' (for the law), but Mark is hardly likely to have intended this more complimentary sense either concerning the priests themselves or concerning Pilate's assessment of them.

28. The full study by M. Hengel, *Crucifixion*, shows that this common generalisation, while not an exhaustive account, fairly represents the balance of evidence.

or strangling, *m. Sanh.* 7:1),[29] but in the *Realpolitik* of Roman occupation they would know that this is what a verdict of guilty of insurrection must amount to; it was already the fate awaiting Barabbas's associates. Jesus' predictions of his death have not specified the manner of execution, but his challenge following the first of those predictions that a faithful disciple ἀράτω τὸν σταυρὸν αὐτοῦ (8:34) has prepared the reader for the reality of what death under official auspices in Jerusalem must mean. The direct singular imperative σταύρωσον, twice repeated (contrast Matthew's third-person imperative σταυρωθήτω), emphasises that this can only be by Pilate's personal decision.

Pilate's question Τί γὰρ ἐποίησεν κακόν; is brushed aside by the crowd and perhaps need not in the narrative context be regarded as a question expecting a reasoned answer. The κακόν has already been spelled out in the accusation that Jesus claims to be ὁ βασιλεὺς τῶν Ἰουδαίων, though v. 11 has shown that Pilate was not impressed by that accusation in the light of what he had seen and heard of Jesus. The question serves here primarily to provide the reader with further confirmation that Jesus' execution was a miscarriage of justice, in that even the 'impartial' Roman governor by whose verdict he was condemned to death was not persuaded that he was really guilty.[30]

15 The idiom τὸ ἱκανὸν ποιῆσαι τινι probably means 'to satisfy' (from the sense of ἱκανός as 'enough', a Latinism corresponding to *satis facere*), though BAGD, 374b, 1.c, find at least one other use of it in the sense 'to do someone a favour'.[31] Pilate is not willing or able to oppose either part of the crowd's demand. The execution of Jesus is not, however, to be a lynching but is to follow due Roman procedure; Barabbas is therefore released αὐτοῖς but Jesus is handed over (for παραδίδωμι see on v. 1) to the official process of execution.[32] That process customarily began with flogging; cf Josephus, *War* 2.306-8; 5.449; 7.200-202 for flogging before crucifixion.[33] φραγελλόω is a loanword from the Latin *flagello,* and denotes flogging with whips normally made of leather and sometimes weighted with pieces of metal or bone, a brutal process which inflicted severe injury and could itself sometimes prove fatal.[34] This

29. See, however, above, p. 616 n. 59, for the possibility of crucifixion as a Jewish means of execution.

30. See J. D. Kingsbury, *Christology,* 126-27, for pointers through this whole section to the fact that 'Mark goes to great lengths to show that Pilate does not believe for a moment that Jesus is in fact the King of the Jews, that is, an insurrectionist'.

31. In the passage they quote from Hermas, *Sim.* 6.5.5, it means to 'give free rein to' sinful desires.

32. The statement of Hooker, 366, that in Mark's account 'sentence is never passed', while formally correct, is an unnecessary argument from silence. Mark's statement that Pilate handed Jesus over (not, like Barabbas, to the Jews but) for scourging and crucifixion presupposes that he has officially authorised the execution, as does also the placing of an official ἐπιγραφή on the cross (v. 26). See further Lane, 558; J. Blinzler, *Trial,* 238-43; R. E. Brown, *Death,* 853-55.

33. For the prevalence of scourging and various other forms of torture before crucifixion see M. Hengel, *Crucifixion,* 25-29.

34. See C. Schneider, *TDNT,* 4.317, 319; J. Blinzler, *Trial,* 222-23.

too,like the 'handing over' to Gentiles, has been part of Jesus' prediction in 10:34.

THE CRUCIFIXION, DEATH, AND BURIAL OF JESUS (15:16-47)

In 14:43–15:15 we have followed the inexorable course of events from Jesus' arrest to the passing of a formal sentence of death by the Roman governor. Various parties have been involved, Judas, the temple guards, the Sanhedrin, the High Priest, the Jerusalem crowd, and the governor himself, each in their own way contributing to the final outcome, and all united in rejecting 'the king of the Jews'. But of the disciples and other supporters who have been so prominent in the earlier part of the story we have heard nothing except the brief note of their dispersal in Gethsemane and the depressing account of Peter's solo but ill-fated attempt to stay close to his master. Jesus is now firmly in the hands of his enemies, and shows no intention to resist their will, even if he could. Already with the passing of the sentence we have marked the beginning of the process leading to his execution, and from 15:16 on that process gathers momentum. The main actors continue to be Jesus' enemies, now augmented by the addition of the Roman soldiers who are to be the actual executioners, while his Jewish opponents join in bitter mockery. Jesus dies abandoned, not only by his human companions but even, we hear with disbelief, apparently by his Father as well.

Yet within this harrowing scene there are gleams of light, pointers to what the Christian reader of course already knows, that this is not the story of the final defeat of God's Messiah, but the moment of his paradoxical victory. A few minor characters pass across the stage, each giving the reader some grounds for hope: Simon, Rufus and Alexander, the Roman centurion with his pregnant exclamation, Joseph of Arimathea, and especially the faithful women who stay around when all the men have gone, and who in the final scene of Mark's story will have the privilege of being the first to witness the dawning of the new age. And within the story line itself there are strong hints that in these terrible events in which God's enemies seem triumphant it is in fact the purpose of God that is being worked out. Echoes of Scripture, especially of Ps. 22, woven into the narrative insistently remind us that 'The Son of Man goes as it is written of him'. The very mockery of Jesus as a failed 'king of the Jews' points, for those who know how the story will end, to truths hidden from the mockers, Roman and Jewish; what they proclaim in jest is actually true.[35] The sarcastically intended writing on the cross in fact declares who Jesus really is, and it is precisely because he is on the cross that it will prove to be true. The tearing of the temple curtain and the words

35. J. D. Kingsbury, *Christology*, 128: 'What Gentile and Jew say "in mockery" (15:20, 31) is — in Marcan perspective — true, namely Jesus is in fact the "King of the Jews," or "the Messiah, the King of Israel".'

of the leader of the execution squad tell the reader that the outrageous claim made in Jesus' last words to the Jewish leaders is already being fulfilled.

We do not have to wait until chapter 16 to discern Mark's message of triumph and hope.

The Soldiers' Mockery (15:16-20)

The sequence of events varies between the gospels, with the soldiers' mockery (which all four gospels record in some form) coming before the sentence (but after the flogging) in Jn. 19:1-3 and transferred to Herod and his soldiers in Lk. 23:11 and therefore preceding the (proposed) flogging. Mark's sequence seems as likely as either of these, but we cannot now be sure.

Just as the passing of the Jewish verdict led to violent mockery of the supposed 'prophet' by the Sanhedrin members and their servants in 14:65, so now after the governor's sentence the Roman soldiers, who for the first time have the supposed royal pretender in their power,[36] enact a mock ceremony of enthronement[37] in which brutality and sarcasm are equally mixed.[38] After the flogging mentioned in v. 15 Jesus must already have been a pitiable sight, probably barely able to stand or walk and certainly incapable of resistance even if he had wished. In any case, he is on his way to execution, so there is nothing to curb their enjoyment of this opportunity to humiliate the 'king of the Jews', and the contempt for Jews in general which is amply illustrated in literature of the Roman empire is eagerly focused on this one ludicrous example of a Jew who had dared to challenge the imperial power.[39] It is not an attractive scene.[40]

36. Belo, 225: 'The body of Jesus is dressed and undressed at the whim of the soldiers, thus calling attention continually to its powerlessness in this space that is dominated by the force of arms.'

37. Philo, *Flacc.* 6.36-39, records a similar incident in Alexandria a few years later when the Jewish King Agrippa I was mocked by the anti-Jewish crowd by setting up a Jewish imbecile as 'king' with robe, crown, and sceptre improvised from everyday materials. For a Jewish semi-parallel, though not in a royal context, see Josephus, *War* 4.155-57, where a group of λῃσταί who had taken over the temple install an ignorant peasant as High Priest in a similar mock ceremony. For other suggested parallels see Taylor, 646-48; R. E. Brown, *Death,* 873-77.

38. Against the view that there was originally only one such mockery, and that one or other of the two scenes is a 'doublet' of the other, see P. Benoit, in W. C. Van Unnik (ed.), *Neotestamentica et Patristica,* 107-10.

39. T. E. Schmidt, *NTS* 41 (1995) 1-18, argues that Mark has related this incident together with the following march to the cross and the mockery that followed with deliberate allusion to a Roman imperial triumph. His argument is, as he acknowledges, strongest with regard to vv. 16-20, in which the parody of Roman imperial regalia is clear whether one speaks specifically of a triumphal procession or not. Beyond that point it is not so obvious that either Mark or his readers would have thought specifically of a triumph; the note of mockery, and of Jesus' paradoxical kingship on the cross, is clear enough in any case.

40. Belo, 330-31 n. 198, draws a modern parallel: 'The scene shows people being unleashed who have been subject to a constricting military discipline. . . . This sort of thing often shows in the ferocity lower-rank police officials demonstrate when dealing with political prisoners.'

16 The στρατιῶται are not now the temple guards who arrested Jesus but members of Pilate's army of occupation. In Judaea at this time the prefect had at his disposal not Roman legionary troops but auxiliaries drawn from the non-Jewish inhabitants of neighbouring areas (in Pilate's case mainly troops from Caesarea and Sebaste [Samaria]).[41] The likelihood of anti-Jewish prejudice among such forces is if anything greater than it would have been with Romans proper. The αὐλή here in Herod's palace[42] would be a larger area than that in which Peter had sat in the High Priest's house (14:54, 66), and ἔσω suggests that it was an enclosed area within the palace used for quartering troops. While πραιτώριον can be used for the governor's headquarters as a whole (so probably Jn. 18:28, 33; 19:9; cf. Acts 23:35), the designation of the αὐλή as the πραιτώριον suggests that the word is here used in a more limited sense such as 'guardroom' or 'barracks'.[43] ἀπήγαγον ἔσω therefore presupposes that the trial (and the flogging?) took place outside the palace[44] (as indeed the presence of the crowd demands), but that now the soldiers have Jesus to themselves inside. If σπεῖρα is used here in its technical military sense for a cohort (as in Acts 10:1; 27:1), there could have been six hundred men involved, though the size of a cohort varied; but the Greek word is not necessarily so specific (we need not believe that it took six hundred men to arrest Jesus, Jn. 18:3, 12), and could mean simply that all the soldiers there on duty gathered round.

17 The rare verb ἐνδιδύσκω (the normal NT verb is ἐνδύω) occurs elsewhere in the NT only in Lk. 16:19, and there, too, it is linked with πορφύρα; perhaps the more elaborate verb carries a grander connotation of 'dressing up'; if so, its use here increases the note of mockery. Matthew offers a more careful account of how the soldiers used commonly available objects (a soldier's cloak, thorn twigs, and a cane) to parody royal regalia (robe, crown, and sceptre). Mark's πορφύρα alone could mean a real purple robe such as a king might wear, but quite apart from the unlikelihood of soldiers coming by such an expensive garment, its combination with a crown made of thorns makes it clear that this, too, was a mockery; Matthew's explanation that they used a red military cloak sounds very likely.[45] Nor does Mark mention that the κάλαμος with which they struck him (v. 19) had previously been put in his hand as a mock sceptre.

---

41. For the military forces in Judaea at this period see Schürer, 1.362-67.

42. See above, p. 625 n. 1, for the location of the trial. Mark's phrasing does not appear to allow for Jesus to be transferred from Herod's Palace to the Antonia, which was the main military base in the city, so that the location described here remains within the palace complex.

43. It is possible, however, that αὐλή is here used in a different sense from 14:54, 66 to designate the palace as a whole (so 1 Macc. 11:46; Josephus, *Life* 66 — though Mann, 642, regards the 1 Maccabees use as 'the only example we have'), in which case πραιτώριον would carry its more normal sense, and the reference would be to a move inside the palace from the open-air setting of the trial.

44. Josephus, *War* 2.301, describes the procurator Florus a generation later setting up a tribunal in front of the palace in Jerusalem for a public trial.

45. BAGD, 694a, mention one use of ἡ πορφύρα to *mean* a soldier's red cloak in the second century A.D., but it is unlikely that taken alone it could have been so understood at the time of Mark. πορφύρα suggests opulence and royalty; it is the context, not the word, which tells us it was a sham.

στέφανος is not so specifically royal a term as our 'crown'; it denotes also a wreath of leaves, such as that awarded to a successful athlete, or more generally a mark of reward or rejoicing. But in this context the royal motif is clear: the wreath of thorn branches symbolises a royal crown. ἀκάνθινος (thorny) does not specify the plant used, and botanical guesses are many;[46] the soldiers used whatever may have been to hand at the time, but the term indicates that it was spiky and therefore presumably intended to cause pain as well as mockery.[47]

To the specific items Mark mentions we must add the fact of Jesus' recent flogging if we are to appreciate the cruelty of the mockery. He must have presented a pathetic and ludicrous picture of a 'king'.

18-19 The mixture of mockery and cruelty in dressing Jesus up is continued in the soldiers' actions, as the homage of royal acclamation and of kneeling before the 'king' is combined with beating and spitting. While ἀσπάζομαι is usually a quite general word for greeting, we have seen ἀσπασμός used for a more formal expression of respect in 12:38 (cf Josephus, *Ant.* 10.211, where it is used of Nebuchadnezzar paying homage to Daniel 'in the way people worship God'); Χαῖρε, βασιλεῦ parodies the customary greeting for the emperor, *Ave, Caesar.* In mocking the title which had formed the basis of Jesus' condemnation the soldiers reflect Pilate's view that he posed no real threat; as members of neighbouring ethnic groups (see on v. 16) they found the idea of a Jewish 'king' (and *such* a king) hilarious. Kneeling (cf. γονυπετέω in 1:40; 10:17; the more elaborate Latinism [so BDF, 5(3b)] here, τίθημι τὰ γόνατα, adds a note of formality) and προσκυνέω (often translated 'worship') sound to us like religious worship, but both terms are commonly used for acts of homage to a social superior, and in this context are a natural part of the mocking recognition of Jesus' royal 'majesty'. In hitting Jesus with a cane the soldiers are merely adding to the brutality of Jesus' earlier flogging (contrast 14:65, where the Jewish beating was linked with the demand Προφήτευσον), perhaps using a cane already supplied to Jesus as a mock sceptre (so Matthew). The spitting further underlines the contempt which their mockery expresses. As in 14:65, the specific mention of spitting reminds the reader again of the violence, insult, and spitting suffered by the Lord's servant in Is. 50:6,[48] as well as of Jesus' own prediction in 10:34.

20 The verb ἐμπαίζω completes the literal fulfilment of Jesus' prediction in 10:34 of what would happen to him in the hands of τὰ ἔθνη: all four

46. R. E. Brown, *Death,* 866-67, discusses some of them.

47. H. St.J. Hart, *JTS* 3 (1952) 66-75, argues that the thorns were intended to imitate the rays like those of the sun which adorned the crowns of several eastern rulers (which he amply illustrates from coins), and suggests that they may have used the long spikes from the base of the leaf of the date palm. In that case the 'thorns' would stick outward from the head rather than inward, and the whole focus would be on mockery, not on torture. It is, however, questionable whether palm leaves, or even parts of them, would be described as ἄκανθαι.

48. See D. J. Moo, *The OT,* 139-44.

verbs (ἐμπαίζω, ἐμπτύω, μαστιγόω, and ἀποκτείνω) have now been reflected in what has happened or is about to happen to Jesus in the hands of the Roman soldiers. It is noteworthy that even though the 'royal' cloak is removed, Jesus is reclothed in his own garments to be taken out for crucifixion. It was normal for people to be crucified naked. Jesus' garments will be removed at the cross (v. 24), but the return of his clothes for the march to Golgotha may have been a concession to Jewish sensibilities, which found public nakedness offensive (see *m. Sanh.* 6:3; *Jub.* 3:30-31). Mark does not say what happened to the crown of thorns. Blinzler (*Trial,* 244-45) argues that it would have to be removed, as the soldiers would not be allowed to mock the Jews (in the person of their 'king') publicly, and that therefore the traditional depiction of Jesus on the cross still wearing the crown is incorrect. But it is doubtful whether the soldiers' cruelty to a condemned man could have been construed as mockery of the Jews in general, and the fact that Mark mentions the removal of the cloak but not of the crown supports the traditional picture.

The Crucifixion (15:21-32)

TEXTUAL NOTE

27. The added v. 28, providing a quotation from Is. 53:12, occurs only in comparatively late witnesses, and is apparently a gloss reflecting Lk. 22:37, though in a different context and with a different introduction.

After the comparatively lengthy account of the soldiers' mockery, Mark's record of the action of crucifixion is economical but powerful.[1] The focus is not so much on the physical suffering involved (though Mark's readers would have been well enough aware of what σταυροῦσιν αὐτόν meant without having it spelled out for them) as on the verbal abuse of Jesus both through the mocking placard on the cross and through the remarks of the various bystanders and even his fellow victims. The irony which we noted in the previous scene continues to run strongly through these verses, both in the association of Jesus as βασιλεὺς τῶν Ἰουδαίων with two convicted λῃσταί and as the reader reflects on the titles of honour which, perverted into sarcastic abuse by Jesus' enemies, nonetheless continue to point to the true nature of his mission as king (Messiah), replacer of the temple, and saviour. His enemies' call to come down from the cross sharply reminds us that it is precisely in order to fulfil these functions that he is there and must remain until the sacrifice he has spoken of at the Passover meal is completed, and his life has been given as a λύτρον ἀντὶ πολλῶν.

---

1. 'The story could not be told any more concisely. . . . It avoids sentimentality and does not seek to arouse sympathy or hatred' (Schweizer, 346). This seems a better perspective than Stock's suggestion (397) that Mark's simple style here 'is the speech of one almost overcome by emotion'.

A further level of reflection is introduced by the clear echo of Ps. 22 in v. 24. Ps. 22 is one of those which depict the suffering of God's faithful servant exposed to the malice of the ungodly, and it was recognised from very early Christian times (following Jesus' use of its opening words on the cross) as a prefiguring of the passion of Jesus. The psalm will not be quoted verbatim until v. 34, but echoes of it run through the Golgotha narrative. Mark does not point them out explicitly, but it is clear that the way he tells the story has been moulded to some extent by the wording of the psalm which will provide Jesus with the only words he speaks from the cross in this gospel. The following echoes are clear:

Mark 15:24	Psalm 22:18
Mark 15:29	Psalm 22:7
Mark 15:34	Psalm 22:1

and further echoes are likely both in the general theme of scorn (cf Ps. 22:6) and in the words of mockery in vv. 30-31 concerning being 'saved' (cf. Ps. 22:8), though this last is not brought out by verbal echo as it is in Matthew.[2] We will consider the allusions in the notes below, but the cumulative effect of this language is to assure the reader who is familiar with Ps. 22 (and surely by the time Mark wrote its relevance to the crucifixion story must already have been widely recognised) that what is happening is, even in detail, 'according to scripture', as Jesus had predicted.[3] An additional echo of Ps. 69 (see below on v. 36), another psalm about the suffering of the faithful servant of God, reinforces the message, while the mockery of God's servant recalls the scorn of the onlookers in Is. 53:3-4.[4]

21 The σταυρός which was carried out to the place of execution was probably the cross-piece, to be slotted into an upright already erected at the site. ἀγγαρεύω, originally a Persian word, denotes the custom, common in the ancient world, whereby the soldiers of an occupying power could commandeer the services of local citizens or their animals for carrying baggage (Mt. 5:41; Josephus, *Ant.* 13.52; cf. on 11:2 for the right of kings to requisition transport, and cf. *m. B. Meṣ.* 6:3, where a form of the same verb is used). Normally the condemned man carried the cross-piece for the cross himself, as Jn. 19:17 says Jesus did (John was presumably either unaware of Simon's role or chose not to

2. For a fuller listing of suggested echoes of Ps. 22 in Mark see F. J. Matera, *Kingship,* 128-29.

3. For an overview of Christian understanding of Ps. 22 and of its use in the passion narratives see R. E. Brown, *Death,* 1455-65; J. H. Reumann, *Int* 28 (1974) 39-58. A. Y. Collins, in C. M. Tuckett (ed.), *Scriptures,* 237-40, provides evidence for a messianic understanding of the psalm by a Jewish group uninfluenced by Christianity 'perhaps as early as the third century CE'.

4. 'The mockery of Christ on the Cross is influenced by the OT to a greater extent perhaps than any other NT passage' (D. J. Moo, *The OT,* 257).

mention it;[5] it is too firmly fixed in the tradition, and too insignificant in itself, to be a later insertion). The need for a porter arose from Jesus' weakened state after the flogging (note his unusually quick death, v. 44); the fact that Simon is described as παράγων suggests that they had already set out from the πραιτώριον with Jesus carrying the beam, but that he proved unable to continue. Σίμων is probably not to be thought of as a Passover visitor, but a member of the community of Cyrenian Jews settled in Jerusalem (cf. Acts 6:9; and for Antioch see Acts 11:20; 13:1).[6] His arrival ἀπ' ἀγροῦ does not mean he was returning from working in the fields (it was still only mid-morning), but merely that he had been out of town and happened to meet the execution squad as he came in. He is not otherwise known (why should he be?), but Mark's apparently unnecessary comment that his sons were Alexander and Rufus suggests that these two men were known to Mark's readers since they (and their father?) had become Christians, perhaps as a result of this involuntary involvement in the story of Jesus. It would be inappropriate to the narrative context to suggest that Simon's 'taking up the cross' (the same verb αἴρω is used here as in 8:34) in itself symbolises his personally entering a life of discipleship, but Mark's readers may well have found in his action a striking illustration of the costly identification with a suffering Messiah which Jesus' earlier saying had called for.

22 The use of φέρουσιν now in place of ἐξάγουσιν for the beginning of the march out of the πραιτώριον (v. 20) has sometimes been taken to indicate increased force,[7] or even that Jesus was no longer capable of walking unaided; but that is probably too much to read out of a verb with a wide range of use, which here need signify no more than their arrival at Golgotha (so Pesch, 2.477-78).[8] If the πραιτώριον was in Herod's palace, the route to the traditional

5. It has been suggested that he suppressed Simon's part in the story because certain Docetic groups were claiming (as some Muslims still believe) that it was Simon who was crucified in place of Jesus (Irenaeus, *Haer.* 1.24.4; *Second Treatise of the Great Seth* [Nag Hammadi Codices VII.2] 56.6-19).

6. For evidence of a cemetery for Cyrenian Jews outside Jerusalem at this period see N. Avigad, *IEJ* 12 (1962) 9-12. The ossuary inscription (in Greek) that particularly interests Avigad is of one 'Alexander son of Simon', who is also described on the ossuary lid in Hebrew as Alexander QRNYT, which *may* mean 'of Cyrene'; the names are common, so that the identity of this man with the Ἀλέξανδρος whom Mark mentions must remain speculative, as must the suggestion that the Ῥοῦφος of Rom. 16:13 is to be identified with Simon's other son.

7. Gundry's suggestion (Gundry, 954) that it refers to the 'executioner's hook for dragging condemned criminals to their place of execution' is perhaps too lurid, but cf. the account in Josephus, *War* 7.154, of the execution of the Jewish rebel leader Simon bar-Giora in Rome after the fall of Jerusalem, 'dragged to the place of execution with a noose round his neck, and simultaneously beaten by his guards'.

8. J. A. Fitzmyer, in E. H. Barth and R. E. Cocroft (ed.), *Festschrift to Honor F. Wilbur Gingrich*, 147-60, surveys in detail (for another purpose) the uses of φέρω and ἄγω in the Synoptics, in the light of the suggestion that 'in Hellenistic times φέρειν was encroaching upon ἄγειν by taking the meaning "lead" or "bring", of animals or persons' in place of its classical meaning 'carry'. He shows that even as early as Homer the two verbs could be used synonymously, and his survey suggests caution in drawing exegetical conclusions from the choice of verb.

site of the crucifixion was not a very long one, not much more than three hundred metres. There are no firm grounds for disputing the traditional site, now enclosed within the Church of the Holy Sepulchre, though there is unlikely ever to be convincing proof; its location just outside the line of the city walls at that time, and the presence of a number of Jewish tombs of the same period close by, are appropriate to a place of public execution, close to the city but outside it (cf. Jn. 19:17, 20). The NT accounts nowhere describe it as a 'hill', merely a τόπος; it is in fourth-century pilgrim records that it is called a small hill *(monticulus)*. The name Γολγοθᾶ represents Aramaic *gulgultā'* (Hebrew *gulgōlet*), which means simply 'skull' (so that Mark's rendering κρανίου τόπος is more an interpretation than an exact translation). The origin of the name is unknown: the nineteenth-century identification of 'Gordon's Calvary' north of the city assumed that it was a hill which was so named because it looked like a skull,[9] but it is at least as likely that the name derived from its use as a place of execution and burial, or even as a 'polling place' (Gundry, 955). For Mark's translation of Aramaic words cf. 5:41; 14:36; 15:34. A place name does not in itself require 'translation', but the sinister implications of the name clearly entered into Christian understanding of the crucifixion story, and Mark does not want his readers to miss that nuance.

23 The subject of ἐδίδουν is not expressed, but since the subjects of the preceding and following verses are clearly the soldiers, that would be the more natural sense here too. This appears to be how Matthew understands the incident, as a hostile act of the soldiers, since he mentions χολή (bile, a bitter substance) rather than myrrh, thus producing an echo of Ps. 69:21 where the action is clearly hostile (and where the LXX χολή translates *rō'š*, normally understood of a poison).[10] Mark will probably allude to the same passage when he mentions the second offer of a drink to Jesus in v. 36, but there is no verbal echo here, and the tone of his account is different from Matthew's.[11]

Mark says specifically that the wine was mixed with myrrh (σμυρνίζω is rare, but seems elsewhere to be used specifically of flavouring with myrrh, σμύρνα, rather than of spicing in a more general sense), a resinous gum used for perfume and flavouring (including of wine) and as an embalming ointment. The combination of wine and myrrh (for which see Pliny, *Nat. Hist.* 14.15, 92-

9. The identification derives from Otto Thenius (1842), but was popularised in a posthumous article of General Charles Gordon in the *Quarterly Statement* of the Palestine Exploration Fund in 1885, which is reprinted in J. Wilkinson, *Jerusalem,* 198-200. Gordon's arguments, which are neither historical nor geographical but derive from a typological understanding of Lv. 1:11 together with other more 'fanciful' (his word) reasons, do not inspire confidence in his historical judgment. It has also often been suggested that the smaller rocky mound (some four metres high) of the traditional site in the Church of the Holy Sepulchre might have been called Golgotha because it resembled (the top of) a skull.

10. W. D. Davies and D. C. Allison, *Matthew,* 3.613, suggest that we take the poison literally and understand the offer in Matthew as 'an invitation to commit suicide', but this depends more on the sense of the Hebrew *rō'š* than on the normal meaning of χολή.

11. The difference is minimised by D. J. Moo, *The OT,* 250-51.

93; it was a luxury, like the 'spiced wine' [οἶνος μυρεψικός] of Ct. 8:2) sounds more like a kind gesture than a hostile one, and it has been suggested that the offer of drugged wine comes not from the soldiers but from sympathetic by-standers, anxious to ease the pain of crucifixion by the use of a crude narcotic. This possibility is supported by the mention in *b. Sanh.* 43a that women of Jerusalem, guided by Pr. 31:6, used to provide for those being led out to execution a drink of 'wine containing a grain of frankincense' in order to dull the pain; the talmudic passage does not say who administered the drug. The specific ingredient mentioned by Mark is not frankincense but myrrh, which is not usually mentioned as a narcotic,[12] but in combination with the wine it might have a similar effect.[13] It is unlikely in the light of vv. 16-20 that a drink intended to ease pain would have been willingly given by the soldiers;[14] so perhaps, despite the unmarked change of subject, we are to understand here the action of sympathisers, perhaps the sort of women mentioned in the talmudic passage (cf. the sympathetic women of Jerusalem in Lk. 23:27-31). The imperfect tense, in contrast with the present tenses of vv. 22 and 24, perhaps points to a 'subplot' alongside the action of the soldiers. It may also have conative force, since Mark tells us that Jesus refused the offer: as the soldiers carried out their task the women were trying (unsuccessfully) to administer the narcotic.

Jesus' refusal of the offer is not explained. It has been linked with his determination since Gethsemane to 'drink the cup' of suffering allotted to him in full measure, his desire to remain in possession of his senses rather than lapse into unconsciousness, or his pledge at the Passover meal not to drink wine again until he drank the new wine of the kingdom of God; any or all of these may have played a part, but Mark does not say so.

24 The means of crucifixion varied,[15] and Mark does not specify. It is from Jn. 20:25 (and possibly the mention of Jesus' hands and feet in Lk. 24:39-40) that we know that nails rather than ropes were used.[16] Mark's interest is not in describing the physical suffering so much as in tracing the fulfilment of Scripture in the disposal of Jesus' clothes[17] after he was stripped for the cross,

---

12. W. Michaelis, *TDNT*, 7.458-59. But Michaelis has missed the reference by the army physician Dioscorides (first century A.D.) to myrrh as having narcotic properties (Dioscorides 1.64.3).

13. See further R. E. Brown, *Death*, 941.

14. W. Michaelis, *TDNT*, 7.458-59, however, thinks it may have been 'a soldiers' wine which executioners handed to the exhausted on the way to the place of execution'. Gundry, 956, suggests that the soldiers gave it as 'a gesture of mockery in connection with his presumed kingship', though Mark does not note their intention.

15. See, e.g., M. Hengel, *Crucifixion*, 24-32, and for earlier scholarship J. Blinzler, *Trial*, 263-65. There is an extensive account also in *ISBE*, 1.825-30.

16. The use of nails at this time in Palestine is vividly illustrated by the nail still fixed through the heel bones in the ossuary of one Jehohanan, who was crucified around the same period in Jerusalem; see N. Hass, *IEJ* 20 (1970) 49-59. See further R. E. Brown, *Death*, 950-51.

17. See A. N. Sherwin-White, *Society*, 46, for 'the accepted right of the executioner's squad to share out the minor possessions of their victim'.

his description of which closely echoes LXX Ps. 21[22]:19[18], with the addition of the explanatory clause τίς τί ἄρῃ to account for the casting of lots which the psalm passage mentioned.

25 Mark's abruptly paratactic summary introduces the first of a series of specific time markers into the crucifixion story, which have the effect of dividing it into three three-hour periods (see above, p. 626). If Mark's story is taken on its own, there is no inherent difficulty in the statement (not found in any other gospel) that Jesus was placed on the cross at the third hour (9 a.m.).[18] The transfer of Jesus to Pilate began πρωΐ (v. 1), which we have seen to mean probably around daybreak, and the trial (which does not seem in Mark's account to have been very protracted), the soldiers' mockery, and the walk to Golgotha would need no more than three hours altogether. The following account of nearly nine hours on the cross, with three hours of darkness from noon to the ninth hour (vv. 33-34) as their middle point, the body being removed ὀψίας γενομένης, before the sabbath began at the twelfth hour (vv. 42-46), is entirely plausible and self-consistent. Even on this time scale Jesus' death before sunset was remarkably soon after he was placed on the cross (v. 44).

While Matthew and Luke do not mention the time of crucifixion, their accounts agree with Mark in presupposing some time on the cross before noon (Mt. 27:45; Lk. 23:44), and convey the same time scale thereafter. The problem posed by this verse then arises not from internal considerations in Mark's own story or within the synoptic tradition but from its conflict with John's statement that it was ὥρα ὡς ἕκτη when Pilate pronounced sentence (Jn. 19:14).[19] The two statements cannot both be right, and the reading ὥρα ἕκτη in this verse in Θ syh.mg is an obvious attempt at harmonisation (as is the rather more widely attested reading of τρίτη in Jn. 19:14).[20] The suggestion of Eusebius that the problem arose from a confusion of the Greek numerals Γ (3) and Ϝ (6), even if plausible in itself,[21] does not remove the discrepancy in what is clearly the original text of the two gospels.

It is possible to argue that it is Mark who is wrong, and to try to find some explanation for his insertion of a mention of the third hour, perhaps along the

18. A. Mahoney, *CBQ* 28 (1966) 292-99, suggests that a harmony with Jn. 19:14 may be achieved by punctuating after τρίτη, so that the time referred to is not that of the crucifixion but of the distribution of Jesus' clothes, which he suggests took place when Jesus was flogged, not at the cross. The result is gratuitously to throw the sequence of Mark's narrative into confusion (including what reads like a direct contradiction of v. 20, where Jesus' clothes were returned to him after flogging and mockery) for the sake of harmony with John.

19. The suggestion of B. F. Westcott, *The Gospel According to St. John* (London: John Murray, 1896), 282, that John used the modern reckoning of hours from midnight to noon, so that the time indicated in Jn. 19:14 is 'about 6.30 *a.m.*', has not found support; see J. V. Miller, *JETS* 26 (1983) 158-63.

20. J. Blinzler, *Trial*, 267-69, solves the problem simply, but without any textual support, by 'the hypothesis that Mark 15:25 was inserted by a reviser'.

21. It should be noted, however, that in NT times the number 6 seems often to have been represented not by the digamma (Ϝ) but by the stigma (for which see BAGD, 335, and critical commentaries on Rev. 13:18), which would remove the basis for Eusebius's proposal.

lines of a deliberate recasting of the whole day into three-hour sections for the purpose of memorisation or to fit some assumed liturgical scheme,[22] or more specifically in order to associate Jesus' sacrifice with the time when the daily *tāmîd* offering was made in the temple.[23] But Mark cannot be isolated in that way, since Matthew and Luke, even though they lack a parallel to this verse (and thus an explicit sequence of three-hour periods through the day), presuppose that Jesus has been on the cross some time before the darkness begins. The general plausibility of the time scale Mark offers is strongly in its favour, particularly in view of the fact that crucified men seldom died quickly, many surviving for days.

The alternative is to try to explain Jn. 19:14 as a deliberate or accidental alteration of the tradition. It might be suggested that John altered the received chronology in order to place the time of Jesus' death as closely as possible to that of the Passover sacrifice. His more extensive account of the Roman trial also seems to require a longer period after dawn than the more perfunctory synoptic version (though Luke's inclusion of a 'trial' before Antipas also runs into problems here, Lk. 23:6-11). On the other hand, it is possible that John's ὥρα ἕκτη derives from the prominence of the same phrase in the synoptic accounts, and has found its way wrongly into the account of the verdict, because someone was unaware that it represented not the beginning of Jesus' time on the cross but the climactic point when the darkness began.[24]

The issue must remain open, but it is important for our reading of Mark to recognise that it is one of gospel harmonisation, not of Mark's own internal consistency.

26 There is evidence in Roman literature that a placard (*titulus,* whence the transliteration τίτλος in Jn. 19:19) detailing the crimes of condemned persons was sometimes tied round their neck or carried before them on the way to execution,[25] and while there is no evidence outside the NT for this placard being attached to the cross there is nothing implausible in this, since the writing was intended to be seen as widely as possible. Mark does not in fact state *where* it was ἐπιγεγραμμένη; it is John who says it was placed on the cross, supported

22. So Stock, 355-56, following the argument of J. Navone, *New Blackfriars* 65 (1984) 125, that Mark was drawing on the three-hourly cycle of Jewish liturgical prayer. Others (e.g., Anderson, 342) have suggested that the scheme was based on or designed for early church liturgy. It should be noted, however, that while the three-hour intervals are mentioned, the story is not constructed in balanced sections to furnish three Good Friday readings, there being no narrative content for the period from the sixth to the ninth hours covered in v. 33.

23. J. Pobee in E. Bammel (ed.), *Trial,* 95.

24. D. A. Carson, *John,* 605, accounts for the discrepancy on the basis of different people's observation of the position of the sun (in a period when there were no clocks): 'If the sun was moving toward mid-heaven, two different observers might well have glanced up and decided, respectively, that it was "the third hour" or "about the sixth hour".' Cf. Mann, 646: 'an approximation at best and a wild guess at worst'. J. V. Miller, *JETS* 26 (1983) 163-166, also prefers a harmonisation based on the view that 'the time notations are approximations'.

25. E. Bammel in E. Bammel and C. F. D. Moule (ed.), *Politics,* 353-54.

by Matthew's statement that it was over Jesus' head (Luke's ἐπ' αὐτῷ could as well mean that it was hung round Jesus' neck). The phrase ὁ βασιλεὺς τῶν Ἰουδαίων is the same as that used at the trial (v. 2) and represents the charge on which Jesus has been convicted. It does not directly describe Jesus as a rebel or insurrectionist, but a claim to be a king under the Roman empire (unless confirmed in such an office by Rome) was treasonable.[26] Placed over a man dying in agony and disgrace it was both a cruel joke and a powerful deterrent.

27 The term λῃστής, which Josephus was later to use almost as a technical term for Jewish freedom fighters under the Roman empire, did not necessarily carry that meaning at the time Mark was writing. It is a general term for a robber or bandit, and we have seen it used in that sense in the LXX quotation from Je. 7:11 in 11:17, and probably also in 14:48 (though a more political note in the latter passage cannot be ruled out). And there is nothing in Mark or, indeed, in any of the gospels to associate these two λῃσταί explicitly with Barabbas or any other nationalist movement. But the coincidence that at the time of Jesus' arrest some men were in fact awaiting execution as insurrectionists, that one of their number was released instead of Jesus, and that Jesus' alleged crime was political treason is enough to convince most interpreters that these were λῃσταί in Josephus's sense, and thus that the βασιλεὺς τῶν Ἰουδαίων was appropriately placed between two other 'revolutionaries' from whom, in Roman eyes, he could be distinguished only in that his claim as βασιλεύς was more audacious than theirs — hence his place in the middle of the group.[27] But ἕνα ἐκ δεξιῶν καὶ ἕνα ἐξ εὐωνύμων[28] αὐτοῦ is a cumbersome way to say 'between', and Mark probably expects his reader to remember the request of James and John to sit at Jesus' right and left in his glory (10:37, 40). If so, there is scope for ironical reflection on the sort of δόξα Jesus now enjoys and on the quality of those who share it with him,[29] and also perhaps on the fact that now the time has come James and John are not there to fulfil their boast of 10:39.

29-30 See the Textual Note for the omission of v. 28. The implied mockery of the *titulus* is now augmented by the overt mockery of onlookers at the cross. The subject in vv. 29-30 is quite general, οἱ παραπορευόμενοι;[30] in

26. E. Bammel, in *Politics,* 357-58, argues that the crime it denotes is *laesa majestas* rather than attempted insurrection.

27. The gospels mention only three people crucified that day, but there may well have been more (so E. Bammel in E. Bammel and C. F. D. Moule [ed.], *Politics,* 443 n. 207), especially as it is unlikely that the στάσις of 15:7 had resulted in only three arrests. But for Mark's purposes only Jesus and his immediate neighbours need be mentioned.

28. For εὐώνυμος see above, p. 415 n. 42.

29. The addition of a reference to Is. 53:12 in many later MSS and versions (see Textual Note) reflects a growing Christian tendency to trace links between the passion story and Is. 53, but nothing in Mark's wording here suggests that he intended such an allusion; see D. J. Moo, *The OT,* 154-55.

30. The phrase is not unnatural, particularly if the place of execution was beside a road, but many commentators suggest that it derives from the mocking of Jerusalem in La. 2:15 (cf 1:12), which also shares the motif of shaking heads; cf. D. J. Moo, *The OT,* 258.

vv. 31-32 more specific groups will be singled out. In recording such general mockery Mark is of course reflecting the effect that public humiliation and punishment have always been able to evoke in any culture, but also indicating that while the priestly authorities have taken the lead in bringing about Jesus' death this has not been done in the face of popular resistance. The popular support which Jesus' teaching had at least begun to gain during the preceding week has now evaporated; his challenge to the powers that be has failed, and he is discredited. βλασφημέω is here used in its more general sense of verbal abuse (see on 3:28-30, and cf. 7:22), not of speaking against God. The apparently unnecessary phrase κινοῦντες τὰς κεφαλὰς αὐτῶν serves to remind the reader again of Ps. 22, where ἐκίνησαν κεφαλήν (LXX Ps. 21[22]:8[7])[31] is part of the description of those who look on while the psalmist suffers and mock him with an assurance of God's deliverance.

οὐά, described by the lexica as an exclamation of astonishment (and used nowhere else in biblical literature, though οὐαί is common as an expression of distress) is the sort of utterance, like 'Ha!', which gains its sense from the tone of voice rather than from a lexical meaning. The following words suggest that it conveys vindictive sarcasm. The echo of the temple charge of 14:58 shows that it was this aspect of Jesus' alleged programme that had particularly impressed and alienated the ordinary population of Jerusalem. It is unlikely that the visible association of Jesus on the cross with two λῃσταί in itself added to that hostility by marking him as 'a man of (potential?) violence against the temple',[32] since for Jewish patriots the temple was more a talisman[33] than a potential target. Jesus' language about the destruction of the temple was no more that of a λῃστής than of any other patriotic Jew.

The connection between the supposed threat/promise with regard to the temple and the invitation to come down from the cross is presumably to be found in that one who has the supernatural ability to do the former must surely be able also to do the latter. The evident helplessness of Jesus on the cross gives the lie to any claim to exercise special powers. The call σῶσον σεαυτόν also picks up the idea of Jesus as a saviour, for which see on the next verse. Mark does not include the direct echo of Ps. 22:8 with which Matthew (27:43) concludes the priests' words of mockery, but after the echo of that psalm in κινοῦντες τὰς κεφαλάς his readers might have remembered that the sufferer there was also mocked with the prospect of being rescued by God.

31 The mockery by the chief priests and scribes (the two groups are mentioned to represent the Sanhedrin establishment as a whole as in 11:18; 14:1) is described using the same verb (ἐμπαίζω) as Mark used for the Roman soldiers in v. 20; the means are different (in this case merely verbal taunts)

31. For the idiom cf. also La. 2:15. A further parallel in Ps. 109:25 is less close in wording (LXX has ἐσάλευσαν), and in view of the other allusions to Ps. 22 is less likely to have been in mind.

32. K. E. Brower in K. E. Brower and M. W. Elliott (ed.), *Reader,* 128-30.

33. N. T. Wright, *Victory,* 420, cited by Brower in this connection.

but the attitude the same. The verb σῴζω and its cognates have not figured previously in Mark either in Jesus' presentation of his own role or in the accounts of him by others, except in the sense of physical healing and restoration. In the priests' words, it would be possible still to take it in that sense:[34] he has been able to restore others' physical well-being but cannot preserve his own life.[35] But Jesus' healings have not been mentioned as an issue in his trial, and it is more likely that Mark intends us to understand σῴζω here in its more theological sense, perhaps as an extrapolation from the title Χριστός (which will be picked up in the next sentence), understood as the God-sent deliverer. In any case, ἄλλους ἔσωσεν functions here not as an affirmation (and therefore does not require that the priests should be able to answer the questions 'when?' and 'how?') but as an ironic foil to the jibe ἑαυτὸν οὐ δύναται σῶσαι. A 'deliverer' who cannot even secure his own survival is a poor sort of Χριστός for others.

32 By linking together the royal title on the placard with the term which had been at the centre of the Sanhedrin hearing, ὁ Χριστός, the priests make clear the basis on which the official charge had been constructed. The form ὁ βασιλεὺς Ἰσραήλ is the more natural way for a Jew to speak, while οἱ Ἰουδαῖοι is the term Gentiles would use of them or they might use to identify themselves to Gentiles. (Mark has used οἱ Ἰουδαῖοι in this way in 7:3 and in 15:2, 9, 12, 18, and 26, where the title ὁ βασιλεὺς τῶν Ἰουδαίων was designed for and used by the Roman prefect and his troops.) ὁ βασιλεὺς Ἰσραήλ thus has a more patriotic, even theological, tone which makes its use in mockery by the leaders of Israel particularly poignant. The proposal that a descent from the cross would cause them to 'see and believe'[36] reminds us of the demand for a σημεῖον in 8:11-12, but also echoes Jesus' challenge in 14:62, ὄψεσθε: if he really is to sit at God's right hand, now is the time to show it. Nothing less is required of a king of Israel.[37]

Themes and titles arising from the Sanhedrin hearing have thus run through this scene of mockery: the replacement of the temple, the title ὁ Χριστός, and the deliverance which it implies, and undergirding it all the royal title which all the time facetiously proclaims from the *titulus* what Jesus claimed to be. The impossibility of any of these proving true of a disgraced and dying man is the basis of the mockery. But Mark's readers are aware that at a

---

34. T. J. Weeden in W. H. Kelber (ed.), *Passion,* 118-19, argues that this sense of miraculous healing power is in focus here, so that '*sozein* in 15:30, 31 bears intentionally a divine man soteriological orientation'.

35. The use of σῴζω in 5:23 in connection with the restoration of life makes this sense especially ironic.

36. C. D. Marshall, *Faith,* 205, comments that 'the phrase "see and believe" . . . reverses the pattern established throughout his entire story where faith is the presupposition of miracle, not its inevitable consequence'.

37. It is possible to see in the demand for a visible sign an echo of the persecution of the righteous in Wis. 2, especially 2:17-18; but Mark, unlike Mt. 27:40, 43, has not drawn attention to that passage by a verbal echo.

deeper level all these are true, and that ironically it is by being where he is that Jesus is fulfilling this mission. It is precisely because he does not come down from the cross that the mockery will prove in time to have missed the mark. If he had saved himself, he could not have saved others. Mark's readers may well be reminded of Jesus' own paradoxical words about losing one's ψυχή in order to save (σώζω) it (8:35).

The final indignity is the insults even of the two λῃσταί.[38] Mark does not, like Luke, tell us what they said, and leaves us to assume that it followed similar lines to the jibes of the bystanders. The mockery of all three groups is expressed in the imperfect tense, suggesting that it may have gone on for some time.

The Death of Jesus (15:33-39)

TEXTUAL NOTES

34. The variety of readings of the Hebrew/Aramaic text of Ps. 22:1 quoted in both Matthew and Mark leaves room for considerable doubt on which form Mark used and what Hebrew/Aramaic words he was transliterating; the ℵ text printed in UBS⁴/NA²⁷ reflects a general agreement that Mark's quotation is intended to be in Aramaic, and that 'Hebraising' readings are due to assimilation to Matthew (though Matthew's ἠλί, often taken to be Hebrew, is in fact the form found in the extant targum of Ps. 22:1); see R. H. Gundry, *Use*, 63-66; J. A. Fitzmyer, *Aramean*, 93. In the Greek rendering it is more likely that the word order ἐγκατέλιπές με, which conforms to LXX Ps 21[22]:2[1], would be altered to agree with Matthew's order με ἐγκατέλιπες than the other way round. The substitution of ὠνείδισάς με in some Western texts may be an attempt to avoid the theological embarrassment of Jesus' desertion by God (on this reading see further D. J. Moo, *The OT*, 269-70).

39. The issue is whether this verse originally contained a reference back to the loud cry of v. 37. The majority of witnesses contain such a reference, in a variety of forms, and it is possible that the Alexandrian witnesses which omit κράξας result from the feeling that a second reference to the cry was redundant at this point (particularly as Matthew does not include it here). But it is perhaps marginally more likely that κράξας was added (perhaps under the influence of Mt. 27:50) because it was felt that an original οὕτως needed to be clarified, and that οὕτως then dropped out of a few texts (but not the majority) because the phrase had become too cumbersome.

In the previous section Jesus has been the passive object of crucifixion and mockery. Now as the passion narrative reaches its climax in his death, while the themes of mockery and perhaps cruelty continue in vv. 35-36, they are overshadowed by the renewed focus on Jesus himself. The unnatural darkness tells us that this is a crucifixion unlike any other, and prepares us to hear Jesus' dreadful last shout from the cross, and then to witness the striking manner in

---

38. 'The two Zealots, who are on the same side as Jesus in relation to the spectators, nonetheless move over to the side of the spectators, and Jesus is strictly *alone*' (Belo, 228).

which he died. His death is as extraordinary as his life, and its far-reaching implications are underlined by the physical symbol of the tearing of the temple curtain and by the astonished declaration of the centurion, whose use of the title υἱὸς θεοῦ rounds off the revelation of the true significance of Jesus which began in Mark's introductory statement in 1:1 and at the narrative level with the voice from heaven in 1:11. The title has come to the surface at several points in the narrative, but this is the first time it has been uttered with conviction (as opposed to the High Priest's scepticism, 14:61) by a human witness. The identity of that witness, a pagan soldier without the benefit either of Jewish theological education or of having been a disciple of Jesus, fits well with Mark's persistent theme of the inability of either the Jewish leadership or even Jesus' own disciples to recognise who he is, and prompts Mark's readers to reflect that what has now taken place is to be the basis for good news εἰς πάντα τὰ ἔθνη (13:10), εἰς ὅλον τὸν κόσμον (14:9).

In v. 39, then, Mark's account of the helpless and humiliating death of Jesus unexpectedly reaches a triumphant christological climax. But this seems the more incongruous in that this final scene is dominated not by a shout of triumph but by what sounds like a cry of despair. Mark has chosen to record as Jesus' last words (though not the last words about Jesus) not a confident address to God as Ἀββά but a tortured cry of abandonment. Perhaps he knew no tradition of other less devastating words from the cross such as Luke and John record. But in recording this last utterance he has set up the supreme paradox of his paradoxical story. The two verses 34 and 39 thus create the two poles of a mind-stretching antinomy, which Mark leaves unresolved for his readers to work at. Nor will he offer much help with its resolution in the remainder of his narrative: the message that the crucified Jesus is alive again (16:6-7) will indeed assure us that all is now well, that whatever was the reality underlying Jesus' cry of despair was not the end of the story. But that cry in itself remains unexplained, unless it be by reflection back over a narrative in which Jesus' death has been repeatedly declared to be the goal of his ministry, in which Scripture must be fulfilled, and the purpose of which has been hinted at in tantalisingly brief statements about a ransom for many (10:45) and about the blood of the covenant (14:24). There are raw materials here for constructing a theological understanding of Jesus' death within which the stark words of v. 34 may find a place, but Mark gives us no help in constructing it. His theology of the cross remains expressed in paradox.

These seven verses consist of a series of brief incidents, a few of which are deliberately linked together (the Elijah episode with the cry of v. 34 on the basis of a supposed mishearing, and the centurion's exclamation based on the account of Jesus' death in v. 37), but mostly following one another without expressed causal links. We shall note below a number of attempts by interpreters to supply such links (notably the assumption by many that the centurion saw the tearing of the temple curtain, though Mark does not say so), but there is need for caution in 'reading Mark's mind' in this way. The overall impact of the series of cameos is powerful, but their structural coherence is less apparent.[39]

33 γενομένης ὥρας ἕκτης, together with the mention of the third hour in 15:25, suggests that all that has been recorded in the preceding verses took place before noon, though the imperfect tenses of vv. 29, 31, and 32 allow for the possibility that the mockery begun in the morning continued. But for the period from noon to the ninth hour no further events are recorded, but merely the passage of time. What is new in this period is not a matter of human activity but an unnatural darkness beginning in the middle of the day and continuing apparently not until sunset, but only until about the time of Jesus' death, which seems to have taken place in Mark's scheme soon after the ninth hour. Darkness during the day is a recognised mark of God's displeasure and judgment (Dt. 28:29; Am. 8:9, Je. 15:9, and cf. on 13:24 above for other such 'cosmic' judgment language in Is. 13:10 etc.),[40] and the supreme example of that phenomenon in the OT, the darkness over Egypt which was the penultimate plague at the time of the first Passover (Ex. 10:21-23), is echoed in Mark's language (LXX Ex. 10:22: ἐγένετο σκότος . . . ἐπὶ πᾶσαν γῆν Αἰγύπτου). That parallel suggests what is in any case more probable, that γῆ is here to be understood in its more limited sense of the land of Judaea rather than of a worldwide darkness (it is so understood by *Gos. Pet.* 5[15]).[41] Given the symbolic significance of the darkness as a divine communication there is little point in speculating on its natural cause: a solar eclipse could not occur at the time of the Passover full moon, though a dust storm ('sirocco') or heavy cloud cover are possible.[42] Mark's language is not precise enough for us to know whether he understands the cry of v. 34 and the events which follow as occurring still within the darkness or after it has passed, though the desolation expressed in v. 34 would be well symbolised by physical darkness.

34 Accounts of ancient crucifixion indicate a gradual loss of strength and consciousness, so that Mark's emphatic statement that these last words of

---

39. For an interesting attempt to fit the whole pericope into an elaborate chiastic structure see K. E. Brower, *JSNT* 18 (1983) 88-93. The outer frame consists of two acts of God (vv. 33, 38), within this are two cries of Jesus (vv. 34, 37), within this two Elijah references (vv. 35, 36b), and at the centre the offer of a drink (v. 36a); the centurion's comment in v. 39 then rounds off the whole section (and, indeed, the whole passion narrative) with a christological summary. This is a valid observation of the contents of the pericope, but it is less easy to demonstrate that Mark so planned it, and it is not encouraging to note that the central point of the suggested structure is the minor episode of the offer of a drink rather than on what is surely the dramatic climax, the death of Jesus.

40. See further D. J. Moo, *The OT,* 342-44. This familiar OT motif makes it unnecessary to search for a background in (mainly) Greek and Roman accounts of eclipses or other unnatural darkness marking the deaths of great men (Davies and Allison, *Matthew* 3.622 nn. 61, 62, list references; Gundry, 963, sets them out more fully).

41. Pesch, 2.493; cf. H. Sasse, *TDNT,* 1.677 (contra H. Conzelmann, *TDNT,* 7.439). More fully S. Légasse, *Procès,* 2.113-15.

42. *Gos. Pet.* 5(18) goes on to embellish the record with an account of people thinking it was night and so lighting lamps and either (probably) going to bed or stumbling (the Greek is not clear).

Jesus were a shout (βοάω is a strong word, 'somewhat obsolescent' according to Gundry, 948, used by Mark elsewhere only in quoting Isaiah's prophecy of the proclamation in the wilderness, 1:3), uttered φωνῇ μεγάλῃ, is to be noted. In v. 37, even at the moment of Jesus' death, he will again speak of a φωνὴ μεγάλη. Jesus is not going out with a whimper but in full possession of his faculties. The loudness of the cry also serves to underline the depth of the emotion it expresses.

Ἐλωῒ ἐλωῒ λεμὰ σαβαχθάνι; is probably (see Textual Note) a transliteration of the opening words of Ps. 22:1 in Aramaic (though not of the extant targum, which has the 'Hebrew' form 'ēlî as in Matthew's version, and mițțûl mâ instead of lᵉmā'), while the Greek translation reflects but does not exactly reproduce the LXX Ὁ θεὸς ὁ θεός μου, πρόσχες μοι· ἵνα τί ἐγκατέλιπές με; The textual confusion does not allow us to be certain, but it seems that Mark's reproduction of the Aramaic form deliberately pictures Jesus in the moment of supreme testing using Scripture in his vernacular rather than in the Hebrew original.[43] This is the third time he has given us Jesus' words in Aramaic as well as in Greek translation, once when exercising divine power over death (5:41), and here and in 14:36 in direct appeal to God in prayer. But this time the contrast with 14:36 is striking: there he could call God Father, and loyally accepted his Father's will; here (for the only time in Jesus' recorded prayers in all four gospels) he calls him not Father but ὁ θεός μου, and his 'prayer' is one of bewilderment and separation. This is, of course, the only time when Jesus' recorded prayer is not in his own words but in the form of a quotation from a psalm, but the fact that such a quotation came to his mind on this occasion, rather than one expressing a trusting relationship with God, speaks for itself. While ὁ θεός μου expresses a continued relationship with God,[44] it is a relationship which feels like abandonment. It is of course true that Ps. 22, having begun on this note of despair, concludes twenty verses later in hope and thanksgiving, but Jesus echoed not the latter part of the psalm but its opening,[45] and to read into these few tortured words an exegesis of the whole psalm is to turn upside down the effect which Mark has created by this pow-

43. For a survey of the debate on whether Mark's quotation is meant to be Hebrew or Aramaic see D. J. Moo, *The OT,* 264-68; R. E. Brown, *Death,* 1051-53, both concluding in favour of Aramaic. M. Casey, *Sources,* 88, concludes that at this 'moment of extreme stress' Jesus used the language in which he was used to *expounding* Scripture: 'He read the scriptures in Hebrew, and expounded them in Aramaic.'

44. Anderson, 346, comments: 'He will not let God go, but dares to cling to him and to name him still "My God, my God".' M. A. Tolbert, *Sowing,* 283, describes the very form of Jesus' cry as ironical in that 'Jesus addresses his words to the very One whom he claims has deserted him. . . . Jesus is forsaken by God, and at the same time God is available to be called upon.'

45. J. Jeremias does not support his suggestion that 'the quotation of the beginning of Ps. 22 is meant to indicate that Jesus prayed the whole psalm' (*Theology,* 189). More normally commentators suggest that Mark (rather than Jesus) intended the whole psalm to be brought to the reader's mind. So, e.g., F. J. Matera, *Kingship,* 132-35. For the reader this 'becomes Jesus' messianic cry' (Matera, *Kingship,* 137).

erful and enigmatic cry of agony.[46] Six hours after he was placed on the cross, and after three hours of darkness, Jesus feels abandoned by God.

We do not know how long the feeling lasted. Mark does not tell us what was the content of Jesus' second loud cry in v. 37 (contrast τετέλεσται, Jn. 19:30), but the centurion's reaction to the manner of his death in v. 39 indicates that by then he gave the impression not of failure and despair, but of being υἱὸς θεοῦ, very different from the tone of this verse. It would be possible to read Mark's notes of time as indicating that the darkness lifted 'at the ninth hour', the time of Jesus' cry, so that that cry marked the end of the time of separation, but that is to read rather a lot between the lines. But if Mark does not tell us how long the sense of abandonment lasted, he gives us no grounds for supposing that it was not, at the time of Jesus' cry, utterly real and all-embracing. He leaves no room for the heroic serenity of Jesus' death in later docetic reconstruction.[47]

A commentary on Mark is not the place to debate how this sense of abandonment fits into the christology and trinitarianism of later Christian orthodoxy. Mark apparently does not find this cry incompatible with Jesus' still being υἱὸς θεοῦ in v. 39. The general Christian instinct is to interpret these words in the light of a doctrine of atonement whereby Jesus enters temporarily into the state of God-forsakenness from which sinful humanity needs to be rescued (cf., e.g., 2 Cor. 5:21; Gal. 3:13), and by tasting that 'cup' (14:36) to the full ἀντὶ πολλῶν (10:45; cf. 14:24) sets them free; thereafter, his redeeming work complete, his relationship with his Father is restored. But this theological reconstruction, though based on hints Mark has given earlier in his story as Jesus has spoken of what lies ahead of him at Jerusalem, goes far beyond anything he is willing to spell out at this point. He wants us to feel Jesus' agony, not to explain it.

35-36 The identity of the παρεστηκότες is not spelled out and is not important. The fact that they instinctively think of Elijah marks them out as Jewish rather than members of the execution squad, but their anonymity puts them

---

46. For some sane comments on this and other attempts to evade the force of Jesus' cry see D. J. Moo, *The OT*, 271-74. See contra J. Marcus, *Way*, 180-82, defending and developing the view of H. Gese that much of the crucifixion account is based on Ps. 22, including its theme of kingship and vindication as well as of suffering. T. E. Schmidt, *BBR* 4 (1994) 145-53, offers the unusual view that the latter part of Ps. 22 focuses on 'judgment issuing in universality', and that in quoting its beginning Jesus intended to express this theme: his own death is the judgment of Israel ('me' thus refers to the Jewish nation), after which salvation will come to all nations, represented by the centurion in v. 39.

47. *Gos. Pet.* 4(10) says that Jesus at the time of crucifixion 'was silent, as if he felt no pain' and gives the present cry in the form (5[19]) ἡ δύναμίς μου, ἡ δύναμις, κατέλειψάς με, after which immediately 'he was taken up', a version which apparently turns abandonment by God into the ebbing of physical strength (or possibly the loss of miraculous power to escape the cross?) as Jesus exchanges earthly life for heavenly. Such an origin for the use of δύναμις seems more likely than the suggestion that it arises from a confusion in this Greek gospel or its source between Hebrew ʾēlî and ḥêlî, 'my strength' (so, e.g., B. Lindars, *Apologetic*, 89-90). See further R. E. Brown, *Death*, 1056-58.

in the category of the παραπορευόμενοι of v. 29 rather than the mocking priests. The idea that Jesus had uttered the name of Elijah would be a more natural mistake if Jesus used the form Ἠλί rather than Mark's Ἐλωΐ, but even the latter (representing Aramaic *'elāhî*) uttered in an agonised shout could perhaps have been heard as the prophet's name.[48] The mistake, if indeed we are to read it as a mistake rather than a malicious twisting of what they had heard,[49] is the more natural in view of the growing belief in an eschatological return of Elijah to 're-store all things' (see on 9:11-13), which in some later Jewish piety included the hope that he might appear from heaven to help in times of need.[50]

The offer of a drink is not necessarily a direct consequence of the supposed appeal to Elijah, but perhaps the idea is that it will enable Jesus to survive until Elijah comes. This would be consistent with the following Ἄφετε, probably used in the sense of 'leave alone',[51] not necessarily to avert any specific interference, but generally asking the bystanders and/or the soldiers to leave the field clear for Elijah to intervene if he so chose. In the narrative context ὄξος was probably the cheap 'wine vinegar' which 'was a favourite beverage of the lower ranks of society and of those in moderate circumstances, esp. of soldiers', and was an effective thirst quencher (BAGD, 574a).[52] John (19:29) says that there was a jar of it standing there, presumably for the use of the soldiers, and Luke (23:36, referring to the period before noon) says the soldiers gave Jesus ὄξος to drink in the course of their mockery. But Mark gives no hint of the involvement of the soldiers, and the τις who offers the drink is more naturally understood to be one of the Jewish παρεστηκότες, especially as he goes on to pick up the Elijah jibe. He could not approach Jesus without the consent of the soldiers, of course, and may indeed have used some of their supply of ὄξος, but

48. So D. J. Moo, *The OT,* 268. R. E. Brown, *Death,* 1061-62, rightly points out that Mark's Greek readers (and Mark himself?) would not be worried about exact Semitic pronunciations, and would simply take Mark's word for it that Ἐλωΐ sounded like Ἠλίας.

49. F. J. Matera, *Kingship,* 122-25, insists that this is not a misunderstanding 'on either the historical or literary level', but a mockery. But in context the nature of the mockery is surely presented in relation to the cry of v. 34, and therefore suggests a deliberate echo, even if not a real belief that Jesus had uttered Elijah's name.

50. J. Jeremias, *TDNT,* 2.930; Str-B, 4/2.769-79. For example, according to *b.'Abod. Zar.* 17b one R. Eleazar was rescued from a Roman trial by Elijah, who (disguised as a Roman official) intercepted an imperial messenger sent for evidence and 'hurled him a distance of 400 parasangs, so that he went and did not return'. Elijah's disguise in some appropriate human form is a regular feature of such stories. Underlying this belief is not only Elijah's role of 'restoration', but also the record of how he helped a woman in distress (1 Ki. 17:8-24); since he was carried to heaven without dying (2 Ki. 2:11), he remains available to help.

51. It is possible to take ἄφετε not as a request to leave Jesus alone but as introducing the deliberative subjunctive ἴδωμεν (so BDF, 364[2]) so that the whole phrase means 'let us see' ('an epexegetical ἵνα having dropped out'; Gundry, 969), though the only NT parallel to this use of ἀφίημι is the singular ἄφες ἐκβάλω in Mt. 7:4/Lk. 6:42. Mark is certainly capable of redundancy, but where the imperative has an appropriate sense of its own in the context this interpretation seems unnecessary.

52. Pliny, *Nat. Hist.* 23.27, lists a wide variety of medicinal uses of vinegar *(acetum),* but his references to its pain-killing effects appear to refer only to external uses.

they would not necessarily object to an act which did not interfere with the process of execution. In that case there is nothing in Mark's narrative to suggest that the ὄξος was meant to be in itself unpleasant, however mocking the context in which it was offered. But the word ὄξος here, together with ποτίζω, echoes LXX Ps. 68[69]:22[21], which, as we have noted above regarding v. 23, speaks of a hostile act and mentions poison in parallel to the ὄξος. If, as his wording suggests, Mark intended such an allusion here (though not in v. 23), it seems that under the influence of the psalm passage he is putting a more sinister construction on what was in itself a harmless and even kindly act, though done in a context of mockery. He does not tell us this time whether Jesus accepted the offer, though the imperfect ἐπότιζεν might perhaps be read like the ἐδίδουν of v. 23 as conative, implying that the attempt was unsuccessful. The need to use a sponge on a cane to reach Jesus' mouth indicates that the cross used was quite a high one, rather than the minimum height to lift the feet clear of the ground,[53] and the κατα- compounds in vv. 30, 32, and 36 suggest the same.

37 Mark does not indicate whether this second loud utterance[54] (Van Iersel's translation 'emitted a deep sigh' is not what Mark says) was in words, as in the different accounts of Lk. 23:46 and Jn. 19:30, or simply an inarticulate cry, and so we cannot say from his account whether it expressed still the desolation of v. 34 or a new mood either of trust (Luke) or triumph (John). The only clue is the reaction of the centurion in v. 39, especially if we accept the reading there (see Textual Note on v. 39) which specifically mentions the cry as the basis of that reaction. The recognition in Jesus of a υἱὸς θεοῦ would follow more naturally from a 'noble' or peaceful death than from one in unrelieved depression, which was surely familiar enough to a centurion used to officiating at crucifixions.

Mark does not specify the time of death, but leaves us to assume that it was soon after the ninth hour; it must in any case be before sunset (v. 42). All four gospels describe Jesus' actual death[55] in πνεῦμα language, though in varying forms. ἐκπνέω, used by Mark and Luke, is the simplest, and offers even less scope than the πνεῦμα phrases of Matthew and John for reading into the scene any reference to the Holy Spirit.[56] It means simply to 'breathe out', and like our

53. So Lane, 565-66; on the height of crosses see also J. Blinzler, *Trial,* 249-50; R. E. Brown, *Death,* 948-49.

54. Against the suggestion that v. 37 refers back to the cry of v. 34, so that there is only one cry in the narrative and that therefore Jesus died before the offer of a drink (so Gundry, 948-49; cf. F. J. Matera, *Kingship,* 125-27; R. E. Brown, *Death,* 1079), see J. D. Kingsbury, *Christology,* 131 n. 221.

55. On the possible physiological cause of death see J. Wilkinson, *ExpTim* 83 (1971/2) 104-7; R. E. Brown, *Death,* 1088-92; the issue is not of interest to the evangelists, and they offer no specific data.

56. See above, p. 74 n. 58. S. Motyer's article there referred to (*NTS* 33 [1987] 155-57) interprets Jesus' 'breathing out his Spirit' as Mark's Pentecost, fulfilling the prophecy of John the Baptist in 1:8. Gundry, 949, speaks mysteriously of 'an exhalation of the Spirit, which is his breath'. Van Iersel, 477, is more inclusive: 'both the breath of life and the Spirit that has been active in him since the beginning of his ministry'.

'expire' is a natural euphemism for dying, used especially in more poetic or solemn contexts. ἀποθνῄσκω would have conveyed the same sense, but perhaps was felt to be too 'ordinary' a verb to narrate so solemn a moment,[57] though there was no hesitation in using it retrospectively of Jesus' death in the epistles. We shall note in a moment (and reject) a suggestion of a further reason for Mark's choice of ἐκπνέω in relation to the temple curtain.

38 In describing the furnishings of the tabernacle the LXX uses καταπέτασμα to denote both the curtain through which one entered from the courtyard into the Holy Place, the place of offering incense (Ex. 26:37), and also the one inside the Holy Place setting off the innermost shrine, the Holy of Holies (Ex. 26:31). In Solomon's temple the corresponding divisions were made by wooden doors, but in Herod's temple Josephus again describes two καταπετάσματα in these two positions (Josephus, *War* 5.212, 219; cf. *Ant.* 8.75); he says that the huge outer curtain hung in front of and was the same height as the doors, which were fifty-five cubits high, but does not give the height of the inner one (though the hall which it divided was sixty cubits high). The outer curtain, which Josephus describes rapturously as a magnificent work of Babylonian tapestry in rich colours symbolising earth, sea, and sky (*War* 5.212-14), was the only one visible to anyone except the priests who served in the Holy Place. Mark does not say which curtain he means, and there is no evidence of the regular use of τὸ καταπέτασμα τοῦ ναοῦ in the singular to denote specifically either the one or the other.[58] The tearing[59] of the outer curtain would be more of a public event, but the symbolism of the violent opening of the Holy of Holies by the tearing of the inner curtain might be thought to be theologically more telling,[60] and it was apparently in this sense that the tradition was understood by the writer of Hebrews, who refers to it as τὸ δεύτερον καταπέτασμα (Heb. 6:19; 9:3; 10:19-20).[61] But we cannot assume that Mark would have

57. J. D. M. Derrett, *Audience,* 195-96, argues that Mark chose the word in order to convey that Jesus 'gave up the spirit', i.e., died prematurely and voluntarily.

58. For a detailed discussion of the two (or perhaps three!) curtains see R. E. Brown, *Death,* 1109-13; Brown concludes by declaring the issue of which curtain was meant to be exegetically insignificant.

59. See above on 1:10 (also p. 74) for the suggestion that σχίζω, used by Mark only in that verse and here, is a deliberate echo of that previous 'tearing open' which was also followed by a revelation of Jesus as the υἱὸς θεοῦ. (See also R. H. Lightfoot, *Message,* 55-56.) But whereas the 'tearing' of heaven is an arresting metaphor, σχίζω is a natural verb for the tearing of a curtain and need carry no further allusion.

60. M. A. Tolbert, *Sowing,* 280-81, notes Josephus's interpretation of the Holy of Holies as representing heaven (*Ant.* 3.123, 181), and suggests that the tearing of its curtain would indicate Jesus' 'transit from the human world to the heavenly', thus creating a 'permanent breach in the divide, allowing freer access to the divine world by the elect'.

61. A related symbolism is discovered in Mark by K. E. Bailey, *ExpTim* 102 (1990/1) 103-4, on the basis of an elaborate chiastic plan which he discerns in the whole of vv. 20-39: Bailey finds the chiastic parallel to the 'unveiling' of the Holy of Holies in the 'unveiling' of Jesus on the cross: 'the new holy of holies is a dying saviour, unveiled on a hill before the entire world'. (For a similar chiastic link see M. A. Tolbert, *Sowing,* 279-80.) A similar conclu-

shared the theological symbolism of Hebrews. Jesus' references to the temple hitherto in this gospel have concerned its destruction and replacement, and the tearing of the more visible and magnificent outer curtain would more naturally pick up this theme. Following the jibe of vv. 29-30, this would be a particularly appropriate divine riposte: the process of the temple's destruction and replacement has indeed begun, even as Jesus continues to hang on the cross.[62] This 'divine vandalism' also appropriately rebuts the mockery by the chief priests (vv. 31-32): the death of Jesus presages the end of the temple on which their power and influence depended. 'The event is for Mark the fulfillment of the "prophecy" made in 14:58 and 15:29. With Jesus' death, the old religious order comes to an end; those who have rejected Jesus, the religious leaders, have now been rejected by God.'[63]

I have referred to the tearing of the curtain as a 'divine riposte' because in stating that the tear was made ἀπ' ἄνωθεν ἕως κάτω Mark indicates that no human being could have torn it that way (especially if we are talking about the outer curtain, some twenty-five metres high). As Jesus dies, God acts to show what is to be the sequel to his death. This seems a more likely explanation of Mark's language than the bizarre suggestion that he used ἐξέπνευσεν in v. 37 to describe a blast of wind (or the release of 'the Spirit') which (along with Jesus' loud cry) tore the curtain, thus making Jesus himself directly responsible for the tearing.[64]

There is no historical record of this event outside the gospels (and in Luke it occurs before, not after, Jesus' death), though a confused echo of it has been claimed in the statement of b. Yoma 39b that 'during the last forty years before the destruction of the temple the doors of the sanctuary would open by themselves'.[65] Less relevant are the similar stories told of events in A.D. 70: Josephus, War 6.293-96, tells how the east gate of the inner court of the temple opened of its own accord at Passover time in that year, and Tacitus, Hist. 5.13, says that the doors of the temple suddenly opened as a superhuman voice cried,

---

sion is reached by a quite different route by H. L. Chronis, JBL 101 (1982) 107-14, who interprets the tearing of the curtain not only as a portent of the destruction and rebuilding of the temple, but as Jesus' divine self-disclosure as the new temple 'not made with hands' which takes its place.

62. Josephus tells us that the spontaneous opening of the temple gate in A.D. 70 (see below) was interpreted as a sign of its coming destruction. Lives of the Prophets 12:12 predicts that the curtain of the Holy of Holies will be torn into small pieces when the temple is destroyed 'by a western nation', but it is not clear whether this was written before or after A.D. 70, nor whether it is influenced by Christian tradition.

63. D. Juel, Messiah, 206.

64. H. M. Jackson, NTS 33 (1987) 27-28; Van Iersel, 477-79. Gundry, 949-50, creatively combines three distinct meanings of πνεῦμα in his assertion that 'Jesus exhales the wind of the Spirit that rends the veil', and goes on to speak of 'the breath-wind-Spirit'. Jackson supports his exegesis from the idea in Is. 11:4 of 'the Messianic figure's punitive use of his breath' (30).

65. So H. W. Montefiore, NovT 4 (1960) 150-51, pointing out that the most likely date of Jesus' death is in fact just forty years before the destruction of the temple.

'The gods are departing'.[66] But Mark's reason for including this apparent digression is clearly not to record a fact interesting for its own sake, but to illuminate the significance of the death of Jesus. Many suggestions have been made as to just what its symbolism was,[67] and in the absence of any indication from Mark they are all necessarily speculative, but something along the lines suggested above seems best to fit into the 'temple theology' which we have seen developing throughout Act Three of Mark's drama, and finds both patristic[68] and modern support.

39 The account of the tearing of the curtain intervenes between Jesus' death and the centurion's reaction to that death (with ἐξέπνευσεν repeated to link the two together). Many interpreters therefore conclude that Mark intends us to include the tearing of the curtain in what the centurion saw which formed the basis for his exclamation.[69] But Mark does not say that the centurion saw it, and at the narrative level this would be impossible since one would have to be standing east of the temple (and nearer to it than any likely location of Golgotha) in order to see the curtain.[70] The account of the curtain is for the benefit of Mark's readers as they think about the significance of Jesus' death, not in relation to the following mention of the centurion; the centurion's comment is evoked simply by how Jesus died.

The centurion (Mark uses the Latin loanword κεντυρίων rather than the Greek forms ἑκατοντάρχης or ἑκατόνταρχος always used by Matthew and Luke), who was παρεστηκὼς ἐξ ἐναντίας αὐτοῦ,[71] was in charge of the execution squad (see vv. 44-45), now keeping watch over the victims as they died. As a low-ranking officer in the auxiliary forces (centurions were normally com-

---

66. Van Iersel, 479, attempts to support the incident from Josephus's statement that the spoils taken to Rome in A.D. 70 included materials needed for repairs to the temple curtain, and even considers the possibility that the torn curtain was publicly displayed in the triumph in Rome, though he admits that this is 'pure speculation'.

67. Geddert, *Watchwords*, 140-45, lists (without documenting) thirty-five suggestions.

68. For example, Tertullian, *Adv. Marc.* 4.42; Chrysostom, *Hom. Mt.* 88.2; *Pseudo-Clementine Recognitions* 1.41. (The last of these speaks of it as a 'lamentation' for the imminent destruction of the temple; D. Daube, *The NT,* 23-25, supports this idea from the tearing εἰς δύο, echoing Elisha's tearing his cloak in mourning for Elijah [2 Ki. 2:12].) Cf. the Christian elements incorporated in *Test. Levi* 10:3; *Test. Ben.* 9:3, and the account of the event in a 'gospel written in Hebrew letters' known to Jerome in which the tearing of the curtain has been replaced by the collapse of a massive lintel, *superliminare* (Jerome, *Ep.* 120.8 and *Comm. Mt.* on 27:51).

69. One of the most forceful recent arguments for this view is that of H. M. Jackson, *NTS* 33 (1987) 16-37. Jackson believes that the tearing of the curtain is not just a cause but *the* cause of the centurion's response.

70. H. M. Jackson, *NTS* 33 (1987) 24-25, argues for a location of Golgotha on the Mount of Olives (in Mark's mind if not in reality) in order to maintain the possibility of the centurion seeing the tearing of the curtain. E. L. Martin, *Secrets,* argues that it was historically so. Contra see R. E. Brown, *Death,* 939. Brown does, however, think (1144-45) that Mark intends us to believe that the centurion saw the tearing of the curtain, and argues that neither Mark nor his audience would be aware of the geographical implausibility of this.

71. Gundry, 950, 973, suggests unusually that the antecedent of αὐτοῦ is the temple, so that Mark describes the centurion as 'standing opposite the temple'.

mon soldiers who had been promoted through the ranks, not 'career officers') he would probably be a non-Jewish member of one of the surrounding nations (see on v. 16). Mark does not make it clear just what in Jesus' manner of death (οὕτως) impressed him so deeply, but his narrative suggests a number of possibilities: the unnatural darkness (v. 33) might suggest to him that Jesus was someone out of the ordinary; the last words of Jesus in v. 34, while far from heroic, might have impressed him with their religious earnestness; the loud cry at the time of death (v. 37; if κράξας is read here, see Textual Note, this aspect would take priority) would be unusual for a crucified man, implying a sudden death in full vigour rather than a slow ebbing of life, and the fact that Jesus died so quickly (v. 44) conveys the same impression. All those hints are in the text; further suggestions are less firmly based, but include the possibility that the unrecorded words of the 'loud cry' expressed either trust in God or even triumph, and that Jesus' demeanour at the time of death (in contrast with his cry at the ninth hour) was noble or even peaceful (see on v. 37).

The centurion's exclamation is the climax of the crucifixion scene, and one of the christological high points of the gospel. I earlier described 14:62 as 'the christological climax of the gospel', and so it was, for at that point Jesus openly declared himself Messiah and Son of God. There is no new christological content here, but what is new is the source from which the declaration comes, the first human witness to describe Jesus as υἱὸς θεοῦ and mean it, and that witness not a disciple or even a Jew at all, but a Gentile army officer with no previous connections with Jesus. What the Jewish leaders have denied and declared to be blasphemy and even the disciples have not yet grasped, this ordinary soldier perceives in the unlikely context of Jesus' final defeat and death. He speaks necessarily in the past tense, since Jesus has now died: his manner of death has proved the truth about what he has been in life. The words ὁ ἄνθρωπος,[72] which are not needed to express the meaning of the sentence, further underline the extraordinary nature of his insight. What he sees in front of him is, of course, a man, and a dying man at that, and yet also the son of God.

For Mark's readers this is a moment of high christological content, and for later theologians the bringing together of ἄνθρωπος and υἱὸς θεοῦ offers attractive raw material for a two-natures christology, but at the narrative level there is no reason to think that the centurion had any such sophisticated ideas, still less that he can be described as the first Christian convert. His words express first of all that Jesus is not what outward appearances would suggest, a mere failed insurrectionary (ἀληθῶς conveys that sense of the triumph of truth

---

72. Is it significant that the only other time in Mark's gospel when Jesus has been described as οὗτος ὁ ἄνθρωπος was in the dismissive language of Peter's final denial (14:71)? P. G. Davis, *JSNT* 35 (1989) 3-18, points out that generally in Mark ἄνθρωπος 'represents opposition to God', while Jesus has been portrayed as one who 'transcends humanity'. He therefore takes the centurion's statement as finally resolving the paradox which has run through Mark's gospel of 'the man who does what only God can do'. 'The man who does divine things is himself divine.'

over appearances)[73] and secondly that religious categories best express the truth about him. υἱὸς θεοῦ from a pagan soldier does not necessarily imply either personal divinity or any specific and unique relationship with God.[74] It goes beyond Luke's δίκαιος only in that it makes explicit the religious connection: the centurion has seen not only that Jesus is innocent and admirable but that his special character derives from his relationship with the God to whom he had appealed in v. 34. But 'son of God' in a pagan context did not carry the theological weight that it did in Judaism.

From the point of view of the narrative context, therefore, there seems little point in debating whether the phrase used by the centurion should be translated 'a son of God' or 'the Son of God', the latter on the basis that the anarthrous construction is syntactically normal where a predicate nominative precedes the verb (as in Jn. 1:1) rather than a deliberate avoidance of the definite article.[75] For the centurion the definite article would probably have meant little and mattered less. It is Mark's readers for whom it matters, and for them, after so many and varied declarations already in this gospel that Jesus is the Son of God in a unique sense (1:1; 1:11; 3:11; 5:7; 9:7; 12:6; 13:32; 14:61-62), there can be no question. Whether or not they realised that the centurion was unlikely to have grasped the theological significance of the words he uttered, for them this is the final declaration, at the moment of his apparent failure, that Jesus is the true Son of God, fulfilling on the cross his Father's will.[76]

73. J. Pobee, in E. Bammel (ed.), *Trial,* 101-2, goes a little too far in describing the centurion's words as a 'cry of defeat for the persecutor': to admit that this one death was an injustice, even a 'martyrdom', to use Pobee's preferred term, is not necessarily an 'admission of the failure of all for which he as a representative of Roman government stood'. In remarkable contrast to Pobee, Myers, 393-94, discusses v. 39 under the heading 'Rome has defeated Jesus', concluding from the centurion's stance 'opposite' Jesus that he is not a 'convert' but a representative of the imperial power who, like the demons who have earlier used υἱὸς θεοῦ, aims to 'gain power over Jesus by "naming" him'. This is an interesting example of how ideology can lead 'exegesis' in opposite directions.

74. See E. S. Johnson, *JSNT* 31 (1987) 12-13, for information on religious beliefs in the Roman army, though his material seems to relate mainly to the Roman legions rather than to the provincial auxiliaries. He points out the importance of the emperor cult, with its description of emperors past and present as sons of God, but rightly questions whether a direct comparison with the emperor is in view here.

75. The issue, and the relevance here of 'Colwell's rule', is well discussed by E. S. Johnson, *JSNT* 31 (1987) 3-7. On the grammatical issue cf. C. F. D. Moule, *Idiom-Book,* 115-16. An interesting article by P. B. Harner, *JBL* 92 (1973) 75-87, goes beyond 'Colwell's rule' by arguing that for the exegesis of Mark the issue is not so much whether an anarthrous predicate preceding the verb is to be taken as 'definite' or 'indefinite', but rather what its function is; he concludes that such predicates serve 'primarily to express the nature or character of the subject', and that for this purpose in some cases the more formal question of whether or not they are 'definite' is secondary and even irrelevant. Harner suggests that 15:39 is therefore best translated, 'Truly this man was God's son'. In response to Harner and Johnson, P. G. Davis, *JSNT* 35 (1989) 11-12, sensibly points out that a reader of Mark would assess the force of the phrase here not by comparing grammatical parallels but by thinking back to previous references to Jesus as the Son of God. For more wide-ranging discussion from the point of view of Mark and his audience see R. E. Brown, *Death,* 1146-50.

76. H. L. Chronis, *JBL* 101 (1982) 101-6, argues that the connotation of υἱὸς θεοῦ in this context is of divinity rather than merely that of a royal-messianic title.

The Burial and the Witnesses (15:40-47)

TEXTUAL NOTE

44. The B D W Θ reading εἰ ἤδη is probably an attempt to smooth out Mark's less elegant idiom εἰ πάλαι by assimilating it to the phrase already used in the preceding clause (an assimilation carried further by D W Θ in also reading the perfect tense again here), but it, like the simple omission of πάλαι in sy^s, weakens the natural progression from the news that he was 'already dead' to the question 'whether he had been dead long'. The Δ reading καὶ εἶπεν, presumably requiring ἀπέθανεν to be read as a direct question, also loses that progression.

The two verses describing the presence of the women at Golgotha (vv. 40-41) are frequently joined with the preceding pericope as the conclusion of the crucifixion scene. Like many such bridging passages in Mark, they can be linked either way. I have linked them rather with the account of the burial of Jesus for two reasons, first because v. 39 brings the story of Jesus' trial and death to so effective a climax that it seems something of an anticlimax to include these additional verses in the same pericope, but secondly and more importantly because the women are introduced here not just as an incidental detail of the crucifixion scene, but as the linking group mentioned again both in v. 47 and in 16:1. Their presence at Golgotha, at the scene of the burial, and again at the discovery of the empty tomb binds the final scenes of the gospel tightly together, and assures the reader that these women, the only human witnesses of the fact of Jesus' resurrection in Mark's gospel, have been closely involved in the whole sequence of events, so that any possibility of a mistake, for instance, over the location of the tomb is ruled out. They saw him die, they saw him buried, and they saw that same tomb empty. The place of vv. 40-41 as Mark's story draws to its close is to introduce this final sequence more than to round off the Golgotha scene. Van Iersel goes so far as to separate 15:40–16:8 from his 'Part III: Passion in Jerusalem' as the 'Epilogue: At the Tomb'.[77]

The appearance at this point in Mark's narrative of a group of women, who will be the narrative focus of the rest of the story, marks a remarkable shift in the gospel's emphasis. The reader of Mark's gospel alone would have concluded up to this point that the movement which Jesus began was an all-male movement. There has been no mention of supporting women as in Lk. 8:2-3, nor of specific women associates like Martha and Mary (Lk. 10:38-42). Women have appeared in Mark's narrative as the recipients of Jesus' ministry of deliverance, but the nearest we have seen to a woman follower has been the woman who anointed Jesus in 14:3-9, and she was an anonymous figure who featured only in that one incident. It is only at this point, when all Jesus' male followers

---

77. Cf. P. L. Danove, *End*, 134-36, though Danove begins the section at 15:42, not 15:40, following Van Iersel's earlier view, *Reading*, 20-22, that 15:40-41 was a 'hinge' rather than part of the 'epilogue'. Danove argues that 15:42–16:8 is designed as a parallel to 1:2-15.

(except the enigmatic Joseph of Arimathaea, if he is to be reckoned as a supporter) have fallen by the wayside, that Mark lets us know that all the time there has been a female element to Jesus' entourage, who are now ready to pick up where the men have left off. The three women named are representative of a wider circle of female followers (γυναῖκες . . . ἐν αἷς . . .) whose close association with the disciple group is marked by the verbs ἀκολουθέω and διακονέω, even though the term μαθητής has been reserved only for the (all-male) Twelve; and in addition there is a wider circle of ἄλλαι πολλαί who have been part of the group coming south to Jerusalem. Only now, when the women come to the centre of the stage for the closing phase of the narrative, does Mark reveal the mixed nature of Jesus' entourage in the Galilean period.

One of the themes of this pericope, then, is the presence at its beginning and end of the women as witnesses. The other is the burial of Jesus, which in the case of a crucified man was by no means to be taken for granted; indeed, in Roman law it was often forbidden (see Tacitus, *Ann.* 6.29, for the situation in Rome at this time), though a local magistrate could give permission. Otherwise, after a slow death the bodies of crucified men were often left to decompose on the cross; or they might be thrown in with a pile of other corpses or left on the ground unburied for scavengers to dispose of.[78] In Judaea there were local sensitivities about bodies left unburied (Dt. 21:22-23), which meant that the soldiers would be likely to give them a quick burial in a mass grave (Josephus, *War* 4.317, attests that in Judaea, exceptionally, crucified men were buried; cf. *m. Sanh.* 6:5 for the tradition of special burial places for executed criminals). Honourable burial in a proper rock tomb was highly unlikely, and in this case it depended on the goodwill of a wealthy and influential member of the Sanhedrin, who apparently dissented from his colleagues' verdict on Jesus and used his social position to gain permission for an individual burial. Joseph of Arimathaea thus enters the Christian tradition not simply as a well-disposed outsider like Simon of Cyrene or the centurion, but as at least a potential disciple (see below for the significance of the description προσδεχόμενος τὴν βασιλείαν τοῦ θεοῦ), and the fact that Mark can introduce him in this commendatory way suggests that he must have remained in good standing with the church within which Mark obtained his information.

The need for speedy burial depended not only on the general requirement that corpses should not remain unburied at nightfall (Dt. 21:23) but on the fact that this was προσάββατον, and sabbath laws forbade burial after sundown. Mark does not mention also here the relevance of the Passover season, but if the chronological scheme followed in this commentary is right, that sabbath was a particularly solemn one since it was also Nisan 15, the day which began after sunset with the Passover meal (Jesus having been crucified on Passover Eve).

---

78. For a cautious summary of the evidence for Roman practice see R. E. Brown, *Death*, 1207-9, and for Jewish attitudes and practice 1209-11. His article in *CBQ* 50 (1988) 234-38 sets out the data.

Joseph's request introduces the issue we have already noted of the speed of Jesus' death on the cross. Pilate's surprise was based no doubt on long experience of crucifixions: death did not normally come so quickly. This fact, coupled with the loud cries recorded in vv. 34 and 37, fills out the sense of an unusual death, as if Jesus remained in control of his fate and died when his work was finished rather than waiting for the natural process to take its slow course.

40-41   The women (and Mark, unlike John, mentions only women disciples at the scene, the men having scattered in Gethsemane) are distinguished from the mocking onlookers and the soldiers in that they are looking on ἀπὸ μακρόθεν.[79] There is nothing they can do but watch, but that watching will prove to be important as the basis of their role as witnesses of what is to follow. They are long-term followers of Jesus, from the Galilean period. Their role in διακονία is more fully spelled out in Luke's description of the group of women who during Jesus' itinerant ministry διηκόνουν αὐτοῖς ἐκ τῶν ὑπαρχόντων αὐταῖς (Lk. 8:3). In Mark's story this is a rare glimpse both of the practical aspect of Jesus' itinerant lifestyle, requiring a support group and the supply of material needs from the contributions of well-wishers, and also of the fact that the group which Mark has so often described as 'Jesus and his disciples' or 'Jesus and the Twelve' was in fact the focus of a larger group of followers who included a good number of women. Moreover, these women had not only provided material help, but also ἠκολούθουν αὐτῷ; this is the language of discipleship, and suggests that they, like the Twelve, were regular members of the group.[80] This long-term group of female supporters was larger than just the three women here named (hence ἐν αἷς), and in addition to this larger group there was a further category of those who had come up to Jerusalem with him, apparently Passover pilgrims from Galilee who had joined forces with Jesus' party on the journey and had thus also become attached to the disciple group. This information enables us to fill in the background to the account of Jesus' arrival at Jerusalem in 11:1-10, particularly the presence of an ὄχλος ἱκανός (10:46) of Galileans who came up with Jesus from Jericho and who were προάγοντες καὶ ἀκολουθοῦντες as they approached the city, shouting their support for Jesus as the coming king (11:8-10). Their enthusiasm has survived sufficiently to keep them even at this gruesome scene, standing apart from the mocking citizens of Jerusalem.

The three women who are specifically named are all mentioned here for the first time in Mark. Μαρία ἡ Μαγδαληνή needed no introduction to Mark's

---

79. This entirely natural note, to distinguish the women from the mockers and the soldiers, does not need to be explained by a supposed allusion to Ps. 38:11 (so Gnilka, 2.325; J. Marcus, *Way*, 174, following R. E. Brown, *John*, 2.904). Nor does the fact that the same word μακρόθεν occurs in 14:54 of Peter before his denial require us to find a similarly negative note here, as J. F. Williams, *Followers*, 188, argues.

80. See R. E. Brown, *Death*, 1155-57, for the question whether these women were 'disciples'. His conclusion is as follows: 'Would Mark consider these women disciples, were he asked? (I suspect so.) Did Mark think of them when in describing the ministry he wrote the word "disciples"? (Perhaps not.)'

readers; she had become well known in the Christian tradition mainly through her part (in all four gospels) in the resurrection narratives, helped no doubt by Luke's account of her notable deliverance by Jesus (Lk. 8:2). Σαλώμη, who will reappear with Mary of Magdala in 16:1, is not mentioned in any other gospel, and Mark gives us no clue to her identity;[81] Matthew's parallel mentions the mother of the sons of Zebedee without naming her, and there is no problem about identifying the two, though the name Σαλώμη, having been borne by the Jewish Queen Alexandra a century earlier, was common.[82] The other Μαρία, who is identified by Mark as ἡ Ἰακώβου τοῦ μικροῦ καὶ Ἰωσῆτος μήτηρ,[83] has sometimes been identified with Mary the mother of Jesus, among whose sons we found the names Ἰάκωβος and Ἰωσῆς in 6:3, but it would be strange for Mark to identify her by these younger and lesser-known sons rather than (as in 6:3) as the mother of Jesus,[84] and to place her second to Mary of Magdala; moreover, what we have heard of Jesus' mother earlier in the gospel (3:21, 31-35) does not suggest that she was among those who were following and serving Jesus in Galilee.[85] The name Ἰάκωβος was common, but his sobriquet ὁ μικρός, which is not used elsewhere in the NT,[86] suggests that this one was generally known in the church, and it is quite possible that he is the son of Alphaeus (see on 3:18), who is so designated to distinguish him from the other and better known Ἰάκωβος among the Twelve, the son of Zebedee — especially if the Salome whose name follows was the mother of the latter.[87] In that case his brother Ἰωσῆς is unknown to us, though presumably not to Mark's readers (cf. the naming of the two sons of Simon in 15:21, probably for the same reason). But all the names in v. 41 are common ones, so that we can have no certainty of

81. For the extraordinary and varied development of later traditions about both this Salome and a sister of Jesus of the same name, see R. J. Bauckham, *NovT* 33 (1991) 245-75.

82. According to T. Ilan, *JJS* 40 (1989) 186-200, Mary (Mariamme) and Salome were by far the most common women's names in Palestine at this time, between them accounting for virtually 50 percent of women named in surviving sources.

83. Pesch, 2.504-7, unusually follows the B reading which places an article before Ἰωσῆτος and thus allows the text to be read as mentioning four women, Mary of Magdala, 'Mary [daughter, mother, wife?] of James the Less', [Mary] mother of Joses, and Salome. He is then able to distinguish between 'Mary of Joses' (15:47) and 'Mary of James' (16:1) as two different women out of this list. But a reading found only in B Ψ 131 and without versional support does not have a strong claim. For contextual arguments against Pesch see Gundry, 976.

84. And even more strange to choose each of those sons once to identify her respectively in 15:47 and in 16:1 still without any mention that she was the mother of Jesus.

85. See further S. C. Barton, *Discipleship,* 68 n. 44. G. W. Trompf, *NTS* 18 (1971/2) 309-11, is among those who maintain that the reference is to Jesus' mother.

86. In later church tradition James the son of Alphaeus became known as 'James the Less', presumably because it was assumed that he was the James whom Mark refers to here.

87. Gundry, 977, arguing that this Mary is the mother of Jesus, suggests that ὁ μικρός derives merely from James being younger than Jesus. But it is not likely that the man who by the time Mark wrote had become a major figure through his leadership of the Jerusalem church, and who is known to patristic writers as 'James the Just', would still have been identified as ὁ μικρός, even if he had been so known during Jesus' lifetime (for which there is no evidence).

the identity of the two companions of Mary of Magdala, even though clearly Mark expected his readers to know them.[88]

The important role played by these women in the closing stages of Mark's narrative (and indeed their earlier role in Galilee, now for the first time revealed) is a pointer to something new in the movement Jesus has begun which contrasts strongly with the male domination of the society of his (and Mark's) time. When all the male disciples have deserted, the women are still there, faithful to the last.[89] And it will be to them first that the message of the resurrection is entrusted. In a society which gave no legal status to the testimony of women (e.g., Josephus, *Ant.* 4.219; *m. Roš HaŠ.* 1:8; *m. Šebu.* 4:1; *Sipre* on Dt. 19:15), everything will nevertheless come to depend on their witness to what they have seen and heard. Thus, as Myers, 396-97, points out with gusto, 'these women now become the "lifeline" of the discipleship narrative. . . . They are the true disciples. . . . This is the last — and, given the highly structured gender roles of the time, surely the most radical — example of Mark's narrative subversion of the canons of social orthodoxy.'

42 For the wide range of times to which ὀψίας γενομένης may apply, see on 6:47; 14:17. If the death of Jesus took place soon after 3 p.m. (see on v. 37), Joseph's initiative would fit within the period of roughly three hours between that and sunset, since the object of his request is to have the body buried before the sabbath begins. For ἡ παρασκευή as meaning Friday see Josephus, *Ant.* 16.163. Mark, aware that his Gentile readers might not know the idiom, explains it with προσάββατον, a term used by the LXX in Jdt. 8:6 and in the title of Ps. 92[93], but whose meaning is in any case obvious even to a non-Jew. This is the first time Mark has indicated that Jesus' death took place on a Friday, a fact on which all the gospels agree. Dt. 21:23 required burial before night, and sabbath regulations would not allow the work involved in burial after sunset.

43 Joseph of Arimathaea (probably a town in the Shephelah northwest of Jerusalem) appears in the gospel accounts (as opposed to the late medieval legend which brought him to Glastonbury) only in connection with the burial of Jesus, for which in John's Gospel he is joined by Nicodemus, another leading member of the Jerusalem establishment. βουλευτής designates a member of a council, in this case presumably the Sanhedrin[90] (as was Nico-

---

88. For a sensible discussion of the names of these women see R. J. Bauckham, *Jude,* 9-19; he concludes that 'no relatives of Jesus appear among the women disciples named by the Synoptic evangelists'. See Taylor, 651-53, for the view that Mark had two different traditions of the women's names which he used in 15:47 and 16:1 respectively, fusing the two traditions to produce the awkward list in 15:40.

89. M. A. Tolbert, *Sowing,* 291-93, who regards the Twelve in Mark's presentation as ultimately total failures ('rocky ground'), points out that not only the women mentioned here, but all the women mentioned by Mark except for Herodias and her daughter, 'represent the good earth'.

90. For βουλευταί used without qualification apparently for Sanhedrin members cf. Josephus, *War* 2.405. There were other, lesser, local councils (13:9), but the Sanhedrin is the only one which has been in view in Mark's narrative; see J. F. Williams, *Followers,* 189.

demus, Jn. 7:50), since he would need significant social standing in Jerusalem to be able to approach Pilate with such an irregular request, and also to have the use of a rock-tomb close to the city. Mark does not say that he owned the tomb (so Mt. 27:60; Matthew also describes Joseph as πλούσιος, as ownership of such a tomb would require),[91] but it is hard to see how else he gained access to an available tomb ready cut. He is further described as εὐσχήμων, 'reputable', a term of social approbation which probably also implies that he was well off.

Joseph is thus a leading figure in Jerusalem, and in the light of the events of the preceding week it is remarkable to find such a man taking a personal and risky initiative in favour of the Galilean prophet whom Joseph's own Sanhedrin had condemned as a blasphemer. Perhaps Mark's πάντες in 14:64 is not to be taken literally (as Lk. 23:51 also supposes), or perhaps Joseph was not present at the hearing. It is possible to attribute his intervention to concern over the impropriety of leaving a corpse on the cross ('traditional Jewish piety'; Gundry, 983) rather than a specific concern for Jesus, though even this would be apparently to step out of line (there is no indication that the establishment as a whole would have provided for a burial). Moreover, Joseph is not said to have concerned himself with the other crucified men, and in any case a less lavish provision than an expensive rock-tomb would have sufficed to meet the law's requirements.[92] Joseph must therefore be seen as a supporter of Jesus,[93] even if not openly a disciple (so Jn. 19:38), and Mark points in this direction with the intriguing phrase προσδεχόμενος τὴν βασιλείαν τοῦ θεοῦ (contrast Mt. 27:57, ἐμαθητεύθη τῷ Ἰησοῦ). See above on 1:15 for the general meaning and usage of ἡ βασιλεία τοῦ θεοῦ in Mark. The term in itself need not imply any connection with Jesus. Every pious Jew would pray regularly in the synagogue for the coming of God's kingdom in the Kaddish prayer: 'May he let his kingdom rule in your lifetime and in the lifetime of the whole house of Israel, speedily and soon.'[94] In such a setting προσδεχόμενος τὴν βασιλείαν τοῦ θεοῦ could mean something like Luke's description of Simeon, προσδεχόμενος παράκλησιν τοῦ Ἰσραήλ (Lk. 2:25). But for Mark the βασιλεία τοῦ θεοῦ is intimately bound up with the mission of Je-

91. Cf. Is. 22:16 for the social implications of cutting out a rock tomb for oneself and one's family.

92. R. E. Brown, *Death,* 1216-19, arguing that Joseph acted as a pious Jew and not as a supporter of Jesus, claims that the 'Achilles' heel' of the view that Joseph was a 'disciple' is the lack of cooperation between Joseph and the Galilean women. This is a remarkable argument from silence, especially when the women are specifically recorded as watching the burial.

93. So J. F. Williams, *Followers,* 189-91, pointing out that Mark presents several of his 'minor characters' in Act Three as exceptions to their group (the understanding scribe of 12:28-34, the centurion of 15:39, and Joseph); in each case the group as a whole has been described as hostile to Jesus. While not 'disciples' as such, these 'minor characters' side with Jesus (cf. Williams, *Followers,* 173, 183).

94. J. Jeremias, *Theology,* 198. For a few other Jewish uses (mostly rather later) of 'kingdom of God' for a hoped-for eschatological event see D. C. Allison, *End,* 103.

sus, so that anyone who has a concern for the βασιλεία τοῦ θεοῦ must be on Jesus' side.[95] Perhaps his choice of this phrase rather than the more explicit language of discipleship implies more a sympathetic fellow traveller than an openly committed member of the group (someone in a situation comparable with that of the scribe in 12:34 who earned the accolade οὐ μακρὰν εἶ ἀπὸ τῆς βασιλείας τοῦ θεοῦ), but he wants us to understand that, whatever the impression we might have gained from the last few chapters, not everyone in Jerusalem, and indeed not everyone in the Sanhedrin, had decided against Jesus.[96] For Joseph, remarkably, even in his humiliating death Jesus remained a figure worthy of respect.[97]

Joseph's request, being irregular, must be made in the highest quarter, and it could not be assumed that it would succeed, as the point of crucifixion was to maximise the deterrent effect of execution, and a quiet and decent burial would reduce this effect. Perhaps Joseph relied on Pilate's not being personally convinced that Jesus should have been executed (vv. 9-15), but even so Pilate's known character would not encourage hope that he would accede to a scrupulous request which might seem to put a question mark against Roman justice. That is why Mark adds τολμήσας: the request took courage.[98]

44-45   Pilate's surprise arose from the fact that death by crucifixion was often a protracted process, lasting days rather than hours, though the severity of the preliminary flogging might shorten it, as it may have done in Jesus' case. But by going into detail over Pilate's enquiry from the centurion, together with his previous account of Jesus' death with a loud cry, Mark intends his readers to be aware that Jesus did not linger on in agony as most others did. How long an interval is implied by πάλαι (see Textual Note) is determined by the context: here the sense is that Pilate, surprised to hear that Jesus was already dead (ἤδη τέθνηκεν, perfect tense) asked how long ago he died (εἰ πάλαι ἀπέθανεν, aorist). The use of δωρέομαι rather than δίδωμι suits the more formal context of official permission granted as a favour.

---

95. It is, however, far too subtle to detect in this phrase 'a characteristically ironic point: Joseph should no longer be waiting, since the kingdom of God has now been revealed with the revelation of the kingship of the crucified Jesus' (J. Marcus, *Way,* 182).

96. Joseph's support for Jesus may be one of the incidental pieces of evidence that, despite Mark's dramatic structure, Jesus had in fact been in Jerusalem before and was known there.

97. As with the centurion (see above, p. 660 n. 73), what most interpreters see as an act of respect, or at least of pious concern, Myers, 394-96, reads as 'a hurried burial, the final indignity', denying Jesus the proper burial rites which his followers would have performed. Joseph's motive was the preservation of the sabbath, and so Jesus 'is subjected to the ultimate insult — improper entombment — for the sake of the Sabbath order' (which he had unsuccessfully challenged). Thus 'Jesus' enemies have had, literally, the last word'. Myers does not explain why in this case Joseph should have made such an extraordinarily lavish provision as a rock-cut tomb rather than the regular burial place for executed criminals.

98. Contrast *Gos. Pet.* 2[3], which escapes the problem by making Joseph 'the friend of Pilate and of the Lord', who arranged to have the body for burial before the crucifixion took place. *Gos. Pet.* 6[23] explains Joseph's action on the basis of his 'having seen all the good [Jesus] had done'.

πτῶμα is rarely used in the NT, and only in connection with corpses requiring burial (cf. 6:29); its use here rather than σῶμα (v. 43) emphasises the fact of death.[99]

46 Apart from the need to 'take Jesus down' from the cross, this verse describes a normal respectful if hurried burial. Mark does not mention the washing of the body, but this was so important a part of Jewish burial ritual (even permitted on the sabbath, *m. Šab.* 23:5) that it is unlikely to have been omitted, however great the hurry. The inclusion of spices or perfuming ointments with the shrouded body would also normally be expected, but was presumably impossible at such short notice, hence the need for the women to repair the omission after the sabbath (16:1). John's mention of the spices at the time of burial (Jn. 19:39-40) represents normal custom, but Mark's specific description of an irregular procedure because of haste rings true to the situation. The σινδών is a natural part of the burial process, and so attracts no special attention and needs no link with 14:51-52 to explain its mention here (see above on 14:51-52); Mark could hardly know that in mentioning it he was setting the scene for the burgeoning science of 'sindonology', the study of the alleged shroud of Jesus now venerated at Turin.

The fact that Joseph was able to buy a piece of cloth, and indeed to undertake all the other 'work' involved in taking Jesus down from the cross and burying him, adds further support to the chronology assumed in this commentary (see the introductory notes on 14:12-25), in that if the Friday was itself the Passover day (Nisan 15) such work and commerce would be forbidden just as they were on the sabbath (*m. Beṣah* 5:2; *m. Meg.* 1:5). But if in that year Nisan 15 coincided with the sabbath, as I have argued, these details cause no problem; Friday was a normal working day.

καθελὼν αὐτόν conceals what must have been quite a formidable operation (since depicted with growing elaboration in Christian art), which would require not only the formal permission which Joseph had obtained from Pilate but also a group of workers, presumably Joseph's servants (note the plural ἔθηκαν in 16:6). Several men would be needed also to put in place the stone which three women knew they would be unable to move (16:3). The presence of such a group (concealed behind Mark's singular verbs) perhaps helps to ease the problem that a member of the Sanhedrin would be unlikely to defile himself for seven days by contact with a dead body (Nu. 19:11) just before the Passover sabbath (a more serious defilement than that feared by the priests in Jn. 18:28): he would not need to touch the body himself.

Anyone who has explored even a few of the many rock-cut tombs still

---

99. F. J. Matera, *Kingship*, 97-100, suggests that its use here is intended to recall its only other Marcan use in 6:29 and thus to establish the link between the suffering of the Son of Man and that of John the Baptist, as predicted in 9:12-13. While the link is certainly there in Mark's thinking, this word alone is hardly enough to carry a conscious echo of an event so much earlier in the book.

accessible in the area around the Old City of Jerusalem today[100] will be aware that the μνήμειον λελατομημένον ἐκ πέτρας is likely to have been a substantial family tomb (Matthew says it was Joseph's own; see on v. 43) rather than an individual burial place. The work involved in cutting a new tomb, and the need to acquire a suitable site, meant that once begun a tomb was normally extended internally, so that some contain several chambers, with shelves or 'tunnels' (*kōkîm*, individual shafts cut back into the rock and large enough to take one body) for dozens of bodies (the largest I have been in had chambers on two levels, in all accommodating more than sixty). The whole complex was entered by a single low tunnel, closed later by huge hinged doors of rock, but in the NT period often by a rolling stone (several of which still survive, while other tombs have channels cut in the rock for the movement of the stone). That the tomb in which Jesus was placed was for multiple occupation is indicated by the fact that in 16:6 the women who have already gone inside the tomb entrance (v. 5) still need to be shown the τόπος ὅπου ἔθηκαν αὐτόν, presumably the specific shelf or 'tunnel' within the burial chamber which had been used on this occasion. If this was Joseph's family tomb, one would expect it to be already occupied by members of the family, but the other gospel writers note that it was a new tomb (Mt. 27:60; Jn. 19:41) where no one had yet been buried (Lk. 23:53; Jn. 19:41); perhaps Joseph and his family had only recently moved to Jerusalem, or indeed did not live there but in Arimathaea.[101]

47 Two of the women who were introduced as witnesses of Jesus' death are now also witnesses of his burial (see the introductory comments on this section for the importance of this theme). They were there not just to watch, however, but so as to know where to return to after the sabbath. Mark's phrase ποῦ τέθειται may intend us to understand that the women actually went into the tomb with the burial group and saw the specific shelf or 'tunnel' where Jesus' body was put, but he may mean no more than that they merely watched the group enter the tomb, which is why they needed to be shown the specific place inside the tomb in 16:6. The omission of Ἰάκωβος ὁ μικρός from the identification of the second Mary is apparently simply to avoid unnecessary repetition after v. 40, and is compensated by the mention of Ἰάκωβος but not Ἰωσῆς in the next verse; it is clearly the same Mary.[102]

---

100. For tomb designs in Palestine see J. Finegan, *Archeology*, 181-202, and for Jerusalem specifically M. Avi-Yonah (ed.), *Encyclopaedia*, 2.627-41.

101. R. E. Brown, *Death*, 1213 n. 17, mentions that some Jews who lived away from Jerusalem nonetheless wished to be buried there and so had tombs near the city.

102. R. E. Brown, *Death*, 1154 n. 34, lists a wide variety of scholarly attempts to account for the different designations in Mark's three mentions of this Mary.

THE EMPTY TOMB (16:1-8)

TEXTUAL NOTES

1. The omission in D and a few OL MSS of the names of the three women may be due to a desire to avoid repetition after 15:47 (though the lists are not the same) and the omission in the same MSS of the genitive absolute διαγενομένου τοῦ σαββάτου may be due to a similar desire to avoid redundancy since the day of the visit to the tomb (but not of the purchase) will be clearly indicated in v. 2. In that case πορευθεῖσαι was included to ease the transition from 15:47, and was then retained in a conflated reading in Θ and a few versions. The text as printed, with its clearer mark of time, is too strongly supported to be easily dismissed, and the fact that the list of women is different indicates that it is not due to repetition from 15:47; nor does it assimilate to Matthew.

2. The textual variants arise from the discrepancy with Jn. 20:1, which states that it was still dark when Mary came to the tomb (and also possibly from the feeling that Mark's λίαν πρωΐ pointed to a time before dawn). D W sy^{s,p} and a few other witnesses omit λίαν, and it^c omits πρωΐ too. Others correct ἀνατείλαντος τοῦ ἡλίου: the present participle ἀνατέλλοντος (D and some OL) is an obvious attempt to make Mark's time earlier, as is the ἔτι of K W Θ etc., though the combination of this with the aorist participle makes a strange phrase. The only external evidence for omitting the phrase ἀνατείλαντος τοῦ ἡλίου altogether (by far the easiest way to harmonise) is the OL Codex Bobbiensis (which also omits λίαν), which is also notable for its more radical approach to the problems of Mark's ending (see below, pp. 684, 685; also p. 675 n. 20); Taylor, 604-5, offers as a 'conjecture' (wrongly stating that it has no textual evidence to support it) the omission of ἀνατείλαντος τοῦ ἡλίου as 'a primitive corruption' or 'a very early scribal gloss'.

8. The textual status of the longer and shorter endings of Mark sometimes found after v. 8 is discussed in an Appended Note after this section.

With this brief and tantalising scene we come (in the view of all but a tiny minority of scholars) to the end of the authentic text of Mark as it has come down to us (see Appended Note). Whether this is also the end of Mark's gospel as he planned it is, however, a different question. The majority of current interpreters think that it is,[1] and that the 'unfinished' feel of the text as it stands which prompted the church from a very early date to provide more 'suitable' endings is a deliberate part of Mark's skilful presentation of the story of Jesus.[2] It is, they argue, appropriate to a gospel which has traded heavily in paradox to end

---

1. It is interesting to observe that this is a relatively recent development, usually traced (at least in English-speaking scholarship) to the influence of R. H. Lightfoot's 1950 study (*Message,* 80-97). Before that time, while few believed that the extant 'endings' of Mark had any claim to authenticity, most believed that Mark did not intend to finish at 16:8. It is tempting to wonder how far this 'modern' swing of opinion derives from a closer understanding of Mark's world and how far from a change in twentieth-century literary fashion.

2. H. Räisänen, *Secret,* 210, even suggests that Mark's opening phrase, Ἀρχὴ τοῦ εὐαγγελίου . . . is a warning that Mark does not intend to finish the story, which is already known to his readers in the liturgy.

on such a paradoxical note, with an appearance of the risen Jesus announced but not narrated, and the central message of the Christian gospel entrusted to a group of demoralised women who are afraid to say anything about it. So we hear much of Mark's 'open-ended' story, which leaves it for readers to work out the implications for themselves:[3] they have in the empty tomb and the young man's message all the raw materials they need to do so, and Mark is not going to spell it all out for them.[4] That is a task left for the preacher.[5]

But ever since the inauthenticity of the received longer ending (vv. 9-20) came to be generally recognised, there have been those who nevertheless believe that Mark cannot have intended to leave it like that, that the early Christians who felt that the gospel needed a more 'satisfying' ending were guided by a right instinct and were closer to the thought-world of Mark than modern scholars.[6] They have argued that the literary taste which finds Mark's mysterious ending more powerful than the more 'obvious' conclusions of the other gospels is a very modern taste, and that ancient authors were more in the habit of saying as clearly as possible what they meant and what conclusions they intended their readers to draw than of teasing the reader[7] with unfulfilled prom-

3. This interpretation is put attractively by E. Best, *Story*, 132: 'By its very nature the conclusion forces us to think out for ourselves the Gospel's challenge. . . . It is like one of Jesus' own parables: the hearer is forced to go on thinking.' But perhaps one should remember that Mark's Jesus did interpret his parables to 'insiders', and that Mark is writing for insiders.

4. J. Camery-Hoggatt, *Irony*, 177, writes: 'Against that catastrophe [the crucifixion], the epilogue provides hardly an adequate closure for the book. And that is precisely the point. The ironies in Mark have left the reader with a deep sense that more is going on than meets the eye, that this story — including its catastrophe — is meaningful in a dimension not readily available on the surface. The reader is forced back into the book again.'

5. A. J. M. Wedderburn, *Resurrection*, 135-44, provides a useful survey of an extraordinarily varied range of recent attempts to explain Mark's abrupt ending on the assumption that this was his intended conclusion. It is tempting to try to envisage Mark's reaction to so many ingenious but conflicting 'readings of his mind' by scholars working within twentieth-century philosophical parameters.

6. This charge has been taken very seriously by J. L. Magness, *Sense*. Magness shows first from modern literature that 'absent endings' can be an effective literary device (ch. 2), and then goes on to suggest examples of 'suspended endings' in classical literature (ch. 3) and in both the OT (ch. 4) and the NT (ch. 5). It must be for the reader to judge whether any of Magness's examples are really parallel in terms of literary effect to the supposed impact of Mark's 'absent ending', but my own impression is that (quite apart from the question of how far it is literarily appropriate to compare Mark with, say, a Greek tragedy, epic, or romance) few if any of them give quite the same jolt and sense of having been cheated which I feel when I reach Mark 16:8 and find nothing to follow. My problem is not so much the omission of the promised resurrection appearance(s), but the sudden and anticlimactic subversion of that promise in v. 8. Even the abrupt ending of Jonah does not do this to the reader; and to compare the triumphantly unfinished ending of Acts with Mk. 16:8 is surely a *tour de force*.

7. M. A. Tolbert, *Sowing*, 297-99, sees this teasing (my term) as exactly the object of this ending: the reader, who had hoped that after the failure of the male disciples at least these faithful women would prove to be 'good earth', is frustrated to find in the end that even they are 'rocky ground'. So who is left to fulfil the task of sowing the word? No one but the readers themselves. And that is just what Mark has prepared for as he 'has created in the role of the authorial audience

ises and undelivered messages.[8] The fact that Mark's story is full of paradox does not mean that it has to conclude on an uncertain note; the Mark who began his story on an overt note of faith in Jesus as the Messiah and the Son of God (1:1) and has reminded his readers quite blatantly from time to time of that faith, is not likely to leave any room for doubt about its reality at the end. By the time Mark wrote his gospel the message of the resurrection and the stories of meetings with the risen Jesus were so widely in circulation and so central to the life of the Christian church that there was in any case nothing to be gained by concealment: what is the point of being coy about what everyone already knows? And Mark himself has given us so many explicit predictions of Jesus' resurrection (8:31; 9:9; 9:31; 10:34) and even more specifically of a future meeting with him in Galilee (14:28; 16:7), and has talked so confidently of good news which must go on being preached throughout the world after the time of Jesus' ministry (13:10; 14:9), that to end his gospel without an account of what everyone knew was the outcome of those predictions would have been an act not of literary artistry or of theological challenge but of frustrating anti-climax, leaving the reader waiting uncomfortably for the other shoe to fall.[9]

Some have added to this argument the literary consideration that to end a book with a two-word clause ending in γάρ is stylistically too clumsy even for Mark. ἐφοβοῦντο γάρ is undoubtedly a strikingly abrupt ending, but there are parallels to such an explanatory clause following a narrative statement in, for example, LXX Gn. 18:15; 45:3, and the search for parallels even to ending a book with γάρ has not been entirely unsuccessful.[10] Mark is a sufficiently un-conventional writer to have been capable of this if he indeed intended to finish here. The clause ἐφοβοῦντο γάρ differs stylistically from the explanatory ἔκφοβοι γὰρ ἐγένοντο of 9:6 only in that the periphrastic formulation of the lat-ter allows the verb to follow the γάρ.[11] For me the 'abruptness' of the ending

---

the perfect disciple', to whom therefore the task is now entrusted. See contra J. F. Williams, *Followers*, 201-2, especially 202 n. 1.

8. The choice between the 'ancient' and 'modern' understandings of a gospel which finished at16:8 is well expressed by F. Kermode, *Genesis*, 68: 'The conclusion is either intolerably clumsy; or it is incredibly subtle.' And by 'incredibly' Kermode intends not the weak sense 'very', but the literal sense, 'unbelievably'. Kermode himself dissents from this judgment, and defends Mark's al-leged subtlety.

9. It was after writing this clause that I found the same analogy used in this connection by N. R. Petersen, *Int* 34 (1980) 154-55. Such coincidence of cliché testifies to the effect of Mark's 'unsatisfying' ending, even though Petersen, unlike me, regards this as deliberate on Mark's part. But he avoids the unsatisfactoriness of this conclusion by arguing that 16:8 is ironical: 'Our narra-tor does not mean what he says in 16:8' (162). (For an exposition of this alleged irony in the lan-guage of structuralism see further P. L. Danove, *End*, 225-28.) Unfortunately, most readers of Mark have not recognised this 'artful substitute for the obvious' (163); it sounds suspiciously like an exegetical counsel of despair on the part of an interpreter who recognises that, taken literally, 16:8 is an impossible ending.

10. BAGD, 151b, 1.a; P. W. Van der Horst, *JTS* 23 (1972) 121-24. See the summary of the debate in P. L. Danove, *End*, 128-29.

11. F. Kermode, *Genesis*, 67, nicely renders ἐφοβοῦντο γάρ, 'They were scared, you see.'

consists not primarily in the stylistic form of its final sentence, but in the 'unfinished' nature of its contents.[12]

The decision between these two understandings of Mark's ending (and to reduce them to only two is of course to oversimplify drastically) is inevitably a matter of literary and theological taste, and in the absence of any authenticated text beyond 16:8 any theory of how else Mark might have intended to finish his book, and of why the text as we have it has no such ending, is speculative. Nonetheless, the choice must be made, even in a commentary which must limit itself to the text we have, since our understanding of what Mark includes in 16:1-8 is inevitably affected by whether or not we think he wrote or intended to write anything beyond those words. And my own inclination is to side with the increasingly unfashionable minority[13] who find an intentional ending at 16:8 an unacceptably 'modern' option.[14]

What, then, happened to Mark's ending? We can only guess. It is possible that it was never written because of adverse circumstances, illness, or death. Or it is possible that it was written but then either accidentally lost[15] or deliberately removed; in that case the loss must have been at a very early stage in order to leave no trace in the manuscript and versional tradition.[16] We simply do not know, and there seems no point in speculating.

12. One of the most elaborate attempts to justify the 'unsatisfying' conclusion of the gospel as Mark's deliberate intention is P. L. Danove, *End*. It is, he argues, precisely as a 'failed story' that the narrative 'entraps' the implied reader (especially pp. 208-10), forcing a re-evaluation of the impressions gained from the story hitherto. The outcome is that the implied reader recognises that he/she him-/herself is the only one through whom the proclamation of the message can now take place, thus presenting the real reader with a challenge to effective discipleship (220-22). This conclusion, which is similar to that of Tolbert, see above, p. 671 n. 7, is reached by taking the structuralist sledgehammer of some 230 pages of closely packed analysis in frequently opaque technical language to crack the Marcan exegetical nut, leaving at least this (real) reader wondering how much of the rhetorical subtlety attributed to him Mark would have been conscious of.

13. Myers, 399, considers this approach 'obsolete', but he still finds it necessary to argue against the ('imperial') attempt to 'betray the gospel by "rewriting" it' (401).

14. Perhaps the term 'post-modern' would be better, both in terms of the nature of the literary arguments used, and also to recognise that it is only in quite recent years that an intentional ending by Mark at 16:8 has become the preferred option (see above, p. 670 n. 1). Hooker, 394, typically expresses the nature of this 'post-modern' interpretation when she claims that even if the reading she has proposed is not what Mark intended 'then at least the gospel's ending offers us a fine example of the value of "reader response" criticism, since it provides us with an interpretation of the text to which author and reader together can contribute — an interpretation which corresponds with the experience of many readers of the gospel, whether or not it was in the mind of the evangelist.' Contrast T. J. Geddert, *Watchwords*, 172: 'There may be several ways of reading a text, but if one of them helps understand why it was written the way it was, that one is to be preferred.'

15. In response to the point often made that the final section of a scroll, being on the inside of the roll, is the least likely to be torn off, Gundry, 1017, replies that it would not be likely to be torn off when the scroll was rolled up, and that the final section might perhaps be 'subjected to the most stress by being rolled up the most tightly'. That manuscripts did become accidentally damaged, and that large sections of many ancient works simply disappeared for this reason, is a fact of classical textual criticism.

16. G. W. Trompf, *NTS* 18 (1971/2) 327-29, explains the loss of the original ending by the sug-

What is perhaps rather more worth speculating about is what the original ending, whether lost or never written, might have contained. On this there are two main clues to be followed. One is the pointers to future events within Mark's existing text, in particular the double indication that the risen Jesus would meet with his disciples again in Galilee (14:28; 16:7) and the fact that the women whose role as witnesses has been so carefully set up in 15:40-41, 47; 16:1-8 have nonetheless not communicated that testimony to anyone by 16:8 (if the latter omission is to be remedied we would have to understand their fearful silence in v. 8 as only temporary, perhaps overcome by a subsequent meeting with Jesus himself and a repetition of the message, as in Mt. 28:9-10). The other clue is the Gospel of Matthew. Mark and Matthew run closely parallel throughout the passion narrative, even though Matthew has a number of independent details not found in Mark. Even his account of the empty tomb, while circumstantially more dramatic with its guard, earthquake, and stone-rolling angel, runs structurally parallel with Mark as far as 28:8, including the angel's message to the disciples to meet Jesus in Galilee. At the point where Mark's text stops, Matthew's resurrection appearances are about to begin, first in Jerusalem to the women and then in Galilee to the eleven disciples. It is thus a reasonable guess (it can be no more) that Mark's original ending (planned or executed) would have followed similar lines[17] (except for Mt. 28:11-15 concerning the guard, who are not part of Mark's scenario), thus fulfilling the promise of 14:28 and 16:7 with an account of a Galilean rendezvous which would suitably round off the marked contrast between Galilee and Jerusalem which has run through this gospel as through Matthew's. To suggest that Matthew's ending was actually based on the original lost ending of Mark is perhaps to push conjecture to the limits, but that Mark at least intended something similar as the conclusion of his work is a suggestion which seems reasonably to fit the features of his gospel and its relation with Matthew.[18]

This commentary will deal, as it must, only with the actual preserved text of Mark, vv. 1-8. But in considering those verses I will bear in mind that they may not have been the end of what Mark at least intended to write.[19]

---

gestion that in the second century a 'second edition' of Mark, with the original ending now replaced by 16:9-20, became the recognised text at the time the four-gospel canon was established, and as a result no MSS of the 'first edition' survived, so that even though some early copyists and patristic writers were aware of the later origin of the longer ending, they did not have the original ending available.

17. G. W. Trompf, *NTS* 18 (1971/2) 315-25, argues strongly for a lost ending of Mark which was the basis of Mt. 28:9-10, and perhaps contained also words of assurance which lie behind the saying Οὔπω ἔχετε πίστιν; ἴδετε, ἐγώ εἰμι found in the fragment Περὶ ἀναστάσεως traditionally attributed to Justin. Trompf does not similarly draw on Mt. 28:16-20, and so strangely fails to provide from Matthew the very appearance which Mark 16:7 appears to require.

18. See Gundry, 1009-11, for a similar argument, with more specific details as to the pointers in the existing text. G. R. Osborne, *Resurrection*, 58-65, argues along similar lines, but goes further in attempting an actual reconstruction of the 'lost' ending from the wording of Mt. 28:9-10 and perhaps 16-20.

19. Gundry, 1009-21, treats v. 8 not as the conclusion to the pericope about the women's

What we find in 16:1-8 is as in the other gospels, though all have different details, an account of women finding that Jesus' tomb was empty and receiving a message that he had risen. None of them includes an account of the actual rising of Jesus from death,[20] and all assume that this has taken place at some time prior to the discovery of the empty tomb.[21] The setting for the discovery is remarkably down-to-earth, with the women coming to fulfil the previously omitted duty of anointing Jesus' body with perfumes, worrying about how they were to get into the tomb, meeting there a young man who tells them that Jesus has risen and gives them a message for the disciples and Peter, and running away frightened from this unexpected encounter. This is not the stuff of a heroic epic, still less of a story of magic and wonder, and yet what underlies it is an event beyond human comprehension: the Jesus they had watched dying and being buried some forty hours earlier is no longer dead but risen, καθὼς εἶπεν ὑμῖν. It is in this incongruous combination of the everyday with the incomprehensible that many have found one of the most powerful and compelling aspects of the NT accounts not of Jesus' resurrection (for there are none) but of how the first disciples discovered that he had risen.

Within this teasing mix of the down-to-earth and the supernatural, where Matthew and John mention one or more angels at the tomb, in Mark we meet the unexpected figure of a νεανίσκος περιβεβλημένος στολὴν λευκήν as the messenger who reveals the truth. Is this, then, a merely human figure who, like the women, has come to visit the tomb and who, having arrived first, is in a position to break the news? And did the whole tradition of angels at the tomb originate from the women's credulous interpretation of the fortuitous presence of this young man in a numinous place and with an extraordinary tale to tell? In the notes on v. 5 I shall discuss a number of reasons for rejecting this reading of the νεανίσκος, but quite apart from its intrinsic improbability, the idea that Mark (or even those from whom he heard the story) intended to describe a mere human being becomes untenable when the nature of his message is taken into account.

---

visit to the tomb but as the opening verse of an account, the remainder of which is now lost, of how their fearful silence was overcome by a meeting with Jesus himself (as in Matthew) and the message duly delivered and fulfilled with a meeting in Galilee. While I agree with his instinct with regard to what may have followed v. 8, it seems to me that to separate v. 8 from its existing context in this way is to allow too much weight to conjectural reconstruction. .

20. Contrast *Gos. Pet.* 9–10 (35–42). OL codex k (Bobbiensis) inserts at the beginning of v. 4 a brief section which appears to describe a scene like that in the *Gospel of Peter*, with angels descending to the tomb and ascending again to heaven taking Jesus with them, though the text is uncertain. D. W. Palmer, *JTS* 27 (1976) 113-22, suggests that the interpolated sentence originally referred not to the resurrection but to 'the assumption of Jesus from the cross', comparable to Jewish traditions about Elijah and Enoch.

21. Van Iersel, 483-84, comments on the 'narrative gap par excellence' between 15:47 and 16:1. He discerns in 15:40–16:8 a 'concentric structure' which unusually has silence at its centre, and regards this 'empty centre' as Mark's invitation to the reader to fill in the gap by envisaging God's 'sabbath work' of raising Jesus. Even if one doubts the structural plan proposed by Van Iersel, the lack of any description of the resurrection itself remains a significant feature of the way the story is narrated.

He does not simply report what he has found, but gives it a simple and authoritative explanation, ἠγέρθη, and he goes on to convey a message from Jesus himself, recapitulating what he had said privately to the Twelve in 14:28, and conveying not comment but command. It would not be the role of an anonymous young man to speak like this. However surprising it may be that Mark uses so low-key a word as νεανίσκος to describe an angel (he talked of ἄγγελοι the only other time he had occasion to mention angels in his narrative, 1:13), in context that must be his meaning, and our surprise may be tempered by observing that Luke in the same place (24:4) uses the phrase ἄνδρες δύο ἐν ἐσθῆτι ἀστραπτούσῃ (not so far from Mark's νεανίσκος περιβεβλημένος στολὴν λευκήν) to describe those whom he later (24:23) calls ἄγγελοι.

The women are the recipients of the young man's message, but its ultimate target is explicitly οἱ μαθηταὶ αὐτοῦ καὶ ὁ Πέτρος. This is a note which the reader needs to hear before the story closes. From Jesus' first recorded public action in Galilee until the débacle in Gethsemane Mark has told the story not of Jesus but of Jesus and his disciples. The experiences and the training of this group of men have been central to the gospel, and Jesus has devoted a large part of his time and effort to training them to become the task force which will take up his proclamation of the kingdom of God. In their fate the future of the εὐαγγέλιον is at stake. For Mark's story to have finished with ten of the Twelve as deserters, one a traitor, and Peter blasphemously dissociating himself from Jesus would have undone all that Mark has tried to do. But in v. 7 (and still more in the account of their reunion with Jesus which I think Mark intended to follow) we come to know that all will yet be well. The hidden growth of the seed has not been thwarted.

1 The sabbath which 15:42 warned us was imminent has now appropriately passed with nothing to record at the level of human activity. As sabbath finished at sunset on the Saturday, the phrase διαγενομένου τοῦ σαββάτου probably refers to the Saturday evening, the first time after Jesus' hasty burial when it would be possible to buy perfumes. (Luke's view that they prepared the anointing oils before the sabbath is less easy to reconcile with the women being present at the burial, given the short time available before sunset on the Friday.) Thus equipped, the women are ready at sunrise the next morning (Sunday) to set out to complete the burial formalities interrupted by the sabbath.[22] The continuity of the witness of the women is confirmed by the listing again of the same three names (see Textual Note) we met in 15:40. Salome, who was apparently absent at the time of the burial (15:47), is now back with the others. The second Mary is now identified by the name of her other son (see on 15:47).

Mark does not specify the nature of the ἀρώματα which they bought, but

---

22. The suggestion that anointing some thirty-six hours after death would be too late because decomposition would already have begun does not take account of the coolness of Jerusalem (and still more of a rock-cut tomb in Jerusalem) at Passover time; see above on the need for a fire, 14:54.

the verb ἀλείφω indicates that they were in the form of ointment or liquid perfume (like that used in 14:3) rather than the λίτραι ἑκατόν (some thirty-three kilos) of solid spices which John says were used at the time of burial. While Jewish corpses were not embalmed in the technical Egyptian sense (see Gn. 50:2-3 for the lengthy process this involved), aromatic spices and ointment (cf. Lk. 23:56: ἀρώματα καὶ μύρα) were used as a mark of respect[23] and perhaps to keep the corpse fresh for as long as possible. The women's intention indicates, *pace* John, that Joseph had been unable to honour Jesus' body in this way in the hurry of Friday evening, and if they knew of the anointing Jesus had received at Bethany while still alive (14:3-9) they would presumably not have thought of this as precluding proper respect for his dead body, despite his enigmatic words at the time (14:8). But Mark's wording here does not suggest that he intends to remind the reader of 14:3-9, where quite different terms are used. The fact that they thought in terms of anointing at all suggests that, if, as 15:41 suggests, they have been with Jesus on the way to Jerusalem and so have heard his passion predictions, they have simply not taken seriously his expectation of rising again after three days.

2 Mark seems to be very particular about the time when the women reached the tomb (ἔρχονται ἐπί; they will not enter it until v. 5), and yet his phrases (see Textual Note) leave commentators confused.[24] λίαν πρωΐ alone could indicate a time before dawn as in Jn. 20:1 (see comments on πρωΐ in 15:1 above), but it does not in itself require this; Matthew (τῇ ἐπιφωσκούσῃ εἰς μίαν σαββάτων) and Luke (ὄρθρου βαθέως) also here imply a very early hour, but are not as specific as John. But Mark's additional phrase ἀνατείλαντος τοῦ ἡλίου assures us that it was already light, so that they could see clearly;[25] even John has Mary 'seeing' the stone on her arrival. Mark goes on to remind us what day of the week it was, even though διαγενομένου τοῦ σαββάτου has already made this information unnecessary (see Textual Note on v. 1). But the phrase ἡ μία τῶν σαββάτων[26] occurs in all the gospel accounts of the discovery of the empty tomb (Mt. 28:1; Lk. 24:1; Jn. 20:1, 19); it had apparently become an essential element in the story, important as the basis for the choice of this as the Christian holy day (Acts 20:7; 1 Cor. 16:2), later to become known as ἡ κυριακή (Rev. 1:10, and regularly in subsequent Christian writings; *Gos. Pet.* 9[35], 12[50] anachronistically uses the term already in its resurrection ac-

---

23. Gundry, 989, argues that the term ἀρώματα implies a 'royal' burial honour rather than the less expensive oil used for commoners, but it is questionable whether the term is as specific as that.

24. Mann, 664-65, devotes considerable space to this 'insoluble problem', but seems to be demanding an unnecessarily pedantic use of language by Mark.

25. The suggestion that λίαν πρωΐ describes the time when they set out (before dawn) and ἀνατείλαντος τοῦ ἡλίου the time when they reached the tomb (just after the sun rose) is plausible in itself, but is not what Mark actually says. For Mark's habit of adding a second clause to define a statement of time cf. 1:32, 35; 14:12; 15:42.

26. For εἷς used instead of the ordinal in expressions of time see BAGD, 231b-32a, 4. It is not only a Semitic idiom.

count). None of the gospels, of course, says that the resurrection *took place* on the first day of the week, only that that was when the empty tomb was discovered, the implication being that it had already been empty some time. Whether Jesus is understood to have risen during the sabbath or only during the night before the women came to the tomb, the interval between death and resurrection was at the most not much more than thirty-six hours. For the compatibility of this with Jewish understanding of the phrase μετὰ τρεῖς ἡμέρας used in Mark's record of Jesus' passion predictions, see above on 8:31. Clearly Mark, with his careful emphasis on the days in 15:42 and here, did not find any discrepancy.

3-4 The women's concern about the stone (which Mark underlines with the comment that it was μέγας σφόδρα, though any stone sufficient to seal a tomb entrance would probably have been beyond the strength of three women) adds an almost humorous, homely touch to the scene: they had made their other preparations but had forgotten this elementary obstacle. Rather than arranging with Joseph's servants to come back with them, they were now trusting to luck that someone would be around to help. But from the dramatic point of view their anxiety is important as the foil to their discovery that the problem was already solved. We are not told how or when the stone had been removed, since the passive ἀποκεκύλισται does not reveal the agency (contrast Mt. 28:2), nor whether it was removed in order for Jesus to come out (as in *Gos. Pet.* 9–10[37–40], whereas in Matthew the tomb was apparently already empty when the stone was removed). But the only other person around in this scene is the νεανίσκος of v. 5. It is perhaps a further pointer to the unlikelihood that Mark intended him to be understood as a merely human character that a single young man would certainly not have been able to move the stone either. The unexplained removal of the stone thus begins to create a sense of superhuman agency in the narrative.

5 The sense of the supernatural continues with the vision of a νεανίσκος in white clothes sitting inside the opened tomb. εἰσελθοῦσαι εἰς τὸ μνημεῖον takes us beyond their previous viewpoint looking at the tomb entrance from outside. They have now gone in through the entrance 'tunnel' into the inner chamber where the bodies would be placed (see above on 15:46). So the νεανίσκος is not just an interested bystander: he is sitting right inside the tomb. We have noted above (introduction to this section) the improbability that the words he is about to utter could come from an anonymous and merely human participant in the discovery. The fact that he is seated (the traditional posture for teaching or speaking with authority) conveys the same impression. Other features of Mark's description add to the supernatural impression: he is wearing white, and the women are terrified. White clothes were, of course, a mark of festivity or of a formal occasion such as a wedding, but for clothes to appear white in the darkness of the burial chamber they would need more than everyday whiteness: Luke's mention of ἐσθὴς ἀστράπτουσα probably picks up the sort of whiteness Mark intended here, and we are reminded of Jesus' clothing at the transfiguration, στίλβοντα λευκὰ λίαν, οἷα γναφεὺς ἐπὶ τῆς γῆς οὐ δύναται οὕτως λευκᾶναι (9:3). For white and/or shining clothes in the NT as the mark of a heavenly visitation see also Mt. 28:3; Jn. 20:12; Acts 1:10; 10:30 and the frequent mention of white clothes for those promoted to join in the worship of heaven in Revelation, and for the wider Jewish background see, for instance, Dn. 7:9; *1 Enoch* 62:15-16; 87:2; 2 Macc. 3:26 (in the latter case it is interesting that what are plainly intended to be heavenly visitants are described, as here in Mark, as young men, νεανίαι).

The reaction of the women, even when due allowance has been made for the 'spooky' effect of the setting, also suggests that they have met someone other than an ordinary young man. For ἐκθαμβέομαι see on 14:33: it conveys a powerful mixture of shock and fear, and this is followed by τρόμος καὶ ἔκστασις leading to a precipitate flight from the tomb in 16:8. Such a reaction is more consonant with a meeting with an angel than with an ordinary young man, and his first words to the women convey the same impression (see on v. 6). νεανίσκος is unusual in such a context, but there are other examples: in 2 Macc. 3:26, 33 the two clearly angelic visitors are described simply as νεανίαι; Josephus, *Ant.* 5.277, speaks of the 'angel of Yahweh', who appeared to Samson's mother as νεανίᾳ καλῷ παραπλήσιον καὶ μεγάλῳ; in Hermas, *Vis.* 3.1.6, the visionary sees six νεανίσκοι, who are later identified as angels (3.4.1). It seems that Mark is doing what Luke does on a number of occasions, using human language to describe the form in which an angel is seen by human witnesses (Lk. 24:4 with 23; Acts 1:10; 10:30; cf. Tob. 5:5, 7, 10 where Tobias addresses the angel Raphael as νεανίσκε because he does not recognise him as an angel and sees only a young man). Cf. *Gos. Pet.* 9(36–37), which describes the angels in the resurrection scene first as ἄνδρες and then as νεανίσκοι.

I have commented above on the suggestion that this νεανίσκος is to be related to the one who ran away at Gethsemane (see on 14:51-52). The two words which link the two passages are νεανίσκος and περιβεβλημένος, both used only in these two places in Mark. But both are quite everyday words (in the NT the 'diminutive' νεανίσκος is used rather than the classical νεανίας with no special diminutive force, and περιβάλλομαι is a frequent word for wearing clothes) so that the fact of their recurrence (even together) once within a work the length of Mark's gospel hardly demands a deliberate link. The term σινδών, often claimed as a further verbal link because it occurs in 14:51-52 and in 15:46, is conspicuously *not* used with reference to this νεανίσκος.[27] Attempts such as those noted above to find a meaningful link between the two young men not only disagree with one another but also by their artificiality serve rather to rein-

27. S. R. Johnson, *Forum* 8 (1992) 125-26, makes a virtue of necessity by discerning 'a motif of being stripped and reclothed, which symbolically connects the νεανίσκος of 14:51-52 with Jesus and the νεανίσκος of 16:5', so that the σινδών taken from the first νεανίσκος is put onto Jesus, while the second νεανίσκος (who is in fact the same one) can be reclothed. 'Thus, as Jesus takes on the σινδών in his own death, he is taking on the symbolic death of the νεανίσκος as well, leading to the latter's transformation (as symbolized by his white robes)'. That is a lot to get out of the fact that the two words νεανίσκος and σινδών recur in two separate passages at the end of the book.

force the conclusion that the common vocabulary between the two passages is a matter of coincidence rather than of literary connection.

6 The message of the νεανίσκος is expressed in this verse in the staccato style of five short utterances without conjunction of any sort. The word of reassurance (even if unsuccessful, v. 8) is a common feature of angelic appearances; cf. Dn. 10:12, 19; Mt. 28:5; Lk. 1:13, 30; 2:10; Acts 27:24. The νεανίσκος speaks from a position of authority and of privileged knowledge, not as an equal. The suggestion that ζητεῖτε implies a rebuke (Lane, 587-88, following R. H. Lightfoot) draws too much out of the fact that most of Mark's uses of this common verb are in negative contexts; their quest may now prove to have been futile, but it was not inappropriate. There seems to be no special significance in his use of the title ὁ Ναζαρηνός; as in 10:47 it simply identifies the Jesus who is referred to. The effect is to confirm the continuity from the Jesus of the ministry (who at the outset was introduced as ἀπὸ Ναζαρέτ, 1:9) to the Jesus of the resurrection. τὸν ἐσταυρωμένον, however, poignantly describes what the women at present believe to be the truth about Jesus. Having themselves watched him die on the cross, they have now come to attend to that tortured body, and that is what they expected to find in the tomb. That whole tragic scenario is reversed in the simple one-word message, ἠγέρθη, though the clauses that follow will spell out more fully what this dramatic verb implies. In Jesus' predictions of his resurrection the verb used has been ἀνιστήμι rather than ἐγείρομαι, except in the promise of a reunion in Galilee (14:28) which will be echoed in the next verse, but in talking about a dead person there is no functional difference (see on 8:31; 14:28), and the appropriateness of ἐγείρομαι to denote life after death is seen in its use in 12:26 for the dead in general.[28] The women, even if they were unaware of Jesus' predictions, could not mistake the meaning of this verb in this context. But the νεανίσκος goes on to make it clear that he is talking not merely about survival beyond death, but about a physical event: the place where Jesus' body had been laid (see above on 15:46 for the τόπος indicating not merely the tomb in general but the specific shelf or 'tunnel' within it which had been used for Jesus' body) is now empty. The body has gone, and from the promise made in the following verse it is plain that it has gone not by passive removal but in the form of a living, travelling Jesus. However philosophy and theology may find it possible to come to terms with the event, it is clear that Mark is describing a bodily resurrection leading to continuing life and activity on earth.[29]

7 The announcement of Jesus' resurrection is not an end in itself, but the basis for action, which for the women is the delivery of an urgent message, and for the disciples to whom that message is sent a journey to Galilee in prepa-

---

28. J. D. Kingsbury, *Christology*, 134-35, suggests that the verb was chosen here to recall Jesus' prediction of the rejected stone being 'raised' to become the cornerstone (12:10-11), but in the absence of a verbal echo this is reading a lot into what is one of the standard NT verbs for resurrection.

29. E. L. Bode, *Easter*, 29-31, demonstrates how the wording of the angel's message corresponds to the kerygma of the early chapters of Acts, notably Acts 4:10, and of Paul's letters.

ration for the promised meeting with Jesus (14:28).[30] Life, discipleship, and the cause of the kingdom of God must go on. The commission to deliver the message presupposes that, despite the scattering in Gethsemane, the disciples including Peter are still to be found together as a group, however demoralised. The fact that Jesus still has a message for them, and still more that it includes the repeated promise of a post-resurrection meeting, may be expected to overcome their self-despair, and they may well remember that the previous prediction of a meeting in Galilee followed directly after Jesus' prediction of their being 'scattered' (14:27). Clearly he had not expected their desertion to be more than temporary. The specific inclusion of Peter reflects not so much his leading role in the group as his specific and more public failure in loyalty to Jesus: even after the curse at the second cockcrow, Peter has not been written off. It is also possible (Gundry, 1003) that Peter needed to be mentioned separately because, smarting after his humiliating failure, he had not yet rejoined the other surviving disciples. Thus both for Peter and for the rest of the eleven remaining μαθηταί, the message sent by the women implies an assurance of forgiveness and restoration, the more impressive for being left unsaid.[31]

It is sometimes suggested that by focusing on the experience of the women and failing to narrate any appearance of Jesus to the disciples Mark is deliberately playing down the significance and leadership of the original disciples in the post-Easter church. But it should be noted that Mark, unlike Matthew, does not have Jesus appearing to the women either (unless, of course, his originally intended ending contained such a meeting, as suggested above), and that the only post-resurrection appearance he does indicate (but not narrate) is precisely to οἱ μαθηταὶ αὐτοῦ καὶ ὁ Πέτρος. Even more questionable is that the location in Galilee is intended to shift the emphasis away from a Jewish church to a Gentile mission:[32]

---

30. Against the once popular suggestion that this verse is to be understood as a prediction of the parousia, not of a resurrection appearance (an idea promoted especially by E. Lohmeyer, R. H. Lightfoot, and W. Marxsen), see A. T. Lincoln, *JBL* 108 (1989) 285; also R. H. Stein, *NTS* 20 (1973/4) 445-52. See further E. Best, *Story,* 76-78, responding to N. Perrin's version of the parousia interpretation.

31. Contrast the view of W. R. Telford, *Theology,* 149-50, who derives from the absence of any resurrection appearances in Mark the conclusion that this gospel 'offers the reader no restoration of Peter after his denial, promises the original disciples no authority to forgive or retain sins, nor grants them any promise or receipt of the Spirit in connection with such a commission'. This is to interpret Mark by his failure to say what others say, rather than by what is actually in his text. A message from the risen Jesus specifically for the disciples and Peter and a promised meeting with them in Galilee seem to me to count for more than what Mark does *not* say.

32. W. R. Telford, *Theology,* 150-51, claiming to 'interpret the reference to Galilee theologically rather than literally'. This view is especially associated with C. F. Evans, *JTS* 5 (1954) 3-18. Evans first argues that προάγω must mean 'lead' rather than 'precede', and since he finds no basis for the idea of the risen Jesus literally leading his disciples northwards, takes the saying as symbolic of the future mission in which he will 'lead' them. He too easily assumes that τῶν ἐθνῶν is naturally understood when Galilee is mentioned, and that therefore 'if the place name is to carry any significance beyond its plain geographical sense there can be no doubt what that significance would be' (p. 13). See contra Gundry, 849.

both the location and the disciples who are to gather there are still Jewish. 'Galilee of the Gentiles' is not a Marcan phrase, nor does it express a Marcan perspective. The very deliberate contrast between Jerusalem and Galilee throughout this gospel is not a contrast between Jew and Gentile.

Προάγει ὑμᾶς εἰς τὴν Γαλιλαίαν exactly repeats the promise of 14:28, apart from the necessary change in the person and tense of the verb. See comments there, especially on the meaning of προάγω;[33] here the following clause makes it clear that there will be no meeting before Galilee, so that προάγω does not refer to Jesus' literally leading them northwards. Rather, once they have left the hostile territory of Jerusalem and returned to their own home province, where the whole story began, they will meet him again, and their role as his disciples can be restored after its temporary failure.[34] αὐτὸν ὄψεσθε belongs, as did v. 6, to the physical dimension rather than promising a visionary experience. The body which the women cannot see in the tomb because it is no longer there will be the one which the disciples will see in Galilee. The concluding clause καθὼς εἶπεν ὑμῖν does not refer specifically to the promise of seeing Jesus, since Mark has recorded no promise in those terms, but rather to the whole prospect of the Galilean rendezvous, in the wording of which in 14:28 the seeing may be implied but is not stated.

8 The account of the women at the tomb so far has not differed substantially in tone (though it has in detail) from those in the other gospels, and we would now expect that, as in Mt. 28:8, they would set out to deliver the message to the disciples, and that its successful delivery would lead, again as in Mt. 28:16, to a Galilean meeting with the risen Jesus to bring the gospel to its climax. Even Luke's account of the disciples' scepticism (Lk. 24:11) is only a temporary setback, and the women's commission is faithfully carried out (cf. also Lk. 24:22-23; Jn. 20:2, 18). So the way Mark concludes the scene (whether or not v. 8 was intended to be the end of his gospel) is extraordinary.

It is no surprise that the women were afraid and ran away; Mt. 28:8 says as much, too. Fear in the presence of the supernatural is to be expected, and is a theme we have met throughout the gospel (4:41; 5:15, 33; 6:50; 9:6), as well as being a recurrent feature of OT theophanies or angelophanies; for running away in such circumstances cf. Dn. 10:7; *1 Enoch* 106:4-6 (and cf. 5:14 above). The nouns τρόμος (cf. 5:33, τρέμουσα) and ἔκστασις (cf. 5:42 and ἐξίστημι in 2:12; 5:42; 6:51) also belong to Mark's vocabulary of the human response to supernatural power. But whereas Mt. 28:8 blends this understandable fear with χαρὰ μεγάλη, in Mark the sense of panic is unrelieved.[35] The words the women have

---

33. See also p. 577 n. 82 for Van Iersel's proposal that εἰς τὴν Γαλιλαίαν be translated 'in Galilee'.

34. T. J. Geddert, *Watchwords*, 166-69, argues persuasively for a motif of 'Discipleship Renewal' in the idea of a return to Galilee. Insofar as there is a call to mission, it is to mission as part of the essential task of discipleship, not as an end in itself. Now is the time for them in their turn to 'take up their cross' and follow Jesus.

35. T. Dwyer, *Wonder*, 185-93, argues that the dominant note in Mark's conclusion is not so

heard were entirely good news, but their immediate response is apparently not to absorb the message of the words but to escape as quickly as possible from the unexpectedly numinous situation in which they have been caught up.[36]

The note of panic is in itself a surprising way for Mark to continue the story, and still more to conclude his whole work. But much more inexplicable is his comment that the women, who have just been given a message of supreme importance to deliver, remained silent. His wording, οὐδενὶ οὐδὲν εἶπαν,[37] could hardly be more definite: the message remained undelivered. We know, of course, and Mark's readers knew, that the message of the resurrection did somehow get out, whether through the three women or despite them, but for Mark to build up so carefully the women's unique role as the first witnesses of the fact of resurrection only to knock it down in his final sentence by insisting on their complete silence seems bizarre. It is one thing to emphasise and exploit paradoxical elements within the story of Jesus' ministry and passion, as we have seen Mark doing again and again, but quite another to conclude his gospel with a note which appears to undermine not only his own message but also the received tradition of the church within which he was writing.

It is this extraordinary *faux pas,* as it seems to be, that has prompted the constantly growing number of attempts nonetheless to find a plausible literary and communicative function of Mark's ending, assuming that 16:8 was where he intended his story to end. I have commented in introducing this section that I do not find any of them persuasive, because they all seem to presuppose an inappropriately 'modern' understanding of literary technique both in terms of how writers wrote and of how readers might be expected to respond.[38] The nat-

---

much fear as wonder, and that in v. 8 'God has broken-in and dramatic amazement results, which should not be overshadowed by the (temporary) silence of the women' (195). Such an interpretation would certainly provide a more satisfying ending to the gospel, but the combination in v. 8 of the themes of running away, trembling, silence (which is *not* said to be temporary and is in direct contradiction of the command of v. 7), and fear seems to me to speak more of panic than of a positive awe at the power of God demonstrated in the resurrection.

36. A. T. Lincoln, *JBL* 108 (1989) 285-87, concludes from a study of Marcan usage that the fear here is to be interpreted as failure, not as proper response; similarly T. J. Geddert, *Watchwords,* 170-71; contra Gundry, 1015.

37. Is there a deliberate echo of 1:44, Ὅρα μηδενὶ μηδὲν εἴπῃς, a command to silence which was disobeyed as blatantly as the women disobeyed the command to speak? (so, e.g., E. L. Bode, *Easter,* 42-43). But to interpret the women's silence as their failure to reveal the 'messianic secret' now that its 'time limit' (9:9) is over (so A. T. Lincoln, *JBL* 108 [1989] 290-91) seems oversubtle, especially since the message entrusted to the women is not an announcement of Jesus' Messiahship.

38. A. T. Lincoln, *JBL* 108 (1989) 283-300, makes an attractive attempt to draw the sting of Mark's ending by insisting that it is vv. 7 and 8 *together* which constitute the ending, and thus set up a typically Marcan 'paradigm for the interplay between divine promise and human failure in Christian existence'. J. F. Williams, *Followers,* 194, regards Lincoln's article as 'the most satisfying solution' to Mark's enigmatic ending. But Lincoln's argument is, in my view, rendered suspect by his recognition (p. 299) that 'whereas for ancient readers it was the notion of the women's failure that was initially alienating, for modern readers it may well be the aspect of failure in the story that is most appealing'. It is precisely the 'alienating' feature which is left in possession of the field if Mark's narrative is intended to end at v. 8, and the divine promise of v. 7 is left unfulfilled within

ural response to v. 8 is surely to assume that this apologetically damaging anti-climax *cannot* be the end. By the time Mark wrote everyone in the churches knew, and therefore Mark's readers must be assumed also to know, that the message of the empty tomb *was* delivered and that the disciples *did* meet with Jesus (whether in Galilee or elsewhere would depend on which traditions you were following).

I therefore think it more likely that Mark did intend his gospel to continue beyond this point, and to contain an account of the fulfilment of the promise of v. 7. But even on that assumption it must be admitted that by writing v. 8 Mark seems to have made things difficult for himself in adding a sequel. If he had included a phrase to indicate that the women's silence was only for the time being, that would have allowed for their subsequent overcoming of their fear and delivery of the message.[39] But οὐδενὶ οὐδὲν εἶπαν does not offer such a handle. It is perhaps not surprising that this uncomfortable clause, together with ἐφοβοῦντο γάρ, is omitted from the OL Codex Bobbiensis, and replaced by the Shorter Ending which directly contradicts it by telling how the women did in fact deliver the message to οἱ περὶ τὸν Πέτρον. It is more surprising that none of the other MSS and versions which contradict the end of v. 8 by going on with the Longer Ending (with or without the Shorter as well) take the further step of removing the offending words.

In the absence of such textual surgery we can only speculate that if Mark did intend any further text it must have included either a statement (which would certainly follow awkwardly) that the women subsequently plucked up courage to pass on the message or more likely an account (underlying Mt. 28:9-10) of a subsequent meeting with Jesus during which the commission was repeated, this time successfully so that the message did reach the disciples and they did find their way to Galilee to meet with Jesus (so Gundry, 1010-11). The latter option, in which the women's disobedience is not simply awkwardly forgotten, but overriden by the force majeure of the command of Jesus himself, seems to me the least unsatisfactory of the proposed understandings of Mark's enigmatic final verse.

Mark's presentation by the women's failure. Lincoln's argument, therefore, like others which treat 16:8 as the intended ending, seems to me to depend too much on what appeals to a modern reader at the expense of Mark's own literary context.

39. Thus T. Dwyer, *Wonder,* 191-92, following J. L. Magness, proposes that the women's silence be understood as 'provisional in the sense that they told no one else, or told no one until they told the disciples'. Magness puts it more concretely: 'They may have said "nothing to anyone" only until, passing soldiers changing the guard and merchants opening their stalls and shoppers heading for the market, they reached the disciples' (J. L. Magness, *Sense,* 100). This is all very plausible in a real-life situation, but unfortunately Mark does not say that.

APPENDED NOTE

THE TEXTUAL EVIDENCE FOR THE ENDING OF MARK

The purpose of this note is not to argue again for what is the virtually unanimous verdict of modern textual scholarship,[40] that the authentic text of Mark available to us ends at 16:8, but rather to set out as simply and clearly as possible (which inevitably will mean some oversimplification) the data which have contributed to that consensus.[41]

A. Textual Evidence

1. The text ends at 16:8 in the major fourth-century codices א and B and in a number of MSS of versions, notably the fourth-century Sinaitic Syriac. Clement of Alexandria and Origen do not appear to have known any text beyond v. 8, and Eusebius and Jerome both state that the traditional Londer Ending (vv. 9-20) was not found in the majority of the Greek MSS available to them. The earliest form of the Eusebian canons (deriving from Ammonius, early third century) made no provision for readings in Mark beyond 16:8.

2. OL Codex Bobbiensis omits the last six words of v. 8 and goes on instead not with vv. 9-20 but with the Shorter Ending which briefly reports (in thirty-four words) how the women took the news to the disciples and how Jesus then sent out by them to all the world 'the holy and immortal proclamation of eternal salvation. Amen'. It includes no account of a resurrection appearance of Jesus, though this is no doubt implied by the statement that αὐτὸς ὁ Ἰησοῦς sent out the gospel proclamation (and a few MSS add ἐφάνη).

---

40. W. R. Farmer, *The Last Twelve Verses of Mark,* stands out as the one serious attempt in recent times to argue for the authenticity of 16:9-20. It has not escaped readers of Farmer's work that a conclusion of Mark which consists largely of what I have called below 'a pastiche of elements drawn from the other gospels and Acts' would fit more comfortably with the Griesbach theory of gospel origins which Farmer champions than with the more common view that Mark was the earliest gospel. For a detailed text-critical review of Farmer's argument see J. N. Birdsall, *JTS* 26 (1975) 151-60.

41. For a recent, well-documented setting forth the data and summary of the debate see P. L. Danove, *End,* 119-31.

3. Without amending v. 8, two seventh-century fragments (099, 0112), two eighth-century MSS (L and Ψ), and a few later uncials use the same Shorter Ending, but then follow it also with some or all of the Longer Ending. The same is found in a few Coptic and Ethiopic MSS and in the margin of the Harcleian Syriac (the main text of which has only the Longer Ending).

4. A number of later minuscule MSS (f^1 22 etc.) give the Longer Ending but mark it off with marginal signs or comments to indicate that its textual status is doubtful.

5. The remaining MSS and versions (which are of course the vast majority, but on the whole are later than those mentioned above) contain the Longer Ending (vv. 9-20), continuing after v. 8 without comment. It was known at least as early as Tatian and Irenaeus in the latter part of the second century.

6. The fifth-century codex W, one of the earliest MSS to have the Longer Ending, has a substantial addition of eighty-nine words (the 'Freer logion') at the beginning of v. 15, described by B. M. Metzger as having an 'obvious and pervasive apocryphal flavour',[42] which consists of a dialogue between Jesus and his disciples concerning the ending of the period of Satan's power and the truth and righteousness now made available through Christ's death. Jerome records the same additional words and says they were found in some Greek MSS.

B. Literary Considerations

1. Most of the content of the Longer Ending (vv. 9-20) echoes, usually in abbreviated form, elements in the resurrection stories of Matthew, Luke, and John, as follows:

v. 9	Appearance to Mary of Magdala	Jn. 20:11-17 (with Lk. 8:2)
v. 10	Mary of Magdala as messenger	Jn. 20:18
vv. 11, 13	Disciples' unbelief	Lk. 24:11, 41
vv. 12-13	Walk to Emmaus	Lk. 24:13-35
v. 14	Appearance to the eleven	Lk. 24:36-49; Jn. 20:19-23
v. 14	Rebuke of unbelief	Jn. 20:24-29 [?]
v. 15	Evangelistic commission	Mt. 28:19; Lk. 24:47
v. 19	Ascension	Lk. 24:50-51 (together with the 'sitting at the right hand' theology of Hebrews etc.)

The parts of the Longer Ending not accounted for in this list are those which go beyond the resurrection appearances as such to describe the subsequent preaching and activity of the church. Thus in v. 16 we have a summary of a basic baptismal soteriology, which has the flavour of Johannine dualism (and

42. B. M. Metzger, *Text,* 227.

possibly draws on the baptism element in Mt. 28:19-20), in vv. 17-18 some of the 'signs' which are related in Acts are summarised, and v. 20 is virtually a summary of the whole book of Acts in a nutshell. In the whole of the Longer Ending the only element which is not easily accounted for on the basis of familiarity with the other gospels and Acts is the emphasis in v. 18 on handling poisonous snakes and drinking poison: the former perhaps reflects the single instance of (involuntary) snake-handling in Acts 28:3-6,[43] but the expectation of these two activities as regular 'signs' is the one distinctive contribution which the Longer Ending makes. In all other respects vv. 9-20 have something of a 'secondhand' flavour, and look like a pastiche of elements drawn from the other gospels and Acts.

2. It is hard to characterise the style of the Longer Ending as a whole since it is such a mixture of elements from other sources, but it certainly reads very differently from Mark's lively and expansive narrative, and contains a notable concentration of words not used elsewhere in Mark.[44] In particular, both v. 20 and the main part of the Shorter Ending read more like pious committee summaries of the post-Easter task and experiences of the church than like the way Mark writes in his gospel.

3. Neither ending follows naturally after v. 8 since both contradict its closing statement (unless the last six words of v. 8 are omitted, as in Codex Bobbiensis but nowhere else). The Longer Ending has further problems in that v. 9 begins with Jesus as subject yet without naming him, when the subject of v. 8 was the women and Jesus was not present in the preceding scene, and goes on to introduce Mary of Magdala as if she had not already been mentioned in 15:40, 47 and 16:1.

For these reasons, the almost unanimous conclusion of modern scholarship is that both the Shorter and Longer Endings, in their different ways, represent well-meaning attempts, probably sometime in the second century,[45] to fill the perceived gap left by the 'unfinished' ending at 16:8, in the case of the Longer Ending by drawing eclectically on what had by then become the familiar traditions of the post-apostolic church, and that these endings, particularly the longer, established themselves in general usage so that by the fourth century they appeared in many MSS, though by no means yet all (so Eusebius and

43. While there is no account of drinking poison with impunity in the NT, later Christian tradition made up the deficit with a story recorded in Eusebius, *H.E.* 3.39.9, about Barsabbas, the unsuccessful candidate for apostleship in Acts 1:23.

44. J. K. Elliott, *TZ* 27 (1971) 258-62, lists the 'distinctive features' of both the Longer and Shorter Endings.

45. See M. Hengel, *Studies* 167-69 (n. 47), for evidence for a date in the early second century for the Longer Ending. In a tenth-century Armenian MS the words 'of the Presbyter Ariston' are inserted between the lines at the beginning of the Longer Ending: some have taken this to attribute its authorship to the presbyter Aristion whom Papias mentioned as a preserver of traditions of the church around the end of the first century (Eusebius, *H.E.* 3.39.5, 14), but this isolated note so many centuries later is no solid basis for attribution, especially as the form of the name is not the same.

Jerome). As time went on, the text concluding at 16:8 was increasingly forgotten, and virtually all later MSS included one (or occasionally both) of the endings. This is an intelligible historical process which accounts as economically as possible for the various data listed above.

INDEX OF MODERN AUTHORS

References to the commentaries on Mark listed on pp. xvii-xviii are not included in this index. (Where the names of authors of those commentaries occur in this list, the reference is to works other than the commentaries.)

INDEX OF GREEK
WORDS AND PHRASES

This index lists only selected exegetical discussions of certain Greek words and phrases, not all citations.

INDEX OF BIBLICAL AND
OTHER ANCIENT SOURCES